THE NEW TESTAMENT

of the
New American Bible

St. Joseph Edition

The Messiah will suffer and will rise from the dead the third day, and in his name repentance leading to remission of sins is to be preached to all nations.

Saint Joseph Edition of
THE NEW AMERICAN BIBLE

THE
New Testament

Revised Edition

AUTHORIZED BY THE BOARD OF TRUSTEES
of the
CONFRATERNITY OF CHRISTIAN DOCTRINE

and

APPROVED BY THE ADMINISTRATIVE COMMITTEE/BOARD
of the
NATIONAL CONFERENCE OF CATHOLIC BISHOPS
and the
UNITED STATES CATHOLIC CONFERENCE

WITH MANY HELPS FOR BIBLE READING

Vatican II Constitution on Divine Revelation, How to Read the Bible, Historical Background to the New Testament, over 30 Photographs and Maps of the Holy Land, Index of Sunday Gospels, Bible Dictionary, Doctrinal Index, and Complete Study Guide by Kathryn Sullivan, R.S.C.J

CATHOLIC BOOK PUBLISHING CO.
NEW YORK

"Let them remember that prayer should accompany the reading of Sacred Scripture, so that God and man may talk together."
(Dogmatic Constitution on Divine Revelation: Second Vatican Council)

Prayer to the Holy Spirit

COME, Holy Spirit, fill the hearts of your faithful and enkindle in them the fire of your love.

Partial Indulgence. *Enchiridion Indulgentiarum,* 1968 edition, no. 62

A partial indulgence is granted to the faithful who use Sacred Scripture for spiritual reading with the veneration due the word of God. A plenary indulgence is granted if the reading continues for at least one half hour.
(Enchiridion Indulgentiarum, 1968 edition, no. 50)

(T-311)

For the faithful in all English-speaking countries the publication of *The New American Bible* represents a notable achievement. Its pages contain a new Catholic version of the Bible in English, along with illustrations and explanations that facilitate the understanding of the text.

For more than a quarter of a century, members of the Catholic Biblical Association of America, sponsored by the Bishops' Committee of the Confraternity of Christian Doctrine, have labored to create this new translation of the Scriptures from the original languages or from the oldest extant form in which the texts exist.

In so doing, the translators have carried out the directive of our predecessor, Pius XII, in his famous Encyclical *Divino Afflante Spiritu,* and the decree of the Second Vatican Council *(Dei Verbum),* which prescribed that "up-to-date and appropriate translations be made in the various languages, by preference from the original texts of the sacred books", and that "with the approval of Church authority, these translations may be produced in cooperation with our separated brethren" so that "all Christians may be able to use them".

The holy task of spreading God's word to the widest possible readership has a special urgency today. Despite all his material achievements, man still struggles with the age-old problems of how to order his life for the glory of God, for the welfare of his fellows and the salvation of his soul. Therefore we are gratified to find in this new translation of the Scriptures a new opportunity for men to give themselves to frequent reading of, and meditation on, the living Word of God. In its pages we recognize His voice, we hear a message of deep significance for every one of us. Through the spiritual dynamism and prophetic force of the Bible, the Holy Spirit spreads his light and his warmth over all men, in whatever historical or sociological situation they find themselves.

On all who have contributed to this translation, and all who seek in its pages the sacred teaching and the promise of salvation of Jesus Christ our Lord, we gladly bestow our paternal Apostolic Blessing.

From the Vatican, September 18, 1970

Paulus PP. VI

[5]

PREFACE

The increasing interest in and love for the Sacred Scriptures can be attributed to the biblical movement, inaugurated and encouraged by our great modern Pontiffs and given even stronger impetus by the Second Vatican Council. Reminded by them of our duty and privilege, as members of the People of God, to disseminate the inspired Word of God, we have spared no effort to produce this improved St. Joseph Edition of the New Testament.

As a sure means of deepening our knowledge of Truth, we have incorporated in this Edition the very latest complete Catholic translation known as "The New American Bible," and produced by members of the Catholic Biblical Association of America under the patronage of the Bishops' Committee of the Confraternity of Christian Doctrine.

We confidently hope that the many distinctive features found only in our Edition of this fine modern translation will add greatly to the enjoyment, understanding, and appreciation of the Sacred Writings.

Among these features, we might mention: the excellent section on the meaning and message of the New Testament by the renowned scripture scholar, Kathryn Sullivan of the Sisters of the Sacred Heart, which is invaluable for serious study of the New Testament, and an easy-to-read sight-saving typeface.

Most important of all, we have included a series of self-explaining Maps showing key events and areas in the Bible—each placed directly near the text which it concerns. In this way, the reader is kept abreast of the history of salvation without needless turning of pages to some other part of the book.

Another series of photographs of important archeological finds offers much light on the Bible and provides impartial confirmation of the events present therein. Finally, the invaluable cross-references and notes at the bottom of each page are all clearly referred to in the text, so that as the reader moves along he or she is constantly kept aware of the wealth of information provided by the latest biblical scholarship.

May God see fit to make this new Edition an instrument for His greater glory and the salvation of souls.

CATHOLIC BOOK PUBLISHING CO.

CONTENTS

THE NEW TESTAMENT

THE GOSPELS

THE NEW TESTAMENT LETTERS

THE CATHOLIC LETTERS

APPENDIX

LIST OF ILLUSTRATIONS

DOGMATIC CONSTITUTION
ON DIVINE REVELATION

PREFACE

1. Hearing the word of God with reverence and proclaiming it with faith, the sacred Synod takes its direction from these words of St. John: "We announce to you the eternal life which dwelt with the Father and was made visible to us. What we have seen and heard we announce to you, so that you may have fellowship with us and our common fellowship be with the Father and His Son Jesus Christ" (1 Jn 1, 2-3). Therefore, following in the footsteps of the Council of Trent and of the First Vatican Council, this present Council wishes to set forth authentic doctrine on divine revelation and how it is handed on, so that by hearing the message of salvation the whole world may believe, by believing it may hope, and by hoping it may love. [1]

1. REVELATION ITSELF

2. In His goodness and wisdom God chose to reveal Himself and to make known to us the hidden purpose of His will (see Eph 1, 9) by which through Christ, the Word made flesh, man might in the Holy Spirit have access to the Father and come to share in the divine nature (see Eph 2, 18; 2 Pt 1, 4). Through this revelation, therefore, the invisible God (see Col 1, 15; 1 Tm 1, 17) out of the abundance of His love speaks to men as friends (see Ex 33, 11; Jn 15, 14-15) and lives among them (see Bar 3, 38), so that He may invite and take them into fellowship with Himself. This plan of revelation is realized by deeds and words having an inner unity: the deeds wrought by God in the history of salvation manifest and confirm the teaching and realities signified by the words, while the words proclaim the deeds and clarify the mystery contained in them. By this revelation then, the deepest truth about God and the salvation of man shines out for our sake in Christ, who is both the mediator and the fullness of all revelation. [2]

3. God, who through the Word creates all things (see Jn 1, 3) and keeps them in existence, gives men an enduring witness to Himself in created realities (see Rom 1, 19-20). Planning to make known the way of heavenly salvation, He went further and from the start manifested Himself to our first parents. Then after their fall His promise of redemption aroused in them the hope of being saved (see Gen 3, 15) and from that time on He ceaselessly kept the human race in His care, to give eternal life to those who perseveringly do good in search of salvation (see Rom 2, 6-7). Then, at the time He had appointed He called Abraham in order to make of him a great nation (see Gn 12, 2). Through the patriarchs, and after them through Moses and the prophets, He taught this people to acknowledge Himself the one living and true God, provident father and just judge, and to wait for the Savior promised by Him, and in this manner prepared the way for the Gospel down through the centuries.

4. Then, after speaking in many and varied ways through the prophets, "now at last in these days God has spoken to us in His Son" (Heb 1, 1-2). For He sent His Son, the eternal Word, who enlightens all men, so that He might dwell among men and tell them of the innermost being of God (see Jn 1, 1-18). Jesus Christ, therefore, the Word made flesh, was sent as "a man to men." [3] He "speaks the words of God" (Jn 3, 34), and completes the work of salvation which His Father gave him to do (see Jn 5, 36; 17, 4). To see Jesus is to see His Father (see Jn 14, 9). For this reason Jesus perfected revela-

[11]

tion by fulfilling it through His whole work of making Himself present and manifesting Himself: through His words and deeds, His signs and wonders, but especially through His death and glorious resurrection from the dead and final sending of the Spirit of truth. Moreover He confirmed with divine testimony what revelation proclaimed, that God is with us to free us from the darkness of sin and death, and to raise us up to life eternal.

The Christian dispensation, therefore, as the new and definitive covenant, will never pass away and we now await no further new public revelation before the glorious manifestation of our Lord Jesus Christ (see 1 Tm 6, 14 and Ti 2, 13).

5. "The obedience of faith" (Rom 13, 26; see Rom 1, 5; 2 Cor 10, 5-6) "is to be given to God who reveals, an obedience by which man commits his whole self freely to God, offering the full submission of intellect and will to God who reveals," [4] and freely assenting to the truth revealed by Him. To make this act of faith, the grace of God and the interior help of the Holy Spirit must precede and assist, moving the heart and turning it to God, opening the eyes of the mind and giving "joy and ease to everyone in assenting to the truth and believing it." [5] To bring about an ever deeper understanding of revelation the same Holy Spirit constantly brings faith to completion by His gifts.

6. Through divine revelation, God chose to show forth and communicate Himself and the eternal decisions of His will regarding the salvation of men. That is to say, He chose to share with them those divine treasures which totally transcend the understanding of the human mind. [6]

As a sacred Synod has affirmed, God, the beginning and end of all things, can be known with certainty from created reality by the light of human reason (see Rom 1, 20); but it teaches that it is through His revelation "that those religious truths which are by their nature accessible to human reason can be known by all men with ease, with solid certitude and with no trace of error, even in this present state of the human race." [7]

2. HANDING ON DIVINE REVELATION

7. In His gracious goodness, God has seen to it that what He had revealed for the salvation of all nations would abide perpetually in its full integrity and be handed on to all generations. Therefore Christ the Lord, in whom the full revelation of the supreme God is brought to completion (see 2 Cor 1, 20; 3, 13; 4, 6), commissioned the Apostles to preach to all men that Gospel which is the source of all saving truth and moral teaching, [1] and to impart to them heavenly gifts. This Gospel had been promised in former times through the prophets, and Christ himself had fulfilled it and promulgated it with His lips. This commission was faithfully fulfilled by the Apostles who, by their oral preaching, by example, and by observances, handed on what they had received from the lips of Christ, from living with Him, and from what He did, or what they had learned through the prompting of the Holy Spirit. The commission was fulfilled, too, by those Apostles and apostolic men who under the inspiration of the same Holy Spirit committed the message of salvation to writing. [2]

But in order to keep the Gospel forever whole and alive within the Church, the Apostles left bishops as their successors, "handing over" to them "the authority to teach in their own place." [3] This sacred tradition, therefore, and Sacred Scripture of both the Old and New Testaments are like a mirror in which the pilgrim Church on earth looks at God, from whom she has received everything, until she is brought finally to see Him as He is, face to face (see 1 Jn 3, 2).

8. And so the apostolic preaching, which is expressed in a special way in the inspired books, was to be preserved by an unending succession of preachers until the end of time. Therefore the Apostles, handing on what they themselves had received, warn the faithful to hold fast to the traditions which they have learned either by word of mouth or by letter (see 2 Thes 2, 15), and to fight in defense of the faith handed on once and for all (see Jude 3). 4 Now what was handed on by the Apostles includes everything which contributes toward the holiness of life and increase in faith of the people of God; and so the Church, in her teaching, life and worship, perpetuates and hands on to all generations all that she herself is, all that she believes.

This tradition which comes from the Apostles develops in the Church with the help of the Holy Spirit. 5 For there is a growth in the understanding of the realities and the words which have been handed down. This happens through the contemplation and study made by believers, who treasure these things in their hearts (see Lk 2, 19. 51), through a penetrating understanding of the spiritual realities which they experience, and through the preaching of those who have received through episcopal succession the sure gift of truth. For as the centuries succeed one another, the Church constantly moves forward toward the fullness of divine truth until the words of God reach their complete fulfillment in her.

The words of the holy Fathers witness to the presence of this living tradition, whose wealth is poured into the practice and life of the believing and praying Church. Through the same tradition the Church's full canon of the sacred books is known, and the sacred writings themselves are more profoundly understood and unceasingly made active in her; and thus God, who spoke of old, uninterruptedly converses with the bride of His beloved Son; and the Holy Spirit, through whom the living voice of the Gospel resounds in the Church, and through her, in the world, leads unto all truth those who believe and makes the word of Christ dwell abundantly in them (see Col 3, 16).

9. Hence there exists a close connection and communication between sacred tradition and Sacred Scripture. For both of them, flowing from the same divine wellspring, in a certain way merge into a unity and tend toward the same end. For Sacred Scripture is the word of God inasmuch as it is consigned to writing under the inspiration of the divine Spirit, while sacred tradition takes the word of God entrusted by Christ the Lord and the Holy Spirit to the Apostles, and hands it on to their successors in its full purity, so that led by the light of the Spirit of truth, they may in proclaiming it preserve this word of God faithfully, explain it, and make it more widely known. Consequently it is not from Sacred Scripture alone that the Church draws her certainty about everything which has been revealed. Therefore both sacred tradition and Sacred Scripture are to be accepted and venerated with the same sense of loyalty and reverence. 6

10. Sacred tradition and Sacred Scripture form one sacred deposit of the word of God, committed to the Church. Holding fast to this deposit the entire holy people united with their shepherds remain always steadfast in the teaching of the Apostles, in the common life, in the breaking of the bread and in prayers (see Acts 2, 42, Greek text), so that holding to, practicing and professing the heritage of the faith, it becomes on the part of the bishops and faithful a single common effort. 7

But the task of authentically interpreting the word of God, whether written or handed on, [8] has been entrusted exclusively to the living teaching office of the Church, [9] whose authority is exercised in the name of Jesus Christ. This teaching office is not above the word of God, but serves it, teaching only what has been handed on, listening to it devoutly, guarding it scrupulously and explaining it faithfully in accord with a divine commission and with the help of the Holy Spirit, it draws from this one deposit of faith everything which it presents for belief as divinely revealed.

It is clear, therefore, that sacred tradition, Sacred Scripture and the teaching authority of the Church, in accord with God's most wise design, are so linked and joined together that one cannot stand without the others, and that all together and each in its own way under the action of the one Holy Spirit contribute effectively to the salvation of souls.

3. SACRED SCRIPTURE, ITS DIVINE INSPIRATION AND INTERPRETATION

11. Those divinely revealed realities which are contained and presented in Sacred Scripture have been committed to writing under the inspiration of the Holy Spirit. For Holy Mother Church, relying on the belief of the Apostles (see Jn 20, 31; 2 Tm 3, 16; 2 Pt 1, 19-20; 3, 15-16), holds that the books of both the Old and New Testaments in their entirety, with all their parts, are sacred and canonical because, written under the inspiration of the Holy Spirit, they have God as their author and have been handed on as such to the Church herself. [1] In composing the sacred books, God chose men and while employed by Him [2] they made use of their powers and abilities, so that with Him acting in them and through them, [3] they, as true authors, consigned to writing everything and only those things which He wanted. [4]

Therefore, since everything asserted by the inspired authors or sacred writers must be held to be asserted by the Holy Spirit, it follows that the books of Scripture must be acknowledged as teaching solidly, faithfully and without error that truth which God wanted put into the sacred writings [5] for the sake of our salvation. Therefore "all Scripture is divinely inspired and has its use for teaching the truth and refuting error, for reformation of manners and discipline in right living, so that the man who belongs to God may be efficient and equipped for good work of every kind" (2 Tm 3, 16-17, Greek text).

12. However, since God speaks in Sacred Scripture through men in human fashion, [6] the interpreter of Sacred Scripture, in order to see clearly what God wanted to communicate to us, should carefully investigate what meaning the sacred writers really intended, and what God wanted to manifest by means of their words.

To search out the intention of the sacred writers, attention should be given, among other things, to "literary forms." For truth is set forth and expressed differently in texts which are variously historical, prophetic, poetic, or of other forms of discourse. The interpreter must investigate what meaning the sacred writer intended to express and actually expressed in particular circumstances by using contemporary literary forms in accordance with the situation of his own time and culture. [7] For the correct understanding of what the sacred author wanted to assert, due attention must be paid to the customary and characteristic styles of feeling, speaking and narrating which prevailed at the time of the sacred writer, and to the patterns men normally employed at that period in their everyday dealings with one another. [8]

But, since holy Scripture must be read and interpreted in the same spirit in which it was written, [9] no less serious attention must be given to the content and unity of the whole of Scripture if the meaning of the sacred texts is to be correctly worked out. The living tradition of the whole Church must be taken into account along with the harmony which exists between elements of the faith. It is the task of exegetes to work according to these rules toward a better understanding and explanation of the meaning of Sacred Scripture, so that through preparatory study the judgment of the Church may mature. For all of what has been said about the way of interpreting Scripture is subject finally to the judgment of the Church, which carries out the divine commission and ministry of guarding and interpreting the word of God. [10]

13. In Sacred Scripture, therefore, while the truth and holiness of God always remains intact, the marvelous "condescension" of eternal wisdom is clearly shown, "that we may learn the gentle kindness of God, which words cannot express, and how far He has gone in adapting His language with thoughtful concern for our weak human nature." [11] For the words of God, expressed in human language, have been made like human discourse, just as the Word of the eternal Father, when He took to Himself the flesh of human weakness, was in every way made like men.

4. THE OLD TESTAMENT

14. In carefully planning and preparing the salvation of the whole human race the God of infinite love, by a special dispensation, chose for Himself a people to whom He would entrust His promises. First He entered into a covenant with Abraham (see Gn 15, 18) and, through Moses, with the people of Israel (see Ex 24, 8). To this people which He had acquired for Himself, He so manifested Himself through words and deeds as the one true and living God that Israel came to know by experience the ways of God with men. Then too, when God Himself spoke to them through the mouth of the prophets, Israel daily gained a deeper and clearer understanding of His ways and made them more widely known among the nations (see Pss 21, 29; 95, 1-3; Is 2, 1-5; Jer 3, 17). The plan of salvation foretold by the sacred authors, recounted and explained by them, is found as the true word of God in the books of the Old Testament: these books, therefore, written under divine inspiration, remain permanently valuable. "For all that was written for our instruction, so that by steadfastness and the encouragement of the Scriptures we might have hope" (Rom 15, 4).

15. The principal purpose to which the plan of the old covenant was directed was to prepare for the coming of Christ, the redeemer of all and of the messianic kingdom, to announce this coming by prophecy (see Lk 24, 44; Jn 5, 39; 1 Pt 1, 10), and to indicate its meaning through various types (see 1 Cor 10, 12). Now the books of the Old Testament, in accordance with the state of mankind before the time of salvation established by Christ, reveal to all men the knowledge of God and of man and the ways in which God, just and merciful, deals with men. These books, though they also contain some things which are incomplete and temporary, nevertheless show us true divine pedagogy. [1] These same books, then, give expression to a lively sense of God, contain a store of sublime teachings about God, sound wisdom about human life, and a wonderful treasury of prayers, and in them the mystery of our salvation is present in a hidden way. Christians should receive them with reverence.

16. God, the inspirer and author of both Testaments, wisely arranged that the New Testament be hidden in the Old and the Old be made manifest in the New. [2] For, though Christ established the new covenant in His blood (see Lk 22, 20; 1 Cor 11, 25), still the books of the Old Testament with all their parts, caught up into the proclamation of the Gospel, [3] acquire and show forth their full meaning in the New Testament (see Mt 5, 17; Lk 24, 27; Rom 16, 25-26; 2 Cor 3, 14-16) and in turn shed light on it and explain it.

5. THE NEW TESTAMENT

17. The word of God, which is the power of God for the salvation of all who believe (see Rom 1, 16), is set forth and shows its power in a most excellent way in the writings of the New Testament. For when the fullness of time arrived (see Gal 4, 4), the Word was made flesh and dwelt among us in His fullness of graces and truth (see Jn 1, 14). Christ established the kingdom of God on earth, manifested His Father and Himself by deeds and words, and completed His work by His death, resurrection and glorious Ascension and by the sending of the Holy Spirit. Having been lifted up from the earth, He draws all men to Himself (see Jn 12, 32, Greek text), He who alone has the words of eternal life (see Jn 6, 68). This mystery had not been manifested to other generations as it was now revealed to His holy Apostles and prophets in the Holy Spirit (see Eph 3, 4-6, Greek text), so that they might preach the Gospel, stir up faith in Jesus, Christ and Lord, and gather together the Church. Now the writings of the New Testament stand as a perpetual and divine witness to these realities.

18. It is common knowledge that among all the Scriptures, even those of the New Testament, the Gospels have a special preeminence, and rightly so, for they are the principal witness for the life and teaching of the incarnate Word, our Savior.

The Church has always and everywhere held and continues to hold that the four Gospels are of apostolic origin. For what the Apostles preached in fulfillment of the commission of Christ, afterwards they themselves and apostolic men, under the inspiration of the divine Spirit, handed on to us in writing: the foundation of faith, namely, the fourfold Gospel, according to Matthew, Mark, Luke and John. [1]

19. Holy Mother Church has firmly and with absolute constancy held, and continues to hold, that the four Gospels just named, whose historical character the Church unhesitatingly asserts, faithfully hand on what Jesus Christ, while living among men, really did and taught for their eternal salvation until the day He was taken up into heaven (see Acts 1, 1). Indeed, after the Ascension of the Lord the Apostles handed on to their hearers what He had said and done. This they did with that clearer understanding which they enjoyed [3] after they had been instructed by the glorious events of Christ's life and taught by the light of the Spirit of truth. [2] The sacred authors wrote the four Gospels, selecting some things from the many which had been handed on by word of mouth or in writing, reducing some of them to a synthesis, explaining some things in view of the situation of their churches, and preserving the form of proclamation but always in such fashion that they told us the honest truth about Jesus. [4] For their intention in writing was that either from their own memory and recollections, or from the witness of those who "themselves from the beginning were eye-witnesses and ministers of the Word" we might know "the truth" concerning those matters about which we have been instructed (see Lk 1, 2-4).

20. Besides the four Gospels, the canon of the New Testament also contains the epistles of St. Paul and other apostolic writings, composed under the inspiration of the Holy Spirit, by which, according to the wise plan of God, those matters which concern Christ the Lord are confirmed, His true teaching is more and more fully stated, the saving power of the divine work of Christ is preached, the story is told of the beginnings of the Church and its marvelous growth, and its glorious fulfillment is foretold.

For the Lord Jesus was with His Apostles as He had promised (see Mt 28, 20) and sent them the advocate Spirit who would lead them into the fullness of truth (see Jn 16, 13).

6. SACRED SCRIPTURE IN THE LIFE OF THE CHURCH

21. The Church has always venerated the divine Scriptures just as she venerates the body of the Lord, since, especially in the sacred liturgy, she unceasingly receives and offers to the faithful the bread of life from the table both of God's word and of Christ's body. She has always maintained them, and continues to do so, together with sacred tradition, as the supreme rule of faith, since, as inspired by God and committed once and for all to writing, they impart the word of God Himself without change, and make the voice of the Holy Spirit resound in the word of the prophets and Apostles. Therefore, like the Christian religion itself, all the preaching of the Church must be nourished and regulated by Sacred Scripture. For in the sacred books, the Father who is in heaven meets His children with great love and speaks with them; and the force and power in the word of God is so great that it stands as the support and energy of the Church, the strength of faith for her sons, the food of the soul, the pure and everlasting source of spiritual life. Consequently these words are perfectly applicable to Sacred Scripture: "For the word of God is living and active" (Heb 4, 12) and "it has power to build you up and give you your heritage among all those who are sanctified" (Acts 20, 32; see 1 Thes 2, 13).

22. Easy access to Sacred Scripture should be provided for all the Christian faithful. That is why the Church from the very beginning accepted as her own that very ancient Greek translation of the Old Testament which is called the Septuagint; and she has always given a place of honor to other Eastern translations and Latin ones, especially the Latin translation known as the Vulgate. But since the word of God should be accessible at all times, the Church by her authority and with maternal concern sees to it that suitable and correct translations are made into different languages, especially from the original texts of the sacred books. And should the opportunity arise and the Church authorities approve, if these translations are produced in cooperation with the separated brethren as well, all Christians will be able to use them.

23. The bride of the incarnate Word, the Church taught by the Holy Spirit, is concerned to move ahead toward a deeper understanding of the Sacred Scriptures so that she may increasingly feed her sons with the divine words. Therefore, she also encourages the study of the holy Fathers of both East and West and of sacred liturgies. Catholic exegetes then and other students of sacred theology, working diligently together and using appropriate means, should devote their energies, under the watchful care of the sacred teaching office of the Church, to an exploration and exposition of the divine writings. This should be so done that as many ministers of the divine word as possible will be able effectively to provide the nourishment of the Scriptures for the people of God, to enlighten their minds, strengthen their wills, and set men's hearts on fire with

the love of God. [1] The sacred Synod encourages the sons of the Church and Biblical scholars to continue energetically, following the mind of the Church, with the work they have so well begun, with a constant renewal of vigor. [2]

24. Sacred theology rests on the written word of God, together with sacred tradition, as its primary and perpetual foundation. By scrutinizing in the light of faith all truth stored up in the mystery of Christ, theology is most powerfully strengthened and constantly rejuvenated by that word. For the Sacred Scriptures contain the word of God and since they are inspired really are the word of God; and so the study of the sacred page is, as it were, the soul of sacred theology. [3] By the same word of Scripture the ministry of the word also, that is, pastoral preaching, catechetics and all Christian instruction, in which the liturgical homily must hold the foremost place, is nourished in a healthy way and flourishes in a holy way.

25. Therefore, all the clergy must hold fast to the Sacred Scriptures through diligent sacred reading and careful study, especially the priests of Christ and others, such as deacons and catechists who are legitimately active in the ministry of the word. This is to be done so that none of them will become "an empty preacher of the word of God outwardly, who is not a listener to it inwardly" [4] since they must share the abundant wealth of the divine word with the faithful committed to them, especially in the sacred liturgy. The sacred Synod also earnestly and especially urges all the Christian faithful, especially Religious, to learn by frequent reading of the divine Scriptures the "excellent knowledge of Jesus Christ" (Phil 3, 8). "For ignorance of the Scriptures is ignorance of Christ." [5] Therefore, they should gladly put themselves in touch with the sacred text itself, whether it be through the liturgy, rich in the divine word, or through devotional reading, or through instructions suitable for the purpose and other aids which, in our time, with approval and active support of the shepherds of the Church, are commendably spread everywhere. And let them remember that prayer should accompany the reading of Sacred Scripture, so that God and man may talk together; for "we speak to Him when we pray; we hear Him when we read the divine saying." [6]

It devolves on sacred bishops "who have the apostolic teaching" [7] to give the faithful entrusted to them suitable instruction in the right use of the divine books, especially the New Testament and above all the Gospels. This can be done through translations of the sacred texts, which are to be provided with the necessary and really adequate explanations so that the children of the Church may safely and profitably become conversant with the Sacred Scriptures and be penetrated with their spirit.

Furthermore, editions of the Sacred Scriptures, provided with suitable footnotes, should be prepared also for the use of non-Christians and adapted to their situation. Both pastors of souls and Christians generally should see to the wise distribution of these in one way or another.

26. In this way, therefore, through the reading and study of the sacred books "the word of God may spread rapidly and be glorified" (2 Thes 3, 1) and the treasure of revelation, entrusted to the Church, may more and more fill the hearts of men. Just as the life of the Church is strengthened through more frequent celebration of the Eucharistic mystery, similarly we may hope for a new stimulus for the life of the Spirit from a growing reverence for the word of God, which "lasts forever" (Is 40, 8; see 1 Pt 1, 23-25).

NOTES

PREFACE:

Article 1: 1. cf. St. Augustine, "De Catechizandis Rudibus," C.IV 8: PL. 40, 316.

CHAPTER I

Article 2: 2. cf. Matt. 11:27; John 1-14 and 17; 14:6; 17:1-3; 2 Cor. 3:16 and 4, 6; Eph. 1, 3-14.

Article 4: 3. Epistle to Diognetus, c. VII, 4: Funk, Apostolic Fathers, I, p. 403.

Article 5: 4. First Vatican Council, Dogmatic Constitution on the Catholic Faith, Chap. 3, "On Faith:" Denzinger 1789 (3008).

5. Second Council of Orange, Canon 7: Denzinger 180 (377); First Vatican Council, loc. cit.: Denzinger 1791 (3010).

Article 6: 6. First Vatican Council, Dogmatic Constitution on the Catholic Faith, Chap. 2, "On Revelation:" Denzinger 1786 (3005).

7. Ibid: Denzinger 1785 and 1786 (3004 and 3005).

CHAPTER II

Article 7: 1. cf. Matt. 28:19-20, and Mark 16:15; Council of Trent, session IV, Decree on Scriptural Canons: Denzinger 783 (1501).

2. cf. Council of Trent, loc. cit.; First Vatican Council, session III, Dogmatic Constitution on the Catholic Faith, Chap. 2, "On Revelation:" Denzinger 1787 (3005).

3. St. Irenaeus, "Against Heretics" III, 3, 1: PG 7, 848; Harvey, 2, p. 9.

Article 8: 4. cf. Second Council of Nicea: Denzinger 303 (602); Fourth Council of Constance, session X, Canon 1: Denzinger 336 (650-652).

5. cf. First Vatican Council, Dogmatic Constitution on the Catholic Faith, Chap. 4, "On Faith and Reason:" Denzinger 1800 (3020).

Article 9: 6. cf. Council of Trent, session IV, loc. cit.: Denzinger 783 (1501).

Article 10: 7. cf. Pius XII, apostolic constitution, "Munificentissimus Deus," Nov. 1, 1950: A.A.S. 42 (1950) p. 756; Collected Writings of St. Cyprian, Letter 66, 8: Hartel, III, B, p. 733; "The Church [is] people united with the priest and the pastor together with his flock."

8. cf. First Vatican Council, Dogmatic Constitution on the Catholic Faith, Chap. 3 "On Faith:" Denzinger 1792 (3011).

9. cf. Pius XII, encyclical "Humani Generis," Aug. 12, 1950: A.A.S. 42 (1950), pp. 568-69: Denzinger 2314 (3886).

CHAPTER III

Article 11: 1. cf. First Vatican Council, Dogmatic Constitution on the Catholic Faith, Chap. 2 "On Revelation:" Denzinger 1787 (3006); Biblical Commission, Decree of June 18, 1915: Denzinger 2180 (3629): EB 420; Holy Office, Epistle of Dec. 22, 1923: EB 499.

2. cf. Pius XII, encyclical "Divino Afflante Spiritu," Sept. 30, 1943: A.A.S. 35 (1943) p. 314; Enchiridion Biblic. (EB) 556.

3. "In" and "for" man: cf. Heb 1, and 4: 7; ("in"): 2 Sm. 23, 2; Matt. 1:22 and various places; ("for"): First Vatican Council, Schema on Catholic Doctrine, note 9: Coll. Lac. VII, 522.

4. Leo XIII, encyclical "Providentissimus Deus," Nov. 18, 1893: Denzinger 1952 (3293); EB 125.

5. cf. St. Augustine, "Gen. ad Litt." 2, 9, 20: PL 34, 270-271; Epistle 82, 3: PL 33, 277: CSEL 34, 2, p. 354.

St. Thomas, "On Truth," Q. 12, A. 2, C.

Council of Trent, session IV, Scriptural Canons: Denzinger 783 (1501).

Leo XIII, encyclical "Providentissimus Deus:" EB 121, 124, 126-127.

Pius XII, encyclical "Divino Afflante Spiritu:" EB 539.

Article 12: 6. St. Augustine, "City of God," XVII, 6, 2: PL 41, 537: CSEL. XL, 2, 228.

7. St. Augustine, "On Christian Doctrine" III, 18, 26; PL 34, 75-76.

8. Pius XII, loc. cit. Denzinger 2294 (3829-3830); EB 557-562.

9. cf. Benedict XV, encyclical "Spiritus Paraclitus" Sept. 15, 1920; EB 469. St. Jerome, "In Galatians" 5, 19-20: PL 26, 417 A.

10. cf. First Vatican Council, Dogmatic Constitution on the Catholic Faith, Chapter 2, "On Revelation:" Denzinger 1788 (3007).

Article 13: 11. St. John Chrysostom, "In Genesis" 3, 8 (Homily 17, 1): PG 53, 134; "Attemperatio [in English "Suitable adjustment"] in Greek "synkatabasis."

CHAPTER IV

Article 15: 1. Pius XI, encyclical "Mit Brennender Sorge," March 14, 1937: A.A.S. 29 (1937) p. 51.

Article 16: 2. St. Augustine, "Quest. in Hept." 2, 73: PL 34, 623.

3. St. Irenaeus, "Against Heretics" III, 21, 3: PG 7, 950; (Same as 25, 1: Harvey 2, p. 115). St. Cyril of Jerusalem, "Catech." 4, 35; PG 33, 497. Theodore of Mopsuestia, "In Soph." 1, 4-6: PG 66, 452D-453A.

CHAPTER V

Article 18: 1. cf. St. Irenaeus, "Against Heretics" III, 11; 8: PG 7, 885, Sagnard Edition, p. 194.

Article 19: (Due to the necessities of translation, footnote 2 follows footnote 3 in text of Article 19.)

2. cf. John 14:26; 16-13.

3. John 2:22; 12:16; cf. 14:26; 16:12-13; 7:39.

4. cf. instruction "Holy Mother Church" edited by Pontifical Consilium for Promotion of Bible Studies: A.A.S. 56 (1964) p. 715.

CHAPTER VI

Article 23: 1. cf. Pius XII, encyclical "Divino Afflante Spiritu:" EB 551, 553, 567.

Pontifical Biblical Commission, Instruction on Proper Teaching of Sacred Scripture in Seminaries and Religious Colleges, May 13, 1950: A.A.S. 42 (1950) pp. 495-505.

2. cf. Pius XII, ibid: EB 569.

Article 24: 3. cf. Leo XIII, encyclical "Providentissimus Deus:" EB 114; Benedict XV, encyclical "Spiritus Paraclitus:" EB 483.

Article 25: 4. St. Augustine, Sermons, 179, 1: PL 38, 966.

5. St. Jerome, Commentary on Isaiah, Prol.: PL 24, 17.

cf. Benedict XV, encyclical "Spiritus Paraclitus:" EB 475-480; Pius XII, encyclical "Divino Afflante Spiritu:" EB 544.

6. St. Ambrose, On the Duties of Ministers I, 20, 88: PL 16, 50.

7. St. Irenaeus, "Against Heretics" IV, 32, 1: PG 7, 1071; (Same as 49, 2) Harvey, 2, p. 255.

HOW TO READ YOUR BIBLE

1. MOST WIDELY DISSEMINATED BOOK

There is no doubt that the Bible is one of the most widely disseminated books. But "most widely disseminated" does not necessarily mean "most read" and "best understood." The Bible is a compilation of many ancient documents stemming from a time and culture which is rather alien to our own. This brings up the question: Why should I read the Bible? It is so old. Why not leave it alone and read contemporary literature, which is more relevant?

2. WHY THE BIBLE?

a. As Americans, we share a rich Judaeo-Christian civilization. Our language, many of our customs and often our outlook on life, love, good and evil are conditioned by the Judaeo-Christian heritage in which we are rooted. You cannot possibly understand them without knowing the Judaeo-Christian classic: the Bible. A few examples will clearly show this. (1) *Customs and practices:* We observe a seven-day week, take an oath with one hand on the Bible, number years as B.C. or A.D., celebrate Christmas and Easter as holidays, print the words "In God we trust" on our money, regard monogamy as a value and accept woman as a companion equal to man. (2) *Sayings of everyday life*: "The patience of Job," "a doubting Thomas," "a Judas," "as old as Methuselah." (3) *Popular songs*: "Tain't Necessarily So" in *Porgy and Bess,* "Miracle of Miracles" in the Broadway musical *Fiddler on the Roof.* (4) *Negro Spirituals and classic Oratoria*: "Let My People Go," and *The Messiah* by Handel. (5) *Classical literature*: *Paradise Lost* by Milton, *East of Eden* by Steinbeck. (6) *Plastic art*: Paintings and statues by Rembrandt, El Greco, Rubens, Michelangelo, Rodin. (7) *Movies: The Ten Commandments, The Robe, Samson and Delilah.* None of these is really understandable without an acquaintance with the literature of the Bible. From our roots, we should understand ourselves.

b. However, besides being an American, you are a Christian. For Christians, the Bible is inspired by God. God chose that time (2000 - 3000 years ago), that people (the Jews) and that culture (Hebrew) to reveal Himself. Guided by God, the Hebrew genius interpreted history, war and peace, birth and death, famine and abundance, happiness and frustration, success and failure, in the light of God's presence to His people. And Christians, regarding themselves as descendants of God's chosen people of ancient times, share this interpretation of life. The Bible reflects the restless search for life's meaning, as the Hebrews wrestled with it. As believers see it, this search was guided by God, which is the reason why we take note of it. Believers understand that ultimately God Himself speaks to them in and through Scripture.

3. BIBLICAL INSPIRATION

Artists, philosophers and even scientists speak of inspiration, which is the urge to create a work of beauty (artists), a constructive outlook on reality (philosophers) or a solution to a problem (scientists). How to explain this inspiration?

First of all, inspiration is related to a certain sensitivity which exists in a society at a given time. This sensitivity inspires gifted individuals in that society. These individuals in turn heighten that sensitivity in their fellow citizens. For example, we would never have produced our Jazz music, which has captured the whole world, without our Negro communities that are so sensitive to music and rhythm. From such communities we have seen arise such men as Louis Armstrong, Duke Ellington and Ray Charles, who in turn have heightened musical sensitivity in this country and all over the world.

More or less by this same process of mutual influence Hebrew literature came into being. We see in the Hebrew people a highly developed sensitivity for God's presence in their lives. From these pious Hebrew communities we see arise prophets, preachers, writers, who offered their (first spoken) reflections on that shared experience of God's presence with His people. In turn these prophets, preachers and writers heightened that religious sensitivity in their people.

There is a similarity between Hebrew literature and all art. Both are inspired. But Hebrew literature is more than just that. It is inspired (breathed upon) in a very special way by almighty God. This does not mean that God dictated His message as a businessman dictates a letter to a secretary. God takes the author as he is and leaves him free to choose his own means of communication. Isaiah was a great poet and composed beautiful poems to convey his message. Ezekiel was not well-versed in letters and his language is rather poor. Some authors chose existing folktales and even beast fables to bring out their point. *Inspiration is guidance.*

4. INSPIRATION AND REVELATION

God Himself guided (inspired) the Hebrew genius in its searching out of the mysteries of the human condition. This guidance is called *inspiration*. When this restless searching for truth and meaning culminates in unfolding one of God's mysteries, we speak of divine *revelation*. This means that God reveals some aspect of Himself or the human condition in and through man's endeavors to find out. Hence, "everything in the Bible is *inspired,* but not everything is *revealed*" (Pierre Benoit). Sometimes inspired searching for meaning leads to conclusions which cannot be qualified as revelation from God. Think of the "holy wars" of total destruction, fought by the Hebrews when they invaded Palestine. The search for meaning in those wars centuries later was inspired, but the conclusions which attributed all those atrocities to the command of God were imperfect and provisional. See Judges 1, 1-8.

5. A LIBRARY OF BOOKS

Ironically, "The Book" is not just *one* book. It is a library of books, put together in one volume. Look at the contents of your Bible! The authors of these books are mostly unknown. Neither were those books composed at one time. Many centuries elapsed between the oldest traditions and the last book of the Bible. Not even the original language of all these books was the same.

A major disadvantage is that these books are not put together systematically as the books of a modern library. All kinds of literary forms: history, historical novels, parables, allegories, poems, midrash (edifying interpretation of events), and more are often intermingled. Even if you read your Bible in an up-to-date American translation, such as this one, you need guidance. Therefore read the introductions to the Bible books and pay attention to the footnotes! Know that, if you want to understand what God has to tell you through Scripture, you must first understand what the writer wants to say. The Bible is God's word and man's word. One must understand man's word first in order to understand the word of God.

Since this collection of books is of such great importance as source book for the humanities and religion (see no. 2), it became known in Western civilization as the "Bible," from the Greek word "biblion" (book); hence, "The Book," which is actually a library of books!

6. LITERARY GENRES OR FORMS

It is very important to know what literary form a writer uses to convey his message. Is it a work of history, a poem, a figure of speech, a parable? If you do not know, you may misunderstand the writer's message. That is why we must pay attention to the literary genres (forms) of the Bible. The following are just a few of them.

a. *The Parable:* A short fictitious narrative from which a moral or spiritual truth is drawn. See Isaiah 5, 1-7 and the parables of the Gospels! Keep in mind that *the point* of the parable (not the details) is God's message to believers.

b. *The Allegory:* A figurative story with a *veiled* meaning. Read Genesis 2, 3; 4, 1-16; 6—8; 11, 1-9. For centuries these chapters have been misunderstood as inspired lessons in science. The Bible does not teach science; it teaches religious values. It uses these folktales to teach a lesson. Again, *the point* of the allegory (not the details) is God's message to you.

c. *The Beast Fable*: See Genesis and Numbers 22, 22-35. (Understand this from Numbers 22, 1-21 and 22, 36-38.) The author chose this literary form to convey his message.

d. *The Short Story and the Historical Novel:* See Genesis 37—50; Judges 13—16; 1 Samuel 17; also Genesis 12—36 and Exodus. The core of these stories is historical, but remember that the author did not intend to write history as we find it in our school books; he simply uses *traditions* and fashions them to bring out a religious lesson. Bible scholars call this edifying interpretation of the past "midrash."

e. *The Problem Story:* The best known problem stories in our contemporary literature are those on the race issue. A Hebrew problem story is the Book of Ruth on intermarriage. The point is a plea for tolerance.

f. *The Speech as a Literary Device:* Read 1 Kings 8, 14-21; Acts 17, 22-31. It is not important whether or not King Solomon or Paul delivered these speeches verbatim as related here. It is the inspired author who wants to state something by putting these words into the mouth of a person with authority. This literary form is often used in the Acts of the Apostles. (See also no. 13.)

7. CONDITIONED THOUGHT PATTERNS

Though inspired (guided) by God, the Hebrew authors were free to choose their literary genres to convey the message. As a matter of fact, these literary forms were conditioned by time and culture. Read the well-known poem on creation in Genesis 1. The ancient Hebrews saw the earth as a large plate with a huge vault over it. Above the vault is God's palace. This outlook conditioned Genesis 1. Do not be shocked about this! We know that the sun neither rises nor sets, nevertheless we go on speaking of sunset and sunrise, since we did not know better for such a long time.

8. THE BIBLE ON GOD

The sacred writers attribute quite a number of human characteristics to God. In fact the Bible does not offer a philosophy on who the "Ultimate Reality" is in Himself; it is mainly concerned about who God is for us. Speaking of God is necessarily limited by the possibilities of human language and conditioned by time and culture. Read Exodus 19, 16-25 and 20, 1-21; Exodus 13, 20-22; Numbers 9, 15-18. Clouds, angels (blasting trumpets!), smoke, fire, earthquake, lightning, thunder, war, calamities, lies and persecution are biblical figures of speech to describe the awe-inspiring greatness of God. As a Jew, who was addressing Jews, Jesus of Nazareth adapted Himself to this biblical way of speaking. Read Matthew 25.

9. POEMS IN THE BIBLE

Poetry, like any other meaningful writing, is a communication from the writer to the reader—usually the communication of a feeling as well as of a thought. The poet wants to pack as much meaning as possible in a few lines. That is why he uses figures of speech, since they involve imaginative comparisons. But biblical poems in particular can easily be misunderstood. Read them as poems and not as scientific or historical reports, in which one tries to explain every detail as a revelation from God. See no. 4 and read Psalm 137: "Ballad of the Exiles," paying special attention to verses 8 and 9. The feeling, the thought, the total poem is inspired (guided) by God, though it is not necessarily revealed truth! Read some psalms!

10. THE PROPHETS

Like other nations in the Middle East, Israel had its *nabis* or prophets. These were groups of ecstatic persons, somehow related to a sanctuary. Music and dance heightened their exotic and vaguely religious activities. Read 1 Samuel 9, 1-10. 16; 1 Kings 22 and 18. From the eighth century B.C. on, we encounter the classical prophets, whose oracles and sayings have been preserved in Sacred Scripture. Prophet means "one who speaks for another," especially for God. It does not necessarily mean that he predicts the future!

The classical prophets' concern focused mainly on such values as *monotheism* (one God, with whom Israel considered itself to live in a sacred partnership or covenant) and *morality as related to religion,* which is seldom found in religions of the ancient world. The "gods" of the ancient world were often anything but morally good, and as such they did not offer any reason to their worshipers to do better. Israel was called to be holy as God Himself!

Another important topic in prophetic preaching is *messianism*. God punishes infidelity to His covenant (partnership). Israel is humiliated for its sins. But at some future date God's kingdom on earth will be restored. God's vicegerent, His Messiah, anointed to royal dignity, will reign in that kingdom. You should pay attention to this messianic expectation in Hebrew literature. This is necessary to understand the literature of the New Testament, which sees the fulfillment of this messianic expectation in Jesus of Nazareth. (See no. 13a.) Read Matthew 23, 33-39; some parts of Amos, Isaiah, Jeremiah.

11.   ATONEMENT AND VICARIOUS SUFFERING

In their search for meaning in our human situation, the Hebrews wrestled with the tantalizing problem of evil and guilt, as we see it in and around us. Is there a way out? In the Old Testament we are often confronted with concepts such as atonement-reconciliation and vicarious satisfaction. Read Isaiah 52, 13-15 and 53. One person could pray, suffer and make up for others. Symbolically, this could be done by "the scapegoat ritual" and other ritual sin-offerings (sacrifices for sin). Read Leviticus 16.

It is important to keep these Old Testament ideas in mind in order to understand the way early theologians of the Church interpreted Jesus' death and resurrection. Who was Jesus of Nazareth? Though innocent, He died a cruel death, but after His death, He was seen by witnesses. What does all this mean? Read how Paul (Philippians 2, 6-11), and the authors of the Epistle to the Hebrews (5, 1-10; 7, 8; 9; 10, 1-18) and the First Epistle of Peter (2, 4-8; 3, 18-22) tried to explain what Jesus of Nazareth means to the new people of God, the Church.

12.   HEBREW PHILOSOPHY

Like all peoples, the Hebrews had their sages or philosophers. In the Bible we find their thoughts mainly in the Wisdom Books. This ancient wisdom is a remarkable mixture of philosophy and poetry. Read it as an inspired search for meaning in life. Do not expect too many ready-made answers. See this literature more as a challenge to a faithful searching for meaning in your own human condition!

13.   THE GOSPELS

a. New Testament literature reflects the Christian interpretation of the Hebrew Bible (Old Testament). It is based on the astonishing fact that a Jew of Galilee applied "messianism," as it was known in Hebrew literature (see no. 10) to Himself. Read Luke 4, 16-30. Jesus quotes the prophet Isaiah and states: "This text is fulfilled in your hearing." New Testament literature can only be understood in the light of this "fulfillment." In other words, the New Testament movement is the fulfillment of the Hebrew Bible. Jesus of Nazareth proclaims that He is the promised Messiah (anointed) king to come, to establish the kingdom (reign) of God, for which the Old Testament was somehow yearning.

b. *Catechisms*. In no. 6 we mentioned how important it is to know what literary form an author is using. If he chooses to use figurative speech, you should understand it as such. A remarkable fact is that for a long time Christians misunderstood the literary genre of the four Gospels. Until recently they thought that the Gospel writers wanted to present us with a biography of Jesus. After much research, Bible scholars agree now that the Gospel writers wanted to write catechisms or digests of Christian teaching concerning the risen Lord Jesus.

c. *Theological Interpretation of History.* Until recently, Catholics learned their religion from the Baltimore Catechism with its questions and answers. Modern catechisms are different. The Gospels are also catechisms, but composed 1900 years ago. In that time they had their own way of making catechisms. The Gospel writers often used a typically Hebrew way of teaching by reflecting on events of the past (see no. 6d). What did the authors of the Gospels do? In the congregations, mainly in the cities around the Mediterranean, they found scores of narratives about Jesus, the beloved Founder of the Christian faith. The writers took those narratives and frequently even remolded and refashioned them to bring out the lesson they wanted to teach.

d. Read Matthew 1, 1-17. What has the sacred writer done? He used a genealogy, probably made available by the family of Joseph and took it for what it was. Then the writer refashioned this document to a list of three times fourteen ancestors. (The Hebrews loved to play with sacred numbers: 14 equal 2 times 7.) The lesson: The Messiah is firmly rooted in the Jewish people; he is the son of David.

e. Reading the Gospels, one should distinguish historical facts from theological elaboration. Take the miracle stories. Catholic Bible scholars accept the fact that Jesus worked miracles. However, the miracle accounts of the Gospel are often more than a record of what actually happened; they also contain theological reflections about what happened in order to bring out its meaning for Christian faith. Moreover, some of these accounts may be adaptations of similar ones in the Old Testament in order to bring out the Christian belief in the importance of Jesus' person and mission. We must keep in mind that the Gospel writers did not intend to write history in the scientific sense; rather they were writing theological reflections on existing traditions (accounts of miracles) in order to teach believing Christians the community's faith in Christ and the Church.

f. *Conflict Stories.* An interesting example of literary form is the conflict story. The author lets his characters debate and thus brings out his lesson. In the conflict stories of the Gospels it is usually Jesus who is in conflict with his opponents, those Jews who did not believe in Him. Read Luke 10, 25-37. One may ask: Was Jesus involved in these conversations? Did He answer exactly as related in the Bible? It is not certain. It is true, Jesus was in conflict with the establishment of His country and this conflict caused His death. There were controversies which supplied the background material for the conflict stories of the Gospels. But as these accounts now stand, they are literary forms used by the Gospel writers in their catechisms to bring out what they had to tell the opponents of early Christianity. Read Matthew 9, 10-13; Luke 7, 36-50; John 10, 22-39; Matthew 12, 1-8.

g. *Infancy Narratives.* The first chapters of Matthew and Luke are dedicated to Jesus' infancy. Both authors have used traditions. How did they handle them? (See no. 13c.) For example take Matthew 2, 1-23. Bible scholars tell us that a horoscope of the expected King-Messiah circulated during the time of Jesus' birth. Astrologers (wise men from the East) were watching the sky for the appearance of the Messiah's star. King Herod, superstitious and upset by these people, killing children of two years and under, is extremely probable. Kings could make and break people! People, leaving Bethlehem to escape the massacre, is equally acceptable. This would be the historical background of this tradition. The rest is interpretation (no. 13c), elaborated by early Jewish-Christian communities and by the author of Matthew. Its purpose is to show Jesus as the true Israel(God's chosen one!), in whose history the history of the old Israel is recapitulated. Note: Israel was in Egypt! God's dealings with Israel in the past are being reproduced in His dealings with Jesus (the new Israel— the new chosen one!). This is a strange literary device, but the ancient writers loved to work with this kind of figurative speech.

h. *On Communication.* Communication is a complicated thing. It is more than just uttering sounds either in English or Chinese. Often barriers must first be taken away. Emotions, hard feelings, prejudice, ignorance, closed-mindedness must be patiently done away with and only then communication becomes possible. Which means should God use to communicate with man? He is so entirely different and so much greater than we are. He is so incomprehensible that we cannot possibly develop an adequate concept of Him. "In our time, God has spoken to us by His Son" (Hebrews 1, 2). God speaks to us through Jesus of Nazareth: a child in a crib, a person, His kindness, goodness, justice, honesty, miracles, parables, death and resurrection. It is this very core of New Testament literature which John tries to explain in the introduction of his Gospel version. He uses figures of speech. He calls Jesus God's *word* to those who are ignorant. He calls Him *light* to people who walk in darkness. Jesus of Nazareth, His charming personality, is God's word to man. Prejudice, lack of interest, closed-mindedness prevent understanding. But could God speak a clearer language than He has done through the appealing personality of Jesus of Nazareth? Read John 1, 1-18.

i. *Sayings of Jesus.* Since we do not possess a biography of Jesus (no. 13b), it is difficult to know whether the words or sayings attributed to Him are written exactly as He spoke them. True, the Gospels are based on sound historical facts as related by eye-witnesses, but both deeds and words of Jesus are offered to us in the framework of theological interpretation (no. 13c). The Church was so firmly convinced that the risen Lord who is the Jesus of history lived in her, and taught through her, that she expressed her teaching in the form of Jesus' sayings. The question is: Can we discover at least some words of Jesus that have escaped such elaboration? Bible scholars point to the very short sayings of Jesus, as for example those put together by Matthew in chapter 5, 1-12. Why? Simply because they are short. Early Christians, who had known Jesus, had His words often on their lips: "The Master used to say . . . " Another question is: Did Jesus sit on a hill and recite this list of sayings on the kingdom of heaven? It is the same question as: Did Moses sit on Mount Sinai writing the law? This composition is figurative. The composer of Matthew, a Jew, wrote his catechism for Christians of Jewish background. He draws a parallel between Moses and Jesus. Moses, the ancient lawmaker, is figuratively related to Mount Sinai. Jesus, the new lawmaker, is figuratively related to a mount in Galilee.

j. Traditions concerning the Resurrection. There is no doubt that Jesus died and was seen alive by witnesses. All reports are unanimous on that. But again the New Testament writers chose theological interpretation to teach what the risen Lord means to believers. Jesus' death, His resurrection, His ascension and the communication of the Spirit are actually *one* Christ-event, that of his glorification. The traditions, told in the Gospels, elucidate the four aspects of the one Christ-event, meaningfully celebrated on four different days. Remember the golden rule: keep historical facts distinct from their theological interpretation.

14. APOCALYPTIC LITERATURE

A real problem for Bible readers is the Book of Revelation. This book is a specimen of a special literary form in vogue just before and in the beginning of the Christian era. It is called apocalyptic literature. In the Old Testament, the Book of Daniel is akin to the Book of Revelation. This literary genre is designated as persecution literature. Its purpose is to console the victims of some crisis by holding out to them the assurance of divine intervention in the near future. The problem for the reader is that apocalyptic literature uses mainly a mysterious or symbolical language, understandable only to one who knows all the ins and outs of the situation. It is in a sense underground literature. The writer wants to console his fellows in suffering in a language understandable to them alone. In our literature we possess this literary form in the Negro spirituals. Take "Let My People Go." The slaves sang it in their wooden plantation churches: "Tell ole Pharaoh, To let my people go." The obvious meaning is a longing for freedom from the bondage of sin, satan, the miseries of life and the hope of a better life hereafter. Obviously genuine biblical piety! But what about "Ole Pharaoh" as the "boss man" of the plantation? Read Revelation 17, 1-8 and 21, 1-4 and see the footnotes for the explanations of the symbolic names used in the text.

15. HOW DO YOU KNOW?

Walking into a modern library, you find all the books neatly arranged under fiction and non-fiction. It is not that simple in the library called the Bible. How does one know whether one deals with history or some form of figurative speech?

To begin with, we should always be disposed to follow the teaching authority of the Church. We should also consult renowned Bible scholars who are experts in Hebrew literature. Sometimes, it is secular science which gives Christians the lead to reconsider their Bible understanding. The discoveries of Copernicus and Galileo made Christians aware that Genesis 1 is not a sacred lesson in science but a poem on creation (no. 7). Most scientists hold that the human species has developed somehow from lower kinds of life. This knowledge helped Christians to rethink the "how" of God's creative activity and to understand that Genesis 2 and 3 is not a lesson in Anthropology, but an allegory, teaching us the lesson that sin is the root of all evil (no. 16b).

However, one problem remains: You may hear interpreters of the Bible who are literalists or fundamentalists. They explain the Bible according to the letter: Eve really ate from the apple and Jonah was miraculously kept alive in the belly of the whale. Then there are ultra-liberal scholars (outside the Catholic Church!), who qualify the whole Bible as another book of fairy tales. Catholic Bible scholars follow the sound middle of the road, keeping a balance between fundamentalists and scholars who are too liberal. You may make your own choice as long as it is not contrary to the teaching authority of the Church. The signature of a bishop in your Bible assures you that opinions, expressed in footnotes and introductions, reflect what is generally accepted as sound doctrine in the Catholic tradition.

16. UNDERSTANDING THE SITUATION

We have stated: One must understand man's word in order to understand the word of God in the Bible. That is why some knowledge of the biblical literary forms is necessary. Of great importance also is some knowledge of the situation in which a Bible passage came into being. You understand the Book of Exodus better if you know something about the slavery in Egypt, have seen pictures of monuments, maps and other background material. Jerusalem was threatened by mighty neighbors when Isaiah spoke his oracles. Knowledge of the history of that time will help you to understand Isaiah better. Historical insight of how the Romans colonized other nations contributes highly to the understanding of "messianism" as reflected in the Gospels. Knowing that early Christians mistakenly expected Christ's second coming during their own lifetime, helps you to understand 1 and 2 Thessalonians. Reading introductions and footnotes in your Bible is very important.

17. GOD'S WORD TO YOU, NOW!

Reading your Bible, you must keep in mind that the Bible is God's word to you, now! Reading can only be valuable to you if you grow in truth through reading. This does not come from a grammatical insight or from an understanding of the literary forms, nor does it come from a reconstruction of the situation which prompted the text (no. 16).

The past is dead. *We* do not expect Christ's second coming as happening tonight; *we* are not an occupied country (no. 16) nor can we artificially recreate this situation of 2000 years ago. Yet there is *something in common,* namely, *we* are captives in our odd and sorry human situation (as the Hebrews in Egypt, in Palestine during the Roman occupation); *we* know about God's coming in Christ and wait for a brighter future through Christ's coming (as the early Christians of 1 and 2 Thessalonians have done it in their way). This *something in common,* found in any passage of Scripture, is called *existential understanding.* This understanding, related to *your* existence or life-situation, is aided by faithful Bible reading. It is the very reason why a Christian can read the same Bible time and again, since it is *his* book! The Hebrews were restless searchers for meaning in our human condition. Reading their inspired literature should challenge you to go on with a faithful search for meaning in your own situation.

HISTORICAL BACKGROUND TO THE NEW TESTAMENT

I. THE ANCIENT NEAR EAST

EGYPT

3200 - 1800 Before Christ

Egypt had thirty dynasties

c 3200   **Predynastic period.** Two kingdoms: the kingdom of the Delta with its capital at Buto; kingdom of Upper Egypt with its capital at Nekhen.

c 2900   **I Dynasty:** rules Egypt for about 100 years.

c 2800   **II Dynasty:** with its residence near Memphis. Rules Egypt for about 200 years.

c 2600   **III Dynasty:** OLD MEMPHITE KINGDOM. It rules Egypt for about 50 years and erects the first pyramid.

c 2550   **IV Dynasty:** signals the apogee of the Memphite Empire. The largest pyramids are constructed. Rules Egypt for about 100 years.

2450   **V Dynasty:** worship of the *"Sun"* god predominates. Rules Egypt for about 100 years.

2350   **VI Dynasty:** marks the end of the Memphite Kingdom. Rules Egypt for about 150 years.

2200   **VII Dynasty:** seems never to have existed: 70 kings in 70 days.

2200   **VIII Dynasty:** finds Egypt divided into three kingdoms: the Delta, Middle Egypt and Upper Egypt.

2150   **IX-X-XI Dynasties:** battle for the unification of Egypt. With the XI Dynasty begins the *Middle Theban Kingdom.*

2000   **XII Dynasty:** Egypt reaches the apogee of its history. It invades Palestine and Syria. Rules Egypt for about 200 years. Classic period of literary Egyptian language.

1800   **XIII Dynasty:** marks the decline of Egypt.

MESOPOTAMIA

3200 - 1800 Before Christ

The Sumerian Empire was made up of the first people of the Ancient Middle East. It had a very high culture and remained in power for more than 1000 years.

c 3200   **Jemdet Nasr period:** at the time of Uruk IV. An era of the expansion and irradiation of the Sumerian culture.

c 2900   **Mesilim period:** dominated by the Lagash dynasties (I, II, III).

c 2650   **I Ur Dynasty period:** an era of struggle for power between the cities of Lagash and Ur. Lugalzaggisi tries to establish a Sumerian Kingdom united to the Uruk capital; but his efforts fail.

c 2350   **Akkadian period:** an age of great expansion. Sargon I unites all Mesopotamia under one kingdom: Akkadians and Sumerians become one people.

2200   **Gutian period:** transformation of the entire Sumerian culture. The king begins to have himself called "god." Sumerian customs, languages and strategies are repressed.

c 2000   **III Ur Dynasty period:** new political and cultural predominance on the part of Sumerians. The efforts of King Ur-Nammu make this the most prosperous kingdom of Sumer; Sumerians and Akkadians become reconciled.

c 1800   The Sumerian Empire disappears with the foundation of the first Babylonian kingdom.

EGYPT

1800-330 before Christ

1750 **XIV-XV-XVI Dynasties:** period of the Hyksos. Occupation of Egypt.

1600 **XVII-XVIII Dynasties: NEW THE-BAN KINGDOM:** battles against the Hyksos — Ahmose I occupies Palestine — Thutmose I conquers Syria — Thutmose III wins the Battle of Megiddo.

1315 **XIX Dynasty:** Seti I defeats the Hittites at Kadesh — Ramesses II again invades Palestine and Syria — Oppression of the Hebrews — Exodus of the Hebrews.

c 1200 **XX Dynasty:** with capital at Thebes — Ramesses III battles against the "Sea Peoples."

c 1050 **XXI Dynasty:** with capital at Tanis — New decline of Egypt.

c 950 **XXII Dynasty:** Influence of Egypt over all of Palestine — Sheshonk I (the biblical Shishak).

c 800 **XXIII Dynasty:** with capital at Bubastis. Egypt is broken up into little states.

c 730 **XXIV Dynasty:** founded by Tefnakht and Bocchoris.

c 715 **XXV Dynasty:** Nubian, founded by the Ethiopian Shabaka: unifies the Egyptian Empire.

c 650 **XXVI Dynasty:** with capital at Sais (Saitic period). Neco invades Palestine and conquers Mari.

c 500 **XXVII Dynasty:** the dynasty of the Persians, from Cambyses to Darius II who govern Egypt as a province of Persian Empire.

c 450 **XXVIII Dynasty:** constituted by the Egyptian Amyrtaeus. Battles Persian domination in Egypt.

c 400 **XXIX Dynasty:** founded by Nepheritis I.

c 360 **XXX Dynasty:** founded by Nectanebo I, enjoys some prosperity until the Persians with Artaxerxes III reconquer Egypt in 342. It is the last indigenous Dynasty. The Persian domination under the XXXI Dynasty lasts only a short time since in 332 Alexander the Great puts an end to Pharaonic civilization.

ASSYRIA

1830-330 before Christ

c 1830 **Assyria** is ruled by a strong indigenous dynasty (Sargon I).

c 1750 Assyria comes under an Amorrite dynasty (Shamshi-Adad I) and then forms part of the Empire of Hammurabi.

c 1700

c 1500 Rise of the **Hurite Kingdom of Mitanni** which subjugates even Assyria.

c 1400 The kingdom of *Mitanni* becomes a vassal of the Hittites.

1266 **Shalmaneser I** proclaims himself king of Assyria.

c 1112 **Tiglath-pileser I** founds the Assyrian power and extends its dominion from the Persian Gulf to the Mediterranean.

883 **Asshurnasirpal II** extends the empire into northern Mesopotamia.

858 **Shalmaneser III** attacks the Arameans of Damascus, the small states of Phoenicia and Israel.

745 **Tiglath-pileser III** intervenes in the war of Damascus and Israel against Judah and reduces them to vassal states.

726 **Shalmaneser V** besieges Samaria.

721 **Sargon II** destroys the kingdom of Israel and deports its inhabitants.

704 **Sennacherib** lays siege to Jerusalem and devastates Babylonia.

680 **Esarhaddon** lifts Assyria's power to its height.

668 **Asshurbanipal:** rules over the most splendid period of Assyrian art and culture.

625-612 Decline of the Assyrian Kingdom and fall of Nineveh.

BABYLONIA

1830-330 before Christ

c 1830 **Start of I Dynasty** (Babylonian-Amorrite) with capital at Babel.

c 1750 **Babylonia reaches the apogee** of its greatness with king Hammurabi. His dominion extends over all of Mesopotamia and part of Assyria and Elam.

c 1700 **II Babylonian Dynasty:** called that of the "Land of the Sea" (that is, near the foci of the Tigris and Euphrates).

c 1500 **III Babylonian Dynasty:** made up of the Kassites stemming from the Iranian highland.

c 1112 **New Babylonian Dynasty:** Nebuchadnezzar I delivers Babylonia from the Elamite invasion.

c 900 Decline in the political power of Babylonia, which falls under the hegemony of Assyria, while retaining autonomous dynasties.

745 The king of Assyria also assumes the title of king of Babylonia.

605 **Nabopolassar** captures Nineveh and initiates the NEO-BABYLONIAN EMPIRE (or Chaldean Empire).

538 **Nebuchadnezzar II** subjugates and then destroys the kingdom of Judah (598-587).
End of the Chaldean Empire under Nabonidas and Balthasar (538).

PERSIAN EMPIRE

Cyrus the Great (559-529)

529	**Cambyses**
521	**Darius I** Hystaspis
485	**Xerxes I** (Ahasuerus in the book of Esther)
464	**Artaxerxes I**
424	**Xerxes II**
424	**Darius II**
404	**Artaxerxes II**
385	**Artaxerxes III**
337	**Arses**
335-330	**Darius III** Codoman
333	EMPIRE OF ALEXANDER THE GREAT

EGYPT

From Alexander the Great to 30 B.C.

333-323 Kingdom of Alexander the Great in Egypt.
With the death of Alexander the Great, in Egypt a new Hellenistic Dynasty begins: that of the "Lagids" with capital at Alexandria. It is composed of nine kings.

c 305 **Ptolemy I Soter:** noble Macedonian, rules Egypt for almost 20 years.

c 285 **Ptolemy II Philadelphus:** son of Soter. Literature and the arts flourish; he rules Egypt for almost 35 years.

c 246 **Ptolemy III Euergetes:** son of Philadelphus. He undertakes an expedition in Syria; but internal troubles in Egypt oblige him to abandon his effort.

c 221 **Ptolemy IV Philopator:** son of Euergetes. He resumes the war in Syria, and defeats the adversary king at Raphia in 217.

c 203 **Ptolemy V Epiphanos:** son of Philopator. He becomes his father's successor at the age of five.

SYRIA - MESOPOTAMIA

From Alexander the Great to 30 B.C.

332-323 Kingdom of Alexander the Great in all Asia.
At the death of Alexander the Great, in Syria the Hellenistic Dynasty of the "Seleucids" is begun with capital at Antioch.

c 312 **Seleucus I Nicator:** founds the Seleucid Dynasty. He dies by assassination.

c 280 **Antiochus I Soter:** son of the preceding. He leaves his power to his son.

c 261 **Antiochus II Theos:** before dying, names his first born as his heir.

c 246 **Seleucus III Callinicus:** undergoes the third Syrian War.

c 226 **Seleucus II Ceraunus:** son of Callinicus. Accomplishes nothing of note.

c 223 **Antiochus III (the Great):** brother of Ceraunus, defeated by the Romans, leaves his kingdom in great poverty.

c 180 **Ptolemy VI Philometor:** son of Epiphanes. Since he is very young, he governs under the tutelage of his mother.

c 145 **Ptolemy VII Physcon:** brother of the preceding, also called Euergetes II, succeeds his brother who has been taken prisoner by Antiochus IV.

c 116 **Ptolemy VIII (Soter II) Lathyrus:** has a most difficult life.

c 108 **Ptolemy IX (Alexander I) Auletes:** illegitimate son of the preceding.

c 51 At the death of Auletes, Cleopatra VII ascends the throne. Protected by Julius Caesar and later by Antony, she kills herself after Antony's defeat at Actium (31); Egypt becomes a Roman province.

c 187 **Seleucus IV Philopator:** son of the preceding, has an insignificant reign.

c 175 **Antiochus IV Epiphanes:** brother of Philopator. Hostile to the Hebrews, he initiates the first religious persecution. He dies during a military expedition in Persia (164 B.C.).

c 164 **Antiochus V Eupator:** succeeds his father at the age of twelve and rules for two years as a mere instrument of Lysias.

c 161 **Demetrius I Soter:** son of Seleucus IV, dies fighting Alexander Balas.

c 150 **Alexander Balas:** usurper, succeeds Demetrius I. Obliged to flee, he is killed.

c 145 **Demetrius II Nicator:** son of Demetrius I, is taken prisoner by the Parthians.

c 145 **Antiochus VI:** son of Alexander Balas, usurps the kingdom while Demetrius is in prison.

c 138 **Antiochus VII Sidetes:** brother of Demetrius II, conquers Gazara, Joppa, Acre; he despoils Jerusalem and is killed by the Parthians.

c 129 **Demetrius II:** returns to power after his imprisonment.

c 125 **Antiochus VIII Gryphus:** brother of Demetrius II, is killed by Heraclone.

c 113 **Antiochus IX Cyzicenus.**

The list of Seleucids goes on. It constitutes one continuous struggle on the part of pretenders to the throne who are ever ready to extend themselves in neighboring lands but inept to defend their own territory from foreign kings and petty local rulers: they fight only for their own personal and family honor, not for the good of their country.

This struggle goes on until the year 65 B.C. when Pompey eliminates the last Seleucid, Antiochus XIII, and declares Syria a Roman province.

II. THE HEBREW PEOPLE

I. FROM ABRAHAM TO MOSES
(Gn 12—25)

c 1850 **Abraham** sets out from Ur; he probably follows the "royal road." This route is most likely: Ur — central Mesopotamia — western bank of the Euphrates — Hit — Abu Kamal — Haran. He remains at Haran until the death of his father Terah.

From Haran through the Euphrates Valley he sets out for Aleppo. From Aleppo he approaches the mountains of Anti-Lebanon, passes through Damascus, crosses the Jordan and heads for the Valley of Shechem. From there he goes to Hebron. In Canaan Abraham and his clan—about 300—dig wells, erect altars and acquire land.

Encountering a great famine in Canaan, Abraham goes to Egypt. Leaving Egypt, he returns in stages to Bethel, where he and his nephew Lot separate. Lot goes down the Jordan Valley as far as Sodom and to the south of the Dead Sea. Abraham remains in the terebinth of Mamre. From here Abraham goes forth with his followers to defeat the Kings of the East who have sacked Sodom and carried off Lot. On his return, he is blessed by Melchizedek, priest and king of Salem (Jerusalem).

During his stay at Mamre, Abraham often emigrates into the Negeb, to Gerar and Beer-sheba. Abraham's offering of Isaac takes place on Mt. Moriah, identified with the site of the temple at Jerusalem. Immediately after the offering, Abraham returns to his home in Hebron.

Sarah dies at Hebron and is buried at Machpelah which Abraham acquires as a tomb for his wife and his other dead. Abraham dies and is buried next to Sarah.

c 1630 **As a result of a prolonged famine**, the "house of Israel" emigrates to Egypt: Joseph, son of Jacob, plays a large role in this emigration. The Israelites settle in the land of Goshen, also called the "land of Raamses" and remain there for about 400 years. During this lengthy period, the "house of Israel" increases ethnically through the annexation of Asiatic Semites who come to Egypt for various reasons. The XIX Dynasty (1315-1224), especially Pharaohs Seti I and Ramesses II, constitute the oppresors of the "house of Israel."

II. FROM EGYPT TO THE PROMISED LAND
(Gn 25—50; Ex 1—18; Nm 33)

c 1230 The most probable date for the exodus of the Hebrews from Egypt is about the year 1230 B.C. The most probable route seems as follows: Rameses — Succoth — Etham — Bitter Lakes — Desert of Etham — Marah — Elim — Dophkah — Rephidim — Mt. Sinai — Ki-brath-hattaavah — Hazeroth — Rithmah — Rimmon-perez — Libnah — Rissah — Makheloth — Hashmonah — Kadesh-barnea — Hor-haggidgad — Jotbathah — Abronah — Eziongeber — Punon — Oboth — Iye-abarim. After many wanderings and battles, the "house of Israel" reaches Mt. Nebo. From there the Lord shows Moses the "promised land." Having accomplished his great mission, Moses dies on Mt. Nebo.

III. FROM JOSHUA TO THE JUDGES
(Jos 1—24)

c 1200 After the Transjordan has been conquered by Moses, Joshua—his successor—crosses the Jordan and conquers Jericho; he defeats the confederated kings of Jerusalem, Hebron, Yarmuth, Lachish and Debir; he extends the Israelite conquests to the whole territory between Gaza and Kadesh-barnea; he conquers central and northern Palestine.

c 1190 After conquering Palestine, Joshua proceeds to the partitioning of the Cisjordan, since the Transjordan has already been divided by Moses among the tribes of Reuben, Gad and the half-tribe of Manasseh. Joshua dies when he is about 120 years old. The "house of Israel," divided into twelve tribes, is harassed by various enemies: the Philistines, Moabites, and Ammonites.

IV. THE SERIES OF 12 JUDGES
(Jgs 1—21)
(An asterisk indicates the 6 "minor" Judges)

c 1130 1) **Othniel** is the first Judge of Israel and the only one from the tribe of Judah. He delivers his people from the oppression of a king of Aram (or Edom). This gives Israel 40 years of peace.

2) **Ehud,** from the tribe of Benjamin. He slays Eglon, king of Moab, assuring peace in that region for 80 years.

3) * **Shamgar** is active at the time of Samson. He saves his people from an attack of the Philistines.

4) **Barak,** from the tribe of Naphtali, is driven by the prophetess Deborah to confront and defeat Sisera, general of the Canaanite army, oppressor of the Israelites.

5) **Gideon,** from the tribe of Manasseh, delivers his people from the Midianites, invaders and oppressors of Israel.

Abimelech, son of Gideon, commits many cruelties; he kills his brothers and proclaims himself king at Shechem, but after 3 years he perishes while battling against his rebelling subjects. He does not have the charisma of a judge nor does he save his people, but he is the first person who in tyrranical fashion seeks to introduce the monarchy in Israel.

6) * **Tola,** from the tribe of Issachar, rules Israel for 23 years.

7) * **Jair,** from the region of Gilead, rules Israel for 22 years.

8) **Jepthah,** from Gilead, one of the greatest warriors; he conquers the Ammonites and rules Israel for 6 years.

9) * **Ibzan,** probably from the tribe of Zebulun; he rules Israel for 7 years.

10) * **Elon,** from the tribe of Zebulun; he judges Israel for 10 years.

11) * **Abdon,** from the territory of Ephraim; he rules Israel for 8 years.

12) **Samson,** from the tribe of Dan, inflicts grave losses on the Philistines. He is famous for his outstanding feats, and rules Israel for 20 years.

Samuel, from the tribe of Levi, although his history is not in the book of Judges, is really the last of the Judges. He leads his people back to the worship of the true God: he fights and defeats the Philistines; he anoints Saul, as the first king of Israel, and then David, destining him for the kingdom (1 Sm 1—16).

V. THE THREE KINGS OF ALL ISRAEL
(1 Sm 13—31; 2 Sm 1—24· 1 Kgs 1—11)

c 1020 1) **Saul** is the first king of Israel — he wars against its enemies: Moabites, Ammonites, Edomites, the kings of Zobah, the Philistines. He dies by his own hand on Mt. Gilboa after reigning for 20 years.

1000 2) **David** is consecrated king of Judah and Hebron. For 7 years he fights against the survivors of the house of Saul and finally becomes king of all Israel. He makes Jerusalem the capital.
David wars against the Philistines in the lowlands of the hills of Judah and confines them to three nearby cities; he reconquers all of the territory of Canaan in the "promised land" and also subjugates the Ammonites, Moabites and Edomites. After reigning 40 years, old and close to death, David names Solomon his successor.

970 3) **Solomon** provides for the safety of his throne; he eliminates his competitors and rules his people in a benevolent manner. He builds the "temple-palace" complex and completes the construction by which the place of the temple and the palace is united to the "city of David." Solomon's private life signals a progressive moral decline; he forms a harem for himself of foreign and idolatrous women; to please them, he builds pagan temples in Jerusalem.
At his death the great kingdom splits into two rural states: the kingdom of Israel, with its capital at Shechem, formed by the northern tribes; the kingdom of Judah, with its capital at Jerusalem, formed by the southern tribes.

THE TWO KINGDOMS

(1 Kgs 12—22; 2 Kgs 1—25)

JUDAH

930-913   **Rehoboam** is the first king; he reinforces the kingdom with many constructions. He distributes the principal fortified cities among his sons and always resides at Jerusalem. He undergoes the invasion of the Pharaoh Sheshonk (1 Kgs 14, 21-31; 2 Chr 11, 1—12, 16).

913-911   **Abijam** wars against Jeroboam. He is buried in the city of David (1 Kgs 15, 1-8).

911-870   **Asa** removes all the idols fashioned by his predecessors; he repels the assaults of Baasha, king of Israel (1 Kgs 15, 9-23).

870-849   **Jehoshaphat** is zealous for religion, weak in confrontations, and unfortunate in politics; he lets himself be drawn by Ahab —his relative—against Damascus and against Moab (1 Kgs 22, 41-51).

849-843   **Jehoram** marries Athaliah, daughter of Ahab. The Edomites rebel against the yoke of Judah; the Philistines make incursion against him (2 Kgs 8, 16-24).

843   **Ahaziah** goes with Joram of Israel to fight against the Arameans; he is killed there by Jehu (2 Kgs 9, 14-30).

ISRAEL

930-910   **Jeroboam I** is the first king of Israel. He erects his capital at Shechem and then at Penuel in Transjordan. He establishes the worship of the "golden calf" at Bethel and Dan, effecting a religious schism (1 Kgs 11, 26ff; 12, 1—14, 20).

910-909   **Nadab**, son of Jeroboam, is slain by Baasha while he is besieging Ghibbethon (1 Kgs 15, 25-31).

909-886   **Baasha** transfers the capital to Tirzah, 7 miles from Shechem. An impious king, he suffers the extermination of his entire family (1 Kgs 15, 28; 16, 1-7).

886-885   **Elah**, in a drunken state, is slain by his general **Zimri**, who then commits suicide after only seven days of rule (1 Kgs 16, 8-20).

885-874   **Omri** founds Samaria and transfers the capital of the kingdom to it. He is one of the most representative figures of Israel (1 Kgs 16, 21-28).

874-853   **Ahab**, son of Omri, repels the invasion of the king of Damascus. After marrying Jezebel, daughter of the king of Sidon, he allows her to introduce the worship of Baal into Israel. He is killed in a war against the Arameans (1 Kgs 16, 29-34; 18; 20, 1—22, 40).

853-852   **Ahaziah**, following the example of his parents, worships Baal, provoking God's wrath (1 Kgs 22, 52; 2 Kgs 1, 1-17).

852-843   **Joram**, the other son of Ahab, takes part in the war against Moab and against the king of Damascus.

The prophet Elisha overthrows the wicked dynasty of the Omrides and consecrates Jehu (2 Kgs 3—8).

843-838 **Athaliah,** queen mother, has the entire royal line murdered (except Joash a year-old baby); she fanatically propagates the worship of Baal until she is killed 7 years later by a usurper whom she placed on the throne of Joash who is still young (2 Kgs 11; 2 Chr 22, 10; 23, 15).

838-800 **Joash** reorganizes the administration of the temple; he delivers himself from the attacks of the king of Damascus with a large contribution. He is killed while descending from his palace at Millo (2 Kgs 11—12; 2 Chr 22—24).

800-785 **Amaziah** succumbs to the king of Israel; he is killed in a plot (2 Kgs 14, 1-21).

785-742 **Uzziah (Azariah)** restores and fortifies Jerusalem; builds up agriculture; reconquers the Negeb and the Philistine plain and controls Edom. Stricken by leprosy, he retires to private life (2 Kgs 15; 2 Chr 26).

742-735 **Jotham** defeats the Ammonites and builds the upper gate of the temple of Jerusalem. Under his rule the prophet Isaiah begins his prophetic ministry (2 Kgs 15; 2 Chr 27).

735-716 **Ahaz** uses gifts to buy the aid of the king of Assyria against the kings of Damascus and of Israel, plotting to harm Judah. He introduces polytheistic worship, institutes religious and political slavery; tramples justice, oppresses the poor to pay the Assyrians (2 Kgs 16; 2 Chr 28).

843-816 **Jehu** has the kings of Israel and Judah killed as well as all the descendants of Ahab; he extirpates the worship of Baal; his kingdom is dismembered by the king of Damascus (2 Kgs 9—11).

816-801 **Jehoahaz** defeated by the king of Damascus loses part of his territory; toward the end of his rule, thanks to the Lord's help, he regains the whole kingdom of Israel (2 Kgs 13, 1-9).

801-786 **Joash** defeats the king of Damascus three times; he obtains victories over Judah (2 Kgs 13, 10-24).

786-746 **Jeroboam II** gives back to the kingdom of Israel its ancient boundaries, reconquering the Transjordan; he increases the richness and power of the kingdom. Under his long rule, Israel reaches its greatest political and territorial power (2 Kgs 14, 23-29).

746 **Zechariah** rules for 6 months, and is assassinated by Shallum (2 Kgs 15, 8-12).

746-745 **Shallum,** murderer of Zechariah and friend of Damascus, rules only for 1 year (2 Kgs 15, 13-16).

745-737 **Menahem** marches against Shallum and kills him; he pays a large amount to Assyria and succeeds in strengthening the kingdom (2 Kgs 15, 17-22).

737-736 **Pekahiah** after a very short reign is killed by his official Pekah (2 Kgs 15, 23-26).

737-732 **Pekah** is responsible for the fact that the kingdom of Israel is reduced solely to the territories of Ephraim and western Manasseh (2 Kgs 15, 27-31).

732-724 **Hoshea** plots against his predecessor, is imprisoned by the Assyrians, who invade Samaria. After 3 years, the kingdom of Israel comes to an end (722/1). (2 Kgs 17).

THE SINGLE KINGDOM OF JUDAH

(721-587/6)

716-687 **Hezekiah** roots out pagan worship and strengthens the State. Sennacherib, king of Assyria, invades Judea and menaces Jerusalem. Hezekiah firmly retains his power; an unforeseen calamity forces Sennacherib to abandon the kingdom of Judah. Hezekiah effects a literary renascence, accomplishes magnificent civil engineering works, and excavates the tunnel destined to bring the waters of Ain Sitti Maryam Gibron to the pool of Siloam built by him (2 Kgs 18; Is 36—39; 2 Chr 29-32).

687 **Manasseh** is the most impious of all Judah's kings. He grants the most favor to foreign cults; he shows himself almost always as a loyal and servile vassal of the Assyrians. He is deported into Babylonia in chains, he is repentant and entirely submissive after a period in prison and is relocated on the throne of Judah by the Assyrian king (2 Kgs 21; 2 Chr 33).

642-640 **Amon** follows in his father's footsteps and is killed, in his home, as a result of a plot on the part of his dependents (2 Kgs 21. (19-26).

640-609 **Josiah**, son of Amon, initiates a radical religious reform; he repairs the temple of God and destroys every sign of idolatry. Opposing a military expedition of Neco, king of Egypt, he is killed in battle (2 Kgs 22—23; 2 Chr 34—35).

609 **Jehoahaz II**, son of Josiah, elected as king of Judah by the people, is taken prisoner by Neco into Egypt, where he dies (2 Kgs 23; 2 Chr 36; Jer 22).

609-598 **Jehoiakim**, the other son of Josiah, rules as a tyrant; he protects the pagan resurgence; he persecutes and kills the prophets; he revolts against the late Babylonian kingdom and dies before Nebuchadnezzar's army reaches Jerusalem (2 Kgs 24; Jer 22).

597 **Jehoiachin called Jeconiah**, son of Jehoiakim, after reigning only 3 months, is deported to Babylon by Nebuchadnezzar (2 Kgs 24; 2 Chr 36).

597-587/6 **Zedekiah**, another son of Josiah, is the last king of Judah. Nebuchadnezzar besieges and destroys Jerusalem; he deports king and people into exile. The kingdom of Judah becomes a Babylonian province (2 Kgs 24, 18—25, 30).

FROM THE BABYLONIAN EXILE TO JUDAS MACCABEUS

(2 Kgs 24—25; Ezr 1—10; Neh 1—10)

c 587-538 **Babylonian captivity** of the Hebrews.

c 538-515 **The Hebrews** return from the exile and begin the reconstruction of the temple.

c 445 **Nehemiah** is sent to Jerusalem and reconstructs the walls of the holy city.

? 458
? 398 **Ezra** is sent to Jerusalem and establishes the observance of the Mosaic law.

c 332 **Alexander the Great** conquers Palestine.

c 305-285 **The Ptolemies** hold dominion over Palestine.

c 199 **The Seleucid kingdom** occupies Palestine.

c 168 **Antiochus IV Epiphanes** proclaims the abolition of the Judaic religion and dedicates the temple of Jerusalem to Olympian Zeus.

THE MACCABEAN DYNASTY

(1 Mc 1—16; 2 Mc 8—15)

Judas Maccabeus, the principal hero of the Jewish revolt against the yoke of Antiochus IV Epiphanes, gives his name to the Maccabean dynasty. It is composed of members of the family of the priest Mattathias.

c 167-165 **Mattathias,** and his sons, from Modein begin the Jewish revolt against Antiochus IV Epiphanes, fierce enemy of the Jews.

c 165-160 **At the death of Mattathias, Judas Maccabeus,** his third-born, takes over the waging of the war. He dies on the field of battle.

c 160-142 **Jonathan,** fifth son of Mattathias, is acknowledged as high priest and leader of the Jews. He begins the struggle against Bacchides. He combats Apollonius and defeats him. Attracted by peace proposals, Jonathan goes to Ptolemais to meet Trypho; but as soon as he arrives, he is taken prisoner and killed.

c 142-134 **Simon Maccabeus,** brother of Jonathan, assumes leadership of the Jews. He wrests Judean independence from Demetrius II. He combats Antiochus VII, defeating him by means of his son John. It turns out to be the final victory of the valorous and aged Simon. He is betrayed and slain during a banquet by a certain Ptolemy, governor of Jericho.

THE HASMONEAN DYNASTY

The Maccabean dynasty is succeeded by the dynasty of the Hasmoneans, descendents of Simon Maccabeus. The Hasmonean dynasty is composed of seven rulers who are also high priests (Hyrcanus II during the reign of Alexander).

135-104 **John Hyrcanus I,** son of Simon Maccabeus, initiates the Hasmonean dynasty. He is an able military man who combats Ptolemy (the slayer of Simon) and Antiochus VII. His reign is a very prosperous one.

104-103 **Aristobulus I Judah,** firstborn son of John Hyrcanus, successor to his father. He annexes to Judah part of the territory of Iturea.

103-76 **Alexander Jannaeus,** son of John Hyrcanus I, succeeds his brother Aristobulus I. He is the first one of his dynasty to use the title of king. Bold and intransigent, and dedicated to adventurous expeditions, he dies in battle.

76-67 **Alexandra Salome,** wife of Aristobulus I, seems to have been an ideal ruler.

67-63 **Aristobulus II,** son of Alexander Jannaeus, leads a very adventurous life and is poisoned to death. The civil war that he undertakes against Hyrcanus II provokes the intervention of Pompey (63) after the latter's conquest of Syria for the Romans (65).

63-40 **Hyrcanus II,** son of Alexander Jannaeus, timid and slothful by nature, is forced after only 3 months to resign in favor of his brother Aristobulus II; but he is then named ethnarch of the Jews by the Romans.

40-36 **Antigonus,** son of Aristobulus II, is the last Hasmonean king. He lives in continuous fighting with the pretender to the throne, Herod. The latter becomes king by the will of Antony and Cleopatra, and brings about the decapitation of Antigonus by the Romans.

FROM HEROD THE GREAT TO HADRIAN

39 B.C. 4 B.C. (or better before the Christian era) **Herod the Great,** governor of Galilee, is proclaimed king of the Jews by Rome. Herod takes Joppa, conquers Medeba, besieges Jerusalem and captures it after a three-month siege; he occupies Samaria and has the temple rebuilt. He dies at Jericho and is buried in the fortress of Herodium near Bethlehem.

Year of Rome 747-748	BIRTH OF JESUS CHRIST IN THE CITY OF BETHLEHEM

Year of Rome 754

BEGINNING OF THE CHRISTIAN ERA (A.D.)

4 B.C.
6 A.D.
Archelaus, son of Herod the Great and Malthace, the Samaritan, succeeds his father with the title of ethnarch of Judea, Idumea, and Samaria. It is a rule without glory. He rules for ten years: from 4 B.C. to 6 A.D. He is then deposed by the Romans and sent into exile.

4 B.C.
39 A.D.
Herod Antipas, son of Herod the Great and Malthace, becomes tetrarch of Galilee and Perea with his capital at Sepphoris, 4 miles from Nazareth and later at Tiberias which he constructs. He is not a wise king. Called a "fox" by Jesus, and reproached repeatedly by John the Baptist for his incestuous adultery, he is sent into exile by Caligula and dies there. His tetrarchy, with that of Philip, passes over to Herod Agrippa I.

4 B.C.
34 A.D.
Philip, son of Herod the Great and Cleopatra of Jerusalem, becomes tetrarch of Batanea, Gaulanitis, Trachonitis, Auranitis, and Ituraea. He lives a peaceful and prosperous life. After 37 years of rule, he dies childless.

6-41 A.D.
Judea becomes part of the Roman province of Syria but is ruled by a Roman Procurator with his seat at the seaport of Caesarea and with an official residence at Jerusalem.

41-44 A.D.
Herod Agrippa I, nephew of Herod and Mariamne, by favor of Claudius becomes king of Judea and of the lands that had belonged to Herod the Great.

44-66 A.D.
All of Palestine becomes at the death of Agrippa I a Roman province, administered by a Procurator.

FROM THE BIRTH OF JESUS TO THE JEWISH WAR
(Mt; Mk; Lk; Jn; Acts)

7-6 B.C.
Jesus Christ is born in Bethlehem during the reign of Herod the Great at the time of the census of Quirinius.

5-6 A.D.
At the age of twelve Jesus is taken to Jerusalem and speaks with the doctors in the temple. Then he returns home to Nazareth until his public ministry.

27
John the Baptist begins his ministry of preaching repentance in the wilderness of Judea, and as a precursor of the Messiah calls upon the Jews to undergo baptism in the Jordan.

Jesus is baptized by John and begins to proclaim in Galilee the near advent of the kingdom of God. He gathers a group of disciples around him.

28
Jesus goes to Jerusalem for the feast of the Passover.

29
John the Baptist is imprisoned as a dangerous agitator for having denounced Herod Antipas' marriage to Herodias, his half-brother's wife.

Shortly before the Passover Jesus multiplies the loaves and promises the Eucharist.

Jesus again goes to Jerusalem for the feasts of Tabernacles and Dedication.

30
Jesus enters Jerusalem in triumph amidst a public demonstration acclaiming him as the Messiah.

At the time of the Passover Jesus is betrayed by one of his disciples, arraigned as a pretender to the Jewish throne and instigator of revolt against Rome, and condemned by Pontius Pilate to be crucified. He rises again on the third day afterward.

The Holy Spirit is poured out on the disciples and the first community of the Church is born.

35
Martyrdom of Stephen, one of the first seven Hellenist deacons.

37
Conversion of Saul on the road to Damascus to persecute the growing Christian Church; retreat to Arabia and then Damascus.

45
Paul's first missionary journey: Cyprus, Antioch in Pisidia, Lystra and back to Antioch.

49
Council of Jerusalem: at the insistence of Paul the converts from paganism are exempted from the Mosaic law.

50-52 Paul's second missionary journey: Lystra, Phrygia, Galatia, Philippi, Thessalonica, Athens.

53-58 Paul's third missionary journey: he visits the same cities as the second journey and stays at Ephesus for three years, laying plans for another missionary journey.

61-63 Paul is imprisoned at Rome, then set free. Possibly he visits Spain.

63 or 67 Martyrdom of Peter at Rome.

67 Martyrdom of Paul at Rome.

THE JEWISH WAR

Date A.D. After the death of Herod Agrippa I in 44, Judea is ruled by Roman procurators. Their cruelties and excesses stimulate the fervent nationalism and messianic expectations of the people and revolt against Rome.

1. THE WAR IN GALILEE

66-70 The Jewish War. Nero entrusts Vespasian with the task of bringing the Jews into complete subjection.

Vespasian sets out from Antioch and joins the Roman army at Ptolemais (Acco) in the spring of 67.

At the same time, from Alexandria Titus goes to meet his father at Ptolemais. In April 67, the Roman army under the command of Trajan and Titus occupies Sepphoris, Gadara, Jotbathah, Jaffa, Tiberias, Tarichaea (Magdala), Gischala (Safed), Tabor, Gamala. In October of 67 all Galilee is conquered by the Romans.

2. THE WAR IN PEREA AND JUDEA

In June of 67 a Roman legion goes up to Mount Gerizim to put down a rebellion of the Samaritans.

In May of 68 Vespasian conquers Perea.

In May of 69 Vespasian occupies all the cities around Jerusalem: Gophna, Akrabattene, Bethel, Ephraim and Hebron.

In December of 69 Vespasian is elected Emperor of Rome (after the turbulent year that sees three emperors succeed Nero: **Galba, Otho** and **Vitellius**). He entrusts his son Titus with the task of ending the war in Judea and returns to Rome.

3. CONQUEST OF JERUSALEM

In March of 70 Titus surrounds the whole city of Jerusalem:

a) **he places part of the army** north of Jerusalem in the region of Gabaa (Tell-el-Ful);

b) **he places another part** on Mount Scopus;

c) **he encamps the X Legion** on Mount Olivet;

d) **he sets up his camp** in front of the Psephinus Tower, at the corner of the Third Wall;

e) **he lets part of the troops pass** and places it at the Hippicus Tower.

Then the battle begins. After fifteen days of fierce fighting, on May 25 of 70, the Romans take the Third Wall, batter it to the ground and enter the quarter of Bethesda. Titus places his command in the region of Gareb.

Since Jewish resistance continues to be fierce, Titus builds a wall about 10 feet high around the city, following the route: Gareb, Bethesda, Mt. Olivet, Kidron Valley, Valley of Gehenna, Abu Tor, and coming back to Gareb. The length is about 4½ miles.

When the construction is finished, Titus attacks the Fortress Antonia; and on July 15, 70 the fortress falls into the hands of the Romans, who raze it to the ground.

Next comes the temple. The struggle is fierce. But on August 9 of 70 the temple goes up in flames and the banners of the Roman legionnaires are raised in front of the Eastern Gate. In this circumstance Titus is proclaimed "emperor."

There only remains the conquest of the "Upper City." This takes place on September 26 of 70: Titus has it razed to the ground.

4. THE SECOND REVOLT

In 135, after the second Jewish revolt is put down with blood (132-135), the Emperor Hadrian rebuilds Jerusalem as a Roman colony.

Aelia Capitolina: on the temple area a statue of Jupiter is erected. Entrance to the city is prohibited to all Jews under penalty of death.

The prophecy of Jesus is fulfilled to the letter: "Jerusalem will be trampled by Gentiles, until the times of the Gentiles are fulfilled" (Lk 21, 24).

The ancient name of Judea is changed to that of **Palestine Syria.**

THE CANON OF THE NEW TESTAMENT

THE CANON

THE book known as the New Testament is a collection of twenty-seven writings differing in style and content. While some of them adopt the historical narrative form (Gospels and Acts of the Apostles), others are letters or epistles, and the last one (the Book of Revelation) utilizes the prophetic style. Within the epistles differing styles and contents can also be distinguished: some respond to very concrete problems (for example, 1 Corinthians, 2 Corinthians), Romans is made up of practically an entire treatise and Hebrews a sermon, while James has more of the aspects of a sapiential work.

This collection constitutes the canon of the writings of the New Testament. The word "canon" in Greek means "rule," "norm" or "standard"; we find ourselves before a group of writings that the Christian Church has considered to be normative or authoritative for knowing the new relation of man and mankind with God, which was inaugurated with Jesus Christ and which we call the New Testament in contrast with the Old (2 Cor 3, 6. 14; cf Lk 22, 20; 1 Cor 11, 25).

ORIGIN AND FORMATION OF THE CANON

In the New Testament, Sacred Scripture is frequently cited or alluded to by referring to the Old Testament (Mk 12, 24). Often it is designated by the titles of the two great collections that constitute it—"Law" and "Prophets" (Mt 5, 17; 11, 13); the collection of Psalms is also mentioned three times (Lk 20, 42; 24, 44; Acts 1, 20).

However, the canon of the Old Testament was not yet defined in all its details at the beginning of Christianity. Only at the end of the 1st century was the Hebrew canon fixed at 39 writings; the Greek-speaking Jews accepted into their canon other works composed in their language, and it was this canon that Christians adopted. In spite of all this, the canon was not fully determined, as is shown by the fact that in the New Testament some works are cited as Scriptures which were afterward not made part of the definitive canon (James 4, 5; Jude 14-15).

In adopting the ancient Scriptures, Christians recognized their authority by their relation to the Lord Jesus and to the Spirit (Mt 5, 21-22. 27-28. 31-32, etc.; Jn 5, 39; 10, 35-36; 2 Cor 3, 12-17; 2 Tm 3, 15; Heb 8, 13). Indeed, there was no thought of a new canon of writings; the word of the Lord Jesus in his earthly life or in his risen life was cited in the same way as the old Scriptures (1 Thes 4, 15; 1 Cor 7, 10. 12. 25; 9, 9. 14; Acts 20, 35; Rv 2, 1. 8. 12. 18; 3, 1-7. 14). Living authority was also owed to the guidance of the Spirit (1 Cor 7, 25. 40), and in virtue of it St. Paul could characterize as illegitimate every Gospel that differed from his own (Gal 1, 6-9).

The writings of the apostles or disciples—even the most occasional ones—circulated and were read as a whole in Christian assemblies, as is shown by the concluding formulas of the liturgy (1 Cor 16, 20-23; Rom 16, 16; 2 Cor 13, 12-13; Col 4, 16; 1 Pt 5, 14). In this way their authority was increasing, even though they were not yet regarded as Scripture on a par with the Old Testament.

As the apostles and witnesses of the first generation began to die off, the urgent need arose to preserve their testimony and hence to decide concerning the authenticity of the writings transmitted. Collections began to be made which enjoyed ever greater authority. By the end of the 1st century, Ignatius of Antioch (d. 107) had already placed the Gospel above the Prophets. By the beginning of the 2nd century the Pauline Epistles were already gathered together—probably in Asia Minor—in a collection, arranged according to length.

The four Gospels appeared as a collection before the middle of the 2nd century, side by side with oral traditions which possessed the identical authority. And the sayings of the Lord began to be cited with the same formula ("it is written") with which the Old Testament was cited.

The heterodox tendencies of the 2nd century contributed to stimulate the formation of the canon. The first was that of Marcion (c. 140) who rejected the Old Testament and accepted only the Gospel of Luke and ten Pauline Epistles (excluding the Pastorals). The other was that of Montanus, in the second half of the century, whose extravagant charismatic movement maintained that inspiration was continuing in its midst and led to the specification that public inspiration had come to an end with the apostles.

No little contribution was made also by the necessity of consolidation and readjustment in times of persecution.

By the end of the 2nd century, the Old Testament was commonly spoken of as a *group* of writings—which presupposed the existence of the New Testament, although the latter was not yet exactly defined. In fact, circulating side by side with the later canonical books were other writings such as, the apocryphal Gospels (never admitted into the canon), the Didache (teaching of the apostles), the Epistle of Barnabas, the Shepherd of Hermas, and the First and Second Epistles of Clement.

At the end of the 2nd century (the time of Irenaeus, Tertullian, Clement of Alexandria), canonical status was accorded to the Gospels and Acts, thirteen Pauline Epistles, 1 Peter, 1 John, and the Book of Revelation. Other epistles and writings were under discussion, among them the Epistle to the Hebrews, while some works were admitted which would later be excluded. At the same time, in Rome according to the Canon of Muratori (or Muratorian Fragment) the ordinary books were recognized except for Hebrews, 1 and 2 Peter, James, and 3 John, and also recognized was the Apocalypse of Peter which was later rejected.

The criterion which came increasingly to be applied was that of apostolic origin. Origen (d. 253/254) for the first time classified the writings—in line with the recognition accorded them in the Churches—into three categories: (1) *undisputed writings*: the four Gospels, 13 Pauline Epistles, 1 Peter, 1 John, Acts, and Book of Revelation; (2) *disputed writings*: 2 Peter, 2 and 3 John, Hebrews, James, Jude, the Shepherd of Hermas, the Epistle of Barnabas, and the Didache; (3) *false writings*: the Gospel according to the Egyptians and the Gospels of Thomas, Basilides, and Matthias.

With diverse vicissitudes, the canon went on being made precise, as is shown by the study of the authors of the time (Dionysius of Alexandria, Eusebius, Cyril of Jerusalem, Gregory Nazianzen, Epiphanius) and the content of the great codices of the 4th century, which already included the entire present canon, although they still added other writings. St. Athanasius in his Easter letter of 367 set down the canon exactly as we have it today, as did a synod of Hippo in 393 and a letter of Innocent I in 405. From that time onward, in the Greek and Latin Churches the question of the canon could be regarded as closed, except for the Book of Revelation whose unanimous admission into the Greek Churches did not take place before the 10th century.

As can be seen, the selection and exclusion of books was not the result of a committee of experts, nor was it a decision of authority. The great writings of the New Testament (some 20 or so) formed an indisputable corpus already from the end of the 2nd century. The Christian Church, whose mission was to bear testimony before the world, intuited the value of such works for supporting and fostering its testimony.

THE DOCUMENTS

The writings of the New Testament have not reached us in the autographs of their authors—an impossibility, considering their antiquity—but in copies and in passages cited by early Christian authors.

These documents are classified according to their antiquity, the material on which they are written (papyrus or parchment), the type of letter used (uncial or minuscule), and their textual affinities (different recensions).

Until the beginning of the 4th century, use was made above all of papyrus, a very unstable material that can be preserved for a long time only in hot and dry climates like that of Egypt. As of 1965 there had been found 72 papyri, some very small fragments and others containing entire books. The oldest (P^{52}), preserved in Manchester, pertains to the first half of the 2nd century and contains excerpts from John (18, 31-33. 37-38); the second oldest (P^{64}) contains fragments of Matthew 26. Others also from the 2nd century reproduce the entire Gospel of John (P^{66}) or those of Luke and John (P^{75}). There are also some from the 2nd and 3rd centuries that contain fragments of the four Gospels and the Acts, the Pauline Epistles, and almost the entire Book of Revelation.

At the beginning of the 4th century, parchment (or vellum) began to be used— a costly but resistent material made from animal skin—and continued until the 13th century when it gave way to paper which had appeared in the 11th century.

The ancient codices in parchment used an uncial alphabet, without punctuation or separation of words (continuous writing), and sometimes uncial *cursive* with letters running into one another as was probably the case with the original texts. There are 242 extant uncial codices, the most ancient of which is the *Codex Vaticanus* written about the beginning of the 4th century, probably at Alexandria, which contains almost the whole of the Old and New Testaments, except for an excerpt from Hebrews, the Pastorals, Philemon, and the Book of Revelation.

The next most ancient is the *Codex Sinaiticus*—so called because it was found in St. Catherine's Monastery on Mount Sinai—which is presently in the British Museum. It contains the whole of the Old and New Testaments plus the Epistle of Barnabas, and part of the Shepherd of Hermas. It dates from the middle of the 4th century and comes from Egypt or Palestine. Another very important witness is the

Codex Alexandrinus, a complete Bible with some lacunae, written in Egypt at the beginning of the 5th century.

Less important are the *minuscule codices,* 2,570 in number, which give the history of the text during the Middle Ages, and sometimes even reproduce very ancient variants. Largely unstudied also are the *lectionaries,* which were found from the beginning of the 5th century on and contain pericopes arranged according to the liturgical year.

The *citations of ancient authors* are numerous but difficult to evaluate, for it is frequently not certain whether they exactly reproduce the text they are using or cite it from memory. The verbal agreement of various authors can, however, lead to certainty.

Also helpful in restoring the text are the *ancient versions,* in particular the *Syriac Version,* dating to the 2nd century, and the *Old Latin Version,* dating to the 3rd century. Of less importance is the *Coptic Version.*

This mass of documents—more than five thousand in all—has transmitted the text across the centuries, forming chains of manuscripts. Since not all the copyists were specialists or endowed with the diligence of scholars, it should come as no surprise that they let errors slip into the copies, and that some endeavored to correct the text where it was obscure, or unwittingly combined parallel passages.

Therefore, in order to restore the original text with the greatest possible exactitude—which is the task of textual criticism—one must classify the documents according to their textual affinities, to deduce what reading has the most probability of being the primitive one. Thus, the manuscripts are divided into three principal recensions:

1) The *Antiochene text* is represented by the greater part of the uncials and almost all the minuscules, by the translations from the 4th century, and by the majority of the writers. This text is clear and elegant, harmonizing passages and integrating variants. From Antioch it passed on to Constantinople and into the whole of the Byzantine East.

2) The *Western text* (also known as the *Received text*) is of Syrian origin and is characterized by its tendency for paraphrasing, clarifying, and harmonizing the texts. It is found in the writers and versions of the 2nd and 3rd centuries.

3) The *Neutral text* is a much purer text, whose principal representatives are the *Codex Vaticanus* and the *Codex Sinaiticus.* With certain variants it is also that of the *Codex Alexandrinus.* Many codices combine variants coming from different recensions.

By dint of an immense labor of selection and rejection, textual criticism succeeds in restoring a text which can be considered certain in almost its totality. The variants—even those that are disputed—do not introduce any change whatever in the meaning of the message of Jesus, which is what these writings intend to transmit.

ABBREVIATIONS OF BOOKS OF THE BIBLE

Acts—Acts of the Apostles
Am—Amos
Bar—Baruch
1 Chr—1 Chronicles
2 Chr—2 Chronicles
Col—Colossians
1 Cor—1 Corinthians
2 Cor—2 Corinthians
Dn—Daniel
Dt—Deuteronomy
Eccl—Ecclesiastes
Eph—Ephesians
Est—Esther
Ex—Exodus
Ez—Ezekiel
Ezr—Ezra
Gal—Galatians
Gn—Genesis
Hb—Habakkuk
Heb—Hebrews
Hg—Haggai
Hos—Hosea
Is—Isaiah
Jas—James
Jb—Job

Jdt—Judith
Jer—Jeremiah
Jgs—Judges
Jl—Joel
Jn—John
1 Jn—1 John
2 Jn—2 John
3 Jn—3 John
Jon—Jonah
Jos—Joshua
Jude—Jude
1 Kgs—1 Kings
2 Kgs—2 Kings
Lam—Lamentations
Lk—Luke
Lv—Leviticus
Mal—Malachi
1 Mc—1 Maccabees
2 Mc—2 Maccabees
Mi—Micah
Mk—Mark
Mt—Matthew
Na—Nahum
Neh—Nehemiah
Nm—Numbers

Ob—Obadiah
Phil—Philippians
Phlm—Philemon
Prv—Proverbs
Ps(s)—Psalms
1 Pt—1 Peter
2 Pt—2 Peter
Rom—Romans
Ru—Ruth
Rv—Revelation
Sir—Sirach
1 Sm—1 Samuel
2 Sm—2 Samuel
Song(Sg)—Song of Songs
Tb—Tobit
1 Thes—1 Thessalonians
2 Thes—2 Thessalonians
Ti—Titus
1 Tm—1 Timothy
2 Tm—2 Timothy
Wis—Wisdom
Zec—Zechariah
Zep—Zephaniah

NOTE: For greater clarity and convenience, the footnotes and cross-references are printed at the bottom of each page and cross-indexed in the text itself. An *asterisk* (*) in the text indicates that there is a footnote to the text in question. Each footnote is in turn clearly marked with the number of the chapter and verse to which it pertains. Similarly, a *superior letter* (ª) in the text indicates that there is a cross-reference to a particular verse. The reference itself is also clearly marked with the same letter. Hence, the reader is always aware of a footnote or a cross-reference simply *by reading the text*.

[ ] Indicates a gloss.
/ = Divides verse
// = Parallel

SIMPLE KEY TO REFERENCES

Gn 1, 1 refers to the Book of Genesis, chapter 1, verse 1.
Gn 1, 1a refers to the Book of Genesis, chapter 1, the first part of verse 1.
Gn 1, 1f refers to the Book of Genesis, chapter 1, verse 1 and the following verse (2).
Gn 1, 1-10 refers to the Book of Genesis, chapter 1, verses 1 to 10 inclusive.
Gn 1, 1-10. 14 refers to the Book of Genesis, chapter 1, verses 1 to 10 inclusive and verse 14.
Gn 1, 1—2, 3 refers to the Book of Genesis, chapter 1, verse 1 to chapter 2, verse 3 inclusive.
Gn 1, 1; 2, 3 refers to the Book of Genesis, chapter 1, verse 1 and chapter 2, verse 3.

Acknowledgments: The section on "How to Read the Bible" has been adapted by John Kersten, S.V.D., from his book *Understanding Hebrew Literature*. The "Historical Background to the New Testament" has been adapted with permission from the book *Atlante Biblico* by Giacomo Pesce, C.P. The section on "The Canon of the New Testament" is reproduced with permission from *Nuevo Testamento* published under the editorship of L. Alonso Schokel and Juan Mateas by Ediciones Cristiandad, 1974.

THE
NEW TESTAMENT

PREFACE TO THE NEW AMERICAN BIBLE
FIRST EDITION OF THE NEW TESTAMENT

On September 30, 1943, His Holiness Pope Pius XII issued his now famous encyclical on scripture studies, *Divino afflante Spiritu*. He wrote: "We ought to explain the original text which was written by the inspired author himself and has more authority and greater weight than any, even the very best, translation whether ancient or modern. This can be done all the more easily and fruitfully if to the knowledge of languages be joined a real skill in literary criticism of the same text."

Early in 1944, in conformity with the spirit of the encyclical, and with the encouragement of Archbishop Cicognani, Apostolic Delegate to the United States, the Bishops' Committee of the Confraternity of Christian Doctrine requested members of The Catholic Biblical Association of America to translate the sacred scriptures from the original languages or from the oldest extant form of the text, and to present the sense of the biblical text in as correct a form as possible.

The New American Bible has accomplished this in response to the need of the church in America today. It is the achievement of some fifty biblical scholars, the greater number of whom, though not all, are Catholics. In particular, the editors-in-chief have devoted twenty-five years to this work. The collaboration of scholars who are not Catholic fulfills the directive of the Second Vatican Council, not only that "correct translations be made into different languages especially from the original texts of the sacred books," but that, "with the approval of the church authority, these translations be produced in cooperation with separated brothers" so that "all Christians may be able to use them."

The text of the books contained in *The New American Bible* is a completely new translation. From the original or the oldest extant texts of the sacred books, it aims to convey as directly as possible the thought and individual style of the inspired writers. The better understanding of Hebrew and Greek, and the steady development of the science of textual criticism, the fruit of patient study since the time of St. Jerome, have allowed the translators and editors in their use of all available materials to approach more closely than ever before the sense of what the sacred authors actually wrote.

The New Testament translation has been approached with essentially the same fidelity to the thought and individual style of the biblical writers as was applied in the Old Testament. In some cases, however, the problem of marked literary peculiarities had to be met. What by any Western standard are the limited vocabularies and stylistic infelicities of the evangelists cannot be retained in the exact form in which they appear in the originals without displeasing the modern ear. A compromise is here attempted whereby some measure of the poverty of the evangelists' expression is kept and placed at the service of their message in its richness. Similarly, the syntactical shortcomings of Paul, his frequent lapses into anacoluthon, and the like, are rendered as they occur in his epistles rather than "smoothed out." Only thus, the translators suppose, will contemporary readers have some adequate idea of the kind of writing they have before them. When the prose of the original flows more smoothly, as in Luke, Acts, and Hebrews, it is reflected in the translation.

The Gospel according to John comprises a special case. Absolute fidelity to his technique of reiterated phrasing would result in an assault on the English ear, yet the softening of the vocal effect by substitution of other words and phrases would destroy the effectiveness of his poetry. Again, resort is had to compromise. This is not an easy matter when the very repetitiousness which the author deliberately employed is at the same time regarded by those who read and speak English to be a serious stylistic defect.

Only those familiar with the Greek originals can know what a relentless tattoo Johannine poetry can produce. A similar observation could be made regarding other New Testament books as well. Matthew and Mark are given to identical phrasing twice and three times in the same sentence. As for the rhetorical overgrowth and mixed figures of speech in the letters of Peter, James, and Jude, the translator must resist a powerful compulsion to tidy them up if only to render these letters intelligibly.

Without seeking refuge in complaints against the inspired authors, however, the translators of *The New American Bible* here state that what they have attempted is a translation rather than a paraphrase. To be sure, all translation can be called paraphrase by definition. Any striving for complete fidelity will shortly end in infidelity. Nonetheless, it must be pointed out that the temptation to improve overladen sentences by the consolidation or elimination of multiplied adjectives, or the simplification of clumsy hendiadys, has been resisted here. For the most part, rhetorically ineffective words and phrases are retained in this translation in some form, even when it is clear that a Western contemporary writer would never have employed them.

The spelling of proper names in *The New American Bible* follows the customary forms found in most English Bibles since the Authorized Version.

Despite the arbitrary character of the divisions into numbered verses (a scheme which in its present form is only four centuries old), the translators have made a constant effort to keep within an English verse the whole verbal content of the Greek verse. At times the effort has not seemed worth the result since it often does violence to the original author's flow of expression, which preceded it by so many centuries. If this translation had been prepared for purposes of public reading only, the editors would have forgone the effort at an early stage. But since they never departed from the threefold objective of preparing a translation suitable for liturgical use, private reading, and the purposes of students, the last-named consideration prevailed. Those familiar with Greek should be able to discover how the translators of the New Testament have rendered any given original verse of scripture, if their exegetical or theological tasks require them to know this. At the same time, the fact should be set down here that the editors did not commit themselves in the synoptic gospels to rendering repeated words or phrases identically.

This leads to a final consideration: the Greek text used for the New Testament. Here, punctuation and verse division are at least as important as variant readings. In general, Nestle-Aland's *Novum Testamentum Graece* (25th edition, 1963) was followed. Additional help was derived from *The Greek New Testament* (Aland, Black, Metzger, Wikgren), produced for the use of translators by the United Bible Societies in 1966. However, the editors did not confine themselves strictly to these texts; at times, they inclined toward readings otherwise attested. The omission of alternative translations does not mean that the translators think them without merit, but only that in every case they had to make a choice.

Poorly attested readings do not occur in this translation. Doubtful readings of some merit appear within brackets; public readers may include such words or phrases, or omit them entirely without any damage to sense. Parentheses are used, as ordinarily in English, as a punctuation device. Material they enclose is in no sense textually doubtful. It is simply thought to be parenthetical in the intention of the biblical author, even though there is no such punctuation mark in Greek. The difficulty in dealing with quotation marks is well known. Since they do not appear in any form in the original text, wherever they occur here they constitute an editorial decision.

The work of translating the Bible has been characterized as "the sacred and apostolic work of interpreting the word of God and of presenting it to the laity in translations as clear as the difficulty of the matter and the limitations of human knowledge permit" (A. G. Cicognani, Apostolic Delegate, in *The Catholic Biblical Quarterly,* 6, [1944], 389-90). In the appraisal of the present work, it is hoped that the words of the encyclical *Divino afflante Spiritu* will serve as a guide: "Let all the sons of the church bear in mind that the efforts of these resolute laborers in the vineyard of the Lord should be judged not only with equity and justice but also with the greatest charity; all moreover should abhor that intemperate zeal which imagines that whatever is new should for that very reason be opposed or suspected."

Conscious of their personal limitations for the task thus defined, those who have prepared this text cannot expect that it will be considered perfect; but they can hope that it may deepen in its readers "the right understanding of the divinely given Scriptures," and awaken in them "that piety by which it behooves us to be grateful to the God of all providence, who from the throne of his majesty has sent these books as so many personal letters to his own children" *(Divino afflante Spiritu).*

PREFACE TO THE REVISED EDITION

The New Testament of *The New American Bible,* a fresh translation from the Greek text, was first published in complete form in 1970, together with the Old Testament translation that had been completed the previous year. Portions of the New Testament had appeared earlier, in somewhat different form, in the provisional Mass lectionary of 1964 and in the *Lectionary for Mass* of 1970.

Since 1970 many different printings of the New Testament have been issued by a number of publishers, both separately and in complete bibles, and the text has become widely known both in the United States and in other English-speaking countries. Most American Catholics have been influenced by it because of its widespread use in the liturgy, and it has received a generally favorable reception from many other Christians as well. It has taken its place among the standard contemporary translations of the New Testament, respected for its fidelity to the original and its attempt to render this into current American English.

Although the scriptures themselves are timeless, translations and explanations of them quickly become dated in an era marked by rapid cultural change to a degree never previously experienced. The explosion of biblical studies that has taken place in our century and the changing nature of our language itself require periodic adjustment both in translations and in the accompanying explanatory materials. The experience of actual use of the New Testament of *The New American Bible,* especially in oral proclamation, has provided a basis for further improvement. Accordingly, it was decided in 1978 to proceed with a thorough revision of the New Testament to reflect advances in scholarship and to satisfy needs identified through pastoral experience.

For this purpose a steering committee was formed to plan, organize, and direct the work of revision, to engage collaborators, and to serve as an editorial board to coordinate the work of the various revisers and to determine the final form of the text and the explanatory materials. Guidelines were drawn up and collaborators selected in 1978 and early 1979, and November of 1980 was established as the deadline for manuscripts. From December 1980 through September 1986 the editorial board met a total of fifty times and carefully reviewed and revised all the material in order to ensure accuracy and consistency of approach. The editors also worked together with the bishops' ad hoc committee that was appointed by the National Conference of Catholic Bishops in 1982 to oversee the revision.

The threefold purpose of the translation that was expressed in the preface to the first edition has been maintained in the revision: to provide a version suitable for liturgical proclamation, for private reading, and for purposes of study. Special attention has been given to the first of these purposes, since oral proclamation demands special qualities in a translation, and experience had provided insights and suggestions that could lead to improvement in this area. Efforts have also been made, however, to facilitate devotional reading by providing suitable notes and introductory materials, and to assist the student by achieving greater accuracy and consistency in the translation and supplying more abundant information in the introductions and notes.

The primary aim of the revision is to produce a version as accurate and faithful to the meaning of the Greek original as is possible for a translation. The editors have consequently moved in the direction of a formal-equivalence approach to translation, matching the vocabulary, structure, and even word order of the original as closely as possible in the receptor language. Some other contemporary biblical versions have adopted, in varying degrees, a dynamic-equivalence approach, which attempts to respect the individuality of each language by expressing the meaning of the original in a linguistic structure suited to English, even though this may be very different from the corresponding Greek structure. While this approach often results in fresh and brilliant renderings, it has the disadvantages of more or less radically abandoning traditional biblical and liturgical terminology and phraseology, of expanding the text to include what more properly belongs in notes, commentaries, or preaching, and of tending toward paraphrase. A more formal approach seems better suited to the specific purposes intended for this translation.

At the same time, the editors have wished to produce a version in English that reflects contemporary American usage and is readily understandable to ordinary educated people, but one that will be recognized as dignified speech, on the level of formal rather than colloquial usage. These aims are not in fact contradictory, for there are different levels of language in current use: the language of formal situations is not that of colloquial conversation, though people understand both and may pass from one to the other without adverting to the transition. The liturgy is a formal situation that requires a level of discourse more dignified, formal, and hieratic than the world of business, sport, or informal communication. People readily understand this more formal level even though they may not often use it; our passive vocabulary is much larger than our active vocabulary. Hence this revision, while avoiding archaisms, does not shrink from traditional biblical terms that are easily understood even though not in common use in everyday speech. The level of language consciously aimed at is one appropriate for liturgical proclamation; this may also permit the translation to serve the purposes of devotional reading and serious study.

A particular effort has been made to ensure consistency of vocabulary. Always to translate a given Greek word by the same English equivalent would lead to ludicrous results and to infidelity to the meaning of the text. But in passages where a particular Greek term retains the same meaning, it has been rendered in the same way insofar as this has been feasible; this is particularly significant in the case of terms that have a specific theological meaning. The synoptic gospels have been carefully translated so as to reveal both the similarities and the differences of the Greek.

An especially sensitive problem today is the question of discrimination in language. In recent years there has been much discussion about allegations of anti-Jewish expressions in the New Testament and of language that discriminates against various minorities. Above all, however, the question of discrimination against women affects the largest number of people and arouses the greatest degree of interest and concern. At present there is little agreement about these problems or about the best way to deal with them. In all these areas the present translation attempts to display a sensitivity appropriate to the present state of the questions under discussion, which are not yet resolved and in regard to which it is impossible to please everyone, since intelligent and sincere participants in the debate hold mutually contradictory views.

The primary concern in this revision is fidelity to what the text says. When the meaning of the Greek is inclusive of both sexes, the translation seeks to reproduce such inclusivity insofar as this is possible in normal English usage, without resort to inelegant circumlocutions or neologisms that would offend against the dignity of the language. Although the generic sense of *man* is traditional in English, many today reject it; its use has therefore generally been avoided, though it is retained in cases where no fully satisfactory equivalent could be found. English does not possess a gender-inclusive third personal pronoun in the singular, and this translation continues to use the masculine resumptive pronoun after *everyone* or *anyone,* in the traditional way, where this cannot be avoided without infidelity to the meaning.

The translation of the Greek word *adelphos,* particularly in the plural form *adelphoi,* poses an especially delicate problem. While the term literally means *brothers* or other male blood relatives, even in profane Greek the plural can designate two persons, one of either sex, who were born of the same parents. It was adopted by the early Christians to designate, in a figurative sense, the members of the Christian community, who were conscious of a new familial relationship to one another by reason of their adoption as children of God. They are consequently addressed as *adelphoi.* This has traditionally been rendered into English by *brothers* or, more archaically, *brethren.* There has never been any doubt that this designation includes *all* the members of the Christian community, both male and female. Given the absence in English of a corresponding term that explicitly includes both sexes, this translation retains the usage of *brothers,* with the inclusive meaning that has been traditionally attached to it in this biblical context.

Since the New Testament is the product of a particular time and culture, the views expressed in it and the language in which they are expressed reflect a particular cultural conditioning, which sometimes makes them quite different from contemporary ideas and concerns. Discriminatory language should be eliminated insofar as possible whenever it is unfaithful to the meaning of the New Testament, but the text should not be altered in order to adjust it to contemporary concerns. This translation does not introduce any changes, expansions, additions to, or subtractions from the text of scripture. It further retains the traditional biblical ways of speaking about God and about Christ, including the use of masculine nouns and pronouns.

The Greek text followed in this translation is that of the third edition of *The Greek New Testament,* edited by Kurt Aland, Matthew Black, Carlo Martini, Bruce Metzger, and Allen Wikgren, and published by the United Bible Societies in 1975. The same text, with a different critical apparatus and variations in punctuation and typography, was published as the twenty-sixth edition of the Nestle-Aland *Novum Testamentum Graece* in 1979 by the Deutsche Bibelstiftung, Stuttgart. This edition has also been consulted. When variant readings occur, the translation, with few exceptions, follows the reading that was placed in the text of these Greek editions, though the occurrence of the principal variants is pointed out in the notes.

The editors of the Greek text placed square brackets around words or portions of words of which the authenticity is questionable because the evidence of textual witnesses is inconclusive. The same has been done in the translation insofar as it is possible to reproduce this convention in English. It should be possible to read the text either with or without the disputed words, but in English it is not always feasible to provide this alternative, and in some passages the bracketed words must be included to make sense. As in the first edition, parentheses do not indicate textual uncertainty, but are simply a punctuation device to indicate a passage that in the editors' judgment appears parenthetical to the thought of the author.

Citations from the Old Testament are placed within quotation marks; longer citations are set off as block quotations in a separate indented paragraph. The sources of such citations, as well as those of many more or less subtle allusions to the Old Testament, are identified in the biblical cross-reference section at the bottom of each page. Insofar as possible, the translation of such Old Testament citations agrees with that of *The New American Bible* Old Testament whenever the underlying Greek agrees with the Hebrew (or, in some cases, the Aramaic or Greek) text from which the Old Testament translation was made. But citations in the New Testament frequently follow the Septuagint or some other version, or were made from memory; hence, in many cases the translation in the New Testament passage will not agree with what appears in the Old Testament. Some of these cases are explained in the notes.

It is a further aim of the revised edition to supply explanatory materials more abundantly than in the first edition. In most cases the introductions and notes have been entirely rewritten and expanded, and the cross-references checked and revised. It is intended that these materials should reflect the present state of sound biblical scholarship and should be presented in such a form that they can be assimilated by the ordinary intelligent reader without specialized biblical training. While they have been written with the ordinary educated Christian in mind, not all technical vocabulary can be entirely dispensed with in approaching the Bible, any more than in any other field. It is the hope of the editors that these materials, even if they sometimes demand an effort, will help the reader to a fuller and more intelligent understanding of the New Testament and a fruitful appropriation of its meaning for personal spiritual growth.

The New American Bible is a Roman Catholic translation. This revision, however, like the first edition, has been accomplished with the collaboration of scholars from other Christian churches, both among the revisers and on the editorial board, in response to the encouragement of Vatican Council II *(Dei Verbum,* 22). The editorial board expresses gratitude to all who have collaborated in the revision: to all the revisers, consultants, and bishops who contributed to it, to reviewers of the first edition, and to those who voluntarily submitted suggestions. May this translation fulfill its threefold purpose, "so that the word of the Lord may speed forward and be glorified" (2 Thes 3, 1).

The Feast of St. Jerome
September 30, 1986

THE REVISED NEW TESTAMENT

BOOKS OF THE NEW TESTAMENT

THE GOSPELS

The collection of writings that constitutes the New Testament begins with four gospels. Next comes the Acts of the Apostles, followed by twenty-one letters that are attributed to Paul, James, Peter, John, and Jude. Finally, at the end of the early church's scriptures stands the Revelation to John. Virtually all Christians agree that these twenty-seven books constitute the "canon," a term that means "rule" and designates the list of writings that are regarded as authoritative for Christian faith and life.

It is the purpose of this Introduction to describe those features that are common to the four gospels. A similar treatment of the letters of the New Testament is provided in the two Introductions that appear before the Letter to the Romans and before the Letter of James, respectively. The Acts of the Apostles, a work that is both historical and theological, and Revelation, an apocalyptic work, have no counterparts in the New Testament; the special Introductions prefixed to these books treat of the literary characteristics proper to each of them.

While the New Testament contains four writings called "gospels," there is in reality only one gospel running through all of the Christian scriptures, the gospel of and about Jesus Christ. Our English word "gospel" translates the Greek term *euangelion,* meaning "good news." This noun was used in the plural by the Greek translators of the Old Testament to render the Hebrew term for "good news" (2 Sm 4, 10; possibly also 18, 22.25). But it is the corresponding verb *euangelizomai,* "to proclaim good news," that was especially significant in preparing for the New Testament idea of "gospel," since this term is used by Deutero-Isaiah for announcing the great victory of God that was to establish his universal kingship and inaugurate the new age (Is 40, 9; 52, 7; 61, 1).

Paul used the word *euangelion* to designate the message that he and the other apostles proclaimed, the "gospel of God" (Rom 1, 1; 15, 16; 2 Cor 11, 7; 1 Thes 2, 2.8.9). He often referred to it simply as "the gospel" (Rom 1, 16; 10, 16; 11, 28; etc) or, because of its content and origin, as "the gospel of Christ" (Rom 15, 19; 1 Cor 9, 12; 1 Thes 3, 2; etc). Because of its personal meaning for him and his own particular manner of telling the story about Jesus Christ and of explaining the significance of his cross and resurrection, Paul also referred to this message as "my gospel" (Rom 2, 16; cf Gal 1, 11; 2, 2) or "our gospel" (2 Cor 4, 3; 1 Thes 1, 5; 2 Thes 2, 14).

It was Mark, as far as we know, who first applied the term "gospel" to a book telling the story of Jesus; see Mk 1, 1 and the note there. This form of presenting Jesus' life, works, teachings, passion, and resurrection was developed further by the other evangelists; see the Introduction to each gospel. The first three of the canonical gospels, Matthew, Mark, and Luke, are so similar at many points when viewed together, particularly when arranged in parallel columns or lines, that they are called "synoptic" gospels, from the Greek word for such a general view. The fourth gospel, John, often differs significantly from the synoptics in outline and approach. This work never uses the word "gospel" or its corresponding verb; nevertheless, its message concerns the same Jesus, and the reader is urged to believe in him as the Messiah, "that through this belief you may have life in his name" (20, 31).

4

From the second century onward, the practice arose of designating each of these four books as a "gospel," understood as a title, and of adding a phrase with a name that identified the traditional author, e.g., "The Gospel according to Matthew." The arrangement of the canon that was adopted, with the four gospels grouped together at the beginning followed by Acts, provides a massive focus upon Jesus and allows Acts to serve as a framework for the letters of the New Testament. This order, however, conceals the fact that Luke's two volumes, a gospel and Acts, were intended by their author to go together. It further obscures the point that Paul's letters were written before any of our gospels, though the sayings and deeds of Jesus stand behind all the New Testament writings.

THE GOSPEL ACCORDING TO MATTHEW

INTRODUCTION

The position of the Gospel according to Matthew as the first of the four gospels in the New Testament reflects both the view that it was the first to be written, a view that goes back to the late second century A.D., and the esteem in which it was held by the church; no other was so frequently quoted in the noncanonical literature of earliest Christianity. Although the majority of scholars now reject the opinion about the time of its composition, the high estimation of this work remains. The reason for that becomes clear upon study of the way in which Matthew presents his story of Jesus, the demands of Christian disciple- ship, and the breaking-in of the new and final age through the ministry but particularly through the death and resurrection of Jesus.

The gospel begins with a narrative prologue (1, 1— 2, 23), the first part of which is a genealogy of Jesus starting with Abraham, the father of Israel (1, 1-17). Yet at the be- ginning of that genealogy Jesus is designated as "the son of David, the son of Abraham" (1, 1). The kingly ancestor who lived about a thousand years after Abraham is named first, for this is the genealogy of Jesus Christ, the Messiah, the royal anointed one (1, 16). In the first of the episodes of the infancy narrative that follow the genealogy, the mystery of Jesus' person is declared. He is conceived of a virgin by the power of the Spirit of God (1, 18-25). The first of the gospel's fulfillment citations, whose purpose it is to show that he was the one to whom the prophecies of Israel were pointing, occurs here (1, 23): he shall be named Emmanuel, for in him God is with us.

The announcement of the birth of this newborn king of the Jews greatly troubles not only King Herod but all Jerusalem (2, 1-3), yet the Gentile magi are overjoyed to find him and offer him their homage and their gifts (2, 10-11). Thus his ultimate rejection by the mass of his own people and his acceptance by the Gentile nations is foreshadowed. He must be taken to Egypt to escape the murderous plan of Herod. By his sojourn there and his subsequent return after the king's death he relives the Exodus experience of Israel. The words of the Lord spoken through the prophet Hosea, "Out of Egypt I called my son," are fulfilled in him (2, 15); if Israel was God's son, Jesus is so in a way far surpassing the dig- nity of that nation, as his marvelous birth and the unfolding of his story show (see 3, 17; 4, 1-11; 11, 27; 14, 33; 16, 16; 27, 54). Back in the land of Israel, he must be taken to Nazareth in Galilee because of the danger to his life in Judea, where Herod's son Arch- elaus is now ruling (2, 22-23). The sufferings of Jesus in the infancy narrative anticipate those of his passion, and if his life is spared in spite of the dangers, it is because his des- tiny is finally to give it on the cross as "a ransom for many" (20, 28). Thus the word of the angel will be fulfilled, ". . . he will save his people from their sins" (1, 21; cf 26, 28).

In 4, 12 Matthew begins his account of the ministry of Jesus, introducing it by the preparatory preaching of John the Baptist (3, 1-12), the baptism of Jesus that culminates in God's proclaiming him his "beloved Son" (3, 13-17), and the temptation in which he proves his true sonship by his victory over the devil's attempt to deflect him from the way of obedience to the Father (4, 1-11). The central message of Jesus' preaching is the com- ing of the kingdom of heaven and the need for repentance, a complete change of heart and conduct, on the part of those who are to receive this great gift of God (4, 17). Galilee is the setting for most of his ministry; he leaves there for Judea only in 19, 1, and his ministry in Jerusalem, the goal of his journey, is limited to a few days (21, 1—25, 46).

In this extensive material there are five great discourses of Jesus, each concluding with the formula "When Jesus finished these words" or one closely similar (7, 28; 11, 1; 13, 53; 19, 1; 26, 1). These are an important structure of the gospel. In every case the dis- course is preceded by a narrative section, each narrative and discourse together constitut-

ing a "book" of the gospel. The discourses are, respectively, the "Sermon on the Mount" (5, 3—7, 27), the missionary discourse (10, 5-42), the parable discourse (13, 3-52), the "church order" discourse (18, 3-35), and the eschatological discourse (24, 4—25, 46). In large measure the material of these discourses came to Matthew from his tradition, but his work in modifying and adding to what he had received is abundantly evident. No other evangelist gives the teaching of Jesus with such elegance and order as he.

In the "Sermon on the Mount" the theme of righteousness is prominent, and even at this early stage of the ministry the note of opposition is struck between Jesus and the Pharisees, who are designated as "the hypocrites" (6, 2.5.16). The righteousness of his disciples must surpass that of the scribes and Pharisees; otherwise, in spite of their alleged following of Jesus, they will not enter into the kingdom of heaven (5, 20). Righteousness means doing the will of the heavenly Father (7, 21), and his will is proclaimed in a manner that is startling to all who have identified it with the law of Moses. The antitheses of the Sermon (5, 21-48) both accept (5, 21-30.43-48) and reject (5, 31-42) elements of that law, and in the former case the understanding of the law's demands is deepened and extended. The antitheses are the best commentary on the meaning of Jesus' claim that he has come not to abolish but to fulfill the law (5, 17). What is meant by fulfillment of the law is not the demand to keep it exactly as it stood before the coming of Jesus, but rather his bringing the law to be a lasting expression of the will of God, and in that fulfillment there is much that will pass away. Should this appear contradictory to his saying that "until heaven and earth pass away" not even the smallest part of the law will pass (5, 18), that time of fulfillment is not the dissolution of the universe but the coming of the new age, which will occur with Jesus' death and resurrection. While righteousness in the new age will continue to mean conduct that is in accordance with the law, it will be conduct in accordance with the law as expounded and interpreted by Jesus (cf 28, 20, ". . . all that I have commanded you").

Though Jesus speaks harshly about the Pharisees in the Sermon, his judgment is not solely a condemnation of them. The Pharisees are portrayed as a negative example for his disciples, and his condemnation of those who claim to belong to him while disobeying his word is no less severe (7, 21-23.26-27).

In 4, 23 a summary statement of Jesus' activity speaks not only of his teaching and proclaiming the gospel but of his "curing every disease and illness among the people"; this is repeated almost verbatim in 9, 35. The narrative section that follows the Sermon on the Mount (8, 1—9, 38) is composed principally of accounts of those merciful deeds of Jesus, but it is far from being simply a collection of stories about miraculous cures. The nature of the community that Jesus will establish is shown; it will always be under the protection of him whose power can deal with all dangers (8, 23-27), but it is only for those who are prepared to follow him at whatever cost (8, 16-22), not only believing Israelites but Gentiles who have come to faith in him (8, 10-12). The disciples begin to have some insight, however imperfect, into the mystery of Jesus' person. They wonder about him whom "the winds and the sea obey" (8, 27), and they witness his bold declaration of the forgiveness of the paralytic's sins (9, 2). That episode of the narrative moves on two levels. When the crowd sees the cure that testifies to the authority of Jesus, the Son of Man, to forgive sins (9, 6), they glorify God "who had given such authority to human beings" (9, 8). The forgiveness of sins is now not the prerogative of Jesus alone but of "human beings," that is, of the disciples who constitute the community of Jesus, the church. The ecclesial character of this narrative section could hardly be more plainly indicated.

The end of the section prepares for the discourse on the church's mission (10, 5-42). Jesus is moved to pity at the sight of the crowds who are like sheep without a shepherd

(9, 36), and he sends out the twelve disciples to make the proclamation with which his own ministry began, "The kingdom of heaven is at hand" (10, 7; cf 4, 17), and to drive out demons and cure the sick as he has done (10, 1). Their mission is limited to Israel (10, 5-6) as Jesus' own was (15, 24), yet in v 16 that perspective broadens and the discourse begins to speak of the mission that the disciples will have after the resurrection and of the severe persecution that will attend it (10, 18). Again, the discourse moves on two levels: that of the time of Jesus and that of the time of the church.

The narrative section of the third book (11, 2—12, 50) deals with the growing opposition to Jesus. Hostility toward him has already been manifested (8, 10; 9, 3.10-13.34), but here it becomes more intense. The rejection of Jesus comes, as before, from Pharisees, who take "counsel against him to put him to death" (12, 14) and repeat their earlier accusation that he drives out demons because he is in league with demonic power (12, 22-24). But they are not alone in their rejection. Jesus complains of the lack of faith of "this generation" of Israelites (11, 16-19) and reproaches the towns "where most of his mighty deeds had been done" for not heeding his call to repentance (11, 20-24). This dark picture is relieved by Jesus' praise of the Father who has enabled "the childlike" to accept him (11, 25-27), but on the whole the story is one of opposition to his word and blindness to the meaning of his deeds. The whole section ends with his declaring that not even the most intimate blood relationship with him counts for anything; his only true relatives are those who do the will of his heavenly Father (12, 48-50).

The narrative of rejection leads up to the parable discourse (13, 3-52). The reason given for Jesus' speaking to the crowds in parables is that they have hardened themselves against his clear teaching, unlike the disciples to whom knowledge of "the mysteries of the kingdom has been granted" (13, 10-16). In 13, 36 he dismisses the crowds and continues the discourse to his disciples alone, who claim, at the end, to have understood all that he has said (13, 51). But, lest the impression be given that the church of Jesus is made up only of true disciples, the explanation of the parable of the weeds among the wheat (13, 37-43), as well as the parable of the net thrown into the sea "which collects fish of every kind" (13, 47-49), shows that it is composed of both the righteous and the wicked, and that separation between the two will be made only at the time of the final judgment.

In the narrative that constitutes the first part of the fourth book of the gospel (13, 54—17, 27), Jesus is shown preparing for the establishment of his church with its teaching authority that will supplant the blind guidance of the Pharisees (15, 13-14), whose teaching, curiously said to be that of the Sadducees also, is repudiated by Jesus as the norm for his disciples (16,6.11-12). The church of Jesus will be built on Peter (16, 18), who will be given authority to bind and loose on earth, an authority whose exercise will be confirmed in heaven (16, 19). The metaphor of binding and loosing has a variety of meanings, among them that of giving authoritative teaching. This promise is made to Peter directly after he has confessed Jesus to be the Messiah, the Son of the living God (16, 16), a confession that he has made as the result of revelation given to him by the heavenly Father (16, 17); Matthew's ecclesiology is based on his high christology.

Directly after that confession Jesus begins to instruct his disciples about how he must go the way of suffering and death (16, 21). Peter, who has been praised for his confession, protests against this and receives from Jesus the sharpest of rebukes for attempting to deflect Jesus from his God-appointed destiny. The future rock upon whom the church will be built is still a man of "little faith" (see 14, 31). Both he and the other disciples must know not only that Jesus will have to suffer and die but that they too will have to follow him on the way of the cross if they are truly to be his disciples (16, 24-25).

The discourse following this narrative (18, 1-35) is often called the "church order" discourse, although that title is perhaps misleading since the emphasis is not on the structure of the church but on the care that the disciples must have for one another in respect to guarding each other's faith in Jesus (18, 6-7), to seeking out those who have wandered from the fold (18, 10-14), and to repeated forgiving of their fellow disciples who have offended them (18, 21-35). But there is also the obligation to correct the sinful fellow Christian and, should one refuse to be corrected, separation from the community is demanded (18, 15-18).

The narrative of the fifth book (19, 1—23, 39) begins with the departure of Jesus and his disciples from Galilee for Jerusalem. In the course of their journey Jesus for the third time predicts the passion that awaits him at Jerusalem and also his resurrection (20, 17-19). At his entrance into the city he is hailed as the Son of David by the crowds accompanying him (21, 9). He cleanses the temple (21, 12-17), and in the few days of his Jerusalem ministry he engages in a series of controversies with the Jewish religious leaders (21, 23-27; 22, 15-22.23-33.34-40.41-46), meanwhile speaking parables against them (21, 28-32.33-46), against all those Israelites who have rejected God's invitation to the messianic banquet (22, 1-10), and against all, Jew and Gentile, who have accepted but have shown themselves unworthy of it (22, 11-14). Once again, the perspective of the evangelist includes not only the time of Jesus' ministry but that of the preaching of the gospel after his resurrection. The narrative culminates in Jesus' denunciation of the scribes and Pharisees, reflecting not only his own opposition to them but that of Matthew's church (23, 1-36), and in Jesus' lament over Jerusalem (23, 37-39).

In the discourse of the fifth book (24, 1—25, 46), the last of the great structural discourses of the gospel, Jesus predicts the destruction of the temple and his own final coming. The time of the latter is unknown (24, 36.44), and the disciples are exhorted in various parables to live in readiness for it, a readiness that entails faithful attention to the duties of the interim period (24, 45—25, 30). The coming of Jesus will bring with it the great judgment by which the everlasting destiny of all will be determined (25, 31-46).

The story of Jesus' passion and resurrection (26, 1—28, 20), the climax of the gospel, throws light on all that has preceded. In Mt "righteousness" means both the faithful response to the will of God demanded of all to whom that will is announced and also the saving activity of God for his people (see 3, 15; 5, 6; 6, 33). The passion supremely exemplifies both meanings of that central Matthean word. In Jesus' absolute faithfulness to the Father's will that he drink the cup of suffering (26, 39), the incomparable model for Christian obedience is given; in his death "for the forgiveness of sins" (26, 28), the saving power of God is manifested as never before.

Matthew's portrayal of Jesus in his passion combines both the majestic serenity of the obedient Son who goes his destined way in fulfillment of the scriptures (26, 52-54), confident of his ultimate vindication by God, and the depths of fear and abandonment that he feels in face of death (26, 38-39; 27, 46). These two aspects are expressed by an Old Testament theme that occurs often in the narrative, i.e., the portrait of the suffering Righteous One who complains to God in his misery, but is certain of eventual deliverance from his terrible ordeal.

The passion-resurrection of God's Son means nothing less than the turn of the ages, a new stage of history, the coming of the Son of Man in his kingdom (28, 18; cf 16, 28). That is the sense of the apocalyptic signs that accompany Jesus' death (27, 51-53) and resurrection (28, 2). Although the old age continues, as it will until the manifestation of Jesus' triumph at his parousia, the final age has now begun. This is known only to those who have seen the Risen One and to those, both Jews and Gentiles, who have believed in *their announcement of Jesus' triumph and have themselves become his disciples (cf 28, 19). To them he is constantly, though invisibly, present (28, 20), verifying the name Emmanuel, "God is with us" (cf 1, 23).*

The questions of authorship, sources, and the time of composition of this gospel have received many answers, none of which can claim more than a greater or lesser degree of probability. The one now favored by the majority of scholars is the following.

The ancient tradition that the author was the disciple and apostle of Jesus named Matthew (see 10, 3) is untenable because the gospel is based, in large part, on the Gospel according to Mark (almost all the verses of that gospel have been utilized in this), and it is hardly likely that a companion of Jesus would have followed so extensively an account that came from one who admittedly never had such an association rather than rely on his own memories. The attribution of the gospel to the disciple Matthew may have been due to his having been responsible for some of the traditions found in it, but that is far from certain.

The unknown author, whom we shall continue to call Matthew for the sake of convenience, drew not only upon the Gospel according to Mark but upon a large body of material (principally, sayings of Jesus) not found in Mk that corresponds, sometimes exactly, to material found also in the Gospel according to Luke. This material, called "Q" (probably from the first letter of the German word Quelle, *meaning "source"), represents traditions, written and oral, used by both Matthew and Luke. Mark and Q are sources common to the two other synoptic gospels; hence the name the "Two-Source Theory" given to this explanation of the relation among the synoptics.*

In addition to what Matthew drew from Mk and Q, his gospel contains material that is found only there. This is often designated "M," written or oral tradition that was available to the author. Since Mk was written shortly before or shortly after A.D. 70 (see Introduction to Mk), Mt was composed certainly after that date, which marks the fall of Jerusalem to the Romans at the time of the First Jewish Revolt (A.D. 66-70), and probably at least a decade later since Matthew's use of Mk presupposes a wide diffusion of that gospel. The post-A.D. 70 date is confirmed within the text by 22, 7, which refers to the destruction of Jerusalem.

As for the place where the gospel was composed, a plausible suggestion is that it was Antioch, the capital of the Roman province of Syria. That large and important city had a mixed population of Greek-speaking Gentiles and Jews. The tensions between Jewish and Gentile Christians there in the time of Paul (see Gal 2, 1-14) in respect to Christian obligation to observe Mosaic law are partially similar to tensions that can be seen between the two groups in Matthew's gospel. The church of Matthew, originally strongly Jewish Christian, had become one in which Gentile Christians were predominant. His gospel answers the question how obedience to the will of God is to be expressed by those who live after the "turn of the ages," the death and resurrection of Jesus.

The principal divisions of the Gospel according to Matthew are the following:

    I.   The Infancy Narrative (1, 1—2, 23)
   II.   The Proclamation of the Kingdom (3, 1—7, 29)
  III.   Ministry and Mission in Galilee (8, 1—11, 1)
  IV.   Opposition from Israel (11, 2—13, 53)
   V.   Jesus, the Kingdom, and the Church (13, 54—18, 35)
  VI.   Ministry in Judea and Jerusalem (19, 1—25, 46)
 VII.   The Passion and Resurrection (26, 1—28, 20)

I. THE INFANCY NARRATIVE*

CHAPTER 1

The Genealogy of Jesus. [1] [a] The book of the genealogy of Jesus Christ, the son of David, the son of Abraham.*

[2] [b] Abraham became the father of Isaac, Isaac the father of Jacob, Jacob the father of Judah and his brothers.[c] [3] Judah became the father of Perez and Zerah, whose mother was Tamar.[d] Perez became the father of Hezron, Hezron the father of Ram, [4] [e] Ram the father of Amminadab. Amminadab became the father of Nahshon, Nahshon the father of Salmon, [5] [f] Salmon the father of Boaz, whose mother was Rahab. Boaz became the father of Obed, whose mother was Ruth. Obed became the father of Jesse, [6] [g] Jesse the father of David the king.

David became the father of Solomon, whose mother had been the wife of Uriah. [7] [h] Solomon became the father of Rehoboam, Rehoboam the father of Abijah, Abijah the father of Asaph.* [8] Asaph became the father of Jehoshaphat, Jehoshaphat the father of Joram, Joram the father of Uzziah. [9] Uzziah became the father of Jotham, Jotham the father of Ahaz, Ahaz the father of Hezekiah. [10] Hezekiah became the father of Manasseh, Manasseh the father of Amos,* Amos the father of Josiah. [11] Josiah became the father of Jechoniah and his brothers at the time of the Babylonian exile.

[12] [i] After the Babylonian exile, Jechoniah became the father of Shealtiel, Shealtiel the father of Zerubbabel, [13] Zerubbabel the father of Abiud. Abiud became the father of Eliakim, Eliakim the father of Azor, [14] Azor the father of Zadok. Zadok became the father of Achim, Achim the father of Eliud, [15] Eliud the father of Eleazar. Eleazar became the father of Matthan, Matthan the father of Jacob, [16] Jacob the father of Joseph, the husband of Mary. Of her was born Jesus who is called the Messiah.

[17] Thus the total number of generations from Abraham to David is fourteen generations; from David to the Babylonian exile, fourteen generations; from the Babylonian exile to the Messiah, fourteen generations.*

The Birth of Jesus.* [18] Now this is how the birth of Jesus Christ came about.

a Gn 5, 1 / 1 Chr 17, 11 / Gn 22, 18.—b 2-17: Lk 3, 23-38.—c Gn 21, 3; 25, 26; 29, 35; 1 Chr 2, 1.—d Gn 38, 29-30; Ru 4, 18; 1 Chr 2, 4-9.—e Ru 4, 19-20; 1 Chr 2, 10-11.—f Ru 4, 21-22; 1 Chr 2, 11-12.—g 2 Sm 12, 24; 1 Chr 2, 15; 3, 5.—h 7-11: 2 Kgs 25, 1-21; 1 Chr 3, 10-15.— i 12-16: 1 Chr 3, 16-19.

1, 1—2, 23: The infancy narrative forms the prologue of the gospel. Consisting of a genealogy and five stories, it presents the coming of Jesus as the climax of Israel's history, and the events of his conception, birth, and early childhood as the fulfillment of Old Testament prophecy. The genealogy is probably traditional material that Matthew edited. In its first two sections (Mt 1, 2-11) it was drawn from Ru 4, 18-22 and 1 Chr 1—3. Except for Jechoniah, Shealtiel, and Zerubbabel, none of the names in the third section (Mt 1, 12-16) is found in any Old Testament genealogy. While the genealogy shows the continuity of God's providential plan from Abraham on, discontinuity is also present. The women Tamar (Mt 1, 3), Rahab and Ruth (Mt 1, 5), and the wife of Uriah, Bathsheba (Mt 1, 6), bore their sons through unions that were in varying degrees strange and unexpected. These "irregularities" culminate in the supreme "irregularity" of the Messiah's birth of a virgin mother; the age of fulfillment is inaugurated by a creative act of God.

Drawing upon both biblical tradition and Jewish stories, Matthew portrays Jesus as reliving the Exodus experience of Israel and the persecutions of Moses. His rejection by his own people and his passion are foreshadowed by the troubled reaction of "all Jerusalem" to the question of the magi who are seeking the "newborn king of the Jews" (Mt 2, 2-3), and by Herod's attempt to have him killed. The magi who do him homage prefigure the Gentiles who will accept the preaching of the gospel. The infancy narrative proclaims who Jesus is, the savior of his people from their sins (Mt 1, 21), Emmanuel in whom "God is with us" (Mt 1, 23), and the Son of God (Mt 2, 15).

1, 1: *The Son of David, the son of Abraham:* two links of the genealogical chain are singled out. Although the later, David is placed first in order to emphasize that Jesus is the royal Messiah. The mention of Abraham may be due not only to his being the father of the nation Israel but to Matthew's interest in the universal scope of Jesus' mission; cf Gn 22, 18, ". . . . in your descendants all the nations of the earth shall find blessing."

1, 7: The successor of Abijah was not Asaph but Asa (see 1 Chr 3, 10). Some textual witnesses read the latter name; however, *Asaph* is better attested. Matthew may have deliberately introduced the psalmist Asaph into the genealogy (and in v 10 the prophet Amos) in order to show that Jesus is the fulfillment not only of the promises made to David (see 2 Sm 7) but of all the Old Testament.

1, 10: *Amos:* some textual witnesses read *Amon,* who was the actual successor of Manasseh (see 1 Chr 3, 14).

1, 17: Matthew is concerned with fourteen generations, probably because fourteen is the numerical value of the Hebrew letters forming the name of David. In the second section of the genealogy (6b-11), three kings of Judah, Ahaziah, Joash, and Amaziah, have been omitted (see 1 Chr 3, 11-12), so that there are fourteen generations in that section. Yet the third (12-16) apparently has only thirteen. Since Matthew here emphasizes that each section has fourteen, it is unlikely that the thirteen of the last was due to his oversight. Some scholars suggest that *Jesus who is called the Messiah* (16b) doubles the final member of the chain: *Jesus,* born within the family of David, opens up the new age as *Messiah,* so that in fact there are fourteen generations in the third section. This is perhaps too subtle, and the hypothesis of a slip not on the part of Matthew but of a later scribe seems likely. On *Messiah,* see the note on Lk 2, 11.

1, 18-25: This first story of the infancy narrative spells out what is summarily indicated in v 16. The virginal conception of Jesus is the work of the Spirit of God. Joseph's decision to divorce Mary is overcome by the heavenly command that he take her into his home and accept the child as his own. The natural genealogical line is broken but the promises to David are fulfilled; through Joseph's adoption the child belongs to the family of David. Matthew sees the virginal conception as the fulfillment of Is 7, 14.

When his mother Mary was betrothed to Joseph,* but before they lived together, she was found with child through the holy Spirit. [19] Joseph her husband, since he was a righteous man,* yet unwilling to expose her to shame, decided to divorce her quietly. [20] j Such was his intention when, behold, the angel of the Lord* appeared to him in a dream and said, "Joseph, son of David, do not be afraid to take Mary your wife into your home. For it is through the holy Spirit that this child has been conceived in her. [21] She will bear a son and you are to name him Jesus,* because he will save his people from their sins." [22] All this took place to fulfill what the Lord had said through the prophet:

[23] k   "Behold, the virgin shall be with child
      and bear a son,
  and they shall name him Emmanuel,"

which means "God is with us."* [24] When Joseph awoke, he did as the angel of the Lord had commanded him and took his wife into his home. [25] He had no relations with her until she bore a son,* and he named him Jesus. l

CHAPTER 2

The Visit of the Magi. *[1] When Jesus was born in Bethlehem of Judea, in the days of King Herod,* behold, magi from the east arrived in Jerusalem, [2] saying, "Where is the newborn king of the Jews? We saw his star* at its rising and have come to do him homage." m [3] When King Herod heard this,

he was greatly troubled, and all Jerusalem with him. [4] Assembling all the chief priests and the scribes of the people, he inquired of them where the Messiah was to be born.* [5] n They said to him, "In Bethlehem of Judea, for thus it has been written through the prophet:

[6]   'And you, Bethlehem, land of Judah,
    are by no means least among the rulers of Judah;
  since from you shall come a ruler,
    who is to shepherd my people Israel.'"

[7] Then Herod called the magi secretly and ascertained from them the time of the star's appearance. [8] He sent them to Bethlehem and said, "Go and search diligently for the child. When you have found him, bring me word, that I too may go and do him homage." [9] After their audience with the king they set out. And behold, the star that they had seen at its rising preceded them, until it came and stopped over the place where the child was. [10] They were overjoyed at seeing the star, [11] o and on entering the house they saw the child with Mary his mother. They prostrated themselves and did him homage. Then they opened their treasures and offered him gifts of gold, frankincense, and myrrh.* [12] And having been warned in a dream not to return to Herod, they departed for their country by another way.

---

j Mt 2, 13.19; Lk 1, 35.—k Is 7, 14 LXX.—l Lk 2, 7.—m Nm 24, 17.—n 5-6: Mi 5, 1; 2 Sm 5, 2.—o Ps 72, 10-11.15; Is 60, 6.

1, 18: *Betrothed to Joseph:* betrothal was the first part of the marriage, constituting a man and woman as husband and wife. Subsequent infidelity was considered adultery. The betrothal was followed some months later by the husband's taking his wife into his home, at which time normal married life began.

1, 19: *A righteous man:* as a devout observer of the Mosaic law, Joseph wished to break his union with someone whom he suspected of gross violation of the law. It is commonly said that the law required him to do so, but the texts usually given in support of that view, e.g., Dt 22, 20-21, do not clearly pertain to Joseph's situation. *Unwilling to expose her to shame:* the penalty for proved adultery was death by stoning; cf Dt 22, 21-23.

1, 20: *The angel of the Lord:* in the Old Testament a common designation of God in communication with a human being. *In a dream:* see Mt 2, 13.19.22. These dreams may be meant to recall the dreams of Joseph, son of Jacob the patriarch (Gn 37, 5-11.19). A closer parallel is the dream of Amram, father of Moses, related by Josephus (*Antiquities* 2, 9, 3 §§212, 215-16).

1, 21: *Jesus:* in first-century Judaism the Hebrew name Joshua (Greek *Iēsous*) meaning "Yahweh helps" was interpreted as "Yahweh saves."

1, 23: *God is with us:* God's promise of deliverance to Judah in Isaiah's time is seen by Matthew as fulfilled in the birth of

Jesus, in whom God is with his people. The name Emmanuel is alluded to at the end of the gospel where the risen Jesus assures his disciples of his continued presence, ". . . I am with you always, until the end of the age" (Mt 28, 20).

1, 25: *Until she bore a son:* the evangelist is concerned to emphasize that Joseph was not responsible for the conception of Jesus. The Greek word translated "until" does not imply normal marital conduct after Jesus' birth, nor does it exclude it.

2, 1-12: The future rejection of Jesus by Israel and his acceptance by the Gentiles are retrojected into this scene of the narrative.

2, 1: *In the days of King Herod:* Herod reigned from 37 to 4 B.C. *Magi:* originally a designation of the Persian priestly caste, the word became used of those who were regarded as having more than human knowledge. Matthew's magi are astrologers.

2, 2: *We saw his star:* it was a common ancient belief that a new star appeared at the time of a ruler's birth. Matthew also draws upon the Old Testament story of Balaam, who had prophesied that "A star shall advance from Jacob" (Nm 24, 17), though there the star means not an astral phenomenon but the king himself.

2, 4: Herod's consultation with the chief priests and scribes has some similarity to a Jewish legend about the child Moses in which the "sacred scribes" warn Pharaoh about the imminent birth of one who will deliver Israel from Egypt and the king makes plans to destroy him.

2, 11: Cf Ps 72, 10.15; Is 60, 6. These Old Testament texts led to the interpretation of the magi as kings.

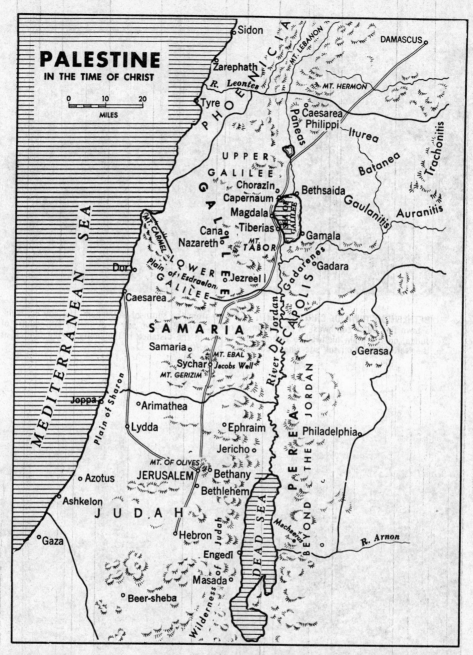

PALESTINE
IN THE TIME OF CHRIST

0   10   20
MILES

Sidon

DAMASCUS

Zarephath

R. Leontes

MT. LEBANON

MT. HERMON

Tyre

Caesarea
Philippi

Paneas

Iturea

Trachonitis

Batanea

UPPER
GALILEE

Chorazin

Bethsaida

Gaulanitis

Auranitis

Capernaum

SEA OF
GALILEE

Magdala

Tiberias

Gamala

Cana

MT. TABOR

Gadara

Nazareth

LOWER

GALILEE

MT. CARMEL

Jezreel

Gadarenes

Dor

Plain of Esdraelon

River Jordan

DECAPOLIS

Caesarea

SAMARIA

MEDITERRANEAN SEA

Samaria

Gerasa

Sychar
Jacobs Well

MT. EBAL

MT. GERIZIM

Joppa

Plain of Sharon

Arimathea

Ephraim

Philadelphia

Lydda

Jericho

PEREA

BEYOND THE JORDAN

MT. OF OLIVES

JERUSALEM

Bethany

Azotus

Bethlehem

Ashkelon

JUDAH

Machaerus

Gaza

Hebron

DEAD SEA

R. Arnon

Engedi

Wilderness of Judah

Masada

Beer-sheba

PALESTINE IN THE TIME OF CHRIST (37 B.C.—36 A.D.) — **(a)** Herod the Great becomes king under the Romans in 37 (and is kept by Caesar Augustus in 29). Herod's reign is one of continual fear of plots and he does not hesitate to execute his own relatives and children, while erecting magnificent edifices. **(b)** Jesus is born sometime before Herod's death (7-6 B.C.?). **(c)** In 4 B.C. Herod's kingdom is divided among his sons. Archelaus becomes ethnarch of Judea but is deposed in 6 A.D. and **Judea** and **Samaria** become part of the Roman province of Syria. Antipas becomes tetrarch of **Galilee** and **Perea** until 39 A.D. Philip becomes tetrarch of **Trachonitis** until his death in 34 A.D. **(d)** In 7 A.D. Annas is made high priest. **(e)** In 15 A.D. Tiberius Caesar becomes Roman Emperor. **(f)** In 26 A.D. Joseph Caiaphas is made high priest. **(g)** In 26 A.D. Pontius Pilate is sent as governor of Judea and outrages the Jews by letting the Romans bring ensigns into the temple.

BETHLEHEM: TOWN OF CHRIST'S BIRTH — A view from the south of Bethlehem, the city of David, a town five miles southwest of Jerusalem. It rises 2550 feet above sea level, in the hill country of Judea, on the main highway to Hebron and Egypt. In the distance is the belfry of the Church of the Nativity built on the site where Christ was born. (See Mt 2, 1)

NAZARETH: SCENE OF CHRIST'S EARLY LIFE — A view of Nazareth (from the east, taken from the ancient bridal-path to Tiberias), a town in lower Galilee located in a geographical basin blocking off the surrounding countryside. However, from the edge of the basin a distance of 30 miles can be seen in each direction. This was the home of the Holy Family after the flight into Egypt. (See Mt 2, 19-23)

The Flight to Egypt. 13 * When they had departed, behold, the angel of the Lord appeared to Joseph in a dream and said, "Rise, take the child and his mother, flee to Egypt,* and stay there until I tell you. Herod is going to search for the child to destroy him." 14 Joseph rose and took the child and his mother by night and departed for Egypt. 15 He stayed there until the death of Herod, that what the Lord had said through the prophet*p* might be fulfilled, "Out of Egypt I called my son."*

The Massacre of the Infants. 16 When Herod realized that he had been deceived by the magi, he became furious. He ordered the massacre of all the boys in Bethlehem and its vicinity two years old and under, in accordance with the time he had ascertained from the magi. 17 Then was fulfilled what had been said through Jeremiah the prophet:

18 *q* "A voice was heard in Ramah,
  sobbing and loud lamentation;
Rachel weeping for her children,
  and she would not be consoled,
  since they were no more."*

The Return from Egypt. 19 When Herod had died, behold, the angel of the Lord appeared in a dream to Joseph in Egypt 20 and said,*r* "Rise, take the child and his mother and go to the land of Israel, for those who sought the child's life are dead."* 21 He rose, took the child and his mother, and went to the land of Israel. 22 But when he heard that Archelaus was ruling over Judea in place of his father Herod,* he was afraid to go back there. And because he had been warned in a dream, he departed for the region of Galilee. 23 *s* He went and dwelt in a town called Nazareth, so that what had been spoken through the prophets might be fulfilled, "He shall be called a Nazorean."*

II. THE PROCLAMATION OF THE KINGDOM

CHAPTER 3

The Preaching of John the Baptist.*t* 1 In those days John the Baptist appeared, preaching in the desert of Judea* 2 [and] saying, "Repent,* for the kingdom of heaven is at hand!"*u* 3 It was of him that the prophet Isaiah*v* had spoken when he said:

"A voice of one crying out in the desert,
'Prepare the way of the Lord,
  make straight his paths.' " *

---

p Hos 11, 1.—q Jer 31, 15.—r Ex 4, 19.—s Mt 13, 54; Mk 1, 9; Lk 2, 39; 4, 34; Jn 19, 19.—t 1-12: Mk 1, 2-8; Lk 3, 2-17.—u Mt 4, 17; 10, 7.—v Is 40, 3.

2, 13-23: Biblical and nonbiblical traditions about Moses are here applied to the child Jesus, though the dominant Old Testament type is not Moses but Israel (see v 15).

2, 13: *Flee to Egypt:* Egypt was a traditional place of refuge for those fleeing from danger in Palestine (see 1 Kgs 11, 40; Jer 26, 21), but the main reason why the child is to be taken to Egypt is that he may relive the Exodus experience of Israel.

2, 15: The fulfillment citation is taken from Hos 11, 1. Israel, God's son, was called out of Egypt at the time of the Exodus; Jesus, the Son of God, will similarly be called out of that land in a new exodus. The father-son relationship between God and the nation is set in a higher key. Here the son is not a group adopted as "son of God," but the child who, as conceived by the holy Spirit, stands in unique relation to God. He is son of David and of Abraham, of Mary and of Joseph, but, above all, of God.

2, 18: Jer 31, 15 portrays Rachel, wife of the patriarch Jacob, weeping for her children taken into exile at the time of the Assyrian invasion of the northern kingdom (722-21 B.C.). Bethlehem was traditionally identified with Ephrath, the place near which Rachel was buried (see Gn 35, 19; 48, 7), and the mourning of Rachel is here applied to her lost children of a later age. *Ramah:* about six miles north of Jerusalem. The lamentation of Rachel is so great as to be heard at a far distance.

2, 20: *For those who sought the child's life are dead:* Moses, who had fled from Egypt because the Pharaoh sought to kill him (see Ex 2, 15), was told to return there, "for all the men who sought your life are dead" (Ex 4, 19).

2, 22: With the agreement of the emperor Augustus, Archelaus received half of his father's kingdom, including Judea, after Herod's death. He had the title "ethnarch" (i.e., "ruler of a nation") and reigned from 4 B.C. to A.D. 6.

2, 23: *Nazareth . . . he shall be called a Nazorean:* the tradition of Jesus' residence in Nazareth was firmly established, and Matthew sees it as being in accordance with the foreannounced plan of God. The town of Nazareth is not mentioned in the Old Testament, and no such prophecy can be found there. The vague expression "through the prophets" may be due to Matthew's seeing a connection between Nazareth and certain texts in which there are words with a remote similarity to the name of that town. Some such Old Testament texts are Is 11, 1 where the Davidic king of the future is called "a bud" (*nēṣer*) that shall blossom from the roots of Jesse, and Jgs 13, 5.7 where Samson, the future deliverer of Israel from the Philistines, is called one who shall be consecrated (a *nāzîr*) to God.

3, 1-12: Here Matthew takes up the order of Jesus' ministry found in the gospel of Mark, beginning with the preparatory preaching of John the Baptist.

3, 1: Unlike Luke, Matthew says nothing of the Baptist's origins and does not make him a relative of Jesus. *The desert of Judea:* the barren region west of the Dead Sea extending up the Jordan valley.

3, 2: *Repent:* the Baptist calls for a change of heart and conduct, a turning of one's life from rebellion to obedience toward God. *The kingdom of heaven is at hand:* "heaven" (literally, "the heavens") is a substitute for the name "God" that was avoided by devout Jews of the time out of reverence. The expression "the kingdom of heaven" occurs only in the gospel of Matthew. It means the effective rule of God over his people. In its fullness it includes not only human obedience to God's word, but the triumph of God over physical evils, supremely over death. In the expectation found in Jewish apocalyptic, the kingdom was to be ushered in by a judgment in which sinners would be condemned and perish, an expectation shared by the Baptist. This was modified in Christian understanding where the kingdom was seen as being established in stages, culminating with the parousia of Jesus.

3, 3: See the note on Jn 1, 23.

4 *w* John wore clothing made of camel's hair and had a leather belt around his waist. His food was locusts and wild honey.* 5 At that time Jerusalem, all Judea, and the whole region around the Jordan were going out to him 6 and were being baptized by him in the Jordan River as they acknowledged their sins.*

7 When he saw many of the Pharisees and Sadducees* coming to his baptism, he said to them, "You brood of vipers! Who warned you to flee from the coming wrath? *x* 8 Produce good fruit as evidence of your repentance. 9 And do not presume to say to yourselves, 'We have Abraham as our father.' For I tell you, God can raise up children to Abraham from these stones. *y* 10 Even now the ax lies at the root of the trees. Therefore every tree that does not bear good fruit will be cut down and thrown into the fire. 11 *z* I am baptizing you with water, for repentance, but the one who is coming after me is mightier than I. I am not worthy to carry his sandals. He will baptize you with the holy Spirit and fire.* 12 *a* His winnowing fan is in his hand. He will clear his threshing floor and gather his wheat into his barn, but the chaff he will burn with unquenchable fire."*

The Baptism of Jesus.* 13 *b* Then Jesus came from Galilee to John at the Jordan to be baptized by him. 14 *John tried to prevent him, saying, "I need to be baptized by you, and yet you are coming to me?" 15 Jesus said to him in reply, "Allow it now, for thus it is fitting for us to fulfill all righteousness." Then he allowed him. 16 *c* After Jesus was baptized, he came up from the water and behold, the heavens were opened [for him], and he saw the Spirit of God descending like a dove [and] coming upon him.* 17 And a voice came from the heavens, saying, "This is my beloved Son,* with whom I am well pleased."*d*

CHAPTER 4

The Temptation of Jesus.* 1 *e* Then Jesus was led by the Spirit into the desert to be tempted by the devil. 2 *f* He fasted for forty days and forty nights,* and afterwards he

---

w Mt 11, 7-8; 2 Kgs 1, 8; Zec 13, 4.—x Mt 12, 34; 23, 33; Is 59, 5.—y Jn 8, 33.39; Rom 9, 7-8; Gal 4, 21-31.—z Jn 1, 26-27.33; Acts 1, 5.—a Mt 13, 30; Is 41, 16; Jer 15, 7.—b 13-17: Mk 1, 9-11; Lk 3, 21-22; Jn 1, 31-34.—c Is 42, 1.—d Mt 12, 18; 17, 5; Gn 22, 2; Ps 2, 7; Is 42, 1.—e 1-11: Mk 1, 12-13; Lk 4, 1-13.—f Ex 24, 18; Dt 8, 2.

3, 4: The clothing of John recalls the austere dress of the prophet Elijah (2 Kgs 1, 8). The expectation of the return of Elijah from heaven to prepare Israel for the final manifestation of God's kingdom was widespread, and according to Matthew this expectation was fulfilled in the Baptist's ministry (Mt 11, 14; 17, 11-13).

3, 6: Ritual washing was practiced by various groups in Palestine between 150 B.C. and A.D. 250. John's baptism may have been related to the purificatory washings of the Essenes at Qumran.

3, 7: *Pharisees and Sadducees:* the former were marked by devotion to the law, written and oral, and the scribes, experts in the law, belonged predominantly to this group. The Sadducees were the priestly aristocratic party, centered in Jerusalem. They accepted as scripture only the first five books of the Old Testament, followed only the letter of the law, rejected the oral legal traditions, and were opposed to teachings not found in the Pentateuch, such as the resurrection of the dead. Matthew links both of these groups together as enemies of Jesus (Mt 16, 1.6.11.12; cf Mk 8, 11-13.15). The threatening words that follow are addressed to them rather than to "the crowds" as in Lk 3, 7. *The coming wrath:* the judgment that will bring about the destruction of unrepentant sinners.

3, 11: *Baptize you with the holy Spirit and fire:* the water baptism of John will be followed by an "immersion" of the repentant in the cleansing power of the Spirit of God, and of the unrepentant in the destroying power of God's judgment. However, some see *the holy Spirit* and *fire* as synonymous, and the effect of this "baptism" as either purification or destruction. See the note on Lk 3, 16.

3, 12: The discrimination between the good and the bad is compared to the procedure by which a farmer separates wheat and chaff. The *winnowing fan* was a forklike shovel with which the threshed wheat was thrown into the air. The kernels fell to the ground; the light chaff, blown off by the wind, was gathered and burned up.

3, 13-17: The baptism of Jesus is the occasion on which he is equipped for his ministry by the holy Spirit and proclaimed to be the Son of God.

3, 14-15: This dialogue, peculiar to Matthew, reveals John's awareness of Jesus' superiority to him as the mightier one who is coming and who will baptize with the holy Spirit (11). His reluctance to admit Jesus among the sinners whom he is baptizing with water is overcome by Jesus' response. *To fulfill all righteousness:* in this gospel to *fulfill* usually refers to fulfillment of prophecy, and *righteousness* to moral conduct in conformity with God's will. Here, however, as in Mt 5, 6 and Mt 6, 33, *righteousness* seems to mean the saving activity of God. *To fulfill all righteousness* is to submit to the plan of God for the salvation of the human race. This involves Jesus' identification with sinners; hence the propriety of his accepting John's baptism.

3, 16: *The Spirit . . . coming upon him:* cf Is 42, 1.

3, 17: *This is my beloved Son:* the Marcan address to Jesus (Mk 1, 11) is changed into a proclamation. The Father's voice speaks in terms that reflect Is 42, 1, Ps 2, 7, and Gn 22, 2.

4, 1-11: Jesus, proclaimed Son of God at his baptism, is subjected to a triple temptation. Obedience to the Father is a characteristic of true sonship, and Jesus is tempted by the devil to rebel against God, overtly in the third case, more subtly in the first two. Each refusal of Jesus is expressed in language taken from the Book of Deuteronomy (Dt 8, 3; 6, 13.16). The testings of Jesus resemble those of Israel during the wandering in the desert and later in Canaan, and the victory of Jesus, the true Israel and the true Son, contrasts with the failure of the ancient and disobedient "son," the old Israel. In the temptation account Matthew is almost identical with Luke; both seem to have drawn upon the same source.

4, 2: *Forty days and forty nights:* the same time as that during which Moses remained on Sinai (Ex 24, 18). The time reference, however, seems primarily intended to recall the forty years during which Israel was tempted in the desert (Dt 8, 2).

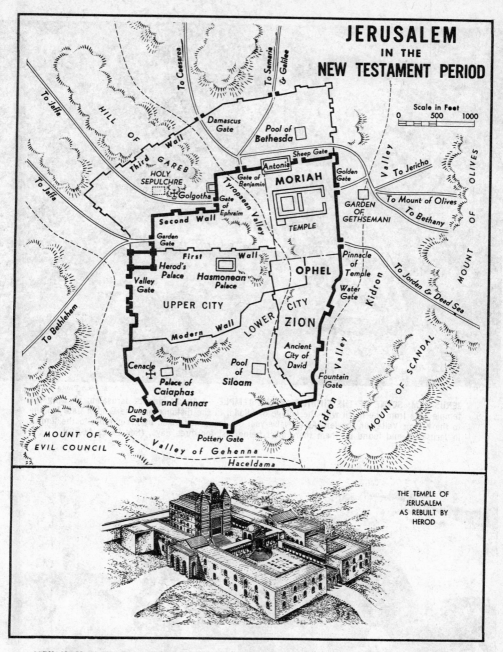

Map labels:

JERUSALEM IN THE NEW TESTAMENT PERIOD

Scale in Feet — 0 500 1000

To Caesarea · To Samaria & Galilee · To Jaffa · HILL OF GAREB · Third Wall · Damascus Gate · Pool of Bethesda · Sheep Gate · To Jericho · HOLY SEPULCHRE · Antonia · Golden Gate · Golgotha · Gate of Benjamin · MORIAH · GARDEN OF GETHSEMANI · To Mount of Olives · To Bethany · Gate of Ephraim · Tyropoeen Valley · TEMPLE · Second Wall · Garden Gate · First Wall · Pinnacle of Temple · MOUNT OF OLIVES · Herod's Palace · Hasmonean Palace · OPHEL · Water Gate · Kidron · To Jordan & Dead Sea · Valley Gate · UPPER CITY · LOWER CITY · ZION · Modern Wall · Ancient City of David · Cenacle · Pool of Siloam · Fountain Gate · Palace of Caiaphas and Annas · Dung Gate · Kidron Valley · MOUNT OF SCANDAL · Pottery Gate · MOUNT OF EVIL COUNCIL · Valley of Gehenna · Haceldama

THE TEMPLE OF JERUSALEM AS REBUILT BY HEROD

JERUSALEM IN THE NEW TESTAMENT PERIOD — **(a)** This period in the history of Jerusalem rivals the Solomonic period in the external glories added to it by Herod the Great. There is the great fortress **Antonia** of the temple enclosure, three great towers, Phasael, Hippicus, and Mariamne, as well as the magnificent **palace**—all at the north-corner. The most splendid addition is the rebuilt **temple** (started in 19 B.C. and finally completed in 62 A.D.). **(b)** It is to this city that Jesus is brought as an infant (Lk 2, 22-38) and as a youth (Lk 2, 41-52). It is here that during his public ministry Jesus cleanses the **temple** (Jn 2, 13-25), heals a man at the pool of **Bethesda** (Jn 5, 1-47), attends the feast of Tabernacles (Jn 7, 2; 10, 21), and the Dedication (Jn 10, 22-39). **(c)** Jesus spends the final week of his life in and around the city (Mt 27; Jn 12, 12—19, 42). **(d)** After his resurrection Jesus appears to various people (Lk 24) and his disciples (Jn 20, 26-29; Lk 24, 49) in Jerusalem and ascends from the **Mount of Olives** nearby (Lk 24, 50-53).

JERUSALEM: SCENE OF THE FINDING IN THE TEMPLE — An air view of Jerusalem showing the temple area from the north with the village of Siloam in the distance and the Golden Gate leading to the Kidron Valley on the left. As a twelve-year-old Jesus was taken by his parents to the temple in Jerusalem and found by them there after being lost for three days. (See Lk 2, 41-50)

MARY'S SPRING IN NAZARETH — View of the only spring located in Nazareth. It has always been considered certain that Jesus and Mary visited this well many times both before and after the finding in the temple. (See Lk 2, 51-52)

was hungry. [3] The tempter approached and said to him, "If you are the Son of God, command that these stones become loaves of bread." [4] He said in reply, "It is written:[g]

> 'One does not live by bread alone,
>> but by every word that comes forth
>> from the mouth of God.' "*

[5] * Then the devil took him to the holy city, and made him stand on the parapet of the temple, [6] and said to him, "If you are the Son of God, throw yourself down. For it is written:

> 'He will command his angels concerning you,'
> and 'with their hands they will support you,
> lest you dash your foot against a stone.' "[h]

[7] Jesus answered him, "Again it is written, 'You shall not put the Lord, your God, to the test.' "[i] [8] Then the devil took him up to a very high mountain, and showed him all the kingdoms of the world in their magnificence, [9] and he said to him, "All these I shall give to you, if you will prostrate yourself and worship me."* [10] At this, Jesus said to him, "Get away, Satan! It is written:

> 'The Lord, your God, shall you worship and him alone shall you serve.' "[j]

[11] Then the devil left him and, behold, angels came and ministered to him.

The Beginning of the Galilean Ministry.* [12] [k] When he heard that John had been arrested, he withdrew to Galilee. [13] He left Nazareth and went to live in Capernaum by the sea, in the region of Zebulun and Naphtali,[l] [14] that what had been said through Isaiah the prophet might be fulfilled:

[15] "Land of Zebulun and land of Naphtali,[m]
> the way to the sea, beyond the Jordan,
> Galilee of the Gentiles,
[16] the people who sit in darkness
> have seen a great light,
> on those dwelling in a land overshadowed by death
> light has arisen."[n]

[17] From that time on, Jesus began to preach and say,[o] "Repent, for the kingdom of heaven is at hand."*

The Call of the First Disciples.* [18] [p] As he was walking by the Sea of Galilee, he saw two brothers, Simon who is called Peter, and his brother Andrew, casting a net into the sea; they were fishermen. [19] He said to them, "Come after me, and I will make you fishers of men." [20] At once they left their nets and followed him.* [21] He walked along from there and saw two other brothers, James, the son of Zebedee, and his brother John. They were in a boat, with their father Zebedee, mending their nets. He called them, [22] and immediately they left their boat and their father and followed him.

Ministering to a Great Multitude.* [23] He went around all of Galilee, teaching in their synagogues,* proclaiming the gospel of the kingdom, and curing every disease and ill-

---

g Dt 8, 3.—h Ps 91, 11-12.—i Dt 6, 16.—j Mt 16, 23; Dt 6, 13.—k 12-13: Mk 1, 14-15; Lk 4, 14.31.—l Jn 2, 12.—m 15-16: Is 8, 23 LXX; 9, 1.—n Lk 1, 79.—o Mt 3, 2.—p 18-22: Mk 1, 16-20; Lk 5, 1-11.

4, 4: Cf Dt 8, 3. Jesus refuses to use his power for his own benefit and accepts whatever God wills.

4, 5-7: The devil supports his proposal by an appeal to the scriptures, Ps 91, 11a.12. Unlike Israel (Dt 6, 16) Jesus refuses to "test" God by demanding from him an extraordinary show of power.

4, 9: The worship of Satan to which Jesus is tempted is probably intended to recall Israel's worship of false gods. His refusal is expressed in the words of Dt 6, 13.

4, 12-17: Isaiah's prophecy of the light rising upon Zebulun and Naphtali (Is 8, 23—9, 1) is fulfilled in Jesus' residence at Capernaum. The territory of these two tribes was the first to be devastated (733-32 B.C.) at the time of the Assyrian invasion. In order to accommodate Jesus' move to Capernaum to the prophecy, Matthew speaks of that town as being "in the region of Zebulun and Naphtali" (13), whereas it was only in the territory of the latter, and he understands the sea of the prophecy, the Mediterranean, as the sea of Galilee.

4, 17: At the beginning of his preaching Jesus takes up the words of John the Baptist (Mt 3, 2) although with a different meaning; in his ministry the kingdom of heaven has already begun to be present (Mt 12, 28).

4, 18-22: The call of the first disciples promises them a share in Jesus' work and entails abandonment of family and former way of life. Three of the four, Simon, James, and John, are distinguished among the disciples by a closer relation with Jesus (Mt 17, 1; 26, 37).

4, 20: Here and in v 22, as in Mark (Mk 1, 16-20) and unlike the Lucan account (Lk 5, 1-11), the disciples' response is motivated only by Jesus' invitation, an element that emphasizes his mysterious power.

4, 23-25: This summary of Jesus' ministry concludes the narrative part of the first book of Matthew's gospel (chs 3-4). The activities of his ministry are teaching, proclaiming the gospel, and healing; cf Mt 9, 35.

4, 23: *Their synagogues:* Matthew usually designates the Jewish synagogues as *their synagogue(s)* (Mt 9, 35; 10, 17; 12, 9; 13, 54) or, in address to Jews, *your synagogues* (Mt 23, 34), an indication that he wrote after the break between church and synagogue.

ness among the people.*q* ²⁴His fame spread to all of Syria,* and they brought to him all who were sick with various diseases and racked with pain, those who were possessed, lunatics, and paralytics, and he cured them. ²⁵And great crowds from Galilee, the Decapolis,* Jerusalem, and Judea, and from beyond the Jordan followed him.*r*

CHAPTER 5

The Sermon on the Mount. ¹ *When he saw the crowds,* he went up the mountain, and after he had sat down, his disciples came to him.²He began to teach them, saying:

The Beatitudes*

³ "Blessed are the poor in spirit,*
    for theirs is the kingdom of heaven.*s*
⁴ Blessed are they who mourn,*t*
    for they will be comforted.*
⁵ Blessed are the meek,*u*
    for they will inherit the land.*
⁶ Blessed are they who hunger and thirst
    for righteousness,*
    for they will be satisfied.
⁷ Blessed are the merciful,
    for they will be shown mercy.*v*

⁸ Blessed are the clean of heart,*w*
    for they will see God.*
⁹ Blessed are the peacemakers,
    for they will be called children of God.
¹⁰ Blessed are they who are persecuted for
    the sake of righteousness,*
    for theirs is the kingdom of heaven.*x*

¹¹Blessed are you when they insult you and persecute you and utter every kind of evil against you [falsely] because of me.*y* ¹²Rejoice and be glad, for your reward will be great in heaven.*z* Thus they persecuted the prophets who were before you.*

The Similes of Salt and Light.* ¹³ *a* "You are the salt of the earth. But if salt loses its taste, with what can it be seasoned? It is no longer good for anything but to be thrown out and trampled underfoot.* ¹⁴You are the light of the world. A city set on a mountain cannot be hidden.*b* ¹⁵Nor do they light a lamp and then put it under a bushel basket; it is set on a lampstand, where it gives light to all in the house.*c* ¹⁶Just so, your light must shine before others, that they may see your good deeds and glorify your heavenly Father.*d*

---

q Mt 9, 35; Mk 1, 39; Lk 4, 15.44.—r Mk 3, 7-8; Lk 6, 17-19.—s 3-12: Lk 6, 20-23.—t Is 61, 2-3; Rv 21, 4.—u Gn 13, 15; Ps 37, 11.—v Mt 18, 33; Jas 2, 13.—w Pss 24, 4-5; 73, 1.—x 1 Pt 2, 20; 3, 14; 4, 14.—y Mt 10, 22; Acts 5, 41.—z 2 Chr 36, 16; Heb 11, 32-38; Jas 5, 10.—a Mk 9, 50; Lk 14, 34-35.—b Jn 8, 12.—c Mk 4, 21; Lk 8, 16; 11, 33.—d Jn 3, 21.

4, 24: *Syria:* the Roman province to which Palestine belonged.

4, 25: *The Decapolis:* a federation of Greek cities in Palestine, originally ten in number, all but one east of the Jordan.

5, 1—7, 29: The first of the five discourses that are a central part of the structure of this gospel. It is the discourse section of the first book and contains sayings of Jesus derived from Q and from M. The Lucan parallel is in that gospel's "Sermon on the Plain" (Lk 6, 20-49), although some of the sayings in Matthew's "Sermon on the Mount" have their parallels in other parts of Luke. The careful topical arrangement of the sermon is probably not due only to Matthew's editing; he seems to have had a structured discourse of Jesus as one of his sources. The form of that source may have been as follows: four beatitudes (Mt 5, 3-4.6.11-12), a section on the new righteousness with illustrations (Mt 5, 17.20-24.27-28.33-48), a section on good works (Mt 6, 1-6.16-18), and three warnings (Mt 7, 1-2.15-21.24-27).

5, 1-2: Unlike Luke's sermon, this is addressed not only to the disciples but to the crowds (see Mt 7, 28).

5, 3-12: The form *Blessed are (is)* occurs frequently in the Old Testament in the Wisdom literature and in the psalms. Although modified by Matthew, the first, second, fourth, and ninth beatitudes have Lucan parallels (Mt 5, 3 // Lk 6, 20; Mt 5, 4 // Lk 6, 21b; Mt 5, 6 // Lk 6, 21a; Mt 5, 11-12 // Lk 5, 22-23). The others were added by the evangelist and are probably his own composition. A few manuscripts, Western and Alexandrian, and many versions and patristic quotations give the second and third beatitudes in inverted order.

5, 3: *The poor in spirit:* in the Old Testament, the *poor* (*'ănāwîm*) are those who are without material possessions and whose confidence is in God (see Is 61, 1; Zep 2, 3; in the NAB the word is translated *lowly* and *humble,* respectively, in those texts). Matthew added *in spirit* in order either to indicate that only the devout poor were meant or to extend the beatitude to all, of whatever social rank, who recognized their complete dependence on God. The same phrase *poor in spirit* is found in the Qumran literature (1QM 14, 7).

5, 4: Cf Is 61, 2, "(The Lord has sent me) . . . to comfort all who mourn." *They will be comforted:* here the passive is a "theological passive" equivalent to the active "God will comfort them"; so also in vv 6 and 7.

5, 5: Cf Ps 37, 11, ". . . the meek shall possess the land." In the psalm "the land" means the land of Palestine; here it means the kingdom.

5, 6: *For righteousness:* a Matthean addition. For the meaning of *righteousness* here, see the note on Mt 3, 14-15.

5, 8: Cf Ps 24, 4. Only one "whose heart is clean" can take part in the temple worship. To be with God in the temple is described in Ps 42, 3 as "beholding his face," but here the promise to *the clean of heart* is that they will *see God* not in the temple but in the coming kingdom.

5, 10: *Righteousness* here, as usually in Matthew, means conduct in conformity with God's will.

5, 12: *The prophets who were before you:* the disciples of Jesus stand in the line of the persecuted prophets of Israel. Some would see the expression as indicating also that Matthew considered all Christian disciples as prophets.

5, 13-16: By their deeds the disciples are to influence the world for good. They can no more escape notice than *a city set on a mountain.* If they fail in good works, they are as useless as flavorless salt or as a lamp whose light is concealed.

5, 13: The unusual supposition of salt losing its flavor has led some to suppose that the saying refers to the salt of the Dead Sea that, because chemically impure, could lose its taste.

Teaching about the Law.* [17]"Do not think that I have come to abolish the law or the prophets. I have come not to abolish but to fulfill. [18]Amen, I say to you, until heaven and earth pass away, not the smallest letter or the smallest part of a letter will pass from the law, until all things have taken place.[e] [19]Therefore, whoever breaks one of the least of these commandments and teaches others to do so will be called least in the kingdom of heaven. But whoever obeys and teaches these commandments will be called greatest in the kingdom of heaven.* [20]I tell you, unless your righteousness surpasses that of the scribes and Pharisees, you will not enter into the kingdom of heaven.

Teaching about Anger. [21] *"You have heard that it was said to your ancestors,[f] 'You shall not kill; and whoever kills will be liable to judgment.'* [22]But I say to you, whoever is angry* with his brother will be liable to judgment,[g] and whoever says to his brother, 'Raqa,' will be answerable to the Sanhedrin, and whoever says, 'You fool,' will be liable to fiery Gehenna.* [23]Therefore, if you bring your gift to the altar, and there recall that your brother has anything against you,[h] [24]leave your gift there at the altar, go first and be reconciled with your brother, and then come and offer your gift. [25]Settle with your opponent quickly while on the way to court with him.[i] Otherwise your opponent will hand you over to the judge, and the judge will hand you over to the guard, and you will be thrown into prison. [26]Amen, I say to you, you will not be released until you have paid the last penny.

Teaching about Adultery. [27]"You have heard that it was said,[j] 'You shall not commit adultery.'* [28]But I say to you, everyone who looks at a woman with lust has already committed adultery with her in his heart. [29] * If your right eye causes you to sin, tear it out and throw it away.[k] It is better for you to lose one of your members than to have your whole body thrown into Gehenna. [30]And if your right hand causes you to sin, cut it off and throw it away. It is better for you to lose one of your members than to have your whole body go into Gehenna.

Teaching about Divorce. [31]"It was also said, 'Whoever divorces his wife must give her a bill of divorce.'[l] [32]But I say to you, whoever divorces his wife (unless the marriage is unlawful) causes her to commit

---

e Lk 16, 17.—f Ex 20, 13; Dt 5, 17.—g Jas 1, 19-20.—h Mk 11, 25.—i 25-26: Mt 18, 34-35; Lk 12, 58-59.—j Ex 20, 14; Dt 5, 18.—k 29-30: Mt 18, 8-9; Mk 9, 43-47.—l Mt 19, 3-9; Dt 24, 1.

5, 17-20: This statement of Jesus' position concerning the Mosaic law is composed of traditional material from Matthew's sermon documentation (see the note on Mt 5, 1—7, 29), other Q material (cf Mt 18 and Lk 16, 17), and the evangelist's own editorial touches. *To fulfill* the law appears at first to mean a literal enforcement of the law in the least detail: *until heaven and earth pass away* nothing of the law *will pass* (18). Yet the "passing away" of heaven and earth is not necessarily the end of the world understood, as in much apocalyptic literature, as the dissolution of the existing universe. The "turning of the ages" comes with the apocalyptic event of Jesus' death and resurrection, and those to whom this gospel is addressed are living in the new and final age, prophesied by Isaiah as the time of "new heavens and a new earth" (Is 65, 17; 66, 22). Meanwhile, during Jesus' ministry when the kingdom is already breaking in, his mission remains within the framework of the law, though with significant anticipation of the age to come, as the following antitheses (vv 21-48) show.

5, 19: Probably *these commandments* means those of the Mosaic law. But this is an interim ethic "until heaven and earth pass away."

5, 21-48: Six examples of the conduct demanded of the Christian disciple. Each deals with a commandment of the law, introduced by *You have heard that it was said to your ancestors* or an equivalent formula, followed by Jesus' teaching in respect to that commandment, *But I say to you;* thus their designation as "antitheses." Three of them accept the Mosaic law but extend or deepen it (21-22; 27-28; 43-44); three reject it as a standard of conduct for the disciples (31-32; 33-37; 38-39).

5, 21: Cf Ex 20, 13; Dt 5, 17. The second part of the verse is not an exact quotation from the Old Testament, but cf Ex 21, 12.

5, 22: Anger is the motive behind murder, as the insulting epithets are steps that may lead to it. They, as well as the deed, are all forbidden. *Raqa:* an Aramaic word *rēqā'* or *rēqâ* probably meaning "imbecile," "blockhead," a term of abuse. The ascending order of punishment, *judgment* (by a local council?), trial before *the Sanhedrin*, condemnation to *Gehenna*, points to a higher degree of seriousness in each of the offenses. *Sanhedrin:* the highest judicial body of Judaism. *Gehenna:* in Hebrew *gê-hinnōm*, "Valley of Hinnom," or *gê ben-hinnōm*, "Valley of the son of Hinnom," southwest of Jerusalem, the center of an idolatrous cult during the monarchy in which children were offered in sacrifice (see 2 Kgs 23, 10; Jer 7, 31). In Jos 18, 16 (Septuagint, Codex Vaticanus) the Hebrew is transliterated into Greek as *gaienna*, which appears in the New Testament as *geenna*. The concept of punishment of sinners by fire either after death or after the final judgment is found in Jewish apocalyptic literature (e.g., Enoch 90, 26) but the name *geenna* is first given to the place of punishment in the New Testament.

5, 22-26: Reconciliation with an offended brother is urged in the admonition of vv 23-24 and the parable of vv 25-26 (// Lk 12, 58-59). The severity of the judge in the parable is a warning of the fate of unrepentant sinners in the coming judgment by God.

5, 27: See Ex 20, 14; Dt 5, 18.

5, 29-30: No sacrifice is too great to avoid total destruction in *Gehenna.*

adultery, and whoever marries a divorced woman commits adultery.*m

Teaching about Oaths. 33 n "Again you have heard that it was said to your ancestors, 'Do not take a false oath, but make good to the Lord all that you vow.'* 34 o But I say to you, do not swear at all;* not by heaven, for it is God's throne; 35 nor by the earth, for it is his footstool; nor by Jerusalem, for it is the city of the great King. 36 Do not swear by your head, for you cannot make a single hair white or black. 37 Let your 'Yes' mean 'Yes,' and your 'No' mean 'No.' Anything more is from the evil one.*

Teaching about Retaliation.* 38 "You have heard that it was said,p 'An eye for an eye and a tooth for a tooth.' 39 q But I say to you, offer no resistance to one who is evil. When someone strikes you on [your] right cheek, turn the other one to him as well. 40 If anyone wants to go to law with you over your tunic, hand him your cloak as well. 41 Should anyone press you into ser-

vice for one mile,* go with him for two miles.r 42 Give to the one who asks of you, and do not turn your back on one who wants to borrow.s

Love of Enemies.* 43 t "You have heard that it was said, 'You shall love your neighbor and hate your enemy.'u 44 But I say to you, love your enemies, and pray for those who persecute you, 45 that you may be children of your heavenly Father, for he makes his sun rise on the bad and the good, and causes rain to fall on the just and the unjust. 46 For if you love those who love you, what recompense will you have? Do not the tax collectors* do the same? 47 And if you greet your brothers only, what is unusual about that? Do not the pagans do the same?* 48 So be perfect,* just as your heavenly Father is perfect.v

CHAPTER 6

Teaching about Almsgiving.* 1 "[But] take care not to perform righteous deeds in order that people may see them;w otherwise, you will have no recompense from

---

m Lk 16, 18; 1 Cor 7, 10-11.—n Lv 19, 12; Nm 30, 3.—o 34-37: Ps 48, 3; Sir 23, 9; Is 66, 1; Jas 5, 12.—p Ex 21, 24; Lv 24, 19-20.—q 39-42: Lk 6, 29-30.—r Lam 3, 30.—s Dt 15, 7-8.—t 43-48: Lk 6, 27.32-36.—u Lv 19, 18.—v Lv 11, 44; 19, 2; Dt 18, 13; Jas 1, 4; 1 Pt 1, 16; 1 Jn 3, 3.—w Mt 23, 5.

5, 31-32: See Dt 24, 1-5. The Old Testament commandment that a bill of divorce be given to the woman assumes the legitimacy of divorce itself. It is this that Jesus denies. *(Unless the marriage is unlawful):* this "exceptive clause," as it is often called, occurs also in Mt 19, 9, where the Greek is slightly different. There are other sayings of Jesus about divorce that prohibit it absolutely (see Mk 10, 11-12; Lk 16, 18; cf 1 Cor 7, 10.11b), and most scholars agree that they represent the stand of Jesus. Matthew's "exceptive clauses" are understood by some as a modification of the absolute prohibition. It seems, however, that the unlawfulness that Matthew gives as a reason why a marriage must be broken refers to a situation peculiar to his community: the violation of Mosaic law forbidding marriage between persons of certain blood and/or legal relationship (Lv 18, 6-18). Marriages of that sort were regarded as incest *(porneia),* but some rabbis allowed Gentile converts to Judaism who had contracted such marriages to remain in them. Matthew's "exceptive clause" is against such permissiveness for Gentile converts to Christianity; cf the similar prohibition of *porneia* in Acts 15, 20.29. In this interpretation, the clause constitutes no exception to the absolute prohibition of divorce when the marriage is lawful.

5, 33: This is not an exact quotation of any Old Testament text, but see Ex 20, 7, Dt 5, 11, and Lv 19, 12. The purpose of an oath was to guarantee truthfulness by one's calling on God as witness.

5, 34-36: The use of these oath formularies that avoid the divine name is in fact equivalent to swearing by it, for all the things sworn by are related to God.

5, 37: *Let your 'Yes' mean 'Yes,' and your 'No' mean 'No':* literally, "let your speech be 'Yes, yes,' 'No, no.' " Some have understood this as a milder form of oath, permitted by Jesus. In view of v 34, "Do not swear at all," that is unlikely. *From the evil one:* i.e., from the devil. Oath-taking presupposes a sinful weakness of the human race, namely, the tendency to lie. Jesus demands of his disciples a truthfulness that makes oaths unnecessary.

5, 38-42: See Lv 24, 20. The Old Testament commandment was meant to moderate vengeance; the punishment should not exceed the injury done. Jesus forbids even this proportionate retaliation. Of the five examples that follow, only the first deals directly with retaliation for evil; the others speak of liberality.

5, 41: Roman garrisons in Palestine had the right to requisition the property and services of the native population.

5, 43-48: See Lv 19, 18. There is no Old Testament commandment demanding hatred of one's enemy, but the "neighbor" of the love commandment was understood as one's fellow countryman. Both in the Old Testament (Ps 139, 19-22) and at Qumran (1QS 9, 21) hatred of evil persons is assumed to be right. Jesus extends the love commandment to the enemy and the persecutor. His disciples, as children of God, must imitate the example of their Father, who grants his gifts of sun and rain to both the good and the bad.

5, 46: *Tax collectors:* Jews who were engaged in the collection of indirect taxes such as tolls and customs. See the note on Mk 2, 14.

5, 47: Jesus' disciples must not be content with merely usual standards of conduct; see v 20 where the verb "surpass" (Greek *perisseuō*) is cognate with the *unusual (perisson)* of this verse.

5, 48: *Perfect:* in the gospels this word occurs only in Matthew, here and in Mt 19, 21. The Lucan parallel (Lk 6, 36) demands that the disciples be *merciful.*

6, 1-18: The sermon continues with a warning against doing good in order to be seen and gives three examples, almsgiving (2-4), prayer (5-15), and fasting (16-18). In each, the conduct of *the hypocrites* (2) is contrasted with that demanded of the disciples. The sayings about *reward* found here and elsewhere (Mt 5, 12.46; 10, 41-42) show that this is a genuine element of Christian moral exhortation. Possibly to underline the difference between the Christian idea of *reward* and that of *the hypocrites,* the evangelist uses two different Greek verbs to express the rewarding of the disciples and that of *the hypocrites;* in the latter case it is the verb *apechō,* a commercial term for giving a receipt for what has been paid in full (2.5.16).

your heavenly Father. [2] When you give alms, do not blow a trumpet before you, as the hypocrites* do in the synagogues and in the streets to win the praise of others. Amen, I say to you, they have received their reward.[x] [3] But when you give alms, do not let your left hand know what your right is doing, [4] so that your almsgiving may be secret. And your Father who sees in secret will repay you.

Teaching about Prayer. [5] "When you pray, do not be like the hypocrites, who love to stand and pray in the synagogues and on street corners so that others may see them. Amen, I say to you, they have received their reward. [6] But when you pray, go to your inner room, close the door, and pray to your Father in secret. And your Father who sees in secret will repay you. [7] * In praying, do not babble like the pagans, who think that they will be heard because of their many words.* [8] Do not be like them. Your Father knows what you need before you ask him.

The Lord's Prayer. [9] * "This is how you are to pray:[y]

Our Father in heaven,*
    hallowed be your name,
[10]   your kingdom come,*
    your will be done,

on earth as in heaven.[z]
[11]   [a] Give us today our daily bread;*
[12]   and forgive us our debts,*
    as we forgive our debtors;[b]
[13]   and do not subject us to the final test,*
    but deliver us from the evil one.[c]

[14] * If you forgive others their transgressions, your heavenly Father will forgive you.[d] [15] But if you do not forgive others, neither will your Father forgive your transgressions.[e]

Teaching about Fasting. [16] "When you fast,* do not look gloomy like the hypocrites. They neglect their appearance, so that they may appear to others to be fasting. Amen, I say to you, they have received their reward. [17] But when you fast, anoint your head and wash your face, [18] so that you may not appear to be fasting, except to your Father who is hidden. And your Father who sees what is hidden will repay you.

Treasure in Heaven. [19] * "Do not store up for yourselves treasures on earth, where moth and decay destroy, and thieves break in and steal.[f] [20] But store up treasures in heaven, where neither moth nor decay de-

---

x Jn 12, 43.—y 9-13: Lk 11, 2-4.—z Mt 26, 42.—a Prv 30, 8-9.—b Mt 18, 21-22; Sir 28, 2.—c Jn 17, 15; 2 Thes 3, 3.—d Mt 18, 35; Sir 28, 1-5; Mk 11, 25.—e Jas 2, 13.—f Jas 5, 2-3.

6, 2: *The hypocrites:* the scribes and Pharisees, see Mt 23, 13.15.23.25.27.29. The designation reflects an attitude resulting not only from the controversies at the time of Jesus' ministry but from the opposition between Pharisaic Judaism and the church of Matthew. *They have received their reward:* they desire praise and have received what they were looking for.

6, 7-15: Matthew inserts into his basic traditional material an expansion of the material on prayer that includes the model prayer, the "Our Father." That prayer is found in Lk 11, 2-4 in a different context and in a different form.

6, 7: The example of what Christian prayer should be like contrasts it now not with the prayer of the hypocrites but with that of *the pagans.* Their babbling probably means their reciting a long list of divine names, hoping that one of them will force a response from the deity.

6, 9-13: Matthew's form of the "Our Father" follows the liturgical tradition of his church. Luke's less developed form also represents the liturgical tradition known to him, but it is probably closer than Matthew's to the original words of Jesus.

6, 9: *Our Father in heaven:* this invocation is found in many rabbinic prayers of the post-New Testament period. *Hallowed be your name:* though the "hallowing" of the divine name could be understood as reverence done to God by human praise and by obedience to his will, this is more probably a petition that God hallow his own name, i.e., that he manifest his glory by an act of power (cf Ez 36, 23), in this case, by the establishment of his kingdom in its fullness.

6, 10: *Your kingdom come:* this petition sets the tone of the prayer, and inclines the balance toward divine rather than human action in the petitions that immediately precede and follow it. *Your will be done, on earth as in heaven:* a petition that the divine purpose to establish the kingdom, a purpose present now *in heaven,* be executed *on earth.*

6, 11: *Give us today our daily bread:* the rare Greek word *epiousios,* here *daily,* occurs in the New Testament only here and in Lk 11, 3. A single occurrence of the word outside of these texts and of literature dependent on them has been claimed, but the claim is highly doubtful. The word may mean *daily* or "future" (other meanings have also been proposed). The latter would conform better to the eschatological tone of the whole prayer. So understood, the petition would be for a speedy coming of the kingdom (*today*), which is often portrayed in both the Old Testament and the New under the image of a feast (Is 25, 6; Mt 8, 11; 22, 1-10; Lk 13, 29; 14, 15-24).

6, 12: *Forgive us our debts:* the word *debts* is used metaphorically of sins, "debts" owed to God (see Lk 11, 4). The request is probably for forgiveness at the final judgment.

6, 13: Jewish apocalyptic writings speak of a period of severe trial before the end of the age, sometimes called the "messianic woes." This petition asks that the disciples be spared that *final test.*

6, 14-15: These verses reflect a set pattern called "Principles of Holy Law." Human action now will be met by a corresponding action of God at the final judgment.

6, 16: The only fast prescribed in the Mosaic law was that of the Day of Atonement (Lv 16, 31), but the practice of regular fasting was common in later Judaism; cf *Didache* 9, 1.

6, 19-34: The remaining material of this chapter is taken almost entirely from Q. It deals principally with worldly possessions, and the controlling thought is summed up in v 24: the disciple can serve only one master and must choose between God and wealth (*mammon*). See further the note on Lk 16, 9.

stroys, nor thieves break in and steal. [21] For where your treasure is, there also will your heart be.[g]

The Light of the Body.* [22] "The lamp of the body is the eye. If your eye is sound, your whole body will be filled with light; [23] but if your eye is bad, your whole body will be in darkness. And if the light in you is darkness, how great will the darkness be.[h]

God and Money. [24] "No one can serve two masters.[i] He will either hate one and love the other, or be devoted to one and despise the other. You cannot serve God and mammon.*

Dependence on God.* [25] [j] "Therefore I tell you, do not worry about your life, what you will eat [or drink], or about your body, what you will wear. Is not life more than food and the body more than clothing? [26] Look at the birds in the sky; they do not sow or reap, they gather nothing into barns, yet your heavenly Father feeds them. Are not you more important than they?[k] [27] Can any of you by worrying add a single moment to your life-span?* [28] Why are you anxious about clothes? Learn from the way the wild flowers grow. They do not work or spin. [29] But I tell you that not even Solomon in all his splendor was clothed like one of them. [30] If God so clothes the grass of the field, which grows today and is thrown into the oven tomorrow, will he not much more provide for you, O you of little faith?* [31] So do not worry and say, 'What are we to eat?' or 'What are we to drink?' or 'What are we to wear?' [32] All these things the pagans seek. Your heavenly Father knows that you need them all. [33] But seek first the kingdom [of God] and his righteousness,* and all these things will be given you besides. [34] Do not worry about tomorrow; tomorrow will take care of itself. Sufficient for a day is its own evil.

CHAPTER 7

Judging Others. [1] * [l] "Stop judging,* that you may not be judged.[m] [2] For as you judge, so will you be judged, and the measure with which you measure will be measured out to you.[n] [3] Why do you notice the splinter in your brother's eye, but do not perceive the wooden beam in your own eye? [4] How can you say to your brother, 'Let me remove that splinter from your eye,' while the wooden beam is in your eye? [5] You hypocrite,* remove the wooden beam from your eye first; then you will see clearly to remove the splinter from your brother's eye.

Pearls before Swine. [6] "Do not give what is holy to dogs,* or throw your pearls before swine, lest they trample them underfoot, and turn and tear you to pieces.[o]

The Answer to Prayers. [7] [p] "Ask and it will be given to you; seek and you will find; knock and the door will be opened to you.[q] [8] For everyone who asks, receives; and the one who seeks, finds; and to the one who knocks, the door will be opened.[r] [9] Which one of you would hand his son a stone when he asks for a loaf of bread,*

---

g 20-21: Lk 12, 33-34.—h 22-23: Lk 11, 34-36.—i Lk 16, 13.—j 25-33: Lk 12, 22-31.—k Pss 145, 15-16; 147, 9.—l 1-5: Lk 6, 37-38.41-42.—m Rom 2, 1-2; 1 Cor 4, 5.—n Wis 12, 22; Mk 4, 24.—o Prv 23, 9.—p 7-11: Mk 11, 24; Lk 11, 9-13.—q Mt 18, 19.—r Lk 18, 1-8; Jn 14, 13.

6, 22-23: In this context the parable probably points to the need for the disciple to be enlightened by Jesus' teaching on the transitory nature of earthly riches.

6, 24: *Mammon:* an Aramaic word meaning wealth or property.

6, 25-34: Jesus does not deny the reality of human needs (32), but forbids making them the object of anxious care and, in effect, becoming their slave.

6, 27: *Life-span:* the Greek word can also mean "stature." If it is taken in that sense, the word here translated *moment* (literally, "cubit") must be translated literally as a unit not of time but of spatial measure. The cubit is about eighteen inches.

6, 30: *Of little faith:* except for the parallel in Lk 12, 28, the word translated *of little faith* is found in the New Testament only in Matthew. It is used by him of those who are disciples of Jesus but whose faith in him is not as deep as it should be (see Mt 8, 26; 14, 31; 16, 8 and the cognate noun in Mt 17, 20).

6, 33: *Righteousness:* see the note on Mt 3, 14-15.

7, 1-12: In v 1 Matthew returns to the basic traditional material of the sermon (Lk 6, 37-38.41-42). The governing thought is the correspondence between conduct toward one's fellows and God's conduct toward the one so acting.

7, 1: This is not a prohibition against recognizing the faults of others, which would be hardly compatible with vv 5 and 6, but against passing judgment in a spirit of arrogance, forgetful of one's own faults.

7, 5: *Hypocrite:* the designation previously given to the scribes and Pharisees is here given to the Christian disciple who is concerned with the faults of another and ignores his own more serious offenses.

7, 6: *Dogs* and *swine* were Jewish terms of contempt for Gentiles. This saying may originally have derived from a Jewish Christian community opposed to preaching the gospel *(what is holy, pearls)* to Gentiles. In the light of Mt 28,19 that can hardly be Matthew's meaning. He may have taken the saying as applying to a Christian dealing with an obstinately impenitent fellow Christian (Mt 18, 17).

7, 9-10: There is a resemblance between a stone and a round loaf of bread and between a serpent and the scaleless fish called *barbut.*

[10] or a snake when he asks for a fish? [11] If you then, who are wicked, know how to give good gifts to your children, how much more will your heavenly Father give good things to those who ask him.[s]

The Golden Rule. [12] "Do to others whatever you would have them do to you.[t] This is the law and the prophets.*

The Narrow Gate. [13] * "Enter through the narrow gate;* for the gate is wide and the road broad that leads to destruction, and those who enter through it are many.[u] [14] How narrow the gate and constricted the road that leads to life. And those who find it are few.

False Prophets.* [15] "Beware of false prophets, who come to you in sheep's clothing, but underneath are ravenous wolves.[v] [16] [w] By their fruits you will know them. Do people pick grapes from thornbushes, or figs from thistles? [17] Just so, every good tree bears good fruit, and a rotten tree bears bad fruit. [18] A good tree cannot bear bad fruit, nor can a rotten tree bear good fruit. [19] Every tree that does not bear good fruit will be cut down and thrown into the fire. [20] So by their fruits you will know them.[x]

The True Disciple.* [21] "Not everyone who says to me, 'Lord, Lord,' will enter the kingdom of heaven, but only the one who does the will of my Father in heaven.[y]

[22] Many will say to me on that day,[z] 'Lord, Lord, did we not prophesy in your name? Did we not drive out demons in your name? Did we not do mighty deeds in your name?'[a] [23] Then I will declare to them solemnly, 'I never knew you.* Depart from me, you evildoers.'[b]

The Two Foundations. [24] * "Everyone who listens to these words of mine and acts on them will be like a wise man who built his house on rock.[c] [25] The rain fell, the floods came, and the winds blew and buffeted the house.[d] But it did not collapse; it had been set solidly on rock. [26] And everyone who listens to these words of mine but does not act on them will be like a fool who built his house on sand. [27] The rain fell, the floods came, and the winds blew and buffeted the house. And it collapsed and was completely ruined."

[28] * When Jesus finished these words, the crowds were astonished at his teaching, [29] [e] for he taught them as one having authority, and not as their scribes.*

III. MINISTRY AND MISSION IN GALILEE*

CHAPTER 8

The Cleansing of a Leper. [1] [f] When Jesus came down from the mountain, great

---

s 1 Jn 5, 14-15.—t Lk 6, 31.—u Lk 13, 24.—v 2 Pt 2, 1.—w 16-17: Mt 12, 33; Lk 6, 43-44.—x Mt 3, 10.—y Is 29, 13; Lk 6, 46.—z 22-23: Lk 13, 26-27.—a Mt 25, 11-12.—b Pss 5, 5; 6, 9.—c 24-27: Lk 6, 47-49.—d 25-26: Prv 10, 25.—e Mk 1, 22; Lk 4, 32.—f 1-4: Mk 1, 40-44; Lk 5, 12-14.

7, 12: See Lk 6, 31. This saying, known since the eighteenth century as the "Golden Rule," is found in both positive and negative form in pagan and Jewish sources, both earlier and later than the gospel. *This is the law and the prophets* is an addition probably due to the evangelist.

7, 13-28: The final section of the discourse is composed of a series of antitheses, contrasting two kinds of life within the Christian community, that of those who obey the words of Jesus and that of those who do not. Most of the sayings are from Q and are found also in Luke.

7, 13-14: The metaphor of the "two ways" was common in pagan philosophy and in the Old Testament. In Christian literature it is found also in the *Didache* (1-6) and the *Epistle of Barnabas* (18-20).

7, 15-20: Christian disciples who claimed to speak in the name of God are called *prophets* (15) in Mt 10, 41 and in Mt 23, 34. They were presumably an important group within the church of Matthew. As in the case of the Old Testament prophets, there were both true and false ones, and for Matthew the difference could be recognized by the quality of their deeds, the *fruits* (16). The mention of *fruits* leads to the comparison with trees, some producing good fruit, others bad.

7, 21-23: The attack on the false prophets is continued, but is broadened to include those disciples who perform works of healing and exorcism in the name of Jesus *(Lord)* but live evil lives. Entrance into the kingdom is only for those who do

the will of the Father. On the day of judgment *(on that day)* the morally corrupt prophets and miracle workers will be rejected by Jesus.

7, 23: *I never knew you:* cf Mt 10, 33. *Depart from me, you evildoers:* cf Ps 6, 9.

7, 24-27: The conclusion of the discourse (cf Lk 6, 47-49). Here the relation is not between saying and doing as in vv 15-23 but between hearing and doing, and the words of Jesus are applied to every Christian *(everyone who listens)*.

7, 28-29: *When Jesus finished these words:* this or a similar formula is used by Matthew to conclude each of the five great discourses of Jesus (cf Mt 11, 1; 13, 53; 19, 1; 26, 1).

7, 29: *Not as their scribes:* scribal instruction was a faithful handing down of the traditions of earlier teachers; Jesus' teaching is based on his own authority. *Their scribes:* for the implications of *their,* see the note on Mt 4, 23.

8, 1—9, 38: This narrative section of the second book of the gospel is composed of nine miracle stories, most of which are found in Mark, although Matthew does not follow the Marcan order and abbreviates the stories radically. The stories are arranged in three groups of three, each group followed by a section composed principally of sayings of Jesus about discipleship. Verse 9, 35 is an almost verbatim repetition of Mt 4, 23. Each speaks of Jesus' teaching, preaching, and healing. The teaching and preaching form the content of chs 5-7; the healing, that of chs 8-9. Some scholars speak of a portrayal of Jesus as "Messiah of the Word" in 5-7 and "Messiah of the Deed" in 8-9. That is accurate so far as it goes, but there is also a strong emphasis on discipleship in 8-9; these chapters have not only christological but ecclesiological import.

crowds followed him. ²And then a leper* approached, did him homage, and said, "Lord, if you wish, you can make me clean." ³He stretched out his hand, touched him, and said, "I will do it. Be made clean." His leprosy was cleansed immediately. ⁴Then Jesus said to him, "See that you tell no one, but go show yourself to the priest, and offer the gift that Moses prescribed;ᵍ that will be proof for them."*

The Healing of a Centurion's Servant.* ⁵ʰWhen he entered Capernaum, a centurion* approached him and appealed to him, ⁶saying, "Lord, my servant is lying at home paralyzed, suffering dreadfully." ⁷He said to him, "I will come and cure him." ⁸The centurion said in reply,* "Lord, I am not worthy to have you enter under my roof; only say the word and my servant will be healed. ⁹For I too am a person subject to authority, with soldiers subject to me. And I say to one, 'Go,' and he goes; and to another, 'Come here,' and he comes; and to my slave, 'Do this,' and he does it." ¹⁰When Jesus heard this, he was amazed and said to those following him, "Amen, I say to you, in no one in Israel* have I found such faith. ¹¹ ᵗ I say to you,* many will come from the east and the west, and will recline with Abraham, Isaac, and Jacob at the banquet in the kingdom of heaven, ¹²but the children of the kingdom will be driven out into the outer darkness, where there will be wailing and grinding of teeth." ¹³And Jesus said to the centurion, "You may go; as you have believed, let it be done for you." And at that very hour [his] servant was healed.

The Cure of Peter's Mother-in-Law.* ¹⁴ ʲ Jesus entered the house of Peter, and saw his mother-in-law lying in bed with a fever. ¹⁵He touched her hand, the fever left her, and she rose and waited on him.ᵏ

Other Healings. ¹⁶When it was evening, they brought him many who were possessed by demons, and he drove out the spirits by a word* and cured all the sick, ¹⁷to fulfill what had been said by Isaiah the prophet:ˡ

"He took away our infirmities
and bore our diseases."*

The Would-be Followers of Jesus.* ¹⁸ ᵐ When Jesus saw a crowd around him, he gave orders to cross to the other side.* ¹⁹ ⁿA scribe approached and said to him, "Teacher,* I will follow you wherever you go." ²⁰Jesus answered him, "Foxes have dens and birds of the sky have nests, but the Son of Man* has nowhere to rest his head." ²¹Another of [his] disciples said to him, "Lord, let me go first and bury my

---

g Lv 14, 2-32; Lk 17, 14.—h 5-13: Lk 7, 1-10; Jn 4, 46-53.—i 11-12: Mt 13, 42.50; 22, 13; 24, 51; 25, 30; Lk 13, 28-29.—j 14-16: Mk 1, 29-34; Lk 4, 38-41.—k Mt 9, 25.—l Is 53, 4.—m Mk 4, 35.—n 19-22: Lk 9, 57-60.

8, 2: *A leper:* see the note on Mk 1, 40.

8, 4: Cf Lv 14, 2-9. *That will be proof for them:* the Greek can also mean "that will be proof against them." It is not clear whether *them* refers to the priests or the people.

8, 5-13: This story comes from Q (see Lk 7, 1-10) and is also reflected in Jn 4, 46-54. The similarity between the Q story and the Johannine is due to a common oral tradition, not to a common literary source. As in the later story of the daughter of the Canaanite woman (Mt 15, 21-28) Jesus here breaks with his usual procedure of ministering only to Israelites and anticipates the mission to the Gentiles.

8, 5: *A centurion:* a military officer commanding a hundred men. He was probably in the service of Herod Antipas, tetrarch of Galilee; see the note on Mt 14, 1.

8, 8-9: Acquainted by his position with the force of a command, the centurion expresses faith in the power of Jesus' mere word.

8, 10: *In no one in Israel:* there is good textual attestation (e.g., Codex Sinaiticus) for a reading identical with that of Lk 7, 9, "not even in Israel." But that seems to be due to a harmonization of Matthew with Luke.

8, 11-12: Matthew inserts into the story a Q saying (see Lk 13, 28-29) about the entrance of Gentiles into the kingdom and the exclusion of those Israelites who, though descended from the patriarchs and members of the chosen nation (*the children of the kingdom*), refused to believe in Jesus. *There will be wail-*

ing and grinding of teeth: the first occurrence of a phrase used frequently in this gospel to describe final condemnation (Mt 13, 42.50; 22, 13; 24, 51; 25, 30). It is found elsewhere in the New Testament only in Lk 13, 28.

8, 14-15: Cf Mk 1, 29-31. Unlike Mark, Matthew has no implied request by others for the woman's cure. Jesus acts on his own initiative, and the cured woman rises and waits not on "them" (Mk 1, 31) but on *him.*

8, 16: *By a word:* a Matthean addition to Mk 1, 34; cf Mt 8, 8.

8, 17: This fulfillment citation from Is 53, 4 follows the MT, not the LXX. The prophet speaks of the Servant of the Lord who suffers vicariously for the sins ("infirmities") of others; Matthew takes the *infirmities* as physical afflictions.

8, 18-22: This passage between the first and second series of miracles about following Jesus is taken from Q (see Lk 9, 57-62). The third of the three sayings found in the source is absent from Matthew.

8, 18: *The other side:* i.e., of the Sea of Galilee.

8, 19: *Teacher:* for Matthew, this designation of Jesus is true, for he has Jesus using it of himself (Mt 10, 24.25; 23, 8; 26, 18), yet when it is used of him by others they are either his opponents (Mt 9, 11; 12, 38; 17, 24; 22, 16.24.36) or, as here and in Mt 19, 16, well-disposed persons who cannot see more deeply. Thus it reveals an inadequate recognition of who Jesus is.

8, 20: *Son of Man:* see the note on Mk 8, 31. This is the first occurrence in Mt of a term that appears in the New Testament only in sayings of Jesus, except for Acts 7, 56 and possibly Mt 9, 6 (// Mk 2, 10; Lk 5, 24). In Mt it refers to Jesus in his ministry (seven times, as here), in his passion and resurrection (nine times, e.g., Mt 17, 22), and in his glorious coming at the end of the age (thirteen times, e.g., Mt 24, 30).

father." 22 But Jesus answered him, "Follow me, and let the dead bury their dead."*

The Calming of the Storm at Sea. 23 [o] He got into a boat and his disciples followed him.* 24 Suddenly a violent storm* came up on the sea, so that the boat was being swamped by waves; but he was asleep. 25 [p] They came and woke him, saying, "Lord, save us!* We are perishing!" 26 He said to them, "Why are you terrified, O you of little faith?"* Then he got up, rebuked the winds and the sea, and there was great calm. 27 The men were amazed and said, "What sort of man is this, whom even the winds and the sea obey?"

The Healing of the Gadarene Demoniacs. 28 [q] When he came to the other side, to the territory of the Gadarenes,* two demoniacs who were coming from the tombs met him. They were so savage that no one could travel by that road. 29 They cried out, "What have you to do with us,* Son of God? Have you come here to torment us before the appointed time?" 30 Some distance away a herd of many swine was feeding.* 31 The demons pleaded with him, "If you drive us out, send us into the herd of swine."[r] 32 And he said to them, "Go then!" They came out and entered the swine, and the whole herd rushed down the steep bank into the sea where they drowned. 33 The swineherds ran away, and when they came to the town they reported everything, including what had happened to the demoniacs. 34 Thereupon the whole town came out to meet Jesus, and when they saw him they begged him to leave their district.

CHAPTER 9

The Healing of a Paralytic. 1 [s] He entered a boat, made the crossing, and came into his own town.* 2 And there people brought to him a paralytic lying on a stretcher. When Jesus saw their faith, he said to the paralytic, "Courage, child, your sins are forgiven."[t] 3 At that, some of the scribes* said to themselves, "This man is blaspheming." 4 Jesus knew what they were thinking, and said, "Why do you harbor evil thoughts? 5 Which is easier, to say, 'Your sins are forgiven,' or to say, 'Rise and walk'? 6 * But that you may know that the Son of Man has authority on earth to forgive sins"—he then said to the paralytic, "Rise, pick up your stretcher, and go home."[u] 7 He rose and went home. 8 When the crowds saw this they were struck with awe and glorified God who had given such authority to human beings.*

---

o 23-27: Mk 4, 35-40; Lk 8, 22-25.—p 25-26: Ps 107, 28-29.—q 28-34: Mk 5, 1-17; Lk 8, 26-37.—r Lk 4, 34.41.—s 1-8: Mk 2, 3-12; Lk 5, 18-26.—t Lk 7, 48.—u Jn 5, 27.

8, 22: *Let the dead bury their dead:* the demand of Jesus overrides what both the Jewish and the Hellenistic world regarded as a filial obligation of the highest importance. See the note on Lk 9, 60.

8, 23: *His disciples followed him:* the first miracle in the second group (Mt 8, 23—9, 8) is introduced by a verse that links it with the preceding sayings by the catchword "follow." In Mk the initiative in entering the boat is taken by the disciples (Mk 4, 35-41); here, Jesus enters first and the disciples follow.

8, 24: *Storm:* literally, "earthquake," a word commonly used in apocalyptic literature for the shaking of the old world when God brings in his kingdom. All the synoptics use it in depicting the events preceding the parousia of the Son of Man (Mt 24, 7; Mk 13, 8; Lk 21, 11). Matthew has introduced it here and in his account of the death and resurrection of Jesus (Mt 27, 51-54; 28, 2).

8, 25: The reverent plea of the disciples contrasts sharply with their reproach of Jesus in Mk 4, 38.

8, 26: *You of little faith:* see the note on Mt 6, 30. *Great calm:* Jesus' calming the sea may be meant to recall the Old Testament theme of God's control over the chaotic waters (Pss 65, 8; 89, 10; 93, 3-4; 107, 29).

8, 28: *Gadarenes:* this is the reading of Codex Vaticanus, supported by other important textual witnesses. The original reading of Codex Sinaiticus was Gazarenes, later changed to Gergesenes, and a few versions have Gerasenes. Each of these readings points to a different territory connected, respectively, with the cities Gadara, Gergesa, and Gerasa (modern Jerash). There is the same confusion of readings in the parallel texts, Mk 5, 1 and Lk 8, 26; there the best reading seems to be "Gerasenes," whereas "Gadarenes" is probably the original reading in Mt. The town of Gadara was about five miles southeast of the Sea of Galilee, and Josephus (*Life* 9 §42) refers to it as possessing territory that lay on that sea. *Two demoniacs:* Mark (5, 1-20) has one.

8, 29: *What have you to do with us?:* see the note on Jn 2, 4. *Before the appointed time:* the notion that evil spirits were allowed by God to afflict human beings until the time of the final judgment is found in Enoch 16, 1 and Jubilees 10, 7-10.

8, 30: The tending of pigs, animals considered unclean by Mosaic law (Lv 11, 6-7), indicates that the population was Gentile.

9, 1: *His own town:* Capernaum; see Mt 4, 13.

9, 3: *Scribes:* see the note on Mk 2, 6. Matthew omits the reason given in the Marcan story for the charge of blasphemy: "Who but God alone can forgive sins?" (Mk 2, 7).

9, 6: It is not clear whether "But that you may know . . . to forgive sins" is intended to be a continuation of the words of Jesus or a parenthetical comment of the evangelist to those who would hear or read this gospel. In any case, Matthew here follows the Marcan text.

9, 8: *Who had given such authority to human beings:* a significant difference from Mk 2, 12 ("They . . . glorified God, saying, 'We have never seen anything like this' "). Matthew's extension to *human beings* of the authority to forgive sins points to the belief that such authority was being claimed by Matthew's church.

The Call of Matthew. 9 * As Jesus passed on from there,[v] he saw a man named Matthew* sitting at the customs post. He said to him, "Follow me." And he got up and followed him. 10 While he was at table in his house,* many tax collectors and sinners came and sat with Jesus and his disciples.[w] 11 The Pharisees saw this and said to his disciples, "Why does your teacher* eat with tax collectors and sinners?" 12 He heard this and said, "Those who are well do not need a physician, but the sick do.* 13 Go and learn the meaning of the words,[x] 'I desire mercy, not sacrifice.'* I did not come to call the righteous but sinners."

The Question about Fasting. 14 [y] Then the disciples of John approached him and said, "Why do we and the Pharisees fast [much], but your disciples do not fast?" 15 Jesus answered them, "Can the wedding guests mourn as long as the bridegroom is with them? The days will come when the bridegroom is taken away from them, and then they will fast.* 16 No one patches an old cloak with a piece of unshrunken cloth,* for its fullness pulls away from the cloak and the tear gets worse. 17 People do not put new wine into old wineskins. Otherwise the skins burst, the wine spills out, and the skins are ruined. Rather, they pour new wine into fresh wineskins, and both are preserved."

The Official's Daughter and the Woman with a Hemorrhage. 18 * While he was saying these things to them,[z] an official* came forward, knelt down before him, and said, "My daughter has just died. But come, lay your hand on her, and she will live." 19 Jesus rose and followed him, and so did his disciples. 20 A woman suffering hemorrhages for twelve years came up behind him and touched the tassel* on his cloak. 21 She said to herself, "If only I can touch his cloak, I shall be cured."[a] 22 Jesus turned around and saw her, and said, "Courage, daughter! Your faith has saved you." And from that hour the woman was cured.

23 When Jesus arrived at the official's house and saw the flute players and the crowd who were making a commotion, 24 he said, "Go away! The girl is not dead but sleeping."* And they ridiculed him. 25 When the crowd was put out, he came and took her by the hand, and the little girl arose. 26 And news of this spread throughout all that land.

The Healing of Two Blind Men. * 27 [b] And as Jesus passed on from there, two blind men

---

v 9-13: Mk 2, 14-17; Lk 5, 27-32.—w Mt 11, 19; Lk 15, 1-2.—x Mt 12, 7; Hos 6, 6.—y 14-17: Mk 2, 18-22; Lk 5, 33-39.—z 18-26: Mk 5, 22-43; Lk 8, 41-56.—a Mt 14, 36; Nm 15, 37.—b 27-31: Mt 20, 29-34.

9, 9-17: In this section the order is the same as that of Mk 2, 13-22.

9, 9: *A man named Matthew:* Mark names this tax collector Levi (Mk 2, 14). No such name appears in the four lists of the twelve who were the closest companions of Jesus (Mt 10, 2-4; Mk 3, 16-19; Lk 6, 14-16; Acts 1, 13 [eleven, because of the defection of Judas Iscariot]), whereas all four list a Matthew, designated in Mt 10, 3 as "the tax collector." The evangelist may have changed the "Levi" of his source to *Matthew* so that this man, whose call is given special notice, like that of the first four disciples (Mt 4, 18-22), might be included among the twelve. Another reason for the change may be that the disciple Matthew was the source of traditions peculiar to the church for which the evangelist was writing.

9, 10: *His house:* it is not clear whether *his* refers to Jesus or Matthew. *Tax collectors:* see the note on Mt 5, 46. Table association with such persons would cause ritual impurity.

9, 11: *Teacher:* see the note on Mt 8, 19.

9, 12: See the note on Mk 2, 17.

9, 13: *Go and learn . . . not sacrifice:* Matthew adds the prophetic statement of Hos 6, 6 to the Marcan account (see also Mt 12, 7). If mercy is superior to the temple sacrifices, how much more to the laws of ritual impurity.

9, 15: Fasting is a sign of mourning and would be as inappropriate at this time of joy, when Jesus is proclaiming the kingdom, as it would be at a marriage feast. Yet the saying looks forward to the time when Jesus will no longer be with the disciples visibly, the time of Matthew's church. *Then they will fast:* see *Didache* 8, 1.

9, 16-17: Each of these parables speaks of the unsuitability of attempting to combine the old and the new. Jesus' teaching is not a patching up of Judaism, nor can the gospel be contained within the limits of Mosaic law.

9, 18-34: In this third group of miracles, the first (18-26) is clearly dependent on Mark (Mk 5, 21-43). Though it tells of two miracles, the cure of the woman had already been included within the story of the raising of the official's daughter, so that the two were probably regarded as a single unit. The other miracles seem to have been derived from Mark and Q respectively, though there Matthew's own editing is much more evident.

9, 18: *Official:* literally, "ruler." Mark calls him "one of the synagogue officials" (Mk 5, 22). *My daughter has just died:* Matthew heightens the Marcan "my daughter is at the point of death" (Mk 5, 23).

9, 20: *Tassel:* possibly "fringe." The Mosaic law prescribed that tassels be worn on the corners of one's garment as a reminder to keep the commandments (see Nm 15, 37-39; Dt 22, 12).

9, 24: *Sleeping:* sleep is a biblical metaphor for death (see Ps 87, 6 LXX; Dn 12, 2; 1 Thes 5, 10). Jesus' statement is not a denial of the child's real death, but an assurance that she will be roused from her sleep of death.

9, 27-31: This story was probably composed by Matthew out of Mark's story of the healing of a blind man named Bartimaeus (Mk 10, 46-52). Mark places the event late in Jesus' ministry, just before his entrance into Jerusalem, and Matthew has followed his Marcan source at that point in his gospel also (see Mt 20, 29-34). In each of the Matthean stories the single blind man of Mark becomes two. The reason why Matthew would have given a double version of the Marcan story and placed the earlier one here may be that he wished to add a story of Jesus' curing the blind at this point in order to prepare for Jesus' answer to the emissaries of the Baptist (Mt 11, 4-6) in which Jesus, recounting his works, begins with his giving sight to the blind.

followed [him], crying out, "Son of David,* have pity on us!"*c* 28 When he entered the house, the blind men approached him and Jesus said to them, "Do you believe that I can do this?" "Yes, Lord," they said to him. 29 Then he touched their eyes and said, "Let it be done for you according to your faith." 30 And their eyes were opened. Jesus warned them sternly, "See that no one knows about this." 31 But they went out and spread word of him through all that land.

The Healing of a Mute Person.* 32 *d* As they were going out, a demoniac who could not speak was brought to him, 33 and when the demon was driven out the mute person spoke. The crowds were amazed and said, "Nothing like this has ever been seen in Israel."*e* 34 But the Pharisees said,*f* "He drives out demons by the prince of demons."*

The Compassion of Jesus. 35 *g* Jesus went around to all the towns and villages, teaching in their synagogues, proclaiming the gospel of the kingdom, and curing every disease and illness.* 36 *h* At the sight of the crowds, his heart was moved with pity for them because they were troubled and abandoned, like sheep without a shepherd.* 37 *i* Then he said to his disciples, "The harvest is abundant but the laborers are few; 38 so ask the master of the harvest to send out laborers for his harvest."*

CHAPTER 10

The Mission of the Twelve. 1 *Then he summoned his twelve disciples* and gave them authority over unclean spirits to drive them out and to cure every disease and every illness.*j* 2 The names of the twelve apostles* are these: first, Simon called Peter, and his brother Andrew; James, the son of Zebedee, and his brother John; 3 Philip and Bartholomew, Thomas and Matthew the tax collector; James, the son of Alphaeus, and Thaddeus; 4 Simon the Cananean, and Judas Iscariot who betrayed him.

The Commissioning of the Twelve. 5 *k* Jesus sent out these twelve* after instructing them thus, "Do not go into pagan territory or enter a Samaritan town. 6 *l* Go rather to the lost sheep of the house of Israel. 7 As you go, make this proclamation: 'The kingdom of heaven is at hand.'*m* 8 * Cure the sick, raise the dead, cleanse lepers, drive out demons. Without cost you have received; without cost you are to give. 9 *n* Do not take gold or silver or copper for your belts; 10 *o* no sack for the journey, or a

---

c Mt 15, 22.—d 32-34: Mt 12, 22-24; Lk 11, 14-15.—e Mk 2, 12; 7, 37.—f Mt 10, 25; Mk 3, 22.—g Mt 4, 23; Lk 8, 1.—h Nm 27, 17; 1 Kgs 22, 17; Jer 50, 6; Ez 34, 5; Mk 6, 34.—i 37-38: Lk 10, 2; Jn 4, 35.—j 1-4: Mk 3, 14-19; Lk 6, 13-16; Acts 1, 13.—k 5-15: Mk 6, 7-13; Lk 9, 1-6.—l Mt 15, 24.—m Mt 3, 2; 4, 17.—n 9-10: Mk 6, 8-9; Lk 9, 3; 10, 4.—o Lk 10, 7; 1 Cor 9, 14; 2 Tm 5, 18.

9, 27: *Son of David:* this messianic title is connected once with the healing power of Jesus in Mark (Mk 10, 47-48) and Luke (Lk 18, 38-39) but more frequently in Matthew (see also Mt 12, 23; 15, 22; 20, 30-31).

9, 32-34: The source of this story seems to be Q (see Lk 11, 14-15). As in the preceding healing of the blind, Matthew has two versions of this healing, the later in Mt 12, 22-24 and the earlier here.

9, 34: This spiteful accusation foreshadows the growing opposition to Jesus in chs 11 and 12.

9, 35: See the notes on Mt 4, 23-25 and Mt 8, 1—9, 38.

9, 36: See Mk 6, 34; Nm 27, 17; 1 Kgs 22, 17.

9, 37-38: This Q saying (see Lk 10, 2) is only imperfectly related to this context. It presupposes that God *(the master of the harvest)* can take the initiative in sending out preachers of the gospel, whereas in Matthew's setting it leads into ch 10, where Jesus does so.

10, 1—11, 1: After an introductory narrative (10, 1-4), the second of the discourses of the gospel. It deals with the mission now to be undertaken by the disciples (5-15), but the perspective broadens and includes the missionary activity of the church between the time of the resurrection and the parousia.

10, 1: *His twelve disciples:* although, unlike Mark (Mk 3, 13-14) and Luke (Lk 6, 12-16), Matthew has no story of Jesus' choosing the Twelve, he assumes that the group is known to the reader. The earliest New Testament text to speak of it is 1 Cor 15, 5. The number probably is meant to recall the twelve tribes of Israel and implies Jesus' authority to call all Israel into the kingdom. While Luke (Lk 6, 13) and probably Mark (Mk 4, 10.34) distinguish between the Twelve and a larger group also termed disciples, Matthew tends to identify the disciples and the Twelve. *Authority . . . every illness:* activities the same as those of Jesus; see Mt 4, 23; 9, 35; 10, 8. The Twelve also share in his proclamation of the kingdom (Mt 10, 7). But although he teaches (Mt 4, 23; 7, 28; 9, 35), they do not. Their commission to teach comes only after Jesus' resurrection, after they have been fully instructed by him (Mt 28, 20).

10, 2-4: Here, for the only time in Matthew, the Twelve are designated *apostles.* The word "apostle" means "one who is sent," and therefore fits the situation here described. In the Pauline letters, the place where the term occurs most frequently in the New Testament, it means primarily one who has seen the risen Lord and has been commissioned to proclaim the resurrection. With slight variants in Luke and Acts, the names of those who belong to this group are the same in the four lists given in the New Testament (see the note on Mt 9, 9). *Cananean:* this represents an Aramaic word meaning "zealot." The meaning of that designation is unclear (see the note on Lk 6, 15).

10, 5-6: Like Jesus (Mt 15, 24), the Twelve are sent only to Israel. This saying may reflect an original Jewish Christian refusal of the mission to the Gentiles, but for Matthew it expresses rather the limitation that Jesus himself observed during his ministry.

10, 8-11: The Twelve have received their own call and mission through God's gift, and the benefits they confer are likewise to be given freely. They are not to take with them money, provisions, or unnecessary clothing; their lodging and food will be provided by those who receive them.

second tunic, or sandals, or walking stick. The laborer deserves his keep. [11] p Whatever town or village you enter, look for a worthy person in it, and stay there until you leave. [12] As you enter a house, wish it peace. [13] If the house is worthy, let your peace come upon it; if not, let your peace return to you.* [14] q Whoever will not receive you or listen to your words—go outside that house or town and shake the dust from your feet.* [15] Amen, I say to you, it will be more tolerable for the land of Sodom and Gomorrah on the day of judgment than for that town. r

Coming Persecutions. [16] s "Behold, I am sending you like sheep in the midst of wolves; so be shrewd as serpents and simple as doves. [17] *But beware of people, t for they will hand you over to courts and scourge you in their synagogues, u [18] and you will be led before governors and kings for my sake as a witness before them and the pagans. [19] When they hand you over, do not worry about how you are to speak or what you are to say. You will be given at that moment what you are to say. v [20] For it will not be you who speak but the Spirit of your Father speaking through you. [21] w Brother will hand over brother to death, and the father his child; children will rise up against parents and have them put to death.* [22] You will be hated by all because of my name, but whoever endures to the end* will be saved. [23] When they persecute you in one town, flee to another. Amen, I say to you, you will not finish the towns of Israel before the Son of Man comes.* [24] x No disciple is above his teacher, no slave above his master. [25] It is enough for the disciple that he become like his teacher, for the slave that he become like his master. If they have called the master of the house Beelzebul,* how much more those of his household!

Courage under Persecution. [26] y "Therefore do not be afraid of them. Nothing is concealed that will not be revealed, nor secret that will not be known.* z [27] What I say to you in the darkness, speak in the light; what you hear whispered, proclaim on the housetops. [28] And do not be afraid of those who kill the body but cannot kill the soul; rather, be afraid of the one who can destroy both soul and body in Gehenna. a [29] Are not two sparrows sold for a small coin? Yet not one of them falls to the ground without your Father's knowledge. [30] Even all the hairs of your head are counted. [31] So do not be afraid; you are worth more than many sparrows. [32] Everyone who acknowledges me before others I will acknowledge before my heavenly Father.* [33] But whoever denies me before others, I will deny before my heavenly Father. b

Jesus: A Cause of Division. [34] c "Do not think that I have come to bring peace upon the earth. I have come to bring not peace but the sword. [35] For I have come to set

> a man 'against his father,
>   a daughter against her mother,
>   and a daughter-in-law against her mother-in-law;
> [36]   and one's enemies will be those of his household.'

---

p 11-15: Mk 6, 10-11; Lk 9, 4-5; 10, 5-12.—q Acts 13, 51; 18, 6.—r Mt 11, 24; Gn 19, 1-29; Jude 7.—s Lk 10, 3.—t 17-22: Mk 13, 9-13; Lk 21, 12-19.—u Acts 5, 40.—v Ex 4, 11-12; Jer 1, 6-10; Lk 12, 11-12.—w 21-22: Mt 24, 9.13.—x 24-25: Lk 6, 40; Jn 13, 16; 15, 20.—y 26-33: Lk 12, 2-9.—z Mk 4, 22; Lk 8, 17; 1 Tm 5, 25.—a Jas 4, 12.—b Mk 8, 38; Lk 9, 26; 2 Tm 2, 12; Rv 3, 5.—c 34-35: Lk 12, 51-53.

10, 13: The greeting of peace is conceived of not merely as a salutation but as an effective word. If it finds no worthy recipient, it will return to the speaker.

10, 14: *Shake the dust from your feet:* this gesture indicates a complete disassociation from such unbelievers.

10, 17: The persecutions attendant upon the post-resurrection mission now begin to be spoken of. Here Matthew brings into the discourse sayings found in Mk 13, which deals with events preceding the parousia.

10, 21: See Mi 7, 6, which is cited in vv 35.36.

10, 22: *To the end:* the original meaning was probably "until the parousia." But it is not likely that Matthew expected no missionary disciples to suffer death before then, since he envisages the martyrdom of other Christians (21). For him, *the end* is probably that of the individual's life (see 28).

10, 23: *Before the Son of Man comes:* since the coming of the Son of Man at the end of the age had not taken place when this gospel was written, much less during the mission of the Twelve during Jesus' ministry, Matthew cannot have meant the coming to refer to the parousia. It is difficult to know what he understood it to be: perhaps the "proleptic parousia" of Mt 28, 16-20, or the destruction of the temple in A.D. 70, viewed as a coming of Jesus in judgment on unbelieving Israel.

10, 25: *Beelzebul:* see Mt 9, 34 for the charge linking Jesus with "the prince of demons," who is named *Beelzebul* in Mt 12, 24. The meaning of the name is uncertain; possibly, "lord of the house."

10, 26: The *concealed* and *secret* coming of the kingdom is to be proclaimed by them, and no fear must be allowed to deter them from that proclamation.

10, 32-33: In the Q parallel (Lk 12, 8-9), the Son of Man will acknowledge those who have acknowledged Jesus, and those who deny him will be denied (by the Son of Man) before the angels of God at the judgment. Here Jesus and the Son of Man are identified, and the acknowledgment or denial will be before his heavenly Father.

Mt

The Conditions of Discipleship. 37 *d* "Whoever loves father or mother more than me is not worthy of me, and whoever loves son or daughter more than me is not worthy of me; 38 and whoever does not take up his cross* and follow after me is not worthy of me. 39 *e* Whoever finds his life will lose it, and whoever loses his life for my sake will find it.*

Rewards. 40 "Whoever receives you receives me,* and whoever receives me receives the one who sent me. *f* 41 Whoever receives a prophet* because he is a prophet will receive a prophet's reward, and whoever receives a righteous man because he is righteous will receive a righteous man's reward. 42 And whoever gives only a cup of cold water to one of these little ones to drink because he is a disciple—amen, I say to you, he will surely not lose his reward." *g*

CHAPTER 11

1 When Jesus finished giving these commands to his twelve disciples,* he went away from that place to teach and to preach in their towns.

IV. OPPOSITION FROM ISRAEL

The Messengers from John the Baptist. 2 * *h* When John heard in prison* of the works of the Messiah, he sent his disciples to him

3 with this question, "Are you the one who is to come, or should we look for another?"* 4 Jesus said to them in reply, "Go and tell John what you hear and see: 5 * the blind regain their sight, the lame walk, lepers are cleansed, the deaf hear, the dead are raised, and the poor have the good news proclaimed to them. *i* 6 And blessed is the one who takes no offense at me."

Jesus' Testimony to John. * 7 As they were going off, Jesus began to speak to the crowds about John, "What did you go out to the desert to see? A reed swayed by the wind? *j* 8 Then what did you go out to see? Someone dressed in fine clothing? Those who wear fine clothing are in royal palaces. 9 Then why did you go out? To see a prophet?* Yes, I tell you, and more than a prophet. 10 This is the one about whom it is written:

'Behold, I am sending my messenger ahead of you;
   he will prepare your way before you.' *k*

11 Amen, I say to you, among those born of women there has been none greater than John the Baptist; yet the least in the kingdom of heaven is greater than he.* 12 From the days of John the Baptist until now, the kingdom of heaven suffers violence,* and

---

d 37-39: Mt 16, 24-25; Lk 14, 26-27.—e Mk 8, 35; Lk 9, 24; Jn 12, 25.—f Lk 10, 16; Jn 12, 44; 13, 20.—g Mt 25, 40; Mk 9, 41.—h 2-11: Lk 7, 18-28.—i Is 26, 19; 29, 18-19; 35, 5-6; 61, 1.—j Mt 3, 3.5.—k Ex 23, 20; Mal 3, 1; Mk 1, 2; Lk 1, 76.

10, 38: The first mention of the cross in Matthew, explicitly that of the disciple, but implicitly that of Jesus *(and follow after me)*. Crucifixion was a form of capital punishment used by the Romans for offenders who were not Roman citizens.

10, 39: One who denies Jesus in order to save one's earthly life will be condemned to everlasting destruction; loss of earthly life for Jesus' sake will be rewarded by everlasting life in the kingdom.

10, 40-42: All who receive the disciples of Jesus receive him, and God who sent him, and will be rewarded accordingly.

10, 41: *A prophet:* one who speaks in the name of God; here, the Christian prophets who proclaim the gospel. *Righteous man:* since righteousness is demanded of all the disciples, it is difficult to take the *righteous man* of this verse and *one of these little ones* (42) as indicating different groups within the followers of Jesus. Probably all three designations are used here of Christian missionaries as such.

11, 1: The closing formula of the discourse refers back to the original addressees, the Twelve.

11, 2—12, 50: The narrative section of the third book deals with the growing opposition to Jesus. It is largely devoted to disputes and attacks relating to faith and discipleship and thus contains much sayings-material, drawn in large part from Q.

11, 2: *In prison:* see Mt 4, 12; 14, 1-12. *The works of the Messiah:* the deeds of chs 8-9.

11, 3: The question probably expresses a doubt of the Baptist that Jesus is *the one who is to come* (cf Mal 3, 1) because his mission has not been one of fiery judgment as John had expected (Mt 3, 2).

11, 5-6: Jesus' response is taken from passages of Isaiah (Is 26, 19; 29, 18-19; 35, 5-6; 61, 1) that picture the time of salvation as marked by deeds such as those that Jesus is doing. The beatitude is a warning to the Baptist not to disbelieve because his expectations have not been met.

11, 7-19: Jesus' rebuke of John is counterbalanced by a reminder of the greatness of the Baptist's function (7-15) that is followed by a complaint about those who have heeded neither John nor Jesus (16-19).

11, 9-10: In common Jewish belief there had been no prophecy in Israel since the last of the Old Testament prophets, Malachi. The coming of a new prophet was eagerly awaited, and Jesus agrees that John was such. Yet he was *more than a prophet,* for he was the precursor of the one who would bring in the new and final age. The Old Testament quotation is a combination of Mal 3, 1 and Ex 23, 20, with the significant change that the *before me* of Malachi becomes *before you.* The messenger now precedes not God, as in the original, but Jesus.

11, 11: John's preeminent greatness lies in his function of announcing the imminence of the kingdom (Mt 3, 1). But to be in the kingdom is so great a privilege that the least who has it is greater than the Baptist.

11, 12: The meaning of this difficult saying is probably that the opponents of Jesus are trying to prevent people from accepting the kingdom and to snatch it away from those who have received it.

the violent are taking it by force.*l* [13] All the prophets and the law* prophesied up to the time of John. [14] And if you are willing to accept it, he is Elijah, the one who is to come.*m* [15] Whoever has ears ought to hear.

[16] *n* "To what shall I compare this generation?* It is like children who sit in marketplaces and call to one another, [17] 'We played the flute for you, but you did not dance, we sang a dirge but you did not mourn.' [18] For John came neither eating nor drinking, and they said, 'He is possessed by a demon.'*o* [19] The Son of Man came eating and drinking and they said, 'Look, he is a glutton and a drunkard, a friend of tax collectors and sinners.' But wisdom is vindicated by her works."*p*

Reproaches to Unrepentant Towns. [20] *q* Then he began to reproach the towns where most of his mighty deeds had been done, since they had not repented. [21] "Woe to you, Chorazin! Woe to you, Bethsaida! For if the mighty deeds done in your midst had been done in Tyre and Sidon,* they would long ago have repented in sackcloth and ashes.*r* [22] But I tell you, it will be more tolerable for Tyre and Sidon on the day of judgment than for you. [23] And as for you, Capernaum:

'Will you be exalted to heaven?*s*

You will go down to the netherworld.'*

For if the mighty deeds done in your midst had been done in Sodom, it would have remained until this day. [24] But I tell you, it will be more tolerable for the land of Sodom on the day of judgment than for you."*t*

The Praise of the Father. [25] *u* At that time Jesus said in reply,* "I give praise to you, Father, Lord of heaven and earth, for although you have hidden these things from the wise and the learned you have revealed them to the childlike. [26] Yes, Father, such has been your gracious will. [27] All things have been handed over to me by my Father. No one knows the Son except the Father, and no one knows the Father except the Son and anyone to whom the Son wishes to reveal him.*v*

The Gentle Mastery of Christ. [28] * "Come to me, all you who labor and are burdened,* and I will give you rest. [29] *w* Take my yoke upon you and learn from me, for I am meek and humble of heart; and you will find rest for yourselves.* [30] For my yoke is easy, and my burden light."

CHAPTER 12

Picking Grain on the Sabbath.[1] *At that time Jesus was going through a field of grain on the sabbath.*x* His disciples were hungry and began to pick the heads of grain and eat them.*y* [2] When the Pharisees saw this, they said to him, "See, your disciples are doing what is unlawful* to do on

---

l Lk 16, 16.—m Mt 17, 10-13; Mal 3, 23; Lk 1, 17.—n 16-19: Lk 7, 31-35.—o Lk 1, 15.—p Mt 9, 10-11.—q 20-24: Lk 10, 12-15.—r Jl 4, 4-7.—s Is 14, 13-15.—t Mt 10, 15.—u 25-27: Lk 10, 21-22.—v Jn 3, 35; 6, 46; 7, 28; 10, 15.—w Sir 51, 26; Jer 6, 16.—x 1-8: Mk 2, 23-28; Lk 6, 1-5.—y Dt 23, 26.

11, 13: *All the prophets and the law:* Matthew inverts the usual order, "law and prophets," and says that both have *prophesied.* This emphasis on the prophetic character of the law points to its fulfillment in the teaching of Jesus and to the transitory nature of some of its commandments (see the note on Mt 5, 17-20).

11, 16-19: See Lk 7, 31-35. The meaning of the parable (16-17) and its explanation (18-19b) is much disputed. A plausible view is that the *children* of the parable are two groups, one of which proposes different entertainments to the other that will not agree with either proposal. The first represents John, Jesus, and their disciples; the second those who reject John for his asceticism and Jesus for his table association with those despised by the religiously observant. Verse 19c *(her works)* forms an inclusion with v 2 ("the works of the Messiah"). The original form of the saying is better preserved in Lk 7, 35, ". . . wisdom is vindicated by all her children." There John and Jesus are the children of Wisdom; here the works of Jesus the Messiah are those of divine Wisdom, of which he is the embodiment. Some important textual witnesses, however, have essentially the same reading as in Luke.

11, 21: Tyre and Sidon were pagan cities denounced for their wickedness in the Old Testament; cf Jl 4, 4-7.

11, 23: Capernaum's pride and punishment are described in language taken from the taunt song against the king of Babylon (Is 14, 13-15).

11, 25-27: This Q saying, identical with Lk 10, 21-22 except for minor variations, introduces a joyous note into this section, so dominated by the theme of unbelief. While *the wise and the learned,* the scribes and Pharisees, have rejected Jesus' preaching and the significance of his mighty deeds, *the childlike* have accepted them. Acceptance depends upon the Father's revelation, but this is granted to those who are open to receive it and refused to the arrogant. Jesus can speak of all mysteries because he is *the Son* and there is perfect reciprocity of knowledge between him and the Father; what has been *handed over* to him is revealed only to those whom he wishes.

11, 28-29: These verses are peculiar to Matthew and are similar to Ben Sirach's invitation to learn wisdom and submit to her yoke (Sir 51, 23.26).

11, 28: *Who labor and are burdened:* burdened by the law as expounded by the scribes and Pharisees (Mt 23, 4).

11, 29: In place of the yoke of the law, complicated by scribal interpretation, Jesus invites the burdened to take the yoke of obedience to his word, under which they *will find rest;* cf Jer 6, 16.

12, 1-14: Matthew here returns to the Marcan order that he left in Mt 9, 18. The two stories depend on Mk 2, 23-28 and Mk 3, 1-6, respectively, and are the only places in either gospel that deal explicitly with Jesus' attitude toward sabbath observance.

12, 1-2: The picking of the heads of grain is here equated with reaping, which was forbidden on the sabbath (Ex 34, 21).

the sabbath." [3] He said to them,* "Have you not read what David[z] did when he and his companions were hungry, [4] how he went into the house of God and ate the bread of offering,[a] which neither he nor his companions but only the priests could lawfully eat? [5] * Or have you not read in the law that on the sabbath the priests serving in the temple violate the sabbath and are innocent?[b] [6] I say to you, something greater than the temple is here. [7] If you knew what this meant, 'I desire mercy, not sacrifice,'[c] you would not have condemned these innocent men.* [8] [d] For the Son of Man is Lord of the sabbath."*

The Man with a Withered Hand. [9] [e] Moving on from there, he went into their synagogue. [10] And behold, there was a man there who had a withered hand. They questioned him, "Is it lawful to cure on the sabbath?"* so that they might accuse him. [11] He said to them, "Which one of you who has a sheep that falls into a pit on the sabbath will not take hold of it and lift it out?* [12] How much more valuable a person is than a sheep. So it is lawful to do good on the sabbath." [13] Then he said to the man, "Stretch out your hand." He stretched it out, and it was restored as sound as the other. [14] But the Pharisees* went out and took counsel against him to put him to death.[f]

z 3-4: 1 Sm 21, 2-7.—a Lv 24, 5-9.—b Lv 24, 8; Nm 28, 9-10.—c Hos 6, 6.—d Jn 5, 16-17.—e 9-15: Mk 3, 1-6; Lk 6, 6-11.—f Jn 5, 18.—g 18-21: Is 42, 1-4.—h 22-24: Mt 9, 32-34; Lk 11, 14-15.—i Mt 9, 27.—j Mt 10, 25; Mk 3, 22.—k 25-29: Mk 3, 23-27; Lk 11, 17-22.

12, 3-4: See 1 Sm 21, 2-7. In the Marcan parallel (Mk 2, 25-26) the high priest is mistakenly called Abiathar, although in 1 Sm this action is attributed to Ahimelech. The Old Testament story is not about a violation of the sabbath rest; its pertinence to this dispute is that a violation of the law was permissible because of David's men being without food.

12, 5-6: This and the following argument (7) are peculiar to Matthew. The temple service seems to be the changing of the showbread on the sabbath (Lv 24, 8) and the doubling on the sabbath of the usual daily holocausts (Nm 28, 9-10). The argument is that the law itself requires work that breaks the sabbath rest, because of the higher duty of temple service. If temple duties outweigh the sabbath law, how much more does the presence of Jesus, with his proclamation of the kingdom (*something greater than the temple*), justify the conduct of his disciples.

12, 7: See the note on Mt 9, 13.

12, 8: The ultimate justification for the disciples' violation of the sabbath rest is that Jesus, the Son of Man, has supreme authority over the law.

12, 10: Rabbinic tradition later than the gospels allowed relief to be given to a sufferer on the sabbath if life was in danger. This may also have been the view of Jesus' Pharisaic contemporaries. But the case here is not about one in danger of death.

12, 11: Matthew omits the question posed by Jesus in Mk 3, 4 and substitutes one about rescuing a sheep on the sabbath, similar to that in Lk 14, 5.

The Chosen Servant.* [15] When Jesus realized this, he withdrew from that place. Many [people] followed him, and he cured them all,* [16] but he warned them not to make him known. [17] This was to fulfill what had been spoken through Isaiah the prophet:

[18] "Behold, my servant whom I have chosen,[g]
    my beloved in whom I delight;
I shall place my spirit upon him,
    and he will proclaim justice to the Gentiles.
[19] He will not contend* or cry out,
    nor will anyone hear his voice in the streets.
[20] A bruised reed he will not break,
    a smoldering wick he will not quench,
until he brings justice to victory.
[21]   And in his name the Gentiles will hope."*

Jesus and Beelzebul.* [22] [h] Then they brought to him a demoniac who was blind and mute. He cured the mute person so that he could speak and see. [23] [i] All the crowd was astounded, and said, "Could this perhaps be the Son of David?"* [24] [j] But when the Pharisees heard this, they said, "This man drives out demons only by the power of Beelzebul, the prince of demons."* [25] [k] But he knew what they were thinking and said to them,* "Every king-

12, 14: See Mk 3, 6. Here the plan to bring about Jesus' death is attributed to the Pharisees only. This is probably due to the situation of Matthew's church, when the sole opponents were the Pharisees.

12, 15-21: Matthew follows Mk 3, 7-12 but summarizes his source in two verses (15.16) that pick up the withdrawal, the healings, and the command for silence. To this he adds a fulfillment citation from the first Servant Song (Is 42, 1-4) that does not correspond exactly to either the Hebrew or the LXX of that passage. It is the longest Old Testament citation in this gospel, emphasizing the meekness of Jesus, the Servant of the Lord, and foretelling the extension of his mission to the Gentiles.

12, 15: Jesus' knowledge of the Pharisees' plot and his healing *all* are peculiar to Matthew.

12, 19: The servant's not contending is seen as fulfilled in Jesus' withdrawal from the disputes narrated in 1-14.

12, 21: Except for a minor detail, Matthew here follows the LXX, although the meaning of the Hebrew ("the coastlands will wait for his teaching") is similar.

12, 22-32: For the exorcism, see the note on Mt 9, 32-34. The long discussion combines Marcan and Q material (Mk 3, 22-30; Lk 11, 19-20.23; 12, 10). Mk 3, 20-21 is omitted, with a consequent lessening of the sharpness of Mt 12, 48.

12, 23: See the note on Mt 9, 27.

12, 24: See the note on Mt 10, 25.

12, 25-26: Jesus' first response to the Pharisees' charge is that if it were true, Satan would be destroying his own kingdom.

dom divided against itself will be laid waste, and no town or house divided against itself will stand. 26 And if Satan drives out Satan, he is divided against himself; how, then, will his kingdom stand? 27 And if I drive out demons by Beelzebul, by whom do your own people* drive them out? Therefore they will be your judges. 28 *l* But if it is by the Spirit of God that I drive out demons, then the kingdom of God has come upon you.* 29 How can anyone enter a strong man's house and steal his property, unless he first ties up the strong man? Then he can plunder his house.* 30 *m* Whoever is not with me is against me, and whoever does not gather with me scatters.* 31 *n* Therefore, I say to you, every sin and blasphemy will be forgiven people, but blasphemy against the Spirit* will not be forgiven. 32 And whoever speaks a word against the Son of Man will be forgiven; but whoever speaks against the holy Spirit will not be forgiven, either in this age or in the age to come.

A Tree and Its Fruits. 33 *o* "Either declare* the tree good and its fruit is good, or declare the tree rotten and its fruit is rotten, for a tree is known by its fruit. 34 *p* You brood of vipers, how can you say good things when you are evil? For from the fullness of the heart the mouth speaks.* 35 A good person brings forth good out of a store of goodness, but an evil person brings forth evil out of a store of evil. 36 *q* I tell you, on the day of judgment people will render an account for every careless word they speak.* 37 By your words you will be acquitted, and by your words you will be condemned."

The Demand for a Sign.* 38 Then some of the scribes and Pharisees said to him, "Teacher,* we wish to see a sign from you."*r* 39 He said to them in reply, "An evil and unfaithful* generation seeks a sign, but no sign will be given it except the sign of Jonah the prophet. 40 Just as Jonah was in the belly of the whale three days and three nights,* so will the Son of Man be in the heart of the earth three days and three nights. 41 * At the judgment, the men of Nineveh will arise with this generation and condemn it, because they repented at the preaching of Jonah; and there is something greater than Jonah here. 42 At the judgment the queen of the south will arise with this generation and condemn it, because she came from the ends of the earth to hear the wisdom of Solomon; and there is something greater than Solomon here.*s*

---

l Lk 11, 20.—m Lk 11, 23.—n 31-32: Mk 3, 28-30; Lk 12, 10.—o 33-35: Lk 6, 43-45.—p Mt 3, 7; 23, 33; 15, 11-12; Lk 3, 7.—q 36-37: Jas 3, 1-2.—r 38-42: Mt 16, 1-4; Jon 2, 1; 3, 1-10; Mk 8, 11-12; Lk 11, 29-32.—s 1 Kgs 10, 1-10.

12, 27: Besides pointing out the absurdity of the charge, Jesus asks how the work of Jewish exorcists *(your own people)* is to be interpreted. Are they, too, to be charged with collusion with Beelzebul? For an example of Jewish exorcism see Josephus, *Antiquities* 8, 2, 5 §§42-49.

12, 28: The Q parallel (Lk 11, 20) speaks of the "finger" rather than of the "spirit" of God. While the difference is probably due to Matthew's editing, he retains *the kingdom of God* rather than changing it to his usual "kingdom of heaven." *Has come upon you:* see Mt 4, 17.

12, 29: A short parable illustrates what Jesus is doing. The *strong man* is Satan, whom Jesus has tied up and whose *house* he is plundering. Jewish expectation was that Satan would be chained up in the last days (Rv 20, 2); Jesus' exorcisms indicate that those days have begun.

12, 30: This saying, already attached to the preceding verses in Q (see Lk 11, 23), warns that there can be no neutrality where Jesus is concerned. Its pertinence in a context where Jesus is addressing not the neutral but the bitterly opposed is not clear. The accusation of scattering, however, does fit the situation. Jesus is the shepherd of God's people (Mt 2, 6), his mission is to the lost sheep of Israel (Mt 15, 24); the Pharisees, who oppose him, are guilty of scattering the sheep.

12, 31: *Blasphemy against the Spirit:* the sin of attributing to Satan (24) what is the work of the Spirit of God (28).

12, 33: *Declare:* literally, "make." The meaning of this verse is obscure. Possibly it is a challenge to the Pharisees either to declare Jesus and his exorcisms good or both of them bad. A tree is known by its fruit; if the fruit is good, so must the tree be. If the driving out of demons is good, so must its source be.

12, 34: The admission of Jesus' goodness cannot be made by the Pharisees, for they are evil, and the words that proceed from their evil hearts cannot be good.

12, 36-37: If on the day of judgment people will be held accountable for even their *careless* words, the vicious accusations of the Pharisees will surely lead to their condemnation.

12, 38-42: This section is mainly from Q (see Lk 11, 29-32). Mk 8, 11-12, which Matthew has followed in Mt 16, 1-4, has a similar demand for a sign. The scribes and Pharisees refuse to accept the exorcisms of Jesus as authentication of his claims and demand a sign that will end all possibility of doubt. Jesus' response is that no such sign will be given. Because his opponents are evil and see him as an agent of Satan, nothing will convince them.

12, 38: *Teacher:* see the note on Mt 8, 19. In Mt 16, 1 the request is for a sign "from heaven" (Mk 8, 11).

12, 39: *Unfaithful:* literally, "adulterous." The covenant between God and Israel was portrayed as a marriage bond, and unfaithfulness to the covenant as adultery; cf Hos 2, 4-15; Jer 3, 6-10.

12, 40: See Jon 2, 1. While in Q the sign was simply Jonah's preaching to the Ninevites (Lk 11, 30.32), Matthew here adds Jonah's sojourn *in the belly of the whale* for *three days and three nights,* a prefigurement of Jesus' sojourn in the abode of the dead and, implicitly, of his resurrection.

12, 41-42: The Ninevites who *repented* (see Jon 3, 1-10) and *the queen of the south* (i.e., of Sheba; see 1 Kgs 10, 1-13) were pagans who responded to lesser opportunities than have been offered to Israel in the ministry of Jesus, *something greater than Jonah* or Solomon. At the final judgment they will condemn the faithless *generation* that has rejected him.

The Return of the Unclean Spirit.* 43 t
"When an unclean spirit goes out of a person it roams through arid regions searching for rest but finds none. 44 Then it says, 'I will return to my home from which I came.' But upon returning, it finds it empty, swept clean, and put in order. 45 Then it goes and brings back with itself seven other spirits more evil than itself, and they move in and dwell there; and the last condition of that person is worse than the first. Thus it will be with this evil generation."

The True Family of Jesus.* 46 u While he was still speaking to the crowds, his mother and his brothers appeared outside, wishing to speak with him. [47 Someone told him, "Your mother and your brothers are standing outside, asking to speak with you."]* 48 But he said in reply to the one who told him, "Who is my mother? Who are my brothers?" 49 And stretching out his hand toward his disciples, he said, "Here are my mother and my brothers. 50 For whoever does the will of my heavenly Father is my brother, and sister, and mother."

t 43-45: Lk 11, 24-26.—u 46-50: Mk 3, 31-35; Lk 8, 19-21.—v 1-15: Mk 4, 1-12; Lk 8, 4-10.—w Mt 25, 29; Mk 4, 25; Lk 8, 18; 19, 26.

12, 43-45: Another Q passage; cf Mt 11, 24-26. Jesus' ministry has broken Satan's hold over Israel, but the refusal of *this evil generation* to accept him will lead to a worse situation than what preceded his coming.

12, 46-50: See Mk 3, 31-35. Matthew has omitted Mk 3, 20-21, which is taken up in Mk 3, 31 (see the note on Mt 12, 22-32), yet the point of the story is the same in both gospels: natural kinship with Jesus counts for nothing; only one who *does the will of his heavenly Father* belongs to his true family.

12, 47: This verse is omitted in some important textual witnesses, including Codex Sinaiticus (original reading) and Codex Vaticanus.

13, 1-53: The discourse in parables is the third great discourse of Jesus in Mt and constitutes the second part of the third book of the gospel. Matthew follows the Marcan outline (Mk 4, 1-35) but has only two of Mark's parables, the five others being from Q and M. In addition to the seven parables, the discourse gives the reason why Jesus uses this type of speech (10-15), declares the blessedness of those who understand his teaching (16-17), explains the parable of the sower (18-23) and of the weeds (36-43), and ends with a concluding statement to the disciples (51-52).

13, 3: *In parables:* the word "parable" (Greek *parabolē*) is used in the LXX to translate the Hebrew *māshāl*, a designation covering a wide variety of literary forms such as axioms, proverbs, similitudes, and allegories. In the New Testament the same breadth of meaning of the word is found, but there it primarily designates stories that are illustrative comparisons between Christian truths and events of everyday life. Sometimes the event has a strange element that is quite different from usual experience (e.g., in v 33, the enormous amount of dough in the parable of the yeast); this is meant to sharpen the curiosity of the hearer. If each detail of such a story is given a figurative meaning, the story is an allegory. Those who maintain a sharp distinction be-

CHAPTER 13

The Parable of the Sower. 1 *On that day, Jesus went out of the house and sat down by the sea.v 2 Such large crowds gathered around him that he got into a boat and sat down, and the whole crowd stood along the shore. 3 And he spoke to them at length in parables,* saying: "A sower went out to sow.* 4 And as he sowed, some seed fell on the path, and birds came and ate it up. 5 Some fell on rocky ground, where it had little soil. It sprang up at once because the soil was not deep, 6 and when the sun rose it was scorched, and it withered for lack of roots. 7 Some seed fell among thorns, and the thorns grew up and choked it. 8 But some seed fell on rich soil, and produced fruit, a hundred or sixty or thirtyfold. 9 Whoever has ears ought to hear."

The Purpose of Parables. 10 The disciples approached him and said, "Why do you speak to them in parables?" 11 He said to them in reply, "Because knowledge of the mysteries of the kingdom of heaven has been granted to you, but to them it has not been granted.* 12 w To anyone who has, more will be given* and he will grow rich; from anyone who has not, even what he

tween parable and allegory insist that a parable has only one point of comparison, and that while parables were characteristic of Jesus' teaching, to see allegorical details in them is to introduce meanings that go beyond their original intention and even falsify it. However, to exclude any allegorical elements from a parable is an excessively rigid mode of interpretation, now abandoned by many scholars.

13, 3-8: Since in Palestine sowing often preceded ploughing, much of the seed is scattered on ground that is unsuitable. Yet while much is wasted, the seed that falls on good ground bears fruit in extraordinarily large measure. The point of the parable is that, in spite of some failure because of opposition and indifference, the message of Jesus about the coming of the kingdom will have enormous success.

13, 11: Since a parable is figurative speech that demands reflection for understanding, only those who are prepared to explore its meaning can come to know it. To understand is a gift of God, granted to the disciples but not to the crowds. In Semitic fashion, both the disciples' understanding and the crowd's obtuseness are attributed to God. The question of human responsibility for the obtuseness is not dealt with, although it is asserted in v 13. *The mysteries:* as in Lk 8, 10; Mk 4, 11 has "the mystery." The word is used in Dn 2, 18.19.27 and in the Qumran literature (1QpHab 7, 8; 1QS 3, 23; 1QM 3, 9) to designate a divine plan or decree affecting the course of history that can be known only when revealed. *Knowledge of the mysteries of the kingdom of heaven* means recognition that the kingdom has become present in the ministry of Jesus.

13, 12: In the New Testament use of this axiom of practical "wisdom" (see Mt 25, 29; Mk 4, 25; Lk 8, 18; 19, 26), the reference transcends the original level. God gives further understanding to one who accepts the revealed mystery; from the one who does not, he will take it away (note the "theological passive," *more will be given, what he has will be taken away*).

has will be taken away. [13] x This is why I speak to them in parables, because 'they look but do not see and hear but do not listen or understand.'* [14] y Isaiah's prophecy is fulfilled in them, which says:

'You shall indeed hear but not understand,
    you shall indeed look but never see.
[15] Gross is the heart of this people,
    they will hardly hear with their ears,
      they have closed their eyes,
    lest they see with their eyes
    and hear with their ears
and understand with their heart and be
      converted
    and I heal them.'

The Privilege of Discipleship.* [16] z "But blessed are your eyes, because they see, and your ears, because they hear. [17] Amen, I say to you, many prophets and righteous people longed to see what you see but did not see it, and to hear what you hear but did not hear it.

The Explanation of the Parable of the Sower.* [18] a "Hear then the parable of the sower. [19] The seed sown on the path is the one who hears the word of the kingdom without understanding it, and the evil one comes and steals away what was sown in his heart. [20] The seed sown on rocky ground is the one who hears the word and receives it at once with joy. [21] But he has no root and lasts only for a time. When some tribulation or persecution comes because

of the word, he immediately falls away. [22] The seed sown among thorns is the one who hears the word, but then worldly anxiety and the lure of riches choke the word and it bears no fruit. [23] But the seed sown on rich soil is the one who hears the word and understands it, who indeed bears fruit and yields a hundred or sixty or thirtyfold."

The Parable of the Weeds among the Wheat.* [24] He proposed another parable to them. "The kingdom of heaven may be likened to a man who sowed good seed in his field. [25] While everyone was asleep his enemy came and sowed weeds* all through the wheat, and then went off. [26] When the crop grew and bore fruit, the weeds appeared as well. [27] The slaves of the householder came to him and said, 'Master, did you not sow good seed in your field? Where have the weeds come from?' [28] He answered, 'An enemy has done this.' His slaves said to him, 'Do you want us to go and pull them up?' [29] He replied, 'No, if you pull up the weeds you might uproot the wheat along with them. [30] Let them grow together until harvest*; then at harvest time I will say to the harvesters, "First collect the weeds and tie them in bundles for burning; but gather the wheat into my barn." ' " b

The Parable of the Mustard Seed.* [31] c He proposed another parable to them. "The kingdom of heaven is like a mustard seed that a person took and sowed in a field. [32]

---

x Jn 9, 39.—y 14-15: Is 6, 9-10; Jn 12, 40; Acts 28, 26-27; Rom 11, 8.—z 16-17: Lk 10, 23-24; 1 Pt 1, 10-12.—a 18-23: Mk 4, 13-20; Lk 8, 11-15.—b Mt 3, 12.—c 31-32: Mk 4, 30-32; Lk 13, 18-19.

13, 13: *Because 'they look . . . or understand':* Matthew softens his Marcan source, which states that Jesus speaks in parables so that the crowds may not understand (Mk 4, 12), and makes such speaking a punishment given *because* they have not accepted his previous clear teaching. However, his citation of Is 6, 9-10 in v 14 supports the harsher Marcan view.

13, 16-17: Unlike the unbelieving crowds, the disciples have seen that which the *prophets* and the *righteous* of the Old Testament *longed to see* without having their longing fulfilled.

13, 18-23: See Mk 4, 14-20; Lk 8, 11-15. In this explanation of the parable the emphasis is on the various types of soil on which the seed falls, i.e., on the dispositions with which the preaching of Jesus is received. The second and third types particularly are explained in such a way as to support the view held by many scholars that the explanation derives not from Jesus but from early Christian reflection upon apostasy from the faith that was the consequence of persecution and worldliness respectively. Others, however, hold that the explanation may come basically from Jesus even though it was developed in the light of later Christian experience. The four types of persons envisaged are (1) those

who never accept *the word of the kingdom* (19); (2) those who believe for a while but fall away because of *persecution* (20-21); (3) those who believe, but in whom *the word* is choked by *worldly anxiety* and the seduction of *riches* (22); (4) those who respond to *the word* and produce *fruit* abundantly (23).

13, 24-30: This parable is peculiar to Matthew. The comparison in v 24 does not mean that *the kingdom of heaven may be likened* simply to the person in question but to the situation narrated in the whole story. The refusal of *the householder* to allow his *slaves* to separate *the wheat* from *the weeds* while they are still growing is a warning to the disciples not to attempt to anticipate the final judgment of God by a definitive exclusion of sinners from the kingdom. In its present stage it is composed of the good and the bad. The judgment of God alone will eliminate the sinful. Until then there must be patience and the preaching of repentance.

13, 25: *Weeds:* darnel, a poisonous weed that in its first stage of growth resembles wheat.

13, 30: *Harvest:* a common biblical metaphor for the time of God's judgment; cf Jer 51, 33; Jl 4, 13; Hos 6, 11.

13, 31-33: See Mk 4, 30-32; Lk 13, 18-21. The parables of the mustard seed and the yeast illustrate the same point: the amazing contrast between the small beginnings of the kingdom and its marvelous expansion.

32 d It is the smallest of all the seeds, yet when full-grown it is the largest of plants. It becomes a large bush, and the 'birds of the sky come and dwell in its branches.' "*

The Parable of the Yeast. 33 He spoke to them another parable. "The kingdom of heaven is like yeast* that a woman took and mixed with three measures of wheat flour until the whole batch was leavened."e

The Use of Parables. 34 f All these things Jesus spoke to the crowds in parables. He spoke to them only in parables,* 35 to fulfill what had been said through the prophet:*

"I will open my mouth in parables,
  I will announce what has lain hidden
    from the foundation [of the
    world]." g

The Explanation of the Parable of the Weeds. 36 Then, dismissing the crowds,* he went into the house. His disciples approached him and said, "Explain to us the parable of the weeds in the field." 37 * He said in reply, "He who sows good seed is the Son of Man, 38 the field is the world,* the good seed the children of the kingdom. The weeds are the children of the evil one, 39 and the enemy who sows them is the devil. The harvest is the end of the age,* and the harvesters are angels. 40 Just as weeds are collected and burned [up] with fire, so will it be at the end of the age.

41 The Son of Man will send his angels, and they will collect out of his kingdom* all who cause others to sin and all evildoers. 42 h They will throw them into the fiery furnace, where there will be wailing and grinding of teeth. 43 i Then the righteous will shine like the sun in the kingdom of their Father. Whoever has ears ought to hear.*

More Parables.* 44 j "The kingdom of heaven is like a treasure buried in a field,* which a person finds and hides again, and out of joy goes and sells all that he has and buys that field. 45 Again, the kingdom of heaven is like a merchant searching for fine pearls. 46 When he finds a pearl of great price, he goes and sells all that he has and buys it. 47 Again, the kingdom of heaven is like a net thrown into the sea, which collects fish of every kind. 48 When it is full they haul it ashore and sit down to put what is good into buckets. What is bad they throw away. 49 Thus it will be at the end of the age. The angels will go out and separate the wicked from the righteous 50 and throw them into the fiery furnace, where there will be wailing and grinding of teeth.

Treasures New and Old. 51 "Do you understand* all these things?" They an-

---

d Ez 17, 23; 31, 6; Dn 4, 7-9.17-19.—e Lk 13, 20-21.—f 34-35: Mk 4, 33-34.—g Ps 78, 2.—h Mt 8, 12; Rv 21, 8.—i Dn 12, 3.—j 44-45: Prv 2, 4; 4, 7.

13, 32: See Dn 4, 7-9.17-19, where the birds nesting in the tree represent the people of Nebuchadnezzar's kingdom. See also Ez 17, 23 and 31, 6.

13, 33: Except in this Q parable and in Mt 16, 12, *yeast* (or "leaven") is, in New Testament usage, a symbol of corruption (see Mt 16, 6.11-12; Mk 8, 15; Lk 12, 1; 1 Cor 5, 6-8; Gal 5, 9). *Three measures:* an enormous amount, enough to feed a hundred people. The exaggeration of this element of the parable points to the greatness of the kingdom's effect.

13, 34: *Only in parables:* see vv 10-15.

13, 35: *The prophet:* some textual witnesses read "Isaiah the prophet." The quotation is actually from Ps 78, 2; the first line corresponds to the LXX text of the psalm. The psalm's title ascribes it to Asaph, the founder of one of the guilds of temple musicians. He is called "the prophet" (NAB "the seer") in 2 Chr 29, 30, but it is doubtful that Matthew adverted to that; for him, any Old Testament text that could be seen as fulfilled in Jesus was prophetic.

13, 36: *Dismissing the crowds:* the return of Jesus to the house marks a break with the crowds, who represent unbelieving Israel. From now on his attention is directed more and more to his disciples and to their instruction. The rest of the discourse is addressed to them alone.

13, 37-43: In the explanation of the parable of the weeds emphasis lies on the fearful end of the wicked, whereas the parable itself concentrates on patience with them until judgment time.

13, 38: *The field is the world:* this presupposes the resurrection of Jesus and the granting to him of "all power in heaven and on earth" (Mt 28, 18).

13, 39: *The end of the age:* this phrase is found only in Mt (13, 40.49; 24, 3; 28, 20).

13, 41: *His kingdom:* the *kingdom* of *the Son of Man* is distinguished from that of the Father (43); see 1 Cor 15, 24-25. The church is the place where Jesus' kingdom is manifested, but his royal authority embraces the entire world; see the note on Mt 13, 38.

13, 43: See Dn 12, 3.

13, 44-50: The first two of the last three parables of the discourse have the same point. The *person* who *finds* a buried *treasure* and the *merchant* who finds a *pearl of great price* sell *all* that they have to acquire these finds; similarly, the one who understands the supreme value of the kingdom gives up whatever he must to obtain it. The *joy* with which this is done is made explicit in the first parable, but it may be presumed in the second also. The concluding parable of the fishnet resembles the explanation of the parable of the weeds with its stress upon the final exclusion of evil persons from the kingdom.

13, 44: In the unsettled conditions of Palestine in Jesus' time, it was not unusual to guard valuables by burying them in the ground.

13, 51: Matthew typically speaks of the understanding of the disciples.

swered, "Yes." [52] And he replied, "Then every scribe who has been instructed in the kingdom of heaven is like the head of a household who brings from his storeroom both the new and the old."* [53] When Jesus finished these parables, he went away from there.

V. JESUS, THE KINGDOM, AND THE CHURCH

The Rejection at Nazareth. [54] * He came to his native place and taught the people in their synagogue.[k] They were astonished* and said, "Where did this man get such wisdom and mighty deeds?[l] [55] Is he not the carpenter's son? Is not his mother named Mary and his brothers James, Joseph, Simon, and Judas?[m] [56] Are not his sisters all with us? Where did this man get all this?" [57] And they took offense at him. But Jesus said to them, "A prophet is not without honor except in his native place and in his own house."[n] [58] And he did not work many mighty deeds there because of their lack of faith.

CHAPTER 14

Herod's Opinion of Jesus. [1] * [o] At that time Herod the tetrarch* [p] heard of the reputation of Jesus[q] [2] and said to his servants, "This man is John the Baptist. He has been raised from the dead; that is why mighty powers are at work in him."

The Death of John the Baptist. [3] [r] Now Herod had arrested John, bound [him], and put him in prison on account of Herodias,* the wife of his brother Philip, [4] for John had said to him, "It is not lawful for you to have her."[s] [5] Although he wanted to kill him, he feared the people, for they regarded him as a prophet.[t] [6] But at a birthday celebration for Herod, the daughter of Herodias performed a dance before the guests and delighted Herod [7] so much that he swore to give her whatever she might ask for. [8] Prompted by her mother, she said, "Give me here on a platter the head of John the Baptist." [9] The king was distressed, but because of his oaths and the guests who were present, he ordered that it be given, [10] and he had John beheaded in the prison. [11] His head was brought in on a platter and given to the girl, who took it to her mother. [12] His disciples came and took away the corpse and buried him; and they went and told Jesus.

The Return of the Twelve and the Feeding of the Five Thousand. * [13] [u] When Jesus heard of it, he withdrew in a boat to a deserted place by himself. The crowds heard of this and followed him on foot from their

k 54-58: Mk 6, 1-6; Lk 4, 16-30.—l Mt 2, 23; Jn 1, 46; 7, 15.—m Mt 12, 46; 27, 56; Jn 6, 42.—n Jn 4, 44.—o 1-12: Mk 6, 14-29.—p Lk 3, 1.—q 1-2: Lk 9, 7-9.—r 3-4: Lk 3, 19-20.—s Lv 18, 16; 20, 21.—t Mt 21, 26.—u 13-21: Mt 15, 32-38; Mk 6, 32-44; Lk 9, 10-17; Jn 6, 1-13.

13, 52: Since Matthew tends to identify the disciples and the Twelve (see the note on Mt 10, 1), this saying about the Christian *scribe* cannot be taken as applicable to all who accept the message of Jesus. While the Twelve are in many ways representative of all who believe in him, they are also distinguished from them in certain respects. The church of Matthew has leaders among whom are a group designated as "scribes" (Mt 23, 34). Like the scribes of Israel, they are teachers. It is the Twelve and these their later counterparts to whom this verse applies. The *scribe . . . instructed in the kingdom of heaven* knows both the teaching of Jesus (*the new*) and the law and prophets (*the old*) and provides in his own teaching *both the new and the old* as interpreted and fulfilled by *the new*. On the translation *head of a household* (for the same Greek word translated *householder* in v 27), see the note on Mt 24, 45-51.

13, 54—17, 27: This section is the narrative part of the fourth book of the gospel.

13, 54-58: After the Sermon on the Mount the crowds are in admiring astonishment at Jesus' teaching (Mt 7, 28); here the astonishment is of those who take *offense at him.* Familiarity with his background and family leads them to regard him as pretentious. Matthew modifies his Marcan source (Mk 6, 1-6). Jesus is not the carpenter but *the carpenter's son* (55), "and among his own kin" is omitted (57), *he did not work many mighty deeds* in face of such unbelief (58) rather than the Marcan ". . . he was not able to perform any mighty deed there" (Mk 6, 5), and there is no mention of his amazement at his townspeople's lack of faith.

14, 1-12: The murder of the Baptist by Herod Antipas prefigures the death of Jesus (see Mt 17, 12). The Marcan source (Mk 6, 14-29) is much reduced and in some points changed. In Mk Herod reveres John as a holy man and the desire to kill him is attributed to Herodias (Mk 6, 19.20), whereas here that desire is Herod's from the beginning (5).

14, 1: *Herod the tetrarch:* Herod Antipas, son of Herod the Great. When the latter died, his territory was divided among three of his surviving sons, Archelaus who received half of it (Mt 2, 23), Herod Antipas who became ruler of Galilee and Perea, and Philip who became ruler of northern Transjordan. Since he received a quarter of his father's domain, Antipas is accurately designated *tetrarch* ("ruler of a fourth [part]"), although in v 9 Matthew repeats the "king" of his Marcan source (Mk 6, 26).

14, 3: Herodias was not the wife of Herod's half-brother Philip but of another half-brother, Herod Boethus. The union was prohibited by Lv 18, 16; 20, 21. According to Josephus (*Antiquities* 18, 5, 2 §§116-19), Herod imprisoned and then executed John because he feared that the Baptist's influence over the people might enable him to lead a rebellion.

14, 13-21: The feeding of the five thousand is the only miracle of Jesus that is recounted in all four gospels. The principal reason for that may be that it was seen as anticipating the Eucharist and the final banquet of Jesus in the kingdom (Mt 8, 11; 26, 29), but it looks not only forward but backward, to the feeding of Israel with manna in the desert at the time of the Exodus (Ex 16), a miracle that in some contemporary Jewish expectation would be repeated in the messianic age (2 Baruch 29, 8). It may also be meant to recall Elisha's feeding a hundred men with small provisions (2 Kgs 4, 42-44).

towns. [14] When he disembarked and saw the vast crowd, his heart was moved with pity for them, and he cured their sick. [15] When it was evening, the disciples approached him and said, "This is a deserted place and it is already late; dismiss the crowds so that they can go to the villages and buy food for themselves." [16] [Jesus] said to them, "There is no need for them to go away; give them some food yourselves." [17] But they said to him, "Five loaves and two fish are all we have here." [18] Then he said, "Bring them here to me," [19] and he ordered the crowds to sit down on the grass. Taking* the five loaves and the two fish, and looking up to heaven, he said the blessing, broke the loaves, and gave them to the disciples, who in turn gave them to the crowds. [20] They all ate and were satisfied, and they picked up the fragments left over*—twelve wicker baskets full. [21] Those who ate were about five thousand men, not counting women and children.

The Walking on the Water.* [22] [v] Then he made the disciples get into the boat and precede him to the other side, while he dismissed the crowds. [23] After doing so, he went up on the mountain by himself to pray. When it was evening he was there alone. [w] [24] Meanwhile the boat, already a few miles offshore, was being tossed about by the waves, for the wind was against it. [25] During the fourth watch of the night,* he came toward them, walking on the sea. [26] When the disciples saw him walking on the sea they were terrified. "It is a ghost," they said, and they cried out in fear. [27] At once [Jesus] spoke to them, "Take courage, it is I;* do not be afraid." [28] Peter said to him in reply, "Lord, if it is you, command me to come to you on the water." [29] He said, "Come." Peter got out of the boat and began to walk on the water toward Jesus. [30] [x] But when he saw how [strong] the wind was he became frightened; and, beginning to sink, he cried out, "Lord, save me!" [31] Immediately Jesus stretched out his hand and caught him, and said to him, "O you of little faith,* why did you doubt?" [32] After they got into the boat, the wind died down. [33] [y] Those who were in the boat did him homage, saying, "Truly, you are the Son of God."*

The Healings at Gennesaret. [34] [z] After making the crossing, they came to land at Gennesaret. [35] When the men of that place recognized him, they sent word to all the surrounding country. People brought to him all those who were sick [36] and begged him that they might touch only the tassel on his cloak, and as many as touched it were healed. [a]

CHAPTER 15

The Tradition of the Elders.* [1] [b] Then Pharisees and scribes came to Jesus from Jerusalem and said, [2] "Why do your disciples break the tradition of the elders?* They do not wash [their] hands when they

---

v 22-33: Mk 6, 45-52; Jn 6, 16-21.—w Mk 1, 35; Lk 5, 16; 6, 12.—x 30-31: Mt 8, 25-26.—y Mt 16, 16.—z 34-36: Mk 6, 53-56.—a Mt 9, 20-22.—b 1-20: Mk 7, 1-23.

14, 19: The *taking*, saying the blessing, breaking, and giving to the disciples correspond to the actions of Jesus over the bread at the Last Supper (Mt 26, 26). Since they were usual at any Jewish meal, that correspondence does not necessarily indicate a eucharistic reference here. Matthew's silence about Jesus' dividing the fish among the people (Mk 6, 41) is perhaps more significant in that regard.

14, 20: *The fragments left over:* as in Elisha's miracle, food was *left over* after all had been fed. The word *fragments* (Greek *klasmata*) is used, in the singular, of the broken bread of the Eucharist in *Didache* 9, 3-4.

14, 22-33: The disciples, laboring against the turbulent sea, are saved by Jesus. For his power over the waters, see the note on Mt 8, 26. Here that power is expressed also by his *walking on the sea* (25; cf Ps 77, 20; Jb 9, 8). Matthew has inserted into the Marcan story (Mk 6, 45-52) material that belongs to his special traditions on Peter (28-31).

14, 25: *The fourth watch of the night:* between 3 a.m. and 6 a.m. The Romans divided the twelve hours between 6 p.m. and 6 a.m. into four equal parts called "watches."

14, 27: *It is I:* see the note on Mk 6, 50.

14, 31: *You of little faith:* see the note on Mt 6, 30. *Why did you doubt?:* the verb is peculiar to Matthew and occurs elsewhere only in Mt 28, 17.

14, 33: This confession is in striking contrast to the Marcan parallel (Mk 6, 51) where the disciples are "completely astounded."

15, 1-20: This dispute begins with the question of the Pharisees and scribes why Jesus' disciples are breaking *the tradition of the elders* about washing one's hands before eating (2). Jesus' counterquestion accuses his opponents of breaking *the commandment of God for the sake of* their *tradition* (3) and illustrates this by their interpretation of the commandment of the Decalogue concerning parents (4-6). Denouncing them as hypocrites, he applies to them a derogatory prophecy of Isaiah (7-8). Then with a wider audience (*the crowd,* 10) he goes beyond the violation of tradition with which the dispute has started. The parable (11) is an attack on the Mosaic law concerning clean and unclean foods, similar to those antitheses that abrogate the law (Mt 5, 31-32.33-34.38-39). After a warning to his disciples not to follow the moral guidance of the Pharisees (13-14), he explains the *parable* (15) to them, saying that defilement comes not from what *enters the mouth* (17) but from the evil thoughts and deeds that rise from within, *from the heart* (18-20). The last verse returns to the starting point of the dispute (eating *with unwashed hands*). Because of Matthew's omission of Mk 7, 19b, some scholars think that Matthew has weakened the Marcan repudiation of the Mosaic food laws. But that half verse is ambiguous in the Greek, which may be the reason for its omission here.

15, 2: *The tradition of the elders:* see the note on Mk 7, 5. The purpose of the handwashing was to remove defilement caused by contact with what was ritually unclean.

eat a meal.'"*c* [3] He said to them in reply, "And why do you break the commandment of God* for the sake of your tradition? [4] For God said, 'Honor your father and your mother,' and 'Whoever curses father or mother shall die.'*d* [5] But you say, 'Whoever says to father or mother, "Any support you might have had from me is dedicated to God,"* [6] need not honor his father.' You have nullified the word of God for the sake of your tradition. [7] Hypocrites, well did Isaiah prophesy about you when he said:

[8] 'This people honors me with their lips,*
   but their hearts are far from me;*e*

[9] in vain do they worship me,
   teaching as doctrines human precepts.' "*f*

[10] He summoned the crowd and said to them, "Hear and understand.*g* [11] It is not what enters one's mouth that defiles that person; but what comes out of the mouth is what defiles one." [12] Then his disciples approached and said to him, "Do you know that the Pharisees took offense when they heard what you said?" [13] He said in reply,* "Every plant that my heavenly Father has not planted will be uprooted. [14] Let them alone; they are blind guides [of the blind]. If a blind person leads a blind person, both will fall into a pit."*h* [15] Then Peter* said to him in reply, "Explain [this] parable to us." [16] He said to them, "Are even you still without understanding? [17] Do you not realize that everything that enters the mouth passes into the stomach and is expelled into the latrine? [18] But the things that come out of the mouth come from the heart, and they defile.*i* [19] For from the heart come evil thoughts, murder, adultery, unchastity, theft, false witness, blasphemy.* [20] These are what defile a person, but to eat with unwashed hands does not defile."

The Canaanite Woman's Faith.* [21]*j* Then Jesus went from that place and withdrew to the region of Tyre and Sidon. [22] And behold, a Canaanite woman of that district came and called out, "Have pity on me, Lord, Son of David! My daughter is tormented by a demon." [23] But he did not say a word in answer to her. His disciples came and asked him, "Send her away, for she keeps calling out after us." [24] He said in reply, "I was sent only to the lost sheep of the house of Israel."* [25] But the woman came and did him homage, saying, "Lord, help me."*k* [26] He said in reply, "It is not right to take the food of the children* and throw it to the dogs." [27] She said, "Please, Lord, for even the dogs eat the scraps that fall from the table of their masters." [28] Then Jesus said to her in reply, "O woman, great is your faith!* Let it be done for you as you wish." And her daughter was healed from that hour.*l*

The Healing of Many People. [29] Moving on from there Jesus walked by the Sea of Galilee, went up on the mountain, and sat down there. [30] Great crowds came to him, having with them the lame, the blind, the deformed, the mute, and many others. They placed them at his feet, and he cured them.*m* [31] The crowds were amazed when they saw the mute speaking, the deformed made whole, the lame walking, and the blind able to see, and they glorified the God of Israel.

The Feeding of the Four Thousand.* [32]*n* Jesus summoned his disciples and said, "My heart is moved with pity for the

---

c Lk 11, 38.—d Ex 20, 12; 21, 17; Lv 20, 9; Dt 5, 16; Prv 20, 20.—e Is 29, 13 LXX.—f Col 2, 23.—g Mk 7, 14.—h Mt 23, 16.19.24; Lk 6, 39; Jn 9, 40.—i Mt 12, 34.—j 21-28: Mk 7, 24-30.—k Mt 10, 6.—l Mt 8, 10.—m Is 35, 5-6.—n 32-39: Mk 8, 1-10.

15, 3-4: For the commandment see Ex 20, 12 (// Dt 5, 16); 21, 17. The honoring of one's parents had to do with supporting them in their needs.

15, 5: See the note on Mk 7, 11.

15, 8: The text of Is 29, 13 is quoted approximately according to the Septuagint.

15, 13-14: Jesus leads his disciples away from the teaching authority of the Pharisees.

15, 15: Matthew specifies *Peter* as the questioner, unlike Mk 7, 17. Given his tendency to present the disciples as more understanding than in his Marcan source, it is noteworthy that here he retains the Marcan rebuke, although in a slightly milder form. This may be due to his wish to correct the Jewish Christians within his church who still held to the food laws and thus separated themselves from Gentile Christians who did not observe them.

15, 19: The Marcan list of thirteen things that defile (Mk 7, 21-22) is here reduced to seven that partially cover the content of the Decalogue.

15, 21-28: See the note on Mt 8, 5-13.

15, 24: See the note on Mt 10, 5-6.

15, 26: *The children:* the people of Israel. *Dogs:* see the note on Mt 7, 6.

15, 28: As in the case of the cure of the centurion's servant (Mt 8, 10), Matthew ascribes Jesus' granting the request to the woman's *great faith,* a point not made equally explicit in the Marcan parallel (Mk 7, 24-30).

15, 32-39: Most probably this story is a doublet of that of the feeding of the five thousand (Mt 14, 13-21). It differs from it notably only in that Jesus takes the initiative, not the disciples (32), and in the numbers: the crowd has been with Jesus *three days* (32), *seven loaves* are multiplied (36), *seven baskets* of *fragments* remain after the feeding (37), and *four thousand* men are fed (38).

crowd, for they have been with me now for three days and have nothing to eat. I do not want to send them away hungry, for fear they may collapse on the way." [33] The disciples said to him, "Where could we ever get enough bread in this deserted place to satisfy such a crowd?" [34] Jesus said to them, "How many loaves do you have?" "Seven," they replied, "and a few fish." [35] He ordered the crowd to sit down on the ground. [36] Then he took the seven loaves and the fish, gave thanks,* broke the loaves, and gave them to the disciples, who in turn gave them to the crowds. [37] They all ate and were satisfied. They picked up the fragments left over—seven baskets full.[o] [38] Those who ate were four thousand men, not counting women and children. [39] And when he had dismissed the crowds, he got into the boat and came to the district of Magadan.

CHAPTER 16

The Demand for a Sign. [1] [p] The Pharisees and Sadducees came and, to test him, asked him to show them a sign from heaven.* [2] He said to them in reply, "[In the evening you say, 'Tomorrow will be fair, for the sky is red'; [3] [q] and, in the

morning, 'Today will be stormy, for the sky is red and threatening.' You know how to judge the appearance of the sky, but you cannot judge the signs of the times.]* [4] An evil and unfaithful generation seeks a sign, but no sign will be given it except the sign of Jonah."* Then he left them and went away.[r]

The Leaven of the Pharisees and Sadducees. * [5] [s] In coming to the other side of the sea, the disciples had forgotten to bring bread. [6] [t] Jesus said to them, "Look out, and beware of the leaven* of the Pharisees and Sadducees." [7] * They concluded among themselves, saying, "It is because we have brought no bread." [8] When Jesus became aware of this he said, "You of little faith, why do you conclude among yourselves that it is because you have no bread? [9] Do you not yet understand, and do you not remember the five loaves for the five thousand, and how many wicker baskets you took up?[u] [10] Or the seven loaves for the four thousand, and how many baskets you took up?[v] [11] How do you not comprehend that I was not speaking to you about bread? Beware of the leaven of the Pharisees and Sadducees." [12] Then they understood* that he was not telling them to beware of the leaven of bread, but of the teaching of the Pharisees and Sadducees.

Peter's Confession about Jesus. * [13] [w] When Jesus went into the region of Caesarea Philippi* he asked his disciples,

---

o Mt 16, 10.—p 1-10: Mk 8, 11-21.—q Lk 12, 54-56.—r Mt 12, 39; Jon 2, 1.—s 5-12: Mk 8, 14-21.—t Lk 12, 1.—u Mt 14, 17-21; Jn 6, 9.—v Mt 15, 34-38.—w 13-16: Mk 8, 27-29; Lk 9, 18-20.

15, 36: *Gave thanks:* see Mt 14, 19, "said the blessing." There is no difference in meaning. The thanksgiving was a blessing of God for his benefits.

16, 1: *A sign from heaven:* see the note on Mt 12, 38-42.

16, 2-3: The answer of Jesus in these verses is omitted in many important textual witnesses, and it is very uncertain that it is an original part of this gospel. It resembles Lk 12, 54-56 and may have been inserted from there. It rebukes the Pharisees and Sadducees who are able to read indications of coming weather but not the indications of the coming kingdom in the signs that Jesus does offer, his mighty deeds and teaching.

16, 4: See the notes on Mt 12, 39.40.

16, 5-12: Jesus' warning his disciples against *the teaching of the Pharisees and Sadducees* comes immediately before his promise to confer on Peter the authority to bind and to loose on earth (19), an authority that will be confirmed in heaven. Such authority most probably has to do, at least in part, with teaching. The rejection of the teaching authority of the Pharisees (see also Mt 12, 12-14) prepares for a new one derived from Jesus.

16, 6: *Leaven:* see the note on Mt 13, 33. *Sadducees:* Matthew's Marcan source speaks rather of "the leaven of Herod" (Mk 8, 15).

16, 7-11: The disciples, men *of little faith,* misunderstand Jesus' metaphorical use of *leaven,* forgetting that, as the feeding of the crowds shows, he is not at a loss to provide them with bread.

16, 12: After his rebuke, the disciples understand that by *leaven* he meant the corrupting influence of *the teaching of the Pharisees and Sadducees.* The evangelist probably understands this *teaching* as common to both groups. Since at the time of Jesus' ministry the two differed widely on points of teaching, e.g., the resurrection of the dead, and at the time of the evangelist the Sadducee party was no longer a force in Judaism, the supposed common *teaching* fits neither period. The disciples' eventual understanding of Jesus' warning contrasts with their continuing obtuseness in the Marcan parallel (Mk 8, 14-21).

16, 13-20: The Marcan confession of Jesus as Messiah, made by Peter as spokesman for the other disciples (Mk 8, 27-29; cf also Lk 9, 18-20), is modified significantly here. The confession is of Jesus both as *Messiah* and as *Son of the living God* (16). Jesus' response, drawn principally from material peculiar to Matthew, attributes the confession to a divine revelation granted to Peter alone (17) and makes him the *rock* on which Jesus *will build* his *church* (18) and the disciple whose authority in the church *on earth* will be confirmed *in heaven,* i.e., by God (19).

16, 13: *Caesarea Philippi:* situated about twenty miles north of the Sea of Galilee in the territory ruled by Philip, a son of Herod the Great, tetrarch from 4 B.C. until his death in A.D. 34 (see the note on Mt 14, 1). He rebuilt the town of Paneas, naming it *Caesarea* in honor of the emperor, and *Philippi* ("of Philip") to distinguish it from the seaport in Samaria that was also called Caesarea. *Who do people say that the Son of Man is?:* although the question differs from the Marcan parallel (Mk 8, 27: "Who . . . that I am?"), the meaning is the same, for Jesus here refers to himself as *the Son of Man* (cf 15).

"Who do people say that the Son of Man is?" [14] They replied, "Some say John the Baptist,* others Elijah, still others Jeremiah or one of the prophets." [x] [15] He said to them, "But who do you say that I am?" [16] [y] Simon Peter said in reply, "You are the Messiah, the Son of the living God."* [17] Jesus said to him in reply, "Blessed are you, Simon son of Jonah. For flesh and blood* has not revealed this to you, but my heavenly Father. [18] And so I say to you, you are Peter, and upon this rock I will build my church,* and the gates of the netherworld shall not prevail against it. [z] [19] I will give you the keys to the kingdom of heaven.* Whatever you bind on earth shall be bound in heaven; and whatever you loose on earth shall be loosed in heaven." [a] [20] [b] Then he strictly ordered his disciples to tell no one that he was the Messiah.*

The First Prediction of the Passion.* [21] [c]

From that time on, Jesus began to show his disciples that he* must go to Jerusalem and suffer greatly from the elders, the chief priests, and the scribes, and be killed and on the third day be raised. [d] [22] * Then Peter took him aside and began to rebuke him, "God forbid, Lord! No such thing shall ever happen to you." [23] He turned and said to Peter, "Get behind me, Satan! You are an obstacle to me. You are thinking not as God does, but as human beings do." [e]

---

x Mt 14, 2.—y Jn 6, 69.—z Jn 1, 42.—a Is 22, 22; Rv 3, 7.—b Mk 8, 30; Lk 9, 21.—c 21-28: Mk 8, 31—9, 1; Lk 9, 22-27.—d Mt 17, 22-23; 20, 17-19.—e Mt 4, 10.

16, 14: *John the Baptist:* see Mt 14, 2. *Elijah:* cf Mal 3, 23-24; Sir 48, 10; and see the note on Mt 3, 4. *Jeremiah:* an addition of Matthew to the Marcan source.

16, 16: *The Son of the living God:* see Mt 2, 15; 3, 17. The addition of this exalted title to the Marcan confession eliminates whatever ambiguity was attached to the title Messiah. This, among other things, supports the view proposed by many scholars that Matthew has here combined his source's confession with a post-resurrectional confession of faith in Jesus as *Son of the living God* that belonged to the appearance of the risen Jesus to Peter; cf 1 Cor 15, 5; Lk 24, 34.

16, 17: *Flesh and blood:* a Semitic expression for human beings, especially in their weakness. *Has not revealed this . . . but my heavenly Father:* that Peter's faith is spoken of as coming not through human means but through a revelation from God is similar to Paul's description of his recognition of who Jesus was; see Gal 1, 15-16, ". . . when he [God] . . . was pleased to reveal his Son to me. . . ."

16, 18: *You are Peter, and upon this rock I will build my church:* the Aramaic word *kēpā'* meaning *rock* and transliterated into Greek as *Kēphas* is the name by which Peter is called in the Pauline letters (1 Cor 1, 12; 3, 22; 9, 5; 15, 4; Gal 1, 18; 2, 9.11.14) except in Gal 2, 7-8 ("Peter"). It is translated as *Petros* ("Peter") in Jn 1, 42. The presumed original Aramaic of Jesus' statement would have been, in English, "You are the Rock *(Kēpā')* and upon this rock *(kēpā')* I will build my church." The Greek text probably means the same, for the difference in gender between the masculine noun *petros,* the disciple's new name, and the feminine noun *petra* (rock) may be due simply to the unsuitability of using a feminine noun as the proper name of a male. Although the two words were generally used with slightly different nuances, they were also used interchangeably with the same meaning, "rock." *Church:* this word (Greek *ekklēsia*) occurs in the gospels only here and in Mt 18, 17 (twice). There are several possibilities for an Aramaic original. Jesus' *church* means the community that he *will* gather and that, like a building, will have Peter as its solid foundation. That function of Peter consists in his being witness to Jesus as *the Messiah, the Son of the living God. The gates of the netherworld shall not prevail against it:* the netherworld (Greek *Hadēs,* the abode of the dead) is conceived of as a walled city whose *gates* will not close in upon the church of Jesus, i.e., it will not be overcome by the power of death.

16, 19: *The keys to the kingdom of heaven:* the image of *the keys* is probably drawn from Is 22, 15-25, where Eliakim, who succeeds Shebnah as master of the palace, is given "the key

of the house of David," which he authoritatively "opens" and "shuts" (Is 22, 22). *Whatever you bind . . . loosed in heaven:* there are many instances in rabbinic literature of the binding-loosing imagery. Of the several meanings given there to the metaphor, two are of special importance here: the giving of authoritative teaching, and the lifting or imposing of the ban of excommunication. It is disputed whether the image of *the keys* and that of binding and loosing are different metaphors meaning the same thing. In any case, the promise of the keys is given to Peter alone. In Mt 18, 18 all the disciples are given the power of binding and loosing, but the context of that verse suggests that there the power of excommunication alone is intended. That *the keys* are those to *the kingdom of heaven* and that Peter's exercise of authority in the church *on earth* will be confirmed *in heaven* show an intimate connection between, but not an identification of, the church and *the kingdom of heaven.*

16, 20: Cf Mk 8, 30. Matthew makes explicit that the prohibition has to do with speaking of Jesus as *the Messiah;* see the note on Mk 8, 27-30.

16, 21-23: This first prediction of the passion follows Mk 8, 31-33 in the main and serves as a corrective to an understanding of Jesus' messiahship as solely one of glory and triumph. By his addition of *from that time on* (21) Matthew has emphasized that Jesus' revelation of his coming suffering and death marks a new phase of the gospel. Neither this nor the two later passion predictions (Mt 17, 22-23; 20, 17-19) can be taken as sayings that, as they stand, go back to Jesus himself. However, it is probable that he foresaw that his mission would entail suffering and perhaps death, but was confident that he would ultimately be vindicated by God (see Mt 26, 29).

16, 21: *He:* the Marcan parallel (Mk 8, 31) has "the Son of Man." Since Matthew has already designated Jesus by that title (13), its omission here is not significant. The Matthean prediction is equally about the sufferings of the Son of Man. *Must:* this necessity is part of the tradition of all the synoptics; cf Mk 8, 31; Lk 9, 21. *The elders, the chief priests, and the scribes:* see the note on Mk 8, 31. *On the third day:* so also Lk 9, 22, against the Marcan "after three days" (Mk 8, 31). Matthew's formulation is, in the Greek, almost identical with the pre-Pauline fragment of the kerygma in 1 Cor 15, 4, and also with Hos 6, 2, which many take to be the Old Testament background to the confession that Jesus was raised on *the third day.* Josephus uses "after three days" and "on the third day" interchangeably (*Antiquities* 7, 11, 6 §§280-81; 8, 8, 1-2 §§214, 218) and there is probably no difference in meaning between the two phrases.

16, 22-23: Peter's refusal to accept Jesus' predicted suffering and death is seen as a satanic attempt to deflect Jesus from his God-appointed course, and the disciple is addressed in terms that recall Jesus' dismissal of the devil in the temptation account (Mt 4, 10: "Get away, Satan!"). Peter's satanic purpose is emphasized by Matthew's addition to the Marcan source of the words *You are an obstacle to me.*

The Conditions of Discipleship.* [24] Then Jesus said to his disciples, "Whoever wishes to come after me must deny himself,* take up his cross, and follow me.[f] [25] For whoever wishes to save his life will lose it,[g] but whoever loses his life for my sake will find it.* [26] What profit would there be for one to gain the whole world and forfeit his life? Or what can one give in exchange for his life? [27] [h] For the Son of Man will come with his angels in his Father's glory, and then he will repay everyone according to his conduct.* [28] Amen, I say to you, there are some standing here who will not taste death until they see the Son of Man coming in his kingdom."*

CHAPTER 17

The Transfiguration of Jesus.* [1] [i] After six days Jesus took Peter, James, and John his brother, and led them up a high mountain by themselves.* [2] And he was transfigured before them; his face shone like the sun* and his clothes became white as light.[j] [3] And behold, Moses and Elijah appeared to them,* conversing with him. [4] Then Peter said to Jesus in reply, "Lord, it is good that we are here. If you wish, I will make three tents* here, one for you, one for Moses, and one for Elijah." [5] [k] While he was still speaking, behold, a bright cloud cast a shadow over them,* then from the cloud came a voice that said, "This is my beloved Son, with whom I am well pleased; listen to him." [6] *When the disciples heard this, they fell prostrate and were very much afraid. [7] But Jesus came and touched them, saying, "Rise, and do not be afraid." [8] And when the disciples raised their eyes, they saw no one else but Jesus alone.

The Coming of Elijah.* [9] [l] As they were coming down from the mountain, Jesus charged them, "Do not tell the vision* to anyone until the Son of Man has been raised from the dead." [10] [m] Then the disciples asked him, "Why do the scribes say that Elijah must come first?"* [11] He said in reply,* "Elijah will indeed come and re-

---

f Lk 14, 27.—g Lk 17, 33; Jn 12, 25.—h Mt 25, 31-33; Jb 34, 11; Ps 62, 13; Jer 17, 10; 2 Thes 1, 7-8.—i 1-8: Mk 9, 2-8; Lk 9, 28-36.—j Mt 28, 3; Dn 7, 9; 10, 6; Rv 4, 4; 7, 9; 19, 14.—k Mt 3, 17; Dt 18, 15; 2 Pt 1, 17.—l 9-13: Mk 9, 9-13.—m Mal 3, 23-24.

16, 24-28: A readiness to follow Jesus even to giving up one's life for him is the condition for true discipleship; this will be repaid by him at the final judgment.

16, 24: *Deny himself:* to deny someone is to disown him (see Mt 10, 33; 26, 34-35) and to deny oneself is to disown oneself as the center of one's existence.

16, 25: See the notes on Mt 10, 38.39.

16, 27: The parousia and final judgment are described in Mt 25, 31 in terms almost identical with these.

16, 28: *Coming in his kingdom:* since the *kingdom of the Son of Man* has been described as "the world" and Jesus' sovereignty precedes his final coming in glory (Mt 13, 38.41), the *coming* in this verse is not the parousia as in the preceding but the manifestation of Jesus' rule after his resurrection; see the notes on Mt 13, 38.41.

17, 1-8: The account of the transfiguration confirms that Jesus is the *Son of God* (5) and points to fulfillment of the prediction that he will come *in his Father's glory* at the end of the age (Mt 16, 27). It has been explained by some as a resurrection appearance retrojected into the time of Jesus' ministry, but that is not probable since the account lacks many of the usual elements of the resurrection-appearance narratives. It draws upon motifs from the Old Testament and noncanonical Jewish apocalyptic literature that express the presence of the heavenly and the divine, e.g., brilliant light, white garments, and the overshadowing cloud.

17, 1: These three disciples are also taken apart from the others by Jesus in Gethsemane (Mt 26, 37). *A high mountain:* this has been identified with Tabor or Hermon, but probably no specific mountain was intended by the evangelist or by his Marcan source (Mk 9, 2). Its meaning is theological rather than geographical, possibly recalling the revelation to Moses on Mount Sinai (Ex 24, 12-18) and to Elijah at the same place (1 Kgs 19, 8-18; Horeb = Sinai).

17, 2: *His face shone like the sun:* this is a Matthean addition; cf Dn 10, 6. *His clothes became white as light:* cf Dn 7, 9, where the clothing of God appears "snow bright." For the *white* garments of other heavenly beings, see Rv 4, 4; 7, 9; 19, 14.

17, 3: See the note on Mk 9, 5.

17, 4: *Three tents:* the booths in which the Israelites lived during the feast of Tabernacles (cf Jn 7, 2) were meant to recall their ancestors' dwelling in booths during the journey from Egypt to the promised land (Lv 23, 39-42). The same Greek word, *skēnē,* here translated *tents,* is used in the LXX for the booths of that feast, and some scholars have suggested that there is an allusion here to that liturgical custom.

17, 5: *Cloud cast a shadow over them:* see the note on Mk 9, 7. *This is my beloved Son . . . listen to him:* cf Mt 3, 17. The voice repeats the baptismal proclamation about Jesus, with the addition of the command *listen to him.* The latter is a reference to Dt 18, 15 in which the Israelites are commanded to *listen to* the prophet like Moses whom God will raise up for them. The command to *listen to* Jesus is general, but in this context it probably applies particularly to the preceding predictions of his passion and resurrection (Mt 16, 21) and of his coming (Mt 16, 27.28).

17, 6-7: A Matthean addition; cf Dn 10, 9-10.18-19.

17, 9-13: In response to the disciples' question about the expected return of Elijah, Jesus interprets the mission of the Baptist as the fulfillment of that expectation. But that was not suspected by those who opposed and finally killed him, and Jesus predicts a similar fate for himself.

17, 9: *The vision:* Matthew alone uses this word to describe the transfiguration. *Until the Son of Man has been raised from the dead:* only in the light of Jesus' resurrection can the meaning of his life and mission be truly understood; until then no testimony to *the vision* will lead people to faith.

17, 10: See the notes on Mt 3, 4; 16, 14.

17, 11-12: The preceding question and this answer may reflect later controversy with Jews who objected to the Christian claims for Jesus that Elijah had not yet come.

store all things;[n] [12]but I tell you that Elijah has already come,[o] and they did not recognize him but did to him whatever they pleased. So also will the Son of Man suffer at their hands." [13]Then the disciples understood that he was speaking to them of John the Baptist.*

The Healing of a Boy with a Demon.* [14] [p] When they came to the crowd a man approached, knelt down before him, [15]and said, "Lord, have pity on my son, for he is a lunatic* and suffers severely; often he falls into fire, and often into water. [16]I brought him to your disciples, but they could not cure him." [17]Jesus said in reply, "O faithless and perverse* generation, how long will I be with you? How long will I endure you? Bring him here to me."[q] [18]Jesus rebuked him and the demon came out of him,* and from that hour the boy was cured. [19]Then the disciples approached Jesus in private and said, "Why could we not drive it out?" [20]*He said to them, "Because of your little faith. Amen, I say to you, if you have faith the size of a mustard seed, you will say to this mountain, 'Move from here to there,' and it will move. Nothing will be impossible for you." [r] [21]*

The Second Prediction of the Passion.* [22] [s] As they were gathering in Galilee, Jesus said to them, "The Son of Man is to be handed over to men, [23]and they will kill him, and he will be raised on the third day." And they were overwhelmed with grief.

Payment of the Temple Tax.* [24]When they came to Capernaum, the collectors of the temple tax* approached Peter and said, "Doesn't your teacher pay the temple tax?"[t] [25]"Yes," he said. When he came into the house, before he had time to speak, Jesus asked him, "What is your opinion, Simon? From whom do the kings of the earth take tolls or census tax? From their subjects or from foreigners?"* [26]When he said, "From foreigners," Jesus said to him, "Then the subjects are exempt.* [27]But that we may not offend

---

n Lk 1, 17.—o 12-13: Mt 11, 14.—p 14-21: Mk 9, 14-29; Lk 9, 37-43.—q Dt 32, 5 LXX.—r Mt 21, 21; Lk 17, 6; 1 Cor 13, 2.—s 22-23: Mt 16, 21; 20, 18-19.—t Ex 30, 11-16; Neh 10, 33.

17, 13: See Mt 11, 14.

17, 14-20: Matthew has greatly shortened the Marcan story (Mk 9, 14-29). Leaving aside several details of the boy's illness, he concentrates on the need for faith, not so much on the part of the boy's father (as does Mark, for Matthew omits Mk 9, 22b-24) but on that of his own disciples whose inability to drive out the demon is ascribed to their *little faith* (20).

17, 15: *A lunatic:* this description of the boy is peculiar to Matthew. The word occurs in the New Testament only here and in Mt 4, 24 and means one affected or struck by the moon. The symptoms of the boy's illness point to epilepsy, and attacks of this were thought to be caused by phases of the moon.

17, 17: *Faithless and perverse:* so Matthew and Luke (Lk 9, 41) against Mark's *faithless* (Mk 9, 19). The Greek word here translated *perverse* is the same as that in Dt 32, 5 LXX, where Moses speaks to his people. There is a problem in knowing to whom the reproach is addressed. Since the Matthean Jesus normally chides his disciples for their *little faith* (as in 20), it would appear that the charge of lack of faith could not be made against them and that the reproach is addressed to unbelievers among the Jews. However in v 20b (*if you have faith the size of a mustard seed*), which is certainly addressed to the disciples, they appear to have not even the smallest faith; if they had, they would have been able to cure the boy. In the light of v 20b the reproach of v 17 could have applied to the disciples. There seems to be an inconsistency between the charge of *little faith* in v 20a and that of not even a little in v 20b.

17, 18: *The demon came out of him:* not until this verse does Matthew indicate that the boy's illness is a case of demoniacal possession.

17, 20: The entire verse is an addition of Matthew who (according to the better attested text) omits the reason given for the disciples' inability in Mk 9, 29. *Little faith:* see the note on Mt 6, 30. *Faith the size of a mustard seed . . . and it will move:* a combination of a Q saying (cf Lk 17, 6) with a Marcan saying (cf Mk 11, 23).

17, 21: Some manuscripts add, "But this kind does not come out except by prayer and fasting"; this is a variant of the better reading of Mk 9, 29.

17, 22-23: The second passion prediction (cf Mt 16, 21-23) is the least detailed of the three and may be the earliest. In the Marcan parallel the disciples do not understand (Mk 9, 32); here they understand and are *overwhelmed with grief* at the prospect of Jesus' death (23).

17, 24-27: Like Mt 14, 28-31 and Mt 16, 16b-19, this episode comes from Matthew's special material on Peter. Although the question of *the collectors* concerns Jesus' payment of *the temple tax,* it is put to *Peter.* It is he who receives instruction from Jesus about freedom from the obligation of payment and yet why it should be made. The means of doing so is provided miraculously. The pericope deals with a problem of Matthew's church, whether its members should pay the temple tax, and the answer is given through a word of Jesus conveyed to Peter. Some scholars see here an example of the teaching authority of Peter exercised in the name of Jesus (see Mt 16, 19). The specific problem was a Jewish Christian one and may have arisen when the Matthean church was composed largely of that group.

17, 24: *The temple tax:* before the destruction of the Jerusalem temple in A.D. 70 every male Jew above nineteen years of age was obliged to make an annual contribution to its upkeep (cf Ex 30, 11-16; Neh 10, 33). After the destruction the Romans imposed upon Jews the obligation of paying that tax for the temple of Jupiter Capitolinus. There is disagreement about which period the story deals with.

17, 25: *From their subjects or from foreigners?:* the Greek word here translated *subjects* literally means "sons."

17, 26: *Then the subjects are exempt:* just as *subjects* are not bound by laws applying to *foreigners,* neither are Jesus and his disciples, who belong to the kingdom of heaven, bound by the duty of paying the temple tax imposed on those who are not of the kingdom. If the Greek is translated "sons," the freedom of Jesus, the Son of God, and of his disciples, children ("sons") of the kingdom (cf Mt 13, 38), is even more clear.

them,* go to the sea, drop in a hook, and take the first fish that comes up. Open its mouth and you will find a coin worth twice the temple tax. Give that to them for me and for you.''

CHAPTER 18*

The Greatest in the Kingdom. [1] u At that time the disciples* approached Jesus and said, ''Who is the greatest in the kingdom of heaven?'' [2] He called a child over, placed it in their midst, [3] and said, ''Amen, I say to you, unless you turn and become like children,* you will not enter the kingdom of heaven. v [4] Whoever humbles himself like this child is the greatest in the kingdom of heaven. w [5] And whoever receives one child such as this in my name receives me.*

Temptations to Sin. [6] x ''Whoever causes one of these little ones* who believe in me

to sin, it would be better for him to have a great millstone hung around his neck and to be drowned in the depths of the sea. [7] Woe to the world because of things that cause sin! Such things must come, but woe to the one through whom they come!* [8] y If your hand or foot causes you to sin,* cut it off and throw it away. It is better for you to enter into life maimed or crippled than with two hands or two feet to be thrown into eternal fire. [9] And if your eye causes you to sin, tear it out and throw it away. It is better for you to enter into life with one eye than with two eyes to be thrown into fiery Gehenna.

The Parable of the Lost Sheep.* [10] z ''See that you do not despise one of these little ones, for I say to you that their angels in heaven always look upon the face of my heavenly Father.* [11]* a [12] What is your opinion? If a man has a hundred sheep and

---

u 1-5: Mk 9, 36-37; Lk 9, 46-48.—v Mt 19, 14; Mk 10, 15; Lk 18, 17.—w Mt 23, 12.—x 6-7: Mk 9, 42; Lk 17, 1-2.—y 8-9: Mt 5, 29-30; Mk 9, 43-47.—z 10-14: Ez 34, 1-3.16; Lk 15, 3-7.—a Lk 19, 10.

17, 27: *That we may not offend them:* though they are *exempt* (26), Jesus and his disciples are to avoid giving offense; therefore the tax is to be paid. *A coin worth twice the temple tax:* literally, ''a stater,'' a Greek coin worth two double drachmas. Two double drachmas were equal to the Jewish shekel and the tax was a half-shekel. *For me and for you:* not only Jesus but Peter pays the tax, and this example serves as a standard for the conduct of all the disciples.

18, 1-35: This discourse of the fourth book of the gospel is often called the ''church order'' discourse, but it lacks most of the considerations usually connected with church order, such as various offices in the church and the duties of each, and deals principally with the relations that must obtain among the members of the church. Beginning with the warning that greatness is not measured by rank or power but by childlikeness (1-5), it deals with the care that the disciples must take not to cause the *little ones to sin* or to neglect them if they stray from the community (6-14), the correction of members who sin (15-18), the efficacy of the prayer of the disciples because of the presence of Jesus (19-20), and the forgiveness that must be repeatedly extended to sinful members who repent (21-35).

18, 1: The initiative is taken not by Jesus as in the Marcan parallel (Mk 9, 33-34) but by the disciples. *Kingdom of heaven:* this may mean *the kingdom* in its fullness, i.e., after the parousia and the final judgment. But what follows about causes of sin, church discipline, and forgiveness, all dealing with the present age, suggests that the question has to do with rank also in the church, where *the kingdom* is manifested here and now, although only partially and by anticipation; see the notes on Mt 3, 2; 4, 17.

18, 3: *Become like children:* the child is held up as a model for the disciples not because of any supposed innocence of children but because of their complete dependence on, and trust in, their parents. So must the disciples be, in respect to God.

18, 5: Cf Mt 10, 40.

18, 6: *One of these little ones:* the thought passes from the child of vv 2-4 to the disciples, *little ones* because of their becoming *like children.* It is difficult to know whether this is a designation of all who are disciples or of those who are insignificant in contrast to others, e.g., the leaders of the community. Since

apart from this chapter the designation *little ones* occurs in Mt only in 10, 42 where it means disciples as such, that is its more likely meaning here. *Who believe in me:* since discipleship is impossible without at least some degree of faith, this further specification seems superfluous. However, it serves to indicate that the warning against causing a *little one* to sin is principally directed against whatever would lead such a one to a weakening or loss of faith. The Greek verb *skandalizein,* here translated *causes . . . to sin,* means literally ''causes to stumble''; what the stumbling is depends on the context. It is used of falling away from faith in Mt 13, 21. According to the better reading of Mk 9, 42, *in me* is a Matthean addition to the Marcan source. *It would be better . . . depths of the sea:* cf Mk 9, 42.

18, 7: This is a Q saying; cf Lk 17, 1. The inevitability of *things that cause sin* (literally, ''scandals'') does not take away the responsibility of *the one through whom they come.*

18, 8-9: These verses are a doublet of Mt 5, 29-30. In that context they have to do with causes of sexual sin. As in the Marcan source from which they have been drawn (Mk 9, 42-48), they differ from the first warning about scandal, which deals with causing another person to sin, for they concern what *causes* oneself *to sin* and they do not seem to be related to another's loss of faith, as the first warning is. It is difficult to know how Matthew understood the logical connection between these verses and vv 6-7.

18, 10-14: The first and last verses are peculiar to Mt. The parable itself comes from Q; see Lk 15, 3-7. In Lk it serves as justification for Jesus' table-companionship with sinners; here, it is an exhortation for the disciples to seek out fellow disciples who have gone *astray.* Not only must no one cause a fellow disciple to sin, but those who have strayed must be sought out and, if possible, brought back to the community. The joy of the shepherd on finding the sheep, though not absent in Mt (13), is more emphasized in Lk. By his addition of vv 10 and 14, Matthew has drawn out explicitly the application of the parable to the care of the *little ones.*

18, 10: *Their angels in heaven . . . my heavenly Father:* for the Jewish belief in angels as guardians of nations and individuals, see Dn 10, 13.20-21; Tb 5, 4-7; 1QH 5, 20-22; as intercessors who present the prayers of human beings to God, see Tb 13, 12.15. The high worth of the *little ones* is indicated by their being represented before God by these heavenly beings.

18, 11: Some manuscripts add, ''For the Son of Man has come to save what was lost''; cf Mt 9, 13. This is practically identical with Lk 19, 10 and is probably a copyist's addition from that source.

one of them goes astray, will he not leave the ninety-nine in the hills and go in search of the stray? [13] And if he finds it, amen, I say to you, he rejoices more over it than over the ninety-nine that did not stray. [14] In just the same way, it is not the will of your heavenly Father that one of these little ones be lost.

A Brother Who Sins.* [15] "If your brother* sins [against you], go and tell him his fault between you and him alone. If he listens to you, you have won over your brother.[b] [16] If he does not listen, take one or two others along with you,[c] so that 'every fact may be established on the testimony of two or three witnesses.'* [17] If he refuses to listen to them, tell the church.* If he refuses to listen even to the church, then treat him as you would a Gentile or a tax collector.[d] [18] [e] Amen, I say to you, whatever you bind on earth shall be bound in heaven, and whatever you loose on earth shall be loosed in heaven.* [19] * Again, [amen,] I say to you, if two of you agree on earth about

anything for which they are to pray, it shall be granted to them by my heavenly Father.[f] [20] [g] For where two or three are gathered together in my name, there am I in the midst of them."*

The Parable of the Unforgiving Servant.* [21] [h] Then Peter approaching asked him, "Lord, if my brother sins against me, how often must I forgive him? As many as seven times?" [22] Jesus answered, "I say to you, not seven times but seventy-seven times.* [23] That is why the kingdom of heaven may be likened to a king who decided to settle accounts with his servants.[i] [24] When he began the accounting, a debtor was brought before him who owed him a huge amount.* [25] Since he had no way of paying it back, his master ordered him to be sold, along with his wife, his children, and all his property, in payment of the debt. [26] At that, the servant fell down, did him homage, and said, 'Be patient with me, and I will pay you back in full.'* [27] Moved with compassion the master of that servant let him go and forgave him the

---

b Lv 19, 17; Sir 19, 13; Gal 6, 1.—c Dt 19, 15; Jn 8, 17; 1 Tm 5, 19.—d 1 Cor 5, 1-13.—e Mt 16, 19; Jn 20, 23.—f Mt 7, 7-8; Jn 15, 7.—g 1 Cor 5, 4.—h 21-22: Mt 6, 12; Lk 17, 4.—i Mt 25, 19.

18, 15-20: Passing from the duty of Christian disciples, toward those who have strayed from their number, the discourse now turns to how they are to deal with one who sins and yet remains within the community. First there is to be private correction (15); if this is unsuccessful, further correction before *two or three witnesses* (16); if this fails, the matter is to be brought before the assembled community (*the church*), and if the sinner refuses to attend to the correction of *the church*, he is to be expelled (17). The church's judgment will be ratified *in heaven*, i.e., by God (18). This three-step process of correction corresponds, though not exactly, to the procedure of the Qumran community; see 1QS 5, 25—6, 1; 6, 24—7, 25; CD 9, 2-8. The section ends with a saying about the favorable response of God to prayer, even to that of a very small number, for Jesus is in the midst of any gathering of his disciples, however small (19-20). Whether this prayer has anything to do with the preceding judgment is uncertain.

18, 15: *Your brother:* a fellow disciple; see Mt 23, 8. The bracketed words, *against you,* are widely attested but they are not in the important codices Sinaiticus and Vaticanus or in some other textual witnesses. Their omission broadens the type of sin in question. *Won over:* literally, "gained."

18, 16: Cf Dt 19, 15.

18, 17: *The church:* the second of the only two instances of this word in the gospels; see the note on Mt 16, 18. Here it refers not to the entire *church* of Jesus, as in Mt 16, 18, but to the local congregation. *Treat him . . . a Gentile or a tax collector:* just as the observant Jew avoided the company of Gentiles and tax collectors, so must the congregation of Christian disciples separate itself from the arrogantly sinful member who refuses to repent even when convicted of his sin by the whole *church*. Such a one is to be set outside the fellowship of the community. The harsh language about *Gentile* and *tax collector* probably reflects a stage of the Matthean *church* when it was principally composed of Jewish Christians. That time had long since passed, but the principle of exclusion for such a sinner remained. Paul makes a similar demand for excommunication in 1 Cor 5, 1-13.

18, 18: Except for the plural of the verbs *bind* and *loose*, this verse is practically identical with Mt 16, 19b, and many scholars understand it as granting to all the disciples what was previously given to Peter alone. For a different view, based on the different contexts of the two verses, see the note on Mt 16, 19.

18, 19-20: Some take these verses as applying to prayer on the occasion of the church's gathering to deal with the sinner of v 17. Unless an *a fortiori* argument is supposed, this seems unlikely. God's answer to the prayer of *two or three* envisages a different situation from one that involves the entire congregation. In addition, the object of this prayer is expressed in most general terms as *anything for which they are to pray.*

18, 20: *For where two or three . . . midst of them:* the presence of Jesus guarantees the efficacy of the prayer. This saying is similar to one attributed to a rabbi executed in A.D. 135 at the time of the second Jewish revolt: ". . . When two sit and there are between them the words of the Torah, the divine presence (Shekinah) rests upon them" (*Pirqê 'Abôt* 3, 3).

18, 21-35: The final section of the discourse deals with the forgiveness that the disciples are to give to their fellow disciples who sin against them. To the question of Peter how often forgiveness is to be granted (21), Jesus answers that it is to be given without limit (22) and illustrates this with the parable of the unmerciful servant (23-34), warning that his *heavenly Father* will give those who do not forgive the same treatment as that given to the unmerciful servant (35). Verses 21-22 correspond to Lk 17, 4; the parable and the final warning are peculiar to Mt. That the parable did not originally belong to this context is suggested by the fact that it really does not deal with repeated forgiveness, which is the point of Peter's question and Jesus' reply.

18, 22: *Seventy-seven times:* the Greek corresponds exactly to the LXX of Gn 4, 24. There is probably an allusion, by contrast, to the limitless vengeance of Lamech in the Gn text. In any case, what is demanded of the disciples is limitless forgiveness.

18, 24: *A huge amount:* literally, "ten thousand talents." The talent was a unit of coinage of high but varying value depending on its metal (gold, silver, copper) and its place of origin. It is mentioned in the New Testament only here and in Mt 25, 14-30.

18, 26: *Pay you back in full:* an empty promise, given the size of the debt.

loan. 28 When that servant had left, he found one of his fellow servants who owed him a much smaller amount.* He seized him and started to choke him, demanding, 'Pay back what you owe.' 29 Falling to his knees, his fellow servant begged him, 'Be patient with me, and I will pay you back.' 30 But he refused. Instead, he had him put in prison until he paid back the debt. 31 Now when his fellow servants saw what had happened, they were deeply disturbed, and went to their master and reported the whole affair. 32 His master summoned him and said to him, 'You wicked servant! I forgave you your entire debt because you begged me to. 33 Should you not have had pity on your fellow servant, as I had pity on you?' j 34 Then in anger his master handed him over to the torturers until he should pay back the whole debt.* 35 k So will my heavenly Father do to you, unless each of you forgives his brother from his heart.''*

j Sir 28, 4.—k Mt 6, 15; Jas 2, 13.—l 3-9: Mk 10, 2-12.—m Gn 1, 27.—n Gn 2, 24; 1 Cor 6, 16; Eph 5, 31.—o Dt 24, 1-4.—p Mt 5, 32; Lk 16, 18; 1 Cor 7, 10-11.

18, 28: *A much smaller amount:* literally, "a hundred denarii." A denarius was the normal daily wage of a laborer. The difference between the two debts is enormous and brings out the absurdity of the conduct of the Christian who has received the great forgiveness of God and yet refuses to forgive the relatively minor offenses done to him.

18, 34: Since the debt is so great as to be unpayable, the punishment will be endless.

18, 35: The Father's forgiveness, already given, will be withdrawn at the final judgment for those who have not imitated his forgiveness by their own.

19, 1—23, 39: The narrative section of the fifth book of the gospel. The first part (Mt 19, 1—20, 34) has for its setting the journey of Jesus from Galilee to Jerusalem; the second (Mt 21, 1—23, 39) deals with Jesus' ministry in Jerusalem up to the final great discourse of the gospel (chs 24-25). Matthew follows the Marcan sequence of events, though adding material both special to this gospel and drawn from Q. The second part ends with the denunciation of the scribes and Pharisees (Mt 23, 1-36) followed by Jesus' lament over Jerusalem (37-39). This long and important speech raises a problem for the view that Mt is structured around five other discourses of Jesus (see Introduction) and that this one has no such function in the gospel. However, it is to be noted that this speech lacks the customary concluding formula that follows the five discourses (see the note on Mt 7, 28), and that those discourses are all addressed either exclusively (chs 10, 18, 24-25) or primarily (chs 5-7, 13) to the disciples, whereas this is addressed primarily to the scribes and Pharisees (13-36). Consequently, it seems plausible to maintain that the evangelist did not intend to give it the structural importance of the five other discourses, and that, in spite of its being composed of sayings-material, it belongs to the narrative section of this book. In that regard, it is similar to the sayings-material of Mt 11, 7-30. Some have proposed that Matthew wished to regard it as part of the final discourse of chs 24-25, but the intervening material (Mt 24, 1-4) and the change in matter and style of those chapters do not support that view.

19, 1-12: In giving Jesus' teaching on divorce (3-9), Matthew here follows his Marcan source (Mk 10, 2-12) as he does Q in Mt 5, 31-32 (cf Lk 16, 18). Verses 10-12 are peculiar to Mt.

VI. MINISTRY IN JUDEA AND JERUSALEM

CHAPTER 19

Marriage and Divorce. 1 *When Jesus* finished these words,* he left Galilee and went to the district of Judea across the Jordan. 2 Great crowds followed him, and he cured them there. 3 l Some Pharisees approached him, and tested him,* saying, "Is it lawful for a man to divorce his wife for any cause whatever?" 4 * He said in reply, "Have you not read that from the beginning the Creator 'made them male and female' m 5 and said, 'For this reason a man shall leave his father and mother and be joined to his wife, and the two shall become one flesh'? n 6 So they are no longer two, but one flesh. Therefore, what God has joined together, no human being must separate." 7 They said to him, "Then why did Moses o command that the man give the woman a bill of divorce and dismiss [her]?"* 8 He said to them, "Because of the hardness of your hearts Moses allowed you to divorce your wives, but from the beginning it was not so. 9 p I say to you,* whoever divorces his wife (unless the marriage

19, 1: *When Jesus finished these words:* see the note on Mt 7, 28-29. *The district of Judea across the Jordan:* an inexact designation of the territory. Judea did not extend *across the Jordan;* the territory east of the river was Perea. The route to Jerusalem by way of Perea avoided passage through Samaria.

19, 3: *Tested him:* the verb is used of attempts of Jesus' opponents to embarrass him by challenging him to do something they think impossible (Mt 16, 1; Mk 8, 11; Lk 11, 16) or by having him say something that they can use against him (Mt 22, 18.35; Mk 10, 2; 12, 15). *For any cause whatever:* this is peculiar to Mt and has been interpreted by some as meaning that Jesus was being asked to take sides in the dispute between the schools of Hillel and Shammai on the reasons for divorce, the latter holding a stricter position than the former. It is unlikely, however, that to ask Jesus' opinion about the differing views of two Jewish schools, both highly respected, could be described as "testing" him, for the reason indicated above.

19, 4-6: Matthew recasts his Marcan source, omitting Jesus' question about Moses' command (Mk 10, 3) and having him recall at once two Genesis texts that show the will and purpose of *the Creator* in making human beings *male and female* (Gn 1, 27), namely, that *a man* may *be joined to his wife* in marriage in the intimacy of *one flesh* (Gn 2, 24). *What God has* thus *joined* must not be separated by any *human being.* (The NAB translation of the Hebrew *bāśār* of Gn 2, 24 as "body" rather than "flesh" obscures the reference of Mt to that text.)

19, 7: See Dt 24, 1-4.

19, 9: Moses' concession to human sinfulness (*the hardness of your hearts,* 8) is repudiated by Jesus, and the original will of the Creator is reaffirmed against that concession. (*Unless the marriage is unlawful*): see the note on Mt 5, 31-32. There is some evidence suggesting that Jesus' absolute prohibition of divorce was paralleled in the Qumran community (see 11QTemple 57, 17-19; CD 4, 12b—5, 14). Matthew removes Mark's setting of this verse as spoken to the disciples alone "in the house" (Mk 10, 10) and also his extension of the divorce prohibition to the case of a woman's divorcing her husband (Mt 10, 12), probably because in Palestine, unlike the places where Roman and Greek law prevailed, the woman was not allowed to initiate the divorce.

is unlawful) and marries another commits adultery." [10] [His] disciples said to him, "If that is the case of a man with his wife, it is better not to marry." [11] He answered, "Not all can accept [this] word,* but only those to whom that is granted. [12] Some are incapable of marriage because they were born so; some, because they were made so by others; some, because they have renounced marriage* for the sake of the kingdom of heaven. Whoever can accept this ought to accept it."

Blessing of the Children.* [13] Then children were brought to him that he might lay his hands on them and pray. q The disciples rebuked them, [14] but Jesus said, "Let the children come to me, and do not prevent them; for the kingdom of heaven belongs to such as these." r [15] After he placed his hands on them, he went away.

The Rich Young Man.* [16] s Now someone approached him and said, "Teacher, what good must I do to gain eternal life?"* [17] He answered him, "Why do you ask me about the good? There is only One who is good.* If you wish to enter into life, keep the commandments." [18] * He asked him, "Which

ones?" And Jesus replied, " 'You shall not kill; t you shall not commit adultery; you shall not steal; you shall not bear false witness; [19] honor your father and your mother'; and 'you shall love your neighbor as yourself.' " [20] The young man* said to him, "All of these I have observed. What do I still lack?" [21] Jesus said to him, "If you wish to be perfect,* go, sell what you have and give to [the] poor, and you will have treasure in heaven. Then come, follow me." u [22] When the young man heard this statement, he went away sad, for he had many possessions. [23] * Then Jesus said to his disciples, "Amen, I say to you, it will be hard for one who is rich to enter the kingdom of heaven. [24] Again I say to you, it is easier for a camel to pass through the eye of a needle than for one who is rich to enter the kingdom of God." v [25] * When the disciples heard this, they were greatly astonished and said, "Who then can be saved?" [26] Jesus looked at them and said, "For human beings this is impossible, but for God all things are possible." w [27] Then Peter said to him in reply, "We have given up everything and followed you. What will

---

q 13-15: Mk 10, 13-16; Lk 18, 15-17.—r Mt 18, 3; Acts 8, 36.—s 16-30: Mk 10, 17-31; Lk 18, 18-30.—t 18-19: Ex 20, 12-16; Dt 5, 16-20 / Lv 19, 18; Rom 13, 9.—u Mt 5, 48; 6, 20.— v Mt 7, 14.—w Gn 18, 14; Jb 42, 2; Lk 1, 37.

19, 11: *[This] word:* probably the disciples' *it is better not to marry* (10). Jesus agrees but says that celibacy is not for all but only for those *to whom that is granted* by God.

19, 12: *Incapable of marriage:* literally, "eunuchs." Three classes are mentioned, eunuchs from birth, eunuchs by castration, and those who have voluntarily *renounced marriage* (literally, "have made themselves eunuchs") *for the sake of the kingdom,* i.e., to devote themselves entirely to its service. Some scholars take the last class to be those who have been divorced by their spouses and have refused to enter another marriage. But it is more likely that it is rather those who have chosen never to marry, since that suits better the optional nature of the decision: *whoever can . . . ought to accept it.*

19, 13-15: This account is understood by some as intended to justify the practice of infant baptism. That interpretation is based principally on the command not to *prevent* the children from coming, since that word sometimes has a baptismal connotation in the New Testament; see Acts 8, 36.

19, 16-30: Cf Mk 10, 17-31. This story does not set up a "two-tier" morality, that of those who seek (only) *eternal life* (16) and that of those who *wish to be perfect* (21). It speaks rather of the obstacle that riches constitute for the following of Jesus and of the impossibility, humanly speaking, for one who has *many possessions* (22) *to enter the kingdom* (24). Actual renunciation of riches is not demanded of all; Matthew counts the rich Joseph of Arimathea as a disciple of Jesus (Mt 27, 57). But only the poor in spirit (Mt 5, 3) can *enter the kingdom* and, as here, such poverty may entail the sacrifice of one's *possessions.* The Twelve, who *have given up everything* (27) to follow Jesus, will have as their reward a share in Jesus' (the Son of

Man's) *judging the twelve tribes of Israel* (28), and all who have similarly sacrificed family or property for his sake *will inherit eternal life* (29).

19, 16: *Gain eternal life:* this is equivalent to "entering into life" (17) and "being saved" (25); the *life* is that of the new age after the final judgment (see Mt 25, 46). It probably is also equivalent here to "entering the kingdom of heaven" (23) or "the kingdom of God" (24), but see the notes on Mt 3, 2; 4, 17; 18, 1 for the wider reference of *the kingdom* in Mt.

19, 17: By Matthew's reformulation of the Marcan question and reply (Mk 10, 17-18) Jesus' repudiation of the term "good" for himself has been softened. Yet the Marcan assertion that "no one is good but God alone" stands, with only unimportant verbal modification.

19, 18-19: The first five commandments cited are from the Decalogue (see Ex 20, 12-16; Dt 5, 16-20). Matthew omits Mark's "you shall not defraud" (Mt 10, 19; see Dt 24, 14) and adds Lv 19, 18. This combination of commandments of the Decalogue with Lv 19, 18 is partially the same as Paul's enumeration of the demands of Christian morality in Rom 13, 9.

19, 20: *Young man:* in Mt alone of the synoptics the questioner is said to be a *young man;* thus the Marcan "from my youth" (Mk 10, 20) is omitted.

19, 21: *If you wish to be perfect: to be perfect* is demanded of all Christians; see Mt 5, 48. In the case of this man, it involves selling his possessions and giving to the poor; only so can he *follow* Jesus.

19, 23-24: Riches are an obstacle to entering *the kingdom* that cannot be overcome by human power. The comparison with the impossibility of a camel's passing *through the eye of a needle* should not be mitigated by such suppositions as that *the eye of a needle* means a low or narrow gate. *The kingdom of God:* as in Mt 12, 28; 21, 31.43, instead of Mt's usual *kingdom of heaven.*

19, 25-26: See the note on Mk 10, 23-27.

there be for us?"ˣ ²⁸ ʸ Jesus said to them, "Amen, I say to you that you who have followed me, in the new age, when the Son of Man is seated on his throne of glory, will yourselves sit on twelve thrones, judging the twelve tribes of Israel.* ²⁹ And everyone who has given up houses or brothers or sisters or father or mother or children or lands for the sake of my name will receive a hundred times more, and will inherit eternal life. ³⁰ ᶻ But many who are first will be last, and the last will be first.*

CHAPTER 20

The Workers in the Vineyard.* ¹ "The kingdom of heaven is like a landowner who went out at dawn to hire laborers for his vineyard. ²After agreeing with them for the usual daily wage, he sent them into his vineyard. ³Going out about nine o'clock, he saw others standing idle in the marketplace, ⁴and he said to them, 'You too go into my vineyard, and I will give you what is just.'* ⁵So they went off. [And] he went out again around noon, and around three o'clock, and did likewise. ⁶Going out about five o'clock, he found others standing around, and said to them, 'Why do you stand here idle all day?' ⁷They answered, 'Because no one has hired us.' He said to them, 'You too go into my vineyard.' ⁸When it was evening the owner of the

vineyard said to his foreman, 'Summon the laborers and give them their pay,ᵃ beginning with the last and ending with the first.'* ⁹When those who had started about five o'clock came, each received the usual daily wage. ¹⁰So when the first came, they thought that they would receive more, but each of them also got the usual wage. ¹¹And on receiving it they grumbled against the landowner, ¹²saying, 'These last ones worked only one hour, and you have made them equal to us, who bore the day's burden and the heat.' ¹³He said to one of them in reply, 'My friend, I am not cheating you.* Did you not agree with me for the usual daily wage? ¹⁴ * Take what is yours and go. What if I wish to give this last one the same as you? ¹⁵[Or] am I not free to do as I wish with my own money? Are you envious because I am generous?' ¹⁶Thus, the last will be first, and the first will be last."*

The Third Prediction of the Passion.* ¹⁷As Jesus was going up to Jerusalem,ᵇ he took the twelve [disciples] aside by themselves, and said to them on the way, ¹⁸ "Behold, we are going up to Jerusalem, and the Son of Man will be handed over to the chief priests and the scribes, and they will condemn him to death, ¹⁹and hand him over to the Gentiles to be mocked and scourged and crucified, and he will be raised on the third day."

---

x Mt 4, 20.22.—y Mt 25, 31; Dn 7, 9.22; Lk 22, 30; Rv 3, 21; 20, 4.—z Mt 20, 16.—a Lv 19, 13; Dt 24, 15.—b 17-19: Mt 16, 21; 17, 22-23; Mk 10, 32-34; Lk 18, 31-33.

19, 28: This saying, directed to the Twelve, is from Q; see Lk 22, 29-30. *The new age:* the Greek word here translated "new age" occurs in the New Testament only here and in Ti 3, 5. Literally, it means "rebirth" or "regeneration," and is used in Ti of spiritual rebirth through baptism. Here it means the "rebirth" effected by the coming of the kingdom. Since that coming has various stages (see the notes on Mt 3, 2; 4, 17), *the new age* could be taken as referring to the time after the resurrection when the Twelve will govern the true Israel, i.e., the church of Jesus. (For "judge" in the sense of "govern," cf Jgs 12, 8.9.11; 15, 20; 16, 31; Ps 2, 10.) But since it is connected here with the time when *the Son of Man* will be *seated on his throne of glory,* language that Matthew uses in Mt 25, 31 for the time of final judgment, it is more likely that what the Twelve are promised is that they will be joined with Jesus then in judging the people of Israel.

19, 30: Different interpretations have been given to this saying, which comes from Mk 10, 31. In view of Matthew's associating it with the following parable (Mt 20, 1-15) and substantially repeating it (in reverse order) at the end of that parable (Mt 20, 16), it may be that his meaning is that all who respond to the call of Jesus, at whatever time (*first* or *last*), will be the same in respect to inheriting the benefits of the kingdom, which is the gift of God.

20, 1-16: This parable is peculiar to Mt. It is difficult to know whether the evangelist composed it or received it as part of his traditional material and, if the latter is the case, what its original reference was. In its present context its close association with Mt 19, 30 suggests that its teaching is the equality of all the disciples in the reward of inheriting eternal life.

20, 4: *What is just:* although the wage is not stipulated as in the case of those first hired, it will be fair.

20, 8: *Beginning with the last . . . the first:* this element of the parable has no other purpose than to show how *the first* knew what *the last* were given (12).

20, 13: *I am not cheating you:* literally, "I am not treating you unjustly."

20, 14-15: The owner's conduct involves no violation of justice (4.13), and that all the workers receive the same wage is due only to his generosity to the latest arrivals; the resentment of the first comes from envy.

20, 16: See the note on Mt 19, 30.

20, 17-19: Cf Mk 10, 32-34. This is the third and the most detailed of the passion predictions (Mt 16, 21-23; 17, 22-23). It speaks of Jesus' being *handed over to the Gentiles* (Mt 27, 2), his being *mocked* (Mt 27, 27-30), *scourged* (Mt 27, 26), and *crucified* (Mt 27, 31.35). In all but the last of these points Matthew agrees with his Marcan source, but whereas Mk speaks of Jesus' being killed (Mk 10, 34), Mt has the specific *to be . . . crucified.*

The Request of James and John.* **20** c Then the mother* of the sons of Zebedee approached him with her sons and did him homage, wishing to ask him for something. **21** He said to her, "What do you wish?" She answered him, "Command that these two sons of mine sit, one at your right and the other at your left, in your kingdom." **22** Jesus said in reply, "You do not know what you are asking.* Can you drink the cup that I am going to drink?" They said to him, "We can." **23** He replied, "My cup you will indeed drink, but to sit at my right and at my left [, this] is not mine to give but is for those for whom it has been prepared by my Father." **24** When the ten heard this, they became indignant at the two brothers.*d* **25** But Jesus summoned them and said, "You know that the rulers of the Gentiles lord it over them, and the great ones make their authority over them felt. **26** But it shall not be so among you. Rather, whoever wishes to be great among you shall be your servant; **27** whoever wishes to be first among you shall be your slave.*e* **28** Just so, the Son of Man did not come to be served but to serve and to give his life as a ransom* for many."*f*

The Healing of Two Blind Men.* **29** As they left Jericho,*g* a great crowd followed him. **30** Two blind men were sitting by the roadside, and when they heard that Jesus was passing by, they cried out, "[Lord,]* Son of David, have pity on us!"*h* **31** The crowd warned them to be silent, but they called out all the more, "Lord, Son of David, have pity on us!" **32** Jesus stopped and called them and said, "What do you want me to do for you?" **33** They answered him, "Lord, let our eyes be opened." **34** Moved with pity, Jesus touched their eyes. Immediately they received their sight, and followed him.

CHAPTER 21

The Entry into Jerusalem.* **1** *i* When they drew near Jerusalem and came to Bethphage* on the Mount of Olives, Jesus sent two disciples, **2** saying to them, "Go into the village opposite you, and immediately you will find an ass tethered, and a colt with her.* Untie them and bring them here to me. **3** And if anyone should say anything to you, reply, 'The master has need of them.' Then he will send them at

---

c 20-28: Mk 10, 35-45.—d 24-27: Lk 22, 25-27.—e Mk 9, 35.—f Mt 26, 28; Is 53, 12; Rom 5, 6; 1 Tm 2, 6.—g 29-34: Mk 10, 46-52; Lk 18, 35-43.—h Mt 9, 27.—i 1-11: Mk 11, 1-11; Lk 19, 28-38; Jn 12, 12-15.

20, 20-28: Cf Mk 10, 35-45. The request of the sons of Zebedee, made through their mother, for the highest places of honor in the *kingdom*, and the indignation of *the* other *ten* disciples at this request, show that neither *the two brothers* nor the others have understood that what makes for greatness in the kingdom is not lordly power but humble service. Jesus gives the example, and his ministry of service will reach its highest point when he gives his life for the deliverance of the human race from sin.

20, 20-21: The reason for Matthew's making *the mother* the petitioner (cf Mk 10, 35) is not clear. Possibly he intends an allusion to Bathsheba's seeking the kingdom for Solomon; see 1 Kgs 1, 11-21. *Your kingdom:* see the note on Mt 16, 28.

20, 22: *You do not know what you are asking:* the Greek verbs are plural and, with the rest of the verse, indicate that the answer is addressed not to the woman but to her sons. *Drink the cup:* see the note on Mk 10, 38-40. Matthew omits the Marcan "or be baptized with the baptism with which I am baptized" (Mk 10, 38).

20, 28: *Ransom:* this noun, which occurs in the New Testament only here and in the Marcan parallel (Mt 10, 45), does not necessarily express the idea of liberation by payment of some price. The cognate verb is used frequently in the LXX of God's liberating Israel from Egypt or from Babylonia after the Exile; see Ex 6, 6; 15, 13; Ps 77 (76 LXX), 16; Is 43, 1; 44, 22. The liberation brought by Jesus' death will be *for many;* cf Is 53, 12. *Many* does not mean that some are excluded, but is a Semitism designating the collectivity who benefit from the service of the one, and is equivalent to "all." While there are few verbal contacts between this saying and the fourth Servant Song (Is 52, 13—53, 12), the ideas of that passage are reflected here.

20, 29-34: The cure of the blind men is probably symbolic of what will happen to the disciples, now blind to the meaning of Jesus' passion and to the necessity of their sharing his suffering.

As the men are given sight, so, after the resurrection, will the disciples come to see that to which they are now blind. Matthew has abbreviated his Marcan source (Mk 10, 46-52) and has made Mk's one man two. Such doubling is characteristic of this gospel; see Mt 8, 28-34 (// Mk 5, 1-20) and the note on Mt 9, 27-31.

20, 30: *[Lord]:* some important textual witnesses omit this, but that may be because copyists assimilated this verse to Mt 9, 27. *Son of David:* see the note on Mt 9, 27.

21, 1-11: Jesus' coming to Jerusalem is in accordance with the divine will that he must go there (cf Mt 16, 21) to suffer, die, and be raised. He prepares for his entry into the city in such a way as to make it a fulfillment of the prophecy of Zec 9, 9 (2) that emphasizes the humility of the *king who comes* (5). That prophecy, absent from the Marcan parallel account (Mk 11, 1-11) although found also in the Johannine account of the entry (Jn 12, 15), is the center of the Matthean story. During the procession from Bethphage to Jerusalem, Jesus is acclaimed as the Davidic messianic king by the crowds who accompany him (9). On his arrival *the whole city was shaken,* and to the inquiry of the amazed populace about Jesus' identity the crowds with him reply that he is *the prophet, from Nazareth in Galilee* (10.11).

21, 1: *Bethphage:* a village that can no longer be certainly identified. Mk mentions it before Bethany (Mk 11, 1), which suggests that it lay to the east of the latter. *The Mount of Olives:* the hill east of Jerusalem that is spoken of in Zec 14, 4 as the place where the Lord will come to rescue Jerusalem from the enemy nations.

21, 2: *An ass tethered, and a colt with her:* instead of the one animal of Mk 11, 2, Mt has two, as demanded by his understanding of Zec 9, 9.

once." [4] This happened so that what had been spoken through the prophet* might be fulfilled:

[5] "Say to daughter Zion,
  'Behold, your king comes to you,
    meek and riding on an ass,
      and on a colt, the foal of a beast of burden.' " [j]

[6] The disciples went and did as Jesus had ordered them. [7] They brought the ass and the colt and laid their cloaks over them, and he sat upon them.* [8] [k] The very large crowd spread their cloaks on the road, while others cut branches from the trees and strewed them on the road.* [9] The crowds preceding him and those following kept crying out and saying:

"Hosanna* to the Son of David;
  blessed is he who comes in the name of the Lord;
  hosanna in the highest." [l]

[10] And when he entered Jerusalem the whole city was shaken* and asked, "Who is this?" [11] And the crowds replied, "This is Jesus the prophet,* from Nazareth in Galilee."

The Cleansing of the Temple.* [12] [m] Jesus entered the temple area and drove out all those engaged in selling and buying there. [n] He overturned the tables of the money changers and the seats of those who were selling doves.* [13] And he said to them, "It is written: [o]

'My house shall be a house of prayer,'*
  but you are making it a den of thieves."

[14] The blind and the lame* approached him in the temple area, and he cured them. [p] [15] When the chief priests and the scribes saw the wondrous things* he was doing, and the children crying out in the temple area, "Hosanna to the Son of David," they were indignant [16] and said to him, "Do you hear what they are saying?" Jesus said to them, "Yes; and have you never read the text, [q] 'Out of the mouths of infants and nurslings you have brought forth praise'?"* [17] And leaving them, he went out of the city to Bethany, and there he spent the night.

---

j Is 62, 11; Zec 9, 9.—k 2 Kgs 9, 13.—l Ps 118, 25-26.—m 12-17: Mk 11, 15-19; Lk 19, 45-48; Jn 2, 14-22.—n Lv 5, 7.—o Is 56, 7; Jer 7, 11.—p 2 Sm 5, 8 LXX.—q Ps 8, 2 LXX; Wis 10, 21.

21, 4-5: *The prophet:* this fulfillment citation is actually composed of two distinct Old Testament texts, Is 62, 11 (*Say to daughter Zion*) and Zec 9, 9. The *ass* and the *colt* are the same animal in the prophecy, mentioned twice in different ways, the common Hebrew literary device of poetic parallelism. That Matthew takes them as two is one of the reasons why some scholars think that he was a Gentile rather than a Jewish Christian who would presumably not make that mistake (see Introduction).

21, 7: *Upon them:* upon the two animals; an awkward picture resulting from Matthew's misunderstanding of the prophecy.

21, 8: *Spread . . . on the road:* cf 2 Kgs 9, 13. There is a similarity between the cutting and strewing of the *branches* and the festivities of Tabernacles (Lv 23, 39-40); see also 2 Mc 10, 5-8 where the celebration of the rededication of the temple is compared to that of Tabernacles.

21, 9: *Hosanna:* the Hebrew means "(O LORD) grant salvation"; see Ps 118, 25, but that invocation had become an acclamation of jubilation and welcome. *Blessed is he . . . in the name of the Lord:* see Ps 118, 26 and the note on Jn 12, 13. *In the highest:* probably only an intensification of the acclamation, although *Hosanna in the highest* could be taken as a prayer, "May God save (him)."

21, 10: *Was shaken:* in the gospels this verb is peculiar to Mt where it is used also of the earthquake at the time of the crucifixion (Mt 27, 51) and of the terror of the guards of Jesus' tomb at the appearance of the angel (Mt 28, 4). For Matthew's use of the cognate noun, see the note on Mt 8, 24.

21, 11: *The prophet:* see Mt 16, 14 ("one of the prophets") and Mt 21, 46.

21, 12-17: Matthew changes the order of Mk (11, 11.12.15) and places the cleansing of the temple on the same day as the entry into Jerusalem, immediately after it. The activities going on in *the temple area* were not secular but connected with the temple worship. Thus Jesus' attack on those so engaged and his charge that they were *making* God's *house of prayer a den of thieves* (12-13) constituted a claim to authority over the religious practices of Israel and were a challenge to the priestly authorities. Verses 14-17 are peculiar to Mt. Jesus' healings and his countenancing the children's cries of praise rouse the indignation of *the chief priests and the scribes* (15). These two groups appear in the infancy narrative (Mt 2, 4) and have been mentioned in the first and third passion predictions (Mt 16, 21; 20, 18). Now, as the passion approaches, they come on the scene again, exhibiting their hostility to Jesus.

21, 12: These activities were carried on in the court of the Gentiles, the outermost court of *the temple area.* Animals for sacrifice were sold; the *doves* were for those who could not afford a more expensive offering; see Lv 5, 7. *Tables of the money changers:* only the coinage of Tyre could be used for the purchases; other money had to be exchanged for that.

21, 13: *'My house . . . prayer':* cf Is 56, 7. Matthew omits the final words of the quotation, "for all peoples" ("all nations"), possibly because for him the worship of the God of Israel by all nations belongs to the time after the resurrection; see Mt 28, 19. *A den of thieves:* the phrase is taken from Jer 7, 11.

21, 14: *The blind and the lame:* according to 2 Sm 5, 8 (LXX) *the blind and the lame* were forbidden to enter "the house of the Lord," the temple. These are the last of Jesus' healings in Mt.

21, 15: *The wondrous things:* the healings.

21, 16: *'Out of the mouths . . . praise':* cf Ps 8, 3 (LXX).

The Cursing of the Fig Tree.* [18] r When he was going back to the city in the morning, he was hungry. [19] Seeing a fig tree by the road, he went over to it, but found nothing on it except leaves. And he said to it, "May no fruit ever come from you again." And immediately the fig tree withered. s [20] When the disciples saw this, they were amazed and said, "How was it that the fig tree withered immediately?" [21] t Jesus said to them in reply, "Amen, I say to you, if you have faith and do not waver, not only will you do what has been done to the fig tree, but even if you say to this mountain, 'Be lifted up and thrown into the sea,' it will be done.* [22] Whatever you ask for in prayer with faith, you will receive." u

The Authority of Jesus Questioned.* [23] v When he had come into the temple area, the chief priests and the elders of the people approached him as he was teaching and said, "By what authority are you doing these things?* And who gave you this authority?" w [24] Jesus said to them in reply, "I shall ask you one question,* and if you answer it for me, then I shall tell you by what authority I do these things. [25] Where was John's baptism from? Was it of heavenly or of human origin?" They discussed this among themselves and said, "If we say 'Of heavenly origin,' he will say to us, 'Then why did you not believe him?' [26] x But if we say, 'Of human origin,' we fear the crowd, for they all regard John as a prophet."* [27] So they said to Jesus in reply, "We do not know." He himself said to them, "Neither shall I tell you by what authority I do these things.*

The Parable of the Two Sons.* [28] "What is your opinion? A man had two sons. He came to the first and said, 'Son, go out and work in the vineyard today.' [29] He said in reply, 'I will not,' but afterwards he changed his mind and went. [30] The man came to the other son and gave the same order. He said in reply, 'Yes, sir,' but did not go. [31] Which of the two did his father's will?" They answered, "The first." Jesus said to them, "Amen, I say to you, tax collectors and prostitutes are entering the kingdom of God before you.* [32] When John came to you in the way of righteousness, you did not believe him; but tax collectors and prostitutes did. y Yet even when you saw that, you did not later change your minds and believe him.*

---

r 18-22: Mk 11, 12-14.20-24.—s Jer 8, 13; Lk 13, 6-9.—t Mt 17, 20; Lk 17, 6.—u Mt 7, 7; 1 Jn 3, 22.—v 23-27: Mk 11, 27-33; Lk 20, 1-8.—w Jn 2, 18.—x Mt 14, 5.—y Lk 7, 29-30.

21, 18-22: In Mk the effect of Jesus' cursing the fig tree is not immediate; see Mk 11, 14.20. By making it so, Matthew has heightened the miracle. Jesus' act seems arbitrary and ill-tempered, but it is a prophetic action similar to those of Old Testament prophets that vividly symbolize some part of their preaching; see, e.g., Ez 12, 1-20. It is a sign of the judgment that is to come upon the Israel that with all its apparent piety lacks the fruit of good deeds (Mt 3, 10) and will soon bear the punishment of its fruitlessness (43). Some scholars propose that this story is the development in tradition of a parable of Jesus about the destiny of a fruitless tree, such as Lk 13, 6-9. Jesus' answer to the question of the amazed disciples (20) makes the miracle an example of the power of prayer made with unwavering *faith* (21-22).

21, 21: See Mt 17, 20.

21, 23-27: Cf Mk 11, 27-33. This is the first of five controversies between Jesus and the religious authorities of Judaism in Mt 21, 23—22, 46, presented in the form of questions and answers.

21, 23: *These things:* probably his entry into the city, his cleansing of the temple, and his healings there.

21, 24: To reply by counterquestion was common in rabbinical debate.

21, 26: *We fear . . . as a prophet:* cf Mt 14, 5.

21, 27: Since through embarrassment on the one hand and fear on the other the religious authorities claim ignorance of the origin of John's baptism, they show themselves incapable of speaking with authority; hence Jesus refuses to discuss with them the grounds of his authority.

21, 28-32: The series of controversies is interrupted by three parables on the judgment of Israel (Mt 21, 28—22, 14) of which this, peculiar to Mt, is the first. The second (Mt 21, 33-46) comes from Mk (12, 1-12), and the third (Mt 22, 1-14) from Q; see Lk 14, 15-24. This interruption of the controversies is similar to that in Mk, although Mk has only one parable between the first and second controversy. As regards Mt's first parable, vv 28-30 if taken by themselves could point simply to the difference between saying and doing, a theme of much importance in this gospel (cf Mt 7, 21; 12, 50); that may have been the parable's original reference. However, it is given a more specific application by the addition of vv 31-32. The two sons represent, respectively, the religious leaders and the religious outcasts who followed John's call to repentance. By the answer they give to Jesus' question (31) the leaders condemn themselves. There is much confusion in the textual tradition of the parable. Of the three different forms of the text given by important textual witnesses, one has the leaders answer that the son who agreed to go but did not was the one who did the father's will. Although some scholars accept that as the original reading, their arguments in favor of it seem unconvincing. The choice probably lies only between a reading that puts the son who agrees and then disobeys before the son who at first refuses and then obeys, and the reading followed in the present translation. The witnesses to the latter reading are slightly better than those that support the other.

21, 31: *Entering . . . before you:* this probably means "they enter; you do not."

21, 32: Cf Lk 7, 29-30. Although the thought is similar to that of the Lucan text, the formulation is so different that it is improbable that the saying comes from Q. *Came to you . . . way of righteousness:* several meanings are possible: that John himself was righteous, that he taught righteousness to others, or that he had an important place in God's plan of salvation. For the last, see the note on Mt 3, 14-15.

Mt

The Parable of the Tenants.* ³³"Hear another parable.ᶻ There was a landowner who planted a vineyard,ᵃ put a hedge around it, dug a wine press in it, and built a tower.* Then he leased it to tenants and went on a journey. ³⁴When vintage time drew near, he sent his servants* to the tenants to obtain his produce. ³⁵But the tenants seized the servants and one they beat, another they killed, and a third they stoned. ³⁶Again he sent other servants, more numerous than the first ones, but they treated them in the same way. ³⁷Finally, he sent his son to them, thinking, 'They will respect my son.' ³⁸But when the tenants saw the son, they said to one another, 'This is the heir. Come, let us kill him and acquire his inheritance.'* ³⁹ᵇ They seized him, threw him out of the vineyard, and killed him.* ⁴⁰What will the owner of the vineyard do to those tenants when he comes?" ⁴¹They answered* him, "He will put those wretched men to a wretched death and lease his vineyard to other tenants who will give him the produce at the proper times." ⁴²Jesus said to them, "Did you never read in the scriptures:ᶜ

'The stone that the builders rejected
    has become the cornerstone;
by the Lord has this been done,
    and it is wonderful in our eyes'?*
⁴³Therefore, I say to you, the kingdom of God will be taken away from you and given to a people that will produce its fruit.* [⁴⁴The one who falls on this stone will be dashed to pieces; and it will crush anyone on whom it falls.]"* ⁴⁵When the chief priests and the Pharisees* heard his parables, they knew that he was speaking about them. ⁴⁶And although they were attempting to arrest him, they feared the crowds, for they regarded him as a prophet.

CHAPTER 22

The Parable of the Wedding Feast.* ¹ᵈ Jesus again in reply spoke to them in parables, saying, ²"The kingdom of heaven may be likened to a king who gave a wedding feast* for his son. ³He dispatched his servants to summon the invited guests to the feast, but they refused to come. ⁴A second time he sent other servants,* saying,

---

z 33-46: Mk 12, 1-12; Lk 20, 9-19.—a Is 5, 1-2.7.—b Heb 13, 12.—c Ps 118, 22-23; Is 28, 16; Acts 4, 11; 1 Pt 2, 7.—d 1-14: Lk 14, 15-24.

21, 33-46: Cf Mk 12, 1-12. In this parable there is a close correspondence between most of the details of the story and the situation that it illustrates, the dealings of God with his people. Because of that heavy allegorizing, some scholars think that it does not in any way go back to Jesus, but represents the theology of the later church. That judgment applies to the Marcan parallel as well, although the allegorizing has gone farther in Mt. There are others who believe that while many of the allegorical elements are due to church sources, they have been added to a basic parable spoken by Jesus. This view is now supported by the Gospel of Thomas, #65, where a less allegorized and probably more primitive form of the parable is found.

21, 33: *Planted a vineyard . . . a tower:* cf Is 5, 1-2. The *vineyard* is defined in Is 5, 7 as "the house of Israel."

21, 34-35: *His servants:* Mt has two sendings of *servants* as against Mk's three sendings of a single servant (Mk 12, 2-5a) followed by a statement about the sending of "many others" (Mk 11, 2.5b). That these *servants* stand for the prophets sent by God to Israel is clearly implied but not made explicit here, but see Mt 23, 37. *His produce:* cf Mk 12, 2, "some of the produce." The *produce* is the good works demanded by God, and his claim to them is total.

21, 38: *Acquire his inheritance:* if a Jewish proselyte died without heir, the tenants of his land would have final claim on it.

21, 39: *Threw him out . . . and killed him:* the change in the Marcan order where the son is killed and his corpse then thrown out (Mk 12, 8) was probably made because of the tradition that Jesus died outside the city of Jerusalem; see Jn 19, 17; Heb 13, 12.

21, 41: *They answered:* in Mk 12, 9 the question is answered by Jesus himself; here the leaders answer and so condemn themselves; cf v 31. Matthew adds that the new *tenants* to whom the vineyard will be transferred *will give* the owner *the produce at the proper times.*

21, 42: Cf Ps 118, 22-23. The psalm was used in the early church as a prophecy of Jesus' resurrection; see Acts 4, 11; 1 Pt 2, 7. If, as some think, the original parable ended at v 39, it was thought necessary to complete it by a reference to Jesus' vindication by God.

21, 43: Peculiar to Mt. *Kingdom of God:* see the note on Mt 19, 23-24. Its presence here instead of Mt's usual "kingdom of heaven" may indicate that the saying came from Matthew's own traditional material. *A people that will produce its fruit:* believing Israelites and Gentiles, the church of Jesus.

21, 44: The majority of textual witnesses omit this verse. It is probably an early addition to Mt from Lk 20, 18 with which it is practically identical.

21, 45: *The Pharisees:* Matthew inserts into the group of Jewish leaders (23) those who represented the Judaism of his own time.

22, 1-14: This parable is from Q; see Lk 14, 15-24. It has been given many allegorical traits by Matthew, e.g., the burning of the *city* of the guests who refused the invitation (7), which corresponds to the destruction of Jerusalem by the Romans in A.D. 70. It has similarities with the preceding parable of the tenants: the sending of two groups of *servants* (3.4), the murder of the *servants* (6), the punishment of the *murderers* (7), and the entrance of a new group into a privileged situation of which the others had proved themselves unworthy (8-10). The parable ends with a section that is peculiar to Mt (11-14), which some take as a distinct parable. Mt presents the *kingdom* in its double aspect, already present and something that can be entered here and now (1-10), and something that will be possessed only by those present members who can stand the scrutiny of the final judgment (11-14). The parable is not only a statement of God's judgment on Israel but a warning to Matthew's church.

22, 2: *Wedding feast:* the Old Testament's portrayal of final salvation under the image of a banquet (Is 25, 6) is taken up also in Mt 8, 11; cf Lk 13, 15.

22, 3-4: *Servants . . . other servants:* probably Christian missionaries in both instances; cf Mt 23, 34.

'Tell those invited: "Behold, I have prepared my banquet, my calves and fattened cattle are killed, and everything is ready; come to the feast." ' ⁵Some ignored the invitation and went away, one to his farm, another to his business. ⁶The rest laid hold of his servants, mistreated them, and killed them.ᵉ ⁷The king was enraged and sent his troops, destroyed those murderers, and burned their city.* ⁸Then he said to his servants, 'The feast is ready, but those who were invited were not worthy to come. ⁹Go out, therefore, into the main roads and invite to the feast whomever you find.' ¹⁰The servants went out into the streets and gathered all they found, bad and good alike,* and the hall was filled with guests. ¹¹But when the king came in to meet the guests he saw a man there not dressed in a wedding garment.* ¹²He said to him, 'My friend, how is it that you came in here without a wedding garment?' But he was reduced to silence. ¹³Then the king said to his attendants, 'Bind his hands and feet, and cast him into the darkness outside,ᶠ where there will be wailing and grinding of teeth.'* ¹⁴Many are invited, but few are chosen."

Paying Taxes to the Emperor.* ¹⁵Then the Pharisees* went off and plotted how they might entrap him in speech.ᵍ ¹⁶They sent their disciples to him, with the Herodians,* saying, "Teacher, we know that you are a truthful man and that you teach the way of God in accordance with the truth. And you are not concerned with anyone's opinion, for you do not regard a person's status. ¹⁷Tell us, then, what is your opinion: Is it lawful* to pay the census tax to Caesar or not?" ¹⁸Knowing their malice, Jesus said, "Why are you testing me, you hypocrites? ¹⁹Show me the coin that pays the census tax." Then they handed him the Roman coin.* ²⁰He said to them, "Whose image is this and whose inscription?" ²¹They replied, "Caesar's."* At that he said to them, "Then repay to Caesar what belongs to Caesar and to God what belongs to God."ʰ ²²When they heard this they were amazed, and leaving him they went away.

The Question about the Resurrection.* ²³ⁱOn that day Sadducees approached him, saying that there is no resurrection.* They put this question to him, ²⁴ʲ saying, "Teacher, Moses said, 'If a man dies* without children, his brother shall marry

---

e Mt 21, 35.—f Mt 8, 12; 25, 30.—g 15-22: Mk 12, 13-17; Lk 20, 20-26.—h Rom 13, 7.—i 23-33: Mk 12, 18-27; Lk 20, 27-40.—j Gn 38, 8; Dt 25, 5-6.

22, 7: See the note on vv 1-14.

22, 10: *Bad and good alike:* cf Mt 13, 47.

22, 11: *A wedding garment:* the repentance, change of heart and mind, that is the condition for entrance into the kingdom (Mt 3, 2; 4, 17) must be continued in a life of good deeds (Mt 7, 21-23).

22, 13: *Wailing and grinding of teeth:* the Christian who lacks the wedding garment of good deeds will suffer the same fate as those Jews who have rejected Jesus; see the note on Mt 8, 11-12.

22, 15-22: The series of controversies between Jesus and the representatives of Judaism (see the note on Mt 21, 23-27) is resumed. As in the first (Mt 21, 23-27), here and in the following disputes Matthew follows his Marcan source with few modifications.

22, 15: *The Pharisees:* while Matthew retains the Marcan union of Pharisees and Herodians in this account, he clearly emphasizes the Pharisees' part. They alone are mentioned here, and the Herodians are joined with them only in a prepositional phrase of v 16. *Entrap him in speech:* the question that they will pose is intended to force Jesus to take either a position contrary to that held by the majority of the people or one that will bring him into conflict with the Roman authorities.

22, 16: *Herodians:* see the note on Mk 3, 6. They would favor payment of the tax; the Pharisees did not.

22, 17: *Is it lawful:* the law to which they refer is the law of God.

22, 19: *They handed him the Roman coin:* their readiness in producing the money implies their use of it and their acceptance of the financial advantages of the Roman administration in Palestine.

22, 21: *Caesar's:* the emperor Tiberius (A.D. 14-37). *Repay to Caesar what belongs to Caesar:* those who willingly use the coin that is Caesar's should *repay* him in kind. The answer avoids taking sides in the question of the lawfulness of the tax. *To God what belongs to God:* Jesus raises the debate to a new level. Those who have hypocritically asked about tax in respect to its relation to the law of God should be concerned rather with repaying God with the good deeds that are his due; cf Mt 21, 41.43.

22, 23-33: Here Jesus' opponents are the *Sadducees,* members of the powerful priestly party of his time; see the note on Mt 3, 7. Denying the resurrection of the dead, a teaching of relatively late origin in Judaism (cf Dn 12, 2), they appeal to a law of the Pentateuch (Dt 25, 5-10) and present a case based on it that would make resurrection from the dead ridiculous (24-28). Jesus chides them for knowing neither *the scriptures* nor *the power of God* (29). His argument in respect to God's *power* contradicts the notion, held even by many proponents as well as by opponents of the teaching, that the life of those raised from the dead would be essentially a continuation of the type of life they had had before death (30). His argument based on the scriptures (31-32) is of a sort that was accepted as valid among Jews of the time.

22, 23: *Saying that there is no resurrection:* in the Marcan parallel (Mk 12, 18) the Sadducees are correctly defined as those "who say there is no resurrection"; see also Lk 20, 27. Matthew's rewording of Mk can mean that these particular Sadducees deny the resurrection, which would imply that he was not aware that the denial was characteristic of the party. For some scholars this is an indication of his being a Gentile Christian; see the note on Mt 21, 4-5.

22, 24: *'If a man dies . . . his brother':* this is known as the "law of the levirate," from the Latin *levir,* "brother-in-law." Its purpose was to continue the family line of the deceased *brother* (Dt 25, 6).

his wife and raise up descendants for his brother.' 25 Now there were seven brothers among us. The first married and died and, having no descendants, left his wife to his brother. 26 The same happened with the second and the third, through all seven. 27 Finally the woman died. 28 Now at the resurrection, of the seven, whose wife will she be? For they all had been married to her." 29 Jesus said to them in reply, "You are misled because you do not know the scriptures or the power of God.* 30 At the resurrection they neither marry nor are given in marriage but are like the angels in heaven. 31 And concerning the resurrection of the dead, have you not read what was said to you* by God, 32 'I am the God of Abraham, the God of Isaac, and the God of Jacob'?[k] He is not the God of the dead but of the living." 33 When the crowds heard this, they were astonished at his teaching.

The Greatest Commandment.* 34 [l] When the Pharisees heard that he had silenced the Sadducees, they gathered together, 35 and one of them [a scholar of the law]* tested him by asking, 36 "Teacher, which commandment in the law is the greatest?"* 37 He said to him,* "You shall love the Lord, your God, with all your heart, with all your soul, and with all your mind.[m] 38 This is the greatest and the first commandment. 39 The second is like it:* You shall love your neighbor as yourself.[n] 40 The whole law and the prophets depend on these two commandments."* [o]

The Question about David's Son.* 41 [p] While the Pharisees were gathered together, Jesus questioned them,* 42 saying, "What is your opinion about the Messiah? Whose son is he?" They replied, "David's."* 43 He said to them, "How, then, does David, inspired by the Spirit, call him 'lord,' saying:

44 'The Lord said to my lord,
"Sit at my right hand
until I place your enemies under your feet" '? [q]

45 If David calls him 'lord,' how can he be his son?"* 46 No one was able to answer him a word, nor from that day on did anyone dare to ask him any more questions.[r]

k Ex 3, 6.—l 34-40: Mk 12, 28-34; Lk 10, 25-28.—m Dt 6, 5.—n Lv 19, 18; Jas 2, 8.—o Rom 13, 8-10; Gal 5, 14.—p 41-46: Mk 12, 35-37; Lk 20, 41-44.—q Ps 110, 1; Acts 2, 35; Heb 1, 13.—r Lk 20, 40.

22, 29: The sexual relationships of this world will be transcended; the risen body will be the work of the creative *power of God.*

22, 31-32: Cf Ex 3, 6. In the Pentateuch, which the Sadducees accepted as normative for Jewish belief and practice, God speaks even now (*to you*) of himself as the God of the patriarchs who died centuries ago. He identifies himself in relation to them, and because of their relation to him, the living God, they too are alive. This might appear no argument for the resurrection, but simply for life after death as conceived in Wis 3, 1-3. But the general thought of early first-century Judaism was not influenced by that conception; for it human immortality was connected with the existence of the body.

22, 34-40: The Marcan parallel (Mk 12, 28-34) is an exchange between Jesus and a scribe who is impressed by the way in which Jesus has conducted himself in the previous controversy (Mk 12, 28), who compliments him for the answer he gives him (Mk 12, 32), and who is said by Jesus to be "not far from the kingdom of God" (Mk 12, 34). Matthew has sharpened that scene. The questioner, as the representative of other Pharisees, tests Jesus by his question (34-35), and both his reaction to Jesus' reply and Jesus' commendation of him are lacking.

22, 35: *[A scholar of the law]:* meaning "scribe." Although this reading is supported by the vast majority of textual witnesses, it is the only time that the Greek word so translated occurs in Mt. It is relatively frequent in Lk, and there is reason to think that it may have been added here by a copyist since it occurs in the Lucan parallel (Lk 10, 25-28). *Tested:* see the note on Mt 19, 3.

22, 36: For the devout Jew all the commandments were to be kept with equal care, but there is evidence of preoccupation in Jewish sources with the question put to Jesus.

22, 37-38: Cf Dt 6, 5. Matthew omits the first part of Mk's fuller quotation (Mk 12, 29; Dt 6, 4-5), probably because he considered its monotheistic emphasis needless for his church. The love of God must engage the total person (*heart, soul, mind*).

22, 39: Jesus goes beyond the extent of the question put to him and joins to *the greatest and the first commandment* a *second,* that of *love* of *neighbor,* Lv 19, 18; see the note on Mt 19, 18-19. This combination of the two commandments may already have been made in Judaism.

22, 40: The double commandment is the source from which *the whole law and the prophets* are derived.

22, 41-46: Having answered the questions of his opponents in the preceding three controversies, Jesus now puts a question to them about the sonship of the Messiah. Their easy response (43a) is countered by his quoting a verse of Ps 110 that raises a problem for their response (43b-45). They are unable to solve it and *from that day on* their questioning of him is ended.

22, 41: *The Pharisees . . . questioned them:* Mk is not specific about who are questioned (Mk 12, 35).

22, 42-44: *David's:* this view of the Pharisees was based on such Old Testament texts as Is 11, 1-9; Jer 23, 5; and Ez 34, 23; see also the extrabiblical Psalms of Solomon 17, 21. *How, then . . . saying:* Jesus cites Ps 110, 1, accepting the Davidic authorship of the psalm, a common view of his time. The psalm was probably composed for the enthronement of a Davidic king of Judah. Matthew assumes that the Pharisees interpret it as referring to the Messiah, although there is no clear evidence that it was so interpreted in the Judaism of Jesus' time. It was widely used in the early church as referring to the exaltation of the risen Jesus. *My lord:* understood as the Messiah.

22, 45: Since Matthew presents Jesus both as Messiah (Mt 16, 16) and as Son of David (Mt 1, 1; see also the note on Mt 9, 27), the question is not meant to imply Jesus' denial of Davidic sonship. It probably means that although he is the Son of David, he is someone greater, Son of Man and Son of God, and recognized as greater by David who calls him my *'lord.'*

CHAPTER 23*

Denunciation of the Scribes and Pharisees. [1] [s] Then Jesus spoke to the crowds and to his disciples, [2] saying, "The scribes and the Pharisees have taken their seat on the chair of Moses.* [3] Therefore, do and observe all things whatsoever they tell you, but do not follow their example. For they preach but they do not practice. [4] [t] They tie up heavy burdens* [hard to carry] and lay them on people's shoulders, but they will not lift a finger to move them. [5] [u] All their works are performed to be seen. They widen their phylacteries and lengthen their tassels.* [6] [v] They love places of honor at banquets,* seats of honor in synagogues, [7] greetings in marketplaces, and the salutation 'Rabbi.' [8] *As for you, do not be called 'Rabbi.' You have but one teacher, and you are all brothers. [9] Call no one on earth your father; you have but one Father in heaven. [10] Do not be called 'Mas-

ter'; you have but one master, the Messiah. [11] The greatest among you must be your servant. [w] [12] Whoever exalts himself will be humbled; but whoever humbles himself will be exalted. [x]

[13] *"Woe to you, scribes and Pharisees, you hypocrites. You lock the kingdom of heaven* before human beings. You do not enter yourselves, nor do you allow entrance to those trying to enter. [y] [14] *

[15] "Woe to you, scribes and Pharisees, you hypocrites. You traverse sea and land to make one convert, and when that happens you make him a child of Gehenna twice as much as yourselves.*

---

s 1-39: Mk 12, 38-39; Lk 11, 37-52; 13, 34-35.—t Lk 11, 46.—u Mt 6, 1-6; Ex 13, 9.16; Nm 15, 38-39; Dt 6, 8; 11, 18.— v 6-7: Mk 12, 38-39; Lk 11, 43; 20, 46.—w Mt 20, 26.—x Lk 14, 11; 18, 14.—y Lk 11, 52.

23, 1-39: The final section of the narrative part of the fifth book of the gospel is a denunciation by Jesus of the scribes and the Pharisees (see the note on Mt 3, 7). It depends in part on Mk and Q (cf Mk 12, 38-39; Lk 11, 37-52; 13, 34-35), but in the main it is peculiar to Mt. (For the reasons against considering this extensive body of sayings-material either as one of the structural discourses of this gospel or as part of the one that follows in chs 24-25, see the note on Mt 19, 1—23, 39.) While the tradition of a deep opposition between Jesus and the Pharisees is well founded, this speech reflects an opposition that goes beyond that of Jesus' ministry and must be seen as expressing the bitter conflict between Pharisaic Judaism and the church of Matthew at the time when the gospel was composed. The complaint often made that the speech ignores the positive qualities of Pharisaism and of its better representatives is true, but the complaint overlooks the circumstances that gave rise to the invective. Nor is the speech purely anti-Pharisaic. The evangelist discerns in his church many of the same faults that he finds in its opponents and warns his fellow Christians to look to their own conduct and attitudes.

23, 2-3: *Have taken their seat . . . Moses:* it is uncertain whether this is simply a .metaphor for Mosaic teaching authority or refers to an actual *chair* on which the teacher sat. It has been proved that there was a seat so designated in synagogues of a later period than that of this gospel. *Do and observe . . . they tell you:* since the Matthean Jesus abrogates Mosaic law (Mt 5, 31-42), warns his disciples against the teaching of the Pharisees (Mt 14, 1-12), and, in this speech, denounces the Pharisees as blind guides in respect to their teaching on oaths (16-22), this commandment to *observe all things whatsoever they* (the scribes and Pharisees) *tell you* cannot be taken as the evangelist's understanding of the proper standard of conduct for his church. The saying may reflect a period when the Matthean community was largely Jewish Christian and was still seeking to avoid a complete break with the synagogue. Matthew has incorporated this traditional material into the speech in accordance with his view of the course of salvation history, in which he portrays the time of Jesus' ministry as marked by the fidelity to the law, although with significant pointers to the new situation that would exist after his death and resurrection (see the note on Mt 5, 17-20). The crowds and the disciples (1) are exhorted not to *follow* the *example* of the Jewish leaders, whose deeds do not conform to their teaching (3).

23, 4: *Tie up heavy burdens:* see the note on Mt 11, 28.

23, 5: To the charge of preaching but not practicing (3), Jesus adds that of acting in order to earn praise. The disciples have already been warned against this same fault (see the note on Mt 6, 1-18). *Phylacteries:* the Mosaic law required that during prayer small boxes containing parchments on which verses of scripture were written be worn on the left forearm and the forehead (see Ex 13, 9.16; Dt 6, 8; 11, 18). *Tassels:* see the note on Mt 9, 20. The widening of *phylacteries* and the lengthening of *tassels* were for the purpose of making these evidences of piety more noticeable.

23, 6-7: Cf Mk 12, 38-39. *'Rabbi':* literally, "my great one," a title of respect for teachers and leaders.

23, 8-12: These verses, warning against the use of various titles, are addressed to the disciples alone. While only the title *'Rabbi'* has been said to be used in addressing the scribes and Pharisees (7), the implication is that *Father* and *'Master'* also were. The prohibition of these titles to the disciples suggests that their use was present in Matthew's church. The Matthean Jesus forbids not only the titles but the spirit of superiority and pride that is shown by their acceptance. *Whoever exalts . . . will be exalted:* cf Lk 14, 11.

23, 13-36: This series of seven "woes," directed against the *scribes and Pharisees* and addressed to them, is the heart of the speech. The phrase *woe to* occurs often in the prophetic and apocalyptic literature, expressing horror of a sin and punishment for those who commit it. *Hypocrites:* see the note on Mt 6, 2. The hypocrisy of the *scribes and Pharisees* consists in the difference between their speech and action (3) and in demonstrations of piety that have no other purpose than to enhance their reputation as religious persons (5).

23, 13: *You lock the kingdom of heaven:* cf Mt 16, 19 where Jesus tells Peter that he will give him the keys to *the kingdom of heaven.* The purpose of the authority expressed by that metaphor is to give entrance into the kingdom (the kingdom is closed only to those who reject the authority); here the charge is made that the authority of the *scribes and Pharisees* is exercised in such a way as to be an obstacle to entrance. Cf Lk 11, 52 where the accusation against the "scholars of the law" (Mt's *scribes*) is that they "have taken away the key of knowledge."

23, 14: Some manuscripts add a verse here or after v 12, "Woe to you, scribes and Pharisees, you hypocrites. You devour the houses of widows and, as a pretext, recite lengthy prayers. Because of this, you will receive a very severe condemnation." Cf Mk 12, 40; Lk 20, 47. This "woe" is almost identical with Mk 12, 40 and seems to be an interpolation derived from that text.

23, 15: In the first century A.D. until the First Jewish Revolt against Rome (A.D. 66-70), many Pharisees conducted a vigorous missionary campaign among Gentiles. *Convert:* literally, "proselyte," a Gentile who accepted Judaism fully by submitting to circumcision and all other requirements of Mosaic law. *Child of Gehenna:* worthy of everlasting punishment; for *Gehenna,* see the note on Mt 5, 22. *Twice as much as yourselves:* possibly this refers simply to the zeal of the *convert,* surpassing that of the one who converted him.

16 * "Woe to you, blind guides, who say, 'If one swears by the temple, it means nothing, but if one swears by the gold of the temple, one is obligated.'ᶻ ¹⁷Blind fools, which is greater, the gold, or the temple that made the gold sacred? ¹⁸And you say, 'If one swears by the altar, it means nothing, but if one swears by the gift on the altar, one is obligated.' ¹⁹You blind ones, which is greater, the gift, or the altar that makes the gift sacred? ²⁰ ᵃ One who swears by the altar swears by it and all that is upon it; ²¹one who swears by the temple swears by it and by him who dwells in it; ²²one who swears by heaven swears by the throne of God and by him who is seated on it.

²³"Woe to you, scribes and Pharisees, you hypocrites. You pay tithes* of mint and dill and cummin, and have neglected the weightier things of the law: judgment and mercy and fidelity. [But] these you should have done, without neglecting the others.ᵇ ²⁴Blind guides, who strain out the gnatᶜ and swallow the camel!*

²⁵ * "Woe to you, scribes and Pharisees, you hypocrites.ᵈ You cleanse the outside of cup and dish, but inside they are full of plunder and self-indulgence. ²⁶Blind Pharisee, cleanse first the inside of the cup, so that the outside also may be clean.

²⁷ * "Woe to you, scribes and Pharisees, you hypocrites. You are like whitewashed tombs, which appear beautiful on the outside, but inside are full of dead men's bones and every kind of filth. ²⁸Even so, on the outside you appear righteous, but inside you are filled with hypocrisy and evildoing.ᵉ

²⁹ * "Woe to you, scribes and Pharisees,* you hypocrites. You build the tombs of the prophets and adorn the memorials of the righteous, ³⁰and you say, 'If we had lived in the days of our ancestors, we would not have joined them in shedding the prophets' blood.'ᶠ ³¹Thus you bear witness against yourselves that you are the children of those who murdered the prophets;ᵍ ³²now fill up what your ancestors measured out! ³³You serpents, you brood of vipers, how can you flee from the judgment of Gehenna?ʰ ³⁴ * Therefore, behold, I send to you prophets and wise men and scribes;ⁱ some of them you will kill and crucify, some of them you will scourge

z Mt 15, 14.—a 20-22: Mt 5, 34-35.—b Lv 27, 30; Dt 14, 22; Lk 11, 42.—c Lv 11, 41-45.—d 25-26: Mk 7, 4; Lk 11, 39.—e Lk 16, 15; 18, 9.—f Lk 11, 47.—g Acts 7, 52.—h Mt 3, 7; 12, 34.—i 34-36: Mt 5, 12; Gn 4, 8; 2 Chr 24, 20-22; Zec 1, 1; Lk 11, 49-51; Rv 18, 24.

ances while inner purity is ignored. The *scribes and Pharisees* are compared to cups carefully washed on the outside but filthy within. *Self-indulgence:* the Greek word here translated means lack of self-control, whether in drinking or in sexual conduct.

23, 27-28: The sixth *woe,* like the preceding one, deals with concern for externals and neglect of what is *inside.* Since contact with dead bodies, even when one was unaware of it, caused ritual impurity (Nm 19, 11-22), tombs were whitewashed so that no one would contract such impurity inadvertently.

23, 29-36: The final *woe* is the most serious indictment of all. It portrays the *scribes and Pharisees* as standing in the same line as their *ancestors* who murdered *the prophets* and *the righteous.*

23, 29-32: In spite of honoring the slain dead by building their *tombs* and adorning their *memorials,* and claiming that they would not have joined in their ancestors' crimes if they *had lived in their days,* the *scribes and Pharisees* are true *children of* their ancestors and are defiantly ordered by Jesus to *fill up* what those *ancestors measured out.* This order reflects the Jewish notion that there was an allotted measure of suffering that had to be completed before God's final judgment would take place.

23, 34-36: There are important differences between the Matthean and the Lucan form of this Q material; cf Lk 11, 49-51. In Lk the one who sends the emissaries is the "wisdom of God." If, as many scholars think, that is the original wording of Q, Matthew, by making Jesus the sender, has presented him as the personified divine wisdom. In Lk, wisdom's emissaries are the Old Testament "prophets" and the Christian "apostles." Mt's *prophets and wise men and scribes* are probably Christian disciples alone; cf Mt 10, 41 and see the note on Mt 13, 52. *You will kill:* see Mt 24, 9. *Scourge in your synagogues . . . town to town:* see Mt 10, 17.23 and the note on Mt 10, 17. *All the righteous blood shed upon the earth:* the slaying of the disciples is in continuity with all the shedding of *righteous blood* beginning with that of *Abel.* The persecution of Jesus' disciples by *this generation* involves the persecutors in the guilt of their murderous ancestors. *The blood of Zechariah:* see the note on Lk 11, 51. By identifying him as *the son of Barachiah* Matthew understands him to be Zechariah the Old Testament minor prophet; see Zec 1, 1.

23, 16-22: An attack on the casuistry that declared some oaths binding (*one is obligated*) and others not (*it means nothing*) and held the binding oath to be the one made by something of lesser value (*the gold; the gift on the altar*). Such teaching, which inverts the order of values, reveals the teachers to be *blind guides;* cf Mt 15, 14. Since the Matthean Jesus forbids all oaths to his disciples (Mt 5, 33-37), this *woe* does not set up a standard for Christian moral conduct, but ridicules the Pharisees on their own terms.

23, 23: The Mosaic law ordered tithing of the produce of the land (Lv 27, 30; Dt 14, 22-23), and the scribal tradition is said here to have extended this law to even the smallest herbs. The practice is criticized not in itself but because it shows the Pharisees' preoccupation with matters of less importance while they neglect *the weightier things of the law.*

23, 24: Cf Lv 11, 41-45 that forbids the eating of any "swarming creature." The Pharisees' scrupulosity about minor matters and neglect of greater ones (23) is further brought out by this contrast between straining liquids that might contain a tiny "swarming creature" and yet swallowing *the camel.* The latter was one of the unclean animals forbidden by the law (Lv 11, 4), but it is hardly possible that the scribes and Pharisees are being denounced as guilty of so gross a violation of the food laws. To *swallow the camel* is only a hyperbolic way of speaking of their neglect of what is important.

23, 25-26: The ritual washing of utensils for dining (cf Mk 7, 4) is turned into a metaphor illustrating a concern for appear-in your synagogues and pursue from town to town, [35] so that there may come upon you all the righteous blood shed upon earth, from the righteous blood of Abel to the blood of Zechariah, the son of Barachiah, whom you murdered between the sanctuary and the altar. [36] Amen, I say to you, all these things will come upon this generation.

The Lament over Jerusalem. * [37] j "Jerusalem, Jerusalem, you who kill the prophets and stone those sent to you, how many times I yearned to gather your children together, as a hen gathers her young under her wings, but you were unwilling! k [38] Behold, your house will be abandoned, desolate. l [39] I tell you, you will not see me again until you say, 'Blessed is he who comes in the name of the Lord.' " m

j 37-39: Lk 13, 34-35; 19, 41-44.—k Mt 21, 35.—l Jer 12, 7.—m Ps 118, 26.—n 1-44: Mk 13, 1-37; Lk 21, 5-36.—o Dn 2, 28 LXX.—p Is 19, 2.—q Mt 10, 17.

23, 37-39: Cf Lk 13, 34-35. The denunciation of Pharisaic Judaism ends with this lament over *Jerusalem,* which has repeatedly rejected and murdered those whom God has *sent* to her. *How many times:* this may refer to various visits of Jesus to the city, an aspect of his ministry found in Jn but otherwise not in the synoptics. *As a hen . . . under her wings:* for imagery similar to this, see Pss 17, 8; 91, 4. *Your house . . . desolate:* probably an allusion to the destruction of the temple in A.D. 70. *You will not see me . . . in the name of the Lord:* Israel will not see Jesus again until he comes in glory for the final judgment. The acclamation has been interpreted in contrasting ways, as an indication that Israel will at last accept Jesus at that time, and as its troubled recognition of him as its dreaded judge who will pronounce its condemnation; in support of the latter view see Mt 24, 30.

24, 1—25, 46: The discourse of the fifth book, the last of the five around which the gospel is structured. It is called the "eschatological" discourse since it deals with the coming of the new age (the *eschaton*) in its fullness, with events that will precede it, and with how the disciples are to conduct themselves while awaiting an event that is as certain as its exact time is unknown to all but the Father (Mt 24, 36). The discourse may be divided into two parts, Mt 24, 1-44 and Mt 24, 45—25, 46. In the first, Matthew follows his Marcan source (Mk 13, 1-37) closely. The second is drawn from Q and from the evangelist's own traditional material. Both parts show Matthew's editing of his sources by deletions, additions, and modifications. The vigilant waiting that is emphasized in the second part does not mean a cessation of ordinary activity and concentration only on what is to come, but a faithful accomplishment of duties at hand, with awareness that the end, for which the disciples must always be ready, will entail the great judgment by which the everlasting destiny of all will be determined.

24, 2: As in Mk, Jesus predicts the destruction of the temple. By omitting the Marcan story of the widow's contribution (Mk 12, 41-44) that immediately precedes the prediction in that gospel, Matthew has established a close connection between it and Mt 23, 38, ". . . your house will be abandoned desolate."

24, 3: *The Mount of Olives:* see the note on Mt 21, 1. *The disciples:* cf Mk 13, 3-4 where only Peter, James, John, and Andrew put the question that is answered by the discourse. In both gospels, however, the question is put *privately:* the ensuing discourse is only for those who are *disciples* of Jesus. *When will this happen . . . end of the age?:* Matthew distinguishes carefully between the destruction of the temple *(this)* and the *coming* of Jesus that will bring *the end of the age.* In Mk the two events are more closely connected, a fact that may be explained by

CHAPTER 24

The Destruction of the Temple Foretold. [1] * n Jesus left the temple area and was going away, when his disciples approached him to point out the temple buildings. [2] * He said to them in reply, "You see all these things, do you not? Amen, I say to you, there will not be left here a stone upon another stone that will not be thrown down."

The Beginning of Calamities. [3] As he was sitting on the Mount of Olives,* the disciples approached him privately and said, "Tell us, when will this happen, and what sign will there be of your coming, and of the end of the age?" [4] * Jesus said to them in reply, "See that no one deceives you. [5] For many will come in my name, saying, 'I am the Messiah,' and they will deceive many. [6] You will hear of wars* and reports of wars; see that you are not alarmed, for these things must happen, but it will not yet be the end. o [7] Nation will rise against nation, and kingdom against kingdom; there will be famines and earthquakes from place to place. p [8] All these are the beginning of the labor pains.* [9] Then they will hand you over to persecution, and they will kill you. q You will be hated by all nations*

Mark's believing that the one would immediately succeed the other. *Coming:* this translates the Greek word *parousia,* which is used in the gospels only here and in vv 27, 37, and 39. It designated the official visit of a ruler to a city or the manifestation of a saving deity, and it was used by Christians to refer to the final coming of Jesus in glory, a term first found in the New Testament with that meaning in 1 Thes 2, 19. *The end of the age:* see the note on Mt 13, 39.

24, 4-14: This section of the discourse deals with calamities in the world (6-7) and in the church (9-12). The former *must happen* before *the end* comes (6), but they are only *the beginning of the labor pains* (8). (It may be noted that the Greek word translated *the end* in v 6 and in vv 13-14 is not the same as the phrase "the end of the age" in v 3, although the meaning is the same.) The latter are sufferings of the church, both from within and without, that will last until the *gospel is preached . . . to all nations. Then the end will come* and those who have endured the sufferings with fidelity *will be saved* (13-14).

24, 6-7: The disturbances mentioned here are a commonplace of apocalyptic language, as is the assurance that they *must happen* (see Dn 2, 28 LXX), for that is the plan of God. *Kingdom against kingdom:* see Is 19, 2.

24, 8: *The labor pains:* the tribulations leading up to the end of the age are compared to the pains of a woman about to give birth. There is much attestation for rabbinic use of the phrase "the woes (or birth pains) of the Messiah" after the New Testament period, but in at least one instance it is attributed to a rabbi who lived in the late first century A.D. In this Jewish usage it meant the distress of the time preceding the coming of the Messiah; here, the *labor pains* precede the coming of the Son of Man in glory.

24, 9-12: Matthew has used Mk 13, 9-12 in his missionary discourse (Mt 10, 17-21) and omits it here. Besides the sufferings, including death, and the hatred of *all nations* that the disciples will have to endure, there will be worse affliction within the church itself. This is described in vv 10-12, which are peculiar to

because of my name. [10] And then many will be led into sin; they will betray and hate one another. [11] Many false prophets will arise and deceive many; [12] and because of the increase of evildoing, the love of many will grow cold. [13] But the one who perseveres to the end will be saved.[r] [14] And this gospel of the kingdom will be preached throughout the world as a witness to all nations,* and then the end will come.[s]

The Great Tribulation.* [15] "When you see the desolating abomination* spoken of through Daniel the prophet standing in the holy place (let the reader understand),[t] [16] then those in Judea must flee* to the mountains, [17] * a person on the housetop must not go down to get things out of his house,[u] [18] a person in the field must not return to get his cloak. [19] Woe to pregnant women and nursing mothers in those days. [20] Pray that your flight not be in winter or on the sabbath,* [21] for at that time there will be great tribulation,[v] such as has not been since the beginning of the world until now, nor ever will be.* [22] And if those days had not been shortened, no one would be

saved; but for the sake of the elect they will be shortened. [23] If anyone says to you then, 'Look, here is the Messiah!' or, 'There he is!' do not believe it.[w] [24] False messiahs and false prophets will arise, and they will perform signs and wonders so great as to deceive, if that were possible, even the elect. [25] Behold, I have told it to you beforehand. [26] So if they say to you, 'He is in the desert,' do not go out there; if they say, 'He is in the inner rooms,' do not believe it.* [27] For just as lightning comes from the east and is seen as far as the west, so will the coming of the Son of Man be.[x] [28] Wherever the corpse is, there the vultures will gather.

The Coming of the Son of Man. [29] "Immediately after the tribulation of those days,

> the sun will be darkened,
>> and the moon will not give its light,
> and the stars will fall from the sky,
>> and the powers of the heavens will be shaken.*[y]

r Mt 10, 22.—s Mt 28, 19; Rom 10, 18.—t Dn 9, 27; 11, 31; 12, 11; Mk 13, 14.—u Lk 17, 31.—v Dn 12, 1.—w Lk 17, 23.—x 27-28: Lk 17, 24.37.—y Is 13, 10.13; Ez 32, 7; Am 8, 9.

Mt. *Will be led into sin:* literally, "will be scandalized," probably meaning that they will become apostates; see Mt 13, 21 where "fall away" translates the same Greek word as here. *Betray:* in the Greek this is the same word as the *hand over* of v 9. The handing over to persecution and hatred from outside will have their counterpart within the church. *False prophets:* these are Christians; see the note on Mt 7, 15-20. *Evildoing:* see Mt 7, 23. Because of the apocalyptic nature of much of this discourse, the literal meaning of this description of the church should not be pressed too hard. However, there is reason to think that Mt's addition of these verses reflects in some measure the condition of his community.

24, 14: Except for the last part *(and then the end will come)*, this verse substantially repeats Mk 13, 10. The Matthean addition raises a problem since what follows in vv 15-23 refers to the horrors of the First Jewish Revolt including the destruction of the temple, and Matthew, writing after that time, knew that the parousia of Jesus was still in the future. A solution may be that the evangelist saw the events of those verses as foreshadowing the cosmic disturbances that he associates with the parousia (29) so that the period in which the former took place could be understood as belonging to *the end.*

24, 15-28: Cf Mk 13, 14-23; Lk 17, 23-24.37. A further stage in the tribulations that will precede the coming of the Son of Man, and an answer to the question of v 3a, "when will this (the destruction of the temple) happen?"

24, 15: *The desolating abomination:* in 167 B.C. the Syrian king Antiochus IV Epiphanes desecrated the temple by setting up in it a statue of Zeus Olympios (see 1 Mc 1, 54). That event is referred to in Dn 12, 11 LXX as the "desolating abomination" (NAB "horrible abomination") and the same Greek term is used here; cf also Dn 9, 27; 11, 31. Although the desecration had taken place before Dn was written, it is presented there as a future event, and Matthew sees that "prophecy" fulfilled in the desecration of the temple by the Romans. *In the holy place:* the temple; more precise than Mk's *where he should not* (Mk 13,

14). *Let the reader understand:* this parenthetical remark, taken from Mk 13, 14, invites *the reader* to realize the meaning of Dn's "prophecy."

24, 16: The tradition that the Christians of Jerusalem fled from that city to Pella, a city of Transjordan, at the time of the First Jewish Revolt is found in Eusebius (*Ecclesiastical History,* 3, 5, 3), who attributes the flight to "a certain oracle given by revelation before the war." The tradition is not improbable but the Matthean command, derived from its Marcan source, is vague in respect to the place of flight *(to the mountains),* although some scholars see it as applicable to the flight to Pella.

24, 17-19: Haste is essential, and the journey will be particularly difficult for women who are burdened with unborn or infant children.

24, 20: *On the sabbath:* this addition to *in winter* (cf Mk 13, 18) has been understood as an indication that Mt was addressed to a church still observing the Mosaic law of sabbath rest and the scribal limitations upon the length of journeys that might lawfully be made on that day. That interpretation conflicts with Mt's view on sabbath observance (cf Mt 12, 1-14). The meaning of the addition may be that those undertaking on the sabbath a journey such as the one here ordered would be offending the sensibilities of law-observant Jews and would incur their hostility.

24, 21: For the unparalleled distress of that time, see Dn 12, 1.

24, 26-28: Claims that the Messiah is to be found in some distant or secret place must be ignored. *The coming of the Son of Man* will be as clear as *lightning* is to all and as *the corpse* of an animal is to *vultures;* cf Lk 17, 24.37. Here there is clear identification of *the Son of Man* and the Messiah; cf v 23.

24, 29: The answer to the question of v 3b, "What will be the sign of your coming?" *Immediately after . . . those days:* the shortening of time between the preceding *tribulation* and the parousia has been explained as Matthew's use of a supposed device of Old Testament prophecy whereby certainty that a predicted event will occur is expressed by depicting it as imminent. While it is questionable that that is an acceptable understanding of the Old Testament predictions, it may be applicable here, for Matthew knew that the parousia had not come *immediately after* the fall of Jerusalem, and it is unlikely that he is attributing a mistaken calculation of time to Jesus. *The sun . . . be shaken:* cf Is 13, 10.13.

30 And then the sign of the Son of Man* will appear in heaven, and all the tribes of the earth will mourn, and they will see the Son of Man coming upon the clouds of heaven with power and great glory.*z* 31 And he will send out his angels* with a trumpet blast, and they will gather his elect from the four winds, from one end of the heavens to the other.*a*

The Lesson of the Fig Tree.* 32 "Learn a lesson from the fig tree. When its branch becomes tender and sprouts leaves, you know that summer is near. 33 In the same way, when you see all these things, know that he is near, at the gates. 34 Amen, I say to you, this generation* will not pass away until all these things have taken place. 35 Heaven and earth will pass away, but my words will not pass away.*b*

The Unknown Day and Hour.* 36 "But of that day and hour no one knows, neither the angels of heaven, nor the Son,* but the Father alone.*c* 37 * For as it was in the days of Noah, so it will be at the coming of the Son of Man.*d* 38 In [those] days before the flood, they were eating and drinking, marrying and giving in marriage, up to the day that Noah entered the ark. 39 They did not know until the flood came and carried them all away. So will it be [also] at the coming of the Son of Man. 40 * Two men will be out in the field; one will be taken,

and one will be left.*e* 41 Two women will be grinding at the mill; one will be taken, and one will be left. 42 * Therefore, stay awake!*f* For you do not know on which day your Lord will come. 43 Be sure of this: if the master of the house had known the hour of night when the thief was coming, he would have stayed awake and not let his house be broken into.*g* 44 So too, you also must be prepared, for at an hour you do not expect, the Son of Man will come.

The Faithful or the Unfaithful Servant.* 45 *h* "Who, then, is the faithful and prudent servant, whom the master has put in charge of his household to distribute to them their food at the proper time?* 46 Blessed is that servant whom his master on his arrival finds doing so. 47 Amen, I say to you, he will put him in charge of all his property. 48 But if that wicked servant says to himself, 'My master is long delayed,'* 49 and begins to beat his fellow servants, and eat and drink with drunkards, 50 the servant's master will come on an unexpected day and at an unknown hour 51 and will punish him severely* and assign him a place with the hypocrites, where there will be wailing and grinding of teeth.*i*

24, 36: Many textual witnesses omit *nor the Son*, which follows Mk 13, 32. Since its omission can be explained by reluctance to attribute this ignorance to *the Son*, the reading that includes it is probably original.

24, 37-39: Cf Lk 17, 26-27. *In the days of Noah:* the Old Testament account of the flood lays no emphasis upon what is central for Matthew, i.e., the unexpected coming of the flood upon those who were unprepared for it.

24, 40-41: Cf Lk 17, 34-35. *Taken . . . left:* the former probably means *taken* into the kingdom; the latter, *left* for destruction. People in the same situation will be dealt with in opposite ways. In this context, the discrimination between them will be based on their readiness for the coming of the Son of Man.

24, 42-44: Cf Lk 12, 39-40. The theme of vigilance and readiness is continued with the bold comparison of the Son of Man to a thief who comes to break into a house.

24, 45-51: The second part of the discourse (see the note on Mt 24, 1 —25, 46) begins with this parable of *the faithful* or unfaithful *servant;* cf Lk 12, 41-46. It is addressed to the leaders of Matthew's church; *the servant has* been *put in charge* of his master's *household* (45) even though that *household* is composed of those who are his *fellow servants* (49).

24, 45: *To distribute . . . proper time:* readiness for the master's return means a vigilance that is accompanied by faithful performance of the duty assigned.

24, 48: *My master . . . delayed:* the note of delay is found also in the other parables of this section; cf Mt 25, 5.19.

24, 51: *Punish him severely:* the Greek verb, found in the New Testament only here and in the Lucan parallel (Lk 12, 46), means, literally, "cut in two." *With the hypocrites:* see the note on Mt 6, 2. Matthew classes the unfaithful Christian leader with the unbelieving leaders of Judaism. *Wailing and grinding of teeth:* see the note on Mt 8, 11-12.

---

z Dn 7, 13; Zec 12, 12-14; Rv 1, 7.—a Is 27, 13; 1 Cor 15, 52; 1 Thes 4, 16.—b Is 40, 8.—c Acts 1, 7.—d 37-39: Gn 6, 5—7, 23; Lk 17, 26-27; 2 Pt 3, 6.—e 40-41: Lk 17, 34-35.—f 42-44: Mt 25, 13; Lk 12, 39-40.—g 1 Thes 5, 2.—h 45-51: Lk 12, 41-46.—i Mt 13, 42; 25, 30.

24, 30: *The sign of the Son of Man:* perhaps this means *the sign* that is the glorious appearance *of the Son of Man;* cf Mt 12, 39-40 where "the sign of Jonah" is Jonah's being in the "belly of the whale." *Tribes of the earth will mourn:* peculiar to Mt; cf Zec 12, 12-14. *Coming upon the clouds . . . glory:* cf Dn 7, 13, although there the "one like a son of man" comes to God to receive kingship; here *the Son of Man* comes from heaven for judgment.

24, 31: *Send out his angels:* cf Mt 13, 41 where they are sent out to collect the wicked for punishment. *Trumpet blast:* cf Is 27, 13; 1 Thes 4, 16.

24, 32-35: Cf Mk 13, 28-31.

24, 34: The difficulty raised by this verse cannot be satisfactorily removed by the supposition that *this generation* means the Jewish people throughout the course of their history, much less the entire human race. Perhaps for Matthew it means the *generation* to which he and his community belonged.

24, 36-44: The statement of v 34 is now counterbalanced by one that declares that the exact time of the parousia is known only to *the Father* (36), and the disciples are warned to be always ready for it. This section is drawn from Mk and Q (cf Lk 17, 26-27.34-35; 12, 39-40).

CHAPTER 25

The Parable of the Ten Virgins.* [1]"Then* the kingdom of heaven will be like ten virgins who took their lamps and went out to meet the bridegroom. [2]Five of them were foolish and five were wise.* [3]The foolish ones, when taking their lamps, brought no oil with them, [4]but the wise brought flasks of oil with their lamps. [5]Since the bridegroom was long delayed, they all became drowsy and fell asleep. [6]At midnight, there was a cry, 'Behold, the bridegroom! Come out to meet him!' [7]Then all those virgins got up and trimmed their lamps. [8]The foolish ones said to the wise, 'Give us some of your oil, for our lamps are going out.' [9]But the wise ones replied, 'No, for there may not be enough for us and you. Go instead to the merchants and buy some for yourselves.' [10]While they went off to buy it, the bridegroom came and those who were ready went into the wedding feast with him. Then the door was locked. [11] * Afterwards the other virgins came and said, 'Lord, Lord, open the door for us!'[j] [12]But he said in reply, 'Amen, I say to you, I do not know you.' [13]Therefore, stay awake,* for you know neither the day nor the hour.[k]

The Parable of the Talents.* [14][l]"It will be as when a man who was going on a journey* called in his servants and entrusted his possessions to them. [15]To one he gave five talents;* to another, two; to a third, one—to each according to his ability. Then he went away. Immediately [16]the one who received five talents went and traded with them, and made another five. [17]Likewise, the one who received two made another two. [18]But the man who received one went off and dug a hole in the ground and buried his master's money.* [19]After a long time the master of those servants came back and settled accounts with them. [20]The one who had received five talents came forward bringing the additional five.* He said, 'Master, you gave me five talents. See, I have made five more.' [21]His master said to him, 'Well done, my good and faithful servant. Since you were faithful in small matters, I will give you great responsibilities. Come, share your master's joy.'[m] [22][Then] the one who had received two talents also came forward and said, 'Master, you gave me two talents. See, I have made two more.' [23]His master said to him, 'Well done, my good and faithful servant. Since you were faithful in small matters, I will give you great responsibilities. Come, share your master's joy.' [24]Then the one who had received the one talent came forward and said, 'Master, I knew you were a demanding person, harvesting where you did not plant and gathering where you did not scatter; [25]so out of fear I went off and buried your talent in the ground. Here it is back.' [26]His master said to him in reply, 'You wicked, lazy servant!* So you knew that I harvest where I did not plant and gather where I did not scatter? [27]Should you not then have put my money in the bank so that I could have got it back with interest on my return? [28]Now then! Take the talent from him and give it to the one with ten. [29] [n] For to everyone who has, more will be given and he will grow rich; but from the one who has not, even what he has will be taken away.* [30]And throw this useless servant into the darkness outside, where there will be wailing and grinding of teeth.'*

---

j 11-12: Mt 7, 21.23; Lk 13, 25.27.—k Mt 24, 42; Mk 13, 33.—l 14-30: Lk 19, 12-27.—m Lk 16, 10.—n Mt 13, 12; Mk 4, 25; Lk 8, 18; 19, 26.

25, 1-13: Peculiar to Mt.

25, 1: *Then:* at the time of the parousia. *Kingdom . . . will be like:* see the note on Mt 13, 24-30.

25, 2-4: *Foolish . . . wise:* cf the contrasted "wise man" and "fool" of Mt 7, 24.26, where the two are distinguished by good deeds and lack of them, and such deeds may be signified by the *oil* of this parable.

25, 11-12: *Lord, Lord:* cf Mt 7, 21. *I do not know you:* cf Mt 7, 23, where the Greek verb is different but synonymous.

25, 13: *Stay awake:* some scholars see this command as an addition to the original parable of Matthew's traditional material, since in v 5 all the virgins, wise and foolish, fall asleep. But the wise virgins are adequately equipped for their task, and *stay awake* may mean no more than to be prepared; cf Mt 24, 42.44.

25, 14-30: Cf Lk 19, 12-27.

25, 14: *It will be as when . . . journey:* literally, "For just as a man who was going on a journey." Although the comparison is not completed, the sense is clear; the kingdom of heaven is like the situation here described. Faithful use of one's gifts will lead to participation in the fullness of the kingdom, lazy inactivity to exclusion from it.

25, 15: *Talents:* see the note on Mt 18, 24.

25, 18: *Buried his master's money:* see the note on Mt 13, 44.

25, 20-23: Although the first two servants have received and doubled large sums, their faithful trading is regarded by the master as fidelity *in small matters* only, compared with the *great responsibilities* now to be given to them. The latter are unspecified. *Share your master's joy:* probably the joy of the banquet of the kingdom; cf Mt 8, 11.

25, 26-28: *Wicked, lazy servant:* this man's inactivity is not negligible but seriously culpable. As punishment, he loses the gift he had received, that is now given to the first servant, whose possessions are already great.

25, 29: See the note on Mt 13, 12 where there is a similar application of this maxim.

25, 30: See the note on Mt 8, 11-12.

The Judgment of the Nations.* 31 "When
the Son of Man comes in his glory, and all
the angels with him,[o] he will sit upon his
glorious throne,* 32 and all the nations*
will be assembled before him. And he will
separate them one from another, as a
shepherd separates the sheep from the
goats.[p] 33 He will place the sheep on his
right and the goats on his left. 34 Then the
king will say to those on his right, 'Come,
you who are blessed by my Father. Inherit
the kingdom prepared for you from the
foundation of the world. 35 [q] For I was
hungry and you gave me food, I was thirsty
and you gave me drink, a stranger and you
welcomed me, 36 naked and you clothed
me, ill and you cared for me, in prison and
you visited me.' 37 Then the righteous* will
answer him and say, 'Lord, when did we
see you hungry and feed you, or thirsty
and give you drink? 38 When did we see
you a stranger and welcome you, or naked
and clothe you? 39 When did we see you ill
or in prison, and visit you?' 40 [r] And the
king will say to them in reply, 'Amen, I say
to you, whatever you did for one of these
least brothers of mine, you did for me.' 41
[s] Then he will say to those on his left, 'Depart from me, you accursed, into the eternal fire prepared for the devil and his
angels.* 42 For I was hungry and you gave
me no food,[t] I was thirsty and you gave me
no drink, 43 a stranger and you gave me no
welcome, naked and you gave me no clothing, ill and in prison, and you did not care
for me.' 44 *Then they will answer and say,
'Lord, when did we see you hungry or
thirsty or a stranger or naked or ill or in
prison, and not minister to your needs?'
45 He will answer them, 'Amen, I say to
you, what you did not do for one of these
least ones, you did not do for me.' 46 And
these will go off to eternal punishment, but
the righteous to eternal life."[u]

VII. THE PASSION AND RESURRECTION

CHAPTER 26

The Conspiracy against Jesus. 1 * When
Jesus finished all these words,* he said to
his disciples, 2 [v] "You know that in two
days' time it will be Passover, and the Son
of Man will be handed over to be
crucified." 3 Then the chief priests and the
elders of the people assembled in the
palace of the high priest, who was called
Caiaphas,* 4 and they consulted together to
arrest Jesus by treachery and put him to
death.[w] 5 But they said, "Not during the
festival,* that there may not be a riot
among the people."

o Mt 16, 27; Dt 33, 2 LXX.—p Ez 34, 17.—q 35-36: Is 58, 7; Ez 18, 7.—r Mt 10, 40.42.—s Mt 7, 23; Lk 13, 27.—t 42-43: Jb 22, 7; Jas 2, 15-16.—u Dn 12, 2.—v 2-5: Mk 14, 1-2; Lk 22, 1-2.—w Jn 11, 47-53.

25, 31-46: The conclusion of the discourse, which is peculiar to Mt, portrays the final judgment that will accompany the parousia. Although often called a "parable," it is not really such, for the only parabolic elements are the depiction of *the Son of Man* as *a shepherd* and of *the righteous* and the wicked as *sheep* and *goats* respectively (32-33). The criterion of judgment will be the deeds of mercy that have been done for the *least* of Jesus' *brothers* (40). A difficult and important question is the identification of these *least brothers.* Are they all people who have suffered hunger, thirst, etc. (35.36) or a particular group of such sufferers? Scholars are divided in their response and arguments can be made for either side. But leaving aside the problem of what the traditional material that Matthew edited may have meant, it seems that a stronger case can be made for the view that in the evangelist's sense the sufferers are Christians, probably Christian missionaries whose sufferings were brought upon them by their preaching of the gospel. The criterion of judgment for *all the nations* is their treatment of those who have borne to the world the message of Jesus, and this means ultimately their acceptance or rejection of Jesus himself; cf Mt 10, 40, "Whoever receives you, receives me."

25, 31: See the note on Mt 16, 27.

25, 32: *All the nations:* before the end the gospel will have been preached throughout the world (Mt 24, 14); thus the Gentiles will be judged on their response to it. But the phrase *all the nations* includes the Jews also, for at the judgment "the Son of Man . . . will repay everyone according to his conduct" (Mt 16, 27).

25, 37-40: *The righteous* will be astonished that in caring for the needs of the sufferers they were ministering to the *Lord* himself. *One of these least brothers of mine:* cf Mt 10, 42.

25, 41: *Fire prepared . . . his angels:* cf 1 Enoch 10, 13 where it is said of the evil angels and Semyaza, their leader, "In those days they will lead them into the bottom of the fire—and in torment—in the prison (where) they will be locked up forever."

25, 44-45: The *accursed* (41) will be likewise astonished that their neglect of the sufferers was neglect of the *Lord* and will receive from him a similar answer.

26, 1—28, 20: The five books with alternating narrative and discourse (Mt 3, 1—25, 46) that give this gospel its distinctive structure lead up to the climactic events that are the center of Christian belief and the origin of the Christian church, the passion and resurrection of Jesus. In his passion narrative (chs 26-27) Matthew follows his Marcan source closely but with omissions (e.g., Mk 14, 51-52) and additions (e.g., Mt 27, 3-10.19). Some of the additions indicate that he utilized traditions that he had received from elsewhere; others are due to his own theological insight (e.g.,Mt 26, 28, ". . . for the forgiveness of sins"; Mt 27, 52). In his editing Matthew also altered Mk in some minor details. But there is no need to suppose that he knew any passion narrative other than Mark's.

26, 1-2: *When Jesus finished all these words:* see the note on Mt 7, 28-29. *"You know . . . crucified":* Matthew turns Mk's statement of the time (Mk 14, 1) into Jesus' final prediction of his passion. *Passover:* see the note on Mk 14, 1.

26, 3: *Caiaphas* was high priest from A.D. 18 to 36.

26, 5: *Not during the festival:* the plan to delay Jesus' arrest and execution until after *the festival* was not carried out, for according to the synoptics he was arrested on the night of Nisan 14 and put to death the following day. No reason is given why the plan was changed.

The Anointing at Bethany.* [6] [x] Now when Jesus was in Bethany in the house of Simon the leper, [7] a woman came up to him with an alabaster jar of costly perfumed oil, and poured it on his head while he was reclining at table. [8] When the disciples saw this, they were indignant and said, "Why this waste? [9] It could have been sold for much, and the money given to the poor." [10] Since Jesus knew this, he said to them, "Why do you make trouble for the woman? She has done a good thing for me. [11] The poor you will always have with you; but you will not always have me.[y] [12] In pouring this perfumed oil upon my body, she did it to prepare me for burial.* [13] Amen, I say to you, wherever this gospel is proclaimed in the whole world, what she has done will be spoken of, in memory of her."

The Betrayal by Judas. [14] [z] Then one of the Twelve, who was called Judas Iscariot,* went to the chief priests [15] [a] and said, "What are you willing to give me if I hand him over to you?"* They paid him thirty pieces of silver, [16] and from that time on he looked for an opportunity to hand him over.

Preparations for the Passover. [17] [b] On the first day of the Feast of Unleavened Bread,* the disciples approached Jesus and said, "Where do you want us to prepare for you to eat the Passover?"[c] [18] * He said, "Go into the city to a certain man and tell him, 'The teacher says, "My appointed time draws near; in your house I shall celebrate the Passover with my disciples." ' " [19] The disciples then did as Jesus had ordered, and prepared the Passover.

The Betrayer. [20] When it was evening, he reclined at table with the Twelve. [21] And while they were eating, he said, "Amen, I say to you, one of you will betray me."* [22] Deeply distressed at this, they began to say to him one after another, "Surely it is not I, Lord?" [23] He said in reply, "He who has dipped his hand into the dish with me is the one who will betray me. [24] The Son of Man indeed goes, as it is written of him,[d] but woe to that man by whom the Son of Man is betrayed. It would be better for that man if he had never been born."* [25] Then Judas, his betrayer, said in reply, "Surely it is not I, Rabbi?" He answered, "You have said so."*

The Lord's Supper. [26] * [e] While they were eating,[f] Jesus took bread, said the blessing, broke it, and giving it to his disciples said, "Take and eat; this is my body."* [27] Then he took a cup, gave thanks,* and

---

x 6-13: Mk 14, 3-9; Jn 12, 1-8.—y Dt 15, 11.—z 14-16: Mk 14, 10-11; Lk 22, 3-6.—a Zec 11, 12.—b 17-25: Mk 14, 12-21; Lk 22, 7-23.—c Ex 12, 14-20.—d Is 53, 8-10—e 26-30: Mk 14, 22-26; Lk 22, 14-23; 1 Cor 11, 23-25.—f 26-27: 1 Cor 10, 16.

26, 6-13: See the notes on Mk 14, 3-9 and Jn 12, 1-8.

26, 12: *To prepare me for burial:* cf Mk 14, 8. In accordance with the interpretation of this act as Jesus' *burial* anointing, Matthew, more consistent than Mark, changes the purpose of the visit of the women to Jesus' tomb; they do not go to anoint him (Mk 16, 1) but "to see the tomb" (Mt 28, 1).

26, 14: *Iscariot:* see the note on Lk 6, 16.

26, 15: The motive of avarice is introduced by Judas's question about the price for betrayal, which is absent in the Marcan source (Mk 14, 10-11). *Hand him over:* the same Greek verb is used to express the saving purpose of God by which Jesus is handed over to death (cf Mt 17, 22; 20, 18; 26, 2) and the human malice that hands him over. *Thirty pieces of silver:* the price of the betrayal is found only in Mt. It is derived from Zec 11, 12 where it is the wages paid to the rejected shepherd, a cheap price (Zec 11, 13). That amount is also the compensation paid to one whose slave has been gored by an ox (Ex 21, 32).

26, 17: *The first day of the Feast of Unleavened Bread:* see the note on Mk 14, 1. Matthew omits Mk's "when they sacrificed the Passover lamb."

26, 18: By omitting much of Mk 14, 13-15, adding *My appointed time draws near,* and turning the question into a statement, *in your house I shall celebrate the Passover,* Matthew has given this passage a solemnity and majesty greater than that of his source.

26, 21: Given Matthew's interest in the fulfillment of the Old Testament, it is curious that he omits the Marcan designation of Jesus' betrayer as "one who is eating with me" (Mk 14, 18), since that is probably an allusion to Ps 41, 10. However, the shocking fact that the betrayer is one who shares table fellowship with Jesus is emphasized in v 23.

26, 24: *It would be better . . . born:* the enormity of the deed is such that it would be better not to exist than to do it.

26, 25: Peculiar to Mt. *You have said so:* cf Mt 26, 64; 27, 11. This is a half-affirmative. Emphasis is laid on the pronoun and the answer implies that the statement would not have been made if the question had not been asked.

26, 26-29: See the note on Mk 14, 22-24. The Marcan-Matthean is one of the two major New Testament traditions of the words of Jesus when instituting the Eucharist. The other (and earlier) is the Pauline-Lucan (1 Cor 11, 23-25; Lk 22, 19-20). Each shows the influence of Christian liturgical usage, but the Marcan-Matthean is more developed in that regard than the Pauline-Lucan. The words over the bread and cup succeed each other without the intervening meal mentioned in 1 Cor 11, 25; Lk 22, 20; and there is parallelism between the consecratory words *(this is my body . . . this is my blood).* Matthew follows Mk closely but with some changes.

26, 26: See the note on Mt 14, 19. *Said the blessing:* a prayer blessing God. *Take and eat:* literally, Take, eat. Eat is an addition to Mk's "take it" (literally, "take"; Mk 14, 22). *This is my body:* the bread is identified with Jesus himself.

26, 27-28: *Gave thanks:* see the note on Mt 15, 36. *Gave it to them . . . all of you:* cf Mk 14, 23-24. In the Marcan sequence the disciples drink and then Jesus says the interpretative words. Matthew has changed this into a command to *drink* followed by those words. *My blood:* see Lv 17, 11 for the concept that the *blood* is "the seat of life" and that when placed on the altar it "makes atonement." *Which will be shed:* the present participle, "being shed" or "going to be shed," is future in relation to the Last Supper. *On behalf of:* Greek *peri;* see the note on Mk 14, 24. *Many:* see the note on Mt 20, 28. *For the forgiveness of sins:* a Matthean addition. The same phrase occurs in Mk 1, 4 in connection with John's baptism but Matthew avoids it there (Mt 3, 11). He places it here probably because he wishes to emphasize that it is the sacrificial death of Jesus that brings *forgiveness of sins.*

gave it to them, saying, "Drink from it, all of you, [28] for this is my blood of the covenant, which will be shed on behalf of many for the forgiveness of sins.[g] [29] I tell you, from now on I shall not drink this fruit of the vine until the day when I drink it with you new in the kingdom of my Father."* [30] Then, after singing a hymn, they went out to the Mount of Olives.*

Peter's Denial Foretold. [31] [h] Then Jesus said to them, "This night all of you will have your faith in me shaken,* for it is written:

'I will strike the shepherd,
    and the sheep of the flock will be dispersed';[i]

[32] but after I have been raised up, I shall go before you to Galilee." [33] Peter said to him in reply, "Though all may have their faith in you shaken, mine will never be." [34] [j] Jesus said to him, "Amen, I say to you, this very night before the cock crows,* you will deny me three times."[k] [35] Peter said to him, "Even though I should have to die with you, I will not deny you." And all the disciples spoke likewise.

The Agony in the Garden. [36] * [l] Then Jesus came with them to a place called Gethsemane,* and he said to his disciples,[m] "Sit here while I go over there and pray." [37] [n] He took along Peter and the two sons of Zebedee,* and began to feel sorrow and distress. [38] Then he said to them, "My soul is sorrowful even to death.* Remain here and keep watch with me."[o] [39] He advanced a little and fell prostrate in prayer, saying, "My Father,* if it is possible, let this cup pass from me; yet, not as I will, but as you will."[p] [40] When he returned to his disciples he found them asleep. He said to Peter, "So you could not keep watch with me for one hour? [41] Watch and pray that you may not undergo the test.* The spirit is willing, but the flesh is weak." [42] Withdrawing a second time, he prayed again, "My Father,[q] if it is not possible that this cup pass without my drinking it, your will be done!"* [43] Then he returned once more and found them asleep, for they could not keep their eyes open. [44] He left them and withdrew again and prayed a third time, saying the same thing again. [45] Then he returned to his disciples and said to them, "Are you still sleeping and taking your rest? Behold, the hour is at hand when the Son of Man is to be handed over to sinners.[r] [46] Get up, let us go. Look, my betrayer is at hand."

The Betrayal and Arrest of Jesus. [47] [s] While he was still speaking, Judas, one of the Twelve, arrived, accompanied by a large crowd, with swords and clubs, who

---

g Ex 24, 8; Is 53, 12.—h 31-35: Mk 14, 7-31.—i Zec 13, 7; Jn 16, 32.—j 34-35: Lk 22, 33-34; Jn 13, 37-38.—k Mt 26, 69-75.—l 36-46: Mk 14, 32-42; Lk 22, 39-46.—m Jn 18, 1.—n 37-39: Heb 5, 7.—o Ps 42, 6.12; Jon 4, 9.—p Jn 4, 34; 6, 38; Phil 2, 8.—q Mt 6, 10; Heb 10, 9.—r Jn 12, 23; 13, 1; 17, 1.—s 47-56: Mk 14, 43-50; Lk 22, 47-53; Jn 18, 3-11.

26, 29: Although his death will interrupt the table fellowship he has had with the disciples, Jesus confidently predicts his vindication by God and a new table fellowship with them at the banquet of the kingdom.

26, 30: See the note on Mk 14, 26.

26, 31: *Will have . . . shaken:* literally, "will be scandalized in me"; see the note on Mt 24, 9-12. *I will strike . . . dispersed:* cf Zec 13, 7.

26, 34: *Before the cock crows:* see the note on Mt 14, 25. The third watch of the night was called "cockcrow." *Deny me:* see the note on Mt 16, 24.

26, 36-56: Cf Mk 14, 32-52. The account of Jesus in Gethsemane is divided between that of his agony (36-46) and that of his betrayal and arrest (47-56). Jesus' *sorrow and distress* (37) in face of death is unrelieved by the presence of his three disciples who, though urged to *watch with* him (38.41), fall asleep (40.43). He prays that *if . . . possible* his death may be avoided (39) but that his Father's will be done (39.42.44). Knowing then that his death must take place, he announces to his companions that *the hour* for his being *handed over* has come (45). Judas arrives with an armed band provided by the Sanhedrin and greets Jesus with a kiss, the prearranged sign for his identification (47-49). After his arrest, he rebukes a disciple who has attacked *the*

high priest's servant with a sword (51-54), and chides those who have come out to seize him with *swords and clubs* as if he were *a robber* (55-56). In both rebukes Jesus declares that the treatment he is now receiving is the fulfillment of the scriptures (55.56). The subsequent flight of *all the disciples* is itself the fulfillment of his own prediction (cf 31). In this episode, Matthew follows Mk with a few alterations.

26, 36: *Gethsemane:* the Hebrew name means "oil press" and designates an olive orchard on the western slope of the Mount of Olives; see the note on Mt 21, 1. The name appears only in Mt and Mk. The place is called a "garden" in Jn 18, 1.

26, 37: *Peter and the two sons of Zebedee:* cf Mt 17, 1.

26, 38: Cf Ps 42, 6.12. In the Septuagint (Ps 41, 5.12) the same Greek word for *sorrowful* is used as here. *To death:* i.e., "enough to die"; cf Jon 4, 9.

26, 39: *My Father:* see the note on Mk 14, 36. Matthew omits the Aramaic *'abbā'* and adds the qualifier *my*. *This cup:* see the note on Mk 10, 38-40.

26, 41: *Undergo the test:* see the note on Mt 6, 13. In that verse "the final test" translates the same Greek word as is here translated *the test,* and these are the only instances of the use of that word in Mt. It is possible that the passion of Jesus is seen here as an anticipation of the great tribulation that will precede the parousia (see the notes on Mt 24, 8; 24, 21) to which Mt 6, 13 refers, and that just as Jesus prays to be delivered from death (39), so he exhorts the disciples to pray that they will not have to *undergo* the great *test* that his passion would be for them. Some scholars, however, understand *not undergo* (literally, "not enter") *the test* as meaning not that the disciples may be spared *the test* but that they may not yield to the temptation of falling away from Jesus because of his passion even though they will have to endure it.

26, 42: *Your will be done:* cf Mt 6, 10.

had come from the chief priests and the elders of the people. [48] His betrayer had arranged a sign with them, saying, "The man I shall kiss is the one; arrest him." [49] Immediately he went over to Jesus and said, "Hail, Rabbi!"* and he kissed him. [50] Jesus answered him, "Friend, do what you have come for." Then stepping forward they laid hands on Jesus and arrested him. [51] And behold, one of those who accompanied Jesus put his hand to his sword, drew it, and struck the high priest's servant, cutting off his ear. [52] Then Jesus said to him, "Put your sword back into its sheath, for all who take the sword will perish by the sword. [53] Do you think that I cannot call upon my Father and he will not provide me at this moment with more than twelve legions of angels? [54] But then how would the scriptures be fulfilled which say that it must come to pass in this way?" [55] At that hour Jesus said to the crowds, "Have you come out as against a robber, with swords and clubs to seize me? Day after day I sat teaching in the temple area, yet you did not arrest me.* [56] But all this has come to pass that the writings of the prophets may be fulfilled." Then all the disciples left him and fled. [t]

Jesus before the Sanhedrin.* [57] [u] Those who had arrested Jesus led him away to Caiaphas* the high priest, where the scribes and the elders were assembled. [58] Peter was following him at a distance as far as the high priest's courtyard, and going inside he sat down with the servants to see the outcome. [59] The chief priests and the entire Sanhedrin* kept trying to obtain false testimony against Jesus in order to put him to death, [60] [v] but they found none, though many false witnesses came forward. Finally two* came forward [61] who stated, "This man said, 'I can destroy the temple of God and within three days rebuild it.' " [62] The high priest rose and addressed him, "Have you no answer? What are these men testifying against you?" [63] But Jesus was silent.* Then the high priest said to him, "I order you to tell us under oath before the living God whether you are the Messiah, the Son of God." [w] [64] Jesus said to him in reply, "You have said so.* But I tell you:

> From now on you will see 'the Son of Man
> seated at the right hand of the Power'
> and 'coming on the clouds of heaven.' " [x]

[65] Then the high priest tore his robes and said, "He has blasphemed!* What further

---

t Mt 26, 31.—u 57-68: Mk 14, 53-65; Lk 22, 54-55.63-71; Jn 18, 12-14.19-24.—v 60-61: Dt 19, 15; Jn 2, 19; Acts 6, 14.—w Is 53, 7.—x Ps 110, 1; Dn 7, 13.

26, 49: *Rabbi:* see the note on Mt 23, 6-7. Jesus is so addressed twice in Mt (cf 25), both times by Judas. For the significance of the closely related address "teacher" in Mt, see the note on Mt 8, 19.

26, 55: *Day after day . . . arrest me:* cf Mk 14, 49. This suggests that Jesus had taught for a relatively long period in Jerusalem, whereas Mt 21, 1-11 puts his coming to the city for the first time only a few days before.

26, 57-68: Following Mk 14, 53-65, Matthew presents the nighttime appearance of Jesus before *the Sanhedrin* as a real trial. After *many false witnesses* bring charges against him that do not suffice for the death sentence (60), *two came forward* who charge him with claiming to be able to *destroy the temple . . . and within three days* to *rebuild it* (60-61). Jesus makes no answer even when challenged to do so by *the high priest,* who then orders him to declare *under oath . . . whether* he is *the Messiah, the Son of God* (62-63). Matthew changes Mk's clear affirmative response (Mk 14, 62) to the same one as that given to Judas (cf 25), but follows Mk almost verbatim in Jesus' predicting that his judges will see him *(the Son of Man) seated at the right hand of* God *and coming on the clouds of heaven* (64). *The high priest* then charges him with blasphemy (65), a charge with which the other members of *the Sanhedrin* agree by declaring that *he deserves to die* (66). They then attack him (67) and mockingly demand that he *prophesy* (68). This account contains elements that are contrary to the judicial procedures prescribed in the Mishnah, the Jewish code of law that dates in written form from ca. A.D. 200, e.g., trial on a feast day, a night session of the court, pronouncement of a verdict of condemnation at the same session at which testimony was re-

ceived. Consequently, some scholars regard the account entirely as a creation of the early Christians without historical value. However, it is disputable whether the norms found in the Mishnah were in force at the time of Jesus. More to the point is the question whether the Matthean-Marcan night trial derives from a combination of two separate incidents, a nighttime preliminary investigation (cf Jn 18, 13.19-24) and a formal trial on the following morning (cf Lk 22, 66-71).

26, 57: *Caiaphas:* see the note on Mt 26, 3.

26, 59: *Sanhedrin:* see the note on Lk 22, 66.

26, 60-61: *Two:* cf Dt 19, 15. *I can destroy . . . rebuild it:* there are significant differences from the Marcan parallel (Mk 14, 58). Matthew omits "made with hands" and "not made with hands" and changes Mk's "will destroy" and "will build another" to *can destroy* and (can) *rebuild.* The charge is probably based on Jesus' prediction of the temple's destruction; see the notes on Mt 23, 37-39; 24, 2; and Jn 2, 19. A similar prediction by Jeremiah was considered as deserving death; cf Jer 7, 1-15; 26, 1-8.

26, 63: *Silent:* possibly an allusion to Is 53, 7. *I order you . . . living God:* peculiar to Mt; cf Mk 14, 61.

26, 64: *You have said so:* see the note on Mt 26, 25. *From now on . . . heaven:* the Son of Man who is to be crucified (cf Mt 20, 19) will be seen in glorious majesty (cf Ps 110, 1) and *coming on the clouds of heaven* (cf Dn 7, 13). *The Power:* see the note on Mk 14, 61-62.

26, 65: *Blasphemed:* the punishment for *blasphemy* was death by stoning (see Lv 24, 10-16). According to the Mishnah, to be guilty of *blasphemy* one had to pronounce "the Name itself," i.e. Yahweh; cf *Sanhedrin* 7, 4.5. Those who judge the gospel accounts of Jesus' trial by the later Mishnah standards point out that Jesus uses the surrogate "the Power," and hence no Jewish court would have regarded him as guilty of *blasphemy;* others hold that the Mishnah's narrow understanding of *blasphemy* was a later development.

need have we of witnesses? You have now heard the blasphemy; [66] what is your opinion?" They said in reply, "He deserves to die!" [67] *Then they spat in his face and struck him, while some slapped him,[y] [68] saying, "Prophesy for us, Messiah: who is it that struck you?"

Peter's Denial of Jesus. [69] [z] Now Peter was sitting outside in the courtyard. One of the maids came over to him and said, "You too were with Jesus the Galilean." [70] But he denied it in front of everyone,* saying, "I do not know what you are talking about!" [71] As he went out to the gate, another girl saw him and said to those who were there, "This man was with Jesus the Nazorean." [72] Again he denied it with an oath, "I do not know the man!" [73] A little later the bystanders came over and said to Peter, "Surely you too are one of them; even your speech gives you away."* [74] At that he began to curse and to swear, "I do not know the man." And immediately a cock crowed. [75] Then Peter remembered the word that Jesus had spoken: "Before the cock crows you will deny me three times." He went out and began to weep bitterly.[a]

CHAPTER 27

Jesus before Pilate. [1] * When it was morning,[b] all the chief priests and the elders of the people took counsel* against Jesus to put him to death. [2] They bound

him, led him away, and handed him over to Pilate, the governor.

The Death of Judas. [3] [c] Then Judas, his betrayer, seeing that Jesus had been condemned, deeply regretted what he had done. He returned the thirty pieces of silver* to the chief priests and elders,[d] [4] saying, "I have sinned in betraying innocent blood." They said, "What is that to us? Look to it yourself." [5] Flinging the money into the temple, he departed and went off and hanged himself.* [6] The chief priests gathered up the money, but said, "It is not lawful to deposit this in the temple treasury, for it is the price of blood." [7] After consultation, they used it to buy the potter's field as a burial place for foreigners. [8] That is why that field even today is called the Field of Blood. [9] Then was fulfilled what had been said through Jeremiah the prophet,* "And they took the thirty pieces of silver, the value of a man with a price on his head, a price set by some of the Israelites, [10] and they paid it out for the potter's field just as the Lord had commanded me."[e]

Jesus Questioned by Pilate. [11] [f] Now Jesus stood before the governor, and he questioned him, "Are you the king of the Jews?"* Jesus said, "You say so." [12] And when he was accused by the chief priests

---

y Wis 2, 19; Is 50, 6.—z 69-75: Mk 14, 66-72; Lk 22, 56-62; Jn 18, 17-18.25-27.—a Mt 26, 34.—b 1-2: Mk 15, 1; Lk 23, 1; Jn 18, 28.—c 3-10: Acts 1, 18-19.—d Mt 26, 15.—e Zec 11, 12-13.—f 11-14: Mk 15, 2-5; Lk 23, 2-3; Jn 18, 29-38.

26, 67-68: The physical abuse, apparently done to Jesus by the members of the Sanhedrin themselves, recalls the sufferings of the Isaian Servant of the Lord; cf Is 50, 6. The mocking challenge to *prophesy* is probably motivated by Jesus' prediction of his future glory (64).

26, 70: *Denied it in front of everyone:* see Mt 10, 33. Peter's repentance (75) saves him from the fearful destiny of which Jesus speaks there.

26, 73: *Your speech . . . away:* Matthew explicates Mk's "you too are a Galilean" (Mk 14, 70).

27, 1-31: Cf Mk 15, 1-20. Matthew's account of the Roman trial before *Pilate* is introduced by a consultation of the Sanhedrin after which Jesus is *handed over to . . . the governor* (1-2). Matthew follows his Marcan source closely but adds some material that is peculiar to him, the death of *Judas* (3-10), possibly the name *Jesus* as the name of *Barabbas* also (16-17), the intervention of Pilate's *wife* (19), Pilate's washing *his hands* in token of his disclaiming responsibility for Jesus' death (24), and the assuming of that responsibility by *the whole people* (25).

27, 1-2: There is scholarly disagreement about the meaning of the Sanhedrin's taking *counsel* (*symboulion elabon*; cf Mt 12, 14; 22, 15; 27, 7; 28, 12); see the note on Mk 15, 1. Some understand it as a discussion about the strategy for putting their death sentence against *Jesus* into effect since they lacked the right to do so themselves. Others see it as the occasion for their passing

that sentence, holding that Matthew, unlike Mark (Mk 14, 64), does not consider that it had been passed in the night session (Mt 26, 66). Even in the latter interpretation, their handing *him over to Pilate* is best explained on the hypothesis that they did not have competence to put their sentence into effect, as is stated in Jn 18, 31.

27, 3: *The thirty pieces of silver:* see Mt 26, 15.

27, 5-8: For another tradition about the death of Judas, cf Acts 1, 18-19. The two traditions agree only in the purchase of a *field* with *the money* paid to Judas for his betrayal of Jesus and the name given to the *field, the Field of Blood.* In Acts Judas himself buys the field and its name comes from his own blood shed in his fatal accident on it. *The potter's field:* this designation of the field is based on the fulfillment citation in v 10.

27, 9-10: Cf Mt 26, 15. Matthew's attributing this text to Jeremiah is puzzling, for there is no such text in that book, and *the thirty pieces of silver* thrown by Judas "into the temple" (5) recall rather Zec 11, 12-13. It is usually said that the attribution of the text to Jeremiah is due to Matthew's combining the Zechariah text with texts from Jeremiah that speak of a *potter* (Jer 18, 2-3), the buying of a *field* (Jer 32, 6-9), or the breaking of a potter's flask at Topheth in the valley of Ben-Hinnom with the prediction that it will become a burial place (Jer 19, 1-13).

27, 11: *King of the Jews:* this title is used of Jesus only by pagans. The Matthean instances are, besides this verse, Mt 2, 2; 27, 29.37. Matthew equates it with "Messiah"; cf Mt 2, 2.4 and Mt 27, 17.22 where he has changed "the king of the Jews" of his Marcan source (Mk 15, 9.12) to "(Jesus) called Messiah." The normal political connotation of both titles would be of concern to the Roman *governor. You say so:* see the note on Mt 26, 25. An unqualified affirmative response is not made because Jesus' kingship is not what Pilate would understand it to be.

and elders,* he made no answer.*g* 13 Then Pilate said to him, "Do you not hear how many things they are testifying against you?" 14 But he did not answer him one word, so that the governor was greatly amazed.

The Sentence of Death.* 15 *h* Now on the occasion of the feast the governor was accustomed to release to the crowd one prisoner whom they wished. 16 And at that time they had a notorious prisoner called [Jesus] Barabbas.* 17 So when they had assembled, Pilate said to them, "Which one do you want me to release to you, [Jesus] Barabbas, or Jesus called Messiah?" 18 For he knew that it was out of envy that they had handed him over.* 19 While he was still seated on the bench, his wife sent him a message, "Have nothing to do with that righteous man. I suffered much in a dream today because of him."* 20 The chief priests and the elders persuaded the crowds to ask for Barabbas but to destroy Jesus.*i* 21 The governor said to them in reply, "Which of the two do you want me to release to you?" They answered, "Barabbas!" 22 Pilate said to them, "Then what shall I do with Jesus called Messiah?"

They all said, "Let him be crucified!"* 23 But he said, "Why? What evil has he done?" They only shouted the louder, "Let him be crucified!" 24 * When Pilate saw that he was not succeeding at all, but that a riot was breaking out instead, he took water and washed his hands in the sight of the crowd, saying, "I am innocent of this man's blood. Look to it yourselves."*j* 25 And the whole people said in reply, "His blood be upon us and upon our children." 26 Then he released Barabbas to them, but after he had Jesus scourged,* he handed him over to be crucified.

Mockery by the Soldiers. 27 *k* Then the soldiers of the governor took Jesus inside the praetorium* and gathered the whole cohort around him. 28 They stripped off his clothes and threw a scarlet military cloak* about him. 29 Weaving a crown out of thorns,* they placed it on his head, and a reed in his right hand. And kneeling before him, they mocked him, saying, "Hail, King of the Jews!"*l* 30 They spat upon him* and took the reed and kept striking him on the head.*m* 31 And when they had mocked him, they stripped him of the cloak, dressed him in his own clothes, and led him off to crucify him.

---

g Is 53, 7.—h 15-26: Mk 15, 6-15; Lk 23, 17-25; Jn 18, 39—19, 16.—i Acts 3, 14.—j Dt 21, 1-8.—k 27-31: Mk 15, 16-20; Jn 19, 2-3.—l Mt 27, 11.—m Is 50, 6.

27, 12-14: Cf Mt 26, 62-63. As in the trial before the Sanhedrin, Jesus' silence may be meant to recall Is 53, 7. *Greatly amazed:* possibly an allusion to Is 52, 14-15.

27, 15-26: The choice that Pilate offers *the crowd* between *Barabbas* and *Jesus* is said to be in accordance with a custom of releasing at the Passover feast *one prisoner* chosen by *the crowd* (15). This custom is mentioned also in Mk 15, 6 and Jn 18, 39 but not in Lk; see the note on Lk 23, 17. Outside of the gospels there is no direct attestation of it, and scholars are divided in their judgment of the historical reliability of the claim that there was such a practice.

27, 16-17: *[Jesus] Barabbas:* it is possible that the double name is the original reading; *Jesus* was a common Jewish name; see the note on Mt 1, 21. This reading is found in only a few textual witnesses, although its absence in the majority can be explained as an omission of *Jesus* made for reverential reasons. That name is bracketed because of its uncertain textual attestation. The Aramaic name *Barabbas* means "son of the father"; the irony of the choice offered between him and Jesus, the true son of the Father, would be evident to those addressees of Mt who knew that.

27, 18: Cf Mk 14, 10. This is an example of the tendency, found in varying degree in all the gospels, to present Pilate in a relatively favorable light and emphasize the hostility of the Jewish authorities and eventually of the people.

27, 19: Jesus' innocence is declared by a Gentile woman. *In a dream:* in Mt's infancy narrative, dreams are the means of divine communication; cf Mt 1, 20; 2, 12.13.19.22.

27, 22: *Let him be crucified:* incited by the chief priests and elders (20), the crowds demand that Jesus be executed by crucifixion, a peculiarly horrible form of Roman capital punishment. The Marcan parallel, "Crucify him" (Mk 15, 3), addressed to Pilate, is changed by Matthew to the passive, probably to emphasize the responsibility of the crowds.

27, 24-25: Peculiar to Mt. *Took water . . . blood:* cf Dt 21, 1-8, the handwashing prescribed in the case of a murder when the killer is unknown. The elders of the city nearest to where the corpse is found must wash their hands, declaring, "Our hands did not shed this blood." *Look to it yourselves:* cf v 4. *The whole people:* Matthew sees in those who speak these words *the* entire *people:* (Greek *laos*) of Israel. *His blood . . . and upon our children:* cf Jer 26, 15. The responsibility for Jesus' death is accepted by the nation that was God's special possession (Ex 19, 5), his own *people* (Hos 2, 25), and they thereby lose that high privilege; see Mt 21, 43 and the note on that verse. The controversy between Matthew's church and Pharisaic Judaism about which was the true people of God is reflected here. As the Second Vatican Council has pointed out, guilt for Jesus' death is not attributable to all the Jews of his time or to any Jews of later times.

27, 26: *He had Jesus scourged:* the usual preliminary to crucifixion.

27, 27: *The praetorium:* the residence of the Roman governor. His usual place of residence was at Caesarea Maritima on the Mediterranean coast, but he went to Jerusalem during the great feasts, when the influx of pilgrims posed the danger of a nationalistic riot. It is disputed whether *the praetorium* in Jerusalem was the old palace of Herod in the west of the city or the fortress of Antonia northwest of the temple area. *The whole cohort:* normally six hundred soldiers.

27, 28: *Scarlet military cloak:* so Mt as against the royal purple of Mk 15, 17 and Jn 19, 2.

27, 29: *Crown out of thorns:* probably of long *thorns* that stood upright so that it resembled the "radiant" *crown,* a diadem with spikes used by Hellenistic kings. The soldiers' purpose was mockery, not torture. *A reed:* peculiar to Mt; a mock scepter.

27, 30: *Spat upon him:* cf Mt 26, 67 where there also is a possible allusion to Is 50, 6.

The Way of the Cross.* [32] As they were going out, they met a Cyrenian named Simon; this man they pressed into service to carry his cross.[n]

The Crucifixion. [33] [o] And when they came to a place called Golgotha (which means Place of the Skull), [34] [p] they gave Jesus wine to drink mixed with gall.* But when he had tasted it, he refused to drink. [35] After they had crucified him, they divided his garments* by casting lots;[q] [36] then they sat down and kept watch over him there. [37] And they placed over his head the written charge* against him: This is Jesus, the King of the Jews. [38] Two revolutionaries* were crucified with him, one on his right and the other on his left. [39] [r] Those passing by reviled him, shaking their heads* [40] and saying, "You who would destroy the temple and rebuild it in three days, save yourself, if you are the Son of God, [and] come down from the cross!"[s] [41] Likewise the chief priests with the scribes and elders mocked him and said,

[42] "He saved others; he cannot save himself. So he is the king of Israel!* Let him come down from the cross now, and we will believe in him. [43] *He trusted in God; let him deliver him now if he wants him. For he said, 'I am the Son of God.' "[t] [44] The revolutionaries who were crucified with him also kept abusing him in the same way.

The Death of Jesus. [45] [u] From noon onward,[v] darkness came over the whole land until three in the afternoon.* [46] And about three o'clock Jesus cried out in a loud voice, "*Eli, Eli, lema sabachthani?*"* which means, "My God, my God, why have you forsaken me?"[w] [47] Some of the bystanders who heard it said, "This one is calling for Elijah."* [48] Immediately one of them ran to get a sponge; he soaked it in wine, and putting it on a reed, gave it to him to drink.[x] [49] But the rest said, "Wait, let us see if Elijah comes to save him." [50] But Jesus cried out again in a loud voice, and gave up his spirit.* [51] [y] And behold, the veil of the sanctuary was torn in two from top to bottom.* The earth quaked, rocks

n Mk 15, 21; Lk 23, 26.—o 33-44: Mk 15, 22-32; Lk 23, 32-38; Jn 19, 17-19.23-24.—p Ps 69, 21.—q Ps 22, 19.—r Ps 22, 8.—s Mt 4, 3.6; 26, 61.—t Ps 22, 9; Wis 2, 12-20.—u 45-46: Mk 15, 33-41; Lk 23, 44-49; Jn 19, 28-30.—v Am 8, 9.—w Ps 22, 2.—x Ps 69, 21.—y Ex 26, 31-36; Ps 68, 9; 77, 19.

27, 32: See note on Mk 15, 21. *Cyrenian named Simon:* Cyrenaica was a Roman province on the north coast of Africa and Cyrene was its capital city. The city had a large population of Greek-speaking Jews. *Simon* may have been living in Palestine or have come there for the Passover as a pilgrim. *Pressed into service:* see the note on Mt 5, 41.

27, 34: *Wine . . . mixed with gall:* cf Mk 15, 23 where the drink is "wine drugged with myrrh," a narcotic. Mt's text is probably an inexact allusion to Ps 69, 22. That psalm belongs to the class called the individual lament, in which a persecuted just man prays for deliverance in the midst of great suffering and also expresses confidence that his prayer will be heard. That theme of the suffering Just One is frequently applied to the sufferings of Jesus in the passion narratives.

27, 35: The clothing of an executed criminal went to his executioner(s), but the description of that procedure in the case of Jesus, found in all the gospels, is plainly inspired by Ps 22, 19. However, that psalm verse is quoted only in Jn 19, 24.

27, 37: The offense of a person condemned to death by crucifixion was written on a tablet that was displayed on his cross. The *charge* against *Jesus* was that he had claimed to be *the King of the Jews* (cf Mt 27, 11), i.e., the Messiah (cf Mt 27, 17.22).

27, 38: *Revolutionaries:* see the note on Jn 18, 40 where the same Greek word as that found here is used for Barabbas.

27, 39-40: *Reviled him . . . heads:* cf Ps 22, 8. *You who would destroy . . . three days:* cf Mt 26, 61. *If you are the Son of God:* the same words as those of the devil in the temptation of Jesus; cf Mt 4, 3.6.

27, 42: *King of Israel:* in their mocking of Jesus the members of the Sanhedrin call themselves and their people not "the Jews" but *Israel.*

27, 43: Peculiar to Mt. *He trusted in God . . . wants him:* cf Ps 22, 9. *He said . . . of God:* probably an allusion to Wis 2, 12-20 where the theme of the suffering Just One appears.

27, 45: Cf Amos 8, 9 where on the day of the Lord "the sun will set at midday."

27, 46: *Eli, Eli, lema sabachthani?:* Jesus cries out in the words of Ps 22, 2a, a psalm of lament that is the Old Testament passage most frequently drawn upon in this narrative. In Mk the verse is cited entirely in Aramaic, which Matthew partially retains but changes the invocation of God to the Hebrew *Eli,* possibly because that is more easily related to the statement of the following verse about Jesus' calling for Elijah.

27, 47: *Elijah:* see the note on Mt 3, 4. This prophet, taken up into heaven (2 Kgs 2, 11), was believed to come to the help of those in distress, but the evidences of that belief are all later than the gospels.

27, 50: *Gave up his spirit:* cf the Marcan parallel (Mk 15, 37), "breathed his last." Matthew's alteration expresses both Jesus' control over his destiny and his obedient giving up of his life to God.

27, 51-53: *Veil of the sanctuary . . . bottom:* cf Mk 15, 38; Lk 23, 45. Lk puts this event immediately before the death of Jesus. There were two veils in the Mosaic tabernacle on the model of which the temple was constructed, the outer one before the entrance of the Holy Place and the inner one before the Holy of Holies (see Ex 26, 31-36). Only the high priest could pass through the latter and that only on the Day of Atonement (see Lv 16, 1-18). Probably the *torn veil* of the gospels is the inner one. The meaning of the scene may be that now, because of Jesus' death, all people have access to the presence of God, or that the temple, its holiest part standing exposed, is now profaned and will soon be destroyed. *The earth quaked . . . appeared to many:* peculiar to Mt. The earthquake, the splitting of the *rocks,* and especially the resurrection of the dead *saints* indicate the coming of the final age. In the Old Testament the coming of God is frequently portrayed with the imagery of an earthquake (see Pss 68, 9; 77, 19), and Jesus speaks of the earthquakes that will accompany the "labor pains" that signify the beginning of the dissolution of the old world (Mt 24, 7-8). For the expectation of the resurrection of the dead at the coming of the new and final age, see Dn 12, 1-3. Matthew knows that the end of the old age has not yet come (Mt 28, 20), but the new age has broken in with the death (and resurrection; cf the earthquake in Mt 28, 2) of Jesus; see the note on Mt 16, 28. *After his resurrection:* this qualification seems to be due to Matthew's wish to assert the primacy of Jesus' *resurrection* even though he has placed the resurrection of the dead *saints* immediately after Jesus' death.

were split, [52] tombs were opened, and the bodies of many saints who had fallen asleep were raised.[z] [53] And coming forth from their tombs after his resurrection, they entered the holy city and appeared to many. [54] *The centurion and the men with him who were keeping watch over Jesus feared greatly when they saw the earthquake and all that was happening, and they said, "Truly, this was the Son of God!" [55] There were many women there, looking on from a distance,* who had followed Jesus from Galilee, ministering to him. [56] Among them were Mary Magdalene and Mary the mother of James and Joseph, and the mother of the sons of Zebedee.[a]

The Burial of Jesus.* [57] [b] When it was evening, there came a rich man from Arimathea named Joseph, who was himself a disciple of Jesus.[c] [58] He went to Pilate and asked for the body of Jesus; then Pilate ordered it to be handed over. [59] Taking the body, Joseph wrapped it [in] clean linen [60] and laid it in his new tomb that he had hewn in the rock. Then he rolled a huge stone across the entrance to the tomb and departed. [61] But Mary Magdalene and the other Mary remained sitting there, facing the tomb.

z Dn 12, 1-3.—a Mt 13, 55.—b 57-61: Mk 15, 42-47; Lk 23, 50-56; Jn 19, 38-42.—c Is 53, 9.—d Mt 12, 40; 16, 21; 17, 23; 20, 19.— e 1-10: Mk 16, 1-8; Lk 24, 1-12; Jn 20, 1-10.

27, 54: Cf Mk 15, 39. The Christian confession of faith is made by Gentiles, not only *the centurion*, as in Mk, but the other soldiers *who were keeping watch over Jesus* (cf 36).

27, 55-56: *Looking on from a distance:* cf Ps 38, 12. *Mary Magdalene . . . Joseph:* these two women are mentioned again in v 61 and Mt 28, 1 and are important as witnesses of the reality of the empty tomb. A *James* and *Joseph* are referred to in Mt 13, 55 as brothers of Jesus.

27, 57-61: Cf Mk 15, 42-47. Matthew drops Mk's designation of *Joseph* of *Arimathea* as "a distinguished member of the council" (the Sanhedrin), and makes him *a rich man* and *a disciple of Jesus.* The former may be an allusion to Is 53, 9 (the Hebrew reading of that text is disputed and the one followed in the NAB OT has nothing about the rich, but they are mentioned in the LXX version). That the tomb was the *new tomb* of *a rich man* and that it was seen by the women are indications of an apologetic intent of Matthew; there could be no question about the identity of Jesus' burial place. *The other Mary:* the mother of James and Joseph (56).

27, 62-66: Peculiar to Mt. The story prepares for Mt 28, 11-15 and the Jewish charge that the tomb was empty because the *disciples* had stolen the body of Jesus (Mt 28, 13.15).

27, 62: *The next day . . . preparation:* the sabbath. According to the synoptic chronology, in that year *the day of preparation* (for the sabbath) was the Passover; cf Mk 15, 42. *The Pharisees:* the principal opponents of Jesus during his ministry and, in Matthew's time, of the Christian church, join with *the chief priests* to guarantee against a possible attempt of Jesus' *disciples* to steal his body.

27, 64: *This last imposture . . . the first:* the claim that Jesus *has been raised from the dead* is clearly the *last imposture; the first* may be either his claim that he would be *raised up* (63) or his claim that he was the one with whose ministry the kingdom of God had come (see Mt 12, 28).

The Guard at the Tomb.* [62] The next day, the one following the day of preparation,* the chief priests and the Pharisees gathered before Pilate [63] and said, "Sir, we remember that this imposter while still alive said, 'After three days I will be raised up.'[d] [64] Give orders, then, that the grave be secured until the third day, lest his disciples come and steal him and say to the people, 'He has been raised from the dead.' This last imposture would be worse than the first."* [65] Pilate said to them, "The guard is yours;* go secure it as best you can." [66] So they went and secured the tomb by fixing a seal to the stone and setting the guard.

CHAPTER 28*

The Resurrection of Jesus. [1] After the sabbath,[e] as the first day of the week was dawning,* Mary Magdalene and the other Mary came to see the tomb. [2] * And behold, there was a great earthquake; for an

27, 65: *The guard is yours:* literally, "have a guard" or "you have a guard." Either the imperative or the indicative could mean that Pilate granted the petitioners some Roman soldiers as guards, which is the sense of the present translation. However, if the verb is taken as an indicative it could also mean that Pilate told them to use their own Jewish guards.

28, 1-20: Except for vv 1-8, based on Mk 16, 1-8, the material of this final chapter is peculiar to Mt. Even where he follows Mk, Matthew has altered his source so greatly that a very different impression is given from that of the Marcan account. The two points that are common to the resurrection testimony of all the gospels are that the tomb of Jesus had been found empty and that the risen Jesus had appeared to certain persons, or, in the original form of Mk, that such an appearance was promised as soon to take place (see Mk 16, 7). On this central and all-important basis, Matthew has constructed an account that interprets the resurrection as the turning of the ages (2-4), shows the Jewish opposition to Jesus as continuing *to the present* in the claim that the resurrection is a deception perpetrated by the *disciples* who stole his body from the tomb (11-15), and marks a new stage in the mission of *the disciples* once limited to Israel (10, 5-6); now they are to *make disciples of all nations.* In this work they will be strengthened by the presence of the exalted Son of Man, who will be with them *until* the kingdom comes in fullness at *the end of the age* (16-20).

28, 1: *After the sabbath . . . dawning:* since the sabbath ended at sunset, this could mean in the early evening, for *dawning* can refer to the appearance of the evening star; cf Lk 23, 54. However, it is probable that Matthew means the morning dawn of the day after the sabbath, as in the similar though slightly different text of Mk, "when the sun had risen" (Mk 16, 2). *Mary Magdalene and the other Mary:* see the notes on Mt 27, 55-56; 57-61. *To see the tomb:* cf Mk 16, 1-2 where the purpose of the women's visit is to anoint Jesus' body.

28, 2-4: Peculiar to Mt. *A great earthquake:* see the note on Mt 27, 51-53. *Descended from heaven:* this trait is peculiar to Mt, although his interpretation of the "young man" of his Marcan source (Mk 16, 5) as an *angel* is probably true to Mk's intention; cf Lk 24, 23 where the "two men" of Mt 24, 4 are said to be "angels." *Rolled back the stone . . . upon it:* not to allow the risen Jesus to leave the tomb but to make evident that the tomb is empty (see 6). Unlike the apocryphal Gospel of Peter (9, 35—11, 44), the New Testament does not describe the resurrection of Jesus, nor is there anyone who sees it. *His appearance was like lightning . . . snow:* see the note on Mt 17, 2.

angel of the Lord descended from heaven, approached, rolled back the stone, and sat upon it.*f* 3 His appearance was like lightning and his clothing was white as snow.*g* 4 The guards were shaken with fear of him and became like dead men. 5 Then the angel said to the women in reply, "Do not be afraid! I know that you are seeking Jesus the crucified. 6 * He is not here, for he has been raised just as he said. Come and see the place where he lay. 7 Then go quickly and tell his disciples, 'He has been raised from the dead, and he is going before you to Galilee; there you will see him.' Behold, I have told you."*h* 8 Then they went away quickly from the tomb, fearful yet overjoyed, and ran to announce* this to his disciples. 9 * And behold, Jesus met them on their way and greeted them.*i* They approached, embraced his feet, and did him homage. 10 Then Jesus said to them, "Do not be afraid. Go tell my brothers to go to Galilee, and there they will see me."

The Report of the Guard. * 11 While they were going, some of the guard went into the city and told the chief priests all that had happened. 12 They assembled with the elders and took counsel; then they gave a large sum of money to the soldiers, 13 telling them, "You are to say, 'His disciples came by night and stole him while we were asleep.' 14 And if this gets to the ears of the governor, we will satisfy [him] and keep you out of trouble." 15 The soldiers took the money and did as they were instructed. And this story has circulated among the Jews to the present [day].

The Commissioning of the Disciples. * 16 *j* The eleven* disciples went to Galilee, to the mountain to which Jesus had ordered them. 17 When they saw him, they worshiped, but they doubted.* 18 Then Jesus approached and said to them, "All power in heaven and on earth*k* has been given to me.* 19 Go, therefore,* and make disciples of all nations, baptizing them in the name of the Father, and of the Son, and of the holy Spirit,*l* 20 teaching them to observe all that I have commanded you.* And behold, I am with you always, until the end of the age."*m*

---

f Mt 25, 51.—g Mt 17, 2.—h Mt 26, 32.—i 9-10: Jn 20, 17.— j 16-20: Mk 16, 14-16; Lk 24, 36-49; Jn 20, 19-23.—k Dn 7, 14 LXX.—l Acts 1, 8.—m Mt 1, 23; 13, 39; 24, 3.

28, 6-7: Cf Mk 16, 6-7. *Just as he said:* a Matthean addition referring to Jesus' predictions of his resurrection, e.g., Mt 16, 21; 17, 23; 20, 19. *Tell his disciples:* like the angel of the Lord of the infancy narrative, the angel interprets a commandment about what is to be done; cf Mt 1, 20-21. Matthew omits Mk's "and Peter" (Mk 16, 7); considering his interest in Peter, this omission is curious. Perhaps the reason is that the Marcan text may allude to a first appearance of Jesus to Peter alone (cf 1 Cor 15, 5; Lk 24, 34) which Matthew has already incorporated into his account of Peter's confession at Caesarea Philippi; see the note on Mt 16, 16. *He is going . . . Galilee:* like Mk 16, 7, a reference to Jesus' prediction at the Last Supper (Mt 26, 32; Mk 14, 28). Matthew changes Mk's "as he told you" to a declaration of the angel.

28, 8: Contrast Mk 16, 8 where the women in their fear "said nothing to anyone."

28, 9-10: Although these verses are peculiar to Mt, there are similarities between them and Jn's account of the appearance of Jesus to Mary Magdalene (Jn 20, 17). In both there is a touching of Jesus' body, and a command of Jesus to bear a message to his disciples, designated as his *brothers.* Matthew may have drawn upon a tradition that appears in a different form in Jn. Jesus' words to the women are mainly a repetition of those of the angel (5a; 7b).

28, 11-15: This account indicates that the dispute between Christians and Jews about the empty tomb was not whether the tomb was empty but why.

28, 16-20: This climactic scene has been called a "proleptic parousia," for it gives a foretaste of the final glorious coming of the Son of Man (Mt 26, 64). Then his triumph will be manifest to all; now it is revealed only to *the disciples,* who are commissioned to announce it to *all nations* and bring them to belief in Jesus and obedience to his commandments.

28, 16: *The eleven:* the number recalls the tragic defection of Judas Iscariot. *To the mountain .. . ordered them:* since the message to *the disciples* was simply that they were to go to Galilee (10), some think that *the mountain* comes from a tradition of the message known to Matthew and alluded to here. For the significance of *the mountain,* see the note on Mt 17, 1.

28, 17: *But they doubted:* the Greek can also be translated, "but some doubted." The verb occurs elsewhere in the New Testament only in Mt 14, 31 where it is associated with Peter's being of "little faith." For the meaning of that designation, see the note on Mt 6, 30.

28, 18: *All power . . . me:* the Greek word here translated *power* is the same as that found in the LXX translation of Dn 7, 13-14 where one "like a son of man" is given *power* and an everlasting kingdom by God. The risen Jesus here claims universal power, i.e., *in heaven and on earth.*

28, 19: *Therefore:* since universal power belongs to the risen Jesus (18), he gives the eleven a mission that is universal. They are to *make disciples of all nations.* While *all nations* is understood by some scholars as referring only to *all* Gentiles, it is probable that it included the Jews as well. *Baptizing them:* baptism is the means of entrance into the community of the risen One, the Church. *In the name of the Father . . . holy Spirit:* this is perhaps the clearest expression in the New Testament of trinitarian belief. It may have been the baptismal formula of Matthew's church, but primarily it designates the effect of baptism, the union of the one baptized with the Father, Son, and holy Spirit.

28, 20: *All that I have commanded you:* the moral teaching found in this gospel, preeminently that of the Sermon on the Mount (chs 5-7). The commandments of Jesus are the standard of Christian conduct, not the Mosaic law as such, even though some of the Mosaic commandments have now been invested with the authority of Jesus. *Behold, I am with you always:* the promise of Jesus' real though invisible presence echoes the name Emmanuel given to him in the infancy narrative; see the note on Mt 1, 23. *End of the age:* see the notes on Mt 13, 39 and Mt 24, 3.

THE GOSPEL ACCORDING TO MARK

INTRODUCTION

This shortest of all New Testament gospels is likely the first to have been written, yet it often tells of Jesus' ministry in more detail than either Matthew or Luke (for example, the miracle stories at 5, 1-20 or 9, 14-29). It recounts what Jesus did in a vivid style, where one incident follows directly upon another. In this almost breathless narrative, Mark stresses Jesus' message about the kingdom of God now breaking into human life as good news (1, 14-15) and Jesus himself as the gospel of God (1, 1; 8, 35; 10, 29). Jesus is the Son whom God has sent to rescue humanity by serving and by sacrificing his life (10, 45).

The opening verse about good news in Mark (1, 1) serves as a title for the entire book. The action begins with the appearance of John the Baptist, a messenger of God attested by scripture. But John points to a mightier one, Jesus, at whose baptism God speaks from heaven, declaring Jesus his Son. The Spirit descends upon Jesus, who eventually, it is promised, will baptize "with the holy Spirit." This presentation of who Jesus really is (1, 1-13) is rounded out with a brief reference to the temptation of Jesus and how Satan's attack fails. Jesus as Son of God will be victorious, a point to be remembered as one reads of Jesus' death and the enigmatic ending to Mark's Gospel.

The key verses at 1, 14-15, which are programmatic, summarize what Jesus proclaims as gospel: fulfillment, the nearness of the kingdom, and therefore the need for repentance and for faith. After the call of the first four disciples, all fishermen (1, 16-20), we see Jesus engaged in teaching (1, 21.22.27), preaching (1, 38.39), and healing (1, 29-31.34.40-45), and exorcising demons (1,22-27.34.39). The content of Jesus' teaching is only rarely stated, and then chiefly in parables (ch 4) about the kingdom. His cures, especially on the sabbath (3, 1-5); his claim, like God, to forgive sins (2, 3-12); his table fellowship with tax collectors and sinners (2, 14-17); and the statement that his followers need not now fast but should rejoice while Jesus is present (2, 18-22), all stir up opposition that will lead to Jesus' death (3, 6).

In Mark, Jesus is portrayed as immensely popular with the people in Galilee during his ministry (2, 2; 3, 7; 4, 1). He appoints twelve disciples to help preach and drive out demons, just as he does (3, 13-19). He continues to work many miracles; the blocks 4, 35—6, 44 and 6, 45—7, 10 are cycles of stories about healings, miracles at the Sea of Galilee, and marvelous feedings of the crowds. Jesus' teaching in ch 7 exalts the word of God over "the tradition of the elders" and sees defilement as a matter of the heart, not of unclean foods. Yet opposition mounts. Scribes charge that Jesus is possessed by Beelzebul (3, 22). His relatives think him "out of his mind" (3, 21). Jesus' kinship is with those who do the will of God, in a new eschatological family, not even with mother, brothers, or sisters by blood ties (3, 31-35; cf 6, 1-6). But all too often his own disciples do not understand Jesus (4, 13.40; 6, 52; 8, 17-21). The fate of John the Baptist (6, 17-29) hints ominously at Jesus' own passion (9, 13; cf 8, 31).

A breakthrough seemingly comes with Peter's confession that Jesus is the Christ (Messiah; 8, 27-30). But Jesus himself emphasizes his passion (8, 31; 9, 31; 10, 33-34), not glory in the kingdom (10, 35-45). Momentarily he is glimpsed in his true identity when he is transfigured before three of the disciples (9, 2-8), but by and large Jesus is depicted in Mark as moving obediently along the way to his cross in Jerusalem. Occasionally there are miracles (9, 17-27; 10, 46-52; 11, 12-14.20-21, the only such account in Jerusalem), sometimes teachings (10, 2-11.23-31), but the greatest concern is with discipleship (8,

34—9, 1; 9, 33-50). For the disciples do not grasp the mystery being revealed (9, 32; 10, 32.38). One of them will betray him, Judas (14, 10-11.43-45); one will deny him, Peter (14, 27.31.54.66-72); all eleven men will desert Jesus (14, 27.50).

The passion account, with its condemnation of Jesus by the Sanhedrin (14, 53.55-65; 15, 1a) and sentencing by Pilate (15, 1b-15), is prefaced with the entry into Jerusalem (11, 1-11), ministry and controversies there (11, 15—12, 44), Jesus' Last Supper with the disciples (14, 1-26), and his arrest at Gethsemane (14, 32-52). A chapter of apocalyptic tone about the destruction of the temple (13, 1-2.14-23) and the coming of the Son of Man (13, 24-27), a discourse filled with promises (13, 11.31) and admonitions to be watchful (13, 2.23.37), is significant for Mark's Gospel, for it helps one see that God, in Jesus, will be victorious after the cross and at the end of history.

The Gospel of Mark ends in the most ancient manuscripts with an abrupt scene at Jesus' tomb, which the women find empty (16, 1-8). His own prophecy of 14, 28 is reiterated, that Jesus goes before the disciples into Galilee; "there you will see him." These words may imply resurrection appearances there, or Jesus' parousia there, or the start of Christian mission, or a return to the roots depicted in 1, 9.14-15 in Galilee. Other hands have attached additional endings after 16, 8; see the note on 16, 9-20.

The framework of Mark's Gospel is partly geographical: Galilee (1, 14—9, 49), through the area "across the Jordan" (10, 1) and through Jericho (10, 46-52), to Jerusalem (11, 1—16, 8). Only rarely does Jesus go into Gentile territory (5, 1-20; 7, 24-37), but those who acknowledge him there and the centurion who confesses Jesus at the cross (15, 39) presage the gospel's expansion into the world beyond Palestine.

Mark's Gospel is even more oriented to christology. Jesus is the Son of God (1, 11; 9, 7; 15, 39; cf 1, 1; 14, 61). He is the Messiah, the anointed king of Davidic descent (12, 35; 15, 32), the Greek for which, Christos, *has, by the time Mark wrote, become in effect a proper name (1, 1; 9, 41). Jesus is also seen as Son of Man, a term used in Mark not simply as a substitute for "I" or for humanity in general (cf 2, 10.27-28; 14, 21) or with reference to a mighty figure who is to come (13, 26; 14, 62), but also in connection with Jesus' predestined, necessary path of suffering and vindication (8, 31; 10, 45).*

The unfolding of Mark's story about Jesus is sometimes viewed by interpreters as centered around the term "mystery." The word is employed just once, at 4, 11, in the singular, and its content there is the kingdom, the open secret that God's reign is now breaking into human life with its reversal of human values. There is a related sense in which Jesus' real identity remained a secret during his lifetime, according to Mark, although demons and demoniacs knew it (1, 24; 3, 11; 5, 7); Jesus warned against telling of his mighty deeds and revealing his identity (1, 44; 3, 12; 5, 43; 7, 36; 8, 26.30), an injunction sometimes broken (1, 45; cf 5, 19-20). Further, Jesus teaches by parables, according to Mark, in such a way that those "outside" the kingdom do not understand, but only those to whom the mystery has been granted by God.

Mark thus shares with Paul, as well as with other parts of the New Testament, an emphasis on election (13, 20.22) and upon the gospel as Christ and his cross (cf 1 Cor 1, 23). Yet in Mark the person of Jesus is also depicted with an unaffected naturalness. He reacts to events with authentic human emotion: pity (1, 44), anger (3, 5), triumph (4, 40), sympathy (5, 36; 6, 34), surprise (6, 9), admiration (7, 29; 10, 21), sadness (14, 33-34), and indignation (14, 48-49).

Although the book is anonymous, apart from the ancient heading "According to Mark" in manuscripts, it has traditionally been assigned to John Mark, in whose mother's house (at Jerusalem) Christians assembled (Acts 12, 12). This Mark was a cousin of Barnabas (Col 4, 10) and accompanied Barnabas and Paul on a missionary journey (Acts 12, 25; 13, 3; 15, 36-39). He appears in Pauline letters (Phlm 24; 2 Tm 4, 11) and with Peter

(1 Pt 5, 13). Papias (ca. A.D. 135) described Mark as Peter's "interpreter," a view found in other patristic writers. Petrine influence should not, however, be exaggerated. The evangelist has put together various oral and possibly written sources—miracle stories, parables, sayings, stories of controversies, and the passion—so as to speak of the crucified Messiah for Mark's own day.

Traditionally, the gospel is said to have been written shortly before A.D. 70 in Rome, at a time of impending persecution and when destruction loomed over Jerusalem. Its audience seems to have been Gentile, unfamiliar with Jewish customs (hence 7, 3-4.11). The book aimed to equip such Christians to stand faithful in the face of persecution (13, 9-13), while going on with the proclamation of the gospel begun in Galilee (13, 10; 14, 9). Modern research often proposes as the author an unknown Hellenistic Jewish Christian, possibly in Syria, and perhaps shortly after the year 70.

The principal divisions of the Gospel according to Mark are the following:

   I.   The Preparation for the Public Ministry of Jesus (1, 1-13)
   II.   The Mystery of Jesus (1, 14—8, 26)
   III.   The Mystery Begins to Be Revealed (8, 27—9, 32)
   IV.   The Full Revelation of the Mystery (9, 33—16, 8)
       The Longer Ending (16, 9-20)
       The Shorter Ending
       The Freer Logion (in the note on 16, 9-20)

I. THE PREPARATION FOR THE PUBLIC MINISTRY OF JESUS*

CHAPTER 1

[1] The beginning of the gospel of Jesus Christ [the Son of God].*

The Preaching of John the Baptist. [2] [a] As it is written in Isaiah the prophet:*

"Behold, I am sending my messenger
    ahead of you;
he will prepare your way. [b]
[3] A voice of one crying out in the desert:
    'Prepare the way of the Lord,
    make straight his paths.' "[c]

[4] John [the] Baptist appeared in the desert proclaiming a baptism of repentance for the forgiveness of sins. [5] People of the whole Judean countryside and all the inhabitants of Jerusalem were going out to him and were being baptized by him in the Jordan River as they acknowledged their sins. [6] John was clothed in camel's hair, with a leather belt around his waist.* He fed on locusts and wild honey. [7] And this is what he proclaimed: "One mightier than I is coming after me. I am not worthy to stoop and loosen the thongs of his sandals. [8] [d] I have baptized you with water; he will baptize you with the holy Spirit."*

The Baptism of Jesus. [9] [e] It happened in those days that Jesus came from Nazareth of Galilee and was baptized in the Jordan by John. [10] On coming up out of the water

---

a 2-8: Mt 3,1-11; Lk 3, 2-16.—b Mal 3, 1.—c Is 40, 3; Jn 1, 23.—d Jn 1, 27; Acts 1, 5; 11, 16.—e 9-11: Mt 3, 13-17; Lk 3, 21-23; Jn 1, 32-33.

1, 1-13: The prologue of the Gospel according to Mark begins with the title (1) followed by three events preparatory to Jesus' preaching: (1) the appearance in the Judean wilderness of John, baptizer, preacher of repentance, and precursor of Jesus (2-8); (2) the baptism of Jesus, at which a voice from heaven acknowledges Jesus to be God's Son, and the holy Spirit descends on him (9-11); (3) the temptation of Jesus by Satan (12-13).

1, 1: The gospel of Jesus Christ [the Son of God]: the "good news" of salvation in and through Jesus, crucified and risen, acknowledged by the Christian community as Messiah (Mk 8, 29; 14, 61-62) and Son of God (Mk 1, 11; 9, 7; 15, 39), although some important manuscripts here omit the Son of God.

1, 2-3: Although Mark attributes the prophecy to Isaiah, the text is a combination of Mal 3, 1; Is 40, 3; and Ex 23, 20; cf Mt 11, 10; Lk 7, 27. John's ministry is seen as God's prelude to the saving mission of his Son. The way of the Lord: this prophecy of Deutero-Isaiah concerning the end of the Babylonian exile is here applied to the coming of Jesus; John the Baptist is to prepare the way for him.

1, 6: Clothed in camel's hair . . . waist: the Baptist's garb recalls that of Elijah in 2 Kgs 1, 8. Jesus speaks of the Baptist as Elijah who has already come (Mk 9, 11-13; Mt 17, 10-12; cf Mal 3, 23-24; Lk 1, 17).

1, 8-9: Through the life-giving baptism with the holy Spirit (8), Jesus will create a new people of God. But first he identifies himself with the people of Israel in submitting to John's baptism of repentance and in bearing on their behalf the burden of God's decisive judgment (9; cf 4). As in the desert of Sinai, so here in the wilderness of Judea, Israel's sonship with God is to be renewed.

he saw the heavens being torn open and the Spirit, like a dove, descending upon him.* [11] And a voice came from the heavens, "You are my beloved Son; with you I am well pleased."[f]

The Temptation of Jesus.* [12] At once the Spirit drove him out into the desert,[g] [13] and he remained in the desert for forty days, tempted by Satan. He was among wild beasts, and the angels ministered to him.

II. THE MYSTERY OF JESUS

The Beginning of the Galilean Ministry. [14] After John had been arrested,* Jesus came to Galilee proclaiming the gospel of God:[h] [15] "This is the time of fulfillment. The kingdom of God is at hand. Repent, and believe in the gospel."[i]

The Call of the First Disciples.* [16] As he passed by the Sea of Galilee,[j] he saw Simon and his brother Andrew casting their nets into the sea; they were fishermen. [17] Jesus said to them, "Come after me, and I will make you fishers of men." [18] Then they left their nets and followed him. [19] He walked along a little farther and saw James, the son of Zebedee, and his brother John. They too were in a boat mending their nets. [20] Then he called them. So they left their father Zebedee in the boat along with the hired men and followed him.

The Cure of a Demoniac. [21] * Then they came to Capernaum, and on the sabbath he entered the synagogue and taught.[k] [22] The people were astonished at his teaching, for he taught them as one having authority and not as the scribes.[l] [23] In their synagogue was a man with an unclean spirit;* [24] he cried out, "What have you to do with us,* Jesus of Nazareth? Have you come to destroy us? I know who you are—the Holy One of God!"* [25] Jesus rebuked him and said, "Quiet! Come out of him!" [26] The unclean spirit convulsed him and with a loud cry came out of him. [27] All were amazed and asked one another, "What is this? A new teaching with authority. He commands even the unclean spirits and they obey him." [28] His fame spread everywhere throughout the whole region of Galilee.

The Cure of Simon's Mother-in-Law. [29] [m] On leaving the synagogue he entered the house of Simon and Andrew with James and John. [30] Simon's mother-in-law lay sick with a fever. They immediately told him about her. [31] He approached, grasped her hand, and helped her up. Then the fever left her and she waited on them.

Other Healings. [32] When it was evening, after sunset, they brought to him all who were ill or possessed by demons. [33] The whole town was gathered at the door. [34] He cured many who were sick with various diseases, and he drove out many demons, not permitting them to speak because they knew him.

---

f Ps 2, 7.—g 12-13: Mt 4, 1-11; Lk 4, 1-13.—h 14-15: Mt 4, 12-17; Lk 4, 14-15.—i Mt 3, 2.—j 16-20: Mt 4, 18-22; Lk 5, 2-11.—k 21-28: Lk 4, 31-37.—l Mt 7, 28-29.—m 29-34: Mt 8, 14-16; Lk 4, 38-41.

1, 10-11: *He saw the heavens . . . and the Spirit . . . upon him:* indicating divine intervention in fulfillment of promise. Here the descent of the Spirit on Jesus is meant, anointing him for his ministry; cf Is 11, 2; 42, 1; 61, 1; 63, 9. *A voice . . . with you I am well pleased:* God's acknowledgment of Jesus as his unique Son, the object of his love. His approval of Jesus is the assurance that Jesus will fulfill his messianic mission of salvation.

1, 12-13: The same Spirit who descended on Jesus in his baptism now drives him into the desert for forty days. The result is radical confrontation and temptation by Satan who attempts to frustrate the work of God. The presence of wild beasts may indicate the horror and danger of the desert regarded as the abode of demons or may reflect the paradise motif of harmony among all creatures; cf Is 11, 6-9. The presence of ministering angels to sustain Jesus recalls the angel who guided the Israelites in the desert in the first Exodus (Ex 14, 19; 23, 20) and the angel who supplied nourishment to Elijah in the wilderness (1 Kgs 19, 5-7). The combined forces of good and evil were present to Jesus in the desert. His sustained obedience brings forth the new Israel of God there where Israel's rebellion had brought death and alienation.

1, 14-15: *After John had been arrested:* in the plan of God, Jesus was not to proclaim the good news of salvation prior to the termination of the Baptist's active mission. *Galilee:* in the Mar-

can account, scene of the major part of Jesus' public ministry before his arrest and condemnation. *The gospel of God:* not only the good news from God but about God at work in Jesus Christ. *This is the time of fulfillment:* i.e., of God's promises. *The kingdom of God . . . repent:* see the note on Mt 3, 2.

1, 16-20: These verses narrate the call of the first disciples. See the notes on Mt 4, 18-22 and Mt 4, 20.

1, 21-45: The account of a single day's ministry of Jesus on a sabbath in and outside the synagogue of Capernaum (21-31) combines teaching and miracles of exorcism and healing. Mention is not made of the content of the teaching but of the effect of astonishment and alarm on the people. Jesus' teaching with authority, making an absolute claim on the hearer, was in the best tradition of the ancient prophets, not of the scribes. The narrative continues with events that evening (32-34; see the notes on Mt 8, 14-17) and the next day (35-39). The cleansing in vv 40-45 stands as an isolated story.

1, 23: *An unclean spirit:* so called because of the spirit's resistance to the holiness of God. The spirit knows and fears the power of Jesus to destroy his influence; cf Mk 1, 32.34; 3, 11; 6, 13.

1, 24: *What have you to do with us?:* see the note on Jn 2, 4.

1, 24-25: *The Holy One of God:* not a confession but an attempt to ward off Jesus' power, reflecting the notion that use of the precise name of an opposing spirit would guarantee mastery over him. Jesus silenced the cry of the unclean spirit and drove him out of the man.

Jesus Leaves Capernaum. [35] [n] Rising very early before dawn, he left and went off to a deserted place, where he prayed. [36] Simon and those who were with him pursued him [37] and on finding him said, "Everyone is looking for you." [38] He told them, "Let us go on to the nearby villages that I may preach there also. For this purpose have I come." [39] So he went into their synagogues, preaching and driving out demons throughout the whole of Galilee.

The Cleansing of a Leper. [40] [o] A leper* came to him [and kneeling down] begged him and said, "If you wish, you can make me clean." [41] Moved with pity, he stretched out his hand, touched him, and said to him, "I do will it. Be made clean." [p] [42] The leprosy left him immediately, and he was made clean. [q] [43] Then, warning him sternly, he dismissed him at once. [44] Then he said to him, "See that you tell no one anything, but go, show yourself to the priest and offer for your cleansing what Moses prescribed; that will be proof for them." [r] [45] The man went away and began to publicize the whole matter. He spread the report abroad so that it was impossible for Jesus to enter a town openly. He remained outside in deserted places, and people kept coming to him from everywhere.

CHAPTER 2

The Healing of a Paralytic. [1] * When Jesus returned to Capernaum [s] after some days, it became known that he was at home.* [2] Many gathered together so that there was no longer room for them, not even around the door, and he preached the word to them. [3] They came bringing to him a paralytic carried by four men. [4] Unable to get near Jesus because of the crowd, they opened up the roof above him. After they had broken through, they let down the mat on which the paralytic was lying. [5] When Jesus saw their faith, he said to the paralytic, "Child, your sins are forgiven."* [6] Now some of the scribes* were sitting there asking themselves, [7] "Why does this man speak that way? He is blaspheming.* Who but God alone can forgive sins?" [t] [8] Jesus immediately knew in his mind what they were thinking to themselves, so he said, "Why are you thinking such things in your hearts? [9] Which is easier, to say to the paralytic, 'Your sins are forgiven,' or to say, 'Rise, pick up your mat and walk'? [10] But that you may know that the Son of Man has authority to forgive sins on earth"*—[11] he said to the paralytic, "I say to you, rise, pick up your mat, and go home." [12] He rose, picked up his mat at once, and went away in the sight of everyone. They were all astounded and glorified God, saying, "We have never seen anything like this."

The Call of Levi. [13] [u] Once again he went out along the sea. All the crowd came to him and he taught them.* [14] [v] As he passed by,* he saw Levi, son of Alphaeus, sitting at the customs post. He said to him, "Follow me." And he got up and followed him. [15] While he was at table in his house,*

---

n 35-39: Lk 4, 42-44.—o 40-44: Mt 8, 2-4; Lk 5, 12-14.—p Mk 5, 30.—q Lk 17, 14.—r Lv 14, 2-32.—s 1-12: Mt 9, 2-8; Lk 5, 18-26.—t Is 43, 25.—u Mk 4, 1.—v 14-17: Mt 9, 9-13; Lk 5, 27-32.

1, 40: *A leper:* for the various forms of skin disease, see Lv 13, 1-50 and the note on Lv 13, 2-4. There are only two instances in the Old Testament in which God is shown to have cured a leper (Nm 12, 10-15 and 2 Kgs 5, 1-14). The law of Moses provided for the ritual purification of a leper. In curing the leper, Jesus assumes that the priests will reinstate the cured man into the religious community. See also the note on Lk 5, 14.

2, 1—3, 6: This section relates a series of conflicts between Jesus and the scribes and Pharisees in which the growing opposition of the latter leads to their plot to put Jesus to death (Mk 3, 6).

2, 1-2: *He was at home:* to the crowds that gathered in and outside the house Jesus *preached the word,* i.e., the gospel concerning the nearness of the kingdom and the necessity of repentance and faith (Mk 1, 14).

2, 5: It was the faith of the paralytic and those who carried him that moved Jesus to heal the sick man. Accounts of other miracles of Jesus reveal more and more his emphasis on faith as the requisite for exercising his healing powers (Mk 5, 34; 9, 23-24; 10, 52).

2, 6: *Scribes:* trained in oral interpretation of the written law; in Mark's gospel, adversaries of Jesus, with one exception (Mk 12, 28.34).

2, 7: *He is blaspheming:* an accusation made here and repeated during the trial of Jesus (Mk 14, 60-64).

2, 10: *But that you may know that the Son of Man . . . on earth:* although vv 8-9 are addressed to the scribes, the sudden interruption of thought and structure in v 10 seems not addressed to them nor to the paralytic. Moreover, the early public use of the designation "Son of Man" to unbelieving scribes is most unlikely. The most probable explanation is that Mark's insertion of v 10 is a commentary addressed to Christians for whom he recalls this miracle and who already accept in faith that Jesus is Messiah and Son of God.

2, 13: *He taught them:* see the note on Mk 1, 21-45.

2, 14: *As he passed by:* see the note on Mk 1, 16-20. *Levi, son of Alphaeus:* see the note on Mt 9, 9. *Customs post:* such tax collectors paid a fixed sum for the right to collect customs duties within their districts. Since whatever they could collect above this amount constituted their profit, the abuse of extortion was widespread among them. Hence, Jewish customs officials were regarded as sinners (16), outcasts of society, and disgraced along with their families. *He got up and followed him:* i.e., became a disciple of Jesus.

2, 15: *In his house:* cf v 1; Mt 9, 10. Lk 5, 29 clearly calls it Levi's house.

many tax collectors and sinners sat with Jesus and his disciples; for there were many who followed him. [16] * Some scribes who were Pharisees saw that he was eating with sinners and tax collectors and said to his disciples, "Why does he eat with tax collectors and sinners?" [17] Jesus heard this and said to them [that], "Those who are well do not need a physician,* but the sick do. I did not come to call the righteous but sinners."

The Question about Fasting. * [18] The disciples of John and of the Pharisees were accustomed to fast. [w] People came to him and objected, "Why do the disciples of John and the disciples of the Pharisees fast, but your disciples do not fast?" [19] Jesus answered them, "Can the wedding guests fast* while the bridegroom is with them? As long as they have the bridegroom with them they cannot fast. [20] But the days will come when the bridegroom is taken away from them, and then they will fast on that day. [21] No one sews a piece of unshrunken cloth on an old cloak. If he does, its fullness pulls away, the new from the old, and the tear gets worse. [22] Likewise, no one pours new wine into old wineskins. Otherwise, the wine will burst the skins, and both the wine and the skins are ruined. Rather, new wine is poured into fresh wineskins."

The Disciples and the Sabbath. * [23] As he was passing through a field of grain on the sabbath, his disciples began to make a path while picking the heads of grain. [x] [24] At this the Pharisees said to him, "Look, why are they doing what is unlawful on the sabbath?" [y] [25] He said to them, "Have you never read what David did* when he was in need and he and his companions were hungry? [26] How he went into the house of God when Abiathar was high-priest and ate the bread of offering that only the priests could lawfully eat, and shared it with his companions?" [z] [27] Then he said to them, "The sabbath was made for man,* not man for the sabbath. [a] [28] That is why the Son of Man is lord even of the sabbath." *

CHAPTER 3

A Man with a Withered Hand. [1] *Again he entered the synagogue. [b] There was a man there who had a withered hand. [2] They watched him closely to see if he would cure him on the sabbath so that they might accuse him. [3] He said to the man with the withered hand, "Come up here before us." [4] Then he said to them, "Is it lawful to do good on the sabbath rather than to do evil, to save life rather than to destroy it?" But they remained silent. [5] Looking around at them with anger and grieved at their hardness of heart, he said to the man, "Stretch out your hand." He stretched it out and his hand was restored. [c] [6] The Pharisees went out and immediately took counsel with the Herodians against him to put him to death. *

---

w 18-22: Mt 9, 14-17; Lk 5, 33-39.—x 23-28: Mt 12, 1-8; Lk 6, 1-5.—y Dt 23, 25.—z 1 Sm 21, 2-7 / Lv 24, 5-9.—a 2 Mc 5, 19.—b 1-6: Mt 12, 9-14; Lk 6, 6-11.—c Lk 14, 4.

2, 16-17: This and the following conflict stories reflect a similar pattern: a statement of fact, a question of protest, and a reply by Jesus.

2, 17: *Do not need a physician:* this maxim of Jesus with its implied irony was uttered to silence his adversaries who objected that he ate with *tax collectors and sinners* (16). Because the scribes and Pharisees were self-righteous, they were not capable of responding to Jesus' call to repentance and faith in the gospel.

2, 18-22: This conflict over the question of fasting has the same pattern as vv 16-17; see the notes on Mt 9, 15 and Mt 9, 16-17.

2, 19: *Can the wedding guests fast?:* the bridal metaphor expresses a new relationship of love between God and his people in the person and mission of Jesus to his disciples. It is the inauguration of the new and joyful messianic time of fulfillment and the passing of the old. Any attempt at assimilating the Pharisaic practice of fasting, or of extending the preparatory discipline of John's disciples beyond the arrival of the bridegroom, would be as futile as sewing *a piece of unshrunken cloth on an old cloak* or pouring *new wine into old wineskins* with the resulting destruction of both cloth and wine (21-22). Fasting is rendered superfluous during the earthly ministry of Jesus; cf v 20.

2, 23-28: This conflict regarding the sabbath follows the same pattern as in vv 18-22.

2, 25-26: *Have you never read what David did?:* Jesus defends the action of his disciples on the basis of 1 Sm 21, 2-7 in which an exception is made to the regulation of Lv 24, 9 because of the extreme hunger of David and his men. According to 1 Sm, the priest who gave the bread to David was Ahimelech, father of Abiathar.

2, 27: *The sabbath was made for man:* a reaffirmation of the divine intent of the sabbath to benefit Israel as contrasted with the restrictive Pharisaic tradition added to the law.

2, 28: *The Son of Man is lord even of the sabbath:* Mark's comment on the theological meaning of the incident is to benefit his Christian readers; see the note on Mk 2, 10.

3, 1-5: Here Jesus is again depicted in conflict with his adversaries over the question of sabbath-day observance. His opponents were already ill disposed toward him because they regarded Jesus as a violator of the sabbath. Jesus' question *Is it lawful to do good on the sabbath rather than to do evil?* places the matter in the broader theological context outside the casuistry of the scribes. The answer is obvious. Jesus heals the man with the withered hand in the sight of all and reduces his opponents to silence; cf Jn 5, 17-18.

3, 6: In reporting the plot of the Pharisees and Herodians to put Jesus to death after this series of conflicts in Galilee, Mark uses a pattern that recurs in his account of later controversies in Jerusalem (Mk 11, 17-18; 12, 13-17). The help of the Herodians, supporters of Herod Antipas, tetrarch of Galilee and Perea, is needed to take action against Jesus. Both series of conflicts point to their gravity and to the impending passion of Jesus.

The Mercy of Jesus. [7] * Jesus withdrew toward the sea with his disciples.[d] A large number of people [followed] from Galilee and from Judea. [8] Hearing what he was doing, a large number of people came to him also from Jerusalem, from Idumea, from beyond the Jordan, and from the neighborhood of Tyre and Sidon. [9] He told his disciples to have a boat ready for him because of the crowd, so that they would not crush him. [10] He had cured many and, as a result, those who had diseases were pressing upon him to touch him.[e] [11] * And whenever unclean spirits saw him they would fall down before him and shout, "You are the Son of God."[f] [12] He warned them sternly not to make him known.

The Mission of the Twelve. [13] [g] He went up the mountain* and summoned those whom he wanted and they came to him. [14] [h] He appointed twelve [whom he also named apostles] that they might be with him* and he might send them forth to preach [15] and to have authority to drive out demons: [16] [he appointed the twelve:] Simon, whom he named Peter;* [17] James, son of Zebedee, and John the brother of James, whom he named Boanerges, that is, sons of thunder;[i] [18] Andrew, Philip, Bartholomew, Matthew, Thomas, James the son of Alphaeus; Thaddeus, Simon the Cananean, [19] and Judas Iscariot who betrayed him.

Blasphemy of the Scribes. [20] * He came home.* Again [the] crowd gathered, making it impossible for them even to eat.[j] [21] When his relatives heard of this they set out to seize him, for they said, "He is out of his mind."[k] [22] The scribes who had come from Jerusalem said, "He is possessed by Beelzebul,"* and "By the prince of demons he drives out demons."[l]

Jesus and Beelzebul. [23] Summoning them, he began to speak to them in parables, "How can Satan drive out Satan? [24] If a kingdom is divided against itself, that kingdom cannot stand. [25] And if a house is divided against itself, that house will not be able to stand. [26] And if Satan has risen up against himself and is divided, he cannot stand; that is the end of him. [27] But no one can enter a strong man's house to plunder his property unless he first ties up the strong man. Then he can plunder his house. [28] Amen, I say to you, all sins and all blasphemies that people utter will be forgiven them.[m] [29] But whoever blasphemes against the holy Spirit* will never have forgiveness, but is guilty of an everlasting sin." [30] For they had said, "He has an unclean spirit."

Jesus and His Family. [31] [n] His mother and his brothers arrived. Standing outside they sent word to him and called him. [32] A crowd seated around him told him, "Your mother and your brothers* [and your sisters] are outside asking for you." [33] But he said to them in reply, "Who are my mother and [my] brothers?" [34] And looking around at those seated in the circle he said, "Here are my mother and my brothers. [35] [For] whoever does the will of God is my brother and sister and mother."

d 7-12: Mt 4, 23-25; 12, 15; Lk 6, 17-19.—e Mk 5, 30.—f Mk 1, 34; Lk 4, 41.—g 13-19: Mk 10, 1-4; Lk 6, 12-16.—h Mk 6, 7.—i Mt 16, 18; Jn 1, 42.—j Mk 2, 2.—k Jn 10, 20.—l 22-30: Mt 12, 24-32; Lk 11, 15-22; 12, 10.—m Lk 12, 10.—n 31-35: Mt 12, 46-50; Lk 8, 19-21.

3, 7-19: This overview of the Galilean ministry manifests the power of Jesus to draw people to himself through his teaching and deeds of power. The crowds of Jews from many regions surround Jesus (7-12). This phenomenon prepares the way for creating a new people of Israel. The choice and mission of the Twelve is the prelude (13-19).

3, 11-12: See the note on Mk 1, 24-25.

3, 13: *He went up the mountain:* here and elsewhere the mountain is associated with solemn moments and acts in the mission and self-revelation of Jesus (Mk 6, 46; 9, 2-8; 13, 3). Jesus acts with authority as he *summoned those whom he wanted and they came to him.*

3, 14-15: *He appointed twelve [whom he also named apostles] that they might be with him:* literally "he made," i.e., instituted them as apostles to extend his messianic mission through them (Mk 6, 7-13). See the notes on Mt 10, 1 and Mt 10, 2-4.

3, 16: *Simon, whom he named Peter:* Mark indicates that Simon's name was changed on this occasion. Peter is first in all lists of the apostles (Mt 10, 2; Lk 6, 14; Acts 1, 13; cf 1 Cor 15, 5-8).

3, 20-35: Within the narrative of the coming of Jesus' relatives (20-21) is inserted the account of the unbelieving scribes from Jerusalem who attributed Jesus' power over demons to Beelzebul (22-30); see the note on Mk 5, 21-43. There were those even among the relatives of Jesus who disbelieved and regarded Jesus as *out of his mind* (21). Against this background, Jesus is informed of the arrival of his mother and brothers [and sisters] (32). He responds by showing that not family ties but doing God's will (35) is decisive in the kingdom; cf the note on Mt 12, 46-50.

3, 20: *He came home:* cf Mk 2, 1-2 and see the note on Mk 2, 15.

3, 22: *By Beelzebul:* see the note on Mt 10, 25. Two accusations are leveled against Jesus: (1) that *he is possessed* by an unclean spirit, and (2) *by the prince of demons he drives out demons.* Jesus answers the second charge by a parable (24-27) and responds to the first charge in vv 28-29.

3, 29: *Whoever blasphemes against the holy Spirit:* this sin is called *an everlasting sin* because it attributes to Satan, who is the power of evil, what is actually the work of the holy Spirit, namely, victory over the demons.

3, 32: *Your brothers:* see the note on Mk 6, 3.

CHAPTER 4

The Parable of the Sower. [1] * On another occasion [o] he began to teach by the sea.* A very large crowd gathered around him so that he got into a boat on the sea and sat down. And the whole crowd was beside the sea on land. [p] [2] And he taught them at length in parables, and in the course of his instruction he said to them, [3] * "Hear this! A sower went out to sow. [4] And as he sowed, some seed fell on the path, and the birds came and ate it up. [5] Other seed fell on rocky ground where it had little soil. It sprang up at once because the soil was not deep. [6] And when the sun rose, it was scorched and it withered for lack of roots. [7] Some seed fell among thorns, and the thorns grew up and choked it and it produced no grain. [8] And some seed fell on rich soil and produced fruit. It came up and grew and yielded thirty, sixty, and a hundredfold." [9] He added, "Whoever has ears to hear ought to hear."

The Purpose of the Parables. [10] And when he was alone, those present along with the Twelve questioned him about the parables. [11] * He answered them, "The mystery of the kingdom of God has been granted to you. But to those outside everything comes in parables, [12] so that

'they may look and see but not perceive,
    and hear and listen but not understand,
in order that they may not be converted and be forgiven.' " [q]

[13] * Jesus said to them, "Do you not understand this parable? [r] Then how will you understand any of the parables? [14] The sower sows the word. [15] These are the ones on the path where the word is sown. As soon as they hear, Satan comes at once and takes away the word sown in them. [16] And these are the ones sown on rocky ground who, when they hear the word, receive it at once with joy. [17] But they have no root; they last only for a time. Then when tribulation or persecution comes because of the word, they quickly fall away. [18] Those sown among thorns are another sort. They are the people who hear the word, [19] but worldly anxiety, the lure of riches, and the craving for other things intrude and choke the word, and it bears no fruit. [20] But those sown on rich soil are the ones who hear the

word and accept it and bear fruit thirty and sixty and a hundredfold."

Parable of the Lamp. [21] [s] He said to them, "Is a lamp brought in to be placed under a bushel basket or under a bed, and not to be placed on a lampstand? [t] [22] For there is nothing hidden except to be made visible; nothing is secret except to come to light. [u] [23] Anyone who has ears to hear ought to hear." [24] He also told them, "Take care what you hear. The measure with which you measure will be measured out to you, and still more will be given to you. [v] [25] To the one who has, more will be given; from the one who has not, even what he has will be taken away." [w]

Seed Grows of Itself. * [26] He said, "This is how it is with the kingdom of God; it is as if a man were to scatter seed [x] on the land [27] and would sleep and rise night and day and the seed would sprout and grow, he knows not how. [28] Of its own accord the land yields fruit, first the blade, then the ear, then the full grain in the ear. [29] And

---

o 1-12: Mt 13, 1-13; Lk 8, 4-10.—p Mk 2, 13; Lk 5, 1.—q Is 6, 9; Jn 12, 40; Acts 28, 26; Rom 11, 8.—r 13-20: Mt 13, 18-23; Lk 8, 11-15.—s 21-25: Lk 8, 16-18.—t Mt 5, 15; Lk 11, 33.—u Mt 10, 26; Lk 12, 2.—v Mt 7, 2; Lk 6, 38.—w Mt 13, 12; Lk 19, 26.—x 26-29: Jas 5, 7.

4, 1-34: *In parables* (2): see the note on Mt 13, 3. The use of parables is typical of Jesus' enigmatic method of teaching the crowds (2-9.12) as compared with the interpretation of the parables he gives to his disciples (10-25.33-34), to each group according to its capacity to understand (9-11). The key feature of the parable at hand is the sowing of the seed (3), representing the breakthrough of the kingdom of God into the world. The various types of soil refer to the diversity of response accorded the word of God (4-7). The climax of the parable is the harvest of thirty, sixty, and a hundredfold, indicating the consummation of the kingdom (8). Thus both the present and the future action of God, from the initiation to the fulfillment of the kingdom, is presented through this and other parables (26-29.30-32).

4, 1: *By the sea:* the shore of the Sea of Galilee or a boat near the shore (Mk 2, 13; 3, 7-8) is the place where Mark depicts Jesus teaching the crowds. By contrast the mountain is the scene of Jesus at prayer (Mk 6, 46) or in the process of forming his disciples (Mk 3, 13; 9, 2).

4, 3-8: See the note on Mt 13, 3-8.

4, 11-12: These verses are to be viewed against their background in Mk 3, 6.22 concerning the unbelief and opposition Jesus encountered in his ministry. It is against this background that the distinction in Jesus' method becomes clear of presenting the kingdom to the disbelieving crowd in one manner and to the disciples in another. To the former it is presented in parables and the truth remains hidden; for the latter the parable is interpreted and the mystery is partially revealed because of their faith; see the notes on Mt 13, 11 and Mt 13, 13.

4, 13-20: See the note on Mt 13, 18-23.

4, 26-29: Only Mark records the parable of the seed's growth. Sower and harvester are the same. The emphasis is on the power of the seed to grow of itself without human intervention (27). Mysteriously it produces *blade* and *ear* and *full grain* (28). Thus the kingdom of God initiated by Jesus in proclaiming the word develops quietly yet powerfully until it is fully established by him at the final judgment (29); cf Rv 14, 15.

when the grain is ripe, he wields the sickle at once, for the harvest has come."

The Mustard Seed. 30 *y* He said, "To what shall we compare the kingdom of God, or what parable can we use for it? 31 It is like a mustard seed that, when it is sown in the ground, is the smallest of all the seeds on the earth. 32 But once it is sown, it springs up and becomes the largest of plants and puts forth large branches, so that the birds of the sky can dwell in its shade." * 33 With many such parables *z* he spoke the word to them as they were able to understand it. 34 Without parables he did not speak to them, but to his own disciples he explained everything in private.

The Calming of a Storm at Sea. 35 * On that day, as evening drew on, he said to them, "Let us cross to the other side." *a* 36 Leaving the crowd, they took him with them in the boat just as he was. And other boats were with him. 37 A violent squall came up and waves were breaking over the boat, so that it was already filling up. 38 Jesus was in the stern, asleep on a cushion. They woke him and said to him, "Teacher, do you not care that we are perishing?" 39 He woke up, rebuked the wind, and said to the sea, "Quiet! Be still!" * The wind ceased and there was great calm. 40 Then he asked them, "Why

---

y 30-32: Mt 13, 31-32; Lk 13, 18-19.—z 33-34: Mt 13, 34.— a 35-40: Mt 8, 18.23-37; Lk 8, 22-25.—b Mk 1, 27.—c 1-20: Mt 8, 28-34; Lk 8, 26-39.—d Mt 12, 45; Lk 8, 2; 11, 26.

4, 32: The universality of the kingdom of God is indicated here; cf Ez 17, 23; 31, 6; Dn 4, 17-19.

4, 35—5, 43: After the chapter on parables, Mark narrates four miracle stories: Mk 4, 35-41; 5, 1-20; and two joined together in Mk 5, 21-43. See also the notes on Mt 8, 23-34 and Mt 9, 8-26.

4, 39: *Quiet! Be still!:* as in the case of silencing a demon (Mk 1, 25), Jesus rebukes the wind and subdues the turbulence of the sea by a mere word; see the note on Mt 8, 26.

4, 41: Jesus is here depicted as exercising power over wind and sea. In the Christian community this event was seen as a sign of Jesus' saving presence amid persecutions that threatened its existence.

5, 1: *The territory of the Gerasenes:* the reference is to pagan territory; cf Is 65, 1. Another reading is "Gadarenes"; see the note on Mt 8, 28.

5, 2-6: The man was an outcast from society, dominated by unclean spirits (8.13), living among the tombs. The prostration before Jesus (6) indicates Jesus' power over evil spirits.

5, 7: *What have you to do with me?:* cf Mk 1, 24 and see the note on Jn 2, 4.

5, 9: *Legion is my name:* the demons were numerous and the condition of the possessed man was extremely serious; cf Mt 12, 45.

5, 11: *Herd of swine:* see the note on Mt 8, 30.

---

are you terrified? Do you not yet have faith?" 41 *b* They were filled with great awe and said to one another, "Who then is this whom even wind and sea obey?" *

CHAPTER 5

The Healing of the Gerasene Demoniac. 1 *c* They came to the other side of the sea, to the territory of the Gerasenes. * 2 When he got out of the boat, at once a man* from the tombs who had an unclean spirit met him. 3 The man had been dwelling among the tombs, and no one could restrain him any longer, even with a chain. 4 In fact, he had frequently been bound with shackles and chains, but the chains had been pulled apart by him and the shackles smashed, and no one was strong enough to subdue him. 5 Night and day among the tombs and on the hillsides he was always crying out and bruising himself with stones. 6 Catching sight of Jesus from a distance, he ran up and prostrated himself before him, 7 crying out in a loud voice, "What have you to do with me,* Jesus, Son of the Most High God? I adjure you by God, do not torment me!" 8 (He had been saying to him, "Unclean spirit, come out of the man!") 9 He asked him, "What is your name?" He replied, "Legion is my name.* There are many of us." *d* 10 And he pleaded earnestly with him not to drive them away from that territory.

11 Now a large herd of swine* was feeding there on the hillside. 12 And they pleaded with him, "Send us into the swine. Let us enter them." 13 And he let them, and the unclean spirits came out and entered the swine. The herd of about two thousand rushed down a steep bank into the sea, where they were drowned. 14 The swineherds ran away and reported the incident in the town and throughout the countryside. And people came out to see what had happened. 15 As they approached Jesus, they caught sight of the man who had been possessed by Legion, sitting there clothed and in his right mind. And they were seized with fear. 16 Those who witnessed the incident explained to them what had happened to the possessed man and to the swine. 17 Then they began to beg him to leave their district. 18 As he was getting into the boat, the man who had been possessed pleaded to remain with him.

Mk

19 But he would not permit him but told him instead, "Go home* to your family and announce to them all that the Lord in his pity has done for you." 20 Then the man went off and began to proclaim in the Decapolis what Jesus had done for him; and all were amazed.

Jairus's Daughter and the Woman with a Hemorrhage.* 21 When Jesus had crossed again [in the boat] to the other side, a large crowd gathered around him, and he stayed close to the sea.*e* 22 One of the synagogue officials, named Jairus, came forward.*f* Seeing him he fell at his feet 23 and pleaded earnestly with him, saying, "My daughter is at the point of death. Please, come lay your hands on her* that she may get well and live." 24 He went off with him, and a large crowd followed him and pressed upon him.

25 There was a woman afflicted with hemorrhages for twelve years. 26 She had suffered greatly at the hands of many doctors and had spent all that she had. Yet she was not helped but only grew worse. 27 She had heard about Jesus and came up behind him in the crowd and touched his cloak. 28 She said, "If I but touch his clothes, I shall be cured."* 29 Immediately her flow of blood dried up. She felt in her body that she was healed of her affliction. 30 Jesus, aware at once that power had gone out from him, turned around in the crowd and asked, "Who has touched my clothes?" 31 But his disciples said to him, "You see how the crowd is pressing upon you, and yet you ask, 'Who touched me?' " 32 And he looked around to see who had done it. 33 The woman, realizing what had happened to her, approached in fear and trembling. She fell down before Jesus and told him the whole truth. 34 He said to her, "Daughter, your faith has saved you. Go in peace and be cured of your affliction."*g*

35 While he was still speaking, people from the synagogue official's house arrived and said, "Your daughter has died; why trouble the teacher any longer?"* 36 Disregarding the message that was reported, Jesus said to the synagogue official, "Do not be afraid; just have faith." 37 He did not allow anyone to accompany him inside except Peter, James, and John, the brother of James. 38 When they arrived at the house of the synagogue official, he caught sight of a commotion, people weeping and wailing loudly. 39 *h* So he went in and said to them, "Why this commotion and weeping? The child is not dead but asleep."* 40 And they ridiculed him. Then he put them all out. He took along the child's father and mother and those who were with him and entered the room where the child was. 41 He took the child by the hand and said to her, *"Talitha koum,"* which means, "Little girl, I say to you, arise!"* 42 The girl, a child of twelve, arose immediately and walked around. [At that] they were utterly astounded. 43 He gave strict orders that no one should know this and said that she should be given something to eat.

CHAPTER 6

The Rejection at Nazareth. 1 *i* He departed from there and came to his native place,* accompanied by his disciples. 2 * When the sabbath came he began to teach in the synagogue, and many who heard him were astonished. They said, "Where did this man get all this? What kind of wisdom has been given him? What mighty

---

e Mk 2, 13.—f 22-43: Mt 9, 18-26; Lk 8, 41-56.—g Lk 7, 30.—h 39-40: Acts 9, 40.—i 1-6: Mt 13, 54-58; Lk 4, 16-30.

5, 19: *Go home:* Jesus did not accept the man's request *to remain with him* as a disciple (18), yet invited him to announce to his own people what the Lord had done for him, i.e., proclaim the gospel message to his pagan family; cf Mk 1, 14.39; 3, 14; 13, 10.

5, 21-43: The story of the raising to life of Jairus's daughter is divided into two parts: vv 21-24 and 35-43. Between these two separated parts the account of the cure of the hemorrhage victim (25-34) is interposed. This technique of intercalating or sandwiching one story within another occurs several times in Mk: 3, 19b-21 (22-30) 31-35; 6, 6b-13 (14-29) 30; 11, 12-14 (15-19) 20-25; 14, 53 (54) 55-65 (66-73).

5, 23: *Lay your hands on her:* this act for the purpose of healing is frequent in Mk (6, 5; 7, 32-35; 8, 23-25; 16, 18) and is also found in Mt 9, 18; Lk 4, 40; 13, 13; Acts 9, 17; 28, 8.

5, 28: Both in the case of Jairus and his daughter (23) and in the case of the hemorrhage victim, the inner conviction that physical contact (30) accompanied by faith in Jesus' saving power could effect a cure was rewarded.

5, 35: The faith of Jairus was put to a twofold test: (1) that his daughter might be cured and, now that she had died, (2) that she might be restored to life. His faith contrasts with the lack of faith of the crowd.

5, 39: *Not dead but asleep:* the New Testament often refers to death as sleep (Mt 27, 52; Jn 11, 11; 1 Cor 15, 6; 1 Thes 4, 13-15); see the note on Mt 9, 24.

5, 41: *Arise:* the Greek verb *egeirein* is the verb generally used to express resurrection from death (Mk 6, 14.16; Mt 11, 5; Lk 7, 14) and Jesus' own resurrection (Mk 16, 6; Mt 28, 6; Lk 24, 6).

6, 1: *His native place:* the Greek word *patris* here refers to Nazareth (cf Mk 1, 9; Lk 4, 16.23-24), though it can also mean native land.

6, 2-6: See the note on Mt 13, 54-58.

deeds are wrought by his hands! [3] [j] Is he not the carpenter,* the son of Mary, and the brother of James and Joses and Judas and Simon? And are not his sisters here with us?" And they took offense at him. [4] [k] Jesus said to them, "A prophet is not without honor except in his native place and among his own kin and in his own house."* [5] So he was not able to perform any mighty deed there,* apart from curing a few sick people by laying his hands on them. [6] He was amazed at their lack of faith.

The Mission of the Twelve. He went around to the villages in the vicinity teaching. [7] [l] He summoned the Twelve* and began to send them out two by two and gave them authority over unclean spirits. [8] * He instructed them to take nothing for the journey but a walking stick—no food, no sack, no money in their belts. [9] They were, however, to wear sandals but not a second tunic. [10] He said to them, "Wherever you enter a house, stay there until you leave from there.* [11] Whatever place does not welcome you or listen to you, leave there and shake the dust off your feet in testimony against them." [12] So they went off and preached repentance. [13] They drove out many demons, and they anointed with oil many who were sick [m] and cured them.*

Herod's Opinion of Jesus.* [14] King Herod* heard about it, for his fame had become widespread, and people were saying, [n] "John the Baptist has been raised from the dead; that is why mighty powers are at work in him." [o] [15] Others were saying, "He is Elijah"; still others, "He is a prophet like any of the prophets." [p] [16] But when Herod learned of it, he said, "It is John whom I beheaded. He has been raised up."

The Death of John the Baptist.* [17] Herod was the one who had John arrested and bound in prison on account of Herodias, the wife of his brother Philip, whom he had married. [q] [18] John had said to Herod, "It is not lawful for you to have your brother's wife." [r] [19] Herodias* harbored a grudge against him and wanted to kill him but was unable to do so. [20] Herod feared John, knowing him to be a righteous and holy man, and kept him in custody. When he heard him speak he was very much perplexed, yet he liked to listen to him. [21] She had an opportunity one day when Herod, on his birthday, gave a banquet for his courtiers, his military officers, and the

---

j Mk 15, 40; Mt 12, 46; Jn 6, 42.—k Jn 4, 44.—l 7-11: Mt 10, 1.9-14; Lk 9, 15; 10, 4-11.—m Jas 5, 14.—n 14-16: Lk 9, 7-8.—o 14-29: Mt 14, 1-12.—p Mt 16, 14.—q Lk 3, 19-20.—r Lv 18, 16.

6, 3: *Is he not the carpenter?:* no other gospel calls Jesus a carpenter. Some witnesses have "the carpenter's son," as in Mt 13, 55. *Son of Mary:* contrary to Jewish custom, which calls a man the son of his father, this expression may reflect Mark's own faith that God is the Father of Jesus (Mk 1, 1.11; 8, 38; 13, 32; 14, 36). *The brother of James . . . Simon:* in Semitic usage, the terms 'brother', 'sister' are applied not only to children of the same parents, but to nephews, nieces, cousins, half-brothers, and half-sisters; cf Gn 14, 16; 29, 15; Lv 10, 4. While one cannot suppose that the meaning of a Greek word should be sought in the first place from Semitic usage, the Septuagint often translates the Hebrew *'āḥ* by the Greek word *adelphos*, "brother," as in the cited passages, a fact that may argue for a similar breadth of meaning in some New Testament passages. For instance, there is no doubt that in v 17, "brother" is used of Philip, who was actually the half-brother of Herod Antipas. On the other hand, Mark may have understood the terms literally; see also Mk 3, 31-32; 12, 46; 13, 55-56; Lk 8, 19; Jn 7, 3.5. The question of meaning here would not have arisen but for the faith of the church in Mary's perpetual virginity.

6, 4: *A prophet is not without honor except . . . in his own house:* a saying that finds parallels in other literatures, especially Jewish and Greek, but without reference to a prophet. Comparing himself to previous Hebrew prophets whom the people rejected, Jesus intimates his own eventual rejection by the nation especially in view of the dishonor his own relatives had shown him (Mk 3, 21) and now his townspeople as well.

6, 5: *He was not able to perform any mighty deed there:* according to Mark, Jesus' power could not take effect because of a person's lack of faith.

6, 7-13: The preparation for the mission of the Twelve is seen in the call (1) of the first disciples to be fishers of men (Mk 1, 16-20), (2) then of the Twelve set apart to be with Jesus and to receive authority to preach and expel demons (Mk 3, 13-19). Now they are given the specific mission to exercise that authority in word and power as representatives of Jesus during the time of their formation.

6, 8-9: In Mk the use of a *walking stick* (8) and *sandals* (9) is permitted, but not in Mt 10, 10 nor in Lk 10, 4. Mark does not mention any prohibition to visit pagan territory and to enter Samaritan towns. These differences indicate a certain adaptation to conditions in and outside of Palestine and suggest in Mark's account a later activity in the church. For the rest, Jesus required of his apostles a total dependence on God for food and shelter; cf Mk 6, 35-44; 8, 1-9.

6, 10-11: Remaining in the same house as a guest (10) rather than moving to another offering greater comfort avoided any impression of seeking advantage for oneself and prevented dishonor to one's host. Shaking the dust off one's feet served as testimony against those who rejected the call to repentance.

6, 13: *Anointed with oil . . . cured them:* a common medicinal remedy, but seen here as a vehicle of divine power for healing.

6, 14-16: The various opinions about Jesus anticipate the theme of his identity that reaches its climax in Mk 8, 27-30.

6, 14: *King Herod:* see the note on Mt 14, 1.

6, 17-29: Similarities are to be noted between Mark's account of the imprisonment and death of John the Baptist in this pericope, and that of the passion of Jesus (Mk 15, 1-47). Herod and Pilate, each in turn, acknowledges the holiness of life of one over whom he unjustly exercises the power of condemnation and death (Mk 6, 26-27; 15, 9-10.14-15). The hatred of Herodias toward John parallels that of the Jewish leaders toward Jesus. After the deaths of John and of Jesus, well-disposed persons request the bodies of the victims of Herod and of Pilate in turn to give them respectful burial (Mk 6, 29; 15, 45-46).

6, 19: *Herodias:* see the note on Mt 14, 3.

leading men of Galilee. [22] Herodias's own daughter came in and performed a dance that delighted Herod and his guests. The king said to the girl, "Ask of me whatever you wish and I will grant it to you." [23] He even swore [many things] to her, "I will' grant you whatever you ask of me, even to half of my kingdom." [s] [24] She went out and said to her mother, "What shall I ask for?" She replied, "The head of John the Baptist." [25] The girl hurried back to the king's presence and made her request, "I want you to give me at once on a platter the head of John the Baptist." [26] The king was deeply distressed, but because of his oaths and the guests he did not wish to break his word to her. [27] [t] So he promptly dispatched an executioner with orders to bring back his head. He went off and beheaded him in the prison. [28] He brought in the head on a platter and gave it to the girl. The girl in turn gave it to her mother. [29] When his disciples heard about it, they came and took his body and laid it in a tomb.

The Return of the Twelve. [30] The apostles* gathered together with Jesus and reported all they had done and taught. [u] [31] * He said to them, "Come away by yourselves to a deserted place and rest a while." People were coming and going in great numbers, and they had no opportunity even to eat. [v] [32] So they went off in the boat by themselves to a deserted place. [w] [33] People saw them leaving and many came to know about it. They hastened there on foot from all the towns and arrived at the place before them.

The Feeding of the Five Thousand. [34] When he disembarked and saw the vast crowd, his heart was moved with pity for them, for they were like sheep without a shepherd; and he began to teach them many things. [35] * By now it was already late and his disciples approached him and said, "This is a deserted place and it is already very late. [36] Dismiss them so that they can go to the surrounding farms and villages and buy themselves something to eat." [37] He said to them in reply, "Give them some food yourselves." But they said to him, "Are we to buy two hundred days' wages worth of food and give it to them to eat?" [38] He asked them, "How many loaves do you have? Go and see." And when they had found out they said, "Five loaves and two fish." [39] So he gave orders to have them sit down in groups on the green grass. [40] The people took their places in rows by hundreds and by fifties.* [41] Then, taking the five loaves and the two fish and looking up to heaven, he said the blessing, broke the loaves, and gave them to [his] disciples to set before the people; he also divided the two fish among them all.* [42] They all ate and were satisfied. [43] And they picked up twelve wicker baskets full of fragments and what was left of the fish. [44] Those who ate [of the loaves] were five thousand men.

The Walking on the Water. * [45] Then he made his disciples get into the boat[x] and precede him to the other side toward Bethsaida,* while he dismissed the crowd. [46] And when he had taken leave of them, he went off to the mountain to pray.* [47] When it was evening, the boat was far out on the sea and he was alone on shore. [48] Then he saw that they were tossed about while rowing, for the wind was against them. About the fourth watch of the night, he came toward them walking on the sea.* He meant to pass by them. [49] But when they saw him walking on the sea, they thought it was a

s Est 5, 3.—t 27-28: Lk 9, 9.—u Lk 9, 10.—v Mk 3, 20; Mt 14, 13; Lk 9, 10.—w 32-44: Mt 14, 13-21; Lk 9, 10-17; Jn 6, 1-13—x 45-51: Mt 14, 22-32; Jn 6, 15-21.

6, 30: *Apostles:* here, and in some manuscripts at 3, 14, Mark calls apostles (i.e., those sent forth) the Twelve whom Jesus sends as his emissaries, empowering them to preach, to expel demons, and to cure the sick (13). Only after Pentecost is the title used in the technical sense.

6, 31-34: The withdrawal of Jesus with his disciples to a desert place to rest attracts a great number of people to follow them. Toward this people of the new exodus Jesus is moved with pity; he satisfies their spiritual hunger by teaching them many things, thus gradually showing himself the faithful shepherd of a new Israel; cf Nm 27, 17; Ez 34, 15.

6, 35-44: See the note on Mt 14, 13-21. Compare this section with Mk 8, 1-9. The various accounts of the multiplication of loaves and fishes, two each in Mark and in Matthew and one each in Luke and in John, indicate the wide interest of the early church in their eucharistic gatherings; see, e.g., Mk 6, 41; 8, 6; 14, 22; and recall also the sign of bread in Ex 16; Dt 8, 3-16; Pss 78, 24-25; 105, 40; Wis 16, 20-21.

6, 40: *The people . . . in rows by hundreds and by fifties:* reminiscent of the groupings of Israelites encamped in the desert (Ex 18, 21-25) and of the wilderness tradition of the prophets depicting the transformation of the wasteland into pastures where the true shepherd feeds his flock (Ez 34, 25-26) and makes his people beneficiaries of messianic grace.

6, 41: On the language of this verse as eucharistic (cf Mk 14, 22), see the notes on Mt 14, 19.20. Jesus observed the Jewish table ritual of blessing God before partaking of food.

6, 45-52: See the note on Mt 14, 22-33.

6, 45: *To the other side toward Bethsaida:* a village at the northeastern shore of the Sea of Galilee.

6, 46: *He went off to the mountain to pray:* see Mk 1, 35-38. In Jn 6, 15 Jesus withdrew to evade any involvement in the false messianic hopes of the multitude.

6, 48: *Walking on the sea:* see the notes on Mt 14, 22-33 and on Jn 6, 19.

ghost and cried out. [50] They had all seen him and were terrified. But at once he spoke with them, "Take courage, it is I, do not be afraid!"* [51] He got into the boat with them and the wind died down. They were [completely] astounded. [52] They had not understood the incident of the loaves.* On the contrary, their hearts were hardened. [y]

The Healings at Gennesaret. [53] [z] After making the crossing, they came to land at Gennesaret and tied up there. [54] As they were leaving the boat, people immediately recognized him. [55] They scurried about the surrounding country and began to bring in the sick on mats to wherever they heard he was. [56] Whatever villages or towns or countryside he entered, they laid the sick in the marketplaces and begged him that they might touch only the tassel on his cloak; and as many as touched it were healed. [a]

---

y Mk 4, 13.—z 53-56: Mt 14, 34-36.—a Mk 5, 27-28; Acts 5, 15.—b 1-23: Mt 15, 1-20.—c Is 29, 13.—d Ex 21, 17; Lv 20, 9; Dt 5, 16; Eph 6, 2.—e 14-23: Mt 15, 10-20.—f Mk 4, 10.13.—g Acts 10, 15.

6, 50: *It is I, do not be afraid!:* literally, "I am." This may reflect the divine revelatory formula of Ex 3, 14; Is 41, 4.10.14; 43, 1-3.10.13. Mark implies the hidden identity of Jesus as Son of God.

6, 52: *They had not understood . . . the loaves:* the revelatory character of this sign and that of the walking on the sea completely escaped the disciples. *Their hearts were hardened:* in Mk 3, 5-6 hardness of heart was attributed to those who did not accept Jesus and plotted his death. Here the same disposition prevents the disciples from comprehending Jesus' self-revelation through signs; cf Mk 8, 17.

7, 1-23: See the note on Mt 15, 1-20. Against the Pharisees' narrow, legalistic, and external practices of piety in matters of purification (2-5), external worship (6-7), and observance of commandments, Jesus sets in opposition the true moral intent of the divine law (8-13). But he goes beyond contrasting the law and Pharisaic interpretation of it. The parable of vv 14-15 in effect sets aside the law itself in respect to clean and unclean food. He thereby opens the way for unity between Jew and Gentile in the kingdom of God, intimated by Jesus' departure into pagan territory beyond Galilee. For similar contrast see Mk 2, 1—3, 6; 3, 20-35; 6, 1-6.

7, 3: *Carefully washing their hands:* refers to ritual purification.

7, 5: *Tradition of the elders:* the body of detailed, unwritten, human laws regarded by the scribes and Pharisees to have the same binding force as that of the Mosaic law; cf Gal 1, 14.

7, 11: *Qorban:* a formula for a gift to God, dedicating the offering to the temple, so that the giver might continue to use it for himself but not give it to others, even needy parents.

7, 16: Verse 16, "Anyone who has ears to hear ought to hear," is omitted because it is lacking in some of the best Greek manuscripts and was probably transferred here by scribes from Mk 4, (9).23.

7, 17: *Away from the crowd . . . the parable:* in this context of privacy the term *parable* refers to something hidden, about to be revealed to the disciples; cf Mk 4, 10-11.34. Jesus sets the Mosaic food laws in the context of the kingdom of God where they are abrogated, and he declares moral defilement the only cause of uncleanness.

7, 19: *(Thus he declared all foods clean):* if this bold declaration goes back to Jesus, its force was not realized among Jewish Christians in the early church; cf Acts 10, 1—11, 18.

CHAPTER 7

The Tradition of the Elders. * [1] Now when the Pharisees with some scribes who had come from Jerusalem gathered around him, [b] [2] they observed that some of his disciples ate their meals with unclean, that is, unwashed, hands. [3] (For the Pharisees and, in fact, all Jews, do not eat without carefully washing their hands,* keeping the tradition of the elders. [4] And on coming from the marketplace they do not eat without purifying themselves. And there are many other things that they have traditionally observed, the purification of cups and jugs and kettles [and beds].) [5] So the Pharisees and scribes questioned him, "Why do your disciples not follow the tradition of the elders* but instead eat a meal with unclean hands?" [6] He responded, "Well did Isaiah prophesy about you hypocrites, as it is written: [c]

'This people honors me with their lips,
    but their hearts are far from me;
[7] In vain do they worship me,
    teaching as doctrines human precepts.'

[8] You disregard God's commandment but cling to human tradition." [9] He went on to say, "How well you have set aside the commandment of God in order to uphold your tradition! [10] For Moses said, 'Honor your father and your mother,' and 'Whoever curses father or mother shall die.' [d] [11] Yet you say, 'If a person says to father or mother, "Any support you might have had from me is *qorban*" '* (meaning, dedicated to God), [12] you allow him to do nothing more for his father or mother. [13] You nullify the word of God in favor of your tradition that you have handed on. And you do many such things." [14] [e] He summoned the crowd again and said to them, "Hear me, all of you, and understand. [15] Nothing that enters one from outside can defile that person; but the things that come out from within are what defile." [16] *

[17] [f] When he got home away from the crowd his disciples questioned him about the parable.* [18] He said to them, "Are even you likewise without understanding? Do you not realize that everything that goes into a person from outside cannot defile, [19] [g] since it enters not the heart but the stomach and passes out into the latrine?" (Thus he declared all foods clean.)* [20] "But what comes out of a person, that is what

defiles. [21] *h* From within people, from their hearts, come evil thoughts, unchastity, theft, murder, [22] adultery, greed, malice, deceit, licentiousness, envy, blasphemy, arrogance, folly. [23] All these evils come from within and they defile."

The Syrophoenician Woman's Faith. [24] *i* From that place he went off to the district of Tyre.* He entered a house and wanted no one to know about it, but he could not escape notice. [25] Soon a woman whose daughter had an unclean spirit heard about him. She came and fell at his feet. [26] The woman was a Greek, a Syrophoenician by birth, and she begged him to drive the demon out of her daughter. *j* [27] He said to her, "Let the children be fed first.* For it is not right to take the food of the children and throw it to the dogs." [28] She replied and said to him, "Lord, even the dogs under the table eat the children's scraps." [29] Then he said to her, "For saying this, you may go. The demon has gone out of your daughter." [30] When the woman went home, she found the child lying in bed and the demon gone.

The Healing of a Deaf Man. [31] *k* Again he left the district of Tyre and went by way of Sidon to the Sea of Galilee, into the district of the Decapolis. [32] And people brought to him a deaf man who had a speech impediment and begged him to lay his hand on him. [33] He took him off by himself away from the crowd. He put his finger into the man's ears and, spitting, touched his tongue; [34] then he looked up to heaven and groaned, and said to him, *"Ephphatha!"* (that is, "Be opened!") [35] And [immediately] the man's ears were opened, his speech impediment was removed, and he spoke plainly. [36] He ordered them not to tell anyone. But the more he ordered them not to, the more they proclaimed it.* [37] They were exceedingly astonished and they said, "He has done all things well. He makes the deaf hear and [the] mute speak." *l*

CHAPTER 8

The Feeding of the Four Thousand.* [1] In those days when there again was a great crowd without anything to eat, *m* he summoned the disciples and said, [2] "My heart is moved with pity for the crowd, because they have been with me now for three days and have nothing to eat. [3] If I send them

away hungry to their homes, they will collapse on the way, and some of them have come a great distance." [4] His disciples answered him, "Where can anyone get enough bread to satisfy them here in this deserted place?" [5] Still he asked them, "How many loaves do you have?" "Seven," they replied. [6] He ordered the crowd to sit down on the ground. Then, taking the seven loaves he gave thanks, broke them, and gave them to his disciples to distribute, and they distributed them to the crowd.* [7] They also had a few fish. He said the blessing over them and ordered them distributed also. [8] They ate and were satisfied. They picked up the fragments left over—seven baskets. [9] There were about four thousand people.

He dismissed them [10] and got into the boat with his disciples and came to the region of Dalmanutha.

The Demand for a Sign. [11] * The Pharisees came forward and began to argue with him, *n* seeking from him a sign from heaven to test him. *o* [12] He sighed from the depth of his spirit and said, "Why does this generation seek a sign? Amen, I say to you, no sign will be given to this generation."

h Jer 17, 9.—i 24-30: Mt 15, 21-28.—j Mt 8, 29.—k 31-37: Mt 15, 29-31.—l Mt 15, 31.—m 1-10: Mk 6, 34-44; Mt 15, 32-39.—n 11-13: Mt 12, 38-39; 16, 1-4.—o Lk 11, 16.

7, 24-37: The withdrawal of Jesus to the district of Tyre may have been for a respite (24), but he soon moved onward to Sidon and, by way of the Sea of Galilee, to the Decapolis. These districts provided a Gentile setting for the extension of his ministry of healing because the people there acknowledged his power (29.37). The actions attributed to Jesus (33-35) were also used by healers of the time.

7, 27-28: The figure of a household in which children at table are fed first and then their leftover food is given to the dogs under the table is used effectively to acknowledge the prior claim of the Jews to the ministry of Jesus; however, Jesus accedes to the Gentile woman's plea for the cure of her afflicted daughter because of her faith.

7, 36: *The more they proclaimed it:* the same verb *proclaim* attributed here to the crowd in relation to the miracles of Jesus is elsewhere used in Mark for the preaching of the gospel on the part of Jesus, of his disciples, and of the Christian community (Mk 1, 14; 13, 10; 14, 9). Implied in the action of the crowd is a recognition of the salvific mission of Jesus; see the note on Mt 11, 5-6.

8, 1-10: The two accounts of the multiplication of loaves and fishes (Mk 8, 1-10 and Mk 6, 31-44) have eucharistic significance. Their similarity of structure and themes but dissimilarity of detail are considered by many to refer to a single event that, however, developed in two distinct traditions, one Jewish Christian and the other Gentile Christian, since Jesus in Mark's presentation (Mk 7, 24-37) has extended his saving mission to the Gentiles.

8, 6: See the note on Mk 6, 41.

8, 11-12: The objection of the Pharisees that Jesus' miracles are unsatisfactory for proving the arrival of God's kingdom is comparable to the request of the crowd for a sign in Jn 6, 30-31. Jesus' response shows that a sign originating in human demand will not be provided; cf Nm 14, 11.22.

13 Then he left them, got into the boat
again, and went off to the other shore.

The Leaven of the Pharisees. 14 [p] They
had forgotten to bring bread, and they had
only one loaf with them in the boat. 15 He
enjoined them, "Watch out, guard against
the leaven of the Pharisees and the leaven
of Herod."* 16 They concluded among
themselves that it was because they had no
bread. 17 When he became aware of this he
said to them, "Why do you conclude that it
is because you have no bread? Do you not
yet understand or comprehend? Are your
hearts hardened? [q] 18 Do you have eyes and
not see, ears and not hear? And do you not
remember, [r] 19 when I broke the five loaves
for the five thousand, how many wicker
baskets full of fragments you picked up?"
They answered him, "Twelve." 20 "When I
broke the seven loaves for the four
thousand, how many full baskets of fragments did you pick up?" They answered
[him], "Seven." 21 He said to them, "Do
you still not understand?"

The Blind Man of Bethsaida.* 22 When
they arrived at Bethsaida, they brought to
him a blind man and begged him to touch
him. 23 He took the blind man by the hand
and led him outside the village. Putting
spittle on his eyes he laid his hands on him
and asked, "Do you see anything?" [s]
24 Looking up he replied, "I see people
looking like trees and walking." 25 Then he
laid hands on his eyes a second time and he
saw clearly; his sight was restored and he
could see everything distinctly. 26 Then he
sent him home and said, "Do not even go
into the village."

Mk

III. THE MYSTERY BEGINS TO BE REVEALED

Peter's Confession about Jesus.* 27 Now
Jesus and his disciples set out for the villages of Caesarea Philippi. [t] Along the way
he asked his disciples, "Who do people say
that I am?" 28 They said in reply, "John the
Baptist, others Elijah, still others one of
the prophets." 29 And he asked them, "But
who do you say that I am?" Peter said to
him in reply, "You are the Messiah."
30 Then he warned them not to tell anyone
about him.

The First Prediction of the Passion. 31 [u]
He began to teach them that the Son of
Man* must suffer greatly and be rejected
by the elders, the chief priests, and the
scribes, and be killed, and rise after three
days. 32 He spoke this openly. Then Peter
took him aside and began to rebuke him.
33 At this he turned around and, looking at
his disciples, rebuked Peter and said, "Get
behind me, Satan. You are thinking not as
God does, but as human beings do."

The Conditions of Discipleship. 34 He summoned the crowd with his disciples and
said* to them, "Whoever wishes to come
after me must deny himself, take up his

p 14-21: Mt 16, 5-12; Lk 12, 1.—q Mk 4, 13.—r Jer 5, 21; Ez 12, 2.—s Mk 7, 33; Jn 9, 6.—t 27-30: Mt 16, 13-20; Lk 9, 18-21.—u 31-38: Mt 16, 21-27; Lk 9, 22-26.

8, 15: *The leaven of the Pharisees . . . of Herod:* the corruptive action of leaven (1 Cor 5, 6-8; Gal 5, 9) was an apt symbol of the evil dispositions both of the Pharisees (Mk 8, 11-13; 7, 5-13) and of Herod (Mk 6, 14-29) toward Jesus. The disciples of Jesus are warned against sharing such rebellious attitudes toward Jesus; cf vv 17, 21.

8, 22-26: Jesus' actions and the gradual cure of the blind man probably have the same purpose as in the case of the deaf man (Mk 7, 31-37). Some commentators regard the cure as an intended symbol of the gradual enlightenment of the disciples concerning Jesus' messiahship.

8, 27-30: This episode is the turning point in Mark's account of Jesus in his public ministry. Popular opinions concur in regarding him as a prophet. The disciples by contrast believe him to be the Messiah. Jesus acknowledges this identification but prohibits them from making his messianic office known to avoid confusing it with ambiguous contemporary ideas on the nature of that office. See further the notes on Mt 16, 13-20.

8, 31: *Son of Man:* an enigmatic title. It is used in Dn 7, 13-14 as a symbol of "the saints of the Most High," the faithful Israelites who receive the everlasting kingdom from the Ancient One (God). They are represented by a human figure that contrasts with the various beasts who represent the previous kingdoms of the earth. In the Jewish apocryphal books of 1 Enoch and 4 Ezra the "Son of Man" is not, as in Dn, a group, but a unique figure of extraordinary spiritual endowments, who will be revealed as the one through whom the everlasting kingdom decreed by God will be established. It is possible though doubtful that this individualization of the Son of Man figure had been made in Jesus' time, and therefore his use of the title in that sense is questionable. Of itself, this expression means simply a human being, or, indefinitely, someone, and there are evidences of this use in pre-Christian times. Its use in the New Testament is probably due to Jesus' speaking of himself in that way, "a human being," and the later church's taking this in the sense of the Jewish apocrypha and applying it to him with that meaning. *Rejected by the elders, the chief priests, and the scribes:* the supreme council called the Sanhedrin was made up of seventy-one members of these three groups and presided over by the high priest. It exercised authority over the Jews in religious matters. See the note on Mt 8, 20.

8, 34-35: This utterance of Jesus challenges all believers to authentic discipleship and total commitment to himself through self-renunciation and acceptance of the cross of suffering, even to the sacrifice of life itself. *Whoever wishes to save his life will lose it . . . will save it:* an expression of the ambivalence of life and its contrasting destiny. Life seen as mere self-centered earthly existence and lived in denial of Christ ends in destruction, but when lived in loyalty to Christ, despite earthly death, it arrives at fullness of life.

cross, and follow me.[v] [35] For whoever wishes to save his life will lose it, but whoever loses his life for my sake and that of the gospel* will save it.[w] [36] What profit is there for one to gain the whole world and forfeit his life? [37] What could one give in exchange for his life? [38] Whoever is ashamed of me and of my words in this faithless and sinful generation, the Son of Man will be ashamed of when he comes in his Father's glory with the holy angels."[x]

CHAPTER 9

[1] [y] He also said to them, "Amen, I say to you, there are some standing here who will not taste death until they see that the kingdom of God has come in power."*

The Transfiguration of Jesus.* [2] After six days Jesus took Peter, James, and John and led them up a high mountain apart by themselves.[z] And he was transfigured before them, [3] and his clothes became dazzling white, such as no fuller on earth could bleach them. [4] Then Elijah appeared to them along with Moses, and they were conversing with Jesus. [5] Then Peter said to Jesus in reply, "Rabbi, it is good that we are here! Let us make three tents: one for you, one for Moses, and one for Elijah."* [6] He hardly knew what to say, they were so terrified. [7] Then a cloud came, casting a shadow over them;* then from the cloud came a voice, "This is my beloved Son. Listen to him." [8] Suddenly, looking around, they no longer saw anyone but Jesus alone with them.

The Coming of Elijah.* [9] As they were coming down from the mountain, he charged them not to relate what they had seen to anyone, except when the Son of Man had risen from the dead.[a] [10] So they kept the matter to themselves, questioning what rising from the dead meant. [11] [b] Then they asked him, "Why do the scribes say that Elijah must come first?" [12] He told them, "Elijah will indeed come first and restore all things, yet how is it written regarding the Son of Man that he must suffer greatly and be treated with contempt? [13] But I tell you that Elijah has come and they did to him whatever they pleased, as it is written of him."[c]

The Healing of a Boy with a Demon.* [14] When they came to the disciples,[d] they saw a large crowd around them and scribes arguing with them. [15] Immediately on seeing him, the whole crowd was utterly amazed. They ran up to him and greeted him. [16] He asked them, "What are you arguing about with them?" [17] Someone from the crowd answered him, "Teacher, I have brought to you my son possessed by a mute spirit. [18] Wherever it seizes him, it throws him down; he foams at the mouth, grinds his teeth, and becomes rigid. I asked your disciples to drive it out, but they were unable to do so." [19] He said to them in reply, "O faithless generation, how long will I be with you? How long will I endure you? Bring him to me." [20] They brought the boy to him. And when he saw him, the spirit immediately threw the boy into convulsions. As he fell to the ground, he began to roll around and foam at the mouth. [21] Then he questioned his father, "How long has this been happening to him?" He replied, "Since childhood. [22] It has often thrown

---

v Mt 10, 38-39; 16, 24-27; Lk 14, 26-27.—w Jn 12, 25.—x Mt 10, 33; Lk 12, 8.—y Mt 16, 28; Lk 9, 27.—z 2-13: Mt 17, 1-13; Lk 9, 28-36.—a Mk 8, 31.—b 11-12: Is 53, 3; Mal 3, 23.—c 1 Kgs 19, 2-10.—d 14-29: Mt 17, 14-21; Lk 9, 37-43.

8, 35: *For my sake and that of the gospel:* Mark here, as at Mk 10, 29, equates Jesus with the gospel.

9, 1: *There are some standing . . . come in power:* understood by some to refer to the establishment by God's power of his kingdom on earth in and through the church; more likely, as understood by others, a reference to the imminent parousia.

9, 2-8: Mk and Mt 17, 1 place the transfiguration of Jesus six days after the first prediction of his passion and death and his instruction to the disciples on the doctrine of the cross; Lk 9, 28 has "about eight days." Thus the transfiguration counterbalances the prediction of the passion by affording certain of the disciples insight into the divine glory that Jesus possessed. His glory will overcome his death and that of his disciples; cf 2 Cor 3, 18; 2 Pt 1, 16-19. The heavenly voice (7) prepares the disciples to understand that in the divine plan Jesus must die ignominiously before his messianic glory is made manifest; cf Lk 24, 25-27. See further the note on Mt 17, 1-8.

9, 5: Moses and Elijah represent respectively law and prophecy in the Old Testament and are linked to Mt. Sinai; cf Ex 19, 16—20, 17; 1 Kgs 19, 2.8-14. They now appear with Jesus as witnesses to the fulfillment of the law and the prophets taking place in the person of Jesus as he appears in glory.

9, 7: *A cloud came, casting a shadow over them:* even the disciples enter into the mystery of his glorification. In the Old Testament the cloud covered the meeting tent, indicating the Lord's presence in the midst of his people (Ex 40, 34-35) and came to rest upon the temple in Jerusalem at the time of its dedication (1 Kgs 8, 10).

9, 9-13: At the transfiguration of Jesus his disciples had seen Elijah. They were perplexed because, according to the rabbinical interpretation of Mal 3, 23-24, Elijah was to come first. Jesus' response shows that Elijah has come, in the person of John the Baptist, to prepare for the day of the Lord. Jesus *must suffer greatly and be treated with contempt* (12) like the Baptist (13); cf Mk 6, 17-29.

9, 14-29: The disciples' failure to effect a cure seems to reflect unfavorably on Jesus (14-18.22). In response Jesus exposes their lack of trust in God (19) and scores their lack of prayer (29), i.e., of conscious reliance on God's power when acting in Jesus' name. For Mt, see the note on Mt 17, 14-20. Luke 9, 37-43 centers attention on Jesus' sovereign power.

him into fire and into water to kill him. But if you can do anything, have compassion on us and help us." ²³ Jesus said to him, " 'If you can!' Everything is possible to one who has faith." ²⁴ Then the boy's father cried out, "I do believe, help my unbelief!" ²⁵ Jesus, on seeing a crowd rapidly gathering, rebuked the unclean spirit and said to it, "Mute and deaf spirit, I command you: come out of him and never enter him again!" ²⁶ Shouting and throwing the boy into convulsions, it came out. He became like a corpse, which caused many to say, "He is dead!" ²⁷ But Jesus took him by the hand, raised him, and he stood up. ²⁸ When he entered the house, his disciples asked him in private, "Why could we not drive it out?" ²⁹ He said to them, "This kind can only come out through prayer."*

The Second Prediction of the Passion. ³⁰ ᵉ They left from there and began a journey through Galilee, but he did not wish anyone to know about it.ᶠ ³¹ He was teaching his disciples and telling them, "The Son of Man is to be handed over to men and they will kill him, and three days after his death he will rise." ³² But they did not understand the saying, and they were afraid to question him.

IV. THE FULL REVELATION OF THE MYSTERY

The Greatest in the Kingdom.* ³³ They came to Capernaum and, once inside the

---

e Jn 7, 1.—f 30-32: Mk 8, 31; Mt 17, 22-23; Lk 9, 43-45.—g 33-37: Mt 18, 1-5; Lk 9, 46-48.—h Mt 20, 27.—i Mt 10, 40; 18, 5; Jn 13, 20.—j 38-41: Nm 11, 28; Lk 9, 49-50; 1 Cor 12, 3.—k Mt 12, 30.—l Mt 10, 42; 1 Cor 3, 23.—m 42-47: Mt 5, 29-30; 18, 6-9; Lk 17, 1-2.—n Is 66, 24.—o Lv 2, 13; Mt 5, 13; Lk 14, 34-35; Col 4, 6.

9, 29: *This kind can only come out through prayer:* a variant reading adds "and through fasting."

9, 33-37: Mark probably intends this incident and the sayings that follow as commentary on the disciples' lack of understanding (32). Their role in Jesus' work is one of service, especially to the poor and lowly. Children were the symbol Jesus used for the *anawim,* the poor in spirit, the lowly in the Christian community.

9, 38-41: Jesus warns against jealousy and intolerance toward others, such as exorcists who do *not follow us.* The saying in v 40 is a broad principle of the divine tolerance. Even the smallest courtesies shown to those who teach in Jesus' name do not go unrewarded.

9, 43.45.47: *Gehenna:* see the note on Mt 5, 22.

9, 44.46: These verses, lacking in some important early manuscripts, are here omitted as scribal additions. They simply repeat v 48, itself a modified citation of Is 66, 24.

9, 49: *Everyone will be salted with fire:* so the better manuscripts. Some add "every sacrifice will be salted with salt." The purifying and preservative use of salt in food (Lv 2, 13) and the refinement effected through fire refer here to comparable effects in the spiritual life of the disciples of Jesus.

---

house, he began to ask them, "What were you arguing about on the way?"ᵍ ³⁴ But they remained silent. They had been discussing among themselves on the way who was the greatest. ³⁵ Then he sat down, called the Twelve, and said to them, "If anyone wishes to be first, he shall be the last of all and the servant of all."ʰ ³⁶ Taking a child he placed it in their midst, and putting his arms around it he said to them, ³⁷ "Whoever receives one child such as this in my name, receives me; and whoever receives not me but the One who sent me."ⁱ

Another Exorcist.* ³⁸ John said to him,ʲ "Teacher, we saw someone driving out demons in your name, and we tried to prevent him because he does not follow us." ³⁹ Jesus replied, "Do not prevent him. There is no one who performs a mighty deed in my name who can at the same time speak ill of me. ⁴⁰ For whoever is not against us is for us.ᵏ ⁴¹ Anyone who gives you a cup of water to drink because you belong to Christ, amen, I say to you, will surely not lose his reward.ˡ

Temptations to Sin.⁴² ᵐ "Whoever causes one of these little ones who believe [in me] to sin, it would be better for him if a great millstone were put around his neck and he were thrown into the sea. ⁴³ If your hand causes you to sin, cut it off. It is better for you to enter into life maimed than with two hands to go into Gehenna,* into the unquenchable fire. [⁴⁴]* ⁴⁵ And if your foot causes you to sin, cut if off. It is better for you to enter into life crippled than with two feet to be thrown into Gehenna. [⁴⁶]* ⁴⁷ And if your eye causes you to sin, pluck it out. Better for you to enter into the kingdom of God with one eye than with two eyes to be thrown into Gehenna, ⁴⁸ where 'their worm does not die, and the fire is not quenched.' ⁿ

The Simile of Salt. ⁴⁹ "Everyone will be salted with fire.* ⁵⁰ Salt is good, but if salt becomes insipid, with what will you restore its flavor? Keep salt in yourselves and you will have peace with one another." ᵒ

CHAPTER 10

Marriage and Divorce. ¹ He set out from there and went into the district of Judea [and] across the Jordan. Again crowds gathered around him and, as was his custom, he again taught them. [2]* The Pharisees approached and asked, "Is it lawful for a husband to divorce his wife?" They were testing him.[p] [3] He said to them in reply, "What did Moses command you?" [4] They replied, "Moses permitted him to write a bill of divorce and dismiss her." [q] [5] But Jesus told them, "Because of the hardness of your hearts he wrote you this commandment. [6] But from the beginning of creation, 'God made them male and female.[r] [7] For this reason a man shall leave his father and mother [and be joined to his wife],[s] [8] and the two shall become one flesh.' So they are no longer two but one flesh. [9] Therefore what God has joined together, no human being must separate." [10] In the house the disciples again questioned him about this. [11] [t] He said to them, "Whoever divorces his wife and marries another commits adultery against her; [12] and if she divorces her husband and marries another, she commits adultery."

Blessing of the Children. [13] [u] And people were bringing children to him that he might touch them, but the disciples rebuked them.[v] [14] When Jesus saw this he became indignant and said to them, "Let the children come to me; do not prevent them, for the kingdom of God belongs to such as these. [15] Amen, I say to you, whoever does not accept the kingdom of God like a child* will not enter it." [w] [16] Then he embraced them and blessed them, placing his hands on them.

The Rich Man. [17] [x] As he was setting out on a journey, a man ran up, knelt down before him, and asked him, "Good teacher, what must I do to inherit eternal life?" [18] Jesus answered him, "Why do you call me good?* No one is good but God alone. [19] You know the commandments: 'You shall not kill; you shall not commit adultery; you shall not steal; you shall not bear false witness; you shall not defraud; honor your father and your mother.'" [y] [20] He replied and said to him, "Teacher, all of these I have observed from my youth." [21] Jesus, looking at him, loved him and said to him, "You are lacking in one thing. Go, sell what you have, and give to [the] poor and you will have treasure in heaven; then come, follow me." [22] At that statement his face fell, and he went away sad, for he had many possessions.

[23]* Jesus looked around and said to his disciples, "How hard it is for those who have wealth to enter the kingdom of God!" [z] [24] The disciples were amazed at his words. So Jesus again said to them in reply, "Children, how hard it is to enter the kingdom of God! [25] It is easier for a camel to pass through [the] eye of [a] needle than for one who is rich to enter the kingdom of God." [26] They were exceedingly astonished and said among themselves, "Then who can be saved?" [27] Jesus looked at them and said, "For human beings it is impossible, but not for God. All things are possible for God." [28] Peter began to say to him, "We have given up everything and followed you." [29] Jesus said, "Amen, I say to you, there is no one who has given up house or brothers or sisters or mother or father or children or lands for my sake and for the sake of the gospel [30] who will not receive a hundred times more now in this present age: houses and brothers and sisters and mothers and children and lands, with persecutions, and eternal life in the age to come. [31] But many that are first will be last, and [the] last will be first." [a]

The Third Prediction of the Passion. [32] [b] They were on the way, going up to Jerusalem, and Jesus went ahead of them. They were amazed, and those who followed were afraid. Taking the Twelve aside again, he began to tell them what was

---

p 2-12: Mt 19, 3-9.—q Dt 24, 1-4.—r Gn 1, 27.—s 7-8: Gn 2, 24; 1 Cor 6, 16; Eph 5, 31.—t 11-12: Mt 5, 32; Lk 16, 18; 1 Cor 7, 10-11.—u 13-16: Mt 19, 13-15; Lk 18, 15-17.—v Lk 9, 47.— w Mt 18, 3.—x 17-31: Mt 19, 16-30; Lk 18, 18-30.—y Ex 20, 12-16; Dt 5, 16-21.—z Prv 11, 28.—a Mt 19, 30; Lk 13, 30.—b 32-34: Mk 8, 31; Mt 20, 17-19; Lk 18, 31-33.

10, 2-9: In the dialogue between Jesus and the Pharisees on the subject of divorce, Jesus declares that the law of Moses permitted divorce (Dt 24, 1) only *because of the hardness of your hearts* (4-5). In citing Gn 1, 27 and Gn 2, 24, Jesus proclaims permanence to be the divine intent from the beginning concerning human marriage (6-8). He reaffirms this with the declaration that *what God has joined together, no human being must separate* (9). See further the notes on Mt 5, 31-32 and Mt 19, 3-9.

10, 15: *Whoever does not accept the kingdom of God like a child:* i.e., in total dependence upon and obedience to the gospel; cf Mt 18, 3-4.

10, 18: *Why do you call me good?:* Jesus repudiates the term "good" for himself and directs it to God, the source of all goodness who alone can grant the gift of eternal life; cf Mt 19, 16-17.

10, 23-27: In the Old Testament wealth and material goods are considered a sign of God's favor (Jb 1, 10; Ps 128, 1-2; Is 3, 10). The words of Jesus in 23-25 provoke astonishment among the disciples because of their apparent contradiction of the Old Testament concept (24.26). Since wealth, power, and merit generate false security, Jesus rejects them utterly as a claim to enter the kingdom. Achievement of salvation is beyond human capability and depends solely on the goodness of God who offers it as a gift (27).

THE GOLDEN GATE — A city gate was very important in the lives of the ancients. Markets were held there and the main item sold gave its name to the gate ("Sheep Gate," etc.); important announcements were made at the city gate; there the law was read, legal business was transacted and public gatherings were held.

The above is a view of "the beautiful gate." This gate in the present wall built by the Turks in the 17th century A.D. overlooks the Kidron Valley and Gethsemani. Christians have traditionally venerated this gate as the place of Jesus' triumphal entry into Jerusalem. It is quite probable that Jesus did enter the city through a gate in the ancient wall located approximately where this Golden Gate (now walled up) stands. (See Mk 11, 11)

PALM SUNDAY IN JERUSALEM — A modern Procession on Palm Sunday from Bethphage, via the Mount of Olives and Gethsemani through St. Stephen's Gate to St. Anne's Convent—in commemoration of Christ's triumphal entry into Jerusalem. In the background is the Church of All Nations directly opposite the Golden Gate through which Christ passed. (See Mk 11, 1-11)

VILLAGE OF BETHANY — View of Bethany, the home of Mary, Martha and Lazarus, situated about two miles southeast of Jerusalem and sometimes referred to as the "Judean home of Jesus." The tower in the center marks the tomb of Lazarus. The ruins at the upper right are the remains of a medieval abbey. It was to this village that Jesus retired after the triumphal entry into Jerusalem. (See Mk 11, 11)

going to happen to him. [33] "Behold, we are going up to Jerusalem, and the Son of Man will be handed over to the chief priests and the scribes, and they will condemn him to death and hand him over to the Gentiles [34] who will mock him, spit upon him, scourge him, and put him to death, but after three days he will rise."

Ambition of James and John. [35] [c] Then James and John, the sons of Zebedee, came to him and said to him, "Teacher, we want you to do for us whatever we ask of you." [36] He replied, "What do you wish [me] to do for you?" [37] They answered him, "Grant that in your glory we may sit one at your right and the other at your left." [38] [d] Jesus said to them, "You do not know what you are asking. Can you drink the cup that I drink or be baptized with the baptism with which I am baptized?"* [39] They said to him, "We can." Jesus said to them, "The cup that I drink, you will drink, and with the baptism with which I am baptized, you will be baptized; [40] but to sit at my right or at my left is not mine to give but is for those for whom it has been prepared." [41] When the ten heard this, they became indignant at James and John. [42] * Jesus summoned them and said to them,[e] "You know that those who are recognized as rulers over the Gentiles lord it over them, and their great ones make their authority over them felt. [43] But it shall not be so among you. Rather, whoever wishes to be great among you will be your servant;

---

c 35-45: Mt 20, 20-28.—d Lk 12, 50.—e 42-45: Lk 22, 25-27.—f 46-52: Mt 20, 29-34; Lk 18, 35-43.—g 1-10: Mt 21, 1-9; Lk 19, 29-38; Jn 12, 12-15.—h 9-10: 2 Sm 7, 16; Ps 118, 26.

10, 38-40: *Can you drink the cup . . . I am baptized?:* the metaphor of drinking the cup is used in the Old Testament to refer to acceptance of the destiny assigned by God; see the note on Ps 11, 6. In Jesus' case, this involves divine judgment on sin that Jesus the innocent one is to expiate on behalf of the guilty (Mk 14, 24; Is 53, 5). His baptism is to be his crucifixion and death for the salvation of the human race; cf Lk 12, 50. The request of James and John for a share in the glory (35-37) must of necessity involve a share in Jesus' sufferings, the endurance of tribulation and suffering for the gospel (39). The authority of assigning places of honor in the kingdom is reserved to God (40).

10, 42-45: Whatever authority is to be exercised by the disciples must, like that of Jesus, be rendered as service to others (45) rather than for personal aggrandizement (42-44). The service of Jesus is his passion and death for the sins of the human race (45); cf Mk 14, 24; Is 53, 11-12; Mt 26, 28; Lk 22, 19-20.

10, 46-52: See the notes on Mt 9, 27-31 and Mt 20, 29-34.

11, 1-11: In Mark's account Jesus takes the initiative in ordering the preparation for his entry into Jerusalem (1-6) even as he later orders the preparation of his last Passover supper (Mk 14, 12-16). In vv 9-10 the greeting Jesus receives stops short of proclaiming him Messiah. He is greeted rather as the prophet of the coming messianic kingdom. Contrast Mt 21, 9.

---

[44] whoever wishes to be first among you will be the slave of all. [45] For the Son of Man did not come to be served but to serve and to give his life as a ransom for many."

The Blind Bartimaeus.* [46] They came to Jericho.[f] And as he was leaving Jericho with his disciples and a sizable crowd, Bartimaeus, a blind man, the son of Timaeus, sat by the roadside begging. [47] On hearing that it was Jesus of Nazareth, he began to cry out and say, "Jesus, son of David, have pity on me." [48] And many rebuked him, telling him to be silent. But he kept calling out all the more, "Son of David, have pity on me." [49] Jesus stopped and said, "Call him." So they called the blind man, saying to him, "Take courage; get up, he is calling you." [50] He threw aside his cloak, sprang up, and came to Jesus. [51] Jesus said to him in reply, "What do you want me to do for you?" The blind man replied to him, "Master, I want to see." [52] Jesus told him, "Go your way; your faith has saved you." Immediately he received his sight and followed him on the way.

CHAPTER 11

The Entry into Jerusalem.* [1] When they drew near to Jerusalem,[g] to Bethphage and Bethany at the Mount of Olives, he sent two of his disciples [2] and said to them, "Go into the village opposite you, and immediately on entering it, you will find a colt tethered on which no one has ever sat. Untie it and bring it here. [3] If anyone should say to you, 'Why are you doing this?' reply, 'The Master has need of it and will send it back here at once.' " [4] So they went off and found a colt tethered at a gate outside on the street, and they untied it. [5] Some of the bystanders said to them, "What are you doing, untying the colt?" [6] They answered them just as Jesus had told them to, and they permitted them to do it. [7] So they brought the colt to Jesus and put their cloaks over it. And he sat on it. [8] Many people spread their cloaks on the road, and others spread leafy branches that they had cut from the fields. [9] Those preceding him as well as those following kept crying out:[h]

"Hosanna!
    Blessed is he who comes in the name
        of the Lord!

10　　Blessed is the kingdom of our father
　　　　David that is to come!
　　Hosanna in the highest!"

[11] He entered Jerusalem and went into the temple area. He looked around at everything and, since it was already late, went out to Bethany with the Twelve.[i]

Jesus Curses a Fig Tree.* [12] The next day as they were leaving Bethany he was hungry.[j] [13] Seeing from a distance a fig tree in leaf, he went over to see if he could find anything on it. When he reached it he found nothing but leaves; it was not the time for figs. [14] And he said to it in reply, "May no one ever eat of your fruit again!" And his disciples heard it.

Cleansing of the Temple.* [15] They came to Jerusalem,[k] and on entering the temple area he began to drive out those selling and buying there. He overturned the tables of the money changers and the seats of those who were selling doves. [16] He did not permit anyone to carry anything through the temple area. [17] Then he taught them saying, "Is it not written:

　　'My house shall be called a house of
　　　　prayer for all peoples'?
　　But you have made it a den of
　　　　thieves."[l]

[18] The chief priests and the scribes came to hear of it and were seeking a way to put him to death, yet they feared him because the whole crowd was astonished at his teaching. [19] When evening came, they went out of the city.[m]

The Withered Fig Tree. [20] [n] Early in the morning, as they were walking along, they saw the fig tree withered to its roots. [21] Peter remembered and said to him, "Rabbi, look! The fig tree that you cursed has withered." [22] Jesus said to them in reply, "Have faith in God. [23] Amen, I say to you, whoever says to this mountain, 'Be lifted up and thrown into the sea,' and does not doubt in his heart but believes that what he says will happen, it shall be done for him.[o] [24] Therefore I tell you, all that you ask for in prayer, believe that you will receive it and it shall be yours.[p] [25] When you stand to pray, forgive anyone against whom you have a grievance, so that your heavenly Father may in turn forgive you your transgressions.[q] [26]"*

The Authority of Jesus Questioned.* [27] They returned once more to Jerusalem.[r]

As he was walking in the temple area, the chief priests, the scribes, and the elders approached him [28] and said to him, "By what authority are you doing these things? Or who gave you this authority to do them?" [29] Jesus said to them, "I shall ask you one question. Answer me, and I will tell you by what authority I do these things. [30] Was John's baptism of heavenly or of human origin? Answer me." [31] They discussed this among themselves and said, "If we say, 'Of heavenly origin,' he will say, '[Then] why did you not believe him?' [32] But shall we say, 'Of human origin'?"—they feared the crowd, for they all thought John really was a prophet. [33] So they said to Jesus in reply, "We do not know." Then Jesus said to them, "Neither shall I tell you by what authority I do these things."

CHAPTER 12

Parable of the Tenants.* [1] He began to speak to them in parables.[s] "A man planted a vineyard, put a hedge around it, dug a wine press, and built a tower. Then he leased it to tenant farmers and left on a journey.[t] [2] At the proper time he sent a servant to the tenants to obtain from them some of the produce of the vineyard. [3] But they seized him, beat him, and sent him away empty-handed. [4] Again he sent them another servant. And that one they beat over the head and treated shamefully. [5] He

i Mt 21, 10.17.—j 12-14: Mt 21, 18-20; Lk 13, 6-9.—k 15-18: Mt 21, 12-13; Lk 19, 45-46; Jn 2, 14-16.—l Is 56, 7; Jer 7, 11.—m Lk 21, 37.—n 20-24: Mt 21, 20-22.—o Mt 17, 20-21; Lk 17, 6.—p Mt 7, 7; Jn 11, 22; 14, 13.—q Mt 6, 14; 18, 35.—r 27-33: Mt 21, 23-27; Lk 20, 1-8.—s 1-12: Mt 21, 33-46; Lk 20, 9-19.—t Is 5, 1-7; Jer 2, 21.

11, 12-14: Jesus' search for fruit on the fig tree recalls the prophets' earlier use of this image to designate Israel; cf Jer 8, 13; 29, 17; Jl 1, 7; Hos 9, 10.16. Cursing the fig tree is a parable in action representing Jesus' judgment (20) on barren Israel and the fate of Jerusalem for failing to receive his teaching; cf Is 34, 4; Hos 2, 14; Lk 13, 6-9.

11, 15-19: See the note on Mt 21, 12-17.

11, 26: This verse, which reads, "But if you do not forgive, neither will your heavenly Father forgive your transgressions," is omitted in the best manuscripts. It was probably added by copyists under the influence of Mt 6, 15.

11, 27-33: The mounting hostility toward Jesus came from the chief priests, the scribes, and the elders (27); the Herodians and the Pharisees (Mk 12, 13); and the Sadducees (Mk 12, 18). By their rejection of God's messengers, John the Baptist and Jesus, they incurred the divine judgment implied in vv 27-33 and confirmed in the parable of the vineyard tenants (Mk 12, 1-12).

12, 1-12: The vineyard denotes Israel (Is 5, 1-7). The tenant farmers are the religious leaders of Israel. God is the owner of the vineyard. His servants are his messengers, the prophets. The beloved son is Jesus (Mk 1, 11; 9, 7; Mt 3, 17; 17, 5; Lk 3, 22; 9, 35). The punishment of the tenants refers to the religious leaders, and the transfer of the vineyard to others refers to the people of the new Israel.

sent yet another whom they killed. So, too, many others; some they beat, others they killed. ⁶He had one other to send, a beloved son. He sent him to them last of all, thinking, 'They will respect my son.' ⁷But those tenants said to one another, 'This is the heir. Come, let us kill him, and the inheritance will be ours.' ⁸So they seized him and killed him, and threw him out of the vineyard. ⁹What [then] will the owner of the vineyard do? He will come, put the tenants to death, and give the vineyard to others. ¹⁰Have you not read this scripture passage: ᵘ

'The stone that the builders rejected
   has become the cornerstone;
¹¹ by the Lord has this been done,
   and it is wonderful in our eyes'?"

¹²They were seeking to arrest him, but they feared the crowd, for they realized that he had addressed the parable to them. So they left him and went away.

Paying Taxes to the Emperor. ¹³ * They sent some Pharisees ᵛ and Herodians to him to ensnare him ʷ in his speech.* ¹⁴They came and said to him, "Teacher, we know that you are a truthful man and that you are not concerned with anyone's opinion. You do not regard a person's status but teach the way of God in accordance with the truth. Is it lawful to pay the census tax to Caesar or not? Should we pay or should we not pay?" ¹⁵Knowing their hypocrisy he said to them, "Why are you testing me? Bring me a denarius to look at." ¹⁶They brought one to him and he said to them, "Whose image and inscription is this?" They replied to him, "Caesar's." ¹⁷So Jesus said to them, "Repay to Caesar what belongs to Caesar and to God what belongs to God." They were utterly amazed at him. ˣ

u 10-11: Ps 118, 22-23; Is 28, 16.—v 13-27: Mt 22, 15-33; Lk 20, 20-39.—w Mk 3, 6.—x Rom 13, 7.—y Dt 25, 5.—z Ex 3, 6.—a 28-34: Mt 22, 34-40; Lk 10, 25-28.—b Dt 6, 4-5.—c Lv 19, 18; Rom 13, 9; Gal 5, 14; Jas 2, 8.—d Dt 6, 4; Ps 40, 7-9.—e Mt 22, 46; Lk 20, 40.—f 35-37: Mt 22, 41-45; Lk 20, 41-44.

12, 13-34: In the ensuing conflicts (cf also Mk 2, 1—3, 6) Jesus vanquishes his adversaries by his responses to their questions and reduces them to silence (34).

12, 13-17: See the note on Mt 22, 15-22.

12, 18-27: See the note on Mt 22, 23-33.

12, 28-34: See the note on Mt 22, 34-40.

12, 35-37: Jesus questions the claim of the scribes about the Davidic descent of the Messiah, not to deny it (Mt 1, 1; Acts 2, 20.34; Rom 1, 3; 2 Tm 2, 8) but to imply that he is more than this. His superiority derives from his transcendent origin, to which David himself attested when he spoke of the Messiah with the name "Lord" (Ps 110, 1). See also the note on Mt 22, 41-46.

The Question about the Resurrection.* ¹⁸Some Sadducees, who say there is no resurrection, came to him and put this question to him, ¹⁹saying, "Teacher, Moses wrote for us, 'If someone's brother dies, leaving a wife but no child, his brother must take the wife and raise up descendants for his brother.' ʸ ²⁰Now there were seven brothers. The first married a woman and died, leaving no descendants. ²¹So the second married her and died, leaving no descendants, and the third likewise. ²²And the seven left no descendants. Last of all the woman also died. ²³At the resurrection [when they arise] whose wife will she be? For all seven had been married to her." ²⁴Jesus said to them, "Are you not misled because you do not know the scriptures or the power of God? ²⁵When they rise from the dead, they neither marry nor are given in marriage, but they are like the angels in heaven. ²⁶As for the dead being raised, have you not read in the Book of Moses, in the passage about the bush, how God told him, 'I am the God of Abraham, [the] God of Isaac, and [the] God of Jacob'? ᶻ ²⁷He is not God of the dead but of the living. You are greatly misled."

The Greatest Commandment.* ²⁸One of the scribes, ᵃ when he came forward and heard them disputing and saw how well he had answered them, asked him, "Which is the first of all the commandments?" ²⁹Jesus replied, "The first is this: 'Hear, O Israel! The Lord our God is Lord alone! ³⁰You shall love the Lord your God with all your heart, with all your soul, with all your mind, and with all your strength.' ᵇ ³¹The second is this: 'You shall love your neighbor as yourself.' There is no other commandment greater than these." ᶜ ³²The scribe said to him, "Well said, teacher. You are right in saying, 'He is One and there is no other than he.' ³³And 'to love him with all your heart, with all your understanding, with all your strength, and to love your neighbor as yourself' is worth more than all burnt offerings and sacrifices." ᵈ ³⁴And when Jesus saw that [he] answered with understanding, he said to him, "You are not far from the kingdom of God." And no one dared to ask him any more questions. ᵉ

The Question about David's Son.* ³⁵As Jesus was teaching in the temple area he said, ᶠ "How do the scribes claim that the

Messiah is the son of David? [36] David himself, inspired by the holy Spirit, said:

'The Lord said to my lord,
"Sit at my right hand
until I place your enemies under your feet." '[g]

[37] David himself calls him 'lord'; so how is he his son?" [The] great crowd heard this with delight.

Denunciation of the Scribes.* [38] In the course of his teaching he said,[h] "Beware of the scribes, who like to go around in long robes and accept greetings in the marketplaces, [39] seats of honor in synagogues, and places of honor at banquets. [40] They devour the houses of widows and, as a pretext, recite lengthy prayers. They will receive a very severe condemnation."

The Poor Widow's Contribution.* [41] He sat down opposite the treasury and observed how the crowd put money into the treasury.[i] Many rich people put in large sums. [42] A poor widow also came and put in two small coins worth a few cents. [43] Calling his disciples to himself, he said to them, "Amen, I say to you, this poor widow put in more than all the other contributors to the treasury. [44] For they have all contributed from their surplus wealth, but she, from her poverty, has contributed all she had, her whole livelihood."

CHAPTER 13

The Destruction of the Temple Foretold.*
[1] As he was making his way out of the temple area one of his disciples said to him, "Look, teacher, what stones and what buildings!"[j] [2] Jesus said to him, "Do you see these great buildings? There will not be one stone left upon another that will not be thrown down."

The Signs of the End. [3] *As he was sitting on the Mount of Olives opposite the temple area, Peter, James, John, and Andrew asked him privately,[k] [4] "Tell us, when will this happen, and what sign will there be when all these things are about to come to an end?" [5] Jesus began to say to them, "See that no one deceives you.[l] [6] Many will come in my name saying, 'I am he,' and they will deceive many. [7] When you hear of wars and reports of wars do not be alarmed; such things must happen, but it will not yet be the end. [8] Nation will rise

against nation and kingdom against kingdom. There will be earthquakes from place to place and there will be famines. These are the beginnings of the labor pains.

The Coming Persecution. [9][m] "Watch out for yourselves. They will hand you over to the courts. You will be beaten in synagogues. You will be arraigned before governors and kings because of me, as a witness before them. [10] But the gospel must first be preached to all nations.* [11] When they lead you away and hand you over, do not worry beforehand about what you are to say.[n] But say whatever will be given to you at that hour. For it will not be you who are speaking but the holy Spirit. [12] Brother will hand over brother to death, and the father his child; children will rise up against parents and have them put to death. [13] You will be hated by all because of my name. But the one who perseveres to the end will be saved.

The Great Tribulation. [14][o] "When you see the desolating abomination standing* where he should not (let the reader understand), then those in Judea must flee to the mountains,[p] [15] [and] a person on a housetop must not go down or enter to get anything out of his house,[q] [16] and a person in

g Ps 110, 1.—h 38-40: Mt 23, 1-7; Lk 11, 43; 20, 45-47.—i 41-44: Lk 21, 1-4.—j 1-2: Mt 24, 1-2; Lk 21, 5-6.—k 3-8: Mt 24, 3-8; Lk 21, 7-11.—l Eph 5, 6; 2 Thes 2, 3.—m 9-13: Mt 24, 9-14; Lk 21, 12-19.—n 11-12: Mt 10, 19-22; Lk 12, 11-12.—o 14-23: Mt 24, 15-22; Lk 21, 20-24.—p Dn 9, 27; Mt 24, 15.—q Lk 17, 31.

12, 38-40: See the notes on Mk 7, 1-23 and Mt 23, 1-39.

12, 41-44: See the note on Lk 21, 1-4.

13, 1-2: The reconstructed temple with its precincts, begun under Herod the Great ca. 20 B.C., was completed only some seven years before it was destroyed by fire in A.D. 70 at the hands of the Romans; cf Jer 26, 18; Mt 24, 1-2. For the dating of the reconstruction of the temple, see further the note on Jn 2, 20.

13, 3-37: Jesus' prediction of the destruction of the temple (2) provoked questions that the four named disciples put to him in private regarding the time and the sign when all *these things are about to come to an end* (3-4). The response to their questions was Jesus' eschatological discourse prior to his imminent death. It contained instruction and consolation exhorting the disciples and the church to faith and obedience through the trials that would confront them (5-13). The sign is the presence of *the desolating abomination* (14; see Dn 9, 27), i.e., of the Roman power profaning the temple. Flight from Jerusalem is urged rather than defense of the city through misguided messianic hope (14-23). Intervention will occur only after destruction (24-27), which will happen before the end of the first Christian generation (28-31). No one but the Father knows the precise time, or that of the parousia (32); hence the necessity of constant vigilance (33-37). Luke sets the parousia at a later date, after "the time of the Gentiles" (Lk 21, 24). See also the notes on Mt 24, 1—25, 46.

13, 10: *The gospel . . . to all nations:* the period of the Christian mission.

13, 14: The participle *standing* is masculine, in contrast to the neuter at Mt 24, 15.

a field must not return to get his cloak. [17] Woe to pregnant women and nursing mothers in those days. [18] Pray that this does not happen in winter. [19] For those times will have tribulation such as has not been since the beginning of God's creation until now, nor ever will be.[r] [20] If the Lord had not shortened those days, no one would be saved; but for the sake of the elect whom he chose, he did shorten the days. [21] If anyone says to you then, 'Look, here is the Messiah! Look, there he is!' do not believe it. [22] False messiahs and false prophets will arise and will perform signs and wonders in order to mislead, if that were possible, the elect. [23] Be watchful! I have told it all to you beforehand.

The Coming of the Son of Man. [24] [s] "But in those days after that tribulation

the sun will be darkened,
    and the moon will not give its light,[t]
[25] and the stars will be falling from the sky,
    and the powers in the heavens will be shaken.

[26] [u] And then they will see 'the Son of Man coming in the clouds' with great power and glory,[*] [27] and then he will send out the angels and gather [his] elect from the four winds, from the end of the earth to the end of the sky.

The Lesson of the Fig Tree. [28] [v] "Learn a lesson from the fig tree. When its branch becomes tender and sprouts leaves, you know that summer is near. [29] In the same way, when you see these things happening, know that he is near, at the gates. [30] Amen, I say to you, this generation will not pass away until all these things have taken place. [31] Heaven and earth will pass away, but my words will not pass away.

Need for Watchfulness. [32] "But of that day or hour, no one knows, neither the angels in heaven, nor the Son, but only the Father. [33] [w] Be watchful! Be alert! You do not know when the time will come. [34] It is like a man traveling abroad. He leaves home and places his servants in charge, each with his work, and orders the gatekeeper to be on the watch.[x] [35] Watch, therefore; you do not know when the lord of the house is coming, whether in the evening, or at midnight, or at cockcrow, or in the morning. [36] May he not come suddenly and find you sleeping. [37] What I say to you, I say to all: 'Watch!' "

CHAPTER 14

The Conspiracy against Jesus. [1] * The Passover and the Feast of Unleavened Bread* were to take place in two days' time.[y] So the chief priests and the scribes were seeking a way to arrest him by treachery and put him to death. [2] They said, "Not during the festival, for fear that there may be a riot among the people."

The Anointing at Bethany. * [3] When he was in Bethany reclining at table in the house of Simon the leper,[z] a woman came with an alabaster jar of perfumed oil, costly genuine spikenard. She broke the alabaster jar and poured it on his head. [4] There were some who were indignant. "Why has there been this waste of perfumed oil? [5] It could have been sold for more than three hundred days' wages and the money given to the poor." They were infuriated with her. [6] Jesus said, "Let her alone. Why do you make trouble for her? She has done a good thing for me. [7] The poor you will always have with you, and whenever you wish you can do good to them, but you will not always have me. [8] She has done what

---

r Dn 12, 1.—s 24-27: Mt 24, 29-31; Lk 21, 25-27.—t Is 13, 10; Ez 32, 7; Jl 2, 10.—u Mk 14, 62; Dn 7, 13-14.—v 28-32: Mt 24, 32-36; Lk 21, 29-33.—w 33-37: Mt 24, 42; 25, 13-15.—x Mt 25, 14-30; Lk 19, 12-27.—y 1-2: Mt 26, 2-5; Lk 22, 1-2; Jn 11, 45-53.—z 3-9: Mt 26, 6-13; Jn 12, 1-8.

13, 26: *Son of Man . . . with great power and glory:* Jesus cites this text from Dn 7, 13 in his response to the high priest, *Are you the Messiah?* (Mk 14, 61). In Ex 34, 5; Lv 16, 2; and Nm 11, 25 the clouds indicate the presence of the divinity. Thus in his role of Son of Man, Jesus is a heavenly being who will come in power and glory.

14, 1—16, 8: In the movement of Mark's gospel the cross is depicted as Jesus' way to glory in accordance with the divine will. Thus the passion narrative is seen as the climax of Jesus' ministry.

14, 1: *The Passover and the Feast of Unleavened Bread:* the connection between the two festivals is reflected in Ex 12, 3-20; 34, 18; Lv 23, 4-8; Nm 9, 2-14; 28, 16-17; Dt 16, 1-8. The Passover commemorated the redemption from slavery and the departure of the Israelites from Egypt by night. It began at sundown after the Passover lamb was sacrificed in the temple in the afternoon of the fourteenth day of the month of Nisan. With the Passover supper on the same evening was associated the eating of unleavened bread. The latter was continued through Nisan 21, a reminder of the affliction of the Israelites and of the haste surrounding their departure. Praise and thanks to God for his goodness in the past were combined at this dual festival with the hope of future salvation. *The chief priests . . . to death:* the intent to put Jesus to death was plotted for a long time but delayed for fear of the crowd (Mk 3, 6; 11, 18; 12, 12).

14, 3-9: At Bethany on the Mount of Olives, a few miles from Jerusalem, *in the house of Simon the leper,* Jesus defends a woman's loving action of anointing his head with perfumed oil in view of his impending death and burial as a criminal, in which case his body would not be anointed. See further the note on Jn 12, 7. He assures the woman of the remembrance of her deed in the worldwide preaching of the good news.

she could. She has anticipated anointing my body for burial. [9]Amen, I say to you, wherever the gospel is proclaimed to the whole world, what she has done will be told in memory of her."

The Betrayal by Judas. [10] [a] Then Judas Iscariot, one of the Twelve, went off to the chief priests to hand him over to them. [11]When they heard him they were pleased and promised to pay him money. Then he looked for an opportunity to hand him over.

Preparations for the Passover. [12] [b] On the first day of the Feast of Unleavened Bread, when they sacrificed the Passover lamb,* his disciples said to him, "Where do you want us to go and prepare for you to eat the Passover?" [13]He sent two of his disciples and said to them, "Go into the city and a man will meet you, carrying a jar of water.* Follow him. [14]Wherever he enters, say to the master of the house, 'The Teacher says, "Where is my guest room where I may eat the Passover with my disciples?" ' [15]Then he will show you a large upper room furnished and ready. Make the preparations for us there." [16]The disciples then went off, entered the city, and found it just as he had told them; and they prepared the Passover.

The Betrayer. [17] [c] When it was evening, he came with the Twelve. [18]And as they reclined at table and were eating, Jesus said, "Amen, I say to you, one of you will betray me, one who is eating with me."* [19]They began to be distressed and to say to him, one by one, "Surely it is not I?" [20]He said to them, "One of the Twelve, the one who dips with me into the dish. [21]For the

Son of Man indeed goes, as it is written of him,* but woe to that man by whom the Son of Man is betrayed. It would be better for that man if he had never been born."

The Lord's Supper. [22]*While they were eating,[d] he took bread, said the blessing, broke it, and gave it to them, and said, "Take it; this is my body." [23]Then he took a cup, gave thanks, and gave it to them, and they all drank from it. [24]He said to them, "This is my blood of the covenant, which will be shed* for many. [25]Amen, I say to you, I shall not drink again the fruit of the vine until the day when I drink it new in the kingdom of God." [26]Then, after singing a hymn,* they went out to the Mount of Olives.[e]

Peter's Denial Foretold.* [27]Then Jesus said to them, "All of you will have your faith shaken, for it is written:

'I will strike the shepherd,
    and the sheep will be dispersed.'[f]

[28]But after I have been raised up, I shall go before you to Galilee." [29]Peter said to him, "Even though all should have their faith shaken, mine will not be." [30]Then Jesus said to him, "Amen, I say to you, this very night before the cock crows twice you will deny me three times." [31]But he vehemently replied, "Even though I should have to die with you, I will not deny you." And they all spoke similarly.

The Agony in the Garden. [32]*Then they came to a place named Gethsemane,[g] and he said to his disciples, "Sit here while I

14, 22-24: The actions and words of Jesus express within the framework of the Passover meal and the transition to a new covenant the sacrifice of himself through the offering of his body and blood in anticipation of his passion and death. His *blood of the covenant* both alludes to the ancient rite of Ex 24, 4-8 and indicates the new community that the sacrifice of Jesus will bring into being (Mt 26, 26-28; Lk 22, 19-20; 1 Cor 11, 23-25).

14, 24: *Which will be shed:* see the note on Mt 26, 27-28. *For many:* the Greek preposition *hyper* is a different one from that at Mt 26, 28 but the same as that found at Lk 22, 19.20 and 1 Cor 11, 24. The sense of both words is vicarious, and it is difficult in Hellenistic Greek to distinguish between them. For *many* in the sense of "all," see the note on Mt 20, 28.

14, 26: *After singing a hymn:* Pss 114-118, thanksgiving songs concluding the Passover meal.

14, 27-31: Jesus predicted that the Twelve would waver in their faith, even abandon him, despite their protestations to the contrary. Yet he reassured them that after his resurrection he would regather them in Galilee (Mk 16, 7; cf Mt 26, 32; 28, 7.10.16; Jn 21), where he first summoned them to be his followers as he began to preach the good news (Mk 1, 14-20).

14, 32-34: The disciples who had witnessed the raising to life of the daughter of Jairus (Mk 5, 37) and the transfiguration of their Master (Mk 9, 2) were now invited to witness his degradation and agony and to watch and pray with him.

a 10-11: Mt 26, 14-16; Lk 22, 3-6.—b 12-16: Mt 26, 17-19; Lk 22, 7-13.—c 17-21: Mt 26, 20-24; Lk 22, 21-23; Jn 13, 21-26.—d 22-25: Mt 26, 26-30; Lk 22, 19-20; 1 Cor 11, 23-25.—e 26-31: Mt 26, 30-35; Lk 22, 34.39; Jn 13, 36-38.—f Zec 13, 7; Jn 16, 32.—g 32-42: Mt 26, 36-46; Lk 22, 40-46.

14, 12: *The first day of the Feast of Unleavened Bread . . . the Passover lamb:* a less precise designation of the day for sacrificing the Passover lamb as evidenced by some rabbinical literature. For a more exact designation, see the note on Mk 14, 1. It was actually Nisan 14.

14, 13: *A man . . . carrying a jar of water:* perhaps a prearranged signal, for only women ordinarily carried water in jars. The Greek word used here, however, implies simply a person and not necessarily a male.

14, 18: *One of you will betray me, one who is eating with me:* contrasts the intimacy of table fellowship at the Passover meal with the treachery of the traitor; cf Ps 41, 10.

14, 21: *The Son of Man indeed goes, as it is written of him:* a reference to Ps 41, 10 cited by Jesus concerning Judas at the Last Supper; cf Jn 13, 18-19.

THE UPPER ROOM — In Jerusalem an "upper room" was frequently built on the roofs of houses and used in summer because it was cooler than the regular living quarters. (Mk 14, 15; Lk 22, 12; Acts 1, 13; 20, 8)

The room above is a medieval structure marking the traditional site in the southwestern corner of the Upper City of Jerusalem where the Last Supper took place as well as the descent of the Holy Spirit on the disciples. (See 14, 14-17; Acts 2, 1-11)

MOUNT OF OLIVES — A range of hills with three peaks rising east of Jerusalem beyond the Kidron Valley. In the foreground is the church of All Nations built in the Garden of Gethsemane; above and to the right of the church of the Agony and in the center on the summit is the tower of the church of the Ascension. This Mount was closely connected with the closing years of our Lord's life and it was here that he retired after the Last Supper. (See Mk 14, 26)

GARDEN OF GETHSEMANE — Close-up of the Garden across the Kidron Valley from Jerusalem; showing the church of All Nations on the left and the city wall with the Golden Gate on the hill beyond. It was in this general area of the Mount of Olives that Christ's Passion began with the agony and arrest. (See Mk 14, 32-52)

pray." [h] [33] He took with him Peter, James, and John, and began to be troubled and distressed. [34] Then he said to them, "My soul is sorrowful even to death. Remain here and keep watch." [35] He advanced a little and fell to the ground and prayed that if it were possible the hour might pass by him; [36] he said, "Abba, Father,* all things are possible to you. Take this cup away from me, but not what I will but what you will." [37] When he returned he found them asleep. He said to Peter, "Simon, are you asleep? Could you not keep watch for one hour? [38] Watch and pray that you may not undergo the test. [i] The spirit is willing but the flesh is weak."* [39] Withdrawing again, he prayed, saying the same thing. [40] Then he returned once more and found them asleep, for they could not keep their eyes open and did not know what to answer him. [41] He returned a third time and said to them, "Are you still sleeping and taking your rest? It is enough. The hour has come. Behold, the Son of Man is to be handed over to sinners. [42] Get up, let us go. See, my betrayer is at hand."

The Betrayal and Arrest of Jesus. [43] [j] Then, while he was still speaking, Judas, one of the Twelve, arrived, accompanied by a crowd with swords and clubs who had come from the chief priests, the scribes, and the elders. [44] His betrayer had arranged a signal with them, saying, "The man I shall kiss is the one; arrest him and lead him away securely." [45] He came and immediately went over to him and said, "Rabbi." And he kissed him. [46] At this they laid hands on him and arrested him. [47] One of the bystanders drew his sword, struck the high priest's servant, and cut off his ear. [48] Jesus said to them in reply, "Have you come out as against a robber, with swords and clubs, to seize me? [49] Day after day I was with you teaching in the temple area, yet you did not arrest me; but that the scriptures may be fulfilled." [50] And they all left him and fled. [51] Now a young man followed him wearing nothing but a linen cloth about his body. They seized him, [52] but he left the cloth behind and ran off naked.

Jesus before the Sanhedrin. [53] [k] They led Jesus away to the high priest, and all the chief priests and the elders and the scribes came together.* [54] Peter followed him at a distance into the high priest's courtyard and was seated with the guards, warming himself at the fire. [55] The chief priests and the entire Sanhedrin kept trying to obtain testimony against Jesus in order to put him to death, but they found none. [56] Many gave false witness against him, but their testimony did not agree. [57]* Some took the stand and testified falsely against him, alleging, [58] "We heard him say, 'I will destroy this temple made with hands and within three days I will build another not made with hands.' " [l] [59] Even so their testimony did not agree. [60] The high priest rose before the assembly and questioned Jesus, saying, "Have you no answer? What are these men testifying against you?" [61] But he was silent and answered nothing. Again the high priest asked him and said to him, "Are you the Messiah, the son of the Blessed One?"* [62] Then Jesus answered, "I am;

and 'you will see the Son of Man
     seated at the right hand of the Power
        and coming with the clouds of
         heaven.' " [m]

[63] At that the high priest tore his garments and said, "What further need have we of witnesses? [64] You have heard the blasphemy. What do you think?" They all condemned him as deserving to die. [65] Some

---

h Jn 18, 1.—i Rom 7, 5.—j 43-50: Mt 26, 47-56; Lk 22, 47-53; Jn 18, 3-11.—k 53-65: Mt 26, 57-68; Lk 22, 54-55.63-65.67-71; Jn 18, 12-13.—l Mk 15, 29; 2 Cor 5, 1.—m Mk 13, 26; Ps 110, 1; Dn 7, 13; Mt 24, 30.

14, 36: *Abba, Father:* an Aramaic term, here also translated by Mark, Jesus' special way of addressing God with filial intimacy. The word *'abbā'* seems not to have been used in earlier or contemporary Jewish sources to address God without some qualifier. Cf Rom 8, 15; Gal 4, 6 for other occurrences of the Aramaic word in the Greek New Testament. *Not what I will but what you will:* note the complete obedient surrender of the human will of Jesus to the divine will of the Father; cf Jn 4, 34; 8, 29; Rom 5, 19; Phil 2, 8; Heb 5, 8.

14, 38: *The spirit is willing but the flesh is weak:* the spirit is drawn to what is good yet found in conflict with the flesh, inclined to sin; cf Ps 51, 7.12. Everyone is faced with this struggle, the full force of which Jesus accepted on our behalf and, through his bitter passion and death, achieved the victory.

14, 53: *They led Jesus away . . . came together:* Mark presents a formal assembly of the whole Sanhedrin (chief priests, elders, and scribes) at night, leading to the condemnation of Jesus (64), in contrast to Lk 22, 66.71, where Jesus is condemned in a daytime meeting of the council; see also Jn 18, 13.19-24.

14, 57-58: See the notes on Mt 26, 60-61 and Jn 2, 19.

14, 61-62: *The Blessed One:* a surrogate for the divine name, which Jews did not pronounce. *I am:* indicates Jesus' acknowledgment that he is the Messiah and Son of God; cf Mk 1, 1. Contrast Mt 26, 64 and Lk 22, 67-70, in which Jesus leaves his interrogators to answer their own question. *You will see the Son of Man . . . with the clouds of heaven:* an allusion to Dn 7, 13 and Ps 110, 1, portending the enthronement of Jesus as judge in the transcendent glory of God's kingdom. *The Power:* another surrogate for the name of God.

began to spit on him. They blindfolded him and struck him and said to him, "Prophesy!" And the guards greeted him with blows.[n]

Peter's Denial of Jesus. 66 [o] While Peter was below in the courtyard, one of the high priest's maids came along. 67 Seeing Peter warming himself, she looked intently at him and said, "You too were with the Nazarene, Jesus." 68 But he denied it saying, "I neither know nor understand what you are talking about." So he went out into the outer court. [Then the cock crowed.]* 69 The maid saw him and began again to say to the bystanders, "This man is one of them." 70 Once again he denied it. A little later the bystanders said to Peter once more, "Surely you are one of them; for you too are a Galilean." 71 He began to curse and to swear, "I do not know this man about whom you are talking." 72 And immediately a cock crowed a second time. Then Peter remembered the word that Jesus had said to him, "Before the cock crows twice you will deny me three times." He broke down and wept.[p]

CHAPTER 15

Jesus before Pilate. 1 [q] As soon as morning came,[r] the chief priests with the elders and the scribes, that is, the whole Sanhedrin, held a council.* They bound Jesus, led him away, and handed him over to Pilate. 2 Pilate questioned him, "Are you the king of the Jews?"* He said to him in reply, "You say so." 3 The chief priests accused him of many things. 4 Again Pilate questioned him, "Have you no answer? See how many things they accuse you of." 5 Jesus gave him no further answer, so that Pilate was amazed.

The Sentence of Death.* 6 Now on the occasion of the feast he used to release to them one prisoner whom they requested.[s] 7 A man called Barabbas* was then in prison along with the rebels who had committed murder in a rebellion. 8 The crowd came forward and began to ask him to do for them as he was accustomed. 9 Pilate answered, "Do you want me to release to you the king of the Jews?" 10 For he knew that it was out of envy that the chief priests had handed him over. 11 But the chief priests stirred up the crowd to have him release Barabbas for them instead. 12 Pilate again said to them in reply, "Then what [do you

want] me to do with [the man you call] the king of the Jews?" 13 They shouted again, "Crucify him."* 14 Pilate said to them, "Why? What evil has he done?" They only shouted the louder, "Crucify him." 15 So Pilate, wishing to satisfy the crowd, released Barabbas to them and, after he had Jesus scourged, handed him over to be crucified.*

Mockery by the Soldiers. 16 [t] The soldiers led him away inside the palace, that is, the praetorium,* and assembled the whole cohort. 17 They clothed him in purple and, weaving a crown of thorns, placed it on him. 18 They began to salute him with, "Hail, King of the Jews!" 19 and kept striking his head with a reed and spitting upon him. They knelt before him in homage. 20 And when they had mocked him, they stripped him of the purple cloak, dressed him in his own clothes, and led him out to crucify him.

The Way of the Cross. 21 They pressed into service a passer-by, Simon, a Cyrenian,* who was coming in from the country, the father of Alexander and Rufus, to carry his cross.[u]

The Crucifixion. 22 [v] They brought him to the place of Golgotha (which is translated

n Lk 22, 63-65.—o 66-72: Mt 26, 69-75; Lk 22, 56-62; Jn 18, 16-18.25-27.—p Jn 13, 38.—q 1-5: Mt 27, 1-2.11-14; Lk 23, 1-3.—r Jn 18, 28.—s 6-15: Mt 27, 15-26; Lk 23, 17-25; Jn 18, 39-40.—t 16-20: Mt 27, 27-31; Jn 19, 2-3.—u Mt 27, 32; Lk 23, 26.—v 22-38: Mt 27, 33-51; Lk 23, 32-46; Jn 19, 17-30.

14, 68: *[Then the cock crowed]:* found in most manuscripts, perhaps in view of vv 30 and 72, but omitted in others.

15, 1: *Held a council:* the verb here, *poieō,* can mean either "convene a council" or "take counsel." This reading is preferred to a variant "reached a decision" (cf Mk 3, 6), which Mk 14, 64 describes as having happened at the night trial; see the note on Mt 27, 1-2. *Handed him over to Pilate:* lacking authority to execute their sentence of condemnation (Mk 14, 64), the Sanhedrin had recourse to Pilate to have Jesus tried and put to death (15); cf Jn 18, 31.

15, 2: *The king of the Jews:* in the accounts of the evangelists a certain irony surrounds the use of this title as an accusation against Jesus (see the note on Mk 15, 26). While Pilate uses this term (2.9.12), he is aware of the evil motivation of the chief priests who handed Jesus over for trial and condemnation (10; Lk 23, 14-16.20; Mt 27, 18.24; Jn 18, 38; 19, 4.6.12).

15, 6-15: See the note on Mt 27, 15-26.

15, 7: *Barabbas:* see the note on Mt 27, 16-17.

15, 13: *Crucify him:* see the note on Mt 27, 22.

15, 15: See the note on Mt 27, 26.

15, 16: *Praetorium:* see the note on Mt 27, 27.

15, 21: *They pressed into service . . . Simon, a Cyrenian:* a condemned person was constrained to bear his own instrument of torture, at least the crossbeam. The precise naming of Simon and his sons is probably due to their being known among early Christian believers to whom Mark addressed his gospel. See also the notes on Mt 27, 32 and Lk 23, 26-32.

Place of the Skull). ²³They gave him wine drugged with myrrh, but he did not take it. ²⁴ *w* Then they crucified him and divided his garments by casting lots for them to see what each should take.* ²⁵It was nine o'clock in the morning* when they crucified him. ²⁶The inscription of the charge against him read, "The King of the Jews."* ²⁷With him they crucified two revolutionaries, one on his right and one on his left. *x* [28]* ²⁹Those passing by reviled him, shaking their heads and saying,*y* "Aha! You who would destroy the temple and rebuild it in three days,* ³⁰save yourself by coming down from the cross." ³¹Likewise the chief priests, with the scribes, mocked him among themselves and said, "He saved others; he cannot save himself. ³²Let the Messiah, the King of Israel, come down now from the cross that we may see and believe." Those who were crucified with him also kept abusing him. *z*

---

w Ps 22, 18.—x Lk 23, 33.—y Jn 2, 19.—z Lk 23, 39.—a Ps 22, 2.—b 39-41: Mt 27, 54-56; Lk 23, 47-49.—c Mk 6, 3; Lk 8, 2-3.—d 42-47: Mt 27, 57-61; Lk 23, 50-56; Jn 19, 38-42.—e 1-8: Mt 28, 1-8; Lk 24, 1-10; Jn 20, 1-10.—f 1-2: Mt 28, 1; Lk 23, 56.

15, 24: See the notes on Mt 27, 35 and Jn 19, 23-25a.

15, 25: *It was nine o'clock in the morning:* literally, "the third hour," thus between 9 a.m. and 12 noon. Cf vv 33.34.42 for Mark's chronological sequence, which may reflect liturgical or catechetical considerations rather than the precise historical sequence of events; contrast the different chronologies in the other gospels, especially Jn 19, 14.

15, 26: *The inscription . . . the King of the Jews:* the political reason for the death penalty falsely charged by the enemies of Jesus. See further the notes on Mt 27, 37 and Jn 19, 19.

15, 28: This verse, "And the scripture was fulfilled that says, 'And he was counted among the wicked,' " is omitted in the earliest and best manuscripts. It contains a citation from Is 53, 12, and was probably introduced from Lk 22, 37.

15, 29: See the note on Mt 27, 39-40.

15, 34: An Aramaic rendering of Ps 22, 2. See also the note on Mt 27, 46.

15, 35: *Elijah:* a verbal link with *Eloi* (34). See the note on Mk 9, 13; cf Mal 3, 23-24. See also the note on Mt 27, 47.

15, 38: See the note on Mt 27, 51-53.

15, 39: The closing portion of Mark's gospel returns to the theme of its beginning in the Gentile centurion's climactic declaration of belief that Jesus *was the Son of God.* It indicates the fulfillment of the good news announced in the prologue (Mk 1, 1) and may be regarded as the firstfruit of the passion and death of Jesus.

15, 40-41: See the note on Mt 27, 55-56.

15, 43: *Joseph of Arimathea:* see the note on Mt 27, 57-61.

16, 1-8: The purpose of this narrative is to show that the tomb is empty and that Jesus *has been raised* (6) and *is going before you to Galilee* (7) in fulfillment of Mk 14, 28. The women find the tomb empty, and an angel stationed there announces to them what has happened. They are told to proclaim the news to Peter and the disciples in order to prepare them for a reunion with him. Mark's composition of the gospel ends at v 8 with the women telling no one, because they were afraid. This abrupt termination causes some to believe that the original ending of this gospel may have been lost. See the following note.

The Death of Jesus. ³³At noon darkness came over the whole land until three in the afternoon. ³⁴And at three o'clock Jesus cried out in a loud voice, *"Eloi, Eloi, lema sabachthani?"* * which is translated, "My God, my God, why have you forsaken me?" *a* ³⁵Some of the bystanders who heard it said, "Look, he is calling Elijah."* ³⁶One of them ran, soaked a sponge with wine, put it on a reed, and gave it to him to drink, saying, "Wait, let us see if Elijah comes to take him down." ³⁷Jesus gave a loud cry and breathed his last. ³⁸The veil of the sanctuary was torn in two from top to bottom.* ³⁹ *b* When the centurion who stood facing him saw how he breathed his last he said, "Truly this man was the Son of God!"* ⁴⁰There were also women looking on from a distance. *c* Among them were Mary Magdalene, Mary the mother of the younger James and of Joses, and Salome.* ⁴¹These women had followed him when he was in Galilee and ministered to him. There were also many other women who had come up with him to Jerusalem.

The Burial of Jesus. ⁴² *d* When it was already evening, since it was the day of preparation, the day before the sabbath, ⁴³Joseph of Arimathea,* a distinguished member of the council, who was himself awaiting the kingdom of God, came and courageously went to Pilate and asked for the body of Jesus. ⁴⁴Pilate was amazed that he was already dead. He summoned the centurion and asked him if Jesus had already died. ⁴⁵And when he learned of it from the centurion, he gave the body to Joseph. ⁴⁶Having bought a linen cloth, he took him down, wrapped him in the linen cloth and laid him in a tomb that had been hewn out of the rock. Then he rolled a stone against the entrance to the tomb. ⁴⁷Mary Magdalene and Mary the mother of Joses watched where he was laid.

CHAPTER 16

The Resurrection of Jesus. * ¹When the sabbath was over,*e* Mary Magdalene, Mary, the mother of James, and Salome bought spices so that they might go and anoint him.*f* ²Very early when the sun had risen, on the first day of the week, they came to the tomb. ³They were saying to one another, "Who will roll back the stone for us from the entrance to the tomb?" ⁴When they looked up, they saw that the stone had been rolled back; it was very large. 5 On entering the tomb they saw a young man sitting on the right side, clothed in a white robe, and they were utterly amazed.g 6 He said to them, "Do not be amazed! You seek Jesus of Nazareth, the crucified. He has been raised; he is not here. Behold, the place where they laid him. 7 But go and tell his disciples and Peter, 'He is going before you to Galilee; there you will see him, as he told you.'"h 8 Then they went out and fled from the tomb, seized with trembling and bewilderment. They said nothing to anyone, for they were afraid.

THE LONGER ENDING*

The Appearance to Mary Magdalene.
[9 i When he had risen, early on the first day of the week, he appeared first to Mary Magdalene, out of whom he had driven seven demons. 10 j She went and told his companions who were mourning and weeping. 11 When they heard that he was alive and had been seen by her, they did not believe.

The Appearance to Two Disciples. 12 k
After this he appeared in another form to two of them walking along on their way to the country. 13 They returned and told the others; but they did not believe them either.

g Jn 20, 12.—h Mk 14, 28.—i 9-20: Mt 28, 1-10; Jn 20, 11-18.—j 10-11: Lk 24, 10-11; Jn 20, 18.—k 12-14: Lk 24, 13-35.—l Lk 24, 36-49; 1 Cor 15, 5.—m 15-16: Mk 13, 10; Mt 28, 18-20; Lk 24, 47; Jn 20, 21.—n Mt 10, 1; Lk 10, 19; Acts 28, 3-6.—o Lk 24, 50-53.—p 1 Tm 3, 16.

16, 9-20: This passage, termed the Longer Ending to the Marcan gospel by comparison with a much briefer conclusion found in some less important manuscripts, has traditionally been accepted as a canonical part of the gospel and was defined as such by the Council of Trent. Early citations of it by the Fathers indicate that it was composed by the second century, although vocabulary and style indicate that it was written by someone other than Mark. It is a general resume of the material concerning the appearances of the risen Jesus, reflecting, in particular, traditions found in Luke (24) and John (20).

The Shorter Ending: Found after v 8 before the Longer Ending in four seventh-to-ninth-century Greek manuscripts as well as in

The Commissioning of the Eleven.
14 l [But] later, as the eleven were at table, he appeared to them and rebuked them for their unbelief and hardness of heart because they had not believed those who saw him after he had been raised. 15 m He said to them, "Go into the whole world and proclaim the gospel to every creature. 16 Whoever believes and is baptized will be saved; whoever does not believe will be condemned. 17 These signs will accompany those who believe: in my name they will drive out demons, they will speak new languages. 18 They will pick up serpents [with their hands], and if they drink any deadly thing, it will not harm them. They will lay hands on the sick, and they will recover."n

The Ascension of Jesus. 19 So then the
Lord Jesus, after he spoke to them, was taken up into heaven and took his seat at the right hand of God.o 20 But they went forth and preached everywhere, while the Lord worked with them and confirmed the word through accompanying signs.]p

THE SHORTER ENDING*

[And they reported all the instructions briefly to Peter's companions. Afterwards Jesus himself, through them, sent forth from east to west the sacred and imperishable proclamation of eternal salvation. Amen.]

one Old Latin version, where it appears alone without the Longer Ending.

The Freer Logion: Found after v 14 in a fourth-fifth century manuscript preserved in the Freer Gallery of Art, Washington, DC, this ending was known to Jerome in the fourth century. It reads: "And they excused themselves, saying, 'This age of lawlessness and unbelief is under Satan, who does not allow the truth and power of God to prevail over the unclean things dominated by the spirits [or, does not allow the unclean things dominated by the spirits] to grasp the truth and power of God]. Therefore reveal your righteousness now.' They spoke to Christ. And Christ responded to them, 'The limit of the years of Satan's power is completed, but other terrible things draw near. And for those who sinned I was handed over to death, that they might return to the truth and no longer sin, in order that they might inherit the spiritual and incorruptible heavenly glory of righteousness. But . . . .'"

THE GOSPEL ACCORDING TO LUKE

INTRODUCTION

The Gospel according to Luke is the first part of a two-volume work that continues the biblical history of God's dealings with humanity found in the Old Testament, showing how God's promises to Israel have been fulfilled in Jesus and how the salvation promised to Israel and accomplished by Jesus has been extended to the Gentiles. The stated purpose of the two volumes is to provide Theophilus and others like him with certainty—assurance— about earlier instruction they have received (1, 4). To accomplish his purpose, Luke shows that the preaching and teaching of the representatives of the early church are grounded in the preaching and teaching of Jesus, who during his historical ministry (Acts 1, 21-22) prepared his specially chosen followers and commissioned them to be witnesses to his resurrection and to all else that he did (Acts 10, 37-42). This continuity between the historical ministry of Jesus and the ministry of the apostles is Luke's way of guaranteeing the fidelity of the church's teaching to the teaching of Jesus.

Luke's story of Jesus and the church is dominated by a historical perspective. This history is first of all salvation history. God's divine plan for human salvation was accomplished during the period of Jesus, who through the events of his life (22, 22) fulfilled the Old Testament prophecies (4, 21; 18, 31; 22, 37; 24, 26-27.44), and this salvation is now extended to all humanity in the period of the church (Acts 4, 12). This salvation history, moreover, is a part of human history. Luke relates the story of Jesus and the church to events in contemporary Palestinian (1, 5; 3, 1-2; Acts 4, 6) and Roman (2, 1-2; 3, 1; Acts 11, 28; 18, 2.12) history, for, as Paul says in Acts 26, 26, "this was not done in a corner." Finally, Luke relates the story of Jesus and the church to contemporaneous church history. Luke is concerned with presenting Christianity as a legitimate form of worship in the Roman world, a religion that is capable of meeting the spiritual needs of a world empire like that of Rome. To this end, Luke depicts the Roman governor Pilate declaring Jesus innocent of any wrongdoing three times (Acts 23, 29; 25, 25; 26, 31-32). At the same time Luke argues in Acts that Christianity is the logical development and proper fulfillment of Judaism and is therefore deserving of the same toleration and freedom traditionally accorded Judaism by Rome (Acts 13, 16-41; 23, 6-9; 24, 10-21; 26, 2-23).

The prominence given to the period of the church in the story has important consequences for Luke's interpretation of the teachings of Jesus. By presenting the time of the church as a distinct phase of salvation history, Luke accordingly shifts the early Christian emphasis away from the expectation of an imminent parousia to the day-to-day concerns of the Christian community in the world. He does this in the gospel by regularly emphasizing the words "each day" (9, 23; cf Mk 8, 34; 11, 3; 16, 19; 19, 47) in the sayings of Jesus. Although Luke still believes the parousia to be a reality that will come unexpectedly (12, 38.45-46), he is more concerned with presenting the words and deeds of Jesus as guides for the conduct of Christian disciples in the interim period between the ascension and the parousia and with presenting Jesus himself as the model of Christian life and piety.

Throughout the gospel, Luke calls upon the Christian disciple to identify with the master Jesus, who is caring and tender toward the poor and lowly, the outcast, the sinner, and the afflicted, toward all those who recognize their dependence on God (4, 18; 6, 20-23; 7, 36-50; 14, 12-14; 15, 1-32; 16, 19-31; 18, 9-14; 19, 1-10; 21, 1-4), but who is severe toward the proud and self-righteous, and particularly toward those who place their material wealth before the service of God and his people (6, 24-26; 12, 13-21; 16, 13-15.19-31; 18, 9-14.15-25; cf 1, 50-53). No gospel writer is more concerned than Luke with the mercy and compassion of Jesus (7, 41-43; 10, 29-37; 13, 6-9; 15, 11-32). No gospel writer is more concerned with the role of the Spirit in the life of Jesus and the Christian disciple (1, 35.41; 2, 25-27; 4, 1.14.18; 10, 21; 11, 13; 24, 49), with the importance of prayer (3, 21; 5, 16; 6, 12; 9, 28; 11, 1-13; 18, 1-8), or with Jesus' concern for women (7, 11-17.36-50; 8, 2-3; 10, 38-42). While Jesus calls all humanity to repent (5, 32; 10, 13; 11, 32; 13, 1-5; 15, 7-10; 16, 30; 17, 3-4; 24, 47), he is particularly demanding of those who would be his disciples. Of them he demands absolute and total detachment from family and material possessions (9, 57-62; 12, 32-34; 14, 25-35). To all who respond in faith and repentance to the word Jesus preaches, he brings salvation (2, 30-32; 3, 6; 7, 50; 8, 48.50; 17, 19; 19, 9) and peace (2, 14; 7, 50; 8, 48; 19, 38.42) and life (10, 25-28; 18, 26-30).

Early Christian tradition, from the late second century on, identifies the author of this gospel and of the Acts of the Apostles as Luke, a Syrian from Antioch, who is mentioned in the New Testament in Col 4, 14, Phlm 24, and 2 Tm 4, 11. The prologue of the gospel makes it clear that Luke is not part of the first generation of Christian disciples but is himself dependent upon the traditions he received from those who were eyewitnesses and ministers of the word (1, 2). His two-volume work marks him as someone who was highly literate both in the Old Testament traditions according to the Greek versions and in Hellenistic Greek writings.

Among the likely sources for the composition of this gospel (1, 3) were the Gospel of Mark, a written collection of sayings of Jesus known also to the author of the Gospel of Matthew (Q; see Introduction to Matthew), and other special traditions that were used by Luke alone among the gospel writers. Some hold that Luke used Mark only as a complementary source for rounding out the material he took from other traditions. Because of its dependence on the Gospel of Mark and because details in Luke's Gospel (13, 35a; 19, 43-44; 21, 20; 23, 28-31) imply that the author was acquainted with the destruction of the city of Jerusalem by the Romans in A.D. 70, the Gospel of Luke is dated by most scholars after that date; many propose A.D. 80-90 as the time of composition.

Luke's consistent substitution of Greek names for the Aramaic or Hebrew names occurring in his sources (e.g., 23, 33 // Mk 15, 22; 18, 41 // Mk 10, 51), his omission from the gospel of specifically Jewish Christian concerns found in his sources (e.g., Mk 7, 1-23), his interest in Gentile Christians (2, 30-32; 3, 6.38; 4, 16-30; 13, 28-30; 14, 15-24; 17, 11-19; 24, 47-48), and his incomplete knowledge of Palestinian geography, customs, and practices are among the characteristics of this gospel that suggest that Luke was a non-Palestinian writing to a non-Palestinian audience that was largely made up of Gentile Christians.

The principal divisions of the Gospel according to Luke are the following:

I. THE PROLOGUE*
CHAPTER 1

[1] Since many have undertaken to compile a narrative of the events that have been fulfilled among us,[a] [2] just as those who were eyewitnesses from the beginning and ministers of the word have handed them down to us,[b] [3] I too have decided, after investigating everything accurately anew, to write it down in an orderly sequence for you, most excellent Theophilus, [4] so that you may realize the certainty of the teachings you have received.

II. THE INFANCY NARRATIVE*
Announcement of the Birth of John.

[5] In the days of Herod, King of Judea,* there was a priest named Zechariah of the priestly division of Abijah; his wife was from the daughters of Aaron, and her name was Elizabeth.[c] [6] Both were righteous in the eyes of God, observing all the commandments and ordinances of the Lord blamelessly. [7] But they had no child,* because Elizabeth was barren and both were advanced in years.[d] [8] Once when he was serving as priest in his division's turn before God, [9] according to the practice of the priestly service, he was chosen by lot to enter the sanctuary of the Lord to burn incense.[e] [10] Then, when the whole assembly of the people was praying outside at the hour of the incense offering, [11] the angel of the Lord appeared to him, standing at the right of the altar of incense. [12] Zechariah was troubled by what he saw, and fear came upon him. [13] But the angel said to him, "Do not be afraid,* Zechariah, because your prayer has been heard. Your wife Elizabeth will bear you a son, and you shall name him John.[f] [14] And you will have joy and gladness, and many will rejoice at his birth, [15] for he will be great in the sight of [the] Lord. He will drink neither wine nor strong drink.* He will be filled with the holy Spirit even from his mother's womb,[g] [16] and he will turn many of the children of Israel to the Lord their God. [17] He will go before him in the spirit and power of Elijah* to turn the hearts of fathers toward children and the disobedient to the understanding of the righteous, to prepare a people fit for the

---

a 1-4: Acts 1, 1; 1 Cor 15, 3.—b Lk 24, 48; Jn 15, 27; Acts 1, 21-22.—c 1 Chr 24, 10.—d Gn 18, 11; Jgs 13, 2-5; 1 Sm 1, 5-6.—e Ex 30, 7.—f Lk 1, 57.60.63; Mt 1, 20-21.—g Lk 7, 33; Nm 6, 1-21; Jgs 13, 4; 1 Sm 1, 11 LXX.

1, 1-4: The Gospel according to Luke is the only one of the synoptic gospels to begin with a literary prologue. Making use of a formal, literary construction and vocabulary, the author writes the prologue in imitation of Hellenistic Greek writers and, in so doing, relates his story about Jesus to contemporaneous Greek and Roman literature. Luke is not only interested in the words and deeds of Jesus, but also in the larger context of the birth, ministry, death, and resurrection of Jesus as the fulfillment of the promises of God in the Old Testament. As a second- or third-generation Christian, Luke acknowledges his debt to earlier *eyewitnesses* and *ministers of the word*, but claims that his contribution to this developing tradition is a complete and accurate account, told in an orderly manner, and intended to provide *Theophilus* ("friend of God," literally) and other readers with certainty about earlier teachings they have received.

1, 5—2, 52: Like the Gospel according to Matthew, this gospel opens with an infancy narrative, a collection of stories about the birth and childhood of Jesus. The narrative uses early Christian traditions about the birth of Jesus, traditions about the birth and circumcision of John the Baptist, and canticles such as the Magnificat (Lk 1, 46-55) and Benedictus (Lk 1, 67-79), composed of phrases drawn from the Greek Old Testament. It is largely, however, the composition of Luke who writes in imitation of Old Testament birth stories, combining historical and legendary details, literary ornamentation and interpretation of scripture, to answer in advance the question, "Who is Jesus Christ?" The focus of the narrative, therefore, is primarily christological. In this section Luke announces many of the themes that will become prominent in the rest of the gospel: the centrality of Jerusalem and the temple, the journey motif, the universality of salvation, joy and peace, concern for the lowly, the importance of women, the presentation of Jesus as savior, Spirit-guided revelation and prophecy, and the fulfillment of Old Testament promises. The account presents parallel scenes (diptychs) of angelic announcements of the birth of John the Baptist and of Jesus, and of

the birth, circumcision, and presentation of John and Jesus. In this parallelism, the ascendency of Jesus over John is stressed: John is prophet of the Most High (Lk 1, 76); Jesus is Son of the Most High (Lk 1, 32). John is great in the sight of the Lord (Lk 1, 15); Jesus will be Great (a LXX attribute, used absolutely, of God) (Lk 1, 32). John will go before the Lord (Lk 1, 16-17); Jesus will be Lord (Lk 1, 43; 2, 11).

1, 5: *In the days of Herod, King of Judea:* Luke relates the story of salvation history to events in contemporary world history. Here and in Lk 3, 1-2, he connects his narrative with events in Palestinian history; in Lk 2, 1-2 and Lk 3, 1, he casts the Jesus story in the light of events of Roman history. Herod the Great, the son of the Idumean Antipater, was declared "King of Judea" by the Roman Senate in 40 B.C., but became the undisputed ruler of Palestine only in 37 B.C. He continued as king until his death in 4 B.C. *Priestly division of Abijah:* a reference to the eighth of the twenty-four divisions of priests who, for a week at a time, twice a year, served in the Jerusalem temple.

1, 7: *They had no child:* though childlessness was looked upon in contemporaneous Judaism as a curse or punishment for sin, it is intended here to present Elizabeth in a situation similar to that of some of the great mothers of important Old Testament figures: Sarah (Gn 15, 3; 16, 1); Rebekah (Gn 25, 21); Rachel (Gn 29, 31; 30, 1); the mother of Samson and wife of Manoah (Jgs 13, 2-3); Hannah (1 Sm 1, 2).

1, 13: *Do not be afraid:* a stereotyped Old Testament phrase spoken to reassure the recipient of a heavenly vision (Gn 15, 1; Jos 1, 9; Dn 10, 12.19 and elsewhere in Lk 1, 30; 2, 10). *You shall name him John:* the name means "Yahweh has shown favor," an indication of John's role in salvation history.

1, 15: *He will drink neither wine nor strong drink:* like Samson (Jgs 13, 4-5) and Samuel (1 Sm 1, 11 LXX and 4QSam[a]), John is to be consecrated by Nazirite vow and set apart for the Lord's service.

1, 17: *He will go before him in the spirit and power of Elijah:* John is to be the messenger sent before Yahweh, as described in Mal 3, 1-2. He is cast, moreover, in the role of the Old Testament fiery reformer, the prophet Elijah, who according to Mal 3, 23 (4, 5) is sent before "the great and terrible day of the Lord comes."

Lord."ʰ ¹⁸Then Zechariah said to the angel, "How shall I know this? For I am an old man, and my wife is advanced in years." ¹⁹And the angel said to him in reply, "I am Gabriel,* who stand before God. I was sent to speak to you and to announce to you this good news.ⁱ ²⁰But now you will be speechless and unable to talk* until the day these things take place, because you did not believe my words, which will be fulfilled at their proper time."ʲ

²¹Meanwhile the people were waiting for Zechariah and were amazed that he stayed so long in the sanctuary. ²²But when he came out, he was unable to speak to them, and they realized that he had seen a vision in the sanctuary. He was gesturing to them but remained mute. ²³Then, when his days of ministry were completed, he went home. ²⁴After this time his wife Elizabeth conceived, and she went into seclusion for five months, saying, ²⁵"So has the Lord done for me at a time when he has seen fit to take away my disgrace before others."ᵏ

Announcement of the Birth of Jesus.* ²⁶In the sixth month, the angel Gabriel was sent from God to a town of Galilee called Nazareth, ²⁷to a virgin betrothed to a man named Joseph, of the house of David, and the virgin's name was Mary.ˡ ²⁸And coming to her, he said, "Hail, favored one! The Lord is with you."ᵐ ²⁹But she was greatly troubled at what was said and pondered what sort of greeting this might be. ³⁰Then the angel said to her, "Do not be afraid, Mary, for you have found favor with God. ³¹ ⁿBehold, you will conceive in your womb and bear a son, and you shall name him Jesus. ³² ᵒHe will be great and will be called Son of the Most High,* and the Lord God will give him the throne of David his father, ³³and he will rule over the house of Jacob forever, and of his kingdom there will be no end."ᵖ ³⁴But Mary said to the angel, "How can this be, since I have no relations with a man?"* ³⁵And the angel said to her in reply, "The holy Spirit will come upon you, and the power of the Most High will overshadow you. Therefore the child to be born will be called holy, the Son of God.�q ³⁶And behold, Elizabeth, your relative, has also conceived* a son in her old age, and this is the sixth month for her who was called barren; ³⁷for nothing will be impossible for God."ʳ ³⁸Mary said, "Behold, I am the handmaid of the Lord. May it be done to me accord-

ing to your word." Then the angel departed from her.

Mary Visits Elizabeth. ³⁹During those days Mary set out and traveled to the hill country in haste to a town of Judah, ⁴⁰where she entered the house of Zechariah and greeted Elizabeth. ⁴¹When Elizabeth heard Mary's greeting, the infant leaped in her womb, and Elizabeth, filled with the holy Spirit,ˢ ⁴²cried out in a loud voice and said, "Most blessed are you among women, and blessed is the fruit of your womb.ᵗ ⁴³And how does this happen to me, that the mother of my Lord* should come to me? ⁴⁴For at the moment the sound of your greeting reached my ears, the infant in my womb leaped for joy.⁴⁵Blessed are you who believed* that

h Sir 48, 10; Mal 3, 1; 3, 23-24; Mt 11, 14; 17, 11-13.—i Dn 8, 16; 9, 21.—j Lk 1, 45.—k Gn 30, 23.—l Lk 2, 5; Mt 1, 16.18.—m Jgs 6, 12; Ru 2, 4; Jdt 13, 18.—n Gn 16, 11; Jgs 13, 3; Is 7, 14; Mt 1, 21-23.—o 32-33: 2 Sm 7, 12.13.16; Is 9, 7.—p Dn 2, 44; 7, 14; Mi 4, 7; Mt 28, 18.—q Mt 1, 20.—r Gn 18, 14; Jer 32, 27; Mt 19, 26.—s Lk 1, 15; Gn 25, 22 LXX.—t Lk 11, 27-28; Jgs 5, 24; Jdt 13, 18 / Dt 28, 4.

1, 19: *I am Gabriel:* "the angel of the Lord" is identified as Gabriel, the angel who in Dn 9, 20-25 announces the seventy weeks of years and the coming of an anointed one, a prince. By alluding to Old Testament themes in vv 17 and 19, such as the coming of the day of the Lord and the dawning of the messianic era, Luke is presenting his interpretation of the significance of the births of John and Jesus.

1, 20: *You will be speechless and unable to talk:* Zechariah's becoming mute is the sign given in response to his question in v 18. When Mary asks a similar question in Lk 1, 34, unlike Zechariah who was punished for his doubt, she, in spite of her doubt, is praised and reassured (35-37).

1, 26-38: The announcement to Mary of the birth of Jesus is parallel to the announcement to Zechariah of the birth of John. In both the angel Gabriel appears to the parent who is troubled by the vision (11-12.26-29) and then told by the angel not to fear (13.30). After the announcement is made (14-17.31-33) the parent objects (18.34) and a sign is given to confirm the announcement (20.36). The particular focus of the announcement of the birth of Jesus is on his identity as Son of David (32-33) and Son of God (32.35).

1, 32: *Son of the Most High:* cf Lk 1, 76 where John is described as "prophet of the Most High." "Most High" is a title for God commonly used by Luke (Lk 1, 35.76; 6, 35; 8, 28; Acts 7, 48; 16, 17).

1, 34: Mary's questioning response is a denial of sexual relations and is used by Luke to lead to the angel's declaration about the Spirit's role in the conception of this child (35). According to Luke, the virginal conception of Jesus takes place through the holy Spirit, the power of God, and therefore Jesus has a unique relationship to Yahweh: he is Son of God.

1, 36-37: The sign given to Mary in confirmation of the angel's announcement to her is the pregnancy of her aged relative Elizabeth. If a woman past the childbearing age could become pregnant, why, the angel implies, should there be doubt about Mary's pregnancy, for *nothing will be impossible for God.*

1, 43: Even before his birth, Jesus is identified in Lk as the *Lord.*

1, 45: *Blessed are you who believed:* Luke portrays Mary as a believer whose faith stands in contrast to the disbelief of Zechariah (Lk 1, 20). Mary's role as believer in the infancy narrative should be seen in connection with the explicit mention of her presence among "those who believed" after the resurrection at the beginning of the Acts of the Apostles (Acts 1, 14).

what was spoken to you by the Lord would be fulfilled." *u*

The Canticle of Mary. 46 *v* And Mary said:*

"My soul proclaims the greatness of the Lord; *w*
47   my spirit rejoices in God my savior. *x*
48 For he has looked upon his handmaid's lowliness;
   behold, from now on will all ages call me blessed. *y*
49 The Mighty One has done great things for me,
   and holy is his name. *z*
50 His mercy is from age to age
   to those who fear him. *a*
51 He has shown might with his arm,
   dispersed the arrogant of mind and heart. *b*
52 He has thrown down the rulers from their thrones
   but lifted up the lowly. *c*
53 The hungry he has filled with good things;
   the rich he has sent away empty. *d*
54 He has helped Israel his servant,
   remembering his mercy, *e*
55 according to his promise to our fathers,
   to Abraham and to his descendants forever." *f*

56 Mary remained with her about three months and then returned to her home.

The Birth of John. * 57 When the time arrived for Elizabeth to have her child she gave birth to a son. 58 Her neighbors and relatives heard that the Lord had shown his great mercy toward her, and they rejoiced with her. *g* 59 When they came on the eighth day to circumcise *h* the child, they were going to call him Zechariah after his father,* 60 but his mother said in reply, "No. He will be called John." *i* 61 But they answered her, "There is no one among your relatives who has this name." 62 So they made signs, asking his father what he wished him to be called. 63 He asked for a tablet and wrote, "John is his name," and all were amazed. 64 Immediately his mouth was opened, his tongue freed, and he spoke blessing God. *j* 65 Then fear came upon all their neighbors, and all these matters were discussed throughout the hill country of Judea. 66 All who heard these things took them to heart, saying, "What, then, will this child be?" For surely the hand of the Lord was with him.

The Canticle of Zechariah. 67 Then Zechariah his father, filled with the holy Spirit, prophesied, saying:

68 "Blessed be the Lord, the God of Israel,*
   for he has visited and brought redemption to his people. *k*
69 He has raised up a horn for our salvation*
   within the house of David his servant, *l*

---

u Lk 1, 20.—v 46-55: 1 Sm 2, 1-10.—w Ps 35, 9; Is 61, 10; Hb 3, 18.—x Ti 3, 4; Jude 25.—y Lk 11, 27; 1 Sm 1, 11; 2 Sm 16, 12; 2 Kgs 14, 26; Ps 113, 7.—z Dt 10, 21; Pss 71, 19; 111, 9; 126, 2-3.—a Pss 89, 2; 103, 13.17.—b Ps 89, 10; 118, 15; Jer 32, 17 (39, 17 LXX).—c 1 Sm 2, 7; 2 Sm 22, 28; Jb 5, 11; 12, 19; Ps 147, 6; Sir 10, 14; Jas 4, 6; 1 Pt 5, 5.—d 1 Sm 2, 5; Ps 107, 9.—e Ps 98, 3; Is 41, 8-9.—f Gn 13, 15; 17, 7; 18, 18; 22, 17-18; Mi 7, 20.—g Lk 1, 14.—h Lk 2, 21; Gn 17, 10.12; Lv 12, 3.—i Lk 1, 13.—j Lk 1, 20.—k Lk 7, 16; Pss 41, 13; 72, 18; 106, 48; 111, 9.—l Ps 18, 3.

1, 46-55: Although Mary is praised for being the mother of the Lord and because of her belief, she reacts as the servant in a psalm of praise, the Magnificat. Because there is no specific connection of the canticle to the context of Mary's pregnancy and her visit to Elizabeth, the Magnificat (with the possible exception of v 48) may have been a Jewish Christian hymn that Luke found appropriate at this point in his story. Even if not composed by Luke, it fits in well with themes found elsewhere in Lk: joy and exultation in the Lord; the lowly being singled out for God's favor; the reversal of human fortunes; the fulfillment of Old Testament promises. The loose connection between the hymn and the context is further seen in the fact that a few Old Latin manuscripts identify the speaker of the hymn as Elizabeth, even though the overwhelming textual evidence makes Mary the speaker.

1, 57-66: The birth and circumcision of John above all emphasize John's incorporation into the people of Israel by the sign of the covenant (Gn 17, 1-12). The narrative of John's circumci-

sion also prepares the way for the subsequent description of the circumcision of Jesus in Lk 2, 21. At the beginning of his two-volume work Luke shows those who play crucial roles in the inauguration of Christianity to be wholly a part of the people of Israel. At the end of the Acts of the Apostles (21, 20; 22, 3; 23, 6-9; 24, 14-16; 26, 2-8.22-23) he will argue that Christianity is the direct descendant of Pharisaic Judaism.

1, 59: The practice of Palestinian Judaism at this time was to name the child at birth; moreover, though naming a male child after the father is not completely unknown, the usual practice was to name the child after the grandfather (see 61). The naming of the child John and Zechariah's recovery from his loss of speech should be understood as fulfilling the angel's announcement to Zechariah in Lk 1, 13 and 20.

1, 68-79: Like the canticle of Mary (46-55) the canticle of Zechariah is only loosely connected with its context. Apart from vv 76-77, the hymn in speaking of *a horn for our salvation* (69) and *the daybreak from on high* (78) applies more closely to Jesus and his work than to John. Again like Mary's canticle, it is largely composed of phrases taken from the Greek Old Testament and may have been a Jewish Christian hymn of praise that Luke adapted to fit the present context by inserting vv 76-77 to give Zechariah's reply to the question asked in v 66.

1, 69: *A horn for our salvation:* the horn is a common Old Testament figure for strength (Pss 18, 3; 75, 5-6; 89, 18; 112, 9; 148, 14). This description is applied to God in Ps 18, 3 and is here transferred to Jesus. The connection of the phrase with *the house of David* gives the title messianic overtones and may indicate an allusion to a phrase in Hannah's song of praise (1 Sm 2, 10), "the horn of his anointed."

70 even as he promised through the mouth
of his holy prophets from of old:

71 salvation from our enemies and from
the hand of all who hate us,*m*

72 to show mercy to our fathers*n*
and to be mindful of his holy
covenant*o*

73 and of the oath he swore to Abraham
our father,*p*
and to grant us that, 74 rescued from
the hand of enemies,
without fear we might worship him 75 in
holiness and righteousness
before him all our days.*q*

76 And you, child, will be called prophet
of the Most High,
for you will go before the Lord* to
prepare his ways,*r*

77 to give his people knowledge of salvation
through the forgiveness of their sins,

78 because of the tender mercy of our
God*s*
by which the daybreak from on high*
will visit us*t*

79 to shine on those who sit in darkness
and death's shadow,
to guide our feet into the path of
peace."

80 The child grew and became strong in
spirit, and he was in the desert until the
day of his manifestation to Israel.*u*

CHAPTER 2

The Birth of Jesus. 1 * In those days a decree went out from Caesar Augustus* that
the whole world should be enrolled. 2 This
was the first enrollment, when Quirinius
was governor of Syria. 3 So all went to be
enrolled, each to his own town. 4 And
Joseph too went up from Galilee from the
town of Nazareth to Judea, to the city of
David that is called Bethlehem, because he
was of the house and family of David,*v* 5 to
be enrolled with Mary, his betrothed, who
was with child.*w* 6 While they were there,
the time came for her to have her child,
7 and she gave birth to her firstborn son.*
She wrapped him in swaddling clothes and
laid him in a manger, because there was no
room for them in the inn.*x*

8 * Now there were shepherds in that region living in the fields and keeping the
night watch over their flock. 9 The angel of
the Lord appeared to them and the glory of
the Lord shone around them, and they
were struck with great fear.*y* 10 The angel
said to them, "Do not be afraid; for behold, I proclaim to you good news of great

---

m Ps 106, 10.—n Ps 106, 45-46.—o 72-73: Gn 17, 7; Lv 26,
42; Ps 105, 8-9; Mi 7, 20.—p 73-74: Gn 22, 16-17.—q Ti 2,
12.—r Is 40, 3; Mal 3, 1; Mt 3, 3; 11, 10.—s Mal 3, 20.—t 78-
79: Is 60, 1-2.—u Lk 2, 40; Mt 3, 1.—v Mi 5, 2; Mt 2, 6.—w Lk
1, 27; Mt 1, 18.—x Mt 1, 25.—y Lk 1, 11.26.

1, 76: *You will go before the Lord:* here *the Lord* is most
likely a reference to Jesus (contrast 15-17 where Yahweh is
meant) and John is presented as the precursor of Jesus.

1, 78: *The daybreak from on high:* three times in the LXX
(Jer 23, 5; Zec 3, 8; 6, 12), the Greek word used here for *day-
break* translates the Hebrew word for "scion, branch," an Old
Testament messianic title.

2, 1-2: Although universal registrations of Roman citizens are
attested in 28 B.C., 8 B.C., and A.D. 14 and enrollments in individual provinces of those who are not Roman citizens are also attested, such a universal census of the Roman world under Caesar
Augustus is unknown outside the New Testament. Moreover,
there are notorious historical problems connected with Luke's
dating the census *when Quirinius was governor of Syria,* and
the various attempts to resolve the difficulties have proved unsuccessful. P. Sulpicius Quirinius became legate of the province of
Syria in A.D. 6-7 when Judea was annexed to the province of
Syria. At that time, a provincial census of Judea was taken up. If
Quirinius had been legate of Syria previously, it would have to
have been before 10 B.C. because the various legates of Syria
from 10 B.C. to 4 B.C. (the death of Herod) are known, and such
a dating for an earlier census under Quirinius would create additional problems for dating the beginning of Jesus' ministry (Lk 3,
1.23). A previous legateship after 4 B.C. (and before A.D. 6)
would not fit with the dating of Jesus' birth in the days of Herod

(Lk 1, 5; Mt 2, 1). Luke may simply be combining Jesus' birth in
Bethlehem with his vague recollection of a census under Quirinius
(see also Acts 5, 37) to underline the significance of this birth for
the whole Roman world: through this child born in Bethlehem
peace and salvation come to the empire.

2, 1: *Caesar Augustus:* the reign of the Roman emperor
Caesar Augustus is usually dated from 27 B.C. to his death in A.D.
14. According to Greek inscriptions, Augustus was regarded in
the Roman Empire as "savior" and "god," and he was credited
with establishing a time of peace, the *pax Augusta,* throughout
the Roman world during his long reign. It is not by chance that
Luke relates the birth of Jesus to the time of Caesar Augustus:
the real savior (11) and peace-bearer (14; see also Lk 19, 38) is
the child born in Bethlehem. The great emperor is simply God's
agent (like the Persian king Cyrus in Is 44, 28—45, 1) who provides the occasion for God's purposes to be accomplished. *The
whole world:* that is, the whole Roman world: Rome, Italy, and
the Roman provinces.

2, 7: *Firstborn son:* the description of Jesus as *firstborn son*
does not necessarily mean that Mary had other sons. It is a legal
description indicating that Jesus possessed the rights and privileges of the firstborn son (Gn 27; Ex 13, 2; Nm 3, 12-13; 18, 15-
16; Dt 21, 15-17). See the notes on Mt 1, 25 and Mk 6, 3.
Wrapped him in swaddling clothes: there may be an allusion
here to the birth of another descendant of David, his son Solomon,
who though a great king was wrapped in swaddling clothes like
any other infant (Wis 7, 4-6). *Laid him in a manger:* a feeding
trough for animals. A possible allusion to Is 1, 3 LXX.

2, 8-20: The announcement of Jesus' birth to the shepherds is in
keeping with Luke's theme that the lowly are singled out as the
recipients of God's favors and blessings (see also Lk 1, 48.52).

THE WAILING WALL OF THE TEMPLE — The gigantic blocks of stone formed part of Herod's temple. It was customary for Jews to insert therein parchments containing their prayers and pleas. This was the temple in which Zechariah was performing his priestly function when he received word he would be the father of the forerunner of the Messiah, John the Baptist. (See Lk 1, 5-19)

DEAD SEA SCROLLS OF ESSENE COMMUNITY — Portions of a very important series of ancient Biblical Manuscripts discovered within recent years in caves near the Dead Sea. On the left (from top to bottom): (1) the Sectarian Document — a non-Biblical book; (2) a complete text of Isaiah ascribed to the second half of the second century B.C.; (3) a commentary on the Book of Habakkuk. On the right: a closer view.

These scrolls were produced in the community of Qumran which was apparently an Essene community. Some scholars believe that John the Baptist was brought up by Essenes. (See Lk 1, 80)

ANCIENT SYNAGOGUE OF CAPERNAUM — Capernaum was a town on the northwest shore of the Sea of Galilee used by Jesus as his headquarters during his Galilean ministry. Extensive ruins have been unearthed there, including those of the 3rd century synagogue which probably stood on the very site of the one Jesus attended and in which he preached. (See Lk 4, 31-32)

VILLAGE OF NAIN — View of the village of Nain, below Mount Tabor. It is located six miles southeast of Nazareth and commands a beautiful view over the hills of lower Galilee and the great plain to Mount Carmel by the sea. This is where Jesus raised a widow's son from the dead. (See Lk 7, 11-17)

joy that will be for all the people. ¹¹ ᶻ For today in the city of David a savior has been born for you who is Messiah and Lord.* ¹² And this will be a sign for you: you will find an infant wrapped in swaddling clothes and lying in a manger." ¹³ And suddenly there was a multitude of the heavenly host with the angel, praising God and saying:

¹⁴   "Glory to God in the highest ᵃ
      and on earth peace to those on whom
      his favor rests."*

The Visit of the Shepherds. ¹⁵ When the angels went away from them to heaven, the shepherds said to one another, "Let us go, then, to Bethlehem to see this thing that has taken place, which the Lord has made known to us." ¹⁶ So they went in haste and found Mary and Joseph, and the infant lying in the manger. ¹⁷ When they saw this, they made known the message that had been told them about this child. ¹⁸ All who heard it were amazed by what had been told them by the shepherds. ¹⁹ And Mary kept all these things, reflecting on them in her heart. ²⁰ Then the shepherds returned, glorifying and praising God for all they had heard and seen, just as it had been told to them.

The Circumcision and Naming of Jesus. ²¹ When eight days were completed for his circumcision,* he was named Jesus, the name given him by the angel before he was conceived in the womb. ᵇ

The Presentation in the Temple. ²² * When the days were completed for their purification* according to the law of Moses, they took him up to Jerusalem to present him to the Lord, ᶜ ²³ just as it is written in the law of the Lord, "Every male that opens the womb shall be consecrated to the Lord," ᵈ ²⁴ and to offer the sacrifice of "a pair of turtledoves or two young pigeons," in accordance with the dictate in the law of the Lord.

²⁵ Now there was a man in Jerusalem whose name was Simeon. This man was righteous and devout, awaiting the consolation of Israel,* and the holy Spirit was upon him. ²⁶ It had been revealed to him by the holy Spirit that he should not see death before he had seen the Messiah of the Lord. ²⁷ He came in the Spirit into the temple; and when the parents brought in the child Jesus to perform the custom of the law in regard to him, ²⁸ he took him into his arms and blessed God, saying:

²⁹   "Now, Master, you may let your ser-
         vant go
      in peace, according to your word, ᵉ
³⁰   for my eyes have seen your salvation, ᵉ

---

z Mt 1, 21; 16, 16; Jn 4, 42; Acts 2, 36; 5, 31; Phil 2, 11.—a Lk 19, 38.—b Lk 1, 31; Gn 17, 12; Mt 1, 21.—c 22-24: Lv 12, 2-8.—d Ex 13, 2.12.—e 30-31: Lk 3, 6; Is 40, 5 LXX; 52, 10.

2, 11: The basic message of the infancy narrative is contained in the angel's announcement: this child is *savior, Messiah,* and *Lord.* Luke is the only synoptic gospel writer to use the title *savior* for Jesus (Lk 2, 11; Acts 5, 31; 13, 23; see also Lk 1, 69; 19, 9; Acts 4, 12). As savior, Jesus is looked upon by Luke as the one who rescues humanity from sin and delivers humanity from the condition of alienation from God. The title *christos,* "Christ," is the Greek equivalent of the Hebrew *māšîaḥ,* "Messiah," "anointed one." Among certain groups in first-century Palestinian Judaism, the title was applied to an expected royal leader from the line of David who would restore the kingdom to Israel (see Acts 1, 6). The political overtones of the title are played down in Lk and instead the Messiah of the Lord (26) or the Lord's anointed is the one who now brings salvation to all humanity, Jew and Gentile (29-32). *Lord* is the most frequently used title for Jesus in Lk and Acts. In the New Testament it is also applied to Yahweh, as it is in the Old Testament. When used of Jesus it points to his transcendence and dominion over humanity.

2, 14: *On earth peace to those on whom his favor rests:* the peace that results from the Christ event is for those whom God has favored with his grace. This reading is found in the oldest representatives of the Western and Alexandrian text traditions and is the preferred one; the Byzantine text tradition, on the other hand, reads: "on earth peace, good will toward men." The peace of which Luke's gospel speaks (Lk 2, 14; 7, 50; 8, 48; 10, 5-6; 19, 38.42; 24, 36) is more than the absence of war or the *pax Augusta;* it also includes the security and well-being characteristic of peace in the Old Testament.

2, 21: Just as John before him had been incorporated into the people of Israel through his circumcision, so too this child (see the note on Lk 1, 57-66).

2, 22-40: The presentation of Jesus in the temple depicts the parents of Jesus as devout Jews, faithful observers of the law of the Lord (23.24.39), i.e., the law of Moses. In this respect, they are described in a fashion similar to the parents of John (Lk 1, 6) and Simeon (25) and Anna (36-37).

2, 22: *Their purification:* syntactically, *their* must refer to Mary and Joseph, even though the Mosaic law never mentions the purification of the husband. Recognizing the problem, some Western scribes have altered the text to read "his purification," understanding the presentation of Jesus in the temple as a form of purification; the Vulgate version has a Latin form that could be either "his" or "her." According to the Mosaic law (Lv 12, 2-8), the woman who gives birth to a boy is unable for forty days to touch anything sacred or to enter the temple area by reason of her legal impurity. At the end of this period she is required to offer a year-old lamb as a burnt offering and a turtledove or young pigeon as an expiation of sin. The woman who could not afford a lamb offered instead two turtledoves or two young pigeons, as Mary does here. *They took him up to Jerusalem to present him to the Lord:* as the firstborn son (Lk 2, 7) Jesus was consecrated to the Lord as the law required (Ex 13, 2.12), but there was no requirement that this be done at the temple. The concept of a presentation at the temple is probably derived from 1 Sm 1, 24-28, where Hannah offers the child Samuel for sanctuary services. The law further stipulated (Nm 3, 47-48) that the firstborn son should be redeemed by the parents through their payment of five shekels to a member of a priestly family. About this legal requirement Luke is silent.

2, 25: *Awaiting the consolation of Israel:* Simeon here and later Anna who speak about the child to all who were awaiting the redemption of Jerusalem represent the hopes and expectations of faithful and devout Jews who at this time were looking forward to the restoration of God's rule in Israel. The birth of Jesus brings these hopes to fulfillment.

31   which you prepared in sight of all the peoples,

32   a light for revelation to the Gentiles, and glory for your people Israel."*f*

33 The child's father and mother were amazed at what was said about him; 34 and Simeon blessed them and said to Mary his mother, "Behold, this child is destined for the fall and rise of many in Israel, and to be a sign that will be contradicted*g* 35 (and you yourself a sword will pierce)* so that the thoughts of many hearts may be revealed." 36 There was also a prophetess, Anna, the daughter of Phanuel, of the tribe of Asher. She was advanced in years, having lived seven years with her husband after her marriage, 37 and then as a widow until she was eighty-four. She never left the temple, but worshiped night and day with fasting and prayer. 38 And coming forward at that very time, she gave thanks to God and spoke about the child to all who were awaiting the redemption of Jerusalem. *h*

The Return to Nazareth. 39 When they had fulfilled all the prescriptions of the law of the Lord, they returned to Galilee, to their own town of Nazareth. *i* 40 The child grew and became strong, filled with wisdom; and the favor of God was upon him.*j*

The Boy Jesus in the Temple.* 41 Each year his parents went to Jerusalem for the feast of Passover,*k* 42 and when he was twelve years old, they went up according to festival custom. 43 After they had com-

pleted its days, as they were returning, the boy Jesus remained behind in Jerusalem, but his parents did not know it. 44 Thinking that he was in the caravan, they journeyed for a day and looked for him among their relatives and acquaintances, 45 but not finding him, they returned to Jerusalem to look for him. 46 After three days they found him in the temple, sitting in the midst of the teachers, listening to them and asking them questions, 47 and all who heard him were astounded at his understanding and his answers. 48 When his parents saw him, they were astonished, and his mother said to him, "Son, why have you done this to us? Your father and I have been looking for you with great anxiety." 49 And he said to them, "Why were you looking for me? Did you not know that I must be in my Father's house?"* 50 But they did not understand what he said to them. 51 He went down with them and came to Nazareth, and was obedient to them; and his mother kept all these things in her heart.*l* 52 And Jesus advanced [in] wisdom and age and favor before God and man.*m*

III. THE PREPARATION FOR THE PUBLIC MINISTRY

CHAPTER 3

The Preaching of John the Baptist.* 1 In the fifteenth year of the reign of Tiberius Caesar,* when Pontius Pilate was governor

---

f Is 42, 6; 46, 13; 49, 6; Acts 13, 47; 26, 23.—g Lk 12, 51; Is 8, 14; Jn 9, 39; Rom 9, 33; 1 Cor 1, 23; 1 Pt 2, 7-8.—h Is 52, 9.—i Mt 2, 23.—j Lk 1, 80; 2, 52.—k Ex 12, 24-27; 23, 15; Dt 16, 1-8.—l Lk 2, 19.—m Lk 1, 80; 2, 40; 1 Sm 2, 26.

2, 35: *(And you yourself a sword will pierce):* Mary herself will not be untouched by the various reactions to the role of Jesus (34). Her blessedness as mother of the Lord will be challenged by her son who describes true blessedness as "hearing the word of God and observing it" (Lk 11, 27-28 and Lk 8, 20-21).

2, 41-52: This story's concern with an incident from Jesus' youth is unique in the canonical gospel tradition. It presents Jesus in the role of the faithful Jewish boy, raised in the traditions of Israel, and fulfilling all that the law requires. With this episode, the infancy narrative ends just as it began, in the setting of the Jerusalem temple.

2, 49: *I must be in my Father's house:* this phrase can also be translated, "I must be about my Father's work." In either translation, Jesus refers to God as his Father. His divine sonship, and his obedience to his heavenly Father's will, take precedence over his ties to his family.

3, 1-20: Although Luke is indebted in this section to his sources, the Gospel of Mark and a collection of sayings of John the Baptist, he has clearly marked this introduction to the ministry of Jesus with his own individual style. Just as the gospel began with a long periodic sentence (Lk 1, 1-4), so too this section (1-2). He casts the call of John the Baptist in the form of an Old Testament prophetic call (2) and extends the quotation from Isaiah found in Mk 1, 3 (Is 40, 3) by the addition of Is 40, 4-5 in vv 5-6.

In doing so, he presents his theme of the universality of salvation, which he has announced earlier in the words of Simeon (Lk 2, 30-32). Moreover, in describing the expectation of the people (15), Luke is characterizing the time of John's preaching in the same way as he had earlier described the situation of other devout Israelites in the infancy narrative (Lk 2, 25-26.37-38). In vv 7-18 Luke presents the preaching of John the Baptist who urges the crowds to reform in view of *the coming wrath* (7.9: eschatological preaching), and who offers the crowds certain standards for reforming social conduct (10-14: ethical preaching), and who announces to the crowds the coming of *one mightier than* he (15-18: messianic preaching).

3, 1: *Tiberius Caesar:* Tiberius succeeded Augustus as emperor in A.D. 14 and reigned until A.D. 37. The fifteenth year of his reign, depending on the method of calculating his first regnal year, would have fallen between A.D. 27 and 29. *Pontius Pilate:* prefect of Judea from A.D. 26 to 36. The Jewish historian Josephus describes him as a greedy and ruthless prefect who had little regard for the local Jewish population and their religious practices (see Lk 13, 1). *Herod:* i.e., Herod Antipas, the son of Herod the Great. He ruled over Galilee and Perea from 4 B.C. to A.D. 39. His official title *tetrarch* means literally, "ruler of a quarter," but came to designate any subordinate prince. *Philip:* also a son of Herod the Great, tetrarch of the territory to the north and east of the Sea of Galilee from 4 B.C. to A.D. 34. Only two small areas of this territory are mentioned by Luke. *Lysanias:* nothing is known about this Lysanias who is said here to have been tetrarch of Abilene, a territory northwest of Damascus.

of Judea,[n] and Herod was tetrarch of Galilee, and his brother Philip tetrarch of the region of Ituraea and Trachonitis, and Lysanias was tetrarch of Abilene, [2] during the high priesthood of Annas and Caiaphas,* the word of God came to John[o] the son of Zechariah in the desert. [3] * He went throughout [the] whole region of the Jordan, proclaiming a baptism of repentance for the forgiveness of sins,[p] [4] as it is written in the book of the words of the prophet Isaiah:[q]

"A voice of one crying out in the desert:
'Prepare the way of the Lord,[r]
    make straight his paths.*
[5] Every valley shall be filled
    and every mountain and hill shall be made low.
The winding roads shall be made straight,
    and the rough ways made smooth,
[6] and all flesh shall see the salvation of God.' "[s]

[7] He said to the crowds who came out to be baptized by him, "You brood of vipers! Who warned you to flee from the coming wrath?[t] [8] Produce good fruits as evidence of your repentance; and do not begin to say to yourselves, 'We have Abraham as our father,' for I tell you, God can raise up children to Abraham from these stones.[u] [9] Even now the ax lies at the root of the trees. Therefore every tree that does not produce good fruit will be cut down and thrown into the fire."[v]

[10] And the crowds asked him, "What then should we do?" [11] He said to them in reply, "Whoever has two cloaks should share with the person who has none. And whoever has food should do likewise." [12] Even tax collectors came to be baptized and they said to him, "Teacher, what should we do?"[w] [13] He answered them, "Stop collecting more than what is prescribed." [14] Soldiers also asked him, "And what is it that we should do?" He told them, "Do not practice extortion, do not falsely accuse anyone, and be satisfied with your wages."

[15] [x] Now the people were filled with expectation, and all were asking in their hearts whether John might be the Messiah. [16] John answered them all, saying,[y] "I am baptizing you with water, but one mightier than I is coming. I am not worthy to loosen the thongs of his sandals. He will baptize you with the holy Spirit and fire.* [17] His winnowing fan* is in his hand to clear his threshing floor and to gather the wheat into his barn, but the chaff he will burn with unquenchable fire."[z] [18] Exhorting them in many other ways, he preached good news to the people. [19] * Now Herod the tetrarch,[a] who had been censured by him because of Herodias, his brother's wife, and because of all the evil deeds Herod had committed, [20] added still another to these by [also] putting John in prison.

n 1-20: Mt 3, 1-12; Mk 1, 1-8; Jn 1, 19-28.—o Lk 1, 80.—p Acts 13, 24; 19, 4.—q 4-6: Is 40, 3-5.—r Jn 1, 23.—s Lk 2, 30-31.—t Mt 12, 34.—u Jn 8, 39.—v Mt 7, 19; Jn 15, 6.—w Lk 7, 29.—x 15-16: Acts 13, 25.—y Lk 7, 19-20; Jn 1, 27; Acts 1, 5; 11, 16.—z Mt 3, 12.—a 19-20: Mt 14, 3-4; Mk 6, 17-18.

3, 2: *During the high priesthood of Annas and Caiaphas:* after situating the call of John the Baptist in terms of the civil rulers of the period, Luke now mentions the religious leadership of Palestine (see the note on Lk 1, 5). Annas had been high priest A.D. 6-15. After being deposed by the Romans in A.D. 15 he was succeeded by various members of his family and eventually by his son-in-law, Caiaphas, who was high priest A.D. 18-36. Luke refers to Annas as high priest at this time (but see Jn 18, 13.19), possibly because of the continuing influence of Annas or because the title continued to be used for the ex-high priest. *The word of God came to John:* Luke is alone among the New Testament writers in associating the preaching of John with a call from God. Luke is thereby identifying John with the prophets whose ministries began with similar calls. In Lk 7, 26 John will be described as "more than a prophet"; he is also the precursor of Jesus (Lk 7, 27), a transitional figure inaugurating the period of the fulfillment of prophecy and promise.

3, 3: See the note on Mt 3, 2.

3, 4: The Essenes from Qumran used the same passage to explain why their community was in the desert studying and observing the law and the prophets (1QS 8, 12-15).

3, 16: *He will baptize you with the holy Spirit and fire:* in contrast to John's baptism with water, Jesus is said to baptize with the holy Spirit and with fire. From the point of view of the early Christian community, the Spirit and fire must have been understood in the light of the fire symbolism of the pouring out of the Spirit at Pentecost (Acts 2, 1-4); but as part of John's preaching, the Spirit and fire should be related to their purifying and refining characteristics (Ez 36, 25-27; Mal 3, 2-3). See the note on Mt 3, 11.

3, 17: *Winnowing fan:* see the note on Mt 3, 12.

3, 19-20: Luke separates the ministry of John the Baptist from that of Jesus by reporting the imprisonment of John before the baptism of Jesus (21-22). Luke uses this literary device to serve his understanding of the periods of salvation history. With John the Baptist, the time of promise, the period of Israel, comes to an end; with the baptism of Jesus and the descent of the Spirit upon him, the time of fulfillment, the period of Jesus, begins. In his second volume, the Acts of the Apostles, Luke will introduce the third epoch in salvation history, the period of the church.

The Baptism of Jesus.* 21 b After all the people had been baptized and Jesus also had been baptized and was praying,* heaven was opened 22 c and the holy Spirit descended upon him in bodily form like a dove. And a voice came from heaven, "You are my beloved Son; with you I am well pleased."*

The Genealogy of Jesus.* 23 d When Jesus began his ministry he was about thirty years of age. He was the son, as was thought, of Joseph, the son of Heli, e 24 the son of Matthat, the son of Levi, the son of Melchi, the son of Jannai, the son of Joseph, 25 the son of Mattathias, the son of Amos, the son of Nahum, the son of Esli, the son of Naggai, 26 the son of Maath, the son of Mattathias, the son of Semein, the son of Josech, the son of Joda, 27 the son of Joanan, the son of Rhesa, the son of Zerubbabel, the son of Shealtiel, the son of Neri, f 28 the son of Melchi, the son of Addi, the son of Cosam, the son of Elmadam, the son of Er, 29 the son of Joshua, the son of Eliezer, the son of Jorim, the son of Matthat, the son of Levi, 30 the son of Simeon, the son of Judah, the son of Joseph, the son of Jonam, the son of Eliakim, 31 g the son of Melea, the son of Menna, the son of Mattatha, the son of Nathan, the son of David,* 32 the son of Jesse, h the son of Obed, the son of Boaz, the son of Sala, the son of Nahshon, 33 the son of Amminadab, the son of Admin, the son of Arni, the son of Hezron, the son of Perez, i

the son of Judah, j 34 the son of Jacob, the son of Isaac, the son of Abraham, k the son of Terah, the son of Nahor, 35 the son of Serug, the son of Reu, the son of Peleg, the son of Eber, the son of Shelah, 36 the son of Cainan, the son of Arphaxad, the son of Shem, l the son of Noah, the son of Lamech, 37 the son of Methuselah, the son of Enoch, the son of Jared, the son of Mahalaleel, the son of Cainan, 38 the son of Enos, the son of Seth, the son of Adam, m the son of God.

CHAPTER 4

The Temptation of Jesus.* 1 n Filled with the holy Spirit,* Jesus returned from the Jordan and was led by the Spirit into the desert 2 for forty days,* to be tempted by the devil. He ate nothing during those days, and when they were over he was hungry. o 3 The devil said to him, "If you are the Son of God, command this stone to become bread." 4 Jesus answered him, "It is written, 'One does not live by bread alone.' " p 5 Then he took him up and showed him all the kingdoms of the world in a single instant. 6 The devil said to him, "I shall give to you all this power and their glory; for it has been handed over to me, and I may give it to whomever I wish. q 7 All this will be yours, if you worship me." 8 Jesus said to him in reply, "It is written:

'You shall worship the Lord, your God,
   and him alone shall you serve.' " r
9 Then he led him to Jerusalem,* made him stand on the parapet of the temple, and

---

b 21-22: Mt 3, 13-17; Mk 1, 9-11.—c Lk 9, 35; Ps 2, 7; Is 42, 1; Mt 12, 18; 17, 5; Mk 9, 7; Jn 1, 32; 2 Pt 1, 17.—d 23-38: Mt 1, 1-17.—e Lk 4, 22; Jn 6, 42.—f 1 Chr 3, 17; Ez 3, 2.—g 2 Sm 5, 14.—h 31-32: 1 Sm 16, 1.18.—i 31-33: Ru 4, 17-22; 1 Chr 2, 1-15.—j Gn 29, 35; 38, 29.—k Gn 21, 3; 25, 26; 1 Chr 1, 34; 28, 34.—l 34-36: Gn 11, 10-26; 1 Chr 1, 24-27.—m 36-38: Gn 4, 25—5, 32; 1 Chr 1, 1-4.—n 1-13: Mt 4, 1-11; Mk 1, 12-13.—o Heb 4, 15.—p Dt 8, 3.—q Jer 27, 5; Mt 28, 18.—r Dt 6, 13.

3, 21-22: This episode in Luke focuses on the heavenly message identifying Jesus as *Son* and, through the allusion to Is 42, 1, as Servant of Yahweh. The relationship of Jesus to the Father has already been announced in the infancy narrative (Lk 1, 32.35; 2, 49); it occurs here at the beginning of Jesus' Galilean ministry and will reappear in Lk 9, 35 before another major section of Luke's gospel, the travel narrative (Lk 9, 51—19, 27). Elsewhere in Luke's writings (Lk 4, 18; Acts 10, 38), this incident will be interpreted as a type of anointing of Jesus.

3, 21: *Was praying:* Luke regularly presents Jesus at prayer at important points in his ministry: here at his baptism; at the choice of the Twelve (Lk 6, 12); before Peter's confession (Lk 9, 18); at the transfiguration (Lk 9, 28); when he teaches his disciples to pray (Lk 11, 1); at the Last Supper (Lk 22, 32); on the Mount of Olives (Lk 22, 41); on the cross (Lk 23, 46).

3, 22: *You are my beloved Son; with you I am well pleased:* this is the best attested reading in the Greek manuscripts. The Western reading, "You are my Son, this day I have begotten you," is derived from Ps 2, 7.

3, 23-38: Whereas Mt 1, 2 begins the genealogy of Jesus with Abraham to emphasize Jesus' bonds with the people of Israel, Luke's universalism leads him to trace the descent of Jesus beyond Israel to Adam and beyond that to God (38) to stress again Jesus' divine sonship.

3, 31: *The son of Nathan, the son of David:* in keeping with Jesus' prophetic role in Lk and Acts (e.g., Lk 7, 16.39; 9, 8; 13, 33; 24, 19; Acts 3, 22-23; 7, 37) Luke traces Jesus' Davidic ancestry through the prophet Nathan (see 2 Sm 7, 2) rather than through King Solomon, as Mt 1, 6-7.

4, 1-13: See the note on Mt 4, 1-11.

4, 1: *Filled with the holy Spirit:* as a result of the descent of the Spirit upon him at his baptism (Lk 3, 21-22), Jesus is now equipped to overcome the devil. Just as the Spirit is prominent at this early stage of Jesus' ministry (1.14.18), so too it will be at the beginning of the period of the church in Acts (Acts 1, 4; 2, 4.17).

4, 2: *For forty days:* the mention of forty days recalls the forty years of the wilderness wanderings of the Israelites during the Exodus (Dt 8, 2).

4, 9: *To Jerusalem:* the Lucan order of the temptations concludes on the parapet of the temple in Jerusalem, the city of destiny in Luke-Acts. It is in Jerusalem that Jesus will ultimately face his destiny (Lk 9, 51; 13, 33).

said to him, "If you are the Son of God, throw yourself down from here, [10] for it is written:

'He will command his angels concerning you,
    to guard you,'[s]

[11] and:

'With their hands they will support you,
    lest you dash your foot against a stone.' "[t]

[12] Jesus said to him in reply, "It also says, 'You shall not put the Lord, your God, to the test.' "[u] [13] When the devil had finished every temptation,[v] he departed from him for a time.*

IV. THE MINISTRY IN GALILEE

The Beginning of the Galilean Ministry. [14] [w] Jesus returned to Galilee in the power of the Spirit, and news of him spread* throughout the whole region.[x] [15] He taught in their synagogues and was praised by all.

The Rejection at Nazareth.* [y] [16] He came to Nazareth, where he had grown up, and went according to his custom* into the synagogue on the sabbath day. He stood up to read [17] and was handed a scroll of the prophet Isaiah. He unrolled the scroll and found the passage where it was written:

[18]   "The Spirit of the Lord is upon me,*
        because he has anointed me
            to bring glad tidings to the poor.[z]

He has sent me to proclaim liberty to captives
    and recovery of sight to the blind,
        to let the oppressed go free,
[19]   and to proclaim a year acceptable to the Lord."

[20] Rolling up the scroll, he handed it back to the attendant and sat down, and the eyes of all in the synagogue looked intently at him. [21] He said to them, "Today this scripture passage is fulfilled in your hearing."* [22] And all spoke highly of him and were amazed at the gracious words that came from his mouth. They also asked, "Isn't this the son of Joseph?"[a] [23] He said to them, "Surely you will quote me this proverb, 'Physician, cure yourself,' and say, 'Do here in your native place the things that we heard were done in Capernaum.' " * [24] And he said, "Amen, I say to you, no prophet is accepted in his own native place. [25] * Indeed, I tell you, there were many widows in Israel in the days of Elijah when the sky was closed for three and a half years and a severe famine spread over the entire land.[b] [26] It was to none of these that Elijah was sent, but only to a widow in Zarephath[c] in the land of Sidon.* [27] Again, there were many lepers in Israel during the time of Elisha the prophet; yet not one of them was cleansed, but only Naaman the Syrian."[d] [28] When the people in the synagogue heard this, they were all filled with fury. [29] They rose up, drove him out of the town, and led him to the brow of the hill on which their town

s Ps 91, 11.—t Ps 91, 12.—u Dt 6, 16; 1 Cor 10, 9.—v Lk 22, 3; Jn 13, 2.27; Heb 4, 15 .—w 14-15: Mt 4, 12-17; Mk 1, 14-15.—x Lk 5, 15; Mt 3, 16.—y 16-30: Mt 13, 53-58; Mk 6, 1-6.—z 18-19: Is 61, 1-2; 58, 6.—a Lk 3, 23; Jn 6, 42.—b 1 Kgs 17, 1-7; 18, 1; Jas 5, 17.—c 1 Kgs 17, 9.—d 2 Kgs 5, 1-14.

4, 13: *For a time:* the devil's opportune time will occur before the passion and death of Jesus (Lk 22, 3.31-32.53).

4, 14: *News of him spread:* a Lucan theme; see Lk 4, 37; 5, 15; 7, 17.

4, 16-30: Luke has transposed to the beginning of Jesus' ministry an incident from his Marcan source, which situated it near the end of the Galilean ministry (Mk 6, 1-6a). In doing so, Luke turns the initial admiration (22) and subsequent rejection of Jesus (28-29) into a foreshadowing of the whole future ministry of Jesus. Moreover, the rejection of Jesus in his own hometown hints at the greater rejection of him by Israel (Acts 13, 46).

4, 16: *According to his custom:* Jesus' practice of regularly attending synagogue is carried on by the early Christians' practice of meeting in the temple (Acts 2, 46; 3, 1; 5, 12).

4, 18: *The Spirit of the Lord is upon me, because he has anointed me:* see the note on Lk 3, 21-22. As this incident develops, Jesus is portrayed as a prophet whose ministry is compared to that of the prophets Elijah and Elisha. Prophetic anointings are known in first-century Palestinian Judaism from the Qumran literature that speaks of prophets as God's anointed ones. *To bring glad tidings to the poor:* more than any other gospel writer Luke is concerned with Jesus' attitude toward the economically and socially poor (see Lk 6, 20.24; 12, 16-21; 14, 12-14;

16, 19-26; 19, 8). At times, the poor in Luke's gospel are associated with the downtrodden, the oppressed and afflicted, the forgotten and the neglected (Lk 4, 18; 6, 20-22; 7, 22; 14, 12-14), and it is they who accept Jesus' message of salvation.

4, 21: *Today this scripture passage is fulfilled in your hearing:* this sermon inaugurates the time of fulfillment of Old Testament prophecy. Luke presents the ministry of Jesus as fulfilling Old Testament hopes and expectations (Lk 7, 22); for Luke, even Jesus' suffering, death, and resurrection are done in fulfillment of the scriptures (Lk 24, 25-27.44-46; Acts 3, 18).

4, 23: *The things that we heard were done in Capernaum:* Luke's source for this incident reveals an awareness of an earlier ministry of Jesus in Capernaum that Luke has not yet made use of because of his transposition of this Nazareth episode to the beginning of Jesus' Galilean ministry. It is possible that by use of the future tense *you will quote me . . . ,* Jesus is being portrayed as a prophet.

4, 25-26: The references to Elijah and Elisha serve several purposes in this episode: they emphasize Luke's portrait of Jesus as a prophet like Elijah and Elisha; they help to explain why the initial admiration of the people turns to rejection; and they provide the scriptural justification for the future Christian mission to the Gentiles.

4, 26: *A widow in Zarephath in the land of Sidon:* like Naaman the Syrian in v 27, a non-Israelite becomes the object of the prophet's ministry.

had been built, to hurl him down headlong. 30 But he passed through the midst of them and went away.

The Cure of a Demoniac. 31 * Jesus then went down to Capernaum,[e] a town of Galilee.[f] He taught them on the sabbath, 32 and they were astonished at his teaching because he spoke with authority.[g] 33 In the synagogue there was a man with the spirit of an unclean demon,[h] and he cried out in a loud voice, 34 "Ha! What have you to do with us, Jesus of Nazareth? Have you come to destroy us?* I know who you are—the Holy One of God!"[i] 35 Jesus rebuked him and said, "Be quiet! Come out of him!" Then the demon threw the man down in front of them and came out of him without doing him any harm. 36 They were all amazed and said to one another, "What is there about his word? For with authority and power he commands the unclean spirits, and they come out." 37 And news of him spread everywhere in the surrounding region.

The Cure of Simon's Mother-in-Law. 38 [j] After he left the synagogue, he entered the house of Simon.* Simon's mother-in-law was afflicted with a severe fever, and they interceded with him about her. 39 He stood over her, rebuked the fever, and it left her. She got up immediately and waited on them.

Other Healings.[k] 40 At sunset, all who had people sick with various diseases brought them to him. He laid his hands on each of them and cured them. 41 And demons also came out from many, shouting, "You are the Son of God."[l] But he rebuked them and did not allow them to speak because they knew that he was the Messiah.*

Jesus Leaves Capernaum.[m] 42 At daybreak, Jesus left and went to a deserted place. The crowds went looking for him, and when they came to him, they tried to prevent him from leaving them.* 43 But he said to them, "To the other towns also I must proclaim the good news of the kingdom of God, because for this purpose I have been sent."[n] 44 And he was preaching in the synagogues of Judea.*

CHAPTER 5

The Call of Simon the Fisherman.*[o] 1 [p] While the crowd was pressing in on Jesus and listening to the word of God, he was standing by the Lake of Gennesaret. 2 He saw two boats there alongside the lake; the fishermen had disembarked and were washing their nets. 3 Getting into one of the boats, the one belonging to Simon, he asked him to put out a short distance from the shore. Then he sat down and taught the crowds from the boat. 4 [q] After he had finished speaking, he said to Simon, "Put out into deep water and lower your nets for a catch." 5 Simon said in reply, "Master,

e 31-37: Mk 1, 21-28.—f Mt 4, 13; Jn 2, 12.—g Mt 7, 28-29.—h 33-34: Lk 8, 28; Mt 8, 29; Mk 1, 23-24; 5, 7.—i Lk 4, 41; Jn 6, 69.—j 38-39: Mt 8, 14-15; Mk 1, 29-31.—k 40-41: Mt 8, 16; Mk 1, 32-34.—l Lk 4, 34; Mt 8, 29; Mk 3, 11-12.—m 42-44: Mk 1, 35-39.—n Lk 8, 1; Mk 1, 14-15.—o 1-11: Mt 4, 18-22; Mk 1, 16-20.—p 1-3: Mt 13, 1-2; Mk 2, 13; 3, 9-10; 4, 1-2.—q 4-9: Jn 21, 1-11.

4, 31-44: The next several incidents in Jesus' ministry take place in Capernaum and are based on Luke's source, Mk 1, 21-39. To the previous portrait of Jesus as prophet (16-30) they now add a presentation of him as teacher (31-32), exorcist (32-37.41), healer (38-40), and proclaimer of God's kingdom (43).

4, 34: *What have you to do with us?:* see the note on Jn 2, 4. *Have you come to destroy us?:* the question reflects the current belief that before the day of the Lord control over humanity would be wrested from the evil spirits, evil destroyed, and God's authority over humanity reestablished. The synoptic gospel tradition presents Jesus carrying out this task.

4, 38: *The house of Simon:* because of Luke's arrangement of material, the reader has not yet been introduced to Simon (cf Mk 1, 16-18.29-31). Situated as it is before the call of Simon (Lk 5, 1-11), it helps the reader to understand Simon's eagerness to do what Jesus says (Lk 5, 5) and to follow him (Lk 5, 11).

4, 41: *They knew that he was the Messiah:* that is, the Christ (see the note on Lk 2, 11).

4, 42: *They tried to prevent him from leaving them:* the reaction of these strangers in Capernaum is presented in contrast to the reactions of those in his hometown who rejected him (28-30).

4, 44: *In the synagogues of Judea:* instead of *Judea,* which is the best reading of the manuscript tradition, the Byzantine text tradition and other manuscripts read "Galilee," a reading that harmonizes Lk with Mt 4, 23 and Mk 1, 39. Up to this point Luke has spoken only of a ministry of Jesus in Galilee. Luke may be using *Judea* to refer to the land of Israel, the territory of the Jews, and not to a specific portion of it.

5, 1-11: This incident has been transposed from his source, Mk 1, 16-20, which places it immediately after Jesus makes his appearance in Galilee. By this transposition Luke uses this example of Simon's acceptance of Jesus to counter the earlier rejection of him by his hometown people, and since several incidents dealing with Jesus' power and authority have already been narrated, Luke creates a plausible context for the acceptance of Jesus by Simon and his partners. Many commentators have noted the similarity between the wondrous catch of fish reported here (4-9) and the post-resurrectional appearance of Jesus in Jn 21, 1-11. There are traces in Luke's story that the post-resurrectional context is the original one: in v 8 Simon addresses Jesus as *Lord* (a post-resurrectional title for Jesus—see Lk 24, 34; Acts 2, 36—that has been read back into the historical ministry of Jesus) and recognizes himself as a sinner (an appropriate recognition for one who has denied knowing Jesus—Lk 22, 54-62). As used by Luke, the incident looks forward to Peter's leadership in Luke-Acts (Lk 6, 14; 9, 20; 22, 31-32; 24, 34; Acts 1, 15; 2, 14-40; 10, 11-18; 15, 7-12) and symbolizes the future success of Peter as fisherman (Acts 2, 41).

we have worked hard all night and have caught nothing, but at your command I will lower the nets." ⁶When they had done this, they caught a great number of fish and their nets were tearing. ⁷They signaled to their partners in the other boat to come to help them. They came and filled both boats so that they were in danger of sinking. ⁸When Simon Peter saw this, he fell at the knees of Jesus and said, "Depart from me, Lord, for I am a sinful man." ⁹For astonishment at the catch of fish they had made seized him and all those with him, ¹⁰and likewise James and John, the sons of Zebedee, who were partners of Simon. Jesus said to Simon, "Do not be afraid; from now on you will be catching men."ʳ ¹¹When they brought their boats to the shore, they left everything* and followed him.ˢ

The Cleansing of a Leper.ᵗ ¹²Now there was a man full of leprosy* in one of the towns where he was; and when he saw Jesus, he fell prostrate, pleaded with him, and said, "Lord, if you wish, you can make me clean." ¹³Jesus stretched out his hand,

---

r Jer 16, 16.—s Mt 19, 27.—t 12-16: Mt 8, 2-4; Mk 1, 40-45.—u Lk 8, 56; Lv 14, 2-32; Mk 7, 36.—v Mk 1, 35.—w 17-26: Mt 9, 1-8; Mk 2, 1-12.—x Lk 7, 49; Is 43, 25.—y Lk 6, 8; 9, 47.—z 24-25: Jn 5, 8-9.27.—a 27-32: Mt 9, 9-13; Mk 2, 13-17.—b 29-30: Lk 15, 1-2.

5, 11: *They left everything:* in Mk 1, 16-20 and Mt 4, 18-22 the fishermen who follow Jesus leave their nets and their father; in Luke, they leave *everything* (see also Lk 5, 28; 12, 33; 14, 33; 18, 22), an indication of Luke's theme of complete detachment from material possessions.

5, 12: *Full of leprosy:* see the note on Mk 1, 40.

5, 14: *Show yourself to the priest .. . what Moses prescribed:* this is a reference to Lv 14, 2-9 that gives detailed instructions for the purification of one who had been a victim of leprosy and thereby excluded from contact with others (see Lv 13, 45-46.49; Nm 5, 2-3). *That will be proof for them:* see the note on Mt 8, 4.

5, 17—6, 11: From his Marcan source, Luke now introduces a series of controversies with Pharisees: controversy over Jesus' power to forgive sins (17-26); controversy over his eating and drinking with tax collectors and sinners (27-32); controversy over not fasting (33-36); and finally two episodes narrating controversies over observance of the sabbath (1-11).

5, 17: *Pharisees:* see the note on Mt 3, 7.

5, 19: *Through the tiles:* Luke has adapted the story found in Mk to his non-Palestinian audience by changing "opened up the roof" (Mk 2, 4, a reference to Palestinian straw and clay roofs) to *through the tiles,* a detail that reflects the Hellenistic Greco-Roman house with tiled roof.

5, 20: *As for you, your sins are forgiven:* literally, "O man, your sins are forgiven you." The connection between the forgiveness of sins and the cure of the paralytic reflects the belief of first-century Palestine (based on the Old Testament: Ex 20, 5; Dt 5, 9) that sickness and infirmity are the result of sin, one's own or that of one's ancestors (see also Lk 13, 2; Jn 5, 14; 9, 2).

5, 21: *The scribes:* see the note on Mk 2, 6.

5, 24: See the notes on Mt 9, 6 and Mk 2, 10.

5, 28: *Leaving everything behind:* see the note on Lk 5, 11.

---

touched him, and said, "I do will it. Be made clean." And the leprosy left him immediately. ¹⁴Then he ordered him not to tell anyone, but "Go, show yourself to the priest and offer for your cleansing what Moses prescribed;* that will be proof for them."ᵘ ¹⁵The report about him spread all the more, and great crowds assembled to listen to him and to be cured of their ailments, ¹⁶but he would withdraw to deserted places to pray.ᵛ

The Healing of a Paralytic.ʷ ¹⁷ * One day as Jesus was teaching, Pharisees* and teachers of the law were sitting there who had come from every village of Galilee and Judea and Jerusalem, and the power of the Lord was with him for healing. ¹⁸And some men brought on a stretcher a man who was paralyzed; they were trying to bring him in and set [him] in his presence. ¹⁹But not finding a way to bring him in because of the crowd, they went up on the roof and lowered him on the stretcher through the tiles* into the middle in front of Jesus. ²⁰When he saw their faith, he said, "As for you, your sins are forgiven."* ²¹Then the scribes* and Pharisees began to ask themselves, "Who is this who speaks blasphemies? Who but God alone can forgive sins?"ˣ ²²Jesus knew their thoughts and said to them in reply, "What are you thinking in your hearts?ʸ ²³Which is easier, to say, 'Your sins are forgiven,' or to say, 'Rise and walk'? ²⁴ ᶻ But that you may know that the Son of Man has authority on earth to forgive sins"—he said to the man who was paralyzed, "I say to you, rise, pick up your stretcher, and go home."* ²⁵He stood up immediately before them, picked up what he had been lying on, and went home, glorifying God. ²⁶Then astonishment seized them all and they glorified God, and, struck with awe, they said, "We have seen incredible things today."

The Call of Levi. ᵃ ²⁷After this he went out and saw a tax collector named Levi sitting at the customs post. He said to him, "Follow me." ²⁸And leaving everything behind,* he got up and followed him. ²⁹ ᵇ Then Levi gave a great banquet for him in his house, and a large crowd of tax collectors and others were at table with them. ³⁰The Pharisees and their scribes complained to his disciples, saying, "Why do you eat and drink with tax collectors and sinners?" ³¹Jesus said to them in reply,

"Those who are healthy do not need a physician, but the sick do. ³²I have not come to call the righteous to repentance but sinners."

The Question about Fasting. *c* ³³And they said to him, "The disciples of John fast often and offer prayers, and the disciples of the Pharisees do the same; but yours eat and drink." ³⁴ * Jesus answered them, "Can you make the wedding guests* fast while the bridegroom is with them? ³⁵But the days will come, and when the bridegroom is taken away from them, then they will fast in those days." ³⁶ *And he also told them a parable. "No one tears a piece from a new cloak to patch an old one. Otherwise, he will tear the new and the piece from it will not match the old cloak. ³⁷Likewise, no one pours new wine into old wineskins. Otherwise, the new wine will burst the skins, and it will be spilled, and the skins will be ruined. ³⁸Rather, new wine must be poured into fresh wineskins. ³⁹[And] no one who has been drinking old wine desires new, for he says, 'The old is good.' "*

CHAPTER 6

Debates about the Sabbath.* ¹ *d* While he was going through a field of grain on a sabbath, his disciples were picking the heads of grain, rubbing them in their hands, and eating them. *e* ²Some Pharisees said, "Why are you doing what is unlawful on the sabbath?" ³ *f* Jesus said to them in reply,

"Have you not read what David did when he and those [who were] with him were hungry? ⁴[How] he went into the house of God, took the bread of offering,* which only the priests could lawfully eat, ate of it, and shared it with his companions."*g* ⁵Then he said to them, "The Son of Man is lord of the sabbath."

⁶ *h* On another sabbath he went into the synagogue and taught, and there was a man there whose right hand was withered. ⁷The scribes and the Pharisees watched him closely to see if he would cure on the sabbath so that they might discover a reason to accuse him.*i* ⁸But he realized their intentions and said to the man with the withered hand, "Come up and stand before us." And he rose and stood there.*j* ⁹Then Jesus said to them, "I ask you, is it lawful to do good on the sabbath rather than to do evil, to save life rather than to destroy it?" ¹⁰Looking around at them all, he then said to him, "Stretch out your hand." He did so and his hand was restored. ¹¹But they became enraged and discussed together what they might do to Jesus.

The Mission of the Twelve.* ¹² *k* In those days he departed to the mountain to pray, and he spent the night in prayer* to God. ¹³When day came, he called his disciples to himself, and from them he chose Twelve,* whom he also named apostles: ¹⁴ *l* Simon, whom he named Peter,* and his brother Andrew, James, John, Philip, Barthol-

---

c 33-39: Mt 9, 14-17; Mk 2, 18-22.—d 1-5: Mt 12, 1-8; Mk 2, 23-28.—e Dt 23, 26.—f 3-4: 1 Sm 21, 1-6.—g Lv 24, 5-9.—h 6-11: Mt 12, 9-14; Mk 3, 1-6.—i Lk 14, 1.—j Lk 5, 22; 9, 47.— k 12-16: Mt 10, 1-4; Mk 3, 13-19.—l 14-16: Acts 1, 13.

5, 34-35: See the notes on Mt 9, 15 and Mk 2, 19.

5, 34: *Wedding guests:* literally, "sons of the bridal chamber."

5, 36-39: See the notes on Mt 9, 16-17 and Mk 2, 19.

5, 39: *The old is good:* this saying is meant to be ironic and offers an explanation for the rejection by some of the new wine that Jesus offers: satisfaction with old forms will prevent one from sampling the new.

6, 1-11: The two episodes recounted here deal with gathering grain and healing, both of which were forbidden on the sabbath. In his defense of his disciples' conduct and his own charitable deed, Jesus argues that satisfying human needs such as hunger and performing works of mercy take precedence even over the sacred sabbath rest. See also the notes on Mt 12, 1-14 and Mk 2, 25-26.

6, 4: *The bread of offering:* see the note on Mt 12, 5-6.

6, 12-16: See the notes on Mt 10, 1—11, 1 and Mk 3, 14-15.

6, 12: *Spent the night in prayer:* see the note on Lk 3, 21.

6, 13: *He chose Twelve:* the identification of this group as the *Twelve* is a part of early Christian tradition (see 1 Cor 15, 5), and in Mt and Lk, the Twelve are associated with the twelve tribes of Israel (Lk 22, 29-30; Mt 19, 28). After the fall of Judas from his position among the Twelve, the need is felt on the part of the early community to reconstitute this group before the Christian mission begins at Pentecost (Acts 1, 15-26). From Luke's perspective, they are an important group who because of their association with Jesus from the time of his baptism to his ascension (Acts 1, 21-22) provide the continuity between the historical Jesus and the church of Luke's day and who as the original eyewitnesses guarantee the fidelity of the church's beliefs and practices to the teachings of Jesus (Lk 1, 1-4). *Whom he also named apostles:* only Luke among the gospel writers attributes to Jesus the bestowal of the name *apostles* upon the Twelve. See the note on Mt 10, 2-4. "Apostle" becomes a technical term in early Christianity for a missionary sent out to preach the word of God. Although Luke seems to want to restrict the title to the Twelve (only in Acts 4, 4.14 are Paul and Barnabas termed apostles), other places in the New Testament show an awareness that the term was more widely applied (1 Cor 15, 5-7; Gal 1, 19; 1 Cor 1, 1; 9, 1; Rom 16, 7).

6, 14: *Simon, whom he named Peter:* see the note on Mk 3, 16.

omew, [15] Matthew, Thomas, James the son of Alphaeus, Simon who was called a Zealot,* [16] and Judas the son of James, and Judas Iscariot,* who became a traitor.

Ministering to a Great Multitude.[m] [17] And he came down with them and stood on a stretch of level ground. A great crowd of his disciples and a large number of the people from all Judea and Jerusalem and the coastal region of Tyre and Sidon* [18] came to hear him and to be healed of their diseases; and even those who were tormented by unclean spirits were cured. [19] Everyone in the crowd sought to touch him because power came forth from him and healed them all.

Sermon on the Plain.[n] [20] * And raising his eyes toward his disciples he said:

"Blessed are you who are poor,*
    for the kingdom of God is yours.
[21] Blessed are you who are now hungry,
    for you will be satisfied.
Blessed are you who are now weeping,
    for you will laugh.[o]
[22] Blessed are you when people hate you,
    and when they exclude and insult you,
    and denounce your name as evil
    on account of the Son of Man.[p]

[23] Rejoice and leap for joy on that day! Behold, your reward will be great in heaven. For their ancestors treated the prophets in the same way.[q]

[24] But woe to you who are rich,
    for you have received your consolation.[r]
[25] But woe to you who are filled now,
    for you will be hungry.

Woe to you who laugh now,
    for you will grieve and weep.[s]
[26] Woe to you when all speak well of you,
    for their ancestors treated the false prophets in this way.[t]

Love of Enemies.* [27] [u] "But to you who hear I say, love your enemies, do good to those who hate you,[v] [28] bless those who curse you, pray for those who mistreat you.[w] [29] To the person who strikes you on one cheek, offer the other one as well, and from the person who takes your cloak, do not withhold even your tunic. [30] Give to everyone who asks of you, and from the one who takes what is yours do not demand it back. [31] Do to others as you would have them do to you.[x] [32] For if you love those who love you, what credit is that to you? Even sinners love those who love them. [33] And if you do good to those who do good to you, what credit is that to you? Even sinners do the same. [34] If you lend money to those from whom you expect repayment, what credit [is] that to you? Even sinners lend to sinners, and get back the same amount.[y] [35] But rather, love your enemies and do good to them, and lend expecting nothing back; then your reward will be great and you will be children of the Most High, for he himself is kind to the ungrateful and the wicked.[z] [36] Be merciful, just as [also] your Father is merciful.

---

m 17-19: Mt 4, 23-25; Mk 3, 7-10.—n 20-26: Mt 5, 1-12.—o Ps 126, 5-6; Is 61, 3; Jer 31, 25; Rv 7, 16-17.—p Jn 15, 19; 16, 2; 1 Pt 4, 14.—q Lk 11, 47-48; 2 Chr 36, 16; Mt 23, 30-31.—r Jas 5, 1.—s Is 65, 13-14.—t Jas 4, 4.—u 27-36: Mt 5, 38-48.— v Prv 25, 21; Rom 12, 20-21.—w Rom 12, 14; 1 Pt 3, 9.—x Mt 7, 12.—y Dt 15, 7-8.—z Lv 25, 35-36.

6, 15: *Simon who was called a Zealot:* the Zealots were the instigators of the First Revolt of Palestinian Jews against Rome in A.D. 66-70. Because the existence of the Zealots as a distinct group during the lifetime of Jesus is the subject of debate, the meaning of the identification of Simon as a Zealot is unclear.

6, 16: *Judas Iscariot:* the name *Iscariot* may mean "man from Kerioth."

6, 17: *The coastal region of Tyre and Sidon:* not only Jews from Judea and Jerusalem, but even Gentiles from outside Palestine come to hear Jesus (see Lk 2, 31-32; 3, 6; 4, 24-27).

6, 20-49: Luke's "Sermon on the Plain" is the counterpart to Mt's "Sermon on the Mount" (Mt 5, 1—7, 27). It is addressed to the disciples of Jesus, and, like the sermon in Mt, it begins with beatitudes (20-22) and ends with the parable of the two houses

(46-49). Almost all the words of Jesus reported by Lk are found in Mt's version, but because Mt includes sayings that were related to specifically Jewish Christian problems (e.g., Mt 5, 17-20; 6, 1-8.16-18) that Luke did not find appropriate for his predominantly Gentile Christian audience, the "Sermon on the Mount" is considerably longer. Lk's sermon may be outlined as follows: an introduction consisting of blessings and woes (20-26); the love of one's enemies (27-36); good deeds as proof of one's goodness (43-45); a parable illustrating the result of listening to and acting on the words of Jesus (46-49). At the core of the sermon is Jesus' teaching on the love of one's enemies (27-36) that has as its source of motivation God's graciousness and compassion for all humanity (35-36) and Jesus' teaching on the love of one's neighbor (37-42) that is characterized by forgiveness and generosity.

6, 20-26: The introductory portion of the sermon consists of blessings and woes that address the real economic and social conditions of humanity (the poor—the rich; the hungry—the satisfied; those grieving—those laughing; the outcast—the socially acceptable). By contrast, Matthew emphasizes the religious and spiritual values of disciples in the kingdom inaugurated by Jesus ("poor in spirit," Mt 5, 5; "hunger and thirst for righteousness," Mt 5, 6). In the sermon, *blessed* extols the fortunate condition of persons who are favored with the blessings of God; the woes, addressed as they are to the disciples of Jesus, threaten God's profound displeasure on those so blinded by their present fortunate situation that they do not recognize and appreciate the real values of God's kingdom. In all the blessings and woes, the present condition of the persons addressed will be reversed in the future.

6, 27-36: See the notes on Mt 5, 43-48 and Mt 5, 48.

Lk

Judging Others.* [37] [a] "Stop judging and you will not be judged. Stop condemning and you will not be condemned. Forgive and you will be forgiven. [b] [38] Give and gifts will be given to you; a good measure, packed together, shaken down, and overflowing, will be poured into your lap. For the measure with which you measure will in return be measured out to you." [c] [39] And he told them a parable, "Can a blind person guide a blind person? Will not both fall into a pit? [d] [40] No disciple is superior to the teacher; but when fully trained, every disciple will be like his teacher. [e] [41] Why do you notice the splinter in your brother's eye, but do not perceive the wooden beam in your own? [42] How can you say to your brother, 'Brother, let me remove that splinter in your eye,' when you do not even notice the wooden beam in your own eye? You hypocrite! Remove the wooden beam from your eye first; then you will see clearly to remove the splinter in your brother's eye.

A Tree Known by Its Fruit. [f] [43] * "A good tree does not bear rotten fruit, nor does a rotten tree bear good fruit. [44] For every tree is known by its own fruit. For people do not pick figs from thornbushes, nor do they gather grapes from brambles. [45] A good person out of the store of goodness in his heart produces good, but an evil person out of a store of evil produces evil; for from the fullness of the heart the mouth speaks.

The Two Foundations. [46] [g] "Why do you call me, 'Lord, Lord,' but not do what I command? [47] * I will show you what someone is like who comes to me, listens to my words, and acts on them. [h] [48] That one is like a person building a house, who dug deeply and laid the foundation on rock; when the flood came, the river burst against that house but could not shake it because it had been well built. [49] But the one who listens and does not act is like a person who built a house on the ground without a foundation. When the river burst against it, it collapsed at once and was completely destroyed."

CHAPTER 7

The Healing of a Centurion's Slave. [i] [1] * When he had finished all his words to the people, he entered Capernaum.* [2] A centurion* there had a slave who was ill and about to die, and he was valuable to him.

[3] When he heard about Jesus, he sent elders of the Jews to him, asking him to come and save the life of his slave. [4] They approached Jesus and strongly urged him to come, saying, "He deserves to have you do this for him, [5] for he loves our nation and he built the synagogue for us." [6] And Jesus went with them, but when he was only a short distance from the house, the centurion sent friends to tell him, "Lord, do not trouble yourself, for I am not worthy to have you enter under my roof.* [7] Therefore, I did not consider myself worthy to come to you; but say the word and let my servant be healed. [8] For I too am a person subject to authority, with soldiers subject to me. And I say to one, 'Go,' and he goes; and to another, 'Come here,' and he comes; and to my slave, 'Do this,' and he does it." [9] When Jesus heard this he was amazed at him and, turning, said to the crowd following him, "I tell you, not even in Israel have I found such faith." [10] When the messengers returned to the house, they found the slave in good health.

Raising of the Widow's Son.* [11] [j] Soon afterward he journeyed to a city called Nain,

---

a 37-42: Mt 7, 1-5.—b Mt 6, 14; Jas 2, 13.—c Mk 4, 24.—d Mt 15, 14; 23, 16-17.24.—e Mt 10, 24-25; Jn 13, 16; 15, 20.—f 43-45: Mt 7, 16-20; 12, 33.35.—g Mt 7, 21; Rom 2, 13; Jas 1, 22.—h 47-49: Mt 7, 24-27.—i 1-10: Mt 8, 5-13; Jn 4, 43-54.—j 11-17: Lk 4, 25-26; 1 Kgs 17, 17-24.

6, 37-42: See the notes on Mt 7, 1-12; 7, 1; 7, 5.

6, 43-46: See the notes on Mt 7, 15-20 and Mt 12, 33.

6, 47-49: See the note on Mt 7, 24-27.

7, 1—8, 3: The episodes in this section present a series of reactions to the Galilean ministry of Jesus and reflect some of Luke's particular interests: the faith of a Gentile (1-10); the prophet Jesus' concern for a widowed mother (11-17); the ministry of Jesus directed to the afflicted and unfortunate of Is 61, 1 (18-23); the relation between John and Jesus and their role in God's plan for salvation (24-35); a forgiven sinner's manifestation of love (36-50); the association of women with the ministry of Jesus (Lk 8, 1-3).

7, 1-10: This story about the faith of the centurion, a Gentile who cherishes the Jewish nation (5), prepares for the story in Acts of the conversion by Peter of the Roman centurion Cornelius who is similarly described as one who is generous to the Jewish nation (Acts 10, 2). See also Acts 10, 34-35 in the speech of Peter: "God shows no partiality . . . the person who fears him and acts righteously is acceptable to him." See also the notes on Mt 8, 5-13 and Jn 4, 43-54.

7, 2: *A centurion:* see the note on Mt 8, 5.

7, 6: *I am not worthy to have you enter under my roof:* to enter the house of a Gentile was considered unclean for a Jew; cf Acts 10, 28.

7, 11-17: In the previous incident Jesus' power was displayed for a Gentile whose servant was dying; in this episode it is displayed toward a widowed mother whose only son has already died. Jesus' power over death prepares for his reply to John's disciples in v 22: "the dead are raised." This resuscitation in alluding to the prophet Elijah's resurrection of the only son of a widow of Zarephath (1 Kgs 7, 8-24) leads to the reaction of the crowd: "A great prophet has arisen in our midst" (16).

and his disciples and a large crowd accompanied him. [12] As he drew near to the gate of the city, a man who had died was being carried out, the only son of his mother, and she was a widow. A large crowd from the city was with her.[k] [13] When the Lord saw her, he was moved with pity for her and said to her, "Do not weep." [14] He stepped forward and touched the coffin; at this the bearers halted, and he said, "Young man, I tell you, arise!" [15] The dead man sat up and began to speak, and Jesus gave him to his mother.[l] [16] Fear seized them all, and they glorified God, exclaiming, "A great prophet has arisen in our midst," and "God has visited his people."[m] [17] This report about him spread through the whole of Judea and in all the surrounding region.

The Messengers from John the Baptist.[*] [18] [n] The disciples of John told him about all these things. John summoned two of his disciples [19] and sent them to the Lord to ask, "Are you the one who is to come, or should we look for another?"[o] [20] When the men came to him, they said, "John the Baptist has sent us to you to ask, 'Are you the one who is to come, or should we look for another?' " [21] At that time he cured many of their diseases, sufferings, and evil

---

k Lk 8, 42; 1 Kgs 17, 17.—l 1 Kgs 17, 23; 2 Kgs 4, 36.—m Lk 1, 68; 19, 44.—n 18-23: Mt 11, 2-6.—o Mal 3, 1; Rv 1, 4.8; 4, 8.—p Lk 4, 18; Is 35, 5-6; 61, 1.—q 24-30: Mt 11, 7-15.—r Lk 1, 76.—s Mal 3, 1 / Is 40, 3.—t 29-30: Lk 3, 7.12; Mt 21, 32.—u 31-35: Mt 11, 16-19.—v Lk 15, 2.—w Lk 11, 37; 14, 1.

7, 18-23: In answer to John's question, *Are you the one who is to come?*—a probable reference to the return of the fiery prophet of reform, Elijah,"before the day of the Lord comes, the great and terrible day" (Mal 3, 23)—Jesus responds that his role is rather to bring the blessings spoken of in Is 61, 1 to the oppressed and neglected of society (22; cf Lk 4, 18).

7, 23: *Blessed is the one who takes no offense at me:* this beatitude is pronounced on the person who recognizes Jesus' true identity in spite of previous expectations of what "the one who is to come" would be like.

7, 24-30: In his testimony to John, Jesus reveals his understanding of the relationship between them: John is the precursor of Jesus (27); John is the messenger spoken of in Mal 3, 1 who in Mal 3, 23 is identified as Elijah. Taken with the previous episode, it can be seen that Jesus identifies John as precisely the person John envisioned Jesus to be: the Elijah who prepares the way for the coming of the day of the Lord.

7, 31-35: See the note on Mt 11, 16-19.

7, 36-50: In this story of the pardoning of the sinful woman Luke presents two different reactions to the ministry of Jesus. A Pharisee, suspecting Jesus to be a prophet, invites Jesus to a festive banquet in his house, but the Pharisee's self-righteousness leads to little forgiveness by God and consequently little love shown toward Jesus. The sinful woman, on the other hand, manifests a faith in God (50) that has led her to seek forgiveness for her sins, and because so much was forgiven, she now overwhelms Jesus with her display of love; cf the similar contrast in attitudes in Lk 18, 9-14. The whole episode is a powerful lesson on the relation between forgiveness and love.

---

spirits; he also granted sight to many who were blind. [22] And he said to them in reply, "Go and tell John what you have seen and heard: the blind regain their sight, the lame walk, lepers are cleansed, the deaf hear, the dead are raised, the poor have the good news proclaimed to them.[p] [23] And blessed is the one who takes no offense at me."[*]

Jesus' Testimony to John. [24] [*] When the messengers of John had left, Jesus began to speak to the crowds about John.[q] "What did you go out to the desert to see—a reed swayed by the wind? [25] Then what did you go out to see? Someone dressed in fine garments? Those who dress luxuriously and live sumptuously are found in royal palaces. [26] Then what did you go out to see? A prophet? Yes, I tell you, and more than a prophet.[r] [27] This is the one about whom scripture says:

'Behold, I am sending my messenger ahead of you,
he will prepare your way before you.'[s]

[28] I tell you, among those born of women, no one is greater than John; yet the least in the kingdom of God is greater than he." [29] [t] (All the people who listened, including the tax collectors, and who were baptized with the baptism of John, acknowledged the righteousness of God; [30] but the Pharisees and scholars of the law, who were not baptized by him, rejected the plan of God for themselves.)

[31] [*] "Then to what shall I compare the people of this generation? What are they like?[u] [32] They are like children who sit in the marketplace and call to one another,

'We played the flute for you, but you did not dance.
We sang a dirge, but you did not weep.'

[33] For John the Baptist came neither eating food nor drinking wine, and you said, 'He is possessed by a demon.' [34] The Son of Man came eating and drinking and you said, 'Look, he is a glutton and a drunkard, a friend of tax collectors and sinners.'[v] [35] But wisdom is vindicated by all her children."

The Pardon of the Sinful Woman. [*] [36] [w] A Pharisee invited him to dine with him, and he entered the Pharisee's house and reclined at table.*[37]Now there was a sinful woman in the city who learned that he was at table in the house of the Pharisee.[x] Bringing an alabaster flask of ointment,[y] [38]she stood behind him at his feet weeping and began to bathe his feet with her tears. Then she wiped them with her hair, kissed them, and anointed them with the ointment. [39]When the Pharisee who had invited him saw this he said to himself, "If this man were a prophet, he would know who and what sort of woman this is who is touching him, that she is a sinner." [40]Jesus said to him in reply, "Simon, I have something to say to you." "Tell me, teacher," he said. [41]"Two people were in debt to a certain creditor; one owed five hundred days' wages* and the other owed fifty. [42]Since they were unable to repay the debt, he forgave it for both. Which of them will love him more?" [43]Simon said in reply, "The one, I suppose, whose larger debt was forgiven." He said to him, "You have judged rightly." [44]Then he turned to the woman and said to Simon, "Do you see this woman? When I entered your house, you did not give me water for my feet, but she has bathed them with her tears and wiped them with her hair. [45]You did not give me a kiss, but she has not ceased kissing my feet since the time I entered. [46]You did not anoint my head with oil, but she anointed my feet with ointment. [47]So I tell you, her many sins have been forgiven; hence, she has shown great love.* But the one to whom little is forgiven, loves little." [48]He said to her, "Your sins are forgiven."[z] [49]The others at table said to themselves, "Who is this who even forgives sins?"[a] [50]But he said to the woman, "Your faith has saved you; go in peace."

CHAPTER 8

Galilean Women Follow Jesus.* [1]Afterward he journeyed from one town and village to another, preaching and proclaiming the good news of the kingdom of God.[b] Accompanying him were the Twelve [2] [c] and some women who had been cured of evil spirits and infirmities, Mary, called Magdalene, from whom seven demons had gone out, [3]Joanna, the wife of Herod's steward Chuza, Susanna, and many others who provided for them out of their resources.

The Parable of the Sower.[d] [4]* When a large crowd gathered, with people from one town after another journeying to him, he spoke in a parable.* [5]"A sower went out to sow his seed. And as he sowed, some seed fell on the path and was trampled, and the birds of the sky ate it up. [6]Some seed fell on rocky ground, and when it grew, it withered for lack of moisture. [7]Some seed fell among thorns, and the thorns grew with it and choked it. [8]And some seed fell on good soil, and when it grew, it produced fruit a hundredfold." After saying this, he called out, "Whoever has ears to hear ought to hear."[e]

The Purpose of the Parables.[f] [9]Then his disciples asked him what the meaning of this parable might be. [10]He answered, "Knowledge of the mysteries of the kingdom of God has been granted to you; but to the rest, they are made known through parables so that 'they may look but not see, and hear but not understand.'[g]

The Parable of the Sower Explained.* [11] [h] "This is the meaning of the parable. The

---

x Mt 26, 7; Mk 14, 3.—y 37-38: Jn 12, 3.—z Lk 5, 20; Mt 9, 20; Mk 2, 5.—a Lk 5, 21.—b Lk 4, 43.—c 2-3: Lk 23, 49; 24, 10; Mt 27, 55-56; Mk 15, 40-41; Jn 19, 5.—d 4-8: Mt 13, 1-9; Mk 4, 1-9.—e Lk 14, 35; Mt 11, 15; 13, 43; Mk 4, 23.—f 9-10: Mt 13, 10-13; Mk 4, 10-12.—g Is 6, 9.—h 11-15: Mt 13, 18-23; Mk 4, 13-20.

7, 36: *Reclined at table:* the normal posture of guests at a banquet. Other oriental banquet customs alluded to in this story include the reception by the host with a kiss (45), washing the feet of the guests (44), and the anointing of the guests' heads (46).

7, 41: *Days' wages:* one denarius is the normal daily wage of a laborer.

7, 47: *Her many sins have been forgiven; hence, she has shown great love:* literally, "her many sins have been forgiven, seeing that she has loved much." That the woman's sins have been forgiven is attested by the great love she shows toward Jesus. Her love is the consequence of her forgiveness. This is also the meaning demanded by the parable in vv 41-43.

8, 1-3: Luke presents Jesus as an itinerant preacher traveling in the company of the Twelve and of the Galilean women who are sustaining them out of their means. These Galilean women will later accompany Jesus on his journey to Jerusalem and become witnesses to his death (Lk 23, 49) and resurrection (Lk 24, 9-11, where Mary Magdalene and Joanna are specifically mentioned; cf also Acts 1, 14). The association of women with the ministry of Jesus is most unusual in the light of the attitude of first-century Palestinian Judaism toward women. The more common attitude is expressed in Jn 4, 27, and early rabbinic documents caution against speaking with women in public.

8, 4-21: The focus in this section is on how one should hear the word of God and act on it. It includes the parable of the sower and its explanation (4-15), a collection of sayings on how one should act on the word that is heard (16-18), and the identification of the mother and brothers of Jesus as the ones who hear the word and act on it (19-21). See also the notes on Mt 13, 1-53 and Mk 4, 1-34.

8, 4-8: See the note on Mt 13, 3-8.

8, 11-15: On the interpretation of the parable of the sower, see the note on Mt 13, 18-23.

seed is the word of God.[i] [12] Those on the path are the ones who have heard, but the devil comes and takes away the word from their hearts that they may not believe and be saved. [13] Those on rocky ground are the ones who, when they hear, receive the word with joy, but they have no root; they believe only for a time and fall away in time of trial. [14] As for the seed that fell among thorns, they are the ones who have heard, but as they go along, they are choked by the anxieties and riches and pleasures of life, and they fail to produce mature fruit. [15] But as for the seed that fell on rich soil, they are the ones who, when they have heard the word, embrace it with a generous and good heart, and bear fruit through perseverance.

The Parable of the Lamp.* [16] [j] "No one who lights a lamp conceals it with a vessel or sets it under a bed; rather, he places it on a lampstand so that those who enter may see the light.[k] [17] For there is nothing hidden that will not become visible, and nothing secret that will not be known and come to light.[l] [18] Take care, then, how you hear. To anyone who has, more will be given, and from the one who has not, even what he seems to have will be taken away."[m]

Jesus and His Family.[n] [19] Then his mother and his brothers* came to him but were unable to join him because of the crowd. [20] [o] He was told, "Your mother and your brothers are standing outside and they wish to see you." [21] He said to them in reply, "My mother and my brothers are those who hear the word of God and act on it."*

The Calming of a Storm at Sea.[p] [22] * One day he got into a boat with his disciples and said to them, "Let us cross to the other side of the lake." So they set sail, [23] and while they were sailing he fell asleep. A squall blew over the lake, and they were taking in water and were in danger. [24] They came and woke him saying, "Master, master, we are perishing!" He awakened, rebuked the wind and the waves, and they subsided and there was a calm. [25] Then he asked them, "Where is your faith?" But they were filled with awe and amazed and said to one another, "Who then is this, who commands even the winds and the sea, and they obey him?"

The Healing of the Gerasene Demoniac.[q] [26] Then they sailed to the territory of the Gerasenes,* which is opposite Galilee. [27] When he came ashore a man from the town who was possessed by demons met him. For a long time he had not worn clothes; he did not live in a house, but lived among the tombs. [28] [r] When he saw Jesus, he cried out and fell down before him; in a loud voice he shouted, "What have you to do with me, Jesus, son of the Most High God? I beg you, do not torment me!" [29] For he had ordered the unclean spirit to come out of the man. (It had taken hold of him many times, and he used to be bound with chains and shackles as a restraint, but he would break his bonds and be driven by the demon into deserted places.) [30] Then Jesus asked him, "What is your name?"* He replied, "Legion," because many demons had entered him. [31] And they pleaded with him not to order them to depart to the abyss.*

[32] A herd of many swine was feeding there on the hillside, and they pleaded with

i 1 Pt 1, 23.—j 16-18: Mk 4, 21-25.—k Lk 11, 33; Mt 5, 15.—l Lk 12, 2; Mt 10, 26.—m Lk 19, 26; Mt 13, 12; 25, 29.— n 19-21: Mt 12, 46-50; Mk 3, 31-35.—o 20-21: Lk 11, 27-28.— p 22-25: Mt 8, 18.23-27; Mk 4, 35-41.—q 26-39: Mt 8, 28-34; Mk 5, 1-20.—r 28-29: Lk 4, 33-35; Mt 8, 29; Mk 1, 23-24.

8, 16-18: These sayings continue the theme of responding to the word of God. Those who hear the word must become a light to others (16); even the mysteries of the kingdom that have been made known to the disciples (9-10) must come to light (17); a generous and persevering response to the word of God leads to a still more perfect response to the word.

8, 19: *His brothers:* see the note on Mk 6, 3.

8, 21: The family of Jesus is not constituted by physical relationship with him but by obedience to the word of God. In this, Luke agrees with the Marcan parallel (Mk 3, 31-35), although by omitting Mk 3, 33 and especially Mk 3, 20-21 Luke has softened the Marcan picture of Jesus' natural family. Probably he did this because Mary has already been presented in Lk 1, 38 as the obedient handmaid of the Lord who fulfills the requirement for belonging to the eschatological family of Jesus; cf also Lk 11, 27-28.

8, 22-56: This section records four miracles of Jesus that manifest his power and authority: (1) the calming of a storm on the lake (22-25); (2) the exorcism of a demoniac (26-39); (3) the cure of a hemorrhaging woman (40-48); (4) the raising of Jairus's daughter to life (49-56). They parallel the same sequence of stories at Mk 4, 35—5, 43.

8, 26: *Gerasenes:* other manuscripts read Gadarenes or Gergesenes. See also the note on Mt 8, 28. *Opposite Galilee:* probably Gentile territory (note the presence in the area of pigs—unclean animals to Jews) and an indication that the person who receives salvation (36) is a Gentile.

8, 30: *What is your name?:* the question reflects the popular belief that knowledge of the spirit's name brought control over the spirit. *Legion:* to Jesus' question the demon replies with a Latin word transliterated into Greek. The Roman legion at this period consisted of 5,000 to 6,000 foot soldiers; hence the name implies a very large number of demons.

8, 31: *Abyss:* the place of the dead (Rom 10, 7) or the prison of Satan (Rv 20, 3) or the subterranean "watery deep" that symbolizes the chaos before the order imposed by creation (Gn 1, 2).

him to allow them to enter those swine; and he let them. [33] The demons came out of the man and entered the swine, and the herd rushed down the steep bank into the lake and was drowned. [34] When the swineherds saw what had happened, they ran away and reported the incident in the town and throughout the countryside. [35] People came out to see what had happened and, when they approached Jesus, they discovered the man from whom the demons had come out sitting at his feet.* He was clothed and in his right mind, and they were seized with fear. [36] Those who witnessed it told them how the possessed man had been saved. [37] The entire population of the region of the Gerasenes asked Jesus to leave them because they were seized with great fear. So he got into a boat and returned. [38] The man from whom the demons had come out begged to remain with him, but he sent him away, saying, [39] "Return home and recount what God has done for you." The man went off and proclaimed throughout the whole town what Jesus had done for him.

Jairus's Daughter and the Woman with a Hemorrhage.* [40] [s] When Jesus returned, the crowd welcomed him, for they were all waiting for him. [41] And a man named Jairus, an official of the synagogue, came forward. He fell at the feet of Jesus and begged him to come to his house, [42] because he had an only daughter,* about twelve years old, and she was dying. As he went, the crowds almost crushed him. [43] And a woman afflicted with hemorrhages for twelve years,* who [had spent her whole livelihood on doctors and] was unable to be cured by anyone, [44] came up behind him and touched the tassel on his cloak. Immediately her bleeding stopped. [45] Jesus then asked, "Who touched me?" While all were denying it, Peter said, "Master, the crowds are pushing and pressing in upon you." [46] But Jesus said, "Someone has touched me; for I know that power has gone out from me." [t] [47] When the woman realized that she had not escaped notice, she came forward trembling. Falling down before him, she explained in the presence of all the people why she had touched him and how she had been healed immediately. [48] He said to her, "Daughter, your faith has saved you; go in peace." [u]

[49] While he was still speaking, someone from the synagogue official's house arrived and said, "Your daughter is dead; do not trouble the teacher any longer." [50] On hearing this, Jesus answered him, "Do not be afraid; just have faith and she will be saved." [51] When he arrived at the house he allowed no one to enter with him except Peter and John and James, and the child's father and mother. [52] [v] All were weeping and mourning for her, when he said, "Do not weep any longer, for she is not dead, but sleeping."* [53] And they ridiculed him, because they knew that she was dead. [54] But he took her by the hand and called to her, "Child, arise!" [55] Her breath returned and she immediately arose. He then directed that she should be given something to eat. [56] Her parents were astounded, and he instructed them to tell no one what had happened.

CHAPTER 9

The Mission of the Twelve.* [1] [w] He summoned the Twelve and gave them power and authority over all demons and to cure diseases, [2] and he sent them to proclaim the kingdom of God and to heal [the sick]. [3] He said to them, "Take nothing for the journey,* neither walking stick, nor sack, nor food, nor money, and let no one take a second tunic. [4] Whatever house you enter,

---

s 40-56: Mt 9, 18-26; Mk 5, 21-43.—t Lk 6, 19.—u Lk 7, 50; 17, 19; 18, 42.—v Lk 7, 13.—w 1-6: Mt 10, 1.5-15; Mk 6, 7-13.

8, 35: *Sitting at his feet:* the former demoniac takes the position of a disciple before the master (Lk 10, 39; Acts 22, 3).

8, 40-56: Two interwoven miracle stories, one a healing and the other a resuscitation, present Jesus as master over sickness and death. In the Lucan account, faith in Jesus is responsible for the cure (48) and for the raising to life (50).

8, 42: *An only daughter:* cf the son of the widow of Nain whom Luke describes as an "only" son (Lk 7, 12; see also Lk 9, 38).

8, 43: *Afflicted with hemorrhages for twelve years:* according to the Mosaic law (Lv 15, 25-30) this condition would render the woman unclean and unfit for contact with other people.

8, 52: *Sleeping:* her death is a temporary condition; cf Jn 11, 11-14.

9, 1-6: Armed with the power and authority that Jesus himself has been displaying in the previous episodes, the Twelve are now sent out to continue the work that Jesus has been performing throughout his Galilean ministry: (1) proclaiming the kingdom (Lk 4, 43; 8, 1); (2) exorcising demons (Lk 4, 33-37.41; 8, 26-39) and (3) healing the sick (Lk 4, 38-40; 5, 12-16.17-26; 6, 6-10; 7, 1-10.17.22; 8, 40-56).

9, 3: *Take nothing for the journey:* the absolute detachment required of the disciple (Lk 14, 33) leads to complete reliance on God (Lk 12, 22-31).

stay there and leave from there.*x* [5] And as for those who do not welcome you, when you leave that town, shake the dust from your feet* in testimony against them."*y* [6] Then they set out and went from village to village proclaiming the good news and curing diseases everywhere.

Herod's Opinion of Jesus. *z* [7] * Herod the tetrarch* heard about all that was happening, and he was greatly perplexed because some were saying, "John has been raised from the dead";*a* [8] others were saying, "Elijah has appeared"; still others, "One of the ancient prophets has arisen." [9] *b* But Herod said, "John I beheaded. Who then is this about whom I hear such things?" And he kept trying to see him.*

The Return of the Twelve and the Feeding of the Five Thousand. *c* [10] When the apostles returned, they explained to him what they had done. He took them and withdrew in private to a town called Bethsaida. [11] The crowds, meanwhile, learned of this and followed him. He received them and spoke to them about the kingdom of God, and he healed those who needed to be cured. [12] As the day was drawing to a close, the Twelve approached him and said, "Dismiss the crowd so that they can go to the surrounding villages and farms and find lodging and provisions; for we are in a deserted place here." [13] *d* He said to them, "Give them some food yourselves." They replied, "Five loaves and two fish are all we have, unless we ourselves go and buy food for all these people." [14] Now the men there numbered about five thousand. Then he said to his disciples, "Have them sit down in groups of [about] fifty." [15] They did so and

made them all sit down. [16] Then taking* the five loaves and the two fish, and looking up to heaven, he said the blessing over them, broke them, and gave them to the disciples to set before the crowd.*e* [17] They all ate and were satisfied. And when the leftover fragments were picked up, they filled twelve wicker baskets.

Peter's Confession about Jesus. *[18] f* Once when Jesus was praying in solitude,* and the disciples were with him, he asked them, "Who do the crowds say that I am?" [19] They said in reply, "John the Baptist; others, Elijah; still others, 'One of the ancient prophets has arisen.' "*g* [20] Then he said to them, "But who do you say that I am?" Peter said in reply, "The Messiah of God."* [21] He rebuked them and directed them not to tell this to anyone.

The First Prediction of the Passion. [22] He said, "The Son of Man must suffer greatly and be rejected by the elders, the chief priests, and the scribes, and be killed and on the third day be raised."*h*

The Conditions of Discipleship. *i* [23] Then he said to all, "If anyone wishes to come after me, he must deny himself and take up his cross daily* and follow me.*j* [24] For whoever wishes to save his life will lose it, but whoever loses his life for my sake will save it.*k* [25] What profit is there for one to gain the whole world yet lose or forfeit himself? [26] Whoever is ashamed of me and of my words, the Son of Man will be ashamed of when he comes in his glory and in the glory of the Father and of the holy angels.*l* [27] Truly I say to you, there are

x Lk 10, 5-7.—y Lk 10, 10-11; Acts 13, 51.—z 7-9: Mt 14, 1-12; Mk 6, 14-29.—a 7-8: Lk 9, 19; Mt 16, 14; Mk 8, 28.—b Lk 23, 8.—c 10-17: Mt 14, 13-21; Mk 6, 30-44; Jn 6, 1-14.—d 13-17: 2 Kgs 4, 42-44.—e Lk 22, 19; 24, 30-31; Acts 2, 42; 20, 11; 27, 35.—f 18-21: Mt 16, 13-20; Mk 8, 27-30.—g Lk 9, 7-8.—h Lk 24, 7.26; Mt 16, 21; 20, 18-19; Mk 8, 31; 10, 33-34.—i 23-27: Mt 16, 24-28; Mk 8, 34—9, 1.—j Lk 14, 27; Mt 10, 38.—k Lk 17, 33; Mt 10, 39; Jn 12, 25.—l Lk 12, 9; Mt 10, 33; 2 Tm 2, 12.

9, 5: *Shake the dust from your feet:* see the note on Mt 10, 14.

9, 7-56: This section in which Luke gathers together incidents that focus on the identity of Jesus is introduced by a question that Herod is made to ask in this gospel: "Who then is this about whom I hear such things?" (9). In subsequent episodes, Luke reveals to the reader various answers to Herod's question: Jesus is one in whom God's power is present and who provides for the needs of God's people (10-17); Peter declares Jesus to be "the Messiah of God" (18-21); Jesus says he is the suffering Son of Man (22.43-45); Jesus is the Master to be followed, even to death (23-27); Jesus is God's Son, his Chosen One (28-36).

9, 7: *Herod the tetrarch:* see the note on Lk 3, 1.

9, 9: *And he kept trying to see him:* this indication of Herod's interest in Jesus prepares for Lk 13, 31-33 and for Lk 23, 8-12 where Herod's curiosity about Jesus' power to perform miracles remains unsatisfied.

9, 16: *Then taking . . . :* the actions of Jesus recall the institution of the Eucharist in Lk 22, 19; see also the note on Mt 14, 19.

9, 18-22: This incident is based on Mk 8, 27-33, but Luke has eliminated Peter's refusal to accept Jesus as suffering Son of Man (Mk 8, 32) and the rebuke of Peter by Jesus (Mk 8, 33). Elsewhere in the gospel, Luke softens the harsh portrait of Peter and the other apostles found in his Marcan source (cf Lk 22, 39-46, which similarly lacks a rebuke of Peter that occurs in the source, Mk 14, 37-38).

9, 18: *When Jesus was praying in solitude:* see the note on Lk 3, 21.

9, 20: *The Messiah of God:* on the meaning of this title in first-century Palestinian Judaism, see the notes on Lk 2, 11 and on Mt 16, 13-20 and Mk 8, 27-30.

9, 23: *Daily:* this is a Lucan addition to a saying of Jesus, removing the saying from a context that envisioned the imminent suffering and death of the disciple of Jesus (as does the saying in Mk 8, 34-35) to one that focuses on the demands of daily Christian existence.

Lk

some standing here who will not taste death until they see the kingdom of God."

The Transfiguration of Jesus.* [28] [m] About eight days after he said this, he took Peter, John, and James and went up the mountain to pray.* [29] While he was praying his face changed in appearance and his clothing became dazzling white. [30] And behold, two men were conversing with him, Moses and Elijah,* [31] [n] who appeared in glory and spoke of his exodus that he was going to accomplish in Jerusalem.* [32] Peter and his companions had been overcome by sleep, but becoming fully awake, they saw his glory* and the two men standing with him. [o] [33] As they were about to part from him, Peter said to Jesus, "Master, it is good that we are here; let us make three tents,* one for you, one for Moses, and one for Elijah." But he did not know what he was saying. [34] While he was still speaking, a cloud came and cast a shadow over them,* and they became frightened when they entered the cloud. [35] [p] Then from the cloud came a voice that said, "This is my chosen Son; listen to him."* [36] After the voice had spoken, Jesus was found alone. They fell silent and did not at that time* tell anyone what they had seen.

The Healing of a Boy with a Demon.* [37] [q] On the next day, when they came down from the mountain, a large crowd met him. [38] There was a man in the crowd who cried out, "Teacher, I beg you, look at my son; he is my only child. [39] For a spirit seizes him and he suddenly screams and it con-

vulses him until he foams at the mouth; it releases him only with difficulty, wearing him out. [40] I begged your disciples to cast it out but they could not." [41] Jesus said in reply, "O faithless and perverse generation, how long will I be with you and endure you? Bring your son here." [42] As he was coming forward, the demon threw him to the ground in a convulsion; but Jesus rebuked the unclean spirit, healed the boy, and returned him to his father. [43] And all were astonished by the majesty of God.

The Second Prediction of the Passion. [r] While they were all amazed at his every deed, he said to his disciples, [44] "Pay attention to what I am telling you. The Son of Man is to be handed over to men." [45] But they did not understand this saying; its meaning was hidden from them so that they should not understand it, and they were afraid to ask him about this saying.

The Greatest in the Kingdom. [s] [46] * An argument arose among the disciples about which of them was the greatest. [t] [47] Jesus realized the intention of their hearts and took a child and placed it by his side [48] and said to them, "Whoever receives this child in my name receives me, and whoever receives me receives the one who sent me. For the one who is least among all of you is the one who is the greatest." [u]

Another Exorcist. [v] [49] Then John said in reply, "Master, we saw someone casting out demons in your name and we tried to prevent him because he does not follow in our company." [50] Jesus said to him, "Do not prevent him, for whoever is not against you is for you."

---

m 28-36: Mt 17, 1-8; Mk 9, 2-8.—n Lk 9, 22; 13, 33.—o Jn 1, 14; 2 Pt 1, 16.—p Lk 3, 22; Dt 18, 15; Ps 2, 7; Is 42, 1; Mt 3, 17; 12, 18; Mk 1, 11; 2 Pt 1, 17-18.—q 37-43: Mt 17, 14-18; Mk 9, 14-27.—r 43-45: Lk 18, 32-34; Mt 17, 22-23; Mk 9, 30-32.—s 46-48: Mt 18, 1-5; Mk 9, 33-37.—t Lk 22, 24.—u Lk 10, 16; Mt 10, 40; Jn 13, 20.—v 49-50: Mk 9, 38-40.

9, 28-36: Situated shortly after the first announcement of the passion, death, and resurrection, this scene of Jesus' transfiguration provides the heavenly confirmation to Jesus' declaration that his suffering will end in glory (32); see also the notes on Mt 17, 1-8 and Mk 9, 2-8.

9, 28: *Up the mountain to pray:* the "mountain" is the regular place of prayer in Lk (see Lk 6, 12; 22, 39-41).

9, 30: *Moses and Elijah:* the two figures represent the Old Testament law and the prophets. At the end of this episode, the heavenly voice will identify Jesus as the one to be listened to now (35). See also the note on Mk 9, 5.

9, 31: *His exodus that he was going to accomplish in Jerusalem:* Luke identifies the subject of the conversation as the *exodus* of Jesus, a reference to the death, resurrection, and ascension of Jesus that will take place in Jerusalem, the city of destiny (see Lk 9, 51). The mention of *exodus*, however, also calls to mind the Israelite Exodus from Egypt to the promised land.

9, 32: *They saw his glory:* the *glory* that is proper to God is here attributed to Jesus (see Lk 24, 26).

9, 33: *Let us make three tents:* in a possible allusion to the feast of Tabernacles, Peter may be likening his joy on the occasion of the transfiguration to the joyful celebration of this harvest festival.

9, 34: *Over them:* it is not clear whether *them* refers to Jesus, Moses, and Elijah, or to the disciples. For the cloud casting its shadow, see the note on Mk 9, 7.

9, 35: Like the heavenly voice that identified Jesus at his baptism prior to his undertaking the Galilean ministry (Lk 3, 22), so too here before the journey to the city of destiny is begun (51) the heavenly voice again identifies Jesus as Son. *Listen to him:* the two representatives of Israel of old depart (33) and Jesus is left alone (36) as the teacher whose words must be heeded (see also Acts 3, 22).

9, 36: *At that time:* i.e., before the resurrection.

9, 37-43a: See the note on Mk 9, 14-29.

9, 46-50: These two incidents focus on attitudes that are opposed to Christian discipleship: rivalry and intolerance of outsiders.

V. THE JOURNEY TO JERUSALEM: LUKE'S TRAVEL NARRATIVE*

Departure for Jerusalem; Samaritan Inhospitality. 51 * When the days for his being taken up* were fulfilled, he resolutely determined to journey to Jerusalem,*w* 52 and he sent messengers ahead of him.*x* On the way they entered a Samaritan* village to prepare for his reception there, 53 but they would not welcome him because the destination of his journey was Jerusalem. 54 When the disciples James and John saw this they asked, "Lord, do you want us to call down fire from heaven to consume them?"*y* 55 Jesus turned and rebuked them, 56 and they journeyed to another village.

The Would-be Followers of Jesus.* 57 *z* As they were proceeding on their journey someone said to him, "I will follow you wherever you go." 58 Jesus answered him, "Foxes have dens and birds of the sky have nests, but the Son of Man has nowhere to rest his head." 59 And to another he said, "Follow me." But he replied, "[Lord,] let me go first and bury my father." 60 But he answered him, "Let the dead bury their dead.* But you, go and proclaim the kingdom of God." 61 *a* And another said, "I will follow you, Lord, but first let me say farewell to my family at home." 62 [To him] Jesus said, "No one who sets a hand to the plow and looks to what was left behind is fit for the kingdom of God."

CHAPTER 10

The Mission of the Seventy-two.* 1 After this the Lord appointed seventy[-two]* others whom he sent ahead of him in pairs to every town and place he intended to visit.*b* 2 He said to them, "The harvest is abundant but the laborers are few; so ask the master of the harvest to send out laborers for his harvest.*c* 3 Go on your way; behold, I am sending you like lambs among wolves.*d* 4 Carry no money bag,*e* no sack, no sandals;*f* and greet no one along the way.* 5 Into whatever house you enter, first say, 'Peace to this household.'* 6 If a peaceful person* lives there, your peace will rest on him; but if not, it will return to you. 7 Stay in the same house and eat and drink what is offered to you, for the la-

---

w Lk 9, 53; 13, 22.33; 17, 11; 18, 31; 19, 28; 24, 51; Acts 1, 2.9-11.22.—x Mal 3, 1.—y 2 Kgs 1, 10.12.—z 57-60: Mt 8, 19-22.—a 61-62: 1 Kgs 19, 20.—b Mk 6, 7.—c Mt 9, 37-38; Jn 4, 35.—d Mt 10, 16.—e Lk 9, 3; 2 Kgs 4, 29.—f 4-11: Mt 10, 7-14.

9, 51—18, 14: The Galilean ministry of Jesus finishes with the previous episode and a new section of Luke's gospel begins, the journey to Jerusalem. This journey is based on Mk 10, 1-52, but Luke uses his Marcan source only in Lk 18, 15—19, 27. Before that point he has inserted into his gospel a distinctive collection of sayings of Jesus and stories about him that he has drawn from Q, a collection of sayings of Jesus used also by Matthew, and from his own special traditions. All of the material collected in this section is loosely organized within the framework of a journey of Jesus to Jerusalem, the city of destiny, where his exodus (suffering, death, resurrection, ascension) is to take place (Lk 9, 31), where salvation is accomplished, and from where the proclamation of God's saving word is to go forth (Lk 24, 47; Acts 1, 8). Much of the material in the Lucan travel narrative is teaching for the disciples. During the course of this journey Jesus is preparing his chosen Galilean witnesses for the role they will play after his exodus (Lk 9, 31): they are to be his witnesses to the people (Acts 10, 39; 13, 31) and thereby provide certainty to the readers of Luke's gospel that the teachings they have received are rooted in the teachings of Jesus (Lk 1, 1-4).

9, 51-55: Just as the Galilean ministry began with a rejection of Jesus in his hometown, so too the travel narrative begins with the rejection of him by Samaritans. In this episode Jesus disassociates himself from the attitude expressed by his disciples that those who reject him are to be punished severely. The story alludes to 2 Kgs 1,10.12, where the prophet Elijah takes the course of action Jesus rejects, and Jesus thereby rejects the identification of himself with Elijah.

9, 51: *Days for his being taken up:* like the reference to his exodus in v 31, this is probably a reference to all the events (suffering, death, resurrection, ascension) of his last days in Jerusalem. *He resolutely determined:* literally, "he set his face."

9, 52: *Samaritan:* Samaria was the territory between Judea and Galilee west of the Jordan river. For ethnic and religious reasons, the Samaritans and the Jews were bitterly opposed to one another (see Jn 4, 9).

9, 57-62: In these sayings Jesus speaks of the severity and the unconditional nature of Christian discipleship. Even family ties and filial obligations, such as burying one's parents, cannot distract one no matter how briefly from proclaiming the kingdom of God. The first two sayings are paralleled in Mt 8, 19-22; see the notes there.

9, 60: *Let the dead bury their dead:* i.e., let the spiritually dead (those who do not follow) bury their physically dead. See also the note on Mt 8, 22.

10, 1-12: Only the Gospel of Luke contains two episodes in which Jesus sends out his followers on a mission: the first (Lk 9,1-6) is based on the mission in Mk 6, 6b-13 and recounts the sending out of the Twelve; here in vv 1-12 a similar report based on Q becomes the sending out of seventy-two in this gospel. The episode continues the theme of Jesus preparing witnesses to himself and his ministry. These witnesses include not only the Twelve but also the seventy-two who may represent the Christian mission in Luke's own day. Note that the instructions given to the Twelve and to the seventy-two are similar and that what is said to the seventy-two in v 4 is directed to the Twelve in Lk 22, 35.

10, 1: *Seventy[-two]:* important representatives of the Alexandrian and Caesarean text types read "seventy," while other important Alexandrian texts and Western readings have "seventy-two."

10, 4: *Carry no money bag . . . greet no one along the way:* because of the urgency of the mission and the singlemindedness required of missionaries, attachment to material possessions should be avoided and even customary greetings should not distract from the fulfillment of the task.

10, 5: *First say, 'Peace to this household':* see the notes on Lk 2, 14 and Mt 10, 13.

10, 6: *A peaceful person:* literally, "a son of peace."

borer deserves his payment. Do not move about from one house to another.[g] [8] Whatever town you enter and they welcome you, eat what is set before you,[h] [9] cure the sick in it and say to them, 'The kingdom of God is at hand for you.'[i] [10] Whatever town you enter and they do not receive you, go out into the streets and say,[j] [11] 'The dust of your town that clings to our feet, even that we shake off against you.' Yet know this: the kingdom of God is at hand.[k] [12] I tell you, it will be more tolerable for Sodom on that day than for that town.[l]

Reproaches to Unrepentant Towns.* [13] [m] "Woe to you, Chorazin! Woe to you, Bethsaida![n] For if the mighty deeds done in your midst had been done in Tyre and Sidon, they would long ago have repented, sitting in sackcloth and ashes. [14] But it will be more tolerable for Tyre and Sidon at the judgment than for you. [15] [o] And as for you, Capernaum, 'Will you be exalted to heaven? You will go down to the netherworld.'* [16] Whoever listens to you listens to me. Whoever rejects you rejects me. And whoever rejects me rejects the one who sent me."[p]

Return of the Seventy-two. [17] The seventy[-two] returned rejoicing, and said, "Lord, even the demons are subject to us because of your name." [18] Jesus said, "I have observed Satan fall like lightning* from the sky.[q] [19] Behold, I have given you the power 'to tread upon serpents' and scorpions and upon the full force of the enemy and nothing will harm you.[r] [20] Nevertheless, do not rejoice because the spirits are subject to you, but rejoice because your names are written in heaven."[s]

Praise of the Father.[t] [21] At that very moment he rejoiced [in] the holy Spirit and said, "I give you praise, Father, Lord of heaven and earth, for although you have hidden these things from the wise and the learned you have revealed them to the childlike.* Yes, Father, such has been your gracious will.[u] [22] All things have been handed over to me by my Father. No one knows who the Son is except the Father, and who the Father is except the Son and anyone to whom the Son wishes to reveal him."[v]

The Privileges of Discipleship.[w] [23] Turning to the disciples in private he said, "Blessed are the eyes that see what you see. [24] For I say to you, many prophets and kings desired to see what you see, but did not see it, and to hear what you hear, but did not hear it."

The Greatest Commandment.[x] [25] * There was a scholar of the law* who stood up to test him and said, "Teacher, what must I do to inherit eternal life?"[y] [26] Jesus said to him, "What is written in the law? How do you read it?" [27] He said in reply, "You shall love the Lord, your God, with all your heart, with all your being, with all your strength, and with all your mind, and your neighbor as yourself."[z] [28] He replied to him, "You have answered correctly; do this and you will live."[a]

The Parable of the Good Samaritan. [29] But because he wished to justify himself, he said to Jesus, "And who is my neighbor?" [30] Jesus replied, "A man fell victim to robbers as he went down from Jerusalem to Jericho. They stripped and beat him and went off leaving him half-dead. [31] * A priest happened to be going down that

---

g Lk 9, 4; Mt 10, 10; 1 Cor 9, 6-14; 1 Tm 5, 18.—h 1 Cor 10, 27.—i Mt 3, 2; 4, 17; Mk 1, 15.—j 10-11: Lk 9, 5.—k Acts 13, 51; 18, 6.—l Mt 10, 15; 11, 24.—m 13-15: Mt 11, 20-24.—n 13-14: Is 23; Ez 26—28; Jl 3, 4-8; Am 1, 1-10; Zec 9, 2-4.—o Is 14, 13-15.—p Mt 10, 40; Jn 5, 23; 13, 20; 15, 23.—q Is 14, 12; Jn 12, 31; Rv 12, 7-12.—r Ps 19, 13; Mk 16, 18.—s Ex 32, 32; Dn 12, 1; Mt 7, 22; Phil 4, 3; Heb 12, 23; Rv 3, 5; 21, 27.—t 21-22: Mt 11, 25-27.—u 1 Cor 1, 26-28.—v Jn 3, 35; 10, 15.—w 23-24: Mt 13, 16-17.—x 25-28: Mt 22, 34-40; Mk 12, 28-34.—y Lk 18, 18; Mt 19, 16; Mk 10, 17.—z Lv 19, 18; Dt 6, 5; 10, 12; Jos 22, 5; Mt 19, 19; 22, 37-39; Rom 13, 9; Gal 5, 14; Jas 2, 8.—a Lv 18, 5; Prv 19, 16; Rom 10, 5; Gal 3, 12.

10, 13-16: The call to repentance that is a part of the proclamation of the kingdom brings with it a severe judgment for those who hear it and reject it.

10, 15: *The netherworld:* the underworld, the place of the dead (Acts 2, 27.31), here contrasted with heaven; see also the note on Mt 11, 23.

10, 18: *I have observed Satan fall like lightning:* the effect of the mission of the seventy-two is characterized by the Lucan Jesus as a symbolic fall of Satan. As the kingdom of God is gradually being established, evil in all its forms is being defeated; the dominion of Satan over humanity is at an end.

10, 21: *Revealed them to the childlike:* a restatement of the theme announced in Lk 8, 10: the mysteries of the kingdom are revealed to the disciples. See also the note on Mt 11, 25-27.

10, 25-37: In response to a question from a Jewish legal expert about inheriting eternal life, Jesus illustrates the superiority of love over legalism through the story of the good Samaritan. The law of love proclaimed in the "Sermon on the Plain" (Lk 6, 27-36) is exemplified by one whom the legal expert would have considered ritually impure (see Jn 4, 9). Moreover, the identity of the "neighbor" requested by the legal expert (29) turns out to be a Samaritan, the enemy of the Jew (see the note on Lk 9, 52).

10, 25: *Scholar of the law:* an expert in the Mosaic law, and probably a member of the group elsewhere identified as the scribes (Lk 5, 21).

10, 31-32: *Priest . . . Levite:* those religious representatives of Judaism who would have been expected to be models of "neighbor" to the victim pass him by.

road, but when he saw him, he passed by on the opposite side. ³²Likewise a Levite came to the place, and when he saw him, he passed by on the opposite side. ³³But a Samaritan traveler who came upon him was moved with compassion at the sight. ³⁴He approached the victim, poured oil and wine over his wounds and bandaged them. Then he lifted him up on his own animal, took him to an inn and cared for him. ³⁵The next day he took out two silver coins and gave them to the innkeeper with the instruction, 'Take care of him. If you spend more than what I have given you, I shall repay you on my way back.' ³⁶Which of these three, in your opinion, was neighbor to the robbers' victim?" ³⁷He answered, "The one who treated him with mercy." Jesus said to him, "Go and do likewise."

Martha and Mary.* ³⁸ ᵇ As they continued their journey he entered a village where a woman whose name was Martha welcomed him. ³⁹She had a sister named Mary [who] sat beside the Lord at his feet* listening to

---

b 38-39: Jn 11, 1; 12, 2-3.—c 1-4: Mt 6, 9-15.—d 5-8: Lk 18, 1-5.—e 9-13: Mt 7, 7-11.—f Mt 21, 22; Mk 11, 24; Jn 14, 13; 15, 7; 1 Jn 5, 14-15.

10, 38-42: The story of Martha and Mary further illustrates the importance of hearing the words of the teacher and the concern with women in Lk.

10, 39: *Sat beside the Lord at his feet:* it is remarkable for first-century Palestinian Judaism that a woman would assume the posture of a disciple at the master's feet (see also Lk 8, 35; Acts 22, 3), and it reveals a characteristic attitude of Jesus toward women in this gospel (see Lk 8, 2-3).

10, 42: *There is need of only one thing:* some ancient versions read, "there is need of few things"; another important, although probably inferior, reading found in some manuscripts is, "there is need of few things, or of one."

11, 1-13: Luke presents three episodes concerned with prayer. The first (1-4) recounts Jesus teaching his disciples the Christian communal prayer, the "Our Father"; the second (5-8), the importance of persistence in prayer; the third (9-13), the effectiveness of prayer.

11, 1-4: The Matthean form of the "Our Father" occurs in the "Sermon on the Mount" (Mt 6, 9-15); the shorter Lucan version is presented while Jesus is at prayer (see the note on Lk 3, 21) and his disciples ask him to teach them to pray just as John taught his disciples to pray. In answer to their question, Jesus presents them with an example of a Christian communal prayer that stresses the fatherhood of God and acknowledges him as the one to whom the Christian disciple owes daily sustenance (3), forgiveness (4), and deliverance from the final trial (4). See also the notes on Mt 6, 9-13.

11, 2: *Your kingdom come:* in place of this petition, some early church Fathers record: "May your holy Spirit come upon us and cleanse us," a petition that may reflect the use of the "Our Father" in a baptismal liturgy.

11, 3-4: *Daily bread:* see the note on Mt 6, 11. *The final test:* see the note on Mt 6, 13.

11, 13: *The holy Spirit:* this is a Lucan editorial alteration of a traditional saying of Jesus (see Mt 7, 11). Luke presents the gift of the holy Spirit as the response of the Father to the prayer of the Christian disciple.

---

him speak. ⁴⁰Martha, burdened with much serving, came to him and said, "Lord, do you not care that my sister has left me by myself to do the serving? Tell her to help me." ⁴¹The Lord said to her in reply, "Martha, Martha, you are anxious and worried about many things. ⁴²There is need of only one thing.* Mary has chosen the better part and it will not be taken from her."

CHAPTER 11

The Lord's Prayer. ᶜ ¹ * He was praying in a certain place, and when he had finished, one of his disciples said to him, "Lord, teach us to pray just as John taught his disciples."* ²He said to them, "When you pray, say:

Father, hallowed be your name,
    your kingdom come.*
3   Give us each day our daily bread*
4   and forgive us our sins
    for we ourselves forgive everyone in
        debt to us,
    and do not subject us to the final
        test."

Further Teachings on Prayer. ᵈ ⁵And he said to them, "Suppose one of you has a friend to whom he goes at midnight and says, 'Friend, lend me three loaves of bread, ⁶for a friend of mine has arrived at my house from a journey and I have nothing to offer him,' ⁷and he says in reply from within, 'Do not bother me; the door has already been locked and my children and I are already in bed. I cannot get up to give you anything.' ⁸I tell you, if he does not get up to give him the loaves because of their friendship, he will get up to give him whatever he needs because of his persistence.

The Answer to Prayer. ᵉ ⁹"And I tell you, ask and you will receive; seek and you will find; knock and the door will be opened to you.ᶠ ¹⁰For everyone who asks, receives; and the one who seeks, finds; and to the one who knocks, the door will be opened. ¹¹What father among you would hand his son a snake when he asks for a fish? ¹²Or hand him a scorpion when he asks for an egg? ¹³If you then, who are wicked, know how to give good gifts to your children, how much more will the Father in heaven give the holy Spirit* to those who ask him?"

Jesus and Beelzebul. [g] [14] He was driving out a demon [that was] mute, and when the demon had gone out, the mute person spoke and the crowds were amazed. [15] Some of them said, "By the power of Beelzebul, the prince of demons, he drives out demons." [h] [16] Others, to test him, asked him for a sign from heaven. [i] [17] But he knew their thoughts and said to them, "Every kingdom divided against itself will be laid waste and house will fall against house. [18] And if Satan is divided against himself, how will his kingdom stand? For you say that it is by Beelzebul that I drive out demons. [19] If I, then, drive out demons by Beelzebul, by whom do your own people* drive them out? Therefore they will be your judges. [20] But if it is by the finger of God that [I] drive out demons, then the kingdom of God has come upon you. [j] [21] When a strong man fully armed guards his palace, his possessions are safe. [22] But when one stronger* than he attacks and overcomes him, he takes away the armor on which he relied and distributes the spoils. [23] Whoever is not with me is against me, and whoever does not gather with me scatters. [k]

The Return of the Unclean Spirit. [l] [24] "When an unclean spirit goes out of someone, it roams through arid regions searching for rest but, finding none, it says, 'I shall return to my home from which I came.' [25] But upon returning, it finds it swept clean and put in order. [26] Then it goes and brings back seven other spirits more wicked than itself who move in and dwell there, and the last condition of that person is worse than the first." [m]

True Blessedness. * [27] While he was speaking, a woman from the crowd called out and said to him, "Blessed is the womb that carried you and the breasts at which you nursed." [n] [28] He replied, "Rather, blessed are those who hear the word of God and observe it."

The Demand for a Sign. * [29] While still more people gathered in the crowd, he said to them, [o] "This generation is an evil generation; it seeks a sign, but no sign will be given it, except the sign of Jonah. [p] [30] Just as Jonah became a sign to the Ninevites, so will the Son of Man be to this generation. [31] At the judgment the queen of the south will rise with the men of this generation and she will condemn them, because she

came from the ends of the earth to hear the wisdom of Solomon, and there is something greater than Solomon here. [q] [32] At the judgment the men of Nineveh will arise with this generation and condemn it, because at the preaching of Jonah they repented, and there is something greater than Jonah here. [r]

The Simile of Light. [33] "No one who lights a lamp hides it away or places it [under a bushel basket], but on a lampstand so that those who enter might see the light. [s] [34] The lamp of the body is your eye. [t] When your eye is sound, then your whole body is filled with light, but when it is bad, then your body is in darkness. [35] Take care, then, that the light in you not become darkness. [36] If your whole body is full of light, and no part of it is in darkness, then it will be as full of light as a lamp illuminating you with its brightness."

Denunciation of the Pharisees and Scholars of the Law. * [37] [u] After he had spoken, a Pharisee invited him to dine at his home. He entered and reclined at table to eat. [v] [38] The Pharisee was amazed to see that he did not observe the prescribed washing before the meal. [w] [39] The Lord said to him, "Oh you Pharisees! [x] Although you cleanse the outside of the cup and the dish, inside you are filled with plunder and evil. [40] You fools! Did not the maker of the outside also

---

g 14-23: Mt 12, 22-30; Mk 3, 20-27.—h Mt 9, 34.—i Mt 12, 38; 16, 1; Mk 8, 11; 1 Cor 1, 22.—j Ex 8, 19.—k Lk 9, 50; Mk 9, 40.—l 24-26: Mt 12, 43-45.—m Jn 5, 14.—n Lk 1, 28.42.48.—o 29-32: Mt 12, 38-42; Mk 8, 12.—p Mt 16, 1.4; Jn 6, 30; 1 Cor 1, 22.—q 1 Kgs 10, 1-10; 2 Chr 9, 1-12.—r Jon 3, 8.10.—s Lk 8, 16; Mt 5, 15; Mk 4, 21.—t 34-36: Mt 6, 22-23.—u 37-54: Lk 20, 45-47; Mt 23, 1-36; Mk 12, 38-40.—v Lk 7, 36; 14, 1.—w Mt 15, 2; Mk 7, 2-5.—x 39-41: Mt 23, 25-26.

11, 19: *Your own people:* the Greek reads "your sons." Other Jewish exorcists (see Acts 19, 13-20), who recognize that the power of God is active in the exorcism, would themselves convict the accusers of Jesus. See also the note on Mt 12, 27.

11, 22: *One stronger:* i.e., Jesus. Cf Lk 3, 16 where John the Baptist identifies Jesus as "more powerful than I."

11, 27-28: The beatitude in v 28 should not be interpreted as a rebuke of the mother of Jesus; see the note on Lk 8, 21. Rather, it emphasizes (like Lk 2, 35) that attentiveness to God's word is more important than biological relationship to Jesus.

11, 29-32: The "sign of Jonah" in Lk is the preaching of the need for repentance by a prophet who comes from afar. Cf Mt 12, 38-42 (and see the notes there) where the "sign of Jonah" is interpreted by Jesus as his death and resurrection.

11, 37-54: This denunciation of the Pharisees (39-44) and the scholars of the law (45-52) is set by Luke in the context of Jesus' dining at the home of a Pharisee. Controversies with or reprimands of Pharisees are regularly set by Luke within the context of Jesus' eating with Pharisees (see Lk 5, 29-39; 7, 36-50; 14, 1-24). A different compilation of similar sayings is found in Mt 23 (see also the notes there).

Lk

make the inside? [41] But as to what is within, give alms, and behold, everything will be clean for you. [42] Woe to you Pharisees! You pay tithes of mint and of rue and of every garden herb, but you pay no attention to judgment and to love for God. These you should have done, without overlooking the others.[y] [43] Woe to you Pharisees! You love the seat of honor in synagogues and greetings in marketplaces.[z] [44] Woe to you! You are like unseen graves* over which people unknowingly walk."[a]

[45] Then one of the scholars of the law* said to him in reply, "Teacher, by saying this you are insulting us too."[b] [46] And he said, "Woe also to you scholars of the law! You impose on people burdens hard to carry, but you yourselves do not lift one finger to touch them. [47] [c] Woe to you! You build the memorials of the prophets whom your ancestors killed. [48] Consequently, you bear witness and give consent to the deeds of your ancestors, for they killed them and you do the building. [49] [d] Therefore, the wisdom of God said, 'I will send to them prophets and apostles;* some of them they

---

y Lv 27, 30; Mt 23, 23.—z Lk 20, 46; Mt 23, 6; Mk 12, 38-39.—a Mt 23, 27.—b Mt 23, 4.—c 47-48: Mt 23, 29-32.—d 49-51: Mt 23, 34-36.—e Gn 4, 8; 2 Chr 24, 20-22.—f Mt 23, 13.—g Lk 6, 11; Mt 22, 15-22.—h Lk 20, 20.—i Mt 16, 6; Mk 8, 15.—j 2-9: Mt 10, 26-33.—k Lk 8, 17; Mk 4, 22.—l Lk 12, 24; 21, 18; Acts 27, 34.—m Lk 9, 26; Mk 8, 38; 2 Tm 2, 12.—n Mt 12, 31-32; Mk 3, 28-29.—o 11-12: Lk 21, 12-15; Mt 10, 17-20; Mk 13, 11.

11, 44: *Unseen graves:* contact with the dead or with human bones or graves (see Nm 19, 16) brought ritual impurity. Jesus presents the Pharisees as those who insidiously lead others astray through their seeming attention to the law.

11, 45: *Scholars of the law:* see the note on Lk 10, 25.

11, 49: *I will send to them prophets and apostles:* Jesus connects the mission of the church (apostles) with the mission of the Old Testament prophets who often suffered the rebuke of their contemporaries.

11, 51: *From the blood of Abel to the blood of Zechariah:* the murder of Abel is the first murder recounted in the Old Testament (Gn 4, 8). The Zechariah mentioned here may be the Zechariah whose murder is recounted in 2 Chr 24, 20-22, the last murder presented in the Hebrew canon of the Old Testament.

12, 1: See the notes on Mk 8, 15 and Mt 16, 5-12.

12, 2-9: Luke presents a collection of sayings of Jesus exhorting his followers to acknowledge him and his mission fearlessly and assuring them of God's protection even in times of persecution. They are paralleled in Mt 10, 26-33.

12, 5: *Gehenna:* see the note on Mt 5, 22.

12, 6: *Two small coins:* the Roman copper coin, the assarion (Latin *as*), was worth about one-sixteenth of a denarius (see the note on Lk 7, 41).

12, 10-12: The sayings about the holy Spirit are set in the context of persecution in the face of persecution (2-9; cf Mt 12, 31-32). The holy Spirit will be presented in Luke's second volume, the Acts of the Apostles, as the power responsible for the guidance of the Christian mission and the source of courage in the face of persecution.

---

will kill and persecute' [50] in order that this generation might be charged with the blood of all the prophets shed since the foundation of the world, [51] from the blood of Abel to the blood of Zechariah* who died between the altar and the temple building. Yes, I tell you, this generation will be charged with their blood! [e] [52] Woe to you, scholars of the law! You have taken away the key of knowledge. You yourselves did not enter and you stopped those trying to enter."[f] [53] When he left, the scribes and Pharisees began to act with hostility toward him and to interrogate him about many things,[g] [54] for they were plotting to catch him at something he might say.[h]

CHAPTER 12

The Leaven of the Pharisees.* [1] Meanwhile, so many people were crowding together that they were trampling one another underfoot.[i] He began to speak, first to his disciples, "Beware of the leaven— that is, the hypocrisy—of the Pharisees.

Courage under Persecution.* [2] [j] "There is nothing concealed that will not be revealed, nor secret that will not be known.[k] [3] Therefore whatever you have said in the darkness will be heard in the light, and what you have whispered behind closed doors will be proclaimed on the housetops. [4] I tell you, my friends, do not be afraid of those who kill the body but after that can do no more. [5] I shall show you whom to fear. Be afraid of the one who after killing has the power to cast into Gehenna;* yes, I tell you, be afraid of that one. [6] Are not five sparrows sold for two small coins?* Yet not one of them has escaped the notice of God. [7] Even the hairs of your head have all been counted. Do not be afraid. You are worth more than many sparrows.[l] [8] I tell you, everyone who acknowledges me before others the Son of Man will acknowledge before the angels of God. [9] But whoever denies me before others will be denied before the angels of God.[m]

Sayings about the holy Spirit.* [10] "Everyone who speaks a word against the Son of Man will be forgiven, but the one who blasphemes against the holy Spirit will not be forgiven.[n] [11] When they take you before synagogues and before rulers and authorities,[o] do not worry about how or what your defense will be or about what you are to say. ¹²For the holy Spirit will teach you at that moment what you should say."

Saying against Greed. 13 * Someone in the crowd said to him, "Teacher, tell my brother to share the inheritance with me." ¹⁴He replied to him, "Friend, who appointed me as your judge and arbitrator?" ᵖ ¹⁵Then he said to the crowd, "Take care to guard against all greed, for though one may be rich, one's life does not consist of possessions." ᑫ

Parable of the Rich Fool. ¹⁶Then he told them a parable. "There was a rich man whose land produced a bountiful harvest. ¹⁷He asked himself, 'What shall I do, for I do not have space to store my harvest?' ¹⁸And he said, 'This is what I shall do: I shall tear down my barns and build larger ones. There I shall store all my grain and other goods ¹⁹ ʳ and I shall say to myself, "Now as for you, you have so many good things stored up for many years, rest, eat, drink, be merry!" ' ˢ ²⁰But God said to him, 'You fool, this night your life will be demanded of you; and the things you have prepared, to whom will they belong?' ²¹Thus will it be for the one who stores up treasure for himself but is not rich in what matters to God."*

Dependence on God. 22 ᵗ He said to [his] disciples, "Therefore I tell you, do not worry about your life and what you will eat, or about your body and what you will wear. ²³For life is more than food and the body more than clothing. ²⁴Notice the ravens: they do not sow or reap; they have neither storehouse nor barn, yet God feeds them. How much more important are you than birds! ᵘ ²⁵Can any of you by worrying add a moment to your life-span? ²⁶If even the smallest things are beyond your control, why are you anxious about the rest? ²⁷Notice how the flowers grow. They do not toil or spin. But I tell you, not even Solomon in all his splendor was dressed like one of them. ᵛ ²⁸If God so clothes the grass in the field that grows today and is thrown into the oven tomorrow, will he not much more provide for you, O you of little faith? ²⁹As for you, do not seek what you are to eat and what you are to drink, and do not worry anymore. ³⁰All the nations of the world seek for these things, and your Father knows that you need them. ³¹Instead, seek his kingdom, and these other things will be given you besides. ³²Do not be afraid any longer, little flock, for your

Father is pleased to give you the kingdom. ʷ ³³Sell your belongings and give alms. Provide money bags for yourselves that do not wear out, an inexhaustible treasure in heaven that no thief can reach nor moth destroy. ˣ ³⁴For where your treasure is, there also will your heart be.

Vigilant and Faithful Servants.* 35 ʸ "Gird your loins and light your lamps ³⁶and be like servants who await their master's return from a wedding, ready to open immediately when he comes and knocks. ᶻ ³⁷Blessed are those servants whom the master finds vigilant on his arrival. Amen, I say to you, he will gird himself, have them recline at table, and proceed to wait on them. ³⁸And should he come in the second or third watch and find them prepared in this way, blessed are those servants. 39 ᵃ Be sure of this: if the master of the house had known the hour when the thief was coming, he would not have let his house be broken into. ⁴⁰You also must be prepared, for at an hour you do not expect, the Son of Man will come."

⁴¹Then Peter said, "Lord, is this parable meant for us or for everyone?" ⁴²And the Lord replied, "Who, then, is the faithful and prudent steward whom the master will put in charge of his servants to distribute [the] food allowance at the proper time? ⁴³Blessed is that servant whom his master on arrival finds doing so. ⁴⁴Truly, I say to you, he will put him in charge of all his property. ⁴⁵But if that servant says to himself, 'My master is delayed in coming,'* and begins to beat the menservants and the maidservants, to eat and drink and get

---

p Ex 2, 14; Acts 7, 27.—q 1 Tm 6, 9-10.—r 19-21: Mt 6, 19-21; 1 Tm 6, 17.—s 19-20: Sir 11, 19.—t 22-32: Mt 6, 25-34.— u Lk 12, 7.—v 1 Kgs 10, 4-7; 2 Chr 9, 3-6.—w Lk 22, 29; Rv 1, 6.—x Lk 18, 22; Mt 6, 20-21; Mk 10, 21.—y 35-46: Mt 24, 45-51.—z Mt 25, 1-13; Mk 13, 35-37.—a 39-40: Mt 24, 43-44; 1 Thes 5, 2.

12, 13-34: Luke has joined together sayings contrasting those whose focus and trust in life is on material possessions, symbolized here by the rich fool of the parable (16-21), with those who recognize their complete dependence on God (21), those whose radical detachment from material possessions symbolizes their heavenly treasure (33-34).

12, 21: *Rich in what matters to God:* literally, "rich for God."

12, 35-48: This collection of sayings relates to Luke's understanding of the end time and the return of Jesus. Luke emphasizes for his readers the importance of being faithful to the instructions of Jesus in the period before the parousia.

12, 45: *My master is delayed in coming:* this statement indicates that early Christian expectations for the imminent return of Jesus had undergone some modification. Luke cautions his readers against counting on such a delay and acting irresponsibly. Cf the similar warning in Mt 24, 48.

drunk, [46] then that servant's master will come on an unexpected day and at an unknown hour and will punish him severely and assign him a place with the unfaithful. [47] That servant who knew his master's will but did not make preparations nor act in accord with his will shall be beaten severely; [b] [48] and the servant who was ignorant of his master's will but acted in a way deserving of a severe beating shall be beaten only lightly. Much will be required of the person entrusted with much, and still more will be demanded of the person entrusted with more.

Jesus: A Cause of Division.* [49] "I have come to set the earth on fire, and how I wish it were already blazing! [50] There is a baptism* with which I must baptized, and how great is my anguish until it is accomplished! [c] [51] Do you think that I have come to establish peace on the earth? [d] No, I tell you, but rather division. [e] [52] From now on a household of five will be divided, three against two and two against three; [53] a father will be divided against his son and a son against his father, a mother against her daughter and a daughter against her

mother, a mother-in-law against her daughter-in-law and a daughter-in-law against her mother-in-law." [f]

Signs of the Times. [g] [54] He also said to the crowds, "When you see [a] cloud rising in the west you say immediately that it is going to rain—and so it does; [55] and when you notice that the wind is blowing from the south you say that it is going to be hot—and so it is. [56] You hypocrites! You know how to interpret the appearance of the earth and the sky; why do you not know how to interpret the present time?

Settlement with an Opponent. [h] [57] "Why do you not judge for yourselves what is right? [58] If you are to go with your opponent before a magistrate, make an effort to settle the matter on the way; otherwise your opponent will turn you over to the judge, and the judge hand you over to the constable, and the constable throw you into prison. [59] I say to you, you will not be released until you have paid the last penny." *

CHAPTER 13

A Call to Repentance.* [1] At that time some people who were present there told him about the Galileans whose blood Pilate* had mingled with the blood of their sacrifices. [2] He said to them in reply, "Do you think that because these Galileans suffered in this way they were greater sinners than all other Galileans? [i] [3] By no means! But I tell you, if you do not repent, [j] you will all perish as they did! [4] Or those eighteen people who were killed when the tower at Siloam fell on them*—do you think they were more guilty than everyone else who lived in Jerusalem? [5] By no means! But I tell you, if you do not repent, you will all perish as they did!"

The Parable of the Barren Fig Tree.* [6] [k] And he told them this parable: "There once was a person who had a fig tree planted in his orchard, and when he came in search of fruit on it but found none, [7] he said to the gardener, 'For three years now I have come in search of fruit on this fig tree but have found none. [So] cut it down. Why should it exhaust the soil?' [8] He said to him in reply, 'Sir, leave it for this year also, and I shall cultivate the ground around it and fertilize it; [9] it may bear fruit in the future. If not you can cut it down.' "

---

b Jas 4, 17.—c Mk 10, 38-39.—d 51-53: Mt 10, 34-35.—e Lk 2, 14.—f Mi 7, 6.—g 54-56: Mt 16, 2-3.—h 57-59: Mt 5, 25-26.—i Jn 9, 2.—j 3-5: Jn 8, 24.—k 6-9: Jer 8, 13; Hb 3, 17; Mt 21, 19; Mk 11, 13.

12, 49-53: Jesus' proclamation of the kingdom is a refining and purifying fire. His message that meets with acceptance or rejection will be a source of conflict and dissension even within families.

12, 50: *Baptism:* i.e., his death.

12, 59: *The last penny:* Greek, *lepton*, a very small amount. Mt 5, 26 has for "the last penny" the Greek word *kodrantēs* (Latin *quadrans*, "farthing").

13, 1-5: The death of the Galileans at the hands of Pilate (1) and the accidental death of those on whom the tower fell (4) are presented by the Lucan Jesus as timely reminders of the need for all to repent, for the victims of these tragedies should not be considered outstanding sinners who were singled out for punishment.

13, 1: The slaughter of the Galileans by Pilate is unknown outside Lk; but from what is known about Pilate from the Jewish historian Josephus, such a slaughter would be in keeping with the character of Pilate. Josephus reports that Pilate had disrupted a religious gathering of the Samaritans on Mt. Gerizim with a slaughter of the participants (*Antiquities* 18, 4, 1 §§86-87), and that on another occasion Pilate had killed many Jews who had opposed him when he appropriated money from the temple treasury to build an aqueduct in Jerusalem (*Jewish War* 2, 9, 4 §§175-77; *Antiquities* 18, 3, 2 §§60-62).

13, 4: Like the incident mentioned in v 1, nothing of this accident in Jerusalem is known outside Lk and the New Testament.

13, 6-9: Following on the call to repentance in vv 1-5, the parable of the barren fig tree presents a story about the continuing patience of God with those who have not yet given evidence of their repentance (see Lk 3, 8). The parable may also be alluding to the delay of the end time, when punishment will be meted out, and the importance of preparing for the end of the age because the delay will not be permanent (8-9).

Cure of a Crippled Woman on the Sabbath.* [10] He was teaching in a synagogue on the sabbath. [11] And a woman was there who for eighteen years had been crippled by a spirit; she was bent over, completely incapable of standing erect. [12] When Jesus saw her, he called to her and said, "Woman, you are set free of your infirmity." [13] He laid his hands on her, and she at once stood up straight and glorified God. [14] [l] But the leader of the synagogue, indignant that Jesus had cured on the sabbath, said to the crowd in reply, "There are six days when work should be done. Come on those days to be cured, not on the sabbath day." [15] * The Lord said to him in reply, "Hypocrites! Does not each one of you on the sabbath untie his ox or his ass from the manger and lead it out for watering?[m] [16] This daughter of Abraham, whom Satan has bound* for eighteen years now, ought she not to have been set free on the sabbath day from this bondage?"[n] [17] When he said this, all his adversaries were humiliated; and the whole crowd rejoiced at all the splendid deeds done by him.

The Parable of the Mustard Seed.[o] [18] * Then he said, "What is the kingdom of God like? To what can I compare it? [19] It is like a mustard seed that a person took and planted in the garden. When it was fully grown, it became a large bush and 'the birds of the sky dwelt in its branches.' "[p]

The Parable of the Yeast.[q] [20] Again he said, "To what shall I compare the kingdom of God? [21] It is like yeast that a woman took and mixed [in] with three measures of wheat flour until the whole batch of dough was leavened."

The Narrow Door; Salvation and Rejection.* [22] He passed through towns and villages, teaching as he went and making his way to Jerusalem. [23] Someone asked him, "Lord, will only a few people be saved?" He answered them, [24] [r] "Strive to enter through the narrow gate, for many, I tell you, will attempt to enter but will not be strong enough.[s] [25] After the master of the house has arisen and locked the door, then will you stand outside knocking and saying, 'Lord, open the door for us.' He will say to you in reply, 'I do not know where you are from.'[t] [26] And you will say, 'We ate and drank in your company and you taught in our streets.' [27] [u] Then he will say to you, 'I do not know where [you] are

from. Depart from me, all you evildoers!' [28] [v] And there will be wailing and grinding of teeth when you see Abraham, Isaac, and Jacob and all the prophets in the kingdom of God and you yourselves cast out. [29] And people will come from the east and the west and from the north and the south and will recline at table in the kingdom of God.[w] [30] For behold, some are last who will be first, and some are first who will be last."[x]

Herod's Desire to Kill Jesus. [31] At that time some Pharisees came to him and said, "Go away, leave this area because Herod wants to kill you." [32] He replied, "Go and tell that fox, 'Behold, I cast out demons and I perform healings today and tomorrow, and on the third day I accomplish my purpose.* [33] Yet I must continue on my way today,[y] tomorrow, and the following day, for it is impossible that a prophet should die outside of Jerusalem.'*

---

l Lk 6, 7; 14, 3; Ex 20, 8-11; Dt 5, 12-15; Mt 12, 10; Mk 3, 2-4; Jn 5, 16; 7, 23; 9, 14.16.—m Lk 14, 5; Dt 22, 4; Mt 12, 11.—n Lk 19, 9.—o 18-19: Mt 13, 31-32; Mk 4, 30-32.—p Ez 17, 23-24; 31, 6.—q 20-21: Mt 13, 33.—r 24-30: Mt 7, 13-14.21-23.—s Mk 10, 25.—t Mt 25, 10-12.—u Ps 6, 9; Mt 7, 23; 25, 41.—v 28-29: Mt 8, 11-12.—w Ps 107, 2-3.—x Mt 19, 20; 20, 16; Mk 10, 31.—y Lk 2, 38; Jn 6, 30; 8, 20.

13, 10-17: The cure of the crippled woman on the sabbath and the controversy that results furnishes a parallel to an incident that will be reported by Lk in 14, 1-6, the cure of the man with dropsy on the sabbath. A characteristic of Luke's style is the juxtaposition of an incident that reveals Jesus' concern for a man with an incident that reveals his concern for a woman; cf, e.g., Lk 7, 11-17 and Lk 8, 49-56.

13, 15-16: If the law as interpreted by Jewish tradition allowed for the untying of bound animals on the sabbath, how much more should this woman who has been bound by Satan's power be freed on the sabbath from her affliction.

13, 16: *Whom Satan has bound:* affliction and infirmity are taken as evidence of Satan's hold on humanity. The healing ministry of Jesus reveals the gradual wresting from Satan of control over humanity and the establishment of God's kingdom.

13, 18-21: Two parables are used to illustrate the future proportions of the kingdom of God that will result from its deceptively small beginning in the preaching and healing ministry of Jesus. They are paralleled in Mt 13, 31-33 and Mk 4, 30-32.

13, 22-30: These sayings of Jesus follow in Lk upon the parables of the kingdom (18-21) and stress that great effort is required for entrance into the kingdom (24) and that there is an urgency to accept the present opportunity to enter because the narrow door will not remain open indefinitely (25). Lying behind the sayings is the rejection of Jesus and his message by his Jewish contemporaries (26) whose places at table in the kingdom will be taken by Gentiles from the four corners of the world (29). Those called last (the Gentiles) will precede those to whom the invitation to enter was first extended (the Jews). See also Lk 14, 15-24.

13, 32: Nothing, not even Herod's desire to kill Jesus, stands in the way of Jesus' role in fulfilling God's will and in establishing the kingdom through his exorcisms and healings.

13, 33: *It is impossible that a prophet should die outside of Jerusalem:* Jerusalem is the city of destiny and the goal of the journey of the prophet Jesus. Only when he reaches the holy city will his work be accomplished.

The Lament over Jerusalem.[z] [34] "Jerusalem, Jerusalem, you who kill the prophets and stone those sent to you, how many times I yearned to gather your children together as a hen gathers her brood under her wings, but you were unwilling! [35] Behold, your house will be abandoned. [But] I tell you, you will not see me until [the time comes when] you say, 'Blessed is he who comes in the name of the Lord.' "[a]

CHAPTER 14

Healing of the Man with Dropsy on the Sabbath.* [1] [b] On a sabbath he went to dine at the home of one of the leading Pharisees, and the people there were observing him carefully.[c] [2] In front of him there was a man suffering from dropsy.* [3] Jesus spoke to the scholars of the law and Pharisees in reply, asking, "Is it lawful to cure on the sabbath or not?"[d] [4] But they kept silent; so he took the man and, after he had healed him, dismissed him. [5] Then he said to them, "Who among you, if your son or ox* falls into a cistern, would not immediately pull him out on the sabbath day?"[e] [6] But they were unable to answer his question.[f]

Conduct of Invited Guests and Hosts.* [7] [g] He told a parable to those who had been invited, noticing how they were choosing the places of honor at the table. [8] [h] "When you are invited by someone to a wedding banquet, do not recline at table in the place of honor. A more distinguished guest than you may have been invited by him, [9] and the host who invited both of you may approach you and say, 'Give your place to this man,' and then you would proceed with embarrassment to take the lowest place. [10] Rather, when you are invited, go and take the lowest place so that when the host comes to you he may say, 'My friend, move up to a higher position.' Then you will enjoy the esteem of your companions at the table. [11] For everyone who exalts himself will be humbled, but the one who humbles himself will be exalted."[i] [12] Then he said to the host who invited him, "When you hold a lunch or a dinner, do not invite your friends or your brothers or your relatives or your wealthy neighbors, in case they may invite you back and you have repayment.[j] [13] Rather, when you hold a banquet, invite the poor, the crippled, the lame, the blind; [14] blessed indeed will you be because of their inability to repay you. For you will be repaid at the resurrection of the righteous."[k]

The Parable of the Great Feast.* [15] One of his fellow guests on hearing this said to him, "Blessed is the one who will dine in the kingdom of God." [16] [l] He replied to him, "A man gave a great dinner to which he invited many. [17] When the time for the dinner came, he dispatched his servant to say to those invited, 'Come, everything is now ready.' [18] But one by one, they all began to excuse themselves. The first said to him, 'I have purchased a field and must go to examine it; I ask you, consider me excused.' [19] And another said, 'I have purchased five yoke of oxen and am on my way to evaluate them; I ask you, consider me excused.' [20] And another said, 'I have just married a woman, and therefore I cannot come.' [21] The servant went and reported this to his master. Then the master of the house in a rage commanded his servant, 'Go out quickly into the streets and alleys of the town and bring in here the poor and the crippled, the blind and the lame.' [22] The servant reported, 'Sir, your orders have been carried out and still there is room.' [23] The master then ordered the servant, 'Go out to the highways and hedgerows and make people come in that my home may be filled. [24] For, I tell you, none of those men who were invited will taste my dinner.' "

---

z 34-35: Lk 19, 41-44; Mt 23, 37-39.—a Lk 19, 38; 1 Kgs 9, 7-8; Ps 118, 26; Jer 7, 4-7.13-15; 12, 7; 22, 5.—b 1-6: Lk 6, 6-11; 13, 10-17.—c Lk 11, 37.—d Lk 6, 9; Mk 3, 4.—e Lk 13, 15; Dt 22, 4; Mt 12, 11.—f Mt 22, 46.—g Lk 11, 43; Mt 23, 6; Mk 12, 38-39.—h 8-10: Prv 25, 6-7.—i Lk 18, 14.—j Lk 6, 32-35.—k Jn 5, 29.—l 16-24: Mt 22, 2-10.

14, 1-6: See the note on Lk 13, 10-17.

14, 2: *Dropsy:* an abnormal swelling of the body because of the retention and accumulation of fluid.

14, 5: *Your son or ox:* this is the reading of many of the oldest and most important New Testament manuscripts. Because of the strange collocation of *son* and *ox,* some copyists have altered it to "your ass or ox," on the model of the saying in Lk 13, 15.

14, 7-14: The banquet scene found only in Luke provides the opportunity for these teachings of Jesus on humility and presents a setting to display Luke's interest in Jesus' attitude toward the rich and the poor (see the notes on Lk 4, 18; 6, 20-26; 12, 13-34).

14, 15-24: The parable of the great dinner is a further illustration of the rejection by Israel, God's chosen people, of Jesus' invitation to share in the banquet in the kingdom and the extension of the invitation to other Jews whose identification as the poor, crippled, blind, and lame (21) classifies them among those who recognize their need for salvation, and to Gentiles (23). A similar parable is found in Mt 22, 1-10.

Sayings on Discipleship.* [25] Great crowds were traveling with him, and he turned and addressed them, [26] m "If anyone comes to me without hating his father* and mother, wife and children, brothers and sisters, and even his own life, he cannot be my disciple.[n] [27] Whoever does not carry his own cross and come after me cannot be my disciple.[o] [28] Which of you wishing to construct a tower does not first sit down and calculate the cost to see if there is enough for its completion? [29] Otherwise, after laying the foundation and finding himself unable to finish the work the onlookers should laugh at him [30] and say, 'This one began to build but did not have the resources to finish.' [31] Or what king marching into battle would not first sit down and decide whether with ten thousand troops he can successfully oppose another king advancing upon him with twenty thousand troops? [32] But if not, while he is still far away, he will send a delegation to ask for peace terms. [33] In the same way, everyone of you who does not renounce all his possessions cannot be my disciple.[p]

The Simile of Salt.* [34] "Salt is good, but if salt itself loses its taste, with what can its flavor be restored?[q] [35] It is fit neither for the soil nor for the manure pile; it is thrown out. Whoever has ears to hear ought to hear."[r]

CHAPTER 15

The Parable of the Lost Sheep.[s] [1] * The tax collectors and sinners were all drawing near to listen to him, [2] but the Pharisees and scribes began to complain, saying, "This man welcomes sinners and eats with them."[t] [3] So to them he addressed this parable. [4] u "What man among you having a hundred sheep and losing one of them would not leave the ninety-nine in the desert and go after the lost one[v] until he finds it?[w] [5] And when he does find it, he sets it on his shoulders with great joy [6] and, upon his arrival home, he calls together his friends and neighbors and says to them, 'Rejoice with me because I have found my lost sheep.' [7] I tell you, in just the same way there will be more joy in heaven over one sinner who repents than over ninety-nine righteous people who have no need of repentance.[x]

The Parable of the Lost Coin. [8] "Or what woman having ten coins* and losing one would not light a lamp and sweep the house, searching carefully until she finds it? [9] And when she does find it, she calls together her friends and neighbors and says to them, 'Rejoice with me because I have found the coin that I lost.' [10] In just the same way, I tell you, there will be rejoicing among the angels of God over one sinner who repents."

The Parable of the Lost Son. [11] Then he said, "A man had two sons, [12] and the younger son said to his father, 'Father, give me the share of your estate that should come to me.' So the father divided the property between them. [13] After a few days, the younger son collected all his belongings and set off to a distant country where he squandered his inheritance on a life of dissipation.[y] [14] When he had freely spent everything, a severe famine struck that country, and he found himself in dire need. [15] So he hired himself out to one of the local citizens who sent him to his farm to tend the swine. [16] And he longed to eat his fill of the pods on which the swine fed, but nobody gave him any. [17] Coming to his senses he thought, 'How many of my father's hired workers have more than enough food to eat, but here am I, dying from hunger. [18] I shall get up and go to my father and I shall say to him, "Father, I

---

m 26-27: Mt 10, 37-38.—n Lk 9, 57-62; 18, 29; Jn 12, 25.—o Lk 9, 23; Mt 16, 24; Mk 8, 34.—p Lk 5, 11.—q Mt 5, 13; Mk 9, 50.—r Lk 8, 8; Mt 11, 15; 13, 9; Mk 4, 9.23.—s 1-7: Mt 9, 10-13.—t Lk 5, 30; 19, 7.—u 4-7: Mt 18, 12-14.—v 4-6: Lk 19, 10.—w Ez 34, 11-12.16.—x Ez 18, 23.—y Prv 29, 3.

14, 25-33: This collection of sayings, most of which are peculiar to Lk, focuses on the total dedication necessary for the disciple of Jesus. No attachment to family (26) or possessions (33) can stand in the way of the total commitment demanded of the disciple. Also, acceptance of the call to be a disciple demands readiness to accept persecution and suffering (27) and a realistic assessment of the hardships and costs (28-32).

14, 26: *Hating his father . . . :* cf the similar saying in Mt 10, 37. The disciple's family must take second place to the absolute dedication involved in following Jesus (see also Lk 9, 59-62).

14, 34-35: The simile of salt follows the sayings of Jesus that demanded of the disciple total dedication and detachment from family and possessions and illustrates the condition of one who does not display this total commitment. The halfhearted disciple is like salt that cannot serve its intended purpose. See the simile of salt in Mt 5, 13 and the note there.

15, 1-32: To the parable of the lost sheep (1-7) that Luke shares with Matthew (Mt 18, 12-14), Luke adds two parables (the lost coin, 8-10; the prodigal son, 11-32) from his own special tradition to illustrate Jesus' particular concern for the lost and God's love for the repentant sinner.

15, 8: *Ten coins:* literally, "ten drachmas." A drachma was a Greek silver coin.

have sinned against heaven and against you. ¹⁹ I no longer deserve to be called your son; treat me as you would treat one of your hired workers." ' ²⁰ So he got up and went back to his father. While he was still a long way off, his father caught sight of him, and was filled with compassion. He ran to his son, embraced him and kissed him. ²¹ His son said to him, 'Father, I have sinned against heaven and against you; I no longer deserve to be called your son.' ²² But his father ordered his servants, 'Quickly bring the finest robe and put it on him; put a ring on his finger and sandals on his feet. ²³ Take the fattened calf and slaughter it. Then let us celebrate with a feast, ²⁴ because this son of mine was dead, and has come to life again; he was lost, and has been found.' Then the celebration began. ²⁵ Now the older son had been out in the field and, on his way back, as he neared the house, he heard the sound of music and dancing. ²⁶ He called one of the servants and asked what this might mean. ²⁷ The servant said to him, 'Your brother has returned and your father has slaughtered the fattened calf because he has him back safe and sound.' ²⁸ He became angry, and when he refused to enter the house, his father

---

z Eph 5, 8; 1 Thes 5, 5.—a Lk 12, 33.—b Lk 19, 17; Mt 25, 20-23.

16, 1-8a: The parable of the dishonest steward has to be understood in the light of the Palestinian custom of agents acting on behalf of their masters and the usurious practices common to such agents. The dishonesty of the steward consisted in the squandering of his master's property (1) and not in any subsequent graft. The master commends the dishonest steward who has forgone his own usurious commission on the business transaction by having the debtors write new notes that reflected only the real amount owed the master (i.e., minus the steward's profit). The dishonest steward acts in this way in order to ingratiate himself with the debtors because he knows he is being dismissed from his position (3). The parable, then, teaches the prudent use of one's material goods in light of an imminent crisis.

16, 6: *One hundred measures:* literally, "one hundred *baths.*" A *bath* is a Hebrew unit of liquid measurement equivalent to eight or nine gallons.

16, 7: *One hundred kors:* a *kor* is a Hebrew unit of dry measure for grain or wheat equivalent to ten or twelve bushels.

16, 8b-13: Several originally independent sayings of Jesus are gathered here by Luke to form the concluding application of the parable of the dishonest steward.

16, 8b-9: The first conclusion recommends the prudent use of one's wealth (in the light of the coming of the end of the age) after the manner of the children of this world, represented in the parable by the dishonest steward.

16, 9: *Dishonest wealth:* literally, "mammon of iniquity." Mammon is the Greek transliteration of a Hebrew or Aramaic word that is usually explained as meaning "that in which one trusts." The characterization of this wealth as *dishonest* expresses a tendency of wealth to lead one to dishonesty. *Eternal dwellings:* or, "eternal tents," i.e., heaven.

16, 10-12: The second conclusion recommends constant fidelity to those in positions of responsibility.

---

came out and pleaded with him. ²⁹ He said to his father in reply, 'Look, all these years I served you and not once did I disobey your orders; yet you never gave me even a young goat to feast on with my friends. ³⁰ But when your son returns who swallowed up your property with prostitutes, for him you slaughter the fattened calf.' ³¹ He said to him, 'My son, you are here with me always; everything I have is yours. ³² But now we must celebrate and rejoice, because your brother was dead and has come to life again; he was lost and has been found.' "

CHAPTER 16

The Parable of the Dishonest Steward. * ¹ Then he also said to his disciples, "A rich man had a steward who was reported to him for squandering his property. ² He summoned him and said, 'What is this I hear about you? Prepare a full account of your stewardship, because you can no longer be my steward.' ³ The steward said to himself, 'What shall I do, now that my master is taking the position of steward away from me? I am not strong enough to dig and I am ashamed to beg. ⁴ I know what I shall do so that, when I am removed from the stewardship, they may welcome me into their homes.' ⁵ He called in his master's debtors one by one. To the first he said, 'How much do you owe my master?' ⁶ He replied, 'One hundred measures* of olive oil.' He said to him, 'Here is your promissory note. Sit down and quickly write one for fifty.' ⁷ Then to another he said, 'And you, how much do you owe?' He replied, 'One hundred kors* of wheat.' He said to him, 'Here is your promissory note; write one for eighty.' ⁸ And the master commended that dishonest steward for acting prudently.

Application of the Parable. * "For the children of this world are more prudent in dealing with their own generation than are the children of light.* ᶻ ⁹ I tell you, make friends for yourselves with dishonest wealth,* so that when it fails, you will be welcomed into eternal dwellings.ᵃ ¹⁰ * The person who is trustworthy in very small matters is also trustworthy in great ones; and the person who is dishonest in very small matters is also dishonest in great ones.ᵇ ¹¹ If, therefore, you are not trustworthy with dishonest wealth, who will trust you with true wealth? [12] If you are not trustworthy with what belongs to another, who will give you what is yours? [13] No servant can serve two masters.* He will either hate one and love the other, or be devoted to one and despise the other. You cannot serve God and mammon." *c*

A Saying against the Pharisees. [14] * The Pharisees, who loved money,* heard all these things and sneered at him. [15] And he said to them, "You justify yourselves in the sight of others, but God knows your hearts; for what is of human esteem is an abomination in the sight of God. *d*

Sayings about the Law. [16] "The law and the prophets lasted until John;* but from then on the kingdom of God is proclaimed, and everyone who enters does so with violence. *e* [17] It is easier for heaven and earth to pass away than for the smallest part of a letter of the law to become invalid. *f*

Sayings about Divorce. [18] "Everyone who divorces his wife and marries another commits adultery, and the one who marries a woman divorced from her husband commits adultery. *g*

The Parable of the Rich Man and Lazarus.* [19] "There was a rich man* who dressed in purple garments and fine linen and dined sumptuously each day. [20] And lying at his door was a poor man named Lazarus, covered with sores, *h* [21] who would gladly have eaten his fill of the scraps that fell from the rich man's table. Dogs even used to come and lick his sores. [22] When the poor man died, he was carried away by angels to the bosom of Abraham. The rich man also died and was buried, [23] and from the netherworld,* where he was in torment, he raised his eyes and saw Abraham far off and Lazarus at his side. [24] And he cried out, 'Father Abraham, have pity on me. Send Lazarus to dip the tip of his finger in water and cool my tongue, for I am suffering torment in these flames.' [25] Abraham replied, 'My child, remember that you received what was good during your lifetime while Lazarus likewise received what was bad; but now he is comforted here, whereas you are tormented. *i* [26] Moreover, between us and you a great chasm is established to prevent anyone from crossing who might wish to go from our side to yours or from your side to ours.' [27] He said, 'Then I beg you, father, send him to my father's house, [28] for I have

five brothers, so that he may warn them, lest they too come to this place of torment.' [29] But Abraham replied, 'They have Moses and the prophets. Let them listen to them.' [30] * He said, 'Oh no, father Abraham, but if someone from the dead goes to them, they will repent.' [31] Then Abraham said, 'If they will not listen to Moses and the prophets, neither will they be persuaded if someone should rise from the dead.' "*j*

CHAPTER 17

Temptations to Sin. [1] *k* He said to his disciples, "Things that cause sin will inevitably occur, but woe to the person through whom they occur. [2] It would be better for him if a millstone were put around his neck and he be thrown into the sea than for him to cause one of these little ones to sin. [3] Be on your guard!* If your brother sins, rebuke him; and if he repents, forgive him. *l* [4] And if he wrongs you seven times in one day and returns to you seven times saying, 'I am sorry,' you should forgive him." *m*

c Mt 6, 24.—d Lk 18, 9-14.—e Mt 11, 12-13.—f Mt 5, 18.—g Mt 5, 32; 19, 9; Mk 10, 11-12; 1 Cor 7, 10-11.—h Mt 15, 27; Mk 7, 28.—i Lk 6, 24-25.—j Jn 5, 46-47; 11, 44-48.—k 1-2: Mt 18, 6-7.—l Mt 18, 15.—m Mt 6, 14; 18, 21-22.35; Mk 11, 25.

16, 13: The third conclusion is a general statement about the incompatibility of serving God and being a slave to riches. To be dependent upon wealth is opposed to the teachings of Jesus who counseled complete dependence on the Father as one of the characteristics of the Christian disciple (Lk 12, 22-39). *God and mammon:* see the note on Lk 16, 9. Mammon is used here as if it were itself a god.

16, 14-18: The two parables about the use of riches in ch 16 are separated by several isolated sayings of Jesus on the hypocrisy of the Pharisees (14-15), on the law (16-17), and on divorce (18).

16, 14-15: The Pharisees are here presented as examples of those who are slaves to wealth (see Lk 16, 13) and, consequently, they are unable to serve God.

16, 16: John the Baptist is presented in Luke's gospel as a transitional figure between the period of Israel, the time of promise, and the period of Jesus, the time of fulfillment. With John, the fulfillment of the Old Testament promises has begun.

16, 19-31: The parable of the rich man and Lazarus again illustrates Luke's concern with Jesus' attitude toward the rich and the poor. The reversal of the fates of the rich man and Lazarus (22-23) illustrates the teachings of Jesus in Luke's "Sermon on the Plain" (Lk 6, 20-21.24-25).

16, 19: The oldest Greek manuscript of Lk dating from ca. A.D. 175-225 records the name of the rich man as an abbreviated form of "Nineveh," but there is very little textual support in other manuscripts for this reading. "Dives" of popular tradition is the Latin Vulgate's translation for "rich man."

16, 23: *The netherworld:* see the note on Lk 10, 15.

16, 30-31: A foreshadowing in Luke's gospel of the rejection of the call to repentance even after Jesus' resurrection.

17, 3a: *Be on your guard:* the translation takes v 3a as the conclusion to the saying on scandal in vv 1-2. It is not impossible that it should be taken as the beginning of the saying on forgiveness in vv 3b-4.

Saying of Faith. [5] And the apostles said to the Lord, "Increase our faith." [6] The Lord replied, "If you have faith the size of a mustard seed, you would say to [this] mulberry tree, 'Be uprooted and planted in the sea,' and it would obey you. [n]

Attitude of a Servant.* [7] "Who among you would say to your servant who has just come in from plowing or tending sheep in the field, 'Come here immediately and take your place at table'? [8] Would he not rather say to him, 'Prepare something for me to eat. Put on your apron and wait on me while I eat and drink. You may eat and drink when I am finished'? [9] Is he grateful to that servant because he did what was commanded? [10] So should it be with you. When you have done all you have been commanded, say, 'We are unprofitable servants; we have done what we were obliged to do.' "

The Cleansing of Ten Lepers.* [11] As he continued his journey to Jerusalem,[o] he traveled through Samaria and Galilee.* [12] As he was entering a village, ten lepers

n Mt 17, 20; 21, 21; Mk 11, 23.—o Lk 9, 51-53; 13, 22.33; 18, 31; 19, 28; Jn 4, 4.—p Lk 18, 38; Mt 9, 27; 15, 22.—q Lk 5, 14; Lv 14, 2-32; Mt 8, 4; Mk 1, 44.—r Lk 7, 50; 18, 42.—s Jn 3, 3.—t Lk 17, 23; Mt 24, 23; Mk 13, 21.—u Lk 17, 21; Mt 24, 23.26; Mk 13, 21.—v Mt 24, 27.—w Lk 9, 22; 18, 32-33; Mt 16, 21; 17, 22-23; 20, 18-19; Mk 8, 31; 9, 31; 10, 33-34.—x 26-27; Gn 6—8; Mt 24, 37-39.—y 28-29; Gn 18, 20-21; 19, 1-29.—z Mt 24, 17-18; Mk 13, 15-16.—a 31-32: Gn 19, 17.26.—b Lk 9, 24; Mt 10, 39; 16, 25; Mk 8, 35; Jn 12, 25.

17, 7-10: These sayings of Jesus, peculiar to Luke, which continue his response to the apostles' request to increase their faith (5-6), remind them that Christian disciples can make no claim on God's graciousness; in fulfilling the exacting demands of discipleship, they are only doing their duty.

17, 11-19: This incident recounting the thankfulness of the cleansed Samaritan leper is narrated only in Luke's gospel and provides an instance of Jesus holding up a non-Jew (18) as an example to his Jewish contemporaries (cf Lk 10, 33 where a similar purpose is achieved in the story of the good Samaritan). Moreover, it is the faith in Jesus manifested by the foreigner that has brought him salvation (19; cf the similar relationship between faith and salvation in Lk 7, 50; 8, 48.50).

17, 11: *Through Samaria and Galilee:* or, "between Samaria and Galilee."

17, 14: See the note on Lk 5, 14.

17, 20-37: To the question of the Pharisees about the time of the coming of God's kingdom, Jesus replies that the kingdom is *among you* (20-21). The emphasis has thus been shifted from an imminent observable coming of the kingdom to something that is already present in Jesus' preaching and healing ministry. Luke has also appended further traditional sayings of Jesus about the unpredictable suddenness of the day of the Son of Man, and assures his readers that in spite of the delay of that day (Lk 12, 45), it will bring judgment unexpectedly on those who do not continue to be vigilant.

17, 21: *Among you:* the Greek preposition translated as *among* can also be translated as "within." In the light of other statements in Luke's gospel about the presence of the kingdom (see Lk 10, 9.11; 11, 20) "among" is to be preferred.

met [him]. They stood at a distance from him [13] and raised their voice, saying, "Jesus, Master! Have pity on us!"[p] [14] And when he saw them, he said, "Go show yourselves to the priests."* As they were going they were cleansed.[q] [15] And one of them, realizing he had been healed, returned, glorifying God in a loud voice; [16] and he fell at the feet of Jesus and thanked him. He was a Samaritan. [17] Jesus said in reply, "Ten were cleansed, were they not? Where are the other nine? [18] Has none but this foreigner returned to give thanks to God?" [19] Then he said to him, "Stand up and go; your faith has saved you." [r]

The Coming of the Kingdom of God. [20] * Asked by the Pharisees when the kingdom of God would come, he said in reply, "The coming of the kingdom of God cannot be observed,[s] [21] and no one will announce, 'Look, here it is,' or, 'There it is.'[t] For behold, the kingdom of God is among you." *

The Day of the Son of Man. [22] Then he said to his disciples, "The days will come when you will long to see one of the days of the Son of Man, but you will not see it. [23] There will be those who will say to you, 'Look, there he is,' [or] 'Look, here he is.' Do not go off, do not run in pursuit.[u] [24] For just as lightning flashes and lights up the sky from one side to the other, so will the Son of Man be [in his day].[v] [25] But first he must suffer greatly and be rejected by this generation.[w] [26] As it was in the days of Noah,[x] so it will be in the days of the Son of Man; [27] they were eating and drinking, marrying and giving in marriage up to the day that Noah entered the ark, and the flood came and destroyed them all. [28] [y] Similarly, as it was in the days of Lot: they were eating, drinking, buying, selling, planting, building; [29] on the day when Lot left Sodom, fire and brimstone rained from the sky to destroy them all. [30] So it will be on the day the Son of Man is revealed. [31] [z] On that day, a person who is on the housetop and whose belongings are in the house must not go down to get them, and likewise a person in the field must not return to what was left behind.[a] [32] Remember the wife of Lot. [33] Whoever seeks to preserve his life will lose it, but whoever loses it will save it.[b] [34] I tell you, on that night there will be two people in one bed;

one will be taken, the other left.[35] *c* And there will be two women grinding meal together; one will be taken, the other left." [36]* [37] They said to him in reply, "Where, Lord?" He said to them, "Where the body is, there also the vultures will gather." *d*

CHAPTER 18

The Parable of the Persistent Widow. [1] * Then he told them a parable about the necessity for them to pray always without becoming weary.*e* He said, [2]"There was a judge in a certain town who neither feared God nor respected any human being. [3]And a widow in that town used to come to him and say, 'Render a just decision for me against my adversary.' [4]For a long time the judge was unwilling, but eventually he thought, 'While it is true that I neither fear God nor respect any human being, [5] *f* because this widow keeps bothering me I shall deliver a just decision for her lest she finally come and strike me.' "* [6]The Lord said, "Pay attention to what the dishonest judge says. [7]Will not God then secure the rights of his chosen ones who call out to him day and night? Will he be slow to answer them? [8]I tell you, he will see to it that justice is done for them speedily. But when the Son of Man comes, will he find faith on earth?"

The Parable of the Pharisee and the Tax Collector. [9]He then addressed this parable to those who were convinced of their own righteousness and despised everyone else.*g* [10]"Two people went up to the temple area to pray; one was a Pharisee and the other was a tax collector. [11]The Pharisee took up his position and spoke this prayer to himself, 'O God, I thank you that I am not like the rest of humanity—greedy, dishonest, adulterous—or even like this tax collector. [12]I fast twice a week, and I pay tithes on my whole income.' *h* [13]But the tax collector stood off at a distance and would not even raise his eyes to heaven but beat his breast and prayed, 'O God, be merciful to me a sinner.' *i* [14]I tell you, the latter went home justified, not the former; for everyone who exalts himself will be humbled, and the one who humbles himself will be exalted." *j*

Saying on Children and the Kingdom. [15] * People were bringing even infants to him that he might touch them,* and when the disciples saw this, they rebuked them.*k*

[16]Jesus, however, called the children to himself and said, "Let the children come to me and do not prevent them; for the kingdom of God belongs to such as these. [17]Amen, I say to you, whoever does not accept the kingdom of God like a child will not enter it." *l*

The Rich Official. [18] *m* An official asked him this question, "Good teacher, what must I do to inherit eternal life?" *n* [19]Jesus answered him, "Why do you call me good? No one is good but God alone. [20]You know the commandments, 'You shall not commit adultery; you shall not kill; you shall not steal; you shall not bear false witness; honor your father and your mother.' " *o* [21]And he replied, "All of these I have observed from my youth." [22] *p* When Jesus heard this he said to him, "There is still one thing left for you: sell all that you have and distribute it to the poor, and you will have a treasure in heaven. Then come, follow me."* [23]But when he heard this he became quite sad, for he was very rich.

---

c Mt 24, 40-41.—d Jb 39, 30; Mt 24, 28.—e Rom 12, 12; Col 4, 2; 1 Thes 5, 17.—f Lk 11, 8.—g Lk 16, 5; Mt 23, 25-28.—h Mt 23, 23.—i Ps 51, 3.—j Lk 14, 11; Mt 23, 12.—k 15-17: Mt 19, 13-15; Mk 10, 13-16.—l Mt 18, 3.—m 18-30: Mt 19, 16-30; Mk 10, 17-31.—n Lk 10, 25.—o Ex 20, 12-16; Dt 5, 16-20.—p Lk 12, 33; Sir 29, 11; Mt 6, 20.

17, 36: The inclusion of v 36, "There will be two men in the field; one will be taken, the other left behind," in some Western manuscripts appears to be a scribal assimilation to Mt 24, 40.

18, 1-14: The particularly Lucan material in the travel narrative concludes with two parables on prayer. The first (1-8) teaches the disciples the need of persistent prayer so that they not fall victims to apostasy (8). The second (9-14) condemns the self-righteous, critical attitude of the Pharisee and teaches that the fundamental attitude of the Christian disciple must be the recognition of sinfulness and complete dependence on God's graciousness. The second parable recalls the story of the pardoning of the sinful woman (Lk 7, 36-50) where a similar contrast is presented between the critical attitude of the Pharisee Simon and the love shown by the pardoned sinner.

18, 5: *Strike me:* the Greek verb translated as *strike* means "to strike under the eye" and suggests the extreme situation to which the persistence of the widow might lead. It may, however, be used here in the much weaker sense of "to wear one out."

18, 15—19, 27: Luke here includes much of the material about the journey to Jerusalem found in his Marcan source (Mk 10, 1-52) and adds to it the story of Zacchaeus (Lk 19, 1-10) from his own particular tradition and the parable of the gold coins (minas) (Lk 19, 11-27) from Q, the source common to Lk and Mt.

18, 15-17: The sayings on children furnish a contrast to the attitude of the Pharisee in the preceding episode (9-14) and that of the wealthy official in the following one (18-23) who think that they can lay claim to God's favor by their own merit. The attitude of the disciple should be marked by the receptivity and trustful dependence characteristic of the child.

18, 22: Detachment from material possessions results in the total dependence on God demanded of one who would inherit eternal life. *Sell all that you have:* the original saying (cf Mk 10, 21) has characteristically been made more demanding by Luke's addition of "all."

On Riches and Renunciation. [24] Jesus looked at him [now sad] and said, "How hard it is for those who have wealth to enter the kingdom of God! [25] For it is easier for a camel to pass through the eye of a needle than for a rich person to enter the kingdom of God." [26] Those who heard this said, "Then who can be saved?" [27] And he said, "What is impossible for human beings is possible for God."[q] [28] Then Peter said, "We have given up our possessions and followed you." [29] [r] He said to them, "Amen, I say to you, there is no one who has given up house or wife or brothers or parents or children for the sake of the kingdom of God [30] who will not receive [back] an overabundant return in this present age and eternal life in the age to come."

The Third Prediction of the Passion.[s] [31] * Then he took the Twelve aside and said to them, "Behold, we are going up to Jerusalem and everything written by the prophets about the Son of Man will be fulfilled.* [32] [t] He will be handed over to the

Gentiles and he will be mocked and insulted and spat upon; [33] and after they have scourged him they will kill him, but on the third day he will rise." [34] But they understood nothing of this; the word remained hidden from them and they failed to comprehend what he said.[u]

The Healing of the Blind Beggar.[v] [35] Now as he approached Jericho a blind man was sitting by the roadside begging, [36] and hearing a crowd going by, he inquired what was happening. [37] They told him, "Jesus of Nazareth is passing by." [38] [w] He shouted, "Jesus, Son of David,* have pity on me!" [39] The people walking in front rebuked him, telling him to be silent, but he kept calling out all the more, "Son of David, have pity on me!" [40] Then Jesus stopped and ordered that he be brought to him; and when he came near, Jesus asked him, [41] "What do you want me to do for you?" He replied, "Lord, please let me see."[x] [42] Jesus told him, "Have sight; your faith has saved you."[y] [43] He immediately received his sight and followed him, giving glory to God. When they saw this, all the people gave praise to God.

q Mk 14, 36.—r 29-30: Lk 14, 26.—s 31-34: Lk 24, 25-27.44; Mt 20, 17-19; Mk 10, 32-34; Acts 3, 18.—t 32-33: Lk 9, 22.44.—u Mk 9, 32.—v 35-43: Mt 20, 29-34; Mk 10, 46-52.—w 38-39: Lk 17, 13; Mt 9, 27; 15, 22.—x Mk 10, 36.—y Lk 7, 50; 17, 19.—z Lk 5, 30; 15, 2.—a Ex 21, 37; Nm 5, 6-7; 2 Sm 12, 6.—b Lk 13, 16; Mt 21, 31.—c Lk 15, 4-10; Ez 34, 16.

18, 31-33: The details included in this third announcement of Jesus' suffering and death suggest that the literary formulation of the announcement has been directed by the knowledge of the historical passion and death of Jesus.

18, 31: *Everything written by the prophets . . . will be fulfilled:* this is a Lucan addition to the words of Jesus found in the Marcan source (Mk 10, 32-34). Luke understands the events of Jesus' last days in Jerusalem to be the fulfillment of Old Testament prophecy, but, as is usually the case in Luke-Acts, the author does not specify which Old Testament prophets he has in mind; cf Lk 24, 25.27.44; Acts 3, 8; 13, 27; 26, 22-23.

18, 38: *Son of David:* the blind beggar identifies Jesus with a title that is related to Jesus' role as Messiah (see the note on Lk 2, 11). Through this Son of David, salvation comes to the blind man. Note the connection between salvation and house of David mentioned earlier in Zechariah's canticle (Lk 1, 69). See also the note on Mt 9, 27.

19, 1-10: The story of the tax collector Zacchaeus is unique to this gospel. While a rich man (2), Zacchaeus provides a contrast to the rich man of Lk 18, 18-23 who cannot detach himself from his material possessions to become a follower of Jesus. Zacchaeus, according to Luke, exemplifies the proper attitude toward wealth: he promises to give half of his possessions to the poor (8) and consequently is the recipient of salvation (9-10).

19, 9: *A descendant of Abraham:* literally, "a son of Abraham." The tax collector Zacchaeus, whose repentance is attested by his determination to amend his former ways, shows himself to be a true descendant of Abraham, the true heir to the promises of God in the Old Testament. Underlying Luke's depiction of Zacchaeus as a descendant of Abraham, the father of the Jews (Lk 1, 73; 16, 22-31), is his recognition of the central place occupied by Israel in the plan of salvation.

19, 10: This verse sums up for Luke his depiction of the role of Jesus as savior in this gospel.

CHAPTER 19

Zacchaeus the Tax Collector.* [1] He came to Jericho and intended to pass through the town. [2] Now a man there named Zacchaeus, who was a chief tax collector and also a wealthy man, [3] was seeking to see who Jesus was; but he could not see him because of the crowd, for he was short in stature. [4] So he ran ahead and climbed a sycamore tree in order to see Jesus, who was about to pass that way. [5] When he reached the place, Jesus looked up and said to him, "Zacchaeus, come down quickly, for today I must stay at your house." [6] And he came down quickly and received him with joy. [7] When they all saw this, they began to grumble, saying, "He has gone to stay at the house of a sinner."[z] [8] But Zacchaeus stood there and said to the Lord, "Behold, half of my possessions, Lord, I shall give to the poor, and if I have extorted anything from anyone I shall repay it four times over."[a] [9] And Jesus said to him, "Today salvation[b] has come to this house because this man too is a descendant of Abraham.* [10] [c] For the Son of Man has come to seek and to save what was lost." *

Lk

The Parable of the Ten Gold Coins.* [11] [d] While they were listening to him speak, he proceeded to tell a parable because he was near Jerusalem and they thought that the kingdom of God would appear there immediately. [12] So he said, "A nobleman went off to a distant country to obtain the kingship for himself and then to return. [e] [13] He called ten of his servants and gave them ten gold coins* and told them, 'Engage in trade with these until I return.' [14] His fellow citizens, however, despised him and sent a delegation after him to announce, 'We do not want this man to be our king.' [15] But when he returned after obtaining the kingship, he had the servants called, to whom he had given the money, to learn what they had gained by trading. [16] The first came forward and said, 'Sir, your gold coin has earned ten additional ones.' [17] He replied, 'Well done, good servant! You have been faithful in this very small matter; take charge of ten cities.' [f] [18] Then the second came and reported, 'Your gold coin, sir, has earned five more.' [19] And to this servant too he said, 'You, take charge of five cities.' [20] Then the other servant came and said, 'Sir, here is your gold coin; I kept it stored away in a handkerchief, [21] for I was afraid of you, because you are a demanding person; you take up what you did not lay down and you harvest what you did not plant.' [22] He said to him, 'With your own words I shall condemn you, you wicked servant. You knew I was a demanding person, taking up what I did not lay down and harvesting what I did not plant; [23] why did you not put my money in a bank? Then on my return I would have collected it with interest.' [24] And to those standing by he said, 'Take the gold coin from him and give it to the servant who has ten.' [25] But they said to him, 'Sir, he has ten gold coins.' [26] 'I tell you, to everyone who has, more will be given, but from the one who has not, even what he has will be taken away. [g] [27] Now as for those enemies of mine who did not want me as their king, bring them here and slay them before me.'"

VI. THE TEACHING MINISTRY IN JERUSALEM*

The Entry into Jerusalem. [h] [28] After he had said this, he proceeded on his journey up to Jerusalem. [29] As he drew near to Bethphage and Bethany at the place called the Mount of Olives, he sent two of his disciples. [i] [30] He said, "Go into the village opposite you, and as you enter it you will find a colt tethered on which no one has ever sat. Untie it and bring it here. [j] [31] And if anyone should ask you, 'Why are you untying it?' you will answer, 'The Master has need of it.'" [32] So those who had been sent went off and found everything just as he had told them. [k] [33] And as they were untying the colt, its owners said to them, "Why are you untying this colt?" [34] They answered, "The Master has need of it." [35] [l] So they brought it to Jesus, threw their cloaks over the colt, and helped Jesus to mount. [36] As he rode along, the people were spreading their cloaks on the road; [37] and now as he was approaching the slope of the Mount of Olives, the whole multitude of his disciples began to praise God aloud with joy for all the mighty deeds they had seen. [38] They proclaimed:

---

d 11-27: Mt 25, 14-30.—e Mk 13, 34.—f Lk 16, 10.—g Lk 8, 18; Mt 13, 12; Mk 4, 25.—h 28-40: Mt 21, 1-11; Mk 11, 1-11; Jn 12, 12-19.—i Zec 14, 4.—j Nm 19, 2; Dt 21, 3, 1 Sm 6, 7; Zec 9, 9.—k Lk 22, 13.—l 35-36: 2 Kgs 9, 13.

19, 11-27: In this parable Luke has combined two originally distinct parables: (1) a parable about the conduct of faithful and productive servants (13.15b-26) and (2) a parable about a rejected king (12.14-15a.27). The story about the conduct of servants occurs in another form in Mt 25, 14-20. The story about the rejected king may have originated with a contemporary historical event. After the death of Herod the Great, his son Archelaus traveled to Rome to receive the title of king. A delegation of Jews appeared in Rome before Caesar Augustus to oppose the request of Archelaus. Although not given the title of king, Archelaus was made ruler over Judea and Samaria. As the story is used by Luke,

however, it furnishes a correction to the expectation of the imminent end of the age and of the establishment of the kingdom in Jerusalem (11). Jesus is not on his way to Jerusalem to receive the kingly power; for that, he must go away and only after returning from the distant country (a reference to the parousia) will reward and judgment take place.

19, 13: *Ten gold coins:* literally, "ten minas." A mina was a monetary unit that in ancient Greece was the equivalent of one hundred drachmas.

19, 28—21, 38: With the royal entry of Jesus into Jerusalem, a new section of Luke's gospel begins, the ministry of Jesus in Jerusalem before his death and resurrection. Luke suggests that this was a lengthy ministry in Jerusalem (Lk 19, 47; 20, 1; 21, 37-38; 22, 53) and it is characterized by Jesus' daily teaching in the temple (Lk 21, 37-38). For the story of the entry of Jesus into Jerusalem, see also Mt 21, 1-11; Mk 11, 1-10; Jn 12, 12-19 and the notes there.

"Blessed is the king who comes
in the name of the Lord.*
Peace in heaven
and glory in the highest." m

39 Some of the Pharisees in the crowd said to him, "Teacher, rebuke your disciples." * 40 He said in reply, "I tell you, if they keep silent, the stones will cry out!"

The Lament for Jerusalem. * 41 n As he drew near, he saw the city and wept over it, o 42 saying, "If this day you only knew what makes for peace—but now it is hidden from your eyes. p 43 * For the days are coming upon you when your enemies will raise a palisade against you; they will encircle you and hem you in on all sides. q 44 They will smash you to the ground and your children within you, and they will not leave one stone upon another within you because you did not recognize the time of your visitation." r

The Cleansing of the Temple. 45 s Then Jesus entered the temple area* and proceeded to drive out those who were selling things, t 46 saying to them, "It is written, 'My house shall be a house of prayer, but you have made it a den of thieves.'" u 47 And every day he was teaching in the temple area. v The chief priests, the scribes, and the leaders of the people, meanwhile, were seeking to put him to death, w 48 but they could find no way to accomplish their purpose because all the people were hanging on his words.

CHAPTER 20*
The Authority of Jesus Questioned. x
1 One day as he was teaching the people in the temple area and proclaiming the good news, the chief priests and scribes, together with the elders, approached him 2 and said to him, "Tell us, by what authority are you doing these things? Or who is the one who gave you this authority?" y 3 He said to them in reply, "I shall ask you a question. Tell me, 4 was John's baptism of heavenly or of human origin?" z 5 They discussed this among themselves, and said, "If we say, 'Of heavenly origin,' he will say, 'Why did you not believe him?' a 6 But if we say, 'Of human origin,' then all the people will stone us, for they are convinced that John was a prophet." 7 So they answered that they did not know from where it came. 8 Then Jesus said to them, "Neither shall I tell you by what authority I do these things."

The Parable of the Tenant Farmers. * 9 b Then he proceeded to tell the people this parable. "[A] man planted a vineyard, leased it to tenant farmers, and then went on a journey for a long time. c 10 At harvest time he sent a servant d to the tenant farmers to receive some of the produce of the vineyard. But they beat the servant and sent him away empty-handed. 11 So he proceeded to send another servant, but him also they beat and insulted and sent away empty-handed. 12 Then he proceeded to send a third, but this one too they wounded and threw out. 13 The owner of the vineyard said, 'What shall I do? I shall

m Lk 2, 14; Ps 118, 26.—n 41-44: Lk 13, 34-35.—o 2 Kgs 8, 11-12; Jer 14, 17; 15, 5.—p Lk 8, 10; Is 6, 9-10; Mt 13, 14; Mk 4, 12; Acts 28, 26-27; Rom 11, 8.10.—q Is 29, 3.—r Lk 1, 68; 21, 6; Ps 137, 9; Mt 24, 2; Mk 13, 2.—s 45-46: Mt 21, 12-13; Mk 11, 15-17; Jn 2, 13-17.—t Mal 3, 1 / Hos 9, 15.—u Is 56, 7; Jer 7, 11.—v 47-48: Lk 20, 19; 22, 2; Mt 21, 46; Mk 11, 18; 12, 12; 14, 1-2; Jn 5, 18; 7, 30.—w Lk 21, 37; 22, 53; Jn 18, 20.—x 1-8: Mt 21, 23-27; Mk 11, 27-33.—y Acts 4, 7.—z Lk 3, 3.16.— a Mt 21, 32.—b 9-19: Mt 21, 33-46; Mk 12, 1-12.—c Is 5, 1-7.—d 10-12: 2 Chr 36, 15-16.

19, 41-44: The lament for Jerusalem is found only in Lk. By not accepting Jesus (the one who mediates peace), Jerusalem will not find peace but will become the victim of devastation.

19, 43-44: Luke may be describing the actual disaster that befell Jerusalem in A.D. 70 when it was destroyed by the Romans during the First Revolt.

19, 45-46: Immediately upon entering the holy city, Jesus in a display of his authority enters the temple (see Mal 3, 1-3) and lays claim to it after cleansing it that it might become a proper place for his teaching ministry in Jerusalem (Lk 19, 47; 20, 1; 21, 37; 22, 53). See Mt 21, 12-17; Mk 11, 15-19; Jn 2, 13-17 and the notes there.

20, 1-47: The Jerusalem religious leaders or their representatives, in an attempt to incriminate Jesus with the Romans and to discredit him with the people, pose a number of questions to him (about his authority, 2; about payment of taxes, 22; about the resurrection, 28-33).

20, 9-19: This parable about an absentee landlord and a tenant farmers' revolt reflects the social and economic conditions of rural Palestine in the first century. The synoptic gospel writers use the parable to describe how the rejection of the landlord's son becomes the occasion for the vineyard to be taken away from those to whom it was entrusted (the religious leadership of Judaism that rejects the teaching and preaching of Jesus; 19).

19, 38: *Blessed is the king who comes in the name of the Lord:* only in Lk is Jesus explicitly given the title *king* when he enters Jerusalem in triumph. Luke has inserted this title into the words of Ps 118, 26 that heralded the arrival of the pilgrims coming to the holy city and to the temple. Jesus is thereby acclaimed as *king* (see Lk 1, 32) and as the one *who comes* (see Mal 3, 1; Lk 7, 19). *Peace in heaven . . . :* the acclamation of the disciples of Jesus in Lk echoes the announcement of the angels at the birth of Jesus (Lk 2, 14). The peace Jesus brings is associated with the salvation to be accomplished here in Jerusalem.

19, 39: *Rebuke your disciples:* this command, found only in Lk, was given so that the Roman authorities would not interpret the acclamation of Jesus as king as an uprising against them; cf Lk 23, 2-3.

send my beloved son; maybe they will respect him.'[e] [14]But when the tenant farmers saw him they said to one another, 'This is the heir. Let us kill him that the inheritance may become ours.' [15]So they threw him out of the vineyard and killed him.* What will the owner of the vineyard do to them? [16]He will come and put those tenant farmers to death and turn over the vineyard to others." When the people heard this, they exclaimed, "Let it not be so!" [17]But he looked at them and asked, "What then does this scripture passage mean:

'The stone which the builders rejected
    has become the cornerstone'?[f]

[18]Everyone who falls on that stone will be dashed to pieces; and it will crush anyone on whom it falls." [19]The scribes and chief priests sought to lay their hands on him at that very hour, but they feared the people, for they knew that he had addressed this parable to them.[g]

Paying Taxes to the Emperor.[h] [20]They watched him closely and sent agents pretending to be righteous who were to trap him in speech,[i] in order to hand him over to the authority and power of the governor.* [21]They posed this question to him, "Teacher, we know that what you say and teach is correct, and you show no partiality, but teach the way of God in accordance with the truth.[j] [22]Is it lawful for us to pay tribute to Caesar or not?"* [23]Recognizing their craftiness he said to them, [24]"Show me a denarius;* whose image and name does it bear?" They replied, "Caesar's." [25]So he said to them, "Then repay to Caesar what belongs to Caesar and to God what belongs to God."[k] [26]They were unable to trap him by something he might say before the people, and so amazed were they at his reply that they fell silent.

The Question about the Resurrection.[l] [27]Some Sadducees,* those who deny that there is a resurrection, came forward and put this question to him,[m] [28] * saying, "Teacher, Moses wrote for us, 'If someone's brother dies leaving a wife but no child, his brother must take the wife and raise up descendants for his brother.'[n] [29]Now there were seven brothers; the first married a woman but died childless. [30]Then the second [31]and the third married her, and likewise all the seven died childless. [32]Finally the woman also died. [33]Now at the resurrection whose wife will

that woman be? For all seven had been married to her." [34]Jesus said to them, "The children of this age marry and remarry; [35]but those who are deemed worthy to attain to the coming age and to the resurrection of the dead neither marry nor are given in marriage. [36]They can no longer die, for they are like angels; and they are the children of God because they are the ones who will rise.* [37]That the dead will rise even Moses made known in the passage about the bush, when he called 'Lord' the God of Abraham, the God of Isaac, and the God of Jacob;[o] [38]and he is not God of the dead, but of the living, for to him all are alive."[p] [39]Some of the scribes said in reply, "Teacher, you have answered well." [40]And they no longer dared to ask him anything.[q]

The Question about David's Son.* [41] [r] Then he said to them, "How do they claim that the Messiah is the Son of David? [42]For David himself in the Book of Psalms says:[s]

e Lk 3, 22.—f Ps 118, 22; Is 28, 16.—g Lk 19, 47-48; 22, 2; Mt 21, 46; Mk 11, 18; 12, 12; 14, 1-2; Jn 5, 18; 7, 30.—h 20-26: Mt 22, 15-22; Mk 12, 13-17.—i Lk 11, 54.—j Jn 3, 2.—k Rom 13, 6-7.—l 27-40: Mt 22, 23-33; Mk 12, 18-27.—m Acts 23, 8.—n Gn 38, 8; Dt 25, 5.—o Ex 3, 2.6.15-16.—p Rom 14, 8-9.—q Mt 22, 46; Mk 12, 34.—r 41-44: Mt 22, 41-45; Mk 12, 35-37.—s 42-43: Ps 110, 1.

20, 15: *They threw him out of the vineyard and killed him:* cf Mk 12, 8. Luke has altered his Marcan source and reports that the murder of the son takes place outside the vineyard to reflect the tradition of Jesus' death outside the walls of the city of Jerusalem (see Heb 13, 12).

20, 20: *The governor:* i.e., Pontius Pilate, the Roman administrator responsible for the collection of taxes and maintenance of order in Palestine.

20, 22: Through their question the agents of the Jerusalem religious leadership hope to force Jesus to take sides on one of the sensitive political issues of first-century Palestine. The issue of nonpayment of taxes to Rome becomes one of the focal points of the First Jewish Revolt (A.D. 66-70) that resulted in the Roman destruction of Jerusalem and the temple. See also the note on Mt 22, 15-22.

20, 24: *Denarius:* a Roman silver coin (see the note on Lk 7, 41).

20, 27: *Sadducees:* see the note on Mt 3, 7.

20, 28-33: The Sadducees' question, based on the law of levirate marriage recorded in Dt 25, 5-10, ridicules the idea of the resurrection. Jesus rejects their naive understanding of the resurrection (35-36) and then argues on behalf of the resurrection of the dead on the basis of the written law (37-38) that the Sadducees accept. See also the notes on Mt 22, 23-33.

20, 36: *Because they are the ones who will rise:* literally, "being sons of the resurrection."

20, 41-44: After successfully answering the three questions of his opponents, Jesus now asks them a question. Their inability to respond implies that they have forfeited their position and authority as the religious leaders of the people because they do not understand the scriptures. This series of controversies between the religious leadership of Jerusalem and Jesus reveals Jesus as the authoritative teacher whose words are to be listened to (see Lk 9, 35). See also the notes on Mt 22, 41-46.

'The Lord said to my lord,
"Sit at my right hand
43   till I make your enemies your footstool." '

⁴⁴Now if David calls him 'lord,' how can he be his son?"

Denunciation of the Scribes. *ᵗ* ⁴⁵Then, within the hearing of all the people, he said to [his] disciples, ⁴⁶"Be on guard against the scribes, who like to go around in long robes and love greetings in marketplaces, seats of honor in synagogues, and places of honor at banquets. *ᵘ* ⁴⁷They devour the houses of widows and, as a pretext, recite lengthy prayers. They will receive a very severe condemnation."

CHAPTER 21

The Poor Widow's Contribution. * ¹ *ᵛ* When he looked up he saw some wealthy people putting their offerings into the treasury ²and he noticed a poor widow putting in two small coins. ³He said, "I tell you truly, this poor widow put in more than all the rest; ⁴for those others have all made offerings from their surplus wealth, but she, from her poverty, has offered her whole livelihood."

The Destruction of the Temple Foretold. *ʷ* ⁵ *While some people were speaking about how the temple was adorned with costly stones and votive offerings, he said, ⁶"All that you see here—the days will come when there will not be left a stone upon another stone that will not be thrown down." *ˣ*

The Signs of the End. ⁷ *ʸ* Then they asked him, "Teacher, when will this happen? And what sign will there be when all these things are about to happen?" ⁸He answered, "See that you not be deceived, for many will come in my name, saying, 'I am he,' and 'The time has come.' * Do not follow them! *ᶻ* ⁹When you hear of wars and insurrections, do not be terrified; for such things must happen first, but it will not immediately be the end." ¹⁰Then he said to them, "Nation will rise against nation, and kingdom against kingdom. *ᵃ* ¹¹There will be powerful earthquakes, famines, and plagues from place to place; and awesome sights and mighty signs will come from the sky.

The Coming Persecution. ¹² *ᵇ* "Before all this happens,* however, they will seize and persecute you, they will hand you over to the synagogues and to prisons, and they will have you led before kings and governors because of my name. *ᶜ* ¹³It will lead to your giving testimony. ¹⁴Remember, you are not to prepare your defense beforehand, ¹⁵ *ᵈ* for I myself shall give you a wisdom in speaking * that all your adversaries will be powerless to resist or refute. ¹⁶ *ᵉ* You will even be handed over by parents, brothers, relatives, and friends, and they will put some of you to death. *ᶠ* ¹⁷You will be hated by all because of my name, ¹⁸but not a hair on your head will be destroyed. *ᵍ* ¹⁹By your perseverance you will secure your lives. *ʰ*

The Great Tribulation. * ²⁰ *ⁱ* "When you see Jerusalem surrounded by armies, know

---

t 45-47: Lk 11, 37-54; Mt 23, 1-36; Mk 12, 38-40.—u Lk 14, 7-11.—v 1-4: Mk 12, 41-44.—w 5-6: Mt 24, 1-2; Mk 13, 1-2.—x Lk 19, 44.—y 7-19: Mt 24, 3-14; Mk 13, 3-13.—z Lk 17, 23; Mk 13, 5.6.21; 1 Jn 2, 18.—a 2 Chr 15, 6; Is 19, 2.—b 12-15: Lk 12, 11-12; Mt 10, 17-20; Mk 13, 9-11.—c Jn 16, 2; Acts 25, 24.—d Acts 6, 10.—e 16-18: Mt 10, 21-22.—f Lk 12, 52-53.—g Lk 12, 7; 1 Sm 14, 45; Mt 10, 30; Acts 27, 34.—h Lk 8, 15.—i 20-24: Mt 24, 15-21; Mk 13, 14-19.

21, 1-4: The widow is another example of the poor ones in this gospel whose detachment from material possessions and dependence on God leads to their blessedness (Lk 6, 20). Her simple offering provides a striking contrast to the pride and pretentiousness of the scribes denounced in the preceding section (Lk 20, 45-47). The story is taken from Mk 12, 41-44.

21, 5-36: Jesus' eschatological discourse in Lk is inspired by Mk 13, but Luke has made some significant alterations to the words of Jesus found there. Luke maintains, though in a modified form, the belief in the early expectation of the end of the age (see 27.28.31.32.36), but, by focusing attention throughout the gospel on the importance of the day-to-day following of Jesus and by reinterpreting the meaning of some of the signs of the end from

Mk 13, he has come to terms with what seemed to the early Christian community to be a delay of the parousia. Mark, for example, described the desecration of the Jerusalem temple by the Romans (Mk 13, 14) as the apocalyptic symbol (see Dn 9, 27; 12, 11) accompanying the end of the age and the coming of the Son of Man. Luke (Lk 21, 20-24), however, removes the apocalyptic setting and separates the historical destruction of Jerusalem from the signs of the coming of the Son of Man by a period that he refers to as "the times of the Gentiles" (Lk 21, 24). See also the notes on Mt 24, 1-36 and Mk 13, 1-37.

21, 8: *The time has come:* in Lk, the proclamation of the imminent end of the age has itself become a false teaching.

21, 12: *Before all this happens . . . :* to Luke and his community, some of the signs of the end just described (10-11) still lie in the future. Now in dealing with the persecution of the disciples (12-19) and the destruction of Jerusalem (20-24) Luke is pointing to eschatological signs that have already been fulfilled.

21, 15: *A wisdom in speaking:* literally, "a mouth and wisdom."

21, 20-24: The actual destruction of Jerusalem by Rome in A.D. 70 upon which Luke and his community look back provides the assurance that, just as Jesus' prediction of Jerusalem's destruction was fulfilled, so too will be his announcement of their final redemption (27-28).

that its desolation is at hand.*j* *21*Then those in Judea must flee to the mountains. Let those within the city escape from it, and let those in the countryside not enter the city,*k* *22*for these days are the time of punishment when all the scriptures are fulfilled. *23*Woe to pregnant women and nursing mothers in those days, for a terrible calamity will come upon the earth and a wrathful judgment upon this people.*l* *24*They will fall by the edge of the sword and be taken as captives to all the Gentiles; and Jerusalem will be trampled underfoot by the Gentiles until the times of the Gentiles* are fulfilled.*m*

The Coming of the Son of Man.n *25*"There will be signs in the sun, the moon, and the stars, and on earth nations will be in dismay, perplexed by the roaring of the sea and the waves.*o* *26*People will die of fright in anticipation of what is coming upon the world, for the powers of the heavens* will be shaken.*p* *27*And then they will see the Son of Man coming in a cloud with power and great glory.*q* *28*But when these signs begin to happen, stand erect and raise your heads because your redemption is at hand."*r*

The Lesson of the Fig Tree.s *29*He taught them a lesson. "Consider the fig tree and all the other trees. *30*When their buds burst open, you see for yourselves and know that summer is now near; *31*in the same way, when you see these things happening, know that the kingdom of God is near. *32*Amen, I say to you, this generation will not pass away until all these things have taken place.*t* *33*Heaven and earth will pass away, but my words will not pass away.*u*

Exhortation to be Vigilant. *34*"Beware that your hearts do not become drowsy from carousing and drunkenness and the anxieties of daily life, and that day catch you by surprise*v* *35*like a trap. For that day will assault everyone who lives on the face of the earth. *36*Be vigilant at all times and pray that you have the strength to escape the tribulations that are imminent and to stand before the Son of Man."*w*

Ministry in Jerusalem. *37*During the day, Jesus was teaching in the temple area, but at night he would leave and stay at the place called the Mount of Olives.*x* *38*And all the people would get up early each morning to listen to him in the temple area.

VII. THE PASSION NARRATIVE*

CHAPTER 22

The Conspiracy against Jesus. *1* *y* Now the feast of Unleavened Bread, called the Passover,* was drawing near, *2* *z* and the chief priests and the scribes were seeking a way to put him to death, for they were afraid of the people. *3* *a* Then Satan entered into Judas,* the one surnamed Iscariot, who was counted among the Twelve,*b* *4*and he went to the chief priests and temple guards to discuss a plan for handing him over to them. *5*They were pleased and agreed to pay him money. *6*He accepted their offer and sought a favorable opportunity to hand him over to them in the absence of a crowd.

Preparations for the Passover.c *7*When the day of the Feast of Unleavened Bread arrived, the day for sacrificing the Passover lamb,*d* *8*he sent out Peter and John, instructing them, "Go and make preparations for us to eat the Passover." *9*They asked him, "Where do you want us to

---

j 20-22: Lk 19, 41-44.—k Lk 17, 31.—l 1 Cor 7, 26.—m Tb 14, 5; Ps 79, 1; Is 63, 18; Jer 21, 7; Rom 11, 25; Rv 11, 2.—n 25-28: Mt 24, 29-31; Mk 13, 24-27.—o Wis 5, 22; Is 13, 10; Ez 32, 7; Jl 2, 10; 3, 3-4; 4, 15; Rv 6, 12-14.—p Hg 2, 6.21.—q Dn 7, 13-14; Mt 26, 64; Rv 1, 7.—r Lk 2, 38.—s 29-33: Mt 24, 32-35; Mk 13, 28-31.—t Lk 9, 27; Mt 16, 28.—u Lk 16, 17.—v Lk 12, 45-46; Mt 24, 48-50; 1 Thes 5, 3.6-7.—w Mk 13, 33.—x Lk 19, 47; 22, 39.—y 1-2: Mt 26, 1-5; Mk 14, 1-2; Jn 11, 47-53.—z Lk 19, 47-48; 20, 19; Mt 21, 46; Mk 12, 12; Jn 5, 18; 7, 30.—a 3-6: Mt 26, 14-16; Mk 14, 10-11; Jn 13, 2.27.—b Acts 1, 17.—c 7-13: Mt 26, 17-19; Mk 14, 12-16.—d Ex 12, 6.14-20.

21, 24: *The times of the Gentiles:* a period of indeterminate length separating the destruction of Jerusalem from the cosmic signs accompanying the coming of the Son of Man.

21, 26: *The powers of the heavens:* the heavenly bodies mentioned in v 25 and thought of as cosmic armies.

22, 1—23, 56a: The passion narrative. Luke is still dependent upon Mk for the composition of the passion narrative but has incorporated much of his own special tradition into the narrative. Among the distinctive sections in Lk are: (1) the tradition of the institution of the Eucharist (Lk 22, 15-20); (2) Jesus' farewell discourse (Lk 22, 21-38); (3) the mistreatment and interrogation of Jesus (Lk 22, 63-71); (4) Jesus before Herod and his second appearance before Pilate (Lk 23, 6-16); (5) words addressed to the women followers on the way to the crucifixion (Lk 23, 27-32); (6) words to the penitent thief (Lk 23, 39-41); (7) the death of Jesus (Lk 23, 46.47b-49). Luke stresses the innocence of Jesus (Lk 23, 4.14-15.22) who is the victim of the powers of evil (Lk 22, 3.31.53) and who goes to his death in fulfillment of his Father's will (Lk 22, 42.46). Throughout the narrative Luke emphasizes the mercy, compassion, and healing power of Jesus (Lk 22, 51; 23, 43) who does not go to death lonely and deserted, but is accompanied by others who follow him on the way of the cross (Lk 23, 26-31.49).

22, 1: *Feast of Unleavened Bread, called the Passover:* see the note on Mk 14, 1.

22, 3: *Satan entered into Judas:* see the note on Lk 4, 13.

make the preparations?" [10] And he answered them, "When you go into the city, a man will meet you carrying a jar of water.* Follow him into the house that he enters [11] and say to the master of the house, 'The teacher says to you, "Where is the guest room where I may eat the Passover with my disciples?" ' [12] He will show you a large upper room that is furnished. Make the preparations there." [13] Then they went off and found everything exactly as he had told them, and there they prepared the Passover.[e]

The Last Supper.[f] [14] When the hour came, he took his place at table with the apostles. [15] He said to them, "I have eagerly desired to eat this Passover* with you before I suffer, [16] for, I tell you, I shall not eat it [again] until there is fulfillment in the kingdom of God."[g] [17] Then he took a cup,* gave thanks, and said, "Take this and share it among yourselves; [18] for I tell you [that] from this time on I shall not drink of the fruit of the vine until the kingdom of God comes." [19] [h] Then he took the bread, said the blessing, broke it, and gave it to them, saying, "This is my body, which will be given for you; do this in memory of me."* [20] And likewise the cup after they had eaten, saying, "This cup is the new covenant in my blood, which will be shed for you.[i]

The Betrayal Foretold.[j] [21] "And yet behold, the hand of the one who is to betray me is with me on the table; [22] for the Son of Man indeed goes as it has been determined; but woe to that man by whom he is betrayed." [23] And they began to debate among themselves who among them would do such a deed.

The Role of the Disciples. [24] * Then an argument broke out among them[k] about which of them should be regarded as the greatest. [25] [l] He said to them, "The kings of the Gentiles lord it over them and those in authority over them are addressed as 'Benefactors';* [26] but among you it shall not be so. Rather, let the greatest among you be as the youngest, and the leader as the servant.[m] [27] For who is greater: the one seated at table or the one who serves? Is it not the one seated at table? I am among you as the one who serves. [28] It is you who have stood by me in my trials; [29] and I confer a kingdom on you, just as my Father has conferred one on me,[n] [30] that you may eat and drink at my table in my kingdom; and you will sit on thrones judging the twelve tribes of Israel.[o]

Peter's Denial Foretold.[p] [31] "Simon, Simon, behold Satan has demanded to sift all of you* like wheat,[q] [32] but I have prayed* that your own faith may not fail; and once you have turned back, you must strengthen your brothers." [33] He said to him, "Lord, I am prepared to go to prison and to die with you."[r] [34] But he replied, "I tell you, Peter, before the cock crows this day, you will deny three times that you know me."[s]

Instructions for the Time of Crisis. [35] [t] He said to them, "When I sent you forth without a money bag or a sack or sandals, were you in need of anything?" "No, nothing," they replied. [36] [u] He said to them,* "But now one who has a money bag should take

---

e Lk 19, 32.—f 14-20: Mt 26, 20.26-30; Mk 14, 17.22-26; 1 Cor 11, 23-25.—g Lk 13, 29.—h Lk 24, 30; Acts 27, 35.—i Ex 24, 8; Jer 31, 31; 32, 40; Zec 9, 11.—j 21-23: Ps 41, 10; Mt 26, 21-25; Mk 14, 18-21; Jn 13, 21-30.—k Lk 9, 46; Mt 18, 1; Mk 9, 34.—l 25-27: Mt 20, 25-27; Mk 10, 42-44; Jn 13, 3-16.—m Mt 23, 11; Mk 9, 35.—n Lk 12, 32.—o Mt 19, 28.—p 31-34: Mt 26, 33-35; Mk 14, 29-31; Jn 13, 37-38.—q Jb 1, 6-12; Am 9, 9.—r Lk 22, 54.—s Lk 22, 54-62.—t Lk 9, 3; 10, 4; Mt 10, 9-10; Mk 6, 7-9.—u Lk 22, 49.

22, 10: *A man will meet you carrying a jar of water:* see the note on Mk 14, 13.

22, 15: *This Passover:* Luke clearly identifies this last supper of Jesus with the apostles as a Passover meal that commemorated the deliverance of the Israelites from slavery in Egypt. Jesus reinterprets the significance of the Passover by setting it in the context of the kingdom of God (16). The "deliverance" associated with the Passover finds its new meaning in the blood that will be shed (20).

22, 17: Because of a textual problem in vv 19 and 20, some commentators interpret this cup as the eucharistic cup.

22, 19c-20: *Which will be given . . . do this in memory of me:* these words are omitted in some important Western text manuscripts and a few Syriac manuscripts. Other ancient text types, including the oldest papyrus manuscript of Lk dating from the late second or early third century, contain the longer reading presented here. The Lucan account of the words of institution of the Eucharist bears a close resemblance to the words of institution in the Pauline tradition (see 1 Cor 11, 23-26). See also the notes on Mt 26, 26-29; 26, 27-28; and Mk 14, 22-24.

22, 24-38: The Gospel of Luke presents a brief farewell discourse of Jesus; compare the lengthy farewell discourses and prayer in Jn, chs 13-17.

22, 25: *'Benefactors':* this word occurs as a title of rulers in the Hellenistic world.

22, 31: *All of you:* literally, "you." The translation reflects the meaning of the Greek text that uses a second person plural pronoun here.

22, 31-32: Jesus' prayer for Simon's faith and the commission to strengthen his brothers anticipates the post-resurrectional prominence of Peter in the first half of Acts, where he appears as the spokesman for the Christian community and the one who begins the mission to the Gentiles (Acts 10—11).

22, 36: In contrast to the ministry of the Twelve and of the seventy-two during the period of Jesus (Lk 9, 3; 10, 4), in the future period of the church the missionaries must be prepared for the opposition they will face in a world hostile to their preaching.

it, and likewise a sack, and one who does not have a sword should sell his cloak and buy one. ³⁷ For I tell you that this scripture must be fulfilled in me, namely, 'He was counted among the wicked'; and indeed what is written about me is coming to fulfillment."*ᵛ ³⁸ Then they said, "Lord, look, there are two swords here." But he replied, "It is enough!"*

The Agony in the Garden. ʷ ³⁹ Then going out he went, as was his custom, to the Mount of Olives, and the disciples followed him. ⁴⁰ When he arrived at the place he said to them, "Pray that you may not undergo the test."ˣ ⁴¹ After withdrawing about a stone's throw from them and kneeling, he prayed,ʸ ⁴² saying, "Father, if you are willing, take this cup away from me; still, not my will but yours be done."ᶻ *[⁴³ And to strengthen him an angel from heaven appeared to him. ⁴⁴ He was in such agony and he prayed so fervently that his sweat became like drops of blood falling on the ground.] ⁴⁵ When he rose from prayer and returned to his disciples, he found them sleeping from grief. ⁴⁶ He said to them, "Why are you sleeping? Get up and pray that you may not undergo the test."ᵃ

The Betrayal and Arrest of Jesus.ᵇ ⁴⁷ While he was still speaking, a crowd approached and in front was one of the Twelve, a man named Judas. He went up to Jesus to kiss him. ⁴⁸ Jesus said to him, "Judas, are you betraying the Son of Man with a kiss?" ⁴⁹ His disciples realized what was about to happen, and they asked, "Lord, shall we strike with a sword?"ᶜ ⁵⁰ And one of them struck the high priest's servant and cut off his right ear.ᵈ ⁵¹ But Jesus said in reply, "Stop, no more of this!" Then he touched the servant's ear and healed him.* ⁵² And Jesus said to the chief priests and temple guards and elders who had come for him, "Have you come out as against a robber, with swords and clubs?ᵉ ⁵³ Day after day I was with you in the temple area, and you did not seize me; but this is your hour, the time for the power of darkness."ᶠ

Peter's Denial of Jesus. ⁵⁴ ᵍ After arresting him they led him away and took him into the house of the high priest; Peter was following at a distance.ʰ ⁵⁵ They lit a fire in the middle of the courtyard and sat around it, and Peter sat down with them. ⁵⁶ When a maid saw him seated in the light, she looked intently at him and said, "This man

too was with him." ⁵⁷ But he denied it saying, "Woman, I do not know him." ⁵⁸ A short while later someone else saw him and said, "You too are one of them"; but Peter answered, "My friend, I am not." ⁵⁹ About an hour later, still another insisted, "Assuredly, this man too was with him, for he also is a Galilean." ⁶⁰ But Peter said, "My friend, I do not know what you are talking about." Just as he was saying this, the cock crowed, ⁶¹ and the Lord turned and looked at Peter;* and Peter remembered the word of the Lord, how he had said to him, "Before the cock crows today, you will deny me three times."ⁱ ⁶² He went out and began to weep bitterly. ⁶³ ʲ The men who held Jesus in custody were ridiculing and beating him. ⁶⁴ They blindfolded him and questioned him, saying, "Prophesy! Who is it that struck you?" ⁶⁵ And they reviled him in saying many other things against him.

Jesus before the Sanhedrin.* ⁶⁶ ᵏ When day came the council of elders of the people met, both chief priests and scribes,ˡ and they brought him before their Sanhedrin.* ⁶⁷ They said, "If you are the Messiah, tell us," but he replied to them, "If I tell you, you will not believe,ᵐ ⁶⁸ and if I question, you will not respond. ⁶⁹ But from this time on the Son of Man will be

---

v Is 53, 12.—w 39-46: Mt 26, 30.36-46; Mk 14, 26.32-42; Jn 18, 1-2.—x Lk 22, 46.—y Heb 5, 7-8.—z Mt 6, 10.—a Lk 22, 40.—b 47-53: Mt 26, 47-56; Mk 14, 43-50; Jn 18, 3-4.—c Lk 22, 36.—d Jn 18, 26.—e Lk 22, 37.—f Lk 19, 47; 21, 37; Jn 7, 30; 8, 20; Col 1, 13.—g 54-62: Mt 26, 57-58.69-75; Mk 14, 53-54.66-72; Jn 18, 12-18.25-27.—h Lk 22, 33.—i Lk 22, 34.—j 63-65: Mt 26, 67-68; Mk 14, 65.—k 66-71: Mt 26, 59-66; Mk 14, 55-64.—l Mt 27, 1; Mk 15, 1.—m Jn 3, 12; 8, 45; 10, 24.

22, 38: *It is enough!*: the farewell discourse ends abruptly with these words of Jesus spoken to the disciples when they take literally what was intended as figurative language about being prepared to face the world's hostility.

22, 43-44: These verses, though very ancient, were probably not part of the original text of Lk. They are absent from the oldest papyrus manuscripts of Lk and from manuscripts of wide geographical distribution.

22, 51: *And healed him:* only Luke recounts this healing of the injured servant.

22, 61: Only Luke recounts that *the Lord turned and looked at Peter.* This look of Jesus leads to Peter's weeping bitterly over his denial (62).

22, 66-71: Luke recounts one daytime trial of Jesus (66-71) and hints at some type of preliminary nighttime investigation (54-65). Mark (and Matthew who follows Mk) has transferred incidents of this day into the nighttime interrogation with the result that there appear to be two Sanhedrin trials of Jesus in Mk (and Mt); see the note on Mk 14, 53.

22, 66: *Sanhedrin:* the word is a Hebraized form of a Greek word meaning a "council," and refers to the elders, chief priests, and scribes who met under the high priest's leadership to decide religious and legal questions that did not pertain to Rome's interests. Jewish sources are not clear on the competence of the Sanhedrin to sentence and to execute during this period.

seated at the right hand of the power of God."n 70 They all asked, "Are you then the Son of God?" He replied to them, "You say that I am." 71 Then they said, "What further need have we for testimony? We have heard it from his own mouth."

CHAPTER 23

Jesus before Pilate.o 1 * Then the whole assembly of them arose and brought him before Pilate. 2 They brought charges against him, saying, "We found this man misleading our people; he opposes the payment of taxes to Caesar and maintains that he is the Messiah, a king."p 3 Pilate asked him, "Are you the king of the Jews?" He said to him in reply, "You say so."q 4 Pilate then addressed the chief priests and the crowds, "I find this man not guilty." 5 But they were adamant and said, "He is inciting the people with his teaching throughout all Judea, from Galilee where he began even to here."r

Jesus before Herod. 6 * On hearing this Pilate asked if the man was a Galilean; 7 and upon learning that he was under Herod's jurisdiction, he sent him to Herod who was in Jerusalem at that time.s 8 Herod was very glad to see Jesus; he had

n Ps 110, 1; Dn 7, 13-14; Acts 7, 56.—o 1-5: Mt 27, 1-2.11-14; Mk 15, 1-5; Jn 18, 28-38.—p Lk 20, 22-25; Acts 17, 7; 24, 5.—q Lk 22, 70; 1 Tm 6, 13.—r Lk 23, 14.22.41; Mt 27, 24; Jn 19, 4.6; Acts 13, 28.—s Lk 3, 1; 9, 7.—t Lk 9, 9; Acts 4, 27-28.—u Mk 15, 5.—v Mt 27, 12; Mk 15, 3.—w Mt 27, 28-30; Mk 15, 17-19; Jn 19, 2-3.—x Lk 23, 4.22.41.—y Lk 23, 22; Jn 19, 12-14.—z 18-25: Mt 27, 20-26; Mk 15, 6-7.11-15; Jn 18, 38b-40; 19, 14-16; Acts 3, 13-14.—a 26-32: Mt 27, 32.38; Mk 15, 21.27; Jn 19, 17.—b 28-31: Lk 19, 41-44; 21, 23-24.

23, 1-5.13-25: Twice Jesus is brought before Pilate in Luke's account, and each time Pilate explicitly declares Jesus innocent of any wrongdoing (4.14.22). This stress on the innocence of Jesus before the Roman authorities is also characteristic of John's gospel (Jn 18, 38; 19, 4.6). Luke presents the Jerusalem Jewish leaders as the ones who force the hand of the Roman authorities (1-2.5.10.13.18.21.23-25).

23, 6-12: The appearance of Jesus before Herod is found only in this gospel. Herod has been an important figure in Lk (Lk 9, 7-9; 13, 31-33) and has been presented as someone who has been curious about Jesus for a long time. His curiosity goes unrewarded. It is faith in Jesus, not curiosity, that is rewarded (Lk 7, 50; 8, 48.50; 17, 19).

23, 17: This verse, "He was obliged to release one prisoner for them at the festival," is not part of the original text of Lk. It is an explanatory gloss from Mk 15, 6 (also Mt 27, 15) and is not found in many early and important Greek manuscripts. On its historical background, see the notes on Mt 27, 15-26.

23, 26-32: An important Lucan theme throughout the gospel has been the need for the Christian disciple to follow in the footsteps of Jesus. Here this theme comes to the fore with the story of Simon of Cyrene who takes up the cross and follows Jesus (see Lk 9, 23; 14, 27) and with the large crowd who likewise follow Jesus on the way of the cross. See also the note on Mk 15, 21.

been wanting to see him for a long time, for he had heard about him and had been hoping to see him perform some sign.t 9 He questioned him at length, but he gave him no answer.u 10 The chief priests and scribes, meanwhile, stood by accusing him harshly.v 11 [Even] Herod and his soldiers treated him contemptuously and mocked him, and after clothing him in resplendent garb, he sent him back to Pilate.w 12 Herod and Pilate became friends that very day, even though they had been enemies formerly. 13 Pilate then summoned the chief priests, the rulers, and the people 14 and said to them, "You brought this man to me and accused him of inciting the people to revolt. I have conducted my investigation in your presence and have not found this man guilty of the charges you have brought against him,x 15 nor did Herod, for he sent him back to us. So no capital crime has been committed by him.16 y Therefore I shall have him flogged and then release him." [17] *

The Sentence of Death. z 18 But all together they shouted out, "Away with this man! Release Barabbas to us." 19 (Now Barabbas had been imprisoned for a rebellion that had taken place in the city and for murder.) 20 Again Pilate addressed them, still wishing to release Jesus, 21 but they continued their shouting, "Crucify him! Crucify him!" 22 Pilate addressed them a third time, "What evil has this man done? I found him guilty of no capital crime. Therefore I shall have him flogged and then release him." 23 With loud shouts, however, they persisted in calling for his crucifixion, and their voices prevailed. 24 The verdict of Pilate was that their demand should be granted. 25 So he released the man who had been imprisoned for rebellion and murder, for whom they asked, and he handed Jesus over to them to deal with as they wished.

The Way of the Cross.* 26 a As they led him away they took hold of a certain Simon, a Cyrenian, who was coming in from the country; and after laying the cross on him, they made him carry it behind Jesus. 27 A large crowd of people followed Jesus, including many women who mourned and lamented him. 28 b Jesus turned to them and said, "Daughters of Jerusalem, do not weep for me; weep instead for yourselves and for your children, 29 for indeed, the days are coming when people will say, 'Blessed are the barren, the wombs that never bore and the breasts that never nursed.' [30] At that time people will say to the mountains, 'Fall upon us!' and to the hills, 'Cover us!'[c] [31] for if these things are done when the wood is green what will happen when it is dry?" [32] Now two others, both criminals, were led away with him to be executed.

The Crucifixion.[d] [33] When they came to the place called the Skull, they crucified him and the criminals there, one on his right, the other on his left.[e] [34] [Then Jesus said, "Father, forgive them, they know not what they do."]* They divided his garments by casting lots.[f] [35] The people stood by and watched; the rulers, meanwhile, sneered at him and said,[g] "He saved others, let him save himself if he is the chosen one, the Messiah of God."[h] [36] Even the soldiers jeered at him. As they approached to offer him wine[i] [37] they called out, "If you are King of the Jews, save yourself." [38] Above him there was an inscription that read, "This is the King of the Jews."

[39] * Now one of the criminals hanging there reviled Jesus, saying, "Are you not the Messiah? Save yourself and us." [40] The other, however, rebuking him, said in reply, "Have you no fear of God, for you are subject to the same condemnation? [41] And indeed, we have been condemned justly, for the sentence we received corresponds to our crimes, but this man has done nothing criminal."[j] [42] Then he said, "Jesus, remember me when you come into your kingdom."[k] [43] He replied to him, "Amen, I say to you, today you will be with me in Paradise."[l]

The Death of Jesus.[m] [44] It was now about noon[n] and darkness came over the whole land until three in the afternoon* [45] because of an eclipse of the sun. Then the veil of the temple was torn down the middle.[o] [46] Jesus cried out in a loud voice, "Father, into your hands I commend my spirit"; and when he had said this he breathed his last.[p] [47] The centurion who witnessed what had happened glorified God and said, "This man was innocent* beyond doubt." [48] When all the people who had gathered for this spectacle saw what had happened, they returned home beating their breasts;[q] [49] but all his acquaintances stood at a distance, including the women who had followed him from Galilee and saw these events.[r]

The Burial of Jesus.[s] [50] Now there was a virtuous and righteous man named Joseph who, though he was a member of the council, [51] had not consented to their plan of action. He came from the Jewish town of Arimathea and was awaiting the kingdom of God.[t] [52] He went to Pilate and asked for the body of Jesus. [53] After he had taken the body down, he wrapped it in a linen cloth and laid him in a rock-hewn tomb in which no one had yet been buried.[u] [54] It was the day of preparation, and the sabbath was about to begin. [55] The women who had come from Galilee with him followed behind, and when they had seen the tomb and the way in which his body was laid in it,[v] [56] they returned and prepared spices and perfumed oils. Then they rested on the sabbath according to the commandment.[w]

VIII. THE RESURRECTION NARRATIVE*

CHAPTER 24

The Resurrection of Jesus. [1] [x] But at daybreak on the first day of the week they took the spices they had prepared and went to

---

c Hos 10, 8; Rv 6, 16.—d 33-43: Mt 27, 33-44; Mk 15, 22-32; Jn 19, 17-24.—e Lk 22, 37; Is 53, 12.—f Nm 15, 27-31; Ps 22, 19; Mt 5, 44; Acts 7, 60.—g 35-36: Ps 22, 8-9.—h Lk 4, 23.—i Ps 69, 22; Mt 27, 48; Mk 15, 36.—j Lk 23, 4.14.22.—k Lk 9, 27; 23, 2.3.38.—l 2 Cor 12, 3; Rv 2, 7.—m 44-49: Mt 27, 45-56; Mk 15, 33-41; Jn 19, 25-30.—n 44-45: Am 8, 9.—o Ex 26, 31-33; 36, 35.—p Ps 31, 6; Acts 7, 59.—q Lk 18, 13; Zec 12, 10.—r Lk 8, 1-3; 23, 55-56; 24, 10; Ps 38, 12.—s 50-56: Mt 27, 57-61; Mk 15, 42-47; Jn 19, 38-42; Acts 13, 29.—t Lk 2, 25.38.—u Lk 19, 30; Acts 13, 29.—v Lk 8, 2; 23, 49; 24, 10.—w Ex 12, 16; 20, 10; Dt 5, 14.—x 1-8: Mt 28, 1-8; Mk 16, 1-8; Jn 20, 1-17.

23, 34a: *[Then Jesus said, "Father, forgive them, they know not what they do."]:* this portion of v 34 does not occur in the oldest papyrus manuscript of Lk and in other early Greek manuscripts and ancient versions of wide geographical distribution.

23, 39-43: This episode is recounted only in this gospel. The penitent sinner receives salvation through the crucified Jesus. Jesus' words to the penitent thief reveal Luke's understanding that the destiny of the Christian is "to be with Jesus."

23, 44: *Noon . . . three in the afternoon:* literally, the sixth and ninth hours. See the note on Mk 15, 25.

23, 47: *This man was innocent:* or, "This man was righteous."

24, 1-53: The resurrection narrative in Lk consists of five sections: (1) the women at the empty tomb (Lk 23, 56b—24, 12); (2) the appearance to the two disciples on the way to Emmaus (Lk 24, 13-35); (3) the appearance to the disciples in Jerusalem (Lk 24, 36-43); (4) Jesus' final instructions (Lk 24, 44-49); (5) the ascension (Lk 24, 50-53). In Lk, all the resurrection appearances take place in and around Jerusalem; moreover, they are all recounted as having taken place on Easter Sunday. A consistent theme throughout the narrative is that the suffering, death, and resurrection of Jesus were accomplished in fulfillment of Old Testament promises and of Jewish hopes (19a.21.26-27.44.46). In his second volume, Acts, Luke will argue that Christianity is the fulfillment of the hopes of Pharisaic Judaism and its logical development (see Acts 24, 10-21).

the tomb. [2] They found the stone rolled away from the tomb; [3] but when they entered, they did not find the body of the Lord Jesus. [4] While they were puzzling over this, behold, two men in dazzling garments appeared to them.[y] [5] They were terrified and bowed their faces to the ground. They said to them, "Why do you seek the living one among the dead?[z] [6] He is not here, but he has been raised.* Remember what he said to you while he was still in Galilee, [7] that the Son of Man must be handed over to sinners and be crucified, and rise on the third day."[a] [8] And they remembered his words.[b] [9] [c] Then they returned from the tomb and announced all these things to the eleven and to all the others.* [10] The women were Mary Magdalene, Joanna, and Mary the mother of James; the others who accompanied them also told this to the apostles,[d] [11] but their story seemed like nonsense and they did not believe them. [12] [e] But Peter got up and ran to the tomb, bent down, and saw the burial cloths alone; then he went home amazed at what had happened.*

---

y 2 Mc 3, 26; Acts 1, 10.—z Acts 2, 9.—a Lk 9, 22.44; 17, 25; 18, 32-33; Mt 16, 21; 17, 22-23; Mk 9, 31; Acts 17, 3.—b Jn 2, 22.—c 9-11: Mk 16, 10-11; Jn 20, 18.—d Lk 8, 2-3; Mk 16, 9.—e Jn 20, 3-7.—f Mk 16, 12-13.—g Jn 20, 14; 21, 4.—h Mt 2, 23; 21, 11; Acts 2, 22.—i Lk 1, 54.68; 2, 38.—j 22-23: Lk 24, 1-11; Mt 28, 1-8; Mk 16, 1-8.—k Jn 20, 3-10.—l 25-26: Lk 9, 22; 18, 31; 24, 44; Acts 3, 24; 17, 3.—m Lk 24, 44; Dt 18, 25; Ps 22, 1-18; Is 53; 1 Pt 1, 10-11.

24, 6a: *He is not here, but he has been raised:* this part of the verse is omitted in important representatives of the Western text tradition, but its presence in other text types and the slight difference in wording from Mt 28, 6 and Mk 16, 6 argue for its retention.

24, 9: The women in this gospel do not flee from the tomb and tell no one, as in Mk 16, 8, but return and tell the disciples about their experience. The initial reaction to the testimony of the women is disbelief (11).

24, 12: This verse is missing from the Western textual tradition but is found in the best and oldest manuscripts of other text types.

24, 13-35: This episode focuses on the interpretation of scripture by the risen Jesus and the recognition of him in the breaking of the bread. The references to the quotations of scripture and explanation of it (25-27), the kerygmatic proclamation (34), and the liturgical gesture (30) suggest that the episode is primarily catechetical and liturgical rather than apologetic.

24, 13: *Seven miles:* literally, "sixty stades." A stade was 607 feet. Some manuscripts read "160 stades" or more than eighteen miles. The exact location of Emmaus is disputed.

24, 16: A consistent feature of the resurrection stories is that the risen Jesus was different and initially unrecognizable (Lk 24, 37; Mk 16, 12; Jn 20, 14; 21, 4).

24, 26: *That the Messiah should suffer . . . :* Luke is the only New Testament writer to speak explicitly of a suffering Messiah (26.46; Acts 3, 18; 17, 3; 26, 23). The idea of a suffering Messiah is not found in the Old Testament or in other Jewish literature prior to the New Testament period, although the idea is hinted at in Mk 8, 31-33. See the notes on Mt 26, 63 and Mt 26, 67-68.

The Appearance on the Road to Emmaus.* [13] Now that very day two of them were going to a village seven miles* from Jerusalem called Emmaus,[f] [14] and they were conversing about all the things that had occurred. [15] And it happened that while they were conversing and debating, Jesus himself drew near and walked with them, [16] [g] but their eyes were prevented from recognizing him.* [17] He asked them, "What are you discussing as you walk along?" They stopped, looking downcast. [18] One of them, named Cleopas, said to him in reply, "Are you the only visitor to Jerusalem who does not know of the things that have taken place there in these days?" [19] And he replied to them, "What sort of things?" They said to him, "The things that happened to Jesus the Nazarene, who was a prophet mighty in deed and word before God and all the people,[h] [20] how our chief priests and rulers both handed him over to a sentence of death and crucified him. [21] [i] But we were hoping that he would be the one to redeem Israel; and besides all this, it is now the third day since this took place. [22] [j] Some women from our group, however, have astounded us: they were at the tomb early in the morning [23] and did not find his body; they came back and reported that they had indeed seen a vision of angels who announced that he was alive. [24] [k] Then some of those with us went to the tomb and found things just as the women had described, but him they did not see." [25] [l] And he said to them, "Oh, how foolish you are! How slow of heart to believe all that the prophets spoke! [26] Was it not necessary that the Messiah should suffer* these things and enter into his glory?" [27] Then beginning with Moses and all the prophets, he interpreted to them what referred to him in all the scriptures.[m] [28] As they approached the village to which they were going, he gave the impression that he was going on farther. [29] But they urged him, "Stay with us, for it is nearly evening and the day is almost over." So he went in to stay with them. [30] And it happened that, while he was with them at table, he took bread, said the blessing, broke it, and gave it to them. [31] With that their eyes were opened and they recognized him, but he vanished from their sight. [32] Then they said to each other, "Were not our hearts burning [within us] while he spoke to us on the way and opened the scriptures to us?"

Lk

33 So they set out at once and returned to Jerusalem where they found gathered together the eleven and those with them 34 who were saying, "The Lord has truly been raised and has appeared to Simon!" *n* 35 Then the two recounted what had taken place on the way and how he was made known to them in the breaking of the bread.

The Appearance to the Disciples in Jerusalem. 36 * While they were still speaking about this,*o* he stood in their midst and said to them, "Peace be with you." *p* 37 But they were startled and terrified and thought that they were seeing a ghost.*q* 38 Then he said to them, "Why are you troubled? And why do questions arise in your hearts? 39 *Look at my hands and my feet, that it is I myself. Touch me and see, because a ghost does not have flesh and bones as you can see I have." 40 *r* And as he said this, he showed them his hands and his feet. 41 While they were still incredulous for joy and were amazed, he asked them, "Have you anything here to eat?" 42 They gave him a piece of baked fish;*s* 43 he took it and ate it in front of them.

n 1 Cor 15, 4-5.—o 36-53: Mk 16, 14-19; Jn 20, 19-20.—p 1 Cor 15, 5.—q Mt 14, 26.—r 40-41: Jn 21, 5.9-10.13.—s Acts 10, 41.—t Lk 18, 31; 24, 27; Mt 16, 21; Jn 5, 39.46.—u Jn 20, 9.—v Lk 9, 22; Is 53; Hos 6, 2.—w Mt 3, 2; 28, 19-20; Mk 16, 15-16; Acts 10, 41.—x Acts 1, 8.—y Jn 14, 26; Acts 1, 4; 2, 3-4.—z 50-51: Mk 16, 19; Acts 1, 9-11.—a Acts 1, 12.

24, 36-43.44-49: The Gospel of Luke, like each of the other gospels (Mt 28, 16-20; Mk 16, 14-15; Jn 20, 19-23), focuses on an important appearance of Jesus to the Twelve in which they are commissioned for their future ministry. As in vv 6 and 12, so in vv 36 and 40 there are omissions in the Western text.

24, 39-42: The apologetic purpose of this story is evident in the concern with the physical details and the report that Jesus ate food.

44 He said to them, "These are my words that I spoke to you while I was still with you, that everything written about me in the law of Moses and in the prophets and psalms must be fulfilled." *t* 45 Then he opened their minds to understand the scriptures. *u* 46 And he said to them,*v* "Thus it is written that the Messiah would suffer and rise from the dead on the third day* 47 and that repentance, for the forgiveness of sins, would be preached in his name to all the nations, beginning from Jerusalem. *w* 48 You are witnesses of these things. *x* 49 And [behold] I am sending the promise of my Father* upon you; but stay in the city until you are clothed with power from on high." *y*

The Ascension. * 50 *z* Then he led them [out] as far as Bethany, raised his hands, and blessed them. 51 As he blessed them he parted from them and was taken up to heaven. 52 They did him homage and then returned to Jerusalem with great joy,*a* 53 and they were continually in the temple praising God.*

24, 46: See the note on Lk 24, 26.

24, 49: *The promise of my Father:* i.e., the gift of the holy Spirit.

24, 50-53: Luke brings his story about the time of Jesus to a close with the report of the ascension. He will also begin the story of the time of the church with a recounting of the ascension. In the gospel, Luke recounts the ascension of Jesus on Easter Sunday night, thereby closely associating it with the resurrection. In Acts (1, 3.9-11; 13, 31) he historicizes the ascension by speaking of a forty-day period between the resurrection and the ascension. The Western text omits some phrases in vv 51 and 52, perhaps to avoid any chronological conflict with Acts 1 about the time of the ascension.

24, 53: The Gospel of Luke ends as it began (Lk 1, 9), in the Jerusalem temple.

THE GOSPEL ACCORDING TO JOHN

INTRODUCTION

The Gospel according to John is quite different in character from the three synoptic gospels. It is highly literary and symbolic. It does not follow the same order or reproduce the same stories as the synoptic gospels. To a much greater degree, it is the product of a developed theological reflection and grows out of a different circle and tradition. It was probably written in the 90s of the first century.

The Gospel of John begins with a magnificent prologue, which states many of the major themes and motifs of the gospel, much as an overture does for a musical work. The prologue proclaims Jesus as the preexistent and incarnate Word of God who has revealed the Father to us. The rest of the first chapter forms the introduction to the gospel proper *and consists of the Baptist's testimony about Jesus (there is no baptism of Jesus in this gospel—John simply points him out as the Lamb of God), followed by stories of the call of the first disciples, in which various titles predicated of Jesus in the early church are presented.*

The gospel narrative contains a series of "signs"—the gospel's word for the wondrous deeds of Jesus. The author is primarily interested in the significance of these deeds, and so interprets them for the reader by various reflections, narratives, and discourses. The first sign is the transformation of water into wine at Cana (2, 1-11); this represents the replacement of the Jewish ceremonial washings and symbolizes the entire creative and transforming work of Jesus. The second sign, the cure of the royal official's son (4, 46-54) simply by the word of Jesus at a distance, signifies the power of Jesus' life-giving word. The same theme is further developed by other signs, probably for a total of seven. The third sign, the cure of the paralytic at the pool with five porticoes in ch 5, continues the theme of water offering newness of life. In the preceding chapter, to the woman at the well in Samaria Jesus had offered living water springing up to eternal life, a symbol of the revelation that Jesus brings; here Jesus' life-giving word replaces the water of the pool that failed to bring life. Chapter 6 contains two signs, the multiplication of loaves and the walking on the waters of the Sea of Galilee. These signs are connected much as the manna and the crossing of the Red Sea are in the Passover narrative and symbolize a new exodus. The multiplication of the loaves is interpreted for the reader by the discourse that follows, where the bread of life is used first as a figure for the revelation of God in Jesus and then for the Eucharist. After a series of dialogues reflecting Jesus' debates with the Jewish authorities at the Feast of Tabernacles in chs 7 and 8, the sixth sign is presented in ch 9, the sign of the young man born blind. This is a narrative illustration of the theme of conflict in the preceding two chapters; it proclaims the triumph of light over darkness, as Jesus is presented as the Light of the world. This is interpreted by a narrative of controversy between the Pharisees and the young man who had been given his sight by Jesus, ending with a discussion of spiritual blindness and spelling out the symbolic meaning of the cure. And finally, the seventh sign, the raising of Lazarus in ch 11, is the climax of signs. Lazarus is presented as a token of the real life that Jesus, the Resurrection and the Life, who will now ironically be put to death because of his gift of life to Lazarus, will give to all who believe in him once he has been raised from the dead.

After the account of the seven signs, the "hour" of Jesus arrives, and the author passes from sign to reality, as he moves into the discourses in the upper room that interpret the meaning of the passion, death, and resurrection narratives that follow. The whole gospel of John is a progressive revelation of the glory of God's only Son, who comes to reveal the Father and then returns in glory to the Father. The author's purpose is clearly expressed in what must have been the original ending of the gospel at the end of ch 20: "Now Jesus did many other signs in the presence of [his] disciples that are not written in this book. But these are written that you may [come to] believe that Jesus is the Messiah, the Son of God, and that through this belief you may have life in his name."

Critical analysis makes it difficult to accept the idea that the gospel as it now stands was written by one person. Chapter 21 seems to have been added after the gospel was completed; it exhibits a Greek style somewhat different from that of the rest of the work. The prologue (1, 1-18) apparently contains an independent hymn, subsequently adapted to serve as a preface to the gospel. Within the gospel itself there are also some inconsistencies, e.g., there are two endings of Jesus' discourse in the upper room (14, 31; 18, 1). To solve these problems, scholars have proposed various rearrangements that would produce a smoother order. However, most have come to the conclusion that the inconsistencies were probably produced by subsequent editing in which homogeneous materials were added to a shorter original.

Other difficulties for any theory of eyewitness authorship of the gospel in its present form are presented by its highly developed theology and by certain elements of its literary style. For instance, some of the wondrous deeds of Jesus have been worked into highly effective dramatic scenes (ch 9); there has been a careful attempt to have these followed by discourses that explain them (chs 5 and 6); and the sayings of Jesus have been woven into long discourses of a quasi-poetic form resembling the speeches of personified Wisdom in the Old Testament.

The gospel contains many details about Jesus not found in the synoptic gospels, e.g., that Jesus engaged in a baptizing ministry (3, 22) before he changed to one of preaching and signs; that Jesus' public ministry lasted for several years (see the note on 2, 13); that he traveled to Jerusalem for various festivals and met serious opposition long before his death (2, 14-25; chs 5 and 7-8); and that he was put to death on the day before Passover (18, 28). These events are not always in chronological order because of the development and editing that took place. However, the accuracy of much of the detail of the fourth gospel constitutes a strong argument that the Johannine tradition rests upon the testimony of an eyewitness. Although tradition identified this person as John, the son of Zebedee, most modern scholars find that the evidence does not support this.

The fourth gospel is not simply history; the narrative has been organized and adapted to serve the evangelist's theological purposes as well. Among them are the opposition to the synagogue of the day and to John the Baptist's followers, who tried to exalt their master at Jesus' expense, the desire to show that Jesus was the Messiah, and the desire to convince Christians that their religious belief and practice must be rooted in Jesus. Such theological purposes have impelled the evangelist to emphasize motifs that were not so clear in the synoptic account of Jesus' ministry, e.g., the explicit emphasis on his divinity.

The polemic between synagogue and church produced bitter and harsh invective, especially regarding the hostility toward Jesus of the authorities—Pharisees and Sadducees—who are combined and referred to frequently as "the Jews" (see the note on 1, 19). These opponents are even described in 8, 44 as springing from their father the devil, whose conduct they imitate in opposing God by rejecting Jesus, whom God has sent. On the other hand, the author of this gospel seems to take pains to show that women are not inferior to men in the Christian community: the woman at the well in Samaria (ch 4) is presented as a prototype of a missionary (4, 4-42), and the first witness of the resurrection is a woman (20, 11-18).

The final editing of the gospel and arrangement in its present form probably dates from between A.D. 90 and 100. Traditionally, Ephesus has been favored as the place of composition, though many support a location in Syria, perhaps the city of Antioch, while some have suggested other places, including Alexandria.

The principal divisions of the Gospel according to John are the following:

I.   Prologue (1, 1-18)

II.   The Book of Signs (1, 19—12, 50)

III. The Book of Glory (13, 1—20, 31)

IV. Epilogue: The Resurrection Appearance in Galilee (21, 1-25)

I. PROLOGUE*

CHAPTER 1

1 In the beginning* was the Word,
and the Word was with God,
and the Word was God.*a*

2 He was in the beginning with God.

3 All things came to be through him,
and without him nothing came to
be.*b*

What came to be* 4through him was
life,
and this life was the light of the
human race;*c*

5 the light shines in the darkness,*d*
and the darkness has not overcome
it.*

6A man named John was sent* from God.*e*
7He came for testimony,* to testify to the
light, so that all might believe through
him.*f* 8He was not the light, but came to
testify to the light.*g* 9The true light, which
enlightens everyone, was coming into the
world.*h*

10 He was in the world,
and the world came to be through
him,
but the world did not know him.

11 He came to what was his own,
but his own people* did not accept
him.

12 *i* But to those who did accept him he
gave power to become children of God, to
those who believe in his name, 13 *j* who
were born not by natural generation nor by
human choice nor by a man's decision but
of God.*

14 And the Word became flesh*
and made his dwelling among us,
and we saw his glory,
the glory as of the Father's only Son,
full of grace and truth.*k*

15John testified to him and cried out, saying, "This was he of whom I said,*l* 'The
one who is coming after me ranks ahead of
me because he existed before me.' " *
16From his fullness we have all received,
grace in place of grace,* 17because while
the law was given through Moses, grace
and truth came through Jesus Christ.*m* 18No

---

a Jn 10, 30; Gn 1, 1-5; Jb 28, 12-27; Prv 8, 22-25; Wis 9, 1-2;
1 Jn 1, 1-2; Col 1, 1.15; Rv 3, 14; 19, 13.—b Ps 33, 9; Wis 9,
1; Sir 42, 15; 1 Cor 8, 6; Col 1, 16; Heb 1, 2; Rv 3, 14.—c Jn 5,
26; 8, 12; 1 Jn 1, 2.—d Jn 3, 19; 8, 12; 9, 5; 12, 35.46; Wis 7,
29-30; 1 Thes 5, 4; 1 Jn 2, 8.—e Mt 3, 1; Mk 1, 4; Lk 3, 2-3.—f
Jn 1, 19-34; 5, 33.—g Jn 5, 35.—h Jn 3, 19; 8, 12; 9, 39; 12,
46.—i Jn 3, 11-12; 5, 43-44; 12, 46-50; Gal 3, 26; 4, 6-7; Eph
1, 5; 1 Jn 3, 2.—j Jn 3, 5-6.—k Ex 16, 10; 24, 17; 25, 8-9; 33,
22; 34, 6; Sir 24, 4.8; Is 60, 1; Ez 43, 7; Jl 4, 17; Hb 2, 14; 1
Jn 1, 2; 4, 2; 2 Jn 7.—l Jn 1, 30; 3, 27-30.—m Jn 7, 19; Ex 31,
18; 34, 28.

1, 1-18: The prologue states the main themes of the gospel:
life, light, truth, the world, testimony, and the preexistence of
Jesus Christ, the incarnate *Logos*, who reveals God the Father. In
origin, it was probably an early Christian hymn. Its closest parallel is in other christological hymns, Col 1, 15-20 and Phil 2, 6-11.
Its core (1-5.10-11.14) is poetic in structure, with short phrases
linked by "staircase parallelism," in which the last word of one
phrase becomes the first word of the next. Prose inserts (at least
6-8 and 15) deal with John the Baptist.

1, 1: *In the beginning:* also the first words of the Old Testament (Gn 1, 1). *Was:* this verb is used three times with different
meanings in this verse: existence, relationship, and predication.
The Word (Greek *logos*): this term combines God's dynamic,
creative word (Genesis), personified preexistent Wisdom as the
instrument of God's creative activity (Proverbs), and the ultimate
intelligibility of reality (Hellenistic philosophy). *With God:* the
Greek preposition here connotes communication with another.
Was God: lack of a definite article with "God" in Greek signifies
predication rather than identification.

1, 3: *What came to be:* while the oldest manuscripts have no
punctuation here, the corrector of Bodmer Papyrus P[75], some
manuscripts, and the Ante-Nicene Fathers take this phrase with
what follows, as staircase parallelism. Connection with v 3 reflects fourth-century anti-Arianism.

1, 5: The ethical dualism of light and darkness is paralleled in
intertestamental literature and in the Dead Sea Scrolls. *Overcome:* "comprehend" is another possible translation, but cf Jn
12, 35; Wis 7, 29-30.

1, 6: John was *sent* just as Jesus was "sent" (Jn 4, 34) in divine mission. Other references to John the Baptist in this gospel
emphasize the differences between them and John's subordinate
role.

1, 7: *Testimony:* the testimony theme of Jn is introduced,
which portrays Jesus as if on trial throughout his ministry. All testify to Jesus: John the Baptist, the Samaritan woman, scripture,
his works, the crowds, the Spirit, and his disciples.

1, 11: *What was his own . . . his own people:* first a neuter,
literally, "his own property/possession" (probably = Israel), then
a masculine, "his own people" (the Israelites).

1, 13: Believers in Jesus become children of God not through
any of the three natural causes mentioned but through God who is
the immediate cause of the new spiritual life. *Were born:* the
Greek verb can mean "begotten" (by a male) or "born" (from a
female or of parents). The variant "he who was begotten," asserting Jesus' virginal conception, is weakly attested in Old Latin
and Syriac versions.

1, 14: *Flesh:* the whole person, used probably against
docetistic tendencies (cf 1 Jn 4, 2; 2 Jn 7). *Made his dwelling:*
literally, "pitched his tent/tabernacle." Cf the tabernacle or tent
of meeting that was the place of God's presence among his people
(Ex 25, 8-9). The incarnate Word is the new mode of God's presence among his people. The Greek verb has the same consonants
as the Aramaic word for God's presence (Shekinah). *Glory:*
God's visible manifestation of majesty in power, which once filled
the tabernacle (Ex 40, 34) and the temple (1 Kgs 8, 10-11.27),
is now centered in Jesus. *Only Son:* Greek, *monogenēs*, but see
the note on Jn 1, 18. *Grace and truth:* these words may represent two Old Testament terms describing Yahweh in covenant relationship with Israel (cf Ex 34, 6), thus God's "love" and "fidelity." The Word shares Yahweh's covenant qualities.

1, 15: This verse, interrupting vv 14 and 16, seems drawn from
v 30.

1, 16: *Grace in place of grace:* replacement of the Old Covenant with the New (cf 17). Other possible translations are
"grace upon grace" (accumulation) and "grace for grace" (correspondence).

one has ever seen God. The only Son, God,* who is at the Father's side, has revealed him.[n]

II. THE BOOK OF SIGNS

John the Baptist's Testimony to Himself. 19 *And this is the testimony of John. When the Jews* from Jerusalem sent priests and Levites [to him] to ask him, "Who are you?" 20 he admitted and did not deny it, but admitted,[o] "I am not the Messiah."* 21 So they asked him, "What are you then? Are you Elijah?"* And he said, "I am not." "Are you the Prophet?" He answered, "No."[p] 22 So they said to him, "Who are you, so we can give an answer to those who sent us? What do you have to say for yourself?" 23 He said:

"I am 'the voice of one crying out in the desert,[q]
"Make straight the way of the Lord," '*

as Isaiah the prophet said." 24 Some Pharisees* were also sent. 25 They asked him, "Why then do you baptize if you are not the Messiah or Elijah or the Prophet?" [r] 26 John answered them, "I baptize with water; * but there is one among you whom you do not recognize,[s] 27 the one who is coming after me, whose sandal strap I am not worthy to untie." 28 This happened in Bethany across the Jordan,* where John was baptizing.

John the Baptist's Testimony to Jesus. 29 The next day he saw Jesus coming toward him and said, "Behold, the Lamb of God,* who takes away the sin of the world.[t] 30 He is the one of whom I said,[u] 'A man is coming after me who ranks ahead of me because he existed before me.'* 31 I did not know him,* but the reason why I came baptizing with water was that he might be made known to Israel." 32 John testified further, saying, "I saw the Spirit come down like a dove* from the sky and remain upon him. 33 I did not know him,[v] but the one who sent me to baptize with water told me, 'On whomever you see the Spirit come down and remain, he is the one who will baptize with the holy Spirit.'[w] 34 [x] Now I have seen and testified that he is the Son of God."*

The First Disciples.[y] 35 The next day John was there again with two of his disciples,

n Jn 5, 37; 6, 46; Ex 33, 20; Jgs 13, 21-22; 1 Tm 6, 16; 1 Jn 4, 12.—o Jn 3, 28; Lk 3, 15; Acts 13, 25.—p Dt 18, 15.18; 2 Kgs 2, 11; Sir 48, 10; Mal 3, 1.23; Mt 11, 14; 17, 11-13; Mk 9, 13; Acts 3, 22.—q Is 40, 3; Mt 3, 3; Mk 1, 2; Lk 3, 4.—r Ez 36, 25; Zec 13, 1; Mt 16, 14.—s Mt 3, 11; Mk 1, 7-8; Lk 3, 16; Acts 13, 25.—t Jn 1, 36; Ex 12; Is 53, 7; Rv 5—7; 17, 14.—u Jn 1, 15; Mt 3, 11; Mk 1, 7; Lk 3, 16.—v Song 5, 2; Is 11, 2; Hos 11, 11; Mt 3, 16; Mk 1, 10; Lk 3, 21-22.—w Is 42, 1; Mt 3, 11; Mk 1, 8; Lk 3, 16.—x Is 42, 1; Mt 3, 17; Mk 1, 11; Lk 9, 35.—y 35-51: Mt 4, 18-22; Mk 1, 16-20; Lk 5, 1-11.

1, 18: *The only Son, God:* while the vast majority of later textual witnesses have another reading, "the Son, the only one" or "the only Son," the translation above follows the best and earliest manuscripts, *monogenēs theos,* but takes the first term to mean not just "Only One" but to include a filial relationship with the Father, as at Lk 9, 38 ("only child") or Heb 11, 17 ("only son") and as translated at Jn 1, 14. The Logos is thus "only Son" and God but not Father/God.

1, 19-51: The testimony of John the Baptist about the Messiah and Jesus' self-revelation to the first disciples. This section constitutes the introduction to the gospel proper and is connected with the prose inserts in the prologue. It develops the major theme of testimony in four scenes: John's negative testimony about himself; his positive testimony about Jesus; the revelation of Jesus to Andrew and Peter; the revelation of Jesus to Philip and Nathanael.

1, 19: *The Jews:* throughout most of the gospel, the "Jews" does not refer to the Jewish people as such but to the hostile authorities, both Pharisees and Sadducees, particularly in Jerusalem, who refuse to believe in Jesus. The usage reflects the atmosphere, at the end of the first century, of polemics between church and synagogue, or possibly it refers to Jews as representative of a hostile world (10-11).

1, 20: *Messiah:* the anointed agent of Yahweh, usually considered to be of Davidic descent. See further the note on Jn 1, 41.

1, 21: *Elijah:* the Baptist did not claim to be Elijah returned to earth (cf Mal 3, 23; Mt 11, 14). *The Prophet:* probably the prophet like Moses (Dt 18, 15; cf Acts 3, 22).

1, 23: This is a repunctuation and reinterpretation (as in the synoptic gospels and Septuagint) of the Hebrew text of Is 40, 3, which reads, "A voice cries out: In the desert prepare the way of the LORD."

1, 24: *Some Pharisees:* other translations, such as "Now they had been sent from the Pharisees," misunderstand the grammatical construction. This is a different group from that in v 19; the priests and Levites would have been Sadducees, not Pharisees.

1, 26: *I baptize with water:* the synoptics add "but he will baptize you with the holy Spirit" (Mk 1, 8) or ". . . holy Spirit and fire" (Mt 3, 11; Lk 3, 16). John's emphasis is on purification and preparation for a better baptism.

1, 28: *Bethany across the Jordan:* site unknown. Another reading is "Bethabara."

1, 29: *The Lamb of God:* the background for this title may be the victorious apocalyptic lamb who would destroy evil in the world (Rv 5—7; 17, 14); the paschal lamb, whose blood saved Israel (Ex 12); and/or the suffering servant led like a lamb to the slaughter as a sin-offering (Is 53, 7.10).

1, 30: *He existed before me:* possibly as Elijah (to come, 27); for the evangelist and his audience, Jesus' preexistence would be implied (see the note on Jn 1, 1).

1, 31: *I did not know him:* this gospel shows no knowledge of the tradition (Lk 1) about the kinship of Jesus and John the Baptist. *The reason why I came baptizing with water:* in this gospel, John's baptism is not connected with forgiveness of sins; its purpose is revelatory, that Jesus may be made known to Israel.

1, 32: *Like a dove:* a symbol of the new creation (Gn 8, 8) or the community of Israel (Hos 11, 11). *Remain:* the first use of a favorite verb in Jn, emphasizing the permanency of the relationship between Father and Son (as here) and between the Son and the Christian. Jesus is the permanent bearer of the Spirit.

1, 34: *The Son of God:* this reading is supported by good Greek manuscripts, including the Chester Beatty and Bodmer Papyri and the Vatican Codex, but is suspect because it harmonizes this passage with the synoptic version: "This is my beloved Son" (Mt 3, 17; Mk 1, 11; Lk 3, 22). The poorly attested alternate reading, "God's chosen One," is probably a reference to the Servant of Yahweh (Is 42, 1).

CANA OF GALILEE — View of the town of Cana in the highlands of Galilee (showing the Nazareth-Tiberias road) about five miles northeast of Nazareth. Here Jesus attended a marriage feast with his mother and disciples and worked his first miracle. (See Jn 2, 1-11)

THE RIVER JORDAN — The most important river in Palestine measures 135 miles in a straight line, but because of its numerous windings covers a distance of about 250 miles. Its width varies from 80 to 180 feet and its depth from 5 to 12 feet. It was at the Jordan that Jesus was pointed out by John the Baptist and eventually baptized by him. (See Jn 1, 19-37 and Mt 3, 13)

TRADITIONAL SITE OF JACOB'S WELL — Both Samaritans and Jews have always believed this to be the well referred to as Jacob's well in John (4, 6). The ground mentioned by John had been purchased by Jacob ((Gn 33, 19) and the area was later forcibly taken away from the Amorites (Gn 48, 22). A narrow opening four feet long led from the floor of the vault into the well which was dug through limestone. The depth has not been determined. The well is near Mount Gerizim, which might have prompted our Lord to use the words "this mountain" in his conversation with the Samaritan woman. (See Jn 4, especially verse 21)

Matson Photo Service

Matson Photo Service

CHURCH OF ST. ANNE IN JERUSALEM — Located in the northeast part of the city, this church dating back to the Crusades commemorates the miracle of the cure effected by Jesus at the Pool of Bethesda. In 1888, while it was being repaired, a reservoir was discovered which is thought to be the ancient pool. (See Jn 5, 2)

Matson Photo Service

THE POOL OF BETHESDA — Reservoir discovered in northeast Jerusalem in 1888, about 55 feet in length and 12 feet in width. It is approached by a steep and winding flight of steps. A fresco on the wall depicts an angel troubling the waters in remembrance of the cure effected by Jesus. (See Jn 5, 2)

[36] and as he watched Jesus walk by, he said, "Behold, the Lamb of God."* [37] The two disciples* heard what he said and followed Jesus. [38] Jesus turned and saw them following him and said to them, "What are you looking for?" They said to him, "Rabbi" (which translated means Teacher), "where are you staying?" [39] He said to them, "Come, and you will see." So they went and saw where he was staying, and they stayed with him that day. It was about four in the afternoon.* [40] Andrew, the brother of Simon Peter, was one of the two who heard John and followed Jesus. [41] He first found his own brother Simon and told him, "We have found the Messiah"* (which is translated Anointed).[z] [42] Then he brought him to Jesus. Jesus looked at him and said, "You are Simon the son of John;* you will be called Kephas" (which is translated Peter).[a]

[43] The next day he* decided to go to Galilee, and he found Philip. And Jesus said to him, "Follow me." [44] Now Philip was from Bethsaida, the town of Andrew and Peter. [45] Philip found Nathanael and told him, "We have found the one about whom Moses wrote in the law, and also the prophets, Jesus son of Joseph, from Nazareth."[b] [46] But Nathanael said to him, "Can anything good come from Nazareth?" Philip said to him, "Come and see." [47] Jesus saw Nathanael coming toward him and said of him, "Here is a true Israelite.* There is no duplicity in him." [48] [c] Nathanael said to him, "How do you know me?" Jesus answered and said to him, "Before Philip called you, I saw you under the fig tree."* [49] Nathanael answered him, "Rabbi, you are the Son of God;* you are the King of Israel." [d] [50] Jesus answered and said to him, "Do you believe because I told you that I saw you under the fig tree?* You will see greater things than this." [51] And he said to him, "Amen, amen,* I say to you, you will see the sky opened and the angels of God ascending and descending on the Son of Man."[e]

CHAPTER 2

The Wedding at Cana. [1] * On the third day there was a wedding* in Cana* in Galilee, and the mother of Jesus was there.[f] [2] Jesus and his disciples were also invited to the wedding. [3] When the wine ran short, the mother of Jesus said to him, "They have no wine." [4] * [And] Jesus said to her, "Woman, how does your concern affect me? My hour has not yet come."[g] [5] His mother said to the servers, "Do what-

---

z Jn 4, 25.—a Mt 16, 18; Mk 3, 16.—b Jn 21, 2.—c Mi 4, 4; Zec 3, 10.—d Jn 12, 13; Ex 4, 22; Dt 14, 1; 2 Sm 7, 14; Jb 1, 6; 2, 1; 38, 7; Pss 2, 7; 29, 1; 89, 27; Wis 2, 18; Sir 4, 10; Dn 3, 25; Hos 11, 1; Mt 14, 33; 16, 16; Mk 13, 32.—e Gn 28, 10-17; Dn 7, 13.—f Jn 4, 46; Jgs 14, 12; Tb 11, 8.—g Jn 7, 30; 8, 20; 12, 23; 13, 1; Jgs 11, 12; 1 Kgs 17, 18; 2 Kgs 3, 13; 2 Chr 35, 21; Hos 14, 9; Mk 1, 24; 5; 7; 7, 30; 8, 20; 12, 23; 13, 1.

1, 36: John the Baptist's testimony makes his disciples' following of Jesus plausible.

1, 37: *The two disciples:* Andrew (40) and, traditionally, John, son of Zebedee (see the note on Jn 13, 23).

1, 39: *Four in the afternoon:* literally, the tenth hour, from sunrise, in the Roman calculation of time. Some suggest that the next day, beginning at sunset, was the sabbath; they would have stayed with Jesus to avoid travel on it.

1, 41: *Messiah:* the Hebrew word *māšîaḥ,* "anointed one" (see the note on Lk 2, 11), appears in Greek as the transliterated *messias* only here and in Jn 4, 25. Elsewhere the Greek translation *christos* is used.

1, 42: *Simon, the son of John:* in Mt 16, 17, Simon is called *Bariōna,* "son of Jonah," a different tradition for the name of Simon's father. *Kephas:* in Aramaic = the Rock; cf Mt 16, 18. Neither the Greek equivalent *Petros* nor, with one isolated exception, *Kephas* is attested as a personal name before Christian times.

1, 43: *He:* grammatically, could be Peter, but logically is probably Jesus.

1, 47: *A true Israelite. There is no duplicity in him:* Jacob was the first to bear the name "Israel" (Gn 32, 29), but Jacob was a man of duplicity (Gn 27, 35-36).

1, 48: *Under the fig tree:* a symbol of messianic peace (cf Mi 4, 4; Zec 3, 10).

1, 49: *Son of God:* this title is used in the Old Testament, among other ways, as a title of adoption for the Davidic king (2 Sm 7, 14; Pss 2, 7; 89, 27), and thus here, with *King of Israel,* in a messianic sense. For the evangelist, Son of God also points to Jesus' divinity (cf Jn 20, 28).

1, 50: Possibly a statement: "You [singular] believe because I saw you under the fig tree."

1, 51: The double "Amen" is characteristic of John. *You* is plural in Greek. The allusion is to Jacob's ladder (Gn 28, 12).

2, 1—6, 71: Signs revealing Jesus as the Messiah to all Israel. "Sign" (*sēmeion*) is John's symbolic term for Jesus' wondrous deeds (see Introduction). The Old Testament background lies in the Exodus story (cf Dt 11, 3; 29, 2). John is interested primarily in what the *sēmeia* signify: God's intervention in human history in a new way through Jesus.

2, 1-11: The first sign. This story of replacement of Jewish ceremonial washings (6) presents the initial revelation about Jesus at the outset of his ministry. He manifests his glory; the disciples believe. There is no synoptic parallel.

2, 1: *Cana:* unknown from the Old Testament. *The mother of Jesus:* she is never named in John.

2, 4: This verse may seek to show that Jesus did not work miracles to help his family and friends, as in the apocryphal gospels. *Woman:* a normal, polite form of address, but unattested in reference to one's mother. Cf also Jn 19, 26. *How does your concern affect me?:* literally, "What is this to me and to you?"—a Hebrew expression either of hostility (Jgs 11, 12; 2 Chr 35, 21; 1 Kgs 17, 18) or of denial of common interest (Hos 14, 9; 2 Kgs 3, 13). Cf Mk 1, 24; 5, 7, used by demons to Jesus. *My hour has not yet come:* the translation as a question ("Has not my hour now come?"), while preferable grammatically and supported by Greek Fathers, seems unlikely from a comparison with Jn 7, 6.30. The "hour" is that of Jesus' passion, death, resurrection, and ascension (Jn 13, 1).

ever he tells you."[h] [6]Now there were six stone water jars there for Jewish ceremonial washings,[i] each holding twenty to thirty gallons.* [7]Jesus told them, "Fill the jars with water." So they filled them to the brim. [8]Then he told them, "Draw some out now and take it to the headwaiter." * So they took it. [9]And when the headwaiter tasted the water that had become wine, without knowing where it came from (although the servers who had drawn the water knew), the headwaiter called the bridegroom [10]and said to him, "Everyone serves good wine first, and then when people have drunk freely, an inferior one; but you have kept the good wine until now." [11]Jesus did this as the beginning of his signs* in Cana in Galilee and so revealed his glory, and his disciples began to believe in him.[j]

[12] * After this, he and his mother, [his] brothers, and his disciples went down to Capernaum and stayed there only a few days.*

Cleansing of the Temple. [13] * Since the Passover* of the Jews was near,[k] Jesus went up to Jerusalem. [14] * He found in the temple area those who sold oxen, sheep, and doves,* as well as the money-changers seated there.[l] [15]He made a whip out of cords and drove them all out of the temple area, with the sheep and oxen, and spilled the coins of the money-changers and over-

turned their tables, [16]and to those who sold doves he said, "Take these out of here, and stop making my Father's house a marketplace."[m] [17]His disciples recalled the words of scripture,[n] "Zeal for your house will consume me." * [18]At this the Jews answered and said to him, "What sign can you show us for doing this?"[o] [19]Jesus answered and said to them,[p] "Destroy this temple and in three days I will raise it up." * [20]The Jews said, "This temple has been under construction for forty-six years,* and you will raise it up in three days?" [21]But he was speaking about the temple of his body. [22]Therefore, when he was raised from the dead, his disciples remembered that he had said this, and they came to believe the scripture and the word Jesus had spoken.[q]

[23]While he was in Jerusalem for the feast of Passover, many began to believe in his name when they saw the signs he was doing.[r] [24]But Jesus would not trust himself to them because he knew them all, [25]and did not need anyone to testify about human nature. He himself understood it well.[s]

CHAPTER 3

Nicodemus. * [1] [t] Now there was a Pharisee named Nicodemus, a ruler of the Jews.* [2]He came to Jesus at night and said

h Gn 41, 55.—i Jn 3, 25; Lv 11, 33; Am 9, 13-14; Mt 15, 2; 23, 25-26; Mk 7, 2-4; Lk 11, 38.—j Jn 4, 54.—k 13-22: Mt 21, 12-13; Mk 11, 15-17; Lk 19, 45-46.—l Ex 30, 11-16; Lv 5, 7.— m Zec 14, 21.—n Ps 69, 9.—o Jn 6, 30.—p Mt 24, 2; 26, 61; 27, 40; Mk 13, 2; 14, 58; 15, 29; Lk 21, 6; Acts 6, 14.—q Jn 5, 39; 12, 16; 14, 26; 20, 9; Mt 12, 6; Lk 24, 6-8; Rv 21, 22.—r Jn 4, 45.—s 1 Kgs 8, 39; Pss 33, 15; 94, 11; Sir 42, 18; Jer 17, 10; 20, 12.—t Jn 7, 50-51; 19, 39.

2, 6: *Twenty to thirty gallons:* literally, "two or three measures"; the Attic liquid measure contained 39.39 liters. The vast quantity recalls prophecies of abundance in the last days; cf Am 9, 13-14; Hos 14, 7; Jer 31, 12.

2, 8: *Headwaiter:* used of the official who managed a banquet, but there is no evidence of such a functionary in Palestine. Perhaps here a friend of the family acted as master of ceremonies; cf Sir 32, 1.

2, 11: *The beginning of his signs:* the first of seven (see Introduction).

2, 12—3, 21: The next three episodes take place in Jerusalem. Only the first is paralleled in the synoptic gospels.

2, 12: This transitional verse may be a harmonization with the synoptic tradition in Lk 4, 31 and Mt 4, 13. There are many textual variants. John depicts no extended ministry in Capernaum as do the synoptics.

2, 13-22: This episode indicates the post-resurrectional replacement of the temple by the person of Jesus.

2, 13: *Passover:* this is the first Passover mentioned in John; a second is mentioned in Jn 6, 4, a third in Jn 13, 1. Taken literally, they point to a ministry of at least two years.

2, 14-22: The other gospels place the cleansing of the temple in the last days of Jesus' life (Mt, on the day Jesus entered

Jerusalem; Mk, on the next day). The order of events in the gospel narratives is often determined by theological motives rather than by chronological data.

2, 14: *Oxen, sheep, and doves:* intended for sacrifice. The doves were the offerings of the poor (Lv 5, 7). *Money-changers:* for a temple tax paid by every male Jew more than nineteen years of age, with a half-shekel coin (Ex 30, 11-16), in Tyrian currency. See the note on Mt 17, 24.

2, 17: Ps 69, 10, changed to future tense to apply to Jesus.

2, 19: This saying about the destruction of the temple occurs in various forms (Mt 24, 2; 27, 40; Mk 13, 2; 15, 29; Lk 21, 6; cf Acts 6, 14). Mt 26, 61 has: "I *can* destroy the temple of God . . . "; see the note there. In Mk 14, 58, there is a metaphorical contrast with a new temple: "I will destroy this temple *made with hands* and within three days I will build another *not made with hands*." Here it is symbolic of Jesus' resurrection and the resulting community (see Jn 2, 21 and Rv 21, 2). *In three days:* an Old Testament expression for a short, indefinite period of time; cf Hos 6, 2.

2, 20: *Forty-six years:* based on references in Josephus (*Jewish Wars* 1, 21, 1 #401; *Antiquities* 15, 11, 1 §380), possibly the spring of A.D. 28. Cf the note on Lk 3, 1.

3, 1-21: Jesus instructs Nicodemus on the necessity of a new birth from above. This scene in Jerusalem at Passover exemplifies the faith engendered by signs (Jn 2, 23). It continues the self-manifestation of Jesus in Jerusalem begun in ch 2. This is the first of the Johannine discourses, shifting from dialogue to monologue (11-15) to reflection of the evangelist (16-21). The shift from singular through v 10 to plural in v 11 may reflect the early church's controversy with the Jews.

3, 1: *A ruler of the Jews:* most likely a member of the Jewish council, the Sanhedrin; see the note on Mk 8, 31.

to him, "Rabbi, we know that you are a teacher who has come from God, for no one can do these signs that you are doing unless God is with him." [u] [3] Jesus answered and said to him, "Amen, amen, I say to you, no one can see the kingdom of God without being born* from above." [4] Nicodemus said to him, "How can a person once grown old be born again? Surely he cannot reenter his mother's womb and be born again, can he?" [v] [5] Jesus answered, "Amen, amen, I say to you, no one can enter the kingdom of God without being born of water and Spirit. [w] [6] What is born of flesh is flesh and what is born of spirit is spirit. [x] [7] Do not be amazed that I told you, 'You must be born from above.' [8] The wind* blows where it wills, and you can hear the sound it makes, but you do not know where it comes from or where it goes; so it is with everyone who is born of the Spirit." [y] [9] Nicodemus answered and said to him, "How can this happen?" [10] Jesus answered and said to him, "You are the teacher of Israel and you do not understand this? [11] Amen, amen, I say to you, we speak of what we know and we testify to what we have seen, but you people do not accept our testimony. [z] [12] If I tell you about earthly things and you do not believe, how will you believe if I tell you about heavenly things? [a] [13] No one has gone up to heaven except the one who has come down from heaven, the Son of Man. [b] [14] And just as Moses lifted up* the serpent in the desert, so must the Son of Man be lifted up, [c] [15] so that everyone who believes in him may have eternal life." *

[16] For God so loved the world that he gave* his only Son, so that everyone who believes in him might not perish but might have eternal life. [d] [17] For God did not send his Son into the world to condemn* the world, but that the world might be saved through him. [e] [18] Whoever believes in him will not be condemned, but whoever does not believe has already been condemned, because he has not believed in the name of the only Son of God. [f] [19] And this is the verdict, [g] that the light came into the world, but people preferred darkness to light, because their works were evil. * [20] For everyone who does wicked things hates the light and does not come toward the light, so that his works might not be exposed. [h] [21] But whoever lives the truth comes to the light, so that his works may be clearly seen as done in God. [i]

Final Witness of the Baptist. [22] * After this, Jesus and his disciples went into the region of Judea, where he spent some time with them baptizing. [j] [23] John was also baptizing in Aenon near Salim,* because there was an abundance of water there, and people came to be baptized, [24] [k] for John had not yet been imprisoned.* [25] Now a dispute arose between the disciples of John and a Jew* about ceremonial washings. [26] So they came to John and said to him, "Rabbi, the one who was with you across the Jordan, to whom you testified, here he is baptizing and everyone is coming to him." [l] [27] John answered and said, "No one can receive anything except what has been given him from heaven. [m] [28] You yourselves can testify that I said [that] I am not the

---

u Jn 9, 4.16.33; 10, 21; 11, 10; 13, 30; Mt 22, 16; Mk 12, 14; Lk 20, 21.—v Jn 1, 13.—w Jn 1, 32; 7, 39; 19, 30.34-35; Is 32, 15; 44, 3; Ez 36, 25-27; Jl 3, 1-2.—x Jn 6, 63; 1 Cor 15, 44-50.—y Eccl 11, 4-5; Acts 2, 2-4.—z Jn 3, 32.34; 8, 14; Mt 11, 27.—a Jn 6, 62-65; Wis 9, 16-17; 1 Cor, 15, 40; 2 Cor 5, 1; Phil 2, 10; 3, 19-20.—b Jn 1, 18; 6, 62; Dn 7, 13; Rom 10, 6; Eph 4, 9.—c Jn 8, 28; 12, 32.34; Nm 21, 4-9; Wis 16, 5-7.—d 1 Jn 4, 9.—e Jn 5, 22.30; 8, 15-18; 12, 47.—f Jn 5, 24; Mk 16, 16.—g Jn 1, 5.9-11; 8, 12; 9, 5.—h Jb 24, 13-17.—i Gn 47, 29 LXX; Jos 2, 14 LXX; 2 Sm 2, 6 LXX; 15, 20 LXX; Tb 4, 6 LXX; 13, 6; Is 26, 10 LXX; Mt 5, 14-16.—j 22-23: Jn 4, 1-2.—k Mt 4, 12; 14, 3; Mk 1, 14; 6, 17; Lk 3, 20.—l Jn 1, 26.32-34.36.—m Jn 19, 11; 1 Cor 4, 7; 2 Cor 3, 5; Heb 5, 4.

3, 3: *Born:* see the note on Jn 1, 13. *From above:* the Greek adverb *anōthen* means both "from above" and "again." Jesus means "from above" (see Jn 3, 31), but Nicodemus misunderstands it as "again." This misunderstanding serves as a springboard for further instruction.

3, 8: *Wind:* the Greek word *pneuma* (as well as the Hebrew *rûah*) means both "wind" and "spirit." In the play on the double meaning, "wind" is primary.

3, 14: *Lifted up:* in Nm 21, 9, Moses simply "mounted" a serpent upon a pole. John here substitutes a verb implying glorification. Jesus, exalted to glory at his cross and resurrection, represents healing for all.

3, 15: *Eternal life:* used here for the first time in John, this term stresses quality of life rather than duration.

3, 16: *Gave:* as a gift in the incarnation, and also "over to death" in the crucifixion; cf Rom 8, 32.

3, 17-19: *Condemn:* the Greek root means both judgment and condemnation. Jesus' purpose is to save, but his coming provokes judgment; some condemn themselves by turning from the light.

3, 19: Judgment not only is future but is partially realized here and now.

3, 22-26: Jesus' ministry in Judea is only loosely connected with Jn 2, 13—3, 21; cf Jn 1, 19-36. Perhaps John the Baptist's further testimony was transposed here to give meaning to "water" in v 5. Jesus is depicted as baptizing (22); contrast Jn 4, 2.

3, 23: *Aenon near Salim:* site uncertain, either in the upper Jordan valley or in Samaria.

3, 24: A remark probably intended to avoid objections based on a chronology like that of the synoptics (Mt 4, 12; Mk 1, 14).

3, 25: *A Jew:* some think Jesus is meant. Many manuscripts read "Jews."

Messiah, but that I was sent before him.[n] [29]The one who has the bride is the bridegroom; the best man,* who stands and listens for him, rejoices greatly at the bridegroom's voice. So this joy of mine has been made complete.[o] [30]He must increase; I must decrease."[p]

The One from Heaven.* [31]The one who comes from above is above all. The one who is of the earth is earthly and speaks of earthly things. But the one who comes from heaven [is above all].[q] [32]He testifies to what he has seen and heard, but no one accepts his testimony.[r] [33]Whoever does accept his testimony certifies that God is trustworthy.[s] [34]For the one whom God sent speaks the words of God. He does not ration his gift* of the Spirit. [35]The Father loves the Son and has given everything over to him.[t] [36]Whoever believes in the Son has eternal life, but whoever disobeys the Son will not see life, but the wrath of God remains upon him.[u]

CHAPTER 4

[1] * Now when Jesus learned that the Pharisees had heard that Jesus was making and baptizing more disciples than John [2](although Jesus himself was not baptizing, just his disciples),* [3]he left Judea and returned to Galilee.

The Samaritan Woman. [4]He had to* pass through Samaria. [5]So he came to a town of Samaria called Sychar,* near the plot of land that Jacob had given to his son

Joseph.[v] [6]Jacob's well was there. Jesus, tired from his journey, sat down there at the well. It was about noon.

[7]A woman of Samaria came to draw water. Jesus said to her, "Give me a drink." [8]His disciples had gone into the town to buy food. [9]The Samaritan woman said to him, "How can you, a Jew, ask me, a Samaritan woman, for a drink?"[w] (For Jews use nothing in common with Samaritans.)* [10]Jesus answered and said to her,[x] "If you knew the gift of God and who is saying to you, 'Give me a drink,' you would have asked him and he would have given you living water."* [11][The woman] said to him, "Sir,* you do not even have a bucket and the cistern is deep; where then can you get this living water? [12]Are you greater than our father Jacob, who gave us this cistern and drank from it himself with his children and his flocks?"[y] [13]Jesus answered and said to her, "Everyone who drinks this water will be thirsty again; [14]but whoever drinks the water I shall give will never thirst; the water I shall give will become in him a spring of water welling up to eternal life."[z] [15]The woman said to him, "Sir, give me this water, so that I may not be thirsty or have to keep coming here to draw water."

[16]Jesus said to her, "Go call your husband and come back." [17]The woman answered and said to him, "I do not have a husband." Jesus answered her, "You are right in saying, 'I do not have a husband.' [18]For you have had five husbands, and the one you have now is not your husband. What you have said is true."[a] [19]The woman said to him, "Sir, I can see that you are a prophet.[b] [20]Our ancestors worshiped on this mountain;* but you people say that

n Jn 1, 20-23; Lk 3, 15.—o Jn 15, 11; 17, 13; Mt 9, 15.—p 2 Sm 3, 1.—q Jn 8, 23.—r Jn 3, 11.—s 33-34: Jn 8, 26; 12, 44-50; 1 Jn 5, 10.—t Jn 13, 3; Mt 11, 27; 28, 18; Lk 10, 22.—u Jn 3, 16; 1 Jn 5, 13.—v Gn 33, 18-19; 48, 22; Jos 24, 32.—w Sir 50, 25-26; Mt 10, 5.—x Sir 24, 20-21; Is 55, 1; Jer 2, 13.—y Jn 8, 53; Mt 12, 41.—z Jn 6, 35.58; 7, 37-39; Is 44, 3; 49, 10; Jl 4, 18; Rv 7, 16; 21, 6.—a 2 Kgs 17, 24-34.—b Jn 9, 17; Hos 1, 3.

3, 29: *The best man:* literally, "the friend of the groom," the *shoshben* of Jewish tradition, who arranged the wedding. Competition between him and the groom would be unthinkable.

3, 31-36: It is uncertain whether these are words by the Baptist, Jesus, or the evangelist. They are reflections on the two preceding scenes.

3, 34: *His gift:* of God or to Jesus, perhaps both. This verse echoes vv 5 and 8.

4, 1-42: Jesus in Samaria. The self-revelation of Jesus continues with his second discourse, on his mission to "half-Jews." It continues the theme of replacement, here with regard to cult (21). Water (7-15) serves as a symbol (as at Cana and in the Nicodemus episode).

4, 2: An editorial refinement of Jn 3, 22, perhaps directed against followers of John the Baptist who claimed that Jesus imitated him.

4, 4: *He had to:* a theological necessity; geographically, Jews often bypassed Samaria by taking a route across the Jordan.

4, 5: *Sychar:* Jerome identifies this with Shechem, a reading found in Syriac manuscripts.

4, 9: Samaritan women were regarded by Jews as ritually impure, and therefore Jews were forbidden to drink from any vessel they had handled.

4, 10: *Living water:* the water of life, i.e., the revelation that Jesus brings; the woman thinks of "flowing water," so much more desirable than stagnant cistern water. On John's device of such misunderstanding, cf the note on Jn 3, 3.

4, 11: *Sir:* the Greek *kyrios* means "master" or "lord," as a respectful mode of address for a human being or a deity; cf Jn 4, 19. It is also the word used in the Septuagint for the Hebrew *'ădōnai,* substituted for the tetragrammaton YHWH.

4, 20: *This mountain:* Gerizim, on which a temple was erected in the fourth century B.C. by Samaritans to rival Mt. Zion in Jerusalem; cf Dt 27, 4 (Mt. Ebal = the Jews' term for Gerizim).

the place to worship is in Jerusalem." *c* [21] Jesus said to her, "Believe me, woman, the hour is coming when you will worship the Father neither on this mountain nor in Jerusalem. [22] You people worship what you do not understand; we worship what we understand, because salvation is from the Jews. *d* [23] But the hour is coming, and is now here, when true worshipers will worship the Father in Spirit and truth;* and indeed the Father seeks such people to worship him. [24] God is Spirit, and those who worship him must worship in Spirit and truth." *e* [25] The woman said to him, "I know that the Messiah is coming, *f* the one called the Anointed; when he comes, he will tell us everything."* [26] Jesus said to her, "I am he,* the one who is speaking with you." *g*

[27] At that moment his disciples returned, and were amazed that he was talking with a woman,* but still no one said, "What are you looking for?" or "Why are you talking with her?" [28] The woman left her water jar and went into the town and said to the people, [29] "Come see a man who told me everything I have done. Could he possibly be the Messiah?" [30] They went out of the town and came to him. [31] Meanwhile, the disciples urged him, "Rabbi, eat." [32] But he said to them, "I have food to eat of which you do not know." [33] So the disciples said to one another, "Could someone have brought him something to eat?" [34] Jesus said to them, "My food is to do the will of the one who sent me and to finish his work. *h* [35] Do you not say, 'In four months* the harvest will be here'? I tell you, look up and see the fields ripe for the harvest. *i* [36] The reaper is already* receiving his payment and gathering crops for eternal life,

so that the sower and reaper can rejoice together. *j* [37] For here the saying is verified that 'One sows and another reaps.' *k* [38] I sent you to reap what you have not worked for; others have done the work, and you are sharing the fruits of their work."

[39] Many of the Samaritans of that town began to believe in him because of the word of the woman* who testified, "He told me everything I have done." [40] When the Samaritans came to him, they invited him to stay with them; and he stayed there two days. [41] Many more began to believe in him because of his word, [42] and they said to the woman, "We no longer believe because of your word; for we have heard for ourselves, and we know that this is truly the savior of the world." *l*

Return to Galilee. [43] * After the two days, he left there for Galilee. [44] *m* For Jesus himself testified that a prophet has no honor in his native place.* [45] When he came into Galilee, the Galileans welcomed him, since they had seen all he had done in Jerusalem at the feast; for they themselves had gone to the feast.

Second Sign at Cana.* [46] *n* Then he returned to Cana in Galilee, where he had made the water wine. Now there was a royal official whose son was ill in Capernaum. [47] When he heard that Jesus had arrived in Galilee from Judea, he went to him and asked him to come down and heal his son, who was near death. [48] Jesus said to him, "Unless you people see signs and wonders, you will not believe." *o* [49] The royal official said to him, "Sir, come down before my child dies." [50] Jesus said to him, "You may go; your son will live." The man believed what Jesus said to him and left. *p* [51] While he was on his way back, his slaves

---

c Dt 11, 29; 27, 4; Jos 8, 33; Ps 122, 1-5.—d 2 Kgs 17, 27; Ps 76, 2-3.—e 2 Cor 3, 17.—f Jn 1, 41.—g Jn 9, 37.—h Jn 5, 30.36; 6, 38; 9, 4; 17, 4.—i Mt 9, 37-38; Lk 10, 2; Rv 14, 15.—j Ps 126, 5-6; Am 9, 13-14.—k Dt 20, 6; 28, 30; Jb 31, 8; Mi 6, 15.—l 1 Jn 4, 14.—m Mt 13, 57; Mk 6, 4; Lk 4, 24.—n 46-54: Jn 2, 1-11; Mt 8, 5-13; 15, 21-28; Mk 7, 24-30; Lk 7, 1-10.—o Jn 2, 18.23; Wis 8, 8; Mt 12, 38; 1 Cor 1, 22.—p 1 Kgs 17, 23.

4, 23: *In Spirit and truth:* not a reference to an interior worship within one's own spirit. The Spirit is the spirit given by God that reveals truth and enables one to worship God appropriately (Jn 14, 16-17). Cf "born of water and Spirit" (Jn 3, 5).

4, 25: The expectations of the Samaritans are expressed here in Jewish terminology. They did not expect a messianic king of the house of David but a prophet like Moses (Dt 18, 15).

4, 26: *I am he:* it could also be translated "I am," an Old Testament self-designation of Yahweh (Is 43, 3, etc.); cf Jn 6, 20; 8, 24.28.58; 13, 19; 18, 5.6.8. See the note on Mk 6, 50.

4, 27: *Talking with a woman:* a religious and social restriction that Jesus is pictured treating as unimportant.

4, 35: *'In four months . . .':* probably a proverb; cf Mt 9, 37-38.

4, 36: *Already:* this word may go with the preceding verse rather than with 36.

4, 39: The woman is presented as a missionary, described in virtually the same words as the disciples are in Jesus' prayer (Jn 17, 20).

4, 43-54: Jesus' arrival in Cana in Galilee; the second sign. This section introduces another theme, that of the life-giving word of Jesus. It is explicitly linked to the first sign (Jn 2, 11). The royal official believes (50). The natural life given his son is a sign of eternal life.

4, 44: Probably a reminiscence of a tradition as in Mk 6, 4. Cf Gospel of Thomas # 31: "No prophet is acceptable in his village, no physician heals those who know him."

4, 46-54: The story of the cure of the royal official's son may be a third version of the cure of the centurion's son (Mt 8, 5-13) or servant (Lk 7, 1-10). Cf also Mt 15, 21-28 // Mk 7, 24-30.

met him and told him that his boy would live. [52] He asked them when he began to recover. They told him, "The fever left him yesterday, about one in the afternoon." [53] The father realized that just at that time Jesus had said to him, "Your son will live," and he and his whole household came to believe. [54] [Now] this was the second sign Jesus did when he came to Galilee from Judea.[q]

CHAPTER 5*

Cure on a Sabbath. [1] After this, there was a feast* of the Jews, and Jesus went up to Jerusalem.[r] [2] Now there is in Jerusalem at the Sheep [Gate]* a pool called in Hebrew Bethesda, with five porticoes.[s] [3] In these lay a large number of ill, blind, lame, and crippled.* [4]* [5] One man was there who had been ill for thirty-eight years. [6] When Jesus saw him lying there and knew that he had been ill for a long time, he said to him, "Do you want to be well?" [7] The sick man answered him, "Sir, I have no one to put me into the pool when the water is stirred up; while I am on my way, someone else gets down there before me." [8] Jesus said to him, "Rise, take up your mat, and walk."[t] [9] Immediately the man became well, took up his mat, and walked.[u]

Now that day was a sabbath. [10] So the Jews said to the man who was cured, "It is the sabbath, and it is not lawful for you to carry your mat."[v] [11] He answered them, "The man who made me well told me, 'Take up your mat and walk.' " [12] They asked him, "Who is the man who told you, 'Take it up and walk'?" [13] The man who was healed did not know who it was, for Jesus had slipped away, since there was a crowd there.[w] [14] After this Jesus found him in the temple area and said to him,[x] "Look, you are well; do not sin anymore, so that nothing worse may happen to you."* [15] The man went and told the Jews that Jesus was the one who had made him well. [16] Therefore, the Jews began to persecute Jesus because he did this on a sabbath.[y] [17] But Jesus answered them,[z] "My Father is at work until now, so I am at work."* [18] For this reason the Jews tried all the more to kill him, because he not only broke the sabbath but he also called God his own father, making himself equal to God.[a]

The Work of the Son. [19] Jesus answered and said to them, "Amen, amen, I say to you, a son cannot do anything on his own, but only what he sees his father doing;[b] for what he does, his son will do also.* [20] For the Father loves his Son and shows him everything that he himself does, and he will show him greater works than these, so that you may be amazed.[c] [21] For just as the Father raises the dead and gives life,* so also does the Son give life to whomever he

q Jn 2, 11.—r Jn 6, 4.—s Neh 3, 1.32; 12, 39.—t Mt 9, 6; Mk 2, 11; Lk 5, 24; Acts 3, 6.—u Mk 2, 12; Lk 5, 25 / Jn 9, 14.—v Ex 20, 8; Jer 17, 21-27; Mk 3, 2; Lk 13, 10; 14, 1.—w Mt 8, 18; 13, 36; Mk 4, 36; 7, 17.—x Jn 8, 11; 9, 2; Ez 18, 20.—y Jn 7, 23; Mt 12, 8.—z Ex 20, 11.—a Jn 7, 1.25; 8, 37.40; 10, 33.36; 14, 28; Gn 3, 5-6; Wis 2, 16; Mt 26, 4; 2 Thes 2, 4.—b Jn 3, 34; 8, 26; 12, 49; 9, 4; 10, 30.—c Jn 3, 35.

5, 1-47: The self-revelation of Jesus continues in Jerusalem at a feast. The third sign (cf Jn 2, 11; 4, 54) is performed, the cure of a paralytic by Jesus' life-giving word. The water of the pool fails to bring life; Jesus' word does.

5, 1: The reference in vv 45-46 to Moses suggests that the feast was Pentecost. The connection of that feast with the giving of the law to Moses on Sinai, attested in later Judaism, may already have been made in the first century. The feast could also be Passover (cf Jn 6, 4). John stresses that the day was a sabbath (9).

5, 2: There is no noun with *Sheep.* "Gate" is supplied on the grounds that there must have been a gate in the NE wall of the temple area where animals for sacrifice were brought in; cf Neh 3, 1.32; 12, 39. *Hebrew:* more precisely, Aramaic. *Bethesda:* preferred to variants "Be(th)zatha" and "Bethsaida"; bêt-'eš-datayin is given as the name of a double pool northeast of the temple area in the Qumran Copper Roll. *Five porticoes:* a pool excavated in Jerusalem actually has five porticoes.

5, 3: The Caesarean and Western recensions, followed by the Vulgate, add "waiting for the movement of the water." Apparently an intermittent spring in the pool bubbled up occasionally (see 7). This turbulence was believed to cure.

5, 4: Toward the end of the second century in the West and among the fourth-century Greek Fathers, an additional verse was known: "For [from time to time] an angel of the Lord used to come down into the pool; and the water was stirred up, so the first one to get in [after the stirring of the water] was healed of whatever disease afflicted him." The angel was a popular explanation of the turbulence and the healing powers attributed to it. This verse is missing from all early Greek manuscripts and the earliest versions, including the original Vulgate. Its vocabulary is markedly non-Johannine.

5, 14: While the cure of the paralytic in Mk 2, 1-12 is associated with the forgiveness of sins, Jesus never drew a one-to-one connection between sin and suffering (cf Jn 9, 3; Lk 12, 1-5), as did Ez 18, 20.

5, 17: Sabbath observance (10) was based on God's resting on the seventh day (cf Gn 2, 2-3; Ex 20, 11). Philo and some rabbis insisted that God's providence remains active on the sabbath, keeping all things in existence, giving life in birth and taking it away in death. Other rabbis taught that God rested from creating, but not from judging (= ruling, governing). Jesus here claims the same authority to work as the Father, and, in the discourse that follows, the same divine prerogatives: power over life and death (21.24-26) and judgment (22.27).

5, 19: This proverb or parable is taken from apprenticeship in a trade: the activity of a son is modeled on that of his father. Jesus' dependence on the Father is justification for doing what the Father does.

5, 21: *Gives life:* in the Old Testament, a divine prerogative (Dt 32, 39; 1 Sm 2, 6; 2 Kgs 5, 7; Tob 13, 2; Is 26, 19; Dan 12, 2).

wishes.*d* [22] Nor does the Father judge anyone, but he has given all judgment* to his Son,*e* [23] so that all may honor the Son just as they honor the Father. Whoever does not honor the Son does not honor the Father who sent him. [24] Amen, amen, I say to you, whoever hears my word and believes in the one who sent me has eternal life and will not come to condemnation, but has passed from death to life.*f* [25] Amen, amen, I say to you, the hour is coming and is now here when the dead will hear the voice of the Son of God, and those who hear will live.*g* [26] For just as the Father has life in himself, so also he gave to his Son the possession of life in himself.*h* [27] And he gave him power to exercise judgment, because he is the Son of Man.*i* [28] * Do not be amazed at this, because the hour is coming in which all who are in the tombs will hear his voice*j* [29] and will come out, those who have done good deeds to the resurrection of life, but those who have done wicked deeds to the resurrection of condemnation.*k*

d Jn 11, 25; Dt 32, 39; 1 Sm 2, 6; 2 Kgs 5, 7; Tb 13, 2; Wis 16, 13; Is 26, 19; Dn 7, 10.13; 12, 2; Rom 4, 17; 2 Cor 1, 9.—e Acts 10, 42; 17, 31.—f Jn 3, 18; 8, 51; 1 Jn 3, 14.—g Jn 5, 28; 8, 51; 11, 25-26; Eph 2, 1; 5, 14; Rv 3, 1.—h Jn 1, 4; 1 Jn 5, 11.—i Jn 5, 22; Dn 7, 13.22; Mt 25, 31; Lk 21, 36.—j Jn 11, 43.—k Dn 12, 2; Mt 16, 27; 25, 46; Acts 24, 15; 2 Cor 5, 10.—l Jn 6, 38.—m 31-32: Jn 8, 13-14.18.—n Jn 1, 19-27; Mt 11, 10-11.—o 1 Jn 5, 9.—p Jn 1, 8; Ps 132, 17; Sir 48, 1.—q Jn 10, 25.—r Jn 8, 18; Dt 4, 12.15; 1 Jn 5, 9.—s 1 Jn 2, 14.—t Jn 12, 16; 19, 28; 20, 9; Lk 24, 27.44; 1 Pt 1, 10.—u 1 Jn 2, 15.—v Mt 24, 5.24.—w Jn 12, 43.—x Dt 31, 26.—y Jn 5, 39; Dt 18, 15; Lk 16, 31; 24, 44.—z 1-13: Mt 14, 13-21; Mk 6, 32-44; Lk 9, 10-17.

5, 22: *Judgment:* another divine prerogative, often expressed as acquittal or condemnation (Dt 32, 36; Ps 43, 1).

5, 28-29: While vv 19-27 present realized eschatology, vv 28-29 are future eschatology; cf Dn 12, 2.

5, 32: *Another:* likely the Father, who in four different ways gives testimony to Jesus, as indicated in the verse groupings 33-34, 36, 37-38, 39-40.

5, 35: *Lamp:* cf Ps 132, 17: "I will place a lamp for my Anointed (= David)," and possibly the description of Elijah in Sir 48, 1. But only *for a while,* indicating the temporary and subordinate nature of John's mission.

5, 39: *You search:* this may be an imperative: "Search the scriptures, because you think that you have eternal life through them."

5, 41: *Praise:* the same Greek word means "praise" or "honor" (from others) and "glory" (from God). There is a play on this in v 44.

6, 1-15: This story of the multiplication of the loaves is the fourth sign (cf the note on Jn 5, 1-47). It is the only miracle story found in all four gospels (occurring twice in Mk and Mt). See the notes on Mt 14, 13-21 and Mt 15, 32-39. John differs on the roles of Philip and Andrew, the proximity of Passover (4), and the allusion to Elisha (see 9). The story here symbolizes the food that is really available through Jesus. It connotes a new exodus and has eucharistic overtones.

6, 1: *[Of Tiberias]:* the awkward apposition represents a later name of the Sea of Galilee. It was probably originally a marginal gloss.

[30] "I cannot do anything on my own; I judge as I hear, and my judgment is just, because I do not seek my own will but the will of the one who sent me.*l*

Witnesses to Jesus. [31] *m* "If I testify on my own behalf, my testimony cannot be verified. [32] But there is another* who testifies on my behalf, and I know that the testimony he gives on my behalf is true. [33] You sent emissaries to John, and he testified to the truth.*n* [34] I do not accept testimony from a human being, but I say this so that you may be saved.*o* [35] He was a burning and shining lamp,* and for a while you were content to rejoice in his light.*p* [36] But I have testimony greater than John's. The works that the Father gave me to accomplish, these works that I perform testify on my behalf that the Father has sent me.*q* [37] Moreover, the Father who sent me has testified on my behalf. But you have never heard his voice nor seen his form,*r* [38] and you do not have his word remaining in you, because you do not believe in the one whom he has sent.*s* [39] You search* the scriptures, because you think you have eternal life through them; even they testify on my behalf.*t* [40] But you do not want to come to me to have life.

Unbelief of Jesus' Hearers. [41] "I do not accept human praise;* [42] moreover, I know that you do not have the love of God in you.*u* [43] I came in the name of my Father, but you do not accept me; yet if another comes in his own name, you will accept him.*v* [44] How can you believe, when you accept praise from one another and do not seek the praise that comes from the only God?*w* [45] Do not think that I will accuse you before the Father: the one who will accuse you is Moses, in whom you have placed your hope.*x* [46] For if you had believed Moses, you would have believed me, because he wrote about me.*y* [47] But if you do not believe his writings, how will you believe my words?"

CHAPTER 6

Multiplication of the Loaves. * [1] *z* After this, Jesus went across the Sea of Galilee [of Tiberias].* [2] A large crowd followed him, because they saw the signs he was performing on the sick. [3] Jesus went up on the mountain, and there he sat down with his disciples. [4] The Jewish feast of Passover was near.*a* 5 When Jesus raised his eyes and saw that a large crowd was coming to him, he said to Philip,*b* "Where can we buy enough food for them to eat?"* 6 He said this to test him, because he himself knew what he was going to do.* 7 Philip answered him, "Two hundred days' wages* worth of food would not be enough for each of them to have a little [bit]."*c* 8 One of his disciples, Andrew, the brother of Simon Peter, said to him, 9 "There is a boy here who has five barley loaves* and two fish; but what good are these for so many?"*d* 10 Jesus said, "Have the people recline." Now there was a great deal of grass* in that place. So the men reclined, about five thousand in number.*e* 11 Then Jesus took the loaves, gave thanks, and distributed them to those who were reclining, and also as much of the fish as they wanted.*f* 12 When they had had their fill, he said to his disciples, "Gather the fragments left over, so that nothing will be wasted." 13 So they collected them, and filled twelve wicker baskets* with fragments from the five barley loaves that had been more than they could eat. 14 When the people saw the sign he had done, they said, "This is truly the Prophet,* the one who is to come into the world."*g* 15 Since Jesus knew that they were going to come and carry him off to make him king, he withdrew again to the mountain alone.*h*

Walking on the Water. * 16 *i* When it was evening, his disciples went down to the sea, 17 embarked in a boat, and went across the sea to Capernaum. It had already grown dark, and Jesus had not yet come to them. 18 The sea was stirred up because a strong wind was blowing. 19 When they had rowed about three or four miles, they saw Jesus walking on the sea* and coming near the boat, and they began to be afraid.*j* 20 But he said to them, "It is I.* Do not be afraid." 21 They wanted to take him into the boat, but the boat immediately arrived at the shore to which they were heading.

The Bread of Life Discourse. 22 *The next day, the crowd that remained across the sea saw that there had been only one boat there, and that Jesus had not gone along with his disciples in the boat, but only his disciples had left. 23 Other boats came from Tiberias near the place where they had eaten the bread when the Lord gave thanks.* 24 When the crowd saw that neither Jesus nor his disciples were there, they themselves got into boats and came to Capernaum looking for Jesus. 25 And when they found him across the sea they said to him, "Rabbi, when did you get here?" 26 Jesus answered them and said, "Amen, amen, I say to you, you are looking for me not because you saw signs but because you ate the loaves and were filled. 27 Do not work for food that perishes but for the food that endures for eternal life,* which the Son of Man will give you. For on him the Father, God, has set his seal."*k* 28 So they said to him, "What can we do to accomplish the works of God?" 29 Jesus answered and said to them, "This is the work of God, that you believe in the one he sent." 30 So they said to him, "What sign can you do, that we may see and believe in you? What can you do?*l* 31 * Our ancestors ate manna in the desert, as it is written: *m*

a Jn 2, 13; 11, 55.—b Nm 11, 13.—c Mt 20, 2.—d 2 Kgs 4, 42-44.—e Mt 14, 21; Mk 6, 44.—f Jn 21, 13.—g Dt 18, 15.18; Mal 3, 1.23; Acts 3, 22.—h Jn 18, 36.—i 16-21: Mt 14, 22-27; Mk 6, 45-52.—j Jb 9, 8; Pss 29, 3-4; 77, 20; Is 43, 16.—k Jn 6, 50.51.54.58.—l Mt 16, 1-4; Lk 11, 29-30.—m Ex 16, 4-5; Nm 11, 7-9; Ps 78, 24.

6, 5: Jesus takes the initiative (in the synoptics, the disciples do), possibly pictured as (cf Jn 6, 14) the new Moses (cf Nm 11, 13).

6, 6: Probably the evangelist's comment; in this gospel Jesus is never portrayed as ignorant of anything.

6, 7: *Days' wages:* literally, "denarii"; a Roman denarius is a day's wage in Mt 20, 2.

6, 9: *Barley loaves:* the food of the poor. There seems an allusion to the story of Elisha multiplying the barley bread in 2 Kgs 4, 42-44.

6, 10: *Grass:* implies springtime, and therefore Passover. *Five thousand:* so Mk 6, 39.44 and parallels.

6, 13: *Baskets:* the word describes the typically Palestinian wicker basket, as in Mk 6, 43 and parallels.

6, 14: *The Prophet:* probably the prophet like Moses (see the note on Jn 1, 21). *The one who is to come into the world:* probably Elijah; cf Mal 3, 1.23.

6, 16-21: The fifth sign is a nature miracle, portraying Jesus sharing Yahweh's power. Cf the parallel stories following the multiplication of the loaves in Mk 6, 45-52 and Mt 14, 22-33.

6, 19: *Walking on the sea:* although the Greek (cf Jn 6, 16) could mean "on the seashore" or "by the sea" (cf Jn 21, 1), the parallels, especially Mt 14, 25, make clear that Jesus walked upon the water. John may allude to Job 9, 8: God "treads upon the crests of the sea."

6, 20: *It is I:* literally, "I am." See also the notes on Jn 4, 26 and Mk 6, 50.

6, 22-71: Discourse on the bread of life; replacement of the manna. Verses 22-34 serve as an introduction, vv 35-59 constitute the discourse proper, vv 60-71 portray the reaction of the disciples and Peter's confession.

6, 23: Possibly a later interpolation, to explain how the crowd got to Capernaum.

6, 27: *The food that endures for eternal life:* cf Jn 4, 14, on water "springing up to eternal life."

6, 31: *Bread from heaven:* cf Ex 16, 4.15.32-34 and the notes there; Ps 78, 24. The manna, thought to have been hidden by Jeremiah (2 Mc 2, 5-8), was expected to reappear miraculously at Passover, in the last days.

'He gave them bread from heaven to eat.' "

[32] So Jesus said to them, "Amen, amen, I say to you, it was not Moses who gave the bread from heaven; my Father gives you the true bread from heaven.[n] [33] For the bread of God is that which comes down from heaven and gives life to the world."

[34] So they said to him, "Sir, give us this bread always." [35] * Jesus said to them, "I am the bread of life; whoever comes to me will never hunger, and whoever believes in me will never thirst.[p] [36] But I told you that although you have seen [me], you do not believe.[q] [37] Everything that the Father gives me will come to me, and I will not reject anyone who comes to me, [38] because I came down from heaven not to do my own will but the will of the one who sent me.[r] [39] And this is the will of the one who sent me, that I should not lose anything of what he gave me, but that I should raise it [on] the last day.[s] [40] For this is the will of my Father, that everyone who sees the Son and believes in him may have eternal life, and I shall raise him [on] the last day."[t]

[41] The Jews murmured about him because he said, "I am the bread that came down from heaven," [42] and they said, "Is this not Jesus, the son of Joseph? Do we not know his father and mother? Then how can he say, 'I have come down from heaven'?"[u] [43] Jesus answered and said to them, "Stop murmuring* among yourselves.[v] [44] No one can come to me unless the Father who sent me draw him, and I will raise him on the last day. [45] It is written in the prophets:

'They shall all be taught by God.'

Everyone who listens to my Father and learns from him comes to me.[w] [46] Not that anyone has seen the Father except the one who is from God; he has seen the Father.[x] [47] Amen, amen, I say to you, whoever believes has eternal life. [48] I am the bread of life. [49] Your ancestors ate the manna in the desert, but they died;[y] [50] this is the bread that comes down from heaven so that one may eat it and not die. [51] I am the living bread that came down from heaven; whoever eats this bread will live forever; and the bread that I will give is my flesh for the life of the world."[z]

[52] The Jews quarreled among themselves, saying, "How can this man give us [his] flesh to eat?" [53] Jesus said to them, "Amen, amen, I say to you, unless you eat the flesh of the Son of Man and drink his blood, you do not have life within you. [54] Whoever eats* my flesh and drinks my blood has eternal life, and I will raise him on the last day. [55] For my flesh is true food, and my blood is true drink. [56] Whoever eats my flesh and drinks my blood remains in me and I in him. [57] Just as the living Father sent me and I have life because of the Father, so also the one who feeds on me will have life because of me.[a] [58] This is the bread that came down from heaven. Unlike your ancestors who ate and still died, whoever eats this bread will live forever." [59] These things he said while teaching in the synagogue in Capernaum.

The Words of Eternal Life. * [60] Then many of his disciples who were listening said, "This saying is hard; who can accept it?" [61] Since Jesus knew that his disciples were murmuring about this, he said to them, "Does this shock you? [62] What if you were to see the Son of Man ascending to where he was before?* [63] It is the spirit that gives life, while the flesh* is of no avail. The words I have spoken to you are spirit and life. [64] But there are some of you who do not believe." Jesus knew from the beginning the ones who would not believe and the one who would betray him.[b] [65] And he said, "For this reason I have told you that

---

n Mt 6, 11.—o Jn 4, 15.—p Is 55, 1-3; Am 8, 11-13.—q Jn 20, 29.—r Jn 4, 34; Mt 26, 39; Heb 10, 9.—s Jn 10, 28-29; 17, 12; 18, 9.—t 1 Jn 2, 25.—u Mt 13, 54-57; Mk 6, 1-4; Lk 4, 22.—v Ex 16, 2.7.8; Lk 4, 22.—w Is 54, 13; Jer 31, 33-34.—x Jn 1, 18; 7, 29; Ex 33, 20.—y 1 Cor 10, 3.5.—z Mt 26, 26-27; Lk 22, 19.—a Jn 5, 26.—b Jn 13, 11.

6, 35-59: Up to v 50, "bread of life" is a figure for God's revelation in Jesus; in vv 51-58, the eucharistic theme comes to the fore. There may thus be a break between vv 50 and 51.

6, 43: *Murmuring:* the word may reflect the Greek of Ex 16, 2.7.8.

6, 54-58: *Eats:* the verb used in these verses is not the classical Greek verb used of human eating, but that of animal eating: "munch," "gnaw." This may be part of John's emphasis on the reality of the flesh and blood of Jesus (cf Jn 6, 55), but the same verb eventually became the ordinary verb in Greek meaning "eat."

6, 60-71: These verses refer more to themes of vv 35-50 than to those of 51-58 and seem to be addressed to members of the Johannine community who found it difficult to accept the high christology reflected in the bread of life discourse.

6, 62: This unfinished conditional sentence is obscure. Probably there is a reference to vv 49-51. Jesus claims to be *the bread that comes down from heaven* (50); this claim provokes incredulity (60); and so Jesus is pictured as asking what his disciples will say when he goes up to heaven.

6, 63: *Spirit . . . flesh:* probably not a reference to the eucharistic body of Jesus but to the supernatural and the natural, as in Jn 3, 6. *Spirit and life:* all Jesus said about the bread of life is the revelation of the Spirit.

no one can come to me unless it is granted
him by my Father."
66 As a result of this, many [of] his disciples returned to their former way of life
and no longer accompanied him. 67 Jesus
then said to the Twelve, "Do you also want
to leave?" 68 Simon Peter answered him,
"Master, to whom shall we go? You have
the words of eternal life. 69 We have come
to believe and are convinced that you are
the Holy One of God."[c] 70 Jesus answered
them, "Did I not choose you twelve? Yet is
not one of you a devil?" 71 He was referring
to Judas, son of Simon the Iscariot; it was
he who would betray him, one of the
Twelve.[d]

CHAPTER 7

The Feast of Tabernacles. 1 * After this,
Jesus moved about within Galilee; but he
did not wish to travel in Judea, because the
Jews were trying to kill him.[e] 2 But the
Jewish feast of Tabernacles was near.[f] 3 So
his brothers* said to him, "Leave here and
go to Judea, so that your disciples also may
see the works you are doing. 4 No one
works in secret if he wants to be known
publicly. If you do these things, manifest
yourself to the world."[g] 5 For his brothers
did not believe in him. 6 So Jesus said to
them, "My time* is not yet here, but the
time is always right for you. 7 The world
cannot hate you, but it hates me, because I
testify to it that its works are evil.[h] 8 You
go up to the feast. I am not going up* to
this feast, because my time has not yet
been fulfilled." 9 After he had said this, he
stayed on in Galilee.
10 But when his brothers had gone up to
the feast, he himself also went up, not
openly but [as it were] in secret. 11 The
Jews were looking for him at the feast and
saying, "Where is he?" 12 And there was
considerable murmuring about him in the
crowds. Some said, "He is a good man,"
[while] others said, "No; on the contrary,
he misleads the crowd." 13 Still, no one
spoke openly about him because they were
afraid of the Jews.[i]

The First Dialogue.* 14 When the feast was
already half over, Jesus went up into the
temple area and began to teach. 15 [j] The
Jews were amazed and said, "How does he
know scripture without having studied?"*
16 Jesus answered them and said, "My
teaching is not my own but is from the one
who sent me. 17 Whoever chooses to do his
will* shall know whether my teaching is
from God or whether I speak on my own.[k]
18 Whoever speaks on his own seeks his
own glory, but whoever seeks the glory of
the one who sent him is truthful, and there
is no wrong in him. 19 Did not Moses give
you the law? Yet none of you keeps the
law. Why are you trying to kill me?"[l]
20 The crowd answered, "You are possessed!* Who is trying to kill you?"[m]
21 Jesus answered and said to them, "I performed one work* and all of you are
amazed[n] 22 because of it. Moses gave you
circumcision—not that it came from
Moses but rather from the patriarchs—and
you circumcise a man on the sabbath.[o] 23 If
a man can receive circumcision on a sabbath so that the law of Moses may not be
broken, are you angry with me because I
made a whole person well on a sabbath?[p]
24 Stop judging by appearances, but judge
justly."[q]

c Jn 11, 27; Mt 16, 16; Mk 1, 24; Lk 4, 34.—d Jn 12, 4; 13, 2.27.—e Jn 5, 18; 8, 37.40.—f Ex 23, 16; Lv 23, 34; Nm 29, 12; Dt 16, 13-16; Zec 14, 16-19.—g Jn 14, 22.—h Jn 15, 18.—i Jn 9, 22; 19, 38; 20, 19.—j Lk 2, 47.—k Jn 6, 29.—l Acts 7, 53.—m Jn 8, 48-49; 10, 20.—n Jn 5, 1-9.—o Gn 17, 10; Lv 12, 3.—p Jn 5, 2-9.16; Mt 12, 11-12; Lk 14, 5.—q Jn 8, 15; Lv 19, 15; Is 11, 3-4.

7—8: These chapters contain events about the feast of Tabernacles (Sukkoth, Ingathering: Ex 23, 16; Tents, Booths: Dt 16, 13-16), with its symbols of booths (originally built to shelter harvesters), rain (water from Siloam poured on the temple altar), and lights (illumination of the four torches in the Court of the Women). They continue the theme of the replacement of feasts (Passover, Jn 2, 13; 6, 4; Hanukkah, Jn 10, 22; Pentecost, Jn 5, 1), here accomplished by Jesus as the Living Water. These chapters comprise seven miscellaneous controversies and dialogues. There is a literary inclusion with Jesus in hiding in Jn 7, 4.10 and 8, 59. There are frequent references to attempts on his life: Jn 7, 1.13.19.25.30.32.44; 8, 37.40.59.

7, 3: *Brothers:* these relatives (cf Jn 2, 12 and see the note on Mk 6, 3) are never portrayed as disciples until after the resurrection (Acts 1, 14). Mt 13, 55 and Mk 6, 3 give the names of four of them. Jesus has already performed works/signs in Judea; cf Jn 2, 23; 3, 2; 4, 45; 5, 8.

7, 6: *Time:* the Greek word means "opportune time," here a synonym for Jesus' "hour" (see the note on Jn 2, 4), his death and resurrection. In the wordplay, any time is suitable for Jesus' brothers, because they are not dependent on God's will.

7, 8: *I am not going up:* an early attested reading "not yet" seems a correction, since Jesus in the story does go up to the feast. "Go up," in a play on words, refers not only to going up to Jerusalem but also to exaltation at the cross, resurrection, and ascension; cf Jn 3, 14; 6, 62; 20, 17.

7, 14-31: Jesus teaches in the temple; debate with the Jews.

7, 15: *Without having studied:* literally, "How does he know letters without having learned?" Children were taught to read and write by means of the scriptures. But here more than Jesus' literacy is being discussed; the people are wondering how he can teach like a rabbi. Rabbis were trained by other rabbis and traditionally quoted their teachers.

7, 17: *To do his will:* presumably a reference back to the "work" of Jn 6, 29: belief in the one whom God has sent.

7, 20: *You are possessed:* literally, "You have a demon." The insane were thought to be possessed by a demoniacal spirit.

7, 21: *One work:* the cure of the paralytic (Jn 5, 1-9) because of the reference to the sabbath (Jn 7, 22; 5, 9-10).

25 So some of the inhabitants of Jerusalem said, "Is he not the one they are trying to kill? 26 And look, he is speaking openly and they say nothing to him. Could the authorities* have realized that he is the Messiah? 27 But we know where he is from. When the Messiah comes, no one will know where he is from." *r* 28 So Jesus cried out in the temple area as he was teaching and said, "You know me and also know where I am from. Yet I did not come on my own, but the one who sent me, whom you do not know, is true. *s* 29 I know him, because I am from him, and he sent me." *t* 30 So they tried to arrest him, but no one laid a hand upon him, because his hour had not yet come. *u* 31 But many of the crowd began to believe in him, and said, "When the Messiah comes, will he perform more signs than this man has done?" *v*

Officers Sent to Arrest Jesus.* 32 The Pharisees heard the crowd murmuring about him to this effect, and the chief priests and the Pharisees sent guards to arrest him. 33 So Jesus said, "I will be with you only a little while longer, and then I will go to the one who sent me. *w* 34 You will look for me but not find [me], and where I am you cannot come." *x* 35 So the Jews said to one another, "Where is he going that we will not find him? Surely he is not going to the dispersion* among the Greeks to teach the Greeks, is he? 36 What is the meaning of his saying, 'You will look for me and not find [me], and where I am you cannot come'?"

Rivers of Living Water.* 37 On the last and greatest day of the feast, Jesus stood up and exclaimed, "Let anyone who thirsts come to me and drink. *y* 38 Whoever believes in me, as scripture says:

'Rivers of living water* will flow from within him.' " *z*

39 He said this in reference to the Spirit that those who came to believe in him were to receive. There was, of course, no Spirit yet,* because Jesus had not yet been glorified. *a*

Discussion about the Origins of the Messiah.* 40 Some in the crowd who heard these words said, "This is truly the Prophet." *b* 41 Others said, "This is the Messiah." But others said, "The Messiah will not come from Galilee, will he? 42 Does not scripture say that the Messiah will be of David's family and come from Bethlehem, the village where David lived?" *c* 43 So a division occurred in the crowd because of him. 44 Some of them even wanted to arrest him, but no one laid hands on him.

45 So the guards went to the chief priests and Pharisees, who asked them, "Why did you not bring him?" 46 The guards answered, "Never before has anyone spoken like this one." 47 So the Pharisees answered them, "Have you also been deceived? 48 Have any of the authorities or the Pharisees believed in him? *d* 49 But this crowd, which does not know the law, is accursed." 50 Nicodemus, one of their members who had come to him earlier, said to them, *e* 51 "Does our law condemn a person before it first hears him and finds out what he is doing?" *f* 52 They answered and said to him, "You are not from Galilee also, are you? Look and see that no prophet arises from Galilee."

CHAPTER 8

A Woman Caught in Adultery.* [53 Then each went to his own house, 1 while Jesus

---

r Heb 7, 3.—s Jn 8, 19.—t Jn 6, 46; 8, 55.—u Jn 7, 44; 8, 20; Lk 4, 29-30.—v Jn 2, 11; 10, 42; 11, 45.—w Jn 13, 33; 16, 16.—x Jn 8, 21; 12, 36; 13, 33.36; 16, 5; Dt 4, 29; Prv 1, 28; Is 55, 6; Hos 5, 6.—y Rv 21, 6.—z Jn 4, 10.14; 19, 34; Is 12, 3; Ez 47, 1.—a Jn 16, 7.—b Dt 18, 15.18.—c 2 Sm 7, 12-14; Pss 89, 3-4; 132, 11; Mi 5, 1; Mt 2, 5-6.—d Jn 12, 42.—e Jn 3, 1; 19, 39.—f Dt 1, 16-17.

7, 26: *The authorities:* the members of the Sanhedrin (same term as Jn 3, 1).

7, 32-36: Jesus announces his approaching departure (cf also Jn 8, 21; 12, 36; 13, 33) and complete control over his destiny.

7, 35: *Dispersion:* or "diaspora": Jews living outside Palestine. *Greeks:* probably refers to the Gentiles in the Mediterranean area; cf Jn 12, 20.

7, 37-39: Promise of living water through the Spirit.

7, 38: *Living water:* not an exact quotation from any Old Testament passage; in the gospel context the gift of the Spirit is meant; cf Jn 3, 5. *From within him:* either Jesus or the believer; if Jesus, it continues the Jesus-Moses motif (water from the rock, Ex 17, 6; Nm 20, 11) as well as Jesus as the new temple (cf Ez 47, 1). Grammatically, it goes better with the believer.

7, 39: *No Spirit yet:* Codex Vaticanus and early Latin, Syriac, and Coptic versions add "given." In this gospel, the sending of the Spirit cannot take place until Jesus' glorification through his death, resurrection, and ascension; cf Jn 20, 22.

7, 40-53: Discussion of the Davidic lineage of the Messiah.

7, 53—8, 11: The story of the woman caught in adultery is a later insertion here, missing from all early Greek manuscripts. A Western text-type insertion, attested mainly in Old Latin translations, it is found in different places in different manuscripts: here, or after Jn 7, 36, or at the end of this gospel, or after Lk 21, 38, or at the end of that gospel. There are many non-Johannine features in the language, and there are also many doubtful readings within the passage. The style and motifs are similar to those of Luke, and it fits better with the general situation at the end of Lk 21, but it was probably inserted here because of the allusion to Jer 17, 13 (cf the note on Jn 8, 6) and the statement, "I do not judge anyone," in Jn 8, 15. The Catholic Church accepts this passage as canonical scripture.

went to the Mount of Olives.* ^g ²But early in the morning he arrived again in the temple area, and all the people started coming to him, and he sat down and taught them. ³Then the scribes and the Pharisees brought a woman who had been caught in adultery and made her stand in the middle. ⁴They said to him, "Teacher, this woman was caught in the very act of committing adultery. ⁵Now in the law, Moses commanded us to stone such women.* So what do you say?"^h ⁶They said this to test him, so that they could have some charge to bring against him. Jesus bent down and began to write on the ground with his finger.* ⁷But when they continued asking him, he straightened up and said to them,ⁱ "Let the one among you who is without sin be the first to throw a stone at her."* ⁸Again he bent down and wrote on the ground. ⁹And in response, they went away one by one, beginning with the elders. So he was left alone with the woman before him. ¹⁰Then Jesus straightened up and said to her, "Woman, where are they? Has no one condemned you?"^j ¹¹She replied, "No one, sir." Then Jesus said, "Neither do I condemn you. Go, [and] from now on do not sin any more."]^k

The Light of the World.* ¹² Jesus spoke to them again, saying, "I am the light of the world. Whoever follows me will not walk in darkness, but will have the light of life."^l ¹³So the Pharisees said to him, "You testify on your own behalf, so your testimony cannot be verified." ¹⁴Jesus answered and said to them, "Even if I do testify on my own behalf, my testimony can be verified,* because I know where I came from and where I am going. But you do not know where I come from or where I am going.^m ¹⁵You judge by appearances,* but I do not judge anyone.ⁿ ¹⁶And even if I should judge, my judgment is valid, because I am not alone, but it is I and the Father who sent me.^o ¹⁷Even in your law* it is written that the testimony of two men can be verified.^p ¹⁸I testify on my behalf and so does the Father who sent me."^q ¹⁹So they said to him, "Where is your father?" Jesus answered, "You know neither me nor my Father. If you knew me, you would know my Father also."^r ²⁰He spoke these words while teaching in the treasury in the temple area. But no one arrested him, because his hour had not yet come.^s

Jesus, the Father's Ambassador.* ²¹He said to them again, "I am going away and you will look for me, but you will die in your sin.* Where I am going you cannot come."^t ²²So the Jews said, "He is not going to kill himself, is he, because he said, 'Where I am going you cannot come'?"* ²³He said to them, "You belong to what is below, I belong to what is above. You belong to this world, but I do not belong to this world.^u ²⁴That is why I told you that you will die in your sins. For if you do not believe that I AM,* you will die in your sins."^v ²⁵So they said to him, "Who are you?"^w Jesus said to them, "What I told you from the beginning.* ²⁶I have much to

---

g 1-2: Lk 21, 37-38.—h Lv 20, 10; Dt 22, 22-29.—i Dt 17, 7.—j Ez 33, 11.—k Jn 5, 14.—l Jn 1, 4-5.9; 12, 46; Ex 13, 22; Is 42, 6; Zec 14, 8.—m Jn 5, 31.—n Jn 12, 47; 1 Sm 16, 7.—o Jn 5, 30.—p Dt 17, 6; 19, 15; Nm 35, 30.—q Jn 5, 23.37.—r Jn 7, 28; 14, 7; 15, 21.—s Jn 7, 30.—t Jn 7, 34; 13, 33.—u Jn 3, 31; 17, 14; 18, 36.—v Ex 3, 14; Dt 32, 39; Is 43, 10.—w Jn 10, 24.

8, 1: *Mount of Olives:* not mentioned elsewhere in the gospel tradition outside of passion week.

8, 5: Lv 20, 10 and Dt 22, 22 mention only death, but Dt 22, 23-24 prescribes stoning for a betrothed virgin.

8, 6: Cf Jer 17, 13 (RSV): "Those who turn away from thee shall be written in the earth, for they have forsaken the LORD, the fountain of living water"; cf Jn 7, 38.

8, 7: The first stones were to be thrown by the witnesses (Dt 17, 7).

8, 12-20: Jesus the light of the world. Jesus replaces the four torches of the illumination of the temple as the light of joy.

8, 14: *My testimony can be verified:* this seems to contradict Jn 5, 31, but the emphasis here is on Jesus' origin from the Father and his divine destiny. *Where I am going:* indicates Jesus' passion and glorification.

8, 15: *By appearances:* literally, "according to the flesh." *I do not judge anyone:* superficial contradiction of Jn 5, 22.27.30; here the emphasis is that the judgment is not by material standards.

8, 17: *Your law:* a reflection of later controversy between church and synagogue.

8, 21-30: He whose ambassador I am is with me. Jesus' origin is from God; he can reveal God.

8, 21: *You will die in your sin:* i.e., of disbelief; cf v 24. *Where I am going you cannot come:* except through faith in Jesus' passion-resurrection.

8, 22: The Jews suspect that he is referring to his death. Johannine irony is apparent here; Jesus' death will not be self-inflicted but destined by God.

8, 24.28: *I AM:* an expression that late Jewish tradition understood as Yahweh's own self-designation (Is 43, 10); see the note on Jn 4, 26. Jesus is here placed on a par with Yahweh.

8, 25: *What I told you from the beginning:* this verse seems textually corrupt, with several other possible translations: "(I am) what I say to you"; "Why do I speak to you at all?" The earliest attested reading (Bodmer Papyrus P⁶⁶) has (in a second hand), "I told you at the beginning what I am also telling you (now)." The answer here (cf Prv 8, 22) seems to hinge on a misunderstanding of v 24 "*that* I AM" as "*what* I am."

say about you in condemnation. But the one who sent me is true, and what I heard from him I tell the world."ˣ ²⁷They did not realize that he was speaking to them of the Father. ²⁸So Jesus said [to them], "When you lift up the Son of Man, then you will realize that I AM, and that I do nothing on my own, but I say only what the Father taught me.ʸ ²⁹The one who sent me is with me. He has not left me alone, because I always do what is pleasing to him." ³⁰Because he spoke this way, many came to believe in him.

Jesus and Abraham.* ³¹Jesus then said to those Jews who believed in him,* "If you remain in my word, you will truly be my disciples, ³²and you will know the truth, and the truth will set you free."ᶻ ³³They answered him, "We are descendants of Abraham and have never been enslaved to anyone.* How can you say, 'You will become free'?"ᵃ ³⁴Jesus answered them, "Amen, amen, I say to you, everyone who commits sin is a slave of sin.ᵇ ³⁵A slave does not remain in a household forever, but a son* always remains.ᶜ ³⁶So if a son frees you, then you will truly be free. ³⁷I know that you are descendants of Abraham. But you are trying to kill me, because my word has no room among you. ³⁸I tell

you what I have seen in the Father's presence; then do what you have heard from the Father."*

³⁹They answered and said to him, "Our father is Abraham." Jesus said to them,ᵈ "If you were Abraham's children, you would be doing the works of Abraham.* ⁴⁰But now you are trying to kill me, a man who has told you the truth that I heard from God; Abraham did not do this. ⁴¹You are doing the works of your father!" [So] they said to him, "We are not illegitimate. We have one Father, God."ᵉ ⁴²Jesus said to them, "If God were your Father, you would love me, for I came from God and am here; I did not come on my own, but he sent me.ᶠ ⁴³Why do you not understand what I am saying? Because you cannot bear to hear my word. ⁴⁴You belong to your father the devil and you willingly carry out your father's desires. He was a murderer from the beginning and does not stand in truth, because there is no truth in him. When he tells a lie, he speaks in character, because he is a liar and the father of lies.ᵍ ⁴⁵But because I speak the truth, you do not believe me. ⁴⁶Can any of you charge me with sin? If I am telling the truth, why do you not believe me?ʰ ⁴⁷Whoever belongs to God hears the words of God; for this reason you do not listen, because you do not belong to God."ⁱ

⁴⁸The Jews answered and said to him, "Are we not right in saying that you are a Samaritan* and are possessed?" ⁴⁹Jesus answered, "I am not possessed; I honor my Father, but you dishonor me. ⁵⁰I do not seek my own glory; there is one who seeks it and he is the one who judges.ʲ ⁵¹Amen, amen, I say to you, whoever keeps my word will never see death."ᵏ ⁵²[So] the Jews said to him, "Now we are sure that you are possessed. Abraham died, as did the prophets, yet you say, 'Whoever keeps my word will never taste death.' ⁵³Are you greater than our father Abraham,* who died? Or the prophets, who died? Who do you make yourself out to be?"ˡ ⁵⁴Jesus answered, "If I glorify myself, my glory is worth nothing; but it is my Father who glorifies me, of whom you say, 'He is our God.' ⁵⁵You do not know him, but I know him. And if I should say that I do not know him, I would be like you a liar. But I do know him and I keep his word.ᵐ ⁵⁶Abraham your father rejoiced to see my day; he

---

x Jn 12, 44-50.—y Jn 3, 14; 12, 32.34.—z Is 42, 7; Gal 4, 31.—a Mt 3, 9.—b Rom 6, 16-17.—c Gn 21, 10; Gal 4, 30; Heb 3, 5-6.—d Gn 26, 5; Rom 4, 11-17; Jas 2, 21-23.—e Mal 2, 10.—f 1 Jn 5, 1.—g Jn 3, 4; Wis 1, 13; 2, 24; Acts 13, 10; 1 Jn 3, 8-15.—h Heb 4, 15; 1 Pt 2, 22; 1 Jn 3, 5.—i Jn 10, 26; 1 Jn 4, 6.—j Jn 7, 18.—k Jn 5, 24-29; 6, 40.47; 11, 25-26.—l Jn 4, 12.—m Jn 7, 28-29.

8, 31-59: Jesus' origin ("before Abraham") and destiny are developed; the truth will free them from sin (34) and death (51).

8, 31: *Those Jews who believed in him:* a rough editorial suture, since in v 37 they are described as trying to kill Jesus.

8, 33: *Have never been enslaved to anyone:* since, historically, the Jews were enslaved almost continuously, this verse is probably Johannine irony, about slavery to sin.

8, 35: *A slave . . . a son:* an allusion to Ishmael and Isaac (Gn 16 and 21), or to the release of a slave after six years (Ex 21, 2; Dt 15, 12).

8, 38: *The Father:* i.e., God. It is also possible, however, to understand the second part of the verse as a sarcastic reference to descent of the Jews from the devil (44), "You do what you have heard from [your] father."

8, 39: *The works of Abraham:* Abraham believed; cf Rom 4, 11-17; Jas 2, 21-23.

8, 48: *Samaritan:* therefore interested in magical powers; cf Acts 7, 14-24.

8, 53: *Are you greater than our father Abraham?:* cf Jn 4, 12.

saw it* and was glad."*n* 57 So the Jews said to him, "You are not yet fifty years old and you have seen Abraham?"* 58 Jesus said to them,*o* "Amen, amen, I say to you, before Abraham came to be, I AM."* 59 So they picked up stones to throw at him; but Jesus hid and went out of the temple area.*p*

CHAPTER 9

The Man Born Blind. 1 *As he passed by he saw a man blind from birth.*q* 2 His disciples asked him,*r* "Rabbi, who sinned, this man or his parents, that he was born blind?"* 3 Jesus answered, "Neither he nor his parents sinned; it is so that the works of God might be made visible through him.*s* 4 We have to do the works of the one who sent me while it is day. Night is coming when no one can work.*t* 5 While I am in the world, I am the light of the world."*u* 6 When he had said this, he spat on the ground and made clay with the saliva, and smeared the clay on his eyes,*v* 7 and said to him, "Go wash* in the Pool of Siloam" (which means Sent). So he went and washed, and came back able to see.*w*

8 His neighbors and those who had seen him earlier as a beggar said, "Isn't this the one who used to sit and beg?" 9 Some said, "It is," but others said, "No, he just looks like him." He said, "I am." 10 So they said to him, "[So] how were your eyes opened?" 11 He replied, "The man called Jesus made clay and anointed my eyes and told me, 'Go to Siloam and wash.' So I went there and washed and was able to see." 12 And they said to him, "Where is he?" He said, "I don't know."

13 They brought the one who was once blind to the Pharisees. 14 Now Jesus had made clay* and opened his eyes on a sabbath.*x* 15 So then the Pharisees also asked him how he was able to see. He said to them, "He put clay on my eyes, and I washed, and now I can see." 16 So some of the Pharisees said, "This man is not from God, because he does not keep the sabbath." [But] others said, "How can a sinful man do such signs?" And there was a division among them.*y* 17 So they said to the blind man again, "What do you have to say about him, since he opened your eyes?" He said, "He is a prophet."*z*

18 Now the Jews did not believe that he had been blind and gained his sight until they summoned the parents of the one who had gained his sight. 19 They asked them, "Is this your son, who you say was born blind? How does he now see?" 20 His parents answered and said, "We know that this is our son and that he was born blind. 21 We do not know how he sees now, nor do we know who opened his eyes. Ask him, he is of age; he can speak for himself." 22 *a* His parents said this because they were afraid of the Jews, for the Jews had already agreed that if anyone acknowledged him as the Messiah, he would be expelled from the synagogue.* 23 For this reason his parents said, "He is of age; question him." *b*

24 So a second time they called the man who had been blind and said to him, "Give God the praise!* We know that this man is a sinner."*c* 25 He replied, "If he is a sinner, I do not know. One thing I do know is that I was blind and now I see." 26 So they said

---

n Gn 17, 17; Mt 13, 17; Lk 17, 22.—o Jn 1, 30; 17, 5.—p Jn 10, 31.39; 11, 8; Lk 4, 29-30.—q 1-2: Is 42, 7.—r Ex 20, 5; Ez 18, 20; Lk 13, 2.—s Jn 5, 14; 11, 4.—t Jn 11, 9-10; 12, 35-36.—u Jn 8, 12.—v Jn 5, 11; Mk 7, 33; 8, 23.—w 2 Kgs 5, 10-14.—x Jn 5, 9.—y Jn 3, 2; Mt 12, 10-11; Lk 13, 10-11; 14, 1-4.—z Jn 4, 19.—a Jn 7, 13; 12, 42; 16, 2; 19, 38.—b Jn 12, 42.—c Jos 7, 19; 1 Sm 6, 5 LXX.

8, 56: *He saw it:* this seems a reference to the birth of Isaac (Gn 17, 7; 21, 6), the beginning of the fulfillment of promises about Abraham's seed.

8, 57: The evidence of the third-century Bodmer Papyrus P75 and the first hand of Codex Sinaiticus indicates that the text originally read: "How can Abraham have seen you?"

8, 58: *Came to be, I AM:* the Greek word used for "came to be" is the one used of all creation in the prologue, while the word used for "am" is the one reserved for the Logos.

9, 1—10, 21: Sabbath healing of the man born blind. This fifth sign is introduced to illustrate the saying, "I am the light of the world" (Jn 8, 12; 9, 5). The narrative of conflict about Jesus contrasts Jesus (light) with the Jews (blindness, 39-41).The theme of water is reintroduced in the reference to the pool of Siloam. Ironically, Jesus is being judged by the Jews, yet the Jews are judged by the Light of the world; cf Jn 3, 19-21.

9, 2: See the note on Jn 5, 14, and Ex 20, 5, that parents' sins were visited upon their children. Jesus denies such a cause and emphasizes the purpose: the infirmity was providential.

9, 7: *Go wash:* perhaps a test of faith; cf 2 Kgs 5, 10-14. The water tunnel Siloam (= Sent) is used as a symbol of Jesus, sent by his Father.

9, 14: In using spittle, kneading clay, and healing, Jesus had broken the sabbath rules laid down by Jewish tradition.

9, 22: This comment of the evangelist (in terms used again in Jn 12, 42 and Jn 16, 2) envisages a situation after Jesus' ministry. Rejection/excommunication from the synagogue of Jews who confessed Jesus as Messiah seems to have begun ca. A.D. 85, when the curse against the *minim* or heretics was introduced into the "Eighteen Benedictions."

9, 24: *Give God the praise!:* an Old Testament formula of adjuration to tell the truth; cf Jos 7, 19; 1 Sm 6, 5 LXX. Cf Jn 5, 41.

to him, "What did he do to you? How did he open your eyes?" [27] He answered them, "I told you already and you did not listen. Why do you want to hear it again? Do you want to become his disciples, too?" [28] They ridiculed him and said, "You are that man's disciple; we are disciples of Moses! [29] We know that God spoke to Moses, but we do not know where this one is from." [d] [30] The man answered and said to them, "This is what is so amazing, that you do not know where he is from, yet he opened my eyes. [31] We know that God does not listen to sinners, but if one is devout and does his will, he listens to him. [e] [32] It is unheard of that anyone ever opened the eyes of a person born blind.* [33] If this man were not from God, he would not be able to do anything." [f] [34] They answered and said to him, "You were born totally in sin, and are you trying to teach us?" Then they threw him out.

[35] When Jesus heard that they had thrown him out, he found him and said, "Do you believe in the Son of Man?" [36] He answered and said, "Who is he, sir, that I may believe in him?" [37] Jesus said to him, "You have seen him and the one speaking with you is he." [g] [38] He said, "I do believe,

Lord," and he worshiped him. [39] * Then Jesus said, "I came into this world for judgment, so that those who do not see might see, and those who do see might become blind." [h]

[40] Some of the Pharisees who were with him heard this and said to him, "Surely we are not also blind, are we?" [i] [41] Jesus said to them, "If you were blind, you would have no sin; but now you are saying, 'We see,' so your sin remains. [j]

CHAPTER 10

The Good Shepherd. [1] * "Amen, amen, I say to you, [k] whoever does not enter a sheepfold* through the gate but climbs over elsewhere is a thief and a robber. [2] But whoever enters through the gate is the shepherd of the sheep. [3] The gatekeeper opens it for him, and the sheep hear his voice, as he calls his own sheep by name and leads them out. [4] When he has driven out all his own, he walks ahead of them, and the sheep follow him, [l] because they recognize his voice.* [5] But they will not follow a stranger; they will run away from him, because they do not recognize the voice of strangers." [6] Although Jesus used this figure of speech,* they did not realize what he was trying to tell them.

[7] * So Jesus said again, "Amen, amen, I say to you, I am the gate for the sheep. [8] All who came [before me]* are thieves and robbers, but the sheep did not listen to them. [9] I am the gate. Whoever enters through me will be saved, and will come in and go out and find pasture. [10] A thief comes only to steal and slaughter and destroy; I came so that they might have life and have it more abundantly. [11] I am the good shepherd. A good shepherd lays down his life for the sheep. [m] [12] A hired man, who is not a shepherd and whose sheep are not his own, sees a wolf coming and leaves the sheep and runs away, and the wolf catches and scatters them. [n] [13] This is because he works for pay and has no concern for the sheep. [14] I am the good shepherd, and I know mine and mine know me, [15] just as the Father knows me and I know the Father; and I will lay down my life for the sheep. [o] [16] I have other sheep* that do not belong to this fold. These also I must lead, and they will hear my voice, and there will be one flock, one

---

d Ex 33, 11.—e Jn 10, 21; Pss 34, 16; 66, 18; Prv 15, 29; Is 1, 15.—f Jn 3, 2.—g Jn 4, 26; Dn 7, 13.—h Mt 13, 33-35.—i Mt 15, 14; 23, 26; Rom 2, 19.—j Jn 15, 22.—k 1-5: Gn 48, 15; 49, 24; Pss 23, 1-4; 80, 2; Jer 23, 1-4; Ez 34, 1-31; Mi 7, 14.—l Mi 2, 12-13.—m Ps 23, 1-4; Is 40, 11; 49, 9-10; Heb 13, 20; Rv 7, 17.—n Zec 11, 17.—o Jn 15, 13; 1 Jn 3, 16.

9, 32: *A person born blind:* the only Old Testament cure from blindness is found in Tobit (cf Tb 7, 7; 11, 7-13; 14, 1-2), but Tobit was not born blind.

9, 39-41: These verses spell out the symbolic meaning of the cure; the Pharisees are not the innocent blind, willing to accept the testimony of others.

10, 1-21: The good shepherd discourse continues the theme of attack on the Pharisees that ends ch 9. The figure is allegorical: the hired hands are the Pharisees who excommunicated the cured blind man. It serves as a commentary on ch 9. For the shepherd motif, used of Yahweh in the Old Testament, cf Ex 34; Gn 48, 15; 49, 24; Mi 7, 14; Pss 23, 1-4; 80, 1.

10, 1: *Sheepfold:* a low stone wall open to the sky.

10, 4: *Recognize his voice:* the Pharisees do not recognize Jesus, but the people of God, symbolized by the blind man, do.

10, 6: *Figure of speech:* John uses a different word for illustrative speech than the "parable" of the synoptics, but the idea is similar.

10, 7-10: In vv 7-8, the figure is of a gate for the shepherd to come to the sheep; in vv 9-10, the figure is of a gate for the sheep to come in and go out.

10, 8: *[Before me]:* these words are omitted in many good early manuscripts and versions.

10, 16: *Other sheep:* the Gentiles, possibly a reference to "God's dispersed children" of Jn 11, 52 destined to be gathered into one, or "apostolic Christians" at odds with the community of the beloved disciple.

shepherd.*p* [17] This is why the Father loves me, because I lay down my life in order to take it up again.*q* [18] No one takes it from me, but I lay it down on my own. I have power to lay it down, and power to take it up again.* This command I have received from my Father."*r*

[19] Again there was a division among the Jews because of these words.*s* [20] Many of them said, "He is possessed and out of his mind; why listen to him?"*t* [21] Others said, "These are not the words of one possessed; surely a demon cannot open the eyes of the blind, can he?"*u*

Feast of the Dedication. [22] The feast of the Dedication* was then taking place in Jerusalem. It was winter.*v* [23] And Jesus walked about in the temple area on the Portico of Solomon.* [24] So the Jews gathered around him and said to him, "How long are you going to keep us in suspense?* If you are the Messiah, tell us plainly."*w* [25] Jesus answered them, "I told you* and you do not believe. The works I do in my Father's name testify to me.*x* [26] But you do not believe, because you are not among my sheep.*y* [27] My sheep hear my voice; I know them, and they follow me. [28] I give them eternal life, and they shall never perish. No one can take them out of my hand. [29] My Father, who has given them to me, is greater than all,* and no one can take them out of the Father's hand.*a* [30] The Father and I are one."*b*

[31] The Jews again picked up rocks to stone him.*c* [13] Jesus answered them, "I

have shown you many good works from my Father. For which of these are you trying to stone me?" [33] The Jews answered him, "We are not stoning you for a good work but for blasphemy. You, a man, are making yourself God."*d* [34] Jesus answered them,*e* "Is it not written in your law, 'I said, "You are gods" '?* [35] If it calls them gods to whom the word of God came, and scripture cannot be set aside, [36] can you say that the one whom the Father has consecrated* and sent into the world blasphemes because I said, 'I am the Son of God'?*f* [37] If I do not perform my Father's works, do not believe me; [38] but if I perform them, even if you do not believe me, believe the works, so that you may realize [and understand] that the Father is in me and I am in the Father."*g* [39] [Then] they tried again to arrest him; but he escaped from their power.

[40] He went back across the Jordan to the place where John first baptized, and there he remained.*h* [41] Many came to him and said, "John performed no sign,* but everything John said about this man was true." [42] And many there began to believe in him.*i*

CHAPTER 11

The Raising of Lazarus. * [1] Now a man was ill, Lazarus from Bethany,*j* the village of

---

p Jn 11, 52; Is 56, 8; Jer 23, 3; Ez 34, 23; 37, 24; Mi 2, 12.— q Heb 10, 10.—r Jn 19, 11.—s Jn 7, 43; 9, 16.—t Jn 7, 20; 8, 48.—u Jn 3, 2.—v 1 Mc 4, 54.59.—w Lk 22, 67.—x Jn 8, 25 / Jn 5, 36; 10, 38.—y Jn 8, 45.47.—z Dt 32, 39.—a Wis 3, 1; Is 43, 13.—b Jn 1, 1; 12, 45; 14, 9; 17, 21.—c Jn 8, 59.—d Jn 5, 18; 19, 7; Lv 24, 16.—e Ps 82, 6.—f Jn 5, 18.—g Jn 14, 10-11.20.—h Jn 1, 28.—i Jn 2, 23; 7, 31; 8, 30.—j 1-2: Jn 12, 1-8; Lk 10, 38-42; 16, 19-31.

10, 18: *Power to take it up again:* contrast the role of the Father as the efficient cause of the resurrection in Acts 2, 24; 4, 10; etc.; Rom 1, 4; 4, 24. Yet even here is added: *This command I have received from my Father.*

10, 22: *Feast of the Dedication:* an eight-day festival of lights (Hebrew, Hanukkah) held in December, three months after the feast of Tabernacles (Jn 7, 2), to celebrate the Maccabees' rededication of the altar and reconsecration of the temple in 164 B.C., after their desecration by Antiochus IV Epiphanes (Dn 8, 13; 9, 27; cf 1 Mc 4, 36-59; 2 Mc 1, 18—2, 19; 10, 1-8).

10, 23: *Portico of Solomon:* on the east side of the temple area, offering protection against the cold winds from the desert.

10, 24: *Keep us in suspense:* literally, "How long will you take away our life?" Cf Jn 11, 48-50. *If you are the Messiah, tell us plainly:* cf Lk 22, 67. This is the climax of Jesus' encounters with the Jewish authorities. There has never yet been an open confession before them.

10, 25: *I told you:* probably at Jn 8, 25, which was an evasive answer.

10, 29: The textual evidence for the first clause is very divided; it may also be translated: "As for the Father, what he has given me is greater than all," or "My Father is greater than all, in what he has given me."

10, 30: This is justification for v 29; it asserts unity of power and reveals that the words and deeds of Jesus are the words and deeds of God.

10, 34: This is a reference to the judges of Israel who, since they exercised the divine prerogative to judge (Dt 1, 17), were called "gods"; cf Ex 21, 6, besides Ps 82, 6, from which the quotation comes.

10, 36: *Consecrated:* this may be a reference to the rededicated altar at the Hanukkah feast; see the note on Jn 10, 22.

10, 41: *Performed no sign:* this is to stress the inferior role of John the Baptist. The Transjordan topography recalls the great witness of John the Baptist to Jesus, as opposed to the hostility of the authorities in Jerusalem.

11, 1-44: The raising of Lazarus, the longest continuous narrative in John outside of the Passion account, is the climax of the signs. It leads directly to the decision of the Sanhedrin to kill Jesus. The theme of life predominates. Lazarus is a token of the real life that Jesus dead and raised will give to all who believe in him. Johannine irony is found in the fact that Jesus' gift of life leads to his own death. The story is not found in the synoptics, but cf Mk 5, 21 and parallels; Lk 7, 11-17. There are also parallels between this story and Luke's parable of the rich man and poor Lazarus (Lk 16, 19-31). In both a man named Lazarus dies; in Luke, there is a request that he return to convince his contemporaries of the need for faith and repentance, while in John, Lazarus does return and some believe but others do not.

Mary and her sister Martha. 2 Mary was the one who had anointed the Lord with perfumed oil and dried his feet with her hair; it was her brother Lazarus who was ill. 3 So the sisters sent word to him, saying, "Master, the one you love is ill." 4 When Jesus heard this he said, "This illness is not to end in death,* but is for the glory of God, that the Son of God may be glorified through it."[k] 5 Now Jesus loved Martha and her sister and Lazarus. 6 So when he heard that he was ill, he remained for two days in the place where he was. 7 Then after this he said to his disciples, "Let us go back to Judea." 8 The disciples said to him, "Rabbi, the Jews were just trying to stone you, and you want to go back there?"[l] 9 Jesus answered, "Are there not twelve hours in a day? If one walks during the day,[m] he does not stumble, because he sees the light of this world.[n] 10 But if one walks at night, he stumbles, because the light is not in him."* 11 He said this, and then told them, "Our friend Lazarus is asleep, but I am going to awaken him." 12 So the disciples said to him, "Master, if he is asleep, he will be saved." 13 But Jesus was talking about his death, while they thought that he meant ordinary sleep.[o] 14 So then Jesus said to them clearly, "Lazarus has died. 15 And I am glad for you that I was not there, that you may believe. Let us go to him." 16 So Thomas, called Didymus,* said to his fellow disciples, "Let us also go to die with him."[p]

17 When Jesus arrived, he found that Lazarus had already been in the tomb for four days. 18 Now Bethany was near Jerusalem, only about two miles* away. 19 And many of the Jews had come to Martha and Mary to comfort them about their brother.[q] 20 When Martha heard that Jesus was coming, she went to meet him; but Mary sat at home. 21 Martha said to Jesus, "Lord, if you had been here, my brother would not have died.[r] 22 [But] even now I know that whatever you ask of God, God will give you." 23 Jesus said to her, "Your brother will rise." 24 Martha said to him, "I know he will rise, in the resurrection on the last day."[s] 25 Jesus told her, "I am the resurrection and the life; whoever believes in me, even if he dies, will live,[t] 26 and everyone who lives and believes in me will never die. Do you believe this?" 27 [u] She said to him, "Yes, Lord. I have come to believe that you are the Messiah, the Son of God, the one who is coming into the world."*

28 When she had said this, she went and called her sister Mary secretly, saying, "The teacher is here and is asking for you." 29 As soon as she heard this, she rose quickly and went to him. 30 For Jesus had not yet come into the village, but was still where Martha had met him. 31 So when the Jews who were with her in the house comforting her saw Mary get up quickly and go out, they followed her, presuming that she was going to the tomb to weep there. 32 When Mary came to where Jesus was and saw him, she fell at his feet and said to him, "Lord, if you had been here, my brother would not have died." 33 When Jesus saw her weeping and the Jews who had come with her weeping, he became perturbed* and deeply troubled, 34 and said, "Where have you laid him?" They said to him, "Sir, come and see." 35 And Jesus wept.[v] 36 So the Jews said, "See how he loved him." 37 But some of them said, "Could not the one who opened the eyes of the blind man have done something so that this man would not have died?"

38 So Jesus, perturbed again, came to the tomb. It was a cave, and a stone lay across it. 39 Jesus said, "Take away the stone." Martha, the dead man's sister, said to him, "Lord, by now there will be a stench; he has been dead for four days." 40 Jesus said to her, "Did I not tell you that if you believe you will see the glory of God?" 41 So they took away the stone. And Jesus raised his eyes and said, "Father,* I thank you

Jn

k Jn 9, 3.24.—l Jn 8, 59; 10, 31.—m Jn 8, 12; 9, 4.—n 9-10: Jn 12, 35; 1 Jn 2, 10.—o Mt 9, 24.—p Jn 14, 5.22.—q Jn 12, 9.17-18.—r Jn 11, 32.—s Jn 5, 29; 6, 39-40.44.54; 12, 48; Is 2, 2; Mi 4, 1; Acts 23, 8; 24, 15.—t Jn 5, 24; 8, 51; 14, 6; Dn 12, 2.—u Jn 1, 9; 6, 69.—v Lk 19, 41.

11, 4: *Not to end in death:* this is misunderstood by the disciples as referring to physical death, but it is meant as spiritual death.

11, 10: *The light is not in him:* the ancients apparently did not grasp clearly the entry of light *through* the eye; they seem to have thought of it as being *in* the eye; cf Lk 11, 34; Mt 6, 23.

11, 16: *Called Didymus: Didymus* is the Greek word for twin. Thomas is derived from the Aramaic word for twin; in an ancient Syriac version and in the Gospel of Thomas (#80, 11-12) his given name, Judas, is supplied.

11, 18: *About two miles:* literally, "about fifteen stades"; a stade was 607 feet.

11, 27: The titles here are a summary of titles given to Jesus earlier in the gospel.

11, 33: *Became perturbed:* a startling phrase in Greek, literally, "He snorted in spirit," perhaps in anger at the presence of evil (death).

11, 41: *Father:* in Aramaic, *'abbā'*. See the note on Mk 14, 36.

for hearing me. ⁴²I know that you always hear me; but because of the crowd here I have said this, that they may believe that you sent me."ʷ ⁴³And when he had said this, he cried out in a loud voice,* "Lazarus, come out!" ⁴⁴The dead man came out, tied hand and foot with burial bands, and his face was wrapped in a cloth. So Jesus said to them, "Untie him and let him go."

Session of the Sanhedrin. ⁴⁵Now many of the Jews who had come to Mary and seen what he had done began to believe in him.ˣ ⁴⁶But some of them went to the Pharisees and told them what Jesus had done. ⁴⁷So the chief priests and the Pharisees convened the Sanhedrin and said, "What are we going to do? This man is performing many signs.ʸ ⁴⁸If we leave him alone, all will believe in him, and the Romans will come* and take away both our land and our nation." ⁴⁹ ᶻ But one of them, Caiaphas, who was high priest that year,* said to them, "You know nothing, ⁵⁰nor do you consider that it is better for you that one man should die instead of the people, so that the whole nation may not perish." ⁵¹He did not say this on his own, but since he was high priest for that year, he prophesied that Jesus was going to die for the nation, ⁵²and not only for the nation, but also to gather into one the dispersed children of God.* ⁵³So from that day on they planned to kill him.ᵃ

⁵⁴So Jesus no longer walked about in public among the Jews, but he left for the region near the desert, to a town called Ephraim,* and there he remained with his disciples.

The Last Passover. ⁵⁵Now the Passover of the Jews was near, and many went up from the country to Jerusalem before Passover to purify* themselves.ᵇ ⁵⁶They looked for Jesus and said to one another as they were in the temple area, "What do you think? That he will not come to the feast?" ⁵⁷For the chief priests and the Pharisees had given orders that if anyone knew where he was, he should inform them, so that they might arrest him.

CHAPTER 12

The Anointing at Bethany.ᶜ ¹ * Six days before Passover Jesus came to Bethany, where Lazarus was, whom Jesus had raised from the dead.ᵈ ²They gave a dinner for

him there, and Martha served, while Lazarus was one of those reclining at table with him.ᵉ ³Mary took a liter of costly perfumed oil made from genuine aromatic nard and anointed the feet of Jesus* and dried them with her hair; the house was filled with the fragrance of the oil.ᶠ ⁴Then Judas the Iscariot, one [of] his disciples, and the one who would betray him, said, ⁵"Why was this oil not sold for three hundred days' wages* and given to the poor?" ⁶He said this not because he cared about the poor but because he was a thief and held the money bag and used to steal the contributions.ᵍ ⁷So Jesus said, "Leave her alone. Let her keep this for the day of my burial.* ⁸You always have the poor with you, but you do not always have me."ʰ

⁹[The] large crowd of the Jews found out that he was there and came, not only because of Jesus, but also to see Lazarus, whom he had raised from the dead.ⁱ ¹⁰And the chief priests plotted to kill Lazarus too, ¹¹because many of the Jews were turning away and believing in Jesus because of him.ʲ

w Jn 12, 30.—x Lk 16, 31.—y Jn 12, 19; Mt 26, 3-5; Lk 22, 2; Acts 4, 16.—z 49-50: Jn 18, 13-14.—a Jn 5, 18; 7, 1; Mt 12, 14.—b Jn 2, 13; 5, 1; 6, 4; 18, 28; Ex 19, 10-11.15; Nm 9, 6-14; 19, 12; Dt 16, 6; 2 Chr 30, 1-3.15-18.—c 1-11: Mt 26, 6-13; Mk 14, 3-9.—d 1-2: Jn 11, 1.—e Lk 10, 38-42.—f Jn 11, 2.—g Jn 13, 29.—h Dt 15, 11.—i Jn 11, 19.—j Jn 11, 45.

11, 43: *Cried out in a loud voice:* a dramatization of Jn 5, 28: "the hour is coming when all who are in the tombs will hear his voice."

11, 48: *The Romans will come:* Johannine irony; this is precisely what happened after Jesus' death.

11, 49: *That year:* emphasizes the conjunction of the office and the year. Actually, Caiaphas was high priest A.D. 18-36. The Jews attributed a gift of prophecy, sometimes unconscious, to the high priest.

11, 52: *Dispersed children of God:* perhaps the "other sheep" of Jn 10, 16.

11, 54: Ephraim is usually located about twelve miles northeast of Jerusalem, where the mountains descend into the Jordan valley.

11, 55: *Purify:* prescriptions for purity were based on Ex 19, 10-11.15; Nm 9, 6-14; 2 Chr 30, 1-3.15-18.

12, 1-8: This is probably the same scene of anointing found in Mk 14, 3-9 (see the note there) and Mt 26, 6-13. The anointing by a penitent woman in Lk 7, 36-38 is different. Details from these various episodes have become interchanged.

12, 3: *The feet of Jesus:* so Mk 14, 3; but in Mt 26, 6, Mary anoints Jesus' head as a sign of regal, messianic anointing.

12, 5: *Days' wages:* literally, "denarii." A denarius is a day's wage in Mt 20, 2; see the note on Jn 6, 7.

12, 7: Jesus' response reflects the rabbinical discussion of what was the greatest act of mercy, almsgiving or burying the dead. Those who favored proper burial of the dead thought it an essential condition for sharing in the resurrection.

The Entry into Jerusalem.* [12] [k] On the next day, when the great crowd that had come to the feast heard that Jesus was coming to Jerusalem, [13] they took palm branches* and went out to meet him, and cried out:

"Hosanna!
Blessed is he who comes in the name of the Lord,
[even] the king of Israel." [l]

[14] Jesus found an ass and sat upon it, as is written:

[15] "Fear no more, O daughter Zion;*
see, your king comes, seated upon an ass's colt." [m]

[16] His disciples did not understand this at first, but when Jesus had been glorified they remembered that these things were written about him and that they had done this* for him. [n] [17] * So the crowd that was with him when he called Lazarus from the tomb and raised him from death continued to testify. [18] This was [also] why the crowd went to meet him, because they heard that he had done this sign. [19] So the Pharisees said to one another, "You see that you are gaining nothing. Look, the whole world* has gone after him." [o]

The Coming of Jesus' Hour.* [20] Now there were some Greeks* among those who had come up to worship at the feast. [p] [21] They came to Philip, who was from Bethsaida in Galilee, and asked him, "Sir, we would like to see Jesus." [q] [22] Philip went and told Andrew; then Andrew* and Philip went and told Jesus. [r] [23] Jesus answered them, [s] "The hour has come for the Son of Man to be glorified.* [24] Amen, amen, I say to you, unless a grain of wheat falls to the ground and dies, it remains just a grain of wheat; [t] but if it dies, it produces much fruit.* [25] Whoever loves his life* loses it, and whoever hates his life in this world will preserve it for eternal life. [u] [26] Whoever serves me must follow me, and where I am, there also will my servant be. The Father will honor whoever serves me. [v]

[27] "I am troubled* now. Yet what should I say? 'Father, save me from this hour'? But it was for this purpose that I came to this hour. [w] [28] Father, glorify your name." Then a voice came from heaven, "I have glorified it and will glorify it again." [x] [29] The crowd there heard it and said it was thunder; but others said, "An angel has spoken to him." [y] [30] Jesus answered and said, "This voice did not come for my sake but for yours. [z] [31] Now is the time of judgment on this world; now the ruler of this world* will be driven out. [a] [32] And when I am lifted up from the earth, I will draw everyone to myself." [b] [33] He said this indi-

---

k 12-19: Mt 21, 1-16; Mk 11, 1-10; Lk 19, 28-40.—l Jn 1, 49; Lv 23, 40; 1 Mc 13, 51; 2 Mc 10, 7; Rv 7, 9.—m Is 40, 9; Zec 9, 9.—n Jn 2, 22.—o Jn 11, 47-48.—p Acts 10, 2.—q Jn 1, 44.—r Jn 1, 40.—s Jn 2, 4.—t Is 53, 10-12; 1 Cor 15, 36.—u Mt 10, 39; 16, 25; Mk 8, 35; Lk 9, 24; 17, 33.—v Jn 14, 3; 17, 24; Mt 16, 24; Mk 8, 34; Lk 9, 23.—w Jn 6, 38; 18, 11; Mt 26, 38-39; Mk 14, 34-36; Lk 22, 42; Heb 5, 7-8.—x Jn 2, 11; 17, 5; Dn 4, 31.34.—y Ex 9, 28; 2 Sm 22, 14; Jb 37, 4; Ps 29, 3; Lk 22, 43; Acts 23, 9.—z Jn 11, 42.—a Jn 16, 11; Lk 10, 18; Rv 12, 9.—b Jn 3, 14; 8, 28; Is 52, 13.

12, 12-19: In Jn, the entry into Jerusalem follows the anointing whereas in the synoptics it precedes. In John, the crowd, not the disciples, are responsible for the triumphal procession.

12, 13: *Palm branches:* used to welcome great conquerors; cf 1 Mc 13, 51; 2 Mc 10, 7. They may be related to the *lûlāb,* the twig bundles used at the feast of Tabernacles. *Hosanna:* see Ps 118, 25-26. The Hebrew word means: "(O Lord), grant salvation." *He who comes in the name of the Lord:* referred in Ps 118, 26 to a pilgrim entering the temple gates, but here a title for Jesus (see the notes on Mt 11, 3 and Jn 6, 14; 11, 27). *The king of Israel:* perhaps from Zep 3, 14-15, in connection with the next quotation from Zec 9, 9.

12, 15: *Daughter Zion:* Jerusalem. *Ass's colt:* symbol of peace, as opposed to the war horse.

12,16: *They had done this:* the antecedent of *they* is ambiguous.

12, 17-18: There seem to be two different crowds in these verses. There are some good witnesses to the text that have an-

other reading for v 17: "Then the crowd that was with him began to testify that he had called Lazarus out of the tomb and raised him from the dead."

12, 19: *The whole world:* the sense is that everyone is following Jesus, but John has an ironic play on *world;* he alludes to the universality of salvation (Jn 3, 17; 4, 42).

12, 20-36: This announcement of glorification by death is an illustration of "the whole world" (19) going after him.

12, 20: *Greeks:* not used here in a nationalistic sense. These are probably Gentile proselytes to Judaism; cf Jn 7, 35.

12, 21-22: *Philip . . . Andrew:* the approach is made through disciples who have distinctly Greek names, suggesting that access to Jesus was mediated to the Greek world through his disciples. Philip and Andrew were from Bethsaida (Jn 1, 44); Galileans were mostly bilingual. *See:* here seems to mean "have an interview with."

12, 23: Jesus' response suggests that only after the crucifixion could the gospel encompass both Jew and Gentile.

12, 24: This verse implies that through his death Jesus will be accessible to all. *It remains just a grain of wheat:* this saying is found in the synoptic triple and double traditions (Mk 8, 35 // Mt 16, 25 // Lk 9, 24; Mt 10, 39 // Lk 17, 33). John adds the phrases (25) *in this world* and *for eternal life.*

12, 25: *His life:* the Greek word *psychē* refers to a person's natural life. It does not mean "soul," for Hebrew anthropology did not postulate body/soul dualism in the way that is familiar to us.

12, 27: *I am troubled:* perhaps an allusion to the Gethsemane agony scene of the synoptics.

12, 31: *Ruler of this world:* Satan.

cating the kind of death he would die. [34] So the crowd answered him, "We have heard from the law that the Messiah remains forever.* Then how can you say that the Son of Man must be lifted up? Who is this Son of Man?"[c] [35] Jesus said to them, "The light will be among you only a little while. Walk while you have the light, so that darkness may not overcome you. Whoever walks in the dark does not know where he is going.[d] [36] While you have the light, believe in the light, so that you may become children of the light."[e]

Unbelief and Belief among the Jews.* After he had said this, Jesus left and hid from them. [37] [f] Although he had performed so many signs in their presence they did not believe in him, [38] * in order that the word which Isaiah the prophet spoke might be fulfilled:

> "Lord, who has believed our preaching,
>> to whom has the might of the Lord
>>> been revealed?"[g]

[39] For this reason they could not believe, because again Isaiah said:

[40] "He blinded their eyes
and hardened their heart,
so that they might not see with their eyes
and understand with their heart and be converted,
and I would heal them."[h]

[41] Isaiah said this because he saw his glory* and spoke about him.[i] [42] Nevertheless, many, even among the authorities, believed in him, but because of the Pharisees they did not acknowledge it openly in order not to be expelled from the synagogue.[j] [43] For they preferred human praise to the glory of God.[k]

Recapitulation. [44] Jesus cried out and said, "Whoever believes in me believes not only in me but also in the one who sent me,[l] [45] and whoever sees me sees the one who sent me.[m] [46] I came into the world as light, so that everyone who believes in me might not remain in darkness.[n] [47] And if anyone hears my words and does not observe them, I do not condemn him, for I did not come to condemn the world but to save the world.[o] [48] Whoever rejects me and does not accept my words has something to judge him: the word that I spoke, it will condemn him on the last day,[p] [49] because I did not speak on my own, but the Father

who sent me commanded me what to say and speak.[q] [50] And I know that his commandment is eternal life. So what I say, I say as the Father told me."

III. THE BOOK OF GLORY*

CHAPTER 13

The Washing of the Disciples' Feet.* [1] Before the feast of Passover,* Jesus knew that his hour had come to pass from this world to the Father. He loved his own in the world and he loved them to the end.[r] [2] The devil had already induced* Judas, son of Simon the Iscariot, to hand him over. So, during supper,[s] [3] fully aware that the Father had put everything into his power and that he had come from God and was returning to God,[t] [4] he rose from supper and took off his outer garments. He took a towel and tied it around his waist. [5] * Then

---

c Pss 89, 5; 110, 4; Is 9, 7; Dn 7, 13-14; Rv 20, 1-6.—d Jn 9, 4; 11, 10; Jb 5, 14.—e Eph 5, 8.—f 37-43: Dt 29, 2-4; Mk 4, 11-12; Rom 9—11.—g Is 53, 1; Rom 10, 16.—h Is 6, 9-10; Mt 13, 13-15; Mk 4, 12.—i Jn 5, 39; Is 6, 1.4.—j Jn 9, 22.—k Jn 5, 44.—l Jn 13, 20; 14, 1.—m Jn 14, 7-9.—n Jn 1, 9; 8, 12.—o Jn 3, 17.—p Lk 10, 16; Heb 4, 12.—q Jn 14, 10.31; Dt 18, 18-19.—r Jn 2, 4; 7, 30; 8, 20; Mt 26, 17.45; Mk 14, 12.41; Lk 22, 7.—s Jn 6, 71; 17, 12; Mt 26, 20-21; Mk 14, 17-18; Lk 22, 3.—t Jn 3, 35.

12, 34: There is no passage in the Old Testament that states precisely that *the Messiah remains forever.* Perhaps the closest is Ps 89, 37.

12, 37-50: These verses, on unbelief of the Jews, provide an epilogue to the Book of Signs.

12, 38-41: John gives a historical explanation of the disbelief of the Jewish people, not a psychological one. The Old Testament had to be fulfilled; the disbelief that met Isaiah's message was a foreshadowing of the disbelief that Jesus encountered. In Jn 12, 42 and also in Jn 3, 20, we see that there is no negation of freedom.

12, 41: *His glory:* Isaiah saw the glory of Yahweh enthroned in the heavenly temple, but in John the antecedent of *his* is Jesus.

13, 1—19, 42: The Book of Glory. There is a major break here; the word "sign" is used again only in Jn 20, 30. In this phase of Jesus' return to the Father, the discourses (chs 13-17) precede the traditional narrative of the passion (chs 18-20) to interpret them for the Christian reader. This is the only extended example of esoteric teaching of disciples in John.

13, 1-20: Washing of the disciples' feet. This episode occurs in John at the place of the narration of the institution of the Eucharist in the synoptics. It may be a dramatization of Lk 22, 27: "I am your servant." It is presented as a "model" ("pattern") of the crucifixion. It symbolizes cleansing from sin by sacrificial death.

13, 1: *Before the feast of Passover:* this would be Thursday evening, before the day of preparation; in the synoptics, the Last Supper is a Passover meal taking place, in John's chronology, on Friday evening. *To the end:* or, "completely."

13, 2: *Induced:* literally, "The devil put into the heart that Judas should hand him over."

13, 5: The act of washing another's feet was one that could not be required of the lowliest Jewish slave. It is an allusion to the humiliating death of the crucifixion.

he poured water into a basin and began to wash the disciples' feet [u] and dry them with the towel around his waist. [6] He came to Simon Peter, who said to him, "Master, are you going to wash my feet?" [7] Jesus answered and said to him, "What I am doing, you do not understand now, but you will understand later." [8] Peter said to him, "You will never wash my feet." Jesus answered him, "Unless I wash you, you will have no inheritance with me." [v] [9] Simon Peter said to him, "Master, then not only my feet, but my hands and head as well." [10] Jesus said to him, "Whoever has bathed* has no need except to have his feet washed, for he is clean all over; so you are clean, but not all." [w] [11] For he knew who would betray him; for this reason, he said, "Not all of you are clean." [x]

[12] So when he had washed their feet [and] put his garments back on and reclined at table again, he said to them, "Do you realize what I have done for you? [13] You call me 'teacher' and 'master,' and rightly so, for indeed I am. [y] [14] If I, therefore, the master and teacher, have washed your feet, you ought to wash one another's feet. [15] I have given you a model to follow, so that as I have done for you, you should

---

u 1 Sm 25, 41.—v 2 Sm 20, 1.—w Jn 15, 3.—x Jn 6, 70.—y Mt 23, 8.10.—z Lk 22, 27; 1 Pt 2, 21.—a Jn 15, 20; Mt 10, 24; Lk 6, 40.—b Ps 41, 10.—c Mt 10, 40; Mk 9, 37; Lk 9, 48.—d 21-30: Mt 26, 21-25; Mk 14, 18-21; Lk 22, 21-23.—e Jn 19, 26; 20, 2; 21, 7.20; Mt 10, 37.—f Jn 21, 20.—g Jn 13, 2; Lk 22, 3.—h Jn 12, 5-6.—i Jn 17, 1-5.—j Jn 7, 33; 8, 21.—k Jn 15, 12-13.17; Lv 19, 18; 1 Thes 4, 9; 1 Jn 2, 7-10; 3, 23; 2 Jn 5.

13, 10: *Bathed:* many have suggested that this passage is a symbolic reference to baptism. The Greek root involved is used in baptismal contexts in 1 Cor 6, 11; Eph 5, 26; Ti 3, 5; Heb 10, 22.

13, 16: *Messenger:* the Greek has *apostolos,* the only occurrence of the term in John. It is not used in the technical sense here.

13, 23: *The one whom Jesus loved:* also mentioned in Jn 19, 26; 20, 2; 21, 7. A disciple, called "another disciple" or "the other disciple," is mentioned in Jn 18, 15 and Jn 20, 2; in the latter reference he is identified with the disciple whom Jesus loved. There is also an unnamed disciple in Jn 1, 35-40; see the note on Jn 1, 37.

13, 26: *Morsel:* probably the bitter herb dipped in salt water.

13, 31—17, 26: Two farewell discourses and a prayer. These seem to be Johannine compositions, including sayings of Jesus at the Last Supper and on other occasions, modeled on similar farewell discourses in Greek literature and the Old Testament (of Moses, Joshua, David).

13, 31-38: Introduction:departure and return. Terms of coming and going predominate. These verses form an introduction to the last discourse of Jesus, which extends through chs 14 to 17. In it John has collected Jesus' words to *his own* (Jn 13, 1). There are indications that separate speeches have been fused together, e.g., in Jn 14, 31 and Jn 17, 1.

13, 34: *I give you a new commandment:* this puts Jesus on a par with Yahweh. The commandment itself is not new; cf Lv 19, 18 and the note there.

---

also do. [z] [16] Amen, amen, I say to you, no slave is greater than his master nor any messenger* greater than the one who sent him. [a] [17] If you understand this, blessed are you if you do it. [18] I am not speaking of all of you. I know those whom I have chosen. But so that the scripture might be fulfilled, 'The one who ate my food has raised his heel against me.' [b] [19] From now on I am telling you before it happens, so that when it happens you may believe that I AM. [20] Amen, amen, I say to you, whoever receives the one I send receives me, and whoever receives me receives the one who sent me." [c]

Announcement of Judas' Betrayal. [d] [21] When he had said this, Jesus was deeply troubled and testified, "Amen, amen, I say to you, one of you will betray me." [22] The disciples looked at one another, at a loss as to whom he meant. [23] One of his disciples, the one whom Jesus loved,* was reclining at Jesus' side. [e] [24] So Simon Peter nodded to him to find out whom he meant. [25] He leaned back against Jesus' chest and said to him, "Master, who is it?" [f] [26] Jesus answered, "It is the one to whom I hand the morsel* after I have dipped it." So he dipped the morsel and [took it and] handed it to Judas, son of Simon the Iscariot. [27] After he took the morsel, Satan entered him. So Jesus said to him, "What you are going to do, do quickly." [g] [28] [Now] none of those reclining at table realized why he said this to him. [29] Some thought that since Judas kept the money bag, Jesus had told him, "Buy what we need for the feast," or to give something to the poor. [h] [30] So he took the morsel and left at once. And it was night.

The New Commandment. [31] * When he had left, Jesus said,* "Now is the Son of Man glorified, and God is glorified in him. [32] [If God is glorified in him,] God will also glorify him in himself, and he will glorify him at once. [i] [33] My children, I will be with you only a little while longer. You will look for me, and as I told the Jews, 'Where I go you cannot come,' so now I say it to you. [j] [34] I give you a new commandment:* love one another. As I have loved you, so you also should love one another. [k] [35] This is how all will know that you are my disciples, if you have love for one another."

Peter's Denial Predicted. [36] Simon Peter said to him, "Master, where are you going?" Jesus answered [him], "Where I am going, you cannot follow me now, though you will follow later." *l* ³⁷Peter said to him, "Master, why can't I follow you now? I will lay down my life for you." ³⁸Jesus answered, "Will you lay down your life for me? Amen, amen, I say to you, the cock will not crow before you deny me three times. *m*

CHAPTER 14

Last Supper Discourses. ¹ * "Do not let your hearts be troubled. You have faith* in God; have faith also in me. ²In my Father's house there are many dwelling places. If there were not, would I have told you that I am going to prepare a place for you? ³And if I go and prepare a place for you, I will come back again* and take you to myself, so that where I am you also may be. *n* ⁴Where [I] am going you know the way." * ⁵Thomas said to him, "Master, we do not know where you are going; how can we know the way?" ⁶Jesus said to him, "I am the way and the truth* and the life. No one comes to the Father except through me. *o* ⁷If you know me, then you will also know my Father.* From now on you do know him and have seen him." *p* ⁸Philip said to him, "Master, show us the Father,* and that will be enough for us." *q* ⁹Jesus said to him, "Have I been with you for so long a time and you still do not know me, Philip? Whoever has seen me has seen the Father.

How can you say, 'Show us the Father'? *r* ¹⁰Do you not believe that I am in the Father and the Father is in me? The words that I speak to you I do not speak on my own. The Father who dwells in me is doing his works. *s* ¹¹Believe me that I am in the Father and the Father is in me, or else, believe because of the works themselves. *t* ¹²Amen, amen, I say to you, whoever believes in me will do the works that I do, and will do greater ones than these, because I am going to the Father. *u* ¹³And whatever you ask in my name, I will do, so that the Father may be glorified in the Son. *v* ¹⁴If you ask anything of me in my name, I will do it.

The Advocate. ¹⁵"If you love me, you will keep my commandments. *w* ¹⁶And I will ask the Father, and he will give you another Advocate* to be with you always, *x* ¹⁷the Spirit of truth,* which the world cannot accept, because it neither sees nor knows it. But you know it, because it remains with you, and will be in you. *y* ¹⁸I will not leave you orphans; I will come to you.* ¹⁹In a little while the world will no longer see me, but you will see me, because I live and you will live. *z* ²⁰On that day you will realize that I am in my Father and you are in me and I in you. *a* ²¹Whoever has my commandments and observes them is the one who loves me. And whoever loves me will be loved by my Father, and I will love him and reveal myself to him." *b* ²²Judas, not the Iscariot,* said to him, "Master, [then] what happened that you will reveal yourself to us and not to the world?" *c*

---

l Mk 14, 27; Lk 22, 23.—m Jn 18, 27; Mt 26, 33-35; Mk 14, 29-31; Lk 22, 33-34.—n Jn 12, 26; 17, 24; 1 Jn 2, 28.—o Jn 8, 31-47.—p Jn 8, 19; 12, 45.—q Ex 24, 9-10; 33, 18.—r Jn 1, 18; 10, 30; 12, 45; 2 Cor 4, 4; Col 1, 15; Heb 1, 3.—s Jn 1, 1; 10, 37-38; 12, 49.—t Jn 10, 38.—u Jn 1, 50; 5, 20.—v Jn 15, 7.16; 16, 23-24; Mt 7, 7-11.—w Jn 15, 10; Dt 6, 4-9; Ps 119; Wis 6, 18; 1 Jn 5, 3; 2 Jn 6.—x Jn 15, 26; Lk 24, 49; 1 Jn 2, 1.—y Jn 16, 13; Mt 28, 20; 2 Jn 1-2.—z Jn 16, 16.—a Jn 10, 38; 17, 21; Is 2, 17; 4, 2-3.—b Jn 16, 27; 1 Jn 2, 5; 3, 24.—c Jn 7, 4; Acts 10, 40-41.

14, 1-31: Jesus' departure and return. This section is a dialogue marked off by a literary inclusion in vv 1 and 27: "Do not let your hearts be troubled."

14, 1: *You have faith:* could also be imperative: "Have faith."

14, 3: *Come back again:* a rare Johannine reference to the parousia; cf 1 Jn 2, 28.

14, 4: *The way:* here, of Jesus himself; also a designation of Christianity in Acts 9, 2; 19, 9.23; 22, 4; 24, 14.22.

14, 6: *The truth:* in John, the divinely revealed reality of the Father manifested in the person and works of Jesus. The possession of truth confers knowledge and liberation from sin (Jn 8, 32).

14, 7: An alternative reading, "If you knew me, then you would have known my Father also," would be a rebuke, as in Jn 8, 19.

14, 8: *Show us the Father:* Philip is pictured asking for a theophany like Ex 24, 9-10; 33,18.

14, 16: *Another Advocate:* Jesus is the first advocate (paraclete); see 1 Jn 2, 1, where Jesus is an advocate in the sense of intercessor in heaven. The Greek term derives from legal terminology for an advocate or defense attorney, and can mean spokesman, mediator, intercessor, comforter, consoler, although no one of these terms encompasses the meaning in John. The Paraclete in John is a teacher, a witness to Jesus, and a prosecutor of the world, who represents the continued presence on earth of the Jesus who has returned to the Father.

14, 17: *The Spirit of truth:* this term is also used at Qumran, where it is a moral force put into a person by God, as opposed to the spirit of perversity. It is more personal in John; it will teach the realities of the new order (26), and testify to the truth (6). While it has been customary to use masculine personal pronouns in English for the Advocate, the Greek word for "spirit" is neuter, and the Greek text and manuscript variants fluctuate between masculine and neuter pronouns.

14, 18: *I will come to you:* indwelling, not parousia.

14, 22: *Judas, not the Iscariot:* probably not the brother of Jesus in Mk 6, 3 // Mt 13, 55 or the apostle named Jude in Lk 6, 16, but Thomas (see the note on Jn 11, 16), although other readings have "Judas the Cananean."

Jn

[23] Jesus answered and said to him, "Whoever loves me will keep my word, and my Father will love him, and we will come to him and make our dwelling with him. [d] [24] Whoever does not love me does not keep my words; yet the word you hear is not mine but that of the Father who sent me.

[25] "I have told you this while I am with you. [26] The Advocate, the holy Spirit that the Father will send in my name—he will teach you everything and remind you of all that [I] told you. [e] [27] Peace* I leave with you; my peace I give to you. Not as the world gives do I give it to you. Do not let your hearts be troubled or afraid. [f] [28] You heard me tell you, 'I am going away and I will come back to you.' [g] If you loved me, you would rejoice that I am going to the Father; for the Father is greater than I.* [29] And now I have told you this before it happens, so that when it happens you may believe. [h] [30] I will no longer speak much with you, for the ruler of the world* is coming. He has no power over me, [31] but the world must know that I love the Father and that I do just as the Father has commanded me. Get up, let us go. [i]

CHAPTER 15

The Vine and the Branches. [1] * "I am the true vine,* and my Father is the vine grower. [j] [2] He takes away every branch in me that does not bear fruit, and everyone that does he prunes* so that it bears more fruit. [3] You are already pruned because of the word that I spoke to you. [k] [4] Remain in me, as I remain in you. Just as a branch cannot bear fruit on its own unless it remains on the vine, so neither can you unless you remain in me. [5] I am the vine, you are the branches. Whoever remains in me and I in him will bear much fruit, because without me you can do nothing. [6] [l] Anyone who does not remain in me will be thrown out like a branch and wither; people will gather them and throw them into a fire and they will be burned.* [7] If you remain in me and my words remain in you, ask for whatever you want and it will be done for you. [m] [8] By this is my Father glorified, that you bear much fruit and become my disciples. [n] [9] As the Father loves me, so I also love you. Remain in my love. [o] [10] If you keep my commandments, you will remain in my love, just as I have kept my Father's commandments and remain in his love. [p]

[11] "I have told you this so that my joy might be in you and your joy might be complete. [q] [12] This is my commandment: love one another as I love you. [r] [13] No one has greater love than this,[s] to lay down one's life for one's friends.* [14] You are my friends if you do what I command you. [15] I no longer call you slaves, because a slave does not know what his master is doing. I have called you friends,* because I have told you everything I have heard from my Father. [t] [16] It was not you who chose me, but I who chose you and appointed you to go and bear fruit that will remain, so that whatever you ask the Father in my name he may give you. [u] [17] This I command you: love one another. [v]

The World's Hatred.* [18] "If the world hates you, realize that it hated me first. [w] [19] If you belonged to the world, the world

d Rv 3, 20.—e Jn 15, 26; 16, 7.13-14; Ps 51, 13; Is 63, 10.—f Jn 16, 33; Eph 2, 14-18.—g Jn 8, 40.—h Jn 13, 19; 16, 4.—i Jn 6, 38.—j Ps 80, 9-17; Is 5, 1-7; Jer 2, 21; Ez 15, 2; 17, 5-10; 19, 10.—k Jn 13, 10.—l Ez 15, 6-7; 19, 10-14.—m Jn 14, 13; Mt 7, 7; Mk 11, 24; 1 Jn 5, 14.—n Mt 5, 16.—o Jn 17, 23.—p Jn 8, 29; 14, 15.—q Jn 16, 22; 17, 13.—r Jn 13, 34.—s Rom 5, 6-8; 1 Jn 3, 16.—t Dt 34, 5; Jos 24, 29; 2 Chr 20, 7; Ps 89, 21; Is 41, 8; Rom 8, 15; Gal 4, 7; Jas 2, 23.—u Jn 14, 13; Dt 7, 6.—v Jn 14, 13; 34; 1 Jn 3, 23; 4, 21.—w Jn 7, 7; 14, 17; Mt 10, 22; 24, 9; Mk 13, 13; Lk 6, 22; 1 Jn 3, 13.

14, 27: *Peace:* the traditional Hebrew salutation *šālôm;* but Jesus' "Shalom" is a gift of salvation, connoting the bounty of messianic blessing.

14, 28: *The Father is greater than I:* because he *sent, gave,* etc., and Jesus is "a man who has told you the truth that I heard from God" (Jn 8, 40).

14, 30: *The ruler of the world:* Satan; cf Jn 12, 31; 16, 11.

15, 1—16, 4: Discourse on the union of Jesus with his disciples. His words become a monologue and go beyond the immediate crisis of the departure of Jesus.

15, 1-17: Like Jn 10, 1-5, this passage resembles a parable. Israel is spoken of as a vineyard at Is 5, 1-7; Mt 21, 33-46 and as a vine at Ps 80, 9-17; Jer 2, 21; Ez 15, 2; 17, 5-10; 19, 10; Hos 10, 1. The identification of the vine as the Son of Man in Ps 80, 16, and Wisdom's description of herself as a vine in Sir 24, 17, are further background for portrayal of Jesus by this figure. There may be secondary eucharistic symbolism here; cf Mk 14, 25, "the fruit of the vine."

15, 2: *Takes away . . . prunes:* in Greek there is a play on two related verbs.

15, 6: Branches were cut off and dried on the wall of the vineyard for later use as fuel.

15, 13: *For one's friends:* or: "those whom one loves." In 9-13a, the words for love are related to the Greek *agapaō.* In 13b-15, the words for love are related to the Greek *phileō.* For John, the two roots seem synonymous and mean "to love"; cf also Jn 21, 15-17. The word *philos* is used here.

15, 15: *Slaves . . . friends:* in the Old Testament, Moses (Dt 34, 5), Joshua (Jos 24, 29), and David (Ps 89, 21) were called "servants" or "slaves of Yahweh"; only Abraham (Is 41, 8; 2 Chr 20, 7; cf Jas 2, 23) was called a "friend of God."

15, 18—16, 4: The hostile reaction of the world. There are synoptic parallels, predicting persecution, especially at Mt 10, 17-25; 24, 9-10.

would love its own; but because you do not belong to the world, and I have chosen you out of the world, the world hates you.ˣ ²⁰Remember the word I spoke to you,* 'No slave is greater than his master.' If they persecuted me, they will also persecute you. If they kept my word, they will also keep yours.ʸ ²¹And they will do all these things to you on account of my name,* because they do not know the one who sent me.ᶻ ²²If I had not come and spoken* to them, they would have no sin; but as it is they have no excuse for their sin.ᵃ ²³Whoever hates me also hates my Father.ᵇ ²⁴If I had not done works among them that no one else ever did, they would not have sin; but as it is, they have seen and hated both me and my Father.ᶜ ²⁵But in order that the word written in their law* might be fulfilled, 'They hated me without cause.'ᵈ

²⁶"When the Advocate comes whom I will send* you from the Father, the Spirit of truth that proceeds from the Father, he will testify to me.ᵉ ²⁷And you also testify, because you have been with me from the beginning.ᶠ

CHAPTER 16

¹"I have told you this so that you may not fall away. ²They will expel you from the synagogues; in fact, the hour* is coming when everyone who kills you will think he is offering worship to God.ᵍ ³They will do this because they have not known either the Father or me.ʰ ⁴I have told you this so that when their hour comes you may remember that I told you.ⁱ

Jesus' Departure; Coming of the Advocate. * "I did not tell you this from the beginning, because I was with you. ⁵But now I am going to the one who sent me, and not one of you asks me,* 'Where are you going?'ʲ ⁶But because I told you this, grief has filled your hearts. ⁷But I tell you the truth, it is better for you that I go. For if I do not go, the Advocate will not come to you.ᵏ But if I go, I will send him to you. ⁸ *And when he comes he will convict the world in regard to sin and righteousness and condemnation: ⁹sin, because they do not believe in me;ˡ ¹⁰righteousness, because I am going to the Father and you will no longer see me; ¹¹condemnation, because the ruler of this world has been condemned.ᵐ

¹²"I have much more to tell you, but you cannot bear it now. ¹³But when he comes, the Spirit of truth, he will guide you to all truth.ⁿ He will not speak on his own, but he will speak what he hears, and will declare to you the things that are coming.* ¹⁴He will glorify me, because he will take from what is mine and declare it to you. ¹⁵Everything that the Father has is mine; for this reason I told you that he will take from what is mine and declare it to you.

¹⁶"A little while and you will no longer see me, and again a little while later and you will see me."ᵒ ¹⁷So some of his disciples said to one another, "What does this mean that he is saying to us, 'A little while and you will not see me, and again a little while and you will see me,' and 'Because I am going to the Father'?" ¹⁸So they said, "What is this 'little while' [of which he

---

x Jn 17, 14-16; 1 Jn 4, 5.—y Jn 13, 16; Mt 10, 24.—z Jn 8, 19; 16, 3.—a Jn 8, 21.24; 9, 41.—b Jn 5, 23; Lk 10, 16; 1 Jn 2, 23.—c Jn 3, 2; 9, 32; Dt 4, 32-33.—d Ps 35, 19; 69, 4.—e Jn 14, 16.26; Mt 10, 19-20.—f Lk 1, 2; Acts 1, 8.—g Jn 9, 22; 12, 42; Mt 10, 17; Lk 21, 12; Acts 26, 11.—h Jn 15, 21.—i Jn 13, 19; 14, 29.—j Jn 7, 33; 13, 36; 14, 5.—k Jn 7, 39; 14, 16-17.26; 15, 26.—l Jn 8, 21-24; 15, 22.—m Jn 12, 31.—n Jn 14, 17.26; 15, 26; Pss 25, 5; 143, 10; 1 Jn 2, 27; Rv 7, 17.—o Jn 7, 33; 14, 19.

15, 20: *The word I spoke to you:* a reference to Jn 13, 16.

15, 21: *On account of my name:* the idea of persecution for Jesus' name is frequent in the New Testament (Mt 10, 22; 24, 9; Acts 9, 14). For John, association with Jesus' name implies union with Jesus.

15, 22.24: Jesus' words *(spoken)* and deeds *(works)* are the great motives of credibility. *They have seen and hated:* probably means that they have seen his works and still have hated; but the Greek can be read: "have seen both me and my Father and still have hated both me and my Father." *Works . . . that no one else ever did:* so Yahweh in Dt 4, 32-33.

15, 25: *In their law:* law is here used as a larger concept than the Pentateuch, for the reference is to Ps 35, 19 or Ps 69, 5. See the notes on Jn 10, 34; 12, 34. *Their* law reflects the argument of the church with the synagogue.

15, 26: *Whom I will send:* in Jn 14, 16.26, the Paraclete is to be sent by the Father, at the request of Jesus. Here the Spirit comes from both Jesus and the Father in mission; there is no reference here to the eternal procession of the Spirit.

16, 2: *Hour:* of persecution, not Jesus' "hour" (see the note on Jn 2, 4).

16, 4b-33: A duplicate of Jn 14, 1-31 on departure and return.

16, 5: *Not one of you asks me:* the difficulty of reconciling this with Simon Peter's question in Jn 13, 36 and Thomas' words in Jn 14, 5 strengthens the supposition that the last discourse has been made up of several collections of Johannine material.

16, 8-11: These verses illustrate the forensic character of the Paraclete's role: in the forum of the disciples' conscience he prosecutes the world. He leads believers to see (a) that the basic sin was and is refusal to believe in Jesus; (b) that, although Jesus was found guilty and apparently died in disgrace, in reality righteousness has triumphed, for Jesus has returned to his Father; (c) finally, that it is *the ruler of this world,* Satan, who has been condemned through Jesus' death (Jn 12, 32).

16, 13: *Declare to you the things that are coming:* not a reference to new predictions about the future, but interpretation of what has already occurred or been said.

speaks]? We do not know what he means." [19] Jesus knew that they wanted to ask him, so he said to them, "Are you discussing with one another what I said, 'A little while and you will not see me, and again a little while and you will see me'? [20] Amen, amen, I say to you, you will weep and mourn, while the world rejoices; you will grieve, but your grief will become joy. [p] [21] When a woman is in labor, she is in anguish because her hour has arrived; but when she has given birth to a child, she no longer remembers the pain because of her joy that a child has been born into the world. [q] [22] So you also are now in anguish. But I will see you again, and your hearts will rejoice, and no one will take your joy away from you. [r] [23] On that day you will not question me about anything. Amen, amen, I say to you, whatever you ask the Father in my name he will give you. [s] [24] Until now you have not asked anything in my name; ask and you will receive, so that your joy may be complete.

[25] [t] "I have told you this in figures of speech. The hour is coming when I will no longer speak to you in figures but I will tell you clearly about the Father.* [26] On that day you will ask in my name, and I do not tell you that I will ask the Father for you. [u] [27] For the Father himself loves you, because you have loved me and have come to believe that I came from God. [28] I came from the Father and have come into the world. Now I am leaving the world and going back to the Father." [v] [29] His disciples said, "Now you are talking plainly, and not in any figure of speech. [30] Now we realize that you know everything and that you do not need to have anyone question you. Because of this we believe that you came from God."* [31] Jesus answered them, "Do you believe now? [32] Behold, the hour is coming and has arrived when each of you will be scattered* to his own home and you will leave me alone. But I am not alone, because the Father is with me. [w] [33] I have told you this so that you might have peace in me. In the world you will have trouble, but take courage, I have conquered the world." [x]

CHAPTER 17

The Prayer of Jesus.* [1] When Jesus had said this, he raised his eyes to heaven* and said, "Father, the hour has come. Give glory to your son, so that your son may glorify you, [y] [2] just as you gave him authority over all people, [z] so that he may give eternal life to all you gave him.* [3] Now this is eternal life, [a] that they should know you, the only true God, and the one whom you sent, Jesus Christ.* [4] I glorified you on earth by accomplishing the work that you gave me to do. [5] Now glorify me, Father, with you, with the glory that I had with you before the world began. [b]

[6] "I revealed your name* to those whom you gave me out of the world. They belonged to you, and you gave them to me, and they have kept your word. [7] Now they know that everything you gave me is from you, [8] because the words you gave to me I have given to them, and they accepted them and truly understood that I came from you, and they have believed that you sent me. [9] I pray for them. I do not pray for the world but for the ones you have given me, because they are yours, [c] [10] and everything of mine is yours and everything of yours is mine, and I have been glorified in them. [d] [11] And now I will no longer be in

p Ps 126, 6.—q Is 26, 17-18; Jer 31, 13; Mic 4, 9.—r Jn 14, 19; 15, 11; 20, 20.—s Jn 14, 13.—t Mt 13, 34-35.—u Jn 14, 13.—v Jn 1, 1.—w Jn 8, 29; Zec 13, 7; Mt 26, 31; Mk 14, 27.—x Jn 14, 27.—y Jn 13, 31.—z Jn 3, 35; Mt 28, 18.—a Jn 1, 17; Wis 14, 7; 15, 3; 1 Jn 5, 20.—b Jn 1, 1.2; 12, 28; Phil 2, 6.9-11.—c Jn 17, 20.—d Jn 16, 15; 2 Thes 1, 10.12.

16, 25: See the note on Jn 10, 6. Here, possibly a reference to Jn 15, 1-16 or Jn 16, 21.

16, 30: The reference is seemingly to the fact that Jesus could anticipate their question in v 19. The disciples naively think they have the full understanding that is the climax of "the hour" of Jesus' death, resurrection, and ascension (25), but the only part of the hour that is at hand for them is their share in the passion (32).

16, 32: *You will be scattered:* cf Mk 14, 27 and Mt 26, 31, where both cite Zec 13, 7 about the sheep being dispersed.

17, 1-26: Climax of the last discourse(s). Since the sixteenth century, this chapter has been called the "high priestly prayer" of Jesus. He speaks as intercessor, with words addressed directly to the Father and not to the disciples, who supposedly only overhear. Yet the prayer is one of petition, for immediate (6-19) and future (20-21) disciples. Many phrases reminiscent of the Lord's Prayer occur. Although still in the world (13), Jesus looks on his earthly ministry as a thing of the past (4.12). Whereas Jesus has up to this time stated that the disciples could follow him (Jn 13, 33.36), now he wishes them to be with him in union with the Father (12-14).

17, 1: The action of looking up to heaven and the address *Father* are typical of Jesus at prayer; cf Jn 11, 41 and Lk 11, 2.

17, 2: Another possible interpretation is to treat the first line of the verse as parenthetical and the second as an appositive to the clause that ends v 1: *so that your son may glorify you (just as . . . all people), so that he may give eternal life. . . .*

17, 3: This verse was clearly added in the editing of the gospel as a reflection on the preceding verse; Jesus nowhere else refers to himself as Jesus Christ.

17, 6: *I revealed your name:* perhaps the name *I AM;* cf Jn 8, 24.28.58; 13, 19.

the world, but they are in the world, while I am coming to you. Holy Father, keep them in your name that you have given me, so that they may be one just as we are. [12] When I was with them I protected them in your name that you gave me, and I guarded them, and none of them was lost except the son of destruction, in order that the scripture might be fulfilled. [e] [13] But now I am coming to you. I speak this in the world so that they may share my joy completely. [f] [14] I gave them your word, and the world hated them, because they do not belong to the world any more than I belong to the world. [g] [15] I do not ask that you take them out of the world [h] but that you keep them from the evil one.* [16] They do not belong to the world any more than I belong to the world. [17] Consecrate them in the truth. Your word is truth. [i] [18] As you sent me into the world, so I sent them into the world. [j] [19] And I consecrate myself for them, so that they also may be consecrated in truth.

[20] "I pray not only for them, but also for those who will believe in me through their word, [21] so that they may all be one, as you, Father, are in me and I in you, that they also may be in us, that the world may believe that you sent me. [k] [22] And I have given them the glory you gave me, so that they may be one, as we are one, [23] I in them and you in me, that they may be brought to perfection as one, that the world may know that you sent me, and that you loved them even as you loved me. [24] Father, they are your gift to me. I wish that where I am* they also may be with me, that they may see my glory that you gave me, because you loved me before the foundation of the world. [l] [25] Righteous Father, the world also does not know you, but I know you, and they know that you sent me. [m] [26] I made known to them your name and I will make it known,* that the love with which you loved me may be in them and I in them."

CHAPTER 18

Jesus Arrested.* [1] When he had said this, Jesus went out* with his disciples across the Kidron valley to where there was a garden, into which he and his disciples entered. [n] [2] Judas his betrayer also knew the place, because Jesus had often met there with his disciples. [3] So Judas got a band of soldiers* and guards from the

chief priests and the Pharisees and went there with lanterns, torches, and weapons. [o] [4] Jesus, knowing everything that was going to happen to him, went out and said to them, "Whom are you looking for?" [5] They answered him, "Jesus the Nazorean."* He said to them, "I AM." Judas his betrayer was also with them. [6] When he said to them, "I AM," they turned away and fell to the ground. [7] So he again asked them, "Whom are you looking for?" They said, "Jesus the Nazorean." [8] Jesus answered, "I told you that I AM. So if you are looking for me, let these men go." [9] [p] This was to fulfill what he had said, "I have not lost any of those you gave me."* [10] Then Simon Peter, who had a sword, drew it, struck the high priest's slave, and cut off his right ear. The slave's name was Malchus.* [11] Jesus said to Peter, "Put your sword into its scabbard. Shall I not drink the cup* that the Father gave me?" [q]

[12] [r] So the band of soldiers, the tribune, and the Jewish guards seized Jesus, bound

---

e Jn 13, 18; 18, 9; Ps 41, 10; Mt 26, 24; Acts 1, 16.—f Jn 15, 11.—g Jn 15, 19.—h Mt 6, 13; 2 Thes 3, 3; 1 Jn 5, 18.—i 1 Pt 1, 22.—j Jn 20, 21-22.—k Jn 10, 30; 14, 10-11.20.—l Jn 14, 3; 1 Thes 4, 17.—m Jn 1, 10.—n 2 Sm 15, 23; Mt 26, 30.36; Mk 14, 26.32; Lk 22, 39.—o Mt 26, 47-51; Mk 14, 43-44; Lk 22, 47.—p Jn 6, 39; 10, 28; 17, 12.—q Mt 20, 22; 26, 39; Mk 10, 38; Lk 22, 42.—r 12-14: Mt 26, 57-58; Mk 14, 53-54; Lk 22, 54-55.

17, 15: Note the resemblance to the petition of the Lord's Prayer, "deliver us from the evil one." Both probably refer to the devil rather than to abstract evil.

17, 24: *Where I am:* Jesus prays for the believers ultimately to join him in heaven. Then they will not see his glory as in a mirror but clearly (2 Cor 3, 18; 1 Jn 3, 2).

17, 26: *I will make it known:* through the Advocate.

18, 1-14: John does not mention the agony in the garden and the kiss of Judas, nor does he identify the place as Gethsemane or the Mount of Olives.

18, 1: *Jesus went out:* see Jn 14, 31, where it seems he is leaving the supper room. *Kidron valley:* literally, "the winter-flowing Kidron"; this wadi has water only during the winter rains.

18, 3: *Band of soldiers:* seems to refer to Roman troops, either the full cohort of 600 men (1/10 of a legion), or more likely the maniple of 200 under their tribune (12). In this case, John is hinting at Roman collusion in the action against Jesus before he was brought to Pilate. The lanterns and torches may be symbolic of the hour of darkness.

18, 5: *Nazorean:* the form found in Mt 26, 71 (see the note on Mt 2, 23) is here used, not *Nazarene* of Mark. *I AM:* or "I am he," but probably intended by the evangelist as an expression of divinity (cf their appropriate response in 6); see the note on Jn 8, 24. John sets the confusion of the arresting party against the background of Jesus' divine majesty.

18, 9: The citation may refer to Jn 6, 39; Jn 10, 28; or Jn 17, 12.

18, 10: Only John gives the names of the two antagonists; both John and Luke mention the right ear.

18, 11: The theme of the cup is found in the synoptic account of the agony (Mk 14, 36 and parallels).

Jn

him, [13] and brought him to Annas* first. He was the father-in-law of Caiaphas, who was high priest that year.[s] [14] It was Caiaphas who had counseled the Jews that it was better that one man should die rather than the people.[t]

Peter's First Denial.[u] [15] Simon Peter and another disciple* followed Jesus. Now the other disciple was known to the high priest, and he entered the courtyard of the high priest with Jesus. [16] But Peter stood at the gate outside. So the other disciple, the acquaintance of the high priest, went out and spoke to the gatekeeper and brought Peter in. [17] Then the maid who was the gatekeeper said to Peter, "You are not one of this man's disciples, are you?" He said, "I am not." [18] Now the slaves and the guards were standing around a charcoal fire that they had made, because it was cold, and were warming themselves. Peter was also standing there keeping warm.

The Inquiry before Annas.[v] [19] The high priest questioned Jesus about his disciples and about his doctrine. [20] Jesus answered him, "I have spoken publicly to the world.

---

s Lk 3, 2.—t Jn 11, 49-50.—u 15-18: Mt 26, 58.69-70; Mk 14, 54.66-68; Lk 22, 54-57.—v 19-24: Mt 26, 59-66; Mk 14, 55-64; Lk 22, 66-71.—w Jn 6, 59; 7, 14.26; Is 48, 16; Mt 26, 55; Mk 4, 23; Lk 19, 47; 22, 53.—x Acts 23, 2.—y Mt 26, 57.— z 25-27: Mt 26, 71-75; Mk 14, 69-72; Lk 22, 58-62.—a 28-38a: Mt 27, 1-2.11-25; Mk 15, 1-5; Lk 23, 1-5.—b Jn 3, 14; 8, 28; 12, 32-33.—c Jn 1, 11.—d Jn 1, 10; 8, 23.

18, 13: *Annas:* only John mentions an inquiry before Annas; cf Jn 18, 16.19-24; see the note on Lk 3, 2. It is unlikely that this nighttime interrogation before Annas is the same as the trial before Caiaphas placed by Matthew and Mark at night and by Luke in the morning.

18, 15-16: *Another disciple . . . the other disciple:* see the note on Jn 13, 23.

18, 20: *I have always taught . . . in the temple area:* cf Mk 14, 49 for a similar statement.

18, 24: *Caiaphas:* see Mt 26, 3.57; Lk 3, 2; and the notes there. John may leave room here for the trial before Caiaphas described in the synoptic gospels.

18, 27: Cockcrow was the third Roman division of the night, lasting from midnight to 3 a.m.

18, 28: *Praetorium:* see the note on Mt 27, 27. *Morning:* literally, "the early hour," or fourth Roman division of the night, 3 to 6 a.m. *The Passover:* the synoptic gospels give the impression that the Thursday night supper was the Passover meal (Mk 14, 12); for John that meal is still to be eaten Friday night.

18, 31: *We do not have the right to execute anyone:* only John gives this reason for their bringing Jesus to Pilate. Jewish sources are not clear on the competence of the Sanhedrin at this period to sentence and to execute for political crimes.

18, 32: The Jewish punishment for blasphemy was stoning (Lv 24, 16). In coming to the Romans to ensure that Jesus would be crucified, the Jewish authorities fulfilled his prophecy that he would be *exalted* (Jn 3, 14; 12, 32-33). There is some historical evidence, however, for Jews crucifying Jews.

18, 37: *You say I am a king:* see Mt 26, 64 for a similar response to the high priest. It is at best a reluctant affirmative.

I have always taught in a synagogue or in the temple area* where all the Jews gather, and in secret I have said nothing.[w] [21] Why ask me? Ask those who heard me what I said to them. They know what I said." [22] When he had said this, one of the temple guards standing there struck Jesus and said, "Is this the way you answer the high priest?"[x] [23] Jesus answered him, "If I have spoken wrongly, testify to the wrong; but if I have spoken rightly, why do you strike me?" [24] Then Annas sent him bound to Caiaphas* the high priest.[y]

Peter Denies Jesus Again.[z] [25] Now Simon Peter was standing there keeping warm. And they said to him, "You are not one of his disciples, are you?" He denied it and said, "I am not." [26] One of the slaves of the high priest, a relative of the one whose ear Peter had cut off, said, "Didn't I see you in the garden with him?" [27] Again Peter denied it. And immediately the cock crowed.*

The Trial before Pilate. [28] [a] Then they brought Jesus from Caiaphas to the praetorium.* It was morning. And they themselves did not enter the praetorium, in order not to be defiled so that they could eat the Passover. [29] So Pilate came out to them and said, "What charge do you bring [against] this man?" [30] They answered and said to him, "If he were not a criminal, we would not have handed him over to you." [31] At this, Pilate said to them, "Take him yourselves, and judge him according to your law." The Jews answered him, "We do not have the right to execute anyone,"* [32] in order that the word of Jesus might be fulfilled that he said indicating the kind of death[b] he would die.* [33] So Pilate went back into the praetorium and summoned Jesus and said to him, "Are you the King of the Jews?" [34] Jesus answered, "Do you say this on your own or have others told you about me?" [35] Pilate answered, "I am not a Jew, am I? Your own nation and the chief priests handed you over to me. What have you done?"[c] [36] Jesus answered, "My kingdom does not belong to this world. If my kingdom did belong to this world, my attendants [would] be fighting to keep me from being handed over to the Jews. But as it is, my kingdom is not here."[d] [37] So Pilate said to him, "Then you are a king?" Jesus answered, "You say I am a king.* For this I was born and for this I came into the world, to testify to the truth. Everyone who belongs to the truth listens to my voice." *e* [38] Pilate said to him, "What is truth?"

When he had said this, he again went out to the Jews and said to them, "I find no guilt in him. *f* [39] But you have a custom that I release one prisoner to you at Passover.* Do you want me to release to you the King of the Jews?" [40] They cried out again, "Not this one but Barabbas!"* Now Barabbas was a revolutionary.

CHAPTER 19

[1] *g* Then Pilate took Jesus and had him scourged.* [2] And the soldiers wove a crown out of thorns and placed it on his head, and clothed him in a purple cloak, [3] and they came to him and said, "Hail, King of the Jews!" And they struck him repeatedly. [4] Once more Pilate went out and said to them, "Look, I am bringing him out to you, so that you may know that I find no guilt in him." *h* [5] So Jesus came out, wearing the crown of thorns and the purple cloak. And he said to them, "Behold, the man!" *i* [6] When the chief priests and the guards saw him they cried out, "Crucify him, crucify him!" Pilate said to them, "Take him yourselves and crucify him. I find no guilt in him." *j* [7] The Jews answered, *k* "We have a law, and according to that law he ought to die, because he made himself the Son of God."* [8] Now when Pilate heard this statement, he became even

more afraid, [9] and went back into the praetorium and said to Jesus, "Where are you from?" Jesus did not answer him. *l* [10] So Pilate said to him, "Do you not speak to me? Do you not know that I have power to release you and I have power to crucify you?" [11] Jesus answered [him], "You would have no power over me if it had not been given to you from above. For this reason the one who handed me over to you has the greater sin." *m* [12] Consequently, Pilate tried to release him; but the Jews cried out, "If you release him, you are not a Friend of Caesar.* Everyone who makes himself a king opposes Caesar." *n*

[13] When Pilate heard these words he brought Jesus out and seated him* on the judge's bench in the place called Stone Pavement, in Hebrew, Gabbatha. [14] It was preparation day for Passover, and it was about noon.* And he said to the Jews, "Behold, your king!" [15] They cried out, "Take him away, take him away! Crucify him!" Pilate said to them, "Shall I crucify your king?" The chief priests answered, "We have no king but Caesar." [16] Then he handed him over to them to be crucified.*

The Crucifixion of Jesus. So they took Jesus, [17] *o* and carrying the cross himself* he went out to what is called the Place of the Skull, in Hebrew, Golgotha. [18] There they crucified him, and with him two others, one on either side, with Jesus in the middle. [19] Pilate also had an inscription written and put on the cross. It read, "Jesus the Nazorean, the King of the Jews."* [20] Now many

e Jn 8, 47; 1 Tm 6, 13.—f 38b-40: Mt 27, 15-26; Mk 15, 6-15; Lk 23, 18-25; Acts 3, 14.—g 1-16: Mt 27, 27-31; Mk 15, 16-20; Lk 23, 13-25.—h Jn 18, 38.—i Is 52, 14.—j Jn 18, 31; 19, 15.—k Jn 10, 33-36; Lv 24, 16.—l Jn 7, 28.—m Jn 3, 27; 10, 18; Rom 13, 1.—n Acts 17, 7.—o 17-22: Mt 27, 32-37; Mk 15, 21-26; Lk 23, 26-35.

18, 39: See the note on Mt 27, 15.

18, 40: *Barabbas:* see the note on Mt 27, 16-17. *Revolutionary:* a guerrilla warrior fighting for nationalistic aims, though the term can also denote a robber. See the note on Mt 27, 38.

19, 1: Luke places the mockery of Jesus at the midpoint in the trial when Jesus was sent to Herod. Mark and Matthew place the scourging and mockery at the end of the trial after the sentence of death. Scourging was an integral part of the crucifixion penalty.

19, 7: *Made himself the Son of God:* this question was not raised in John's account of the Jewish interrogations of Jesus as it was in the synoptic account. Nevertheless, see Jn 5, 18; 8, 53; 10, 36.

19, 12: *Friend of Caesar:* a Roman honorific title bestowed upon high-ranking officials for merit.

19, 13: *Seated him:* others translate "(Pilate) sat down." In John's thought, Jesus is the real judge of the world, and John may here be portraying him seated on the judgment bench. *Stone Pavement:* in Greek *lithostrotos;* under the fortress Antonia, one of the conjectured locations of the praetorium, a massive

stone pavement has been excavated. *Gabbatha* (Aramaic rather than Hebrew) probably means "ridge, elevation."

19, 14: *Noon:* Mk 15, 25 has Jesus crucified "at the third hour," which means either 9 a.m. or the period from 9 to 12. Noon, the time when, according to John, Jesus was sentenced to death, was the hour at which the priests began to slaughter Passover lambs in the temple; see Jn 1, 29.

19, 16: *He handed him over to them to be crucified:* in context this would seem to mean "handed him over to the chief priests." Lk 23, 25 has a similar ambiguity. There is a polemic tendency in the gospels to place the guilt of the crucifixion on the Jewish authorities and to exonerate the Romans from blame. But John later mentions the Roman soldiers (23), and it was to these soldiers that Pilate handed Jesus over.

19, 17: *Carrying the cross himself:* a different picture from that of the synoptics, especially Lk 23, 26, where Simon of Cyrene is made to carry the cross, walking behind Jesus. In John's theology, Jesus remained in complete control and master of his destiny (cf Jn 10, 18). *Place of the Skull:* the Latin word for skull is *Calvaria;* hence "Calvary." *Golgotha* is actually an Aramaic rather than a Hebrew word.

19, 19: The inscription differs with slightly different words in each of the four gospels. John's form is fullest and gives the equivalent of the Latin *INRI = Iesus Nazarenus Rex Iudaeorum.* Only John mentions its polyglot character (20) and Pilate's role in keeping the title unchanged (21-22).

WAY OF THE CROSS (VIA DOLOROSA) — The location of Pilate's judgment hall in which Jesus was sentenced to death is uncertain. Very probably it was in the fortress Antonia at the northwest angle of the temple area.

Pictured above is the street leading from the ruins of the fortress to the traditional site of Calvary in the church of the Holy Sepulchre. In the background is the "fifth station," the little chapel of Simon the Cyrenian who helped Jesus carry the cross. (See Jn 19, 13-18 and Mt 27, 32-34)

ANCIENT JEWISH TOMB — The tomb pictured above is located a few miles west of Jerusalem. Note the large circular stone (some stones are said to have weighed one or more tons) used to seal the entrance to the tomb. The tomb in which Jesus was laid was probably similar to this one. (See Jn 19, 42)

TOMB OF OUR LORD — A continuous tradition going back to the time of Constantine identifies Calvary and the tomb of Jesus with the site of the church of the Holy Sepulchre in Jerusalem. The Tomb itself is preceded by a vestibule called the Chapel of the Angel to commemorate the angel who rolled back the stone and announced to the women that Jesus had risen as he had said. (See Jn 20, 1 and Mt 28, 2. 5. 6)

of the Jews read this inscription, because the place where Jesus was crucified was near the city; and it was written in Hebrew, Latin, and Greek. 21 So the chief priests of the Jews said to Pilate, "Do not write 'The King of the Jews,' but that he said, 'I am the King of the Jews.' " *p* 22 Pilate answered, "What I have written, I have written."

23 * When the soldiers had crucified Jesus,*q* they took his clothes and divided them into four shares, a share for each soldier.*r* They also took his tunic, but the tunic was seamless, woven in one piece from the top down. 24 So they said to one another, "Let's not tear it, but cast lots for it to see whose it will be," in order that the passage of scripture might be fulfilled [that says]:

"They divided my garments among them,
and for my vesture they cast lots."

This is what the soldiers did. 25 *s* Standing by the cross of Jesus were his mother and his mother's sister, Mary the wife of Clopas, and Mary of Magdala.* 26 When Jesus saw his mother* and the disciple there whom he loved, he said to his mother, "Woman, behold, your son."*t* 27 Then he said to the disciple, "Behold, your mother." And from that hour the disciple took her into his home.

28 *u* After this, aware that everything was now finished, in order that the scripture might be fulfilled,* Jesus said, "I thirst."*v* 29 There was a vessel filled with common wine.* So they put a sponge soaked in wine on a sprig of hyssop and put it up to his mouth. 30 When Jesus had taken the wine, he said, "It is finished."*w* And bowing his head, he handed over the spirit.*

The Blood and Water. 31 Now since it was preparation day, in order that the bodies might not remain on the cross on the sabbath, for the sabbath day of that week was a solemn one, the Jews asked Pilate that their legs be broken and they be taken down.*x* 32 So the soldiers came and broke the legs of the first and then of the other one who was crucified with Jesus. 33 But when they came to Jesus and saw that he was already dead, they did not break his legs, 34 *y* but one soldier thrust his lance into his side, and immediately blood and water flowed out.* 35 An eyewitness has testified, and his testimony is true; he knows* that he is speaking the truth, so that you also may [come to] believe.*z* 36 For this happened so that the scripture passage might be fulfilled:

"Not a bone of it will be broken."*a*

37 And again another passage says:

"They will look upon him whom they have pierced."*b*

The Burial of Jesus.* 38 *c* After this, Joseph of Arimathea, secretly a disciple of

---

p Jn 18, 33; Lk 19, 14.—q 23-27: Mt 27, 38-44; Mk 15, 27-32; Lk 23, 36-43.—r 23-24: Ps 22, 19; Mt 27, 35; Mk 15, 24; Lk 23, 34.—s Mt 27, 55; Mk 15, 40-41; Lk 8, 2; 23, 49.—t Jn 13, 23.—u 28-30: Mt 27, 45-56; Mk 15, 33-41; Lk 23, 44-49.—v Pss 22, 16; 69, 22.—w Jn 4, 34; 10, 18; 17, 4; Lk 23, 46.—x Ex 12, 16; Dt 21, 23.—y Nm 20, 11; 1 Jn 5, 6.—z Jn 7, 37-39; 21, 24.—a Ex 12, 46; Nm 9, 12; Ps 34, 21.—b Nm 21, 9; Zec 12, 10; Rv 1, 7.—c 38-42: Mt 27, 57-60; Mk 15, 42-46; Lk 34, 50-54.

19, 23-25a: While all four gospels describe the soldiers casting lots to divide Jesus' garments (see the note on Mt 27, 35), only John quotes the underlying passage from Ps 22, 19, and only John sees each line of the poetic parallelism literally carried out in two separate actions (23a; 23b-24).

19, 25: It is not clear whether four women are meant, or three (i.e., *Mary the wife of Cl[e]opas* [cf Lk 24, 18] is in apposition with *his mother's sister*) or two (his mother and his mother's sister, i.e., Mary of Cl[e]opas and Mary of Magdala). Only John mentions the mother of Jesus here. The synoptics have a group of women looking on from a distance at the cross (Mk 15, 40).

19, 26-27: This scene has been interpreted literally, of Jesus' concern for his mother; and symbolically, e.g., in the light of the Cana story in ch 2 (the presence of the mother of Jesus, the address *woman*, and the mention of the *hour)* and of the upper room in ch 13 (the presence of the beloved disciple; the *hour).* Now that the hour has come (28), Mary (a symbol of the church?) is given a role as the mother of Christians (personified by the beloved disciple); or, as a representative of those seeking salvation,

she is supported by the disciple who interprets Jesus' revelation; or Jewish and Gentile Christianity (or Israel and the Christian community) are reconciled.

19, 28: *The scripture . . . fulfilled:* either in the scene of vv 25-27, or in the *I thirst* of v 28. If the latter, Pss 22, 16 and 69, 22 deserve consideration.

19, 29: *Wine:* John does not mention the drugged wine, a narcotic that Jesus refused as the crucifixion began (Mk 15, 23), but only this final gesture of kindness at the end (Mk 15, 36). *Hyssop,* a small plant, is scarcely suitable for carrying a sponge (Mark mentions a reed) and may be a symbolic reference to the hyssop used to daub the blood of the paschal lamb on the doorpost of the Hebrews (Ex 12, 22).

19, 30: *Handed over the spirit:* there is a double nuance of dying (giving up the last breath or spirit) and that of passing on the holy Spirit; see Jn 7, 39, which connects the giving of the Spirit with Jesus' glorious return to the Father, and Jn 20, 22, where the author portrays the conferral of the Spirit.

19, 34-35: John probably emphasizes these verses to show the reality of Jesus' death, against the Docetist heretics. In the blood and water there may also be a symbolic reference to the Eucharist and baptism.

19, 35: *He knows:* it is not certain from the Greek that this *he* is the *eyewitness* of the first part of the sentence. *May [come to] believe:* see the note on Jn 20, 31.

19, 38-42: In the first three gospels there is no anointing on Friday. In Mt and Lk, the women come to the tomb on Sunday morning precisely to anoint Jesus.

Jesus for fear of the Jews, asked Pilate if he could remove the body of Jesus. And Pilate permitted it. So he came and took his body. [39] Nicodemus, the one who had first come to him at night, also came bringing a mixture of myrrh and aloes weighing about one hundred pounds.[d] [40] They took the body of Jesus and bound it with burial cloths along with the spices, according to the Jewish burial custom. [41] Now in the place where he had been crucified there was a garden, and in the garden a new tomb, in which no one had yet been buried. [42] So they laid Jesus there because of the Jewish preparation day; for the tomb was close by.

CHAPTER 20*

The Empty Tomb.* [1] On the first day of the week,[e] Mary of Magdala came to the tomb early in the morning, while it was still dark,* and saw the stone removed from the tomb.[f] [2] So she ran* and went to Simon Peter and to the other disciple whom Jesus loved, and told them, "They have taken the Lord from the tomb, and we don't know where they put him." [3] *So Peter and the other disciple went out and came to the tomb. [4] They both ran, but the other disciple ran faster than Peter and arrived at the tomb first; [5] he bent down and saw the burial cloths there, but did not go in. [6] [g] When Simon Peter arrived after him, he went into the tomb and saw the burial cloths* there, [7] and the cloth that had covered his head, not with the burial cloths but rolled up in a separate place.[h] [8] Then the other disciple also went in, the one who had arrived at the tomb first, and he saw and believed. [9] [i] For they did not yet understand the scripture that he had to rise from the dead.* [10] Then the disciples returned home.

The Appearance to Mary of Magdala.* [11] But Mary stayed outside the tomb weeping.[j] And as she wept, she bent over into the tomb [12] and saw two angels in white sitting there, one at the head and one at the feet where the body of Jesus had been. [13] And they said to her, "Woman, why are you weeping?" She said to them, "They have taken my Lord, and I don't know where they laid him." [14] When she had said this, she turned around and saw Jesus there, but did not know it was Jesus.[k] [15] Jesus said to her, "Woman, why are you weeping? Whom are you looking for?"[l] She thought it was the gardener and said to him, "Sir, if you carried him away, tell me where you laid him, and I will take him." [16] Jesus said to her, "Mary!" She turned and said to him in Hebrew, "Rabbouni,"* which means Teacher. [17] Jesus said to her, "Stop holding on to me,* for I have not yet ascended to the Father. But go to my brothers and tell them, 'I am going to my Father and your Father, to my God and your God.' "[m] [18] Mary of Magdala went and announced to the disciples, "I have seen the Lord," and what he told her.

---

d Jn 3, 1-2; 7, 50; Ps 45, 9.—e 1-10: Mt 28, 1-10; Mk 16, 1-11; Lk 24, 1-12.—f Jn 19, 25.—g Lk 24, 12.—h Jn 11, 44; 19, 40.—i Acts 2, 26-27; 1 Cor 15, 4.—j 11-18: Mk 16, 9-11.—k Jn 21, 4; Mk 16, 12; Lk 24, 16; 1 Cor 15, 43-44.—l 15-17: Mt 28, 9-10.—m Acts 1, 9.

20, 1-31: The risen Jesus reveals his glory and confers the Spirit. This story fulfills the basic need for testimony to the resurrection. What we have here is not a record but a series of single stories.

20, 1-10: The story of the empty tomb is found in both the Matthean and the Lucan traditions; John's version seems to be a fusion of the two.

20, 1: *Still dark:* according to Mark the sun had risen, Matthew describes it as "dawning," and Luke refers to early dawn. Mary sees the stone removed, not the empty tomb.

20, 2: Mary runs away, not directed by an angel/young man as in the synoptic accounts. The plural "we" in the second part of her statement might reflect a tradition of more women going to the tomb.

20, 3-10: The basic narrative is told of Peter alone in Lk 24, 12, a verse missing in important manuscripts and which may be borrowed from tradition similar to John. Cf also Lk 24, 24.

20, 6-8: Some special feature about the state of the burial cloths caused the beloved disciple to believe. Perhaps the details emphasized that the grave had not been robbed.

20, 9: Probably a general reference to the scriptures is intended, as in Lk 24, 26 and 1 Cor 15, 4. Some individual Old Testament passages suggested are Ps 16, 10; Hos 6, 2; Jon 2, 1.2.11.

20, 11-18: This appearance to Mary is found only in Jn, but cf Mt 28, 8-10 and Mk 16, 9-11.

20, 16: *Rabbouni:* Hebrew or Aramaic for "my master."

20, 17: *Stop holding on to me:* see Mt 28, 9, where the women take hold of his feet. *I have not yet ascended:* for John and many of the New Testament writers, the ascension in the theological sense of going to the Father to be glorified took place with the resurrection as one action. This scene in John dramatizes such an understanding, for by Easter night Jesus is glorified and can give the Spirit. Therefore his ascension takes place immediately after he has talked to Mary. In such a view, the ascension after forty days described in Acts 1, 1-11 would be simply a termination of earthly appearances or, perhaps better, an introduction to the conferral of the Spirit upon the early church, modeled on Elisha's being able to have a (double) share in the spirit of Elijah if he saw him being taken up (same verb as ascending) into heaven (2 Kgs 2, 9-12). *To my Father and your Father, to my God and your God:* this echoes Ru 1, 16: "Your people shall be my people, and your God my God." The Father of Jesus will now become the Father of the disciples because, once ascended, Jesus can give them the Spirit that comes from the Father and they can be reborn as God's children (Jn 3, 5). That is why he calls them *my brothers.*

Appearance to the Disciples.* [19]On the evening of that first day of the week,[n] when the doors were locked, where the disciples* were, for fear of the Jews, Jesus came and stood in their midst and said to them, "Peace be with you." [20]When he had said this, he showed them his hands and his side.* The disciples rejoiced when they saw the Lord.[o] [21][Jesus] said to them again,[p] "Peace be with you. As the Father has sent me, so I send you."* [22]And when he had said this, he breathed on them and said to them,[q] "Receive the holy Spirit.* [23] [r] Whose sins you forgive are forgiven them, and whose sins you retain are retained."*

Thomas. [24]Thomas, called Didymus, one of the Twelve, was not with them when Jesus came. [25]So the other disciples said to him, "We have seen the Lord." But he said to them, "Unless I see the mark of the nails in his hands and put my finger into the nailmarks and put my hand into his side, I will not believe." [s][26]Now a week later his disciples were again inside and Thomas was with them. Jesus came, although the doors were locked, and stood in their midst and said, "Peace be with you." [t] [27]Then he said to Thomas, "Put your finger here and see my hands, and bring your hand and put it into my side, and do not be unbelieving, but believe." [28] [u] Thomas answered and said to him, "My Lord and my God!"* [29]Jesus said to him, "Have you come to believe because you have seen me?[v] Blessed are those who have not seen and have believed."*

Conclusion.* [30]Now Jesus did many other signs in the presence of [his] disciples that are not written in this book.[w] [31]But these are written that you may [come to] believe that Jesus is the Messiah, the Son of God, and that through this belief you may have life in his name.[x]

IV. EPILOGUE

THE RESURRECTION APPEARANCE IN GALILEE

CHAPTER 21

The Appearance to the Seven Disciples. [1] * After this, Jesus revealed himself again to his disciples at the Sea of Tiberias. He revealed himself in this way.[y] [2]Together were Simon Peter, Thomas called Didymus, Nathanael from Cana in Galilee, Zebedee's sons,* and two others of his disciples. [3] * Simon Peter said to them, "I am going fishing." They said to him, "We also will come with you." So they went out and got into the boat, but that night they caught nothing.[z] [4]When it was already dawn, Jesus was standing on the shore; but the disciples did not realize that it was Jesus.[a] [5]Jesus said to them, "Children, have you caught anything to eat?" They

---

n 19-23: Mt 28, 16-20; Mk 16, 14-18; Lk 24, 36-44.—o Jn 14, 27.—p Jn 17, 18; Mt 28, 19; Mk 16, 15; Lk 24, 47-48.—q Gn 2, 7; Ez 37, 9; 1 Cor 15, 45.—r Mt 16, 19; 18, 18.—s 1 Jn 1, 1.—t Jn 21, 14.—u Jn 1, 1.—v Jn 4, 48; Lk 1, 45; 1 Pt 1, 8.—w Jn 21, 25.—x Jn 3, 14.15; 1 Jn 5, 13.—y Mt 26, 32; 28, 7.—z Mt 4, 18; Lk 5, 4-10.—a Jn 20, 14; Mt 28, 17; Lk 24, 16.

20, 19-29: The appearances to the disciples, without or with Thomas (cf Jn 11, 16; 14, 5), have rough parallels in the other gospels only for vv 19-23; cf Lk 24, 36-39; Mk 16, 14-18.

20, 19: *The disciples:* by implication from v 24, this means ten of the Twelve, presumably in Jerusalem. *Peace be with you:* although this could be an ordinary greeting, John intends here to echo Jn 14, 27. The theme of rejoicing in v 20 echoes Jn 16, 22.

20, 20: *Hands and . . . side:* Lk 24, 39-40 mentions "hands and feet," based on Ps 22, 17.

20, 21: By means of this sending, the Eleven were made apostles, that is, "those sent" (cf Jn 17, 18), though John does not use the noun in reference to them (see the note on Jn 13, 16). A solemn mission or "sending" is also the subject of the post-resurrection appearances to the Eleven in Mt 28, 19; Lk 24, 47; Mk 16, 15.

20, 22: This action recalls Gn 2, 7, where God breathed on the first man and gave him life; just as Adam's life came from God, so now the disciples' new spiritual life comes from Jesus. Cf also the revivification of the dry bones in Ez 37. This is the author's version of Pentecost. Cf also the note on Jn 19, 30.

20, 23: The Council of Trent defined that this power to forgive sins is exercised in the sacrament of penance. See Mt 16, 19 and Mt 18, 18.

20, 28: *My Lord and my God:* this forms a literary inclusion with the first verse of the gospel: "and the Word was God."

20, 29: This verse is a beatitude on future generations; faith, not sight, matters.

20, 30-31: These verses are clearly a conclusion to the gospel and express its purpose. While many manuscripts read *come to believe*, possibly implying a missionary purpose for John's gospel, a small number of quite early ones read "continue to believe," suggesting that the audience consists of Christians whose faith is to be deepened by the book; cf Jn 19, 35.

21, 1-23: There are many non-Johannine peculiarities in this chapter, some suggesting Lucan Greek style; yet this passage is closer to John than Jn 7, 53—8, 11. There are many Johannine features as well. Its closest parallels in the synoptic gospels are found in Lk 5, 1-11 and Mt 14, 28-31. Perhaps the tradition was ultimately derived from John but preserved by some disciple other than the writer of the rest of the gospel. The appearances narrated seem to be independent of those in ch 20. Even if a later addition, the chapter was added before publication of the gospel, for it appears in all manuscripts.

21, 2: *Zebedee's sons:* the only reference to James and John in this gospel (but see the note on Jn 1, 37). Perhaps the phrase was originally a gloss to identify, among the five, the *two others of his disciples.* The anonymity of the latter phrase is more Johannine (Jn 1, 35). The total of seven may suggest the community of the disciples in its fullness.

21, 3-6: This may be a variant of Luke's account of the catch of fish; see the note on Lk 5, 1-11.

answered him, "No." *b* 6 So he said to them, "Cast the net over the right side of the boat and you will find something." So they cast it, and were not able to pull it in because of the number of fish. 7 So the disciple whom Jesus loved said to Peter, "It is the Lord." When Simon Peter heard that it was the Lord, he tucked in his garment, for he was lightly clad, and jumped into the sea. 8 The other disciples came in the boat, for they were not far from shore, only about a hundred yards, dragging the net with the fish. 9 *c* When they climbed out on shore, they saw a charcoal fire with fish on it and bread.* 10 Jesus said to them, "Bring some of the fish you just caught." 11 So Simon Peter went over and dragged the net ashore full of one hundred fifty-three* large fish. Even though there were so many, the net was not torn. *d* 12 Jesus said to them, "Come, have breakfast." And none of the disciples dared to ask him,* "Who are you?" because they realized it was the Lord. 13 Jesus came over and took the bread and gave it to them, and in like manner the fish. *e* 14 This was now the third time *f* Jesus was revealed to his disciples after being raised from the dead.*

Jesus and Peter.* 15 When they had finished breakfast, Jesus said to Simon Peter,* "Simon, son of John, do you love me more than these?"* He said to him, "Yes, Lord, you know that I love you." He said to him, "Feed my lambs." 16 He then said to him a second time, "Simon, son of John, do you love me?" He said to him, "Yes, Lord, you know that I love you." He said to him, "Tend my sheep." 17 He said to him the third time, "Simon, son of John, do you love me?" Peter was distressed that he had said to him a third time, "Do you love me?" and he said to him, "Lord, you know everything; you know that I love you." [Jesus] said to him, "Feed my sheep. *g* 18 Amen, amen, I say to you, *h* when you were younger, you used to dress yourself and go where you wanted; but when you grow old, you will stretch out your hands, and someone else will dress you and lead you where you do not want to go."* 19 He said this signifying by what kind of death he would glorify God. And when he had said this, he said to him, "Follow me." *i*

The Beloved Disciple. 20 Peter turned and saw the disciple following whom Jesus loved, the one who had also reclined upon his chest during the supper and had said, "Master, who is the one who will betray you?" *j* 21 When Peter saw him, he said to Jesus, "Lord, what about him?" 22 Jesus said to him, "What if I want him to remain until I come?* What concern is it of yours? You follow me." *k* 23 So the word spread among the brothers that that disciple would not die. But Jesus had not told him that he would not die, just "What if I want him to remain until I come? [What concern is it of yours?]"*

Conclusion. 24 It is this disciple who testifies to these things and has written them,* and we know that his testimony is true. *l* 25 There are also many other things that Jesus did, but if these were to be described individually, I do not think the whole world would contain the books that would be written. *m*

b Lk 24, 41.—c Lk 24, 41-43.—d 2 Chr 2, 16.—e Lk 24, 42.—f Jn 20, 19.26.—g Jn 13, 37-38; 18, 15-18.25-27; Mt 26, 69-75; Mk 14, 66-72; Lk 22, 55-62.—h Acts 21, 11.14; 2 Pt 1, 14.—i Jn 13, 36.—j Jn 13, 25.—k Mt 16, 28.—l Jn 19, 35.—m Jn 20, 30.

21, 9.12-13: It is strange that Jesus already has fish since none have yet been brought ashore. This meal may have had eucharistic significance for early Christians since v 13 recalls Jn 6, 11, which uses the vocabulary of Jesus' action at the Last Supper; but see also the note on Mt 14, 19.

21, 11: The exact number 153 is probably meant to have a symbolic meaning in relation to the apostles' universal mission; Jerome claims that Greek zoologists catalogued 153 species of fish. Or 153 is the sum of the numbers from 1 to 17. Others invoke Ez 47, 10.

21, 12: *None . . . dared to ask him:* is Jesus' appearance strange to them? Cf Lk 24, 16; Mk 16, 12; Jn 20, 14. The disciples do, however, recognize Jesus *before* the breaking of the bread (opposed to Lk 24, 35).

21, 14: This verse connects chs 20 and 21; cf Jn 20, 19.26.

21, 15-23: This section constitutes Peter's rehabilitation and emphasizes his role in the church.

21, 15-17: In these three verses there is a remarkable variety of synonyms: two different Greek verbs for *love* (see the note on Jn 15, 13); two verbs for *feed/tend;* two nouns for *sheep;* two verbs for *know.* But apparently there is no difference of meaning. The threefold confession of Peter is meant to counteract his earlier threefold denial (Jn 18, 17.25.27). The First Vatican Council cited these verses in defining that Jesus after his resurrection gave Peter the jurisdiction of supreme shepherd and ruler over the whole flock.

21, 15: *More than these:* probably "more than these disciples do" rather than "more than you love them" or "more than you love these things [fishing, etc.]."

21, 18: Originally probably a proverb about old age, now used as a figurative reference to the crucifixion of Peter.

21, 22: *Until I come:* a reference to the parousia.

21, 23: This whole scene takes on more significance if the disciple is already dead. The death of the apostolic generation caused problems in the church because of a belief that Jesus was to have returned first. Loss of faith sometimes resulted; cf 2 Pt 3, 4.

21, 24: *Who . . . has written them:* this does not necessarily mean he wrote them with his own hand. The same expression is used in Jn 19, 22 of Pilate, who certainly would not have written the inscription himself. *We know:* i.e., the Christian community; cf Jn 1, 14.16.

THE ACTS OF THE APOSTLES

INTRODUCTION

The Acts of the Apostles, the second volume of Luke's two-volume work, continues Luke's presentation of biblical history, describing how the salvation promised to Israel in the Old Testament and accomplished by Jesus has now under the guidance of the holy Spirit been extended to the Gentiles. This was accomplished through the divinely chosen representatives (10, 41) whom Jesus prepared during his historical ministry (1, 21-22) and commissioned after his resurrection as witnesses to all that he taught (1, 8; 10, 37-43; Lk 24, 48). Luke's preoccupation with the Christian community as the Spirit-guided bearer of the word of salvation rules out of his book detailed histories of the activity of most of the preachers. Only the main lines of the roles of Peter and Paul serve Luke's interest.

Peter was the leading member of the Twelve (1, 13.15), a miracle worker like Jesus in the gospel (3, 1-10; 5, 1-11.15; 9, 32-35.36-42), the object of divine care (5, 17-21; 12, 6-11), and the spokesman for the Christian community (2, 14-36; 3, 12-26; 4, 8-12; 5, 29-32; 10, 34-43; 15, 7-11), who, according to Luke, was largely responsible for the growth of the community in the early days (2, 4; 4, 4). Paul eventually joined the community at Antioch (11, 25-26), which subsequently commissioned him and Barnabas to undertake the spread of the gospel to Asia Minor. This missionary venture generally failed to win the Jews of the diaspora to the gospel but enjoyed success among the Gentiles (13, 14—14, 27).

Paul's refusal to impose the Mosaic law upon his Gentile converts provoked very strong objection among the Jewish Christians of Jerusalem (15, 1), but both Peter and James supported his position (15, 6-21). Paul's second and third missionary journeys (16, 36—21, 16) resulted in the same pattern of failure among the Jews generally but of some success among the Gentiles. Paul, like Peter, is presented as a miracle worker (14, 8-18; 19, 12; 20, 7-12; 28, 7-10) and the object of divine care (16, 25-31).

In Acts, Luke has provided a broad survey of the church's development from the resurrection of Jesus to Paul's first Roman imprisonment, the point at which the book ends. In telling this story, Luke describes the emergence of Christianity from its origins in Judaism to its position as a religion of worldwide status and appeal. Originally a Jewish Christian community in Jerusalem, the church was placed in circumstances impelling it to include within its membership people of other cultures: the Samaritans (8, 4-25), at first an occasional Gentile (8, 26-30; 10, 1-48), and finally the Gentiles on principle (11, 20-21). Fear on the part of the Jewish people that Christianity, particularly as preached to the Gentiles, threatened their own cultural heritage caused them to be suspicious of Paul's gospel (13, 42-45; 15, 1-5; 28, 17-24). The inability of Christian missionaries to allay this apprehension inevitably created a situation in which the gospel was preached more and more to the Gentiles. Toward the end of Paul's career, the Christian communities, with the exception of those in Palestine itself (9, 31), were mainly of Gentile membership. In tracing the emergence of Christianity from Judaism, Luke is insistent upon the prominence of Israel in the divine plan of salvation (see the note on 1, 26; see also 2, 5-6; 3, 13-15; 10, 36; 13, 16-41; 24, 14-15) and that the extension of salvation to the Gentiles has been a part of the divine plan from the beginning (see 15, 13-18; 26, 22-23).

In the development of the church from a Jewish Christian origin in Jerusalem, with its roots in Jewish religious tradition, to a series of Christian communities among the Gentiles of the Roman empire, Luke perceives the action of God in history laying open the heart of all humanity to the divine message of salvation. His approach to the history of the

179

church is motivated by his theological interests. His history of the apostolic church is the story of a Spirit-guided community and a Spirit-guided spread of the Word of God (1, 8). The travels of Peter and Paul are in reality the travels of the Word of God as it spreads from Jerusalem, the city of destiny for Jesus, to Rome, the capital of the civilized world of Luke's day. Nonetheless, the historical data he utilizes are of value for the understanding of the church's early life and development and as general background to the Pauline epistles. In the interpretation of Acts, care must be exercised to determine Luke's theological aims and interests and to evaluate his historical data without either exaggerating their literal accuracy or underestimating their factual worth.

Finally, an apologetic concern is evident throughout Acts. By stressing the continuity between Judaism and Christianity (13, 16-41; 23, 6-9; 24, 10-21; 26, 2-23), Luke argues that Christianity is deserving of the same toleration accorded Judaism by Rome. Part of Paul's defense before Roman authorities is to show that Christianity is not a disturber of the peace of the Roman Empire (24, 5.12-13; 25, 7-8). Moreover, when he stands before Roman authorities, he is declared innocent of any crime against the empire (18, 13-15; 23, 29; 25, 25-27; 26, 31-32). Luke tells his story with the hope that Christianity will be treated as fairly.

Concerning the date of Acts, see the Introduction to the Gospel according to Luke.

The principal divisions of the Acts of the Apostles are the following:

    I.   The Preparation for the Christian Mission (1, 1—2, 13)
   II.   The Mission in Jerusalem (2, 14—8, 3)
  III.   The Mission in Judea and Samaria (8, 4—9, 43)
  IV.   The Inauguration of the Gentile Mission (10, 1—15, 35)
   V.   The Mission of Paul to the Ends of the Earth (15, 36— 28, 31)

I. THE PREPARATION FOR THE CHRISTIAN MISSION

CHAPTER 1*

The Promise of the Spirit. [1] In the first book,[a] Theophilus, I dealt with all that Jesus did and taught [2] until the day he was taken up, after giving instructions through the holy Spirit to the apostles whom he had chosen.[b] [3] He presented himself alive to them by many proofs after he had suffered, appearing to them during forty days* and speaking about the kingdom of God.[c] [4] While meeting with them, he enjoined them not to depart from Jerusalem, but to wait for "the promise of the Father* about which you have heard me speak;[d] [5] for John baptized with water, but in a few days you will be baptized with the holy Spirit."[e]

The Ascension of Jesus. [6] When they had gathered together they asked him, "Lord, are you at this time going* to restore the

---

a Lk 1, 1-4.—b Mt 28, 19-20; Lk 24, 44-49; Jn 20, 22; 1 Tm 3, 16.—c Acts 10, 41; 13, 31.—d Jn 14, 16.17.26.—e Acts 11, 16; Mt 3, 11; Mk 1, 8; Lk 3, 16; Jn 1, 26; Eph 1, 13.

1, 1-26: This introductory material (1-2) connects Acts with the Gospel of Luke, shows that the apostles were instructed by the risen Jesus (3-5), points out that the parousia or second coming in glory of Jesus will occur as certainly as his ascension occurred (6-11), and lists the members of the Twelve, stressing their role as a body of divinely mandated witnesses to his life, teaching, and resurrection (12-26).

1, 3: *Appearing to them during forty days:* Luke considered especially sacred the interval in which the appearances and instructions of the risen Jesus occurred and expressed it therefore in terms of the sacred number forty (cf Dt 8, 2). In his gospel, however, Luke connects the ascension of Jesus with the resurrection by describing the ascension on Easter Sunday evening (Lk 24, 50-53). What should probably be understood as one event (resurrection, glorification, ascension, sending of the Spirit—the

paschal mystery) has been historicized by Luke when he writes of a visible ascension of Jesus after forty days and the descent of the Spirit at Pentecost. For Luke, the ascension marks the end of the appearances of Jesus except for the extraordinary appearance to Paul. With regard to Luke's understanding of salvation history, the ascension also marks the end of the time of Jesus (Lk 24, 50-53) and signals the beginning of the time of the church.

1, 4: *The promise of the Father:* the holy Spirit, as is clear from the next verse. This gift of the Spirit was first promised in Jesus' final instructions to his chosen witnesses in Luke's gospel (Lk 24, 49) and formed part of the continuing instructions of the risen Jesus on the kingdom of God, of which Luke speaks in v 3.

1, 6: The question of the disciples implies that in believing Jesus to be the Christ (see the note on Lk 2, 11) they had expected him to be a political leader who would restore self-rule to Israel during his historical ministry. When this had not taken place, they ask if it is to take place at this time, the period of the church.

BETHSAIDA-SEA OF GALILEE — View of the Sea of Galilee (which is an expansion of the Jordan River) with the Plain of Gennesaret and the Mount of Beatitudes in the distance. This might have been the scene of the breakfast that Jesus took with his disciples after his resurrection. (See Jn 21, 1. 15)

MOUNT OF THE ASCENSION — An overall view of the Mount of Olives and surroundings where Jesus led his disciples before his ascension forty days after his resurrection. The Church of the Ascension rises in the background. There is little doubt that though he described the ascension in physical terms, Luke meant to emphasize our Lord's exaltation. (Acts 1, 11)

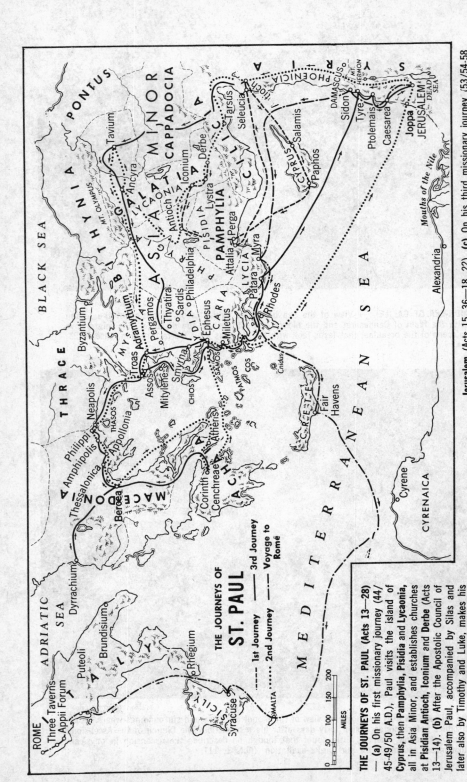

THE JOURNEYS OF ST. PAUL (Acts 13—28) — **(a)** On his first missionary journey (44/45-49/50 A.D.), Paul visits the island of **Cyprus**, then **Pamphylia, Pisidia** and **Lycaonia,** all in Asia Minor, and establishes churches at **Pisidian Antioch, Iconium** and **Derbe** (Acts 13—14). **(b)** After the Apostolic Council of Jerusalem Paul, accompanied by Silas and later also by Timothy and Luke, makes his second missionary journey (50-53 A.D.), first revisiting the churches previously established by him in Asia Minor and then the region of **Galatia** (Acts 16, 6). At **Troas** Paul has a vision in which a man from Macedonia invites him to preach the gospel to his countrymen. Paul accordingly sails for **Europe** and preaches the gospel in **Philippi, Thessalonica, Beroea,** and then in **Athens** and **Corinth.** Then he returns to **Antioch** by way of **Ephesus** and

Jerusalem (Acts 15, 36—18, 22). **(c)** On his third missionary journey (53/54-58 A.D.) Paul visits nearly the same regions as on the second, but makes **Ephesus,** where he remains nearly three years, the center of his missionary activity. He lays plans also for another missionary journey, intending to leave **Jerusalem** for **Rome** and Spain. But persecutions by the Jews hinder him from accomplishing his purpose. After two years of imprisonment at **Caesarea** he finally reaches **Rome,** where he is kept another two years in chains (Acts 18, 23—28, 31).

THE JOURNEYS OF
ST. PAUL

1st Journey ---- 3rd Journey ———
2nd Journey ····· Voyage to Rome —·—·

MILES
0 50 100 150 200

kingdom to Israel?" [7] He answered them,[f] "It is not for you to know the times or seasons that the Father has established by his own authority.* [8] But you will receive power when the holy Spirit comes upon you,[g] and you will be my witnesses in Jerusalem, throughout Judea and Samaria, and to the ends of the earth."* [9] When he had said this, as they were looking on, he was lifted up, and a cloud took him from their sight.[h] [10] While they were looking intently at the sky as he was going, suddenly two men dressed in white garments stood beside them.[i] [11] They said, "Men of Galilee, why are you standing there looking at the sky? This Jesus who has been taken up from you into heaven will return in the same way as you have seen him going into heaven."[j] [12] [k] Then they returned to Jerusalem from the mount called Olivet, which is near Jerusalem, a sabbath day's journey away.

The First Community in Jerusalem. [13] When they entered the city they went to the upper room where they were staying,

---

f Mt 24, 36; 1 Thes 5, 1-2.—g Acts 2, 1-13; 10, 39; Is 43, 10; Mt 28, 19; Lk 24, 47-48.—h 2 Kgs 2, 11; Mk 16, 19; Lk 24, 51.—i Jn 20, 17.—j Lk 24, 51; Eph 4, 8-10; 1 Pt 3, 22; Rv 1, 7.—k 12-14: Lk 6, 14-16.—l Lk 23, 49.—m Ps 41, 10; Lk 22, 47.—n Mt 27, 3-10.—o Pss 69, 26; 109, 8; Jn 17, 12.—p Acts 1, 8-9; 10, 39.—q Prv 16, 33.—r Lv 23, 15-21; Dt 16, 9-11.—s 2-3: Jn 3, 8.

1, 7: This verse echoes the tradition that the precise time of the parousia is not revealed to human beings; cf Mk 13, 32; 1 Thes 5, 1-3.

1, 8: Just as Jerusalem was the city of destiny in the Gospel of Luke (the place where salvation was accomplished), so here at the beginning of Acts, Jerusalem occupies a central position. It is the starting point for the mission of the Christian disciples to "the ends of the earth," the place where the apostles were situated and the doctrinal focal point in the early days of the community (Acts 15, 2.6). *The ends of the earth:* for Luke, this means Rome.

1, 18: Luke records a popular tradition about the death of Judas that differs from the one in Mt 27, 5, according to which Judas hanged himself. Here, although the text is not certain, Judas is depicted as purchasing a piece of property with the betrayal money and being killed on it in a fall.

1, 26: The need to replace Judas was probably dictated by the symbolism of the number twelve, recalling the twelve tribes of Israel. This symbolism also indicates that for Luke (see Lk 22, 30) the Christian church is a reconstituted Israel.

2, 1-41: Luke's pentecostal narrative consists of an introduction (1-13), a speech ascribed to Peter declaring the resurrection of Jesus and its messianic significance (14-36), and a favorable response from the audience (37-41). It is likely that the narrative telescopes events that took place over a period of time and on a less dramatic scale. The Twelve were not originally in a position to proclaim publicly the messianic office of Jesus without incurring immediate reprisal from those religious authorities in Jerusalem who had brought about Jesus' death precisely to stem the rising tide in his favor.

2, 2: *There came from the sky a noise like a strong driving wind:* wind and spirit are associated in Jn 3, 8. The sound of a great rush of wind would herald a new action of God in the history of salvation.

Peter and John and James and Andrew, Philip and Thomas, Bartholomew and Matthew, James son of Alphaeus, Simon the Zealot, and Judas son of James. [14] All these devoted themselves with one accord to prayer, together with some women, and Mary the mother of Jesus, and his brothers.[l]

The Choice of Judas's Successor. [15] During those days Peter stood up in the midst of the brothers (there was a group of about one hundred and twenty persons in the one place). He said, [16] "My brothers, the scripture had to be fulfilled which the holy Spirit spoke beforehand through the mouth of David, concerning Judas, who was the guide for those who arrested Jesus.[m] [17] He was numbered among us and was allotted a share in this ministry. [18] [n] He bought a parcel of land with the wages of his iniquity, and falling headlong, he burst open in the middle, and all his insides spilled out.* [19] This became known to everyone who lived in Jerusalem, so that the parcel of land was called in their language 'Akeldama,' that is, Field of Blood. [20] For it is written in the Book of Psalms:

'Let his encampment become desolate, and may no one dwell in it.'

And:

'May another take his office.'[o]

[21] Therefore, it is necessary that one of the men who accompanied us the whole time the Lord Jesus came and went among us, [22] beginning from the baptism of John until the day on which he was taken up from us, become with us a witness to his resurrection."[p] [23] So they proposed two, Joseph called Barsabbas, who was also known as Justus, and Matthias. [24] Then they prayed, "You, Lord, who know the hearts of all, show which one of these two you have chosen [25] to take the place in this apostolic ministry from which Judas turned away to go to his own place." [26] [q] Then they gave lots to them, and the lot fell upon Matthias, and he was counted with the eleven apostles.*

CHAPTER 2

The Coming of the Spirit. [1] * When the time for Pentecost was fulfilled, they were all in one place together.[r] [2] And suddenly there came from the sky a noise like a strong driving wind,* and it filled the entire house in which they were.[s]

³Then there appeared to them tongues as of fire,* which parted and came to rest on each one of them.ᵗ ⁴And they were all filled with the holy Spirit and began to speak in different tongues,* as the Spirit enabled them to proclaim.ᵘ

⁵Now there were devout Jews from every nation under heaven staying in Jerusalem. ⁶At this sound, they gathered in a large crowd, but they were confused because each one heard them speaking in his own language. ⁷They were astounded, and in amazement they asked, "Are not all these people who are speaking Galileans?ᵛ ⁸Then how does each of us hear them in his own native language? ⁹We are Parthians, Medes, and Elamites, inhabitants of Mesopotamia, Judea and Cappadocia, Pontus and Asia, ¹⁰Phrygia and Pamphylia, Egypt and the districts of Libya near Cyrene, as well as travelers from Rome, ¹¹both Jews and converts to Judaism, Cretans and Arabs, yet we hear them speaking in our own tongues of the mighty acts of God."ʷ ¹²They were all astounded and bewildered, and said to one another, "What does this mean?" ¹³But others said, scoffing, "They have had too much new wine."ˣ

II. THE MISSION IN JERUSALEM

Peter's Speech at Pentecost. ¹⁴ * Then Peter stood up with the Eleven, raised his voice, and proclaimed to them, "You who are Jews, indeed all of you staying in Jerusalem. Let this be known to you, and listen to my words. ¹⁵These people are not drunk, as you suppose, for it is only nine o'clock in the morning. ¹⁶No, this is what was spoken through the prophet Joel:

¹⁷ 'It will come to pass in the last days,'
　　　God says,
　　'that I will pour out a portion of my
　　　　spirit
　　　upon all flesh.
　　Your sons and your daughters shall
　　　　prophesy,
　　　your young men shall see visions,
　　　your old men shall dream dreams.ʸ
¹⁸ Indeed, upon my servants and my
　　　　handmaids
　　I will pour out a portion of my spirit
　　　in those days,
　　　and they shall prophesy.
¹⁹ And I will work wonders in the heavens
　　　above

and signs on the earth below:
　　blood, fire, and a cloud of smoke.
²⁰ The sun shall be turned to darkness,
　　　and the moon to blood,
　　　before the coming of the great and
　　　　splendid day of the Lord,
²¹ and it shall be that everyone shall be
　　　saved who calls on the name of
　　　the Lord.'ᶻ

²²You who are Israelites, hear these words. Jesus the Nazorean was a man commended to you by God with mighty deeds, wonders, and signs, which God worked through him in your midst, as you yourselves know.ᵃ ²³This man, delivered up by the set plan and foreknowledge of God, you killed, using lawless men to crucify him.ᵇ ²⁴But God raised him up, releasing him from the throes of death, because it was impossible for him to be held by it.ᶜ ²⁵For David says of him:

'I saw the Lord ever before me,ᵈ
　　with him at my right hand I shall not
　　　be disturbed.
²⁶ Therefore my heart has been glad and
　　　my tongue has exulted;
　　my flesh, too, will dwell in hope,
²⁷ because you will not abandon my soul
　　　to the nether world,
　　nor will you suffer your holy one to
　　　see corruption.ᵉ
²⁸ You have made known to me the paths
　　　of life;
　　you will fill me with joy in your presence.'

²⁹My brothers, one can confidently say to you about the patriarch David that he died and was buried, and his tomb is in our

---

t Lk 3, 16.—u Acts 1, 5; 4, 31; 8, 15.17; 10, 44; 11, 15-16; 15, 8; 19, 6; Ps 104, 30; Jn 20, 33.—v Acts 1, 11.—w Acts 10, 46.—x 1 Cor 14, 23.—y Is 2, 2; 44, 3; Jl 3, 1-5.—z Rom 10, 13.—a Acts 10, 38; Lk 24, 19.—b 1 Thes 2, 15.—c Acts 13, 34.—d 25-28: Ps 16, 8-11.—e Acts 13, 35.

2, 3: *Tongues as of fire:* see Ex 19, 18 where fire symbolizes the presence of God to initiate the covenant on Sinai. Here the holy Spirit acts upon the apostles, preparing them to proclaim the new covenant with its unique gift of the Spirit (38).

2, 4: *To speak in different tongues:* ecstatic prayer in praise of God, interpreted in vv 6 and 11 as speaking in foreign languages, symbolizing the worldwide mission of the church.

2, 14-36: The first of six discourses in Acts (along with Acts 3, 12-26; 4, 8-12; 5, 29-32; 10, 34-43; 13, 16-41) dealing with the resurrection of Jesus and its messianic import. Five of these are attributed to Peter, the final one to Paul. Modern scholars term these discourses in Acts the "kerygma," the Greek word for proclamation (cf 1 Cor 15, 11).

midst to this day. ³⁰But since he was a prophet and knew that God had sworn an oath to him that he would set one of his descendants upon his throne,^f ³¹he foresaw and spoke of the resurrection of the Messiah, that neither was he abandoned to the netherworld nor did his flesh see corruption.^g ³²God raised this Jesus; of this we are all witnesses. ³³Exalted at the right hand of God,* he received the promise of the holy Spirit from the Father and poured it forth, as you [both] see and hear.^h ³⁴For David did not go up into heaven, but he himself said:

'The Lord said to my Lord,ⁱ

"Sit at my right hand

³⁵   until I make your enemies your footstool." '

³⁶Therefore let the whole house of Israel know for certain that God has made him both Lord and Messiah, this Jesus whom you crucified."^j

³⁷Now when they heard this, they were cut to the heart, and they asked Peter and the other apostles, "What are we to do, my brothers?"^k ³⁸Peter [said] to them, "Repent and be baptized,* every one of you, in the name of Jesus Christ for the forgiveness of your sins; and you will receive the gift of the holy Spirit.^l ³⁹For the promise is made to you and to your children and to all those far off, whomever the Lord our God will call."^m ⁴⁰He testified with many other arguments, and was exhorting them, "Save yourselves from this corrupt generation."ⁿ ⁴¹Those who accepted his message

were baptized, and about three thousand persons were added that day.^o

Communal Life.* ⁴² ^p They devoted themselves to the teaching of the apostles and to the communal life, to the breaking of the bread and to the prayers.^q ⁴³Awe came upon everyone, and many wonders and signs were done through the apostles.^r ⁴⁴All who believed were together and had all things in common;^s ⁴⁵they would sell their property and possessions and divide them among all according to each one's need. ⁴⁶Every day they devoted themselves to meeting together in the temple area and to breaking bread in their homes. They ate their meals with exultation and sincerity of heart, ⁴⁷praising God and enjoying favor with all the people. And every day the Lord added to their number those who were being saved.

CHAPTER 3

Cure of a Crippled Beggar. ¹ * Now Peter and John were going up to the temple area for the three o'clock hour of prayer.* ² ^t And a man crippled from birth was carried and placed at the gate of the temple called "the Beautiful Gate" every day to beg for alms from the people who entered the temple. ³When he saw Peter and John about to go into the temple, he asked for alms. ⁴But Peter looked intently at him, as did John, and said, "Look at us." ⁵He paid attention to them, expecting to receive something from them. ⁶ * Peter said, "I have neither silver nor gold, but what I do have I give

---

f 2 Sm 7, 12; Ps 132, 11.—g Acts 13, 35; Ps 16, 10.—h Acts 1, 4-5.—i 34-35: Ps 110, 1.—j Acts 9, 22; Rom 10, 9; Phil 2, 11.—k Lk 3, 10.—l Acts 3, 19; 16, 31; Lk 3, 3.—m Is 57, 19; Jl 3, 5; Eph 2, 17.—n Dt 32, 5; Ps 78, 8; Lk 9, 41; Phil 2, 15.—o Acts 2, 47; 4, 4; 5, 14; 6, 7; 11, 21.24; 21, 20.—p 42-47: Acts 4, 32-35.—q Acts 1, 14; 6, 4.—r Acts 5, 12-16.—s Acts 4, 32.34-35.—t 2-8: Acts 14, 8-10.

2, 33: *At the right hand of God:* or "by the right hand of God."

2, 38: *Repent and be baptized:* repentance is a positive concept, a change of mind and heart toward God reflected in the actual goodness of one's life. It is in accord with the apostolic teaching derived from Jesus (42) and ultimately recorded in the four gospels. Luke presents baptism in Acts as the expected response to the apostolic preaching about Jesus and associates it with the conferring of the Spirit (Acts 1, 5; 10, 44-48; 11, 16).

2, 42-47: The first of three summary passages (along with Acts 4, 32-37 and 5, 12-16) that outline, somewhat idyllically, the chief characteristics of the Jerusalem community: adherence to the teachings of the Twelve and the centering of its religious life in the eucharistic liturgy (42); a system of distribution of goods that led wealthier Christians to sell their possessions when the needs of the community's poor required it (44 and the note on Acts 4, 32-37); and continued attendance at the temple, since in this initial stage there was little or no thought of any dividing line between Christianity and Judaism (46).

3, 1—4, 31: This section presents a series of related events: the dramatic cure of a lame beggar (Acts 3, 1-10) produces a large audience for the kerygmatic discourse of Peter (Acts 3, 11-26). The Sadducees, taking exception to the doctrine of resurrection, have Peter, John, and apparently the beggar as well, arrested (Acts 4, 1-4) and brought to trial before the Sanhedrin. The issue concerns the authority by which Peter and John publicly teach religious doctrine in the temple (Acts 4, 5-7). Peter replies with a brief summary of the kerygma, implying that his authority is prophetic (Acts 4, 8-12). The court warns the apostles to abandon their practice of invoking prophetic authority in the name of Jesus (Acts 4, 13-18). When Peter and John reply that the prophetic role cannot be abandoned to satisfy human objections, the court nevertheless releases them, afraid to do otherwise since the beggar, lame from birth and over forty years old, is a well-known figure in Jerusalem and the facts of his cure are common property (Acts 4, 19-22). The narrative concludes with a prayer of the Christian community imploring divine aid against threats of persecution (Acts 4, 23-31).

3, 1: *For the three o'clock hour of prayer:* literally, "at the ninth hour of prayer." With the day beginning at 6 a.m., the ninth hour would be 3 p.m.

3, 6-10: The miracle has a dramatic cast; it symbolizes the saving power of Christ and leads the beggar to enter the temple, where he hears Peter's proclamation of salvation through Jesus.

you: in the name of Jesus Christ the Nazorean, [rise and] walk." [u] [7] Then Peter took him by the right hand and raised him up, and immediately his feet and ankles grew strong. [8] He leaped up, stood, and walked around, and went into the temple with them, walking and jumping and praising God. [v] [9] When all the people saw him walking and praising God, [10] they recognized him as the one who used to sit begging at the Beautiful Gate of the temple, and they were filled with amazement and astonishment at what had happened to him.

Peter's Speech. [11] As he clung to Peter and John, all the people hurried in amazement toward them in the portico called "Solomon's Portico." [w] [12] When Peter saw this, he addressed the people, "You Israelites, why are you amazed at this, and why do you look so intently at us as if we had made him walk by our own power or piety? [x] [13] The God of Abraham, [the God] of Isaac, and [the God] of Jacob, the God of our ancestors, has glorified* his servant Jesus whom you handed over and denied in Pilate's presence, when he had decided to release him. [y] [14] You denied the Holy and Righteous One* and asked that a murderer be released to you. [z] [15] The author of life* you put to death, but God raised him from the dead; of this we are witnesses. [a] [16] And by faith in his name, this man, whom you see and know, his name has made strong, and the faith that comes

through it has given him this perfect health, in the presence of all of you. [17] Now I know, brothers, that you acted out of ignorance,* just as your leaders did; [b] [18] but God has thus brought to fulfillment what he had announced beforehand through the mouth of all the prophets,* that his Messiah would suffer. [c] [19] Repent, therefore, and be converted, that your sins may be wiped away, [d] [20] and that the Lord may grant you times of refreshment and send you the Messiah already appointed for you, Jesus,* [21] whom heaven must receive until the times of universal restoration* of which God spoke through the mouth of his holy prophets from of old. [22] For Moses said:*

'A prophet like me will the Lord, your
　　God, raise up for you
　　from among your own kinsmen;
to him you shall listen in all that he may
　　say to you. [e]
[23] Everyone who does not listen to that
　　prophet
　　will be cut off from the people.' [f]

[24] Moreover, all the prophets who spoke, from Samuel and those afterwards, also announced these days. [25] You are the children of the prophets and of the covenant that God made with your ancestors when he said to Abraham, 'In your offspring all the families of the earth shall be blessed.' [g] [26] For you first, God raised up his servant and sent him to bless you by turning each of you from your evil ways." [h]

---

u Acts 4, 10.—v Is 35, 6; Lk 7, 22.—w Acts 5, 12; Jn 10, 23.—x Acts 14, 15.—y Ex 3, 6.15; Is 52, 13; Lk 23, 14-25.—z Mt 27, 20-21; Mk 15, 11; Lk 23, 18; Jn 18, 40.—a Acts 4, 10; 5, 31 / Acts 1, 8; 2, 32.—b Acts 13, 27; Lk 23, 34; 1 Cor 2, 8; 1 Tm 1, 13.—c Lk 18, 31.—d Acts 2, 38.—e Acts 7, 37; Dt 18, 15.18.—f Lv 23, 29; Dt 18, 19.—g Gn 12, 3; 18, 18; 22, 18; Sir 44, 19-21; Gal 3, 8-9.—h Acts 13, 46; Rom 1, 16.

3, 13: *Has glorified:* through the resurrection and ascension of Jesus, God reversed the judgment against him on the occasion of his trial. *Servant:* the Greek word can also be rendered as "son" or even "child" here and also in Acts 3, 26; Acts 4, 25 (applied to David); Acts 4, 27; and Acts 4, 30. Scholars are of the opinion, however, that the original concept reflected in the words identified Jesus with the suffering Servant of the Lord of Is 52, 13—53, 12.

3, 14: *The Holy and Righteous One:* so designating Jesus emphasizes his special relationship to the Father (see Lk 1, 35; 4, 34) and emphasizes his sinlessness and religious dignity that are placed in sharp contrast with the guilt of those who rejected him in favor of Barabbas.

3, 15: *The author of life:* other possible translations of the Greek title are "leader of life" or "pioneer of life." The title clearly points to Jesus as the source and originator of salvation.

3, 17: *Ignorance:* a Lucan motif, explaining away the actions not only of the people but also of their leaders in crucifying Jesus. On this basis the presbyters in Acts could continue to appeal to the Jews in Jerusalem to believe in Jesus, even while affirming their involvement in his death because they were unaware of his messianic dignity. See also Acts 13, 27 and Lk 23, 34.

3, 18: *Through the mouth of all the prophets:* Christian prophetic insight into the Old Testament saw the crucifixion and death of Jesus as the main import of messianic prophecy. The Jews themselves did not anticipate a suffering Messiah; they usually understood the Servant Song in Is 52, 13—53, 12 to signify their own suffering as a people. In his typical fashion (cf Lk 18, 31; 24, 25.27.44), Luke does not specify the particular Old Testament prophecies that were fulfilled by Jesus. See also the note on Lk 24, 26.

3, 20: *The Lord . . . and send you the Messiah already appointed for you, Jesus:* an allusion to the parousia or second coming of Christ, judged to be imminent in the apostolic age. This reference to its nearness is the only explicit one in Acts. Some scholars believe that this verse preserves a very early christology, in which the title "Messiah" (Greek "Christ") is applied to him as of his parousia, his second coming (contrast Acts 2, 36). This view of a future messiahship of Jesus is not found elsewhere in the New Testament.

3, 21: *The times of universal restoration:* like "the times of refreshment" (20), an apocalyptic designation of the messianic age, fitting in with the christology of v 20 that associates the messiahship of Jesus with his future coming.

3, 22: A loose citation of Dt 18, 15, which teaches that the Israelites are to learn the will of Yahweh from no one but their prophets. At the time of Jesus, some Jews expected a unique prophet to come in fulfillment of this text. Early Christianity applied this tradition and text to Jesus and used them especially in defense of the divergence of Christian teaching from traditional Judaism.

CHAPTER 4

[1] While they were still speaking to the people, the priests, the captain of the temple guard, and the Sadducees* confronted them, [2] disturbed that they were teaching the people and proclaiming in Jesus the resurrection of the dead.[i] [3] They laid hands on them and put them in custody until the next day, since it was already evening. [4] But many of those who heard the word came to believe and [the] number of men grew to [about] five thousand.

Before the Sanhedrin. [5] On the next day, their leaders, elders, and scribes were assembled in Jerusalem, [6] with Annas the high priest, Caiaphas, John, Alexander, and all who were of the high-priestly class. [7] They brought them into their presence and questioned them, "By what power or by what name have you done this?" [8] Then Peter, filled with the holy Spirit, answered them, "Leaders of the people and elders:[j] [9] If we are being examined today about a good deed done to a cripple, namely, by what means he was saved, [10] then all of you and all the people of Israel should know that it was in the name of Jesus Christ the Nazorean whom you crucified, whom God raised from the dead; in his name this man stands before you healed. [11] [k] He is 'the stone rejected by you, the builders, which has become the cornerstone.'* [12] [l] There is no salvation through anyone else, nor is there any other name under heaven given to the human race by which we are to be saved."*

[13] Observing the boldness of Peter and John and perceiving them to be unedu-cated, ordinary men, they were amazed, and they recognized them as the companions of Jesus. [14] Then when they saw the man who had been cured standing there with them, they could say nothing in reply. [15] So they ordered them to leave the Sanhedrin, and conferred with one another, saying, [16] "What are we to do with these men? Everyone living in Jerusalem knows that a remarkable sign was done through them, and we cannot deny it. [17] But so that it may not be spread any further among the people, let us give them a stern warning never again to speak to anyone in this name."[m]

[18] So they called them back and ordered them not to speak or teach at all in the name of Jesus. [19] Peter and John, however, said to them in reply, "Whether it is right in the sight of God for us to obey you rather than God, you be the judges.[n] [20] It is impossible for us not to speak about what we have seen and heard." [21] After threatening them further, they released them, finding no way to punish them, on account of the people who were all praising God for what had happened. [22] For the man on whom this sign of healing had been done was over forty years old.

Prayer of the Community. [23] After their release they went back to their own people and reported what the chief priests and elders had told them. [24] And when they heard it, they raised their voices to God with one accord and said, "Sovereign Lord, maker of heaven and earth and the sea and all that is in them, [25] you said by the holy Spirit through the mouth of our father David, your servant:

'Why did the Gentiles rage[o]
    and the peoples entertain folly?
[26] The kings of the earth took their stand
    and the princes gathered together
        against the Lord and against his
            anointed.'

[27] Indeed they gathered in this city against your holy servant Jesus whom you anointed, Herod* and Pontius Pilate, together with the Gentiles and the peoples of Israel,[p] [28] to do what your hand and [your] will had long ago planned to take place. [29] And now, Lord, take note of their threats, and enable your servants to speak your word with all boldness, [30] as you stretch forth [your] hand to heal, and signs

---

i Acts 23, 6-8; 24, 21.—j Mt 10, 20.—k Ps 118, 22; Is 28, 16; Mt 21, 42; Mk 12, 10; Lk 20, 17; Rom 9, 33; 1 Pt 2, 7.—l Mt 1, 21; 1 Cor 3, 11.—m Acts 5, 28.—n Acts 5, 29-32.—o 25-26: Ps 2, 1-2.—p Lk 23, 12-13.

4, 1: *The priests, the captain of the temple guard, and the Sadducees:* the priests performed the temple liturgy; the temple guard was composed of Levites, whose captain ranked next after the high priest. The Sadducees, a party within Judaism at this time, rejected those doctrines, including bodily resurrection, which they believed alien to the ancient Mosaic religion. The Sadducees were drawn from priestly families and from the lay aristocracy.

4, 11: Early Christianity applied this citation from Ps 118, 22 to Jesus; cf Mk 12, 10; 1 Pt 2, 7.

4, 12: In the Roman world of Luke's day, salvation was often attributed to the emperor who was hailed as "savior" and "god." Luke, in the words of Peter, denies that deliverance comes through anyone other than Jesus.

4, 27: *Herod:* Herod Antipas, ruler of Galilee and Perea from 4 B.C. to A.D. 39, who executed John the Baptist and before whom Jesus was arraigned; cf Lk 23, 6-12.

and wonders are done through the name of your holy servant Jesus." 31 As they prayed, the place where they were gathered shook,* and they were all filled with the holy Spirit and continued to speak the word of God with boldness.[q]

Life in the Christian Community.* 32 The community of believers was of one heart and mind, and no one claimed that any of his possessions was his own, but they had everything in common. 33 With great power the apostles bore witness to the resurrection of the Lord Jesus, and great favor was accorded them all. 34 [r] There was no needy person among them, for those who owned property or houses would sell them, bring the proceeds of the sale, 35 and put them at the feet of the apostles, and they were distributed to each according to need.

36 [s] Thus Joseph, also named by the apostles Barnabas (which is translated "son of encouragement"), a Levite, a Cypriot by birth, 37 sold a piece of property that he owned, then brought the money and put it at the feet of the apostles.

CHAPTER 5

Ananias and Sapphira. * 1 A man named Ananias, however, with his wife Sapphira, sold a piece of property. 2 He retained for himself, with his wife's knowledge, some of the purchase price, took the remainder, and put it at the feet of the apostles. 3 But Peter said, "Ananias, why has Satan filled your heart so that you lied to the holy Spirit and retained part of the price of the land?[t] 4 While it remained unsold, did it not remain yours? And when it was sold, was it not still under your control? Why did you contrive this deed? You have lied not to human beings, but to God." 5 When Ananias heard these words, he fell down and breathed his last, and great fear came upon all who heard of it. 6 The young men came and wrapped him up, then carried him out and buried him.

7 After an interval of about three hours, his wife came in, unaware of what had happened. 8 Peter said to her, "Tell me, did you sell the land for this amount?" She answered, "Yes, for that amount." 9 Then Peter said to her, "Why did you agree to test the Spirit of the Lord? Listen, the footsteps of those who have buried your husband are at the door, and they will carry you out." 10 At once, she fell down at his feet and breathed her last. When the young men entered they found her dead, so they carried her out and buried her beside her husband. 11 And great fear came upon the whole church and upon all who heard of these things.[u]

Signs and Wonders of the Apostles.* 12 Many signs and wonders were done among the people at the hands of the apostles. They were all together in Solomon's portico.[v] 13 None of the others dared to join them, but the people esteemed them. 14 Yet more than ever, believers in the Lord, great numbers of men and women, were added to them. 15 Thus they even carried the sick out into the streets and laid them on cots and mats so that when Peter came by, at least his shadow might fall on one or another of them.[w] 16 A large number of people from the towns in the vicinity of Jerusalem also gathered, bringing the sick and those disturbed by unclean spirits, and they were all cured.

q Acts 2, 4.—r 34-35: Acts 2, 44-45.—s 36-37: Acts 9, 27; 11, 22.30; 12, 25; 13, 15; 1 Cor 9, 6; Gal 2, 1.9.13; Col 4, 10.—t Lk 22, 3; Jn 13, 2.—u Acts 2, 43; 5, 5; 19, 17.—v Acts 2, 43; 6, 8; 14, 3; 15, 12.—w Acts 19, 11-12; Mk 6, 56.

4, 31: *The place . . . shook:* the earthquake is used as a sign of the divine presence in Ex 19, 18; Is 6, 4. Here the shaking of the building symbolizes God's favorable response to the prayer. Luke may have had as an additional reason for using the symbol in this sense the fact that it was familiar in the Hellenistic world. Ovid and Virgil also employ it.

4, 32-37: This is the second summary characterizing the Jerusalem community (see the note on Acts 2, 42-47). It emphasizes the system of the distribution of goods and introduces Barnabas, who appears later in Acts as the friend and companion of Paul, and who, as noted here (37), endeared himself to the community by a donation of money through the sale of property. This sharing of material possessions continues a practice that Luke describes during the historical ministry of Jesus (Lk 8, 3) and is in accord with the sayings of Jesus in Luke's gospel (Lk 12, 33; 16, 9.11.13).

5, 1-11: The sin of Ananias and Sapphira did not consist in the withholding of part of the money but in their deception of the community. Their deaths are ascribed to a lie to the holy Spirit (3.9), i.e., they accepted the honor accorded them by the community for their generosity, but in reality they were not deserving of it.

5, 12-16: This, the third summary portraying the Jerusalem community, underscores the Twelve as its bulwark, especially because of their charismatic power to heal the sick; cf Acts 2, 42-47; 4, 32-37.

Trial before the Sanhedrin.* 17 Then the high priest rose up and all his companions, that is, the party of the Sadducees, and, filled with jealousy,ˣ 18 laid hands upon the apostles and put them in the public jail. 19 But during the night, the angel of the Lord opened the doors of the prison, led them out, and said,ʸ 20 "Go and take your place in the temple area, and tell the people everything about this life." 21 When they heard this, they went to the temple early in the morning and taught. When the high priest and his companions arrived, they convened the Sanhedrin, the full senate of the Israelites, and sent to the jail to have them brought in. 22 But the court officers who went did not find them in the prison, so they came back and reported, 23 "We found the jail securely locked and the guards stationed outside the doors, but when we opened them, we found no one inside." 24 When they heard this report, the captain of the temple guard and the chief priests were at a loss about them, as to what this would come to. 25 Then someone came in and reported to them, "The men whom you put in prison are in the temple area and are teaching the people." 26 Then the captain and the court officers went and brought them in, but without force, because they were afraid of being stoned by the people.ᶻ

27 When they had brought them in and made them stand before the Sanhedrin, the high priest questioned them, 28 "We gave you strict orders [did we not?] to stop teaching in that name. Yet you have filled Jerusalem with your teaching and want to bring this man's blood upon us."ᵃ 29 But Peter and the apostles said in reply, "We must obey God rather than men.ᵇ 30 The God of our ancestors raised Jesus,ᶜ though you had him killed by hanging him on a tree.* 31 God exalted him at his right hand * as leader and savior to grant Israel repentance and forgiveness of sins.ᵈ 32 We are witnesses of these things, as is the holy Spirit that God has given to those who obey him."ᵉ

33 When they heard this, they became infuriated and wanted to put them to death. 34 But a Pharisee in the Sanhedrin named Gamaliel,* a teacher of the law, respected by all the people, stood up, ordered the men to be put outside for a short time,ᶠ 35 and said to them, "Fellow Israelites, be careful what you are about to do to these men. 36 * Some time ago, Theudas appeared, claiming to be someone important, and about four hundred men joined him, but he was killed, and all those who were loyal to him were disbanded and came to nothing. 37 After him came Judas the Galilean at the time of the census. He also drew people after him, but he too perished and all who were loyal to him were scattered. 38 So now I tell you, have nothing to do with these men, and let them go. For if this endeavor or this activity is of human origin, it will destroy itself. 39 But if it comes from God, you will not be able to destroy them; you may even find yourselves fighting against God." They were persuaded by him. 40 After recalling the apostles, they had them flogged, ordered them to stop speaking in the name of Jesus, and dismissed them.ᵍ 41 So they left the presence of the Sanhedrin, rejoicing that they had been found worthy to suffer dishonor for the sake of the name.ʰ 42 And all day long, both at the temple and in their homes, they did not stop teaching and proclaiming the Messiah, Jesus.ⁱ

x Acts 4, 1-3.6.—y Acts 12, 7-10; 16, 25-26.—z Lk 20, 19.—a Mt 27, 25.—b Acts 4, 19.—c Acts 2, 23-24.—d Acts 2, 38.—e Lk 24, 48; Jn 15, 26.—f Acts 22, 3.—g Mt 10, 17; Acts 4, 17-18.—h Mt 5, 10-11; 1 Pt 4, 13.—i Acts 2, 46; 5, 20-21.25; 8, 35; 17, 3; 18, 5.28; 19, 4-5.

5, 17-42: A second action against the community is taken by the Sanhedrin in the arrest and trial of the Twelve; cf Acts 4, 1-3. The motive is the jealousy of the religious authorities over the popularity of the apostles (17) who are now charged with the defiance of the Sanhedrin's previous order to them to abandon their prophetic role (28; cf Acts 4, 18). In this crisis the apostles are favored by a miraculous release from prison (18-24). (For similar incidents involving Peter and Paul, see Acts 12, 6-11; 16, 25-29.) The real significance of such an event, however, would be manifest only to people of faith, not to unbelievers; since the Sanhedrin already judged the Twelve to be inauthentic prophets, it could disregard reports of their miracles. When the Twelve immediately resumed public teaching, the Sanhedrin determined to invoke upon them the penalty of death (33) prescribed in Dt 13, 6-10. Gamaliel's advice against this course finally prevailed, but it did not save the Twelve from the punishment of scourging (40) in a last endeavor to shake their conviction of their prophetic mission.

5, 30: *Hanging him on a tree:* that is, crucifying him (cf also Gal 3, 13).

5, 31: *At his right hand:* see the note on Acts 2, 33.

5, 34: *Gamaliel:* in Acts 22, 3, Paul identifies himself as a disciple of this Rabbi Gamaliel I who flourished in Jerusalem between A.D. 25 and 50.

5, 36-37: Gamaliel offers examples of unsuccessful contemporary movements to argue that if God is not the origin of this movement preached by the apostles it will perish by itself. The movement initiated by Theudas actually occurred when C. Cuspius Fadus was governor, A.D. 44-46. Luke's placing of Judas the Galilean after Theudas and at the time of the census (see the note on Lk 2, 1-2) is an indication of the vagueness of his knowledge of these events.

CHAPTER 6

The Need for Assistants. [1] At that time, as the number of disciples continued to grow, the Hellenists complained against the Hebrews* because their widows were being neglected in the daily distribution.*j* [2] * So the Twelve called together the community of the disciples and said, "It is not right for us to neglect the word of God to serve at table.* [3] Brothers, select from among you seven reputable men, filled with the Spirit and wisdom, whom we shall appoint to this task, [4] whereas we shall devote ourselves to prayer and to the ministry of the word." [5] The proposal was acceptable to the whole community, so they chose Stephen, a man filled with faith and the holy Spirit, also Philip, Prochorus, Nicanor, Timon, Parmenas, and Nicholas of Antioch, a convert to Judaism. [6] *k* They presented these men to the apostles who prayed and laid hands on them.* [7] The word of God continued to spread, and the number of the disciples in Jerusalem increased greatly; even a large group of priests were becoming obedient to the faith.*l*

Accusation against Stephen. [8] * Now Stephen, filled with grace and power, was working great wonders and signs among the people. [9] Certain members of the so-called Synagogue of Freedmen, Cyrenians, and Alexandrians, and people from Cilicia and Asia, came forward and debated with Stephen, [10] but they could not withstand the wisdom and the spirit with which he spoke.*m* [11] Then they instigated some men to say, "We have heard him speaking blasphemous words against Moses and God." *n* [12] They stirred up the people, the elders, and the scribes, accosted him, seized him, and brought him before the Sanhedrin. [13] They presented false witnesses* who testified, "This man never stops saying things against [this] holy place and the law. [14] For we have heard him claim that this Jesus the Nazorean will destroy this place and change the customs that Moses handed down to us." *o* [15] All those who sat in the Sanhedrin looked intently at him and saw that his face was like the face of an angel.

CHAPTER 7

Stephen's Discourses. [1] Then the high priest asked, "Is this so?" [2] *p* And he replied,* "My brothers and fathers, listen. The God of glory appeared to our father Abraham while he was in Mesopotamia,* before he had settled in Haran, [3] and said to him, 'Go forth from your land and

---

j Acts 2, 45; 4, 34-35.—k Acts 1, 24; 13, 3; 14, 23.—l Acts 9, 31; 12, 24; 16, 5; 19, 20; 28, 30-31.—m Lk 21, 15.—n Mt 26, 59-61; Mk 14, 55-58; Acts 21, 21.—o Mt 26, 59-61; 27, 40; Jn 2, 19.—p Gn 11, 31; 12, 1; Ps 29, 3.

6, 1-7: *The Hellenists . . . the Hebrews:* the Hellenists were not necessarily Jews from the diaspora, but were more probably Palestinian Jews who spoke only Greek. The Hebrews were Palestinian Jews who spoke Hebrew or Aramaic and who may also have spoken Greek. Both groups belong to the Jerusalem Jewish Christian community. The conflict between them leads to a restructuring of the community that will better serve the community's needs. The real purpose of the whole episode, however, is to introduce Stephen as a prominent figure in the community whose long speech and martyrdom will be recounted in ch 7.

6, 2-4: The essential function of the Twelve is the "service of the word," including development of the kerygma by formulation of the teachings of Jesus.

6, 2: *To serve at table:* some commentators think that it is not the serving of food that is described here but rather the keeping of the accounts that recorded the distribution of food to the needy members of the community. In any case, after Stephen and the others are chosen, they are never presented carrying out the task for which they were appointed (2-3). Rather, two of their number, Stephen and Philip, are presented as preachers of the Christian message. They, the Hellenist counterpart of the Twelve, are active in the ministry of the word.

6, 6: *They . . . laid hands on them:* the customary Jewish way of designating persons for a task and invoking upon them the divine blessing and power to perform it.

6, 8—8, 1: The summary (Acts 6, 7) on the progress of the Jerusalem community, illustrated by the conversion of the priests, is followed by a lengthy narrative regarding Stephen. Stephen's

defense is not a response to the charges made against him but takes the form of a discourse that reviews the fortunes of God's word to Israel and leads to a prophetic declaration: a plea for the hearing of that word as announced by Christ and now possessed by the Christian community.

The charges that Stephen depreciated the importance of the temple and the Mosaic law and elevated Jesus to a stature above Moses (Acts 6, 13-14) were in fact true. Before the Sanhedrin, no defense against them was possible. With Stephen, who thus perceived the fuller implications of the teachings of Jesus, the differences between Judaism and Christianity began to appear. Luke's account of Stephen's martyrdom and its aftermath shows how the major impetus behind the Christian movement passed from Jerusalem, where the temple and law prevailed, to Antioch in Syria, where these influences were less pressing.

6, 13: *False witnesses:* here, and in his account of Stephen's execution (Acts 7, 54-60), Luke parallels the martyrdom of Stephen with the death of Jesus.

7, 2-53: Stephen's speech represents Luke's description of Christianity's break from its Jewish matrix. Two motifs become prominent in the speech: (1) Israel's reaction to God's chosen leaders in the past reveals that the people have consistently rejected them; and (2) Israel has misunderstood God's choice of the Jerusalem temple as the place where he is to be worshiped.

7, 2: *God . . . appeared to our father Abraham . . . in Mesopotamia:* the first of a number of minor discrepancies between the data of the Old Testament and the data of Stephen's discourse. According to Gn 12, 1, God first spoke to Abraham in Haran. The main discrepancies are these: in v 16 it is said that Jacob was buried in Shechem, whereas Gn 50, 13 says he was buried at Hebron; in the same verse it is said that the tomb was purchased by Abraham, but in Gn 33, 19 and Jos 24, 32 the purchase is attributed to Jacob himself.

[from] your kinsfolk to the land that I will show you.'�q ⁴So he went forth from the land of the Chaldeans and settled in Haran. And from there, after his father died, he made him migrate to this land where you now dwell.ʳ ⁵Yet he gave him no inheritance in it, not even a foot's length, but he did promise to give it to him and his descendants as a possession, even though he was childless.ˢ ⁶And God spoke thus,ᵗ 'His descendants shall be aliens in a land not their own, where they shall be enslaved and oppressed for four hundred years; ⁷but I will bring judgment on the nation they serve,' God said, 'and after that they will come out and worship me in this place.'ᵘ ⁸Then he gave him the covenant of circumcision, and so he became the father of Isaac, and circumcised him on the eighth day, as Isaac did Jacob, and Jacob the twelve patriarchs.ᵛ

⁹"And the patriarchs, jealous of Joseph, sold him into slavery in Egypt; but God was with himʷ ¹⁰and rescued him from all his afflictions. He granted him favor and wisdom before Pharaoh, the king of Egypt, who put him in charge of Egypt and [of] his entire household.ˣ ¹¹Then a famine and great affliction struck all Egypt and Canaan, and our ancestors could find no food;ʸ ¹²but when Jacob heard that there was grain in Egypt, he sent our ancestors there a first time.ᶻ ¹³The second time, Joseph made himself known to his brothers, and Joseph's family became known to Pharaoh.ᵃ ¹⁴Then Joseph sent for his father Jacob, inviting him and his whole clan, seventy-five persons;ᵇ ¹⁵and Jacob went down to Egypt. And he and our ancestors diedᶜ ¹⁶and were brought back to Shechem and placed in the tomb that Abraham had purchased for a sum of money from the sons of Hamor at Shechem.ᵈ

¹⁷"When the time drew near for the fulfillment of the promise that God pledged to Abraham, the people had increased and become very numerous in Egypt,ᵉ ¹⁸until another king who knew nothing of Joseph came to power [in Egypt].ᶠ ¹⁹He dealt shrewdly with our people and oppressed [our] ancestors by forcing them to expose their infants, that they might not survive. ²⁰At this time Moses was born, and he was extremely beautiful. For three months he was nursed in his father's house;ᵍ ²¹but when he was exposed, Pharaoh's daughter adopted him and brought him up as her own son.ʰ ²²Moses was educated [in] all the wisdom of the Egyptians and was powerful in his words and deeds.

²³ⁱ"When he was forty years old, he decided to visit his kinsfolk, the Israelites. ²⁴When he saw one of them treated unjustly, he defended and avenged the oppressed man by striking down the Egyptian. ²⁵He assumed [his] kinsfolk would understand that God was offering them deliverance through him, but they did not understand. ²⁶ʲ The next day he appeared to them as they were fighting and tried to reconcile them peacefully, saying, 'Men, you are brothers. Why are you harming one another?' ²⁷Then the one who was harming his neighbor pushed him aside, saying, 'Who appointed you ruler and judge over us? ²⁸Are you thinking of killing me as you killed the Egyptian yesterday?' ²⁹Moses fled when he heard this and settled as an alien in the land of Midian, where he became the father of two sons.ᵏ

³⁰ˡ "Forty years later, an angel appeared to him in the desert near Mount Sinai in the flame of a burning bush. ³¹When Moses saw it, he was amazed at the sight, and as he drew near to look at it, the voice of the Lord came, ³²'I am the God of your fathers, the God of Abraham, of Isaac, and of Jacob.' Then Moses, trembling, did not dare to look at it. ³³But the Lord said to him, 'Remove the sandals from your feet, for the place where you stand is holy ground. ³⁴I have witnessed the affliction of my people in Egypt and have heard their groaning, and I have come down to rescue them. Come now, I will send you to Egypt.' ³⁵This Moses, whom they had rejected with the words, 'Who appointed you ruler and judge?' God sent as [both] ruler and deliverer, through the angel who appeared to him in the bush.ᵐ ³⁶This man led them out, performing wonders and signs in the land of Egypt, at the Red Sea, and in the desert for forty years.ⁿ ³⁷It was this Moses who said to the Israel-

q Gn 12, 1.—r Gn 12, 5; 15, 7.—s Gn 12, 7; 13, 15; 15, 2; 16, 1; Dt 2, 5.—t 6-7: Gn 15, 13-14.—u Ex 3, 12.—v Gn 17, 10-14; 21, 2-4.—w Gn 37, 11.28; 39, 2.3.21.23.—x Gn 41, 37-43; Ps 105, 21; Wis 10, 13-14.—y Gn 41, 54-57; 42, 5.—z Gn 42, 1-2.—a Gn 45, 3-4.16.—b Gn 45, 9-11.18-19; 46, 27; Ex 1, 5 LXX; Dt 10, 22.—c Gn 46, 5-6; 49, 33.—d Gn 23, 3-20; 33, 19; 49, 29-30; 50, 13; Jos 24, 32.—e Ex 1, 7.—f Ex 1, 8.—g Ex 2, 2; Heb 11, 23.—h Ex 2, 3-10.—i 23-24: Ex 2, 11-12.—j 26-28: Ex 2, 13-14.—k Ex 2, 15.21-22; 18, 3-4.—l 30-34: Ex 3, 2-3.—m Ex 2, 14.—n Ex 7, 3.10; 14, 21; Nm 14, 33.

ites, 'God will raise up for you, from among your own kinsfolk, a prophet like me.'[o] [38] It was he who, in the assembly in the desert, was with the angel who spoke to him on Mount Sinai and with our ancestors, and he received living utterances to hand on to us.[p]

[39] "Our ancestors were unwilling to obey him; instead, they pushed him aside and in their hearts turned back to Egypt,[q] [40] saying to Aaron, 'Make us gods who will be our leaders. As for that Moses who led us out of the land of Egypt, we do not know what has happened to him.'[r] [41] So they made a calf in those days, offered sacrifice to the idol, and reveled in the works of their hands.[s] [42] Then God turned and handed them over to worship the host of heaven, as it is written in the book of the prophets:[t]

'Did you bring me sacrifices and offerings
    for forty years in the desert, O house of Israel?[u]
[43] No, you took up the tent of Moloch
    and the star of [your] god Rephan,
      the images that you made to worship.
So I shall take you into exile beyond Babylon.'

[44] Our ancestors had the tent of testimony in the desert just as the One who spoke to Moses directed him to make it according to the pattern he had seen.[v] [45] Our ancestors who inherited it brought it with Joshua when they dispossessed the nations that God drove out from before our ancestors, up to the time of David,[w] [46] who found favor in the sight of God and asked that he might find a dwelling place for the house of Jacob.[x] [47] But Solomon built a house for him.[y] [48] Yet the Most High does not dwell in houses made by human hands. As the prophet says:[z]

[49] 'The heavens are my throne,
    the earth is my footstool.
What kind of house can you build for me?
    says the Lord,
    or what is to be my resting place?[a]
[50] Did not my hand make all these things?'

Conclusion. [51] "You stiff-necked people, uncircumcised in heart and ears, you always oppose the holy Spirit; you are just like your ancestors. [52] Which of the proph-

ets did your ancestors not persecute? They put to death those who foretold the coming of the righteous one, whose betrayers and murderers you have now become.[b] [53] You received the law as transmitted by angels, but you did not observe it."[c]

Stephen's Martyrdom. [54] When they heard this, they were infuriated, and they ground their teeth at him. [55] [d] But he, filled with the holy Spirit, looked up intently to heaven and saw the glory of God and Jesus standing at the right hand of God,* [56] and he said, "Behold, I see the heavens opened and the Son of Man standing at the right hand of God." [57] But they cried out in a loud voice, covered their ears,* and rushed upon him together. [58] They threw him out of the city, and began to stone him. The witnesses laid down their cloaks at the feet of a young man named Saul.[e] [59] As they were stoning Stephen,[f] he called out, "Lord Jesus, receive my spirit."* [60] Then he fell to his knees and cried out in a loud voice, "Lord, do not hold this sin against them"; and when he said this, he fell asleep.[g]

CHAPTER 8

[1] Now Saul was consenting to his execution.[h]

Persecution of the Church. On that day, there broke out a severe persecution* of the church in Jerusalem, and all were scattered throughout the countryside of Judea and Samaria, except the apostles.* [2] De-

---

o Dt 18, 15; Acts 3, 22.—p Ex 19, 3; 20, 1-17; Dt 5, 4-22; 6, 4-25.—q Nm 14, 3.—r Ex 32, 1.23.—s Ex 32, 4-6.—t 42-43: Am 5, 25-27.—u Jer 7, 18; 8, 2; 19, 13.—v Ex 25, 9.40.—w Jos 3, 14-17; 18, 1; 2 Sm 7, 5-7.—x 2 Sm 7, 1-2; 1 Kgs 8, 17; Ps 132, 1-5.—y 1 Kgs 6, 1; 1 Chr 17, 12.—z Acts 17, 24.—a Is 66, 1-2.—b 2 Chr 36, 16; Mt 23, 31.34.—c Gal 3, 19; Heb 2, 2.—d 55-56: Mt 26, 64; Mk 14, 62; Lk 22, 69; Acts 2, 34.—e Acts 22, 20.—f Ps 31, 6; Lk 23, 46.—g Mt 27, 46.50; Mk 15, 34; Lk 23, 46.—h Acts 22, 20.

7, 55: *He . . . saw . . . Jesus standing at the right hand of God:* Stephen affirms to the Sanhedrin that the prophecy Jesus made before them has been fulfilled (Mk 14, 62).

7, 57: *Covered their ears:* Stephen's declaration, like that of Jesus, is a scandal to the court, which regards it as blasphemy.

7, 59: Compare Lk 23, [34].46.

8, 1-40: Some idea of the severity of the persecution that now breaks out against the Jerusalem community can be gathered from Acts 22, 4 and Acts 26, 9-11. Luke, however, concentrates on the fortunes of the word of God among people, indicating how the dispersal of the Jewish community resulted in the conversion of the Samaritans (4-17.25). His narrative is further expanded to include the account of Philip's acceptance of an Ethiopian (26-39).

8, 1: *All were scattered . . . except the apostles:* this observation leads some modern scholars to conclude that the persecution was limited to the Hellenist Christians and that the Hebrew Christians were not molested, perhaps because their attitude to-

vout men buried Stephen and made a loud lament over him. ³Saul, meanwhile, was trying to destroy the church;* entering house after house and dragging out men and women, he handed them over for imprisonment.ⁱ

III. THE MISSION IN JUDEA AND SAMARIA

Philip in Samaria. ⁴Now those who had been scattered went about preaching the word.ʲ ⁵Thus Philip went down to [the] city of Samaria and proclaimed the Messiah to them.ᵏ ⁶With one accord, the crowds paid attention to what was said by Philip when they heard it and saw the signs he was doing. ⁷For unclean spirits, crying out in a loud voice, came out of many possessed people, and many paralyzed and crippled people were cured.ˡ ⁸There was great joy in that city.

Simon the Magician. ⁹A man named Simon used to practice magic* in the city and astounded the people of Samaria, claiming to be someone great. ¹⁰All of them, from the least to the greatest, paid attention to him, saying, "This man is the 'Power of God' that is called 'Great.' " ¹¹They paid attention to him because he had astounded them by his magic for a long time, ¹²but once they began to believe Philip as he preached the good news about the kingdom of God and the name of Jesus Christ, men and women alike were baptized.ᵐ ¹³Even Simon himself believed and, after being baptized, became devoted to Philip; and when he saw the signs and mighty deeds that were occurring, he was astounded.

¹⁴Now when the apostles in Jerusalem heard that Samaria had accepted the word of God, they sent them Peter and John, ¹⁵who went down and prayed for them, that they might receive the holy Spirit, ¹⁶for it had not yet fallen upon any of them; they had only been baptized in the name of the Lord Jesus.* ¹⁷Then they laid hands on them and they received the holy Spirit.ⁿ

¹⁸ *When Simon saw that the Spirit was conferred by the laying on of the apostles' hands, he offered them money ¹⁹and said, "Give me this power too, so that anyone upon whom I lay my hands may receive the holy Spirit." ²⁰But Peter said to him, "May your money perish with you, because you thought that you could buy the gift of God with money. ²¹You have no share or lot in this matter, for your heart is not upright before God. ²²Repent of this wickedness of yours and pray to the Lord that, if possible, your intention may be forgiven. ²³For I see that you are filled with bitter gall and are in the bonds of iniquity." ²⁴Simon said in reply, "Pray for me to the Lord, that nothing of what you have said may come upon me." ²⁵So when they had testified and proclaimed the word of the Lord, they returned to Jerusalem and preached the good news to many Samaritan villages.

Philip and the Ethiopian.* ²⁶Then the angel of the Lord spoke to Philip, "Get up and head south on the road that goes down from Jerusalem to Gaza, the desert route."

i Acts 9, 1.13; 22, 4; 26, 9-11; 1 Cor 5, 9; Gal 1, 13.—j Acts 11, 19.—k Acts 6, 5; 21, 8-9.—l Mk 16, 17.—m Acts 1, 3; 19, 8; 28, 23.31.—n Acts 2, 4; 4, 31; 10, 44-47; 15, 8-9; 19, 2.6.

8, 16: Here and in Acts 10, 44-48 and Acts 19, 1-6, Luke distinguishes between baptism in the name of the Lord Jesus and the reception of the Spirit. In each case, the Spirit is conferred through members of the Twelve (Peter and John) or their representative (Paul). This may be Luke's way of describing the role of the church in the bestowal of the Spirit. Elsewhere in Acts, baptism and the Spirit are more closely related (Acts 1, 5; 11, 16).

8, 18-20: Simon attempts to buy the gift of God (20) with money. Peter's cursing of Simon's attempt so to use his money expresses a typically Lucan attitude toward material wealth (cf Lk 6, 24; 12, 16-21; 16, 13).

8, 26-40: In the account of the conversion of the Ethiopian eunuch, Luke adduces additional evidence to show that the spread of Christianity outside the confines of Judaism itself was in accord with the plan of God. He does not make clear whether the Ethiopian was originally a convert to Judaism or, as is more probable, a "God-fearer" (Acts 10, 1), i.e., one who accepted Jewish monotheism and ethic and attended the synagogue but did not consider himself bound by other regulations such as circumcision and observance of the dietary laws. The story of his conversion to Christianity is given a strong supernatural cast by the introduction of an angel (26), instruction from the holy Spirit (29), and the strange removal of Philip from the scene (39).

ward the law and temple was still more in line with that of their fellow Jews (see the charge leveled against the Hellenist Stephen in Acts 6, 13-14). Whatever the facts, it appears that the Twelve took no public stand regarding Stephen's position, choosing, instead, to await the development of events.

8, 3: *Saul . . . was trying to destroy the church:* like Stephen, Saul was able to perceive that the Christian movement contained the seeds of doctrinal divergence from Judaism. A pupil of Gamaliel, according to Acts 22, 3, and totally dedicated to the law as the way of salvation (Gal 1, 13-14), Saul accepted the task of crushing the Christian movement, at least insofar as it detracted from the importance of the temple and the law. His vehement opposition to Christianity reveals how difficult it was for a Jew of his time to accept a messianism that differed so greatly from the general expectation.

8, 9-13.18-24: Sorcerers were well known in the ancient world. Probably the incident involving Simon and his altercation with Peter is introduced to show that the miraculous charisms possessed by members of the Christian community (6-7) were not to be confused with the magic of sorcerers.

27 So he got up and set out. Now there was an Ethiopian eunuch, a court official of the Candace,* that is, the queen of the Ethiopians, in charge of her entire treasury, who had come to Jerusalem to worship,° 28 and was returning home. Seated in his chariot, he was reading the prophet Isaiah. 29 The Spirit said to Philip, "Go and join up with that chariot." 30 * Philip ran up and heard him reading Isaiah the prophet and said, "Do you understand what you are reading?" 31 He replied, "How can I, unless someone instructs me?" So he invited Philip to get in and sit with him.º 32 This was the scripture passage he was reading: ⁹

> "Like a sheep he was led to the slaughter,
> and as a lamb before its shearer is silent,
> so he opened not his mouth.

33 In [his] humiliation justice was denied him.
> Who will tell of his posterity?
> For his life is taken from the earth."

34 Then the eunuch said to Philip in reply, "I beg you, about whom is the prophet saying this? About himself, or about someone else?" 35 Then Philip opened his mouth and, beginning with this scripture passage, he proclaimed Jesus to him. 36 ʳ As they traveled along the road they came to some water, and the eunuch said, "Look, there is water. What is to prevent my being baptized?" [37] * 38 Then he ordered the chariot to stop, and Philip and the eunuch both went down into the water, and he baptized him. 39 When they came out of the water, the Spirit of the Lord snatched Philip away, and the eunuch saw him no more, but continued on his way rejoicing.ˢ 40 Philip came to Azotus, and went about proclaiming the good news to all the towns until he reached Caesarea.ᵗ

CHAPTER 9

Saul's Conversion. 1 * Now Saul, still breathing murderous threats against the disciples of the Lord,ᵘ went to the high priestᵛ 2 and asked him for letters to the synagogues in Damascus, that, if he should find any men or women who belonged to the Way,* he might bring them back to Jerusalem in chains. 3 On his journey, as he was nearing Damascus, a light from the sky suddenly flashed around him.ʷ 4 He

fell to the ground and heard a voice saying to him, "Saul, Saul, why are you persecuting me?"ˣ 5 He said, "Who are you, sir?" The reply came, "I am Jesus, whom you are persecuting.ʸ 6 Now get up and go into the city and you will be told what you must do."ᶻ 7 The men who were traveling with him stood speechless, for they heard the voice but could see no one.ᵃ 8 Saul got up from the ground, but when he opened his eyes he could see nothing;* so they led him by the hand and brought him to Damascus.ᵇ 9 For three days he was unable to see, and he neither ate nor drank.

Saul's Baptism. 10 ᶜ There was a disciple in Damascus named Ananias, and the Lord said to him in a vision, "Ananias." He answered, "Here I am, Lord." 11 The Lord said to him, "Get up and go to the street called Straight and ask at the house of Judas for a man from Tarsus named Saul. He is there praying,ᵈ 12 and [in a vision] he has seen a man named Ananias

---

o Is 56, 3-5.—p Jn 16, 13.—q 32-33: Is 53, 7-8 LXX.—r Acts 10, 47.—s 1 Kgs 18, 12.—t Acts 21, 8.—u Acts 8, 3; 9, 13; 22, 4; 1 Cor 15, 9; Gal 1, 13-14.—v 1-2: Acts 9, 14; 26, 10.—w 1 Cor 9, 1; 15, 8; Gal 1, 16.—x Acts 22, 6; 26, 14.—y Acts 22, 8; 26, 15; Mt 25, 40.—z Acts 22, 10; 26, 16.—a Acts 22, 9; 26, 13-14.—b Acts 22, 11.—c 10-19: Acts 22, 12-16.—d Acts 21, 39.

8, 27: *The Candace:* Candace is not a proper name here but the title of a Nubian queen.

8, 30-34: Philip is brought alongside the carriage at the very moment when the Ethiopian is pondering the meaning of Is 53, 7-8, a passage that Christianity, from its earliest origins, has applied to Jesus; cf the note on Acts 3, 13.

8, 37: The oldest and best manuscripts of Acts omit this verse, which is a Western text reading: "And Philip said, 'If you believe with all your heart, you may.' And he said in reply, 'I believe that Jesus Christ is the Son of God.' "

9, 1-19: This is the first of three accounts of Paul's conversion (with Acts 22, 3-16 and Acts 26, 2-18) with some differences of detail owing to Luke's use of different sources. Paul's experience was not visionary but was precipitated by the appearance of Jesus, as he insists in 1 Cor 15, 8. The words of Jesus, "Saul, Saul, why are you persecuting me?" related by Luke with no variation in all three accounts, exerted a profound and lasting influence on the thought of Paul. Under the influence of this experience he gradually developed his understanding of justification by faith (see the letters to the Galatians and Romans) and of the identification of the Christian community with Jesus Christ (see 1 Cor 12, 27). That Luke would narrate this conversion three times is testimony to the importance he attaches to it. This first account occurs when the word is first spread to the Gentiles. At this point, the conversion of the hero of the Gentile mission is recounted. The emphasis in the account is on Paul as a divinely chosen instrument (15).

9, 2: *The Way:* a name used by the early Christian community for itself (Acts 18, 26; 19, 9.23; 22, 4; 24, 14.22). The Essene community at Qumran used the same designation to describe its mode of life.

9, 8: *He could see nothing:* a temporary blindness (18) symbolizing the religious blindness of Saul as persecutor (cf Acts 26, 18).

Ewing Galloway

THE STREET CALLED STRAIGHT — View of one of the oldest streets in the world. In St. Paul's time Damascus was laid out in the form of a rectangle intersected by "straight streets." The longest of them all was the "Street called Straight." When Paul was blinded on the way to Damascus, his companions took him into the city to the house of Judas where Ananias called for him. (See Acts 9, 11ff)

Matson Photo Service

THE OLD WALL OF DAMASCUS — View of the Bab Kisar Gate (now boarded up) in the old wall of Damascus 300 yards south of the Easter Gate at the end of the "Street called Straight." It was here that tradition says the disciples lowered Paul in a basket through a window in the wall to enable him to escape his enemies. (See Acts 9, 25)

H. H. Kok

ARTEMIS OF THE EPHESIANS — Ephesian goddess counterpart of the Roman Diana, regarded as the great Asiatic nursing mother of gods, men, animals and plants. Her worship was centered in the great temple at Ephesus and her feast was highly commercialized. (See Acts 19, 26-28)

THE FORTRESS ANTONIA IN JERUSALEM — A fortress connected with the temple at Jerusalem and housing a Roman legion to guard against excesses on the part of the people. When Paul was seized in the temple by the Jews, he was taken to this fortress and addressed the people from its stairs. (See Acts 21, 30ff)

THE THEATER AT EPHESUS — View of excavation of the theater at Ephesus. Visible are the ruins of the stage and the orchestra, with some of the seats rising tier upon tier behind them (which could reportedly hold 24,000 people). It was here that the silversmiths incited the worshipers of Artemis to gather and riot because of the words of Paul. (See Acts 19, 28ff)

come in and lay [his] hands on him, that he may regain his sight." [13] But Ananias replied, "Lord, I have heard from many sources about this man, what evil things he has done to your holy ones* in Jerusalem.[e] [14] And here he has authority from the chief priests to imprison all who call upon your name."[f] [15] But the Lord said to him, "Go, for this man is a chosen instrument of mine to carry my name before Gentiles, kings, and Israelites,[g] [16] and I will show him what he will have to suffer for my name." [17] So Ananias went and entered the house; laying his hands on him, he said, "Saul, my brother, the Lord has sent me, Jesus who appeared to you on the way by which you came, that you may regain your sight and be filled with the holy Spirit." [18] Immediately things like scales fell from his eyes and he regained his sight. He got up and was baptized, [19] and when he had eaten, he recovered his strength.

Saul Preaches in Damascus.* He stayed some days with the disciples in Damascus, [20] and he began at once to proclaim Jesus in the synagogues, that he is the Son of God.* [21] All who heard him were astounded and said, "Is not this the man who in Jerusalem ravaged those who call upon this name, and came here expressly to take them back in chains to the chief priests?" [22] But Saul grew all the stronger and confounded [the] Jews who lived in Damascus, proving that this is the Messiah.

---

e Acts 8, 3; 9, 1.—f Acts 9, 1-2; 26, 10; 1 Cor 1, 2; 2 Tm 2, 22.—g Acts 22, 15; 26, 1; 27, 24.—h 24-25: 2 Cor 11, 32-33.— i 26-27: Gal 1, 18.—j Acts 11, 25.

9, 13: *Your holy ones:* literally, "your saints."

9, 19-30: This is a brief resume of Paul's initial experience as an apostolic preacher. At first he found himself in the position of being regarded as an apostate by the Jews and suspect by the Christian community of Jerusalem. His acceptance by the latter was finally brought about through his friendship with Barnabas (27).

9, 20: *Son of God:* the title "Son of God" occurs in Acts only here, but cf the citation of Ps 2, 7 in Paul's speech at Antioch in Pisidia (Acts 13, 33).

9, 26: This visit of Paul to Jerusalem is mentioned by Paul in Gal 1, 18.

9, 29: *Hellenists:* see the note on Acts 6, 1-7.

9, 31-43: In the context of the period of peace enjoyed by the community through the cessation of Paul's activities against it, Luke introduces two traditions concerning the miraculous power exercised by Peter as he was making a tour of places where the Christian message had already been preached. The towns of Lydda, Sharon, and Joppa were populated by both Jews and Gentiles and their Christian communities may well have been mixed.

9, 36: *Tabitha (Dorcas),* respectively the Aramaic and Greek words for "gazelle," exemplifies the right attitude toward material possessions expressed by Jesus in the Lucan Gospel (Lk 6, 30; 11, 41; 12, 33; 18, 22; 19, 8).

Saul Visits Jerusalem. [23] After a long time had passed, the Jews conspired to kill him, [24] [h] but their plot became known to Saul. Now they were keeping watch on the gates day and night so as to kill him, [25] but his disciples took him one night and let him down through an opening in the wall, lowering him in a basket.

[26] [i] When he arrived in Jerusalem* he tried to join the disciples, but they were all afraid of him, not believing that he was a disciple. [27] Then Barnabas took charge of him and brought him to the apostles, and he reported to them how on the way he had seen the Lord and that he had spoken to him, and how in Damascus he had spoken out boldly in the name of Jesus. [28] He moved about freely with them in Jerusalem, and spoke out boldly in the name of the Lord. [29] He also spoke and debated with the Hellenists,* but they tried to kill him. [30] And when the brothers learned of this, they took him down to Caesarea and sent him on his way to Tarsus.[j]

The Church at Peace. [31] * The church throughout all Judea, Galilee, and Samaria was at peace. It was being built up and walked in the fear of the Lord, and with the consolation of the holy Spirit it grew in numbers.

Peter Heals Aeneas at Lydda. [32] As Peter was passing through every region, he went down to the holy ones living in Lydda. [33] There he found a man named Aeneas, who had been confined to bed for eight years, for he was paralyzed. [34] Peter said to him, "Aeneas, Jesus Christ heals you. Get up and make your bed." He got up at once. [35] And all the inhabitants of Lydda and Sharon saw him, and they turned to the Lord.

Peter Restores Tabitha to Life. [36] Now in Joppa there was a disciple named Tabitha (which translated means Dorcas).* She was completely occupied with good deeds and almsgiving. [37] Now during those days she fell sick and died, so after washing her, they laid [her] out in a room upstairs. [38] Since Lydda was near Joppa, the disciples, hearing that Peter was there, sent two men to him with the request, "Please come to us without delay." [39] So Peter got up and went with them. When he arrived, they took him to the room upstairs where all the widows came to him weeping and showing him the tunics and cloaks that Dorcas had made while she was with them. [40]Peter sent them all out and knelt down and prayed. Then he turned to her body and said, "Tabitha, rise up." She opened her eyes, saw Peter, and sat up.[k] [41]He gave her his hand and raised her up, and when he had called the holy ones and the widows, he presented her alive. [42]This became known all over Joppa, and many came to believe in the Lord. [43] [l] And he stayed a long time in Joppa with Simon, a tanner.*

IV. THE INAUGURATION OF THE GENTILE MISSION

CHAPTER 10

The Vision of Cornelius.[m] [1] * Now in Caesarea there was a man named Cornelius, a centurion of the Cohort called the Italica,* [2]devout and God-fearing along with his whole household, who used to give alms generously* to the Jewish people and pray to God constantly. [3]One afternoon about three o'clock,* he saw plainly in a vision an angel of God come in to him and say to him, "Cornelius." [4]He looked intently at him and, seized with fear, said, "What is it, sir?" He said to him, "Your prayers and almsgiving have ascended as a memorial offering before God. [5]Now send some men to Joppa and summon one Simon who is called Peter. [6]He is staying with another Simon, a tanner, who has a house by the sea."[n] [7]When the angel who spoke to him had left, he called two of his servants and a devout soldier* from his staff, [8]explained everything to them, and sent them to Joppa.

The Vision of Peter. [9] * The next day, while they were on their way and nearing the city, Peter went up to the roof terrace to pray at about noontime.* [10]He was hungry and wished to eat, and while they were making preparations he fell into a trance. [11] [o] He saw heaven opened and something resembling a large sheet coming down, lowered to the ground by its four corners. [12]In it were all the earth's four-legged animals and reptiles and the birds of the sky. [13]A voice said to him, "Get up, Peter. Slaughter and eat." [14]But Peter said, "Certainly not, sir. For never have I eaten anything profane and unclean."[p] [15]The voice spoke to him again, a second time, "What God has made clean, you are not to call profane."[q] [16]This happened three times, and then the object was taken up into the sky.

[17] * While Peter was in doubt about the meaning of the vision he had seen, the men sent by Cornelius asked for Simon's house and arrived at the entrance. [18]They called out inquiring whether Simon, who is called Peter, was staying there. [19]As Peter was pondering the vision, the Spirit said [to him], "There are three men here looking for you.[r] [20]So get up, go downstairs, and accompany them without hesitation, because I have sent them." [21]Then Peter went down to the men and said, "I am the one you are looking for. What is the reason for your being here?" [22]They answered, "Cornelius, a centurion, an upright and God-fearing man, respected by the whole Jewish nation, was directed by a holy angel to summon you to his house and to hear what you have to say."[s] [23]So he invited them in and showed them hospitality.

The next day he got up and went with them, and some of the brothers from Joppa

k Mk 5, 40-41.—l Acts 10, 6.—m 1-8: Acts 10, 30-33.—n Acts 9, 43.—o 11-20: Acts 11, 5-12.—p Lv 11, 1-47; Ez 4, 14.—q Mk 7, 15-19; Gal 2, 12.—r Acts 13, 2.—s Lk 7, 4-5.

9, 43: The fact that Peter lodged with a tanner would have been significant to both the Gentile and the Jewish Christians, for Judaism considered the tanning occupation unclean.

10, 1-48: The narrative centers on the conversion of Cornelius, a Gentile and a "God-fearer" (see the note on Acts 8, 26-40). Luke considers the event of great importance, as is evident from his long treatment of it. The incident is again related in Acts 11, 1-18 where Peter is forced to justify his actions before the Jerusalem community and alluded to in Acts 15, 7-11 where at the Jerusalem "Council" Peter supports Paul's missionary activity among the Gentiles. The narrative divides itself into a series of distinct episodes, concluding with Peter's presentation of the Christian kerygma (34-43) and a pentecostal experience undergone by Cornelius's household preceding their reception of baptism (44-48).

10, 1: *The Cohort called the Italica:* this battalion was an auxiliary unit of archers formed originally in Italy but transferred to Syria shortly before A.D. 69.

10, 2: *Used to give alms generously:* like Tabitha (Acts 9, 36), Cornelius exemplifies the proper attitude toward wealth (see the note on Acts 9, 36).

10, 3: *About three o'clock:* literally, "about the ninth hour." See the note on Acts 3, 1.

10, 7: *A devout soldier:* by using this adjective, Luke probably intends to classify him as a "God-fearer" (see the note on Acts 8, 26-40).

10, 9-16: The vision is intended to prepare Peter to share the food of Cornelius's household without qualms of conscience (48). The necessity of such instructions to Peter reveals that at first not even the apostles fully grasped the implications of Jesus' teaching on the law. In Acts, the initial insight belongs to Stephen.

10, 9: *At about noontime:* literally, "about the sixth hour."

10, 17-23: The arrival of the Gentile emissaries with their account of the angelic apparition illuminates Peter's vision: he is to be prepared to admit Gentiles, who were considered unclean like the animals of his vision, into the Christian community.

went with him. ²⁴ * On the following day he entered Caesarea. Cornelius was expecting them and had called together his relatives and close friends. ²⁵ ᵗ When Peter entered, Cornelius met him and, falling at his feet, paid him homage. ²⁶ Peter, however, raised him up, saying, "Get up. I myself am also a human being." ²⁷ While he conversed with him, he went in and found many people gathered together ²⁸ ᵘ and said to them, "You know that it is unlawful for a Jewish man to associate with, or visit, a Gentile, but God has shown me that I should not call any person profane or unclean.* ²⁹ And that is why I came without objection when sent for. May I ask, then, why you summoned me?"

³⁰ Cornelius replied, "Four days ago* at this hour, three o'clock in the afternoon, I was at prayer in my house when suddenly a man in dazzling robes stood before me and said, ³¹ 'Cornelius, your prayer has been heard and your almsgiving remembered before God. ³² Send therefore to Joppa and summon Simon, who is called Peter. He is a guest in the house of Simon, a tanner, by the sea.' ³³ So I sent for you immediately, and you were kind enough to come. Now therefore we are all here in the presence of God to listen to all that you have been commanded by the Lord."

Peter's Speech.* ³⁴ Then Peter proceeded to speak and said,* "In truth, I see that God shows no partiality. ᵛ ³⁵ Rather, in every nation whoever fears him and acts uprightly is acceptable to him. ³⁶ * You

know the word [that] he sent to the Israelites* as he proclaimed peace through Jesus Christ, who is Lord of all, ʷ ³⁷ what has happened all over Judea, beginning in Galilee after the baptism that John preached, ˣ ³⁸ how God anointed Jesus of Nazareth* with the holy Spirit and power. He went about doing good and healing all those oppressed by the devil, for God was with him. ʸ ³⁹ We are witnesses* of all that he did both in the country of the Jews and [in] Jerusalem. They put him to death by hanging him on a tree. ⁴⁰ This man God raised [on] the third day and granted that he be visible, ⁴¹ not to all the people, but to us, the witnesses chosen by God in advance, who ate and drank with him after he rose from the dead. ᶻ ⁴² He commissioned us ᵃ to preach to the people and testify that he is the one appointed by God as judge of the living and the dead.* ⁴³ To him all the prophets bear witness, that everyone who believes in him will receive forgiveness of sins through his name."

The Baptism of Cornelius. ⁴⁴ ᵇ While Peter was still speaking these things, the holy Spirit fell upon all who were listening to the word.* ⁴⁵ The circumcised believers who had accompanied Peter were astounded that the gift of the holy Spirit should have been poured out on the Gentiles also, ⁴⁶ for they could hear them speaking in tongues and glorifying God. Then Peter responded, ⁴⁷ "Can anyone

t 25-26: Acts 14, 13-15; Rv 19, 10.—u Gal 2, 11-16.—v Dt 17, 2; 2 Chr 19, 7; Jb 34, 19; Wis 6, 7; Rom 2, 11; Gal 2, 6; Eph 6, 9; 1 Pt 1, 17.—w Is 52, 7; Na 2, 1.—x Mt 4, 12; Mk 1, 14; Lk 4, 14.—y Is 61, 1; Lk 4, 18.—z Lk 24, 41-43.—a Acts 1, 8; 3, 15; 17, 31; Lk 24, 48; Rom 14, 9; 2 Tm 4, 1.—b Acts 11, 15; 15, 8.

10, 24-27: So impressed is Cornelius with the apparition that he invites close personal friends to join him in his meeting with Peter. But his understanding of the person he is about to meet is not devoid of superstition, suggested by his falling down before him. For a similar experience of Paul and Barnabas, see Acts 14, 11-18.

10, 28: Peter now fully understands the meaning of his vision; see the note on Acts 10, 17-23.

10, 30: *Four days ago:* literally, "from the fourth day up to this hour."

10, 34-43: Peter's speech to the household of Cornelius typifies early Christian preaching to Gentiles.

10, 34-35: The revelation of God's choice of Israel to be the people of God did not mean he withheld the divine favor from other people.

10, 36-43: These words are more directed to Luke's Christian readers than to the household of Cornelius, as indicated by the opening words, "You know." They trace the continuity between the preaching and teaching of Jesus of Nazareth and the procla-

mation of Jesus by the early community. The emphasis on this divinely ordained continuity (41) is meant to assure Luke's readers of the fidelity of Christian tradition to the words and deeds of Jesus.

10, 36: *To the Israelites:* Luke, in the words of Peter, speaks of the prominent position occupied by Israel in the history of salvation.

10, 38: *Jesus of Nazareth:* God's revelation of his plan for the destiny of humanity through Israel culminated in Jesus of Nazareth. Consequently, the ministry of Jesus is an integral part of God's revelation. This viewpoint explains why the early Christian communities were interested in conserving the historical substance of the ministry of Jesus, a tradition leading to the production of the four gospels.

10, 39: *We are witnesses:* the apostolic testimony was not restricted to the resurrection of Jesus but also included his historical ministry. This witness, however, was theological in character; the Twelve, divinely mandated as prophets, were empowered to interpret his sayings and deeds in the light of his redemptive death and resurrection. The meaning of these words and deeds was to be made clear to the developing Christian community as the bearer of the word of salvation (cf Acts 1, 21-26). *Hanging him on a tree:* see the note on Acts 5, 30.

10, 42: *As judge of the living and the dead:* the apostolic preaching to the Jews appealed to their messianic hope, while the preaching to Gentiles stressed the coming divine judgment; cf 1 Thes 1, 10.

10, 44: Just as the Jewish Christians received the gift of the Spirit, so too do the Gentiles.

Acts

withhold the water for baptizing these people, who have received the holy Spirit even as we have?"[c] [48] He ordered them to be baptized in the name of Jesus Christ. [49] Then they invited him to stay for a few days.

CHAPTER 11

The Baptism of the Gentiles Explained.*

[1] Now the apostles and the brothers who were in Judea heard that the Gentiles too had accepted the word of God. [2] So when Peter went up to Jerusalem the circumcised believers confronted him, [3] saying, "You entered* the house of uncircumcised people and ate with them." [4] Peter began and explained it to them step by step, saying, [5] [d] "I was at prayer in the city of Joppa when in a trance I had a vision, something resembling a large sheet coming down, lowered from the sky by its four corners, and it came to me. [6] Looking intently into it, I observed and saw the four-legged animals of the earth, the wild beasts, the reptiles, and the birds of the sky. [7] I also heard a voice say to me, 'Get up, Peter. Slaughter and eat.' [8] But I said, 'Certainly not, sir, because nothing profane or unclean has ever entered my mouth.' [9] But a second time a voice from heaven answered, 'What God has made clean, you are not to call profane.' [10] This happened three times, and then everything was drawn up again into the sky. [11] Just then three men appeared at the house where we were, who had been sent to me from Caesarea. [12] The Spirit told me to accompany them without discriminating. These six brothers* also went with me, and we entered the man's house. [13] He related to us how he had seen [the] angel standing in his house, saying, 'Send someone to Joppa and summon Simon, who is called Peter,[e] [14] who will speak words to you by which you and all your household will be saved.' [15] As I began to speak, the holy Spirit fell upon them as it had upon us at the beginning,[f] [16] and I remembered the word of the Lord, how he had said, 'John baptized with water but you will be baptized with the holy Spirit.'[g] [17] If then God gave them the same gift he gave to us when we came to believe in the Lord Jesus Christ, who was I to be able to hinder God?"[h] [18] When they heard this, they stopped objecting and glorified God, saying, "God has then granted life-giving repentance to the Gentiles too."

The Church at Antioch.* [19] Now those who had been scattered by the persecution that arose because of Stephen went as far as Phoenicia, Cyprus, and Antioch, preaching the word to no one but Jews.[i] [20] There were some Cypriots and Cyrenians among them, however, who came to Antioch and began to speak to the Greeks as well, proclaiming the Lord Jesus. [21] The hand of the Lord was with them and a great number who believed turned to the Lord. [22] The news about them reached the ears of the church in Jerusalem, and they sent Barnabas [to go] to Antioch. [23] When he arrived and saw the grace of God, he rejoiced and encouraged them all to remain faithful to the Lord in firmness of heart, [24] for he was a good man, filled with the holy Spirit and faith. And a large number of people was added to the Lord. [25] Then he went to Tarsus to look for Saul, [26] and when he had found him he brought him to Antioch. For a whole year they met with the church and taught a large number of people, and it was in Antioch that the disciples were first called Christians.*

The Prediction of Agabus.* [27] At that time some prophets came down from Jerusalem

c Acts 8, 36.—d 5-12: Acts 10, 11-20.—e Acts 10, 3-5.22.30-32.—f Acts 10, 44.—g Acts 1, 5; 19, 4; Lk 3, 16.—h Acts 15, 8-9.—i Acts 8, 1-4.

11, 1-18: The Jewish Christians of Jerusalem were scandalized to learn of Peter's sojourn in the house of the Gentile Cornelius. Nonetheless, they had to accept the divine directions given to both Peter and Cornelius. They concluded that the setting aside of the legal barriers between Jew and Gentile was an exceptional ordinance of God to indicate that the apostolic kerygma was also to be directed to the Gentiles. Only in ch 15 at the "Council" in Jerusalem does the evangelization of the Gentiles become the official position of the church leadership in Jerusalem.

11, 3: *You entered . . . :* alternatively, this could be punctuated as a question.

11, 12: *These six brothers:* companions from the Christian community of Joppa (see Acts 10, 23).

11, 19-26: The Jewish Christian antipathy to the mixed community was reflected by the early missionaries generally. The few among them who entertained a different view succeeded in introducing Gentiles into the community at Antioch (in Syria). When the disconcerted Jerusalem community sent Barnabas to investigate, he was so favorably impressed by what he observed that he persuaded his friend Saul to participate in the Antioch mission.

11, 26: *Christians:* "Christians" is first applied to the members of the community at Antioch because the Gentile members of the community enable it to stand out clearly from Judaism.

11, 27-30: It is not clear whether the prophets from Jerusalem came to Antioch to request help in view of the coming famine or whether they received this insight during their visit there. The former supposition seems more likely. Suetonius and Tacitus speak of famines during the reign of Claudius (A.D. 41-54), while the Jewish historian Josephus mentions a famine in Judea in A.D. 46-48. Luke is interested, rather, in showing the charity of the Antiochene community toward the Jewish Christians of Jerusalem despite their differences on mixed communities.

to Antioch, [28]and one of them named Agabus stood up and predicted by the Spirit that there would be a severe famine all over the world, and it happened under Claudius.[j] [29]So the disciples determined that, according to ability,[k] each should send relief to the brothers who lived in Judea. [30]This they did, sending it to the presbyters* in care of Barnabas and Saul.

CHAPTER 12

Herod's Persecution of the Christians.* [1]About that time King Herod laid hands upon some members of the church to harm them. [2]He had James, the brother of John,* killed by the sword, [3]and when he saw that this was pleasing to the Jews he proceeded to arrest Peter also. (It was [the] feast of Unleavened Bread.) [4]He had him taken into custody and put in prison under the guard of four squads of four soldiers each. He intended to bring him before the people after Passover.* [5]Peter thus was being kept in prison, but prayer by the church was fervently being made to God on his behalf.[l]

[6]On the very night before Herod was to bring him to trial, Peter, secured by double chains, was sleeping between two soldiers, while outside the door guards kept watch on the prison. [7]Suddenly the angel

---

j Acts 21, 10.—k 29-30: Acts 12, 25.—l Jas 5, 16.—m Acts 12, 25; 15, 37.—n Acts 5, 22-24.

11, 30: *Presbyters:* this is the same Greek word that elsewhere is translated "elders," primarily in reference to the Jewish community.

12, 1-19: Herod Agrippa ruled Judea A.D. 41-44. While Luke does not assign a motive for his execution of James and his intended execution of Peter, the broad background lies in Herod's support of Pharisaic Judaism. The Jewish Christians had lost the popularity they had had in Jerusalem (Acts 2, 47), perhaps because of suspicions against them traceable to the teaching of Stephen.

12, 2: *James, the brother of John:* this James, the son of Zebedee, was beheaded by Herod Agrippa ca. A.D. 44.

12, 3.4: *Feast of Unleavened Bread . . . Passover:* see the note on Lk 22, 1.

12, 17: *To James:* this James is not the son of Zebedee mentioned in v 2, but is James, the "brother of the Lord" (Gal 1, 19), who in chs 15 and 21 is presented as leader of the Jerusalem Christian community. *He left and went to another place:* the conjecture that Peter left for Rome at this time has nothing to recommend it. His chief responsibility was still the leadership of the Jewish Christian community in Palestine (see Gal 2, 7). The concept of the great missionary effort of the church was yet to come (see Acts 13, 1-3).

12, 20-23: Josephus gives a similar account of Herod's death that occurred in A.D. 44. Early Christian tradition considered the manner of it to be a divine punishment upon his evil life. See 2 Kgs 19, 35 for the figure of the angel of the Lord in such a context.

of the Lord stood by him and a light shone in the cell. He tapped Peter on the side and awakened him, saying, "Get up quickly." The chains fell from his wrists. [8]The angel said to him, "Put on your belt and your sandals." He did so. Then he said to him, "Put on your cloak and follow me." [9]So he followed him out, not realizing that what was happening through the angel was real; he thought he was seeing a vision. [10]They passed the first guard, then the second, and came to the iron gate leading out to the city, which opened for them by itself. They emerged and made their way down an alley, and suddenly the angel left him. [11]Then Peter recovered his senses and said, "Now I know for certain that [the] Lord sent his angel and rescued me from the hand of Herod and from all that the Jewish people had been expecting." [12]When he realized this, he went to the house of Mary, the mother of John who is called Mark, where there were many people gathered in prayer.[m] [13]When he knocked on the gateway door, a maid named Rhoda came to answer it. [14]She was so overjoyed when she recognized Peter's voice that, instead of opening the gate, she ran in and announced that Peter was standing at the gate. [15]They told her, "You are out of your mind," but she insisted that it was so. But they kept saying, "It is his angel." [16]But Peter continued to knock, and when they opened it, they saw him and were astounded. [17]He motioned to them with his hand to be quiet and explained [to them] how the Lord had led him out of the prison, and said, "Report this to James* and the brothers." Then he left and went to another place. [18]At daybreak there was no small commotion among the soldiers over what had become of Peter.[n] [19]Herod, after instituting a search but not finding him, ordered the guards tried and executed. Then he left Judea to spend some time in Caesarea.

Herod's Death. [20]* He had long been very angry with the people of Tyre and Sidon, who now came to him in a body. After winning over Blastus, the king's chamberlain, they sued for peace because their country was supplied with food from the king's territory. [21]On an appointed day, Herod, attired in royal robes, [and] seated on the rostrum, addressed them publicly. [22]The assembled crowd cried out, "This is the voice of a god, not of a man." 23 At once the angel of the Lord struck him down because he did not ascribe the honor to God, and he was eaten by worms and breathed his last. 24 But the word of God continued to spread and grow.*o*

Mission of Barnabas and Saul. 25 After Barnabas and Saul completed their relief mission, they returned to Jerusalem,* taking with them John, who is called Mark.*p*

CHAPTER 13

1 * Now there were in the church at Antioch prophets and teachers: Barnabas, Symeon who was called Niger, Lucius of Cyrene, Manaen who was a close friend of Herod the tetrarch, and Saul. 2 While they were worshiping the Lord and fasting, the holy Spirit said, "Set apart for me Barnabas and Saul for the work to which I have called them." 3 Then, completing their fasting and prayer, they laid hands on them and sent them off.

First Mission Begins in Cyprus. 4 * So they, sent forth by the holy Spirit, went down to Seleucia and from there sailed to Cyprus. 5 When they arrived in Salamis, they proclaimed the word of God in the Jewish synagogues. They had John* also as their assistant. 6 When they had traveled through the whole island as far as Paphos, they met a magician named Bar-Jesus who was a Jewish false prophet.* 7 He was with the proconsul Sergius Paulus, a man of intelligence, who had summoned Barnabas and Saul and wanted to hear the word of God. 8 But Elymas the magician (for that is

what his name means) opposed them in an attempt to turn the proconsul away from the faith. 9 But Saul, also known as Paul,* filled with the holy Spirit, looked intently at him 10 and said, "You son of the devil, you enemy of all that is right, full of every sort of deceit and fraud. Will you not stop twisting the straight paths of [the] Lord? 11 Even now the hand of the Lord is upon you. You will be blind, and unable to see the sun for a time." Immediately a dark mist fell upon him, and he went about seeking people to lead him by the hand. 12 When the proconsul saw what had happened, he came to believe, for he was astonished by the teaching about the Lord.

Paul's Arrival at Antioch in Pisidia. 13 From Paphos, Paul and his companions set sail and arrived at Perga in Pamphylia. But John left them and returned to Jerusalem.*q* 14 They continued on from Perga and reached Antioch in Pisidia. On the sabbath they entered [into] the synagogue and took their seats. 15 After the reading of the law and the prophets, the synagogue officials sent word to them, "My brothers, if one of you has a word of exhortation for the people, please speak."

Paul's Address in the Synagogue. 16 * So Paul got up, motioned with his hand, and said, "Fellow Israelites and you others who are God-fearing,* listen. 17 The God of this people Israel chose our ancestors and exalted the people during their sojourn in the land of Egypt.*r* With uplifted arms he led them out of it 18 and for about forty years he put up with* them in the desert.*s* 19 When he had destroyed seven nations in the land of Canaan, he gave them their

---

o Acts 6, 7.—p Acts 11, 29-30.—q Acts 15, 38.—r Ex 6, 1.6; 12, 51.—s Ex 16, 1.35; Nm 14, 34.

12, 25: *They returned to Jerusalem:* many manuscripts read "from Jerusalem," since Acts 11, 30 implies that Paul and Barnabas are already in Jerusalem. This present verse could refer to a return visit or subsequent relief mission.

13, 1-3: The impulse for the first missionary effort in Asia Minor is ascribed to the prophets of the Antiochene community, under the inspiration of the holy Spirit. Just as the Jerusalem community had earlier been the center of missionary activity, so too Antioch becomes the center from which the missionaries Barnabas and Saul are sent out.

13, 4—14, 27: The key event in Luke's account of the first missionary journey is the experience of Paul and Barnabas at Pisidian Antioch (Acts 13, 14-52). The Christian kerygma proclaimed by Paul in the synagogue was favorably received. Some Jews and "God-fearers" (see the note on Acts 8, 26-40) became interested and invited the missionaries to speak again on the following sabbath (Acts 13, 42). By that time, however, the appearance of a large number of Gentiles from the city had so discon-

certed the Jews that they became hostile toward the apostles (Acts 13, 44-50). This hostility of theirs appears in all three accounts of Paul's missionary journeys in Acts, the Jews of Iconium (Acts 14, 1-2) and Beroea (Acts 17, 11) being notable exceptions.

13, 5: *John:* that is, John Mark (see Acts 12, 12.25).

13, 6: *A magician named Bar-Jesus who was a Jewish false prophet:* that is, he posed as a prophet. Again Luke takes the opportunity to dissociate Christianity from the magical acts of the time (7-11); see also Acts 8, 18-24.

13, 9: *Saul, also known as Paul:* there is no reason to believe that his name was changed from Saul to Paul upon his conversion. The use of a double name, one Semitic (Saul), the other Greco-Roman (Paul), is well attested (cf Acts 1, 23, Joseph Justus; Acts 12, 12.25, John Mark).

13, 16-41: This is the first of several speeches of Paul to Jews proclaiming that the Christian church is the logical development of Pharisaic Judaism (see also Acts 24, 10-21; 26, 2-23).

13, 16: *Who are God-fearing:* see the note on Acts 8, 26-40.

13, 18: *Put up with:* some manuscripts read "sustained."

land as an inheritance[t] [20] at the end of about four hundred and fifty years.* After these things he provided judges up to Samuel [the] prophet.[u] [21] Then they asked for a king. God gave them Saul, son of Kish, a man from the tribe of Benjamin, for forty years.[v] [22] Then he removed him and raised up David as their king; of him he testified, 'I have found David, son of Jesse, a man after my own heart; he will carry out my every wish.'[w] [23] From this man's descendants God, according to his promise, has brought to Israel a savior, Jesus.[x] [24] John heralded his coming by proclaiming a baptism of repentance to all the people of Israel;[y] [25] and as John was completing his course, he would say, 'What do you suppose that I am? I am not he. Behold, one is coming after me; I am not worthy to unfasten the sandals of his feet.'[z]

[26] "My brothers, children of the family of Abraham, and those others among you who are God-fearing, to us this word of salvation has been sent. [27] The inhabitants of Jerusalem and their leaders failed to recognize him, and by condemning him they fulfilled the oracles of the prophets that are read sabbath after sabbath. [28] For even

---

t Dt 7, 1; Jos 14, 1-2.—u Jgs 2, 16; 1 Sm 3, 20.—v 1 Sm 8, 5.19; 9, 16; 10, 1.20-21.24; 11, 15.—w 1 Sm 13, 14; 16, 12-13; Ps 89, 20-21.—x Is 11, 1.—y Mt 3, 1-2; Mk 1, 4-5; Lk 3, 2-3.— z Mt 3, 11; Mk 1, 7; Lk 3, 16; Jn 1, 20.27.—a Mt 27, 20.22-23; Mk 15, 13-14; Lk 23, 4.14-15. 21-23; Jn 19, 4-6.15.—b Mt 27, 59-60; Mk 16, 46; Lk 23, 53; Jn 19, 38.41-42.—c Acts 2, 24.32; 3, 15; 4, 10; 17, 31.—d Acts 1, 3.8; 10, 39.41; Mt 28, 8-10.16-20; Mk 16, 9.12-20; Lk 24, 13-53; Jn 20, 11-29; 21, 1-23.—e Ps 2, 7.—f Is 55, 3.—g Ps 16, 10.—h Acts 2, 29; 1 Kgs 2, 10.—i Rom 3, 20.—j Hb 1, 5.—k Acts 3, 26; Rom 1, 16.

13, 20: *At the end of about four hundred and fifty years:* the manuscript tradition makes it uncertain whether the mention of four hundred and fifty years refers to the sojourn in Egypt before the Exodus, the wilderness period and the time of the conquest (see Ex 12, 40-41), as the translation here suggests, or to the time between the conquest and the time of Samuel, the period of the judges, if the text is read, "After these things, for about four hundred and fifty years, he provided judges."

13, 31: The theme of the Galilean witnesses is a major one in the Gospel of Luke and in Acts and is used to signify the continuity between the teachings of Jesus and the teachings of the church and to guarantee the fidelity of the church's teachings to the words of Jesus.

13, 38-39: *Justified:* the verb is the same as that used in Paul's letters to speak of the experience of justification and, as in Paul, is here connected with the term "to have faith" ("every believer"). But this seems the only passage about Paul in Acts where justification is mentioned. In Lucan fashion it is paralleled with "forgiveness of sins" (a theme at Acts 2, 38; 3, 19; 5, 31; 10, 43) based on Jesus' resurrection (37) rather than his cross, and is put negatively (38). Therefore, some would translate, "in regard to everything from which you could not be acquitted . . . every believer is acquitted."

though they found no grounds for a death sentence, they asked Pilate to have him put to death,[a] [29] and when they had accomplished all that was written about him, they took him down from the tree and placed him in a tomb.[b] [30] But God raised him from the dead,[c] [31] and for many days he appeared to those who had come up with him from Galilee to Jerusalem.[d] These are [now] his witnesses before the people.* [32] We ourselves are proclaiming this good news to you that what God promised our ancestors [33] he has brought to fulfillment for us, [their] children, by raising up Jesus, as it is written in the second psalm, 'You are my son; this day I have begotten you.'[e] [34] And that he raised him from the dead never to return to corruption he declared in this way, 'I shall give you the benefits assured to David.'[f] [35] That is why he also says in another psalm, 'You will not suffer your holy one to see corruption.'[g] [36] Now David, after he had served the will of God in his lifetime, fell asleep, was gathered to his ancestors, and did see corruption.[h] [37] But the one whom God raised up did not see corruption. [38] You must know, my brothers, that through him forgiveness of sins is being proclaimed to you, [and] in regard to everything from which you could not be justified* under the law of Moses, [39] in him every believer is justified.[i] [40] Be careful, then, that what was said in the prophets not come about:

[41] 'Look on, you scoffers,
    be amazed and disappear.
For I am doing a work in your days,
    a work that you will never believe
      even if someone tells you.' "[j]

[42] As they were leaving, they invited them to speak on these subjects the following sabbath. [43] After the congregation had dispersed, many Jews and worshipers who were converts to Judaism followed Paul and Barnabas, who spoke to them and urged them to remain faithful to the grace of God.

Address to the Gentiles. [44] On the following sabbath almost the whole city gathered to hear the word of the Lord. [45] When the Jews saw the crowds, they were filled with jealousy and with violent abuse contradicted what Paul said. [46] [k] Both Paul and Barnabas spoke out boldly and said, "It was necessary that the word of God be spoken to you first, but since you reject it and condemn yourselves as unworthy of eternal life, we now turn to the Gentiles.* [47] For so the Lord has commanded us, 'I have made you a light to the Gentiles, that you may be an instrument of salvation to the ends of the earth.' "[l]

[48] The Gentiles were delighted when they heard this and glorified the word of the Lord. All who were destined for eternal life came to believe, [49] and the word of the Lord continued to spread through the whole region. [50] The Jews, however, incited the women of prominence who were worshipers and the leading men of the city, stirred up a persecution against Paul and Barnabas, and expelled them from their territory. [51] [m] So they shook the dust from their feet in protest against them and went to Iconium.* [52] The disciples were filled with joy and the holy Spirit.

CHAPTER 14

Paul and Barnabas at Iconium. [1] In Iconium they entered the Jewish synagogue together and spoke in such a way that a great number of both Jews and Greeks came to believe, [2] although the disbelieving Jews stirred up and poisoned the minds of the Gentiles against the brothers. [3] So they stayed for a considerable period, speaking out boldly for the Lord, who confirmed the word about his grace by granting signs and wonders to occur through their hands.[n] [4] The people of the city were divided: some were with the Jews; others, with the apostles. [5] When there was an attempt by both the Gentiles and the Jews, together with their leaders, to attack and stone them,[o] [6] they realized it and fled to the Lycaonian cities of Lystra and Derbe and to the surrounding countryside, [7] where they continued to proclaim the good news.

Paul and Barnabas at Lystra. [8] * At Lystra there was a crippled man, lame from birth, who had never walked. [9] He listened to Paul speaking, who looked intently at him, saw that he had the faith to be healed, [10] and called out in a loud voice, "Stand up straight on your feet." He jumped up and began to walk about. [11] When the crowds saw what Paul had done, they cried out in Lycaonian, "The gods have come down to us in human form."[p] [12] They called Barnabas "Zeus" and Paul "Hermes,"* because he was the chief speaker. [13] And the priest of Zeus, whose temple was at the entrance to the city, brought oxen and garlands to the gates, for he together with the people intended to offer sacrifice.

[14] The apostles Barnabas and Paul tore their garments* when they heard this and rushed out into the crowd, shouting, [15] * "Men, why are you doing this? We are of the same nature as you, human beings. We proclaim to you good news that you should turn from these idols to the living God, 'who made heaven and earth and sea and all that is in them.'[q] [16] In past generations he allowed all Gentiles to go their own ways;[r] [17] yet, in bestowing his goodness, he did not leave himself without witness, for he gave you rains from heaven and fruitful seasons, and filled you with nourishment and gladness for your hearts."[s] [18] Even with these words, they scarcely restrained the crowds from offering sacrifice to them.

[19] [t] However, some Jews from Antioch and Iconium arrived and won over the crowds. They stoned Paul and dragged him out of the city, supposing that he was dead. [20] But when the disciples gathered around him, he got up and entered the city. On the following day he left with Barnabas for Derbe.

End of the First Mission. [21] After they had proclaimed the good news to that city and

---

l Is 49, 6.—m Mt 10, 14; Mk 6, 11; Lk 9, 5; 10, 11.—n Mk 16, 17-20.—o 2 Tm 3, 11.—p Acts 28, 6.—q Acts 3, 12; 10, 26; Ex 20, 11; Ps 146, 6.—r Acts 17, 30.—s Wis 13, 1.—t 19-20: 2 Cor 11, 25; 2 Tm 3, 11.

13, 46: The refusal to believe frustrates God's plan for his chosen people; however, no adverse judgment is made here concerning their ultimate destiny. Again, Luke, in the words of Paul, speaks of the priority of Israel in the plan for salvation (see Acts 10, 36).

13, 51: See the note on Lk 9, 5.

14, 8-18: In an effort to convince his hearers that the divine power works through his word, Paul cures the cripple. However, the pagan tradition of the occasional appearance of gods among human beings leads the people astray in interpreting the miracle. The incident reveals the cultural difficulties with which the church had to cope. Note the similarity of the miracle worked here by Paul to the one performed by Peter in Acts 3, 2-10.

14, 12: *Zeus . . . Hermes:* in Greek religion, Zeus was the chief of the Olympian gods, the "father of gods and men"; Hermes was a son of Zeus and was usually identified as the herald and messenger of the gods.

14, 14: *Tore their garments:* a gesture of protest.

14, 15-17: This is the first speech of Paul to Gentiles recorded by Luke in Acts (cf Acts 17, 22-31). Rather than showing how Christianity is the logical outgrowth of Judaism, as he does in speeches before Jews, Luke says that God excuses past Gentile ignorance and then presents a natural theology arguing for the recognition of God's existence and presence through his activity in natural phenomena.

made a considerable number of disciples, they returned to Lystra and to Iconium and to Antioch. [22] They strengthened the spirits of the disciples and exhorted them to persevere in the faith, saying, "It is necessary for us to undergo many hardships to enter the kingdom of God." [u] [23] They appointed presbyters* for them in each church and, with prayer and fasting, commended them to the Lord in whom they had put their faith. [24] Then they traveled through Pisidia and reached Pamphylia. [25] After proclaiming the word at Perga they went down to Attalia. [26] From there they sailed to Antioch, where they had been commended to the grace of God for the work they had now accomplished. [v] [27] And when they arrived, they called the church together and reported what God had done with them and how he had opened the door of faith to the Gentiles. [28] Then they spent no little time with the disciples.

CHAPTER 15

Council of Jerusalem. [1] * Some who had come down from Judea were instructing the brothers, [w] "Unless you are circumcised according to the Mosaic practice, [x] you cannot be saved."* [2] Because there arose no little dissension and debate by Paul and Barnabas with them, it was decided that Paul, Barnabas, and some of the others should go up to Jerusalem to the apostles and presbyters about this question. [3] They were sent on their journey by the church, and passed through Phoenicia and Samaria telling of the conversion of the Gentiles, and brought great joy to all the brothers. [4] When they arrived in Jerusalem, they were welcomed by the church, as well as by the apostles and the presbyters, and they reported what God had done with them. [5] But some from the party of the Pharisees who had become believers stood up and said, "It is necessary to circumcise them and direct them to observe the Mosaic law."

[6] * The apostles and the presbyters met together to see about this matter. [7] * After much debate had taken place, Peter got up and said to them, "My brothers, you are well aware that from early days God made his choice among you that through my mouth the Gentiles would hear the word of the gospel and believe. [y] [8] And God, who knows the heart, bore witness by granting them the holy Spirit just as he did us. [z] [9] He made no distinction between us and them, for by faith he purified their hearts. [a] [10] Why, then, are you now putting God to the test by placing on the shoulders of the disciples a yoke that neither our ancestors nor we have been able to bear? [b] [11] On the contrary, we believe that we are saved through the grace of the Lord Jesus, [c] in the same way as they."* [12] The whole assembly fell silent, and they listened while Paul and Barnabas described the signs and wonders God had worked among the Gentiles through them.

James on Dietary Law. [13] * After they had fallen silent, James responded, "My

---

u 1 Thes 3, 3.—v Acts 13, 1-3.—w 1-4: Gal 2, 1-9.—x Lv 12, 3; Gal 5, 2.—y Acts 10, 27-43.—z Acts 10, 44-48.—a Acts 10, 34-35.—b Mt 23, 4; Gal 5, 1.—c Gal 2, 16; 3, 11; Eph 2, 5-8.

14, 23: *They appointed presbyters:* the communities are given their own religious leaders by the traveling missionaries. The structure in these churches is patterned on the model of the Jerusalem community (Acts 11, 30; 15, 2.5.22; 21, 18).

15, 1-35: The Jerusalem "Council" marks the official rejection of the rigid view that Gentile converts were obliged to observe the Mosaic law completely. From here to the end of Acts, Paul and the Gentile mission become the focus of Luke's writing.

15, 1-5: When some of the converted Pharisees of Jerusalem discover the results of the first missionary journey of Paul, they urge that the Gentiles be taught to follow the Mosaic law. Recognizing the authority of the Jerusalem church, Paul and Barnabas go there to settle the question of whether Gentiles can embrace a form of Christianity that does not include this obligation.

15, 6-12: The gathering is possibly the same as that recalled by Paul in Gal 2, 1-10. Note that in v 2 it is only the apostles and presbyters, a small group, with whom Paul and Barnabas are to meet. Here Luke gives the meeting a public character because he wishes to emphasize its doctrinal significance (see Acts 15, 22).

15, 7-11: Paul's refusal to impose the Mosaic law on the Gentile Christians is supported by Peter on the ground that within his own experience God bestowed the holy Spirit upon Cornelius and his household without preconditions concerning the adoption of the Mosaic law (see Acts 10, 44-47).

15, 11: In support of Paul, Peter formulates the fundamental meaning of the gospel: that all are invited to be saved through faith in the power of Christ.

15, 13-35: Some scholars think that this apostolic decree suggested by James, the immediate leader of the Jerusalem community, derives from another historical occasion than the meeting in question. This seems to be the case if the meeting is the same as the one related in Gal 2, 1-10. According to that account, nothing was imposed upon Gentile Christians in respect to Mosaic law; whereas the decree instructs Gentile Christians of mixed communities to abstain from meats sacrificed to idols and from blood-meats, and to avoid marriage within forbidden degrees of consanguinity and affinity (Lv 18), all of which practices were especially abhorrent to Jews. Luke seems to have telescoped two originally independent incidents here: the first a Jerusalem "Council" that dealt with the question of circumcision, and the second a Jerusalem decree dealing mainly with Gentile observance of dietary laws (see Acts 21, 25 where Paul seems to be learning of the decree for the first time).

brothers, listen to me. [14] Symeon* has described how God first concerned himself with acquiring from among the Gentiles a people for his name. [15] The words of the prophets agree with this, as is written:

[16] 'After this I shall return[d]
     and rebuild the fallen hut of David;
  from its ruins I shall rebuild it
     and raise it up again,
[17] so that the rest of humanity may seek
     out the Lord,
     even all the Gentiles on whom my
     name is invoked.
  Thus says the Lord who accomplishes
     these things,
[18] known from of old.'

[19] [e] It is my judgment, therefore, that we ought to stop troubling the Gentiles who turn to God, [20] but tell them by letter to avoid pollution from idols, unlawful marriage, the meat of strangled animals, and blood.[f] [21] For Moses, for generations now, has had those who proclaim him in every town, as he has been read in the synagogues every sabbath."

Letter of the Apostles. [22] Then the apostles and presbyters, in agreement with the whole church, decided to choose representatives and to send them to Antioch with Paul and Barnabas. The ones chosen were Judas, who was called Barsabbas, and Silas, leaders among the brothers. [23] This is the letter delivered by them: "The apostles and the presbyters, your brothers, to the brothers in Antioch, Syria, and Cilicia of Gentile origin: greetings. [24] Since we have heard that some of our number [who went out] without any mandate from us have upset you with their teachings and disturbed your peace of mind, [25] we have with one accord decided to choose representatives and to send them to you along with our beloved Barnabas and Paul, [26] who have dedicated their lives to the name of our Lord Jesus Christ. [27] So we are sending Judas and Silas who will also convey this same message by word of mouth: [28] [g]'It is the decision of the holy Spirit and of us not to place on you any burden beyond these necessities, [29] namely, to abstain from meat sacrificed to idols, from blood, from meats of strangled animals, and from unlawful marriage. If you keep free of these, you will be doing what is right. Farewell.'"[h]

Delegates at Antioch. [30] And so they were sent on their journey. Upon their arrival in Antioch they called the assembly together and delivered the letter. [31] When the people read it, they were delighted with the exhortation. [32] Judas and Silas, who were themselves prophets, exhorted and strengthened the brothers with many words. [33] After they had spent some time there, they were sent off with greetings of peace from the brothers to those who had commissioned them. [34] * [35] But Paul and Barnabas remained in Antioch, teaching and proclaiming with many others the word of the Lord.

V. THE MISSION OF PAUL TO THE ENDS OF THE EARTH

Paul and Barnabas Separate. [36] * After some time, Paul said to Barnabas, "Come, let us make a return visit to see how the brothers are getting on in all the cities where we proclaimed the word of the Lord." [37] Barnabas wanted to take with them also John, who was called Mark, [38] but Paul insisted that they should not take with them someone who had deserted them at Pamphylia and who had not continued with them in their work.[i] [39] So sharp was their disagreement that they separated. Barnabas took Mark and sailed to Cyprus. [40] But Paul chose Silas and departed after being commended by the brothers to the grace of the Lord. [41] He traveled through Syria and Cilicia bringing strength to the churches.

---

d 16-17: Am 9, 11-12.—e 19-20: Acts 15, 28-29; 21, 25.—f Gn 9, 4; Lv 3, 17; 17, 10-14.—g 28-29: Acts 15, 19-20.—h Gn 9, 4; Lv 3, 17; 17, 10-14.—i Acts 13, 13.

15, 14: *Symeon:* elsewhere in Acts he is called either Peter or Simon. The presence of the name Symeon here suggests that, in the source Luke is using for this part of the Jerusalem "Council" incident, the name may have originally referred to someone other than Peter (see Acts 13, 1 where the Antiochene Symeon Niger is mentioned). As the text now stands, however, it is undoubtedly a reference to Simon Peter (7).

15, 34: Some manuscripts add, in various wordings, "But Silas decided to remain there."

15, 36—18, 22: This continuous narrative recounts Paul's second missionary journey. On the internal evidence of the Lucan account, it lasted about three years. Paul first visited the communities he had established on his first journey (Acts 16, 1-5), then pushed on into Macedonia, where he established communities at Philippi, Thessalonica, and Beroea (Acts 16, 7—17, 5). To escape the hostility of the Jews of Thessalonica, he left for Greece and while resident in Athens attempted, without success, to establish an effective Christian community there. From Athens he proceeded to Corinth and, after a stay of a year and a half, returned to Antioch by way of Ephesus and Jerusalem (Acts 17, 16—18, 22). Luke does not concern himself with the structure or statistics of the communities but aims to show the general progress of the gospel in the Gentile world as well as its continued failure to take root in the Jewish community.

CHAPTER 16

Paul in Lycaonia: Timothy. [1] He reached [also] Derbe and Lystra where there was a disciple named Timothy, the son of a Jewish woman who was a believer, but his father was a Greek.[j] [2] The brothers in Lystra and Iconium spoke highly of him,[k] [3] and Paul wanted him to come along with him. On account of the Jews of that region, Paul had him circumcised,* for they all knew that his father was a Greek. [4] As they traveled from city to city, they handed on to the people for observance the decisions reached by the apostles and presbyters in Jerusalem. [5] Day after day the churches grew stronger in faith and increased in number.

Through Asia Minor. [6] They traveled through the Phrygian and Galatian territory because they had been prevented by the holy Spirit from preaching the message in the province of Asia. [7] When they came to Mysia, they tried to go on into Bithynia, but the Spirit of Jesus* did not allow them, [8] so they crossed through Mysia and came down to Troas. [9] During [the] night Paul had a vision. A Macedonian stood before him and implored him with these words, "Come over to Macedonia and help us."

j 1 Tm 1, 2; 2 Tm 1, 5.—k Phil 2, 20.—l 22-23: 2 Cor 11, 25; Phil 1, 30; 1 Thes 2, 2.

16, 3: *Paul had him circumcised:* he did this in order that Timothy might be able to associate with the Jews and so perform a ministry among them. Paul did not object to the Jewish Christians' adherence to the law. But he insisted that the law could not be imposed on the Gentiles. Paul himself lived in accordance with the law, or as exempt from the law, according to particular circumstances (see 1 Cor 9, 19-23).

16, 7: *The Spirit of Jesus:* this is an unusual formulation in Luke's writings. The parallelism with v 6 indicates its meaning, the holy Spirit.

16, 10-17: This is the first of the so-called "we-sections" in Acts, where Luke writes as one of Paul's companions. The other passages are Acts 20, 5-15; 21, 1-18; 27, 1—28, 16. Scholars debate whether Luke may not have used the first person plural simply as a literary device to lend color to the narrative. The realism of the narrative, however, lends weight to the argument that the "we" includes Luke or another companion of Paul whose data Luke used as a source.

16, 11-40: The church at Philippi became a flourishing community to which Paul addressed one of his letters (see Introduction to the Letter to the Philippians).

16, 14: *A worshiper of God:* a "God-fearer." See the note on Acts 8, 26-40.

16, 16: *With an oracular spirit:* literally, "with a Python spirit." The Python was the serpent or dragon that guarded the Delphic oracle. It later came to designate a "spirit that pronounced oracles" and also a ventriloquist who, it was thought, had such a spirit in the belly.

16, 20: *Magistrates:* in Greek, *stratēgoi,* the popular designation of the *duoviri,* the highest officials of the Roman colony of Philippi.

[10] When he had seen the vision, we* sought passage to Macedonia at once, concluding that God had called us to proclaim the good news to them.

Into Europe. [11] * We set sail from Troas, making a straight run for Samothrace, and on the next day to Neapolis, [12] and from there to Philippi, a leading city in that district of Macedonia and a Roman colony. We spent some time in that city. [13] On the sabbath we went outside the city gate along the river where we thought there would be a place of prayer. We sat and spoke with the women who had gathered there. [14] One of them, a woman named Lydia, a dealer in purple cloth, from the city of Thyatira, a worshiper of God,* listened, and the Lord opened her heart to pay attention to what Paul was saying. [15] After she and her household had been baptized, she offered us an invitation, "If you consider me a believer in the Lord, come and stay at my home," and she prevailed on us.

Imprisonment at Philippi. [16] As we were going to the place of prayer, we met a slave girl with an oracular spirit,* who used to bring a large profit to her owners through her fortune-telling. [17] She began to follow Paul and us, shouting, "These people are slaves of the Most High God, who proclaim to you a way of salvation." [18] She did this for many days. Paul became annoyed, turned, and said to the spirit, "I command you in the name of Jesus Christ to come out of her." Then it came out at that moment.

[19] When her owners saw that their hope of profit was gone, they seized Paul and Silas and dragged them to the public square before the local authorities. [20] They brought them before the magistrates* and said, "These people are Jews and are disturbing our city [21] and are advocating customs that are not lawful for us Romans to adopt or practice." [22] [l] The crowd joined in the attack on them, and the magistrates had them stripped and ordered them to be beaten with rods. [23] After inflicting many blows on them, they threw them into prison and instructed the jailer to guard them securely. [24] When he received these instructions, he put them in the innermost cell and secured their feet to a stake.

Deliverance from Prison. [25] About midnight, while Paul and Silas were praying and singing hymns to God as the prisoners listened, [26] there was suddenly such a severe earthquake that the foundations of the jail shook; all the doors flew open, and the chains of all were pulled loose. [27] When the jailer woke up and saw the prison doors wide open, he drew [his] sword and was about to kill himself, thinking that the prisoners had escaped. [28] But Paul shouted out in a loud voice, "Do no harm to yourself; we are all here." [29] He asked for a light and rushed in and, trembling with fear, he fell down before Paul and Silas. [30] Then he brought them out and said, "Sirs, what must I do to be saved?" [31] And they said, "Believe in the Lord Jesus and you and your household will be saved." [32] So they spoke the word of the Lord to him and to everyone in his house. [33] He took them in at that hour of the night and bathed their wounds; then he and all his family were baptized at once. [34] He brought them up into his house and provided a meal and with his household rejoiced at having come to faith in God.

[35] But when it was day, the magistrates sent the lictors* with the order, "Release those men." [36] The jailer reported the[se] words to Paul, "The magistrates have sent orders that you be released. Now, then, come out and go in peace." [37] But Paul said to them, "They have beaten us publicly, even though we are Roman citizens and have not been tried, and have thrown us into prison.[m] And now, are they going to release us secretly? By no means. Let them come themselves and lead us out."* [38] The lictors reported these words to the magistrates, and they became alarmed when they heard that they were Roman citizens.[n] [39] So they came and placated them, and led them out and asked that they leave the city. [40] When they had come out of the prison, they went to Lydia's house where they saw and encouraged the brothers, and then they left.

CHAPTER 17

Paul in Thessalonica. [1] When they took the road through Amphipolis and Apollonia, they reached Thessalonica, where there was a synagogue of the Jews.[o] [2] Following his usual custom, Paul joined them, and for three sabbaths he entered into discussions with them from the scriptures, [3] expounding and demonstrating that the Messiah had to suffer and rise from the

dead, and that "This is the Messiah, Jesus, whom I proclaim to you."[p] [4] Some of them were convinced and joined Paul and Silas; so, too, a great number of Greeks who were worshipers, and not a few of the prominent women. [5] But the Jews became jealous and recruited some worthless men loitering in the public square, formed a mob, and set the city in turmoil. They marched on the house of Jason,[q] intending to bring them before the people's assembly. [6] * When they could not find them, they dragged Jason and some of the brothers before the city magistrates, shouting, "These people who have been creating a disturbance all over the world have now come here, [7] and Jason has welcomed them.[r] They all act in opposition to the decrees of Caesar and claim instead that there is another king, Jesus."* [8] They stirred up the crowd and the city magistrates who, upon hearing these charges, [9] took a surety payment from Jason and the others before releasing them.

Paul in Beroea. [10] The brothers immediately sent Paul and Silas to Beroea during the night. Upon arrival they went to the synagogue of the Jews. [11] These Jews were more fair-minded than those in Thessalonica, for they received the word with all willingness and examined the scriptures daily to determine whether these things were so.[s] [12] Many of them became believers, as did not a few of the influential Greek women and men. [13] But when the Jews of Thessalonica learned that the word of God had now been proclaimed by Paul in Beroea also, they came there too to cause a commotion and stir up the crowds. [14] So the brothers at once sent Paul on his way to the seacoast, while Silas and Timothy remained behind.[t] [15] After Paul's escorts had taken him to Athens, they came away with instructions for Silas and Timothy to join him as soon as possible.

---

m Acts 22, 25.—n Acts 22, 29.—o 1 Thes 2, 1-2.—p Acts 3, 18; Lk 24, 25-26.46.—q Rom 16, 21.—r Lk 23, 2; Jn 19, 12-15.—s Jn 5, 39.—t 1 Thes 3, 1-2.

16, 35: *The lictors:* the equivalent of police officers, among whose duties were the apprehension and punishment of criminals.

16, 37: Paul's Roman citizenship granted him special privileges in regard to criminal process. Roman law forbade under severe penalty the beating of Roman citizens (see also Acts 22, 25).

17, 6-7: The accusations against Paul and his companions echo the charges brought against Jesus in Lk 23, 2.

17, 7: *There is another king, Jesus:* a distortion into a political sense of the apostolic proclamation of Jesus and the kingdom of God (see Acts 8, 12).

Paul in Athens.* [16]While Paul was waiting for them in Athens, he grew exasperated at the sight of the city full of idols. [17]So he debated in the synagogue with the Jews and with the worshipers, and daily in the public square with whoever happened to be there. [18]Even some of the Epicurean and Stoic philosophers* engaged him in discussion. Some asked, "What is this scavenger trying to say?" Others said, "He sounds like a promoter of foreign deities," because he was preaching about 'Jesus' and 'Resurrection.' [19]They took him and led him to the Areopagus* and said, "May we learn what this new teaching is that you speak of? [20]For you bring some strange notions to our ears; we should like to know what these things mean." [21]Now all the Athenians as well as the foreigners residing there used their time for nothing else but telling or hearing something new.

Paul's Speech at the Areopagus. [22]Then Paul stood up at the Areopagus and said:*

"You Athenians, I see that in every respect you are very religious. [23]For as I walked around looking carefully at your shrines, I even discovered an altar inscribed, 'To an Unknown God.'* What therefore you unknowingly worship, I proclaim to you. [24]The God who made the world and all that is in it, the Lord of heaven and earth, does not dwell in sanctuaries made by human hands,ᵛ [25]nor is he served by human hands because he needs anything. Rather it is he who gives to everyone life and breath and everything. [26]He made from one* the whole human race to dwell on the entire surface of the earth, and he fixed the ordered seasons and the boundaries of their regions, [27]so that people might seek God, even perhaps grope for him and find him, though indeed he is not far from any one of us.ʷ [28]For 'In him we live and move and have our being,'* as even some of your poets have said, 'For we too are his offspring.' [29]Since therefore we are the offspring of God, we ought not to think that the divinity is like an image fashioned from gold, silver, or stone by human art and imagination.ˣ [30]God has overlooked the times of ignorance, but now he demands that all people everywhere repent [31]because he has established a day on which he will 'judge the world with justice' through a man he has appointed, and he has provided confirmation for all by raising him from the dead."ʸ

[32]When they heard about resurrection of the dead, some began to scoff, but others said, "We should like to hear you on this some other time." [33]And so Paul left them. [34]But some did join him, and became believers. Among them were Dionysius, a member of the Court of the Areopagus, a woman named Damaris, and others with them.

---

u 1 Cor 1, 22.—v Acts 7, 48-50; Gn 1, 1; 1 Kgs 8, 27; Is 42, 5.—w Jer 23, 23; Wis 13, 6; Rom 1, 19.—x Acts 19, 26; Is 40, 18-20; 44, 10-17; Rom 1, 22-23.—y Acts 10, 42.

17, 16-21: Paul's presence in Athens sets the stage for the great discourse before a Gentile audience in vv 22-31. Although Athens was a politically insignificant city at this period, it still lived on the glories of its past and represented the center of Greek culture. The setting describes the conflict between Christian preaching and Hellenistic philosophy.

17, 18: *Epicurean and Stoic philosophers:* for the followers of Epicurus (342-271 B.C.), the goal of life was happiness attained through sober reasoning and the searching out of motives for all choice and avoidance. The Stoics were followers of Zeno, a younger contemporary of Alexander the Great. Zeno and his followers believed in a type of pantheism that held that the spark of divinity was present in all reality and that, in order to be free, each person must live "according to nature." *This scavenger:* literally, "seed-picker," as of a bird that picks up grain. The word is later used of scrap collectors and of people who take other people's ideas and propagate them as if they were their own. *Promoter of foreign deities:* according to Xenophon, Socrates was accused of promoting new deities. The accusation against Paul echoes the charge against Socrates. *'Jesus' and 'Resurrection':* the Athenians are presented as misunderstanding Paul from the outset; they think he is preaching about Jesus and a goddess named *Anastasis*, i.e., Resurrection.

17, 19: *To the Areopagus:* the "Areopagus" refers either to the Hill of Ares west of the Acropolis or to the Council of Athens, which at one time met on the hill but which at this time assembled in the Royal Colonnade (*Stoa Basileios*).

17, 22-31: In Paul's appearance at the Areopagus he preaches his climactic speech to Gentiles in the cultural center of the ancient world. The speech is more theological than christological. Paul's discourse appeals to the Greek world's belief in divinity as responsible for the origin and existence of the universe. It contests the common belief in a multiplicity of gods supposedly exerting their powers through their images. It acknowledges that the attempt to find God is a constant human endeavor. It declares, further, that God is the judge of the human race, that the time of the judgment has been determined, and that it will be executed through a man whom God raised from the dead. The speech reflects sympathy with pagan religiosity, handles the subject of idol worship gently, and appeals for a new examination of divinity, not from the standpoint of creation but from the standpoint of judgment.

17, 23: *'To an Unknown God':* ancient authors such as Pausanias, Philostratus, and Tertullian speak of Athenian altars with no specific dedication as altars of "unknown gods" or "nameless altars."

17, 26: *From one:* many manuscripts read "from one blood." *Fixed . . . seasons:* or "fixed limits to the epochs."

17, 28: *'In him we live and move and have our being':* some scholars understand this saying to be based on an earlier saying of Epimenides of Knossos (6th century B.C.). *'For we too are his offspring':* here Paul is quoting Aratus of Soli, a third-century B.C. poet from Cilicia.

CHAPTER 18

Paul in Corinth. [1]After this he left Athens and went to Corinth. [2]There he met a Jew named Aquila,[z] a native of Pontus, who had recently come from Italy with his wife Priscilla* because Claudius had ordered all the Jews to leave Rome. He went to visit them [3]and, because he practiced the same trade, stayed with them and worked, for they were tentmakers by trade. [4]Every sabbath, he entered into discussions in the synagogue, attempting to convince both Jews and Greeks.

[5]When Silas and Timothy came down from Macedonia, Paul began to occupy himself totally with preaching the word, testifying to the Jews that the Messiah was Jesus. [6]When they opposed him and reviled him, he shook out his garments* and said to them, "Your blood be on your heads! I am clear of responsibility. From now on I will go to the Gentiles." [a] [7]So he left there and went to a house belonging to a man named Titus Justus, a worshiper of God;* his house was next to a synagogue.[b] [8]Crispus,* the synagogue official,[c] came to believe in the Lord along with his entire household, and many of the Corinthians who heard believed and were baptized. [9] [d] One night in a vision the Lord said to Paul, "Do not be afraid. Go on speaking, and do not be silent, [10]for I am with you. No one will attack and harm you, for I have many people in this city." [11]He settled there for a year and a half and taught the word of God among them.

Accusations before Gallio. [12]But when Gallio was proconsul of Achaia,* the Jews rose up together against Paul and brought him to the tribunal, [13]saying, "This man is inducing people to worship God contrary

to the law."* [14]When Paul was about to reply, Gallio spoke to the Jews, "If it were a matter of some crime or malicious fraud, I should with reason hear the complaint of you Jews; [15]but since it is a question of arguments over doctrine and titles and your own law, see to it yourselves. I do not wish to be a judge of such matters." [16]And he drove them away from the tribunal. [17]They all seized Sosthenes, the synagogue official, and beat him in full view of the tribunal. But none of this was of concern to Gallio.

Return to Syrian Antioch. [18]Paul remained for quite some time, and after saying farewell to the brothers he sailed for Syria, together with Priscilla and Aquila. At Cenchreae he had his hair cut[e] because he had taken a vow.* [19]When they reached Ephesus, he left them there, while he entered the synagogue and held discussions with the Jews. [20]Although they asked him to stay for a longer time, he did not consent, [21]but as he said farewell he promised, "I shall come back to you again, God willing." Then he set sail from Ephesus. [22]Upon landing at Caesarea, he went up and greeted the church* and then went down to Antioch. [23] *. After staying there some time, he left and traveled in orderly sequence through the Galatian country and Phrygia, bringing strength to all the disciples.

Apollos. [24]A Jew named Apollos,[f] a native of Alexandria, an eloquent speaker, arrived in Ephesus. He was an authority on the scriptures.* [25]He had been instructed in the Way of the Lord and, with ardent spirit, spoke and taught accurately about Jesus, although he knew only the baptism

---

z Rom 16, 3.—a Acts 13, 51; Mt 10, 14; 27, 24-25; Mk 6, 11; Lk 9, 5; 10, 10-11.—b Acts 13, 46-47; 28, 28.—c 1 Cor 1, 14.—d 9-10: Jer 1, 8.—e Acts 21, 24; Nm 6, 18.—f 1 Cor 1, 12.

18, 2: *Aquila . . . Priscilla:* both may already have been Christians at the time of their arrival in Corinth (see Acts 18, 26). According to 1 Cor 16, 19, their home became a meeting place for Christians. *Claudius:* the Emperor Claudius expelled the Jews from Rome ca. A.D. 40. The Roman historian Suetonius gives as reason for the expulsion disturbances among the Jews "at the instigation of Chrestos," probably meaning disputes about the messiahship of Jesus.

18, 6: *Shook out his garments:* a gesture indicating Paul's repudiation of his mission to the Jews there; cf Acts 28, 17-31.

18, 7: *A worshiper of God:* see the note on Acts 8, 26-40.

18, 8: *Crispus:* in 1 Cor 1, 14, Paul mentions that Crispus was one of the few he himself baptized at Corinth.

18, 12: *When Gallio was proconsul of Achaia:* Gallio's proconsulship in Achaia is dated to A.D. 51-52 from an inscription discovered at Delphi. This has become an important date in establishing a chronology of the life and missionary work of Paul.

18, 13: *Contrary to the law:* Gallio (15) understands this to be a problem of Jewish, not Roman, law.

18, 18: *He had his hair cut because he had taken a vow:* a reference to a Nazirite vow (see Nm 6, 1-21, especially, 6, 18) taken by Paul (see also Acts 21, 23-27).

18, 22: *He went up and greeted the church:* "going up" suggests a visit to the church in Jerusalem.

18, 23—21, 16: Luke's account of Paul's third missionary journey devotes itself mainly to his work at Ephesus (Acts 19, 1—20, 1). There is a certain restiveness on Paul's part and a growing conviction that the Spirit bids him return to Jerusalem and prepare to go to Rome (Acts 19, 21).

18, 24-25: Apollos appears as a preacher who knows the teaching of Jesus in the context of John's baptism of repentance. Aquila and Priscilla instruct him more fully. He is referred to in 1 Cor 1, 12; 3, 5-6.22.

of John. 26 He began to speak boldly in the synagogue; but when Priscilla and Aquila heard him, they took him aside and explained to him the Way [of God]* more accurately. 27 And when he wanted to cross to Achaia, the brothers encouraged him and wrote to the disciples there to welcome him. After his arrival he gave great assistance to those who had come to believe through grace. 28 He vigorously refuted the Jews in public, establishing from the scriptures that the Messiah is Jesus.

CHAPTER 19

Paul in Ephesus. 1 * While Apollos was in Corinth, Paul traveled through the interior of the country and came [down] to Ephesus where he found some disciples. 2 He said to them, "Did you receive the holy Spirit when you became believers?" They answered him, "We have never even heard that there is a holy Spirit." 3 He said, "How were you baptized?" They replied, "With the baptism of John." 4 Paul then said, "John baptized with a baptism of repentance, telling the people to believe in the one who was to come after him, that is, in Jesus." g 5 When they heard this, they were baptized in the name of the Lord Jesus. 6 And when Paul laid [his] hands on them, the holy Spirit came upon them, and they spoke in tongues and prophesied. h 7 Altogether there were about twelve men.

8 He entered the synagogue, and for three months debated boldly with persuasive arguments about the kingdom of God. 9 But when some in their obstinacy and disbelief disparaged the Way before the assembly, he withdrew and took his disciples with him and began to hold daily discussions in the lecture hall of Tyrannus.

10 This continued for two years with the result that all the inhabitants of the province of Asia heard the word of the Lord, Jews and Greeks alike. 11 So extraordinary were the mighty deeds God accomplished at the hands of Paul 12 that when face cloths or aprons that touched his skin were applied to the sick, their diseases left them and the evil spirits came out of them. i

The Jewish Exorcists. 13 Then some itinerant Jewish exorcists tried to invoke the name of the Lord Jesus over those with evil spirits, saying, "I adjure you by the Jesus whom Paul preaches." 14 When the seven sons of Sceva, a Jewish high priest, tried to do this, 15 the evil spirit said to them in reply, "Jesus I recognize, Paul I know, but who are you?" 16 The person with the evil spirit then sprang at them and subdued them all. He so overpowered them that they fled naked and wounded from that house. 17 When this became known to all the Jews and Greeks who lived in Ephesus, fear fell upon them all, and the name of the Lord Jesus was held in great esteem. 18 Many of those who had become believers came forward and openly acknowledged their former practices. 19 Moreover, a large number of those who had practiced magic collected their books and burned them in public. They calculated their value and found it to be fifty thousand silver pieces. 20 Thus did the word of the Lord continue to spread with influence and power.

Paul's Plans. 21 When this was concluded, Paul made up his mind to travel through Macedonia and Achaia, and then to go on to Jerusalem, saying, "After I have been there, I must visit Rome also." j 22 Then he sent to Macedonia two of his assistants, Timothy and Erastus, while he himself stayed for a while in the province of Asia.

The Riot of the Silversmiths. 23 About that time a serious disturbance broke out concerning the Way. 24 There was a silversmith named Demetrius who made miniature silver shrines of Artemis* and provided no little work for the craftsmen. 25 He called a meeting of these and other workers in related crafts and said, "Men, you know well that our prosperity derives from this work. 26 As you can now see and hear, not only in Ephesus but throughout most of the province of Asia this Paul has persuaded and misled a great number of people by saying that gods made by hands

---

g Acts 1, 5; 11, 16; 13, 24-25; Mt 3, 11; Mk 1, 8; Lk 3, 16.—h Acts 8, 15-17; 10, 44.46.—i Acts 5, 15-16; Lk 8, 44-47.—j Acts 23, 11; Rom 1, 13; 15, 22-32.

18, 26: *The Way [of God]:* for the Way, see the note on Acts 9, 2. Other manuscripts here read "the Way of the Lord," "the word of the Lord," or simply "the Way."

19, 1-6: Upon his arrival in Ephesus, Paul discovers other people at the same religious stage as Apollos, though they seem to have considered themselves followers of Christ, not of the Baptist. On the relation between baptism and the reception of the Spirit, see the note on Acts 8, 16.

19, 24: *Miniature silver shrines of Artemis:* the temple of Artemis at Ephesus was one of the seven wonders of the ancient world. Artemis, originally the Olympian virgin hunter, moon goddess, and goddess of wild nature, was worshiped at Ephesus as an Asian mother goddess and goddess of fertility. She was one of the most widely worshiped female deities in the Hellenistic world (see Acts 18, 27).

are not gods at all.[k] 27 The danger grows, not only that our business will be discredited, but also that the temple of the great goddess Artemis will be of no account, and that she whom the whole province of Asia and all the world worship will be stripped of her magnificence."

28 When they heard this, they were filled with fury and began to shout, "Great is Artemis of the Ephesians!" 29 The city was filled with confusion, and the people rushed with one accord into the theater, seizing Gaius and Aristarchus, the Macedonians, Paul's traveling companions.[l] 30 Paul wanted to go before the crowd, but the disciples would not let him, 31 and even some of the Asiarchs* who were friends of his sent word to him advising him not to venture into the theater. 32 Meanwhile, some were shouting one thing, others something else; the assembly was in chaos, and most of the people had no idea why they had come together. 33 Some of the crowd prompted Alexander, as the Jews pushed him forward, and Alexander signaled with his hand that he wished to explain something to the gathering. 34 But when they recognized that he was a Jew, they all shouted in unison, for about two hours, "Great is Artemis of the Ephesians!" 35 Finally the town clerk restrained the crowd and said, "You Ephesians, what person is there who does not know that the city of the Ephesians is the guardian of the temple* of the great Artemis and of her image that fell from the sky? 36 Since these things are undeniable, you must calm yourselves and not do anything rash. 37 The men you brought here are not temple robbers, nor have they insulted our goddess. 38 If Demetrius and his fellow craftsmen have a complaint against anyone, courts are in session, and there are proconsuls. Let them bring charges against one another. 39 If you have anything further to investigate, let the matter be settled in the lawful assembly, 40 for, as it is, we are in danger of being charged with rioting because of today's conduct. There is no cause for it. We shall [not]* be able to give a reason for this demonstration." With these words he dismissed the assembly.

CHAPTER 20

Journey to Macedonia and Greece. 1 When the disturbance was over, Paul had the disciples summoned and, after encouraging them, he bade them farewell and set out on his journey to Macedonia.[m] 2 As he traveled throughout those regions, he provided many words of encouragement for them. Then he arrived in Greece, 3 where he stayed for three months. But when a plot was made against him by the Jews as he was about to set sail for Syria, he decided to return by way of Macedonia.

Return to Troas. 4 [n] Sopater, the son of Pyrrhus, from Beroea, accompanied him, as did Aristarchus and Secundus from Thessalonica, Gaius from Derbe, Timothy, and Tychicus and Trophimus from Asia 5 who went on ahead and waited for us* at Troas.[o] 6 We sailed from Philippi after the feast of Unleavened Bread,* and rejoined them five days later in Troas, where we spent a week.

Eutychus Restored to Life. 7 On the first day of the week* when we gathered to break bread, Paul spoke to them because he was going to leave on the next day, and he kept on speaking until midnight. 8 There were many lamps in the upstairs room where we were gathered, 9 and a young man named Eutychus who was sitting on the window sill was sinking into a deep sleep as Paul talked on and on. Once overcome by sleep, he fell down from the third story and when he was picked up, he was dead. 10 [p] Paul went down,* threw

k Acts 17, 29.—l Col 4, 10.—m 1 Cor 16, 1.—n Rom 16, 21.—o Acts 21, 29; 2 Tm 4, 20.—p 1 Kgs 17, 17-24; 2 Kgs 4, 30-37; Mt 9, 24; Mk 5, 39; Lk 8, 52.

19, 31: *Asiarchs:* the precise status and role of the Asiarchs is disputed. They appear to have been people of wealth and influence who promoted the Roman imperial cult and who may also have been political representatives in a league of cities in the Roman province of Asia.

19, 35: *Guardian of the temple:* this title was accorded by Rome to cities that provided a temple for the imperial cult. Inscriptional evidence indicates that Ephesus was acknowledged as the temple keeper of Artemis and of the imperial cult. *That fell from the sky:* many scholars think that this refers to a meteorite that was worshiped as an image of the goddess.

19, 40: Some manuscripts omit the negative in *[not] be able,* making the meaning, "There is no cause for which we shall be able to give a reason for this demonstration."

20, 5: The second "we-section" of Acts begins here. See the note on Acts 16, 10-17.

20, 6: *Feast of Unleavened Bread:* see the note on Lk 22, 1.

20, 7: *The first day of the week:* the day after the sabbath and the first day of the Jewish week, apparently chosen originally by the Jerusalem community for the celebration of the liturgy of the Eucharist in order to relate it to the resurrection of Christ.

20, 10: The action of Paul in throwing himself upon the dead boy recalls that of Elijah in 1 Kgs 17, 21 where the son of the widow of Zarephath is revived and that of Elisha in 2 Kgs 4, 34 where the Shunamite woman's son is restored to life.

himself upon him, and said as he embraced him, "Don't be alarmed; there is life in him." [11] Then he returned upstairs, broke the bread, and ate; after a long conversation that lasted until daybreak, he departed. [12] And they took the boy away alive and were immeasurably comforted.

Journey to Miletus. [13] We went ahead to the ship and set sail for Assos where we were to take Paul on board, as he had arranged, since he was going overland. [14] When he met us in Assos, we took him aboard and went on to Mitylene. [15] We sailed away from there on the next day and reached a point off Chios, and a day later we reached Samos, and on the following day we arrived at Miletus. [16] * Paul had decided to sail past Ephesus in order not to lose time in the province of Asia, for he was hurrying to be in Jerusalem, if at all possible, for the day of Pentecost.

Paul's Farewell Speech at Miletus. [17] From Miletus he had the presbyters of the church at Ephesus summoned. [18] When they came to him, he addressed them, "You know how I lived among you the whole time from the day I first came to the province of Asia. [19] I served the Lord with all humility and with the tears and trials that came to me because of the plots of the Jews, [20] and I did not at all shrink from telling you what was for your benefit, or from teaching you in public or in your homes. [21] I earnestly bore witness for both Jews and Greeks to repentance before God and to faith in our Lord Jesus. [22] But now, compelled by the Spirit, I am going to Jerusalem. What will happen to me there I do not know, [23] except that in one city after another the holy Spirit has been warning me that imprisonment and hardships await me.[q] [24] Yet I consider life of no importance to me, if only I may finish my course and the ministry that I received from the Lord Jesus, to bear witness to the gospel of God's grace.[r]

[25] "But now I know that none of you to whom I preached the kingdom during my travels will ever see my face again. [26] And so I solemnly declare to you this day that I am not responsible for the blood of any of you, [27] for I did not shrink from proclaiming to you the entire plan of God. [28] [s] Keep watch over yourselves and over the whole flock of which the holy Spirit has appointed you overseers,* in which you tend the church of God that he acquired with his own blood. [29] I know that after my departure savage wolves will come among you, and they will not spare the flock.[t] [30] And from your own group, men will come forward perverting the truth to draw the disciples away after them.[u] [31] So be vigilant and remember that for three years, night and day, I unceasingly admonished each of you with tears.[v] [32] And now I commend you to God and to that gracious word of his that can build you up and give you the inheritance among all who are consecrated. [33] I have never wanted anyone's silver or gold or clothing. [34] You know well that these very hands have served my needs and my companions.[w] [35] In every way I have shown you that by hard work of that sort we must help the weak, and keep in mind the words of the Lord Jesus who himself said, 'It is more blessed to give than to receive.' "[x]

[36] When he had finished speaking he knelt down and prayed with them all. [37] They were all weeping loudly as they threw their arms around Paul and kissed him, [38] for they were deeply distressed that he had said that they would never see his face again. Then they escorted him to the ship.

CHAPTER 21

Arrival at Tyre. [1] * When we had taken leave of them we set sail, made a straight run for Cos, and on the next day for Rhodes, and from there to Patara. [2] Finding a ship crossing to Phoenicia, we went on board and put out to sea. [3] We caught sight of Cyprus but passed by it on our left and sailed on toward Syria and put in at Tyre where the ship was to unload cargo.

---

q Acts 9, 16.—r 2 Tm 4, 7.—s Jn 21, 15-17; 1 Pt 5, 2.—t Jn 10, 12.—u Mt 7, 15; 2 Pt 2, 1-3; 1 Jn 2, 18-19.—v 1 Thes 2, 11.—w 1 Cor 4, 12; 1 Thes 2, 9; 2 Thes 3, 8.—x Sir 4, 31.

20, 16-35: Apparently aware of difficulties at Ephesus and neighboring areas, Paul calls the presbyters together at Miletus, about thirty miles from Ephesus. He reminds them of his dedication to the gospel (18-21), speaks of what he is about to suffer for the gospel (22-27), and admonishes them to guard the community against false prophets, sure to arise upon his departure (28-31). He concludes by citing a saying of Jesus (35) not recorded in the gospel tradition. Luke presents this farewell to the Ephesian presbyters as Paul's last will and testament.

20, 28: *Overseers:* see the note on Phil 1, 1. *The church of God:* because the clause "that he acquired with his own blood" following "the church of God" suggests that "his own blood" refers to God's blood, some early copyists changed "the church of God" to "the church of the Lord." Some prefer the translation "acquired with the blood of his own," i.e., Christ.

21, 1-18: The third "we-section" of Acts (see the note on Acts 16, 10-17).

[4] There we sought out the disciples and stayed for a week. They kept telling Paul through the Spirit not to embark for Jerusalem. [5] At the end of our stay we left and resumed our journey. All of them, women and children included, escorted us out of the city, and after kneeling on the beach to pray, [6] we bade farewell to one another. Then we boarded the ship, and they returned home.

Arrival at Ptolemais and Caesarea. [7] We continued the voyage and came from Tyre to Ptolemais, where we greeted the brothers and stayed a day with them. [8] On the next day we resumed the trip and came to Caesarea, where we went to the house of Philip the evangelist, who was one of the Seven,* and stayed with him.[y] [9] He had four virgin daughters gifted with prophecy. [10] We had been there several days when a prophet named Agabus* came down from Judea. [11] [z] He came up to us, took Paul's belt, bound his own feet and hands with it, and said, "Thus says the holy Spirit: This is the way the Jews will bind the owner of this belt in Jerusalem, and they will hand him over to the Gentiles."* [12] When we heard this, we and the local residents begged him not to go up to Jerusalem. [13] Then Paul replied, "What are you doing, weeping and breaking my heart? I am prepared not only to be bound but even to die in Jerusalem for the name of the Lord Jesus." [14] [a] Since he would not be dissuaded we let the matter rest, saying,[b] "The Lord's will be done."*

Paul and James in Jerusalem. [15] After these days we made preparations for our journey, then went up to Jerusalem. [16] Some of the disciples from Caesarea came along to lead us to the house of Mnason, a Cypriot, a disciple of long standing, with whom we were to stay. [17] * When we reached Jerusalem the brothers welcomed us warmly. [18] The next day, Paul accompanied us on a visit to James, and all the presbyters were present. [19] He greeted them, then proceeded to tell them in detail what God had accomplished among the Gentiles through his ministry. [20] They praised God when they heard it but said to him, "Brother, you see how many thousands of believers there are from among the Jews, and they are all zealous observers of the law. [21] They have been informed that you are teaching all the Jews who live among the Gentiles to abandon Moses and that you are telling them not to circumcise their children or to observe their customary practices. [22] What is to be done? They will surely hear that you have arrived. [23] * So do what we tell you. We have four men who have taken a vow.[c] [24] Take these men and purify yourself with them, and pay their expenses* that they may have their heads shaved. In this way everyone will know that there is nothing to the reports they have been given about you but that you yourself live in observance of the law. [25] [d] As for the Gentiles who have come to believe, we sent them our decision that they abstain from meat sacrificed to idols, from blood, from the meat of strangled animals, and from unlawful marriage."* [26] So Paul took the men, and on the next day after purifying himself together with them entered the temple to give notice of the day when the purification would be completed and the offering made for each of them.[e]

Paul's Arrest. [27] When the seven days were nearly completed, the Jews from the province of Asia noticed him in the temple, stirred up the whole crowd, and laid hands

---

y Acts 6, 5; 8, 5-6.—z Acts 11, 28; 20, 23.—a Acts 19, 15-16.—b Mt 6, 10; 26, 39; Mk 14, 36; Lk 22, 42.—c 23-27: Acts 18, 18; Nm 6, 1-21.—d Acts 15, 19-20.28-29.—e 1 Cor 9, 20.

21, 8: *One of the Seven:* see the note on Acts 6, 2-4.

21, 10: *Agabus:* mentioned in Acts 11, 28 as the prophet who predicted the famine that occurred when Claudius was emperor.

21, 11: The symbolic act of Agabus recalls those of Old Testament prophets. Compare Is 20, 2; Ez 4, 1; Jer 13, l.

21, 14: The Christian disciples' attitude reflects that of Jesus (see Lk 22, 42).

21, 17-26: The leaders of the Jewish Christians of Jerusalem inform Paul that the Jews there believe he has encouraged the Jews of the diaspora to abandon the Mosaic law. According to Acts, Paul had no objection to the retention of the law by the Jewish Christians of Jerusalem and left the Jews of the diaspora who accepted Christianity free to follow the same practice.

21, 23-26: The leaders of the community suggest that Paul, on behalf of four members of the Jerusalem community, make the customary payment for the sacrifices offered at the termination of the Nazirite vow (see Nm 6, 1-24) in order to impress favorably the Jewish Christians in Jerusalem with his high regard for the Mosaic law. Since Paul himself had once made this vow (Acts 18, 18), his respect for the law would be on public record.

21, 24: *Pay their expenses:* according to Nm 6, 14-15 the Nazirite had to present a yearling lamb for a holocaust, a yearling ewe lamb for a sin offering, and a ram for a peace offering, along with food and drink offerings, upon completion of the period of the vow.

21, 25: Paul is informed about the apostolic decree, seemingly for the first time (see the note on Acts 15, 13-35). The allusion to the decree was probably introduced here by Luke to remind his readers that the Gentile Christians deriving from the law.

on him, [28] f shouting, "Fellow Israelites, help us. This is the man who is teaching everyone everywhere against the people and the law and this place, and what is more, he has even brought Greeks into the temple and defiled this sacred place."* [29] For they had previously seen Trophimus the Ephesian in the city with him and supposed that Paul had brought him into the temple. [30] The whole city was in turmoil with people rushing together. They seized Paul and dragged him out of the temple, and immediately the gates were closed. [31] While they were trying to kill him, a report reached the cohort commander* that all Jerusalem was rioting. [32] He immediately took soldiers and centurions and charged down on them. When they saw the commander and the soldiers they stopped beating Paul. [33] The cohort commander came forward, arrested him, and ordered him to be secured with two chains; he tried to find out who he might be and what he had done. [34] Some in the mob shouted one thing, others something else; so, since he was unable to ascertain the truth because of the uproar, he ordered Paul to be brought into the compound. [35] When he reached the steps, he was carried by the soldiers because of the violence of the mob,

f Rom 15, 31.—g Acts 22, 22; Lk 23, 18; Jn 19, 15.—h Acts 5, 36-37.—i Acts 5, 34; 26, 4-5; 2 Cor 11, 22; Gal 1, 13-14; Phil 3, 5-6.—j Acts 8, 3; 9, 1-2; 22, 19; 26, 9-11; Phil 3, 6.—k Acts 9, 3; 26, 13; 1 Cor 15, 8.—l Acts 9, 4; 26, 14.—m Acts 9, 5; 26, 15; Mt 25, 40.—n Acts 9, 7; 26, 13-14.—o Acts 9, 6; 26, 16.—p Acts 9, 8.—q 12-16: Acts 9, 10-19.

21, 28: The charges against Paul by the diaspora Jews are identical to the charges brought against Stephen by diaspora Jews in Acts 6, 13. *Brought Greeks into the temple:* non-Jews were forbidden, under penalty of death, to go beyond the Court of the Gentiles. Inscriptions in Greek and Latin on a stone balustrade marked off the prohibited area.

21, 31: *Cohort commander:* literally, "the leader of a thousand in a cohort." At this period the Roman cohort commander usually led six hundred soldiers, a tenth of a legion; but the number in a cohort varied.

21, 36: *Away with him:* at the trial of Jesus before Pilate in Lk 23, 18, the people similarly shout, "Away with this man."

21, 38: *The Egyptian:* according to the Jewish historian Josephus, an Egyptian gathered a large crowd on the Mount of Olives to witness the destruction of the walls of Jerusalem that would fall at the Egyptian "prophet's" word. The commotion was put down by the Roman authorities and the Egyptian escaped, but only after thousands had been killed. *Four thousand assassins:* literally, *sicarii.* According to Josephus, these were political nationalists who removed their opponents by assassination with a short dagger, called in Latin a *sica.*

21, 40: *In Hebrew:* meaning, perhaps, in Aramaic, which at this time was the Semitic tongue in common use.

22, 1-21: Paul's first defense speech is presented to the Jerusalem crowds. Luke here presents Paul as a devout Jew (3) and zealous persecutor of the Christian community (4-5) and then recounts the conversion of Paul for the second time in Acts (see the note on Acts 9, 1-19).

[36] g for a crowd of people followed and shouted, "Away with him!"*

[37] Just as Paul was about to be taken into the compound, he said to the cohort commander, "May I say something to you?" He replied, "Do you speak Greek? [38] So then you are not the Egyptian* who started a revolt some time ago and led the four thousand assassins into the desert?" h [39] Paul answered, "I am a Jew, of Tarsus in Cilicia, a citizen of no mean city; I request you to permit me to speak to the people." [40] When he had given his permission, Paul stood on the steps and motioned with his hand to the people; and when all was quiet he addressed them in Hebrew.*

CHAPTER 22

Paul's Defense before the Jerusalem Jews. * [1] "My brothers and fathers, listen to what I am about to say to you in my defense." [2] When they heard him addressing them in Hebrew they became all the more quiet. And he continued, [3] "I am a Jew, born in Tarsus in Cilicia, but brought up in this city. At the feet of Gamaliel I was educated strictly in our ancestral law and was zealous for God, just as all of you are today. i [4] I persecuted this Way to death, binding both men and women and delivering them to prison. j [5] Even the high priest and the whole council of elders can testify on my behalf. For from them I even received letters to the brothers and set out for Damascus to bring back to Jerusalem in chains for punishment those there as well.

[6] "On that journey as I drew near to Damascus, about noon a great light from the sky suddenly shone around me. k [7] I fell to the ground and heard a voice saying to me, 'Saul, Saul, why are you persecuting me?' l [8] I replied, 'Who are you, sir?' And he said to me, 'I am Jesus the Nazorean whom you are persecuting.' m [9] My companions saw the light but did not hear the voice of the one who spoke to me. n [10] I asked, 'What shall I do, sir?' The Lord answered me, 'Get up and go into Damascus, and there you will be told about everything appointed for you to do.' o [11] Since I could see nothing because of the brightness of that light, I was led by hand by my companions and entered Damascus. p

[12] q "A certain Ananias, a devout observer of the law, and highly spoken of by

all the Jews who lived there, [13] came to me and stood there and said, 'Saul, my brother, regain your sight.' And at that very moment I regained my sight and saw him. [14] Then he said, 'The God of our ancestors designated you to know his will, to see the Righteous One, and to hear the sound of his voice; [15] for you will be his witness* before all to what you have seen and heard. [16] Now, why delay? Get up and have yourself baptized and your sins washed away, calling upon his name.'

[17] "After I had returned to Jerusalem and while I was praying in the temple, I fell into a trance [18] and saw the Lord saying to me, 'Hurry, leave Jerusalem at once, because they will not accept your testimony about me.' [19] But I replied, 'Lord, they themselves know that from synagogue to synagogue I used to imprison and beat those who believed in you.[r] [20] And when the blood of your witness Stephen was being shed, I myself stood by giving my approval and keeping guard over the cloaks of his murderers.'[s] [21] Then he said to me,[t] 'Go, I shall send you far away to the Gentiles.' "*

Paul Imprisoned. [22] [u] They listened to him until he said this, but then they raised their voices and shouted, "Take such a one as this away from the earth. It is not right that he should live."* [23] And as they were yelling and throwing off their cloaks and flinging dust into the air, [24] the cohort commander ordered him to be brought into the compound and gave instruction that he be interrogated under the lash to determine the reason why they were making such an outcry against him. [25] [v] But when they had stretched him out for the whips, Paul said to the centurion on duty, "Is it lawful for you to scourge a man who is a Roman citizen and has not been tried?"* [26] When the centurion heard this, he went to the cohort commander and reported it, saying, "What are you going to do? This man is a Roman citizen." [27] Then the commander came and said to him, "Tell me, are you a Roman citizen?" "Yes," he answered. [28] The commander replied, "I acquired this citizenship for a large sum of money." Paul said, "But I was born one." [29] At once those who were going to interrogate him backed away from him, and the commander became alarmed when he realized that he was a Roman citizen and that he had had him bound.

Paul before the Sanhedrin. [30] The next day, wishing to determine the truth about why he was being accused by the Jews, he freed him and ordered the chief priests and the whole Sanhedrin to convene. Then he brought Paul down and made him stand before them.

CHAPTER 23

[1] Paul looked intently at the Sanhedrin and said, "My brothers, I have conducted myself with a perfectly clear conscience before God to this day."[w] [2] The high priest Ananias* ordered his attendants to strike his mouth. [3] Then Paul said to him, "God will strike you,* you whitewashed wall. Do you indeed sit in judgment upon me according to the law and yet in violation of the law order me to be struck?"[x] [4] The attendants said, "Would you revile God's high priest?" [5] Paul answered, "Brothers, I did not realize he was the high priest. For it is written,[y] 'You shall not curse a ruler of your people.' "*

[6] Paul was aware that some were Sadducees and some Pharisees, so he called out before the Sanhedrin, "My brothers, I am a Pharisee, the son of Pharisees; [I] am on trial for hope in the resurrection of the dead."[z] [7] When he said this, a dispute

---

r Acts 8, 3; 9, 1-2; 22, 4-5; 26, 9-11.—s Acts 7, 58; 8, 1.—t Acts 9, 15; Gal 2, 7-9.—u Acts 21, 36; Lk 23, 18; Jn 19, 15.—v Acts 16, 37.—w Acts 24, 16.—x Ez 13, 10-15; Mt 23, 27.—y Ex 22, 27.—z Acts 24, 15.21; 26, 5; Phil 3, 5.

22, 15: *His witness:* like the Galilean followers during the historical ministry of Jesus, Paul too, through his experience of the risen Christ, is to be a witness to the resurrection (compare Acts 1, 8; 10, 39-41; Lk 24, 48).

22, 21: Paul endeavors to explain that his position on the law has not been identical with that of his audience because it has been his prophetic mission to preach to the Gentiles to whom the law was not addressed and who had no faith in it as a way of salvation.

22, 22: Paul's suggestion that his prophetic mission to the Gentiles did not involve his imposing the law on them provokes the same opposition as occurred in Pisidian Antioch (Acts 13, 45).

22, 25: *Is it lawful for you to scourge a man who is a Roman citizen and has not been tried?:* see the note on Acts 16, 37.

23, 2: *The high priest Ananias:* Ananias, son of Nedebaeus, was high priest from A.D. 47 to 59.

23, 3: *God will strike you:* Josephus reports that Ananias was later assassinated in A.D. 66 at the beginning of the First Revolt.

23, 5: Luke portrays Paul as a model of one who is obedient to the Mosaic law. Paul, because of his reverence for the law (Ex 22, 27), withdraws his accusation of hypocrisy, "whitewashed wall" (cf Mt 23, 27), when he is told Ananias is the high priest.

broke out between the Pharisees and Sadducees, and the group became divided. [8] For the Sadducees say that there is no resurrection or angels or spirits, while the Pharisees acknowledge all three.[a] [9] A great uproar occurred, and some scribes belonging to the Pharisee party stood up and sharply argued, "We find nothing wrong with this man. Suppose a spirit or an angel has spoken to him?" [10] The dispute was so serious that the commander, afraid that Paul would be torn to pieces by them, ordered his troops to go down and rescue him from their midst and take him into the compound. [11] [b] The following night the Lord stood by him and said, "Take courage. For just as you have borne witness to my cause in Jerusalem, so you must also bear witness in Rome."*

Transfer to Caesarea. [12] When day came, the Jews made a plot and bound themselves by oath not to eat or drink until they had killed Paul. [13] There were more than forty who formed this conspiracy. [14] They went to the chief priests and elders and said, "We have bound ourselves by a solemn oath to taste nothing until we have killed Paul. [15] You, together with the Sanhedrin, must now make an official request to the commander to have him bring him down to you, as though you meant to investigate his case more thoroughly. We on our part are prepared to kill him before he arrives." [16] The son of Paul's sister, however, heard about the ambush; so he went and entered the compound and reported it to Paul. [17] Paul then called one of the centurions* and requested, "Take this young man to the commander; he has something to report to him." [18] So he took him and brought him to the commander and explained, "The prisoner Paul called me and asked that I bring this young man to you; he has something to say to you." [19] The commander took him by the hand, drew him aside, and asked him privately, "What is it you have to report to me?" [20] He replied, "The Jews have conspired to ask you to bring Paul down to the Sanhedrin tomorrow, as though they meant to inquire about him more thoroughly, [21] but do not believe them. More than forty of them are lying in wait for him; they have bound themselves by oath not to eat or drink until they have killed him. They are now ready and only wait for your consent." [22] As the commander dismissed the young man he directed him, "Tell no one that you gave me this information."

[23] Then he summoned two of the centurions and said, "Get two hundred soldiers ready to go to Caesarea by nine o'clock tonight,* along with seventy horsemen and two hundred auxiliaries. [24] Provide mounts for Paul to ride and give him safe conduct to Felix the governor." [25] Then he wrote a letter with this content: [26] * "Claudius Lysias to his excellency the governor Felix, greetings.* [27] This man, seized by the Jews and about to be murdered by them, I rescued after intervening with my troops when I learned that he was a Roman citizen.[c] [28] I wanted to learn the reason for their accusations against him so I brought him down to their Sanhedrin. [29] I discovered that he was accused in matters of controversial questions of their law and not of any charge deserving death or imprisonment.[d] [30] Since it was brought to my attention that there will be a plot against the man, I am sending him to you at once, and have also notified his accusers to state [their case] against him before you."

[31] So the soldiers, according to their orders, took Paul and escorted him by night to Antipatris. [32] The next day they returned to the compound, leaving the horsemen to complete the journey with him. [33] When they arrived in Caesarea they delivered the letter to the governor and presented Paul to him. [34] When he had read it and asked to what province he belonged, and learned that he was from

---

a Mt 22, 23; Lk 20, 27.—b Acts 19, 21.—c Acts 21, 30-34; 22, 27.—d Acts 18, 14-15; 25, 18-19.

23, 11: The occurrence of the vision of Christ consoling Paul and assuring him that he will be his witness in Rome prepares the reader for the final section of Acts: the journey of Paul and the word he preaches to Rome under the protection of the Romans.

23, 17: *Centurions:* a centurion was a military officer in charge of one hundred soldiers.

23, 23: *By nine o'clock tonight:* literally, "by the third hour of the night." The night hours began at 6 p.m. *Two hundred auxiliaries:* the meaning of the Greek is not certain. It seems to refer to spearmen from the local police force and not from the cohort of soldiers, which would have numbered only 500-1000 men.

23, 26-30: The letter emphasizes the fact that Paul is a Roman citizen and asserts the lack of evidence that he is guilty of a crime against the empire. The tone of the letter implies that the commander became initially involved in Paul's case because of his Roman citizenship, but this is not an exact description of what really happened (see Acts 21, 31-33; 22, 25-29).

23, 26: M. Antonius Felix was procurator of Judea from A.D. 52 to 60. His procuratorship was marked by cruelty toward and oppression of his Jewish subjects.

Cilicia, [35] he said, "I shall hear your case when your accusers arrive." Then he ordered that he be held in custody in Herod's praetorium.

CHAPTER 24

Trial before Felix. [1] Five days later the high priest Ananias came down with some elders and an advocate, a certain Tertullus, and they presented formal charges against Paul to the governor. [2] When he was called, Tertullus began to accuse him, saying, "Since we have attained much peace through you, and reforms have been accomplished in this nation through your provident care, [3] we acknowledge this in every way and everywhere, most excellent Felix, with all gratitude. [4] But in order not to detain you further, I ask you to give us a brief hearing with your customary graciousness. [5] *e* We found this man to be a pest; he creates dissension among Jews all over the world and is a ringleader of the sect of the Nazoreans.* [6] He even tried to desecrate our temple, but we arrested him. *f* [7] * [8] If you examine him you will be able to learn from him for yourself about everything of which we are accusing him." [9] The Jews also joined in the attack and asserted that these things were so.

[10] * Then the governor motioned to him to speak and Paul replied, "I know that you have been a judge over this nation for many years and so I am pleased to make my defense before you. [11] As you can verify, not more than twelve days have passed since I went up to Jerusalem to worship. [12] Neither in the temple, nor in the synagogues, nor anywhere in the city did they find me arguing with anyone or instigating a riot among the people. [13] Nor can they prove to you the accusations they are now making against me. [14] But this I do admit to you, that according to the Way, which they call a sect, I worship the God of our ancestors and I believe everything that is in accordance with the law and written in the prophets. *g* [15] I have the same hope in God as they themselves have that there will be a resurrection of the righteous and the unrighteous. *h* [16] Because of this, I always strive to keep my conscience clear before God and man. *i* [17] After many years, I came to bring alms for my nation and offerings. *j* [18] While I was so engaged, they found me,

after my purification, in the temple without a crowd or disturbance. *k* [19] But some Jews from the province of Asia, who should be here before you to make whatever accusation they might have against me— [20] or let these men themselves state what crime they discovered when I stood before the Sanhedrin, [21] unless it was my one outcry as I stood among them, that 'I am on trial before you today for the resurrection of the dead.' "*l*

[22] Then Felix, who was accurately informed about the Way, postponed the trial, saying, "When Lysias the commander comes down, I shall decide your case." [23] He gave orders to the centurion that he should be kept in custody but have some liberty, and that he should not prevent any of his friends from caring for his needs.

Captivity in Caesarea. [24] * Several days later Felix came with his wife Drusilla, who was Jewish. He had Paul summoned and listened to him speak about faith in Christ Jesus. [25] But as he spoke about righteousness and self-restraint and the coming judgment, Felix became frightened and said, "You may go for now; when I find an opportunity I shall summon you again." [26] At the same time he hoped that a bribe would be offered him by Paul, and so he sent for him very often and conversed with him.

[27] Two years passed and Felix was succeeded by Porcius Festus. Wishing to ingratiate himself with the Jews, Felix left Paul in prison.*

---

e Acts 24, 14; Lk 23, 2.—f Acts 21, 28.—g Acts 24, 5.—h Dn 12, 2; Jn 5, 28-29.—i Acts 23, 1.—j Rom 15, 25-26; Gal 2, 10.—k 18-19: Acts 21, 26-30.—l Acts 23, 6; 24, 15.

24, 5: *Nazoreans:* that is, followers of Jesus of Nazareth.

24, 7: The Western text has added here a verse (really 6b-8a) that is not found in the best Greek manuscripts. It reads, "and would have judged him according to our own law, but the cohort commander Lysias came and violently took him out of our hands and ordered his accusers to come before you."

24, 10-21: Whereas the advocate Tertullus referred to Paul's activities on his missionary journeys, the apostle narrowed the charges down to the riot connected with the incident in the temple (see Acts 21, 27-30; 24, 17-20). In his defense, Paul stresses the continuity between Christianity and Judaism.

24, 24-25: The way of Christian discipleship greatly disquiets Felix, who has entered into an adulterous marriage with Drusilla, daughter of Herod Agrippa I. This marriage provides the background for the topics Paul speaks about and about which Felix does not want to hear.

24, 27: Very little is known of Porcius Festus who was a procurator of Judea from A.D. 60 to 62.

CHAPTER 25

Appeal to Caesar. [1] Three days after his arrival in the province, Festus went up from Caesarea to Jerusalem [2] where the chief priests and Jewish leaders presented him their formal charges against Paul.* They asked him [3] as a favor to have him sent to Jerusalem, for they were plotting to kill him along the way. [4] Festus replied that Paul was being held in custody in Caesarea and that he himself would be returning there shortly. [5] He said, "Let your authorities come down with me, and if this man has done something improper, let them accuse him."

[6] After spending no more than eight or ten days with them, he went down to Caesarea, and on the following day took his seat on the tribunal and ordered that Paul be brought in. [7] When he appeared, the Jews who had come down from Jerusalem surrounded him and brought many serious charges against him, which they were unable to prove. [8] In defending himself Paul said, "I have committed no crime either against the Jewish law or against the temple or against Caesar." [9] * Then Festus, wishing to ingratiate himself with the Jews, said to Paul in reply, "Are you willing to go up to Jerusalem and there stand trial before me on these charges?" [10] Paul answered, "I am standing before the tribunal of Caesar; this is where I should be tried. I have committed no crime against the Jews, as you very well know. [11] If I have committed a crime or done anything deserving death, I do not seek to escape the death penalty; but if there is no substance to the charges they are bringing against me, then no one has the right to hand me over to them. I appeal to Caesar." [12] Then Festus, after conferring with his council, replied, "You have appealed to Caesar. To Caesar you will go."

Paul before King Agrippa. [13] When a few days had passed, King Agrippa and Bernice* arrived in Caesarea on a visit to Festus. [14] Since they spent several days there, Festus referred Paul's case to the king, saying, "There is a man here left in custody by Felix.[m] [15] When I was in Jerusalem the chief priests and the elders of the Jews brought charges against him and demanded his condemnation. [16] I answered them that it was not Roman practice to hand over an accused person before he has faced his accusers and had the opportunity to defend himself against their charge. [17] So when [they] came together here, I made no delay; the next day I took my seat on the tribunal and ordered the man to be brought in. [18] [n] His accusers stood around him, but did not charge him with any of the crimes I suspected. [19] Instead they had some issues with him about their own religion and about a certain Jesus who had died but who Paul claimed was alive. [20] Since I was at a loss how to investigate this controversy, I asked if he were willing to go to Jerusalem and there stand trial on these charges. [21] And when Paul appealed that he be held in custody for the Emperor's decision, I ordered him held until I could send him to Caesar." [22] Agrippa said to Festus, "I too should like to hear this man." He replied, "Tomorrow you will hear him."

[23] The next day Agrippa and Bernice came with great ceremony and entered the audience hall in the company of cohort commanders and the prominent men of the city and, by command of Festus, Paul was brought in. [24] And Festus said, "King Agrippa and all you here present with us, look at this man about whom the whole Jewish populace petitioned me here and in Jerusalem, clamoring that he should live no longer. [25] I found, however, that he had done nothing deserving death, and so when he appealed to the Emperor, I decided to send him. [26] But I have nothing definite to write about him to our sovereign; therefore I have brought him before all of you, and particularly before you, King Agrippa, so that I may have something to write as a result of this investigation. [27] For it seems senseless to me to send up a prisoner without indicating the charges against him."

---

m Acts 24, 27.—n 18-19: Acts 18, 14-15; 23, 29.

25, 2: Even after two years the animosity toward Paul in Jerusalem had not subsided (see Acts 24, 27).

25, 9-12: Paul refuses to acknowledge that the Sanhedrin in Jerusalem has any jurisdiction over him now (11). Paul uses his right as a Roman citizen to appeal his case to the jurisdiction of the Emperor (Nero, ca. A.D. 60) (12). This move broke the deadlock between Roman protective custody of Paul and the plan of his enemies to kill him (3).

25, 13: *King Agrippa and Bernice:* brother and sister, children of Herod Agrippa I whose activities against the Jerusalem community are mentioned in Acts 12, 1-19. Agrippa II was a petty ruler over small areas in northern Palestine and some villages in Perea. His influence on the Jewish population of Palestine was insignificant.

CHAPTER 26

King Agrippa Hears Paul. [1] Then Agrippa said to Paul, "You may now speak on your own behalf." So Paul stretched out his hand and began his defense. [2] * "I count myself fortunate, King Agrippa, that I am to defend myself before you today against all the charges made against me by the Jews, [3] especially since you are an expert in all the Jewish customs and controversies. And therefore I beg you to listen patiently. [4] My manner of living from my youth, a life spent from the beginning among my people* and in Jerusalem, all [the] Jews know. [5] o They have known about me from the start, if they are willing to testify, that I have lived my life as a Pharisee, the strictest party of our religion. [6] p But now I am standing trial because of my hope in the promise made by God to our ancestors. [7] Our twelve tribes hope to attain to that promise as they fervently worship God day and night; and on account of this hope I am accused by Jews, O king. [8] Why is it thought unbelievable among you that God raises the dead? [9] q I myself once thought that I had to do many things against the name of Jesus the Nazorean, [10] and I did so in Jerusalem. I imprisoned many of the holy ones with the authorization I received from the chief priests, and when they were to be put to death I cast my vote against them. [r] [11] Many times, in synagogue after synagogue, I punished them in an attempt to force them to blaspheme; I was so enraged against them that I pursued them even to foreign cities.

[12] "On one such occasion I was traveling to Damascus with the authorization and commission of the chief priests. [13] s At midday, along the way, O king, I saw a light from the sky, brighter than the sun, shining around me and my traveling companions. [t] [14] We all fell to the ground and I heard a voice saying to me in Hebrew, 'Saul, Saul, why are you persecuting me?[u] It is hard for you to kick against the goad.'* [15] And I said, 'Who are you, sir?' And the Lord replied, 'I am Jesus whom you are persecuting. [v] [16] Get up now, and stand on your feet. [w] I have appeared to you for this purpose, to appoint you as a servant and witness of what you have seen [of me] and what you will be shown.* [17] I shall deliver you from this people and from the Gentiles to whom I send you, [x] [18] to

open their eyes* that they may turn from darkness to light and from the power of Satan to God, so that they may obtain forgiveness of sins and an inheritance among those who have been consecrated by faith in me.' [y]

[19] "And so, King Agrippa, I was not disobedient to the heavenly vision. [20] On the contrary, first to those in Damascus and in Jerusalem and throughout the whole country of Judea, and then to the Gentiles, I preached the need to repent and turn to God, and to do works giving evidence of repentance. [21] z That is why the Jews seized me [when I was] in the temple and tried to kill me. [22] a But I have enjoyed God's help to this very day, and so I stand here testifying to small and great alike, saying nothing different from what the prophets and Moses foretold,* [23] that the Messiah must suffer* and that, as the first to rise from the dead, he would proclaim light both to our people and to the Gentiles." [b]

Reactions to Paul's Speech. [24] While Paul was so speaking in his defense, Festus said in a loud voice, "You are mad, Paul; much learning is driving you mad." [25] But Paul replied, "I am not mad, most excellent Festus; I am speaking words of truth and

---

o Phil 3, 5-6; Gal 1, 13-14; 2 Cor 11, 22.—p 6-8: Acts 23, 6; 24, 15.21; 28, 20.—q 9-11: Acts 8, 3; 9, 1-2; 22, 19; Phil 3, 6.—r Acts 9, 14.—s 13-14: Acts 9, 7.—t Acts 9, 3; 22, 6.—u Acts 9, 4; 22, 7.—v Acts 9, 5; 22, 8; Mt 25, 40.—w Acts 9, 6; 22, 10; Ez 2, 1.—x Jer 1, 7.—y Is 42, 7.16; 61, 1 LXX; Col 1, 13.—z Acts 21, 31.—a 22-23: Acts 3, 18; Lk 24, 26-27.44-47.—b Is 42, 6; 49, 6; Lk 2, 32; 1 Cor 15, 20-23.

26, 2-23: Paul's final defense speech in Acts is now made before a king (see Acts 9, 15). In the speech Paul presents himself as a zealous Pharisee and Christianity as the logical development of Pharisaic Judaism. The story of his conversion is recounted for the third time in Acts in this speech (see the note on Acts 9, 1-19).

26, 4: *Among my people:* that is, among the Jews.

26, 14: *In Hebrew:* see the note on Acts 21, 40. *It is hard for you to kick against the goad:* this proverb is commonly found in Greek literature and in this context signifies the senselessness and ineffectiveness of any opposition to the divine influence in his life.

26, 16: The words of Jesus directed to Paul here reflect the dialogues between Christ and Ananias (Acts 9, 15) and between Ananias and Paul (Acts 22, 14-15) in the two previous accounts of Paul's conversion.

26, 18: *To open their eyes:* though no mention is made of Paul's blindness in this account (cf Acts 9, 8-9.12.18; 22, 11-13), the task he is commissioned to perform is the removal of other people's spiritual blindness.

26, 22: *Saying nothing different from what the prophets and Moses foretold:* see the note on Lk 18, 31.

26, 23: *That the Messiah must suffer:* see the note on Lk 24, 26.

reason. [26] The king knows about these matters and to him I speak boldly, for I cannot believe that [any] of this has escaped his notice; this was not done in a corner.* [27] King Agrippa, do you believe the prophets?* I know you believe." [28] Then Agrippa said to Paul, "You will soon persuade me to play the Christian." [29] Paul replied, "I would pray to God that sooner or later not only you but all who listen to me today might become as I am except for these chains."

[30] Then the king rose, and with him the governor and Bernice and the others who sat with them. [31] * And after they had withdrawn they said to one another, "This man is doing nothing [at all] that deserves death or imprisonment." [32] And Agrippa said to Festus, "This man could have been set free if he had not appealed to Caesar." *c*

CHAPTER 27

Departure for Rome. [1] * When it was decided that we should sail to Italy, they handed Paul and some other prisoners over to a centurion named Julius of the Cohort Augusta.* [2] We went on board a ship from Adramyttium bound for ports in the province of Asia and set sail. Aristarchus, a

---

c Acts 25, 11-12.—d Acts 19, 29; 20, 4.—e Lv 16, 29-31.

26, 26: *Not done in a corner:* for Luke, this Greek proverb expresses his belief that he is presenting a story about Jesus and the church that is already well known. As such, the entire history of Christianity is public knowledge and incontestable. Luke presents his story in this way to provide "certainty" to his readers about the instructions they have received (Lk 1, 4).

26, 27-28: If the Christian missionaries proclaim nothing different from what the Old Testament prophets had proclaimed (22-23), then the logical outcome for the believing Jew, according to Luke, is to become a Christian.

26, 31-32: In recording the episode of Paul's appearance before Agrippa, Luke wishes to show that, when Paul's case was judged impartially, no grounds for legal action against him were found (see Acts 23, 29; 25, 25).

27, 1—28, 16: Here Luke has written a stirring account of adventure on the high seas, incidental to his main purpose of showing how well Paul got along with his captors and how his prophetic influence saved the lives of all on board. The recital also establishes the existence of Christian communities in Puteoli and Rome. This account of the voyage and shipwreck also constitutes the final "we-section" in Acts (see the note on Acts 16, 10-17).

27, 1: *Cohort Augusta:* the presence of a Cohort Augusta in Syria during the first century A.D. is attested in inscriptions. Whatever the historical background to this information given by Luke may be, the name Augusta serves to increase the prominence and prestige of the prisoner Paul whose custodians bear so important a Roman name.

27, 9: *The time of the fast:* the fast kept on the occasion of the Day of Atonement (Lv 16, 29-31), which occurred in late September or early October.

Macedonian from Thessalonica, was with us. *d* [3] On the following day we put in at Sidon where Julius was kind enough to allow Paul to visit his friends who took care of him. [4] From there we put out to sea and sailed around the sheltered side of Cyprus because of the headwinds, [5] and crossing the open sea off the coast of Cilicia and Pamphylia we came to Myra in Lycia.

Storm and Shipwreck. [6] There the centurion found an Alexandrian ship that was sailing to Italy and put us on board. [7] For many days we made little headway, arriving at Cnidus only with difficulty, and because the wind would not permit us to continue our course we sailed for the sheltered side of Crete off Salmone. [8] We sailed past it with difficulty and reached a place called Fair Havens, near which was the city of Lasea.

[9] Much time had now passed and sailing had become hazardous because the time of the fast* had already gone by, so Paul warned them, *e* [10] "Men, I can see that this voyage will result in severe damage and heavy loss not only to the cargo and the ship, but also to our lives." [11] The centurion, however, paid more attention to the pilot and to the owner of the ship than to what Paul said. [12] Since the harbor was unfavorably situated for spending the winter, the majority planned to put out to sea from there in the hope of reaching Phoenix, a port in Crete facing west-northwest, there to spend the winter.

[13] A south wind blew gently, and thinking they had attained their objective, they weighed anchor and sailed along close to the coast of Crete. [14] Before long an offshore wind of hurricane force called a "Northeaster" struck. [15] Since the ship was caught up in it and could not head into the wind we gave way and let ourselves be driven. [16] We passed along the sheltered side of an island named Cauda and managed only with difficulty to get the dinghy under control. [17] They hoisted it aboard, then used cables to undergird the ship. Because of their fear that they would run aground on the shoal of Syrtis, they lowered the drift anchor and were carried along in this way. [18] We were being pounded by the storm so violently that the next day they jettisoned some cargo, [19] and on the third day with their own hands they threw even the ship's tackle overboard. [20] Neither the

sun nor the stars were visible for many days, and no small storm raged. Finally, all hope of our surviving was taken away.

21 When many would no longer eat, Paul stood among them and said, "Men, you should have taken my advice and not have set sail from Crete and you would have avoided this disastrous loss. 22 I urge you now to keep up your courage; not one of you will be lost, only the ship. 23 For last night an angel of the God to whom [I] belong and whom I serve stood by me 24 and said, 'Do not be afraid, Paul. You are destined to stand before Caesar; and behold, for your sake, God has granted safety to all who are sailing with you.' f 25 Therefore, keep up your courage, men; I trust in God that it will turn out as I have been told. 26 We are destined to run aground on some island."

27 On the fourteenth night, as we were still being driven about on the Adriatic Sea, toward midnight the sailors began to suspect that they were nearing land. 28 They took soundings and found twenty fathoms; a little farther on, they again took soundings and found fifteen fathoms. 29 Fearing that we would run aground on a rocky coast, they dropped four anchors from the stern and prayed for day to come. 30 The sailors then tried to abandon ship; they lowered the dinghy to the sea on the pretext of going to lay out anchors from the bow. 31 But Paul said to the centurion and the soldiers, "Unless these men stay with the ship, you cannot be saved." 32 So the soldiers cut the ropes of the dinghy and set it adrift.

33 Until the day began to dawn, Paul kept urging all to take some food. He said, "Today is the fourteenth day that you have been waiting, going hungry and eating nothing. 34 I urge you, therefore, to take some food; it will help you survive. Not a hair of the head of anyone of you will be lost." 35 When he said this, he took bread,* gave thanks to God in front of them all, broke it, and began to eat. g 36 They were all encouraged, and took some food themselves. 37 In all, there were two hundred seventy-six of us on the ship. 38 After they had eaten enough, they lightened the ship by throwing the wheat into the sea.

39 When day came they did not recognize the land, but made out a bay with a beach. They planned to run the ship ashore on it,

if they could. 40 So they cast off the anchors and abandoned them to the sea, and at the same time they unfastened the lines of the rudders, and hoisting the foresail into the wind, they made for the beach. 41 But they struck a sandbar and ran the ship aground. The bow was wedged in and could not be moved, but the stern began to break up under the pounding [of the waves]. 42 The soldiers planned to kill the prisoners so that none might swim away and escape, 43 but the centurion wanted to save Paul and so kept them from carrying out their plan. He ordered those who could swim to jump overboard first and get to the shore, 44 and then the rest, some on planks, others on debris from the ship. In this way, all reached shore safely.

CHAPTER 28

Winter in Malta. 1 Once we had reached safety we learned that the island was called Malta. 2 The natives showed us extraordinary hospitality; they lit a fire and welcomed all of us because it had begun to rain and was cold. 3 Paul had gathered a bundle of brushwood and was putting it on the fire when a viper, escaping from the heat, fastened on his hand. 4 When the natives saw the snake hanging from his hand, they said to one another, "This man must certainly be a murderer; though he escaped the sea, Justice* has not let him remain alive." 5 But he shook the snake off into the fire and suffered no harm. 6 They were expecting him to swell up or suddenly to fall down dead but, after waiting a long time and seeing nothing unusual happen to him, they changed their minds and began to say that he was a god. h 7 In the vicinity of that place were lands belonging to a man named Publius, the chief of the island. He welcomed us and received us cordially as his guests for three days. 8 It so happened that the father of Publius was sick with a fever and dysentery. Paul visited him and, after praying, laid his hands on him and healed him. 9 After this had taken place, the rest of the sick on the island came to Paul and were cured. 10 They paid us great honor

---

f Acts 23, 11.—g Mt 15, 36; Mk 6, 41; 8, 6; Lk 22, 19; 1 Cor 11, 23-24.—h Acts 14, 11.

27, 35: *He took bread . . . . :* the words recall the traditional language of the celebration of the Eucharist (see Lk 22, 19).

28, 4: *Justice:* in Greek mythology, the pursuing goddess of vengeance and justice.

and when we eventually set sail they brought us the provisions we needed.

Arrival in Rome. [11] Three months later we set sail on a ship that had wintered at the island. It was an Alexandrian ship with the Dioscuri* as its figurehead. [12] We put in at Syracuse and stayed there three days, [13] and from there we sailed round the coast and arrived at Rhegium. After a day, a south wind came up and in two days we reached Puteoli. [14] There we found some brothers and were urged to stay with them for seven days. And thus we came to Rome. [15] The brothers from there heard about us and came as far as the Forum of Appius and Three Taverns to meet us. On seeing them, Paul gave thanks to God and took courage. [16] When he entered Rome,* Paul was allowed to live by himself, with the soldier who was guarding him.

Testimony to Jews in Rome. [17] * Three days later he called together the leaders of the Jews. When they had gathered he said to them, "My brothers, although I had

i Acts 24, 12-13; 25, 8.—j Acts 23, 29; 25, 25; 26, 31-32.—k Acts 25, 11.—l Acts 23, 6; 24, 15.21; 26, 6-8.—m Acts 24, 5.14.—n Is 6, 9-10; Mt 13, 14-15; Mk 4, 12; Lk 8, 10; Jn 12, 40; Rom 11, 8.—o Acts 13, 46; 18, 6; Ps 67, 2; Is 40, 5 LXX; Lk 3, 6.

28, 11: *Dioscuri:* that is, the Twin Brothers, Castor and Pollux, the sons of Zeus and the patrons of the sailors.

28, 16: With Paul's arrival in Rome, the programmatic spread of the word of the Lord to "the ends of the earth" (Acts 1, 8) is accomplished. In Rome, Paul is placed under house arrest, and under this mild form of custody he is allowed to proclaim the word in the capital of the civilized world of his day.

28, 17-22: Paul's first act in Rome is to learn from the leaders of the Jewish community whether the Jews of Jerusalem plan to pursue their case against him before the Roman jurisdiction. He is informed that no such plan is afoot, but that the Jews of Rome have heard the Christian teaching denounced. Paul's offer to explain it to them is readily accepted.

28, 20: *The hope of Israel:* in the words of Paul (Acts 23, 6), Luke has identified this hope as hope in the resurrection of the dead.

28, 25-28: Paul's final words in Acts reflect a major concern of Luke's writings: how the salvation promised in the Old Testament, accomplished by Jesus, and offered first to Israel (Acts 13, 26), has now been offered to and accepted by the Gentiles. Quoting Is 6, 9-10, Paul presents the scriptural support for his indictment of his fellow Jews who refuse to accept the message he proclaims. Their rejection leads to its proclamation among the Gentiles.

28, 29: The Western text has added here a verse that is not found in the best Greek manuscripts: "And when he had said this, the Jews left, seriously arguing among themselves."

28, 30-31: Although the ending of Acts may seem to be abrupt, Luke has now completed his story with the establishment of Paul and the proclamation of Christianity in Rome. Paul's confident and unhindered proclamation of the gospel in Rome forms the climax to the story whose outline was provided in Acts 1, 8: "You will be my witnesses in Jerusalem . . . and to the ends of the earth."

done nothing against our people or our ancestral customs, I was handed over to the Romans as a prisoner from Jerusalem. [i] [18] After trying my case the Romans wanted to release me, because they found nothing against me deserving the death penalty. [j] [19] But when the Jews objected, I was obliged to appeal to Caesar, even though I had no accusation to make against my own nation. [k] [20] This is the reason, then, I have requested to see you and to speak with you, for it is on account of the hope of Israel* that I wear these chains." [l] [21] They answered him, "We have received no letters from Judea about you, nor has any of the brothers arrived with a damaging report or rumor about you. [22] But we should like to hear you present your views, for we know that this sect is denounced everywhere." [m]

[23] So they arranged a day with him and came to his lodgings in great numbers. From early morning until evening, he expounded his position to them, bearing witness to the kingdom of God and trying to convince them about Jesus from the law of Moses and the prophets. [24] Some were convinced by what he had said, while others did not believe. [25] Without reaching any agreement among themselves they began to leave; then Paul made one final statement.* "Well did the holy Spirit speak to your ancestors through the prophet Isaiah, saying:

[26] 'Go to this people and say: [n]
    You shall indeed hear but not understand.
        You shall indeed look but never see.
[27] Gross is the heart of this people;
        they will not hear with their ears;
        they have closed their eyes,
            so they may not see with their eyes
        and hear with their ears
    and understand with their heart and be converted,
        and I heal them.'

[28] [o] Let it be known to you that this salvation of God has been sent to the Gentiles; they will listen." [29] *

[30] * He remained for two full years in his lodgings. He received all who came to him, [31] and with complete assurance and without hindrance he proclaimed the kingdom of God and taught about the Lord Jesus Christ.

Acts

NEW TESTAMENT LETTERS

In the New Testament canon, between the Acts of the Apostles and Revelation, there are twenty-one documents that take the form of letters or epistles. Most of these are actual letters, but some are more like treatises in the guise of letters. In a few cases even some of the more obvious elements of the letter form are absent; see the Introductions to Hebrews and to 1 John.

The virtually standard form found in these documents, though with some variation, is dependent upon the conventions of letter writing common in the ancient world, but these were modified to suit the purposes of Christian writers. The New Testament letters usually begin with a greeting including an identification of the sender or senders and of the recipients. Next comes a prayer, usually in the form of a thanksgiving. The body of the letter provides an exposition of Christian teaching, usually provoked by concrete circumstances, and generally also draws conclusions regarding ethical behavior. There often follows a discussion of practical matters, such as the writer's travel plans, and the letter concludes with further advice and a formula of farewell.

Fourteen of the twenty-one letters have been traditionally attributed to Paul. One of these, the Letter to the Hebrews, does not itself claim to be the work of Paul; when it was accepted into the canon after much discussion, it was attached at the very end of the Pauline corpus. The other thirteen identify Paul as their author, but most scholars believe that some of them were actually written by his disciples; see the Introductions to Ephesians, Colossians, 2 Thessalonians, and 1 Timothy.

Four of the letters in the Pauline corpus (Ephesians, Philippians, Colossians, and Philemon) are called the "Captivity Epistles" because in each of them the author speaks of being in prison at the time of writing. Three others (1-2 Timothy and Titus) are known as the "Pastoral Epistles" because, addressed to individuals rather than communities, they give advice to disciples about caring for the flock. The letters of the Pauline corpus are arranged in roughly descending order of length from Romans to Philemon, with Hebrews added at the end.

The other seven letters of the New Testament that follow the Pauline corpus are collectively referred to as the "Catholic Epistles." This term, which means "universal," refers to the fact that most of them are directed not to a single Christian community, as are most of the Pauline letters, but to a wider audience; see the Introduction to the catholic letters. Three of them (1-2-3 John) are closely related to the fourth gospel and thus belong to the Johannine corpus. The catholic letters, like those of the Pauline corpus, are also arranged in roughly descending order of length, but the three Johannine letters are kept together and Jude is placed at the end.

The genuine letters of Paul are earlier in date than any of our written gospels. The dates of the other New Testament letters are more difficult to determine, but for the most part they belong to the second and third Christian generations rather than to the first.

THE LETTER TO THE ROMANS

INTRODUCTION

Of all the letters of Paul, that to the Christians at Rome has long held pride of place. It is the longest and most systematic unfolding of the apostle's thought, expounding the gospel of God's righteousness that saves all who believe (1, 16-17); it reflects a universal outlook, with special implications for Israel's relation to the church (chs 9-11). Yet, like all Paul's letters, Romans too arose out of a specific situation, when the apostle wrote from Greece, likely Corinth, between A.D. 56 and 58 (cf Acts 20, 2-3).

Paul at that time was about to leave for Jerusalem with a collection of funds for the impoverished Jewish Christian believers there, taken up from his predominantly Gentile congregations (15, 25-27). He planned then to travel on to Rome and to enlist support there for a mission to Spain (15, 24.28). Such a journey had long been on his mind (1, 9-13; 15, 23). Now, with much missionary preaching successfully accomplished in the East (15, 19), he sought new opportunities in the West (15, 20-21), in order to complete the divine plan of evangelization in the Roman world. Yet he recognized that the visit to Jerusalem would be hazardous (15, 30-32), and we know from Acts that Paul was arrested there and came to Rome only in chains, as a prisoner (Acts 21—28, especially 21, 30-33 and 28, 14.30-31).

The existence of a Christian community in Rome antedates Paul's letter there. When it arose, likely within the sizable Jewish population at Rome, and how, we do not know. The Roman historian Suetonius mentions an edict of the Emperor Claudius about A.D. 49 ordering the expulsion of Jews from Rome in connection with a certain "Chrestus," probably involving a dispute in the Jewish community over Jesus as the Messiah ("Christus"). According to Acts 18, 2, Aquila and Priscilla (or Prisca, as in Rom 16, 3) were among those driven out; from them, in Corinth, Paul may have learned about conditions in the church at Rome.

Opinions vary as to whether Jewish or Gentile Christians predominated in the house churches (cf 16, 5) in the capital city of the empire at the time Paul wrote. Perhaps already by then Gentile Christians were in the majority. Paul speaks in Romans of both Jews and Gentiles (3, 9.29; see the note on 1, 14). The letter also refers to those "weak in faith" (14, 1) and those "who are strong" (15, 1); this terminology may reflect not so much differences between believers of Jewish and of Gentile background, respectively, as an ascetic tendency in some converts (14, 2) combined with Jewish laws about clean and unclean foods (14, 14.20). The issues were similar to problems that Paul had faced in Corinth (1 Cor 8). If Romans 16 is part of the letter to Rome (see the note on 16, 1-23), then Paul had considerable information about conditions in Rome through all these people there whom he knew, and our letter does not just reflect a generalized picture of an earlier situation in Corinth.

In any case, Paul writes to introduce himself and his message to the Christians at Rome, seeking to enlist their support for the proposed mission to Spain. He therefore employs formulations likely familiar to the Christians at Rome; see the note on the confessional material at 1, 3-4 and compare 3, 25-26 and 4, 25. He cites the Old Testament frequently (1, 17; 3, 10-18; ch 4; 9, 7.12-13.15.17.25-29.33; 10, 5-13.15-21; 15, 9-12). The gospel Paul presents is meant to be a familiar one to those in Rome, even though they heard it first from other preachers.

As the outline below shows, this gospel of Paul (see 16, 25) finds its center in salvation and justification through faith in Christ (1, 16-17). While God's wrath is revealed against all sin and wickedness of Gentile and Jew alike (1, 18—3, 20), God's power to save by divine righteous or justifying action in Christ is also revealed (1, 16-17; 3, 21—5, 21). The consequences and implications for those who believe are set forth (6, 1—8, 39), as are results for those in Israel (chs 9-11) who, to Paul's great sorrow (9, 1-5), disbelieve. The apostle's hope is that, just as rejection of the gospel by some in Israel has led to a ministry of salvation for non-Jews, so one day, in God's mercy, "all Israel" will be saved (11, 11-15.25-29.30-32). The fuller ethical response of believers is also drawn out, both with reference to life in Christ's body (ch 12) and with regard to the world (13, 1-7), on the basis of the eschatological situation (13, 11-14) and conditions in the community (14, 1—15, 13).

Others have viewed Romans more in the light of Paul's earlier, quite polemical Letter to the Galatians and so see the theme as the relationship between Judaism and Christianity, a topic judged to be much in the minds of the Roman Christians. Each of these religious faiths claimed to be the way of salvation based upon a covenant between God and a people chosen and made the beneficiary of divine gifts. But Christianity regarded itself as the prophetic development and fulfillment of the faith of the Old Testament, declaring that the preparatory Mosaic covenant must now give way to the new and more perfect covenant in Jesus Christ. Paul himself had been the implacable advocate of freedom of Gentiles from the laws of the Mosaic covenant and, especially in Galatia, had refused to allow attempts to impose them on Gentile converts to the gospel. He had witnessed the personal hostilities that developed between the adherents of the two faiths and had written his strongly worded letter to the Galatians against those Jewish Christians who were seeking to persuade Gentile Christians to adopt the religious practices of Judaism. For him, the purity of the religious understanding of Jesus as the source of salvation would be seriously impaired if Gentile Christians were obligated to amalgamate the two religious faiths.

Still others find the theme of Israel and the church as expressed in Romans 9—11 to be the heart of Romans. Then the implication of Paul's exposition of justification by faith rather than by means of law is that the divine plan of salvation works itself out on a broad theological plane to include the whole of humanity, despite the differences in the content of the given religious system to which a human culture is heir. Romans presents a plan of salvation stretching from Adam through Abraham and Moses to Christ (chs 4 and 5) and on to the future revelation at Christ's parousia (8, 18-25). Its outlook is universal.

Paul's Letter to the Romans is a powerful exposition of the doctrine of the supremacy of Christ and of faith in Christ as the source of salvation. It is an implicit plea to the Christians at Rome, and to all Christians, to hold fast to that faith. They are to resist any pressure put on them to accept a doctrine of salvation through works of the law (see the note on 10, 4). At the same time they are not to exaggerate Christian freedom as an abdication of responsibility for others (12, 1-2) or as a repudiation of God's law and will (see the notes on 3, 9-26; 3, 31; 7, 7-12.13-25).

The principal divisions of the Letter to the Romans are the following:

I. *Address (1, 1-15)*
II. *Humanity Lost without the Gospel (1, 16—3, 20)*
III. *Justification through Faith in Christ (3, 21—5, 21)*
IV. *Justification and the Christian Life (6, 1—8, 39)*
V. *Jews and Gentiles in God's Plan (9, 1—11, 36)*
VI. *The Duties of Christians (12, 1—15, 13)*
VII. *Conclusion (15, 14—16, 27)*

I. ADDRESS

CHAPTER 1

Greeting.* [1] Paul, a slave of Christ Jesus,* called to be an apostle and set apart for the gospel of God,[a] [2] which he promised previously through his prophets in the holy scriptures,[b] [3] * the gospel about his Son, descended from David according to the flesh,[c] [4] but established as Son of God in power according to the spirit of holiness through resurrection from the dead, Jesus Christ our Lord.[d] [5] * Through him we have received the grace of apostleship, to bring about the obedience of faith, for the sake of his name, among all the Gentiles,[e] [6] among whom are you also, who are called to belong to Jesus Christ;[f] [7] to all the beloved of God in Rome, called to be holy.* Grace to you and peace from God our Father and the Lord Jesus Christ.[g]

Thanksgiving. [8] First, I give thanks* to my God through Jesus Christ for all of you, because your faith is heralded throughout the world.[h] [9] God is my witness, whom I serve with my spirit in proclaiming the gospel of his Son, that I remember you constantly,[i] [10] * always asking in my prayers that somehow by God's will I may at last find my way clear to come to you.[j] [11] For I long to see you, that I may share with you some spiritual gift so that you may be strengthened,[k] [12] that is, that you and I may be mutually encouraged by one another's faith, yours and mine. [13] I do not want you to be unaware, brothers,* that I often planned to come to you, though I was prevented until now, that I might harvest some fruit among you, too, as among the rest of the Gentiles.[l] [14] To Greeks and non-Greeks* alike, to the wise and the ignorant, I am under obligation; [15] that is why I am eager to preach the gospel also to you in Rome.[m]

---

a Gal 1, 10; Phil 1, 1; Jas 1, 1 / Acts 9, 15; 13, 2; 1 Cor 1, 1; Gal 1, 15; Ti 1, 1.—b Rom 16, 25-26; Ti 1, 2.—c Rom 9, 5; 2 Sm 7, 12; Mt 1, 1; Mk 12, 35; Jn 7, 42; Acts 13, 22-23; 2 Tm 2, 8; Rv 22, 16.—d Rom 10, 9; Acts 13, 33; Phil 3, 10.—e Rom 15, 15; Gal 2, 7.9 / Rom 15, 18; Acts 9, 15; 26, 16-18; Gal 1, 16; 2, 7.9.—f 1 Cor 1, 9.—g Nm 6, 25-26; 1 Cor 1, 2-3; 2 Cor 1, 1-2.— h Rom 16, 19; 1 Thes 1, 8.—i 2 Cor 1, 23; Eph 1, 16; Phil 1, 8; 1 Thes 1, 2; 2, 5.10; 2 Tm 1, 3.—j Rom 15, 23.32; Acts 18, 21; 1 Cor 4, 19; 1 Thes 2, 17.—k 1 Thes 2, 17; 3, 10.—l Rom 15, 22; Jn 15, 16; Acts 19, 21.—m Acts 28, 30-31.

1, 1-7: In Paul's letters the greeting or *praescriptio* follows a standard form, though with variations. It is based upon the common Greco-Roman epistolary practice, but with the addition of Semitic and specifically Christian elements. The three basic components are: name of sender; name of addressee; greeting. In identifying himself, Paul often adds phrases to describe his apostolic mission; this element is more developed in Rom than in any other letter. Elsewhere he associates co-workers with himself in the greeting: Sosthenes (1 Cor), Timothy (2 Cor; Phil; Phlm), Silvanus (1-2 Thes). The standard secular greeting was the infinitive *chairein*, "greetings." Paul uses instead the similar-sounding *charis*, "grace," together with the Semitic greeting *šālôm* (Greek *eirēnē*), "peace." These gifts, foreshadowed in God's dealings with Israel (see Nm 6, 24-26), have been poured out abundantly in Christ, and Paul wishes them to his readers. In Rom the Pauline *praescriptio* is expanded and expressed in a formal tone; it emphasizes Paul's office as apostle to the Gentiles. Verses 3-4 stress the gospel or kerygma, v 2 the fulfillment of God's promise, and vv 1 and 5 Paul's office. On his call, see Gal 1, 15-16; 1 Cor 9, 1; 15, 8-10; Acts 9, 1-22; 22, 3-16; 26, 4-18.

1, 1: *Slave of Christ Jesus:* Paul applies the term slave to himself in order to express his undivided allegiance to the Lord of the church, the Master of all, including slaves and masters. "No one can serve (i.e., be a slave to) two masters," said Jesus (Mt 6, 24). It is this aspect of the slave-master relationship rather than its degrading implications that Paul emphasizes when he discusses Christian commitment.

1, 3-4: Paul here cites an early confession that proclaims Jesus' sonship as messianic descendant of David (cf Mt 22, 42; 2 Tm 2, 8; Rv 22, 16) and as Son of God by the resurrection. As "life-giving spirit" (1 Cor 15, 45), Jesus Christ is able to communicate the Spirit to those who believe in him.

1, 5: Paul recalls his apostolic office, implying that the Romans know something of his history. *The obedience of faith:* as Paul will show at length in chs 6-8 and 12-15, faith in God's justifying action in Jesus Christ relates one to God's gift of the new life that is made possible through the death and resurrection of Jesus Christ and the activity of the holy Spirit (see especially Rom 8, 1-11).

1, 7: *Called to be holy:* Paul often refers to Christians as "the holy ones" or "the saints." The Israelite community was called a "holy assembly" because they had been separated for the worship and service of the Lord (see Lv 11, 44; 23, 1-44). The Christian community regarded its members as sanctified by baptism (Rom 6, 22; 15, 16; 1 Cor 6, 11; Eph 5, 26-27). Christians are called to holiness (1 Cor 1, 2; 1 Thes 4, 7), that is, they are called to make their lives conform to the gift they have already received.

1, 8: In Greco-Roman letters, the greeting was customarily followed by a prayer. The Pauline letters usually include this element (except Gal and Ti), expressed in Christian thanksgiving formulas and usually stating the principal theme of the letter. In 2 Cor the thanksgiving becomes a blessing, and in Eph it is preceded by a lengthy blessing. Sometimes the thanksgiving is blended into the body of the letter, especially in 1 Thes. In Rom it is stated briefly.

1, 10-12: Paul lays the groundwork for his more detailed statement in Rom 15, 22-24 about his projected visit to Rome.

1, 13: *Brothers* is idiomatic for all Paul's "kin in Christ," all those who believe in the gospel; it includes women as well as men (cf Rom 4, 3).

1, 14: *Greeks and non-Greeks:* literally, "Greeks and barbarians." As a result of Alexander's conquests, Greek became the standard international language of the Mediterranean world. *Greeks* in Paul's statement therefore means people who know Greek or who have been influenced by Greek culture. *Non-Greeks* were people whose cultures remained substantially unaffected by Greek influences. Greeks called such people "barbarians" (cf Acts 28, 2), meaning people whose speech was foreign. Roman citizens would scarcely classify themselves as such, and Nero, who was reigning when Paul wrote this letter, prided himself on his admiration for Greek culture. *Under obligation:* Paul will expand on the theme of obligation in Rom 13, 8; 15, 1.27.

II. HUMANITY LOST WITHOUT
THE GOSPEL

God's Power for Salvation.* [16] For I am not ashamed of the gospel. It is the power of God for the salvation of everyone who believes: for Jew first, and then Greek.[n] [17] For in it is revealed the righteousness of God from faith to faith;* as it is written, "The one who is righteous by faith will live."[o]

Punishment of Idolaters. [18] * The wrath* of God* is indeed being revealed from heaven against every impiety and wickedness[p] of those who suppress the truth by their wickedness. [19] For what can be known about God is evident to them, because God made it evident to them.[q] [20] Ever since the creation of the world, his invisible attributes of eternal power and divinity have been able to be understood and perceived in what he has made.[r] As a result, they have no excuse; [21] for although they knew God they did not accord him glory as God or give him thanks. Instead, they became vain in their reasoning, and their senseless minds were darkened.[s] [22] While claiming to be wise,[t] they became fools [23] and exchanged the glory of the immortal God for the likeness of an image of mortal man or of birds or of four-legged animals or of snakes.[u]

[24] Therefore, God handed them over to impurity through the lusts of their hearts* for the mutual degradation of their bodies.[v] [25] They exchanged the truth of God for a lie and revered and worshiped the creature rather than the creator, who is blessed forever. Amen.[w] [26] Therefore, God handed them over to degrading passions. Their females exchanged natural relations for unnatural, [27] and the males likewise gave up natural relations with females and burned with lust for one another. Males did shameful things with males and thus received in their own persons the due penalty for their perversity.[x] [28] And since they did not see fit to acknowledge God, God handed them over to their undiscerning mind to do what is improper. [29] [y] They are filled with every form of wickedness, evil, greed, and malice; full of envy, murder, rivalry, treachery, and spite. They are gossips [30] and scandalmongers and they hate God. They are insolent, haughty, boastful, ingenious in their wickedness, and rebellious toward their parents. [31] They are senseless, faithless, heartless, ruthless. [32] Although they know the just decree of God that all who practice such things deserve death, they not only do them but give approval to those who practice them.[z]

---

n Ps 119, 46; 1 Cor 1, 18.24 / Rom 2, 9; Acts 3, 26; 13, 46.—o Rom 3, 21-22; Hb 2, 4; Gal 3, 11; Heb 10, 38.—p Rom 2, 5.8-9; Is 66, 15; Eph 5, 6; Col 3, 6.—q 19-32: Wis 13, 1-9; Acts 14, 15-17; 17, 23-29.—r Jb 12, 7-9; Pss 8, 4; 19, 2; Sir 17, 7-9; Is 40, 26; Acts 14, 17; 17, 25-28.—s Eph 4, 17-18.—t Wis 13, 1-9; Is 5, 21; Jer 10, 14; Acts 17, 29-30; 1 Cor 1, 19-21.—u Dt 4, 15-19; Ps 106, 20; Wis 11, 15; 12, 24; 13, 10-19; Jer 2, 11.—v Wis 12, 25; 14, 22-31; Acts 7, 41-42; Eph 4, 19.—w Rom 9, 5; Jer 13, 25-27.—x Lv 18, 22; 20, 13; Wis 14, 26; 1 Cor 6, 9; 1 Tm 1, 10.—y 29-31: Rom 13, 13; Mt 15, 19; Mk 7, 21-22; Gal 5, 19-21; 2 Tm 3, 2-4.—z Acts 8, 1; 2.Thes 2, 12.

1, 16-17: The principal theme of the letter is salvation through faith. *I am not ashamed of the gospel:* Paul is not ashamed to proclaim the gospel, despite the criticism that Jews and Gentiles leveled against the proclamation of the crucified savior; cf 1 Cor 1, 23-24. Paul affirms, however, that it is precisely through the crucifixion and resurrection of Jesus that God's saving will and power become manifest. *Jew first* (cf Rom 2, 9-10) means that Jews especially, in view of the example of Abraham (ch 4), ought to be the leaders in the response of faith.

1, 17: *In it is revealed the righteousness of God from faith to faith:* the gospel centers in Jesus Christ, in whom God's saving presence and righteousness in history have been made known. Faith is affirmation of the basic purpose and meaning of the Old Testament as proclamation of divine promise (Rom 1, 2; 4, 13) and exposure of the inability of humanity to effect its salvation even through covenant law. Faith is the gift of the holy Spirit and denotes acceptance of salvation as God's righteousness, that is, God's gift of a renewed relationship in forgiveness and power for a new life. Faith is response to God's total claim on people and their destiny. *The one who is righteous by faith will live:* see the note on Hb 2, 4.

1, 18—3, 20: Paul aims to show that all humanity is in a desperate plight and requires God's special intervention if it is to be saved.

1, 18-32: In this passage Paul uses themes and rhetoric common in Jewish-Hellenistic mission proclamation (cf Wis 13, 1—14, 31) to indict especially the non-Jewish world. The close association of idolatry and immorality is basic, but the generalization needs in all fairness to be balanced against the fact that non-Jewish Christian society on many levels displayed moral attitudes and performance whose quality would challenge much of contemporary Christian culture. Romans themselves expressed abhorrence over devotion accorded to animals in Egypt. Paul's main point is that the wrath of God does not await the end of the world but goes into action at each present moment in humanity's history when misdirected piety serves as a facade for self-interest.

1, 18: *The wrath of God:* God's reaction to human sinfulness, an Old Testament phrase that expresses the irreconcilable opposition between God and evil (see Is 9, 11.16.18.20; 10, 4; 30, 27). It is not contrary to God's universal love for his creatures, but condemns Israel's turning aside from the covenant obligations. Hosea depicts Yahweh as suffering intensely at the thought of having to punish Israel (Hos 11, 8-9). God's wrath was to be poured forth especially on the "Day of Yahweh" and thus took on an eschatological connotation (see Zep 1, 15).

1, 24: In order to expose the depth of humanity's rebellion against the Creator, *God handed them over to impurity through the lusts of their hearts.* Instead of curbing people's evil interests, God abandoned them to self-indulgence, thereby removing the facade of apparent conformity to the divine will. Subsequently Paul will show that the Mosaic law produces the same effect; cf Rom 5, 20; 7, 13-24. The divine judgment expressed here is related to the theme of hardness of heart described in Rom 9, 17-18.

CHAPTER 2

God's Just Judgment. [1] * Therefore, you are without excuse,[a] every one of you who passes judgment.* For by the standard by which you judge another you condemn yourself, since you, the judge, do the very same things. [2] We know that the judgment of God on those who do such things is true. [3] Do you suppose, then, you who judge those who engage in such things and yet do them yourself, that you will escape the judgment of God?[b] [4] Or do you hold his priceless kindness, forbearance, and patience in low esteem, unaware that the kindness of God would lead you to repentance?[c] [5] By your stubbornness and impenitent heart,[d] you are storing up wrath for yourself for the day of wrath and revelation of the just judgment of God, [6] [e] who will repay everyone according to his works:* [7] eternal life to those who seek glory, honor, and immortality through perseverance in good works, [8] but wrath and fury to those who selfishly disobey the truth and obey wickedness.[f] [9] Yes, affliction and distress will come upon every human being who does evil, Jew first and then Greek. [10] [g] But there will be glory, honor, and peace for everyone who does good, Jew first and then Greek. [11] [h] There is no partiality with God.*

Judgment by the Interior Law. * [12] All who sin outside the law will also perish without reference to it, and all who sin under the law will be judged in accordance with it.[i] [13] For it is not those who hear the law who are just in the sight of God; rather, those who observe the law will be justified.[j] [14] For when the Gentiles who do not have the law by nature observe the prescriptions of the law, they are a law for themselves even though they do not have the law.[k] [15] They show that the demands of the law are written in their hearts,* while their conscience also bears witness and their conflicting thoughts accuse or even defend them [16] on the day when, according to my gospel, God will judge people's hidden works through Christ Jesus.[l]

Judgment by the Mosaic Law. * [17] Now if you call yourself a Jew and rely on the law and boast of God[m] [18] and know his will and are able to discern what is important since you are instructed from the law,[n] [19] and if you are confident that you are a guide for the blind and a light for those in darkness,[o] [20] that you are a trainer of the foolish and teacher of the simple,[p] because in the law you have the formulation of knowledge and truth— [21] then you who teach another, are you failing to teach yourself? You who preach against stealing, do you steal?[q] [22] You who forbid adultery, do you commit adultery? You who detest idols, do you rob temples? [23] You who boast of the law, do you dishonor God by breaking the law? [24] [r] For, as it is written, "Because of you the name of God is reviled among the Gentiles."*

[25] [s] Circumcision, to be sure, has value if you observe the law; but if you break the law, your circumcision has become uncir-

---

a Mt 7, 1-2.—b Wis 16, 15-16.—c Rom 3, 25-26; 9, 22; Wis 11, 23; 15, 1; 2 Pt 3, 9.15.—d Ex 33, 3; Acts 7, 51; Rv 6, 17; 11, 18.—e Ps 62, 12; Prv 24, 12; Sir 16, 14; Mt 16, 27; Jn 5, 29; 2 Cor 5, 10.—f 2 Thes 1, 8.—g Rom 1, 16; 3, 9.—h Dt 10, 17; 2 Chr 19, 7; Sir 35, 12-13; Acts 10, 34; Gal 2, 6; Eph 6, 9; Col 3, 25; 1 Pt 1, 17.—i Rom 3, 19.—j Mt 7, 21; Lk 6, 46-49; 8, 21; Jas 1, 22-25; 1 Jn 3, 7.—k Acts 10, 35.—l Acts 10, 42; 17, 31.—m Is 48, 1-2; Mi 3, 11; Phil 3, 4-6.—n Phil 1, 10.—o Mt 15, 14; Lk 6, 39.—p 2 Tm 3, 15.—q Ps 50, 16-21; Mt 23, 3-4.—r Is 52, 5; Ez 36, 20; 2 Pt 2, 2.—s 25-29: Jer 4, 4; 9, 24-25.

2, 1—3, 20: After his general indictment of the Gentile, Paul shows that in spite of special revelation Jews enjoy no advantage in moral status before God (Rom 3, 1-8). With the entire human race now declared guilty before God (Rom 3, 9-20), Paul will then be able to display the solution for the total problem: salvation through God's redemptive work that is revealed in Christ Jesus for all who believe (Rom 3, 21-31).

2, 1-11: As a first step in his demonstration that Jews enjoy no real moral supremacy over Gentiles, Paul explains that the final judgment will be a review of performance, not of privilege. From this perspective Gentiles stand on an equal footing with Jews, and Jews cannot condemn the sins of Gentiles without condemning themselves.

2, 6: *Will repay everyone according to his works:* Paul reproduces the Septuagint text of Ps 62, 12 and Prv 24, 12.

2, 11: *No partiality with God:* this sentence is not at variance with the statements in vv 9-10. Since Jews are the first to go under indictment, it is only fair that they be given first consideration in the distribution of blessings. Basic, of course, is the understanding that God accepts no bribes (Dt 10, 17).

2, 12-16: Jews cannot reasonably demand from Gentiles the standard of conduct inculcated in the Old Testament since God did not address its revelation to them. Rather, God made it possible for Gentiles to know instinctively the difference between right and wrong. But, as Paul explained in Rom 1, 18-32, humanity misread the evidence of God's existence, power, and divinity, and "while claiming to be wise, they became fools" (Rom 1, 22).

2, 15: Paul expands on the thought of Jer 31, 33; Wis 17, 11.

2, 17-29: Mere possession of laws is no evidence of virtue. By eliminating circumcision as an elitist moral sign, Paul clears away the last obstacle to his presentation of justification through faith without claims based on the receipt of circumcision and its attendant legal obligations.

2, 24: According to Is 52, 5 the suffering of Israel prompts her enemies to revile God. Paul uses the passage in support of his point that the present immorality of Israelites is the cause of such defamation.

cumcision.[t] [26]Again, if an uncircumcised man keeps the precepts of the law, will he not be considered circumcised?[u] [27]Indeed, those who are physically uncircumcised but carry out the law will pass judgment on you, with your written law and circumcision, who break the law. [28]One is not a Jew outwardly. True circumcision is not outward, in the flesh.[v] [29]Rather, one is a Jew inwardly, and circumcision is of the heart, in the spirit, not the letter; his praise is not from human beings but from God.[w]

CHAPTER 3

Answers to Objections. [1] * What advantage is there then in being a Jew? Or what is the value of circumcision? [2]Much, in every respect. [For] in the first place, they were entrusted with the utterances of God.[x] [3]What if some were unfaithful? Will their infidelity nullify the fidelity of God?[y] [4]Of course not! God must be true, though every human being is a liar,* as it is written:

"That you may be justified in your words,
and conquer when you are judged."[z]

[5]But if our wickedness provides proof of God's righteousness, what can we say? Is God unjust, humanly speaking, to inflict his wrath?[a] [6]Of course not! For how else is God to judge the world? [7]But if God's truth redounds to his glory through my falsehood, why am I still being condemned as a sinner? [8]And why not say—as we are

accused and as some claim we say—that we should do evil that good may come of it? Their penalty is what they deserve.[b]

Universal Bondage to Sin. * [9]Well, then, are we better off? Not entirely, for we have already brought the charge against Jews and Greeks alike that they are all under the domination of sin,[c] [10]as it is written:[d]

"There is no one just, not one,
[11]   there is no one who understands,
        there is no one who seeks God.
[12] All have gone astray; all alike are worthless;
        there is not one who does good,
        [there is not] even one.
[13] Their throats are open graves;
        they deceive with their tongues;
    the venom of asps is on their lips;[e]
[14]   their mouths are full of bitter cursing.[f]
[15] Their feet are quick to shed blood;[g]
[16]   ruin and misery are in their ways,
[17] and the way of peace they know not.
[18]   There is no fear of God before their eyes."[h]

[19]Now we know that what the law* says is addressed to those under the law, so that every mouth may be silenced and the whole world stand accountable to God,[i] [20]since no human being will be justified in his sight* by observing the law; for through the law comes consciousness of sin.[j]

III. JUSTIFICATION THROUGH FAITH IN CHRIST

Justification apart from the Law. * [21]But now* the righteousness of God has been manifested apart from the law, though tes-

t 1 Cor 7, 19; Gal 5, 3.—u Gal 5, 6.—v Jn 7, 24; 8, 15.39.—w Dt 30, 6; Jer 4, 4; 9, 25; Col 2, 11 / 1 Cor 4, 5; 2 Cor 10, 18.—x Rom 9, 4; Dt 4, 7-8; Pss 103, 7; 147, 19-20.—y Rom 9, 6; 11, 1.29; Ps 89, 30-37; 2 Tm 2, 13.—z Ps 116, 11 / Ps 51, 6.—a Rom 9, 14; Jb 34, 12-17.—b Rom 6, 1.—c Rom 1, 18—2, 25; 3, 23; Sir 8, 5.—d 10-11: Pss 14, 1-3; 53, 2-4; Eccl 7, 20.—e Pss 5, 10; 140, 4.—f Ps 10, 7.—g 15-17: Prv 1, 16; Is 59, 7-8.—h Ps 36, 2.—i Rom 7, 7.—j Ps 143, 2; Gal 2, 16 / Rom 7, 7.

3, 1-4: In keeping with the popular style of diatribe, Paul responds to the objection that his teaching on the sinfulness of all humanity detracts from the religious prerogatives of Israel. He stresses that Jews have remained the vehicle of God's revelation despite their sins, though this depends on the fidelity of God.

3, 4: *Though every human being is a liar:* these words reproduce the Greek text of Ps 116, 11. The rest of the verse is from Ps 51, 6.

3, 9-20: *Well, then, are we better off?:* this phrase can also be translated "Are we at a disadvantage?" but the latter version does not substantially change the overall meaning of the passage. Having explained that Israel's privileged status is guaranteed by God's fidelity, Paul now demonstrates the infidelity of the Jews by a catena of citations from scripture, possibly derived from an existing collection of *testimonia*. These texts show that all human beings share the common burden of sin. They are linked together by mention of organs of the body: throat, tongue, lips, mouth, feet, eyes.

3, 19: *The law:* Paul here uses the term in its broadest sense to mean all of the scriptures; none of the preceding texts is from the Torah or Pentateuch.

3, 20: *No human being will be justified in his sight:* these words are freely cited from Ps 143, 2. In place of the psalmist's "no living person," Paul substitutes "no human being" (literally "no flesh," a Hebraism), and he adds "by observing the law."

3, 21-31: These verses provide a clear statement of Paul's "gospel," i.e., the principle of justification by faith in Christ. God has found a means of rescuing humanity from its desperate plight: Paul's general term for this divine initiative is *the righteousness of God* (21). Divine mercy declares the guilty innocent and makes them so. God does this not as a result of the law but apart from it (21), and not because of any merit in human beings but through forgiveness of their sins (24), in virtue of the redemption wrought in Christ Jesus for all who believe (22.24-25). God has manifested his righteousness in the coming of Jesus Christ, whose saving activity inaugurates a new era in human history.

3, 21: *But now:* Paul adopts a common phrase used by Greek authors to describe movement from disaster to prosperity. The expressions indicate that vv 21-26 are the consolatory answer to vv 9-20.

tified to by the law and the prophets,[k] [22] the righteousness of God through faith in Jesus Christ for all who believe.[l] For there is no distinction; [23] all have sinned and are deprived of the glory of God.[m] [24] They are justified freely by his grace through the redemption in Christ Jesus,[n] [25] whom God set forth as an expiation,* through faith, by his blood, to prove his righteousness because of the forgiveness of sins previously committed,[o] [26] through the forbearance of God—to prove his righteousness in the present time, that he might be righteous and justify the one who has faith in Jesus.

[27] [p] What occasion is there then for boasting?* It is ruled out. On what principle, that of works? No, rather on the principle of faith.* [28] For we consider that a person is justified by faith apart from works of the law.[q] [29] Does God belong to Jews alone? Does he not belong to Gentiles, too? Yes, also to Gentiles,[r] [30] for God is one and will justify the circumcised on the basis of faith and the uncircumcised through faith.[s] [31] Are we then annulling the law by this faith? Of course not![t] On the contrary, we are supporting the law.*

CHAPTER 4*

Abraham Justified by Faith. [1] What then can we say that Abraham found, our ancestor according to the flesh?[u] [2] * Indeed, if Abraham was justified on the basis of his

works, he has reason to boast; but this was not so in the sight of God. [3] [v] For what does the scripture say? "Abraham believed God, and it was credited to him as righteousness."* [4] A worker's wage is credited not as a gift, but as something due.[w] [5] But when one does not work, yet believes in the one who justifies the ungodly, his faith is credited as righteousness. [6] So also David declares the blessedness of the person to whom God credits righteousness apart from works:

[7] "Blessed are they whose iniquities are forgiven[x]
    and whose sins are covered.
[8] Blessed is the man whose sin the Lord does not record."

[9] Does this blessedness* apply only to the circumcised, or to the uncircumcised as well? Now we assert that "faith was credited to Abraham as righteousness."[y] [10] Under what circumstances was it credited? Was he circumcised or not? He was not circumcised, but uncircumcised. [11] And he received the sign of circumcision as a seal on the righteousness received through faith while he was uncircumcised. Thus he was to be the father of all the uncircumcised who believe, so that to them [also] righteousness might be credited,[z] [12] as well as the father of the circumcised who not only are circumcised but also follow the path of faith that our father Abraham walked while still uncircumcised.

---

k Is 51, 6-8; Acts 10, 43.—l Rom 1, 17; Gal 2, 16; Phil 3, 9.—m Rom 3, 9; 5, 12.—n Eph 2, 8; Ti 3, 7 / Rom 5, 1-2; Eph 1, 7.—o Lv 16, 12-15; Acts 17, 31; 1 Jn 4, 10.—p Rom 8, 2; 1 Cor 1, 29-31.—q Rom 5, 1; Gal 2, 16.—r Rom 10, 12.—s Dt 6, 4; Gal 3, 20; Jas 2, 19 / Rom 4, 11-12.—t Rom 8, 4; Mt 5, 17.—u Gal 3, 6-9.—v Gn 15, 6; Gal 3, 6; Jas 2, 14.20-24.—w Rom 11, 6.—x 7-8: Ps 32, 1-2.—y Rom 4, 3.—z Gn 17, 10-11; Gal 3, 6-8.

3, 25: *Expiation:* this rendering is preferable to "propitiation," which suggests hostility on the part of God toward sinners. As Paul will be at pains to point out (Rom 5, 8-10), it is humanity that is hostile to God.

3, 27-31: People cannot boast of their own holiness, since it is God's free gift (27), both to the Jew who practices circumcision out of faith and to the Gentile who accepts faith without the Old Testament religious culture symbolized by circumcision (29-30).

3, 27: *Principle of faith:* literally, "law of faith." Paul is fond of wordplay involving the term "law"; cf Rom 7, 21.23; 8, 2. Since "law" in Greek may also connote "custom" or "principle," his readers and hearers would have sensed no contradiction in the use of the term after the negative statement concerning law in v 20.

3, 31: *We are supporting the law:* giving priority to God's intentions. God is the ultimate source of law, and the essence of law is fairness. On the basis of the Mosaic covenant, God's justice is in question if those who sinned against the law are permitted to go free (see Rom 3, 23-26). In order to rescue all humanity rather than condemn it, God thinks of an alternative: the law or

"principle" of faith (Rom 3, 27). What can be more fair than to admit everyone into the divine presence on the basis of forgiveness grasped by faith? Indeed, this principle of faith antedates the Mosaic law, as Paul will demonstrate in ch 4, and does not therefore mark a change in divine policy.

4, 1-25: This is an expanded treatment of the significance of Abraham's faith, which Paul discusses in Gal 3, 6-18; see the notes there.

4, 2-5: Verse 2 corresponds to v 4, and v 3 to v 5. The Greek term here rendered *credited* means "made an entry." The context determines whether it is credit or debit. Verse 8 speaks of "recording sin" as a debit. Paul's repeated use of accountants' terminology in this and other passages can be traced both to the Old Testament texts he quotes and to his business activity as a tentmaker. The commercial term in Gn 15, 6, "credited it to him," reminds Paul in vv 7-8 of Ps 32, 2, in which the same term is used and applied to forgiveness of sins. Thus Paul is able to argue that Abraham's faith involved receipt of forgiveness of sins and that all believers benefit as he did through faith.

4, 3: Jas 2, 24 appears to conflict with Paul's statement. However, James combats the error of extremists who used the doctrine of justification through faith as a screen for moral self-determination. Paul discusses the subject of holiness in greater detail than does James and beginning with ch 6 shows how justification through faith introduces one to the gift of a new life in Christ through the power of the holy Spirit.

4, 9: *Blessedness:* evidence of divine favor.

Inheritance through Faith. [13] It was not through the law that the promise was made to Abraham and his descendants that he would inherit the world, but through the righteousness that comes from faith.[a] [14] For if those who adhere to the law are the heirs, faith is null and the promise is void.[b] [15] For the law produces wrath;[c] but where there is no law, neither is there violation.* [16] For this reason, it depends on faith, so that it may be a gift, and the promise may be guaranteed to all his descendants, not to those who only adhere to the law but to those who follow the faith of Abraham, who is the father of all of us,[d] [17] as it is written, "I have made you father of many nations." He is our father in the sight of God, in whom he believed, who gives life to the dead and calls into being what does not exist.[e] [18] He believed, hoping against hope,[f] that he would become "the father of many nations," according to what was said, "Thus shall your descendants be." [19] [g] He did not weaken in faith when he considered his own body as [already] dead (for he was about a hundred years old) and the dead womb of Sarah. [20] He did not doubt God's promise in unbelief;* rather, he was empowered by faith and gave glory to God [21] and was fully convinced that what he had promised he was also able to do.[h] [22] That is why "it was credited to him as righteousness."[i] [23] But it was not for him alone that it was written that "it was credited to him"; [24] it was also for us, to whom it will be credited, who believe in the one who raised Jesus our Lord from the dead,[j] [25] who was handed over for our transgressions and was raised for our justification.[k]

CHAPTER 5

Faith, Hope, and Love.* [1] Therefore, since we have been justified by faith, we have peace* with God through our Lord Jesus Christ,[l] [2] through whom we have gained access [by faith] to this grace in which we stand, and we boast in hope of the glory of God.[m] [3] Not only that, but we even boast of our afflictions, knowing that affliction produces endurance, [4] and endurance, proven character, and proven character, hope,[n] [5] and hope does not disappoint, because the love of God has been poured out into our hearts through the holy Spirit that has been given to us.[o] [6] For Christ, while we were still helpless, yet died at the appointed time for the ungodly. [7] Indeed, only with difficulty does one die for a just person, though perhaps for a good person one might even find courage to die.* [8] But God proves his love for us in that while we were still sinners Christ died for us.[p] [9] How much more then, since we are now justified by his blood, will we be saved through him from the wrath.[q] [10] Indeed, if, while we were enemies, we were reconciled to God through the death of his Son, how much more, once reconciled, will we be saved by his life.[r] [11] Not only that, but we also boast of God through our Lord Jesus Christ, through whom we have now received reconciliation.

---

a Gn 12, 7; 18, 18; 22, 17-18; Sir 44, 21; Gal 3, 16-18.29.—b Gal 3, 18.—c Rom 3, 20; 5, 13; 7, 8; Gal 3, 19.—d Sir 44, 19; Gal 3, 7-9.—e Gn 17, 5; Heb 11, 19 / Is 48, 13.—f Gn 15, 5.—g 19-20: Gn 17, 17; Heb 11, 11.—h Gn 18, 14; Lk 1, 37.—i Gn 15, 6.—j Rom 10, 9; 1 Pt 1, 21.—k Is 53, 4-5.12; 1 Cor 15, 17; 1 Pt 1, 3 / Rom 8, 11.—l Rom 3, 24-28; Gal 2, 16.—m Eph 2, 18; 3, 12.—n 2 Cor 12, 9-10; Jas 1, 2-4; 1 Pt 1, 5-7; 4, 12-14.—o Rom 8, 14-16; Pss 22, 5-6; 25, 20.—p Jn 3, 16; 1 Jn 4, 10.19.—q Rom 1, 18; 1 Thes 1, 10.—r Rom 8, 7-8; 2 Cor 5, 18; Col 1, 21-22.

4, 15: Law has the negative function of bringing the deep-seated rebellion against God to the surface in specific sins; see the note on Rom 1, 18-32.

4, 20: *He did not doubt God's promise in unbelief:* any doubts Abraham might have had were resolved in commitment to God's promise. Heb 11, 8-12 emphasizes the faith of Abraham and Sarah.

5, 1-11: Popular piety frequently construed reverses and troubles as punishment for sin; cf Jn 9, 2. Paul therefore assures believers that God's justifying action in Jesus Christ is a declaration of peace. The crucifixion of Jesus Christ displays God's initiative in certifying humanity for unimpeded access into the divine presence. Reconciliation is God's gift of pardon to the entire human race. Through faith one benefits personally from this pardon or, in Paul's term, is justified. The ultimate aim of God is to liberate believers from the pre-Christian self as described in chs 1-3. Since this liberation will first find completion in the believer's resurrection, salvation is described as future in Rom 5, 10. Because this fullness of salvation belongs to the future it is called the Christian *hope*. Paul's Greek term for *hope* does not, however, suggest a note of uncertainty, to the effect: "I wonder whether God really means it." Rather, God's promise in the gospel fills believers with expectation and anticipation for the climactic gift of unalloyed commitment in the holy Spirit to the performance of the will of God. The persecutions that attend Christian commitment are to teach believers patience and to strengthen this hope, which will not disappoint them because the holy Spirit dwells in their hearts and imbues them with God's love (5).

5, 1: *We have peace:* a number of manuscripts, versions, and church Fathers read "Let us have peace"; cf Rom 14, 19.

5, 7: In the world of Paul's time the *good person* is especially one who is magnanimous to others.

Humanity's Sin through Adam. 12 * Therefore, just as through one person sin entered the world,[s] and through sin, death, and thus death came to all, inasmuch as all sinned*—13 for up to the time of the law, sin was in the world, though sin is not accounted when there is no law.[t] 14 But death reigned from Adam to Moses, even over those who did not sin after the pattern of the trespass of Adam, who is the type of the one who was to come.[u]

Grace and Life through Christ. 15 But the gift is not like the transgression. For if by that one person's transgression the many died, how much more did the grace of God and the gracious gift of the one person Jesus Christ overflow for the many. 16 And the gift is not like the result of the one person's sinning. For after one sin there was the judgment that brought condemnation; but the gift, after many transgressions, brought acquittal. 17 For if, by the transgression of one person, death came to reign through that one, how much more will those who receive the abundance of grace and of the gift of justification come to reign in life through the one person Jesus Christ. 18 In conclusion, just as through one transgression condemnation came upon all, so through one righteous act acquittal and life came to all.[v] 19 For just as through the disobedience of one person the many were made sinners, so through the obedience of one the many will be made righteous.[w] 20 The law entered in* so that transgression might increase but, where sin increased, grace overflowed all the more,[x] 21 so that, as sin reigned in death, grace also might

reign through justification for eternal life through Jesus Christ our Lord.[y]

IV. JUSTIFICATION AND THE CHRISTIAN LIFE

CHAPTER 6

Freedom from Sin; Life in God. 1 * What then shall we say? Shall we persist in sin that grace may abound? Of course not![z] 2 How can we who died to sin yet live in it?[a] 3 Or are you unaware that we who were baptized into Christ Jesus were baptized into his death?[b] 4 We were indeed buried with him through baptism into death, so that, just as Christ was raised from the dead by the glory of the Father, we too might live in newness of life.[c]

5 For if we have grown into union with him through a death like his, we shall also be united with him in the resurrection.[d] 6 We know that our old self was crucified with him, so that our sinful body might be done away with, that we might no longer be in slavery to sin.[e] 7 For a dead person has been absolved from sin. 8 If, then, we have died with Christ, we believe that we shall also live with him.[f] 9 We know that Christ, raised from the dead, dies no more; death no longer has power over him.[g] 10 As to his death, he died to sin once and for all; as to his life, he lives for God.[h] 11 Consequently, you too must think of yourselves as [being] dead to sin and living for God in Christ Jesus.[i]

s Gn 2, 17; 3, 1-19; Wis 2, 24 / Rom 3, 19.23.—t Rom 4, 15.—u 1 Cor 15, 21.—v 1 Cor 15, 21-22.—w Is 53, 11; Phil 2, 8-9.—x Rom 4, 15; 7, 7-8; Gal 3, 19.—y Rom 6, 23.—z Rom 3, 5-8.—a 1 Pt 4, 1.—b Gal 3, 27.—c Col 2, 12; 1 Pt 3, 21-22.—d Phil 3, 10-11; 2 Tm 2, 11.—e Gal 5, 24; 6, 14; Eph 4, 22-23.—f 1 Thes 4, 17.—g Acts 13, 34; 1 Cor 15, 26; 2 Tm 1, 10; Rv 1, 18.—h Heb 9, 26-28; 1 Pt 3, 18.—i 2 Cor 5, 15; 1 Pt 2, 24.

5, 12-21: Paul reflects on the sin of Adam (Gn 3, 1-13) in the light of the redemptive mystery of Christ. Sin, as used in the singular by Paul, refers to the dreadful power that has gripped humanity, which is now in revolt against the Creator and engaged in the exaltation of its own desires and interests. But no one has a right to say, "Adam made me do it," for all are culpable (12): Gentiles under the demands of the law written in their hearts (Rom 2, 14-15), and Jews under the Mosaic covenant. Through the Old Testament law, the sinfulness of humanity that was operative from the beginning (13) found further stimulation, with the result that sins were generated in even greater abundance. According to vv 15-21, God's act in Christ is in total contrast to the disastrous effects of the virus of sin that invaded humanity through Adam's crime.

5, 12: *Inasmuch as all sinned:* others translate "because all sinned," and understand v 13 as a parenthetical remark. Unlike Wis 2, 24, Paul does not ascribe the entry of death to the devil.

5, 20: *The law entered in:* sin had made its entrance (12); now the law comes in alongside sin. See the notes on Rom 1, 18-32; 5, 12-21. *Where sin increased, grace overflowed all the more:* Paul declares that grace outmatches the productivity of sin.

6, 1-11: To defend the gospel against the charge that it promotes moral laxity (cf Rom 3, 5-8), Paul expresses himself in the typical style of spirited diatribe. God's display of generosity or grace is not evoked by sin but, as stated in Rom 5, 8, is the expression of God's love, and this love pledges eternal life to all believers (Rom 5, 21). Paul views the present conduct of the believers from the perspective of God's completed salvation when the body is resurrected and directed totally by the holy Spirit. Through baptism believers share the death of Christ and thereby escape from the grip of sin. Through the resurrection of Christ the power to live anew becomes reality for them, but the fullness of participation in Christ's resurrection still lies in the future. But life that is lived in dedication to God now is part and parcel of that future. Hence anyone who sincerely claims to be interested in that future will scarcely be able to say, "Let us sin so that grace may prosper" (cf Rom 6, 1).

12 * Therefore, sin must not reign over your mortal bodies so that you obey their desires.*j* 13 And do not present the parts of your bodies to sin as weapons for wickedness, but present yourselves to God as raised from the dead to life and the parts of your bodies to God as weapons for righteousness.*k* 14 For sin is not to have any power over you, since you are not under the law but under grace.*l*

15 What then? Shall we sin because we are not under the law but under grace? Of course not!*m* 16 Do you not know that if you present yourselves to someone as obedient slaves,*n* you are slaves of the one you obey, either of sin, which leads to death, or of obedience, which leads to righteousness?*o* 17 But thanks be to God that, although you were once slaves of sin, you have become obedient from the heart to the pattern of teaching to which you were entrusted.* 18 Freed from sin, you have become slaves of righteousness. 19 I am speaking in human terms because of the weakness of your nature. For just as you presented the parts of your bodies as slaves to impurity and to lawlessness for lawlessness, so now present them as slaves to righteousness for sanctification. 20 *p* For when you were slaves of sin, you were free from righteousness.* 21 But what profit did you get then from the things of which you are now ashamed? For the end of those things is death.*q* 22 But now that you have been freed from sin and have become slaves of God, the benefit that you have leads to sanctification,* and its end is eternal life.*r* 23 For the wages of sin is death,

but the gift of God is eternal life in Christ Jesus our Lord.*s*

CHAPTER 7

Freedom from the Law.* 1 Are you unaware, brothers (for I am speaking to people who know the law), that the law has jurisdiction over one as long as one lives? 2 Thus a married woman is bound by law to her living husband; but if her husband dies, she is released from the law in respect to her husband.*t* 3 Consequently, while her husband is alive she will be called an adulteress if she consorts with another man. But if her husband dies she is free from that law, and she is not an adulteress if she consorts with another man.

4 In the same way, my brothers, you also were put to death to the law through the body of Christ, so that you might belong to another, to the one who was raised from the dead in order that we might bear fruit for God. 5 For when we were in the flesh, our sinful passions, awakened by the law, worked in our members to bear fruit for death.*u* 6 But now we are released from the law, dead to what held us captive, so that we may serve in the newness of the spirit and not under the obsolete letter.*v*

Acquaintance with Sin through the Law. 7 * What then can we say? That the law is sin? Of course not!* Yet I did not know sin except through the law, and I did not know what it is to covet except that the law said, "You shall not covet."*w* 8 But sin, finding an opportunity in the commandment, produced in me every kind of covetousness. Apart from the law sin is dead.*x* 9 I once lived outside the law, but when the commandment came, sin became alive; 10 then

---

j Gn 4, 7.—*k* Rom 12, 1; Eph 2, 5; 5, 14 / Col 3, 5.—*l* Gal 5, 18; 1 Jn 3, 6.—*m* Rom 5, 17.21.—*n* Jn 8, 31-34; 2 Pt 2, 19.—*o* 16-18: Jn 8, 32-36.—*p* Jn 8, 34.—*q* Rom 8, 6.13; Prv 12, 28; Ez 16, 61.63.—*r* 1 Pt 1, 9.—*s* Gn 2, 17; Gal 6, 7-9; Jas 1, 15.—*t* 1 Cor 7, 39.—*u* Rom 6, 21; 8, 6.13.—*v* Rom 8, 2; 2 Cor 3, 6.—*w* Rom 3, 20; Ex 20, 17; Dt 5, 21.—*x* Rom 5, 13.20; 1 Cor 15, 56 / Rom 4, 15.

6, 12-19: Christians have been released from the grip of sin, but sin endeavors to reclaim its victims. The antidote is constant remembrance that divine grace has claimed them and identifies them as people who are alive only for God's interests.

6, 17: In contrast to humanity, which was handed over to self-indulgence (Rom 1, 24-32), believers are *entrusted* ("handed over") to God's *pattern of teaching,* that is, the new life God aims to develop in Christians through the productivity of the holy Spirit. Throughout this passage Paul uses the slave-master model in order to emphasize the fact that one cannot give allegiance to both God and sin.

6, 20: *You were free from righteousness:* expressed ironically, for such freedom is really tyranny. The commercial metaphors in vv 21-23 add up only one way: sin is a bad bargain.

6, 22: *Sanctification:* or holiness.

7, 1-6: Paul reflects on the fact that Christians have a different understanding of the law because of their faith in Christ. Law binds the living, not the dead, as exemplified in marriage, which binds in life but is dissolved through death. Similarly, Christians who through baptism have died with Christ to sin (cf Rom 6, 2-4) are freed from the law that occasioned transgressions, which in turn were productive of death. Now that Christians are joined to Christ, the power of Christ's resurrection makes it possible for them to bear the fruit of newness of life for God.

7, 7-25: In this passage Paul uses the first person singular in the style of diatribe for the sake of argument. He aims to depict the disastrous consequences when a Christian reintroduces the law as a means to attain the objective of holiness pronounced in Rom 6, 22.

7, 7-12: The apostle defends himself against the charge of identifying the law with sin. Sin does not exist in law but in human beings, whose sinful inclinations are not overcome by the proclamation of law.

I died, and the commandment that was for life turned out to be death for me.[y] [11]For sin, seizing an opportunity in the commandment, deceived me and through it put me to death.[z] [12]So then the law is holy, and the commandment is holy and righteous and good.[a]

Sin and Death.* [13]Did the good, then, become death for me? Of course not! Sin, in order that it might be shown to be sin, worked death in me through the good, so that sin might become sinful beyond measure through the commandment.[b] [14]We know that the law is spiritual; but I am carnal, sold into slavery to sin.[c] [15]What I do, I do not understand. For I do not do what I want, but I do what I hate. [16]Now if I do what I do not want, I concur that the law is good. [17]So now it is no longer I who do it, but sin that dwells in me. [18]For I know that good does not dwell in me, that is, in my flesh. The willing is ready at hand, but doing the good is not.[d] [19]For I do not do the good I want, but I do the evil I do not want. [20]Now if [I] do what I do not want, it is no longer I who do it, but sin that dwells in me. [21]So, then, I discover the principle that when I want to do right, evil is at hand. [22]For I take delight in the law of God, in my inner self, [23] [e] but I see in my members another principle at war with the law of my mind, taking me captive to the law of sin that dwells in my members.* [24]Miserable one that I am! Who will deliver me from this mortal body? [25]Thanks be to God through Jesus Christ our Lord. Therefore, I myself, with my mind, serve the law of God but, with my flesh, the law of sin.[f]

CHAPTER 8

The Flesh and the Spirit.* [1]Hence, now there is no condemnation for those who are in Christ Jesus. [2]For the law of the spirit of life in Christ Jesus has freed you from the law of sin and death.[g] [3]For what the law, weakened by the flesh, was powerless to do, this God has done: by sending his own Son in the likeness of sinful flesh and for the sake of sin, he condemned sin in the flesh,[h] [4]so that the righteous decree of the law might be fulfilled in us, who live not according to the flesh but according to the spirit.[i] [5]For those who live according to the flesh are concerned with the things of the flesh, but those who live according to the spirit with the things of the spirit. [6]The concern of the flesh is death, but the concern of the spirit is life and peace.[j] [7]For the concern of the flesh is hostility toward God; it does not submit to the law of God, nor can it;[k] [8]and those who are in the flesh cannot please God.[l] [9]But you are not in the flesh; on the contrary, you are in the spirit, if only the Spirit of God dwells in you. Whoever does not have the Spirit of Christ does not belong to him.[m] [10]But if Christ is in you, although the body is dead because of sin, the spirit is alive because of righteousness.[n] [11]If the Spirit of the one who raised Jesus from the dead dwells in you, the one who raised Christ from the dead will give life to your mortal bodies also, through his Spirit that dwells in you. [12]Consequently, brothers, we are not debtors to the flesh, to live according to the flesh. [13]For if you live according to the flesh, you will die, but if by the spirit you put to death the deeds of the body, you will live.[o]

---

y Lv 18, 5.—z Gn 3, 13; Heb 3, 13.—a 1 Tm 1, 8.—b Rom 4, 15; 5, 20.—c Rom 8, 7-8; Ps 51, 7.—d Gn 6, 5; 8, 21; Phil 2, 13.—e Gal 5, 17; 1 Pt 2, 11.—f 1 Cor 15, 57.—g Rom 7, 23-24; 2 Cor 3, 17.—h Acts 13, 38; 15, 10 / Jn 3, 16-17; 2 Cor 5, 21; Gal 3, 13; 4, 4; Phil 2, 7; Col 1, 22; Heb 2, 17; 4, 15; 1 Jn 4, 9.—i Gal 5, 16-25.—j Rom 6, 21; 7, 5; 8, 13; Gal 6, 8.—k Rom 5, 10; Jas 4, 4.—l 1 Jn 2, 16.—m 1 Cor 3, 16.—n Gal 2, 20; 1 Pt 4, 6.—o Gal 5, 24; 6, 8; Eph 4, 22-24.

7, 13-25: Far from improving the sinner, law encourages sin to expose itself in transgressions or violations of specific commandments (see Rom 1, 24; 5, 20). Thus persons who do not experience the justifying grace of God, and Christians who revert to dependence on law as the criterion for their relationship with God, will recognize a rift between their reasoned desire for the goodness of the law and their actual performance that is contrary to the law. Unable to free themselves from the slavery of sin and the power of death, they can only be rescued from defeat in the conflict by the power of God's grace working through Jesus Christ.

7, 23: As in Rom 3, 27, Paul plays on the term *law*, which in Greek can connote custom, system, or *principle*.

8, 1-13: After his warning in ch 7 against the wrong route to fulfillment of the objective of holiness expressed in Rom 6, 22, Paul points his addressees to the correct way. Through the redemptive work of Christ, Christians have been liberated from the terrible forces of sin and death. Holiness was impossible so long as the *flesh* (or our "old self"), that is, self-interested hostility toward God (7), frustrated the divine objectives expressed in the law. What is worse, sin used the law to break forth into all manner of lawlessness (8). All this is now changed. At the cross God broke the power of sin and pronounced sentence on it (3). Christians still retain the flesh, but it is alien to their new being, which is life in the spirit, namely the new self, governed by the holy Spirit. Under the direction of the holy Spirit Christians are able to fulfill the divine will that formerly found expression in the law (4). The same Spirit who enlivens Christians for holiness will also resurrect their bodies at the last day (11). Christian life is therefore the experience of a constant challenge to put to death the evil deeds of the body through life of the spirit (13).

Children of God through Adoption.* [14] For those who are led by the Spirit of God are children of God.[p] [15] For you did not receive a spirit of slavery to fall back into fear, but you received a spirit of adoption, through which we cry, *Abba,** "Father!"[q] [16] The Spirit itself bears witness with our spirit that we are children of God,[r] [17] and if children, then heirs, heirs of God and joint heirs with Christ, if only we suffer with him so that we may also be glorified with him.[s]

Destiny of Glory.* [18] I consider that the sufferings of this present time are as nothing compared with the glory to be revealed for us.[t] [19] For creation awaits with eager expectation the revelation of the children of God; [20] for creation was made subject to futility, not of its own accord but because of the one who subjected it,[u] in hope [21] that creation itself would be set free from slavery to corruption and share in the glorious freedom of the children of God.[v] [22] We know that all creation is groaning in labor pains even until now;[w] [23] and not only that, but we ourselves, who have the firstfruits of the Spirit, we also groan within ourselves as we wait for adoption, the redemption of our bodies.[x] [24] For in hope we were saved. Now hope that sees for itself is not hope. For who hopes for what one sees?[y] [25] But if we hope for what we do not see, we wait with endurance.

[26] In the same way, the Spirit too comes to the aid of our weakness; for we do not know how to pray as we ought, but the Spirit itself intercedes with inexpressible groanings. [27] And the one who searches hearts knows what is the intention of the Spirit, because it intercedes for the holy ones according to God's will.[z]

God's Indomitable Love in Christ. [28] * We know that all things work for good for those who love God,* who are called according to his purpose.[a] [29] For those he foreknew he also predestined to be conformed to the image* of his Son, so that he might be the firstborn among many brothers.[b] [30] And those he predestined he also called; and those he called he also justified; and those he justified he also glorified.[c]

[31] * What then shall we say to this? If God is for us, who can be against us?[d] [32] He who did not spare his own Son but handed him over for us all, how will he not also give us everything else along with him?[e] [33] Who will bring a charge against God's chosen ones?[f] It is God who acquits us. [34] Who will condemn? It is Christ [Jesus] who died, rather, was raised, who also is at the right hand of God, who indeed intercedes for us.[g] [35] What will separate us from the love of Christ? Will anguish, or distress, or persecution, or famine, or nakedness, or peril, or the sword? [36] As it is written:[h]

"For your sake we are being slain all the day;
    we are looked upon as sheep to be slaughtered."

[37] No, in all these things we conquer overwhelmingly through him who loved us.[i]

p Gal 5, 18.—q Mk 14, 36; Gal 4, 5-6; 2 Tm 1, 7.—r Jn 1, 12; Gal 3, 26-29.—s Gal 4, 7; 1 Pt 4, 13; 5, 1.—t 2 Cor 4, 17.—u Gn 3, 17-19.—v 2 Pt 3, 12-13; Rv 21, 1.—w 2 Cor 5, 2-5.—x 2 Cor 1, 22; Gal 5, 5.—y 2 Cor 5, 7; Heb 11, 1.—z Ps 139, 1; 1 Cor 4, 5.—a 28-29: Eph 1, 4-14; 3, 11.—b Eph 1, 5; 1 Pt 1, 2.—c Is 45, 25; 2 Thes 2, 13-14.—d Ps 118, 6; Heb 13, 6.—e Jn 3, 16.—f 33-34: Is 50, 8.—g Ps 110, 1; Heb 7, 25; 1 Jn 2, 1.—h Ps 44, 23; 1 Cor 4, 9; 15, 30; 2 Cor 4, 11; 2 Tm 3, 12.—i 1 Jn 5, 4.

8, 14-17: Christians, by reason of the Spirit's presence within them, enjoy not only new life but also a new relationship to God, that of adopted children and heirs through Christ, whose sufferings and glory they share.

8, 15: *Abba:* see the note on Mk 14, 36.

8, 18-27: The glory that believers are destined to share with Christ far exceeds the sufferings of the present life. Paul considers the destiny of the created world to be linked with the future that belongs to the believers. As it shares in the penalty of corruption brought about by sin, so also will it share in the benefits of redemption and future glory that comprise the ultimate liberation of God's people (19-22). After patient endurance in steadfast expectation, the full harvest of the Spirit's presence will be realized. On earth believers enjoy the firstfruits, i.e., the Spirit, as a guarantee of the total liberation of their bodies from the influence of the rebellious old self (23).

8, 28-30: These verses outline the Christian vocation as it was designed by God: *to be conformed to the image of his Son,* who is to *be the firstborn among many brothers* (29). God's redemptive action on behalf of the believers has been in process before the beginning of the world. Those whom God chooses are *those he foreknew* (29) or elected. Those who are *called* (30) are *predestined* or predetermined. These expressions do not mean that God is arbitrary. Rather, Paul uses them to emphasize the thought and care that God has taken for the Christian's salvation.

8, 28: *We know that all things work for good for those who love God:* a few ancient authorities have God as the subject of the verb, and some translators render: "We know that God makes everything work for good for those who love God. . . ."

8, 29: *Image:* while man and woman were originally created in God's image (Gn 1, 26-27), it is through baptism into Christ, the image of God (2 Cor 4, 4; Col 1, 15), that we are renewed according to the image of the Creator (Col 3, 10).

8, 31-39: The all-conquering power of God's love has overcome every obstacle to Christians' salvation and every threat to separate them from God. That power manifested itself fully when God's own Son was delivered up to death for their salvation. Through him Christians can overcome all their afflictions and trials.

[38] For I am convinced that neither death, nor life, nor angels, nor principalities, nor present things,* nor future things, nor powers,[j] [39] nor height, nor depth,* nor any other creature will be able to separate us from the love of God in Christ Jesus our Lord.

V. JEWS AND GENTILES IN GOD'S PLAN*

CHAPTER 9

Paul's Love for Israel.* [1] I speak the truth in Christ, I do not lie; my conscience joins with the holy Spirit in bearing me witness[k] [2] that I have great sorrow and constant anguish in my heart. [3] For I could wish that I myself were accursed and separated from Christ for the sake of my brothers, my kin according to the flesh.[l] [4] They are Israelites; theirs the adoption, the glory, the covenants, the giving of the law, the worship, and the promises;[m] [5] theirs the patriarchs, and from them, according to the flesh, is the Messiah. God who is over all* be blessed forever. Amen.[n]

God's Free Choice. [6] But it is not that the word of God has failed. For not all who are of Israel are Israel,[o] [7] nor are they all children of Abraham because they are his descendants; but "It is through Isaac that descendants shall bear your name."[p] [8] This means that it is not the children of the flesh who are the children of God, but the children of the promise are counted as descendants.[q] [9] For this is the wording of the promise, "About this time I shall return and Sarah will have a son."[r] [10] And not only that,[s] but also when Rebecca had conceived children by one husband, our father Isaac*—[11] before they had yet been born or had done anything, good or bad, in order that God's elective plan might continue, [12] not by works but by his call—she was told, "The older shall serve the younger."[t] [13] As it is written:[u]

"I loved Jacob
but hated Esau."*

[14] * What then are we to say? Is there injustice on the part of God? Of course not![v] [15] For he says to Moses:

"I will show mercy to whom I will,
I will take pity on whom I will."[w]

[16] So it depends not upon a person's will or exertion, but upon God, who shows mercy.[x] [17] For the scripture says to Pharaoh, "This is why I have raised you up, to show my power through you that my name may be proclaimed throughout

j 38-39: 1 Cor 3, 22; Eph 1, 21; 1 Pt 3, 22.—k 2 Cor 11, 31; 1 Tm 2, 7.—l Ex 32, 32.—m 4-5: Rom 3, 2; Ex 4, 22; Dt 7, 6; 14, 1-2.—n Mt 1, 1-16; Lk 3, 23-38 / Rom 1, 25; Ps 41, 14.—o Nm 23, 19 / Mt 3, 9.—p Gn 21, 12; Gal 3, 29.—q Gal 4, 23.28.—r Gn 18, 10.14.—s Gn 25, 21.—t Rom 11, 5-6 / Gn 25, 23-24.—u Mal 1, 3.—v Dt 32, 4.—w Ex 33, 19.—x Eph 2, 8; Ti 3, 5.

8, 38: *Present things* and *future things* may refer to astrological data. Paul appears to be saying that the gospel liberates believers from dependence on astrologers.

8, 39: *Height, depth* may refer to positions in the zodiac, positions of heavenly bodies relative to the horizon. In astrological documents the term for "height" means "exaltation" or the position of greatest influence exerted by a planet. Since hostile spirits were associated with the planets and stars, Paul includes *powers* (38) in his list of malevolent forces.

9, 1—11, 36: Israel's unbelief and its rejection of Jesus as savior astonished and puzzled Christians. It constituted a serious problem for them in view of God's specific preparation of Israel for the advent of the Messiah. Paul addresses himself here to the essential question of how the divine plan could be frustrated by Israel's unbelief. At the same time, he discourages both complacency and anxiety on the part of Gentiles. To those who might boast of their superior advantage over Jews, he warns that their enjoyment of the blessings assigned to Israel can be terminated. To those who might anxiously ask, "How can we be sure that Israel's fate will not be ours?" he replies that only unbelief can deprive one of salvation.

9, 1-5: The apostle speaks in strong terms of the depth of his grief over the unbelief of his own people. He would willingly undergo a curse himself for the sake of their coming to the knowledge of Christ (3; cf Lv 27, 28-29). His love for them derives from God's continuing choice of them and from the spiritual benefits that God bestows on them and through them on all of humanity (4-5).

9, 5: Some editors punctuate this verse differently and prefer the translation, "Of whom is Christ according to the flesh, who is God over all." However, Paul's point is that *God who is over all* aimed to use Israel, which had been entrusted with every privilege, in outreach to the entire world through the Messiah.

9, 10: *Children by one husband, our father Isaac:* Abraham had two children, Ishmael and Isaac, by two wives, Hagar and Sarah, respectively. In that instance Isaac, although born later than Ishmael, became the bearer of the messianic promise. In the case of twins born to Rebecca, God's elective procedure is seen even more dramatically, and again the younger, contrary to Semitic custom, is given the preference.

9, 13: The literal rendering, *"Jacob I loved, but Esau I hated,"* suggests an attitude of divine hostility that is not implied in Paul's statement. In Semitic usage "hate" means to love less; cf Lk 14, 26 with Mt 10, 37. Israel's unbelief reflects the mystery of the divine election that is always operative within it. Mere natural descent from Abraham does not ensure the full possession of the divine gifts; it is God's sovereign prerogative to bestow this fullness upon, or to withhold it from, whomsoever he wishes; cf Mt 3, 9; Jn 8, 39. The choice of Jacob over Esau is a case in point.

9, 14-18: The principle of divine election does not invite Christians to theoretical inquiry concerning the nonelected, nor does this principle mean that God is unfair in his dealings with humanity. The instruction concerning divine election is a part of the gospel and reveals that the gift of faith is the enactment of God's mercy (16). God raised up Moses to display that mercy, and Pharaoh to display divine severity in punishing those who obstinately oppose their Creator.

Rom

the earth."[y] [18] Consequently, he has mercy upon whom he wills,[z] and he hardens whom he wills.*

[19] * You will say to me then, "Why [then] does he still find fault? For who can oppose his will?"[a] [20] But who indeed are you, a human being, to talk back to God?[b] Will what is made say to its maker, "Why have you created me so?" [21] Or does not the potter have a right over the clay, to make out of the same lump one vessel for a noble purpose and another for an ignoble one? [22] What if God, wishing to show his wrath and make known his power, has endured with much patience the vessels of wrath made for destruction?[c] [23] This was to make known the riches of his glory to the vessels of mercy, which he has prepared previously for glory, [24] namely, us whom he has called, not only from the Jews but also from the Gentiles.

Witness of the Prophets. [25] As indeed he says in Hosea:

"Those who were not my people I will
    call 'my people,'
and her who was not beloved* I will
    call 'beloved.'[d]
[26] And in the very place where it was said
    to them, 'You are not my people,'
    there they shall be called children of
    the living God."[e]

[27] [f] And Isaiah cries out concerning Israel, "Though the number of the Israelites were

like the sand of the sea, only a remnant will be saved; [28] for decisively and quickly will the Lord execute sentence upon the earth." [29] And as Isaiah predicted:

"Unless the Lord of hosts had left us
    descendants,
we would have become like Sodom
    and have been made like Gomor-
    rah."[g]

Righteousness Based on Faith.* [30] What then shall we say? That Gentiles, who did not pursue righteousness, have achieved it, that is, righteousness that comes from faith;[h] [31] but that Israel, who pursued the law of righteousness, did not attain to that law?[i] [32] Why not? Because they did it not by faith, but as if it could be done by works.[j] They stumbled over the stone that causes stumbling,* [33] as it is written:

"Behold, I am laying a stone in Zion
    that will make people stumble
    and a rock that will make them fall,
and whoever believes in him shall not
    be put to shame."[k]

CHAPTER 10

[1] * Brothers, my heart's desire and prayer to God on their behalf is for salvation.[l] [2] I testify with regard to them that they have zeal for God, but it is not discerning.[m] [3] For, in their unawareness of the righteousness that comes from God and their attempt to establish their own [righteousness], they did not submit to the righteousness of God.[n] [4] For Christ is the end* of the law for the justification of everyone who has faith.[o]

y Ex 9, 16.—z Rom 11, 30-32; Ex 4, 21; 7, 3.—a Rom 3, 7; Wis 12, 12.—b 20-21: Wis 15, 7; Is 29, 16; 45, 9; Jer 18, 6.—c Rom 2, 4; Wis 12, 20-21; Jer 50, 25.—d Hos 2, 25.—e Hos 2, 1.—f 27-28: Is 10, 22-23; Hos 2, 1 / Rom 11, 5 / Is 28, 22.—g Is 1, 9; Mt 10, 15.—h Rom 10, 4.20.—i Rom 10, 3.—j Is 8, 14.—k Is 28, 16; 1 Pt 2, 6-8.—l Rom 9, 1.3.—m Acts 22, 3.—n Rom 9, 31-32; Phil 3, 9.—o Acts 13, 38-39; 2 Cor 3, 14; Heb 8, 13.

9, 18: The basic biblical principle is: those who will not see or hear *shall* not see or hear. On the other hand, the same God who thus makes stubborn or hardens the heart can reconstruct it through the work of the holy Spirit.

9, 19-29: The apostle responds to the objection that if God rules over faith through the principle of divine election, God cannot then accuse unbelievers of sin (19). For Paul, this objection is in the last analysis a manifestation of human insolence, and his "answer" is less an explanation of God's ways than the rejection of an argument that places humanity on a level with God. At the same time, Paul shows that God is far less arbitrary than appearances suggest, for God endures *with much patience* (22) a person like the Pharaoh of the Exodus.

9, 25: *Beloved:* in Semitic discourse means "preferred" or "favorite" (cf 13). See Hos 2, 1, which is transposed after Hos 3, 5 in the NAB.

9, 30-33: In the conversion of the Gentiles and, by contrast, of relatively few Jews, the Old Testament prophecies are seen to be fulfilled; cf 25-29. Israel feared that the doctrine of justification through faith would jeopardize the validity of the Mosaic law, and so they never reached their goal of righteousness that they had

sought to attain through meticulous observance of the law (31). Since Gentiles, including especially Greeks and Romans, had a great regard for righteousness, Paul's statement concerning Gentiles in v 30 is to be understood from a Jewish perspective: quite evidently they had not been interested in "God's" righteousness, for it had not been revealed to them; but now in response to the proclamation of the gospel they respond in faith.

9, 32: Paul discusses Israel as a whole from the perspective of contemporary Jewish rejection of Jesus as Messiah. The Old Testament and much of Jewish noncanonical literature in fact reflect a fervent faith in divine mercy.

10, 1-13: Despite Israel's lack of faith in God's act in Christ, Paul does not abandon hope for her salvation (1). However, Israel must recognize that the Messiah's arrival in the person of Jesus Christ means the termination of the Mosaic law as the criterion for understanding oneself in a valid relationship to God. Faith in God's saving action in Jesus Christ takes precedence over any such legal claim (6).

10, 4: The Mosaic legislation has been superseded by God's action in Jesus Christ. Others understand *end* here in the sense that Christ is the goal of the law, i.e., the true meaning of the Mosaic law, which cannot be correctly understood apart from him. Still others believe that both meanings are intended.

5 * Moses writes about the righteousness that comes from [the] law, "The one who does these things will live by them."*p* 6 But the righteousness that comes from faith says,*q* "Do not say in your heart, 'Who will go up into heaven?' (that is, to bring Christ down) 7 * or 'Who will go down into the abyss?' (that is, to bring Christ up from the dead)."*r* 8 But what does it say?

"The word is near you,
    in your mouth and in your heart"*s*

(that is, the word of faith that we preach), 9 for, if you confess* with your mouth that Jesus is Lord and believe in your heart that God raised him from the dead, you will be saved.*t* 10 For one believes with the heart and so is justified, and one confesses with the mouth and so is saved. 11 For the scripture says, "No one who believes in him will be put to shame."*u* 12 For there is no distinction between Jew and Greek; the same Lord is Lord of all, enriching all who call upon him.*v* 13 For "everyone who calls on the name of the Lord will be saved."*w*

14 * But how can they call on him in whom they have not believed? And how can they believe in him of whom they have not heard? And how can they hear without

---

p Lv 18, 5; Gal 3, 12.—q Dt 9, 4; 30, 12.—r Dt 30, 13; 1 Pt 3, 19.—s Dt 30, 14.—t 1 Cor 12, 3.—u Rom 9, 33; Is 28, 16.—v Rom 1, 16; 3, 22.29; Acts 10, 34; 15, 9.11; Gal 3, 28; Eph 2, 14.—w Jl 3, 5; Acts 2, 21.—x Acts 8, 31.—y Is 52, 7; Na 2, 1; Eph 6, 15.—z Is 53, 1; Jn 12, 38.—a Jn 17, 20.—b Ps 19, 5; Mt 24, 14.—c Rom 11, 11.14; Dt 32, 21.—d 20- 21: Rom 9, 30; Is 65, 1-2.—e 2 Cor 11, 22; Phil 3, 5.—f 1-2: 1 Sm 12, 22; Ps 94, 14.—g 1 Kgs 19, 10.14.—h 1 Kgs 19, 18.—i Rom 9, 27.—j Rom 4, 4; Gal 3, 18.—k Rom 9, 31.—l Dt 29, 3; Is 29, 10; Mt 13, 13-15; Acts 28, 26-27.

10, 5-6: The subject of the verb *says* (6) is *righteousness* personified. Both of the statements in vv 5 and 6 derive from Moses, but Paul wishes to contrast the language of law and the language of faith.

10, 7: Here Paul blends Dt 30, 13 and Ps 107, 26.

10, 9-11: To confess Jesus as Lord was frequently quite hazardous in the first century (cf Mt 10, 18; 1 Thes 2, 2; 1 Pt 2, 18-21; 3, 14). For a Jew it could mean disruption of normal familial and other social relationships, including great economic sacrifice. In the face of penalties imposed by the secular world, Christians are assured that *no one who believes in Jesus will be put to shame* (11).

10, 14-21: The gospel has been sufficiently proclaimed to Israel, and Israel has adequately understood God's plan for the messianic age, which would see the gospel brought to the uttermost parts of the earth. As often in the past, Israel has not accepted the prophetic message; cf Acts 7, 51-53.

10, 15: *How beautiful are the feet of those who bring [the] good news:* in Semitic fashion, the parts of the body that bring the messenger with welcome news are praised; cf Lk 11, 27.

11, 1-10: Although Israel has been unfaithful to the prophetic message of the gospel (Rom 10, 14-21), God remains faithful to Israel. Proof of the divine fidelity lies in the existence of Jewish Christians like Paul himself. The unbelieving Jews, says Paul, have been blinded by the Christian teaching concerning the Messiah.

---

someone to preach?*x* 15 And how can people preach unless they are sent? As it is written,*y* "How beautiful are the feet of those who bring [the] good news!"* 16 But not everyone has heeded the good news; for Isaiah says, "Lord, who has believed what was heard from us?"*z* 17 Thus faith comes from what is heard, and what is heard comes through the word of Christ.*a* 18 But I ask, did they not hear? Certainly they did; for

"Their voice has gone forth to all the earth,
    and their words to the ends of the world."*b*

19 But I ask, did not Israel understand?*c* First Moses says:

"I will make you jealous of those who are not a nation;
    with a senseless nation I will make you angry."

20 *d* Then Isaiah speaks boldly and says:

"I was found [by] those who were not seeking me;
    I revealed myself to those who were not asking for me."

21 But regarding Israel he says, "All day long I stretched out my hands to a disobedient and contentious people."

CHAPTER 11

The Remnant of Israel. * 1 I ask, then, has God rejected his people? Of course not!*e* For I too am an Israelite, a descendant of Abraham, of the tribe of Benjamin.*f* 2 God has not rejected his people whom he foreknew. Do you not know what the scripture says about Elijah, how he pleads with God against Israel? 3 "Lord, they have killed your prophets, they have torn down your altars, and I alone am left, and they are seeking my life."*g* 4 But what is God's response to him? "I have left for myself seven thousand men who have not knelt to Baal."*h* 5 So also at the present time there is a remnant, chosen by grace.*i* 6 But if by grace, it is no longer because of works; otherwise grace would no longer be grace.*j* 7 What then? What Israel was seeking it did not attain, but the elect attained it; the rest were hardened,*k* 8 as it is written:

"God gave them a spirit of deep sleep,
    eyes that should not see
    and ears that should not hear,
down to this very day."*l*

[9] And David says: [m]

"Let their table become a snare and a trap,
    a stumbling block and a retribution for them;
[10] let their eyes grow dim so that they may not see,
    and keep their backs bent forever."

The Gentiles' Salvation. [11] * Hence I ask, did they stumble so as to fall? Of course not! But through their transgression salvation has come to the Gentiles, so as to make them jealous. [n] [12] Now if their transgression is enrichment for the world, and if their diminished number is enrichment for the Gentiles, how much more their full number.

[13] Now I am speaking to you Gentiles. Inasmuch then as I am the apostle to the Gentiles, I glory in my ministry [o] [14] in order to make my race jealous and thus save some of them. [15] For if their rejection is the reconciliation of the world, what will their acceptance be but life from the dead? [16] * If the firstfruits are holy, so is the whole batch of dough; and if the root is holy, so are the branches. [p]

[17] But if some of the branches were broken off, and you, a wild olive shoot, were grafted in their place and have come to share in the rich root of the olive tree, [q] [18] do not boast against the branches. If you do boast, consider that you do not support the root; the root supports you. [r] [19] Indeed you will say, "Branches were broken off so that I might be grafted in." [20] That is so. They were broken off because of unbelief, but you are there because of faith. So do not become haughty, but stand in awe. [s]

[21] For if God did not spare the natural branches, [perhaps] he will not spare you either. [t] [22] See, then, the kindness and severity of God: severity toward those who fell, but God's kindness to you, provided you remain in his kindness; otherwise you too will be cut off. [u] [23] And they also, if they do not remain in unbelief, will be grafted in, for God is able to graft them in again. [v] [24] For if you were cut from what is by nature a wild olive tree, and grafted, contrary to nature, into a cultivated one, how much more will they who belong to it by nature be grafted back into their own olive tree.

God's Irrevocable Call. * [25] I do not want you to be unaware of this mystery, brothers, so that you will not become wise [in] your own estimation: a hardening has come upon Israel in part, until the full number of the Gentiles comes in, [w] [26] and thus all Israel will be saved, [x] as it is written: [y]

"The deliverer will come out of Zion,
    he will turn away godlessness from Jacob;
[27] and this is my covenant with them
    when I take away their sins." [z]

[28] In respect to the gospel, they are enemies on your account; but in respect to election, they are beloved because of the patriarchs. [a] [29] For the gifts and the call of God are irrevocable. [b]

Triumph of God's Mercy. [30] * Just as you once disobeyed God but have now received mercy because of their disobedience, [31] so they have now disobeyed in order that, by virtue of the mercy shown to you, they too may [now] receive mercy. [32] For God delivered all to disobedience, that he might have mercy upon all. [c]

---

m 9-10: Pss 69, 23-24; 35, 8.—n Acts 13, 46; 18, 6; 28, 28 / Rom 10, 19; Dt 32, 21.—o Rom 1, 5.—p Nm 15, 17-21; Ez 44, 30; Neh 10, 36-38.—q Eph 2, 11-19.—r 1 Cor 1, 31.—s Rom 12, 16.—t 1 Cor 10, 12.—u Jn 15, 2.4; Heb 3, 14.—v 2 Cor 3, 16.—w Prv 3, 7 / Rom 12, 16; Mk 13, 10; Lk 21, 24; Jn 10, 16.—x Mt 23, 39.—y 26-27: Ps 14, 7; Is 59, 20-21.—z Is 27, 9; Jer 31, 33-34.—a Rom 15, 8; 1 Thes 2, 15-16.—b Rom 9, 6; Nm 23, 19; Is 54, 10.—c Gal 3, 22; 1 Tm 2, 4.

11, 11-15: The unbelief of the Jews has paved the way for the preaching of the gospel to the Gentiles and for their easier acceptance of it outside the context of Jewish culture. Through his mission to the Gentiles Paul also hopes to fill his fellow Jews with jealousy. Hence he hastens to fill the entire Mediterranean world with the gospel. Once all the Gentile nations have heard the gospel, Israel as a whole is expected to embrace it. This will be tantamount to resurrection of the dead, that is, the reappearance of Jesus Christ with all the believers at the end of time.

11, 16-24: Israel remains holy in the eyes of God and stands as a witness to the faith described in the Old Testament because of *the firstfruits* (or the first piece baked) (16), that is, the converted remnant, and *the root* that *is holy,* that is, the patriarchs (16). The Jews' failure to believe in Christ is a warning to Gentile Christians to be on guard against any semblance of anti-Jewish arrogance, that is, failure to recognize their total dependence on divine grace.

11, 25-29: In God's design, Israel's unbelief is being used to grant the light of faith to the Gentiles. Meanwhile, Israel remains dear to God (cf Rom 9, 13), still the object of special providence, the mystery of which will one day be revealed.

11, 30-32: Israel, together with the Gentiles who have been handed over to all manner of vices (ch 1), has been *delivered . . . to disobedience.* The conclusion of v 32 repeats the thought of Rom 5, 20, "Where sin increased, grace overflowed all the more."

33 * Oh, the depth of the riches and wisdom and knowledge of God! How inscrutable are his judgments and how unsearchable his ways!*d*

34 "For who has known the mind of the Lord*
     or who has been his counselor?"*e*

35 "Or who has given him anything*f*
     that he may be repaid?"*

36 For from him and through him and for him are all things. To him be glory forever. Amen.*g*

VI. THE DUTIES OF CHRISTIANS*

CHAPTER 12

Sacrifice of Body and Mind. 1 *I urge you therefore, brothers, by the mercies of God, to offer your bodies as a living sacrifice, holy and pleasing to God, your spiritual worship.*h* 2 Do not conform yourself to this age but be transformed by the renewal of your mind, that you may discern what is the will of God, what is good and pleasing and perfect.*i*

Many Parts in One Body. 3 *j* For by the grace given to me I tell everyone among you not to think of himself more highly than one ought to think, but to think soberly, each according to the measure of faith that God has apportioned. 4 *k* For as in one body we have many parts, and all the parts do not have the same function, 5 so we, though many, are one body in Christ* and individually parts of one another. 6 *l* Since we have gifts that differ according to the grace given to us, let us exercise them:* if prophecy, in proportion to the faith; 7 if ministry, in ministering; if one is a teacher, in teaching; 8 if one exhorts, in exhortation; if one contributes, in generosity; if one is over others,* with diligence; if one does acts of mercy, with cheerfulness.

Mutual Love. 9 Let love be sincere; hate what is evil, hold on to what is good;*m* 10 love one another with mutual affection; anticipate one another in showing honor.*n* 11 Do not grow slack in zeal, be fervent in spirit, serve the Lord.*o* 12 Rejoice in hope, endure in affliction, persevere in prayer.*p* 13 Contribute to the needs of the holy ones,*q* exercise hospitality. 14 * Bless those who persecute [you],*r* bless and do not curse them.*s* 15 Rejoice with those who rejoice, weep with those who weep.*t* 16 Have the same regard for one another; do not be haughty but associate with the lowly; do not be wise in your own estimation.*u* 17 Do not repay anyone evil for evil; be con-

d Jb 11, 7-8; Ps 139, 6.17-18; Wis 17, 1; Is 55, 8-9.—e Jb 15, 8; Wis 9, 13; Is 40, 13; Jer 23, 18; 1 Cor 2, 11-16.—f Jb 41, 3; Is 40, 14.—g 1 Cor 8, 6; Col 1, 16-17.—h 2 Cor 1, 3 / Rom 6, 13; 1 Pt 2, 5.—i Eph 4, 17.22-23; 1 Pt 1, 14 / Eph 5, 10.17; Phil 1, 10.—j Rom 15, 15 / Phil 2, 3 / 1 Cor 12, 11; Eph 4, 7.—k 4-5: 1 Cor 12, 12.27; Eph 4, 25.—l 6-8: 1 Cor 12, 4-11.28-31; Eph 4, 7-12; 1 Pt 4, 10-11 / 2 Cor 9, 7.—m 2 Cor 6, 6; 1 Tm 1, 5; 1 Pt 1, 22 / Am 5, 15.—n Jn 13, 34; 1 Thes 4, 9; 1 Pt 2, 17; 2 Pt 1, 7 / Phil 2, 3.—o Acts 18, 25.—p Rom 5, 2-3; Col 4, 2; 1 Thes 5, 17.—q Heb 13, 2; 1 Pt 4, 9.—r 14-21: Mt 5, 38-48; 1 Cor 4, 12; 1 Pt 3, 9.—s Lk 6, 27-28.—t Ps 35, 13; Sir 7, 34; 1 Cor 12, 26.—u Rom 15, 5; Phil 2, 2-3 / Rom 11, 20; Prv 3, 7; Is 5, 21.

11, 33-36: This final reflection celebrates the wisdom of God's plan of salvation. As Paul has indicated throughout these chapters, both Jew and Gentile, despite the religious recalcitrance of each, have received the gift of faith. The methods used by God in making this outreach to the world stagger human comprehension but are at the same time a dazzling invitation to abiding faith.

11, 34: The citation is from the Greek text of Is 40, 13. Paul does not explicitly mention Isaiah in this verse, nor Job in v 35.

11, 35: Paul quotes from an old Greek version of Jb 41, 3a, which differs from the Hebrew text (Jb 41, 11a).

12, 1—13, 14: Since Christ marks the termination of the Mosaic law as the primary source of guidance for God's people (Rom 10, 4), the apostle explains how Christians can function, in the light of the gift of justification through faith, in their relation to one another and the state.

12, 1-8: The Mosaic code included elaborate directions on sacrifices and other cultic observances. The gospel, however, invites believers to present their *bodies as a living sacrifice* (1). Instead of being limited by specific legal maxims, Christians are lib-

erated for the exercise of good judgment as they are confronted with the many and varied decisions required in the course of daily life. To assist them, God distributes a variety of gifts to the fellowship of believers, including those of prophecy, teaching, and exhortation (6-8). Prophets assist the community to understand the will of God as it applies to the present situation (6). Teachers help people to understand themselves and their responsibilities in relation to others (7). One who *exhorts* offers encouragement to the community to exercise their faith in the performance of all that is pleasing to God (8). Indeed, this very section, beginning with v 1, is a specimen of Paul's own style of exhortation.

12, 5: *One body in Christ:* on the church as the body of Christ, see 1 Cor 12, 12-27.

12, 6: Everyone has some gift that can be used for the benefit of the community. When the instruction on justification through faith is correctly grasped, the possessor of a gift will understand that it is not an instrument of self-aggrandizement. Possession of a gift is not an index to quality of faith. Rather, the gift is a challenge to faithful use.

12, 8: *Over others:* usually taken to mean "rule over" but possibly "serve as a patron." Wealthier members in Greco-Roman communities were frequently asked to assist in public service projects. In view of the references to contributing *in generosity* and to *acts of mercy*, Paul may have in mind people like Phoebe (Rom 16, 1-2), who is called a *benefactor* (or "patron") because of the services she rendered to many Christians, including Paul.

12, 14-21: Since God has justified the believers, it is not necessary for them to take justice into their own hands by taking vengeance. God will ultimately deal justly with all, including those who inflict injury on the believers. This question of personal rights as a matter of justice prepares the way for more detailed consideration of the state as adjudicator.

Rom

cerned for what is noble in the sight of all.[v] [18]If possible, on your part, live at peace with all.[w] [19]Beloved, do not look for revenge but leave room for the wrath; for it is written, "Vengeance is mine, I will repay, says the Lord."[x] [20]Rather, "if your enemy is hungry, feed him; if he is thirsty, give him something to drink; for by so doing you will heap burning coals upon his head."[y] [21]Do not be conquered by evil but conquer evil with good.

CHAPTER 13

Obedience to Authority.[*] [1]Let every person be subordinate to the higher authorities, for there is no authority except from God, and those that exist have been established by God.[z] [2]Therefore, whoever resists authority opposes what God has appointed, and those who oppose it will bring judgment upon themselves. [3]For rulers are not a cause of fear to good conduct, but to evil.[a] Do you wish to have no fear of authority? Then do what is good and you will receive approval from it, [4]for it is a servant of God for your good. But if you do evil, be afraid, for it does not bear the sword without purpose; it is the servant of God to inflict wrath on the evildoer.[b] [5]Therefore, it is necessary to be subject not only because of the wrath but also because of conscience.[c] [6]This is why you also pay taxes, for the authorities are ministers of God, devoting themselves to this very thing. [7]Pay to all their dues, taxes to whom taxes are

due, toll to whom toll is due, respect to whom respect is due, honor to whom honor is due.[d]

Love Fulfills the Law.[*] [8]Owe nothing to anyone, except to love one another; for the one who loves another has fulfilled the law.[e] [9]The commandments, "You shall not commit adultery; you shall not kill; you shall not steal; you shall not covet," and whatever other commandment there may be, are summed up in this saying, [namely] "You shall love your neighbor as yourself."[f] [10]Love does no evil to the neighbor; hence, love is the fulfillment of the law.[g]

Awareness of the End of Time.[*] [11]And do this because you know the time; it is the hour now for you to awake from sleep. For our salvation is nearer now than when we first believed;[h] [12]the night is advanced, the day is at hand. Let us then throw off the works of darkness [and] put on the armor of light;[i] [13]let us conduct ourselves properly as in the day,[*] not in orgies and drunkenness, not in promiscuity and licentiousness, not in rivalry and jealousy.[j] [14]But put on the Lord Jesus Christ, and make no provision for the desires of the flesh.[k]

CHAPTER 14

To Live and Die for Christ. [1] [*] Welcome anyone who is weak in faith,[l] but not for disputes over opinions.[m] [2]One person be-

v Prv 3, 4; 1 Thes 5, 15; 1 Pt 3, 9.—w Heb 12, 14.—x Lv 19, 18; Dt 32, 35.41; Mt 5, 39; 1 Cor 6, 6-7; Heb 10, 30.—y Prv 25, 21-22; Mt 5, 44.—z Prv 8, 15-16; Wis 6, 3; Jn 19, 11; 1 Pt 2, 13-17; Ti 3, 1.—a 1 Pt 2, 13-14; 3, 13.—b Rom 12, 19.—c 1 Pt 2, 19.—d Mt 22, 21; Mk 12, 17; Lk 20, 25.—e Jn 13, 34; Gal 5, 14.—f Ex 20, 13-17 / Lv 19, 18; Dt 5, 17-21; Mt 5, 43-44; 19, 18-19; 22, 39; Mk 12, 31; Lk 10, 27; Gal 5, 14; Jas 2, 8.—g Mt 22, 40; 1 Cor 13, 4-7.—h Eph 5, 8-16; 1 Thes 5, 5-7.—i Jn 8, 12; 1 Thes 5, 4-8; 1 Jn 2, 8 / 2 Cor 6, 7; 10, 4; Eph 5, 11; 6, 13-17.—j Lk 21, 34; Eph 5, 18.—k Gal 3, 27; 5, 16; Eph 4, 24; 6, 11.—l 1-23: 1 Cor 8, 1-13.—m Rom 15, 1.7; 1 Cor 9, 22.

13,1-7: Paul must come to grips with the problem raised by a message that declares people free from the law. How are they to relate to Roman authority? The problem was exacerbated by the fact that imperial protocol was interwoven with devotion to various deities. Paul builds on the traditional instruction exhibited in Wis 6, 1-3, according to which kings and magistrates rule by consent of God. From this perspective, then, believers who render obedience to the governing authorities are obeying the one who is highest in command. At the same time, it is recognized that Caesar has the responsibility to make just ordinances and to commend uprightness; cf Wis 6, 4-21. That Caesar is not entitled to obedience when such obedience would nullify God's prior claim to the believers' moral decision becomes clear in the light of the following verses.

13, 8-10: When love directs the Christian's moral decisions, the interest of law in basic concerns, such as familial relationships, sanctity of life, and security of property, is safeguarded (9).

Indeed, says Paul, the same applies to any *other commandment* (9), whether one in the Mosaic code or one drawn up by local magistrates under imperial authority. Love anticipates the purpose of public legislation, namely, to secure the best interests of the citizenry. Since Caesar's obligation is to punish the wrongdoer (4), the Christian who acts in love is free from all legitimate indictment.

13, 11-14: These verses provide the motivation for the love that is encouraged in vv 8-10.

13, 13: *Let us conduct ourselves properly as in the day:* the behavior described in Rom 1, 29-30 is now to be reversed. Secular moralists were fond of making references to people who could not wait for nightfall to do their carousing. Paul says that Christians claim to be people of the new day that will dawn with the return of Christ. Instead of planning for nighttime behavior they should be concentrating on conduct that is consonant with avowed interest in the Lord's return.

14, 1—15, 6: Since Christ spells termination of the law, which included observance of specific days and festivals as well as dietary instruction, the jettisoning of long-practiced customs was traumatic for many Christians brought up under the Mosaic code. Although Paul acknowledges that in principle no food is a source of moral contamination (14), he recommends that the consciences of Christians who are scrupulous in this regard be respected by other Christians (21). On the other hand, those who have scruples are not to sit in judgment on those who know that the gospel has liberated them from such ordinances (10). See 1 Cor 8 and 10.

lieves that one may eat anything, while the weak person eats only vegetables.*ⁿ* ³ The one who eats must not despise the one who abstains, and the one who abstains must not pass judgment on the one who eats; for God has welcomed him.*ᵒ* ⁴ Who are you to pass judgment on someone else's servant? Before his own master he stands or falls. And he will be upheld, for the Lord is able to make him stand.*ᵖ* ⁵ [For] one person considers one day more important than another, while another person considers all days alike.*q* Let everyone be fully persuaded in his own mind.* ⁶ Whoever observes the day, observes it for the Lord. Also whoever eats, eats for the Lord, since he gives thanks to God; while whoever abstains, abstains for the Lord and gives thanks to God. ⁷ None of us lives for oneself, and no one dies for oneself. ⁸ For if we live, we live for the Lord,* and if we die, we die for the Lord; so then, whether we live or die, we are the Lord's.*ʳ* ⁹ For this is why Christ died and came to life, that he might be Lord of both the dead and the living.*ˢ* ¹⁰ Why then do you judge your brother? Or you, why do you look down on your brother? For we shall all stand before the judgment seat of God;*t* ¹¹ for it is written:

n Gn 1, 29; 9, 3; 1 Cor 8, 1-13; 10, 14-33.—o Col 2, 16.—p Rom 2, 1; Mt 7, 11; Jas 4, 11-12.—q Gal 4, 10.—r Lk 20, 38; 2 Cor 5, 15; Gal 2, 20; 1 Thes 5, 10.—s Acts 10, 42.—t Acts 17, 31; 2 Cor 5, 10.—u Is 49, 18 / Is 45, 23; Phil 2, 10-11.—v Gal 6, 5.—w 1 Cor 8, 9.13.—x Mk 7, 5.20; Acts 10, 15; 1 Cor 10, 25-27; 1 Tm 4, 4.—y 1 Cor 8, 11-13.—z Rom 2, 24; Ti 2, 5.—a 1 Cor 8, 8.—b Rom 12, 18 / Rom 5, 2.—c 20-21: 1 Cor 8, 11-13; 10, 28-29; Ti 1, 15.—d Ti 1, 15; Jas 4, 17.—e Rom 14, 1-2.—f Rom 14, 1.19; 1 Cor 9, 19; 10, 24.33.—g Ps 69, 10.—h Rom 4, 23-24; 1 Mc 12, 9; 1 Cor 10, 11; 2 Tm 3, 16.—i Rom 12, 16; Phil 2, 2; 4, 2.

14, 5: Since the problem to be overcome was humanity's perverted mind or judgment (Rom 1, 28), Paul indicates that the *mind* of the Christian is now able to function with appropriate discrimination (cf Rom 12, 2).

14, 8: *The Lord:* Jesus, our Master. The same Greek word, *kyrios,* was applied to both rulers and holders of slaves. Throughout the Letter to the Romans Paul emphasizes God's total claim on the believer; see the note on Rom 1, 1.

14, 19: Some manuscripts, versions, and church Fathers read, "We then pursue . . ."; cf Rom 5, 1.

14, 23: *Whatever is not from faith is sin:* Paul does not mean that all the actions of unbelievers are sinful. He addresses himself to the question of intracommunity living. *Sin* in the singular is the dreadful power described in Rom 5, 12-14.

15, 3: Liberation from the law of Moses does not make the scriptures of the old covenant irrelevant. Much consolation and motivation for Christian living can be derived from the Old Testament, as in the citation from Ps 69, 10. Because this psalm is quoted several times in the New Testament, it has been called indirectly messianic.

15, 5: *Think in harmony:* a Greco-Roman ideal. Not rigid uniformity of thought and expression but thoughtful consideration of other people's views finds expression here.

"As I live, says the Lord, every knee shall bend before me,
and every tongue shall give praise to God."*u*
¹² So [then] each of us shall give an account of himself [to God].*v*

Consideration for the Weak Conscience. ¹³ Then let us no longer judge one another, but rather resolve never to put a stumbling block or hindrance in the way of a brother.*w* ¹⁴ I know and am convinced in the Lord Jesus that nothing is unclean in itself; still, it is unclean for someone who thinks it unclean.*x* ¹⁵ If your brother is being hurt by what you eat, your conduct is no longer in accord with love. Do not because of your food destroy him for whom Christ died.*y* ¹⁶ So do not let your good be reviled.*z* ¹⁷ For the kingdom of God is not a matter of food and drink, but of righteousness, peace, and joy in the holy Spirit;*a* ¹⁸ whoever serves Christ in this way is pleasing to God and approved by others. ¹⁹ Let us* then pursue what leads to peace and to building up one another.*b* ²⁰ For the sake of food, do not destroy the work of God.*c* Everything is indeed clean, but it is wrong for anyone to become a stumbling block by eating; ²¹ it is good not to eat meat or drink wine or do anything that causes your brother to stumble. ²² Keep the faith [that] you have to yourself in the presence of God; blessed is the one who does not condemn himself for what he approves. ²³ *d* But whoever has doubts is condemned if he eats, because this is not from faith; for whatever is not from faith is sin.*

CHAPTER 15

Patience and Self-Denial. ¹ We who are strong ought to put up with the failings of the weak and not to please ourselves;*e* ² let each of us please our neighbor for the good, for building up.*f* ³ For Christ did not please himself; but, as it is written,*g* "The insults of those who insult you fall upon me."* ⁴ For whatever was written previously was written for our instruction, that by endurance and by the encouragement of the scriptures we might have hope.*h* ⁵ May the God of endurance and encouragement grant you to think in harmony* with one another, in keeping with Christ Jesus,*i* ⁶ that with one accord you may with one voice glorify the God and Father of our Lord Jesus Christ.

God's Fidelity and Mercy.* [7]Welcome one another, then, as Christ welcomed you, for the glory of God.[j] [8]For I say that Christ became a minister of the circumcised to show God's truthfulness, to confirm the promises to the patriarchs,[k] [9]but so that the Gentiles might glorify God for his mercy. As it is written:

"Therefore, I will praise you among the Gentiles
and sing praises to your name."[l]

[10]And again it says:[m]

"Rejoice, O Gentiles, with his people."*

[11]And again:

"Praise the Lord, all you Gentiles,
and let all the peoples praise him."[n]

[12]And again Isaiah says:

"The root of Jesse shall come,
raised up to rule the Gentiles;
in him shall the Gentiles hope."[o]

[13]May the God of hope fill you with all joy and peace in believing, so that you may abound in hope by the power of the holy Spirit.[p]

VII. CONCLUSION

Apostle to the Gentiles. [14] * I myself am convinced about you, my brothers, that you yourselves are full of goodness,* filled with all knowledge, and able to admonish one another. [15]But I have written to you rather boldly in some respects to remind you, because of the grace given me by God[q] [16]to be a minister of Christ Jesus to the Gentiles in performing the priestly service of the gospel of God, so that the offering up of the Gentiles may be acceptable, sanctified by the holy Spirit.[r] [17]In Christ Jesus, then, I have reason to boast in what pertains to God. [18]For I will not dare to speak of anything except what Christ has accomplished through me to lead the Gentiles to obedience by word and deed,[s] [19]by the power of signs and wonders, by the power of the Spirit [of God], so that from Jerusalem all the way around to Illyricum* I have finished preaching the gospel of Christ. [20]Thus I aspire* to proclaim the gospel not where Christ has already been named, so that I do not build on another's foundation,[t] [21]but as it is written:[u]

"Those who have never been told of him shall see,
and those who have never heard of him shall understand."*

Paul's Plans; Need for Prayers. [22]That is why I have so often been prevented from coming to you. [23]But now, since I no longer have any opportunity in these regions and since I have desired to come to you for many years,[v] [24]I hope to see you in passing as I go to Spain and to be sent on my way there by you, after I have enjoyed being with you for a time.[w] [25] * Now, however, I am going to Jerusalem to minister to the holy ones.[x] [26]For Macedonia and Achaia* have decided to make some contribution for the poor among the holy ones in Jerusalem;[y] [27]they decided to do it, and in fact they are indebted to them, for if the Gentiles have come to share in their spiritual blessings, they ought also to serve them in material blessings.[z] [28]So when I

---

j Rom 14, 1.—k Mt 15, 24 / Mi 7, 20; Acts 3, 25.—l Rom 11, 30 / 2 Sm 22, 50; Ps 18, 50.—m Dt 32, 43.—n Ps 117, 1.—o Is 11, 10; Rv 5, 5; 22, 16.—p Rom 5, 1-2.—q Rom 1, 5; 12, 3.—r Rom 11, 13; Phil 2, 17.—s Acts 15, 12; 2 Cor 12, 12.—t 2 Cor 10, 13-18.—u Is 52, 15.—v Rom 1, 10-13; Acts 19, 21-22.—w 1 Cor 16, 6.—x Acts 19, 21; 20, 22.—y 1 Cor 16, 1; 2 Cor 8, 1-4; 9, 2.12.—z Rom 9, 4 / 1 Cor 9, 11.

15, 7-13: True oneness of mind is found in pondering the ultimate mission of the church: to bring it about that God's name be glorified throughout the world and that Jesus Christ be universally recognized as God's gift to all humanity. Paul here prepares his addressees for the climactic appeal he is about to make.

15, 10: Paul's citation of Dt 32, 43 follows the Greek version.

15, 14-33: Paul sees himself as apostle and benefactor in the priestly service of the gospel and so sketches plans for a mission in Spain, supported by those in Rome.

15, 14: *Full of goodness:* the opposite of what humanity was filled with according to Rom 1, 29-30.

15, 19: *Illyricum:* Roman province northwest of Greece on the eastern shore of the Adriatic.

15, 20: *I aspire:* Paul uses terminology customarily applied to philanthropists. Unlike some philanthropists of his time, Paul does not engage in cheap competition for public acclaim. This explanation of his missionary policy is to assure the Christians in Rome that he is also not planning to remain in that city and build on other people's foundations (cf 2 Cor 10, 12-18). However, he does solicit their help in sending him on his way to Spain, which was considered the limit of the western world. Thus Paul's addressees realize that evangelization may be understood in the broader sense of mission or, as in Rom 1, 15, of instruction within the Christian community that derives from the gospel.

15, 21: The citation from Is 52, 15 concerns the Servant of the Lord. According to Isaiah, the Servant is first of all Israel, which was to bring the knowledge of Yahweh to the nations. In chs 9-11 Paul showed how Israel failed in this mission. Therefore, he himself undertakes almost singlehandedly Israel's responsibility as the Servant and moves as quickly as possible with the gospel through the Roman empire.

15, 25-27: Paul may have viewed the contribution he was gathering from Gentile Christians for the poor in Jerusalem (cf 2 Cor 8 and 9) as a fulfillment of the vision of Is 60, 5-6. In confidence that the messianic fulfillment was taking place, Paul stresses in chs 14-16 the importance of harmonious relationships between Jews and Gentiles.

15, 26: *Achaia:* the Roman province of southern Greece.

have completed this and safely handed over this contribution to them, I shall set out by way of you to Spain; [29] and I know that in coming to you I shall come in the fullness of Christ's blessing.

[30] I urge you, [brothers,] by our Lord Jesus Christ and by the love of the Spirit, to join me in the struggle by your prayers to God on my behalf,[a] [31] that I may be delivered from the disobedient in Judea, and that my ministry for Jerusalem may be acceptable to the holy ones, [32] so that I may come to you with joy by the will of God and be refreshed together with you. [33] The God of peace be with all of you. Amen.[b]

CHAPTER 16

Phoebe Commended. [1] * I commend to you Phoebe our sister, who is [also] a minister* of the church at Cenchreae,[c] [2] that you may receive her in the Lord in a manner worthy of the holy ones, and help her in whatever she may need from you, for she has been a benefactor to many and to me as well.

Paul's Greetings. [3] Greet Prisca and Aquila,* my co-workers in Christ Jesus,[d] [4] who risked their necks for my life, to whom not only I am grateful but also all the churches of the Gentiles; [5] greet also the church at their house.* Greet my beloved Epaenetus, who was the firstfruits in Asia for Christ.[e] [6] Greet Mary, who has worked hard for you. [7] Greet Andronicus and Junia,* my relatives and my fellow prisoners; they are prominent among the apostles and they were in Christ before me.

[8] Greet Ampliatus, my beloved in the Lord. [9] Greet Urbanus, our co-worker in Christ, and my beloved Stachys. [10] Greet Apelles, who is approved in Christ. Greet those who belong to the family of Aristobulus. [11] Greet my relative Herodion. Greet those in the Lord who belong to the family of Narcissus. [12] Greet those workers in the Lord, Tryphaena and Tryphosa. Greet the beloved Persis, who has worked hard in the Lord. [13] Greet Rufus,* chosen in the Lord, and his mother and mine.[f] [14] Greet Asyncritus, Phlegon, Hermes, Patrobas, Hermas, and the brothers who are with them. [15] Greet Philologus, Julia, Nereus and his sister, and Olympas, and all the holy ones who are with them. [16] Greet one another with a holy kiss. All the churches of Christ greet you.[g]

Against Factions. [17] * I urge you, brothers, to watch out for those who create dissensions and obstacles, in opposition to the teaching that you learned; avoid them.[h] [18] For such people do not serve our Lord Christ but their own appetites, and by fair and flattering speech they deceive the hearts of the innocent.[i] [19] For while your obedience is known to all, so that I rejoice over you, I want you to be wise as to what is good, and simple as to what is evil;[j] [20] then the God of peace will quickly crush Satan* under your feet. The grace of our Lord Jesus be with you.[k]

Greetings from Corinth. [21] Timothy, my co-worker, greets you; so do Lucius and Jason and Sosipater, my relatives.[l] [22] I, Tertius, the writer of this letter, greet you in the Lord. [23] [m] Gaius, who is host to me

---

a 2 Cor 1, 11; Phil 1, 27; Col 4, 3; 2 Thes 3, 1.—b Rom 16, 20; 2 Cor 13, 11; Phil 4, 9; 1 Thes 5, 23; 2 Thes 3, 16; Heb 13, 20.—c Acts 18, 18.—d Acts 18, 2.18-26; 1 Cor 16, 19; 2 Tm 4, 19.—e 1 Cor 16, 19; Col 4, 15; Phlm 2 / 1 Cor 16, 15.—f Mk 15, 21.—g 1 Cor 16, 20; 2 Cor 13, 12; 1 Thes 5, 26; 1 Pt 5, 14.—h Mt 7, 15; Ti 3, 10.—i Phil 3, 18-19 / Col 2, 4; 2 Pt 2, 3.—j Rom 1, 8; Mt 10, 16; 1 Cor 14, 20.—k Rom 15, 33; Gn 3, 15; Lk 10, 19 / 1 Cor 16, 23; 1 Thes 5, 28; 2 Thes 3, 18.—l Acts 16, 1-2; 19, 22; 20, 4; 1 Cor 4, 17; 16, 10; Phil 2, 19-22; Heb 13, 23.—m Acts 19, 29; 1 Cor 1, 14 / 2 Tm 4, 20.

16, 1-23: Some authorities regard these verses as a later addition to the letter, but in general the evidence favors the view that they were included in the original. Paul endeavors through the long list of greetings (3-16; 21-23) to establish strong personal contact with congregations that he has not personally encountered before. The combination of Jewish and Gentile names dramatically attests the unity in the gospel that transcends previous barriers of nationality, religious ceremony, or racial status.

16, 1: *Minister:* in Greek, *diakonos;* see the note on Phil 1, 1.

16, 3: *Prisca and Aquila:* presumably the couple mentioned at Acts 18, 2; 1 Cor 16, 19; 2 Tm 4, 19.

16, 5: *The church at their house:* i.e., that meets there. Such local assemblies (cf 1 Cor 16, 19; Col 4, 15; Phlm 2) might consist of only one or two dozen Christians each. It is understandable, therefore, that such smaller groups might experience difficulty in relating to one another on certain issues. *Firstfruits:* cf Rom 8, 23; 11, 16; 1 Cor 16, 15.

16, 7: The name Junia is a woman's name. One ancient Greek manuscript and a number of ancient versions read the name "Julia." Most editors have interpreted it as a man's name, Junias.

16, 13: This Rufus cannot be identified to any degree of certainty with the Rufus of Mk 15, 21.

16, 17-18: Paul displays genuine concern for the congregations in Rome by warning them against self-seeking teachers. It would be a great loss, he intimates, if their obedience, which is known to all (cf Rom 1, 8), would be diluted.

16, 20: This verse contains the only mention of Satan in Romans.

and to the whole church, greets you. Erastus,* the city treasurer, and our brother Quartus greet you. [24]*

Doxology.* [25 Now to him who can strengthen you, according to my gospel and the proclamation of Jesus Christ,ⁿ according to the revelation of the mystery

kept secret for long ages* 26 but now manifested through the prophetic writings and, according to the command of the eternal God, made known to all nations to bring about the obedience of faith,ᵒ 27 to the only wise God, through Jesus Christ be glory forever and ever. Amen.]ᵖ

---

n 1 Cor 2, 7; Eph 1, 9; 3, 3-9; Col 1, 26.—o 2 Tm 1, 10 / Rom 1, 5; Eph 3, 4-5.9; 1 Pt 1, 20.—p Rom 11, 36; Gal 1, 5; Eph 3, 20-21; Phil 4, 20; 1 Tm 1, 17; 2 Tm 4, 18; Heb 13, 21; 1 Pt 4, 11; 2 Pt 3, 18; Jude 25; Rv 1, 6.

16, 23: This Erastus is not necessarily to be identified with the Erastus of Acts 19, 22 or of 2 Tm 4, 20.

16, 24: Some manuscripts add, similarly to v 20, "The grace of our Lord Jesus Christ be with you all. Amen."

16, 25-27: This doxology is assigned variously to the end of chs 14, 15, and 16 in the manuscript tradition. Some manuscripts omit it entirely. Whether written by Paul or not, it forms an admirable conclusion to the letter at this point.

16, 25: Paul's gospel reveals *the mystery kept secret for long ages:* justification and salvation through faith, with all the implications for Jews and Gentiles that Paul has developed in the letter.

THE FIRST LETTER TO THE CORINTHIANS

INTRODUCTION

Paul's first letter to the church of Corinth provides us with a fuller insight into the life of an early Christian community of the first generation than any other book of the New Testament. Through it we can glimpse both the strengths and the weaknesses of this small group in a great city of the ancient world, men and women who had accepted the good news of Christ and were now trying to realize in their lives the implications of their baptism. Paul, who had founded the community and continued to look after it as a father, responds both to questions addressed to him and to situations of which he had been informed. In doing so, he reveals much about himself, his teaching, and the way in which he conducted his work of apostleship. Some things are puzzling because we have the correspondence only in one direction. For the person studying this letter, it seems to raise as many questions as it answers, but without it our knowledge of church life in the middle of the first century would be much poorer.

Paul established a Christian community in Corinth about the year 51, on his second missionary journey. The city, a commercial crossroads, was a melting pot full of devotees of various pagan cults and marked by a measure of moral depravity not unusual in a great seaport. The Acts of the Apostles suggests that moderate success attended Paul's efforts among the Jews in Corinth at first, but that they soon turned against him (Acts 18, 1-8). More fruitful was his year and a half spent among the Gentiles (Acts 18, 11), which won to the faith many of the city's poor and underprivileged (1, 26). After his departure the eloquent Apollos, an Alexandrian Jewish Christian, rendered great service to the community, expounding "from the scriptures that the Messiah is Jesus" (Acts 18, 24-28).

While Paul was in Ephesus on his third journey (16, 8; Acts 19, 1-20), he received disquieting news about Corinth. The community there was displaying open factionalism, as certain members were identifying themselves exclusively with individual Christian leaders and interpreting Christian teaching as a superior wisdom for the initiated few (1, 10—4, 21). The community lacked the decisiveness to take appropriate action against one of its members who was living publicly in an incestuous union (5, 1-13). Other members engaged in legal conflicts in pagan courts of law (6, 1-11); still others may have participated in religious prostitution (6, 12-20) or temple sacrifices (10, 14-22).

The community's ills were reflected in its liturgy. In the celebration of the Eucharist certain members discriminated against others, drank too freely at the agape, or fellowship meal, and denied Christian social courtesies to the poor among the membership (11, 17-22). Charisms such as ecstatic prayer, attributed freely to the impulse of the holy Spirit, *were more highly prized than works of charity (13, 1-2.8), and were used at times in a disorderly way (14, 1-40). Women appeared at the assembly without the customary head-covering (11, 3-16), and perhaps were quarreling over their right to address the assembly (14, 34-35).*

Still other problems with which Paul had to deal concerned matters of conscience discussed among the faithful members of the community: the eating of meat that had been sacrificed to idols (8, 1-13), the use of sex in marriage (7, 1-7), and the attitude to be taken by the unmarried toward marriage in view of the possible proximity of Christ's second coming (7, 25-40). There was also a doctrinal matter that called for Paul's attention, for some members of the community, despite their belief in the resurrection of Christ, were denying the possibility of general bodily resurrection.

To treat this wide spectrum of questions, Paul wrote this letter from Ephesus about the year 56. The majority of the Corinthian Christians may well have been quite faithful. Paul writes on their behalf to guard against the threats posed to the community by the views and conduct of various minorities. He writes with confidence in the authority of his apostolic mission, and he presumes that the Corinthians, despite their deficiencies, will recognize and accept it. On the other hand, he does not hesitate to exercise his authority as his judgment dictates in each situation, even going so far as to promise a direct confrontation with recalcitrants, should the abuses he scores remain uncorrected (4, 18-21).

The letter illustrates well the mind and character of Paul. Although he is impelled to insist on his office as founder of the community, he recognizes that he is only one servant of God among many and generously acknowledges the labors of Apollos (3, 5-8). He provides us in this letter with many valuable examples of his method of theological reflection and exposition. He always treats the questions at issue on the level of the purity of Christian teaching and conduct. Certain passages of the letter are of the greatest importance for the understanding of early Christian teaching on the Eucharist (10, 14-22; 11, 17-34) and on the resurrection of the body (15, 1-58).

Paul's authorship of 1 Corinthians, apart from a few verses that some regard as later interpolations, has never been seriously questioned. Some scholars have proposed, however, that the letter as we have it contains portions of more than one original Pauline letter. We know that Paul wrote at least two other letters to Corinth (see 5, 9; 2 Cor 2, 3-4) in addition to the two that we now have; this theory holds that the additional letters are actually contained within the two canonical ones. Most commentators, however, find 1 Corinthians quite understandable as a single coherent work.

The principal divisions of the First Letter to the Corinthians are the following:

I. ADDRESS*

CHAPTER 1

Greeting. [1] Paul, called to be an apostle of Christ Jesus by the will of God,* and Sosthenes our brother,[a] [2] to the church of God that is in Corinth, to you who have been sanctified in Christ Jesus, called to be holy, with all those everywhere who call upon the name of our Lord Jesus Christ, their Lord and ours.[b] [3] Grace to you and peace from God our Father and the Lord Jesus Christ.

Thanksgiving. [4] I give thanks to my God always on your account for the grace of God bestowed on you in Christ Jesus, [5] that in him you were enriched in every way, with all discourse and all knowledge, [6] as the testimony* to Christ was confirmed among you, [7] so that you are not lacking in any spiritual gift as you wait for the revelation of our Lord Jesus Christ.[c] [8] He will keep you firm to the end, irreproachable on the day of our Lord Jesus [Christ].[d] [9] God is faithful, and by him you were called to fellowship with his Son, Jesus Christ our Lord.[e]

---

a Rom 1, 1.—b Acts 18, 1-11.—c Ti 2, 13.—d Phil 1, 6.—e 1 Jn 1, 3.—f Phil 2, 2.—g 1 Cor 3, 4.22; 16, 12; Acts 18, 24-28.—h Acts 18, 8 / Rom 16, 23.—i 1 Cor 16, 15-17.—j 1 Cor 2, 1.4.—k 1 Cor 2, 14 / Rom 1, 16.—l Is 29, 14.

1, 1-9: Paul follows the conventional form for the opening of a Hellenistic letter (cf Rom 1, 1-7), but expands the opening with details carefully chosen to remind the readers of their situation and to suggest some of the issues the letter will discuss.

1, 1: *Called . . . by the will of God:* Paul's mission and the church's existence are grounded in God's initiative. God's call, grace, and fidelity are central ideas in this introduction, emphasized by repetition and wordplays in the Greek.

1, 6: *The testimony:* this defines the purpose of Paul's mission (see also 1 Cor 15, 15 and the note on 1 Cor 2, 1). The forms of his testimony include oral preaching and instruction, his letters, and the life he leads as an apostle.

1, 10—4, 21: The first problem Paul addresses is that of divisions within the community. Although we are unable to reconstruct the situation in Corinth completely, Paul clearly traces the divisions back to a false self-image on the part of the Corinthians, coupled with a false understanding of the apostles who preached to them (cf 1 Cor 4, 6.9; 9, 1-5) and of the Christian message itself. In these chapters he attempts to deal with those underlying factors and to bring the Corinthians back to a more correct perspective.

1, 12: *I belong to:* the activities of Paul and Apollos in Corinth are described in Acts 18. *Kephas* (i.e., "the Rock," a name by which Paul designates Peter also in 1 Cor 3, 22; 9, 5; 15, 5 and in Gal 1, 18; 2, 9.11.14) may well have passed through Corinth; he could have baptized some members of the community either there or elsewhere. The reference to *Christ* may be intended ironically here.

1, 13-17: The reference to baptism and the contrast with preaching the gospel in v 17a suggest that some Corinthians were paying special allegiance to the individuals who initiated them into the community.

II. DISORDERS IN THE CORINTHIAN COMMUNITY

A. Divisions in the Church*

Groups and Slogans. [10] I urge you, brothers, in the name of our Lord Jesus Christ, that all of you agree in what you say, and that there be no divisions among you, but that you be united in the same mind and in the same purpose.[f] [11] For it has been reported to me about you, my brothers, by Chloe's people, that there are rivalries among you. [12] I mean that each of you is saying, "I belong to* Paul," or "I belong to Apollos," or "I belong to Kephas," or "I belong to Christ."[g] [13] * Is Christ divided? Was Paul crucified for you? Or were you baptized in the name of Paul? [14] I give thanks [to God] that I baptized none of you except Crispus and Gaius,[h] [15] so that no one can say you were baptized in my name. [16] (I baptized the household of Stephanas also; beyond that I do not know whether I baptized anyone else.)[i] [17] For Christ did not send me to baptize but to preach the gospel, and* not with the wisdom of human eloquence,* so that the cross of Christ might not be emptied of its meaning.[j]

Paradox of the Cross. [18] The message of the cross is foolishness to those who are perishing, but to us who are being saved it is the power of God.[k] [19] For it is written:

> "I will destroy the wisdom of the wise,
> and the learning of the learned I will set aside."[l]

1, 17b-18: The basic theme of chs 1-4 is announced. Adherence to individual leaders has something to do with differences in rhetorical ability and also with certain presuppositions regarding wisdom, eloquence, and effectiveness (power), which Paul judges to be in conflict with the gospel and the cross.

1, 17b: *Not with the wisdom of human eloquence:* both of the nouns employed here involve several levels of meaning, on which Paul deliberately plays as his thought unfolds. *Wisdom* (*sophia*) may be philosophical and speculative, but in biblical usage the term primarily denotes practical knowledge such as is demonstrated in the choice and effective application of means to achieve an end. The same term can designate the arts of building (cf 1 Cor 3, 10) or of persuasive speaking (cf 1 Cor 2, 4) or effectiveness in achieving salvation. *Eloquence* (*logos*): this translation emphasizes one possible meaning of the term *logos* (cf the references to rhetorical style and persuasiveness in 1 Cor 2, 1.4). But the term itself may denote an internal reasoning process, plan, or intention, as well as an external word, speech, or message. So by his expression *ouk en sophia logou* in the context of gospel preaching, Paul may intend to exclude both human ways of reasoning or thinking about things and human rhetorical technique. *Human:* this adjective does not stand in the Greek text but is supplied from the context. Paul will begin immediately to distinguish between *sophia* and *logos* from their divine counterparts and play them off against each other.

20 Where is the wise one? Where is the scribe? Where is the debater of this age? Has not God made the wisdom of the world foolish?[m] 21 * For since in the wisdom of God the world did not come to know God through wisdom, it was the will of God through the foolishness of the proclamation to save those who have faith. 22 For Jews demand signs and Greeks look for wisdom,[n] 23 but we proclaim Christ crucified, a stumbling block to Jews and foolishness to Gentiles,[o] 24 but to those who are called, Jews and Greeks alike, Christ the power of God and the wisdom of God. 25 For the foolishness of God is wiser than human wisdom, and the weakness of God is stronger than human strength.

The Corinthians and Paul.* 26 Consider your own calling, brothers. Not many of you were wise by human standards, not many were powerful, not many were of noble birth. 27 Rather, God chose the foolish of the world to shame the wise, and God chose the weak of the world to shame the strong,[p] 28 and God chose the lowly and despised of the world, those who count for nothing, to reduce to nothing those who are something, 29 so that no human being might boast* before God.[q] 30 It is due to him that you are in Christ Jesus, who became for us wisdom from God, as well as righteousness, sanctification, and redemption,[r] 31 so that, as it is written, "Whoever boasts, should boast in the Lord."[s]

---

m Is 19, 12.—n Mt 12, 38; 16, 1 / Acts 17, 18-21.—o 1 Cor 2, 2; Gal 3, 1 / Gal 5, 11.—p Jas 2, 5.—q Eph 2, 9.—r Rom 4, 17 / 1 Cor 6, 11; Rom 3, 24-26; 2 Cor 5, 21 / Eph 1, 7; Col 1, 14; 1 Thes 5, 23.—s Jer 9, 23; 2 Cor 10, 17.—t 1 Cor 1, 17.—u 1 Cor 1, 23; Gal 6, 14.—v 1 Cor 4, 20; Rom 15, 19; 1 Thes 1, 5.—w 2 Cor 4, 7.—x Is 64, 3.—y Mt 11, 25; 13, 11; 16, 17.

1, 21-25: True wisdom and power are to be found paradoxically where one would least expect them, in the place of their apparent negation. To human eyes the crucified Christ symbolizes impotence and absurdity.

1, 26—2, 5: The pattern of God's wisdom and power is exemplified in their own experience, if they interpret it rightly (1 Cor 1, 26-31), and can also be read in their experience of Paul as he first appeared among them preaching the gospel (I Cor 2, 1-5).

1, 29-31: "Boasting (about oneself)" is a Pauline expression for the radical sin, the claim to autonomy on the part of a creature, the illusion that we live and are saved by our own resources. "Boasting in the Lord" (31), on the other hand, is the acknowledgment that we live only from God and for God.

2, 1: *The mystery of God:* God's secret, known only to himself, is his plan for the salvation of his people; it is clear from 1 Cor 1, 18-25; 2, 2.8-10 that this secret involves Jesus and the cross. In place of *mystery*, other good manuscripts read "testimony" (cf 1 Cor 1, 6).

2, 3: The *weakness* of the crucified Jesus is reflected in Paul's own bearing (cf 2 Cor 10—13). *Fear and much trembling:* reverential fear based on a sense of God's transcendence

---

CHAPTER 2

1 When I came to you, brothers, proclaiming the mystery of God,* I did not come with sublimity of words or of wisdom.[t] 2 For I resolved to know nothing while I was with you except Jesus Christ, and him crucified.[u] 3 I came to you in weakness* and fear and much trembling, 4 and my message and my proclamation were not with persuasive [words of] wisdom,* but with a demonstration of spirit and power,[v] 5 so that your faith might rest not on human wisdom but on the power of God.[w]

The True Wisdom.* 6 Yet we do speak a wisdom to those who are mature, but not a wisdom of this age, nor of the rulers of this age who are passing away. 7 Rather, we speak God's wisdom,* mysterious, hidden, which God predetermined before the ages for our glory, 8 and which none of the rulers of this age* knew for, if they had known it, they would not have crucified the Lord of glory. 9 But as it is written:

"What eye has not seen, and ear has not heard,
     and what has not entered the human heart,
          what God has prepared for those who love him,"[x]

10 [y] this God has revealed to us through the Spirit.

---

permeates Paul's existence and preaching. Compare his advice to the Philippians to work out their salvation with "fear and trembling" (Phil 2, 12), because God is at work in them just as his exalting power was paradoxically at work in the emptying, humiliation, and obedience of Jesus to death on the cross (Phil 2, 6-11).

2, 4: Among many manuscript readings here the best is either "not with the persuasion of wisdom" or "not with persuasive words of wisdom," which differ only by a nuance. Whichever reading is accepted, the inefficacy of human wisdom for salvation is contrasted with the power of the cross.

2, 6—3, 4: Paul now asserts paradoxically what he has previously been denying. To the Greeks who "are looking for wisdom" (1 Cor 1, 22), he does indeed bring a wisdom, but of a higher order and an entirely different quality, the only wisdom really worthy of the name. The Corinthians would be able to grasp Paul's preaching as wisdom and enter into a wisdom-conversation with him if they were more open to the Spirit and receptive to the new insight and language that the Spirit teaches.

2, 7-10a: *God's wisdom:* his plan for our salvation. This was his own eternal secret that no one else could fathom, but in this new age of salvation he has graciously revealed it to us. For the pattern of God's secret, hidden to others and now revealed to the Church, cf also Rom 11, 25-36; 16, 25-27; Eph 1, 3-10; 3, 3-11; Col 1, 25-28.

2, 8: *The rulers of this age:* this suggests not only the political leaders of the Jews and Romans under whom Jesus was crucified (cf Acts 4, 25-28) but also the cosmic powers behind them (cf Eph 1, 20-23; 3, 10). *They would not have crucified the Lord of glory:* they became the unwitting executors of God's plan, which will paradoxically bring about their own conquest and submission (1 Cor 15, 24-28).

1Cor

For the Spirit scrutinizes everything, even the depths of God. [11]Among human beings, who knows what pertains to a person except the spirit of the person that is within? Similarly, no one knows what pertains to God except the Spirit of God. [12]We have not received the spirit of the world but the Spirit that is from God, so that we may understand the things freely given us by God. [13]And we speak about them not with words taught by human wisdom, but with words taught by the Spirit, describing spiritual realities in spiritual terms.*

[14]Now the natural person* does not accept what pertains to the Spirit of God, for to him it is foolishness, and he cannot understand it, because it is judged spiritually. [15]The spiritual person, however, can judge everything but is not subject to judgment* by anyone.

[16]For "who has known the mind of the Lord, so as to counsel him?" But we have the mind of Christ.[z]

CHAPTER 3

[1] * Brothers, I could not talk to you as spiritual people, but as fleshly people,* as infants in Christ. [2]I fed you milk, not solid food, because you were unable to take it. Indeed, you are still not able, even now,[a]

[3]for you are still of the flesh. While there is jealousy and rivalry among you,* are you not of the flesh and behaving in an ordinary human way?[b] [4]Whenever someone says, "I belong to Paul," and another, "I belong to Apollos," are you not merely human?[c]

The Role of God's Ministers.* [5]What is Apollos, after all, and what is Paul? Ministers* through whom you became believers, just as the Lord assigned each one. [6]I planted, Apollos watered, but God caused the growth.[d] [7]Therefore, neither the one who plants nor the one who waters is anything, but only God, who causes the growth. [8]The one who plants and the one who waters are equal, and each will receive wages in proportion to his labor. [9]For we are God's co-workers; you are God's field, God's building.[e]

[10] * According to the grace of God given to me, like a wise master builder I laid a foundation, and another is building upon it. But each one must be careful how he builds upon it, [11]for no one can lay a foundation other than the one that is there, namely, Jesus Christ. [12]If anyone builds on this foundation with gold, silver, precious stones, wood, hay, or straw, [13]the work of each will come to light, for the Day* will disclose it. It will be revealed with fire, and the fire [itself] will test the

---

z Wis 9, 13; Is 40, 13; Rom 11, 34.—a Heb 5, 12-14.—b Jas 3, 13-16.—c 1 Cor 1, 12.—d Acts 18, 1-11.24-28.—e Eph 2, 20-22; 1 Pt 2, 5.

2, 13: *In spiritual terms:* the Spirit teaches spiritual people a new mode of perception (12) and an appropriate language by which they can share their self-understanding, their knowledge about what God has done in them. The final phrase in v 13 can also be translated "describing spiritual realities to spiritual people," in which case it prepares for vv 14-16.

2, 14: *The natural person:* see the note on 1 Cor 3, 1.

2, 15: *The spiritual person . . . is not subject to judgment:* since spiritual persons have been given knowledge of what pertains to God (11-12), they share in God's own capacity to judge. One to whom the mind of the Lord (and of Christ) is revealed (16) can be said to share in some sense in God's exemption from counseling and criticism.

3, 1-4: The Corinthians desire a sort of wisdom dialogue or colloquy with Paul; they are looking for solid, adult food, and he appears to disappoint their expectations. Paul counters: if such a dialogue has not yet taken place, the reason is that they are still at an immature stage of development (cf 1 Cor 2, 6).

3, 1: *Spiritual people . . . fleshly people:* Paul employs two clusters of concepts and terms to distinguish what later theology will call the "natural" and the "supernatural." (1) The natural person (1 Cor 2, 14) is one whose existence, perceptions, and behavior are determined by purely natural principles, the *psychē* (1 Cor 2, 14) and the *sarx* (flesh, a biblical term that connotes creatureliness, 1 Cor 3, 1.3). Such persons are only infants (1 Cor 3, 1); they remain on a purely human level *(anthrōpoi,* 1 Cor 3, 4). (2) On the other hand, they are called to be animated by a

higher principle, the *pneuma,* God's spirit. They are to become spiritual *(pneumatikoi,* 1 Cor 3, 1) and mature (1 Cor 2, 6) in their perceptions and behavior (cf Gal 5, 16-26). The culmination of existence in the Spirit is described in 1 Cor 15, 44-49.

3, 3-4: Jealousy, rivalry, and divisions in the community are symptoms of their arrested development; they reveal the immaturity both of their self-understanding (4) and of the judgments about their apostles (21).

3, 5—4, 5: The Corinthians tend to evaluate their leaders by the criteria of human wisdom and to exaggerate their importance. Paul views the role of the apostles in the light of his theology of spiritual gifts (cf chs 12-14, where the charism of the apostle heads the lists). The essential aspects of all spiritual gifts (1 Cor 12, 4-6 presents them as gifts of grace, as services, and as modes of activity) are exemplified by the apostolate, which is a gift of grace (1 Cor 3, 10) through which God works (1 Cor 3, 9) and a form of service (1 Cor 3, 5) for the common good (elsewhere expressed by the verb "build up," suggested here by the image of the building, 1 Cor 3, 9). The apostles serve the church, but their accountability is to God and to Christ (1 Cor 4, 1-5).

3, 5: *Ministers:* for other expressions of Paul's understanding of himself as minister or steward to the church, cf 1 Cor 4, 1; 9, 17.19-27; 2 Cor 3, 6-9; 4, 1; 5, 18; 6, 3-4; and 2 Cor 11, 23 (the climax of Paul's defense).

3, 10-11: There are diverse functions in the service of the community, but each individual's task is serious, and each will stand accountable for the quality of his contribution.

3, 13: *The Day:* the great day of Yahweh, the day of judgment, which can be a time of either gloom or joy. *Fire* both destroys and purifies.

quality of each one's work.*f* ¹⁴ If the work stands that someone built upon the foundation, that person will receive a wage. ¹⁵ But if someone's work is burned up, that one will suffer loss; the person will be saved,* but only as through fire. ¹⁶ Do you not know that you are the temple of God, and that the Spirit of God dwells in you?*g* ¹⁷ If anyone destroys God's temple, God will destroy that person; for the temple of God, which you are, is holy.*

¹⁸ Let no one deceive himself. If anyone among you considers himself wise in this age, let him become a fool so as to become wise.*h* ¹⁹ For the wisdom of this world is foolishness in the eyes of God, for it is written:*i*

> "He catches the wise in their own ruses,"

²⁰ and again:

> "The Lord knows the thoughts of the wise, that they are vain."*j*

²¹ * So let no one boast about human beings, for everything belongs to you,*k* ²² Paul or Apollos or Kephas, or the world or life or death, or the present or the future: all belong to you, ²³ and you to Christ, and Christ to God.

---

f Mt 3, 11-12; 2 Thes 1, 7-10.—g 1 Cor 6, 19; 2 Cor 6, 16; Eph 2, 20-22.—h 1 Cor 8, 2; Is 5, 21; Gal 6, 3.—i 1 Cor 1, 20 / Jb 5, 13.—j Ps 94, 11.—k 1 Cor 4, 6 / Rom 8, 32.—l Ti 1, 7; 1 Pt 4, 10.—m 2 Cor 1, 12 / Rom 2, 16; 2 Cor 5, 10.

3, 15: *Will be saved:* although Paul can envision very harsh divine punishment (cf 1 Cor 3, 17), he appears optimistic about the success of divine corrective means both here and elsewhere (cf 1 Cor 5, 5; 11, 32 [discipline]). The text of v 15 has sometimes been used to support the notion of purgatory, though it does not envisage this.

3, 17: *Holy:* i.e., "belonging to God." The cultic sanctity of the community is a fundamental theological reality to which Paul frequently alludes (cf 1 Cor 1, 2.30; 6, 11; 7, 14).

3, 21-23: These verses pick up the line of thought of 1 Cor 1, 10-13. If the Corinthians were genuinely wise (18-20), their perceptions would be reversed, and they would see everything in the world and all those with whom they exist in the church in their true relations with one another. Paul assigns all the persons involved in the theological universe a position on a scale: God, Christ, church members, church leaders. Read from top to bottom, the scale expresses ownership; read from bottom to top, the obligation to serve. This picture should be complemented by similar statements such as those in 1 Cor 8, 6 and 1 Cor 15, 20-28.

4, 6-21: This is an emotionally charged peroration to the discussion about divisions. It contains several exhortations and statements of Paul's purpose in writing (cf 6.14-17.21) that counterbalance the initial exhortation at 1 Cor 1, 10.

4, 6: *That you may learn from us not to go beyond what is written:* the words "to go" are not in the Greek, but have here been added as the minimum necessary to elicit sense from this difficult passage. It probably means that the Corinthians should avoid the false wisdom of vain speculation, contenting themselves with Paul's proclamation of the cross, which is the fulfillment of

---

¹ Thus should one regard us: as servants of Christ and stewards of the mysteries of God.*l* ² Now it is of course required of stewards that they be found trustworthy. ³ It does not concern me in the least that I be judged by you or any human tribunal; I do not even pass judgment on myself; ⁴ I am not conscious of anything against me, but I do not thereby stand acquitted; the one who judges me is the Lord.*m* ⁵ Therefore, do not make any judgment before the appointed time, until the Lord comes, for he will bring to light what is hidden in darkness and will manifest the motives of our hearts, and then everyone will receive praise from God.

Paul's Life as Pattern.* ⁶ I have applied these things to myself and Apollos for your benefit, brothers, so that you may learn from us not to go beyond what is written,* so that none of you will be inflated with pride in favor of one person over against another. ⁷ Who confers distinction upon you? What do you possess that you have not received? But if you have received it, why are you boasting as if you did not receive it? ⁸ You are already satisfied; you have already grown rich; you have become kings* without us! Indeed, I wish that you had become kings, so that we also might become kings with you.

⁹ * For as I see it, God has exhibited us apostles as the last of all, like people sen-

---

God's promises in the Old Testament (what is written). *Inflated with pride:* literally, "puffed up," i.e., arrogant, filled with a sense of self-importance. The term is particularly Pauline, found in the New Testament only in 1 Cor 4, 6.18-19; 5, 2; 8, 1; 13, 4; Col 2, 18 (cf the related noun at 2 Cor 12, 20). It sometimes occurs in conjunction with the theme of "boasting," as in vv 6-7 here.

4, 8: *Satisfied . . . rich . . . kings:* these three statements could also be punctuated as questions continuing the series begun in v 7. In any case these expressions reflect a tendency at Corinth toward an overrealized eschatology, a form of self-deception that draws Paul's irony. The underlying attitude has implications for the Corinthians' thinking about other issues, notably morality and the resurrection, that Paul will address later in the letter.

4, 9-13: A rhetorically effective catalogue of the circumstances of apostolic existence, in the course of which Paul ironically contrasts his own sufferings with the Corinthians' illusion that they have passed beyond the folly of the passion and have already reached the condition of glory. His language echoes that of the beatitudes and woes, which assert a future reversal of present conditions. Their present sufferings ("to this very hour," 11) place the apostles in the class of those to whom the beatitudes promise future relief (Mt 5, 3-11; Lk 6, 20-23); whereas the Corinthians' image of themselves as "already" filled, rich, ruling (8), as wise, strong, and honored (10) places them paradoxically in the position of those whom the woes threaten with future undoing (Lk 6, 24-26). They have lost sight of the fact that the reversal is predicted for the future.

tenced to death, since we have become a spectacle to the world, to angels and human beings alike.[n] [10] We are fools on Christ's account, but you are wise in Christ; we are weak, but you are strong; you are held in honor, but we in disrepute.[o] [11] To this very hour we go hungry and thirsty, we are poorly clad and roughly treated, we wander about homeless[p] [12] and we toil, working with our own hands. When ridiculed, we bless; when persecuted, we endure;[q] [13] when slandered, we respond gently. We have become like the world's rubbish, the scum of all, to this very moment.

[14] I am writing you this not to shame you, but to admonish you as my beloved children.* [15] Even if you should have countless guides to Christ, yet you do not have many fathers, for I became your father in Christ Jesus through the gospel.[r] [16] Therefore, I urge you, be imitators of me.[s] [17] For this reason I am sending you Timothy, who is my beloved and faithful son in the Lord; he will remind you of my ways in Christ [Jesus], just as I teach them everywhere in every church.[t]

[18] * Some have become inflated with pride, as if I were not coming to you. [19] But I will come to you soon, if the Lord is willing, and I shall ascertain not the talk of these inflated people but their power.

[20] For the kingdom of God is not a matter of talk but of power.[u] [21] Which do you prefer? Shall I come to you with a rod, or with love and a gentle spirit?[v]

B. Moral Disorders*

CHAPTER 5

A Case of Incest.* [1] It is widely reported that there is immorality among you, and immorality of a kind not found even among pagans—a man living with his father's wife.[w] [2] And you are inflated with pride.* Should you not rather have been sorrowful? The one who did this deed should be expelled from your midst. [3] I, for my part, although absent in body but present in spirit, have already, as if present, pronounced judgment on the one who has committed this deed,[x] [4] in the name of [our] Lord Jesus: when you have gathered together and I am with you in spirit with the power of the Lord Jesus, [5] you are to deliver this man to Satan* for the destruction of his flesh, so that his spirit may be saved on the day of the Lord.[y]

[6] [z] Your boasting is not appropriate. Do you not know that a little yeast* leavens all the dough? [7] * Clear out the old yeast, so

---

n 1 Cor 15, 31; Rom 8, 36; 2 Cor 4, 8-12; 11, 23 / Heb 10, 33.—o 1 Cor 1, 18; 3, 18; 2 Cor 11, 19 / 1 Cor 2, 3; 2 Cor 13, 9.—p Rom 8, 35; 2 Cor 11, 23-27.—q Acts 9, 6-14; 18, 3; 20, 34; 1 Thes 2, 9 / 1 Pt 3, 9.—r Gal 4, 19; Phlm 10.—s 1 Cor 11, 1; Phil 3, 17; 4, 9; 1 Thes 1, 6; 2 Thes 3, 7.9.—t 1 Cor 16, 10; Acts 19, 22.—u 1 Cor 2, 4; 1 Thes 1, 5.—v 2 Cor 1, 23; 10, 2.—w Lv 18, 7-8; 20, 11; Dt 27, 20.—x Col 2, 5.—y 1 Tm 1, 20.—z Gal 5, 9.

4, 14-17: *My beloved children:* the close of the argument is dominated by the tender metaphor of the father who not only gives his children life but also educates them. Once he has begotten them through his preaching, Paul continues to present the gospel to them existentially, by his life as well as by his word, and they are to learn, as children do, by imitating their parents (16). The reference to the *rod* in v 21 belongs to the same image-complex. So does the image of the *ways* in v 17: the ways that Paul teaches everywhere, "his ways in Christ Jesus," mean a behavior pattern quite different from the human ways along which the Corinthians are walking (1 Cor 3, 3).

4, 18-21: Verse 20 picks up the contrast between a certain kind of talk (*logos*) and true power (*dynamis*) from 1 Cor 1, 17-18 and 1 Cor 2, 4-5. The kingdom, which many of them imagine to be fully present in their lives (8), will be rather unexpectedly disclosed in the strength of Paul's encounter with them, if they make a powerful intervention on his part necessary. Compare the similar ending to an argument in 2 Cor 13, 1-4.10.

5, 1—6, 20: Paul now takes up a number of other matters that require regulation. These have come to his attention by hearsay (1 Cor 5, 1), probably in reports brought by "Chloe's people" (1 Cor 1, 11).

5, 1-13: Paul first deals with the incestuous union of a man with his stepmother (1-8) and then attempts to clarify general admonitions he has given about associating with fellow Christians guilty of immorality (9-13). Each of these three brief paragraphs expresses the same idea: the need of separation between the holy and the unholy.

5, 2: *Inflated with pride:* this remark and the reference to *boasting* in v 6 suggest that they are proud of themselves despite the infection in their midst, tolerating and possibly even approving the situation. The attitude expressed in 1 Cor 6, 2.13 may be influencing their thinking in this case.

5, 5: *Deliver this man to Satan:* once the sinner is expelled from the church, the sphere of Jesus' lordship and victory over sin, he will be in the region outside over which Satan is still master. *For the destruction of his flesh:* the purpose of the penalty is medicinal: through affliction, sin's grip over him may be destroyed and the path to repentance and reunion laid open. With Paul's instructions for an excommunication ceremony here, contrast his recommendations for the reconciliation of a sinner in 2 Cor 2, 5-11.

5, 6: *A little yeast:* yeast, which induces fermentation, is a natural symbol for a source of corruption that becomes all-pervasive. The expression is proverbial.

5, 7-8: In the Jewish calendar, Passover was followed immediately by the festival of Unleavened Bread. In preparation for this feast all traces of old bread were removed from the house, and during the festival only unleavened bread was eaten. The sequence of these two feasts provides Paul with an image of Christian existence: Christ's death (the true Passover celebration) is followed by the life of the Christian community, marked by newness, purity, and integrity (a perpetual feast of unleavened bread). Paul may have been writing around Passover time (cf 1 Cor 16, 5); this is a little Easter homily, the earliest in Christian literature.

that you may become a fresh batch of dough, inasmuch as you are unleavened. For our paschal lamb, Christ, has been sacrificed.*a* [8] Therefore, let us celebrate the feast, not with the old yeast, the yeast of malice and wickedness, but with the unleavened bread of sincerity and truth.*b*

[9] * I wrote you in my letter not to associate with immoral people, [10] not at all referring to the immoral of this world or the greedy and robbers or idolaters; for you would then have to leave the world.*c* [11] But I now write to you not to associate with anyone named a brother, if he is immoral, greedy, an idolater, a slanderer, a drunkard, or a robber, not even to eat with such a person.*d* [12] For why should I be judging outsiders? Is it not your business to judge those within? [13] God will judge those outside. "Purge the evil person from your midst."*e*

CHAPTER 6

Lawsuits before Unbelievers. * [1] How can any one of you with a case against another dare to bring it to the unjust for judgment instead of to the holy ones? [2] * Do you not know that the holy ones will judge the world? If the world is to be judged by you, are you unqualified for the lowest law courts?*f* [3] Do you not know that we will judge angels? Then why not everyday matters? [4] If, therefore, you have courts for everyday matters, do you seat as judges

people of no standing in the church? [5] I say this to shame you. Can it be that there is not one among you wise enough to be able to settle a case between brothers? [6] But rather brother goes to court against brother, and that before unbelievers?

[7] Now indeed [then] it is, in any case, a failure on your part that you have lawsuits against one another. Why not rather put up with injustice? Why not rather let yourselves be cheated?*g* [8] Instead, you inflict injustice and cheat, and this to brothers. [9] * Do you not know that the unjust will not inherit the kingdom of God? Do not be deceived; neither fornicators nor idolaters nor adulterers nor boy prostitutes* nor practicing homosexuals*h* [10] nor thieves nor the greedy nor drunkards nor slanderers nor robbers will inherit the kingdom of God. [11] That is what some of you used to be; but now you have had yourselves washed, you were sanctified, you were justified in the name of the Lord Jesus Christ and in the Spirit of our God.*i*

Sexual Immorality. * [12] "Everything is lawful for me,"* but not everything is beneficial. "Everything is lawful for me," but I will not let myself be dominated by anything.*j* [13] "Food for the stomach and the stomach for food," but God will do away with both the one and the other. The body, however, is not for immorality, but for the Lord, and the Lord is for the body; [14] God raised the Lord and will also raise us by his power.*k*

1Cor

---

a Ex 12, 1-13; Dt 16, 1-2; 1 Pt 1, 19.—b Ex 12, 15-20; 13, 7; Dt 16, 3.—c 1 Cor 10, 27; Jn 17, 15.—d Mt 18, 17; 2 Thes 3, 6.14; 2 Jn 10.—e Dt 13, 6; 17, 7; 22, 24.—f Wis 3, 8; Mt 19, 28; Rv 20, 4.—g Mt 5, 38-42; Rom 12, 17-21; 1 Thes 5, 15.—h 1 Cor 15, 50; Gal 5, 19-21; Eph 5, 5.—i Ti 3, 3-7.—j 1 Cor 10, 23.—k Rom 8, 11; 2 Cor 4, 14.

5, 9-13: Paul here corrects a misunderstanding of his earlier directives against associating with immoral fellow Christians. He concedes the impossibility of avoiding contact with sinners in society at large but urges the Corinthians to maintain the inner purity of their own community.

6, 1-11: Christians at Corinth are suing one another before pagan judges in Roman courts. A barrage of rhetorical questions (1-9) betrays Paul's indignation over this practice, which he sees as an infringement upon the holiness of the Christian community.

6, 2-3: The principle to which Paul appeals is an eschatological prerogative promised to Christians: they are to share with Christ the judgment of the world (cf Dn 7, 22.27). Hence they ought to be able to settle minor disputes within the community.

6, 9-10: A catalogue of typical vices that exclude from the kingdom of God and that should be excluded from God's church. Such lists (cf 1 Cor 5, 10) reflect the common moral sensibility of the New Testament period.

6, 9: The Greek word translated as *boy prostitutes* designated catamites, i.e., boys or young men who were kept for purposes of prostitution, a practice not uncommon in the Greco-Roman world. In Greek mythology this was the function of Ganymede, the "cupbearer of the gods," whose Latin name was Catamitus. The term translated *practicing homosexuals* refers to adult males who indulged in homosexual practices with such boys. See similar condemnations of such practices in Rom 1, 26-27; 1 Tm 1, 10.

6, 12-20: Paul now turns to the opinion of some Corinthians that sexuality is a morally indifferent area (12-13). This leads him to explain the mutual relation between the Lord Jesus and our bodies (13b) in a densely packed paragraph that contains elements of a profound theology of sexuality (15-20).

6, 12-13: *Everything is lawful for me:* the Corinthians may have derived this slogan from Paul's preaching about Christian freedom, but they mean something different by it: they consider sexual satisfaction a matter as indifferent as food, and they attribute no lasting significance to bodily functions (13a). Paul begins to deal with the slogan by two qualifications, which suggest principles for judging sexual activity. *Not everything is beneficial:* cf 1 Cor 10, 23, and the whole argument of chs 8-10 on the finality of freedom and moral activity. *Not let myself be dominated:* certain apparently free actions may involve in fact a secret servitude in conflict with the lordship of Jesus.

15 Do you not know that your bodies are members of Christ? Shall I then take Christ's members and make them the members of a prostitute?* Of course not![l] 16 [Or] do you not know that anyone who joins himself to a prostitute becomes one body with her? For "the two," it says, "will become one flesh."[m] 17 But whoever is joined to the Lord becomes one spirit with him.[n] 18 Avoid immorality. Every other sin a person commits is outside the body, but the immoral person sins against his own body.* 19 Do you not know that your body is a temple* of the holy Spirit within you, whom you have from God, and that you are not your own?[o] 20 For you have been purchased at a price. Therefore glorify God in your body.[p]

III. ANSWERS TO THE CORINTHIANS' QUESTIONS

A. Marriage and Virginity*

CHAPTER 7

Advice to the Married.* 1 Now in regard to the matters about which you wrote: "It is a good thing for a man not to touch a woman,"* 2 but because of cases of immorality every man should have his own wife, and every woman her own husband. 3 The husband should fulfill his duty toward his wife, and likewise the wife toward her husband. 4 A wife does not have authority over her own body, but rather her husband, and similarly a husband does not have authority over his own body, but rather his wife. 5 Do not deprive each other, except perhaps by mutual consent for a time, to be free for prayer, but then return to one another, so that Satan may not tempt you through your lack of self-control. 6 This I say by way of concession,* however, not as a command. 7 Indeed, I wish everyone to be as I am, but each has a particular gift from God,* one of one kind and one of another.[q]

8 [r] Now to the unmarried and to widows I say: it is a good thing for them to remain as they are, as I do,* 9 but if they cannot exercise self-control they should marry, for it is better to marry than to be on fire. 10 [s] To the married, however, I give this instruction (not I, but the Lord):* a wife should not separate from her husband 11 —and if she does separate she must either remain single or become reconciled

l 1 Cor 12, 27; Rom 6, 12-13; 12, 5; Eph 5, 30.—m Gn 2, 24; Mt 19, 5; Mk 10, 8; Eph 5, 31.—n Rom 8, 9-10; 2 Cor 3, 17.—o 1 Cor 3, 16-17; Rom 5, 5.—p 1 Cor 3, 23; 7, 23; Acts 20, 28 / Rom 12, 1; Phil 1, 20.—q Mt 19, 11-12.—r 1 Tm 5, 11-16 / 1 Cor 9, 5.—s 10-11: Mt 5, 32; 19, 9.

6, 15b-16: *A prostitute:* the reference may be specifically to religious prostitution, an accepted part of pagan culture at Corinth and elsewhere; but the prostitute also serves as a symbol for any sexual relationship that conflicts with Christ's claim over us individually. *The two . . . will become one flesh:* the text of Gn 2, 24 is applied positively to human marriage in Mt and Mk, and in Eph 5, 29-32: love of husband and wife reflect the love of Christ for his church. The application of the text to union with a prostitute is jarring, for such a union is a parody, an antitype of marriage, which does conflict with Christ's claim over us. This explains the horror expressed in 15b.

6, 18: *Against his own body:* expresses the intimacy and depth of sexual disorder, which violates the very orientation of our bodies.

6, 19-20: Paul's vision becomes trinitarian. *A temple:* sacred by reason of God's gift, his indwelling Spirit. *Not your own:* but "for the Lord," who acquires ownership by the act of redemption. *Glorify God in your body:* the argument concludes with a positive imperative to supplement the negative "avoid immorality" of v 18. Far from being a terrain that is morally indifferent, the area of sexuality is one in which our relationship with God (and his Christ and his Spirit) is very intimately expressed: he is either highly glorified or deeply offended.

7, 1-40: Paul now begins to answer questions addressed to him by the Corinthians (1 Cor 7, 1—11, 1). The first of these concerns marriage. This chapter contains advice both to the married (1-16) and to the unmarried (25-38) or widowed (39-40); these two parts are separated by vv 17-24, which enunciate a principle applicable to both.

7, 1-16: It seems that some Christians in Corinth were advocating asceticism in sexual matters. The pattern *it is a good thing . . . , but* occurs twice (1-2.8-9; cf 1 Cor 7, 26), suggesting that in this matter as in others the Corinthians have seized upon a genuine value but are exaggerating or distorting it in some way. Once again Paul calls them to a more correct perspective and a better sense of their own limitations. The phrase *it is a good thing* (1) may have been the slogan of the ascetic party at Corinth.

7, 1-7: References to Paul's own behavior (7-8) suggest that his celibate way of life and his preaching to the unmarried (cf 1 Cor 7, 25-35) have given some the impression that asceticism within marriage, i.e., suspension of normal sexual relations, would be a laudable ideal. Paul points to their experience of widespread immorality to caution them against overestimating their own strength (2); as individuals they may not have the particular gift that makes such asceticism feasible (7) and hence are to abide by the principle to be explained in vv 17-24.

7, 6: *By way of concession:* this refers most likely to the concession mentioned in v 5a: temporary interruption of relations for a legitimate purpose.

7, 7: *A particular gift from God:* use of the term *charisma* suggests that marriage and celibacy may be viewed in the light of Paul's theology of spiritual gifts (chs 12-14).

7, 8: Paul was obviously unmarried when he wrote this verse. Some interpreters believe that he had previously been married and widowed; there is no clear evidence either for or against this view, which was expressed already at the end of the second century by Clement of Alexandria.

7, 10-11: *(Not I, but the Lord):* Paul reminds the married of Jesus' principle of nonseparation (Mk 10, 9). This is one of his rare specific references to the teaching of Jesus.

to her husband—and a husband should not divorce his wife.

¹²To the rest* I say (not the Lord): if any brother has a wife who is an unbeliever, and she is willing to go on living with him, he should not divorce her; ¹³and if any woman has a husband who is an unbeliever, and he is willing to go on living with her, she should not divorce her husband. ¹⁴For the unbelieving husband is made holy through his wife, and the unbelieving wife is made holy through the brother. Otherwise your children would be unclean, whereas in fact they are holy.ᵗ

¹⁵If the unbeliever separates,* however, let him separate. The brother or sister is not bound in such cases; God has called you to peace. ¹⁶For how do you know, wife, whether you will save your husband; or how do you know, husband, whether you will save your wife?

The Life That the Lord Has Assigned.*
¹⁷Only, everyone should live as the Lord has assigned, just as God called each one. I give this order in all the churches. ¹⁸Was someone called after he had been circumcised? He should not try to undo his circumcision. Was an uncircumcised person called? He should not be circumcised.ᵘ

---

t Rom 11, 16.—u 1 Mc 1, 15 / Acts 15, 1-2.—v Rom 2, 25.29; Gal 5, 6; 6, 15.—w Eph 6, 5-9; Col 3, 11; Phlm 16.—x 1 Cor 6, 20.—y 1 Cor 7, 8.—z Rom 13, 11.—a Lk 14, 20.—b 1 Tm 5, 5.—c Lk 10, 39-42.

7, 12-14: *To the rest:* marriages in which only one partner is a baptized Christian. Jesus' prohibition against divorce is not addressed to them, but Paul extends the principle of nonseparation to such unions, provided they are marked by peacefulness and shared sanctification.

7, 15-16: *If the unbeliever separates:* the basis of the "Pauline privilege" in Catholic marriage legislation.

7, 17-24: On the ground that distinct human conditions are less significant than the whole new existence opened up by God's call, Paul urges them to be less concerned with changing their states of life than with answering God's call where it finds them. The principle applies both to the married state (1 Cor 7, 1-16) and to the unmarried (1 Cor 7, 25-38).

7, 25-28: Paul is careful to explain that the principle of v 17 does not bind under sin but that present earthly conditions make it advantageous for the unmarried to remain as they are (28). These remarks must be complemented by the statement about "particular gifts" from v 7.

7, 29-31: *The world . . . is passing away:* Paul advises Christians to go about the ordinary activities of life in a manner different from those who are totally immersed in them and unaware of their transitoriness.

¹⁹Circumcision means nothing, and uncircumcision means nothing; what matters is keeping God's commandments.ᵛ ²⁰Everyone should remain in the state in which he was called.

²¹Were you a slave when you were called? Do not be concerned but, even if you can gain your freedom, make the most of it. ²²For the slave called in the Lord is a freed person in the Lord, just as the free person who has been called is a slave of Christ.ʷ ²³You have been purchased at a price. Do not become slaves to human beings.ˣ ²⁴Brothers, everyone should continue before God in the state in which he was called.

Advice to Virgins and Widows. ²⁵Now in regard to virgins I have no commandment from the Lord,* but I give my opinion as one who by the Lord's mercy is trustworthy. ²⁶So this is what I think best because of the present distress: that it is a good thing for a person to remain as he is.ʸ ²⁷Are you bound to a wife? Do not seek a separation. Are you free of a wife? Then do not look for a wife. ²⁸If you marry, however, you do not sin, nor does an unmarried woman sin if she marries; but such people will experience affliction in their earthly life, and I would like to spare you that.

²⁹*I tell you, brothers, the time is running out. From now on, let those having wives act as not having them,ᶻ ³⁰those weeping as not weeping, those rejoicing as not rejoicing, those buying as not owning, ³¹those using the world as not using it fully. For the world in its present form is passing away.

³²I should like you to be free of anxieties. An unmarried man is anxious about the things of the Lord, how he may please the Lord. ³³But a married man is anxious about the things of the world, how he may please his wife,ᵃ ³⁴and he is divided. An unmarried woman or a virgin is anxious about the things of the Lord, so that she may be holy in both body and spirit. A married woman, on the other hand, is anxious about the things of the world, how she may please her husband.ᵇ ³⁵I am telling you this for your own benefit, not to impose a restraint upon you, but for the sake of propriety and adherence to the Lord without distraction.ᶜ

1Cor

36 * If anyone thinks he is behaving improperly toward his virgin, and if a critical moment has come* and so it has to be, let him do as he wishes. He is committing no sin; let them get married. **37** The one who stands firm in his resolve, however, who is not under compulsion but has power over his own will, and has made up his mind to keep his virgin, will be doing well. **38** So then, the one who marries his virgin does well; the one who does not marry her will do better.

39 * A wife is bound to her husband as long as he lives. But if her husband dies, she is free to be married to whomever she wishes, provided that it be in the Lord.*d* **40** She is more blessed, though, in my opinion, if she remains as she is, and I think that I too have the Spirit of God.*e*

B. Offerings to Idols*

CHAPTER 8

Knowledge Insufficient. **1** Now in regard to meat sacrificed to idols:* we realize that "all of us have knowledge"; knowledge inflates with pride, but love builds up.*f* **2** If anyone supposes he knows something, he does not yet know as he ought to know. **3** But if one loves God, one is known by him.*g*

4 So about the eating of meat sacrificed to idols: we know that "there is no idol in the world," and that "there is no God but one."*h* **5** Indeed, even though there are so-called gods in heaven and on earth (there are, to be sure, many "gods" and many "lords"), **6** * yet for us there is

one God, the Father,
> from whom all things are and for whom we exist,

and one Lord, Jesus Christ,
> through whom all things are and through whom we exist.*i*

Practical Rules. **7** But not all have this knowledge. There are some who have been so used to idolatry up until now that, when they eat meat sacrificed to idols, their conscience, which is weak, is defiled.*j* **8** * Now food will not bring us closer to God. We are no worse off if we do not eat, nor are we better off if we do.*k* **9** But make sure that this liberty of yours in no way becomes a stumbling block to the weak.*l* **10** If someone sees you, with your knowledge, reclining at table in the temple of an idol, may not his conscience too, weak as it is, be "built up" to eat the meat sacrificed to idols? **11** Thus through your knowledge, the weak person is brought to destruction, the brother for whom Christ died.*m*

---

d Rom 7, 2.—e 1 Cor 7, 25.—f Rom 15, 14 / 1 Cor 13, 1-13; Rom 14, 15.19.—g Rom 8, 29; Gal 4, 9.—h 1 Cor 10, 19; Dt 6, 4.—i Mal 2, 10 / Rom 11, 36; Eph 4, 5-6 / 1 Cor 1, 2-3 / Jn 1, 3; Col 1, 16.—j 1 Cor 10, 28; Rom 14, 23 / Rom 14, 1; 15, 1.—k Rom 14, 17.—l Rom 14, 13.20-21.—m Rom 14, 15.20.

7, 36-38: The passage is difficult to interpret, because it is unclear whether Paul is thinking of a father and his unmarried daughter (or slave), or of a couple engaged in a betrothal or spiritual marriage. The general principles already enunciated apply: there is no question of sin, even if they should marry, but staying as they are is "better" (for the reasons mentioned in 1 Cor 7, 28-35). Once again the *charisma* of v 7, which applies also to the unmarried (1 Cor 7, 8-9), is to be presupposed.

7, 36: *A critical moment has come:* either because the woman will soon be beyond marriageable age, or because their passions are becoming uncontrollable (cf 1 Cor 7, 9).

7, 39-40: Application of the principles to the case of widows. If they do choose to remarry, they ought to prefer Christian husbands.

8, 1—11, 1: The Corinthians' second question concerns meat that has been sacrificed to idols; in this area they were exhibiting a disordered sense of liberation that Paul here tries to rectify. These chapters contain a sustained and unified argument that illustrates Paul's method of theological reflection on a moral dilemma. Although the problem with which he is dealing is dated, the guidelines for moral decisions that he offers are of lasting validity.

Essentially Paul urges them to take a communitarian rather than an individualistic view of their Christian freedom. Many decisions that they consider pertinent only to their private relationship with God have, in fact, social consequences. Nor can moral decisions be determined by merely theoretical considerations; they must be based on concrete circumstances, specifically on the value and needs of other individuals and on mutual responsibility within the community. Paul here introduces the theme of "building up" *(oikodomē)*, i.e., of contributing by individual action to the welfare and growth of the community. This theme will be further developed in ch 14; see the note on 1 Cor 14, 3b-5. Several years later Paul would again deal with the problem of meat sacrificed to idols in Rom 14, 1—15, 6.

8, 1a: *Meat sacrificed to idols:* much of the food consumed in the city could have passed through pagan religious ceremonies before finding its way into markets and homes. "*All of us have knowledge*": a slogan, similar to 1 Cor 6, 12, which reveals the self-image of the Corinthians. Verse 4 will specify the content of this knowledge.

8, 6: This verse rephrases the monotheistic confession of v 4 in such a way as to contrast it with polytheism (5) and to express our relationship with the one God in concrete, i.e., in personal and Christian terms. *And for whom we exist:* since the Greek contains no verb here and the action intended must be inferred from the preposition *eis*, another translation is equally possible: "toward whom we return." *Through whom all things:* the earliest reference in the New Testament to Jesus' role in creation.

8, 8-9: Although the food in itself is morally neutral, extrinsic circumstances may make the eating of it harmful. *A stumbling block:* the image is that of tripping or causing someone to fall (cf 1 Cor 8, 13; 9, 12; 10, 12.32; 2 Cor 6, 3; Rom 14, 13.20-21). This is a basic moral imperative for Paul, a counterpart to the positive imperative to "build one another up"; compare the expression "giving offense" as opposed to "pleasing" in 1 Cor 10, 32-33.

¹²When you sin in this way against your brothers and wound their consciences, weak as they are, you are sinning against Christ. ¹³ ⁿ Therefore, if food causes my brother to sin, I will never eat meat again, so that I may not cause my brother to sin.*

CHAPTER 9*

Paul's Rights as an Apostle. ¹Am I not free? Am I not an apostle? Have I not seen Jesus our Lord? Are you not my work in the Lord?ᵒ ²Although I may not be an apostle for others, certainly I am for you, for you are the seal of my apostleship in the Lord.

³My defense against those who would pass judgment on me* is this. ⁴ * Do we not have the right to eat and drink? ⁵Do we not have the right to take along a Christian wife, as do the rest of the apostles, and the brothers of the Lord, and Kephas? ⁶Or is it only myself and Barnabas who do not have the right not to work?ᵖ ⁷Who ever serves as a soldier at his own expense? Who plants a vineyard without eating its produce? Or who shepherds a flock without using some of the milk from the flock?�q ⁸Am I saying this on human authority, or does not the law also speak of these things? ⁹It is written in the law of Moses, "You shall not muzzle an ox while it is treading out the grain."ʳ Is God concerned about oxen, ¹⁰or is he not really speaking for our sake? It was written for our sake, because the plowman should plow in hope, and the thresher in hope of receiving a share.ˢ ¹¹If we have sown spiritual seed for you, is it a great thing that we reap a material harvest from you?ᵗ ¹²If others share this rightful claim on you, do not we still more?ᵘ

Reason for Not Using His Rights. Yet we have not used this right.* On the contrary, we endure everything so as not to place an obstacle to the gospel of Christ. ¹³ * Do you not know that those who perform the temple services eat [what] belongs to the temple, and those who minister at the altar share in the sacrificial offerings?ᵛ ¹⁴In the same way, the Lord ordered that those who preach the gospel should live by the gospel.ʷ

¹⁵ * I have not used any of these rights, however, nor do I write this that it be done so in my case. I would rather die. Certainly no one is going to nullify my boast.ˣ ¹⁶If I preach the gospel, this is no reason for me to boast, for an obligation has been imposed on me, and woe to me if I do not preach it!ʸ ¹⁷If I do so willingly, I have a recompense, but if unwillingly, then I have been entrusted with a stewardship.ᶻ ¹⁸What then is my recompense? That, when I preach, I offer the gospel free of charge so as not to make full use of my right in the gospel.ᵃ

1Cor

n Mt 18, 6; Rom 14, 20-21.—o 1 Cor 9, 19 / 2 Cor 12, 12 / 1 Cor 15, 8-9; Acts 9, 17; 26, 16.—p Acts 4, 36-37; 13, 1-2; Gal 2, 1.9.13; Col 4, 10.—q 2 Tm 2, 3-4.—r Dt 25, 4; 1 Tm 5, 18.—s 2 Tm 2, 6.—t Rom 15, 27.—u 2 Cor 11, 7-12; 12, 13-18; 2 Thes 3, 6-12.—v Nm 18, 8.31; Dt 18, 1-5.—w Mt 10, 10; Lk 10, 7-8.—x 2 Cor 11, 9-10.—y Acts 26, 14-18.—z 1 Cor 4, 1; Gal 2, 7.—a 2 Cor 11, 7-12.

8, 13: His own course is clear: he will avoid any action that might harm another Christian. This statement prepares for the paradigmatic development in ch 9.

9, 1-27: This chapter is an emotionally charged expansion of Paul's appeal to his own example in 1 Cor 8, 13; its purpose is to reinforce the exhortation of 1 Cor 8, 9. The two opening questions introduce the themes of Paul's freedom and his apostleship (1), themes that the chapter will develop in reverse order, vv 1-18 treating the question of his apostleship and the rights that flow from it, and vv 19-27 exploring dialectically the nature of Paul's freedom. The language is highly rhetorical, abounding in questions, wordplays, paradoxes, images, and appeals to authority and experience. The argument is unified by repetitions; its articulations are highlighted by inclusions and transitional verses.

9, 3: *My defense against those who would pass judgment on me:* the reference to a defense *(apologia)* is surprising, and suggests that Paul is incorporating some material here that he has previously used in another context. The defense will touch on two points: the fact of Paul's rights as an apostle (4-12a and 13-14) and his nonuse of those rights (12b and 15-18).

9, 4-12a: Apparently some believe that Paul is not equal to the other apostles and therefore does not enjoy equal privileges. His defense on this point (here and in 13-14) reinforces the assertion of his apostolic character in v 2. It consists of a series of analogies from natural equity (7) and religious custom (13) designed to establish his equal right to support from the churches (4-6.11-12a); these analogies are confirmed by the authority of the law (8-10) and of Jesus himself (14).

9, 12b: It appears, too, that suspicion or misunderstanding has been created by Paul's practice of not living from his preaching. The first reason he asserts in defense of this practice is an entirely apostolic one; it anticipates the developments to follow in vv 19-22. He will give a second reason in vv 15-18.

9, 13-14: The position of these verses produces an interlocking of the two points of Paul's defense. These arguments by analogy (13) and from authority (14) belong with those of vv 7-10 and ground the first point. But Paul defers them until he has had a chance to mention "the gospel of Christ" (12b), after which it is more appropriate to mention Jesus' injunction to his preachers and to argue by analogy from the sacred temple service to his own liturgical service, the preaching of the gospel (cf Rom 1, 9; 15, 16).

9, 15-18: Paul now assigns a more personal motive to his nonuse of his right to support. His preaching is not a service spontaneously undertaken on his part but a stewardship imposed by a sort of divine compulsion. Yet to merit any reward he must bring some spontaneous quality to his service, and this he does by freely renouncing his right to support. The material here is quite similar to that contained in Paul's "defense" at 2 Cor 11, 5-12; 12, 11-18.

All Things to All. [19] * Although I am free in regard to all, I have made myself a slave to all so as to win over as many as possible. [b] [20] To the Jews I became like a Jew to win over Jews; to those under the law I became like one under the law—though I myself am not under the law—to win over those under the law. [21] To those outside the law I became like one outside the law—though I am not outside God's law but within the law of Christ—to win over those outside the law. [22] To the weak I became weak, to win over the weak. I have become all things to all, to save at least some. [c] [23] All this I do for the sake of the gospel, so that I too may have a share in it.

[24] * Do you not know that the runners in the stadium all run in the race, but only one wins the prize? Run so as to win. [d] [25] Every athlete exercises discipline in every way. They do it to win a perishable crown, but we an imperishable one. [e] [26] Thus I do not run aimlessly; I do not fight as if I were shadowboxing. [27] No, I drive my body and train it, for fear that, after having preached to others, I myself should be disqualified. *

CHAPTER 10

Warning against Overconfidence. [1] * I do not want you to be unaware, brothers, that our ancestors were all under the cloud and all passed through the sea, [f] [2] and all of them were baptized into Moses in the cloud and in the sea. [g] [3] All ate the same spiritual food, [4] and all drank the same spiritual drink, for they drank from a spiritual rock that followed them,* and the rock was the Christ. [h] [5] Yet God was not pleased with most of them, for they were struck down in the desert. [i]

[6] * These things happened as examples for us, so that we might not desire evil things, as they did. [j] [7] And do not become idolaters, as some of them did, as it is written, "The people sat down to eat and drink, and rose up to revel." [k] [8] Let us not indulge in immorality as some of them did, and twenty-three thousand fell within a single day. [l] [9] Let us not test Christ* as some of them did, and suffered death by serpents. [m] [10] Do not grumble as some of them did, and suffered death by the destroyer. [n] [11] These things happened to them as an example, and they have been written down as a warning to us, upon whom the end of the ages has come.* [12] Therefore, whoever thinks he is standing secure should take care not to fall.* [13] No trial has come to you but what is human. God is faithful and will not let you be tried beyond your strength; but with the trial he will also provide a way out, so that you may be able to bear it. [o]

b Mt 20, 26-27.—c 1 Cor 10, 33; Rom 15, 1; 2 Cor 11, 29.—d Heb 12, 1.—e 2 Tm 2, 5 / 2 Tm 4, 7-8; Jas 1, 12; 1 Pt 5, 4.—f Ex 13, 21-22; 14, 19-20 / Ex 14, 21-22.26-30.—g Rom 6, 3; Gal 3, 27 / Ex 16, 4-35.—h Ex 17, 1-7; Nm 20, 7-11; Dt 8, 15.—i Nm 14, 28-38; Jude 5.—j Nm 11, 4.34.—k Ex 32, 6.—l Nm 25, 1-9.—m Nm 21, 5-9.—n Nm 14, 2-37; 16, 1-35.—o Mt 6, 13; Jas 1, 13-14 / 1 Cor 1, 9.

9, 19-23: In a rhetorically balanced series of statements Paul expands and generalizes the picture of his behavior and explores the paradox of apostolic freedom. It is not essentially freedom *from* restraint but freedom *for* service—a possibility of constructive activity.

9, 24-27: A series of miniparables from sports, appealing to readers familiar with Greek gymnasia and the nearby Isthmian games.

9, 27: *For fear that . . . I myself should be disqualified:* a final paradoxical turn to the argument: what appears at first a free, spontaneous renunciation of rights (12-18) seems subsequently to be required for fulfillment of Paul's stewardship (to preach effectively he must reach his hearers wherever they are, 19-22), and finally is seen to be necessary for his own salvation (23-27). Mention of the possibility of disqualification provides a transition to ch 10.

10, 1-5: Paul embarks unexpectedly upon a panoramic survey of the events of the Exodus period. The privileges of Israel in the wilderness are described in terms that apply strictly only to the realities of the new covenant ("baptism," "spiritual food and drink"); interpreted in this way they point forward to the Christian experience (1-4). But those privileges did not guarantee God's permanent pleasure (5).

10, 4: *A spiritual rock that followed them:* the Torah speaks only about a rock from which water issued, but rabbinic legend amplified this into a spring that followed the Israelites throughout their migration. Paul uses this legend as a literary type: he makes the rock itself accompany the Israelites, and he gives it a spiritual sense. *The rock was the Christ:* in the Old Testament, Yahweh is the Rock of his people (cf Dt 32, Moses' song to Yahweh the Rock). Paul now applies this image to the Christ, the source of the living water, the true Rock that accompanied Israel, guiding their experiences in the desert.

10, 6-13: This section explicitates the typological value of these Old Testament events: the desert experiences of the Israelites are examples, meant as warnings, to deter us from similar sins (idolatry, immorality, etc.) and from a similar fate.

10, 9: *Christ:* to avoid Paul's concept of Christ present in the wilderness events, some manuscripts read "the Lord."

10, 11: *Upon whom the end of the ages has come:* it is our period in time toward which past ages have been moving and in which they arrive at their goal.

10, 12-13: *Take care not to fall:* the point of the whole comparison with Israel is to caution against overconfidence, a sense of complete security (12). This warning is immediately balanced by a reassurance, based, however, on God (13).

Warning against Idolatry.* [14] Therefore, my beloved, avoid idolatry.[p] [15] I am speaking as to sensible people; judge for yourselves what I am saying. [16] The cup of blessing that we bless, is it not a participation in the blood of Christ? The bread that we break, is it not a participation in the body of Christ?[q] [17] Because the loaf of bread is one, we, though many, are one body, for we all partake of the one loaf.[r]

[18] Look at Israel according to the flesh; are not those who eat the sacrifices participants in the altar?[s] [19] So what am I saying? That meat sacrificed to idols is anything? Or that an idol is anything? [20] No, I mean that what they sacrifice, [they sacrifice] to demons,* not to God, and I do not want you to become participants with demons.[t] [21] You cannot drink the cup of the Lord and also the cup of demons. You cannot partake of the table of the Lord and of the table of demons.[u] [22] Or are we provoking the Lord to jealous anger? Are we stronger than he?[v]

Seek the Good of Others.* [23] "Everything is lawful," but not everything is beneficial.* "Everything is lawful," but not everything builds up.[w] [24] No one should seek his own advantage, but that of his neighbor.[x] [25] * Eat anything sold in the market, without raising questions on grounds of conscience, [26] for "the earth and its fullness are the Lord's."[y] [27] If an unbeliever invites you and you want to go, eat whatever is placed before you, without raising questions on grounds of conscience. [28] But if someone says to you, "This was offered in sacrifice," do not eat it on account of the one who called attention to it and on account of conscience; [29] I mean not your own conscience, but the other's. For why should my freedom be determined by someone else's conscience? [30] If I partake thankfully, why am I reviled for that over which I give thanks?[z]

[31] So whether you eat or drink, or whatever you do, do everything for the glory of God. [32] * Avoid giving offense, whether to Jews or Greeks or the church of God, [33] just as I try to please everyone in every way, not seeking my own benefit but that of the many, that they may be saved.[a]

CHAPTER 11

[1] Be imitators of me, as I am of Christ.[b]

IV. PROBLEMS IN LITURGICAL ASSEMBLIES*

[2] I praise you because you remember me in everything and hold fast to the traditions, just as I handed them on to you.[c]

---

p 1 Jn 5, 21.—q Mt 26, 26-29; Acts 2, 42.—r Rom 12, 5; Eph 4, 4.—s Lv 7, 6.—t Dt 32, 17.—u 2 Cor 6, 14-18.—v Dt 32, 21 / Eccl 6, 10.—w 1 Cor 6, 12.—x Rom 15, 2; Phil 2, 4.21.—y Pss 24, 1; 50, 12.—z Rom 14, 6; 1 Tm 4, 3-4.—a 1 Cor 9, 22; Rom 15, 2.—b 1 Cor 4, 16; Phil 3, 17.—c 1 Cor 15, 3; 2 Thes 2, 15.

10, 14-22: The warning against idolatry from v 7 is now repeated (14) and explained in terms of the effect of sacrifices: all sacrifices, Christian (16-17), Jewish (18), or pagan (20), establish communion. But communion with Christ is exclusive, incompatible with any other such communion (21). Compare the line of reasoning at 1 Cor 6, 15.

10, 20: *To demons:* although Jews denied divinity to pagan gods, they often believed that there was some nondivine reality behind the idols, such as the dead, or angels, or demons. The explanation Paul offers in v 20 is drawn from Dt 32, 7: the power behind the idols, with which the pagans commune, consists of demonic powers hostile to God.

10, 23—11, 1: By way of peroration Paul returns to the opening situation (ch 8) and draws conclusions based on the intervening considerations (chs 9-10).

10, 23-24: He repeats in the context of this new problem the slogans of liberty from 1 Cor 6, 12, with similar qualifications. Liberty is not merely an individual perfection, nor an end in itself, but is to be used for the common good. The language of v 24 recalls the description of Jesus' self-emptying in Phil 2.

10, 25-30: A summary of specific situations in which the eating of meat sacrificed to idols could present problems of conscience. Three cases are considered. In the first (the marketplace, 25-26) and the second (at table, 27), there is no need to be concerned with whether food has passed through a pagan sacrifice or not, for the principle of 1 Cor 8, 4-6 still stands, and the whole creation belongs to the one God. But in the third case (28), the situation changes if someone present explicitly raises the question of the sacrificial origin of the food; eating in such circumstances may be subject to various interpretations, some of which could be harmful to individuals. Paul is at pains to insist that the enlightened Christian conscience need not change its judgment about the neutrality, even the goodness, of the food in itself (29-30); yet the total situation is altered to the extent that others are potentially endangered, and this calls for a different response, for the sake of others.

10, 32—11, 1: In summary, the general rule of mutually responsible use of their Christian freedom is enjoined first negatively (32), then positively, as exemplified in Paul (33), and finally grounded in Christ, the pattern for Paul's behavior and theirs (1 Cor 11, 1; cf Rom 15, 1-3).

11, 2—14, 40: This section of the letter is devoted to regulation of conduct at the liturgy. The problems Paul handles have to do with the dress of women in the assembly (1 Cor 11, 3-16), improprieties in the celebration of community meals (1 Cor 11, 17-34), and the use of charisms and spiritual gifts (1 Cor 12, 1—14, 40). The statement in 1 Cor 11, 2 introduces all of these discussions, but applies more appropriately to the second (cf the mention of praise in 1 Cor 11, 17 and of tradition in 1 Cor 11, 23).

A. Women's Headdresses*

Man and Woman. 3 But I want you to know that Christ is the head of every man, and a husband the head of his wife,* and God the head of Christ.*d* 4 * Any man who prays or prophesies with his head covered brings shame upon his head. 5 But any woman who prays or prophesies with her head unveiled brings shame upon her head, for it is one and the same thing as if she had had her head shaved. 6 For if a woman does not have her head veiled, she may as well have her hair cut off. But if it is shameful for a woman to have her hair cut off or her head shaved, then she should wear a veil.

7 * A man, on the other hand, should not cover his head, because he is the image and glory of God, but woman is the glory of man.*e* 8 For man did not come from woman, but woman from man;*f* 9 nor was man created for woman, but woman for man;*g* 10 for this reason a woman should have a sign of authority* on her head, because of the angels. 11 * Woman is not independent of man or man of woman in the Lord.*h* 12 For just as woman came from man, so man is born of woman; but all things are from God.*i*

13 * Judge for yourselves: is it proper for a woman to pray to God with her head unveiled? 14 Does not nature itself teach you that if a man wears his hair long it is a disgrace to him, 15 whereas if a woman has long hair it is her glory, because long hair has been given [her] for a covering? 16 But if anyone is inclined to be argumentative, we do not have such a custom, nor do the churches of God.

B. The Lord's Supper*

An Abuse at Corinth. 17 In giving this instruction, I do not praise the fact that your meetings are doing more harm than good. 18 First of all, I hear that when you meet as a church there are divisions among you, and to a degree I believe it;*j* 19 there have to be factions among you in order that [also] those who are approved among you may become known.* 20 When you meet in one place, then, it is not to eat the Lord's supper, 21 for in eating, each one goes ahead with his own supper, and one goes hungry while another gets drunk. 22 Do you not have houses in which you can eat and drink? Or do you show contempt for the church of God and make those who have nothing feel ashamed? What can I say to

---

d Eph 5, 23.—e Gn 1, 26-27; 5, 1.—f Gn 2, 21-23.—g Gn 2, 18.—h Gal 3, 27-28.—i 1 Cor 8, 6; Rom 11, 36.—j 1 Cor 1, 10-12; Gal 5, 20.

11, 3-16: Women have been participating in worship at Corinth without the head-covering normal in Greek society of the period. Paul's stated goal is to bring them back into conformity with contemporary practice and propriety. In his desire to convince, he reaches for arguments from a variety of sources, though he has space to develop them only sketchily and is perhaps aware that they differ greatly in persuasiveness.

11, 3: *A husband the head of his wife:* the specific problem suggests to Paul the model of the head as a device for clarifying relations within a hierarchical structure. The model is similar to that developed later in greater detail and nuance in Eph 5, 21-33. It is a hybrid model, for it grafts onto a strictly theological scale of existence (cf 1 Cor 3, 21-23) the hierarchy of sociosexual relations prevalent in the ancient world: men, dominant, reflect the active function of Christ in relation to his church; women, submissive, reflect the passive role of the church with respect to its savior. This gives us the functional scale: God, Christ, man, woman.

11, 4-6: From man's direct relation to Christ, Paul infers that his head should not be covered. But woman, related not directly to Christ on the scale but to her husband, requires a covering as a sign of that relationship. *Shameful . . . to have her hair cut off:* certain less honored classes in society, such as lesbians and prostitutes, are thought to have worn their hair close-cropped.

11, 7-9: The hierarchy of v 3 is now expressed in other metaphors: the image (*eikōn*) and the reflected glory (*doxa*). Paul is alluding basically to the text of Gn 1, 27, in which mankind as a whole, the male-female couple, is created in God's image and given the command to multiply and together dominate the lower creation. But Gn 1, 24 is interpreted here in the light of the sec-

ond creation narrative in Gn 2, in which each of the sexes is created separately (first the man and then the woman *from* man and *for* him, to be his helpmate, Gn 2, 20-23), and under the influence of the story of the fall, as a result of which the husband rules over the woman (Gn 3, 16). This interpretation splits the single image of God into two, at different degrees of closeness.

11, 10: *A sign of authority:* "authority" (*exousia*) may possibly be due to mistranslation of an Aramaic word for "veil"; in any case, the connection with v 9 indicates that the covering is a sign of woman's subordination. *Because of the angels:* a surprising additional reason, which the context does not clarify. Presumably the reference is to cosmic powers who might inflict harm on women or whose function is to watch over women or the cult.

11, 11-12: These parenthetical remarks relativize the argument from Gn 2—3. *In the Lord:* in the Christian economy the relation between the sexes is characterized by a mutual dependence, which is not further specified. And even in the natural order conditions have changed: the mode of origin described in Gn 2 has been reversed (12a). But the ultimately significant fact is the origin that all things have in common (12b).

11, 13-16: The argument for conformity to common church practice is summed up and pressed home. Verses 14-15 contain a final appeal to the sense of propriety that contemporary Greek society would consider "natural" (cf 1 Cor 11, 5-6).

11, 17-34: Paul turns to another abuse connected with the liturgy, and a more serious one, for it involves neglect of basic Christian tradition concerning the meaning of the Lord's Supper. Paul recalls that tradition for them and reminds them of its implications.

11, 19: *That . . . those who are approved among you may become known:* Paul situates their divisions within the context of the eschatological separation of the authentic from the inauthentic and the final revelation of the difference. The notion of authenticity-testing recurs in the injunction to self-examination in view of present and future judgment (28-32).

you? Shall I praise you? In this matter I do not praise you.[k]

Tradition of the Institution. [23] * For I received from the Lord what I also handed on to you,[l] that the Lord Jesus, on the night he was handed over, took bread, [24]and, after he had given thanks, broke it and said, "This is my body that is for you. Do this in remembrance of me." [25]In the same way also the cup, after supper, saying, "This cup is the new covenant in my blood. Do this, as often as you drink it, in remembrance of me."[m] [26]For as often as you eat this bread and drink the cup, you proclaim the death of the Lord until he comes.

[27]Therefore whoever eats the bread or drinks the cup of the Lord unworthily will have to answer for the body and blood of the Lord.* [28]A person should examine himself,* and so eat the bread and drink the cup. [29]For anyone who eats and drinks without discerning the body, eats and drinks judgment* on himself. [30]That is why many among you are ill and infirm, and a considerable number are dying. [31]If we discerned ourselves, we would not be under judgment; [32]but since we are judged by [the] Lord, we are being disciplined so that we may not be condemned along with the world.[n]

[33]Therefore, my brothers, when you come together to eat, wait for one another. [34]If anyone is hungry, he should eat at home, so that your meetings may not result in judgment. The other matters I shall set in order when I come.

C. Spiritual Gifts*

CHAPTER 12

Unity and Variety. [1]Now in regard to spiritual gifts, brothers, I do not want you to be unaware. [2] * You know how, when you were pagans, you were constantly attracted and led away to mute idols.[o] [3]Therefore, I tell you that nobody speaking by the spirit of God says, "Jesus be accursed." And no one can say, "Jesus is Lord," except by the holy Spirit.[p]

[4] * There are different kinds of spiritual gifts but the same Spirit;[q] [5]there are different forms of service but the same Lord; [6]there are different workings but the same God who produces all of them in everyone. [7]To each individual the manifestation of the Spirit is given for some benefit. [8]To one is given through the Spirit the expression of wisdom; to another the expression of knowledge according to the same Spirit;[r] [9]to another faith by the same Spirit; to another gifts of healing by the one Spirit; [10]to another mighty deeds; to another prophecy; to another discernment of spirits; to another varieties of tongues; to another interpretation of tongues.[s] [11]But one and the same Spirit produces all

---

k Jas 2, 1-7.—l 1 Cor 11, 2; 15, 3 / 1 Cor 10, 16-17; Mt 26, 26-29; Mk 14, 22-25; Lk 22, 14-20.—m Ex 24, 8; 2 Cor 3, 6; Heb 8, 6-13.—n Dt 8, 5; Heb 12, 5-11.—o Eph 2, 11-18.—p Rom 10, 9; 1 Jn 4, 2-3.—q Rom 12, 6; Eph 4, 7.11.—r 1 Cor 2, 6-13.—s 1 Cor 14, 5.26.39; Acts 2, 4.

11, 23-25: This is the earliest written account of the institution of the Lord's Supper in the New Testament. The narrative emphasizes Jesus' action of self-giving (expressed in the words over the bread and the cup) and his double command to repeat his own action.

11, 27: It follows that the only proper way to celebrate the Eucharist is one that corresponds to Jesus' intention, which fits with the meaning of his command to reproduce his action in the proper spirit. If the Corinthians eat and drink unworthily, i.e., without having grasped and internalized the meaning of his death for them, they *will have to answer for the body and blood*, i.e., will be guilty of a sin against the Lord himself (cf 1 Cor 8, 12).

11, 28: *Examine himself:* the Greek word is similar to that for "approved" in v 19, which means "having been tested and found true." The self-testing required for proper eating involves *discerning the body* (29), which, from the context, must mean understanding the sense of Jesus' death (26), perceiving the imperative to unity that follows from the fact that Jesus gives himself to all and requires us to repeat his sacrifice in the same spirit (18-25).

11, 29-32: *Judgment:* there is a series of wordplays in these verses that would be awkward to translate literally into English; it includes all the references to judgment (*krima*, 29.34; *krinō*, 31.32), discernment (*diakrinō*, 29.31), and condemnation (*katakrinō*, 32). The judgment is concretely described as the illness, infirmity, and death that have visited the community. These are signs that the power of Jesus' death is not yet completely recognized and experienced. Yet even the judgment incurred is an expression of God's concern; it is a medicinal measure meant to rescue us from condemnation with God's enemies.

12, 1—14, 40: Ecstatic activity and charismatic activity were common in early Christian experience, as they were in other ancient religions. But the Corinthians seem to have developed a disproportionate esteem for certain phenomena, especially tongues, to the detriment of order in the liturgy. Paul's response to this development provides us with the fullest exposition we have of his theology of the charisms.

12, 2-3: There is an experience of the Spirit and an understanding of ecstatic phenomena that are specifically Christian and that differ, despite apparent similarities, from those of the pagans. It is necessary to discern which spirit is leading one; ecstatic phenomena must be judged by their effect (2). Verse 3 illustrates this by an example: power to confess Jesus as Lord can come only from the Spirit, and it is inconceivable that the Spirit would move anyone to curse the Lord.

12, 4-6: There are some features common to all charisms, despite their diversity: all are *gifts (charismata)*, grace from outside ourselves; all are *forms of service (diakoniai)*, an expression of their purpose and effect; and all are *workings (energēmata)*, in which God is at work. Paul associates each of these aspects with what later theology will call one of the persons of the Trinity, an early example of "appropriation."

of these, distributing them individually to each person as he wishes.[1]

One Body, Many Parts.* [12] As a body is one though it has many parts, and all the parts of the body, though many, are one body, so also Christ.[u] [13] For in one Spirit we were all baptized into one body, whether Jews or Greeks, slaves or free persons, and we were all given to drink of one Spirit.[v]

[14] Now the body is not a single part, but many. [15] If a foot should say, "Because I am not a hand I do not belong to the body," it does not for this reason belong any less to the body. [16] Or if an ear should say, "Because I am not an eye I do not belong to the body," it does not for this reason belong any less to the body. [17] If the whole body were an eye, where would the hearing be? If the whole body were hearing, where would the sense of smell be? [18] But as it is, God placed the parts, each one of them, in the body as he intended. [19] If they were all one part, where would the body be? [20] But as it is, there are many parts, yet one body. [21] The eye cannot say to the hand, "I do not need you," nor again the head to the feet, "I do not need you." [22] Indeed, the parts of the body that seem to be weaker are all the more necessary, [23] and those parts of the body that we consider less honorable we surround with greater honor, and our less presentable parts are treated with greater propriety, [24] whereas our more presentable parts do not need this. But God has so constructed the body as to give greater honor to a part

that is without it, [25] so that there may be no division in the body, but that the parts may have the same concern for one another. [26] If [one] part suffers, all the parts suffer with it; if one part is honored, all the parts share its joy.

Application to Christ.* [27] Now you are Christ's body, and individually parts of it.[w] [28] Some people God has designated in the church to be, first, apostles;* second, prophets; third, teachers; then, mighty deeds; then gifts of healing, assistance, administration, and varieties of tongues.[x] [29] Are all apostles? Are all prophets? Are all teachers? Do all work mighty deeds? [30] Do all have gifts of healing? Do all speak in tongues? Do all interpret? [31] Strive eagerly for the greatest spiritual gifts.

The Way of Love. But I shall show you a still more excellent way.

CHAPTER 13*

[1] If I speak in human and angelic tongues* but do not have love, I am a resounding gong or a clashing cymbal.[y] [2] And if I have the gift of prophecy and comprehend all mysteries and all knowledge; if I have all faith so as to move mountains but do not have love, I am nothing.[z] [3] If I give away everything I own, and if I hand my body over so that I may boast but do not have love, I gain nothing.[a]

[4] * Love is patient, love is kind. It is not jealous, [love] is not pompous, it is not inflated,[b] [5] it is not rude, it does not seek its own interests, it is not quick-tempered, it does not brood over injury,[c] [6] it does not rejoice over wrongdoing but rejoices with the truth. [7] It bears all things, believes all

t 1 Cor 7, 7; Eph 4, 7.—u 1 Cor 10, 17; Rom 12, 4-5; Eph 2, 16; Col 3, 15.—v Gal 3, 28; Eph 2, 13-18; Col 3, 11 / Jn 7, 37-39.—w Rom 12, 5-8; Eph 1, 23; 4, 12; 5, 30; Col 1, 18.24.—x Eph 2, 20; 3, 5; 4, 11.—y 1 Cor 8, 1; 16, 14; Rom 12, 9-10; 13, 8-10.—z 1 Cor 4, 1; 14, 2 / 1 Cor 1, 5; 8, 1-3; 12, 8 / Mt 17, 20; 21, 21; Col 2, 3.—a Mt 6, 2.—b Eph 4, 2 / 1 Cor 4, 6.18; 5, 2; 8, 1.—c 1 Cor 10, 24.33; Phil 2, 4.21; 1 Thes 5, 15.

12, 12-26: The image of *a body* is introduced to explain Christ's relationship with believers (12). Verse 13 applies this model to the church: by baptism all, despite diversity of ethnic or social origins, are integrated into one organism. Verses 14-26 then develop the need for diversity of function among the parts of a body without threat to its unity.

12, 27-30: Paul now applies the image again to the church as a whole and its members (27). The lists in vv 28-30 spell out the parallelism by specifying the diversity of functions found in the church (cf Rom 12, 6-8; Eph 4, 11).

12, 28: *First, apostles:* apostleship was not mentioned in vv 8-10, nor is it at issue in these chapters, but Paul gives it pride of place in his listing. It is not just one gift among others but a prior and fuller gift that includes the others. They are all demonstrated in Paul's apostolate, but he may have developed his theology of charisms by reflecting first of all on his own grace of apostleship

(cf 1 Cor 3, 5—4, 14; 9, 1-27; 2 Cor 2, 14—6, 13; 10, 1—13, 30, esp. 11, 23 and 12, 12).

13, 1-13: This chapter involves a shift of perspective and a new point. All or part of the material may once have been an independent piece in the style of Hellenistic eulogies of virtues, but it is now integrated, by editing, into the context of chs 12-14 (cf the reference to tongues and prophecy) and into the letter as a whole (cf the references to knowledge and to behavior). The function of ch 13 within the discussion of spiritual gifts is to relativize all the charisms by contrasting them with the more basic, pervasive, and enduring value that gives them their purpose and their effectiveness. The rhetoric of this chapter is striking.

13, 1-3: An inventory of gifts, arranged in careful gradation: neither tongues (on the lowest rung), nor prophecy, knowledge, or faith, nor even self-sacrifice has value unless informed by love.

13, 4-7: This paragraph is developed by personification and enumeration, defining love by what it does or does not do. The Greek contains fifteen verbs; it is natural to translate many of them by adjectives in English.

things, hopes all things, endures all things.*d*

8 * Love never fails. If there are prophecies, they will be brought to nothing; if tongues, they will cease; if knowledge, it will be brought to nothing. ⁹For we know partially and we prophesy partially, ¹⁰but when the perfect comes, the partial will pass away. ¹¹When I was a child, I used to talk as a child, think as a child, reason as a child; when I became a man, I put aside childish things. ¹²At present we see indistinctly, as in a mirror, but then face to face. At present I know partially; then I shall know fully, as I am fully known.*e* ¹³So faith, hope, love remain, these three;*f* but the greatest of these is love.*

CHAPTER 14

Prophecy Greater than Tongues. ¹ * Pursue love, but strive eagerly for the spiritual gifts, above all that you may prophesy.*g* ² * For one who speaks in a tongue does not speak to human beings but to God, for no one listens; he utters mysteries in spirit. ³On the other hand, one who prophesies does speak to human beings, for their building up,* encouragement, and solace.*h* ⁴Whoever speaks in a tongue builds himself up, but whoever prophesies builds up the church. ⁵Now I should like all of you to speak in tongues, but even more to prophesy. One who prophesies is greater

than one who speaks in tongues, unless he interprets, so that the church may be built up.

⁶ * Now, brothers, if I should come to you speaking in tongues, what good will I do you if I do not speak to you by way of revelation, or knowledge, or prophecy, or instruction? ⁷Likewise, if inanimate things that produce sound, such as flute or harp, do not give out the tones distinctly, how will what is being played on flute or harp be recognized? ⁸And if the bugle gives an indistinct sound, who will get ready for battle? ⁹Similarly, if you, because of speaking in tongues, do not utter intelligible speech, how will anyone know what is being said? For you will be talking to the air. ¹⁰It happens that there are many different languages in the world, and none is meaningless; ¹¹but if I do not know the meaning of a language, I shall be a foreigner to one who speaks it, and one who speaks it a foreigner to me. ¹²So with yourselves: since you strive eagerly for spirits, seek to have an abundance of them for building up the church.

Need for Interpretation.* ¹³Therefore, one who speaks in a tongue should pray to be able to interpret. ¹⁴[For] if I pray in a tongue, my spirit* is at prayer but my mind is unproductive. ¹⁵So what is to be done? I will pray with the spirit, but I will also pray with the mind. I will sing praise

d Prv 10, 12; 1 Pt 4, 8.—e 2 Cor 5, 7; Heb 11, 1/2 Tm 2, 19; 1 Jn 3, 2.—f Col 1, 4; 1 Thes 1, 3; 5, 8.—g 1 Cor 14, 5.12.39.— h 1 Cor 14, 4-5.12.17.26; 3, 9; 8, 1.10; 10, 23.

13, 8-13: The final paragraph announces its topic, *Love never fails* (8), then develops the permanence of love in contrast to the charisms (9-12), and finally asserts love's superiority even over the other "theological virtues" (13).

13, 13: In speaking of love, Paul is led by spontaneous association to mention faith and hope as well. They are already a well-known triad (cf 1 Thes 1, 3), three interrelated (cf 1 Cor 13, 7) features of Christian life, more fundamental than any particular charism. *The greatest . . . is love:* love is operative even within the other members of the triad (7), so that it has a certain primacy among them. Or, if the perspective is temporal, love will remain (cf "never fails," 8) even when faith has yielded to sight and hope to possession.

14, 1-5: Verse 1b returns to the thought of 1 Cor 12, 31a and reveals Paul's primary concern. The series of contrasts in vv 2-5 discloses the problem at Corinth: a disproportionate interest in tongues, with a corresponding failure to appreciate the worth of prophecy. Paul attempts to clarify the relative values of those gifts by indicating the kind of communication achieved in each and the kind of effect each produces.

14, 2-3a: They involve two kinds of communication: tongues, private speech toward God in inarticulate terms that need interpretation to be intelligible to others (see 1 Cor 14, 27-28); prophecy, communication with others in the community.

14, 3b-5: They produce two kinds of effect. One who speaks in tongues *builds himself up;* it is a matter of individual experience and personal perfection, which inevitably recalls Paul's previous remarks about being inflated, seeking one's own good, pleasing oneself. But a prophet *builds up the church:* the theme of "building up" or "edifying" others, the main theme of the letter, comes to clearest expression in this chapter (3.4.5.12.17). It has been anticipated at 1 Cor 8, 1 and 1 Cor 10, 23, and by the related concept of "the beneficial" in 1 Cor 6, 12; 10, 23; 12, 7; etc.

14, 6-12: Sound, in order to be useful, must be intelligible. This principle is illustrated by a series of analogies from music (7-8) and from ordinary human speech (10-11); it is applied to the case at hand in v 9 and v 12.

14, 13-19: The charism of interpretation lifts tongues to the level of intelligibility, enabling them to produce the same effect as prophecy (cf 1 Cor 14, 5.26-28).

14, 14-15: *My spirit:* Paul emphasizes the exclusively ecstatic, nonrational quality of tongues. The tongues at Pentecost are also described as an ecstatic experience (Acts 2, 4.12-13), though Luke superimposes further interpretations of his own. *My mind:* the ecstatic element, dominant in earliest Old Testament prophecy as depicted in 1 Sam 10, 5-13; 19, 20-24, seems entirely absent from Paul's notion of prophecy and completely relegated to tongues. He emphasizes the role of reason when he specifies instruction as a function of prophecy (6.19.31). But he does not exclude intuition and emotion; cf references to encouragement and consolation (3.31) and the scene describing the ideal exercise of prophecy (24-25).

with the spirit, but I will also sing praise with the mind.[i] [16]Otherwise, if you pronounce a blessing [with] the spirit, how shall one who holds the place of the uninstructed say the "Amen" to your thanksgiving, since he does not know what you are saying? [17]For you may be giving thanks very well, but the other is not built up. [18]I give thanks to God that I speak in tongues more than any of you, [19]but in the church I would rather speak five words with my mind, so as to instruct others also, than ten thousand words in a tongue.

Functions of These Gifts. [20] * Brothers, stop being childish in your thinking. In respect to evil be like infants, but in your thinking be mature.[j] [21]It is written in the law:

"By people speaking strange tongues
    and by the lips of foreigners
I will speak to this people,
    and even so they will not listen to
    me,[k]

says the Lord." [22]Thus, tongues are a sign not for those who believe but for unbelievers, whereas prophecy is not for unbelievers but for those who believe.

[23] * So if the whole church meets in one place and everyone speaks in tongues, and then uninstructed people or unbelievers should come in, will they not say that you are out of your minds?[l] [24]But if everyone is prophesying, and an unbeliever or uninstructed person should come in, he will be convinced by everyone and judged by everyone, [25]and the secrets of his heart will be disclosed, and so he will fall down and worship God, declaring, "God is really in your midst."[m]

Rules of Order. [26] * So what is to be done, brothers? When you assemble, one has a psalm, another an instruction, a revelation, a tongue, or an interpretation. Everything should be done for building up.[n] [27]If anyone speaks in a tongue, let it be two or at most three, and each in turn, and one should interpret. [28]But if there is no interpreter, the person should keep silent in the church and speak to himself and to God.

[29]Two or three prophets should speak, and the others discern. [30]But if a revelation is given to another person sitting there, the first one should be silent. [31]For you can all prophesy one by one, so that all may learn and all be encouraged. [32]Indeed, the spirits of prophets are under the prophets' control, [33]since he is not the God of disorder but of peace.

As in all the churches of the holy ones,* [34]women should keep silent in the churches, for they are not allowed to speak, but should be subordinate, as even the law says.[o] [35]But if they want to learn anything, they should ask their husbands at home. For it is improper for a woman to speak in the church. [36]Did the word of God go forth from you? Or has it come to you alone?

[37]If anyone thinks that he is a prophet or a spiritual person, he should recognize that what I am writing to you is a commandment of the Lord. [38]If anyone does not acknowledge this, he is not acknowledged.

---

i Eph 5, 19; Col 3, 16.—j Mt 10, 16; Rom 16, 19; Eph 4, 14.—k Is 28, 11-12; Dt 28, 49.—l Acts 2, 6.13.—m 1 Cor 4, 5 / Is 45, 14; Zec 8, 23.—n Eph 4, 12.—o 1 Tm 2, 11-15; 1 Pt 3, 1.

14, 20-22: The Corinthians pride themselves on tongues as a sign of God's favor, a means of direct communication with him (2.28). To challenge them to a more mature appraisal, Paul draws from scripture a less flattering explanation of what speaking in tongues may signify. Isaiah threatened the people that if they failed to listen to their prophets, the Lord would speak to them (in punishment) through the lips of Assyrian conquerors (Is 28, 11-12). Paul compresses Isaiah's text and makes God address his people directly. Equating tongues with foreign languages (cf 1 Cor 14, 10-11), Paul concludes from Isaiah that *tongues are a sign not for those who believe*, i.e., not a mark of God's pleasure for those who listen to him but a mark of his displeasure with those in the community who are faithless, who have not heeded the message that he has sent through the prophets.

14, 23-25: Paul projects the possible missionary effect of two hypothetical liturgical experiences, one consisting wholly of tongues, the other entirely of prophecy. *Uninstructed (idiōtai):* the term may simply mean people who do not speak or understand tongues, as in v 16, where it seems to designate Christians. But coupled with the term "unbelievers" it may be another way of designating those who have not been initiated into the community of faith; some believe it denotes a special class of non-Christians who are close to the community, such as catechumens. *Unbelievers (apistoi):* he has shifted from the inner-community perspective of v 22; the term here designates non-Christians (cf 1 Cor 6, 6; 7, 15; 10, 27).

14, 26-33a: Paul concludes with specific directives regarding exercise of the gifts in their assemblies. Verse 26 enunciates the basic criterion in the use of any gift: it must contribute to "building up."

14, 33b-36: Verse 33b may belong with what precedes, so that the new paragraph would begin only with v 34. Verses 34-35 change the subject. These two verses have the theme of submission in common with ch 11, despite differences in vocabulary, and a concern with what is or is not becoming; but it is difficult to harmonize the injunction to silence here with ch 11, which appears to take it for granted that women do pray and prophesy aloud in the assembly (cf 1 Cor 11, 5.13). Hence the verses are often considered an interpolation, reflecting the discipline of later churches; such an interpolation would have to have antedated our manuscripts, all of which contain them, though some transpose them to the very end of the chapter.

[39] So, [my] brothers, strive eagerly to prophesy, and do not forbid speaking in tongues, [40] but everything must be done properly and in order.

V. THE RESURRECTION
A. The Resurrection of Christ
CHAPTER 15*

The Gospel Teaching.* [1] Now I am reminding you, brothers, of the gospel I preached to you, which you indeed received and in which you also stand. [2] Through it you are also being saved, if you hold fast to the word I preached to you, unless you believed in vain. [3] * For I handed on to you as of first importance what I also received: that Christ died for our sins in accordance with the scriptures;[p] [4] that he was buried; that he was raised on the third day in accordance with the scriptures;[q] [5] that he appeared to Kephas, then to the Twelve.[r] [6] After that, he appeared to more than five hundred brothers at once, most of whom are still living, though some have fallen asleep. [7] After that he appeared to James, then to all the apostles. [8] Last of all, as to one born abnormally, he appeared to me.[s] [9] For I am the least* of the apostles, not fit to be called an apostle, because I persecuted the church of God.[t] [10] But by the grace of God I am what I am, and his grace to me has not been ineffective. Indeed, I have toiled harder than all of them; not I, however, but the grace of God [that is] with me. [11] Therefore, whether it be I or they, so we preach and so you believed.

B. The Resurrection of the Dead

Results of Denial.* [12] But if Christ is preached as raised from the dead, how can some among you say there is no resurrection of the dead? [13] If there is no resurrection of the dead, then neither has Christ been raised.[u] [14] And if Christ has not been raised, then empty [too] is our preaching; empty, too, your faith. [15] Then we are also false witnesses to God, because we testified against God that he raised Christ, whom he did not raise if in fact the dead are not raised.[v] [16] For if the dead are not raised, neither has Christ been raised, [17] and if Christ has not been raised,* your faith is vain; you are still in your sins. [18] Then those who have fallen asleep in Christ have perished. [19] If for this life only we have hoped in Christ, we are the most pitiable people of all.

Christ the Firstfruits.* [20] *w* But now Christ has been raised from the dead, the firstfruits* of those who have fallen asleep.

---

p 1 Cor 11, 23 / 1 Pt 2, 24; 3, 18 / Is 53, 4-12.—q Acts 2, 23-24 / Ps 16, 8-11; Hos 6, 1-2; Jon 2, 1.—r Mk 16, 14; Mt 28, 16-17; Lk 24, 36; Jn 20, 19.—s 1 Cor 9, 1; Acts 9, 3-6; Gal 1, 16.—t Acts 8, 3; 9, 1-2; Gal 1, 23; Eph 3, 8; 1 Tm 1, 15.—u 1 Thes 4, 14.—v Acts 5, 32.—w Rom 8, 11; Col 1, 18; 1 Thes 4, 14.

15, 1-58: Some consider this chapter an earlier Pauline composition inserted into the present letter. The problem that Paul treats is clear to a degree: some of the Corinthians are denying the resurrection of the dead (12), apparently because of their inability to imagine how any kind of bodily existence could be possible after death (35). It is plausibly supposed that their attitude stems from Greek anthropology, which looks with contempt upon matter and would be content with the survival of the soul, and perhaps also from an overrealized eschatology of gnostic coloration, such as that reflected in 2 Tm 2, 18, which considers the resurrection a purely spiritual experience already achieved in baptism and in the forgiveness of sins. Paul, on the other hand, will affirm both the essential corporeity of the resurrection and its futurity.

His response moves through three steps: a recall of the basic kerygma about Jesus' resurrection (1-11), an assertion of the logical inconsistencies involved in denial of the resurrection (12-34), and an attempt to perceive theologically what the properties of the resurrected body must be (35-58).

15, 1-11: Paul recalls the tradition (3-7), which he can presuppose as common ground and which provides a starting point for his argument. This is the fundamental content of all Christian preaching and belief (1-2.11).

15, 3-7: The language by which Paul expresses the essence of the "gospel" (1) is not his own but is drawn from older credal formulas. This credo highlights Jesus' death for our sins (confirmed by his burial) and Jesus' resurrection (confirmed by his appearances) and presents both of them as fulfillment of prophecy. *In accordance with the scriptures:* conformity of Jesus' passion with the scriptures is asserted in Mt 16, 1; Lk 24, 25-27.32.44-46. Application of some Old Testament texts (Pss 2, 7; 16, 8-11) to his resurrection is illustrated by Acts 2, 27-31; 13, 29-39; and Is 52, 13—53, 12 and Hos 6, 2 may also have been envisaged.

15, 9-11: A persecutor may have appeared disqualified (*ouk . . . hikanos*) from apostleship, but in fact God's grace has qualified him. Cf the remarks in 2 Cor about his qualifications (2 Cor 2, 16; 3, 5) and his greater labors (2 Cor 11, 23). These verses are parenthetical, but a nerve has been touched (the references to his abnormal birth and his activity as a persecutor may echo taunts from Paul's opponents), and he is instinctively moved to self-defense.

15, 12-19: Denial of the resurrection (12) involves logical inconsistencies. The basic one, stated twice (13.16), is that if there is no such thing as (bodily) resurrection, then it has not taken place even in Christ's case.

15, 17-18: The consequences for the Corinthians are grave: both forgiveness of sins and salvation are an illusion, despite their strong convictions about both. Unless Christ is risen, their faith does not save.

15, 20-28: After a triumphant assertion of the reality of Christ's resurrection (20a), Paul explains its positive implications and consequences. As a soteriological event of both human (20-23) and cosmic (24-28) dimensions, Jesus' resurrection logically and necessarily involves ours as well.

15, 20: *The firstfruits:* the portion of the harvest offered in thanksgiving to God implies the consecration of the entire harvest to come. Christ's resurrection is not an end in itself; its finality lies in the whole harvest, ourselves.

21 * For since death came through a human being, the resurrection of the dead came also through a human being. 22 For just as in Adam all die, so too in Christ shall all be brought to life,ˣ 23 but each one in proper order: Christ the firstfruits; then, at his coming, those who belong to Christ;ʸ 24 then comes the end,* when he hands over the kingdom to his God and Father, when he has destroyed every sovereignty and every authority and power.ᶻ 25 For he must reign until he has put all his enemies under his feet.ᵃ 26 The last enemyᵇ to be destroyed is death,* 27 for "he subjected everything under his feet."ᶜ But when it says that everything has been subjected, it is clear that it excludes the one who subjected everything to him.* 28 When everything is subjected to him, then the Son himself will [also] be subjected to the one who subjected everything to him, so that God may be all in all.ᵈ

Practical Arguments.* 29 Otherwise, what will people accomplish by having themselves baptized for the dead?* If the dead are not raised at all, then why are they having themselves baptized for them?

30 * Moreover, why are we endangering ourselves all the time?ᵉ 31 Every day I face death; I swear it by the pride in you [brothers] that I have in Christ Jesus our Lord.ᶠ 32 If at Ephesus I fought with beasts, so to speak, what benefit was it to me? If the dead are not raised:

"Let us eat and drink,
　　for tomorrow we die."ᵍ

33 Do not be led astray:

"Bad company corrupts good morals."

34 Become sober as you ought and stop sinning. For some have no knowledge of God; I say this to your shame.ʰ

C. The Manner of the Resurrection*

35 * But someone may say, "How are the dead raised? With what kind of body will they come back?"

The Resurrection Body. 36 * You fool! What you sow is not brought to life unless it dies.ⁱ 37 And what you sow is not the body that is to be but a bare kernel of wheat, perhaps, or of some other kind; 38 ʲ but God gives it a body as he chooses, and to each of the seeds its own body. 39 * Not all flesh is the same, but there is one kind

---

x Gn 3, 17-19; Rom 5, 12-19.—y 1 Thes 4, 15-17.—z Eph 1, 22.—a Ps 110, 1.—b Rom 6, 9; 2 Tm 1, 10; Rv 20, 14; 21, 4.—c Ps 8, 7; Eph 1, 22; Phil 3, 21.—d Eph 4, 6; Col 3, 11.—e 2 Cor 4, 8-12; 11, 23-27.—f Ps 44, 23; Rom 8, 36.—g 1 Cor 4, 9; 2 Cor 4, 10-11 / Wis 2, 5-7; Is 22, 13.—h Mt 22, 29; Mk 12, 24.—i Jn 12, 24.—j Gn 1, 11.

15, 21-22: Our human existence, both natural and supernatural, is corporate, involves solidarity. *In Adam . . . in Christ:* the Hebrew word *'ādām* in Genesis is both a common noun for mankind and a proper noun for the first man. Paul here presents Adam as at least a literary type of Christ; the parallelism and contrast between them will be developed further in vv 45-49 and in Rom 5, 12-21.

15, 24-28: Paul's perspective expands to cosmic dimensions, as he describes the climax of history, *the end.* His viewpoint is still christological, as in vv 20-23. Verses 24 and 28 describe Christ's final relations to his enemies and his Father in language that is both royal and military; vv 25-28 insert a proof from scripture (Pss 110, 1; 8, 7) into this description. But the viewpoint is also theological, for God is the ultimate agent and end, and likewise soteriological, for we are the beneficiaries of all the action.

15, 26: *The last enemy . . . is death:* a parenthesis that specifies the final fulfillment of the two Old Testament texts just referred to, Ps 110, 1 and Ps 8, 7. Death is not just one cosmic power among many, but the ultimate effect of sin in the universe (cf 1 Cor 15, 56; Rom 5, 12). Christ defeats death where it prevails, in our bodies. The destruction of the last enemy is concretely the "coming to life" (22) of "those who belong to Christ" (23).

15, 27b-28: *The one who subjected everything to him:* the Father is the ultimate agent in the drama, and the final end of the process, to whom the Son and everything else is ordered (24.28). *That God may be all in all:* his reign is a dynamic exercise of creative power, an outpouring of life and energy through the uni-universe, with no further resistance. This is the supremely positive meaning of "subjection": that God may fully be God.

15, 29-34: Paul concludes his treatment of logical inconsistencies with a listing of miscellaneous Christian practices that would be meaningless if the resurrection were not a fact.

15, 29: *Baptized for the dead:* this practice is not further explained here, nor is it necessarily mentioned with approval, but Paul cites it as something in their experience that attests in one more way to belief in the resurrection.

15, 30-34: A life of sacrifice, such as Paul describes in 1 Cor 4, 9-13 and 2 Cor, would be pointless without the prospect of resurrection; a life of pleasure, such as that expressed in the Epicurean slogan of v 32, would be far more consistent. *I fought with beasts:* since Paul does not elsewhere mention a combat with beasts at Ephesus, he may be speaking figuratively about struggles with adversaries.

15, 35-58: Paul imagines two objections that the Corinthians could raise: one concerning the manner of the resurrection (*how?*), the other pertaining to the qualities of the risen body (*what kind?*). These questions probably lie behind their denial of the resurrection (12), and seem to reflect the presumption that no kind of body other than the one we now possess would be possible. Paul deals with these objections in inverse order, in vv 36-49 and vv 50-58. His argument is fundamentally theological and its appeal is to the understanding.

15, 35-49: Paul approaches the question of the nature of the risen body (*what kind of body?*) by means of two analogies: the seed (36-44) and the first man, Adam (45-49).

15, 36-38: The analogy of the seed: there is a change of attributes from seed to plant; the old life-form must be lost for the new to emerge. By speaking about the seed as a *body* that dies and comes to life, Paul keeps the point of the analogy before the reader's mind.

15, 39-41: The expression "its own body" (38) leads to a development on the marvelous diversity evident in bodily life.

for human beings, another kind of flesh for animals, another kind of flesh for birds, and another for fish. [40] There are both heavenly bodies and earthly bodies, but the brightness of the heavenly is one kind and that of the earthly another. [41] The brightness of the sun is one kind, the brightness of the moon another, and the brightness of the stars another. For star differs from star in brightness.

[42] * So also is the resurrection of the dead. It is sown corruptible; it is raised incorruptible. [43] It is sown dishonorable; it is raised glorious. It is sown weak; it is raised powerful.[k] [44] It is sown a natural body; it is raised a spiritual body. If there is a natural body, there is also a spiritual one.

[45] So, too, it is written, "The first man, Adam,* became a living being," the last Adam a life-giving spirit.[l] [46] But the spiritual was not first; rather the natural and then the spiritual. [47] The first man was from the earth, earthly; the second man, from heaven. [48] As was the earthly one, so also are the earthly, and as is the heavenly one, so also are the heavenly. [49] Just as we have borne the image of the earthly one, we shall also bear the image* of the heavenly one.[m]

The Resurrection Event. [50] * This I declare, brothers: flesh and blood cannot inherit the kingdom of God, nor does corruption* inherit incorruption.[n] [51] * Behold, I tell you a mystery. We shall not all fall asleep, but we will all be changed,[o] [52] in an instant, in the blink of an eye, at the last trumpet. For the trumpet will sound, the dead will be raised incorruptible, and we shall be changed.[p] [53] For that which is corruptible must clothe itself with incorruptibility, and that which is mortal must clothe itself with immortality.[q] [54] And when this which is corruptible clothes itself with incorruptibility and this which is mortal clothes itself with immortality, then the word that is written shall come about:[r]

"Death is swallowed up in victory.*
[55] Where, O death, is your victory?
Where, O death, is your sting?"[s]

[56] The sting of death is sin,* and the power of sin is the law.[t] [57] But thanks be to God who gives us the victory through our Lord Jesus Christ.[u]

[58] Therefore, my beloved brothers, be firm, steadfast, always fully devoted to the work of the Lord, knowing that in the Lord your labor is not in vain.

1Cor

---

k Phil 3, 20-21; Col 3, 4.—l Gn 2, 7 / Jn 5, 21-29; 2 Cor 3, 6.17.—m Gn 5, 3 / Rom 8, 29; Phil 3, 21.—n Jn 3, 3-6.—o 1 Thes 4, 14-17.—p Jl 2, 1; Zec 9, 14; Mt 24, 31; Rv 11, 15-18.—q 2 Cor 5, 2-4.—r Is 25, 8; 2 Cor 5, 4; 2 Tm 1, 10; Heb 2, 14-15.—s Hos 13, 14.—t Rom 4, 15; 7, 7.13.—u Jn 16, 33; 1 Jn 5, 4.

15, 42-44: The principles of qualitative difference before and after death (36-38) and of diversity on different levels of creation (39-41) are now applied to the human body. Before: a body animated by a lower, natural life-principle *(psychē)* and endowed with the properties of natural existence (corruptibility, lack of glory, weakness). After: a body animated by a higher life-principle *(pneuma;* cf 45) and endowed with other qualities (incorruptibility, glory, power, spirituality), which are properties of God himself.

15, 45: The analogy of *the first man, Adam,* is introduced by a citation from Gn 2, 7. Paul alters the text slightly, adding the adjective *first,* and translating the Hebrew *'ādām* twice, so as to give it its value both as a common noun *(man)* and as a proper name *(Adam).* Verse 45b then specifies similarities and differences between the two Adams. *The last Adam,* Christ (cf 1 Cor 15, 21-22) has become *a . . . spirit (pneuma),* a life-principle transcendent with respect to the natural soul *(psychē)* of the first Adam (on the terminology here, cf the note on 1 Cor 3, 1). Further, he is not just alive, but *life-giving,* a source of life for others.

15, 49: *We shall also bear the image:* although it has less manuscript support, this reading better fits the context's emphasis on futurity and the transforming action of God; on future transformation as conformity to the image of the Son, cf Rom

8, 29; Phil 3, 21. The majority reading, "let us bear the image," suggests that the image of the heavenly man is already present and exhorts us to conform to it.

15, 50-57: These verses, an answer to the first question of v 35, explain theologically how the change of properties from one image to another will take place: God has the power to transform, and he will exercise it.

15, 50-53: *Flesh and blood . . . corruption:* living persons and the corpses of the dead, respectively. In both cases, the gulf between creatures and God is too wide to be bridged unless God himself transforms us.

15, 51-52: *A mystery:* the last moment in God's plan is disclosed; cf the notes on 1 Cor 2, 1.7-10a. The final trumpet and the awakening of the dead are stock details of the apocalyptic scenario. *We shall not all fall asleep:* Paul expected that some of his contemporaries might still be alive at Christ's return; after the death of Paul and his whole generation, copyists altered this statement in various ways. *We will all be changed:* the statement extends to all Christians, for Paul is not directly speaking about anyone else. Whether they have died before the end or happen still to be alive, all must be transformed.

15, 54-55: *Death is swallowed up in victory:* scripture itself predicts death's overthrow. *O death:* in his prophetic vision Paul may be making Hosea's words his own, or imagining this cry of triumph on the lips of the risen church.

15, 56: *The sting of death is sin:* an explanation of Hosea's metaphor. Death, scorpion-like, is equipped with a sting, sin, by which it injects its poison. Christ defeats sin, the cause of death (Gn 3, 19; Rom 5, 12).

VI. CONCLUSION

CHAPTER 16

The Collection.* [1] Now in regard to the collection* for the holy ones, you also should do as I ordered the churches of Galatia.[v] [2] On the first day of the week each of you should set aside and save whatever he can afford, so that collections will not be going on when I come. [3] And when I arrive, I shall send those whom you have approved with letters of recommendation to take your gracious gift to Jerusalem. [4] If it seems fitting that I should go also,* they will go with me.

Paul's Travel Plans.* [5] I shall come to you after I pass through Macedonia (for I am going to pass through Macedonia),[w] [6] and perhaps I shall stay or even spend the winter with you, so that you may send me on my way wherever I may go. [7] For I do not wish to see you now just in passing, but I hope to spend some time with you, if the Lord permits.[x] [8] I shall stay in Ephesus[y] until Pentecost,* [9] because a door has opened for me wide and productive for work, but there are many opponents.[z]

[10] If Timothy comes, see that he is without fear in your company, for he is doing the work of the Lord just as I am.[a] [11] Therefore, no one should disdain him.

Rather, send him on his way in peace that he may come to me, for I am expecting him with the brothers. [12] Now in regard to our brother Apollos, I urged him strongly to go to you with the brothers, but it was not at all his will that he go now. He will go when he has an opportunity.[b]

Exhortation and Greetings. [13] Be on your guard, stand firm in the faith, be courageous, be strong. [14] Your every act should be done with love.

[15] I urge you, brothers—you know that the household of Stephanas[c] is the firstfruits of Achaia and that they have devoted themselves to the service of the holy ones—[16] be subordinate to such people and to everyone who works and toils with them. [17] I rejoice in the arrival of Stephanas, Fortunatus, and Achaicus, because they made up for your absence, [18] for they refreshed my spirit as well as yours. So give recognition to such people.[d]

[19] * The churches of Asia send you greetings. Aquila and Prisca together with the church at their house send you many greetings in the Lord.[e] [20] All the brothers greet you. Greet one another with a holy kiss.[f]

[21] I, Paul, write you this greeting in my own hand.[g] [22] If anyone does not love the Lord, let him be accursed.* *Marana tha*.[h] [23] The grace of the Lord Jesus be with you. [24] My love to all of you in Christ Jesus.[i]

v Acts 24, 17; Rom 15, 25-32; 2 Cor 8-9; Gal 2, 10.—w Acts 19, 21; Rom 15, 26; 2 Cor 1, 15-16.—x Acts 18, 21.—y 1 Cor 15, 32; Acts 18, 19; 19, 1-10.—z Acts 14, 27; 2 Cor 2, 12.—a 1 Cor 4, 17; Acts 16, 1; 19, 22; Phil 2, 19-23.—b 1 Cor 1, 12; 3, 4-6.22; Acts 18, 24-28.—c 1 Cor 1, 16.—d 1 Thes 5, 12-13.—e Acts 18, 2.18.26; Rom 16, 3-5.—f Rom 16, 16; 2 Cor 13, 12; 1 Thes 5, 26; 1 Pt 5, 14.—g Gal 6, 11; Col 4, 18; 2 Thes 3, 17.—h 1 Cor 12, 3; Rom 9, 3; Gal 1, 8-9; Rv 22, 20.—i Rom 16, 20.

16, 1-4: This paragraph contains our earliest evidence for a project that became a major undertaking of Paul's ministry. The collection for the church at Jerusalem was a symbol in his mind for the unity of Jewish and Gentile Christianity. Cf Gal 2, 10; Rom 15, 25-29; 2 Cor 8—9 and the notes to this last passage.

16, 1: *In regard to the collection:* it has already begun in Galatia and Macedonia (cf 2 Cor 8), and presumably he has already instructed the Corinthians about its purpose.

16, 4: *That I should go also:* presumably Paul delivered the collection on his final visit to Jerusalem; cf Rom 15, 25-32; Acts 24, 14.

16, 5-12: The travel plans outlined here may not have materialized precisely as Paul intended; cf 2 Cor 1, 8—2, 13; 7, 4-16.

16, 8: *In Ephesus until Pentecost:* this tells us the place from which he wrote the letter and suggests he may have composed it about Easter time (cf 1 Cor 5, 7-8).

16, 19-24: These paragraphs conform to the normal epistolary conclusion, but their language is overlaid with liturgical coloration as well. The *greetings* of the Asian churches are probably to be read, along with the letter, in the liturgy at Corinth, and the union of the church is to be expressed by *a holy kiss* (19-20). Paul adds to this his own greeting (21) and blessings (23-24).

16, 22: *Accursed:* literally, "anathema." This expression (cf 1 Cor 12, 3) is a formula for exclusion from the community; it may imply here a call to self-examination before celebration of the Eucharist, in preparation for the Lord's coming and judgment (cf 1 Cor 11, 17-34). *Marana tha:* an Aramaic expression, probably used in the early Christian liturgy. As understood here ("O Lord, come!"), it is a prayer for the early return of Christ. If the Aramaic words are divided differently *(Maran atha,* "Our Lord has come"), it becomes a credal declaration. The former interpretation is supported by what appears to be a Greek equivalent of this acclamation in Rv 22, 20: "Amen. Come, Lord Jesus!"

THE SECOND LETTER TO THE CORINTHIANS

INTRODUCTION

The Second Letter to the Corinthians is the most personal of all of Paul's extant writings, and it reveals much about his character. In it he deals with one or more crises that have arisen in the Corinthian church. The confrontation with these problems caused him to reflect deeply on his relationship with the community and to speak about it frankly. One moment he is venting his feelings of frustration and uncertainty, the next he is pouring out his relief and affection. The importance of the issues at stake between them calls forth from him an enormous effort of personal persuasion, as well as doctrinal considerations that are of great value for us. Paul's ability to produce profound theological foundations for what may at first sight appear to be rather commonplace circumstances is perhaps nowhere better exemplified than in Second Corinthians. The emotional tone of the letter, its lack of order, and our ignorance of some of its background do not make it easy to follow, but it amply repays the effort required of the reader.

Second Corinthians is rich and varied in content. The interpretation of Exodus in chapter 3, for instance, offers a striking example of early apologetic use of the Old Testament. Paul's discussion of the collection in chs 8-9 contains a theology of sharing of possessions, of community of goods among Christian churches, which is both balanced and sensitive. Furthermore, the closing chapters provide an illustration of early Christian invective and polemic, because the conflict with intruders forces Paul to assert his authority. But in those same chapters Paul articulates the vision and sense of values that animate his own apostolate, revealing his faith that Jesus' passion and resurrection are the pattern for all Christian life and expressing a spirituality of ministry unsurpassed in the New Testament.

The letter is remarkable for its rhetoric. Paul falls naturally into the style and argumentation of contemporary philosophic preachers, employing with ease the stock devices of the "diatribe." By a barrage of questions, by challenges both serious and ironic, by paradox heaped upon paradox, even by insults hurled at his opponents, he strives to awaken in his hearers a true sense of values and an appropriate response. All his argument centers on the destiny of Jesus, in which a paradoxical reversal of values is revealed. But Paul appeals to his own personal experience as well. In passages of great rhetorical power (4, 7-15; 6, 3-10; 11, 21-29; 12, 5-10; 13, 3-4) he enumerates the circumstances of his ministry and the tribulations he has had to endure for Jesus and the gospel, in the hope of illustrating the pattern of Jesus' existence in his own and of drawing the Corinthians into a reappraisal of the values they cherish. Similar passages in the same style in his other letters (cf especially Rom 8, 31-39; 1 Cor 1, 26-31; 4, 6-21; 9, 1-27; 13, 1-13; Phil 4, 10-19) confirm Paul's familiarity with contemporary rhetoric and demonstrate how effectively it served to express his vision of Christian life and ministry.

Second Corinthians was occasioned by events and problems that developed after Paul's first letter reached Corinth. We have no information about these circumstances except what is contained in the letter itself, which of course supposes that they are known to the readers. Consequently the reconstruction of the letter's background is an uncertain enterprise about which there is not complete agreement.

The letter deals principally with these three topics: (1) a crisis between Paul and the Corinthians, occasioned at least partially by changes in his travel plans (1, 12—2, 13), and the successful resolution of that crisis (7, 5-16); (2) further directives and encouragement in regard to the collection for the church in Jerusalem (8, 1—9, 15); (3) the definition and defense of Paul's ministry as an apostle. Paul's reflections on this matter are oc-

265

casioned by visitors from other churches who passed through Corinth, missionaries who differed from Paul in a variety of ways, both in theory and in practice. Those differences led to comparisons. Either the visitors themselves or some of the local church members appear to have sown confusion among the Corinthians with regard to Paul's authority or his style, or both. Paul deals at length with aspects of this situation in 2, 14—7, 4 and again in 10, 1—13, 10, though the manner of treatment and the thrust of the argument differ in each of these sections.

Scholars have noticed a lack of continuity in this document. For example, the long section of 2, 14—7, 4 seems abruptly spliced into the narrative of a crisis and its resolution. Identical or similar topics, moreover, seem to be treated several times during the letter (compare 2, 14—7, 4 with 10, 1—13, 10, and 8, 1-24 with 9, 1-15). Many judge, therefore, that this letter as it stands incorporates several briefer letters sent to Corinth over a certain span of time. If this is so, then Paul himself or, more likely, some other editor clearly took care to gather those letters together and impose some literary unity upon the collection, thus producing the document that has come down to us as the Second Letter to the Corinthians. Others continue to regard it as a single letter, attributing its inconsistencies to changes of perspective in Paul that may have been occasioned by the arrival of fresh news from Corinth during its composition. The letter, or at least some sections of it, appears to have been composed in Macedonia (2, 12-13; 7, 5-6; 8, 1-4; 9, 2-4). It is generally dated about the autumn of A.D. 57; if it is a compilation, of course, the various parts may have been separated by intervals of at least some months.

The principal divisions of the Second Letter to the Corinthians are the following:

I. ADDRESS

CHAPTER 1

Greeting. [1] * Paul, an apostle of Christ Jesus by the will of God, and Timothy our brother, to the church of God that is in Corinth, with all the holy ones throughout Achaia: [a] [2] grace to you and peace from God our Father and the Lord Jesus Christ.

Thanksgiving. [3] [b] Blessed be the God and Father of our Lord Jesus Christ, the Father of compassion and God of all encouragement,* [4] who encourages us in our every affliction, so that we may be able to encourage those who are in any affliction with the encouragement with which we ourselves are encouraged by God. [c] [5] For as Christ's sufferings overflow to us, so

through Christ* does our encouragement also overflow. [6] If we are afflicted, it is for your encouragement and salvation; if we are encouraged, it is for your encouragement, which enables you to endure the

a Eph 1, 1; Col 1, 1 / 2 Cor 1, 19; Acts 16 / Rom 1, 7; 1 Cor 1, 2.—b 1 Cor 15, 24; Eph 1, 3; 1 Pt 1, 3 / Rom 15, 5.—c 2 Cor 7, 6-7.13; 1 Thes 3, 6-8; 2 Thes 2, 16.

1, 1-11: The opening follows the usual Pauline form, except that the thanksgiving takes the form of a doxology or glorification of God (3). This introduces a meditation on the experience of suffering and encouragement shared by Paul and the Corinthians (4-7), drawn, at least in part, from Paul's reflections on a recent affliction (8-10). The section ends with a modified and delayed allusion to thanksgiving (11).

1, 3: *God of all encouragement:* Paul expands a standard Jewish blessing so as to state the theme of the paragraph. The theme of "encouragement" or "consolation" *(paraklēsis)* occurs ten times in this opening, against a background formed by multiple references to "affliction" and "suffering."

1, 5: *Through Christ:* the Father of compassion is the Father of our Lord Jesus (3); Paul's sufferings and encouragement (or "consolation") are experienced in union with Christ. Cf Lk 2, 25: the "consolation of Israel" is Jesus himself.

same sufferings that we suffer. [7]Our hope for you is firm, for we know that as you share in the sufferings, you also share in the encouragement.*

[8]We do not want you to be unaware, brothers, of the affliction that came to us in the province of Asia;* we were utterly weighed down beyond our strength, so that we despaired even of life.[d] [9]Indeed, we had accepted within ourselves the sentence of death,* that we might trust not in ourselves but in God who raises the dead.[e] [10]He rescued us from such great danger of death, and he will continue to rescue us; in him we have put our hope [that] he will also rescue us again,[f] [11]as you help us with prayer, so that thanks may be given by many on our behalf for the gift granted us through the prayers of many.[g]

II. THE CRISIS BETWEEN PAUL AND THE CORINTHIANS
A. Past Relationships*

Paul's Sincerity and Constancy. [12] * For our boast is this, the testimony of our conscience that we have conducted ourselves in the world, and especially toward you, with the simplicity and sincerity of God, [and] not by human wisdom but by the grace of God. [13]For we write you nothing but what you can read and understand, and I hope that you will understand completely, [14]as you have come to understand us partially, that we are your boast as you also are ours, on the day of [our] Lord Jesus.[h]

[15]With this confidence I formerly intended to come* to you so that you might receive a double favor, [16]namely, to go by way of you to Macedonia, and then to come to you again on my return from Macedonia, and have you send me on my way to Judea.[i] [17]So when I intended this, did I act lightly?* Or do I make my plans according to human considerations, so that with me it is "yes, yes" and "no, no"?[j] [18]As God is faithful,* our word to you is not "yes" and "no." [19]For the Son of God, Jesus Christ, who was proclaimed to you by us, Silvanus and Timothy and me, was not "yes" and "no," but "yes" has been in him.[k] [20]For however many are the promises of God, their Yes is in him;[l] therefore, the Amen from us also goes through him to God for glory. [21] * But the one who gives us security with you in Christ and who anointed us is God;[m] [22]he has also put his seal upon us and given the Spirit in our hearts as a first installment.[n]

---

d Acts 20, 18-19; 1 Cor 15, 32.—e 2 Cor 4, 7-11; Rom 4, 17.—f 2 Tm 4, 18.—g 2 Cor 4, 15; 9, 12.—h Phil 2, 16; 1 Thes 2, 19-20.—i 1 Cor 16, 5-9; Acts 19, 21.—j Mt 5, 37; Jas 5, 12.—k Acts 16, 1-3; 1 Thes 1, 1; 2 Thes 1, 1.—l 1 Cor 14, 16; Rv 3, 14.—m 1 Jn 2, 20.27.—n Eph 1, 13-14; 4, 30 / 2 Cor 5, 5; Rom 5, 5; 8, 16.23.

1, 7: *You also share in the encouragement:* the eschatological reversal of affliction and encouragement that Christians expect (cf Mt 5, 4; Lk 6, 24) permits some present experience of reversal in the Corinthians' case, as in Paul's.

1, 8: *Asia:* a Roman province in western Asia Minor, the capital of which was Ephesus.

1, 9-10: *The sentence of death:* it is unclear whether Paul is alluding to a physical illness or to an external threat to life. The result of the situation was to produce an attitude of faith in God alone. *God who raises the dead:* rescue is the constant pattern of God's activity; his final act of encouragement is the resurrection.

1, 12—2, 13: The autobiographical remarks about the crisis in Asia Minor lead into consideration of a crisis that has arisen between Paul and the Corinthians. Paul will return to this question, after a long digression, in 2 Cor 7, 5-16. Both of these sections deal with travel plans Paul had made, changes in the plans, alternative measures adopted, a breach that opened between him and the community, and finally a reconciliation between them.

1, 12-14: Since Paul's own conduct will be under discussion here, he prefaces the section with a statement about his habitual behavior and attitude toward the community. He protests his openness, single-mindedness, and conformity to God's grace; he hopes that his relationship with them will be marked by mutual understanding and pride, which will constantly increase until it reaches its climax at the judgment. Two references to boasting

frame this paragraph (12.14), the first appearances of a theme that will be important in the letter, especially in chs 10-13; the term is used in a positive sense here (cf the note on 1 Cor 1, 29-31).

1, 15: *I formerly intended to come:* this plan reads like a revision of the one mentioned in 1 Cor 16, 5. Not until 2 Cor 1, 23—2, 1 will Paul tell us something his original readers already knew, that he has canceled one or the other of these projected visits.

1, 17: *Did I act lightly?:* the subsequent change of plans casts suspicion on the original intention, creating the impression that Paul is vacillating and inconsistent or that *human considerations* keep dictating shifts in his goals and projects (cf the counterclaim of 12). *"Yes, yes" and "no, no":* stating something and denying it in the same or the next breath; being of two minds at once, or from one moment to the next.

1, 18-22: *As God is faithful:* unable to deny the change in plans, Paul nonetheless asserts the firmness of the original plan and claims a profound constancy in his life and work. He grounds his defense in God himself, who is firm and reliable; this quality can also be predicated in various ways of those who are associated with him. Christ, Paul, and the Corinthians all participate in analogous ways in the constancy of God. A number of the terms here, which appear related only conceptually in Greek or English, would be variations of the same root, *'mn,* in a Semitic language, and thus naturally associated in a Semitic mind, such as Paul's. These include the words *yes* (17-20), *faithful* (18), *Amen* (20), *gives us security* (21), *faith, stand firm* (24).

1, 21-22: The commercial terms *gives us security, seal, first installment* are here used analogously to refer to the process of initiation into the Christian life, perhaps specifically to baptism. The Spirit is the *first installment* or "down payment" of the full messianic benefits that God guarantees to Christians. Cf Eph 1, 13-14.

Paul's Change of Plan. [23] o But I call upon God as witness, on my life, that it is to spare you that I have not yet gone to Corinth.* [24] Not that we lord it over your faith; rather, we work together for your joy, for you stand firm in the faith.

CHAPTER 2

[1] For I decided not to come to you again in painful circumstances. [2] For if I inflict pain upon you, then who is there to cheer me except the one pained by me? [3] And I wrote as I did* so that when I came I might not be pained by those in whom I should have rejoiced, confident about all of you that my joy is that of all of you. [4] For out of much affliction and anguish of heart I wrote to you with many tears, not that you might be pained but that you might know the abundant love I have for you.

The Offender.* [5] If anyone has caused pain, he has caused it not to me, but in some measure (not to exaggerate) to all of you. [6] This punishment by the majority is enough for such a person, [7] so that on the contrary you should forgive and encourage him instead, or else the person may be overwhelmed by excessive pain.*p* [8] Therefore, I urge you to reaffirm your love for him. [9] For this is why I wrote, to know your proven character, whether you were obedient in everything.*q* [10] Whomever you forgive anything, so do I. For indeed what I have forgiven, if I have forgiven anything, has been for you in the presence of Christ, [11] so that we might not be taken advantage of by Satan, for we are not unaware of his purposes.*r*

Paul's Anxiety.* [12] When I went to Troas for the gospel of Christ, although a door was opened for me in the Lord,*s* [13] I had no relief in my spirit because I did not find my brother Titus.*t* So I took leave of them and went on to Macedonia.*

B. Paul's Ministry*

Ministers of a New Covenant. [14] * But thanks be to God,* who always leads us in triumph in Christ* and manifests through

---

o 2 Cor 13, 2.—p Col 3, 13.—q 2 Cor 7, 15.—r Eph 4, 27.—s Acts 16, 8.—t 2 Cor 7, 6; 1 Tm 1, 3.

1, 23-24: *I have not yet gone to Corinth:* some suppose that Paul received word of some affair in Corinth, which he decided to regulate by letter even before the first of his projected visits (cf 2 Cor 1, 16). Others conjecture that he did pay the first visit, was offended there (cf 2 Cor 2, 5), returned to Ephesus, and sent a letter (2 Cor 2, 3-9) in place of the second visit. The expressions *to spare you* (23) and *work together for your joy* (24) introduce the major themes of the next two paragraphs, which are remarkable for insistent repetition of key words and ideas. These form two clusters of terms in the English translation: (1) cheer, rejoice, encourage, joy; (2) pain, affliction, anguish. These clusters reappear when Paul resumes treatment of this subject in 2 Cor 7, 5-16.

2, 3-4: *I wrote as I did:* we learn for the first time about the sending of a letter in place of the proposed visit. Paul mentions the letter in passing, but emphasizes his motivation in sending it: to avoid being saddened by them (cf 2 Cor 2, 1), and to help realize the depth of his love. Another motive will be added in 2 Cor 7, 12: to bring to light their own concern for him. *With many tears:* it has been suggested that we may have all or part of this "tearful letter" somewhere in the Corinthian correspondence, either in 1 Cor 5 (the case of the incestuous man), or in 1 Cor as a whole, or in 2 Cor 10—13. None of these hypotheses is entirely convincing. See the note on 2 Cor 13, 1.

2, 5-11: The nature of the *pain* (5) is unclear, though some believe an individual at Corinth rejected Paul's authority, thereby scandalizing many in the community. In any case, action has been taken, and Paul judges the measures adequate to right the situation (6). The follow-up directives he now gives are entirely positive: forgive, encourage, love. *Overwhelmed* (7): a vivid metaphor (literally "swallowed") that Paul employs positively at 2 Cor 5, 4 and in 1 Cor 15, 54 (7). It is often used to describe satanic activity (cf 1 Pt 5, 8); note the reference to Satan here in v 11.

2, 12-13: *I had no relief:* Paul does not explain the reason for his anxiety until he resumes the thread of his narrative at 2 Cor 7, 5: he was waiting to hear how the Corinthians would respond to his letter. Since 2 Cor 7, 5-16 describes their response in entirely positive terms, we never learn in detail why he found it necessary to defend and justify his change of plans, as in 2 Cor 1, 15-24. Was this portion of the letter written before the arrival of Titus with his good news (2 Cor 7, 6-7)?

2, 13: *Macedonia:* a Roman province in northern Greece.

2, 14—7, 4: This section constitutes a digression within the narrative of the crisis and its resolution (2 Cor 1, 12—2, 13 and 2 Cor 7, 5-16). The main component (2 Cor 2, 14—6, 10) treats the nature of Paul's ministry and his qualifications for it; this material bears some similarity to the defense of his ministry in chs 10-13, but it may well come from a period close to the crisis. This is followed by a supplementary block of material quite different in character and tone (2 Cor 6, 14—7, 1). These materials may have been brought together into their present position during final editing of the letter; appeals to the Corinthians link them to one another (2 Cor 6, 11-13) and lead back to the interrupted narrative (2 Cor 7, 2-4).

2, 14—6, 10: The question of Paul's adequacy (2 Cor 2, 16; cf 2 Cor 3, 5) and his credentials (2 Cor 3, 1-2) has been raised. Paul responds by an extended treatment of the nature of his ministry. It is a ministry of glory (2 Cor 3, 7—4, 6), of life (2 Cor 4, 7—5, 10), of reconciliation (2 Cor 5, 11—6, 10).

2, 14-16a: The initial statement plunges us abruptly into another train of thought. Paul describes his personal existence and his function as a preacher in two powerful images (14) that constitute a prelude to the development to follow.

2, 14a: *Leads us in triumph in Christ:* this metaphor of a festive parade in honor of a conquering military hero can suggest either a positive sharing in Christ's triumph or an experience of defeat, being led in captivity and submission (cf 2 Cor 4, 8-11; 1 Cor 4, 9). Paul is probably aware of the ambiguity, as he is in the case of the next metaphor.

us the odor of the knowledge of him* in every place. [15] For we are the aroma of Christ for God among those who are being saved and among those who are perishing,[u] [16] to the latter an odor of death that leads to death, to the former an odor of life that leads to life. Who is qualified* for this? [17] For we are not like the many who trade on the word of God; but as out of sincerity, indeed as from God and in the presence of God, we speak in Christ.[v]

CHAPTER 3

[1] [w] Are we beginning to commend ourselves again? Or do we need, as some do, letters of recommendation to you or from you?* [2] You are our letter,* written on our hearts, known and read by all, [3] [x] shown to be a letter of Christ administered by us, written not in ink but by the Spirit of the living God, not on tablets of stone but on tablets that are hearts of flesh.*

---

u 2 Cor 4, 3; 1 Cor 1, 18.—v 2 Cor 4, 2; 1 Cor 5, 8.—w Acts 18, 27; Rom 16, 1; 1 Cor 16, 3.—x Ex 24, 12; 31, 18; 32, 15-19 / Jer 31, 33; Ez 11, 19; 36, 26-27.—y Jn 3, 27.—z Eph 3, 7 / Jer 31, 31-34.—a Ex 34, 29-35.

2, 14b-16a: *The odor of the knowledge of him:* incense was commonly used in triumphal processions. The metaphor suggests the gradual diffusion of the knowledge of God through the apostolic preaching. *The aroma of Christ:* the image shifts from the fragrance Paul diffuses to the aroma that he is. Paul is probably thinking of the "sweet odor" of the sacrifices in the Old Testament (e.g., Gn 8, 21; Ex 29, 18) and perhaps of the metaphor of wisdom as a sweet odor (Sir 24, 15). *Death . . . life:* the aroma of Christ that comes to them through Paul is perceived differently by various classes of people. To some his preaching and his life (cf 1 Cor 1, 17—2, 6) are perceived as *death*, and the effect is death for them; others perceive him, despite appearances, as *life*, and the effect is life for them. This fragrance thus produces a separation and a judgment (cf the function of the "light" in John's gospel).

2, 16b-17: *Qualified:* Paul may be echoing either the self-satisfied claims of other preachers or their charges about Paul's deficiencies. No one is really qualified, but the apostle contrasts himself with those who dilute or falsify the preaching for personal advantage and insists on his totally good conscience: his ministry is from God, and he has exercised it with fidelity and integrity (cf 2 Cor 3, 5-6).

3, 1: Paul seems to allude to certain preachers who pride themselves on their written credentials. Presumably they reproach him for not possessing similar credentials and compel him to spell out his own qualifications (2 Cor 4, 2; 5, 12; 6, 4). The Corinthians themselves should have performed this function for Paul (2 Cor 5, 12; cf 2 Cor 12, 11). Since he is forced to find something that can recommend him, he points to them: their very existence constitutes his *letter* of recommendation (1-2). Others who engage in self-commendation will also be mentioned in 2 Cor 10, 12-18.

3, 2-3: Mention of "letters of recommendation" generates a series of metaphors in which Paul plays on the word "letter": (1) the community is Paul's letter of recommendation (2a); (2) they are a letter engraved on his affections for all to see and read (2b); (3) they are a letter from Christ that Paul merely delivers (3a); (4) they are a letter written by the Spirit on the tablets of human hearts (3b). One image dissolves into another.

[4] * Such confidence we have through Christ toward God. [5] Not that of ourselves we are qualified to take credit for anything as coming from us; rather, our qualification comes from God,[y] [6] who has indeed qualified us as ministers of a new covenant, not of letter but of spirit;[z] for the letter brings death, but the Spirit gives life.*

Contrast with the Old Covenant. [7] * Now if the ministry of death,* carved in letters on stone, was so glorious that the Israelites could not look intently at the face of Moses because of its glory that was going to fade,[a] [8] how much more* will the ministry of the Spirit be glorious? [9] For if the ministry of condemnation was glorious, the ministry of righteousness will abound much more in glory. [10] Indeed, what was endowed with glory has come to have no glory in this respect because of the glory that surpasses it.

3, 3b: This verse contrasts Paul's letter with those *written . . . in ink* (like the credentials of other preachers) and those *written . . . on tablets of stone* (like the law of Moses). These contrasts suggest that the other preachers may have claimed special relationship with Moses. If they were Judaizers zealous for the Mosaic law, that would explain the detailed contrast between the old and the new covenants (2 Cor 3, 6; 4, 7—6, 10). If they were charismatics who claimed Moses as their model, that would explain the extended treatment of Moses himself and his glory (2 Cor 3, 7—4, 6). *Hearts of flesh:* cf Ezekiel's contrast between the heart of flesh that the Spirit gives and the heart of stone that it replaces (Ez 36, 26); the context is covenant renewal and purification that makes observance of the law possible.

3, 4-6: These verses resume 2 Cor 2, 1—3, 3. Paul's confidence (4) is grounded in his sense of God-given mission (2 Cor 2, 17), the specifics of which are described in vv 1-3. Verses 5-6 return to the question of his qualifications (2 Cor 2, 16), attributing them entirely to God. Verse 6 further spells out the situation described in v 3b and "names" it: Paul is living within a *new covenant*, characterized by the Spirit, which *gives life*. The usage of a *new covenant* is derived from Jer 31, 31-33, a passage that also speaks of writing on the heart; cf 2 Cor 3, 2.

3, 6b: This verse serves as a topic sentence for 2 Cor 3, 7—6, 10. For the contrast between *letter* and *spirit*, cf Rom 2, 29; 7, 5-6.

3, 7—4, 6: Paul now develops the contrast enunciated in 2 Cor 3, 6b in terms of the relative glory of the two covenants, insisting on the greater glory of the new. His polemic seems directed against individuals who appeal to the glorious Moses and fail to perceive any comparable glory either in Paul's life as an apostle or in the gospel he preaches. He asserts in response that Christians have a glory of their own that far surpasses that of Moses.

3, 7: *The ministry of death:* from his very first words, Paul describes the Mosaic covenant and ministry from the viewpoint of their limitations. They lead to *death* rather than life (6-7; cf 2 Cor 4, 7—5, 10), to *condemnation* rather than reconciliation (9; cf 2 Cor 5, 11 —6, 10). *Was so glorious:* the basic text to which Paul alludes is Ex 34, 29-35, to which his opponents have undoubtedly laid claim. *Going to fade:* Paul concedes the glory of Moses' covenant and ministry, but grants them only temporary significance.

3, 8-11: *How much more:* the argument "from the less to the greater" is repeated three times (8.9.11). Verse 10 expresses another point of view: the difference in glory is so great that only the new covenant and ministry can properly be called "glorious" at all.

11 For if what was going to fade was glorious, how much more will what endures be glorious.

12 Therefore, since we have such hope,* we act very boldly 13 and not like Moses,* who put a veil over his face so that the Israelites could not look intently at the cessation of what was fading. 14 Rather, their thoughts were rendered dull, for to this present day* the same veil remains unlifted when they read the old covenant, because through Christ it is taken away. 15 To this day, in fact, whenever Moses is read, a veil lies over their hearts,*b* 16 but whenever a person turns to the Lord the veil is removed.*c* 17 Now the Lord is the Spirit,* and where the Spirit of the Lord is, there is freedom. 18 * All of us, gazing with unveiled face on the glory of the Lord, are being transformed into the same image from glory to glory, as from the Lord who is the Spirit.*d*

CHAPTER 4

Integrity in the Ministry. 1 * Therefore, since we have this ministry through the mercy shown us, we are not discouraged. 2 Rather, we have renounced shameful, hidden things; not acting deceitfully or falsifying the word of God, but by the open declaration of the truth we commend ourselves to everyone's conscience in the sight of God.*e* 3 And even though our gospel is veiled,* it is veiled for those who are perishing,*f* 4 in whose case the god of this age has blinded the minds of the unbelievers, so that they may not see the light of the gospel of the glory of Christ, who is the image of God.*g* 5 For we do not preach ourselves* but Jesus Christ as Lord, and ourselves as your slaves for the sake of Jesus. 6 * For God who said, "Let light shine out of darkness," has shone in our hearts to bring to light the knowledge of the glory of God on the face of [Jesus] Christ.*h*

---

b Rom 11, 7-10.—c Ex 34, 34.—d Rom 8, 29-30; 12, 2; Gal 4, 19; Phil 3, 10.20-21 / 2 Cor 4, 4-6; 1 Cor 15, 49; Col 1, 15; 3, 9-11; 1 Jn 3, 2.—e 2 Cor 2, 17; 1 Thes 2, 4-7.—f 2 Cor 2, 15-16; 2 Thes 2, 10.—g Jn 12, 31-36 / 1 Tm 1, 11.—h Gn 1, 3; Is 9, 1; Acts 26, 13-23; Gal 1, 15-16 / Jn 8, 12; Heb 1, 3.

3, 12: *Such hope:* the glory is not yet an object of experience, but that does not lessen Paul's confidence. *Boldly:* the term *parrēsia* expresses outspoken declaration of Christian conviction (cf 2 Cor 4, 1-2). Paul has nothing to hide and no reason for timidity.

3, 13-14a: *Not like Moses:* in Exodus Moses veiled his face to protect the Israelites from God's reflected glory. Without impugning Moses' sincerity, Paul attributes another effect to the veil. Since it lies between God's glory and the Israelites, it explains how they could fail to notice the glory disappearing. *Their thoughts were rendered dull:* the problem lay with their understanding. This will be expressed in vv 14b-16 by a shift in the place of the veil: it is no longer over Moses' face but over their perception.

3, 14b-16: The parallelism in these verses makes it necessary to interpret corresponding parts in relation to one another. *To this present day:* this signals the shift of Paul's attention to his contemporaries; his argument is typological, as in 1 Cor 10. The Israelites of Moses' time typify the Jews of Paul's time, and perhaps also Christians of Jewish origin or mentality who may not recognize the temporary character of Moses' glory. *When they read the old covenant:* the lasting dullness prevents proper appraisal of Moses' person and covenant. When his writings are read in the synagogue, a veil still impedes their understanding. *Through Christ:* i.e., in the new covenant. *Whenever a person turns to the Lord:* Moses in Exodus appeared before God without the veil and gazed on his face unprotected. Paul applies that passage to converts to Christianity: when they turn to the Lord fully and authentically, the impediment to their understanding is removed.

3, 17: *The Lord is the Spirit:* the "Lord" to whom the Christian turns (16) is the Spirit of whom Paul has been speaking, the life-giving Spirit of the living God (6.8), the inaugurator of the new covenant and ministry, who is also the Spirit of Christ. *The Spirit of the Lord:* the Lord here is the living God (3), but there may also be an allusion to Christ as Lord (14.16). *Freedom:* i.e., from the ministry of death (7) and the covenant that condemned (9).

3, 18: Another application of the veil image. *All of us . . . with unveiled face:* Christians (Israelites from whom the veil has been removed) are like Moses, standing in God's presence, beholding and reflecting his glory. *Gazing:* the verb may also be translated "contemplating as in a mirror"; 2 Cor 4, 6 would suggest that the mirror is Christ himself. *Are being transformed:* elsewhere Paul speaks of transformation, conformity to Jesus, God's image, as a reality of the end time, and even v 12 speaks of the glory as an object of hope. But the life-giving Spirit, the distinctive gift of the new covenant, is already present in the community (cf 2 Cor 1, 22, the "first installment"), and the process of transformation has already begun. *Into the same image:* into the image of God, which is Christ (2 Cor 4, 4).

4, 1-2: A ministry of this sort generates confidence and forthrightness; cf 2 Cor 1, 12-14; 2, 17.

4, 3-4: *Though our gospel is veiled:* the final application of the image. Paul has been reproached either for obscurity in his preaching or for his manner of presenting the gospel. But he confidently asserts that there is no veil over his gospel. If some fail to perceive its light, that is because of unbelief. The veil lies over their eyes (2 Cor 3, 14), a blindness induced by Satan, and a sign that they are headed for destruction (cf 2 Cor 2, 15).

4, 5: *We do not preach ourselves:* the light seen in his gospel is the glory of Christ (4). Far from preaching himself, the preacher should be a transparent medium through whom Jesus is perceived (cf 2 Cor 4, 10-11). *Your slaves:* Paul draws attention away from individuals as such and toward their role in relation to God, Christ, and the community; cf 1 Cor 3, 5; 4, 1.

4, 6: Autobiographical allusion to the episode at Damascus clarifies the origin and nature of Paul's service; cf Acts 9, 1-19; 22, 3-16; 26, 2-18. *"Let light shine out of darkness":* Paul seems to be thinking of Gn 1, 3 and presenting his apostolic ministry as a new creation. There may also be an allusion to Is 9, 1, suggesting his prophetic calling as servant of the Lord and light to the nations; cf Is 42, 6.16; 49, 6; 60, 1-2, and the use of light imagery in Acts 26, 13-23. *To bring to light the knowledge:* Paul's role in the process of revelation, expressed at the beginning under the image of the odor and aroma (2 Cor 2, 14-15), is restated now, at the end of this first moment of the development, in the imagery of light and glory (3-6).

The Paradox of the Ministry. 7 * But we hold this treasure* in earthen vessels, that the surpassing power may be of God and not from us. 8 * We are afflicted in every way, but not constrained; perplexed, but not driven to despair;*i* 9 persecuted, but not abandoned; struck down, but not destroyed; 10 * always carrying about in the body the dying of Jesus, so that the life of Jesus may also be manifested in our body.*j* 11 For we who live are constantly being given up to death for the sake of Jesus, so that the life of Jesus may be manifested in our mortal flesh. *k*

12 * So death is at work in us, but life in you. 13 * Since, then, we have the same spirit of faith, according to what is written, "I believed, therefore I spoke," we too believe and therefore speak,*l* 14 knowing that the one who raised the Lord Jesus will raise us also with Jesus and place us with you in his presence.*m* 15 Everything indeed is for you, so that the grace bestowed in abundance on more and more people may cause the thanksgiving to overflow for the glory of God.*n*

16 * Therefore, we are not discouraged;* rather, although our outer self is wasting away, our inner self is being renewed day by day.*o* 17 For this momentary light affliction is producing for us an eternal weight of glory beyond all comparison,*p* 18 as we look not to what is seen but to what is unseen; for what is seen is transitory, but what is unseen is eternal.*q*

CHAPTER 5

Our Future Destiny. 1 *r* For we know that if our earthly dwelling,* a tent, should be destroyed, we have a building from God, a dwelling not made with hands, eternal in heaven. 2 * For in this tent we groan, longing to be further clothed with our heavenly habitation*s* 3 if indeed, when we have taken it off,* we shall not be found naked. 4 For while we are in this tent we groan and are

2Cor

---

i 2 Cor 6, 4-10; 1 Cor 4, 9-13.—j Col 1, 24.—k Rom 8, 36; 1 Cor 15, 31.—l Ps 116, 10.—m Rom 4, 24-25; 8, 11; 1 Cor 6, 14; 1 Thes 4, 14.—n 2 Cor 1, 11.—o 2 Cor 4, 11.—p Mt 5, 11-12; Rom 8, 18.—q Rom 8, 24-25; Heb 11, 1.—r Is 38, 12 / Col 3, 1-4 / Mk 14, 58; Col 2, 11; Heb 9, 11.24.—s Rom 8, 23 / 1 Cor 15, 51-54.

4, 7—5, 10: Paul now confronts the difficulty that his present existence does not appear glorious at all; it is marked instead by suffering and death. He deals with this by developing the topic already announced in 2 Cor 3, 3.6, asserting his faith in the presence and ultimate triumph of life, in his own and every Christian existence, despite the experience of death.

4, 7: *This treasure:* the glory that he preaches and into which they are being transformed. *In earthen vessels:* the instruments God uses are human and fragile; some imagine small terracotta lamps in which light is carried.

4, 8-9: A catalogue of his apostolic trials and afflictions. Yet in these the negative never completely prevails; there is always some experience of rescue, of salvation.

4, 10-11: Both the negative and the positive sides of the experience are grounded christologically. The logic is similar to that of 2 Cor 1, 3-11. His sufferings are connected with Christ's, and his deliverance is a sign that he is to share in Jesus' resurrection.

4, 12-15: His experience does not terminate in himself, but in others (12.15; cf 2 Cor 1, 4-5). Ultimately, everything is ordered even beyond the community, toward God (15; cf 2 Cor 1, 11).

4, 13-14: Like the Psalmist, Paul clearly proclaims his faith, affirming life within himself despite death (10-11) and the life-giving effect of his experience upon the church (12.14-15). *And place us with you in his presence:* Paul imagines God presenting him and them to Jesus at the parousia and the judgment; cf 2 Cor 11, 2; Rom 14, 10.

4, 16-18: In a series of contrasts Paul explains the extent of his faith in life. Life is not only already present and revealing itself (8-11.16) but will outlast his experience of affliction and dying: it is eternal (17-18).

4, 16: *Not discouraged:* i.e., despite the experience of death. Paul is still speaking of himself personally, but he assumes his faith and attitude will be shared by all Christians. *Our outer self:* the individual subject of ordinary perception and observation, in contrast to the interior and hidden self, which undergoes renewal. *Is being renewed day by day:* this suggests a process that has already begun; cf 2 Cor 3, 18.The renewal already taking place even in Paul's dying is a share in the life of Jesus, but this is recognized only by faith (13.18; 2 Cor 5, 7).

5, 1: *Our earthly dwelling:* the same contrast is restated in the imagery of a dwelling. The language recalls Jesus' saying about the destruction of the temple and the construction of another building *not made with hands* (Mk 14, 58), a prediction later applied to Jesus' own body (Jn 2, 20).

5, 2-5: Verses 2-3 and 4 are largely parallel in structure. *We groan, longing:* see the note on 2 Cor 5, 5. *Clothed with our heavenly habitation:* Paul mixes his metaphors, adding the image of the garment to that of the building. *Further clothed:* the verb means strictly "to put one garment on over another." Paul may desire to put the resurrection body on over his mortal body, without dying; vv 2 and 4 permit this meaning but do not impose it. Or perhaps he imagines the resurrection body as a garment put on over the Christ-garment first received in baptism (Gal 3, 27) and preserved by moral behavior (Rom 13, 12-14; Col 3, 12; cf Mt 22, 11-13). Some support for this interpretation may be found in the context; cf the references to baptism (5), to judgment according to works (10), and to present renewal (2 Cor 4, 16), an idea elsewhere combined with the image of "putting on" a new nature (Eph 4, 22-24; Col 3, 1-5.9-10).

5, 3: *When we have taken it off:* the majority of witnesses read "when we have put it on," i.e., when we have been clothed (in the resurrection body), then we shall not be without a body (naked). This seems tautology, though some understand it to mean: whether we are "found" (by God at the judgment) clothed or naked depends upon whether we have preserved or lost our original investiture in Christ (cf the previous note). In this case to "put it on" does not refer to the resurrection body, but to keeping intact the Christ-garment of baptism. The translation follows the western reading (Codex Bezae, Tertullian), the sense of which is clear: to "take it off" is to shed our mortal body in death, after which we shall be clothed in the resurrection body and hence not "naked" (cf 1 Cor 15, 51-53).

weighed down, because we do not wish to be unclothed* but to be further clothed, so that what is mortal may be swallowed up by life.[t] [5]Now the one who has prepared us for this very thing is God,[u] who has given us the Spirit as a first installment.*

[6] * So we are always courageous, although we know that while we are at home in the body we are away from the Lord, [7]for we walk by faith, not by sight. [8]Yet we are courageous, and we would rather leave the body and go home to the Lord.[v] [9]Therefore, we aspire to please him, whether we are at home or away. [10]For we must all appear* before the judgment seat of Christ, so that each one may receive recompense, according to what he did in the body, whether good or evil.[w]

The Ministry of Reconciliation. [11] * Therefore, since we know the fear of the Lord, we try to persuade others; but we are clearly apparent to God, and I hope we are also apparent to your consciousness.[x] [12]We are not commending ourselves to you again but giving you an opportunity to boast of us, so that you may have something to say to those who boast of external appearance rather than of the heart.[y] [13]For

if we are out of our minds,* it is for God; if we are rational, it is for you. [14] * For the love of Christ impels us, once we have come to the conviction that one died for all; therefore, all have died.[z] [15]He indeed died for all, so that those who live might no longer live for themselves but for him who for their sake died and was raised.[a]

[16]Consequently,* from now on we regard no one according to the flesh; even if we once knew Christ according to the flesh, yet now we know him so no longer. [17] [b] So whoever is in Christ is a new creation: the old things have passed away; behold, new things have come. [18] * And all this is from God, who has reconciled us to himself through Christ and given us the ministry of reconciliation, [19]namely, God was reconciling the world to himself in Christ, not counting their trespasses against them and entrusting to us the message of reconciliation.[c] [20]So we are ambassadors for Christ, as if God were appealing through us. We implore you on behalf of Christ, be reconciled to God.[d] [21]For our sake he made him to be sin who did not know sin,[e] so that we might become the righteousness of God in him.*

t Is 25, 8; 1 Cor 15, 54.—u 2 Cor 1, 22.—v Phil 1, 21-23.—w Mt 16, 27; 25, 31-46; Rom 2, 16; 14, 10-11.—x 2 Cor 1, 12-14.—y 2 Cor 3, 1 / 2 Cor 1, 14; Phil 1, 26.—z Rom 6, 1-6.—a Rom 4, 25; 6, 4-11; 14, 9; Col 3, 3-4.—b Gal 6, 15; Eph 2, 15 / Is 43, 18-21; Rv 21, 5.—c Rom 5, 10-11; Col 1, 20.—d Eph 6, 20; Phlm 9.—e Is 53, 6-9; Gal 3, 13 / Rom 3, 24-26; 1 Cor 1, 30; 1 Pt 2, 24; 1 Jn 3, 5-8.

5, 4: *We do not wish to be unclothed:* a clear allusion to physical death (2 Cor 4, 16; 5, 1). Unlike the Greeks, who found dissolution of the body desirable (cf Socrates), Paul has a Jewish horror of it. He seems to be thinking of the "intermediate period," an interval between death and resurrection. *Swallowed up by life:* cf 1 Cor 15, 54.

5, 5: God has created us for resurrected bodily life and already prepares us for it by the gift of the Spirit in baptism. *The Spirit as a first installment:* the striking parallel to 2 Cor 5, 1-5 in Rom 8, 17-30 describes Christians who have received the "firstfruits" (cf "first installment" here) of the Spirit as "groaning" (cf 2.4 here) for the resurrection, the complete redemption of their bodies. In place of clothing and building, Rom 8 uses other images for the resurrection: adoption and conformity to the image of the Son.

5, 6-9: Tension between present and future is expressed by another spatial image, the metaphor of the country and its citizens. At present we are like citizens in exile or far away from home. The Lord is the distant homeland, believed in but unseen (7).

5, 10: *We must all appear:* the verb is ambiguous: we are scheduled to "appear" for judgment, at which we will be "revealed" as we are (cf 2 Cor 5, 11; 2, 14; 4, 10-11).

5, 11-15: This paragraph is transitional. Paul sums up much that has gone before. Still playing on the term "appearance," he reasserts his transparency before God and the Corinthians, in contrast to the self-commendation, boasting, and preoccupation with externals that characterize some others (cf 2 Cor 1, 12-14; 2, 14; 3, 1; 3, 7—4, 6). Verse 14 recalls 2 Cor 3, 7—4, 6, and sums up 2 Cor 4, 7—5, 10.

5, 13: *Out of our minds:* this verse confirms that a concern for ecstasy and charismatic experience may lie behind the discussion about "glory" in 2 Cor 3, 7—4, 6. Paul also enjoys such experiences but, unlike others, does not make a public display of them or consider them ends in themselves. *Rational:* the Greek virtue *sōphrosynē*, to which Paul alludes, implies reasonableness, moderation, good judgment, self-control.

5, 14-15: These verses echo 2 Cor 4, 14 and resume the treatment of "life despite death" from 2 Cor 4, 7—5, 10.

5, 16-17: *Consequently:* the death of Christ described in vv 14-15 produces a whole new order (17) and a new mode of perception (16). *According to the flesh:* the natural mode of perception, characterized as "fleshly," is replaced by a mode of perception proper to the Spirit. Elsewhere Paul contrasts what Christ looks like according to the old criteria (weakness, powerlessness, folly, death) and according to the new (wisdom, power, life); cf 2 Cor 5, 15.21; 1 Cor 1, 17—3, 3. Similarly, he describes the paradoxical nature of Christian existence, e.g., in 2 Cor 4, 10-11.14. *A new creation:* rabbis used this expression to describe the effect of the entrance of a proselyte or convert into Judaism or of the remission of sins on the Day of Atonement. The new order created *in Christ* is the new covenant (2 Cor 3, 6).

5, 18-21: Paul attempts to explain the meaning of God's action by a variety of different categories; his attention keeps moving rapidly back and forth from God's act to his own ministry as well. *Who has reconciled us to himself:* i.e., he has brought all into oneness. *Not counting their trespasses:* the reconciliation is described as an act of justification (cf "righteousness," 21); this contrasts with the covenant that condemned (2 Cor 3, 8). *The ministry of reconciliation:* Paul's role in the wider picture is described: entrusted with the message of reconciliation (19), he is Christ's ambassador, through whom God appeals (20a). In v 20b Paul acts in the capacity just described.

5, 21: This is a statement of God's purpose, expressed paradoxically in terms of sharing and exchange of attributes. As Christ became our righteousness (1 Cor 1, 30), we become God's righteousness (cf 2 Cor 5, 14-15).

CHAPTER 6

The Experience of the Ministry. 1 * Working together,*f* then, we appeal to you not to receive the grace of God in vain.* 2 For he says:

"In an acceptable time* I heard you,
    and on the day of salvation I helped
      you."*g*

Behold, now is a very acceptable time; behold, now is the day of salvation. 3 *h* We cause no one to stumble* in anything, in order that no fault may be found with our ministry; 4 * on the contrary, in everything we commend ourselves as ministers of God, through much endurance,* in afflictions, hardships, constraints,*i* 5 beatings, imprisonments, riots, labors, vigils, fasts;*j* 6 * by purity, knowledge, patience, kindness, in a holy spirit, in unfeigned love,*k* 7 in truthful speech, in the power of God; with weapons of righteousness at the right and at the left;*l* 8 through glory and dishonor, insult and praise. We are treated as deceivers and yet are truthful;* 9 as unrec-

ognized and yet acknowledged; as dying and behold we live; as chastised and yet not put to death;*m* 10 as sorrowful yet always rejoicing; as poor yet enriching many; as having nothing and yet possessing all things.*n*

11 * We have spoken frankly to you, Corinthians; our heart is open wide. 12 You are not constrained by us; you are constrained by your own affections.*o* 13 As recompense in kind (I speak as to my children), be open yourselves.*p*

Call to Holiness. 14 * Do not be yoked with those who are different, with unbelievers.* For what partnership do righteousness and lawlessness have? Or what fellowship does light have with darkness? 15 What accord has Christ with Beliar? Or what has a believer in common with an unbeliever? 16 *q* What agreement has the temple of God with idols? For we are the temple of the living God; as God said:

"I will live with them and move among
      them,*
    and I will be their God
    and they shall be my people.

2Cor

---

f 1 Cor 3, 9; 1 Thes 3, 2.—g Is 49, 8.—h 1 Cor 9, 12; 10, 32 / 2 Cor 8, 20-21.—i 2 Cor 4, 8-11; 11, 23-27; 1 Cor 4, 9-13.—j Acts 16, 23.—k Gal 5, 22-23.—l 2 Cor 10, 4; Rom 13, 12; Eph 6, 11-17.—m 2 Cor 4, 10-11; Rom 8, 36.—n Rom 8, 32; 1 Cor 3, 21.—o 2 Cor 7, 3.—p Gal 4, 19.—q 1 Cor 10, 20-21 / 1 Cor 3, 16-17; 6, 19 / Ex 25, 8; 29, 45; Lv 26, 12; Jer 31, 1; 32, 38; Ez 37, 27.

6, 1-10: This paragraph is a single long sentence in the Greek, interrupted by the parenthesis of v 2. The one main verb is "we appeal." In this paragraph Paul both exercises his ministry of reconciliation (cf 2 Cor 5, 20) and describes how his ministry is exercised: the "message of reconciliation" (2 Cor 5, 19) is lived existentially in his apostolic experience.

6, 1: *Not to receive . . . in vain:* i.e., conform to the gift of justification and new creation. The context indicates how this can be done concretely: become God's righteousness (2 Cor 5, 21), not live for oneself (2 Cor 5, 15), be reconciled with Paul (2 Cor 6, 11-13; 7, 2-3).

6, 2: *In an acceptable time:* Paul cites the Septuagint text of Is 49, 8; the Hebrew reads "in a time of favor"; it is parallel to "on the day of salvation." *Now:* God is bestowing favor and salvation at this very moment, as Paul is addressing his letter to them.

6, 3: *Cause no one to stumble:* the language echoes that of 1 Cor 8—10, as does the expression "no longer live for themselves" in 2 Cor 5, 15. *That no fault may be found:* i.e., at the eschatological judgment (cf 1 Cor 4, 2-5).

6, 4a: This is the central assertion, the topic statement for the catalogue that follows. *We commend ourselves:* Paul's self-commendation is ironical (with an eye on the charges mentioned in 2 Cor 3, 1-3) and paradoxical (pointing mostly to experiences that would not normally be considered points of pride but are perceived as such by faith). Cf also the self-commendation in 2 Cor 11, 23-29. *As ministers of God:* the same Greek word, *diakonos,* means "minister" and "servant"; cf 2 Cor 11, 23, the central assertion in a similar context, and 1 Cor 3, 5.

6, 4b-5: *Through much endurance:* this phrase functions as a subtitle; it is followed by an enumeration of nine specific types of trials endured.

6, 6-7a: A list of virtuous qualities in two groups of four, the second fuller than the first.

6, 8b-10: A series of seven rhetorically effective antitheses, contrasting negative external impressions with positive inner reality. Paul perceives his existence as a reflection of Jesus' own and affirms an inner reversal that escapes outward observation. The final two members illustrate two distinct kinds of paradox or apparent contradiction that are characteristic of apostolic experience.

6, 11-13: Paul's tone becomes quieter, but his appeal for acceptance and affection is emotionally charged. References to the heart and their mutual relations bring the development begun in 2 Cor 2, 14—3, 3 to an effective conclusion.

6, 14—7, 1: Language and thought shift noticeably here. Suddenly we are in a different atmosphere, dealing with a quite different problem. Both the vocabulary and the thought, with their contrast between good and evil, are more characteristic of Qumran documents or the Book of Revelation than they are of Paul. Hence, critics suspect that this section was inserted by another hand.

6, 14-16a: The opening injunction to separate from unbelievers is reinforced by five rhetorical questions to make the point that Christianity is not compatible with paganism. Their opposition is emphasized also by the accumulation of five distinct designations for each group. These verses are a powerful statement of God's holiness and the exclusiveness of his claims.

6, 16c-18: This is a chain of scriptural citations carefully woven together. God's covenant relation to his people and his presence among them (16) is seen as conditioned on cultic separation from the profane and cultically impure (17); that relation is translated into the personal language of the parent-child relationship, an extension to the community of the language of 2 Sm 7, 14 (18). Some remarkable parallels to this chain are found in the final chapters of Revelation. God's presence among his people (Rv 21, 22) is expressed there, too, by applying 2 Sm 7, 14 to the community (Rv 21, 7). There is a call to separation (Rv 18, 4) and exclusion of the unclean from the community and its liturgy (Rv 21, 27). The title "Lord Almighty" *(Pantokratōr)* occurs in the New Testament only here in 18 and nine times in Rv.

¹⁷ Therefore, come forth from them
  and be separate," says the Lord,
"and touch nothing unclean;
  then I will receive you[r]
¹⁸ and I will be a father to you,
  and you shall be sons and daughters
   to me,
  says the Lord Almighty."[s]

CHAPTER 7

¹ Since we have these promises, beloved, let us cleanse ourselves from every defilement of flesh and spirit, making holiness perfect in the fear of God.

² * Make room for us; we have not wronged anyone, or ruined anyone, or taken advantage of anyone. ³ I do not say this in condemnation, for I have already said that you are in our hearts, that we may die together and live together.[t] ⁴ I have great confidence in you, I have great pride in you; I am filled with encouragement, I am overflowing with joy all the more because of all our affliction.

C. Resolution of the Crisis*

Paul's Joy in Macedonia. ⁵ * For even when we came into Macedonia,* our flesh had no rest, but we were afflicted in every way—external conflicts, internal fears.[u] ⁶ But God, who encourages the downcast, encouraged us by the arrival of Titus,[v] ⁷ and not only by his arrival but also by the encouragement with which he was encouraged in regard to you, as he told us of your yearning, your lament, your zeal for me, so that I rejoiced even more. ⁸ * For even if I saddened you by my letter, I do not regret it; and if I did regret it ([for] I see that that letter saddened you, if only for a while),[w] ⁹ I rejoice now, not because you were saddened, but because you were saddened into repentance; for you were saddened in a godly way, so that you did not suffer loss in anything because of us. ¹⁰ For godly sorrow produces a salutary repentance without regret, but worldly sorrow produces death. ¹¹ For behold what earnestness this godly sorrow has produced for you, as well as readiness for a defense, and indignation, and fear, and yearning, and zeal, and punishment. In every way you have shown yourselves to be innocent in the matter. ¹² So then even though I wrote to you, it was not on account of the one who did the wrong, or on account of the one who suffered the wrong, but in order that your concern for us might be made plain to you in the sight of God.[x] ¹³ For this reason we are encouraged.

And besides our encouragement,* we rejoice even more because of the joy of Titus, since his spirit has been refreshed by all of you. ¹⁴ For if I have boasted to him about you, I was not put to shame. No, just as everything we said to you was true, so our boasting before Titus proved to be the truth. ¹⁵ And his heart goes out to you all the more, as he remembers the obedience of all of you, when you received him with fear and trembling.[y] ¹⁶ I rejoice, because I have confidence in you in every respect.

---

r Is 52, 11; Ez 20, 34.41; Rv 18, 4; 21, 27.—s 2 Sm 7, 14; Ps 2, 7; Is 43, 6; Jer 31, 9; Rv 21, 7 / Rv 4, 8; 11, 17; 15, 3; 21, 22.—t 2 Cor 6, 11-13.—u 2 Cor 2, 13.—v 2 Cor 7, 13-14; 1 Thes 3, 6-8.—w 2 Cor 2, 2-4; Heb 12, 11.—x 2 Cor 2, 3.9; 7, 8.—y 2 Cor 2, 9.

7, 2-4: These verses continue the thought of 2 Cor 6, 11-13, before the interruption of 2 Cor 6, 14—7, 1. Verse 4 serves as a transition to the next section: the four themes it introduces (confidence; pride or "boasting"; encouragement; joy in affliction) are developed in vv 5-16. All have appeared previously in the letter.

7, 5-16: This section functions as a peroration or formal summing up of the whole first part of the letter, chs 1-7. It deals with the restoration of right relations between Paul and the Corinthians, and it is marked by fullness and intensity of emotion.

7, 5-7: Paul picks up the thread of the narrative interrupted at 2 Cor 2, 13 (5) and describes the resolution of the tense situation there depicted (6-7). Finally Titus arrives and his coming puts an end to Paul's restlessness (2 Cor 2, 13; 7, 5), casts out his fears,

and reverses his mood. The theme of encouragement and affliction is reintroduced (cf 2 Cor 1, 3-11); here, too, encouragement is traced back to God and is described as contagious (6). The language of joy and sorrow also reappears in v 7 (cf 2 Cor 1, 23—2, 1 and the note on 2 Cor 1, 23-24).

7, 5: *Macedonia:* see the note on 2 Cor 2, 13.

7, 8-12: Paul looks back on the episode from the viewpoint of its ending. The goal of their common activity, promotion of their joy (2 Cor 1, 24), has been achieved, despite and because of the sorrow they felt. That sorrow was God-given. Its salutary effects are enumerated fully and impressively in vv 10-11; not the least important of these is that it has revealed to them the attachment they have to Paul.

7, 13-16: Paul summarizes the effect of the experience on Titus: encouragement, joy, love, relief. Finally, he describes its effects on himself: encouragement, joy, confidence, pride or "boasting" (i.e., the satisfaction resulting from a boast that proves well-founded; cf 2 Cor 7, 4; 1, 12.14).

III. THE COLLECTION FOR JERUSALEM*

CHAPTER 8

Generosity in Giving. ¹ * We want you to know, brothers,* of the grace of God* that has been given to the churches of Macedonia,ᶻ ² * for in a severe test of affliction, the abundance of their joy and their profound poverty overflowed in a wealth of generosity on their part. ³ * For according to their means, I can testify, and beyond their means, spontaneously, ⁴ they begged us insistently for the favor of taking part in the service to the holy ones,ᵃ ⁵ and this, not as we expected, but they gave themselves first to the Lord and to us* through the will of God, ⁶ so that we urged Titus* that, as he had already begun, he should also complete for you this gracious act also.ᵇ ⁷ Now as you excel in every respect, in faith, discourse, knowledge, all earnestness, and in the love we have for you,ᶜ may you excel in this gracious act also.*

⁸ I say this not by way of command, but to test the genuineness of your love by your concern for others. ⁹ ᵈ For you know the gracious act of our Lord Jesus Christ, that for your sake he became poor although he was rich, so that by his poverty you might become rich.* ¹⁰ And I am giving counsel in this matter, for it is appropriate for you who began not only to act but to act willingly last year:ᵉ ¹¹ complete it now, so that your eager* willingness may be matched by your completion of it out of what you have. ¹² * For if the eagerness is there, it is acceptable according to what one has, not according to what one does not have; ¹³ not that others should have re-

---

z 2 Cor 11, 9; Rom 15, 26.—a Acts 24, 17; Rom 15, 31.—b 2 Cor 2, 13; 7, 6-7.13-14; 8, 16.23; 12, 18.—c 1 Cor 1, 5.—d 2 Cor 6, 10; Phil 2, 6-8.—e 2 Cor 9, 2; 1 Cor 16, 1-4.

8, 1—9, 15: Paul turns to a new topic, the collection for the church in Jerusalem. There is an early precedent for this project in the agreement mentioned in Gal 2, 6-10. According to Acts, the church at Antioch had sent Saul and Barnabas to Jerusalem with relief (Acts 11, 27-30). Subsequently Paul organized a project of relief for Jerusalem among his own churches. Our earliest evidence for it comes in 1 Cor 16, 1-4, after it had already begun (see the notes there); by the time Paul wrote Rom 15, 25-28 the collection was completed and ready for delivery. Chapters 8 and 9 contain what appear to be two letters on the subject. In them Paul gives us his fullest exposition of the meaning he sees in the enterprise, presenting it as an act of Christian charity and as an expression of the unity of the church, both present and eschatological. These chapters are especially rich in the recurrence of key words, on which Paul plays; it is usually impossible to do justice to these wordplays in the translation.

8, 1-24: This is a letter of recommendation for Titus and two unnamed companions, written from Macedonia probably at least a year later than 1 Cor 16. The recommendation proper is prefaced by remarks about the ideals of sharing and equality within the Christian community (1-15). Phil 4, 10-20 shows that Paul has reflected on his personal experience of need and relief in his relations with the community at Philippi; he now develops his reflections on the larger scale of relations between his Gentile churches and the mother church in Jerusalem.

8, 1-5: The example of the Macedonians, a model of what ought to be happening at Corinth, provides Paul with the occasion for expounding his theology of "giving."

8, 1: *The grace of God:* the fundamental theme is expressed by the Greek noun *charis,* which will be variously translated throughout these chapters as "grace" (2 Cor 8, 1; 9, 8.14), "favor" (2 Cor 8, 4), "gracious act" (2 Cor 8, 6.7.9) or "gracious work" (2 Cor 8, 19), to be compared to "gracious gift" (1 Cor 16, 3). The related term, *eucharistia,* "thanksgiving," also occurs at 2 Cor 9, 11.12. The wordplay is not superficial; various mutations of the same root signal inner connection between aspects of a single reality, and Paul consciously exploits the similarities in vocabulary to highlight that connection.

8, 2: Three more terms are now introduced. *Test (dokimē):* the same root is translated as "to test" (8) and "evidence" (2 Cor 9, 13); it means to be tried and found genuine. *Abundance:* variations on the same root lie behind "overflow" (2 Cor 8, 2; 9, 12), "excel" (2 Cor 8, 7), "surplus" (2 Cor 8, 14), "superfluous" (2 Cor 9, 1), "make abundant" and "have an abundance" (2 Cor 9, 8). These expressions of fullness contrast with references to need (2 Cor 8, 14; 9, 12). *Generosity:* the word *haplotēs* has nuances of both simplicity and sincerity; here and in 2 Cor 9, 11.13 it designates the singleness of purpose that manifests itself in generous giving.

8, 3-4: Paul emphasizes the spontaneity of the Macedonians and the nature of their action. *They begged us insistently:* the same root is translated as "urge," "appeal," "encourage" (2 Cor 8, 6.17; 9, 5). *Taking part:* the same word is translated "contribution" in 2 Cor 9, 13 and a related term as "partner" in 2 Cor 8, 23. *Service (diakonia):* this word occurs also in 2 Cor 9, 1.13 as "service"; in 2 Cor 9, 12 it is translated "administration," and in 2 Cor 8, 19.20 the corresponding verb is rendered "administer."

8, 5: *They gave themselves . . . to the Lord and to us:* on its deepest level their attitude is one of self-giving.

8, 6: *Titus:* 1 Cor 16 seemed to leave the organization up to the Corinthians, but apparently Paul has sent Titus to initiate the collection as well; 2 Cor 8, 16-17 will describe Titus' attitude as one of shared concern and cooperation.

8, 7: The charitable service Paul is promoting is seen briefly and in passing within the perspective of Paul's theology of the charisms. *Earnestness (spoudē):* this or related terms occur also in v 22 ("earnest") and 2 Cor 8, 8.16.17 ("concern").

8, 9: The dialectic of Jesus' experience, expressed earlier in terms of life and death (2 Cor 5, 15), sin and righteousness (2 Cor 5, 21), is now rephrased in terms of poverty and wealth. Many scholars think this is a reference to Jesus' preexistence with God (his "wealth") and to his incarnation and death (his "poverty"), and they point to the similarity between this verse and Phil 2, 6-8. Others interpret the wealth and poverty as succeeding phases of Jesus' earthly existence, e.g., his sense of intimacy with God and then the desolation and the feeling of abandonment by God in his death (cf Mk 15, 34).

8, 11: *Eager:* the word *prothymia* also occurs in 2 Cor 8, 12.19; 9, 2.

8, 12-15: Paul introduces the principle of *equality* into the discussion. The goal is not impoverishment but sharing of resources; balance is achieved at least over the course of time. In v 15 Paul grounds his argument unexpectedly in the experience of Israel gathering manna in the desert: equality was achieved, independently of personal exertion, by God, who gave with an even hand according to need. Paul touches briefly here on the theme of "living from God."

lief while you are burdened, but that as a matter of equality [14] your surplus at the present time should supply their needs, so that their surplus may also supply your needs, that there may be equality. [15] As it is written:

"Whoever had much did not have more,
and whoever had little did not have less."[f]

Titus and His Collaborators.* [16] But thanks be to God who put the same concern for you into the heart of Titus, [17] for he not only welcomed our appeal but, since he is very concerned, he has gone to you of his own accord. [18] With him we have sent the brother* who is praised in all the churches for his preaching of the gospel.[g] [19] And not only that, but he has also been appointed our traveling companion by the churches in this gracious work administered by us for the glory of the Lord [himself] and for the expression of our eagerness.[h] [20] This we desire to avoid, that anyone blame us* about this lavish gift administered by us, [21] for we are concerned for what is honorable not only in the sight of the Lord but also in the sight of others.[i] [22] And with them we have sent our brother whom we often tested in many ways and found earnest, but who is now much more earnest because of his great confidence in you. [23] As for Titus, he is my partner and co-worker for you; as for our brothers, they are apostles of the churches, the glory of Christ. [24] So give proof before the churches of your love and of our boasting about you to them.*

CHAPTER 9

God's Indescribable Gift.* [1] Now about the service to the holy ones, it is superfluous for me to write to you, [2] for I know your eagerness, about which I boast of you to the Macedonians, that Achaia* has been ready since last year; and your zeal has stirred up most of them.[j] [3] Nonetheless, I sent the brothers* so that our boast about you might not prove empty in this case, so that you might be ready, as I said, [4] for fear that if any Macedonians come with me and find you not ready we might be put to shame (to say nothing of you) in this conviction. [5] So I thought it necessary to encourage the brothers to go on ahead to you and arrange in advance for your promised gift, so that in this way it might be ready as a bountiful gift and not as an exaction.

[6] Consider this: whoever sows sparingly will also reap sparingly, and whoever sows bountifully will also reap bountifully.[k] [7] Each must do as already determined, without sadness or compulsion, for God loves a cheerful giver.[l] [8] * Moreover, God is able to make every grace abundant for you, so that in all things, always having all you need, you may have an abundance for every good work. [9] As it is written:

"He scatters abroad, he gives to the poor;
his righteousness endures forever."[m]

[10] The one who supplies seed to the sower and bread for food will supply and multiply your seed and increase the harvest of your righteousness.[n]

---

f Ex 16, 18.—g 2 Cor 12, 18.—h 1 Cor 16, 3-4.—i Rom 12, 17.—j 2 Cor 8, 10; Rom 15, 26.—k Prv 11, 24-25.—l Prv 22, 8 LXX.—m Ps 112, 9.—n Is 55, 10.

8, 16-24: In recommending Titus and his companions, Paul stresses their personal and apostolic qualities, their good dispositions toward the Corinthians, and their authority as messengers of the churches and representatives of Christ.

8, 18: *The brother:* we do not know the identity of this co-worker of Paul, nor of the third companion mentioned below in v 22.

8, 20-22: *That anyone blame us:* 2 Cor 12, 16-18 suggests that misunderstandings may indeed have arisen concerning Paul's management of the collection through the messengers mentioned here, but those same verses seem to imply that the Corinthians by and large would recognize the honesty of Paul's conduct in this area as in others (cf 2 Cor 6, 3).

8, 24: As Paul began by holding up the Macedonians as examples to be imitated, he closes by exhorting the Corinthians to show their love (by accepting the envoys and by cooperating as the Macedonians do), thus justifying the pride Paul demonstrates because of them before other churches.

9, 1-15: Quite possibly this was originally an independent letter, though it deals with the same subject and continues many of the same themes. In that case, it may have been written a few weeks later than ch 8, while the delegation there mentioned was still on its way.

9, 2: *Achaia:* see the note on Rom 15, 26.

9, 3: *I sent the brothers:* the Greek aorist tense here could be epistolary, referring to the present; in that case Paul would be sending them now, and ch 9 would merely conclude the letter of recommendation begun in ch 8. But the aorist may also refer to a sending that is past as Paul writes; then ch 9, with its apparently fresh beginning, is a follow-up message entrusted to another carrier.

9, 8-10: The behavior to which he exhorts them is grounded in God's own pattern of behavior. God is capable of overwhelming generosity, as scripture itself attests (9), so that they need not fear being short. He will provide in abundance, both supplying their natural needs and increasing their righteousness. Paul challenges them to godlike generosity and reminds them of the fundamental motive for encouragement: God himself cannot be outdone.

11 * You are being enriched in every way
for all generosity, which through us produces thanksgiving to God, 12 for the administration of this public service is not
only supplying the needs of the holy ones
but is also overflowing in many acts of
thanksgiving to God. 13 Through the evidence of this service, you are glorifying
God for your obedient confession of the
gospel of Christ and the generosity of your
contribution to them and to all others,[o]
14 while in prayer on your behalf they long
for you, because of the surpassing grace of
God upon you. 15 Thanks be to God for his
indescribable gift![p]

IV. PAUL'S DEFENSE OF HIS MINISTRY*

CHAPTER 10

Accusation of Weakness.* 1 Now I myself, Paul, urge you through the gentleness
and clemency of Christ,* I who am humble
when face to face with you, but brave toward you when absent, 2 [q] I beg you that,
when present, I may not have to be brave
with that confidence with which I intend to
act boldly against some who consider us as
acting according to the flesh.* 3 For, although we are in the flesh, we do not battle
according to the flesh,* 4 for the weapons
of our battle* are not of flesh but are enor-
mously powerful, capable of destroying
fortresses.[r] We destroy arguments 5 and
every pretension raising itself against the
knowledge of God, and take every thought
captive in obedience to Christ, 6 and we are
ready to punish every disobedience, once
your obedience is complete.[s]

7 [t] Look at what confronts you. Whoever is confident of belonging to Christ
should consider that as he belongs to
Christ, so do we.* 8 [u] And even if I should
boast a little too much of our authority,
which the Lord gave for building you up
and not for tearing you down, I shall not be
put to shame. 9 * May I not seem as one
frightening you through letters. 10 For
someone will say, "His letters are severe
and forceful, but his bodily presence is
weak, and his speech contemptible."[v]
11 Such a person must understand that
what we are in word through letters when

o 2 Cor 8, 4; Rom 15, 31.—p Rom 5, 15-16.—q 2 Cor 13, 2.10; 1 Cor 4, 21.—r 2 Cor 6, 7; 13, 2-3; 1 Cor 1, 25; Eph 6, 10-14.—s 2 Cor 2, 9.—t 1 Cor 1, 12.—u 2 Cor 13, 10.—v 1 Cor 2, 3.

9, 11-15: Paul's vision broadens to take in all the interested parties in one dynamic picture. His language becomes liturgically colored and conveys a sense of fullness. With a final play on the words *charis* and *eucharistia* (see the note on 2 Cor 8, 1), he describes a circle that closes on itself: the movement of grace overflowing from God to them and handed on from them through Paul to others is completed by the prayer of praise and thanksgiving raised on their behalf to God.

10, 1—13, 10: These final chapters have their own unity of structure and theme and could well have formed the body of a separate letter. They constitute an *apologia* on Paul's part, i.e., a legal defense of his behavior and his ministry; the writing is emotionally charged and highly rhetorical. In the central section (2 Cor 11, 16—12, 10), the *apologia* takes the form of a boast. This section is prepared for by a prologue (2 Cor 11, 1-15) and followed by an epilogue (2 Cor 12, 11-18), which are similar in content and structure. These sections, in turn, are framed by an introduction (2 Cor 10, 1-18) and a conclusion (2 Cor 12, 19—13, 10), both of which assert Paul's apostolic authority and confidence and define the purpose of the letter. The structure that results from this disposition of the material is chiastic, i.e., the first element corresponds to the last, the second to the second last, etc., following the pattern *a b c b*[1] *a*[1].

10, 1-18: Paul asserts his apostolic authority and expresses the confidence this generates in him. He writes in response to certain opinions that have arisen in the community and certain charges raised against him and in preparation for a forthcoming visit in which he intends to set things in order. This section gives us an initial glimpse of the situation in Corinth that Paul must address; much of its thematic material will be taken up again in the finale (2 Cor 12, 19—13, 10).

10, 1-2: A strong opening plunges us straight into the conflict. Contrasts dominate here: presence versus absence, gentleness-clemency-humility versus boldness-confidence-bravery. *Through the gentleness and clemency of Christ:* the figure of the gentle Christ, presented in a significant position before any specifics of the situation are suggested, forms a striking contrast to the picture of the bold and militant Paul (2-6); this tension is finally resolved in 2 Cor 13, 3-4. *Absent . . . present:* this same contrast, with a restatement of the purpose of the letter, recurs in 2 Cor 13, 10, which forms an inclusion with 2 Cor 10, 1-2.

10, 2b-4a: *Flesh:* the Greek word *sarx* can express both the physical life of the body without any pejorative overtones (as in "we are in the flesh," 3) and our natural life insofar as it is marked by limitation and weakness (as in the other expressions) in contrast to the higher life and power conferred by the Spirit; cf the note on 1 Cor 3, 1. The wordplay is intended to express the paradoxical situation of a life already taken over by the Spirit but not yet seen as such except by faith. Lack of empirical evidence of the Spirit permits misunderstanding and misjudgment, but Paul resolutely denies that his behavior and effectiveness are as limited as some suppose.

10, 3b-6: Paul is involved in combat. The strong military language and imagery are both an assertion of his confidence in the divine power at his disposal and a declaration of war against those who underestimate his resources. The threat is echoed in 2 Cor 13, 2-3.

10, 7-8: *Belonging to Christ . . . so do we:* these phrases already announce the pattern of Paul's boast in 2 Cor 11, 21b-29, especially 2 Cor 11, 22-23. *For building you up and not for tearing you down:* Paul draws on the language by which Jeremiah described the purpose of the prophetic power the Lord gave to him (Jer 1, 9-10; 12, 16-17; 24, 6). Though Paul's power may have destructive effects on others (2-6), its intended effect on the community is entirely constructive (cf 2 Cor 13, 10). *I shall not be put to shame:* his assertions will not be refuted; they will be revealed as true at the judgment.

10, 9-10: Paul cites the complaints of some who find him lacking in personal forcefulness and holds out the threat of a personal *parousia* (both "return" and "presence") that will be forceful, indeed will be a demonstration of Christ's own power (cf 2 Cor 13, 2-4).

absent, that we also are in action when present. *w*

¹² * Not that we dare to class or compare ourselves with some of those who recommend themselves. But when they measure themselves by one another and compare themselves with one another, they are without understanding. *x* ¹³ But we will not boast beyond measure but will keep to the limits* God has apportioned us, namely, to reach even to you. ¹⁴ For we are not overreaching ourselves, as though we did not reach you; we indeed first came to you with the gospel of Christ. ¹⁵ We are not boasting beyond measure, in other people's labors; yet our hope is that, as your faith increases, our influence among you may be greatly enlarged, within our proper limits, ¹⁶ so that we may preach the gospel even beyond you, not boasting of work already done in another's sphere. *y* ¹⁷ *z* "Whoever boasts, should boast in the Lord."* ¹⁸ For it is not the one who recommends himself who is approved,* but the one whom the Lord recommends. *a*

---

w 2 Cor 13, 1-2.—x 2 Cor 3, 1-2; 4, 2; 5, 12; 6, 4; 10, 18; 12, 11.—y Rom 15, 20-21.—z Jer 9, 22-23; 1 Cor 1, 31.—a 2 Cor 13, 3-9.—b 2 Cor 11, 21; 12, 11.—c Hos 2, 21-22; Eph 5, 26-27.—d Gn 3, 1-6.—e Gal 1, 6-9.—f 2 Cor 12, 11.—g 1 Cor 1, 5.17; 2, 1-5.

10, 12-18: Paul now qualifies his claim to boldness, indicating its limits. He distinguishes his own behavior from that of others, revealing those "others" as they appear to him: as self-recommending, immoderately boastful, encroaching on territory not assigned to them, and claiming credit not due to them.

10, 13: *Will keep to the limits:* the notion of proper limits is expressed here by two terms with overlapping meanings, *metron* and *kanōn,* which are played off against several expressions denoting overreaching or expansion beyond a legitimate sphere.

10, 17: *Boast in the Lord:* there is a legitimate boasting, in contrast to the immoderate boasting to which vv 13 and 15 allude. God's work through Paul in the community is the object of his boast (13-16; 2 Cor 1, 12-14) and constitutes his recommendation (2 Cor 3, 1-3). Cf the notes on 2 Cor 1, 12-14 and 1 Cor 1, 29-31.

10, 18: *Approved:* to be approved is to come successfully through the process of testing for authenticity (cf 2 Cor 13, 3-7 and the note on 2 Cor 8, 2). *Whom the Lord recommends:* self-commendation is a premature and unwarranted anticipation of the final judgment, which the Lord alone will pass (cf 1 Cor 4, 3-5). Paul alludes to this judgment throughout chs 10-13, frequently in final or transitional positions; cf 2 Cor 11, 15; 12, 19a; 13, 3-7.

11, 1-15: Although these verses continue to reveal information about Paul's opponents and the differences he perceives between them and himself, 2 Cor 11, 1 signals a turn in Paul's thought. This section constitutes a prologue to the boasting that he will undertake in 2 Cor 11, 16—12, 10, and it bears remarkable similarities to the section that follows the central boast, 2 Cor 12, 11-18.

11, 1: *Put up with a little foolishness from me:* this verse indicates more clearly than the general statement of intent in 2 Cor 10, 13 the nature of the project Paul is about to undertake. He alludes ironically to the Corinthians' toleration for others.

CHAPTER 11

Preaching without Charge. * ¹ If only you would put up with a little foolishness from me!* Please put up with me. *b* ² * For I am jealous of you with the jealousy of God, since I betrothed you to one husband to present you as a chaste virgin to Christ. *c* ³ But I am afraid that, as the serpent deceived Eve* by his cunning, your thoughts may be corrupted from a sincere [and pure] commitment to Christ. *d* ⁴ For if someone comes and preaches another Jesus* than the one we preached, *e* or if you receive a different spirit from the one you received or a different gospel from the one you accepted, you put up with it well enough. ⁵ *f* For I think that I am not in any way inferior to these "superapostles."* ⁶ Even if I am untrained in speaking, I am not so in knowledge; *g* in every way we have made this plain to you in all things.*

Foolishness: Paul qualifies his project as folly from beginning to end; see the note on 2 Cor 11, 16—12, 10.

11, 2: Paul gives us a sudden glimpse of the theological values that are at stake. *The jealousy of God:* the perspective is that of the covenant, described in imagery of love and marriage, as in the prophets; cf 1 Cor 10, 22. *I betrothed you:* Paul, like a father (cf 2 Cor 12, 14), betroths the community to Christ as his bride (cf Eph 5, 21-33) and will present her to him at his second coming. Cf Mt 25, 1-13 and the nuptial imagery in Rv 21.

11, 3: *As the serpent deceived Eve:* before Christ can return for the community Paul fears a repetition of the primal drama of seduction. Corruption of minds is satanic activity (see 2 Cor 2, 11; 4, 4). Satanic imagery recurs in 2 Cor 11, 13-15.20; 12, 7b.16-17; see the notes on these passages.

11, 4: *Preaches another Jesus:* the danger is specified, and Paul's opponents are identified with the cunning serpent. The battle for minds has to do with the understanding of Jesus, the Spirit, the gospel; the Corinthians have flirted with another understanding than the one that Paul handed on to them as traditional and normative.

11, 5: *These "superapostles":* this term, employed again in 2 Cor 12, 11b, designates the opponents of whom Paul has spoken in 2 Cor 10 and again in 2 Cor 11, 4. They appear to be intruders at Corinth. Their preaching is marked at least by a different emphasis and style, and they do not hesitate to accept support from the community. Perhaps these itinerants appeal to the authority of church leaders in Jerusalem and even carry letters of recommendation from them. But it is not those distant leaders whom Paul is attacking here. The intruders are "superapostles" not in the sense of the "pillars" at Jerusalem (Gal 2), but in their own estimation. They consider themselves superior to Paul as apostles and ministers of Christ, and they are obviously enjoying some success among the Corinthians. Paul rejects their claim to be apostles in any superlative sense (*hyperlian*), judging them bluntly as "false apostles," ministers of Satan masquerading as apostles of Christ (13-15). On the contrary, he himself will claim to be a superminister of Christ (*hyper egō,* 23).

11, 6: Apparently found deficient in both rhetorical ability (cf 2 Cor 10, 10) and knowledge (cf 2 Cor 10, 5), Paul concedes the former charge but not the latter. *In every way:* in all their contacts with him revelation has been taking place. Paul, through whom God reveals the knowledge of himself (2 Cor 2, 14), and in whom the death and life of Jesus are revealed (2 Cor 4, 10-11; cf 2 Cor 6, 4), also demonstrates his own role as the bearer of true knowledge. Cf 1 Cor 1, 18—2, 16.

⁷ * Did I make a mistake when I humbled myself so that you might be exalted, because I preached the gospel of God to you without charge?ʰ ⁸ I plundered other churches by accepting from them in order to minister to you. ⁹ And when I was with you and in need, I did not burden anyone, for the brothers who came from Macedonia supplied my needs. So I refrained and will refrain from burdening you in any way.ⁱ ¹⁰ By the truth of Christ in me, this boast of mine shall not be silenced in the regions of Achaia.ʲ ¹¹ * And why? Because I do not love you? God knows I do!ᵏ

¹² And what I do I will continue to do, in order to end this pretext of those who seek a pretext for being regarded as we are in the mission of which they boast. ¹³ * For such people are false apostles, deceitful workers, who masquerade as apostles of Christ. ¹⁴ And no wonder, for even Satan masquerades as an angel of light. ¹⁵ So it is not strange that his ministers also masquerade as ministers of righteousness. Their end will correspond to their deeds.

Paul's Boast: His Labors. ¹⁶ * I repeat, no one should consider me foolish;* but if you do, accept me as a fool, so that I too may boast a little.* ¹⁷ What I am saying I am not saying according to the Lord but as in foolishness, in this boastful state. ¹⁸ Since many boast according to the flesh, I too will boast. ¹⁹ For you gladly put up with fools, since you are wise yourselves. ²⁰ * For you put up with it if someone enslaves you, or devours you, or gets the better of you, or puts on airs, or slaps you in the face. ²¹ To my shame I say that we were too weak!*

But what anyone dares to boast of (I am speaking in foolishness) I also dare. ²² * Are they Hebrews? So am I. Are they Israelites? So am I. Are they descendants of Abraham? So am I.ˡ ²³ Are they ministers of Christ? (I am talking like an insane person.)ᵐ I am still more,* with far greater labors, far more imprisonments, far worse beatings, and numerous brushes with death.* ²⁴ Five times at the hands of the Jews I received forty lashes minus one.ⁿ ²⁵ Three times I was beaten with rods, once I was stoned, three times I was shipwrecked, I passed a night and a day on the deep;ᵒ ²⁶ on frequent journeys, in dangers from rivers, dangers from robbers, dangers from my own race, dangers from Gentiles, dangers in the city, dangers in the wilder-

---

h 2 Cor 12, 13-18; Acts 18, 3; 1 Cor 9, 6-18.—i Phil 4, 15.18.—j 1 Cor 9, 15.—k 2 Cor 12, 15.—l Acts 22, 3 / Rom 11, 1; Phil 3, 5-6.—m 2 Cor 6, 5; Acts 16, 22-24; 1 Cor 15, 31-32.— n Dt 25, 2-3.—o Acts 14, 19; 27, 43-44.

11, 7-10: Abruptly Paul passes to another reason for complaints: his practice of preaching without remuneration (cf 1 Cor 9, 3-18). He deftly defends his practice by situating it from the start within the pattern of Christ's own self-humiliation (cf 2 Cor 10, 1) and reduces objections to absurdity by rhetorical questions (cf 2 Cor 12, 13).

11, 11-12: Paul rejects lack of affection as his motive (possibly imputed to him by his opponents) and states his real motive, a desire to emphasize the disparity between himself and the others (cf 2 Cor 11, 19-21). The topic of his gratuitous service will be taken up once more in 2 Cor 12, 13-18. 1 Cor 9, 15-18 gives a different but complementary explanation of his motivation.

11, 13-15: Paul picks up again the imagery of v 3 and applies it to the opponents: they are false apostles of Christ, really serving another master. *Deceitful . . . masquerade:* deception and simulation, like cunning (3), are marks of the satanic. *Angel of light:* recalls the contrast between light and darkness, Christ and Beliar at 2 Cor 6, 14-15. *Ministers of righteousness:* recalls the earlier contrast between the ministry of condemnation and that of righteousness (2 Cor 3, 9). *Their end:* the section closes with another allusion to the judgment, when all participants in the final conflict will be revealed or unmasked and dealt with as they deserve.

11, 16—12, 10: Paul now accepts the challenge of his opponents and indulges in boasting similar to theirs, but with differences that he has already signaled in 2 Cor 10, 12-18 and that become clearer as he proceeds. He defines the nature of his project and unmistakably labels it as folly at the beginning and the end (2 Cor 11, 16-23; 12, 11). Yet his boast does not spring from ignorance (2 Cor 11, 21; 12, 6) nor is it concerned merely with human distinctions (2 Cor 11, 18). Paul boasts "in moderation" (2 Cor 10, 13.15) and "in the Lord" (2 Cor 10, 17).

11,16-29: The first part of Paul's boast focuses on labors and afflictions, in which authentic service of Christ consists.

11, 16-21: These verses recapitulate remarks already made about the foolishness of boasting and the excessive toleration of the Corinthians. They form a prelude to the boast proper.

11, 20: Paul describes the activities of the "others" in terms that fill out the picture drawn in vv 3-4.13-15. Much of the vocabulary suggests fleshly or even satanic activity. *Enslaves:* cf Gal 2, 4. *Devours:* cf 1 Pt 5, 8. *Gets the better:* the verb *lambanō* means "to take," but is used in a variety of senses; here it may imply financial advantage, as in the English colloquialism "to take someone." It is similarly used at 2 Cor 12, 16 and is there connected with cunning and deceit. *Puts on airs:* the same verb is rendered "raise oneself" (2 Cor 10, 5) and "be too elated" (2 Cor 12, 7).

11, 21: Paul ironically concedes the charge of personal weakness from 2 Cor 10, 1-18 but will refute the other charge there mentioned, that of lack of boldness, accepting the challenge to demonstrate it by his boast.

11, 22: The opponents apparently pride themselves on their "Jewishness." Paul, too, can claim to be a Jew by race, religion, and promise. *Descendants of Abraham:* elsewhere Paul distinguishes authentic from inauthentic heirs of Abraham and the promise (Rom 4, 13-18; 9, 7-13; 11, 1; Gal 3, 9.27-29; cf Jn 8, 33-47). Here he grants his opponents this title in order to concentrate on the principal claim that follows.

11, 23a: *Ministers of Christ . . . I am still more:* the central point of the boast (cf the note on 2 Cor 11, 5). *Like an insane person:* the climax of his folly.

11, 23b-29: Service of the humiliated and crucified Christ is demonstrated by trials endured for him. This rhetorically impressive catalogue enumerates many of the labors and perils Paul encountered on his missionary journeys.

2Cor

ness, dangers at sea, dangers among false brothers; [27] in toil and hardship, through many sleepless nights, through hunger and thirst, through frequent fastings, through cold and exposure.[p] [28] And apart from these things, there is the daily pressure upon me of my anxiety for all the churches. [29] Who is weak, and I am not weak? Who is led to sin, and I am not indignant?[q]

Paul's Boast: His Weakness.* [30] If I must boast, I will boast of the things that show my weakness. [31] * The God and Father of the Lord Jesus knows, he who is blessed forever, that I do not lie. [32] At Damascus, the governor under King Aretas guarded the city of Damascus, in order to seize me, [33] but I was lowered in a basket through a window in the wall and escaped his hands.[r]

CHAPTER 12

[1] I * must boast; not that it is profitable, but I will go on to visions and revelations of the Lord. [2] I know someone in Christ who, fourteen years ago (whether in the body or out of the body I do not know,

God knows), was caught up to the third heaven. [3] And I know that this person (whether in the body or out of the body I do not know, God knows) [4] was caught up into Paradise and heard ineffable things, which no one may utter.[s] [5] About this person* I will boast, but about myself I will not boast, except about my weaknesses. [6] Although if I should wish to boast, I would not be foolish, for I would be telling the truth. But I refrain, so that no one may think more of me than what he sees in me or hears from me [7] because of the abundance of the revelations. Therefore, that I might not become too elated,* a thorn in the flesh was given to me, an angel of Satan, to beat me, to keep me from being too elated.[t] [8] Three times* I begged the Lord about this, that it might leave me,[u] [9] but he said to me,* "My grace is sufficient for you, for power is made perfect in weakness." I will rather boast most gladly of my weaknesses,* in order that the power of Christ may dwell with me.[v] [10] Therefore, I am content with weaknesses, insults, hardships, persecutions, and constraints,

---

p 1 Cor 4, 11.—q 1 Cor 9, 22.—r Acts 9, 23-25.—s Lk 23, 43; Rv 2, 7.—t Nm 33, 55; Jos 23, 13; Ez 28, 24.—u Mt 26, 39-44.—v 2 Cor 4, 7.

11, 30—12, 10: The second part of Paul's boast, marked by a change of style and a shift in focus. After recalling the project in which he is engaged, he states a new topic: his weaknesses as matter for boasting. Everything in this section, even the discussion of privileges and distinctions, will be integrated into this perspective.

11, 31-32: The episode at Damascus is symbolic. It aptly illustrates Paul's weakness but ends in deliverance (cf 2 Cor 4, 7-11).

12, 1-4: *In the body or out of the body:* he seemed no longer confined to bodily conditions, but he does not claim to understand the mechanics of the experience. *Caught up:* i.e., in ecstasy. *The third heaven . . . Paradise:* ancient cosmologies depicted a multitiered universe. Jewish intertestamental literature contains much speculation about the number of heavens. Seven is the number usually mentioned, but the Testament of Levi (2, 7-10; 3, 1-4) speaks of three; God himself dwelt in the third of these. Without giving us any clear picture of the cosmos, Paul indicates a mental journey to a nonearthly space, set apart by God, in which secrets were revealed to him. *Ineffable things:* i.e., privileged knowledge, which it was not possible or permitted to divulge.

12, 5-7: *This person:* the indirect way of referring to himself has the effect of emphasizing the distance between that experience and his everyday life, just as the indirect *someone in Christ* (2) and all the passive verbs emphasize his passivity and recep-

tivity in the experience. The revelations were not a personal achievement, nor were they meant to draw attention to any quality of his own.

12, 7b: *That I might not become too elated:* God assures that there is a negative component to his experience, so that he cannot lose proper perspective; cf 2 Cor 1, 9; 4, 7-11. *A thorn in the flesh:* variously interpreted as a sickness or physical disability, a temptation, or a handicap connected with his apostolic activity. But since Hebrew "thorn in the flesh," like English "thorn in my side," refers to persons (cf Nm 33, 55; Ez 28, 24), Paul may be referring to some especially persistent and obnoxious opponent. The language of vv 7-8 permits this interpretation. If this is correct, the frequent appearance of singular pronouns in depicting the opposition may not be merely a stylistic variation; the singular may be provoked and accompanied by the image of one individual in whom criticism of Paul's preaching, way of life, and apostolic consciousness is concentrated, and who embodies all the qualities Paul attributes to the group. *An angel of Satan:* a personal messenger from Satan; cf the satanic language already applied to the opponents in 2 Cor 11, 3.13-15.20.

12, 8: *Three times:* his prayer was insistent, like that of Jesus in Gethsemane, a sign of how intolerable he felt the thorn to be.

12, 9: *But he said to me:* Paul's petition is denied; release and healing are withheld for a higher purpose. The Greek perfect tense indicates that Jesus' earlier response still holds at the time of writing. *My grace is sufficient for you:* this is not a statement about the sufficiency of grace in general. Jesus speaks directly to Paul's situation. *Is made perfect:* i.e., is given most fully and manifests itself fully.

12, 9b-10a: Paul draws the conclusion from the autobiographical anecdote and integrates it into the subject of this part of the boast. *Weaknesses:* the apostolic hardships he must endure, including active personal hostility, as specified in a final catalogue (10a). *That the power of Christ may dwell with me:* Paul pinpoints the ground for the paradoxical strategy he has adopted in his self-defense.

for the sake of Christ;*w* for when I am weak, then I am strong.*

Selfless Concern for the Church.* [11] I have been foolish. You compelled me, for I ought to have been commended by you. For I am in no way inferior to these "superapostles,"*x* even though I am nothing. [12] * The signs of an apostle were performed among you with all endurance, signs and wonders, and mighty deeds.*y* [13] * In what way were you less privileged than the rest of the churches, except that on my part I did not burden you? Forgive me this wrong!*z*

[14] Now I am ready to come to you this third time. And I will not be a burden, for I want not what is yours, but you. Children ought not to save for their parents, but parents for their children. [15] I will most gladly spend and be utterly spent for your sakes. If I love you more, am I to be loved less? [16] But granted that I myself did not burden you, yet I was crafty and got the better of you by deceit.*a* [17] Did I take advantage of you through any of those I sent to you? [18] I urged Titus to go and sent the brother with him. Did Titus take advantage of you? Did we not walk in the same spirit? And in the same steps?*b*

Final Warnings and Appeals.* [19] Have you been thinking all along that we are defending* ourselves before you? In the sight of God we are speaking in Christ, and all for building you up, beloved. [20] For I fear that* when I come I may find you not such as I wish, and that you may find me not as you wish; that there may be rivalry, jealousy, fury, selfishness, slander, gossip, conceit, and disorder.*c* [21] I fear that when I come again* my God may humiliate me before you, and I may have to mourn over many of those who sinned earlier and have not repented of the impurity, immorality, and licentiousness they practiced.

CHAPTER 13

[1] This third time I am coming* to you. "On the testimony of two or three witnesses a

---

w 2 Cor 6, 4-5; Rom 5, 3 / Phil 4, 13.—x 2 Cor 11, 5.—y Rom 15, 19; 1 Thes 1, 5.—z 2 Cor 11, 9-12.—a 2 Cor 11, 3.13.—b 2 Cor 2, 13; 8, 16.23.—c 1 Cor 1, 11; 3, 3.

12, 10b: *When I am weak, then I am strong:* Paul recognizes a twofold pattern in the resolution of the weakness-power (and death-life) dialectic, each of which looks to Jesus as the model and is experienced in him. The first is personal, involving a reversal in oneself (Jesus, 2 Cor 13, 4a; Paul, 2 Cor 1, 9-10; 4, 10-11; 6, 9). The second is apostolic, involving an effect on others (Jesus, 2 Cor 5, 14-15; Paul, 2 Cor 1, 6; 4, 12; 13, 9). The specific kind of "effectiveness in ministry" that Paul promises to demonstrate on his arrival (2 Cor 13, 4b; cf 2 Cor 10, 1-11) involves elements of both; this, too, will be modeled on Jesus' experience and a participation in that experience (2 Cor 12, 9; 13, 3b).

12, 11-18: This brief section forms an epilogue or concluding observation to Paul's boast, corresponding to the prologue in 2 Cor 11, 1-15. A four-step sequence of ideas is common to these two sections: Paul qualifies his boast as folly (2 Cor 11, 1; 12, 11a), asserts his noninferiority to the "superapostles" (2 Cor 11, 5; 12, 11b), exemplifies this by allusion to charismatic endowments (2 Cor 11, 6; 12, 12), and finally denies that he has been a financial burden to the community (2 Cor 11, 7-12; 12, 13-18).

12, 12: Despite weakness and affliction (suggested by the mention of *endurance*), his ministry has been accompanied by demonstrations of power (cf 1 Cor 2, 3-4). *Signs of an apostle:* visible proof of belonging to Christ and of mediating Christ's power, which the opponents require as touchstones of apostleship (2 Cor 12, 11; cf 2 Cor 13, 3).

12, 13-18: Paul insists on his intention to continue refusing support from the community (cf 2 Cor 11, 8-12). In defending his practice and his motivation, he once more protests his love (cf 2 Cor 11, 11) and rejects the suggestion of secret self-enrichment. He has recourse here again to language applied to his opponents earlier: "cunning" (2 Cor 11, 3), "deceit" (2 Cor 11, 13), "got the better of you" (see the note on 2 Cor 11, 20), "take advantage" (2 Cor 2, 11).

12, 19—13, 10: This concludes the development begun in ch 10. In the chiastic arrangement of the material (see the note on 2 Cor 10, 1—13, 10), this final part corresponds to the opening; there are important similarities of content between the two sections as well.

12, 19: This verse looks back at the previous chapters and calls them by their proper name, a defense, an *apologia* (cf 1 Cor 9, 3). Yet Paul insists on an important distinction: he has indeed been speaking for their benefit, but the ultimate judgment to which he submits is God's (cf 1 Cor 4, 3-5). This verse also leads into the final section, announcing two of its themes: judgment and building up.

12, 20: *I fear that . . . .:* earlier Paul expressed fear that the Corinthians were being victimized, exploited, seduced from right thinking by his opponents (2 Cor 11, 3-4.19-21). Here he alludes unexpectedly to moral disorders among the Corinthians themselves. The catalogue suggests the effects of factions that have grown up around rival apostles.

12, 21: *Again:* one can also translate, "I fear that when I come my God may again humiliate me." Paul's allusion to the humiliation and mourning that may await him recall the mood described in 2 Cor 2, 1-4, but there is no reference here to any individual such as there is in 2 Cor 2, 5-11. The crisis of ch 2 has happily been resolved by integration of the offender and repentance (2 Cor 7, 4-16), whereas 2 Cor 12, 21 is preoccupied with still unrepentant sinners. The sexual sins recall 1 Cor 5—7.

13, 1: *This third time I am coming:* designation of the forthcoming visit as the "third" (cf 2 Cor 12, 14) may indicate that, in addition to his founding sojourn in Corinth, Paul had already made the first of two visits mentioned as planned in 2 Cor 1, 15, and the next visit will be the long-postponed second of these. If so, the materials in 2 Cor 1, 12—2, 13 plus 2 Cor 7, 4-16 and chs 10-13 may date from the same period of time, presumably of some duration, between Paul's second and third visit, though it is not clear that they are addressing the same crisis. The chronology is too unsure and the relations between sections of 2 Cor too unclear to yield any certainty. The hypothesis that chs 10-13 are themselves the "tearful letter" mentioned at 2 Cor 2, 3-4 creates more problems than it solves.

fact shall be established."[d] [2] I warned those who sinned earlier* and all the others, and I warn them now while absent, as I did when present on my second visit, that if I come again I will not be lenient, [3] * since you are looking for proof of Christ speaking in me. He is not weak toward you but powerful in you. [4] For indeed he was crucified out of weakness, but he lives by the power of God. So also we are weak in him, but toward you we shall live with him by the power of God.

[5] * Examine yourselves to see whether you are living in faith. Test yourselves. Do you not realize that Jesus Christ is in you?—unless, of course, you fail the test. [6] I hope you will discover that we have not failed. [7] But we pray to God that you may not do evil, not that we may appear to have passed the test but that you may do what is right, even though we may seem to have failed. [8] For we cannot do anything against the truth, but only for the truth. [9] For we rejoice when we are weak but you are strong. What we pray for is your improvement.

[10] [e] I am writing this while I am away, so that when I come I may not have to be severe in virtue of the authority that the Lord has given me to build up and not to tear down.*

V. CONCLUSION*

[11] Finally, brothers, rejoice. Mend your ways, encourage one another, agree with one another, live in peace, and the God of love and peace will be with you. [12] Greet one another with a holy kiss. All the holy ones greet you.[f]

[13] The grace of the Lord Jesus Christ and the love of God and the fellowship of the holy Spirit be with all of you.[g]

---

d Dt 19, 15; Mt 18, 16; Jn 8, 17; Heb 10, 28.—e 2 Cor 10, 8.—f Rom 16, 16; 1 Cor 16, 20 / Phil 4, 22; 1 Thes 5, 26; 1 Pt 5, 14.—g Rom 16, 20; 1 Cor 16, 23.

13, 2: *I warned those who sinned earlier:* mention of unrepentant sinners (2 Cor 12, 21 and here) and of an oral admonition given them on an earlier visit complicates the picture at the very end of Paul's development. It provides, in fact, a second explanation for the show of power that has been threatened from the beginning (2 Cor 10, 1-6), but a different reason for it, quite unsuspected until now. It is not clear whether Paul is merely alluding to a dimension of the situation that he has not previously had occasion to mention, or whether some other community crisis, not directly connected with that behind chs 10-13, has influenced the final editing. *I will not be lenient:* contrast Paul's hesitation and reluctance to inflict pain in 2 Cor 1, 23 and 2 Cor 2, 1-4. The next visit will bring the showdown.

13, 3-4: Paul now gives another motive for severity when he comes, the charge of weakness leveled against him as an apostle. The motive echoes more closely the opening section (2 Cor 10, 1-18) and the intervening development (especially 2 Cor 11, 30—12, 10). *Proof of Christ speaking in me:* the threat of 2 Cor 10, 1-2 is reworded to recall Paul's conformity with the pattern of Christ, his insertion into the interplay of death and life, weakness and power (cf the note on 2 Cor 12, 10b).

13, 5-9: Paul turns the challenge mentioned in v 3 on them: they are to put themselves to the test to demonstrate whether Christ is in them. These verses involve a complicated series of plays on the theme of *dokimē* (testing, proof, passing and failing a test). Behind this stands the familiar distinction between present human judgment and final divine judgment. This is the final appearance of the theme (cf 2 Cor 10, 18; 11, 15; 12, 19).

13, 10: *Authority . . . to build up and not to tear down:* Paul restates the purpose of his letter in language that echoes 2 Cor 10, 2.8, emphasizing the positive purpose of his authority in their regard. This verse forms an inclusion with the topic sentence of the section (2 Cor 12, 19), as well as with the opening of this entire portion of the letter (2 Cor 10, 1-2).

13, 11-13: These verses may have originally concluded chs 10-13, but they have nothing specifically to do with the material of that section. It is also possible to consider them a conclusion to the whole of 2 Cor in its present edited form. The exhortations are general, including a final appeal for peace in the community. The letter ends calmly, after its many storms, with the prospect of ecclesial unity and divine blessing. The final verse is one of the clearest trinitarian passages in the New Testament.

THE LETTER TO THE GALATIANS

INTRODUCTION

The Galatians to whom the letter is addressed were Paul's converts, most likely among the descendants of Celts who had invaded western and central Asia Minor in the third century B.C. and had settled in the territory around Ancyra (modern Ankara, Turkey). Paul had passed through this area on his second missionary journey (Acts 16, 6) and again on his third (Acts 18, 23). It is less likely that the recipients of this letter were Paul's churches in the southern regions of Pisidia, Lycaonia, and Pamphylia where he had preached earlier in the Hellenized cities of Perge, Iconium, Pisidian Antioch, Lystra, and Derbe (Acts 13, 13—14, 27); this area was part of the Roman province of Galatia, and some scholars think that South Galatia was the destination of this letter.

If it is addressed to the Galatians in the north, the letter was probably written around A.D. 54 or 55, most likely from Ephesus after Paul's arrival there for a stay of several years on his third missionary journey (Acts 19; 20, 31). On the South Galatian theory, the date would be earlier, perhaps A.D. 48-50. Involved is the question of how one relates the events of 2, 1-10 to the "Council of Jerusalem" described in Acts 15 (see the notes on each passage).

In any case, the new Christians whom Paul is addressing were converts from paganism (4, 8-9) who were now being enticed by other missionaries to add the observances of the Jewish law, including the rite of circumcision, to the cross of Christ as a means of salvation. For, since Paul's visit, some other interpretation of Christianity had been brought to these neophytes, probably by converts from Judaism (the name "Judaizers" is sometimes applied to them); it has specifically been suggested that they were Jewish Christians who had come from the austere Essene sect.

These interlopers insisted on the necessity of following certain precepts of the Mosaic law along with faith in Christ. They were undermining Paul's authority also, asserting that he had not been trained by Jesus himself, that his gospel did not agree with that of the original and true apostles in Jerusalem, that he had kept from his converts in Galatia the necessity of accepting circumcision and other key obligations of the Jewish law, in order more easily to win them to Christ, and that his gospel was thus not the full and authentic one held by "those of repute" in Jerusalem (2, 2). Some scholars also see in chapters 5 and 6 another set of opponents against whom Paul writes, people who in their emphasis on the Spirit set aside all norms for conduct and became libertines in practice.

When Paul learned of the situation, he wrote this defense of his apostolic authority and of the correct understanding of the faith. He set forth the unique importance of Christ and his redemptive sacrifice on the cross, the freedom that Christians enjoy from the old burdens of the law, the total sufficiency of Christ and of faith in Christ as the way to God and to eternal life, and the beauty of the new life of the Spirit. Galatians is thus a summary of basic Pauline theology. Its themes were more fully and less polemically developed in the Letter to the Romans.

Autobiographically, the letter gives us Paul's own accounts of how he came to faith (1, 15-24), the agreement in "the truth of the gospel" (2, 5.14) that he shared with the Jewish Christian leaders in Jerusalem, James, Kephas, and John (2, 1-10), and the rebuke he had to deliver to Kephas in Antioch for inconsistency, contrary to the gospel, on the issue of table fellowship in the racially mixed church of Jewish and Gentile Christians

283

in Antioch (2, 11-14; cf 15-21). At the conclusion of the letter (6, 11-18), Paul wrote in his own hand (cf 2 Thes 3, 17-18) a vivid summary of the message to the Galatians.

In his vigorous emphasis on the absolute preeminence of Christ and his cross as God's way to salvation and holiness, Paul stresses Christian freedom and the ineffectiveness of the Mosaic law for gaining divine favor and blessings (3, 19-29). The pious Jew saw in the law a way established by God to win divine approval by a life of meticulous observance of ritual, social, and moral regulations. But Paul's profound insight into the higher designs of God in Christ led him to understand and welcome the priority of promise and faith (shown in the experience of Abraham, 3, 6-18) and the supernatural gifts of the Spirit (3, 2-5; 5, 16—6, 10). His enthusiasm for this new vision of the life of grace in Christ and of the uniquely salvific role of Christ's redemptive death on the cross shines through this whole letter.

The principal divisions of the Letter to the Galatians are the following:

I. *Address (1, 1-5)*
II. *Loyalty to the Gospel (1, 6-10)*
III. *Paul's Defense of His Gospel and His Authority (1, 11— 2, 21)*
IV. *Faith and Liberty (3, 1—4, 31)*
V. *Exhortation to Christian Living (5, 1—6, 10)*
VI. *Conclusion (6, 11-18)*

I. ADDRESS

CHAPTER 1

Greeting.* [1] *a* Paul, an apostle* not from human beings nor through a human being but through Jesus Christ and God the Father who raised him from the dead,*b* [2] and all the brothers* who are with me, to the churches of Galatia: [3] grace to you and peace from God our Father and the Lord Jesus Christ, [4] * who gave himself for our sins that he might rescue us from the present evil age in accord with the will of our God and Father,*c* [5] to whom be glory forever and ever. Amen.*d*

II. LOYALTY TO THE GOSPEL*

[6] *e* I am amazed that you are so quickly forsaking the one who called you* by [the] grace [of Christ] for a different gospel [7] (not that there is another). But there are some who are disturbing you and wish to pervert the gospel of Christ. [8] *f* But even if we or an angel from heaven should preach [to you] a gospel other than the one that we preached to you, let that one be accursed!* [9] As we have said before, and now I say again, if anyone preaches to you a gospel other than the one that you received, let that one be accursed!

[10] *g* Am I now currying favor with human beings or God? Or am I seeking to please people? If I were still trying to please people, I would not be a slave of Christ.*

---

a 1-3: Rom 1, 1-7; 1 Cor 1, 1-3.—b Gal 1, 11-12.—c Gal 2, 20; Eph 5, 2; 1 Tm 2, 6 / 1 Jn 5, 19 / Rom 12, 2; Eph 5, 16; Heb 10, 10.—d Rom 16, 27; 2 Tm 4, 18.—e 6-7: Gal 5, 8.10; Acts 15, 1.24; 2 Cor 11, 4.—f 8-9: 1 Cor 16, 22 / Gal 5, 3.21; 2 Cor 13, 2.—g 2 Cor 5, 11 / 1 Thes 2, 4.

1, 1-5: See the note on Rom 1, 1-7, concerning the greeting.

1, 1: *Apostle:* because of attacks on his authority in Galatia, Paul defends his apostleship. He is not an apostle commissioned by a congregation (Phil 2, 25; 2 Cor 8, 23) or even by prophets (1 Tm 1, 18 and 1 Tm 4, 14) but *through Jesus Christ and God the Father.*

1, 2: *All the brothers:* fellow believers in Christ, male and female; cf Gal 3, 27-28. Paul usually mentions the co-sender(s) at the start of a letter, but the use of *all* is unique, adding weight to the letter. *Galatia:* central Turkey more likely than the Roman province of Galatia; see Introduction.

1, 4: The greeting in v 3 is expanded by a christological formula that stresses deliverance through the Lord Jesus from a world dominated by Satan; cf 2 Cor 4, 4; Eph 2, 2; 6, 12.

1, 6-10: In place of the usual thanksgiving (see the note on Rom 1, 8), Paul, with little to be thankful for in the Galatian situation, expresses amazement at the way his converts are deserting the gospel of Christ for a perverted message. He reasserts the one gospel he has preached (7-9) and begins to defend himself (10).

1, 6: *The one who called you:* God or Christ, though in actuality Paul was the divine instrument to call the Galatians.

1, 8: *Accursed:* in Greek, *anathema;* cf Rom 9, 3; 1 Cor 12, 3; 16, 22.

1, 10: This charge by Paul's opponents, that he sought to conciliate people with flattery and to curry favor with God, might refer to his mission practices (cf 1 Cor 9, 19-23) but the word *still* suggests it refers to his pre-Christian days (cf Gal 1, 14; Phil 3, 6). The self-description *slave of Christ* is one Paul often uses in a greeting (Rom 1, 1).

III. PAUL'S DEFENSE OF HIS GOSPEL AND HIS AUTHORITY*

His Call by Christ. [11] *h* Now I want you to know, brothers, that the gospel preached by me is not of human origin. [12] For I did not receive it from a human being, nor was I taught it, but it came through a revelation of Jesus Christ.*

[13] * For you heard of my former way of life in Judaism, how I persecuted the church of God beyond measure and tried to destroy it,*i* [14] and progressed in Judaism beyond many of my contemporaries among my race, since I was even more a zealot for my ancestral traditions.*j* [15] But when [God], who from my mother's womb had set me apart and called me through his grace, was pleased*k* [16] to reveal his Son to me,*l* so that I might proclaim him to the Gentiles, I did not immediately consult flesh and blood,* [17] nor did I go up to Jerusalem to those who were apostles be-fore me; rather, I went into Arabia* and then returned to Damascus.

[18] * Then after three years* I went up to Jerusalem to confer with Kephas and re-mained with him for fifteen days.*m* [19] But I did not see any other of the apostles,*n* only James the brother of the Lord.* [20] (As to what I am writing to you, behold, before God, I am not lying.)*o* [21] Then I went into the regions of Syria and Cilicia.*p* [22] And I was unknown personally to the churches of Judea that are in Christ; [23] they only kept hearing that "the one who once was perse-cuting us is now preaching the faith he once tried to destroy."*q* [24] So they glorified God because of me.

CHAPTER 2

The Council of Jerusalem.* [1] Then after fourteen years* I again went up to Jerusalem with Barnabas, taking Titus along also.*r* [2] I went up in accord with a revelation,* and I presented to them the

h 11-12: 1 Cor 15, 1 / Gal 1, 1; Eph 3, 3.—i Acts 8, 1-3; 9, 1-2; 1 Cor 15, 9.—j Acts 26, 4-5.—k Is 49, 1; Jer 1, 4.—l Gal 1, 11-12; Rom 1, 5; 1 Cor 15, 10; Acts 9, 3-9 / Gal 2, 2.7 / Mt 16, 17.—m Acts 9, 26-30 / Jn 1, 42.—n Gal 2, 9; Mt 13, 55; Acts 12, 17.—o Rom 9, 1; 2 Cor 11, 31.—p Acts 9, 30.—q Gal 1, 13.—r Acts 15, 2.

1, 11—2, 21: Paul's presentation on behalf of his message and of his apostleship reflects rhetorical forms of his day: he first narrates the facts about certain past events (Gal 1, 12—2, 14) and then states his contention regarding justification by faith as the gospel message (Gal 2, 15-21). Further arguments follow from both experience and scripture in chs 3 and 4, before he draws out the ethical consequences (Gal 5, 1—6, 10). The specific facts that he takes up here to show that his gospel is not a human invention (Gal 1, 11) but *came through a revelation of Jesus Christ* (Gal 1, 12) deal with his own calling as a Christian missionary (Gal 1, 13-17), his initial relations with the apostles in Jerusalem (Gal 1, 18-24), a later journey to Jerusalem (Gal 2, 1-10), and an incident in Antioch involving Kephas and persons from James (Gal 2, 11-14). The content of Paul's revealed gospel is then set forth in the heart of the letter (Gal 2, 15-21).

1, 12: Although Paul received his gospel *through a revelation* from Christ, this did not exclude his use of early Christian confessional formulations. See the note on Gal 1, 4.

1, 13-17: Along with Phil 3, 4-11, which also moves from au-tobiography to its climax in a discussion on justification by faith (cf Gal 2, 15-21), this passage is Paul's chief account of the change from his *former way of life* (13) to service as a Christian missionary (16); cf Acts 9, 1-22; 22, 4-16; 26, 9-18. Paul himself does not use the term "conversion" but stresses revelation (12.16). In v 15 his language echoes the Old Testament prophetic call of Jeremiah. Unlike the account in Acts (cf Acts 22, 4-16), the calling of Paul here includes the mission to proclaim Christ *to the Gentiles* (16).

1, 16: *Flesh and blood:* human authorities (cf Mt 16, 17; 1 Cor 15, 50). Paul's apostleship comes from God (1).

1, 17: *Arabia:* probably the region of the Nabataean Arabs, east and south of Damascus.

1, 18-24: Paul's first journey to Jerusalem as a Christian, ac-cording to Galatians (cf Acts 9, 23-31 and the note on Acts 12, 25). He is quite explicit about contacts there, testifying under oath (20). On returning to *Syria* (perhaps specifically Damascus,

cf Gal 1, 17) *and Cilicia* (including his home town Tarsus, cf Acts 9, 30; 22, 3), Paul most likely engaged in missionary work. He underscores the fact that Christians in Judea knew of him only by reputation.

1, 18: *After three years:* two years and more, since Paul's call. To *confer with* Kephas may mean simply "pay a visit" or more specifically "get information from" him about Jesus, over a two-week period. *Kephas:* Aramaic name of Simon (Peter); cf Mt 16, 16-18 and the notes there.

1, 19: *James the brother of the Lord:* not one of the twelve, but a brother of Jesus (see the note on Mk 6, 3). He played an im-portant role in the Jerusalem church (see the note on Gal 2, 9), the leadership of which he took over from Peter (Acts 12, 17). Paul may have regarded James as an apostle.

2, 1-10: Paul's second journey to Jerusalem, according to Ga-latians, involved a private meeting with *those of repute* (2). At issue was a Gentile, Titus, and the question of circumcision, which *false brothers* (4) evidently demanded for him. Paul insists that the gospel he preaches (2; cf Gal 1, 9.11) remained intact with no addition by those of repute (6); that *Titus* was not *compelled* to accept circumcision (3); and that he and the reputed *pillars* in Jerusalem agreed on how each would advance the missionary task (7-10). Usually, 1-10 is equated with the "Council of Jerusalem," as it is called, described in Acts 15. See the notes on Acts 15, 6-12 and Acts 15, 13-35, the latter concerning the "decree" that Paul does not mention.

2, 1: *After fourteen years:* thirteen or more years, probably reckoned from the return to Syria and Cilicia (Gal 1, 21), though possibly from Paul's calling as a Christian (Gal 1, 15). *Bar-nabas:* cf Gal 2, 9.13; 1 Cor 9, 6. A Jewish Christian missionary, with whom Paul worked (Acts 4, 36-37; 11, 22.25.30; 12, 25; 13, 1-3; 15, 2). *Titus:* a missionary companion of Paul (2 Cor 2, 13; 7, 6.13-15; 8, 6.16.23; 12, 18), non-Jewish (Gal 2, 3), never mentioned in Acts.

2, 2: *A revelation:* cf Gal 1, 1.12. Paul emphasizes it was God's will, not Jerusalem authority, that led to the journey. Acts 15, 2 states that the church in Antioch appointed Paul and Bar-nabas for the task. *Those of repute:* leaders of the Jerusalem church; the term, while positive, may be slightly ironic (cf Gal 2, 6.9). *Run, in vain:* while Paul presents a positive picture in what follows, his missionary work in Galatia would have been to no pur-pose if his opponents were correct that circumcision is needed for complete faith in Christ.

gospel that I preach to the Gentiles—but privately to those of repute—so that I might not be running, or have run, in vain.[s] 3 Moreover, not even* Titus, who was with me, although he was a Greek, was compelled to be circumcised,[t] 4 but because of the false brothers* secretly brought in, who slipped in to spy on our freedom that we have in Christ Jesus,[u] that they might enslave us—5 to them we did not submit even for a moment, so that the truth of the gospel* might remain intact for you.[v] 6 But from those who were reputed to be important (what they once were makes no difference to me; God shows no partiality)—those of repute made me add nothing.[w] 7 * On the contrary, when they saw that I had been entrusted with the gospel to the uncircumcised, just as Peter to the circumcised,[x] 8 for the one who worked in Peter for an apostolate to the circumcised worked also in me for the Gentiles, 9 and when they recognized the grace bestowed upon me, James and Kephas and John,* who were reputed to be pillars, gave me and Barnabas their right hands in partnership, that we should go to the Gentiles and they to the circumcised.[y] 10 Only, we were to be mindful of the poor,* which is the very thing I was eager to do.[z]

Peter's Inconsistency at Antioch.* 11 [a] And when Kephas came to Antioch, I opposed him to his face because he clearly was wrong.* 12 For, until some people came from James,* he used to eat with the Gentiles; but when they came, he began to draw back and separated himself, because he was afraid of the circumcised.[b] 13 And the rest of the Jews* [also] acted hypocritically along with him, with the result that even Barnabas was carried away by their hypocrisy.[c] 14 But when I saw that they were not on the right road in line with the truth of the gospel, I said to Kephas in front of all,[d] "If you, though a Jew, are living like a Gentile and not like a Jew, how can you compel the Gentiles to live like Jews?"*

Faith and Works.* 15 We, who are Jews by nature and not sinners from among the Gentiles, 16 [e] [yet] who know that a person is not justified by works of the law but through faith in Jesus Christ, even we have believed in Christ Jesus that we may be justified by faith in Christ and not by works of the law, because by works of the

s Gal 1, 11-12.16 / Gal 1, 16 / Phil 2, 16.—t 2 Cor 2, 13; 7, 6-7; 8, 16-17; 12, 18; Ti 1, 4 / Gal 2, 14; 6, 12.—u Gal 5, 1; Acts 15, 1.24.—v Gal 2, 14; 4, 16.—w Dt 10, 17; Rom 2, 11.—x Gal 1, 15-16; Acts 9, 15; 15, 12; 22, 21; Rom 1, 5.—y Rom 15, 15 / Gal 1, 18-19; Jn 1, 42; Acts 12, 17 / Gal 2, 1.—z Acts 11, 29-30; Rom 15, 25-28; 1 Cor 16, 1-4; 2 Cor 8, 9.—a Gal 1, 18 / Acts 11, 19-30; 15, 1-2.—b Acts 10, 15.28; 11, 3.—c Gal 2, 1.9.—d Gal 2, 5 / Gal 1, 18; Gal 2, 9 / Gal 2, 3.—e Gal 3, 2.11; Ps 143, 1-2; Rom 3, 20.28; 4, 5; 11, 6; Eph 2, 8-9; Phil 3, 9.

2, 3: *Not even* a Gentile Christian like Titus was compelled to receive the rite of circumcision. The Greek text could be interpreted that he voluntarily accepted circumcision, but this is unlikely in the overall argument.

2, 4: *False brothers:* Jewish Christians who took the position that Gentile Christians must first become Jews through circumcision and observance of the Mosaic law in order to become Christians; cf Acts 15, 1.

2, 5: *The truth of the gospel:* the true gospel, in contrast to the false one of the opponents (Gal 1, 6-9); the gospel of grace, used as a norm (14).

2, 7-9: Some think that actual "minutes" of the meeting are here quoted. Paul's apostleship to the Gentiles (Gal 1, 16) is recognized alongside that of Peter to the Jews. Moreover, the right to proclaim the gospel without requiring circumcision and the Jewish law is sealed by a handshake. That Paul and colleagues *should go to the Gentiles* did not exclude his preaching to the Jews as well (Rom 1, 13-16) or Kephas to Gentile areas.

2, 9: *James and Kephas and John:* see the notes on Gal 1, 18 and 19; on Peter and John as leaders in the Jerusalem church, cf Acts 3, 1 and Acts 8, 14. The order here, with James first, may reflect his prominence in Jerusalem after Peter (Kephas) departed (Acts 12, 17).

2, 10: *The poor:* Jerusalem Christians or a group within the church there (cf Rom 15, 26). The collection for them was extremely important in Paul's thought and labor (cf Rom 15, 25-28; 1 Cor 16, 1-4; 2 Cor 8 and 9).

2, 11-14: The decision reached in Jerusalem (3-7) recognized the freedom of Gentile Christians from the Jewish law. But the problem of table fellowship between Jewish Christians, who possibly still kept kosher food regulations, and Gentile believers was not yet settled. When Kephas first came to the racially mixed community of Jewish and Gentile Christians in Antioch (12), he ate with non-Jews. Pressure from persons arriving later from Jerusalem caused him and Barnabas to draw back. Paul therefore publicly rebuked Peter's inconsistency toward the gospel (14). Some think that what Paul said on that occasion extends through v 16 or v 21.

2, 11: *Clearly was wrong:* literally, "stood condemned," by himself and also by Paul. His action in breaking table fellowship was especially grievous if the eating involved the meal at the Lord's supper (cf 1 Cor 11, 17-25).

2, 12: *Some people came from James:* strict Jewish Christians (cf Acts 15, 1.5; 21, 20-21), either sent by James (Gal 1, 19; 2, 9) or claiming to be from the leader of the Jerusalem church. *The circumcised:* presumably Jewish Christians, not Jews.

2, 13: *The Jews:* Jewish Christians, like Barnabas. *Hypocrisy:* literally, "pretense," "play-acting"; moral insincerity.

2, 14: *Compel the Gentiles to live like Jews:* that is, conform to Jewish practices, such as circumcision (3-5) or regulations about food (12).

2, 15-21: Following on the series of incidents cited above, Paul's argument, whether spoken to Kephas at Antioch or only now articulated, is pertinent to the Galatian situation, where believers were having themselves circumcised (Gal 6, 12-13) and obeying other aspects of Jewish law (Gal 4, 9-10; 5, 1-4). He insists that salvation is by faith in Christ, not by works of the law. His teaching on the gospel concerns justification by faith (16) in relation to sin (17), law (19), life in Christ (19-20), and grace (21).

law no one will be justified.* [17]But if, in seeking to be justified in Christ, we ourselves are found to be sinners, is Christ then a minister of sin?* Of course not! [18]But if I am building up again those things that I tore down, then I show myself to be a transgressor.* [19]For through the law I died to the law,* that I might live for God. I have been crucified with Christ;[f] [20]yet I live, no longer I, but Christ lives in me; insofar as I now live in the flesh, I live by faith in the Son of God who has loved me and given himself up for me.[g] [21]I do not nullify the grace of God; for if justification comes through the law, then Christ died for nothing.[h]

IV. FAITH AND LIBERTY

CHAPTER 3

Justification by Faith.* [1]O stupid* Galatians! Who has bewitched you, before whose eyes Jesus Christ was publicly portrayed as crucified?[i] [2]I want to learn only this from you:[j] did you receive the Spirit from works of the law, or from faith in what you heard?* [3]Are you so stupid?[k] After beginning with the Spirit, are you now ending with the flesh?* [4]Did you ex-

perience so many things* in vain?—if indeed it was in vain. [5]Does, then, the one who supplies the Spirit to you and works mighty deeds among you do so from works of the law or from faith in what you heard?[l] [6]Thus Abraham "believed God,[m] and it was credited to him as righteousness."*

[7] * Realize then that it is those who have faith who are children of Abraham.[n] [8]Scripture, which saw in advance that God would justify the Gentiles by faith, foretold the good news to Abraham, saying, "Through you shall all the nations be blessed."[o] [9]Consequently, those who have faith are blessed along with Abraham who had faith.[p] [10] * For all who depend on works of the law are under a curse; for it is written, "Cursed be everyone who does not persevere in doing all the things written in the book of the law."[q] [11]And that no one is justified before God by the law is clear, for "the one who is righteous by faith will live."[r] [12]But the law does not depend on faith; rather, "the one who does these things will live by them."[s] [13]Christ ransomed us from the curse of the law by becoming a curse for us, for it is written, "Cursed be everyone who hangs on a

---

f Gal 6, 14; Rom 6, 6.8.10; 7, 6.—g Gal 1, 4; Rom 8, 10-11; Col 3, 3-4.—h Gal 5, 2.—i Gal 5, 7; 1 Cor 1, 23.—j Gal 2, 16 / Gal 3, 14; Rom 10, 17.—k Gal 5, 16-18.—l Gal 2, 16.—m Gn 15, 6; Rom 4, 3; Jas 2, 23.—n Gal 3, 29; Rom 4, 11-12 / Sir 44, 19-21.—o Gn 12, 3; 18, 17-19; Acts 3, 25.—p Rom 4, 16.—q Dt 27, 26; Jas 2, 10.—r Gal 2, 16; Hb 2, 4; Rom 1, 17.—s Lv 18, 5; Rom 10, 5.

2, 16: *No one will be justified:* Ps 143, 2 is reflected.

2, 17: *A minister of sin:* literally, "a servant of sin" (cf Rom 15, 8), an agent of sin, one who promotes it. This is possibly a claim by opponents that justification on the basis of faith in Christ makes Christ an abettor of sin when Christians *are found to be sinners.* Paul denies the conclusion (cf Rom 6, 1-4).

2, 18: To return to observance of the law as the means to salvation would entangle one not only in inevitable transgressions of it but also in the admission that it was wrong to have abandoned the law in the first place.

2, 19: *Through the law I died to the law:* this is variously explained: the law revealed sin (Rom 7, 7-9) and led to death and then to belief in Christ; or, the law itself brought the insight that law cannot justify (Gal 2, 16; Ps 143, 2); or, the "law of Christ" (Gal 6, 2) led to abandoning the Mosaic law; or, the law put Christ to death (cf Gal 3, 13) and so provided a way to our salvation, through baptism into Christ, through which we die (*crucified with Christ;* see Rom 6, 6). Cf also Gal 3, 19-25 on the role of the law in reference to salvation.

3, 1-14: Paul's contention that justification comes not through the law or the works of the law but by faith in Christ and in his death (Gal 2, 16.21) is supported by appeals to Christian experience (1-5) and to scripture (6-14). The gift of God's Spirit to the Galatians came from the gospel received in faith, not from doing

what the law enjoins. The story of Abraham shows that faith in God brings *righteousness* (6; Gn 15, 6). The promise to Abraham (8; Gn 12, 3) extends to the Gentiles (14).

3, 1: *Stupid:* not just senseless, for they were in danger of deserting their salvation.

3, 2: *Faith in what you heard:* Paul's message received with faith. The Greek can also mean "the proclamation of the faith" or "a hearing that comes from faith."

3, 3: On the contrast of *Spirit* and *flesh,* cf Rom 8, 1-11. Having received the Spirit, they need not be circumcised now.

3, 4: *Experience so many things:* probably the *mighty deeds* of v 5 but possibly the experience of sufferings.

3, 6: *Abraham . . . righteousness:* see Gn 15, 6; Rom 4, 3. The Galatians like Abraham heard with faith and experienced justification. This first argument forms the basis for the further scriptural evidence that follows.

3, 7-9: *Faith* is what matters, for *Abraham* and the *children of Abraham,* in contrast to the claims of the opponents that circumcision and observance of the law are needed to bring the promised blessing of Gn 12, 3; cf Gn 18, 18; Sir 44, 21; Acts 3, 25.

3, 10-14: Those *who depend* not on promise and faith but *on works of the law are under a curse* because they do *not persevere in doing all the things written in the book of the law* (10; Dt 27, 26) in order to gain life (12; Lv 18, 5; cf Rom 10, 5). But scripture teaches that *no one is justified before God by the law* (11; Hb 2, 4, adapted from the Greek version of Habakkuk; cf Rom 1, 17; Heb 10, 38). Salvation, then, depends on faith in Christ who died on the cross (13), taking upon himself a curse found in Dt 21, 23 (about executed criminals hanged in public view), to free us from *the curse of the law* (13). That the Gentile Galatians have received the promised Spirit (14) by faith and in no other way returns the argument to the experience cited in vv 1-5.

tree,"*t* [14] that the blessing of Abraham might be extended to the Gentiles through Christ Jesus, so that we might receive the promise of the Spirit through faith.*u*

The Law Did Not Nullify the Promise. [15] * Brothers, in human terms I say that no one can annul or amend even a human will once ratified.*v* [16] Now the promises were made to Abraham and to his descendant.* It does not say, "And to descendants," as referring to many, but as referring to one, "And to your descendant," who is Christ.*w* [17] This is what I mean: the law, which came four hundred and thirty years afterward,* does not annul a covenant previously ratified by God, so as to cancel the promise.*x* [18] For if the inheritance comes from the law,*y* it is no longer from a promise; but God bestowed it on Abraham through a promise.*

[19] * Why, then, the law? It was added for transgressions, until the descendant* came to whom the promise had been made; it was promulgated by angels at the hand of a mediator.*z* [20] Now there is no mediator when only one party is involved, and God is one.*a* [21] Is the law then opposed to the promises [of God]? Of course not! For if a law had been given that could bring life,

then righteousness would in reality come from the law.*b* [22] But scripture confined all things under the power of sin, that through faith in Jesus Christ the promise might be given to those who believe.*c*

What Faith Has Brought Us. * [23] Before faith came, we were held in custody under law, confined for the faith that was to be revealed.*d* [24] Consequently, the law was our disciplinarian* for Christ, that we might be justified by faith.*e* [25] But now that faith has come, we are no longer under a disciplinarian.*f* [26] For through faith you are all children of God* in Christ Jesus.*g* [27] * For all of you who were baptized into Christ*h* have clothed yourselves with Christ.* [28] There is neither Jew nor Greek, there is neither slave nor free person, there is not male and female; for you are all one in Christ Jesus.*i* [29] And if you belong to Christ, then you are Abraham's descendant, heirs according to the promise.*j*

CHAPTER 4

God's Free Children in Christ. * [1] I mean that as long as the heir is not of age,* he is no different from a slave, although he is

---

t Dt 21, 23; Rom 8, 3; 2 Cor 5, 21.—u Gal 3, 2-3.5; Is 44, 3; Jl 3, 1-2; Acts 2, 33.—v Rom 3, 5 / Heb 9, 16-17.—w Gn 12, 7; 13, 15; 17, 8; 22, 17; 24, 7; Mt 1, 1.—x Ex 12, 40.—y Rom 4, 16; 11, 6.—z Rom 4, 15; 5, 20; 7, 7.13 / Acts 7, 38.53.—a Dt 6, 4.—b Rom 7, 7.10; 8, 2-4.—c Rom 3, 9-20.23; 11, 32.—d Gal 4, 3-5; 5, 18.—e Gal 2, 16.—f Rom 10, 4.—g Gal 4, 5-7; Jn 1, 12; Rom 8, 14-17.—h Rom 6, 3; 13, 14; Eph 4, 24.—i Rom 10, 12; 1 Cor 12, 13; Col 3, 11.—j Gal 3, 7.14.16.18; Rom 4, 16-17; 9, 7 / Gal 4, 1.7; Rom 4, 13-14; 8, 17; Heb 6, 12; Jas 2, 5.

3, 15-18: A third argument to support Paul's position that salvation is not through the law but by promise (1-14) comes from legal practice and scriptural history. A legal agreement or *human will*, duly *ratified*, is unalterable (15). God's *covenant* with *Abraham* and its repeated promises (Gn 12, 2-3.7; 13, 15; 17, 7-8; 22, 16-18; 24, 7) is not superseded by *the law*, which came much later, in the time of Moses. *The inheritance* (of the Spirit and the blessings) is by promise, not by law (18). Paul's argument hinges on the fact that the same Greek word, *diathēkē*, can be rendered as *will* or testament (15) and as *covenant* (17).

3, 16: *Descendant:* literally, "and to his seed." The Hebrew, as in Gn 12, 7; 15, 18; 22, 17-18, is a collective singular, traditionally rendered as a plural, *descendants*, but taken by Paul in its literal sense to refer to *Christ* as descendant of Abraham.

3, 17: *Four hundred and thirty years afterward:* follows Ex 12, 40 in the Greek (Septuagint) version, in contrast to Gn 15, 13 and Acts 7, 6, for chronology.

3, 18: This refutes the opponents' contention that the promises of God are fulfilled only as a reward for human observance of the law.

3, 19-22: A digression: if the Mosaic law, then, does not save or *bring life*, why was it given? Elsewhere, Paul says the law served to show what sin is (Rom 3, 20; 7, 7-8). Here the further implication is that the law in effect served to produce transgressions. Moreover, it was received at second hand *by angels*, through a *mediator*, not directly from God (19). The law does

not, however, oppose God's purposes, for it carries out its function (22), so that *righteousness* comes by *faith* and *promise*, not by human works of the law.

3, 19: *The descendant:* Christ (16). *By angels:* Dt 33, 2-4 stressed their presence as enhancing the importance of the law; Paul uses their role to diminish its significance (cf Acts 7, 38.53). *A mediator:* Moses. But in a covenant of promise, where all depends on the one God, no mediator is needed (20).

3, 23-29: Paul adds a further argument in support of righteousness or justification by faith and through God's promise rather than by works of the law (Gal 2, 16; 3, 22): as *children of God, baptized into Christ*, the Galatians are all *Abraham's descendant* and *heirs* of *the promise* to Abraham (8.14.16-18.29). The teaching in 23-25, that since *faith* (Christianity) *has come, we are no longer under* the law, could be taken with the previous paragraph on the role of the Mosaic law, but it also fits here as a contrast between the situation *before faith* (23) and the results after faith has come (25-29).

3, 24-25: *Disciplinarian:* the Greek *paidagōgos* referred to a slave who escorted a child to school but did not teach or tutor; hence, a guardian or monitor. Applying this to the law fits the role of the law described in vv 19-25.

3, 26: *Children of God:* literally "sons," in contrast to the young child under the disciplinarian in vv 24-25. The term includes males and females (28).

3, 27-28: Likely a formula used at baptism that expresses racial, social-economic, and sexual equality in Christ (cf Col 3, 11).

3, 27: *Clothed yourselves with Christ:* literally, "have put on Christ"; cf Rom 13, 14; Eph 4, 24; Col 3, 10. Baptismal imagery, traceable to the Old Testament (Jb 29, 14; Is 59, 17) but also found in pagan mystery cults.

4, 1-7: What Paul has argued in Gal 3, 26-29 is now elaborated in terms of the Christian as *the heir* (1.7; cf Gal 3, 18.29) freed from control by others. Again, as in Gal 3, 2-5, the proof that Christians are children of God is the gift of the Spirit of Christ relating them intimately to God.

4, 1.3: *Not of age:* an infant or minor.

the owner of everything, [2] but he is under the supervision of guardians and administrators until the date set by his father. [3] [k] In the same way we also, when we were not of age, were enslaved to the elemental powers of the world.* [4] But when the fullness of time had come, God sent his Son, born of a woman, born under the law, [l] [5] to ransom those under the law, so that we might receive adoption. [m] [6] As proof that you are children,* God sent the spirit of his Son into our hearts, crying out, "Abba, Father!" [n] [7] So you are no longer a slave but a child, and if a child then also an heir, through God. [o]

Do Not Throw This Freedom Away.* [8] [p] At a time when you did not know God, you became slaves to things that by nature are not gods;* [9] but now that you have come to know God, or rather to be known by God, how can you turn back again to the weak and destitute elemental powers? Do you want to be slaves to them all over again? [q] [10] You are observing days, [r] months, seasons, and years.* [11] I am afraid on your account that perhaps I have labored for you in vain.*

Appeal to Former Loyalty.* [12] I implore you, brothers, be as I am, because I have also become as you are.* You did me no wrong; [s] [13] you know that it was because of a physical illness* that I originally preached the gospel to you, [14] and you did not show disdain or contempt because of the trial caused you by my physical condition, but rather you received me as an angel of God, as Christ Jesus. [15] Where now is that blessedness of yours?* Indeed, I can testify to you that, if it had been possible, you would have torn out your eyes and given them to me. [16] So now have I become your enemy by telling you the truth? [17] They show interest in you, but not in a good way; they want to isolate you,* so that you may show interest in them. [t] [18] Now it is good to be shown interest for good reason at all times, and not only when I am with you. [u] [19] My children, for whom I am again in labor until Christ be formed in you! [20] I would like to be with you now and to change my tone, for I am perplexed because of you.

An Allegory on Christian Freedom.* [21] Tell me, you who want to be under the law, do you not listen to the law? [22] For it is written that Abraham had two sons, one by the slave woman and the other by the freeborn woman. [v] [23] The son of the slave woman was born naturally, the son of the freeborn through a promise. [w] [24] Now this is an al-

---

k Gal 3, 23 / Gal 4, 9; Col 2, 20.—l Mk 1, 15.—m Gal 3, 13.26.—n Gal 3, 26; Rom 8, 15.—o Gal 3, 29; Rom 8, 16-17.—p 1 Cor 12, 2.—q Gal 4, 3; Col 2, 20.—r Col 2, 16-20.—s 1 Cor 11, 1.—t Gal 1, 7; 6, 12; Acts 20, 30.—u 1 Cor 4, 14-15; 2 Cor 6, 13; 1 Thes 2, 7-8.—v Gn 16, 15; 21, 2-3.—w Gn 17, 16; Rom 4, 19-20; 9, 7-9.

4, 3: *The elemental powers of the world:* while the term can refer to the "elements" like earth, air, fire, and water or to elementary forms of religion, the sense here is more likely that of celestial beings that were thought in pagan circles to control the world; cf Gal 4, 8; Col 2, 8.20.

4, 6: *Children:* see the note on Gal 3, 26; here in contrast to the infant or young person *not of age* (1.3). *Abba:* cf Mk 14, 36 and the note; Rom 8, 15.

4, 8-11: On the basis of the arguments advanced from Gal 3, 1 through Gal 4, 7, Paul now launches his appeal to the Galatians with the question, *how can you turn back* to the slavery of the law (9)? The question is posed with reference to bondage to the *elemental powers* (see the note on Gal 4, 3) because the Galatians had originally been converted to Christianity from paganism, not Judaism (8). The use of the direct question is like Gal 3, 3-5.

4, 8: *Things that by nature are not gods:* or "gods that by nature do not exist."

4, 10: This is likely a reference to ritual observances from the Old Testament, promoted by opponents: sabbaths or Yom Kippur, new moon, Passover or Pentecost, sabbatical years.

4, 11: Cf Gal 2, 2. If the Galatians become *slaves . . . all over again* to the law (9), Paul will have worked in vain among them.

4, 12-20: A strongly personal section. Paul appeals to past ties between the Galatians and himself. He speaks sharply of the opponents (17-18) and pastorally to the Galatians (19-20).

4, 12: *Because I have also become as you are:* a terse phrase in Greek, meaning "Be as I, Paul, am," i.e., living by faith, independent of the law, for, in spite of my background in Judaism (Gal 1, 13), I have become as you Galatians are now, a brother in Christ.

4, 13: *Physical illness:* because its nature is not described, some assume an eye disease (15); others, epilepsy; some relate it to 2 Cor 12, 7-9. *Originally:* this may also be translated "formerly" or "on the first (of two) visit(s)"; cf Acts 16, 6; 18, 23.

4, 15: *That blessedness of yours:* possibly a reference to the Galatians' initial happy reception of Paul (14) and of his gospel (Gal 1, 6; 3, 1-4) and their felicitation at such blessedness, but the phrase could also refer ironically to earlier praise by Paul of the Galatians, no longer possible when they turn from the gospel to the claims of the opponents (Gal 4, 17-18; 1, 7). If the word is a more literal reference to a beatitude, Gal 3, 26-28 may be in view.

4, 17: *Isolate you:* that is, from the blessings of the gospel and/or from Paul.

4, 21-31: Paul supports his appeal for the gospel (Gal 4, 9; 1, 6-9; 2, 16; 3, 2) by a further argument from scripture (cf Gal 3, 6-18). It involves the relationship of *Abraham* (Gal 3, 6-16) to his wife, Sarah, the *freeborn woman,* and to Hagar, *the slave woman,* and the contrast between the sons born to each, *Isaac,* child of promise, and *Ishmael,* son of Hagar (Gn 16 and 21). Only through Isaac is the promise of God preserved. This *allegory* (24), with its equation of the Sinai covenant and Mosaic law with slavery and of the promise of God with freedom, Paul uses only in light of previous arguments. His quotation of Gn 21, 10 at v 30 suggests on a scriptural basis that the Galatians should expel those who are troubling them (Gal 1, 7).

Gal

legory. These women represent two covenants. One was from Mount Sinai, bearing children for slavery; this is Hagar.[x] [25] Hagar represents Sinai,* a mountain in Arabia; it corresponds to the present Jerusalem, for she is in slavery along with her children. [26] But the Jerusalem above is freeborn, and she is our mother.[y] [27] For it is written:

"Rejoice, you barren one who bore no children;[z]
break forth and shout, you who were not in labor;
for more numerous are the children of the deserted one
than of her who has a husband."*

[28] Now you, brothers, like Isaac, are children of the promise.[a] [29] But just as then the child of the flesh persecuted the child of the spirit, it is the same now. [30] But what does the scripture say?

"Drive out the slave woman and her son!
For the son of the slave woman shall not share the inheritance with the son"[b]

of the freeborn. [31] Therefore, brothers, we are children not of the slave woman but of the freeborn woman.[c]

V. EXHORTATION TO CHRISTIAN LIVING

CHAPTER 5

The Importance of Faith.* [1] For freedom* Christ set us free; so stand firm and do not submit again to the yoke of slavery.[d]

[2] It is I, Paul, who am telling you that if you have yourselves circumcised, Christ will be of no benefit to you.[e] [3] Once again I declare to every man who has himself circumcised[f] that he is bound to observe the entire law.* [4] You are separated from Christ, you who are trying to be justified by law; you have fallen from grace. [5] [g] For through the Spirit, by faith, we await the hope of righteousness. [6] [h] For in Christ Jesus, neither circumcision nor uncircumcision counts for anything, but only faith working through love.*

Be Not Misled.* [7] You were running well;* who hindered you from following [the] truth? [8] [i] That enticement does not come from the one who called you.* [9] A little yeast leavens the whole batch of dough.[j] [10] I am confident of you in the Lord that you will not take a different view, and that the one who is troubling you will bear the condemnation, whoever he may be.[k] [11] As for me, brothers, if I am still preaching circumcision,* why am I still being persecuted? In that case, the stumbling block of the cross has been abolished.[l] [12] Would that those who are upsetting you might also castrate themselves!*

Freedom for Service.* [13] For you were called for freedom, brothers.[m] But do not use this freedom as an opportunity for the flesh; rather, serve* one another through

---

x Gal 3, 17 / Ex 19, 20 / Gn 16, 1.—y Heb 12, 22; Rv 21, 2.—z Is 54, 1.—a Rom 9, 8.—b Gn 21, 10.—c Gal 3, 29; Jn 8, 35.—d Gal 2, 4; 4, 5.9; Jn 8, 32.36.—e Gal 2, 21; Acts 15, 1-29.—f Gal 3, 10; Rom 2, 25; Jas 2, 10.—g Rom 8, 23.25.—h Gal 3, 28; 6, 15; 1 Cor 7, 19.—i Gal 1, 6.—j 1 Cor 5, 6.—k Gal 1, 7.—l Gal 6, 12.14; 1 Cor 1, 23.—m Gal 5, 1 / Rom 6, 18; 1 Cor 8, 9; 1 Pt 2, 16.

4, 25: *Hagar represents Sinai . . . :* some manuscripts have what seems a geographical note, "For Sinai is a mountain in Arabia."

4, 27: Is 54, 1 in the Septuagint translation is applied to Sarah as the *barren one* (in Gn 15) who ultimately becomes the mother not only of Isaac but now of numerous children, i.e., of all those who believe, the *children of the promise* (28).

5, 1-6: Paul begins the exhortations, continuing through Gal 6, 10, with an appeal to the Galatians to side with freedom instead of slavery (1). He reiterates his message of justification or righteousness by faith instead of law and circumcision (2-5); cf Gal 2, 16; 3, 3. Faith, not circumcision, is what counts (6).

5, 1: *Freedom:* Paul stresses as the conclusion from the allegory in Gal 4, 21-31 this result of Christ's work for us. It is a principle previously mentioned (Gal 2, 4), the responsible use of which v 13 will emphasize.

5, 3: Cf Gal 3, 10-12. Just as those who seek to live by the law must carry out all its contents, so those who have faith and live by promise must stand firm in their freedom (1.13).

5, 6: Cf Rom 2, 25-26; 1 Cor 7, 19; Gal 6, 15. The Greek for *faith working through love* or "faith expressing itself through love" can also be rendered as "faith energized by (God's) love."

5, 7-12: Paul addresses the Galatians directly: with questions (7.11), a proverb (9), a statement (8), and biting sarcasm (12), seeking to persuade the Galatians to break with those trying to add law and circumcision to Christ as a basis for salvation.

5, 7: *Running well:* as in an athletic contest; cf Gal 2, 2; 1 Cor 9, 24-26; Phil 2, 16; 3, 14.

5, 8: *The one who called you:* see the note on Gal 1, 6.

5, 11: *Preaching circumcision:* this could refer to Paul's pre-Christian period (possibly as a missionary for Judaism); more probably it arose as a charge from opponents, based perhaps on the story in Acts 16, 1-3 that Paul had circumcised Timothy "on account of the Jews." Unlike the Gentile Titus in Gal 2, 3, Timothy was the son of a Jewish mother. *The stumbling block of the cross:* cf 1 Cor 1, 23.

5, 12: A sarcastic half-wish that their knife would go beyond mere circumcision; cf Phil 3, 2 and the note there.

5, 13-26: In light of another reminder of the freedom of the gospel (13; cf Gal 5, 1), Paul elaborates on what believers are called to do and be: they fulfill the law by love of neighbor (14-15), walking in the Spirit (16-26), as is illustrated by concrete *fruit of the Spirit* in their lives.

5, 13: *Serve . . . through love:* cf Gal 5, 6.

love. [14] For the whole law[n] is fulfilled in one statement, namely, "You shall love your neighbor as yourself."* [15] But if you go on biting and devouring one another, beware that you are not consumed by one another.

[16] [o] I say, then: live by the Spirit and you will certainly not gratify the desire of the flesh.* [17] For the flesh has desires against the Spirit, and the Spirit against the flesh; these are opposed to each other, so that you may not do what you want.[p] [18] But if you are guided by the Spirit, you are not under the law.[q] [19] * Now the works of the flesh are obvious: immorality, impurity, licentiousness,[r] [20] idolatry, sorcery, hatreds, rivalry, jealousy, outbursts of fury, acts of selfishness, dissensions, factions,[s] [21] occasions of envy,* drinking bouts, orgies, and the like. I warn you, as I warned you before, that those who do such things will not inherit the kingdom of God. [22] In contrast, the fruit of the Spirit is love, joy, peace, patience, kindness, generosity, faithfulness,[t] [23] gentleness, self-control. Against such there is no law.[u] [24] Now those who belong to Christ [Jesus] have crucified their flesh with its passions and desires.[v] [25] If we live in the Spirit, let us also follow the Spirit.[w] [26] Let us not be conceited, provoking one another, envious of one another.[x]

CHAPTER 6

Life in the Community of Christ.* [1] Brothers, even if a person is caught in some transgression, you who are spiritual should correct that one in a gentle spirit, looking to yourself, so that you also may not be tempted.[y] [2] Bear one another's burdens,[z] and so you will fulfill the law of Christ.* [3] [a] For if anyone thinks he is something when he is nothing, he is deluding himself. [4] * Each one must examine his own work, and then he will have reason to boast with regard to himself alone, and not with regard to someone else; [5] for each will bear his own load.[b]

[6] [c] One who is being instructed in the word should share all good things with his instructor.* [7] Make no mistake: God is not mocked, for a person will reap only what he sows, [8] because the one who sows for his flesh will reap corruption from the flesh, but the one who sows for the spirit will reap eternal life from the spirit.[d] [9] Let us not grow tired of doing good, for in due time we shall reap our harvest, if we do not give up.[e] [10] So then, while we have the opportunity, let us do good to all,[f] but especially to those who belong to the family of the faith.*

VI. CONCLUSION

Final Appeal.* [11] See with what large letters* I am writing to you in my own hand![g]

n Lv 19, 18; Mt 22, 39; Rom 13, 8-10.—o Gal 5, 24-25; Rom 8, 5.—p Rom 7, 15.23; 8, 6.—q Rom 6, 14; 8, 14.—r 19-21: Rom 1, 29-31; 1 Cor 6, 9-10; Col 3, 5-6.8.—s Rv 22, 15.—t Eph 5, 9 / 1 Cor 13, 4-7; 2 Cor 6, 6; 1 Tm 4, 12; 2 Pt 1, 6.—u 1 Tm 1, 9.—v Gal 2, 19; Rom 6, 6; 8, 13.—w Gal 5, 16.—x Phil 2, 3.—y Mt 18, 15; Jas 5, 19 / 1 Cor 10, 12-13.—z Col 3, 13 / 1 Cor 9, 21.—a 3-4: 1 Cor 3, 18; 8, 2; 2 Cor 12, 11.—b Rom 14, 12.— c 1 Cor 9, 14.—d Prv 11, 18; Rom 8, 6.13.—e 2 Thes 3, 13; Heb 12, 1-3.—f 1 Thes 5, 15.—g 1 Cor 16, 21.

5, 14: Lv 19, 18, emphasized by Jesus (Mt 22, 39; Lk 10, 27); cf Rom 13, 8-10.

5, 16-25: *Spirit . . . flesh:* cf Gal 3, 3 and the note on Rom 8, 1-13.

5, 19-23: Such lists of vices and virtues (cf Rom 1, 29-31; 1 Cor 6, 9-10) were common in the ancient world. Paul contrasts *works of the flesh* (19) with *fruit* (not "works") *of the Spirit* (22). Not law, but the Spirit, leads to such traits.

5, 21: *Occasions of envy:* after the Greek word *phthonoi,* "envies," some manuscripts add a similar sounding one, *phonoi,* "murders."

6, 1-10: The ethical exhortations begun at Gal 5, 1 continue with a variety of admonitions to the community (*brothers:* see the note on Gal 1, 2). Nearly every sentence contains a separate item of practical advice; the faith and freedom of the gospel underlie each maxim. Tensions and temptation within communal life have previously been addressed in Gal 5, 15.26, and v 1 continues with a case in which *a person is caught in some transgression* such as those in Gal 5, 19-21; cf Gal 2, 17.

6, 2: *The law of Christ:* cf Rom 8, 2; 1 Cor 9, 21; Gal 5, 14. The principle of love for others is meant. To *bear one another's burdens* is to "serve one another through love" (Gal 5, 13).

6, 4-5: Self-examination is the cure for self-deception. Compare what you are with what you were before, and give the glory to God; cf Rom 6, 19-22. *Load:* used elsewhere of a soldier's pack. Correcting one's own conduct avoids burdening others with it.

6, 6: Implies oral instruction in the faith by catechists; these are to be remunerated for their service; cf Rom 15, 27.

6, 10: *The family of the faith:* the Christian household or church. Doing good has a universal object (*to all*), but the local community makes specific the reality of those to be served.

6, 11-18: A postscript in Paul's own hand, as was his practice (see 1 Cor 16, 21; 2 Thes 3, 17). Paul summarizes his appeal against his opponents (12-13), then returns to his message of glorying in the cross, not in circumcision, as the means of salvation (14-15); cf Gal 5, 11. A benediction follows at v. 16. In the polemical spirit that the attack on his apostleship called forth (Gal 1, 11—2, 21), Paul reasserts his missionary credentials (17) before giving a final benediction (18).

6, 11: *Large letters:* in contrast to the finer hand of the scribe who wrote the letter up to this point. The larger Greek letters make Paul's message even more emphatic. Some find a hint of poor eyesight on Paul's part. See the note on Gal 4, 13.

12 * It is those who want to make a good appearance in the flesh who are trying to compel you to have yourselves circumcised, only that they may not be persecuted for the cross of Christ. [h] 13 Not even those having themselves circumcised* observe the law themselves; they only want you to be circumcised so that they may boast of your flesh. 14 But may I never boast except in the cross of our Lord Jesus Christ, through which* the world has been crucified to me, and I to the world. [i] 15 For neither does circumcision mean anything, nor does uncircumcision, [j] but only a new creation.* 16 Peace and mercy be to all who follow this rule* and to the Israel of God. [k]

17 From now on, let no one make troubles for me; for I bear the marks of Jesus* on my body. [l]

18 The grace of our Lord Jesus Christ be with your spirit, brothers. Amen. [m]

---

h Gal 5, 2.11.—i Gal 2, 20; 1 Cor 2, 2.—j Gal 5, 6; 1 Cor 7, 19 / 2 Cor 5, 17.—k Pss 125, 5; 128, 6.—l 2 Cor 4, 10.—m Phil 4, 23; 2 Tm 4, 22; Phlm 25.

6, 12-15: The Jewish Christian opponents wished *not to be persecuted*, possibly by Jews. But since Judaism seems to have had a privileged status as a religion in the Roman empire, circumcised Christians might, if taken as Jews, thereby avoid persecution from the Romans. In any case, Paul instead stresses conformity with *the cross of our Lord Jesus Christ*; cf Gal 2, 19-21; 5, 11.

6, 13: *Those having themselves circumcised:* other manuscripts read, "those who have had themselves circumcised."

6, 14: *Through which:* or "through whom."

6, 15: *New creation:* or "new creature"; cf 2 Cor 5, 17.

6, 16: *This rule:* the principle in vv 14 and 15. *The Israel of God:* while the church may be meant (the phrase can be translated "to all who follow this rule, even the Israel of God"; cf Gal 6, 10; 1 Cor 10, 18), the reference may also be to God's ancient people, Israel; cf Pss 125, 5; 128, 6.

6, 17: *The marks of Jesus:* slaves were often branded by marks (*stigmata*) burned into their flesh to show to whom they belonged; so also were devotees of pagan gods. Paul implies that instead of outdated circumcision, his body bears the scars of his apostolic labors (2 Cor 11, 22-31), such as floggings (Acts 16, 22; 2 Cor 11, 25) and stonings (Acts 14, 19), that mark him as belonging to the Christ who suffered (cf Rom 6, 3; 2 Cor 4, 10; Col 1, 24) and will protect his own.

THE LETTER TO THE EPHESIANS

INTRODUCTION

Ephesians is the great Pauline letter about the church. It deals, however, not so much with a congregation in the city of Ephesus in Asia Minor as with the worldwide church, the head of which is Christ (4, 15), the purpose of which is to be the instrument for making God's plan of salvation known throughout the universe (3, 9-10). Yet this ecclesiology is anchored in God's saving love, shown in Jesus Christ (2, 4-10), and the whole of redemption is rooted in the plan and accomplishment of the triune God (1, 3-14). The language is often that of doxology (1, 3-14) and prayer (cf 1, 15-23; 3, 14-19), indeed of liturgy and hymns (3, 20-21; 5, 14).

The majestic chapters of Ephesians emphasize the unity in the church of Christ that has come about for both Jews and Gentiles within God's household (1, 15—2, 22, especially 2, 11-22) and indeed the "seven unities" of church, Spirit, hope; one Lord, faith, and baptism; and the one God (4, 4-6). Yet the concern is not with the church for its own sake but rather as the means for mission in the world (3, 1—4, 24). The gifts Christ gives its members are to lead to growth and renewal (4, 7-24). Ethical admonition is not lacking either; all aspects of human life and relationships are illumined by the light of Christ (4, 25—6, 20).

The letter is seemingly addressed by Paul to Christians in Ephesus (1, 1), a place where the apostle labored for well over two years (Acts 19, 10). Yet there is a curiously impersonal tone to the writing for a community with which Paul was so intimately acquainted (cf 3, 2 and 4, 21). There are no personal greetings (cf 6, 23). More significantly, important early manuscripts omit the words "in Ephesus" (see the note on 1, 1). Many therefore regard the letter as an encyclical or "circular letter" sent to a number of churches in Asia Minor, the addressees to be designated in each place by its bearer,

Tychicus (6, 21-22). Others think that Ephesians is the letter referred to in Colossians 4, 16 as "to the Laodiceans."

Paul, who is designated as the sole author at 1, 1, is described in almost unparalleled terms with regard to the significant role he has in God's plan for bringing the Gentiles to faith in Christ (3, 1-12). Yet at the time of writing he is clearly in prison (3, 1; 4, 1; 6, 20), suffering afflictions (3, 13). Traditionally this "Captivity Epistle" has, along with Colossians, Philippians, and Philemon, been dated to an imprisonment in Rome, likely in A.D. 61-63. Others appeal to an earlier imprisonment, perhaps in Caesarea (Acts 23, 27—27, 2). Since the early nineteenth century, however, much of critical scholarship has considered the letter's style and use of words (especially when compared with Colossians), its concept of the church, and other points of doctrine put forward by the writer as grounds for serious doubt about authorship by Paul. The letter may then be the work of a secretary writing at the apostle's direction or of a later disciple who sought to develop Paul's ideas for a new situation around A.D. 80-100.

The principal divisions of the Letter to the Ephesians are the following:

   I.   *Address (1, 1-14)*
   II.   *Unity of the Church in Christ (1, 15—2, 22)*
   III.   *World Mission of the Church (3, 1—4, 24)*
   IV.   *Daily Conduct, an Expression of Unity (4, 25—6, 20)*
   V.   *Conclusion (6, 21-24)*

I. ADDRESS

CHAPTER 1

Greeting.* [1] Paul, an apostle of Christ Jesus by the will of God, to the holy ones who are [in Ephesus]* faithful in Christ Jesus:[a] [2] grace to you and peace from God our Father and the Lord Jesus Christ.[b]

The Father's Plan of Salvation. [3] * Blessed be the God and Father of our Lord Jesus Christ,[c] who has blessed us in Christ with every spiritual blessing in the heavens,* [4] as he chose us in him, before the founda-tion of the world, to be holy and without blemish before him.[d] In love [5] he destined us for adoption to himself through Jesus Christ, in accord with the favor of his will,[e] [6] for the praise of the glory of his grace that he granted us in the beloved.[f]

Fulfillment through Christ. [7] In him we have redemption by his blood, the forgive-ness of transgressions, in accord with the riches of his grace[g] [8] that he lavished upon us. In all wisdom and insight,[h] [9] he has made known to us the mystery* of his will in accord with his favor that he set forth in

---

a Rom 1, 7; 1 Cor 1, 1-2; Col 1, 1.—b Col 1, 2.—c Eph 2, 6; 2 Cor 1, 3.—d Eph 5, 27; Jn 15, 16; 17, 24; Rom 8, 29; 2 Thes 2, 13.—e Jn 1, 12; 1 Jn 3, 1.—f Mt 3, 17; Col 1, 13.—g Eph 2, 7-13; Rom 3, 24; Col 1, 14.20.—h Col 1, 9.

1, 1-2: For the epistolary form used at the beginning of letters, see the note on Rom 1, 1-7. Twenty-two of the thirty Greek words in vv 1-2 also occur in Col 1, 1-2.

1, 1: *[In Ephesus]:* the phrase is lacking in important early witnesses such as P46 (3rd cent.), and Sinaiticus and Vaticanus (4th cent.), appearing in the latter two as a fifth-century addition. Basil and Origen mention its absence from manuscripts. See Introduction. Without the phrase, the Greek can be rendered, as in Col 1, 2, "to the holy ones and faithful brothers in Christ."

1, 3-14: While a Pauline letter usually continues after the greeting with a prayer of thanksgiving, as in 15-23 below, Ephesians first inserts a blessing of God for the blessings Christians have experienced, as in 2 Cor 1, 3-4 and 1 Pt 1, 3-12. The blessing here, akin to a Jewish *berakah*, is rich in images almost certainly drawn from hymns and liturgy. Many ideas here are also found in Col 1, 3-23. Certain phrases are frequently repeated, such as *in Christ* (3.10.12) or *in him* (4.7.9.11.13) or *in the Beloved* (6) and *(for) the praise of (his) glory* (6.12.14). Some

terms like *chose* (4) and *destined* (5) reflect Old Testament theology (Dt 7, 7; 9, 4-6; 23, 5) or Pauline themes (*redemption*, 7.14; *grace*, 6.7) or specific emphases in Col (*forgiveness*, Col 1, 14).

A triadic structure is discernible in vv 3-14: *God the Father* (3-6.8.11), *Christ* (3.5.7-10.12), and the *Spirit* (13-14). The spiritual blessings Christians have received through Christ (3) are gratefully enumerated: the call to holiness (4; cf Col 1, 22); the gift of divine *adoption* establishing a unique spiritual relationship with God the Father through Christ (5; cf Gal 4, 5); liberation from sin through Christ's sacrificial death (7); revelation of God's plan of salvation in Christ (9; cf Eph 3, 3-4; Rom 16, 25); the gift of election and faith in Christ bestowed upon Jewish Christians (see the note on 12, *we who first hoped in Christ*); and finally, the same gift granted to Gentiles (13, *you also*). In the Christ-centered faith and existence of the Christian communities the apostle sees the predetermined *plan* of God to bring all creation under the final rule of Christ (4-5.9-10) being *made known* (9) and carried through, to God's *glory* (6.12.14).

1, 3: *In the heavens:* literally, "in the heavenlies" or "in the heavenly places," a term in Eph for the divine realm.

1, 9: *Mystery:* as in Rom 16, 25; Col 1, 26.27 and elsewhere, a secret of God now revealed in the *plan* to save and *sum up all things in Christ* (10); cf Eph 3, 3-6.

him[i] [10]as a plan for the fullness of times, to sum up all things in Christ, in heaven and on earth.[j]

Inheritance through the Spirit. [11]In him we were also chosen, destined in accord with the purpose of the One who accomplishes all things according to the intention of his will,[k] [12]so that we might exist for the praise of his glory, we who first hoped* in Christ. [13]In him you also, who have heard the word of truth, the gospel of your salvation, and have believed in him, were sealed* with the promised holy Spirit,[l] [14]which is the first installment* of our inheritance toward redemption as God's possession, to the praise of his glory.[m]

II. UNITY OF THE CHURCH IN CHRIST

The Church as Christ's Body.* [15]Therefore, I, too, hearing of your faith in the Lord Jesus and of your love* for all the holy ones,[n] [16]do not cease giving thanks for you, remembering you in my prayers,[o] [17]that the God of our Lord Jesus Christ, the Father of glory, may give you a spirit of

wisdom and revelation resulting in knowledge of him.[p] [18]May the eyes of [your] hearts be enlightened, that you may know what is the hope that belongs to his call, what are the riches of glory in his inheritance among the holy ones,[q] [19]and what is the surpassing greatness of his power for us who believe, in accord with the exercise of his great might,[r] [20]which he worked in Christ, raising him from the dead and seating him at his right hand in the heavens,[s] [21]far above every principality, authority, power, and dominion, and every name that is named not only in this age but also in the one to come.[t] [22]And he put all things beneath his feet and gave him as head over all things to the church,[u] [23]which is his body,* the fullness of the one who fills all things in every way.[v]

CHAPTER 2*

Generosity of God's Plan.* [1] [w] You were dead in your transgressions and sins* [2]in which you once lived following the age of this world,* following the ruler of the power of the air, the spirit that is now at

---

i Eph 3, 3.9; Rom 16, 25.—j Gal 4, 4; Col 1, 16.20.—k Is 46, 10; Rom 8, 28; Col 1, 12; Rv 4, 11.—l Eph 4, 30; Acts 2, 33; Col 1, 5-6.—m 2 Cor 1, 22; 5, 5.—n Col 1, 3-4; Phlm 4-5.—o Col 1, 3.9.—p Eph 3, 14.16; Col 1, 9-10; 1 Jn 5, 20.—q Eph 4, 4; Col 1, 12.27.—r 2 Cor 13, 4; Col 1, 11; 2, 12.—s Ps 110, 1; Heb 1, 3.—t Phil 2, 9; Col 1, 16; 1 Pt 3, 22.—u Eph 4, 15; Ps 8, 7; Mt 28, 18; Col 1, 18.—v Eph 4, 10.12; Rom 12, 5; 1 Cor 12, 27; Col 1, 19.—w Col 1, 21; 2, 13.

1, 12: *We who first hoped:* probably Jewish Christians (contrast 13, *you*, the Gentiles); possibly the people of Israel, "we who already enjoyed the hope of Christ," or perhaps present hope in contrast to future redemption (cf Eph 1, 14).

1, 13: *Sealed:* by God, in baptism; cf Eph 4, 30; 2 Cor 1, 22.

1, 14: *First installment:* down payment by God on full salvation, as at 2 Cor 1, 22.

1, 15-23: See the note on Rom 1, 8 for the thanksgiving form in a letter. Much of the content parallels thoughts in Col 1, 3-20. The prayer moves from God and Christ (17.20-21) to the Ephesians (17-19) and the church (22-23). Paul asks that the blessing imparted by God the Father (3) to the Ephesians will be strengthened in them through the message of the gospel (13.17-19). Those blessings are seen in the context of God's *might* in establishing the sovereignty of Christ over all other creatures (19-21) and in appointing him *head* of the church (22-23). For the allusion to angelic spirits in v 21, see Rom 8, 38 and Col 1, 16. Here, as in 1 Cor 15, 24-25 and Col 2, 15, every such *principality* and *power* is made subject to Christ.

1, 15: *Your faith . . . your love:* some manuscripts omit the latter phrase, but cf Col 1, 4.

1, 23: *His body:* the church (22); cf the note on Col 1, 18. Only in Eph and Col is Christ the *head* of the *body*, in contrast to the view in 1 Cor 12 and Rom 12, 4-8 where Christ is equated with the entire body or community. *Fullness:* see the note on Col 1, 19. Some take *the one who fills* as God, others as Christ (cf Eph 4, 10). If in Christ "dwells the fullness of the deity bodily" (Col 2, 9), then, as God "fills" Christ, Christ in turn fills the church and the believer (Eph 3, 19; 5, 18). But the difficult

phrases here may also allow the church to be viewed as the "complement" of Christ who is "being filled" as God's plan for the universe is carried out through the church (cf Eph 3, 9-10).

2, 1-22: The gospel of *salvation* (Eph 1, 13) that God *worked in Christ* (Eph 1, 20) is reiterated in terms of what God's *great love* (4), expressed in Christ, means for us. The passage sometimes addresses *you*, Gentiles (1-2.8.11-13.19.22), but other times speaks of *all of us* who believe (3-7.10.14.18). In urging people to *remember* their grim past when they were *dead* in sins (1-3.11-12) and what they are *now in Christ* (4-10.13), the author sees both Jew and Gentile reconciled with God, now *one new person*, a new humanity, *one body*, the *household of God*, a *temple* and *dwelling place* of God's Spirit (15-16.19-22). The presentation falls into two parts, the second stressing more the meaning for the church.

2, 1-10: The recipients of Paul's letter have experienced, in their redemption from *transgressions and sins*, the effect of Christ's supremacy over the power of the devil (1-2; cf Eph 6, 11-12), who rules not from the netherworld but from the *air* between God in heaven and human beings on earth. Both Jew and Gentile have experienced, through Christ, God's free gift of salvation that already marks them for a future heavenly destiny (3-7). The language *dead, raised us up,* and *seated us . . . in the heavens* closely parallels Jesus' own passion and Easter experience. The terms in vv 8-9 describe salvation in the way Paul elsewhere speaks of justification: *by grace, through faith, the gift of God, not from works;* cf Gal 2, 16-21; Rom 3, 24-28. Christians are a newly created people in Christ, fashioned by God for a life of goodness (10).

2, 1-7: These verses comprise one long sentence in Greek, the main verb coming in v 5, God *brought us to life,* the object you/us *dead in . . . transgressions* being repeated in 1 and 5; cf Col 2, 13.

2, 2: *Age of this world:* or "aeon," a term found in gnostic thought, possibly synonymous with *the rulers of this world,* but also reflecting the Jewish idea of "two ages," this present evil age and "the age to come"; cf 1 Cor 3, 19; 5, 10; 7, 31; Gal 1, 4; Ti 2, 12. *The disobedient:* literally, "the sons of disobedience," a Semitism as at Is 30, 9.

work in the disobedient.[x] [3]All of us once lived among them in the desires of our flesh, following the wishes of the flesh and the impulses, and we were by nature children of wrath, like the rest.[y] [4]But God, who is rich in mercy, because of the great love he had for us, [5] [z] even when we were dead in our transgressions, brought us to life with Christ* (by grace you have been saved), [6]raised us up with him, and seated us with him in the heavens in Christ Jesus,[a] [7]that in the ages to come he might show the immeasurable riches of his grace in his kindness to us in Christ Jesus.[b] [8]For by grace you have been saved through faith, and this is not from you; it is the gift of God;[c] [9]it is not from works, so no one may boast.[d] [10]For we are his handiwork, created in Christ Jesus for the good works that God has prepared in advance, that we should live in them.[e]

One in Christ.* [11]Therefore, remember that at one time you, Gentiles in the flesh, called the uncircumcision by those called the circumcision, which is done in the flesh by human hands, [12]were at that time without Christ, alienated from the community of Israel* and strangers to the covenants of promise, without hope and without God in the world.[f] [13]But now in Christ Jesus you who once were far off have become near by the blood of Christ.[g]

[14] * For he is our peace, he who made both one and broke down the dividing wall of enmity, through his flesh,[h] [15]abolishing the law with its commandments and legal claims, that he might create in himself one new person* in place of the two, thus establishing peace,[i] [16]and might reconcile both with God, in one body, through the cross, putting that enmity to death by it.[j] [17]He came and preached peace to you who were far off and peace to those who were near,[k] [18]for through him we both have access in one Spirit to the Father.[l]

[19]So then you are no longer strangers and sojourners, but you are fellow citizens with the holy ones and members of the household of God,[m] [20]built upon the foundation of the apostles and prophets,[n] with Christ Jesus himself as the capstone.* [21]Through him the whole structure is held together and grows into a temple sacred in the Lord;[o] [22]in him you also are being built together into a dwelling place of God in the Spirit.[p]

III. WORLD MISSION OF THE CHURCH

CHAPTER 3

Commission to Preach God's Plan.* [1]Because of this,[q] I, Paul, a prisoner of Christ* [Jesus] for you Gentiles— [2]if, as I suppose, you have heard of the stewardship* of God's grace that was given to me

x Eph 6, 12; Jn 12, 31; Col 1, 13.—y Col 3, 6-7.—z Rom 5, 8; 6, 13; Col 2, 13.—a Rom 8, 10-11; Phil 3, 20; Col 2, 12.—b Eph 1, 7.—c Rom 3, 24; Gal 2, 16.—d 1 Cor 1, 29.—e Eph 4, 24; Ti 2, 14.—f Rom 9, 4; Col 1, 21.27.—g Eph 2, 17; Is 57, 19; Col 1, 20.—h Gal 3, 28.—i 2 Cor 5, 17; Col 2, 14.—j Col 1, 20.22.—k Is 57, 19; Zec 9, 10.—l Eph 3, 12.—m Heb 12, 22-23.—n Is 28, 16; Rv 21, 14.—o 1 Cor 3, 16; Col 2, 19.—p 1 Pt 2, 5.—q Phil 1, 7.13; Col 1, 24-29; 4, 18; Phlm 1.9; 2 Tm 2, 9.

2, 5: Our relation through baptism *with Christ*, the risen Lord, is depicted in terms of realized eschatology, as already exaltation, though v 7 brings in the future aspect too.

2, 11-22: The Gentiles lacked Israel's messianic expectation, lacked the various *covenants* God made with *Israel*, lacked *hope* of salvation and knowledge of the true *God* (11-12); but through Christ all these religious barriers between Jew and Gentile have been transcended (13-14) by the abolition of the Mosaic covenant-law (15) for the sake of uniting Jew and Gentile into a single religious community (15-16), imbued with the same holy *Spirit* and worshiping the same *Father* (18). The Gentiles are now included in God's *household* (19) as it arises upon the *foundation* of *apostles* assisted by those endowed with the prophetic gift (Eph 3, 5), the preachers of Christ (20; cf 1 Cor 12, 28). With Christ as the *capstone* (20; cf Is 28, 16; Mt 21, 42), they are being built into the holy *temple* of God's people where the divine presence dwells (21-22).

2, 12: *The community of Israel:* or "commonwealth"; cf Eph 4, 18. *The covenants:* cf Rom 9, 4: with Abraham, with Moses, with David.

2, 14-16: The elaborate imagery here combines pictures of Christ as *our peace* (Is 9, 5), his crucifixion, the ending of the Mosaic law (cf Col 2, 14), reconciliation (2 Cor 5, 18-21), and

the destruction of *the dividing wall* such as kept people from God in the temple or a barrier in the heavens.

2, 15: *One new person:* a corporate body, the Christian community, made up of Jews and Gentiles, replacing ancient divisions; cf Rom 1, 16.

2, 20: *Capstone:* the Greek can also mean cornerstone or keystone.

3, 1-13: Paul reflects on his mission to the Gentiles. He alludes to his call and appointment to the apostolic office (2-3) and how his *insight* through revelation, as well as that of the other apostles and charismatic prophets in the church (4-5), has deepened understanding of God's plan of salvation in Christ. Paul is the special herald (7) of a new *promise* to the *Gentiles* (6): that the divine plan includes them in the spiritual benefits promised to Israel. Not only is this unique apostolic role his; Paul also has been given the task of explaining to all the divine *plan* of salvation (8-9), once *hidden*. Through *the church*, God's plan to save through Christ is becoming manifest to angelic beings (10; cf Eph 1, 21), in accord with God's *purpose* (11). The fulfillment of the plan in Christ gives the whole church more *confidence* through *faith* in God (12). The readers of this letter are also thereby encouraged to greater confidence despite Paul's imprisonment (13).

3, 1: *A prisoner of Christ:* see Introduction. Paul abruptly departs from his train of thought at the end of v 1, leaving an incomplete sentence.

3, 2: *Stewardship:* the Greek is the same term employed at Eph 1, 10 for the *plan* that God administers (Col 1, 25) and in which Paul plays a key role.

Eph

for your benefit,[r] [3][namely, that] the mystery* was made known to me by revelation, as I have written briefly earlier.[s] [4]When you read this you can understand my insight into the mystery of Christ, [5]which was not made known to human beings in other generations as it has now been revealed to his holy apostles and prophets by the Spirit,[t] [6]that the Gentiles are coheirs, members of the same body, and copartners in the promise in Christ Jesus through the gospel.[u]

[7]Of this I became a minister by the gift of God's grace that was granted me in accord with the exercise of his power.[v] [8]To me, the very least of all the holy ones, this grace was given, to preach to the Gentiles the inscrutable riches of Christ,[w] [9]and to bring to light [for all]* what is the plan of the mystery hidden from ages past in God who created all things,[x] [10]so that the manifold wisdom of God might now be made known through the church to the principalities and authorities* in the heavens.[y] [11]This was according to the eternal purpose that he accomplished in Christ Jesus our Lord, [12]in whom we have boldness of speech and confidence of access through faith in him.[z] [13]So I ask you not to lose heart over my afflictions for you; this is your glory.[a]

Prayer for the Readers.* [14]For this reason I kneel before the Father, [15]from whom every family* in heaven and on earth is named, [16]that he may grant you in accord with the riches of his glory to be strengthened with power through his Spirit in the inner self,[b] [17]and that Christ may dwell in your hearts through faith; that you, rooted and grounded in love,[c] [18]may have strength to comprehend with all the holy ones what is the breadth and length and height and depth,[d] [19]and to know the love of Christ that surpasses knowledge, so that you may be filled with all the fullness of God.[e]

[20]Now to him who is able to accomplish far more than all we ask or imagine, by the power at work within us,[f] [21]to him be glory in the church and in Christ Jesus to all generations, forever and ever. Amen.

CHAPTER 4

Unity in the Body. [1]* I, then, a prisoner for the Lord, urge you to live in a manner worthy of the call you have received,[g] [2]with all humility and gentleness, with patience, bearing with one another through love,[h] [3]striving to preserve the unity of the spirit through the bond of peace:[i] [4] * one body and one Spirit, as you were also called to the one hope of your call;[j] [5]one Lord, one faith, one baptism;[k] [6]one God and Father of all, who is over all and through all and in all.[l]

Diversity of Gifts. [7]But grace was given to each of us according to the measure of Christ's gift.[m] [8]Therefore, it says:

r Col 1, 25.—s Eph 1, 9-10; Col 1, 26.—t Col 1, 26.—u Eph 2, 13.18-19.—v Rom 15, 15; Col 1, 25.29.—w 1 Cor 15, 8-10; Gal 1, 16; 2, 7-9.—x Rom 16, 25; Col 1, 26-27.—y 1 Pt 1, 12.—z Rom 5, 1-2; Heb 4, 16.—a Col 1, 22.24; 2 Tm 2, 10.—b Eph 6, 10; Rom 7, 22; 2 Cor 4, 16; Col 1, 11.—c Jn 14, 23; Col 1, 23; 2, 7.—d Col 2, 2.—e Col 2, 3.9.—f Rom 16, 25-27; Col 1, 29.— g Eph 3, 1; Col 1, 10.—h Col 3, 12-13.—i Col 3, 14-15.—j Rom 12, 5; 1 Cor 10, 17; 12, 12-13.—k 1 Cor 8, 6.—l 1 Cor 12, 6.— m Rom 12, 3.6; 1 Cor 12, 28.

3, 3-4: *The mystery:* God's resolve to deliver Gentiles along with Israel through Christ; cf the notes on Eph 1, 10; 3, 9.

3, 9: *[For all]:* while some think this phrase was added so as to yield the sense "to enlighten all about the plan . . . ," it is more likely that some manuscripts and Fathers omitted it accidentally or to avoid the idea that *all* conflicted with Paul's assignment to preach to *the Gentiles* (8) specifically.

3, 10: *Principalities and authorities:* see the note on Eph 1, 15-23 regarding v 21.

3, 14-21: The apostle prays that those he is addressing may, like the rest of the church, deepen their understanding of God's plan of salvation in Christ. It is a plan that affects the whole universe (15) with *the breadth and length and height and depth* of God's love in Christ (18) or possibly the universe in all its dimensions. The apostle prays that they may perceive the redemptive love of Christ for them and be completely immersed in the fullness of God (19). The prayer concludes with a doxology to God (20-21).

3, 14-15: *Every family:* in the Greek there is wordplay on the word for *the Father (patria, patēr).* The phrase could also mean "God's whole family" (cf Eph 2, 21).

4, 1-16: A general plea for unity in the church. Christians have been fashioned through the *Spirit* into a single harmonious religious community *(one body,* 4.12; cf Eph 4, 16), belonging to a single *Lord* (in contrast to the many gods of the pagan world), and by one way of salvation through *faith,* brought out especially by the significance of *baptism* (1-6; cf Rom 6, 1-11). But Christian unity is more than adherence to a common belief. It is manifested in the exalted Christ's gifts to individuals to serve so as to make the community more Christlike (11-16). This teaching on Christ as the source of the gifts is introduced in v 8 by a citation of Ps 68, 18, which depicts Yahweh triumphantly leading Israel to salvation in Jerusalem. It is here understood of Christ, ascending *above all the heavens,* the *head* of the church; through his redemptive death, resurrection, and ascension he has become the source of the church's spiritual gifts. The "descent" of Christ (9-10) refers more probably to the incarnation (cf Phil 2, 6-8) than to Christ's presence after his death in the world of the dead (cf 1 Pt 3, 19).

4, 4-6: The "seven unities" (church, *Spirit, hope; Lord, faith* in Christ [Eph 1, 13], *baptism; one God)* reflect the triune structure of later creeds in reverse.

"He ascended* on high and took prisoners captive;

he gave gifts to men."[n]

9 What does "he ascended" mean except that he also descended into the lower [regions] of the earth? 10 The one who descended is also the one who ascended far above all the heavens, that he might fill all things.

11 * And he gave some as apostles, others as prophets, others as evangelists, others as pastors and teachers,[o] 12 to equip the holy ones for the work of ministry,* for building up the body of Christ, 13 until we all attain to the unity of faith and knowledge of the Son of God, to mature manhood,* to the extent of the full stature of Christ,[p] 14 so that we may no longer be infants, tossed by waves and swept along by every wind of teaching arising from human trickery, from their cunning in the interests of deceitful scheming.[q] 15 Rather, living the truth in love, we should grow in every way into him who is the head,[r] Christ,* 16 from whom the whole body, joined and held together by every supporting ligament, with the proper functioning of each part, brings about the body's growth and builds itself up in love.[s]

Renewal in Christ.* 17 So I declare and testify in the Lord that you must no longer live as the Gentiles do, in the futility of their minds;[t] 18 darkened in understanding, alienated from the life of God because of their ignorance, because of their hardness of heart,[u] 19 they have become callous and have handed themselves over to licentiousness for the practice of every kind of impurity to excess.[v] 20 That is not how you learned Christ, 21 assuming that you have heard of him and were taught in him, as truth is in Jesus, 22 that you should put away the old self of your former way of life, corrupted through deceitful desires,[w] 23 and be renewed in the spirit of your minds,[x] 24 and put on* the new self, created in God's way in righteousness and holiness of truth.[y]

IV. DAILY CONDUCT, AN EXPRESSION OF UNITY*

Rules for the New Life. 25 Therefore, putting away falsehood, speak the truth, each one to his neighbor, for we are members one of another.[z] 26 Be angry but do not sin;[a] do not let the sun set on your anger,* 27 and do not leave room for the devil.[b] 28 The thief must no longer steal, but rather labor, doing honest work* with his [own] hands, so that he may have something to share with one in need.[c] 29 No foul language should come out of your mouths, but only such as is good for needed edification, that it may impart grace to those who hear.[d] 30 And do not grieve the holy Spirit of God, with which you were sealed for the day of redemption.* 31 All bitterness, fury, anger, shouting, and reviling must be removed from you, along with all malice.[e] 32 [And] be kind to one another, compassionate, forgiving one another as God has forgiven you in Christ.[f]

Eph

---

n Ps 68, 19; Col 2, 15.—o 1 Cor 12, 28.—p Col 1, 28.—q 1 Cor 14, 20; Col 2, 4.8; Heb 13, 9; Jas 1, 6.—r 1 Cor 11, 3; Col 1, 18; 2, 19.—s Col 2, 19.—t Rom 1, 21.—u Col 1, 21; 1 Pt 1, 14.—v Col 3, 5.—w Rom 8, 13; Gal 6, 8; Col 3, 9.—x Rom 12, 2.—y Gn 1, 26-27; Col 3, 10.—z Zec 8, 16.—a Ps 4, 5 LXX; Mt 5, 22.—b 2 Cor 2, 11.—c 1 Thes 4, 11.—d Eph 5, 4; Col 3, 16; 4, 6.—e Col 3, 8.—f Mt 6, 14; Col 3, 12-13.

4, 8-10: While the emphasis is on an ascension and gift-giving by Christ, there is also a reference in taking *prisoners captive* to the aeons and powers mentioned at Eph 1, 21; 2, 2; 3, 10; and 6, 12.

4, 11: Concerning this list of ministers, cf 1 Cor 12, 28 and Rom 12, 6-8. *Evangelists:* missionary preachers (cf Acts 21, 8 and 2 Tm 4, 5), not those who wrote gospels. *Pastors and teachers:* a single group in the Greek, shepherding congregations.

4, 12: The ministerial leaders in v 11 are to equip the whole people of God for their *work of ministry.*

4, 13: *Mature manhood:* literally, "a perfect man" (cf Col 1, 28), possibly the "one new person" of Eph 2, 15, though there *anthrōpos* suggests humanity, while here *anēr* is the term for male. This personage becomes visible in the church's growing to its fullness in the unity of those who believe in Christ.

4, 15-16: *The head, Christ:* cf Col 1, 18 and contrast 1 Cor 12, 12-27 and Rom 12, 4-5 where Christ is identified with the whole body, including the head. The imagery may derive from ancient views in medicine, the *head* coordinating and caring for the body, each *ligament* (perhaps the ministers of v 11) supporting the whole. But as at Eph 2, 19-22, where the temple is depicted as a growing organism, there may also be the idea here of growing toward the capstone, Christ.

4, 17-24: Paul begins to indicate how the new life in Christ contrasts with the Gentiles' old way of existence. Literally, the *old self* (22) and the *new self* (24) are "the old man" and "the new man" (*anthrōpos*, person), as at Eph 2, 15; cf the note on Eph 4, 13.

4, 24: *Put on:* in baptism. See the note on Gal 3, 27.

4, 25—6, 20: For similar exhortations to a morally good life in response to God's gift of faith, see the notes on Rom 12, 1—13, 14 and Gal 5, 13-26.

4, 26: If angry, seek reconciliation that day, not giving the devil (Eph 6, 11) opportunity to lead into sin.

4, 28: *Honest work:* literally, "the good." *His [own] hands:* some manuscripts have the full phrase as in 1 Cor 4, 12.

4, 30: See the note on Eph 1, 13.

CHAPTER 5

[1] So be imitators of God,* as beloved children,[g] [2] and live in love, as Christ loved us and handed himself over for us as a sacrificial offering to God for a fragrant aroma.[h] [3] Immorality or any impurity or greed must not even be mentioned among you, as is fitting among holy ones,[i] [4] no obscenity or silly or suggestive talk, which is out of place, but instead, thanksgiving.[j] [5] Be sure of this, that no immoral or impure or greedy person, that is, an idolater, has any inheritance in the kingdom of Christ and of God.[k]

Duty to Live in the Light. [6] [l] Let no one deceive you with empty arguments, for because of these things the wrath of God is coming upon the disobedient.* [7] So do not be associated with them. [8] For you were once darkness, but now you are light in the Lord. Live as children of light,[m] [9] for light produces every kind of goodness and righteousness and truth.[n] [10] Try to learn what is pleasing to the Lord.[o] [11] Take no part in the fruitless works of darkness; rather expose them,[p] [12] for it is shameful even to mention the things done by them in secret; [13] but everything exposed by the light becomes visible,[q] [14] for everything that becomes visible is light. Therefore, it says:[r]

"Awake, O sleeper,
  and arise from the dead,
  and Christ will give you light."*

[15] * Watch carefully then how you live, not as foolish persons but as wise,[s] [16] making the most of the opportunity, because the days are evil. [17] Therefore, do not continue in ignorance, but try to understand what is the will of the Lord. [18] And do not get drunk on wine, in which lies debauchery, but be filled with the Spirit,[t] [19] addressing one another [in] psalms and hymns and spiritual songs, singing and playing to the Lord in your hearts,[u] [20] giving thanks always and for everything in the name of our Lord Jesus Christ to God the Father.[v]

Wives and Husbands. [21] * Be subordinate to one another[w] out of reverence for Christ.* [22] Wives should be subordinate to their husbands as to the Lord.[x] [23] For the husband is head of his wife just as Christ is head of the church, he himself the savior of the body.[y] [24] As the church is subordinate to Christ, so wives should be subordinate to their husbands in everything. [25] Husbands, love your wives, even as Christ loved the church and handed himself over for her[z] [26] to sanctify her, cleansing her by the bath of water with the word,[a] [27] that he might present to himself the church in splendor, without spot or wrinkle or any such thing, that she might be holy and without blemish.[b] [28] So [also] husbands should love their wives as their own bodies. He who loves his wife loves himself. [29] For no one hates his own flesh but rather nourishes and cherishes it, even as Christ does the church, [30] because we are members of his body.[c]

[31] "For this reason a man shall leave [his]
    father and [his] mother
    and be joined to his wife,
    and the two shall become one flesh."[d]

[32] This is a great mystery, but I speak in reference to Christ and the church.[e] [33] In any case, each one of you should love his wife as himself, and the wife should respect her husband.

g Mt 5, 45.48.—h Ex 29, 18; Ps 40, 7; Gal 2, 20; 1 Jn 3, 16.—i Gal 5, 19; Col 3, 5.—j Eph 4, 29; Col 3, 8.—k 1 Cor 6, 9-10; Gal 5, 21; Col 3, 5.—l Rom 1, 18; Col 2, 4.8.—m Eph 2, 11-13; Jn 12, 36; Col 1, 12-13.—n Gal 5, 22.—o Rom 12, 2.—p Rom 13, 12.—q Jn 3, 20-21.—r Is 26, 19; 60, 1.—s 15-16: Col 4, 5.—t Prv 23, 31 LXX; Lk 21, 34.—u Ps 33, 2-3; Col 3, 16.—v Col 3, 17.—w 1 Pt 5, 5.—x Col 3, 18—4, 1; 1 Pt 3, 1.7.—y 1 Cor 11, 3; Col 1, 18.—z Col 3, 19; 1 Tm 2, 6.—a Rom 6, 4; Ti 3, 5-7.—b 2 Cor 11, 2; Col 1, 22.—c Rom 12, 5; 1 Cor 6, 15.—d Gn 2, 24; Mt 19, 5; Mk 10, 7-8.—e Rv 19, 7.

5, 1: *Imitators of God:* in forgiving (Eph 4, 32) and in loving (as exhibited in how *Christ loved us*).

5, 6: See the note on Eph 2, 2.

5, 14: An early Christian hymn, possibly from a baptismal liturgy. For the content compare Eph 2, 5-6; 3, 9 and Is 60, 1.

5, 15-16.19-20: The wording is similar to Col 4, 5 and Eph 3, 16-17.

5, 21—6, 9: Cf the notes on Col 3, 18—4, 1 and 1 Pt 2, 18—3, 7 for a similar listing of household duties where the inferior is admonished first *(wives,* Eph 5, 22; *children,* Eph 6, 1; *slaves,* Eph 6, 5), then the superior *(husbands,* Eph 5, 25; *fathers,* Eph 6, 4; *masters,* Eph 6, 9). Paul varies this pattern by an emphasis on mutuality (see Eph 5, 20); use of Old Testament material about *father and mother* in Eph 6, 2; the judgment to come for slave-owners *(you have a Master in heaven,* Eph 6, 9); and above all the initial principle of subordination *to one another* under *Christ,* thus effectively undermining exclusive claims to domination by one party. Into the section on *wives* and *husbands* an elaborate teaching on *Christ* and *the church* has been woven (Eph 5, 22-33).

5, 21-33: The apostle exhorts married Christians to a strong mutual love. Holding with Gn 2, 24 that marriage is a divine institution (31), Paul sees Christian marriage as taking on a new meaning symbolic of the intimate relationship of love between Christ and the church. The wife should serve her husband in the same spirit as that of the church's service to Christ (22.24), and the husband should care for his wife with the devotion of Christ to the church (25-30). Paul gives to the Genesis passage its highest meaning in the light of the union of Christ and the church, of which Christlike loyalty and devotion in Christian marriage are a clear reflection (31-33).

CHAPTER 6

Children and Parents. [1]Children, obey your parents [in the Lord], for this is right.[f] [2]"Honor your father and mother."[g] This is the first commandment with a promise, [3]"that it may go well with you and that you may have a long life on earth." [4]Fathers, do not provoke your children to anger, but bring them up with the training and instruction of the Lord.[h]

Slaves and Masters. [5]Slaves, be obedient to your human masters with fear and trembling, in sincerity of heart, as to Christ,[i] [6]not only when being watched, as currying favor, but as slaves of Christ, doing the will of God from the heart,[j] [7]willingly serving the Lord and not human beings, [8]knowing that each will be requited from the Lord for whatever good he does, whether he is slave or free. [9]Masters, act in the same way toward them, and stop bullying, knowing that both they and you have a Master in heaven and that with him there is no partiality.[k]

Battle against Evil. [10] * Finally, draw your strength from the Lord and from his mighty power. [11]Put on the armor of God so that you may be able to stand firm against the tactics of the devil.[l] [12]For our struggle is not with flesh and blood but with the principalities, with the powers, with the world rulers of this present darkness, with the evil spirits in the heavens.[m] [13]Therefore, put on the armor of God, that you may be able to resist on the evil day and, having done everything, to hold your ground.[n] [14]So stand fast with your loins girded in truth, clothed with righteousness as a breastplate,[o] [15]and your feet shod in readiness for the gospel of peace.[p] [16]In all circumstances, hold faith as a shield, to quench all [the] flaming arrows of the evil one.[q] [17]And take the helmet of salvation and the sword of the Spirit, which is the word of God.[r]

Constant Prayer. [18]With all prayer and supplication, pray at every opportunity in the Spirit. To that end, be watchful with all perseverance and supplication for all the holy ones[s] [19]and also for me, that speech may be given me to open my mouth, to make known with boldness the mystery of the gospel[t] [20]for which I am an ambassador in chains, so that I may have the courage to speak as I must.[u]

V. CONCLUSION

A Final Message. * [21]So that you also may have news of me and of what I am doing, Tychicus, my beloved brother and trustworthy minister in the Lord, will tell you everything.[v] [22]I am sending him to you for this very purpose, so that you may know about us and that he may encourage your hearts.[w]

[23]Peace be to the brothers, and love with faith, from God the Father and the Lord Jesus Christ. [24]Grace be with all who love our Lord Jesus Christ in immortality.[x]

---

f Prv 6, 20; Sir 3, 1-6; Col 3, 20.—g 2-3: Ex 20, 12; Dt 5, 16.—h Col 3, 21-22.—i Col 3, 22-25; 1 Tm 6, 1-2; Ti 2, 9-10.— j 1 Pt 2, 18.—k Col 4, 1.—l Rom 13, 12; 2 Cor 6, 7; 10, 4; Jas 4, 7.—m Eph 1, 21; 2, 2; Col 1, 13.—n Rom 13, 12.—o Wis 5, 17-20; Is 11, 5; Lk 12, 35; 1 Thes 5, 8.—p Is 52, 7.—q 1 Pt 5, 9.—r Is 59, 17; 1 Thes 5, 8.—s Mt 26, 41; Col 4, 2-3.—t Acts 4, 29; Col 4, 3; 2 Thes 3, 1.—u 2 Cor 5, 20; Col 4, 4.—v Acts 20, 4; Col 4, 7; 2 Tm 4, 12.—w Col 4, 8.—x 1 Pt 1, 8.

6, 10-20: A general exhortation to courage and prayer. Drawing upon the imagery and ideas of Is 11, 5; 59, 16-17; and Wis 5, 17-23, Paul describes the Christian in terms of the dress and equipment of Roman soldiers. He observes, however, that the Christian's readiness for combat is not directed against human beings but against the spiritual powers of evil (10-17; cf Eph 1, 21; 2, 2; 3, 10). Unique importance is placed upon prayer (18-20).

6, 21-24: *Tychicus:* the bearer of the letter; see the note on Col 4, 7. Verses 21-22 parallel Col 4, 7-8, often word for word. If Ephesians is addressed to several Christian communities (see Introduction), it is understandable that no greetings to individual members of these communities should have been included in it.

THE LETTER TO THE PHILIPPIANS

INTRODUCTION

Philippi, in northeastern Greece, was a city of some importance in the Roman province of Macedonia. Lying on the great road from the Adriatic coast to Byzantium, the Via Egnatia, and in the midst of rich agricultural plains near the gold deposits of Mt. Pangaeus, it was in Paul's day a Roman town (Acts 16, 21), with a Greek-Macedonian population and a small group of Jews (see Acts 16, 13). Originally founded in the sixth century B.C. as Krenides by the Thracians, the town was taken over after 360 B.C. by Philip II of Macedon, the father of Alexander the Great, and was renamed for himself, "Philip's City." The area became Roman in the second century B.C. On the plains near Philippi in October 42 B.C., Antony and Octavian decisively defeated the forces of Brutus and Cassius, the slayers of Julius Caesar. Octavian (Augustus) later made Philippi a Roman colony and settled many veterans of the Roman armies there.

Paul, according to Acts (16, 9-40), established at Philippi the first Christian community in Europe. He came to Philippi, via its harbor town of Neapolis (modern Kavalla), on his second missionary journey, probably in A.D. 49 or 50, accompanied by Silas and Timothy (Acts 15, 40; 16, 3; cf Phil 1, 1) and Luke, if he is to be included in the "we" references of Acts 16, 10-17. The Acts account tells of the conversion of a business woman, Lydia; the exorcism of a slave girl; and, after an earthquake, while Paul and Silas were imprisoned in Philippi, the faith and baptism of a jailer and his family. None of these persons, however, is directly mentioned in Philippians (cf the notes on 4, 2 and 4, 3). Acts 16 concludes its account by describing how Paul (and Silas), asked by the magistrates to leave Philippi, went on to Thessalonica (Acts 17, 1-10), where several times his loyal Philippians continued to support him with financial aid (Phil 4, 16). Later, Paul may have passed through Philippi on his way from Ephesus to Greece (Acts 20, 1-2), and he definitely stopped there on his fateful trip to Jerusalem (Acts 20, 6).

Paul's letter to the Christians at Philippi was written while he was in a prison somewhere (1, 7.13.14.17), indeed in danger of death (1, 20-23). Although under guard for preaching Christ, Paul rejoices at the continuing progress of the gospel (1, 12-26) and expresses gratitude for the Philippians' renewed concern and help in an expression of thanks most clearly found at 4, 10-20. Much of the letter is devoted to instruction about unity and humility within the Christian community at Philippi (1, 27—2, 18) and exhortations to growth, joy, and peace in their life together (4, 1-9). The letter seems to be drawing to a close at the end of what we number as ch 2, as Paul reports the plans of his helper Timothy and of Epaphroditus (whom the Philippians had sent to aid Paul) to come to Philippi (2, 19—3, 1), and even Paul's own expectation that he will go free and come to Philippi (1, 25-26; 2, 24). Yet quite abruptly at 3, 2, Paul erupts into warnings against false teachers who threaten to impose on the Philippians the burdens of the Mosaic law, including circumcision. The section that follows, 3, 2-21, is a vigorous attack on these Judaizers (cf Gal 2, 11—3, 29) or Jewish Christian teachers (cf 2 Cor 11, 12-23), giving us insights into Paul's own life story (3, 4-6) and into the doctrine of justification, the Christian life, and ultimate hope (3, 7-21).

The location of Paul's imprisonment when he wrote to the Philippians, and thus the date of the letter, are uncertain. The traditional view has been that it stems from Paul's confinement in Rome, between A.D. 59 and 63 (cf Acts 28, 14-31). One modern view suggests the period when he was imprisoned at Caesarea, on the coast of Palestine, A.D.

57 or 58 (Acts 23, 23—26, 32); another suggests Corinth (cf 2 Cor 11, 9). Much recent scholarship favors Ephesus, around A.D. 55, a situation referred to in 2 Cor 1, 8 concerning "the affliction that came to us" in Asia Minor (cf also 1 Cor 15, 32). The reference at 1, 13 to the "praetorium" (cf also 4, 22) can be understood to mean the imperial guard or government house at Ephesus (or Caesarea), or the praetorian camp in Rome. Involved in a decision are the several journeys back and forth between Philippi and wherever Paul is imprisoned, mentioned in the letter (2, 25-28; 4, 14); this factor causes many to prefer Ephesus because of its proximity to Philippi. The Ephesian hypothesis dates the composition of Philippians to the mid-50s when most of Paul's major letters were written.

There is also a likelihood, according to some scholars, that the letter as we have it is a composite from parts of three letters by Paul to the Philippians. Seemingly 4, 10-20 is a brief note of appreciation for help sent through Epaphroditus. The long section from 1, 3 to 3, 1 is then another letter, with news of Paul's imprisonment and reports on Timothy and Epaphroditus (who has fallen ill while with Paul), along with exhortations to the Philippians about Christian conduct; and 3, 2-21 a third communication warning about threats to Philippian Christianity. The other verses in ch 4 and 1, 1-2, are variously assigned by critics to these three underlying letters, which an editor presumably put together to produce a picture of Paul writing earnestly from prison (chs 1-2), facing opponents of the faith (ch 3), and with serene joy advising and thanking his Philippians (ch 4). If all four chapters were originally a unity, then one must assume that a break occurred between the writing of 3, 1 and 3, 2, possibly involving the receipt of bad news from Philippi, and that Paul had some reasons for delaying his words of thanks for the aid brought by Epaphroditus till the end of his letter.

This beautiful letter is rich in insights into Paul's theology and his apostolic love and concern for the gospel and his converts. In Philippians, Paul reveals his human sensitivity and tenderness, his enthusiasm for Christ as the key to life and death (1, 21), and his deep feeling for those in Christ who dwell in Philippi. With them he shares his hopes and convictions, his anxieties and fears, revealing the total confidence in Christ that constitutes faith (3, 8-10). The letter incorporates a hymn about the salvation that God has brought about through Christ (2, 6-11), applied by Paul to the relations of Christians with one another (2, 1-5). Philippians has been termed "the letter of joy" (4, 4.10). It is the rejoicing of faith, based on true understanding of Christ's unique role in the salvation of all who profess his lordship (2, 11; 3, 8-12.14.20-21).

The principal divisions of the Letter to the Philippians are the following:

    I.   Address (1, 1-11)
   II.   Progress of the Gospel (1, 12-26)
  III.   Instructions for the Community (1, 27—2, 18)
  IV.   Travel Plans of Paul and His Assistants (2, 19—3, 1)
   V.   Polemic: Righteousness and the Goal in Christ (3, 2-21)
  VI.   Instructions for the Community (4, 1-9)
 VII.   Gratitude for the Philippians' Generosity (4, 10-20)
VIII.   Farewell (4, 21-23)

I. ADDRESS

CHAPTER 1

Greeting.* [1] Paul and Timothy, slaves* of Christ Jesus, to all the holy ones in Christ Jesus who are in Philippi, with the overseers and ministers:[a] [2] [b] grace to you and peace from God our Father and the Lord Jesus Christ.*

Thanksgiving.* [3] I give thanks to my God at every remembrance of you,[c] [4] praying always with joy in my every prayer for all of you, [5] because of your partnership for the gospel from the first day until now. [6] [d] I am confident of this, that the one who began a good work in you will continue to complete it until the day of Christ Jesus.* [7] It is right that I should think this way about all of you, because I hold you in my heart, you who are all partners with me in grace, both in my imprisonment and in the defense and confirmation of the gospel. [8] For God is my witness, how I long for all of you with the affection of Christ Jesus.[e] [9] And this is my prayer: that your love may increase ever more and more in knowledge and every kind of perception,[f] [10] to discern what is of value, so that you may be pure and blameless for the day of Christ, [g] [11] filled with the fruit of righteousness that comes through Jesus Christ for the glory and praise of God.[h]

II. PROGRESS OF THE GOSPEL*

[12] [i] I want you to know, brothers, that my situation has turned out rather to advance the gospel, [13] so that my imprisonment has become well known in Christ throughout the whole praetorium* and to all the rest,[j] [14] * and so that the majority of the brothers, having taken encouragement in the Lord from my imprisonment, dare more than ever to proclaim the word fearlessly.

[15] Of course, some preach Christ from envy and rivalry, others from good will. [16] The latter act out of love, aware that I am here for the defense of the gospel; [17] the former proclaim Christ out of selfish ambition, not from pure motives, thinking that they will cause me trouble in my imprisonment. [18] What difference does it make, as long as in every way, whether in pretense or in truth, Christ is being proclaimed?[k] And in that I rejoice.*

---

a Rom 1, 1; 2 Cor 1, 1; 1 Thes 1, 1; Phlm 1 / 1 Tm 3, 1-13.—b Rom 1, 7; Gal 1, 3; Phlm 3.—c Rom 1, 8; 1 Cor 1, 4; 1 Thes 1, 2.—d Phil 2, 13 / Phil 1, 10; 2, 16; 1 Cor 1, 8.—e Rom 1, 9; 2 Cor 1, 23; 1 Thes 2, 5.—f Eph 3, 14-19; Col 1, 9-10; Phlm 6.—g Rom 2, 18; 12, 2 / Phil 1, 6.—h Jn 15, 8.—i 12-13: Eph 3, 1; 6, 20; 2 Tm 2, 9; Phlm 9.—j Phil 4, 22.—k Phil 4, 10.

1, 1-2: See the note on Rom 1, 1-7, concerning the greeting.

1, 1: *Slaves:* Paul usually refers to himself at the start of a letter as an apostle. Here he substitutes a term suggesting the unconditional obligation of himself and Timothy to the service of Christ, probably because, in view of the good relationship with the Philippians, he wishes to stress his status as a co-servant rather than emphasize his apostolic authority. Reference to Timothy is a courtesy: Paul alone writes the letter, as the singular verb throughout shows (Phil 1, 3-26), and the reference (Phil 2, 19-24) to Timothy in the third person. *Overseers:* the Greek term *episkopos* literally means "one who oversees" or "one who supervises," but since the second century it has come to designate the "bishop," the official who heads a local church. In New Testament times this office had not yet developed into the form that it later assumed, though it seems to be well on the way to such development in the Pastorals; see 1 Tm 3, 2 and Ti 1, 7, where it is translated *bishop*. At Philippi, however (and at Ephesus, according to Acts 20, 28), there was more than one *episkopos*, and the precise function of these officials is uncertain. In order to distinguish this office from the later stages into which it developed, the term is here translated as *overseers*. *Ministers:* the Greek term *diakonos* is used frequently in the New Testament to designate "servants," "attendants," or "ministers." Paul refers to himself and to other apostles as "ministers of God" (2 Cor 6, 4) or "ministers of Christ" (2 Cor 11, 23). In the Pastorals (1 Tm 3, 8.12) the *diakonos* has become an established official in the local church; hence the term is there translated as *deacon*. The *diakonoi* at Philippi seem to represent an earlier stage of development of the office; we are uncertain about their precise functions. Hence the term is here translated as *ministers*. See Rom 16, 1, where Phoebe is described as a *diakonos* (*minister*) of the church of Cenchreae.

1, 2: The gifts come *from* Christ the Lord, not simply through him from the Father; compare the christology in Phil 2, 6-11.

1, 3-11: As in Rom 1, 8-15 and all the Pauline letters except Galatians, a thanksgiving follows, including a direct prayer for the Philippians (9-11); see the note on Rom 1, 8. On their *partnership for the gospel* (5), cf Phil 1, 29-30; 4, 10-20. Their devotion to the faith and to Paul made them his pride and joy (Phil 4, 1). The characteristics thus manifested are evidence of the community's continuing preparation for the Lord's parousia (6.10). Paul's especially warm relationship with the Philippians is suggested here (7.8) as elsewhere in the letter. The eschatology serves to underscore a concern for ethical growth (9-11), which appears throughout the letter.

1, 6: *The day of Christ Jesus:* the parousia or triumphant return of Christ, when those loyal to him will be with him and share in his eternal glory; cf Phil 1, 10; 2, 16; 3, 20-21; 1 Thes 4, 17; 5, 10; 2 Thes 1, 10; 1 Cor 1, 8.

1, 12-26: The body of the letter begins with an account of Paul's present *situation,* i.e., his *imprisonment* (12-13; see Introduction), and then goes on with advice for the Philippians (Phil 1, 27—2, 18). The *advance of the gospel* (12) and the *progress* of the Philippians *in the faith* (25) frame what is said.

1, 13: *Praetorium:* either the praetorian guard in the city where Paul was imprisoned or the governor's official residence in a Roman province (cf Mk 15, 16; Acts 23, 35). See Introduction on possible sites.

1, 14-18: Although Paul is imprisoned, Christians there nonetheless go on preaching Christ. But they do so with varied motives, *some* with personal hostility toward Paul, others out of personal ambition.

1, 18: *Rejoice:* a major theme in the letter; see Introduction.

Indeed I shall continue to rejoice, [19] * for I know that this will result in deliverance for me* through your prayers and support from the Spirit of Jesus Christ.[l] [20] My eager expectation and hope is that I shall not be put to shame in any way, but that with all boldness, now as always, Christ will be magnified in my body, whether by life or by death.[m] [21] For to me life is Christ, and death is gain.[n] [22] If I go on living in the flesh, that means fruitful labor for me. And I do not know which I shall choose.[o] [23] I am caught between the two. I long to depart this life and be with Christ, [for] that is far better.[p] [24] Yet that I remain [in] the flesh is more necessary for your benefit. [25] And this I know with confidence, that I shall remain and continue in the service of all of you for your progress and joy in the faith, [26] so that your boasting in Christ Jesus may abound on account of me when I come to you again.

III. INSTRUCTIONS FOR THE COMMUNITY

Steadfastness in Faith.* [27] Only, conduct yourselves in a way worthy of the gospel of Christ, so that, whether I come and see you or am absent, I may hear news of you, that you are standing firm in one spirit, with one mind struggling together for the faith of the gospel,[q] [28] not intimidated in any way by your opponents. This is proof to them of destruction, but of your salvation. And this is God's doing. [29] For to you has been granted, for the sake of Christ, not only to believe in him but also to suffer for him.[r] [30] Yours is the same struggle[s] as you saw in me and now hear about me.*

CHAPTER 2

Plea for Unity and Humility.* [1] If there is any encouragement in Christ, any solace in love, any participation in the Spirit, any compassion and mercy, [2] complete my joy by being of the same mind, with the same love, united in heart, thinking one thing.[t] [3] Do nothing out of selfishness or out of vainglory; rather, humbly regard others as more important than yourselves,[u] [4] each looking out not for his own interests, but [also] everyone for those of others.[v]

[5] Have among yourselves the same attitude that is also yours in Christ Jesus,*

[6] Who,* though he was in the form of God,[w]

did not regard equality with God something to be grasped.*

---

l Jb 13, 16 / 2 Cor 1, 11.—m 1 Cor 6, 20; 1 Pt 4, 16.—n Gal 2, 20.—o Rom 1, 13.—p 2 Cor 5, 8.—q Eph 4, 1; Col 1, 10; 1 Thes 2, 12 / Phil 4, 3.—r Mt 5, 10; 10, 38; Mk 8, 34; Acts 5, 41.—s Phil 1, 13; Acts 16, 22-24.—t Rom 15, 5; 1 Cor 1, 10.—u Rom 12, 3.10; Gal 5, 26.—v 1 Cor 10, 24.33; 13, 5.—w Jn 1, 1-2; 17, 5; Col 2, 9; Heb 1, 3.

1, 19-25: Paul earnestly debates his prospects of martyrdom or continued missionary labor. While he may *long to depart this life* and thus *be with Christ* (23), his overall and final expectation is that he will be delivered from this imprisonment and *continue in the service* of the Philippians and of others (19.25; Phil 2, 24). In either case, Christ is central (20.21); if to live means Christ for Paul, death means to be united with Christ in a deeper sense.

1, 19: *Result in deliverance for me:* an echo of Jb 13, 16, hoping that God will turn suffering to ultimate good and deliverance from evil.

1, 27-30: Ethical admonition begins at this early point in the letter, emphasizing steadfastness and congregational unity in the face of possible suffering. The *opponents* (28) are those in Philippi, probably pagans, who oppose the gospel cause. *This is proof* . . . (28) may refer to the whole outlook and conduct of the Philippians, turning out for their salvation but to the judgment of the opponents (cf 2 Cor 2, 15-16), or possibly the sentence refers to the opinion of the opponents, who hold that the obstinacy of the Christians points to the destruction of such people as defy Roman authority (though in reality, Paul holds, such faithfulness leads to salvation).

1, 30: A reference to Paul's earlier imprisonment in Philippi (Acts 16, 19-24; 1 Thes 2, 2) and to his present confinement.

2, 1-11: The admonition to likemindedness and unity (2-5) is based on the believers' threefold experience with Christ, God's love, and the Spirit. The appeal to humility (3) and to obedience (12) is rooted in christology, specifically in a statement about Christ Jesus (6-11) and his humbling of self and obedience to the point of death (8).

2, 5: *Have . . . the same attitude that is also yours in Christ Jesus:* or, "that also Christ Jesus had." While it is often held that Christ here functions as a model for moral imitation, it is not the historical Jesus but the entire Christ event that vv 6-11 depict. Therefore, the appeal is to have in relations among yourselves that same relationship you have in Jesus Christ, i.e., serving one another as you serve Christ (4).

2, 6-11: Perhaps an early Christian hymn quoted here by Paul. The short rhythmic lines fall into two parts, vv 6-8 where the subject of every verb is Christ, and vv 9-11 where the subject is God. The general pattern is thus of Christ's humiliation and then exaltation. More precise analyses propose a division into six three-line stanzas (6; 7abc; 7d-8; 9; 10; 11) or into three stanzas (6-7ab; 7cd-8; 9-11). Phrases such as *even death on a cross* (8c) are considered by some to be additions (by Paul) to the hymn, as are vv 10c and 11c.

2, 6: Either a reference to Christ's preexistence and those aspects of divinity that he was willing to give up in order to serve in human form, or to what the man Jesus refused to grasp at to attain divinity. Many see an allusion to the Genesis story: unlike Adam, Jesus, *though . . . in the form of God* (Gn 1, 26-27), did not reach out for *equality with God*, in contrast with the first Adam in Gn 3, 5-6.

7 Rather, he emptied himself,
   taking the form of a slave,
   coming in human likeness;*
   and found human in appearance,ˣ
8 he humbled himself,ʸ
   becoming obedient to death,
      even death on a cross.*
9 Because of this, God greatly exalted
      him
   and bestowed on him the name*
   that is above every name,ᶻ
10 that at the name of Jesus
   every knee should bend,*
   of those in heaven and on earth and
      under the earth,ᵃ
11 and every tongue confess that
   Jesus Christ is Lord,*
   to the glory of God the Father.ᵇ

Obedience and Service in the World.* ¹² ᶜ So then, my beloved, obedient as you have always been, not only when I am present but all the more now when I am absent, work out your salvation with fear and trembling.* ¹³ For God is the one who, for his good purpose, works in you both to desire and to work.ᵈ ¹⁴ Do everything without grumbling or questioning,ᵉ ¹⁵ that you may be blameless and innocent, children of God without blemish in the midst of a crooked and perverse generation,* among whom you shine like lights in the world,ᶠ ¹⁶ as you hold on to the word of life, so that

my boast for the day of Christ may be that I did not run in vain or labor in vain.ᵍ ¹⁷ But, even if I am poured out as a libation* upon the sacrificial service of your faith, I rejoice and share my joy with all of you.ʰ ¹⁸ In the same way you also should rejoice and share your joy with me.ⁱ

IV. TRAVEL PLANS OF PAUL AND HIS ASSISTANTS*

Timothy and Paul. ¹⁹ I hope, in the Lord Jesus, to send Timothy* to you soon, so that I too may be heartened by hearing news of you.ʲ ²⁰ For I have no one comparable to him for genuine interest in whatever concerns you. ²¹ For they all seek their own interests, not those of Jesus Christ.ᵏ ²² But you know his worth, how as a child with a father he served along with me in the cause of the gospel. ²³ He it is, then, whom I hope to send as soon as I see how things go with me, ²⁴ but I am confident in the Lord that I myself will also come soon.*

Epaphroditus. ²⁵ With regard to Epaphroditus,* my brother and co-worker and fellow soldier, your messenger and minister in my need, I consider it necessary to send him to you.ˡ ²⁶ For he has been longing for all of you and was distressed because you heard that he was ill. ²⁷ He was indeed ill, close to death; but God had mercy on him, not just on him but also on me, so that I might not have sorrow upon

---

x Is 53, 3.11; Jn 1, 14; Rom 8, 3; 2 Cor 8, 9; Gal 4, 4; Heb 2, 14.17.—y Mt 26, 39; Jn 10, 17; Heb 5, 8; 12, 2.—z Acts 2, 33; Mt 23, 12; Eph 1, 20-21; Heb 1, 3-4.—a Is 45, 23; Jn 5, 23; Rom 14, 11; Rv 5, 13.—b Acts 2, 36; Rom 10, 9; 1 Cor 12, 3.—c Ps 2, 11; 1 Cor 2, 3; 2 Cor 7, 15.—d Phil 1, 6; 1 Cor 12, 6; 15, 10; 2 Cor 3, 5.—e 1 Cor 10, 10; 1 Pt 4, 9.—f 1 Thes 3, 13 / Dt 32, 5; Mt 10, 16; Acts 2, 40 / Dn 12, 3; Mt 5, 14.16; Eph 5, 8.—g 1 Thes 2, 19 / Is 49, 4; 65, 23; Gal 2, 2.—h Rom 15, 16; 2 Tm 4, 6.—i Phil 3, 1; 4, 4.—j Acts 16, 1-3; 17, 14-15; 1 Cor 4, 17; 16, 10.—k 1 Cor 13, 5; 2 Tm 4, 10.—l Phil 4, 10-11.15-16.18.

2, 7: *Taking the form of a slave, coming in human likeness:* or "... taking the form of a slave. // Coming in human likeness, and found human in appearance." While it is common to take vv 6 and 7 as dealing with Christ's preexistence and v 8 with his incarnate life, so that lines 7b and c are parallel, it is also possible to interpret so as to exclude any reference to preexistence (see the note on Phil 2, 6) and to take vv 6-8 as presenting two parallel stanzas about Jesus' human state (6-7b; 7cd-8); in the latter alternative, *coming in human likeness* begins the second stanza and parallels 6a to some extent.

2, 8: There may be reflected here language about the servant of the Lord, Is 52, 13—53, 12, especially Is 53, 12.

2, 9: *The name:* "Lord" (11), revealing the true nature of the one who is named.

2, 10-11: *Every knee should bend . . . every tongue confess:* into this language of Is 45, 23 there has been inserted a reference to the three levels in the universe, according to ancient thought, *heaven, earth, under the earth.*

2, 11: *Jesus Christ is Lord:* a common early Christian acclamation; cf 1 Cor 12, 3; Rom 10, 9. But doxology to God the Father is not overlooked here (11c) in the final version of the hymn.

2, 12-18: Paul goes on to draw out further ethical implications for daily life (14-18) from the salvation God works in Christ.

2, 12: *Fear and trembling:* a common Old Testament expression indicating awe and seriousness in the service of God (cf Ex 15, 16; Jdt 2, 28; Ps 2, 11; Is 19, 16).

2, 15-16: *Generation . . . as you hold on to . . . :* or ". . . generation. Among them shine like lights in the world because you hold the word of life. . . ."

2, 17: *Libation:* in ancient religious ritual, the pouring out on the ground of a liquid offering as a sacrifice. Paul means that he may be facing death.

2, 19—3, 1: The plans of Paul and his assistants for future travel are regularly a part of a Pauline letter near its conclusion; cf Rom 15, 22-29; 1 Cor 16, 5-12.

2, 19: *Timothy:* already known to the Philippians (Acts 16, 1-15; cf 1 Cor 4, 17; 16, 10).

2, 24: *I myself will also come soon:* cf Phil 1, 19-25 for the significance of this statement.

2, 25: *Epaphroditus:* sent by the Philippians as their *messenger* (literally, "apostle") to aid Paul in his imprisonment, he had fallen seriously ill; Paul commends him as he sends him back to Philippi.

sorrow. [28] I send him therefore with the greater eagerness, so that, on seeing him, you may rejoice again, and I may have less anxiety. [29] Welcome him then in the Lord with all joy and hold such people in esteem,[m] [30] because for the sake of the work of Christ he came close to death, risking his life to make up for those services to me that you could not perform.

CHAPTER 3

Concluding Admonitions. [1] Finally, my brothers, rejoice* in the Lord. Writing the same things to you is no burden for me but is a safeguard for you.[n]

V. POLEMIC: RIGHTEOUSNESS AND THE GOAL IN CHRIST*

Against Legalistic Teachers. [2] * Beware of the dogs! Beware of the evil-workers![o] Beware of the mutilation!* [3] For we are the circumcision,* we who worship through the Spirit of God, who boast in Christ Jesus and do not put our confidence in flesh,[p] [4] although I myself have grounds for confidence even in the flesh.[q]

Paul's Autobiography. If anyone else thinks he can be confident in flesh, all the more can I. [5] Circumcised on the eighth day,* of the race of Israel, of the tribe of Benjamin, a Hebrew of Hebrew parentage, in observance of the law a Pharisee,[r] [6] in

zeal I persecuted the church, in righteousness based on the law I was blameless.[s]

Righteousness from God. [7] [But] whatever gains I had, these I have come to consider a loss* because of Christ.[t] [8] More than that, I even consider everything as a loss because of the supreme good of knowing Christ Jesus my Lord. For his sake I have accepted the loss of all things and I consider them so much rubbish, that I may gain Christ [9] and be found in him, not having any righteousness of my own based on the law but that which comes through faith in Christ,[u] the righteousness from God, depending on faith [10] to know him and the power of his resurrection and [the] sharing of his sufferings by being conformed to his death,[v] [11] if somehow I may attain the resurrection from the dead.[w]

Forward in Christ.* [12] x It is not that I have already taken hold of it or have already attained perfect maturity,* but I continue my pursuit in hope that I may possess it, since I have indeed been taken possession of by Christ [Jesus]. [13] Brothers, I for my part do not consider myself to have taken possession. Just one thing: forgetting what lies behind but straining forward to what lies ahead, [14] I continue my pursuit toward the goal, the prize of

m 1 Cor 16, 18.—n Phil 2, 18; 4, 4.—o Ps 22, 17.21; Rv 22, 15 / 2 Cor 11, 13 / Gal 5, 6.12.—p Rom 2, 28-29; Col 2, 11.—q 2 Cor 11, 18.21-23.—r Lk 1, 59; 2, 21 / Acts 22, 3; 23, 6; 26, 5.—s Acts 8, 3; 22, 4; 26, 9-11.—t Mt 13, 44.46; Lk 14, 33.—u Rom 3, 21-22.—v Rom 6, 3-5; 8, 17; Gal 6, 17.—w Jn 11, 23-26; Acts 4, 2; Rv 20, 5-6.—x 1 Tm 6, 12.19.

3, 1: *Finally . . . rejoice:* the adverb often signals the close of a letter; cf Phil 4, 8; 2 Cor 13, 11. While the verb could also be translated "good-bye" or "farewell," although it is never so used in Greek epistolography, the theme of joy has been frequent in the letter (Phil 1, 18; 2, 2.18); note also Phil 4, 4 and the addition of "always" there as evidence for the meaning "rejoice." To write *the same things* may refer to what Paul has previously taught in Philippi or to what he has just written or to what follows.

3, 2-21: An abrupt change in content and tone, either because Paul at this point responds to disturbing news he has just heard about a threat to the faith of the Philippians in the form of false teachers, or because part of another Pauline letter was inserted here; see Introduction. The chapter describes these teachers in strong terms as *dogs.* The persons meant are evidently different from the rival preachers of Phil 1, 14-18 and the opponents of Phil 1, 28. Since vv 2-4 emphasize Jewish terms like *circumcision* (2-3.5), some relate them to the "Judaizers" of the Letter to the Galatians. Other phrases make them appear more like the false teachers of 2 Cor 11, 12-15, the *evil-workers.* The latter part of the chapter depicts the *many* who are *enemies* of

Christ's cross in terms that may sound more Gentile or even "gnostic" than Jewish (18-19). Accordingly, some see two groups of false teachers in ch 3, others one group characterized by a claim of having attained "perfect maturity" (12-15).

3, 2-11: Paul sets forth the Christian claim, especially using personal, autobiographical terms that are appropriate to the situation. He presents his own experience in coming to know Christ Jesus in terms of *righteousness* or justification (cf Rom 1, 16-17; 3, 21—5, 11; Gal 2, 5-11), contrasting *the righteousness from God* through faith and that of one's own *based on the law* as two exclusive ways of pleasing God.

3, 2: *Beware of the mutilation:* literally, "incision," an ironic wordplay on "circumcision"; cf Gal 5, 12. There may be an association with the self-inflicted mutilations of the prophets of Baal (1 Kgs 18, 28) and of devotees of Cybele who slashed themselves in religious frenzy.

3, 3: *We are the circumcision:* the true people of God, seed and offspring of Abraham (Gal 3, 7.29; 6, 15). *Spirit of God:* some manuscripts read "worship God by the Spirit."

3, 5: *Circumcised on the eighth day:* as the law required (Gn 17, 12; Lv 12, 3).

3, 7: *Loss:* his knowledge of Christ led Paul to reassess the ways of truly pleasing and serving God. His reevaluation indicates the profound and lasting effect of his experience of the meaning of Christ on the way to Damascus some twenty years before (Gal 1, 15-16; Acts 9, 1-22).

3, 12-16: To be *taken possession of by Christ* does not mean that one has already arrived at perfect spiritual maturity. Paul and the Philippians instead press on, trusting in God.

3, 12: *Attained perfect maturity:* possibly an echo of the concept in the mystery religions of being an initiate, admitted to divine secrets.

God's upward calling, in Christ Jesus.[y] [15] Let us, then, who are "perfectly mature" adopt this attitude. And if you have a different attitude, this too God will reveal to you. [16] Only, with regard to what we have attained, continue on the same course.*

Wrong Conduct and Our Goal.* [17] Join with others in being imitators of me,* brothers, and observe those who thus conduct themselves according to the model you have in us.[z] [18] For many, as I have often told you and now tell you even in tears, conduct themselves as enemies of the cross of Christ.[a] [19] Their end is destruction. Their God is their stomach; their glory is in their "shame." Their minds are occupied with earthly things.[b] [20] But our citizenship* is in heaven, and from it we also await a savior, the Lord Jesus Christ.[c] [21] He will change our lowly body to conform with his glorified body by the power that enables him also to bring all things into subjection to himself.[d]

VI. INSTRUCTIONS FOR THE COMMUNITY*

CHAPTER 4

Live in Concord. [1] Therefore, my brothers, whom I love and long for, my joy and crown, in this way stand firm in the Lord, beloved.[e]

[2] I urge Euodia and I urge Syntyche* to come to a mutual understanding in the Lord. [3] Yes, and I ask you also, my true yokemate,* to help them, for they have struggled at my side in promoting the gospel, along with Clement and my other co-workers, whose names are in the book of life.[f]

Joy and Peace. [4] Rejoice* in the Lord always. I shall say it again: rejoice![g] [5] Your kindness* should be known to all. The Lord is near.[h] [6] Have no anxiety at all, but in everything, by prayer and petition, with thanksgiving, make your requests known to God.[i] [7] Then the peace of God that surpasses all understanding will guard your hearts and minds in Christ Jesus.[j]

[8] [k] Finally, brothers, whatever is true, whatever is honorable, whatever is just, whatever is pure, whatever is lovely, whatever is gracious, if there is any excellence and if there is anything worthy of praise, think about these things.* [9] Keep on doing what you have learned and received and heard and seen in me.[l] Then the God of peace will be with you.*

VII. GRATITUDE FOR THE PHILIPPIANS' GENEROSITY*

[10] I rejoice greatly in the Lord that now at last you revived your concern for me. You were, of course, concerned about me but lacked an opportunity.[m] [11] Not that I say this because of need, for I have

y 1 Cor 9, 24-25; 2 Tm 4, 7.—z 1 Cor 4, 16; 11, 1; 1 Thes 1, 7; 1 Pt 5, 3.—a 1 Cor 1, 17.23; Gal 6, 12.—b Rom 8, 5-6; 16, 18.—c Eph 2, 6.19; Col 3, 1-3; Heb 12, 22.—d Rom 8, 23.29; 1 Cor 15, 42-57; 2 Cor 3, 18; 5, 1-5 / 1 Cor 15, 27-28.—e 1 Thes 2, 19-20.—f Ex 32, 32-33; Ps 69, 29; Dn 12, 1; Lk 10, 20; Rv 3, 5; 13, 8; 17, 8; 20, 12.15; 21, 27.—g Phil 2, 18; 3, 1.—h Ti 3, 2 / Ps 145, 18; Heb 10, 37; Jas 5, 8-9.—i Mt 6, 25-34; 1 Pt 5, 7 / Col 4, 2.—j Jn 14, 27; Col 3, 15.—k Rom 12, 17.—l 1 Thes 4, 1 / Rom 15, 33; 16, 20; 1 Cor 14, 33; 1 Thes 5, 23.—m Phil 1, 18; 2, 25; 1 Cor 9, 11; 2 Cor 11, 9.

3, 16: Some manuscripts add, probably to explain Paul's cryptic phrase, "thinking alike."

3, 17-21: Paul and those who live a life centered in Christ, envisaging both his suffering and his resurrection, provide a model that is the opposite of opponents who reject Christ's cross (cf 1 Cor 1, 23).

3, 17: *Being imitators of me:* not arrogance, but humble simplicity, since all his converts know that Paul is wholly dedicated to imitating Christ (1 Cor 11, 1; cf also Phil 4, 9; 1 Thes 1, 6; 2 Thes 3, 7.9; 1 Cor 4, 6).

3, 20: *Citizenship:* Christians constitute a colony of heaven, as Philippi was a *colonia* of Rome (Acts 16, 12). The hope Paul expresses involves the final coming of Christ, not a status already attained, such as the opponents claim.

4, 1-9: This series of ethical admonitions rests especially on the view of Christ and his coming (cf 5) in Phil 3, 20-21. Paul's instructions touch on unity within the congregation, joy, prayer, and the Christian outlook on life.

4, 2: *Euodia . . . Syntyche:* two otherwise unknown women in the Philippian congregation; on the advice to them, cf Phil 2, 2-4.

4, 3: *Yokemate:* or "comrade," although the Greek *syzygos* could also be a proper name. *Clement:* otherwise unknown, although later writers sought to identify him with Clement, bishop of Rome (Eusebius, *Ecclesiastical History* 3.15.1).

4, 4: *Rejoice:* see the note on Phil 3, 1.

4, 5: *Kindness:* considerateness, forbearance, fairness. *The Lord is near:* most likely a reference to Christ's parousia (Phil 1, 6.10; 3, 20-21; 1 Cor 16, 22), although some sense an echo of Ps 119, 151 and the perpetual presence of the Lord.

4, 8: The language employs terms from Roman Stoic thought.

4, 9: Cf the note on Phil 3, 17.

4, 10-20: Paul, more directly than anywhere else in the letter (cf Phil 1, 3-5), here thanks the Philippians for their gift of money sent through Epaphroditus (Phil 2, 25). Paul's own policy was *to be self-sufficient* as a missionary, supporting himself by his own labor (1 Thes 2, 5-9; 1 Cor 9, 15-18; cf Acts 18, 2-3). In spite of this reliance on self and on God to provide (11-13), Paul accepted gifts from the Philippians *not only once but more than once* (16) when he was in Thessalonica (Acts 17, 1-9), as he does now, in prison (*my distress,* 14). While commercial terms appear in the passage, like *an account of giving and receiving* (15) and *received full payment* (18), Paul is most concerned about the spiritual growth of the Philippians (10.17.19); he emphasizes that God will care for their needs, through Christ.

learned, in whatever situation I find myself, to be self-sufficient.[n] [12]I know indeed how to live in humble circumstances; I know also how to live with abundance. In every circumstance and in all things I have learned the secret of being well fed and of going hungry, of living in abundance and of being in need. [13]I have the strength for everything through him who empowers me.[o] [14]Still, it was kind of you to share in my distress.

[15]You Philippians indeed know that at the beginning of the gospel,* when I left Macedonia, not a single church shared with me in an account of giving and receiving, except you alone. [16]For even when I was at Thessalonica you sent me something for my needs, not only once but more than once. [17]It is not that I am eager for the gift; rather, I am eager for the profit that accrues to your account. [18]I have received full payment and I abound. I am very well supplied because of what I received from you through Epaphroditus, "a fragrant aroma," an acceptable sacrifice,* pleasing to God.[p] [19]My God will fully supply whatever you need, in accord with his glorious riches in Christ Jesus.[q] [20]To our God and Father, glory for ever and ever. Amen.[r]

VIII. FAREWELL*

[21]Give my greetings to every holy one in Christ Jesus. The brothers who are with me send you their greetings; [22] [s] all the holy ones send you their greetings, especially those of Caesar's household.* [23]The grace of the Lord Jesus Christ be with your spirit.

---

n 11-12: 1 Cor 4, 11; 2 Cor 6, 10; 11, 27 / 2 Cor 12, 9-10.—o Col 1, 29; 2 Tm 4, 17.—p Gn 8, 21; Ex 29, 18; Eph 5, 2; Heb 13, 16.—q 1 Thes 3, 11.13.—r Rom 16, 27; Eph 5, 20.—s Phil 1, 13.

4, 15: *The beginning of the gospel:* it was at Philippi that Paul first preached Christ in Europe, going on from there to Thessalonica and Beroea (Acts 16, 9—17, 14).

4, 18: *Aroma . . . sacrifice:* Old Testament cultic language (cf Gn 8, 21; Ex 29, 18.25.41; Lv 1, 9.13; Ez 20, 41) applied to the Philippians' gift; cf Eph 5, 2; 2 Cor 2, 14-16.

4, 21-23: On the usual greetings at the conclusion of a letter, see the note on 1 Cor 16, 19-24. Inclusion of greetings from *all the holy ones* in the place from which Paul writes would involve even the Christians of Phil 1, 14-18 who had their differences with Paul.

4, 22: *Those of Caesar's household:* minor officials or even slaves and freedmen, found in Ephesus or Rome, among other places.

THE LETTER TO THE COLOSSIANS
INTRODUCTION

This letter is addressed to a congregation at Colossae in the Lycus Valley in Asia Minor, east of Ephesus. At the time of writing, Paul had not visited there, the letter says (1, 4; 2, 1). The community had apparently been established by Epaphras of Colossae (1, 7; 4, 12; Phlm 23). Problems, however, had arisen, brought on by teachers who emphasized Christ's relation to the universe (cosmos). Their teachings stressed angels (2, 18; "principalities and powers," 2, 15), which were connected with astral powers and cultic practices (see the note on 2, 16) and rules about food and drink and ascetical disciplines (2, 16.18). These teachings, Paul insists, detract from the person and work of Christ for salvation as set forth magnificently in a hymnic passage at 1, 15-20 and reiterated throughout the letter. Such teachings are but "shadows"; Christ is "reality" (2, 17).

For help in dealing with these problems that the new teachers posed at Colossae, Epaphras sought out Paul, who was then imprisoned (4, 10.18) at a place that the letter does not mention. Paul, without entering into debate over the existence of angelic spirits or their function, simply affirms that Christ possesses the sum total of redemptive power (1, 19) and that the spiritual renewal of the human person occurs through contact in baptism with the person of Christ, who died and rose again (2, 9-14). It is unnecessary for the Christian to be concerned about placating spirits (2, 15) or avoiding imagined defilement through ascetical practices in regard to food and drink (2, 20-23). True Christian asceticism consists in the conquering of personal sins (3, 5-10) and the practice of love of neighbor in accordance with the standard set by Christ (3, 12-16).

Paul commends the community as a whole (1, 3-8); this seems to indicate that, though the Colossians have been under pressure to adopt the false doctrines, they have not yet succumbed. The apostle expresses his prayerful concern for them (1, 9-14). His preaching has cost him persecution, suffering, and imprisonment, but he regards these as reflective of the sufferings of Christ, a required discipline for the sake of the gospel (see the note on 1, 24; cf 1, 29; 2, 1). His instructions to the Christian family and to slaves and masters require a new spirit of reflection and action. Love, obedience, and service are to be rendered "in the Lord" (3, 18—4, 1).

Colossians follows the outline of a typical Pauline letter. It is distinguished by the poetic lines in 1, 15-20 concerning who Christ is and what Christ means in creation and redemption. This hymn may be compared with similar passages in Philippians 2, 6-11; 1 Timothy 3, 16; and John 1, 1-18. It was apparently familiar liturgical material to the author, the audience, and the false teachers. In 1, 21—2, 7, however, Paul interprets the relation between the body of Christ, which he insists is the church (1, 18), and the world or cosmos to be one not simply of Christ's preexistence and rule but one of missionary advance into the world by the spreading of the word (1, 25.28). In this labor of the missionary body of Christ, Paul as a minister plays a prime part in bringing Christ and the gospel as hope to the Gentiles (1, 23.25.27). To "every creature under heaven" the word is to be proclaimed, so that everyone receives Christ, is established in faith, and walks in Christ (1, 28; 2, 6.7).

Paul wrote the Letter to the Colossians while in prison, but his several imprisonments leave the specific place and date of composition uncertain. On this point the same problem exists as with Ephesians and Philippians (see the Introductions to these letters). Traditionally the house arrest at Rome, in which Paul enjoyed a certain restricted freedom in preaching (see Acts 28, 16-28), or a second Roman imprisonment has been claimed as the setting. Others suggest a still earlier imprisonment at Caesarea (see Acts 23, 12—27, 1) or in Ephesus (see Acts 19). Still others regard the letter as the work of some pupil or follower of Paul, writing in his name. In any case, the contents are often closely paralleled by thoughts in Ephesians.

The principal divisions of the Letter to the Colossians are the following:

   I. Address (1, 1-14)
  II. The Preeminence of Christ (1, 15—2, 3)
 III. Warnings against False Teachers (2, 4-23)
 IV. The Ideal Christian Life in the World (3, 1—4, 6)
  V. Conclusion (4, 7-18)

I. ADDRESS
CHAPTER 1

Greeting.* [1] Paul, an apostle of Christ Jesus by the will of God, and Timothy our brother,[a] [2] to the holy ones and faithful brothers in Christ in Colossae: grace to you and peace from God our Father.

Thanksgiving.* [3] We always give thanks to God, the Father of our Lord Jesus Christ, when we pray for you,[b] [4] for we have heard of your faith in Christ Jesus and the love that you have for all the holy ones [5] because of the hope reserved for you in heaven. Of this you have already heard through the word of truth, the gospel,[c]

a Eph 1, 1.—b Eph 1, 15-16; Phlm 4-5.—c Eph 1, 13.18; 1 Pt 1, 4.

1, 1-2: For the epistolary form used by Paul at the beginning of his letters, see the note on Rom 1, 1-7. On *holy ones* or "God's people," see the note on Rom 1, 7. Awareness of their calling helps this group to be *faithful brothers* and sisters *in Christ,* i.e., dedicated to the tasks implied in their calling.

1, 3-8: On thanksgiving at the start of a letter, see the note on Rom 1, 8. The apostle, recalling his own prayers for them and the

good report about them he has received (3-4), congratulates the Colossians upon their acceptance of Christ and their faithful efforts to live the gospel (Col 3, 6-8). To encourage them he mentions the success of the gospel elsewhere (6) and assures them that his knowledge of their community is accurate, since he has been in personal contact with Epaphras (7-8), who likely had evangelized Colossae and other cities in the Lycus Valley of Asia Minor (cf Col 4, 12.13; Phlm 23). On *faith, love,* and *hope* (4.5.8), see the note on 1 Cor 13, 13; cf 1 Thes 1, 3; 5, 8.

[6]that has come to you. Just as in the whole world it is bearing fruit and growing, so also among you, from the day you heard it and came to know the grace of God in truth, [7] *d* as you learned it from Epaphras* our beloved fellow slave, who is a trustworthy minister of Christ on your behalf [8] and who also told us of your love in the Spirit.

Prayer for Continued Progress. * [9]Therefore, from the day we heard this, we do not cease praying for you and asking that you may be filled with the knowledge of his will through all spiritual wisdom and understanding*e* [10]to live in a manner worthy of the Lord, so as to be fully pleasing, in every good work bearing fruit and growing in the knowledge of God, [11]strengthened with every power, in accord with his glorious might, for all endurance and patience, with joy [12] * giving thanks to the Father, who has made you fit to share in the inheritance of the holy ones in light.*f* [13]He delivered us from the power of darkness and transferred us to the kingdom of his beloved Son, [14]in whom we have redemption, the forgiveness of sins.*g*

---

d Phlm 23.—e Eph 1, 15-17; 5, 17; Phil 1, 9.—f Col 3, 17; Jn 8, 12; Acts 26, 18; 1 Tm 6, 16; 1 Pt 2, 9.—g Eph 1, 7.—h Ps 89, 28; Jn 1, 3.18; 2 Cor 4, 4.—i 1 Cor 8, 6; Eph 1, 10.21.—j 1 Cor 11, 3; 12, 12.27; 15, 20; Eph 1, 22-23; Rv 1, 5.—k 2 Cor 5, 18-19; Eph 1, 10.—l Eph 2, 14-16.

1, 7: *Epaphras:* now with Paul but a Colossian, founder of the church there.

1, 9-14: Moved by Epaphras' account, the apostle has prayed and continues to pray fervently for the Colossians that, in their response to the gospel, they *may be filled with the knowledge of God's will* (9; cf Col 3, 10). Paul expects a mutual interaction between their life according to the gospel and this knowledge (10), yielding results (*fruit,* 10; cf Col 1, 6) *in every good work:* growth, strength, *endurance, patience, with joy* (11), and the further giving of thanks (12).

1, 12-14: A summary about *redemption* by *the Father* precedes the statement in vv 15-20 about the *beloved Son* who is God's love in person (13). Christians share *the inheritance . . . in light* with *the holy ones,* here probably the angels (12). The imagery reflects the Exodus (*delivered . . . transferred*) and Jesus' theme of *the kingdom. Redemption* is explained as *forgiveness of sins* (cf Acts 2, 38; Rom 3, 24-25; Eph 1, 7).

1, 15-20: As the poetic arrangement indicates, these lines are probably an early Christian hymn, known to the Colossians and taken up into the letter from liturgical use (cf Phil 2, 6-11; 1 Tm 3, 16). They present Christ as the mediator of creation (15-18a) and of redemption (18b-20). There is a parallelism between *firstborn of all creation* (15) and *firstborn from the dead* (18). While many of the phrases were at home in Greek philosophical use and even in gnosticism, the basic ideas also reflect Old Testament themes about Wisdom found in Prv 8, 22-31; Wis 7, 22—8, 1; and Sir 1, 4. See also the notes on what is possibly a hymn in Jn 1, 1-18.

1, 15: *Image:* cf Gn 1, 27. Whereas the man and the woman were originally created in the image and likeness of God (see also Gn 1, 26), Christ as image (2 Cor 4, 4) *of the invisible God* (Jn 1, 18) now shares this new nature in baptism with those redeemed (cf Col 3, 10-11).

II. THE PREEMINENCE OF CHRIST
His Person and Work

[15] * He is the image* of the invisible God,
    the firstborn of all creation.*h*

[16] For in him* were created all things in
    heaven and on earth,
    the visible and the invisible,
    whether thrones or dominions or
    principalities or powers;
    all things were created through him
    and for him.*i*

[17] He is before all things,
    and in him all things hold together.

[18] He is the head of the body, the
    church.*
    He is the beginning, the firstborn from
    the dead,
    that in all things he himself might be
    preeminent.*j*

[19] For in him all the fullness* was pleased
    to dwell,

[20]   and through him to reconcile all
    things for him,
    making peace by the blood of his
    cross*
    [through him], whether those on
    earth or those in heaven.*k*

[21] * And you who once were alienated and hostile in mind because of evil deeds*l* [22]he

---

1, 16-17: Christ (though not mentioned by name) is preeminent and supreme as God's agent in the creation of *all things* (cf Jn 1, 3), as prior to *all things* (17; cf Heb 1, 3).

1, 18: *Church:* such a reference seemingly belongs under "redemption" in the following lines, not under the "creation" section of the hymn. Stoic thought sometimes referred to the world as "the body of Zeus." Pauline usage is to speak of the church as the body of Christ (1 Cor 12, 12-27; Rom 12, 4-5). Some think that the author of Colossians has inserted the reference to the church here so as to define "head of the body" in Paul's customary way. See v 24. *Preeminent:* when Christ was raised by God as *firstborn from the dead* (cf Acts 26, 23; Rv 1, 5), he was placed over the community, the church, that he had brought into being, but he is also indicated as crown of the whole new creation, over *all things.* His further role is to *reconcile all things* (20) for God or possibly "to himself."

1, 19: *Fullness:* in gnostic usage this term referred to a spiritual world of beings above, between God and the world; many later interpreters take it to refer to *the fullness of the deity* (Col 2, 9); the reference could also be to the fullness of grace (cf Jn 1, 16).

1, 20: *The blood of his cross:* the most specific reference in the hymn to redemption through Christ's death, a central theme in Paul; cf Col 2, 14-15; 1 Cor 1, 17.18.23. *[Through him]:* the phrase, lacking in some manuscripts, seems superfluous but parallels the reference to reconciliation through Christ earlier in the verse.

1, 21-23: Paul, in applying this hymn to the Colossians, reminds them that they have experienced the reconciling effect of Christ's death. He sees the effects of the cross in the redemption of human beings, not cosmic powers such as those referred to in vv 16 and 20 (*all things*). Paul also urges adherence to Christ in faith and begins to point to his own role as minister (23), sufferer (24), and proclaimer (27-28) of this gospel.

has now reconciled in his fleshly body through his death, to present you holy, without blemish, and irreproachable before him, [23] provided that you persevere in the faith, firmly grounded, stable, and not shifting from the hope of the gospel that you heard, which has been preached to every creature under heaven, of which I, Paul, am a minister.

Christ in Us.* [24] Now I rejoice in my sufferings for your sake, and in my flesh I am filling up what is lacking* in the afflictions of Christ on behalf of his body, which is the church, [25] of which I am a minister in accordance with God's stewardship given to me to bring to completion for you the word of God, [26] the mystery hidden from ages and from generations past. But now it has been manifested to his holy ones,[m] [27] to whom God chose to make known the riches of the glory of this mystery among the Gentiles; it is Christ in you, the hope for glory.[n] [28] It is he whom we proclaim, admonishing everyone and teaching everyone with all wisdom, that we may present everyone perfect in Christ.[o] [29] For this I labor and struggle, in accord with the exercise of his power working within me.[p]

CHAPTER 2

[1] For I want you to know how great a struggle I am having for you and for those in

Laodicea* and all who have not seen me face to face, [2] that their hearts may be encouraged as they are brought together in love, to have all the richness of fully assured understanding, for the knowledge of the mystery of God, Christ,[q] [3] in whom are hidden all the treasures of wisdom and knowledge.[r]

III. WARNINGS AGAINST FALSE TEACHERS*

A General Admonition. [4] I say this so that no one may deceive you by specious arguments.[s] [5] For even if I am absent in the flesh, yet I am with you in spirit, rejoicing as I observe your good order and the firmness of your faith in Christ.[t] [6] So, as you received Christ Jesus the Lord, walk in him, [7] rooted in him and built upon him and established in the faith as you were taught, abounding in thanksgiving.[u] [8] See to it that no one captivate you with an empty, seductive philosophy according to human tradition, according to the elemental powers of the world* and not according to Christ.[v]

Sovereign Role of Christ. [9] [w] For in him dwells the whole fullness of the deity* bodily, [10] and you share in this fullness in him, who is the head of every principality and power. [11] [x] In him* you were also circumcised with a circumcision not adminis-

---

m Rom 16, 25-26; 1 Cor 2, 7; Eph 3, 3.9.—n Col 3, 4; Rom 8, 10.—o Eph 4, 13.—p Col 2, 1; 4, 12; Phil 4, 13.—q Col 1, 26-27; Eph 3, 18-19.—r Prv 2, 4-5; Is 45, 3; Rom 11, 33; 1 Cor 1, 30.—s Eph 4, 14.—t 1 Cor 5, 3; Phil 1, 27.—u Eph 2, 20-22; 3, 17.—v Gal 4, 3; Eph 5, 6.—w Col 1, 19; Eph 3, 19.—x Col 1, 22; Jer 4, 4; Rom 2, 25-29; Phil 3, 3.

1, 24—2, 1: As the community at Colossae was not personally known to Paul (see Introduction), he here invests his teaching with greater authority by presenting a brief sketch of his apostolic ministry and sufferings as they reflect those of Christ on behalf of the church (24). The preaching of God's word (25) carries out the divine plan (*the mystery*, 26) to make Christ known to the Gentiles (27). It teaches the God-given wisdom about Christ (28), whose power works mightily in the apostle (29). Even in those communities that do not know him personally (Col 2, 1), he can increase the perception of God in Christ, unite the faithful more firmly in love, and so bring encouragement to them (Col 2, 2). He hopes that his apostolic authority will make the Colossians perceive more readily the defects in the teaching of others who have sought to delude them, the next concern in the letter.

1, 24: *What is lacking:* although variously interpreted, this phrase does not imply that Christ's atoning death on the cross was defective. It may refer to the apocalyptic concept of a quota of "messianic woes" to be endured before the end comes; cf Mk 13, 8.19-20.24 and the note on Mt 23, 29-32. Others suggest that Paul's mystical unity with Christ allowed him to call his own *sufferings the afflictions of Christ.*

2, 1: *Laodicea:* chief city in Phrygia, northwest of Colossae; cf Col 4, 13.16; Rv 3, 14-22.

2, 4-23: In face of the threat posed by false teachers (4), the Colossians are admonished to adhere to the gospel as it was first preached to them (6), steeping themselves in it with grateful hearts (7). They must reject religious teachings originating in any source except the gospel (8) because in Christ alone will they have access to God, *the deity* (9). So fully has Christ enlightened them that they need no other source of religious knowledge or virtue (10). They do not require *circumcision* (11), for *in baptism* their whole being has been affected by Christ (12) through forgiveness of sin and resurrection to a new life (13; cf Col 3, 1 and Rom 6, 1-11).

On the cross Christ canceled the record of the debt that stood against us with all its claims (14), i.e., he eliminated the law (cf Eph 2, 15) that human beings could not observe—and that could not save them. He forgave sins against the law (14) and exposed as false and misleading (15) all other powers (cf Col 1, 16) that purport to offer salvation. Therefore, the Colossians are not to accept judgments from such teachers on *food and drink* or to keep certain religious festivals or engage in certain cultic practices (16), for the Colossians would thereby risk severing themselves from Christ (19). If, when they accepted the gospel, they believed in Christ as their savior, they must be convinced that their salvation cannot be achieved by appeasing ruling spirits through dietary practices or through a wisdom gained simply by means of harsh asceticism (20-23).

2, 8: *Elemental powers of the world:* see the note on Gal 4, 3.

2, 9: *Fullness of the deity:* the divine nature, not just attributes; see the note on Col 1, 19.

2, 11: A description of baptism (12) in symbolic terms of the Old Testament rite for entry into the community. The false teachers may have demanded physical circumcision of the Colossians.

tered by hand, by stripping off the carnal body, with the circumcision of Christ. [12] You were buried with him in baptism, in which you were also raised with him through faith in the power of God, who raised him from the dead.[y] [13] [z] And even when you were dead [in] transgressions and the uncircumcision of your flesh, he brought you to life along with him, having forgiven us all our transgressions; [14] * obliterating the bond against us, with its legal claims, which was opposed to us, he also removed it from our midst, nailing it to the cross;[a] [15] despoiling the principalities and the powers, he made a public spectacle of them,[b] leading them away in triumph by it.*

Practices Contrary to Faith. [16] [c] Let no one, then, pass judgment on you in matters of food and drink or with regard to a festival or new moon or sabbath.* [17] These are shadows of things to come; the reality belongs to Christ.[d] [18] Let no one disqualify you, delighting in self-abasement and worship of angels, taking his stand on visions,* inflated without reason by his fleshly mind,[e] [19] and not holding closely to the head, from whom the whole body, supported and held together by its ligaments and bonds, achieves the growth that comes from God.[f]

[20] If you died with Christ to the elemental powers of the world, why do you submit to regulations as if you were still living in the world? [21] "Do not handle! Do not taste! Do not touch!" [22] These are all things

destined to perish with use; they accord with human precepts and teachings.[g] [23] While they have a semblance of wisdom in rigor of devotion and self-abasement [and] severity to the body, they are of no value against gratification of the flesh.

IV. THE IDEAL CHRISTIAN LIFE IN THE WORLD

CHAPTER 3

Mystical Death and Resurrection. * [1] If then you were raised with Christ, seek what is above, where Christ is seated at the right hand of God.[h] [2] Think of what is above, not of what is on earth. [3] For you have died, and your life is hidden with Christ in God.[i] [4] When Christ your life appears, then you too will appear with him in glory.

Renunciation of Vice. * [5] Put to death, then, the parts of you that are earthly:[j] immorality, impurity, passion, evil desire, and the greed that is idolatry.* [6] Because of these the wrath of God* is coming [upon the disobedient].[k] [7] By these you too once conducted yourselves, when you lived in that way. [8] But now you must put them all away:* anger, fury, malice, slander, and obscene language out of your mouths.[l] [9] Stop lying to one another, since you have taken off the old self with its practices[m] [10] and have put on the new self, which is being renewed, for knowledge, in the image* of its creator.[n] [11] Here there is not Greek and Jew, circumcision and uncircumcision, barbarian, Scythian,* slave, free; but Christ is all and in all.[o]

Col

---

y Rom 6, 3-4.—z Eph 2, 1.5.—a Eph 2, 14-15.—b Col 1, 16.20; 2 Cor 2, 14; Eph 1, 21.—c Rom 14, 3-4; 1 Tm 4, 3.—d Heb 8, 5; 10, 1.—e Col 2, 23; Mt 24, 4.—f Eph 2, 21-22; 4, 16.—g Is 29, 13.—h Col 2, 12; Ps 110, 1; Phil 3, 20; Eph 2, 6.—i Rom 6, 2-5.—j Mt 15, 19; Rom 1, 29-30; Gal 5, 19-21; Eph 5, 3.5.—k Rom 1, 18.—l Eph 4, 22.25.31.—m Rom 6, 4.6; Eph 4, 22-25; Heb 12, 1; 1 Pt 2, 1; 4, 2.—n Gn 1, 26-27.—o 1 Cor 12, 13; Gal 3, 27-28.

2, 14: The elaborate metaphor here about how God canceled the legal claims against us through Christ's cross depicts not Christ being nailed to the cross by men but *the bond . . . with its legal claims* being nailed to the cross by God.

2, 15: The picture derives from the *public spectacle* and *triumph* of a Roman emperor's victory parade, where captives marched in subjection. *The principalities and the powers* are here conquered, not reconciled (cf Col 1, 16.20). An alternate rendering for *by it* (the cross) is "by him" (Christ).

2, 16: *Festival or new moon or sabbath:* yearly, monthly, and weekly observances determined by religious powers associated with a calendar set by the heavenly bodies, sun, moon, and stars (cf Col 2, 8).

2, 18: Ascetic practices encouraged by the false teachers included subjection of self humbly to their rules, worship of angels, and cultivation of visions, though exact details are unclear.

3, 1-4: By retaining the message of the gospel that the risen, living Christ is the source of their salvation, the Colossians will be free from false religious evaluations of the things of the world (1-2). They have died to these; but one day *when Christ . . . appears,* they will live with Christ in the presence of God (3-4).

3, 5-17: In lieu of false asceticism and superstitious festivals, the apostle reminds the Colossians of the moral life that is to characterize their response to God through Christ. He urges their participation in the liturgical hymns and prayers that center upon God's plan of salvation in Christ (16).

3, 5.8: The two lists of five vices each are similar to enumerations at Rom 1, 29-31 and Gal 5, 19-21.

3, 6: *The wrath of God:* see the note on Rom 1, 18. Many manuscripts add, as at Eph 5, 6, "upon the disobedient."

3, 8-10: *Put . . . away; have taken off; have put on:* the terms may reflect baptismal practice, taking off garments and putting on new ones after being united with Christ, here translated into ethical terms.

3, 10: *Image:* see the note on Col 1, 15.

3, 11: *Scythian:* a barbarous people from north of the Black Sea.

[12]Put on then, as God's chosen ones, holy and beloved, heartfelt compassion, kindness, humility, gentleness, and patience,[p] [13]bearing with one another and forgiving one another, if one has a grievance against another; as the Lord has forgiven you, so must you also do.[q] [14]And over all these put on love, that is, the bond of perfection.[r] [15]And let the peace of Christ control your hearts, the peace into which you were also called in one body. And be thankful.[s] [16]Let the word of Christ dwell in you richly, as in all wisdom you teach and admonish one another, singing psalms, hymns, and spiritual songs with gratitude in your hearts to God.[t] [17]And whatever you do, in word or in deed, do everything in the name of the Lord Jesus, giving thanks to God the Father through him.[u]

The Christian Family. [18] * Wives, be subordinate to your husbands, as is proper in the Lord.[v] [19]Husbands, love your wives, and avoid any bitterness toward them. [20]Children, obey your parents in everything, for this is pleasing to the Lord.[w] [21]Fathers, do not provoke your children, so they may not become discouraged.[x]

Slaves and Masters. [22]Slaves,* obey your human masters in everything, not only when being watched, as currying favor, but in simplicity of heart, fearing the Lord.[y] [23]Whatever you do, do from the heart, as for the Lord and not for others, [24]knowing that you will receive from the Lord the due payment of the inheritance; be slaves of the Lord Christ. [25]For the wrongdoer will receive recompense for the wrong he committed, and there is no partiality.[z]

CHAPTER 4

[1]Masters, treat your slaves justly and fairly, realizing that you too have a Master in heaven.

Prayer and Apostolic Spirit. [2]Persevere in prayer, being watchful in it with thanksgiving;[a] [3]at the same time, pray for us, too, that God may open a door to us for the word, to speak of the mystery of Christ, for which I am in prison,[b] [4]that I may make it clear, as I must speak. [5]Conduct yourselves wisely toward outsiders, making the most of the opportunity.[c] [6]Let your speech always be gracious, seasoned with salt, so that you know how you should respond to each one.

V. CONCLUSION*

Tychicus and Onesimus. [7]Tychicus,* my beloved brother, trustworthy minister, and fellow slave in the Lord, will tell you all the news of me.[d] [8]I am sending him to you for this very purpose, so that you may know about us and that he may encourage your hearts, [9]together with Onesimus, a trustworthy and beloved brother, who is one of you. They will tell you about everything here.[e]

From Paul's Co-Workers. [10]Aristarchus,* my fellow prisoner, sends you greetings, as does Mark the cousin of Barnabas (concerning whom you have received instructions; if he comes to you, receive him),[f] [11]and Jesus,* who is called Justus, who are of the circumcision; these alone are my co-workers for the kingdom of God, and they have been a comfort to me. [12]Epaphras* sends you greetings; he is one of you, a slave of Christ [Jesus], always striving for you in his prayers so that you may be perfect and fully assured in all the will of

p Eph 4, 1-2.32; 1 Thes 5, 15.—q Mt 6, 14; 18, 21-35; Eph 4, 32.—r Rom 13, 8-10.—s Rom 12, 5; 1 Cor 12, 12; Eph 2, 16; 4, 3-4; Phil 4, 7.—t Eph 5, 19-20.—u 1 Cor 10, 31.—v Eph 5, 22; Ti 2, 5; 1 Pt 3, 1.—w Eph 6, 1.—x Eph 6, 4.—y Eph 6, 5; 1 Tm 6, 1; Ti 2, 9-10; 1 Pt 2, 18.—z Rom 2, 11.—a Lk 18, 1; Rom 12, 12; Eph 6, 18-20; 1 Thes 5, 17.—b Rom 15, 30; 1 Cor 16, 9; Eph 6, 19; 2 Thes 3, 1.—c Eph 5, 15-16.—d Acts 20, 4; Eph 6, 21-22; Phil 1, 12.—e Phlm 10-11.—f Acts 19, 29; 20, 4; 27, 2 / Acts 12, 12.25; 13, 13; 15, 37.40; 2 Tm 4, 11; Phlm 24; 1 Pt 5, 13.

3, 18—4, 6: After general recommendations that connect family life and the social condition of slavery with the service of Christ (Col 3, 18—4, 1), Paul requests prayers for himself, especially in view of his imprisonment (2-3), and recommends friendly relations and meaningful discussions of Christian teaching with *outsiders,* i.e., non-Christians (5-6). See the note on Eph 5, 21—6, 9.

3, 22-25: *Slaves:* within this table of duties in family and societal relations, involving wives and husbands, children and parents (18-21), such as also appears in Eph 5, 22—6, 9, slaves here receive special attention because of the case of Onesimus the slave returning to his master (Col 4, 9; Phlm 10-12).

4, 7-18: Paul concludes with greetings and information concerning various Christians known to the Colossians.

4, 7: *Tychicus:* Acts 20, 4 mentions his role in the collection for Jerusalem; Eph 6, 21 repeats what is said here; see also 2 Tm 4, 12; Ti 3, 12.

4, 10: *Aristarchus:* a Thessalonian who was with Paul at Ephesus and Caesarea and on the voyage to Rome (Acts 19, 29; 20, 4; 27, 2). *Mark:* also referred to at Phlm 24 and 2 Tm 4, 11 and, as "John Mark," in Acts (Acts 12, 12.25; 13, 13; 15, 37-40). See also 1 Pt 5, 13 and the note there. Traditionally the author of the second gospel.

4, 11: *Jesus:* a then common Jewish name, the Greek form of Joshua.

4, 12: *Epaphras:* see the notes on Col 1, 3-8 and Col 1, 7.

God.*g* ¹³For I can testify that he works very hard for you and for those in Laodicea* and those in Hierapolis. ¹⁴Luke* the beloved physician sends greetings, as does Demas.*h*

A Message for the Laodiceans. ¹⁵Give greetings to the brothers in Laodicea and to Nympha and to the church in her house.* ¹⁶And when this letter is read be-fore you, have it read also in the church of the Laodiceans, and you yourselves read the one from Laodicea.* ¹⁷And tell Archippus, "See that you fulfill the ministry* that you received in the Lord."*i*

¹⁸The greeting is in my own hand,* Paul's. Remember my chains. Grace be with you.*j*

---

g Col 1, 7; Rom 15, 30.—h Phlm 24; 2 Tm 4, 10-11.—i Phlm 2.—j 1 Cor 16, 21; Gal 6, 11; Eph 3, 1; 2 Thes 3, 17.

4, 13: *Laodicea:* see the note on Col 2, 1. *Hierapolis:* a city northeast of Laodicea and northwest of Colossae.

4, 14: *Luke:* only here described as a medical doctor; cf Phlm 24 and 2 Tm 4, 11. Traditionally the author of the third gospel. *Demas:* cf Phlm 24; he later deserted Paul (2 Tm 4, 10).

4, 15: *Nympha and . . . her house:* some manuscripts read a masculine for the house-church leader, "Nymphas and . . . his house."

4, 16: *The one from Laodicea:* either a letter by Paul that has been lost or the Letter to the Ephesians (cf the note on Eph 1, 1, *in Ephesus*).

4, 17: *Fulfill the ministry:* usually taken to mean that *Archippus,* the son of Philemon and Apphia (Phlm 1-2), is "pastor" at Colossae. An alternate interpretation is that Archippus, not Philemon, is the owner of the slave Onesimus and that Paul is asking Archippus to complete the service he has received in the Lord by sending Onesimus back to minister to Paul in his captivity (cf Phlm 20).

4, 18: *My own hand:* a postscript in Paul's own hand was his custom; cf Gal 6, 11-18 and 2 Thes 3, 17-18.

THE FIRST LETTER TO THE THESSALONIANS

INTRODUCTION

1Thes

When Paul parted from Barnabas (Acts 15, 36-41) at the beginning of what is called his second missionary journey, he chose Silvanus (Silas) as his traveling companion. Soon afterwards he took Timothy along with him (Acts 16, 1-3). Paul was now clearly at the head of his own missionary band. About A.D. 50, he arrived in Greece for the first time. In making converts in Philippi and, soon afterwards, in Thessalonica, he was beset by persecution from Jews and Gentiles alike. Moving on to Beroea, he was again harassed by enemies from Thessalonica and hurriedly left for Athens (Acts 16, 11—17, 15). Silvanus and Timothy remained behind for a while. Paul soon sent Timothy back to Thessalonica to strengthen that community in its trials (3, 1-5). Timothy and Silvanus finally returned to Paul when he reached Corinth (Acts 18, 1-18), probably in the early summer of A.D. 51. Timothy's return with a report on conditions at Thessalonica served as the occasion for Paul's first letter (3, 6-8).

The letter begins with a brief address (1, 1) and concludes with a greeting (5, 26-28). The body of the letter consists of two major parts. The first (1, 2—3, 13) is a set of three sections of thanksgiving connected by two apologiae (defenses) dealing, respectively, with the missionaries' previous conduct and their current concerns. Paul's thankful optimism regarding the Thessalonians' spiritual welfare is tempered by his insistence on their recognition of the selfless love shown by the missionaries. In an age of itinerant peddlers of new religions, Paul found it necessary to emphasize not only the content of his gospel but also his manner of presenting it, for both attested to God's grace as freely bestowed and powerfully effected.

The second part of the letter (4, 1—5, 25) is specifically hortatory or parenetic. The superabundant love for which Paul has just prayed (3, 12-13) is to be shown practically by living out the norms of conduct that he has communicated to them. Specific "imperatives" of Christian life, principles for acting morally, stem from the "indicative" of one's relationship to God through Christ by the sending of the holy Spirit. Thus, moral conduct is the practical, personal expression of one's Christian faith, love, and hope.

The principal divisions of the First Letter to the Thessalonians are the following:

I.   *Address (1, 1-10)*
II. *Previous Relations with the Thessalonians (2, 1—3, 13)*
III. *Specific Exhortations (4, 1—5, 25)*
IV. *Final Greeting (5, 26-28)*

I. ADDRESS

CHAPTER 1

Greeting. [1] [a] Paul, Silvanus, and Timothy to the church of the Thessalonians in God the Father and the Lord Jesus Christ: grace to you and peace.*

Thanksgiving for Their Faith. [2] We give thanks to God always for all of you, remembering you in our prayers, unceasingly[b] [3] calling to mind your work of faith and labor of love and endurance in hope* of our Lord Jesus Christ, before our God and Father, [4] knowing, brothers loved by God, how you were chosen.[c] [5] For our gospel did not come to you in word alone, but also in power and in the holy Spirit and [with] much conviction. You know what sort of people we were [among] you for your sake.[d] [6] And you became imitators* of us and of the Lord, receiving the word in great affliction, with joy from the holy Spirit, [7] so that you became a model for all the believers in Macedonia and in Achaia.[e] [8] For from you the word of the Lord has sounded forth not only in Macedonia and [in] Achaia, but in every place your faith in God has gone forth, so that we have no need to say anything.[f] [9] For they themselves openly declare about us what sort of reception we had among you, and how you turned to God from idols to serve the living and true God[g] [10] and to await his Son from heaven, whom he raised from [the] dead, Jesus, who delivers us from the coming wrath.[h]

II. PREVIOUS RELATIONS WITH THE THESSALONIANS

CHAPTER 2

Paul's Ministry Among Them. [1] For you yourselves know, brothers, that our reception among you was not without effect. [2] Rather, after we had suffered and been insolently treated, as you know, in Philippi, we drew courage through our God to speak to you the gospel of God with much struggle.[i] [3] Our exhortation was not from delusion or impure motives, nor did it work through deception. [4] But as we were judged worthy* by God to be entrusted with the gospel, that is how we speak, not as trying to please human beings, but rather God, who judges our hearts.[j] [5] Nor, indeed, did we ever appear with flattering speech, as you know, or with a pretext for greed—God is witness—[6] nor did we seek praise from human beings, either from you or from others,[k] [7] although we were able to impose our weight as apostles of Christ. Rather, we were gentle* among you, as a nursing mother cares for her children. [8] With such affection for you, we were determined to share with you not only the gospel of God, but our very selves as well, so dearly beloved had you become to us. [9] You recall, brothers, our toil and drudgery. Working night and day in order not to burden any of you, we proclaimed to you the gospel of God.[l] [10] You are witnesses, and so is God, how devoutly and justly and blamelessly we behaved toward you

---

a Acts 15, 40; 16, 1-3.19; 17, 14-15; 2 Thes 1, 1-2.—b 2 Thes 1, 3.—c 2 Thes 2, 13.—d Acts 13, 52; 17, 1-9.—e 2 Thes 1, 4; 1 Cor 4, 16; 11, 1 / 1 Thes 2, 14; Phil 3, 17.—f Rom 1, 8.—g Acts 14, 15; Gal 4, 8 / 1 Thes 4, 5.—h Rom 2, 1-16; 5, 9; 13, 4 / 1 Thes 5, 9.—i Acts 16, 19—17, 10.—j Gal 1, 10.—k Jn 5, 41.44; 1 Cor 10, 31; 2 Cor 4, 17.—l Acts 20, 34; 1 Cor 4, 12; 9, 3-18; 2 Thes 3, 7-9.

1, 1: On the address, see the note on Rom 1, 1-7.

1, 3: *Faith . . . love . . . hope:* this, along with 1 Thes 5, 8, is the earliest mention in Christian literature of the three "theological virtues" (see 1 Cor 13, 13). The order here stresses eschatological hope, in line with the letter's emphasis on the Lord's

second, triumphal coming, or parousia (1 Thes 1, 10; 2, 12.19; 3, 13; 4, 13—5, 11; 5, 23).

1, 6: *Imitators:* the Pauline theme of "imitation" (see 1 Thes 2, 14; 1 Cor 4, 16; 11, 1; 2 Thes 3, 9) is rooted in Paul's view of solidarity in Christ through sharing in Jesus' cross and in the Spirit of the risen Lord.

2, 4: *Judged worthy:* Paul regards "worthiness" not as grounded in one's own talent or moral self-righteousness but in God's discernment of genuinely selfless attitudes and actions (see 2 Cor 10, 17-18).

2, 7: *Gentle:* many excellent manuscripts read "infants" (nēpioi), but "gentle" (ēpioi) better suits the context here.

believers. [11] As you know, we treated each one of you as a father treats his children,[m] [12] exhorting and encouraging you and insisting that you conduct yourselves as worthy of the God who calls you into his kingdom and glory.[n]

Further Thanksgiving. [13] And for this reason we too give thanks to God unceasingly, that, in receiving the word of God from hearing us, you received not a human word but, as it truly is, the word of God, which is now at work in you who believe. [14] * For you, brothers, have become imitators of the churches of God that are in Judea in Christ Jesus. For you suffer the same things from your compatriots as they did from the Jews, [15] * who killed both the Lord Jesus and the prophets and persecuted us; they do not please God, and are opposed to everyone,[o] [16] trying to prevent us from speaking to the Gentiles that they may be saved, thus constantly filling up the measure of their sins. But the wrath of God has finally begun to come upon them.[p]

Paul's Recent Travel Plans. [17] Brothers, when we were bereft of you for a short time, in person, not in heart, we were all the more eager in our great desire to see you in person.[q] [18] We decided to go to you—I, Paul, not only once but more than once—yet Satan thwarted us.[r] [19] For what is our hope or joy or crown to boast of in the presence of our Lord Jesus at his coming if not you yourselves?[s] [20] For you are our glory and joy.

CHAPTER 3

[1] That is why, when we could bear it no longer, we decided to remain alone in Athens[t] [2] and sent Timothy, our brother

and co-worker for God in the gospel of Christ, to strengthen and encourage you in your faith,[u] [3] so that no one be disturbed in these afflictions. For you yourselves know that we are destined* for this. [4] For even when we were among you, we used to warn you in advance that we would undergo affliction, just as has happened, as you know.[v] [5] For this reason, when I too could bear it no longer, I sent to learn about your faith, for fear that somehow the tempter had put you to the test and our toil might come to nothing.

[6] But just now Timothy has returned to us from you, bringing us the good news of your faith and love, and that you always think kindly of us and long to see us as we long to see you. [7] Because of this, we have been reassured about you, brothers, in our every distress and affliction, through your faith. [8] For we now live, if you stand firm in the Lord.

Concluding Thanksgiving and Prayer. [9] * What thanksgiving, then, can we render to God for you, for all the joy we feel on your account before our God? [10] Night and day we pray beyond measure to see you in person and to remedy the deficiencies of your faith. [11] Now may God himself, our Father, and our Lord Jesus direct our way to you, [12] and may the Lord make you increase and abound in love for one another and for all, just as we have for you,[w] [13] so as to strengthen your hearts, to be blameless in holiness before our God and Father at the coming of our Lord Jesus with all his holy ones. [Amen.][x]

III. SPECIFIC EXHORTATIONS

CHAPTER 4

General Exhortations. [1] Finally, brothers, we earnestly ask and exhort you in the Lord Jesus that, as you received from us

---

m Acts 20, 31.—n 1 Pt 5, 10 / 1 Thes 4, 7; 2 Thes 2, 14.—o Acts 2, 23; 7, 52.—p Gn 15, 16; 2 Mc 6, 14 / Rom 1, 18; 2, 5-6.—q 1 Thes 3, 10; Rom 1, 10-11.—r Rom 15, 22.—s 2 Cor 1, 14; Phil 2, 16; 4, 1.—t Acts 17, 14.—u Acts 16, l-2; 1 Cor 3, 5-9.—v Acts 14, 22; 2 Thes 2, 5-7; 2 Tm 3, 12.—w 1 Thes 4, 9-10; 2 Thes 1, 3.—x 1 Thes 5, 23; 1 Cor 1, 8.

2, 14: Luke's picture of the persecutions at Philippi (by Gentiles) and in Thessalonica and Beroea (by Jews) seems to be considerably schematized (Acts 16, 11-40; 17, 1-15). Paul pictures the Thessalonian community as composed of converts from paganism (1 Thes 1, 9) and speaks here of persecution by their (pagan) compatriots rather than by Jews.

2, 15-16: Paul is speaking of historical opposition on the part of Palestinian Jews in particular and does so only some twenty years after Jesus' crucifixion. Even so, he quickly proceeds to depict the persecutors typologically, in apocalyptic terms. His remarks give no grounds for anti-Semitism to those willing to understand him, especially in view of Paul's pride in his own ethnic and religious background (Rom 9, 1-5; 10, 1; 11, 1-3; Phil

3, 4-6). Sinful conduct (16) is itself an anticipation of the ultimate wrath or judgment of God (Rom 1, 18—2, 5), whether or not it is perceived as such.

3, 3: *We are destined:* the Greek phraseology and the context suggest Paul's concern to alert his readers to difficulties he knew they would necessarily face and to enable them to see their present experience in the light of what he warned them would happen in the future. This line of thought is followed in 2 Thes 2, 1-15.

3, 9-10: The tension between Paul's optimism concerning the Thessalonians' faith and his worries about their perseverance remains unresolved. Perhaps this is accounted for not only by the continuing harassment but also by the shortness of his own stay in Thessalonica (even if that were over twice as long as the conventional three weeks that Luke assigns to it, Acts 17, 2).

how you should conduct yourselves to please God—and as you are conducting yourselves—you do so even more. ²For you know what instructions* we gave you through the Lord Jesus.

Holiness in Sexual Conduct.* ³This is the will of God, your holiness: that you refrain from immorality, ⁴that each of you know how to acquire a wife for himself in holiness and honor, ⁵not in lustful passion as do the Gentiles who do not know God;ʸ ⁶not to take advantage of or exploit a brother in this matter, for the Lord is an avenger in all these things, as we told you before and solemnly affirmed. ⁷For God did not call us to impurity but to holiness. ⁸Therefore, whoever disregards this, disregards not a human being but God, who [also] gives his holy Spirit to you.ᶻ

Mutual Charity. ⁹On the subject of mutual charity you have no need for anyone to write you, for you yourselves have been taught by God to love one another.ᵃ ¹⁰Indeed, you do this for all the brothers throughout Macedonia. Nevertheless we urge you, brothers, to progress even more,ᵇ ¹¹and to aspire to live a tranquil life, to mind your own affairs, and to work with your [own] hands, as we instructed you, ¹²that you may conduct yourselves properly toward outsiders and not depend on anyone.

Hope for the Christian Dead. ¹³We do not want you to be unaware, brothers, about those who have fallen asleep, so that you may not grieve like the rest, who have no hope. ¹⁴For if we believe that Jesus died and rose, so too will God, through Jesus, bring with him those who have fallen asleep.ᶜ ¹⁵Indeed, we tell you this, on the word of the Lord, that we who are alive, who are left until the coming of the Lord,* will surely not precede those who have fallen asleep.ᵈ ¹⁶For the Lord himself, with a word of command, with the voice of an archangel and with the trumpet of God, will come down from heaven, and the dead in Christ will rise first.ᵉ ¹⁷Then we who are alive, who are left, will be caught up together* with them in the clouds to meet the Lord in the air. Thus we shall always be with the Lord. ¹⁸Therefore, console one another with these words.

CHAPTER 5

Vigilance. ¹Concerning times and seasons, brothers, you have no need for anything to be written to you.ᶠ ²For you yourselves know very well that the day of the Lord will come like a thief at night.ᵍ ³When people are saying, "Peace and security," then sudden disaster comes upon them, like labor pains upon a pregnant woman, and they will not escape.

⁴But you, brothers, are not in darkness, for that day to overtake you like a thief.ʰ ⁵For all of you are children of the light* and children of the day. We are not of the night or of darkness. ⁶Therefore, let us not sleep as the rest do, but let us stay alert and sober.ⁱ ⁷Those who sleep go to sleep at night, and those who are drunk get drunk at night. ⁸But since we are of the day, let us be sober, putting on the breastplate of faith and love and the helmet that is hope for salvation.ʲ ⁹For God did not destine us for wrath, but to gain salvation through

---

perhaps thereby occasion divorce. In that case, "immorality" (3) should be rendered as "unlawful marriage" and "this matter" (6) as "a lawsuit." The phrase in v 4, "acquire a wife for himself," has often been interpreted to mean "control one's body."

y Ps 79, 6; Jer 10, 25; 2 Thes 1, 8; 1 Pt 3, 7.—z Lk 10, 16.—a Jn 6, 45; 13, 34; 1 Jn 2, 20-21.27; 4, 7.—b 2 Thes 3, 6-12.—c 1 Cor 15, 3-4.12.20.—d 1 Cor 15, 51; Rv 14, 13; 20, 4-6.—e Mt 24, 31; 1 Cor 15, 23.52.—f Mt 24, 36-45.—g 2 Pt 3, 10.—h Eph 5, 8-9.—i Mt 24, 42; Rom 13, 12-13; 1 Pt 5, 8.—j Is 59, 17; Rom 13, 11-14; Eph 6, 11.14-17.

4, 2: *Instructions:* these include specific guidelines on the basis of the Lord's authority, not necessarily sayings Jesus actually uttered. More profoundly, as v 8 implies, the instructions are practical principles that Paul worked out in accordance with his understanding of the role of the Spirit.

4, 3-8: Many think that this passage deals with a variety of moral regulations (fornication, adultery, sharp business practices). It can be more specifically interpreted as bringing general norms to bear on a specific problem, namely, marriage within degrees of consanguinity (as between uncle and niece) forbidden in Jewish law but allowed according to a Greek heiress law, which would insure retention of an inheritance within the family and

4, 15: *Coming of the Lord:* Paul here assumes that the second coming, or parousia, will occur within his own lifetime but insists that the time or season is unknown (1 Thes 5, 1-2). Nevertheless, the most important aspect of the parousia for him was the fulfillment of union with Christ. His pastoral exhortation focuses first on hope for the departed faithful, then (1 Thes 5, 1-3) on the need of preparedness for those who have to achieve their goal.

4, 17: *Will be caught up together:* literally, snatched up, carried off; cf 2 Cor 12, 2; Rv 12, 5. From the Latin verb here used, *rapiemur*, has come the idea of "the rapture," when believers will be transported away from the woes of the world; this construction combines this verse with Mt 24, 40-41 (see the note there) // Lk 17, 34-35 and passages from Rv in a scheme of millennial dispensationalism.

5, 5: *Children of the light:* that is, belonging to the daylight of God's personal revelation and expected to achieve it (an analogous development of imagery that appears in Jn 12, 36).

our Lord Jesus Christ, [10]who died for us, so that whether we are awake or asleep we may live together with him.* [11]Therefore, encourage one another and build one another up, as indeed you do.[k]

Church Order. [12]We ask you, brothers, to respect those who are laboring among you and who are over you in the Lord and who admonish you, [13]and to show esteem for them with special love on account of their work. Be at peace among yourselves.

[14]We urge you, brothers, admonish the idle, cheer the fainthearted, support the weak, be patient with all. [15]See that no one returns evil for evil; rather, always seek what is good [both] for each other and for all.[l] [16]Rejoice always. [17]Pray without ceasing. [18]In all circumstances give thanks, for this is the will of God for you in Christ Jesus.[m] [19] * Do not quench the Spirit. [20]Do not despise prophetic utterances. [21]Test everything; retain what is good. [22]Refrain from every kind of evil.

Concluding Prayer. [23] * May the God of peace himself make you perfectly holy and may you entirely, spirit, soul, and body, be preserved blameless for the coming of our Lord Jesus Christ.[n] [24]The one who calls you is faithful, and he will also accomplish it. [25]Brothers, pray for us [too].

IV. FINAL GREETING

[26]Greet all the brothers with a holy kiss.* [27]I adjure you by the Lord that this letter be read to the brothers. [28]The grace of our Lord Jesus Christ be with you.

---

k Rom 15, 2; 1 Cor 8, 1; 14, 12.26; Eph 4, 29.—l Prv 20, 22; Mt 5, 38-42; Rom 12, 17.—m Eph 5, 20.—n 2 Thes 3, 16.

5, 10: Characteristically, Paul plays on words suggesting ultimate and anticipated death and life. Union with the crucified and risen Lord at his parousia is anticipated in some measure in contrasted states of our temporal life. The essential element he urges is our indestructible personal union in Christ's own life (see Rom 5, 1-10).

5, 19-21: Paul's buoyant encouragement of charismatic freedom sometimes occasioned excesses that he or others had to remedy (see 1 Cor 14; 2 Thes 2, 1-15; 2 Pt 3, 1-16).

5, 23: Another possible translation is, "May the God of peace himself make you perfectly holy and sanctify your spirit fully, and may both soul and body be preserved blameless for the coming of our Lord Jesus Christ." In either case, Paul is not offering an anthropological or philosophical analysis of human nature. Rather, he looks to the wholeness of what may be called the supernatural and natural aspects of a person's service of God.

5, 26: *Kiss:* the holy embrace (see Rom 16, 16; 1 Cor 16, 20; 2 Cor 13, 12; 1 Pt 5, 14) was a greeting of respect and affection, perhaps given during a liturgy at which Paul's letter would have been read.

2Thes

THE SECOND LETTER TO THE THESSALONIANS
INTRODUCTION

This letter is addressed to the same church as the letter that precedes it in the canon and contains many expressions parallel to those in the First Letter to the Thessalonians, indeed verbatim with them. Yet other aspects of the contents of the Second Letter to the Thessalonians suggest a more impersonal tone and changed circumstances in the situation at Thessalonica.

The letter begins with an address (1, 1-2) that expands only slightly on that of 1 Thes 1, 1. It ends with a greeting insisting on its Pauline authority in the face of false claims made in Paul's name (see the note on 2, 2). The body of the letter falls into three short parts, of which the second is notoriously difficult (ch 2).

The opening thanksgiving and prayer (1, 3-12) speak of the Thessalonians' increasing faith and love in the face of outside persecution. God's eventual judgment against persecutors and his salvation for the faithful are already evidenced by the very fact of persecution. The second part (2, 1-17), the heart of the letter, deals with a problem threatening the faith of the community. A message involving a prophetic oracle and apparently a forged letter, possibly presented at a liturgical gathering (cf 2, 2 and 1 Cor 14, 26-33), to the effect that the day of the Lord and all that it means have already come, has upset the life of the Thessalonian church.

The writer counters their preoccupation with the date of the parousia (or coming again of the Lord Jesus from heaven, 2, 1) by recalling Paul's teaching concerning what must happen first and by going on to describe what will happen at the Lord's coming (2, 8); he indicates the twofold process by which the "activity of Satan" and God's actions (2, 9-11) are working out, namely, a growing division between believers and those who succumb to false prophecy and "the lie." He concludes by insisting on Pauline traditions and by praying for divine strength (2, 13-17). The closing part of the letter (3, 1-16) deals in particular with the apostle's directives and model style of life and with correction of disorderly elements within the community.

Traditional opinion holds that this letter was written shortly after 1 Thessalonians. Occasionally it has been argued that 2 Thessalonians was written first or that the two letters are addressed to different segments within the church at Thessalonica (2 Thessalonians being directed to the Jewish Christians there) or even that 2 Thessalonians was originally written to some other nearby place where Paul carried out mission work, such as Philippi or Beroea. Increasingly in recent times, however, the opinion has been advanced that 2 Thessalonians is a pseudepigraph, that is, a letter written authoritatively in Paul's name, to maintain apostolic traditions in a later period, perhaps during the last two decades of the first century.

In any case, the presumed audience of Second Thessalonians and certain features of its style and content require that it be read and studied in a Pauline context, particularly that provided by 1 Thessalonians. At the same time, and especially if the letter is regarded as not by Paul himself, its apocalyptic presentation of preconditions for the parousia (2, 1-12) may profit from and require recourse to a wider biblical basis for interpretation, namely Old Testament books such as Daniel and Isaiah and especially, in the New Testament, the synoptic apocalyptic discourse (Mk 13; Mt 24—25; Lk 21, 5-36) and the Book of Revelation.

The principal divisions of the Second Letter to the Thessalonians are the following:

I. ADDRESS

CHAPTER 1

Greeting.* [1] Paul, Silvanus, and Timothy to the church of the Thessalonians in God our Father and the Lord Jesus Christ:[a] [2] grace to you and peace from God [our] Father and the Lord Jesus Christ.

Thanksgiving. [3] * We ought to thank God always for you, brothers, as is fitting, because your faith flourishes ever more, and the love of every one of you for one another grows ever greater.[b] [4] Accordingly, we ourselves boast of you in the churches of God regarding your endurance and faith in all your persecutions and the afflictions you endure.

[5] This is evidence of the just judgment of God, so that you may be considered worthy of the kingdom of God for which you are suffering.[c] [6] For it is surely just on God's part to repay with afflictions those who are afflicting you, [7] and to grant rest along with us to you who are undergoing afflictions, at the revelation of the Lord Jesus from heaven with his mighty angels, [8] in blazing fire, inflicting punishment on those who do not acknowledge God and on those who do not obey the gospel of our

a 1 Thes 1, 1.—b 1 Cor 1, 4; 1 Thes 1, 2; 3, 12.—c Phil 1, 28; 1 Thes 2, 12.

1, 1-2: On the address, see the note on Rom 1, 1-7 and cf 1 Thes 1, 1.

1, 3-12: On the thanksgiving, see the note on Rom 1, 8 and cf 1 Thes 1, 2-10. Paul's gratitude to God for the faith and love of the Thessalonians (3) and his Christian pride in their faithful endurance (4-5) contrast with the condemnation announced for those who afflict them, a judgment to be carried out at the parousia (6-10), which is described in vivid language drawn from Old Testament apocalyptic. A prayer for the fulfillment of God's purpose in the Thessalonians (11-12) completes the section, as is customary in a Pauline letter (cf 1 Thes 1, 2-3).

Lord Jesus.*d* *9*These will pay the penalty of eternal ruin, separated from the presence of the Lord and from the glory of his power,*e* *10*when he comes to be glorified among his holy ones* and to be marveled at on that day among all who have believed, for our testimony to you was believed.*f*

Prayer. *11*To this end, we always pray for you, that our God may make you worthy of his calling and powerfully bring to fulfillment every good purpose and every effort of faith,*g* *12*that the name of our Lord Jesus may be glorified in you, and you in him,*h* in accord with the grace of our God and Lord Jesus Christ.*

II. WARNING AGAINST DECEPTION CONCERNING THE PAROUSIA
CHAPTER 2

Christ and the Lawless One. *1*We ask you, brothers, with regard to the coming of our Lord Jesus Christ and our assembling

with him,*i* *2*not to be shaken out of your minds suddenly, or to be alarmed either by a "spirit,"* or by an oral statement, or by a letter allegedly from us to the effect that the day of the Lord is at hand.*j* *3*Let no one deceive you in any way. For unless the apostasy comes first and the lawless one is revealed,* the one doomed to perdition, *4* *k* who opposes and exalts himself above every so-called god and object of worship, so as to seat himself in the temple of God,* claiming that he is a god—*5*do you not recall that while I was still with you I told you these things? *6*And now you know what is restraining,* that he may be re-

---

d Ps 79, 5-6; Is 66, 15; Jer 10, 25.—e Is 2, 10.19.21.—f Ps 89, 8; Dn 7, 18-22.27; 1 Thes 3, 13.—g 1 Thes 1, 2-3.—h Is 66, 5.—i 1 Thes 4, 13-17.—j Mt 24, 6; 1 Cor 14, 26.32-33; 1 Thes 5, 1-2.—k Dn 11, 36-37; Ez 28, 2.

1, 10: *Among his holy ones:* in the Old Testament, this term can refer to an angelic throng (cf also Jude 14), but here, in parallel with *among all who have believed,* it can refer to the triumphant people of God.

1, 12: *The grace of our God and Lord Jesus Christ:* the Greek can also be translated, "the grace of our God and of the Lord Jesus Christ."

2, 1-17: The Thessalonians have been *shaken* by a message purporting to come from Paul himself that *the day of the Lord* is already present. He warns against this deception in eschatology by citing a scenario of events that must first occur (3-12) before the end will come. The overall point Paul makes is the need to reject such lies as Satan sends; he also reaffirms the Thessalonians in their calling (13-14). They are to uphold what Paul himself has taught (15). There is a concluding prayer for their strengthening (16-17). As in 2 Thes 1, 8-10, the Old Testament provides a good deal of coloring; cf especially Is 14, 13-14; 66, 15.18-21; Ez 28, 2-9; Dn 11, 36-37. The contents of 2 Thes 2, 3b-8 may come from a previously existing apocalypse. The details have been variously interpreted.

An alternative to the possibilities noted below understands that an oracular utterance, supposedly coming from a prophetic spirit (2-3a), has so disrupted the community's thinking that its effects may be compared to those of the mania connected with the worship of the Greek god Dionysus. On this view, the writer seems to allude in vv 6-8 to Dionysiac "seizure," although, of course, ironically, somewhat as Paul alludes to witchcraft ("an evil eye") in Gal 3, 1 in speaking of the threat to faith posed by those disturbing the Galatians (Gal 1, 6-7; 5, 10b). On this view of 2 Thes 2, the Greek participles *katechon* (rendered above as *what is restraining)* and *katechōn (the one who restrains)* are to be translated "the seizing power" in v 6 and "the seizer" in v 7. They then allude to a pseudocharismatic force or spirit of Dionysiac character that has suddenly taken hold of the Thessalonian community (see 2). The addressees *know* (6) this force or

spirit because of the problem it is causing. This pseudocharismatic force or spirit is a kind of anticipation and advance proof of the ultimate, climactic figure (*the lawless one* or the rebel, 3), of which the community has been warned (see the note on 1 Thes 3, 3). It is, however, only the beginning of the end that the latter's manifestation entails; the end is not yet. For in the course of *the mystery of lawlessness* (7), false prophetism, after it ceases in the Thessalonian community, will be manifested in the world at large (8-12), where it will also be eliminated in turn by the Lord Jesus.

2, 2: *"Spirit":* a Spirit-inspired utterance or ecstatic revelation. *An oral statement:* literally, a "word" or pronouncement, not necessarily of ecstatic origin. *A letter allegedly sent by us:* possibly a forged letter, so that Paul calls attention in 2 Thes 3, 17 to his practice of concluding a genuine letter with a summary note or greeting in his own hand, as at Gal 6, 11-18 and elsewhere.

2, 3b-5: This incomplete sentence (anacoluthon, 4) recalls what the Thessalonians had already been taught, an apocalyptic scenario depicting, in terms borrowed especially from Dn 11, 36-37 and related verses, human self-assertiveness against God in *the temple of God* itself. *The lawless one* represents the climax of such activity in history.

2, 4: *Seat himself in the temple of God:* a reflection of the language in Dn 7, 23-25; 8, 9-12; 9, 27; 11, 36-37; and 12, 11 about the attempt of Antiochus IV Epiphanes to set up a statue of Zeus in the Jerusalem temple and possibly of the Roman emperor Caligula to do a similar thing (Mk 13, 14). Here the imagery suggests an attempt to install someone in the place of God, *claiming that he is a god* (cf Ez 28, 2). Usually, it is the Jerusalem temple that is assumed to be meant; on the alternative view sketched above (see the note on 2 Thes 2, 1-17), *the temple* refers to the Christian community.

2, 6-7: *What is restraining ... the one who restrains:* neuter and masculine, respectively, of a force and person holding back the lawless one. The Thessalonians know what is meant (6), but the terms, seemingly found only in this passage and in writings dependent on it, have been variously interpreted. Traditionally, v 6 has been applied to the Roman empire and v 7 to the Roman emperor (in Paul's day, Nero) as bulwarks holding back chaos (cf Rom 13, 1-7). A second interpretation suggests that cosmic or angelic powers are binding Satan (9) and so restraining him; some relate this to an anti-Christ figure (1 Jn 2, 18) or to Michael the archangel (Rv 12, 7-9; 20, 1-3). A more recent view suggests that it is the preaching of the Christian gospel that restrains the end, for in God's plan the end cannot come until the gospel is preached to all nations (Mk 13, 10); in that case, Paul as missionary preacher par excellence is "the one who restrains," whose removal (death) will bring the end (7). On the alternative view (see the note on 2 Thes 2, 1-17), the phrases should be referred to that which and to him who seizes (a prophet) in ecstasy so as to have him speak pseudo-oracles.

vealed in his time. 7 * For the mystery of lawlessness is already at work. But the one who restrains is to do so only for the present, until he is removed from the scene.[l] 8 And then the lawless one will be revealed, whom the Lord [Jesus] will kill with the breath of his mouth and render powerless by the manifestation of his coming,[m] 9 the one whose coming springs from the power of Satan in every mighty deed and in signs and wonders that lie,[n] 10 and in every wicked deceit for those who are perishing because they have not accepted the love of truth so that they may be saved. 11 Therefore, God is sending them a deceiving power so that they may believe the lie, 12 that all who have not believed the truth but have approved wrongdoing may be condemned.

13 But we ought to give thanks to God for you always, brothers loved by the Lord, because God chose you as the firstfruits* for salvation through sanctification by the Spirit and belief in truth.[o] 14 To this end he has [also] called you through our gospel to possess the glory of our Lord Jesus Christ.[p] 15 Therefore, brothers, stand firm and hold fast to the traditions that you were taught, either by an oral statement or by a letter of ours.*

16 May our Lord Jesus Christ himself and God our Father, who has loved us and given us everlasting encouragement and good hope through his grace, 17 encourage your hearts and strengthen them in every good deed and word.

III. CONCLUDING EXHORTATIONS

CHAPTER 3*

Request for Prayers. 1 Finally, brothers, pray for us, so that the word of the Lord may speed forward and be glorified, as it did among you,[q] 2 and that we may be delivered from perverse and wicked people, for not all have faith. 3 But the Lord is faithful; he will strengthen you and guard you from the evil one.[r] 4 We are confident of you in the Lord that what we instruct you, you [both] are doing and will continue to do.[s] 5 May the Lord direct your hearts to the love of God and to the endurance of Christ.

Neglect of Work. 6 We instruct you, brothers, in the name of [our] Lord Jesus Christ, to shun any brother who conducts himself in a disorderly way and not according to the tradition they received from us.* 7 For you know how one must imitate us. For we did not act in a disorderly way among you, 8 nor did we eat food received free from anyone. On the contrary, in toil and drudgery, night and day we worked, so as not to burden any of you.[t] 9 Not that we do not have the right. Rather, we wanted to present ourselves as a model for you, so that you might imitate us.[u] 10 In fact, when we were with you, we instructed you that if anyone was unwilling to work, neither should that one eat.[v] 11 We hear that some are conducting themselves among you in a disorderly way, by not keeping busy but minding the business of others.[w] 12 Such people we instruct and urge in the Lord Jesus Christ to work quietly and to eat their own food. 13 But

---

l Mt 13, 36-43; Acts 20, 29; Gal 5, 10; 2 Pt 2, 1; Rv 22, 11.— m Is 11, 4; Rv 19, 15.—n Mt 24, 24; Rv 13, 13.—o 1 Thes 2, 13; 5, 9.—p Rom 5, 1-10; 8, 29-30; 1 Thes 4, 7; 5, 9.—q Eph 6, 19; Col 4, 3.—r 1 Thes 5, 24 / 1 Cor 16, 13 / Mt 6, 13.—s 2 Cor 7, 16; 1 Thes 4, 1-2.—t 1 Thes 2, 9.—u Mt 10, 10; Phil 3, 17.—v 1 Thes 4, 11.—w 1 Thes 5, 14.

2, 7-12: *The lawless one* and *the one who restrains* are involved in an activity or process, *the mystery of lawlessness,* behind which *Satan* stands (9). The action of *the Lord [Jesus]* in overcoming the lawless one is described in Old Testament language (*with the breath of his mouth;* cf Is 11, 4; Jb 4, 9; Rv 19, 15). His *coming* is literally the Lord's "parousia." The biblical concept of the "holy war," eschatologically conceived, may underlie the imagery.

2, 13: *As the firstfruits:* there is also strong manuscript evidence for the reading, "God chose you from the beginning," thus providing a focus on God's activity from beginning to end; *firstfruits* is a Pauline term, however; cf Rom 8, 23; 11, 16; 16, 5, among other references.

2, 15: Reference to *an oral statement* and *a letter* (2) and the content here, including a formula of conclusion (cf 1 Cor 16, 13; Gal 5, 1), suggest that vv 1-15 or even 1-17 are to be taken

as a literary unit, notwithstanding the incidental thanksgiving formula in v 13.

3, 1-18: The final chapter urges the Thessalonians to pray for Paul and his colleagues (1-2) and reiterates confidence in the Thessalonians (3-5), while admonishing them about a specific problem in their community that has grown out of the intense eschatological speculation, namely, not to work but to become instead disorderly busybodies (6-15). A benediction (16) and postscript in Paul's own hand round out the letter. On vv 17-18, cf the note on 2 Thes 2, 2.

3, 6: Some members of the community, probably because they regarded the parousia as imminent or the new age of the Lord to be already here (2 Thes 2, 2), had apparently ceased to work for a living. The disciplinary problem they posed could be rooted in distorted thinking about Paul's own teaching (cf 1 Thes 2, 16; 3, 3-4; 5, 4-5) or, more likely, in a forged letter (2 Thes 2, 2) and the type of teaching dealt with in 2 Thes 2, 1-15. The apostle's own moral teaching, reflected in his selfless labors for others, was rooted in a deep doctrinal concern for the gospel message (cf 1 Thes 2, 3-10).

you, brothers, do not be remiss in doing good. [14] If anyone does not obey our word as expressed in this letter, take note of this person not to associate with him, that he may be put to shame. [15] Do not regard him as an enemy but admonish him as a brother.[x] [16] May the Lord of peace himself give you peace at all times and in every way. The Lord be with all of you.[y]

IV. FINAL GREETINGS

[17] This greeting is in my own hand, Paul's. This is the sign in every letter; this is how I write.[z] [18] The grace of our Lord Jesus Christ be with all of you.

x 2 Cor 2, 7; Gal 6, 1.—y Jn 14, 27; Rom 15, 33.—z 1 Cor 16, 21; Gal 6, 11.

THE FIRST LETTER TO TIMOTHY

INTRODUCTION

The three letters, First and Second Timothy and Titus, form a distinct group within the Pauline corpus. In the collection of letters by the Apostle to the Gentiles, they differ from the others in form and contents. All three suggest they were written late in Paul's career. The opponents are not "Judaizers" as in Galatians but false teachers stressing "knowledge" (gnōsis; see the note on 1 Tm 6, 20-21). Attention is given especially to correct doctrine and church organization. Jesus' second coming recedes into the background compared to references in Paul's earlier letters (though not Colossians and Ephesians). The three letters are addressed not to congregations but to those who shepherd congregations (Latin, pastores). These letters were first named "Pastoral Epistles" in the eighteenth century because they all are concerned with the work of a pastor in caring for the community or communities under his charge.

The first of the Pastorals, 1 Timothy, is presented as having been written from Macedonia. Timothy, whom Paul converted, was of mixed Jewish and Gentile parentage (Acts 16, 1-3). He was the apostle's companion on both the second and the third missionary journeys (Acts 16, 3; 19, 22) and was often sent by him on special missions (Acts 19, 22; 1 Cor 4, 17; 1 Thes 3, 2). In 1 Timothy (1, 3), he is described as the administrator of the entire Ephesian community.

The letter instructs Timothy on his duty to restrain false and useless teaching (1, 3-11; 4, 1-5; 6, 3-16) and proposes principles pertaining to his relationship with the older members of the community (5, 1-2) and with the presbyters (5, 17-22). It gives rules for aid to widows (5, 3-8) and their selection for charitable ministrations (5, 9-16) and also deals with liturgical celebrations (2, 1-15), selections for the offices of bishop and deacon (3, 1-13), relation of slaves with their masters (6, 1-2), and obligations of the wealthier members of the community (6, 17-19). This letter also reminds Timothy of the prophetic character of his office (1, 12-20) and encourages him in his exercise of it (4, 6-16). The central passage of the letter (3, 14-16) expresses the principal motive that should guide the conduct of Timothy—preservation of the purity of the church's doctrine against false teaching. On this same note the letter concludes (6, 20-21).

From the late second century to the nineteenth, Pauline authorship of the three Pastoral Epistles went unchallenged. Since then, the attribution of these letters to Paul has been questioned. Most scholars are convinced that Paul could not have been responsible for the vocabulary and style, the concept of church organization, or the theological expressions found in these letters. A second group believes, on the basis of statistical evidence, that the vocabulary and style are Pauline, even if at first sight the contrary seems

1Tm

to be the case. They state that the concept of church organization in the letters is not as advanced as the questioners of Pauline authorship hold since the notion of hierarchical order in a religious community existed in Israel before the time of Christ, as evidenced in the Dead Sea Scrolls. Finally, this group sees affinities between the theological thought of the Pastorals and that of the unquestionably genuine letters of Paul. Other scholars, while conceding a degree of validity to the positions mentioned above, suggest that the apostle made use of a secretary who was responsible for the composition of the letters. A fourth group of scholars believes that these letters are the work of a compiler, that they are based on traditions about Paul in his later years, and that they include, in varying amounts, actual fragments of genuine Pauline correspondence.

If Paul is considered the more immediate author, the Pastorals are to be dated between the end of his first Roman imprisonment (Acts 28, 16) and his execution under Nero (A.D. 63-67); if they are regarded as only more remotely Pauline, their date may be as late as the early second century. In spite of these problems of authorship and dating, the Pastorals are illustrative of early Christian life and remain an important element of canonical scripture.

The principal divisions of the First Letter to Timothy are the following:

   I.   Address (1, 1-2)
   II.   Sound Teaching (1, 3-20)
  III. Problems of Discipline (2, 1—4, 16)
  IV. Duties toward Others (5, 1—6, 2a)
   V. False Teaching and True Wealth (6, 2b-19)
  VI. Final Recommendation and Warning (6, 20-21)

I. ADDRESS

CHAPTER 1

Greeting.* [1] Paul, an apostle of Christ Jesus by command of God our savior and of Christ Jesus our hope,[a] [2] to Timothy, my true child in faith: grace, mercy, and peace from God the Father and Christ Jesus our Lord.[b]

II. SOUND TEACHING

Warning against False Doctrine. [3] * I repeat the request I made of you when I was on my way to Macedonia,[c] that you stay in Ephesus to instruct certain people not to teach false doctrines [4] [d] or to concern themselves with myths and endless genealogies, which promote speculations rather than the plan of God that is to be re-

ceived by faith.* [5] The aim of this instruction is love from a pure heart, a good conscience, and a sincere faith.[e] [6] Some people have deviated from these and turned to meaningless talk,[f] [7] wanting to be teachers of the law, but without understanding either what they are saying or what they assert with such assurance.

[8] * We know that the law is good, provided that one uses it as law,[g] [9] with the understanding that law is meant not for a righteous person but for the lawless and unruly, the godless and sinful, the unholy and profane, those who kill their fathers or mothers, murderers, [10] the unchaste, practicing homosexuals,* kidnapers, liars, perjurers, and whatever else is opposed to sound teaching,[h] [11] according to the glorious gospel of the blessed God, with which I have been entrusted.[i]

---

a 1 Tm 2, 3; Lk 1, 47; Ti 1, 3; 2, 10 / Col 1, 27.—b 2 Tm 1, 2; Ti 1, 4.—c Acts 20, 1.—d 1 Tm 4, 7; Ti 1, 14; 3, 9; 2 Pt 1, 16.—e Rom 13, 10.—f 1 Tm 6, 4.20; Ti 1, 10.—g Rom 7, 12.16.—h 1 Tm 4, 6; 6, 3; 2 Tm 4, 3; Ti 1, 9; 2, 1.—i Ti 1, 3.

1, 1-2: For the Pauline use of the conventional epistolary form, see the note on Rom 1, 1-7.

1, 3-7: Here Timothy's initial task *in Ephesus* (cf Acts 20, 17-35) is outlined: to suppress the idle religious speculations, probably about Old Testament figures (3-4, but see the note on 1 Tm 6, 20-21), which do not contribute to the development of love within the community (5) but rather encourage similar useless conjectures (6-7).

1, 4: *The plan of God that is to be received by faith:* the Greek may also possibly mean "God's trustworthy plan" or "the training in faith that God requires."

1, 8-11: Those responsible for the speculations that are to be suppressed by Timothy do not present the Old Testament from the Christian viewpoint. The Christian values the Old Testament not as a system of law but as the first stage in God's revelation of his saving plan, which is brought to fulfillment in the good news of salvation through faith in Jesus Christ.

1, 10: *Practicing homosexuals:* see 1 Cor 6, 9 and the note there.

Gratitude for God's Mercy.* [12] I am grateful to him who has strengthened me, Christ Jesus our Lord, because he considered me trustworthy in appointing me to the ministry.[j] [13] I was once a blasphemer and a persecutor and an arrogant man, but I have been mercifully treated because I acted out of ignorance in my unbelief.[k] [14] Indeed, the grace of our Lord has been abundant, along with the faith and love that are in Christ Jesus.[l] [15] This saying is trustworthy* and deserves full acceptance: Christ Jesus came into the world to save sinners. Of these I am the foremost.[m] [16] But for that reason I was mercifully treated, so that in me, as the foremost, Christ Jesus might display all his patience as an example for those who would come to believe in him for everlasting life. [17] To the king of ages,* incorruptible, invisible, the only God, honor and glory forever and ever. Amen.[n]

Responsibility of Timothy.* [18] I entrust this charge to you, Timothy, my child, in accordance with the prophetic words once spoken about you.* Through them may you fight a good fight[o] [19] by having faith and a good conscience. Some, by rejecting conscience, have made a shipwreck of their faith,[p] [20] among them Hymenaeus* and Alexander, whom I have handed over to Satan to be taught not to blaspheme.[q]

III. PROBLEMS OF DISCIPLINE

CHAPTER 2

Prayer and Conduct. [1] * First of all, then, I ask that supplications, prayers, petitions, and thanksgivings be offered for everyone,[r] [2] for kings and for all in authority, that we may lead a quiet and tranquil life in all devotion and dignity. [3] This is good and pleasing to God our savior,[s] [4] who wills everyone to be saved and to come to knowledge of the truth.[t]

[5] For there is one God.
There is also one mediator between God and the human race,
Christ Jesus, himself human,[u]
[6] who gave himself as ransom for all.

This was the testimony* at the proper time.[v] [7] For this I was appointed preacher and apostle (I am speaking the truth, I am not lying), teacher of the Gentiles in faith and truth.[w]

j Phil 4, 13 / Acts 9, 15; Gal 1, 15-16.—k Acts 8, 3; 9, 1-2; 1 Cor 15, 9; Gal 1, 13.—l Rom 5, 20; 2 Tm 1, 13.—m Lk 15, 2; 19, 10.—n Rom 16, 27.—o 1 Tm 4, 14 / 1 Tm 6, 12; 2 Tm 4, 7; Jude 3.—p 1 Tm 3, 9.—q 2 Tm 2, 17; 4, 14 / 1 Cor 5, 5.—r Eph 6, 18; Phil 4, 6.—s 1 Tm 1, 1; 4, 10.—t 2 Tm 3, 7; 2 Pt 3, 9.—u 1 Cor 8, 6; Heb 8, 6; 9, 15; 12, 24 / Rom 5, 15.—v Mk 10, 45; Gal 1, 4; 2, 20; Eph 5, 25; Ti 2, 14.—w Acts 9, 15; 1 Cor 9, 1; Gal 2, 7-8.

1, 12-17: Present gratitude for the Christian apostleship leads Paul to recall an earlier time when he had been a fierce persecutor of the Christian communities (cf Acts 26, 9-11) until his conversion by intervention of divine mercy through the appearance of Jesus. This and his subsequent apostolic experience testify to the saving purpose of Jesus' incarnation. The fact of his former ignorance of the truth has not kept the apostle from regarding himself as having been the worst of sinners (15). Yet he was chosen to be an apostle, that God might manifest his firm will to save sinful humanity through Jesus Christ (16). The recounting of so great a mystery leads to a spontaneous outpouring of adoration (17).

1, 15: *This saying is trustworthy:* this phrase regularly introduces in the Pastorals a basic truth of early Christian faith; cf 1 Tm 3, 1; 4, 9; 2 Tm 2, 11; Ti 3, 8.

1, 17: *King of ages:* through Semitic influence, the Greek expression could mean "everlasting king"; it could also mean "king of the universe."

1, 18-20: Timothy is to be mindful of his calling, which is here compared to the way Barnabas and Saul were designated by Christ as prophets for missionary service; cf Acts 13, 1-3. Such is probably the sense of the allusion to the prophetic words (18). His task is not to yield, whether in doctrine or in conduct, to erroneous opinions, taking warning from what has already happened at Ephesus in the case of Hymenaeus and Alexander (19-20).

1Tm

1, 18: *The prophetic words once spoken about you:* the Greek may also be translated, "the prophecies that led (me) to you." It probably refers to testimonies given by charismatic figures in the Christian communities. *Fight a good fight:* this translation preserves the play on words in Greek. The Greek terms imply a lengthy engagement in battle and might well be translated "wage a good campaign."

1, 20: *Hymenaeus:* mentioned in 2 Tm 2, 17 as saying that the resurrection has already taken place (in baptism). *Alexander:* probably the Alexander mentioned in 2 Tm 4, 14 as the coppersmith who "did me a great deal of harm." *Whom I have handed over to Satan:* the same terms are used in the condemnation of the incestuous man in 1 Cor 5, 5.

2, 1-7: This marked insistence that the liturgical prayer of the community concern itself with the needs of all, whether Christian or not, and especially of those in authority, may imply that a disposition existed at Ephesus to refuse prayer for pagans. In actuality, such prayer aids the community to achieve peaceful relationships with non-Christians (2) and contributes to salvation, since it derives its value from the presence within the community of Christ, who is the one and only savior of all (3-6). The vital apostolic mission to the Gentiles (7) reflects Christ's purpose of universal salvation.

Verse 5 contains what may well have been a very primitive creed. Some interpreters have called it a Christian version of the Jewish *shema:* "Hear, O Israel, the LORD is our God, the LORD alone . . ." (Dt 6, 4-5). The assertion in v 7, "I am speaking the truth, I am not lying," reminds one of similar affirmations in Rom 9, 1; 2 Cor 11, 31; and Gal 1, 20.

2, 6: *The testimony:* to make sense of this overly concise phrase, many manuscripts supply "to which" (or "to whom"); two others add "was given." The translation has supplied "this was."

8 * It is my wish, then, that in every place the men should pray, lifting up holy hands, without anger or argument. 9 Similarly, [too,] women should adorn themselves with proper conduct, with modesty and self-control, not with braided hairstyles and gold ornaments, or pearls, or expensive clothes,ˣ 10 but rather, as befits women who profess reverence for God, with good deeds.ʸ 11 A woman must receive instruction silently and under complete control.ᶻ 12 I do not permit a woman to teach or to have authority over a man.* She must be quiet. 13 For Adam was formed first, then Eve.ᵃ 14 Further, Adam was not deceived, but the woman was deceived and transgressed.ᵇ 15 But she will be saved through motherhood, provided women persevere in faith and love and holiness, with self-control.ᶜ

CHAPTER 3

Qualifications of Various Ministers. 1 * This saying is trustworthy:* whoever aspires to the office of bishop desires a noble task.ᵈ 2 Therefore, a bishop must be irreproachable, married only once, temperate, self-controlled, decent, hospitable, able to teach, 3 not a drunkard, not aggressive, but gentle, not contentious, not a lover of money.ᵉ 4 He must manage his own household well, keeping his children under control with perfect dignity; 5 for if a man does not know how to manage his own household, how can he take care of the church of God? 6 He should not be a recent convert, so that he may not become conceited and thus incur the devil's punishment.* 7 He must also have a good reputation among outsiders, so that he may not fall into disgrace, the devil's trap.ᶠ

8 * Similarly, deacons must be dignified, not deceitful, not addicted to drink, not greedy for sordid gain, 9 holding fast to the mystery of the faith with a clear conscience. 10 Moreover, they should be tested first; then, if there is nothing against them, let them serve as deacons. 11 Women,* similarly, should be dignified, not slanderers, but temperate and faithful in everything.ᵍ 12 Deacons may be married only once and must manage their children and their households well. 13 Thus those who serve well as deacons gain good standing and much confidence in their faith in Christ Jesus.

The Mystery of Our Religion. * 14 I am writing you about these matters, although I hope to visit you soon. 15 But if I should be delayed, you should know how to behave in the household of God, which is the

x 1 Pt 3, 3-5.—y 1 Tm 5, 10; 1 Pt 3, 1.—z 11-12: 1 Cor 14, 34-35.—a Gn 1, 27; 2, 7.22; 1 Cor 11, 8-9.—b Gn 3, 6.13; 2 Cor 11, 3.—c 1 Tm 5, 14.—d 1-7: Ti 1, 6-9.—e Heb 13, 5.—f 2 Cor 8, 21; 2 Tm 2, 26.—g Ti 2, 3.

2, 8-15: The prayer of the community should be unmarred by internal dissension (8); cf Mt 5, 21-26; 6, 14; Mk 11, 25. At the liturgical assembly the dress of women should be appropriate to the occasion (9); their chief adornment is to be reputation for good works (10). Women are not to take part in the charismatic activity of the assembly (11-12; cf 1 Cor 14, 34) or exercise authority; their conduct there should reflect the role of man's helpmate (13; cf Gn 2, 18) and not the later relationship of Eve to Adam (14; cf Gn 3, 6-7). As long as women perform their role as wives and mothers in faith and love, their salvation is assured (15).

2, 12: *A man:* this could also mean "her husband."

3, 1-7: The passage begins by commending those who aspire to the office of bishop *(episkopos;* see the note on Phil 1, 1) within the community, but this first sentence (1) may also imply a warning about the great responsibilities involved. The writer proceeds to list the qualifications required: personal stability and graciousness; talent for teaching (2); moderation in habits and temperament (3); managerial ability (4); and experience in Christian living (5-6). Moreover, the candidate's previous life should provide no grounds for the charge that he did not previously practice what he now preaches. No list of qualifications for presbyters appears in 1 Tm. The presbyter-bishops here and in Ti (see the note on Ti 1, 5-9) lack certain functions reserved here for Paul and Timothy.

3, 1: *This saying is trustworthy:* the saying introduced is so unlike others after this phrase that some later Western manuscripts read, "This saying is popular." It is understood by some interpreters as concluding the preceding section (1 Tm 2, 8-15). *Bishop:* literally, "overseer"; see the note on Phil 1, 1.

3, 6: *The devil's punishment:* this phrase could mean the punishment once incurred by the devil (objective genitive) or a punishment brought about by the devil (subjective genitive).

3, 8-13: Deacons, besides possessing the virtue of moderation (8), are to be outstanding for their faith (9) and well respected within the community (10). Women in the same role, although some interpreters take them to mean wives of deacons, must be dignified, temperate, dedicated, and not given to malicious talebearing (11). Deacons must have shown stability in marriage and have a good record with their families (12), for such experience prepares them well for the exercise of their ministry on behalf of the community (13). See further the note on Phil 1, 1.

3, 11: *Women:* this seems to refer to women deacons but may possibly mean wives of deacons. The former is preferred because the word is used absolutely; if deacons' wives were meant, a possessive "their" would be expected. Moreover, they are also introduced by the word "similarly," as in v 8; this parallel suggests that they too exercised ecclesiastical functions.

3, 14-16: In case there is some delay in the visit to Timothy at Ephesus planned for the near future, the present letter is being sent on ahead to arm and enlighten him in his task of preserving sound Christian conduct in the Ephesian church. The care he must exercise over this community is required by the profound nature of Christianity. It centers in Christ, appearing in human flesh, vindicated by the holy Spirit; the mystery of his person was revealed to the angels, announced to the Gentiles, and accepted by them in faith. He himself was taken up (through his resurrection and ascension) to the divine glory (16). This passage apparently includes part of a liturgical hymn used among the Christian communities in and around Ephesus. It consists of three couplets in typical Hebrew balance: flesh-spirit (contrast), seen-proclaimed (complementary), world-glory (contrast).

church of the living God, the pillar and foundation of truth.[h] [16]Undeniably great is the mystery of devotion,

> Who* was manifested in the flesh,
> vindicated in the spirit,
> seen by angels,
> proclaimed to the Gentiles,
> believed in throughout the world,
> taken up in glory.[i]

CHAPTER 4

False Asceticism.* [1]Now the Spirit explicitly says that in the last times some will turn away from the faith by paying attention to deceitful spirits and demonic instructions[j] [2]through the hypocrisy of liars with branded consciences. [3]They forbid marriage and require abstinence from foods that God created to be received with thanksgiving by those who believe and know the truth.[k] [4]For everything created by God is good, and nothing is to be rejected when received with thanksgiving,[l] [5]for it is made holy by the invocation of God in prayer.*

Counsel to Timothy. [6] * If you will give these instructions to the brothers, you will be a good minister of Christ Jesus, nourished on the words of the faith and of the sound teaching you have followed. [7]Avoid profane and silly myths. Train

yourself for devotion,[m] [8]for, while physical training is of limited value, devotion is valuable in every respect, since it holds a promise of life both for the present and for the future.[n] [9]This saying is trustworthy and deserves full acceptance.[o] [10]For this we toil and struggle,* because we have set our hope on the living God, who is the savior of all, especially of those who believe.[p]

[11] * Command and teach these things. [12]Let no one have contempt for your youth,* but set an example for those who believe, in speech, conduct, love, faith, and purity.[q] [13]Until I arrive, attend to the reading,* exhortation, and teaching. [14]Do not neglect the gift you have, which was conferred on you through the prophetic word* with the imposition of hands of the presbyterate.[r] [15]Be diligent in these matters, be absorbed in them, so that your progress may be evident to everyone. [16]Attend to yourself and to your teaching; persevere in both tasks, for by doing so you will save both yourself and those who listen to you.

IV. DUTIES TOWARD OTHERS
CHAPTER 5

[1] * Do not rebuke an older man, but appeal to him as a father. Treat younger men

1Tm

---

h Eph 2, 19-22.—i Jn 1, 14; Rom 1, 3-4.—j 2 Tm 3, 1; 4, 3; 2 Pt 3, 3; Jude 18.—k Gn 9, 3; Rom 14, 6; 1 Cor 10, 30-31.—l Gn 1, 31; Acts 10, 15.—m 1 Tm 1, 4; 2 Tm 2, 16; Ti 1, 14.—n 1 Tm 6, 6.—o 1 Tm 1, 15; 2 Tm 2, 11; Ti 3, 8.—p 1 Tm 2, 4; Ti 2, 11.—q 1 Cor 16, 11; Ti 2, 15 / Phil 3, 17.—r 1 Tm 5, 22; Acts 6, 6; 8, 17; 2 Tm 1, 6.

3, 16: *Who:* the reference is to Christ, who is himself "the mystery of our devotion." Some predominantly Western manuscripts read "which," harmonizing the gender of the pronoun with that of the Greek word for mystery; many later (eighth/ninth century on), predominantly Byzantine manuscripts read "God," possibly for theological reasons.

4, 1-5: Doctrinal deviations from the true Christian message within the church have been prophesied, though the origin of the prophecy is not specified (1-2); cf Acts 20, 29-30. The letter warns against a false asceticism that prohibits marriage and regards certain foods as forbidden, though they are part of God's good creation (3).

4, 5: *The invocation of God in prayer:* literally, "the word of God and petition." The use of "word of God" without an article in Greek suggests that it refers to the name of God being invoked in blessing rather than to the "word of God" proclaimed to the community.

4, 6-10: Timothy is urged to be faithful, both in his teaching and in his own life, as he looks only to God for salvation.

4, 10: *Struggle:* other manuscripts and patristic witnesses read "suffer reproach."

4, 11-16: Timothy is urged to preach and teach with confidence, relying on the gifts and the mission that God has bestowed on him.

4, 12: *Youth:* some commentators find this reference a sign of pseudepigraphy. Timothy had joined Paul as a missionary already in A.D. 49, some fifteen years before the earliest supposed date of composition.

4, 13: *Reading:* the Greek word refers to private or public reading. Here, it probably designates the public reading of scripture in the Christian assembly.

4, 14: *Prophetic word:* this may mean the utterance of a Christian prophet designating the candidate or a prayer of blessing accompanying the rite. *Imposition of hands:* this gesture was used in the Old Testament to signify the transmission of authority from Moses to Joshua (Nm 27, 18-23; Dt 34, 9). The early Christian community used it as a symbol of installation into an office: the Seven (Acts 6, 6) and Paul and Barnabas (Acts 13, 3). *Of the presbyterate:* this would mean that each member of the college of presbyters imposed hands and appears to contradict 2 Tm 1, 6, in which Paul says that he imposed hands on Timothy. This latter text, however, does not exclude participation by others in the rite. Some prefer to translate "for the presbyterate," and thus understand it to designate the office into which Timothy was installed rather than the agents who installed him.

5, 1-16: After a few words of general advice based on common sense (1-2), the letter takes up, in its several aspects, the subject of widows. The first responsibility for their care belongs to the family circle, not to the Christian community as such (3-4.16). The widow left without the aid of relatives may benefit the community by her prayer, and the community should consider her material sustenance its responsibility (5-8). Widows who wish to work directly for the Christian community should not be accepted unless they are well beyond the probability of marriage, i.e., sixty years of age, married only once, and with a reputation for good works (9-10). Younger widows are apt to be troublesome and should be encouraged to remarry (11-15).

as brothers,[s] [2] older women as mothers, and younger women as sisters with complete purity.

Rules for Widows. [3] Honor widows who are truly widows. [4] But if a widow has children or grandchildren, let these first learn to perform their religious duty to their own family and to make recompense to their parents, for this is pleasing to God. [5] The real widow, who is all alone, has set her hope on God and continues in supplications and prayers night and day.[t] [6] But the one who is self-indulgent is dead while she lives. [7] Command this, so that they may be irreproachable. [8] And whoever does not provide for relatives and especially family members has denied the faith and is worse than an unbeliever.

[9] Let a widow be enrolled if she is not less than sixty years old, married only once, [10] with a reputation for good works, namely, that she has raised children, practiced hospitality, washed the feet of the holy ones, helped those in distress, involved herself in every good work.[u] [11] But exclude younger widows, for when their sensuality estranges them from Christ, they want to marry [12] and will incur condemnation for breaking their first pledge. [13] And furthermore, they learn to be idlers, going about from house to house, and not only idlers but gossips and busybodies as well, talking about things that ought not to be mentioned.[v] [14] So I would like younger widows to marry, have children, and manage a home, so as to give the adversary no pretext for maligning us.[w] [15] For some have already turned away to follow Satan. [16] If any woman believer* has widowed relatives, she must assist them; the church is not to be burdened, so that it will be able to help those who are truly widows.

Rules for Presbyters.* [17] Presbyters who preside well deserve double honor, especially those who toil in preaching and teaching.[x] [18] For the scripture says, "You shall not muzzle an ox when it is threshing," and, "A worker deserves his pay."[y] [19] Do not accept an accusation against a presbyter unless it is supported by two or three witnesses.[z] [20] Reprimand publicly those who do sin, so that the rest also will be afraid.[a] [21] I charge you before God and Christ Jesus and the elect angels to keep these rules without prejudice, doing nothing out of favoritism. [22] Do not lay hands too readily on anyone, and do not share in another's sins. Keep yourself pure.[b] [23] Stop drinking only water, but have a little wine for the sake of your stomach and your frequent illnesses.

[24] Some people's sins are public, preceding them to judgment; but other people are followed by their sins. [25] Similarly, good works are also public; and even those that are not cannot remain hidden.

CHAPTER 6

Rules for Slaves. [1] * Those who are under the yoke of slavery must regard their masters as worthy of full respect, so that the name of God and our teaching* may not suffer abuse.[c] [2] Those whose masters are believers must not take advantage of them because they are brothers but must give better service because those who will profit from their work are believers and are beloved.[d]

---

s Lv 19, 32; Ti 2, 2.—t Jer 49, 11; Lk 2, 37; 18, 7.—u Jn 13, 14; Heb 13, 2.—v 2 Thes 3, 11.—w 1 Cor 7, 9.—x 1 Cor 16, 18; Phil 2, 29.—y Dt 25, 4; 1 Cor 9, 8 / Mt 10, 10; Lk 10, 7.—z Dt 17, 6; 19, 15; Mt 18, 16; 2 Cor 13, 1.—a Gal 2, 14; Eph 5, 11; 2 Tm 4, 2; Ti 1, 9.13.—b 1 Tm 4, 14; 2 Tm 1, 6.—c Eph 6, 5; Ti 2, 9-10.—d Phlm 16.

5, 16: *Woman believer:* some early Latin manuscripts and Fathers have a masculine here, while most later manuscripts and patristic quotations conflate the two readings, perhaps to avoid unfair restriction to women.

5, 17-25: The function of presbyters is not exactly the same as that of the *episkopos*, "bishop" (1 Tm 3, 1); in fact, the relation of the two at the time of this letter is obscure (but cf the note on Ti 1, 5-9). The Pastorals seem to reflect a transitional stage that developed in many regions of the church into the monarchical episcopate of the second and third centuries. The presbyters possess the responsibility of preaching and teaching, for which functions they are supported by the community (17-18). The realization that their position subjects them to adverse criticism is implied in the direction to Timothy (19-20) to make sure of the truth of any accusation against them before public reproof is given. He must be as objective as possible in weighing charges against presbyters (21), learning from his experience to take care in selecting them (22). Some scholars take v 22 as a reference not to ordination of presbyters but to reconciliation of public sinners. The letter now sounds an informal note of personal concern in its advice to Timothy not to be so ascetic that he even avoids wine (23). Judgment concerning the fitness of candidates to serve as presbyters is easy with persons of open conduct, more difficult and prolonged with those of greater reserve (24-25).

6, 1-2: Compare the tables for household duties, such as that of Col 3, 18—4, 1. Domestic relationships derive new meaning from the Christian faith.

6, 1: *Our teaching:* this refers to the teaching of the Christian community.

V. FALSE TEACHING AND TRUE WEALTH

Teach and urge these things.* ³Whoever teaches something different and does not agree with the sound words of our Lord Jesus Christ and the religious teaching*e* ⁴is conceited, understanding nothing, and has a morbid disposition for arguments and verbal disputes. From these come envy, rivalry, insults, evil suspicions, ⁵and mutual friction among people with corrupted minds, who are deprived of the truth, supposing religion to be a means of gain.*f* ⁶Indeed, religion with contentment* is a great gain.*g* ⁷For we brought nothing into the world, just as we shall not be able to take anything out of it.*h* ⁸If we have food and clothing, we shall be content with that.*i* ⁹Those who want to be rich are falling into temptation and into a trap and into many foolish and harmful desires, which plunge them into ruin and destruction.*j* ¹⁰For the love of money is the root of all evils, and some people in their desire for it have strayed from the faith and have pierced themselves with many pains.

Exhortations to Timothy.* ¹¹But you, man of God,* avoid all this. Instead, pursue righteousness, devotion, faith, love, patience, and gentleness.*k* ¹²Compete well for the faith. Lay hold of eternal life, to which you were called when you made the noble confession in the presence of many witnesses.*l* ¹³I charge [you] before God, who gives life to all things, and before Christ Jesus, who gave testimony under Pontius Pilate for the noble confession,*m* ¹⁴to keep the commandment without stain or reproach until the appearance of our Lord Jesus Christ ¹⁵that the blessed and only ruler will make manifest at the proper time, the King of kings and Lord of lords,*n* ¹⁶who alone has immortality, who dwells in unapproachable light, and whom no human being has seen or can see. To him be honor and eternal power. Amen.*o*

Right Use of Wealth.* ¹⁷Tell the rich in the present age not to be proud and not to rely on so uncertain a thing as wealth but rather on God, who richly provides us with all things for our enjoyment.*p* ¹⁸Tell them to do good, to be rich in good works, to be generous, ready to share, ¹⁹thus accumulating as treasure a good foundation for the future, so as to win the life that is true life.*q*

VI. FINAL RECOMMENDATION AND WARNING*

²⁰O Timothy, guard what has been entrusted to you. Avoid profane babbling and the absurdities of so-called knowledge.*r* ²¹By professing it, some people have deviated from the faith.

Grace be with all of you.*s*

1Tm

---

e Gal 1, 6-9; 2 Tm 1, 13; Ti 1, 1.—f 2 Tm 3, 8; 4, 4; Ti 1, 14.—g 1 Tm 4, 8; Phil 4, 11-12; Heb 13, 5.—h Jb 1, 21; Eccl 5, 14.—i Prv 30, 8.—j Prv 23, 4; 28, 22.—k 2 Tm 2, 22.—l 1 Cor 9, 26; 2 Tm 4, 7.—m Jn 18, 36-37; 19, 11.—n 2 Mc 13, 4; Rv 17, 14.—o Ex 33, 20; Ps 104, 2.—p Ps 62, 11; Lk 12, 20.—q Mt 6, 20.—r 2 Tm 1, 14 / 1 Tm 4, 7.—s 1 Tm 1, 6; 2 Tm 2, 18.

6, 2b-10: Timothy is exhorted to maintain steadfastly the position outlined in this letter, not allowing himself to be pressured into any other course. He must realize that false teachers can be discerned by their pride, envy, quarrelsomeness, and greed for material gain. Verse 6 is rather obscure and is interpreted, and therefore translated, variously. The suggestion seems to be that the important gain that religion brings is spiritual, but that there is material gain, too, up to the point of what is needed for physical sustenance (cf 1 Tm 6, 17-19).

6, 6: *Contentment:* the word *autarkeia* is a technical Greek philosophical term for the virtue of independence from material goods (Aristotle, Cynics, Stoics).

6, 11-16: Timothy's position demands total dedication to God and faultless witness to Christ (11-14) operating from an awareness, through faith, of the coming revelation in Jesus of the invisible God (15-16).

6, 11: *Man of God:* a title applied to Moses and the prophets (Dt 33,1; 1 Sm 2, 27; 1 Kgs 12, 22; 13, 1; etc.).

6, 17-19: Timothy is directed to instruct the rich, advising them to make good use of their wealth by aiding the poor.

6, 20-21: A final solemn warning against the heretical teachers, with what seems to be a specific reference to gnosticism, the great rival and enemy of the church for two centuries and more (the Greek word for "knowledge" is *gnōsis*). If gnosticism is being referred to here, it is probable that the warnings against "speculations" and "myths and genealogies" (cf especially 1 Tm 1, 4; Ti 3, 9) involve allusions to that same kind of heresy. Characteristic of the various gnostic systems of speculation was an elaborate mythology of innumerable superhuman intermediaries, on a descending scale ("genealogies"), between God and the world. Thus would be explained the emphasis upon Christ's being the *one* mediator (as in 1 Tm 2, 5). Although fully developed gnosticism belonged to the second and later centuries, there are signs that incipient forms of it belonged to Paul's own period.

THE SECOND LETTER TO TIMOTHY

INTRODUCTION

The authorship and date of this letter, as one of the Pastoral Epistles, are discussed in the Introduction to the First Letter to Timothy.

The tone here is more personal than in First Timothy, for this letter addresses Timothy in vivid terms (1, 6-14; 2, 1-13) and depicts Paul's courage and hope in the face of discouragements late in the course of his apostolic ministry (1, 15-18; 3, 10-17; 4, 9-18). Indeed, the letter takes on the character of a final exhortation and testament from Paul to the younger Timothy (4, 1-8). Paul is portrayed as a prisoner (1, 8.16; 2, 9) in Rome (1, 17), and there is a hint that Timothy may be in Ephesus (2, 17). The letter reveals that, with rare exceptions, Christians have not rallied to Paul's support (1, 15-18) and takes a pessimistic view of the outcome of his case (4, 6). It describes Paul as fully aware of what impends, looking to God, not to human beings, for his deliverance (4, 3-8.18). It recalls his mission days with Timothy (1, 3-5; cf Acts 16, 1-4). It points to his preaching of the gospel as the reason for his imprisonment and offers Timothy, as a motive for steadfastness, his own example of firmness in faith despite adverse circumstances (1, 6-14). The letter suggests that Timothy should prepare others to replace himself as Paul has prepared Timothy to replace him (2, 1-2). Paul urges him not to desist out of fear from preserving and spreading the Christian message (2, 3-7). It presents the resurrection of Jesus and his messianic role as the heart of the gospel for which Paul has been ready to lay down his life (2, 8-9) and thus not only to express his own conviction fully but to support the conviction of others (2, 10-13).

This letter, like the preceding one, urges Timothy to protect the community from the inevitable impact of false teaching (2, 14—3, 9), without fear of the personal attacks that may result (3, 10-13). It recommends that he rely on the power of the scriptures, on proclamation of the word, and on sound doctrine (3, 14—4, 2), without being troubled by those who do not accept him (4, 3-5). The letter poignantly observes in passing that Paul has need of his reading materials and his cloak (4, 13) and, what will be best of all, a visit from Timothy.

On the theory of authorship by Paul himself, Second Timothy appears to be the last of the three Pastoral Epistles. The many scholars who argue that the Pastorals are products of the Pauline school often incline toward Second Timothy as the earliest of the three and the one most likely to have actual fragments of material from Paul himself.

The principal divisions of the Second Letter to Timothy are the following:

I. *Address (1, 1-5)*
II. *Exhortations to Timothy (1, 6—2, 13)*
III. *Instructions Concerning False Teaching (2, 14—4, 8)*
IV. *Personal Requests and Final Greetings (4, 9-22)*

I. ADDRESS

CHAPTER 1

Greeting.* [1] Paul, an apostle of Christ Jesus by the will of God[a] for the promise of life in Christ Jesus,* [2] to Timothy, my dear child: grace, mercy, and peace from God the Father and Christ Jesus our Lord.

Thanksgiving. [3] [b] I am grateful to God, whom I worship with a clear conscience as my ancestors did,* as I remember you con-

---

a 1 Tm 4, 8.—b 1 Tm 3, 9 / Phil 3, 5.

1, 1-2: For the formula of address and greeting, see the note on Rom 1, 1-7.

1, 1: *The promise of life in Christ Jesus:* that God grants through union with Christ in faith and love; cf Col 3, 4; 1 Tm 4, 8.

1, 3: *As my ancestors did:* this emphasizes the continuity of Judaism and Christianity; for a similar view, see Rom 9, 3-5; Phil 3, 4-6.

stantly in my prayers, night and day. [4] * I yearn to see you again, recalling your tears, so that I may be filled with joy, [5] as I recall your sincere faith that first lived in your grandmother Lois and in your mother Eunice and that I am confident lives also in you. [c]

II. EXHORTATIONS TO TIMOTHY

The Gifts Timothy Has Received. [6] For this reason, I remind you to stir into flame the gift of God* that you have through the imposition of my hands. [d] [7] For God did not give us a spirit of cowardice but rather of power and love and self-control. [e] [8] So do not be ashamed of your testimony to our Lord,* nor of me, a prisoner for his sake; but bear your share of hardship for the gospel with the strength that comes from God. [f]

[9] * He saved us and called us to a holy life, not according to our works but according to his own design and the grace bestowed on us in Christ Jesus before time began, [g] [10] but now made manifest through the appearance of our savior Christ Jesus, who destroyed death and brought life and immortality to light through the gospel, [h] [11] for which I was appointed preacher and apostle [i] and teacher.* [12] On this account I am suffering these things; but I am not ashamed, [j] for I know him in whom I have believed and am confident that he is able to guard what has been entrusted to me until that day.* [13] Take as your norm the sound words that you heard from me, in the faith and love that are in Christ Jesus. [k] [14] Guard this rich trust with the help of the holy Spirit that dwells within us. [l]

Paul's Suffering. [15] [m] You know that everyone in Asia deserted me, including Phygelus and Hermogenes.* [16] May the Lord grant mercy to the family of Onesiphorus [n] because he often gave me new heart and was not ashamed of my chains.* [17] But when he came to Rome, he promptly searched for me and found me. [18] May the Lord grant him to find mercy from the Lord* on that day. And you know very well the services he rendered in Ephesus. [o]

CHAPTER 2

Timothy's Conduct. [1] * So you, my child, be strong in the grace that is in Christ Jesus. [2] And what you heard from me through many witnesses entrust to faithful people who will have the ability to teach others as well. [3] Bear your share of hardship along with me like a good soldier of Christ Jesus. [p] [4] To satisfy the one who recruited him, a soldier does not become entangled in the business affairs of life. [q] [5] Similarly, an athlete cannot receive the winner's crown except by competing according to the rules. [r] [6] The hardworking farmer ought to have the first share of the crop. [s] [7] Reflect on what I am saying, for

2Tm

---

c 1 Tm 1, 5 / Acts 16, 1.—d 1 Tm 4, 14; 5, 22 / Acts 6, 6; 8, 17.—e Rom 5, 5; 8, 15; 1 Cor 2, 4.—f 2 Tm 2, 3.15; Rom 1, 16.—g Eph 2, 8-9; Ti 3, 5 / Eph 1, 4; Ti 1, 2.—h Rom 16, 26; 1 Pt 1, 20 / 1 Tm 6, 14 / Phil 3, 20; Ti 1, 4; 2, 13; 2 Pt 1, 11 / 1 Cor 15, 54-55; Heb 2, 14 / 1 Cor 15, 53-54.—i 1 Tm 2, 7.—j 1 Pt 4, 16 / 1 Tm 1, 10-11.—k 1 Tm 1, 14.—l 1 Tm 6, 20 / Rom 8, 11.—m 2 Tm 4, 16.—n 2 Tm 4, 19.—o Jude 21.—p 2 Tm 1, 8; 4, 5; Phlm 2.—q 1 Cor 9, 6.—r 1 Cor 9, 25.—s 1 Cor 9, 7-10.

1, 4-5: Purportedly written from prison in Rome (2 Tm 1, 8.17; 4, 6-8) shortly before the writer's death, the letter recalls the earlier sorrowful parting from Timothy, commending him for his faith and expressing the longing to see him again.

1, 6: *The gift of God:* the grace resulting from the conferral of an ecclesiastical office. *The imposition of my hands:* see the note on 1 Tm 4, 14.

1, 8: *Do not be ashamed of your testimony to our Lord:* i.e., of preaching and suffering for the sake of the gospel.

1, 9-10: Redemption from sin and the call to holiness of life are not won by personal deeds but are freely and graciously bestowed according to God's eternal plan; cf Eph 1, 4.

1, 11: *Teacher:* the overwhelming majority of manuscripts and Fathers read "teacher of the nations," undoubtedly a harmonization with 1 Tm 2, 7.

1, 12: *He is able to guard . . . until that day:* the intervening words can also be translated "what I have entrusted to him" (i.e., the fruit of his ministry) as well as "what has been entrusted

to me" (i.e., the faith). The same difficult term occurs in v 14, where it is modified by the adjective "rich" and used without a possessive.

1, 15: Keen disappointment is expressed, here and later (2 Tm 4, 16), that the Christians of the province of Asia, especially Phygelus and Hermogenes, should have abandoned the writer and done nothing to defend his case in court.

1, 16-18: *The family of Onesiphorus because he . . . of my chains:* Onesiphorus seems to have died before this letter was written. His family is mentioned twice (here and in 2 Tm 4, 19), though it was Onesiphorus himself who was helpful to Paul in prison and rendered much service to the community of Ephesus. Because the apostle complains of abandonment by all in Asia during his second imprisonment and trial, the assistance of Onesiphorus seems to have been given to Paul during his first Roman imprisonment (A.D. 61-63).

1, 18: *Lord . . . Lord:* the first "Lord" here seems to refer to Christ, the second "Lord" to the Father.

2, 1-7: This passage manifests a characteristic deep concern for safeguarding the faith and faithfully transmitting it through trustworthy people (1-2; cf 2 Tm 1, 14; 1 Tm 6, 20; Ti 1, 9). Comparisons to the soldier's detachment, the athlete's sportsmanship, and the farmer's arduous work as the price of recompense (4-6) emphasize the need of singleness of purpose in preaching the word, even at the cost of hardship, for the sake of Christ (3).

the Lord will give you understanding in everything.[*t*]

8 * Remember Jesus Christ, raised from the dead, a descendant of David: such is my gospel,[*u*] 9 for which I am suffering, even to the point of chains, like a criminal. But the word of God is not chained.[*v*] 10 Therefore, I bear with everything for the sake of those who are chosen, so that they too may obtain the salvation that is in Christ Jesus, together with eternal glory.[*w*] 11 This saying is trustworthy:

If we have died with him
    we shall also live with him;[*x*]
12 if we persevere
    we shall also reign with him.
But if we deny him
    he will deny us.[*y*]
13 If we are unfaithful
    he remains faithful,
    for he cannot deny himself.[*z*]

III. INSTRUCTIONS CONCERNING FALSE TEACHING

Warning against Useless Disputes. 14 * Remind people of these things and charge them before God* to stop disputing about words. This serves no useful purpose since it harms those who listen.[*a*] 15 Be eager to present yourself as acceptable to God, a workman who causes no disgrace, imparting the word of truth without deviation.[*b*] 16 Avoid profane, idle talk, for such people will become more and more godless,[*c*] 17 and their teaching will spread like gangrene. Among them are Hymenaeus and Philetus,[*d*] 18 who have deviated from the

truth by saying that [the] resurrection has already taken place and are upsetting the faith of some.[*e*] 19 Nevertheless, God's solid foundation stands, bearing this inscription, "The Lord knows those who are his"; and, "Let everyone who calls upon the name of the Lord avoid evil."[*f*]

20 In a large household there are vessels not only of gold and silver but also of wood and clay, some for lofty and others for humble use. 21 If anyone cleanses himself of these things, he will be a vessel for lofty use, dedicated, beneficial to the master of the house, ready for every good work.[*g*] 22 So turn from youthful desires and pursue righteousness, faith, love, and peace, along with those who call on the Lord* with purity of heart.[*h*] 23 Avoid foolish and ignorant debates, for you know that they breed quarrels.[*i*] 24 A slave of the Lord should not quarrel, but should be gentle with everyone, able to teach, tolerant,[*j*] 25 correcting opponents with kindness. It may be that God will grant them repentance that leads to knowledge of the truth,[*k*] 26 and that they may return to their senses out of the devil's snare,[*l*] where they are entrapped by him, for his will.*

CHAPTER 3

The Dangers of the Last Days.* 1 But understand this: there will be terrifying times in the last days.[*m*] 2 People will be self-centered and lovers of money, proud, haughty, abusive, disobedient to their parents, ungrateful, irreligious,[*n*] 3 callous, im-

---

Hymenaeus and Philetus (17), while accepting the Christian's mystical death and resurrection in Christ through baptism, claimed that baptized Christians are already risen with Christ in this life and thus that there is no future bodily resurrection or eternal glory to come. The first quotation in v 19 is from Nm 16, 5; the other quotation is from some unidentified Jewish or Christian writing.

2, 14: *Before God:* many ancient manuscripts read "before the Lord."

2, 22: *Those who call on the Lord:* those who believe in Christ and worship him as Lord, i.e., Christians (Acts 9, 14-16.20-21; Rom 10, 12-13; cf 19, literally, "Everyone who names the name of the Lord").

2, 26: Some interpreters would render this passage, "Thus they may come to their senses and, forced to do his (i.e., God's) will, may escape the devil's trap." This interpretation of the Greek is possible, but the one accepted in the text seems more likely.

3, 1-9: The moral depravity and false teaching that will be rampant in the last days are already at work (1-5). The frivolous and superficial, too, devoid of the true spirit of religion, will be easy victims of those who pervert them by falsifying the truth (6-8), just as Jannes and Jambres, Pharaoh's magicians of Egypt (Ex 7, 11-12.22), discredited the truth in Moses' time. Exodus does not name the magicians, but the two names are widely found in much later Jewish, Christian, and even pagan writings. Their origins are legendary.

---

t Prv 2, 6.—u Rom 1, 3; 1 Cor 15, 4.20 / Rom 2, 16; Gal 1, 11; 2, 2.—v Phil 1, 12-14.—w Col 1, 24; 1 Tm 1, 15.—x Rom 6, 8.—y Mt 10, 22.33; Lk 12, 9.—z Nm 23, 19; Rom 3, 3-4; 1 Cor 10, 13; Ti 1, 2.—a 1 Tm 6, 4.—b 2 Tm 1, 8; 2 Cor 6, 7; Eph 1, 13; Col 1, 5.—c 1 Tm 4, 7.—d 1 Tm 1, 20.—e 2 Thes 2, 2.—f Is 28, 16; 1 Cor 3, 10-15 / Nm 16, 5; Jn 10, 14.—g 2 Tm 3, 17.—h Gal 5, 22; 1 Tm 6, 11 / Rom 10, 13; 1 Cor 1, 2.—i 1 Tm 1, 4; 4, 7; 6, 4; Ti 3, 9.—j 1 Tm 3, 2-3.—k 2 Tm 3, 7; 1 Tm 2, 4.—l 1 Tm 3, 7.—m 1 Tm 4, 1; 2 Pt 3, 3; Jude 18.—n 2-4: Rom 1, 29-31.

2, 8-13: The section begins with a sloganlike summary of Paul's gospel about Christ (8) and concludes with what may be part of an early Christian hymn (11b-12a; most exegetes include the rest of v 12 and all of v 13 as part of the quotation). The poetic lines suggest that through baptism Christians die spiritually with Christ and hope to live with him and reign with him forever, but the Christian life includes endurance, witness, and even suffering, as the final judgment will show and as Paul's own case makes clear; while he is imprisoned for preaching the gospel (9), his sufferings are helpful to the elect for obtaining the salvation and glory available in Christ (10), who will be true to those who are faithful and will disown those who deny him (12-13).

2, 14-19: For those who dispute about mere words (cf 2 Tm 2, 23-24) and indulge in irreligious talk to the detriment of their listeners (16-19), see the notes on 1 Tm 1, 3-7; 6, 20-21.

placable, slanderous, licentious, brutal, hating what is good, [4]traitors, reckless, conceited, lovers of pleasure rather than lovers of God, [5]as they make a pretense of religion but deny its power. Reject them.[o] [6]For some of these slip into homes and make captives of women weighed down by sins, led by various desires,[p] [7]always trying to learn but never able to reach a knowledge of the truth.[q] [8]Just as Jannes and Jambres opposed Moses, so they also oppose the truth—people of depraved mind, unqualified in the faith.[r] [9]But they will not make further progress, for their foolishness will be plain to all, as it was with those two.

Paul's Example and Teaching.* [10]You have followed my teaching, way of life, purpose, faith, patience, love, endurance, [11]persecutions, and sufferings, such as happened to me in Antioch, Iconium, and Lystra, persecutions that I endured. Yet from all these things the Lord delivered me.[s] [12]In fact, all who want to live religiously in Christ Jesus will be persecuted.[t] [13]But wicked people and charlatans will go from bad to worse, deceivers and deceived. [14]But you, remain faithful to what you have learned and believed, because you know from whom you learned it,[u] [15]and that from infancy you have known [the] sacred scriptures, which are capable of giving you wisdom for salvation through faith in Christ Jesus.[v] [16]All scripture[w] is inspired by God* and is useful for teaching, for refutation, for correction, and for train-ing in righteousness,* [17]so that one who belongs to God may be competent, equipped for every good work.[x]

CHAPTER 4

Solemn Charge.* [1]I charge you in the presence of God and of Christ Jesus, who will judge the living and the dead, and by his appearing and his kingly power:[y] [2]proclaim the word; be persistent whether it is convenient or inconvenient; convince, reprimand, encourage through all patience and teaching.[z] [3]For the time will come when people will not tolerate sound doctrine but, following their own desires and insatiable curiosity,* will accumulate teachers[a] [4]and will stop listening to the truth and will be diverted to myths.[b] [5]But you, be self-possessed in all circumstances; put up with hardship; perform the work of an evangelist; fulfill your ministry.

Reward for Fidelity. [6][c] For I am already being poured out like a libation, and the time of my departure is at hand.* [7]I have competed well; I have finished the race;[d] I have kept the faith.* [8]From now on the crown of righteousness awaits me, which the Lord, the just judge, will award to me on that day,[e] and not only to me, but to all who have longed for his appearance.*

IV. PERSONAL REQUESTS AND FINAL GREETINGS

2Tm

Paul's Loneliness. [9] * Try to join me soon, [10]for Demas, enamored of the pres-

---

o Rom 2, 20-22; Ti 1, 16.—p Ti 1, 11.—q 2 Tm 2, 25.—r Ex 7, 11.22; 1 Tm 6, 5.—s Acts 13, 50; 14, 5.19 / Ps 34, 20.—t Jn 15, 20; Acts 14, 22.—u 2 Tm 2, 2.—v Jn 5, 39.—w Rom 15, 4; 2 Pt 1, 19-21.—x 2 Tm 2, 21.—y 1 Tm 5, 21; 6, 14 / Acts 10, 42; Rom 14, 9-10; 1 Pt 4, 5.—z Acts 20, 20.31; 1 Tm 5, 20.—a 1 Tm 4, 1.—b 1 Tm 1, 4; 4, 7; Ti 1, 14.—c Phil 2, 17.—d 1 Tm 1, 18; 6, 12; Jude 3 / Acts 20, 24; 1 Cor 9, 24; Heb 12, 1.—e 2 Tm 2, 5; Wis 5, 16; 1 Cor 9, 25; Phil 3, 14; Jas 1, 12; 1 Pt 5, 4; Rv 2, 10.

3, 10-17: Paul's example for Timothy includes persecution, a frequent emphasis in the Pastorals. Timothy is to be steadfast to what he has been taught and to scripture. The scriptures are the source of wisdom, i.e., of belief in and loving fulfillment of God's word revealed in Christ, through whom salvation is given.

3, 16: *All scripture is inspired by God:* this could possibly also be translated, "All scripture inspired by God is useful for. . . ." In this classic reference to inspiration, God is its principal author, with the writer as the human collaborator. Thus the scriptures are the word of God in human language. See also 2 Pt 1, 20-21.

3, 16-17: *Useful for teaching . . . every good work:* because as God's word the scriptures share his divine authority. It is exercised through those who are ministers of the word.

4, 1-5: The gravity of the obligation incumbent on Timothy to preach the word can be gauged from the solemn adjuration: in the presence of God, and of Christ coming as universal judge, and by his appearance and his kingly power (1). Patience, courage, constancy, and endurance are required despite the opposition, hostility, indifference, and defection of many to whom the truth has been preached (2-5).

4, 3: *Insatiable curiosity:* literally, "with itching ears."

4, 6: The apostle recognizes his death through martyrdom to be imminent. He regards it as an act of worship in which his blood will be poured out in sacrifice; cf Ex 29, 38-40; Phil 2, 17.

4, 7: At the close of his life Paul could testify to the accomplishment of what Christ himself foretold concerning him at the time of his conversion, "I will show him what he will have to suffer for my name" (Acts 9, 16).

4, 8: When the world is judged at the parousia, all who have eagerly looked for the Lord's appearing and have sought to live according to his teachings will be rewarded. The crown is a reference to the laurel wreath placed on the heads of victorious athletes and conquerors in war; cf 2 Tm 2, 5; 1 Cor 9, 25.

4, 9-13: Demas either abandoned the work of the ministry for worldly affairs or, perhaps, gave up the faith itself (10). Luke (11) may have accompanied Paul on parts of his second and third missionary journeys (Acts 16, 10-12; 20, 5-7). Notice the presence of the first personal pronoun "we" in these Acts passages, suggesting to some that Luke (or at least some traveling companion of Paul's) was the author of Acts. Mark, once rejected by Paul (Acts 13, 13; 15, 39), is now to render him a great service (11); cf Col 4, 10; Phlm 24. For Tychicus, see Eph 6, 21; cf also Acts 20, 4; Col 4, 7.

ent world, deserted me and went to Thessalonica, Crescens to Galatia,* and Titus to Dalmatia.*f* [11] Luke is the only one with me. Get Mark and bring him with you, for he is helpful to me in the ministry.*g* [12] I have sent Tychicus to Ephesus.*h* [13] When you come, bring the cloak I left with Carpus in Troas, the papyrus rolls, and especially the parchments.*i*

[14] Alexander* the coppersmith did me a great deal of harm; the Lord will repay him according to his deeds.*j* [15] You too be on guard against him, for he has strongly resisted our preaching.

[16] At my first defense no one appeared on my behalf, but everyone deserted me. May it not be held against them!*k* [17] But the Lord stood by me and gave me strength, so that through me the proclamation might be completed and all the Gentiles might hear it. And I was rescued from the lion's mouth.*l* [18] The Lord will rescue me from every evil threat and will bring me safe to his heavenly kingdom. To him be glory forever and ever. Amen.*m*

Final Greeting. [19] Greet Prisca and Aquila* and the family of Onesiphorus.*n* [20] Erastus* remained in Corinth, while I left Trophimus sick at Miletus.*o* [21] Try to get here before winter. Eubulus, Pudens, Linus,* Claudia, and all the brothers send greetings.

[22] The Lord be with your spirit. Grace be with all of you.*p*

---

f Col 4, 14; Phlm 24 / 2 Cor 2, 13; 7, 6-7; 8, 23; Gal 2, 3; Ti 1, 4.—g Col 4, 14; Phlm 24 / Col 4, 10; Phlm 24.—h Acts 20, 4; Eph 6, 21; Col 4, 7.—i Acts 16, 8; 20, 6.—j 1 Tm 1, 20 / 2 Sm 3, 39; Pss 28, 4; 62, 12; Prv 24, 12; Rom 2, 6.—k 2 Tm 1, 15.—l Acts 23, 11; 27, 23; Phil 4, 13 / 1 Mc 2, 60; Ps 22, 22; Dn 6, 23.—m 2 Cor 1, 10 / Rom 16, 27.—n Acts 18, 2; Rom 16, 3; 1 Cor 16, 19 / 2 Tm 1, 16.—o Acts 19, 22; Rom 16, 24 / Acts 20, 4; 21, 29.—p Gal 6, 18; Phil 4, 23; Col 4, 18; 1 Tm 6, 21; Ti 3, 15.

4, 10: *Galatia:* some manuscripts read "Gaul" or "Gallia."

4, 14-18: *Alexander:* an opponent of Paul's preaching (14-15), perhaps the one who is mentioned in 1 Tm 1, 20. Despite Paul's abandonment by his friends in the province of Asia (cf 2 Tm 1, 15-16), the divine assistance brought this first trial to a successful issue, even to the point of making the gospel message known to those who participated in or witnessed the trial (16-17).

4, 19: *Prisca and Aquila:* they assisted Paul in his ministry in Corinth (Acts 18, 2-3) and Ephesus (Acts 18, 19.26; 1 Cor 16, 19). They risked death to save his life, and all the Gentile communities are indebted to them (Rom 16, 3-5).

4, 20: *Erastus:* he was the treasurer of the city of Corinth (Rom 16, 24); cf also Acts 19, 22. *Trophimus:* from the province of Asia, he accompanied Paul from Greece to Troas (Acts 20, 4-5).

4, 21: *Linus:* Western tradition sometimes identified this Linus with the supposed successor of Peter as bishop of Rome, and Claudia as the mother of Linus (*Apostolic Constitutions*, fourth century).

THE LETTER TO TITUS

INTRODUCTION

The third of the Pastoral Epistles in the New Testament is addressed to a different co-worker of Paul than are First and Second Timothy. The situation is different, too, for Titus is addressed as the person in charge of developing the church on the large Mediterranean island of Crete (1, 5), a place Paul had never, according to the New Testament, visited. The tone is closer to that of First Timothy as three topics of church life and structure are discussed: presbyter-bishops (see the note on 1, 5-9), groups with which one must work in the church (2, 1-10), and admonitions for conduct based on the grace and love of God that appeared in Jesus Christ (2, 11—3, 10). The warmer personal tone of Second Timothy is replaced by emphasis on church office and on living in the society of the day, in which deceivers and heretics abound (1, 10-16; 3, 9-10).

The Pauline assistant who is addressed, Titus, was a Gentile Christian, but we are nowhere informed of his place of birth or residence. He went from Antioch with Paul and Barnabas to Jerusalem (Gal 2, 1; cf Acts 15, 2). According to 2 Corinthians (2, 13; 7, 6.13-14), he was with Paul on his third missionary journey; his name, however, does not appear in Acts. Besides being the bearer of Paul's severe letter to the Corinthians (2 Cor 7, 6-8), he had the responsibility of taking up the collection in Corinth for the Christian community of Jerusalem (2 Cor 8, 6.16-19.23). In the present letter (1, 5), he is mentioned as the administrator of the Christian community in Crete, charged with the task of *organizing it through the appointment of presbyters and bishops (1, 5-9; here the two terms refer to the same personages).*

The letter instructs Titus about the character of the assistants he is to choose in view of the pastoral difficulties peculiar to Crete (1, 5-16). It suggests the special individual and social virtues that the various age groups and classes in the Christian community should be encouraged to acquire (2, 1-10). The motivation for transformation of their lives comes from christology, especially the redemptive sacrifice of Christ and his future coming, as applied through baptism and justification (2, 11-14; 3, 4-8). The community is to serve as a leaven for Christianizing the social world about it (3, 1-3). Good works are to be the evidence of their faith in God (3, 8); those who engage in religious controversy are, after suitable warning, to be ignored (3, 9-11).

The authorship and date of the Letter to Titus are discussed in the Introduction to 1 Timothy. Those who assume authorship by Paul himself usually place Titus after 1 Timothy and before 2 Timothy. Others see it as closely related to 1 Timothy, in a growing emphasis on church structure and opposition to heresy, later than the letters of Paul himself and 2 Timothy. It has also been suggested that, if the three Pastorals once circulated as a literary unit, Titus was meant to be read ahead of 1 and 2 Timothy.

The principal divisions of the Letter to Titus are the following:

   I.   Address (1, 1-4)
  II.   Pastoral Charge (1, 5-16)
 III.   Teaching the Christian Life (2, 1—3, 15)

I. ADDRESS

CHAPTER 1

Greeting.* ¹Paul, a slave of God and apostle of Jesus Christ for the sake of the faith of God's chosen ones and the recognition of religious truth,ᵃ ²in the hope of eternal life that God, who does not lie, promised before time began,ᵇ ³who indeed at the proper time revealed his word in the proclamation with which I was entrusted by the command of God our savior,ᶜ ⁴to Titus, my true child in our common faith: grace and peace from God the Father and Christ Jesus our savior.ᵈ

II. PASTORAL CHARGE

Titus in Crete. ⁵ * For this reason I left you in Crete so that you might set right what remains to be done and appoint pres-byters in every town, as I directed you, ⁶ ᵉ on condition that a man be blameless, married only once, with believing children who are not accused of licentiousness or rebellious. ⁷For a bishop as God's steward must be blameless, not arrogant, not irritable, not a drunkard, not aggressive, not greedy for sordid gain, ⁸but hospitable, a lover of goodness, temperate, just, holy, and self-controlled, ⁹holding fast to the true message as taught so that he will be able both to exhort with sound doctrine and to refute opponents.ᶠ ¹⁰ * For there are also many rebels, idle talkers and deceivers, especially the Jewish Christians.* ¹¹It is imperative to silence them, as they are upsetting whole families by teaching for sordid gain what they should not. ¹²One of them, a prophet of their own, once said, "Cretans have always been liars, vicious beasts, and lazy gluttons."* ¹³That

a 1 Tm 2, 4; 4, 3; 2 Tm 2, 25; 3, 7; Heb 10, 26.—b Ti 3, 7; 2 Tm 1, 1; 1 Jn 2, 25.—c Ti 2, 10; 3, 4; Ps 24, 5; 1 Tm 1, 1; 2, 3; 4, 10; Jude 25.—d Ti 2, 13; 3, 6; Phil 3, 20; 2 Tm 1, 10; 2 Pt 1, 1.11; 2, 20; 3, 2.18.—e 6-7: 1 Tm 3, 2-7; 2 Tm 2, 24-26.—f Ti 1, 13; 2, 1-2.8; 1 Tm 1, 10; 6, 3; 2 Tm 1, 13; 4, 3.

Acts 20, 17.28, the terms *episkopos* and *presbyteros* ("bishop" and "presbyter") refer to the same persons. Deacons are not mentioned in Titus. See also the note on Phil 1, 1.

1, 10-16: This adverse criticism of the defects within the community is directed especially against certain Jewish Christians, who busy themselves with useless speculations over persons mentioned in the Old Testament, insist on the observance of Jewish ritual purity regulations, and thus upset whole families by teaching things they have no right to teach; cf Ti 3, 9; 1 Tm 1, 3-10.

1, 10: *Jewish Christians:* literally, "those of the circumcision."

1, 12: *Cretans . . . gluttons:* quoted from Epimenides, a Cretan poet of the sixth century B.C.

1, 1-4: On the epistolary form, see the note on Rom 1, 1-7. The apostolate is the divinely appointed mission to lead others to the true faith and through it to eternal salvation (1-3).

1, 5-9: This instruction on the selection and appointment of presbyters, substantially identical with that in 1 Tm 3, 1-7 on a bishop (see the note there), was aimed at strengthening the authority of Titus by apostolic mandate; cf Ti 2, 15. In vv 5.7 and

testimony is true. Therefore, admonish them sharply, so that they may be sound in the faith,[g] [14]instead of paying attention to Jewish myths and regulations of people who have repudiated the truth.[h] [15]To the clean all things are clean, but to those who are defiled and unbelieving nothing is clean; in fact, both their minds and their consciences are tainted.[i] [16]They claim to know God, but by their deeds they deny him. They are vile and disobedient and unqualified for any good deed.

III. TEACHING THE CHRISTIAN LIFE

CHAPTER 2

Christian Behavior. * [1]As for yourself, you must say what is consistent with sound doctrine, namely,[j] [2]that older men should be temperate, dignified, self-controlled, sound in faith, love, and endurance. [3]Similarly, older women should be reverent in their behavior, not slanderers, not addicted to drink, teaching what is good, [4]so that they may train younger women to love their husbands and children, [5]to be self-controlled, chaste, good homemakers, under the control of their husbands, so that the word of God may not be discredited.[k]

[6]Urge the younger men, similarly, to control themselves, [7]showing yourself as a model of good deeds in every respect, with integrity in your teaching, dignity, [8]and sound speech that cannot be criticized, so that the opponent will be put to shame without anything bad to say about us.

[9]Slaves are to be under the control of their masters in all respects, giving them satisfaction, not talking back to them[l] [10]or

stealing from them, but exhibiting complete good faith, so as to adorn the doctrine of God our savior in every way.[m]

Transformation of Life. [11] * For the grace of God has appeared, saving all[n] [12]and training us to reject godless ways and worldly desires and to live temperately, justly, and devoutly in this age, [13]as we await the blessed hope, the appearance* of the glory of the great God and of our savior Jesus Christ,[o] [14]who gave himself for us to deliver us from all lawlessness and to cleanse for himself a people as his own, eager to do what is good.[p]

[15]Say these things. Exhort and correct with all authority. Let no one look down on you.[q]

CHAPTER 3

[1] * Remind them to be under the control of magistrates and authorities,* to be obedient, to be open to every good enterprise.[r] [2]They are to slander no one, to be peaceable, considerate, exercising all graciousness toward everyone. [3]For we ourselves were once foolish, disobedient, deluded, slaves to various desires and pleasures, living in malice and envy, hateful ourselves and hating one another.[s]

[4] But when the kindness and generous love
of God our savior appeared,[t]
[5] not because of any righteous deeds we had done
but because of his mercy,
he saved us through the bath of rebirth and renewal by the holy Spirit,[u]
[6] whom he richly poured out on us
through Jesus Christ our savior,[v]

---

g Ti 1, 9.—h Ti 3, 9; 1 Tm 1, 4; 4, 7; 2 Tm 4, 4; 2 Pt 1, 16.—i Mk 7, 18-23; Acts 10, 15; Rom 14, 14-23.—j Ti 1, 9.13; 2, 8; 1 Tm 1, 10; 6, 3; 2 Tm 1, 13; 4, 3.—k 1 Cor 11, 3; 14, 34; Eph 5, 22-24; Col 3, 18; 1 Tm 2, 11-15; 1 Pt 3, 1-6.—l 1 Cor 7, 21-22; Eph 6, 5-8; Col 3, 22-25; 1 Tm 6, 1-2; 1 Pt 2, 18.—m Ti 1, 3; 3, 4; Ps 24, 5; 1 Tm 1, 1; 2, 3; 4, 10; Jude 25.—n 1 Tm 2, 4; 4, 10.—o 1 Cor 1, 7; Phil 3, 20; 1 Thes 1, 10 / 2 Tm 1, 10 / Ti 1, 4; 3, 6; 2 Pt 1, 1.11; 2, 20; 3, 2.18.—p Gal 1, 4; 2, 20; Eph 5, 2.25; 1 Tm 2, 6; 1 Pt 1, 18-19 / Ps 130, 8.—q 1 Tm 4, 12.—r Rom 13, 1-7; 1 Tm 2, 1-2; 1 Pt 2, 13-14.—s 1 Cor 6, 9-11; Eph 2, 1-3; 5, 8; Col 3, 5-7; 1 Pt 4, 3.—t Ti 1, 3; 2, 10; Ps 24, 5; 1 Tm 1, 1; 2, 3; 4, 10; Jude 25.—u Dt 9, 5; Eph 2, 4-5.8-9; 2 Tm 1, 9.—v Ti 1, 4; 2, 13; Phil 3, 20; 2 Tm 1, 10; 2 Pt 1, 1.11; 2, 20; 3, 2.18.

2, 1-10: One of Titus' main tasks in Crete is to become acquainted with the character of the Cretans and thereby learn to cope with its deficiencies (see Ti 1, 12). The counsel is not only for Titus himself but for various classes of people with whom he must deal: older men and women (2-4), younger women and men (4-7), and slaves (9-10); cf Eph 6, 1-9; Col 3, 18—4, 1.

2, 11-15: Underlying the admonitions for moral improvement in Ti 2, 1-10 as the moving force is the constant appeal to God's revelation of salvation in Christ, with its demand for transformation of life.

2, 13: *The blessed hope, the appearance:* literally, "the blessed hope and appearance," but the use of a single article in Greek strongly suggests an epexegetical, i.e., explanatory sense. *Of the great God and of our savior Jesus Christ:* another possible translation is "of our great God and savior Jesus Christ."

3, 1-8: The list of Christian duties continues from Ti 2, 9-10, undergirded again as in Ti 2, 11-13 by appeal to what God in Christ has done (4-7; cf Ti 2, 11-14). The spiritual renewal of the Cretans, signified in God's merciful gift of baptism (4-7), should be reflected in their improved attitude toward civil authority and in their Christian relationship with all (1-3).

3, 1: *Magistrates and authorities:* some interpreters understand these terms as referring to the principalities and powers of the heavenly hierarchy. *To be open to every good enterprise:* this implies being good citizens. It could also be translated "ready to do every sort of good work" (as Christians); cf Ti 3, 14.

[7] so that we might be justified by his grace
and become heirs in hope of eternal life. [w]

[8] This saying is trustworthy.

Advice to Titus.* I want you to insist on these points, that those who have believed in God be careful to devote themselves to good works; these are excellent and benefi-

---

w Ti 1, 2; 2 Tm 1, 1; 1 Jn 2, 25.—x 1 Tm 1, 15; 3, 1; 4, 9; 2 Tm 2, 11.—y 1 Tm 1, 4; 4, 7; 2 Tm 2, 23.—z Mt 18, 15-18; Rom 16, 17; 1 Cor 5, 11; 2 Thes 3, 6.14-15.—a Acts 20, 4; Eph 6, 21; Col 4, 7; 2 Tm 4, 12.—b Acts 18, 24-26; 1 Cor 1, 12; 3, 4-6.22; 4, 6; 16, 12.—c Ti 2, 14; 3, 8; Heb 10, 24; 1 Pt 3, 13.—d Heb 13, 25.

3, 8-11: In matters of good conduct and religious doctrine, Titus is to stand firm.

3, 9: See the note on 1 Tm 6, 20-21.

3, 12-15: *Artemas* or *Tychicus* (2 Tm 4, 12) is to replace Titus, who will join Paul in his winter sojourn at Nicopolis in Epirus, on the western coast of Greece.

---

cial to others. [x] [9] Avoid foolish arguments, genealogies, rivalries, and quarrels about the law, [y] for they are useless and futile.* [10] After a first and second warning, break off contact with a heretic, [z] [11] realizing that such a person is perverted and sinful and stands self-condemned.

Directives, Greetings, and Blessing.* [12] When I send Artemas to you, or Tychicus, try to join me at Nicopolis, where I have decided to spend the winter. [a] [13] Send Zenas the lawyer and Apollos on their journey soon, and see to it that they have everything they need. [b] [14] But let our people, too, learn to devote themselves to good works to supply urgent needs, so that they may not be unproductive. [c]

[15] All who are with me send you greetings. Greet those who love us in the faith. Grace be with all of you. [d]

THE LETTER TO PHILEMON

INTRODUCTION

This short letter addressed to three specific individuals was written by Paul during an imprisonment, perhaps in Rome between A.D. 61 and 63 (see the Introduction to Colossians for other possible sites). It concerns Onesimus, a slave from Colossae (Col 4, 9), who had run away from his master, perhaps guilty of theft in the process (18). Onesimus was converted to Christ by Paul (10). Paul sends him back to his master (12) with this letter asking that he be welcomed willingly by his old master (8-10.14.17) not just as a slave but as a brother in Christ (16). Paul uses very strong arguments (especially 19) in his touching appeal on behalf of Onesimus. It is unlikely that Paul is subtly hinting that he would like to retain Onesimus as his own slave, lent to Paul by his master. Rather, he suggests he would like to have Onesimus work with him for the gospel (13.20-21). There is, however, little evidence connecting this Onesimus with a bishop of Ephesus of the same name mentioned by Ignatius of Antioch (ca. A.D. 110).

Paul's letter deals with an accepted institution of antiquity, human slavery. But Paul breathes into this letter the spirit of Christ and of equality within the Christian community. He does not attack slavery directly, for this is something the Christian communities of the first century were in no position to do, and the expectation that Christ would soon come again militated against social reforms. Yet Paul, by presenting Onesimus as "brother, beloved . . . to me, but even more so to you" (16), voiced an idea revolutionary in that day and destined to break down worldly barriers of division "in the Lord."

Address and Greeting. [1] Paul, a prisoner* for Christ Jesus, and Timothy our brother, to Philemon, our beloved and our co-worker, [a] [2] to Apphia our sister,* to Archippus our fellow soldier, and to the

---

a Phlm 9; Eph 3, 1; 4, 1; Phil 1, 7.13.

1: *Prisoner:* as often elsewhere (cf Rom, 1 Cor, Gal especially), the second word in Greek enunciates the theme and sets the tone of the letter. Here it is the prisoner appealing rather than the apostle commanding.

2: *Apphia our sister:* sister is here used (like brother) to indicate a fellow Christian. *The church at your house: your* here is singular. It more likely refers to Philemon than to the last one named, Archippus; Philemon is then the owner of the slave Onesimus (10). An alternate view is that the actual master of the slave is Archippus and that the one to whom the letter is addressed, Philemon, is the most prominent Christian there; see the note on Col 4, 17.

church at your house.[b] [3]Grace to you and peace* from God our Father and the Lord Jesus Christ.[c]

Thanksgiving. [4] [d] I give thanks to my God always, remembering you in my prayers,* [5]as I hear of the love and the faith you have in the Lord Jesus and for all the holy ones,* [6]so that your partnership in the faith may become effective in recognizing every good there is in us* that leads to Christ.[e]

Plea for Onesimus. [7]For I have experienced much joy and encouragement* from your love, because the hearts of the holy ones have been refreshed by you, brother.[f] [8]Therefore, although I have the full right* in Christ to order you to do what is proper, [9]I rather urge you out of love, being as I am, Paul, an old man,* and now also a prisoner for Christ Jesus.[g] [10]I urge you on behalf of my child Onesimus, whose father I have become in my imprisonment,[h] [11]who was once useless to you but is now useful* to [both] you and me. [12]I am sending him, that is, my own heart, back to you. [13]I should have liked to retain him for myself, so that he might serve* me on your behalf in my imprisonment for the gospel,[i] [14]but I did not want to do anything without your consent, so that the good you do might not be forced but voluntary.[j] [15]Perhaps this is why he was away from* you for a while, that you might have him back forever, [16]no longer as a slave but more than a slave, a brother, beloved especially to me, but even more so to you, as a man* and in the Lord.[k] [17]So if you regard me as a partner, welcome him as you would me. [18] * And if he has done you any injustice or owes you anything, charge it to me. [19]I, Paul, write this in my own hand: I will pay. May I not tell you that you owe me your very self.[l] [20]Yes, brother, may I profit from you in the Lord. Refresh my heart in Christ.

[21]With trust in your compliance I write to you, knowing that you will do even more than I say. [22]At the same time prepare a guest room for me, for I hope to be granted to you through your prayers.[m]

Final Greetings. [23]Epaphras,* my fellow prisoner in Christ Jesus, greets you,[n] [24]as well as Mark, Aristarchus, Demas, and Luke, my co-workers. [25]The grace of the Lord Jesus Christ be with your spirit.[o]

---

b Col 4, 17.—c Rom 1, 7; Gal 1, 3; Phil 1, 2.—d 4-5: Rom 1, 8-9; Eph 1, 15-16.—e Phil 1, 9; Col 1, 9.—f 2 Cor 7, 4.—g Phlm 1; Eph 3, 1; 4, 1; Phil 1, 7.13.—h 1 Cor 4, 14-15; Gal 4, 19; Col 4, 9.—i Phil 2, 30.—j 2 Cor 9, 7; 1 Pt 5, 2.—k 1 Tm 6, 2.—l Gal 6, 11; 2 Thes 3, 17.—m Heb 13, 19.—n Col 1, 7; 4, 12-13.—o Acts 12, 12.15; 13, 13; 15, 37-39; 19, 29; 20, 4; 27, 2; Col 4, 10.14; 2 Tm 4, 10-13.

3: *Grace . . . and peace:* for this greeting, which may be a combination of Greek and Aramaic epistolary formulae, see the note on Rom 1, 1-7.

4: *In my prayers:* literally, "at the time of my prayers."

5: *Holy ones:* a common term for members of the Christian community (so also 7).

6: *In us:* some good ancient manuscripts have *in you* (plural). *That leads to Christ: leads to* translates the Greek preposition *eis,* indicating direction or purpose.

7: *Encouragement:* the Greek word *paraklēsis* is cognate with the verb translated "urge" in vv 9.10, and serves as an introduction to Paul's plea. *Hearts:* literally, "bowels," expressing in Semitic fashion the seat of the emotions, one's "inmost self." The same Greek word is used in v 12 and again in v 20, where it forms a literary inclusion marking off the body of the letter.

8: *Full right:* often translated "boldness," the Greek word *parrēsia* connotes the full franchise of speech, as the right of a citizen to speak before the body politic, claimed by the Athenians as their privilege (Euripides).

9: *Old man:* some editors conjecture that Paul here used a similar Greek word meaning "ambassador" (cf Eph 6, 20). This conjecture heightens the contrast with "prisoner" but is totally without manuscript support.

11: *Useless . . . useful:* here Paul plays on the name Onesimus, which means "useful" or "beneficial." The verb translated "profit" in v 20 is cognate.

13: *Serve:* the Greek *diakoneō* could connote a ministry.

15: *Was away from:* literally, "was separated from," but the same verb means simply "left" in Acts 18, 1. It is a euphemism for his running away.

16: *As a man:* literally, "in the flesh." With this and the following phrase, Paul describes the natural and spiritual orders.

18-19: *Charge it to me . . . I will pay:* technical legal and commercial terms in account keeping and acknowledgment of indebtedness.

23-24: *Epaphras:* a Colossian who founded the church there (Col 1, 7) and perhaps also in Laodicea and Hierapolis (Col 2, 1; 4, 12-13). *Aristarchus:* a native of Thessalonica and fellow worker of Paul (Acts 19, 29; 20, 4; 27, 2). For Mark, Demas, and Luke, see 2 Tm 4, 9-13 and the note there.

THE LETTER TO THE HEBREWS

INTRODUCTION

As early as the second century, this treatise, which is of great rhetorical power and force in its admonition to faithful pilgrimage under Christ's leadership, bore the title "To the Hebrews." It was assumed to be directed to Jewish Christians. Usually Hebrews was attached in Greek manuscripts to the collection of letters by Paul. Although no author is mentioned (for there is no address), a reference to Timothy (13, 23) suggested connections to the circle of Paul and his assistants. Yet the exact audience, the author, and even whether Hebrews is a letter have long been disputed.

The author saw the addressees in danger of apostasy from their Christian faith. This danger was due not to any persecution from outsiders but to a weariness with the demands of Christian life and a growing indifference to their calling (2, 1; 4, 14; 6, 1-12; 10, 23-32). The author's main theme, the priesthood and sacrifice of Jesus (chs 3-10), is not developed for its own sake but as a means of restoring their lost fervor and strengthening them in their faith. Another important theme of the letter is that of the pilgrimage of the people of God to the heavenly Jerusalem (11, 10; 12, 1-3.18-29; 13, 14). This theme is intimately connected with that of Jesus' ministry in the heavenly sanctuary (9, 11—10, 22).

The author calls this work a "message of encouragement" (13, 22), a designation that is given to a synagogue sermon in Acts 13, 15. Hebrews is probably therefore a written homily, to which the author gave an epistolary ending (13, 22-25).

The author begins with a reminder of the preexistence, incarnation, and exaltation of Jesus (1, 3) that proclaimed him the climax of God's word to humanity (1, 1-3). He dwells upon the dignity of the person of Christ, superior to the angels (1, 4—2, 2). Christ is God's final word of salvation communicated (in association with accredited witnesses to his teaching: cf 2, 3-4) not merely by word but through his suffering in the humanity common to him and to all others (2, 5-16). This enactment of salvation went beyond the pattern known to Moses, faithful prophet of God's word though he was, for Jesus as high priest expiated sin and was faithful to God with the faithfulness of God's own Son (2, 17—3, 6).

Just as the infidelity of the people thwarted Moses' efforts to save them, so the infidelity of any Christian may thwart God's plan in Christ (3, 6—4, 13). Christians are to reflect that it is their humanity that Jesus took upon himself, with all its defects save sinfulness, and that he bore the burden of it until death out of obedience to God. God declared this work of his Son to be the cause of salvation for all (4, 14—5, 10). Although Christians recognize this fundamental teaching, they may grow weary of it and of its implications, and therefore require other reflections to stimulate their faith (5, 11—6, 20).

Therefore, the author presents to the readers for their reflection the everlasting priesthood of Christ (7, 1-28), a priesthood that fulfills the promise of the Old Testament (8, 1-13). It also provides the meaning God ultimately intended in the sacrifices of the Old Testament (9, 1-28): these pointed to the unique sacrifice of Christ, which alone obtains forgiveness of sins (10, 1-18). The trial of faith experienced by the readers should resolve itself through their consideration of Christ's ministry in the heavenly sanctuary and his perpetual intercession there on their behalf (7, 25; 8, 1-13). They should also be *strengthened by the assurance of his foreordained parousia, and by the fruits of faith that they have already enjoyed (10, 19-39).*

It is in the nature of faith to recognize the reality of what is not yet seen and is the object of hope, and the saints of the Old Testament give striking example of that faith (11, 1-40). The perseverance to which the author exhorts the readers is shown forth in the early life of Jesus. Despite the afflictions of his ministry and the supreme trial of his suffering and death, he remained confident of the triumph that God would bring him (12, 1-3). The difficulties of human life have meaning when they are accepted as God's discipline (12, 4-13), and if Christians persevere in fidelity to the word in which they have believed, they are assured of possessing forever the unshakable kingdom of God (12, 14-29).

The letter concludes with specific moral commandments (13, 1-17), in the course of which the author recalls again his central theme of the sacrifice of Jesus and the courage needed to associate oneself with it in faith (13, 9-16).

As early as the end of the second century, the church of Alexandria in Egypt accepted Hebrews as a letter of Paul, and that became the view commonly held in the East. Pauline authorship was contested in the West into the fourth century, but then accepted. In the six-teenth century, doubts about that position were again raised, and the modern consensus is that the letter was not written by Paul. There is, however, no widespread agreement on any of the other suggested authors, e.g., Barnabas, Apollos, or Prisc(ill)a and Aquila. The document itself has no statement about its author.

Among the reasons why Pauline authorship has been abandoned are the great differ-ence of vocabulary and style between Hebrews and Paul's letters, the alternation of doc-trinal teaching with moral exhortation, the different manner of citing the Old Testament, and the resemblance between the thought of Hebrews and that of Alexandrian Judaism. The Greek of the letter is in many ways the best in the New Testament.

Since the letter of Clement of Rome to the Corinthians, written about A.D. 96, most probably cites Hebrews, the upper limit for the date of composition is reasonably certain. While the letter's references in the present tense to the Old Testament sacrificial worship do not necessarily show that temple worship was still going on, many older commentators and a growing number of recent ones favor the view that it was and that the author wrote before the destruction of the temple of Jerusalem in A.D. 70. In that case, the argument of the letter is more easily explained as directed toward Jewish Christians rather than those of Gentile origin, and the persecutions they have suffered in the past (cf 10, 32-34) may have been connected with the disturbances that preceded the expulsion of the Jews from Rome in A.D. 49 under the emperor Claudius. These were probably caused by dis-putes between Jews who accepted Jesus as the Messiah and those who did not.

The principal divisions of the Letter to the Hebrews are the following:

  I.   Introduction (1, 1-4)
 II.   The Son Higher than the Angels (1, 5—2, 18)
III.   Jesus, Faithful and Compassionate High Priest (3, 1—5, 10)
 IV.   Jesus' Eternal Priesthood and Eternal Sacrifice (5, 11—10, 39)
  V.   Examples, Discipline, Disobedience (11, 1—12, 29)
 VI.   Final Exhortation, Blessing, Greetings (13, 1-25)

I. INTRODUCTION*

CHAPTER 1

[1] In times past, God spoke in partial and various ways to our ancestors through the prophets; [2] in these last days, he spoke to us through a son, whom he made heir of all things and through whom he created the universe, [a]

[3] who is the refulgence of his glory,
the very imprint of his being,
and who sustains all things by his mighty word.
When he had accomplished purification from sins,
he took his seat at the right hand of the Majesty on high, [b]
[4] as far superior to the angels
as the name he has inherited is more excellent than theirs. [c]

II. THE SON HIGHER THAN THE ANGELS

Messianic Enthronement.* [5] For to which of the angels did God ever say:

"You are my son; this day I have begotten you"? [d]

Or again:

"I will be a father to him, and he shall be a son to me"?

[6] And again, when he leads* the first-born into the world, he says:

"Let all the angels of God worship him." [e]

[7] Of the angels he says:

"He makes his angels winds
and his ministers a fiery flame"; [f]

[8] but of the Son:

"Your throne, O God,* stands forever and ever;
and a righteous scepter is the scepter of your kingdom. [g]
[9] You loved justice and hated wickedness;
therefore God, your God, anointed you
with the oil of gladness above your companions";
[10] and:
"At the beginning, O Lord, you established the earth, [h]
and the heavens are the works of your hands.
[11] They will perish, but you remain;
and they will all grow old like a garment.
[12] You will roll them up like a cloak,
and like a garment they will be changed.
But you are the same, and your years will have no end."

---

a Is 2, 2; Jer 23, 20; Ez 38, 16; Dn 10, 14 / Jn 3, 17; Rom 8, 3; Gal 4, 4 / Prv 8, 30; Wis 7, 22; Jn 1, 3; 1 Cor 8, 6; Col 1, 16.— b Wis 7, 26; 2 Cor 4, 4; Col 1, 15 / Heb 8, 1; 10, 12; 12, 2; Mk 16, 19; Acts 2, 33; 7, 55-56; Rom 8, 34; Eph 1, 20; Col 3, 1; 1 Pt 3, 22.—c Eph 1, 21; Phil 2, 9-11.—d Ps 2, 7 / 2 Sm 7, 14.—e Dt 32, 43 LXX; Ps 97, 7.—f Ps 104, 4 LXX.—g Ps 45, 7-8.—h 10-12: Ps 102, 26-28.

1, 1-4: The letter opens with an introduction consisting of a reflection on the climax of God's revelation to the human race in his Son. The divine communication was initiated and maintained during Old Testament times in fragmentary and varied ways through *the prophets* (1), including Abraham, Moses, and all through whom God spoke. But now *in these last days* (2), the final age, God's revelation of his saving purpose is achieved *through a son,* i.e., one who is Son, whose role is redeemer and mediator of creation. He was made *heir of all things* through his death and exaltation to glory, yet he existed before he appeared as man; through him God *created the universe.* Verses 3-4, which may be based upon a liturgical hymn, assimilate the Son to the personified Wisdom of the Old Testament as *refulgence of God's glory* and *imprint of his being* (3; cf Wis 7, 26). These same terms are used of the Logos in Philo. The author now turns from the cosmological role of the preexistent Son to the redemptive work of Jesus: he brought about purification from sins and has been exalted to the right hand of God (see Ps 110, 1). The once-humiliated and crucified Jesus has been declared God's Son, and

this name shows his superiority to the angels. The reason for the author's insistence on that superiority is, among other things, that in some Jewish traditions angels were mediators of the old covenant (see Acts 7, 53; Gal 3, 19). Finally, Jesus' superiority to the angels emphasizes the superiority of the new covenant to the old because of the heavenly priesthood of Jesus.

1, 5-14: Jesus' superiority to the angels is now demonstrated by a series of seven Old Testament texts. Some scholars see in the stages of Jesus' exaltation an order corresponding to that of enthronement ceremonies in the ancient Near East, especially in Egypt, namely, elevation to divine status (5-6); presentation to the angels and proclamation of everlasting lordship (7-12); enthronement and conferral of royal power (13). The citations from the Psalms in vv 5 and 13 were traditionally used of Jesus' messianic sonship (cf Acts 13, 33) through his resurrection and exaltation (cf Acts 2, 33-35); those in vv 8 and 10-12 are concerned with his divine kingship and his creative function. The central quotation in v 7 serves to contrast the angels with the Son. The author quotes it according to the Septuagint translation, which is quite different in meaning from that of the Hebrew ("You make the winds your messengers, and flaming fire your ministers"). The angels are only *sent to serve . . . those who are to inherit salvation* (14).

1, 6: *And again, when he leads:* the Greek could also be translated "And when he again leads" in reference to the parousia.

1, 8-12: *O God:* the application of the name "God" to the Son derives from the preexistence mentioned in vv 2-3; the psalmist had already used it of the Hebrew king in the court style of the original. See the note on Ps 45, 7. It is also important for the author's christology that in vv 10-12 an Old Testament passage addressed to God is redirected to Jesus.

Heb

13 But to which of the angels has he ever said:

"Sit at my right hand
until I make your enemies your footstool"?[i]

14 Are they not all ministering spirits sent to serve, for the sake of those who are to inherit salvation?[j]

CHAPTER 2

Exhortation to Faithfulness.* 1 Therefore, we must attend all the more to what we have heard, so that we may not be carried away. 2 For if the word announced through angels proved firm, and every transgression and disobedience received its just recompense,[k] 3 how shall we escape if we ignore so great a salvation? Announced originally through the Lord, it was confirmed for us by those who had heard.[l] 4 God added his testimony by signs, wonders, various acts of power, and distribution of the gifts of the holy Spirit according to his will.[m]

Exaltation through Abasement.* 5 For it was not to angels that he subjected the world to come, of which we are speaking. 6 Instead, someone has testified somewhere:

"What is man that you are mindful of him,
     or the son of man that you care for him?[n]

7 You made him for a little while lower than the angels;
     you crowned him with glory and honor,
8   subjecting all things under his feet."

In "subjecting" all things [to him], he left nothing not "subject to him." Yet at present we do not see "all things subject to him,"[o] 9 but we do see Jesus "crowned with glory and honor" because he suffered death, he who "for a little while" was made "lower than the angels," that by the grace of God he might taste death for everyone.[p]

10 For it was fitting that he, for whom and through whom all things exist, in bringing many children to glory, should make the leader to their salvation perfect through suffering.[q] 11 He who consecrates and those who are being consecrated all have one origin. Therefore, he is not ashamed to call them "brothers," 12 saying:

"I will proclaim your name to my brothers,
     in the midst of the assembly I will praise you";[r]

13 and again:

"I will put my trust in him";

and again:

"Behold, I and the children God has given me."[s]

14 Now since the children share in blood and flesh, he likewise shared in them, that through death he might destroy the one

i Ps 110, 1.—j Ps 91, 11; Dn 7, 10.—k Acts 7, 38.53; Gal 3, 19.—l Heb 10, 29; 12, 25.—m Mk 16, 20; Acts 14, 3; 19, 11.—n Ps 8, 5-7.—o Mt 28, 18; 1 Cor 15, 25-28; Eph 1, 20-23; Phil 3, 21; 1 Pt 3, 22.—p Phil 2, 6-11.—q Heb 12, 2; Is 53, 4 / Rom 11, 36; 1 Cor 8, 6.—r Ps 22, 23.—s Is 8, 17.18.

2, 1-4: The author now makes a transition into exhortation, using an a fortiori argument (as at Heb 7, 21-22; 9, 13-14; 10, 28-29; 12, 25). The *word announced through angels* (2), the Mosaic law, is contrasted with the more powerful word that Christians have received (3-4). Christ's supremacy strengthens Christians against being *carried away* from their faith.

2, 5-18: The humanity and the suffering of Jesus do not constitute a valid reason for relinquishing the Christian faith. Ps 8 (6-7) is also applied to Jesus in 1 Cor 15, 27; Eph 1, 22; and probably 1 Pt 3, 22. This christological interpretation, therefore, probably reflects a common early Christian tradition, which may have originated in the expression *the son of man* (6). The psalm contrasts God's greatness with man's relative insignificance but also stresses the superiority of man to the rest of creation, of which he is lord. Heb applies this christologically: Jesus lived a truly human existence, *lower than the angels*, in the days of his earthly life, particularly in his suffering and death; now, *crowned with glory and honor*, he is raised above all creation. The author considers all things as already *subject to him* because of his exaltation (8-9), though *we do not see* this yet. The reference to Jesus as

leader (10) sounds the first note of an important leitmotif in Heb: the journey of the people of God to the sabbath rest (Heb 4, 9), the heavenly sanctuary, following Jesus, their "forerunner" (Heb 6, 20). It was fitting that God should make him *perfect through suffering*, consecrated by obedient suffering. Because he is perfected as high priest, Jesus is then able to consecrate his people (11); access to God is made possible by each of these two consecrations. If Jesus is able to help human beings, it is because he has become one of us; we are his "brothers." The author then cites three Old Testament texts as proofs of this unity between ourselves and the Son. Psalm 22, 23 is interpreted so as to make Jesus the singer of this lament, which ends with joyful praise of the Lord in the assembly of "brothers." The other two texts are from Is 8, 17.18. The first of these seems intended to display in Jesus an example of the trust in God that his followers should emulate. The second curiously calls these followers "children"; probably this is to be understood to mean children of Adam, but the point is our solidarity with Jesus. By sharing human nature, including the ban of death, Jesus broke the power of the devil over death (14); the author shares the view of Hellenistic Judaism that death was not intended by God and that it had been introduced into the world by the devil. The *fear of death* (15) is a religious fear based on the false conception that death marks the end of a person's relations with God (cf Ps 115, 17-18; Is 38, 18). Jesus deliberately allied himself with *the descendants of Abraham* (16) in order to be *a merciful and faithful high priest*. This is the first appearance of the central theme of Heb, Jesus the great high priest expiating *the sins of the people* (17), as one who experienced the same tests as they (18).

who has the power of death, that is, the devil,[t] 15 and free those who through fear of death had been subject to slavery all their life. 16 Surely he did not help angels but rather the descendants of Abraham; 17 therefore, he had to become like his brothers in every way, that he might be a merciful and faithful high priest before God to expiate the sins of the people.[u] 18 Because he himself was tested through what he suffered, he is able to help those who are being tested.

III. JESUS, FAITHFUL AND COMPASSIONATE HIGH PRIEST

CHAPTER 3

Jesus, Superior to Moses.* 1 Therefore, holy "brothers," sharing in a heavenly calling, reflect on Jesus, the apostle and high priest of our confession, 2 who was faithful to the one who appointed him, just as Moses was "faithful in [all] his house."[v] 3 But he is worthy of more "glory" than Moses, as the founder of a house has more "honor" than the house itself.[w] 4 Every house is founded by someone, but the founder of all is God. 5 Moses was "faithful in all his house" as a "servant" to testify to what would be spoken, 6 [x] but Christ was faithful as a son placed over his house. We are his house, if [only] we hold fast to our confidence and pride in our hope.*

t Is 25, 8; Hos 13, 14; Jn 12, 31; Rom 6, 9; 1 Cor 15, 54-55; 2 Tm 1, 10; Rv 12, 10.—u Heb 4, 15; 5, 1-3.—v Nm 12, 7.—w 2 Cor 3, 7-8.—x Heb 10, 21; Eph 2, 19; 1 Tm 3, 15; 1 Pt 4, 17.—y 7-11 Ps 95, 7-11.—z Ex 17, 7; Nm 20, 2-5.—a Rom 8, 17.—b Ps 95, 7-8.—c 16-19: Nm 14, 1-38; Dt 1, 19-40.

3, 1-6: The author now takes up the two qualities of Jesus mentioned in Heb 2, 17, but in inverse order: faithfulness (Heb 3, 1—4, 13) and mercy (Heb 4, 14—5, 10). Christians are called *holy "brothers"* because of their common relation to him (Heb 2, 11), the *apostle*, a designation for Jesus used only here in the New Testament (cf Jn 13, 16; 17, 3), meaning one sent as God's final word to us (Heb 1, 2). He is compared with Moses probably because he is seen as mediator of the new covenant (Heb 9, 15) just as Moses was of the old (Heb 9, 19-22, including his sacrifice). But when the author of Heb speaks of Jesus' sacrifice, he does not consider Moses as the Old Testament antitype, but rather the high priest on the Day of Atonement (Heb 9, 6-15). Moses' faithfulness *"in [all] his house"* refers back to Nm 12, 7, on which this section is a midrashic commentary. In vv 3-6, the author does not indicate that he thinks of either Moses or Christ as the founder of the household. *His house* (2.5.6) means God's house, not that of Moses or Christ; in the case of Christ, compare v 6 with Heb 10, 21. The *house* of v 6 is the Christian community; the author suggests its continuity with Israel by speaking not of two houses but of only one. Verse 6 brings out the reason why Jesus is superior to Moses: the latter was the faithful *servant* laboring *in* the house founded by God, but Jesus is God's *son*, placed *over* the house.

3, 6: The majority of manuscripts add "firm to the end," but these words are not found in the three earliest and best witnesses and are probably an interpolation derived from v 14.

Israel's Infidelity a Warning. 7 * Therefore, as the holy Spirit says:

"Oh, that today you would hear his voice,[y]
8 'Harden not your hearts as at the rebellion
in the day of testing in the desert,
9 where your ancestors tested and tried me
and saw my works[z] 10 for forty years.
Because of this I was provoked with that generation
and I said, "They have always been of erring heart,
and they do not know my ways."
11 As I swore in my wrath,
"They shall not enter into my rest."'"

12 Take care, brothers, that none of you may have an evil and unfaithful heart, so as to forsake the living God. 13 Encourage yourselves daily while it is still "today," so that none of you may grow hardened by the deceit of sin. 14 We have become partners of Christ if only we hold the beginning of the reality firm until the end,[a] 15 for it is said:

"Oh, that today you would hear his voice:
'Harden not your hearts as at the rebellion.' "[b]

16 [c] Who were those who rebelled when they heard? Was it not all those who came

3, 7—4, 13: The author appeals for steadfastness of faith in Jesus, basing his warning on the experience of Israel during the Exodus. In the Old Testament the Exodus had been invoked as a symbol of the return of Israel from the Babylonian exile (Is 42, 9; 43, 16-21; 51, 9-11). In the New Testament the redemption was similarly understood as a new exodus, both in the experience of Jesus himself (Lk 9, 31) and in that of his followers (1 Cor 10, 1-4). The author cites Ps 95, 7-11, a salutary example of hardness of heart, as a warning against the danger of growing weary and giving up the journey. To call God *living* (12) means that he reveals himself in his works (cf Jos 3, 10; Jer 10, 10). The *rest* (11) into which Israel was to enter was only a foreshadowing of that rest to which Christians are called. They are to remember the example of Israel's revolt in the desert that cost a whole generation the loss of the promised land (15-19; cf Nm 14, 20-29). In Heb 4, 1-11, the symbol of *rest* is seen in deeper dimension: because the promise to the ancient Hebrews foreshadowed that given to Christians, it is *good news;* and because the promised land was the place of rest that God provided for his people, it was a share in his own rest, which he enjoyed after he had finished his creative work (3-4; cf Gn 2, 2). The author attempts to read this meaning of God's rest into Ps 95, 7-11 (6-9). The Greek form of the name of Joshua, who led Israel into the promised land, is Jesus (8). The author plays upon the name but stresses the superiority of Jesus, who leads his followers into heavenly rest. Verses 12 and 13 are meant as a continuation of the warning, for the word of God brings judgment as well as salvation. Some would capitalize *the word of God* and see it as a personal title of Jesus, comparable to that of Jn 1, 1-18.

Heb

out of Egypt under Moses? [17] With whom was he "provoked for forty years"? Was it not those who had sinned, whose corpses fell in the desert?[d] [18] And to whom did he "swear that they should not enter into his rest," if not to those who were disobedient?[e] [19] And we see that they could not enter for lack of faith.

CHAPTER 4

The Sabbath Rest. [1] Therefore, let us be on our guard while the promise of entering into his rest remains, that none of you seem to have failed. [2] For in fact we have received the good news just as they did. But the word that they heard did not profit them, for they were not united in faith with those who listened. [3] For we who believed enter into [that] rest, just as he has said:[f]

"As I swore in my wrath,
 'They shall not enter into my rest,' "
and yet his works were accomplished at the foundation of the world. [4] For he has spoken somewhere about the seventh day in this manner, "And God rested on the seventh day from all his works";[g] [5] and again, in the previously mentioned place, "They shall not enter into my rest."[h] [6] Therefore, since it remains that some will enter into it, and those who formerly received the good news did not enter because of disobedience, [7] he once more set a day, "today," when long afterwards he spoke through David, as already quoted:[i]

"Oh, that today you would hear his voice:
 'Harden not your hearts.' "

[8] Now if Joshua had given them rest, he would not have spoken afterwards of another day.[j] [9] Therefore, a sabbath rest still remains for the people of God. [10] And whoever enters into God's rest, rests from his own works as God did from his. [11] Therefore, let us strive to enter into that rest, so that no one may fall after the same example of disobedience.

[12] Indeed, the word of God is living and effective, sharper than any two-edged sword, penetrating even between soul and spirit, joints and marrow, and able to discern reflections and thoughts of the heart.[k] [13] No creature is concealed from him, but everything is naked and exposed to the eyes of him to whom we must render an account.[l]

Jesus, Compassionate High Priest. [14] * Therefore, since we have a great high priest who has passed through the heavens, Jesus, the Son of God, let us hold fast to our confession.[m] [15] For we do not have a high priest who is unable to sympathize with our weaknesses, but one who has similarly been tested in every way, yet without sin.[n] [16] So let us confidently approach the throne of grace to receive mercy and to find grace for timely help.[o]

CHAPTER 5

[1] * Every high priest is taken from among men and made their representative before God, to offer gifts and sacrifices for sins.* [2] He is able to deal patiently* with the ignorant and erring, for he himself is beset by weakness [3] and so, for this reason, must make sin offerings for himself as well as for the people.[p] [4] No one takes this honor

---

d Nm 14, 29.—e Nm 14, 22-23; Dt 1, 35.—f Heb 3, 11; Ps 95, 11.—g Gn 2, 2.—h Ps 95, 11.—i Heb 3, 7-8.15; Ps 95, 7-8.—j Dt 31, 7; Jos 22, 4.—k Wis 18, 15-16; Is 49, 2; Eph 6, 17; Rv 1, 16; 2, 12.—l Jb 34, 21-22; Pss 90, 8; 139, 2-4.—m Heb 9, 11.24.—n Heb 2, 17-18; 5, 2.—o Heb 8, 1; 10, 19.22.35; 12, 2; Eph 3, 12.—p Lv 9, 7; 16, 15-17.30.34.

4, 14-16: These verses, which return to the theme first sounded in Heb 2, 16—3, 1, serve as an introduction to the section that follows. The author here alone calls Jesus *a great high priest* (14), a designation used by Philo for the Logos; perhaps he does so in order to emphasize Jesus' superiority over the Jewish high priest. He *has been tested in every way, yet without sin* (15); this indicates an acquaintance with the tradition of Jesus' temptations, not only at the beginning (as in Mk 1, 13) but throughout his public life (cf Lk 22, 28). Although the reign of the exalted Jesus is a theme that occurs elsewhere in Heb, and Jesus' throne is mentioned in Heb 1, 8, *the throne of grace* (16) refers to the throne of God. The similarity of v 16 to Heb 10, 19-22 indicates that the author is thinking of our confident access to God, made possible by the priestly work of Jesus.

5, 1-10: The true humanity of Jesus (see the note on Heb 2, 5-18) makes him a more rather than a less effective high priest to the Christian community. In Old Testament tradition, the high priest was identified with the people, guilty of personal sin just as they were (1-3). Even so, the office was of divine appointment (4), as was also the case with the sinless Christ (5). For v 6, see the note on Ps 110, 4. Although Jesus was Son of God, he was destined as a human being to learn obedience by accepting the suffering he had to endure (8). Because of his perfection through this experience of human suffering, he is the cause of salvation for all (9), a *high priest according to the order of Melchizedek* (10; cf Heb 5, 6 and Heb 7, 3).

5, 1: *To offer gifts and sacrifices for sins:* the author is thinking principally of the Day of Atonement rite, as is clear from Heb 9, 7. This ritual was celebrated to atone for "all the sins of the Israelites" (Lv 16, 34).

5, 2: *Deal patiently:* the Greek word *metriopathein* occurs only here in the Bible; this term was used by the Stoics to designate the golden mean between excess and defect of passion. Here it means rather the ability to sympathize.

upon himself but only when called by God, just as Aaron was.[q] [5]In the same way, it was not Christ who glorified himself in becoming high priest, but rather the one who said to him:

> "You are my son;
> this day I have begotten you";[r]

[6]just as he says in another place:*

> "You are a priest forever
> according to the order of Melchizedek."[s]

[7]In the days when he was in the flesh, he offered prayers and supplications with loud cries and tears to the one who was able to save him from death,* and he was heard because of his reverence.[t] [8]Son though he was,* he learned obedience from what he suffered;[u] [9]and when he was made perfect, he became the source of eternal salvation for all who obey him,[v] [10]declared by God high priest according to the order of Melchizedek.[w]

IV. JESUS' ETERNAL PRIESTHOOD AND ETERNAL SACRIFICE

Exhortation to Spiritual Renewal. [11] * About this we have much to say, and it is difficult to explain, for you have become sluggish in hearing. [12]Although you should be teachers by this time, you need to have someone teach you again the basic elements of the utterances of God. You need milk, [and] not solid food.[x] [13]Everyone who lives on milk lacks experience of the word of righteousness, for he is a child. [14]But solid food is for the mature, for those whose faculties are trained by practice to discern good and evil.

CHAPTER 6

[1]Therefore, let us leave behind the basic teaching about Christ and advance to maturity, without laying the foundation all over again: repentance from dead works and faith in God,[y] [2]instruction about baptisms* and laying on of hands, resurrection of the dead and eternal judgment.[z] [3]And we shall do this, if only God permits. [4]For it is impossible in the case of those who have once been enlightened and tasted the heavenly gift* and shared in the holy Spirit[a] [5]and tasted the good word of God and the powers of the age to come,* [6]and then have fallen away, to bring them to repentance again, since they are recrucifying the Son of God for themselves* and holding him up to contempt.[b] [7]Ground that has absorbed the rain falling upon it repeatedly and brings forth crops useful to those for whom it is cultivated receives a blessing from God.[c] [8]But if it produces thorns and thistles, it is rejected; it will soon be cursed and finally burned.[d]

---

q Ex 28, 1.—r Ps 2, 7.—s Ps 110, 4.—t Mt 26, 38-44; Mk 14, 34-40; Lk 22, 41-46; Jn 12, 27.—u Rom 5, 19; Phil 2, 8.—v Heb 7, 24-25.28.—w Heb 6, 20; Ps 110, 4.—x 1 Cor 3, 1-3.—y Heb 9, 14.—z Heb 9, 10; Mk 7, 4 / Acts 6, 6; 8, 17; 13, 3; 19, 6; 1 Tm 4, 14; 5, 22; 2 Tm 1, 6.—a Heb 10, 26.32; Ps 34, 6; 2 Cor 4, 6.—b 2 Pt 2, 21.—c Gn 1, 11-12; Dt 11, 11.—d Gn 3, 17-18; Mt 7, 16; 13, 7; Mk 4, 7; Lk 8, 7.

5, 6-8: The author of Heb is the only New Testament writer to cite v 4 of Ps 110, here and in Heb 7, 17.21, to show that Jesus has been called by God to his role as priest. Verses 7-8 deal with his ability to sympathize with sinners, because of his own experience of the trials and weakness of human nature, especially fear of death. In his present exalted state, weakness is foreign to him, but he understands what we suffer because of his previous earthly experience.

5, 7: *He offered prayers . . . to the one who was able to save him from death:* at Gethsemane (cf Mk 14, 35), though some see a broader reference (see the note on Jn 12, 27).

5, 8: *Son though he was:* two different though not incompatible views of Jesus' sonship coexist in Heb, one associating it with his exaltation, the other with his preexistence. The former view is the older one (cf Rom 1, 4).

5, 11—6, 20: The central section of Heb (5, 11—10, 39) opens with a reprimand and an appeal. Those to whom the author directs his teaching about Jesus' priesthood, which is *difficult to explain,* have become *sluggish in hearing* and forgetful of even *the basic elements* (Heb 5, 12). But rather than treating of basic teachings, the author apparently believes that the challenge of more advanced ones may shake them out of their inertia (*therefore,* Heb 6, 1). The six examples of *basic teaching* in Heb 6, 1-3 are probably derived from a traditional catechetical list. No effort is made to address apostates, for their very hostility to the Christian message cuts them off completely from Christ (Heb 6, 4-8). This harsh statement seems to rule out repentance after apostasy, but perhaps the author deliberately uses hyperbole in order to stress the seriousness of abandoning Christ. With Heb 6, 9 a milder tone is introduced, and the criticism of the community (Heb 6, 1-3.9) is now balanced by an expression of confidence that its members are living truly Christian lives, and that God will justly reward their efforts (10). The author is concerned especially about their persevering (11-12), citing in this regard the achievement of Abraham, who relied on God's promise and on God's oath (13-18; cf Gn 22, 16), and proposes to them as a firm anchor of Christian hope the high priesthood of Christ, who is now living with God (19-20).

6, 2: *Instruction about baptisms:* not simply about Christian baptism but about the difference between it and similar Jewish rites, such as proselyte baptism, John's baptism, and the washings of the Qumran sectaries. *Laying on of hands:* in Acts 8, 17; 19, 6 this rite effects the infusion of the holy Spirit; in Acts 6, 6; 13, 3; 1 Tm 4, 14; 5, 22; 2 Tm 1, 6 it is a means of conferring some ministry or mission in the early Christian community.

6, 4: *Enlightened and tasted the heavenly gift:* this may refer to baptism and the Eucharist, respectively, but more probably means the neophytes' enlightenment by faith and their experience of salvation.

6, 5: *Tasted the good word of God and the powers of the age to come:* the proclamation of the *word of God* was accompanied by signs of the Spirit's power (1 Thes 1, 5; 1 Cor 2, 4).

6, 6: *They are recrucifying the Son of God for themselves:* a colorful description of the malice of apostasy, which is portrayed as again crucifying and deriding the Son of God.

Heb

[9] But we are sure in your regard, beloved, of better things related to salvation, even though we speak in this way. [10] For God is not unjust so as to overlook your work and the love you have demonstrated for his name by having served and continuing to serve the holy ones. [11] We earnestly desire each of you to demonstrate the same eagerness for the fulfillment of hope until the end,[e] [12] so that you may not become sluggish, but imitators of those who, through faith and patience,[f] are inheriting the promises.*

God's Promise Immutable. [13] [g] When God made the promise to Abraham, since he had no one greater by whom to swear, "he swore by himself,"* [14] and said, "I will indeed bless you and multiply" you.[h] [15] And so, after patient waiting,[i] he obtained the promise.* [16] Human beings swear by someone greater than themselves; for them an oath serves as a guarantee and puts an end to all argument. [17] So when God wanted to give the heirs of his promise an even clearer demonstration of the immutability of his purpose, he intervened with an oath,[j] [18] so that by two immutable things,* in which it was impossible for God to lie, we who have taken refuge might be strongly encouraged to hold fast to the hope that lies before us.[k] [19] This we have as

an anchor of the soul,[l] sure and firm, which reaches into the interior behind the veil,* [20] where Jesus has entered on our behalf as forerunner, becoming high priest forever according to the order of Melchizedek.[m]

CHAPTER 7

Melchizedek, a Type of Christ. [1] * This "Melchizedek, king of Salem and priest of God Most High,"* "met Abraham as he returned from his defeat of the kings" and "blessed him."[n] [2] And Abraham apportioned to him "a tenth of everything." His name first means righteous king, and he was also "king of Salem," that is, king of peace.* [3] Without father, mother, or ancestry, without beginning of days or end of life,* thus made to resemble the Son of God, he remains a priest forever.[o]

[4] * See how great he is to whom the patriarch "Abraham [indeed] gave a tenth" of his spoils.[p] [5] The descendants of Levi who receive the office of priesthood have a commandment according to the law to exact tithes from the people, that is, from their brothers, although they also have come from the loins of Abraham.[q] [6] But he who was not of their ancestry received tithes from Abraham and blessed him who had received the promises. [7] Unquestionably, a lesser person is blessed by a greater.* [8] In

e Heb 3, 14.—f Heb 5, 11; Gal 3, 14; Eph 1, 13-14.—g Gn 22, 16.—h Gn 22, 17.—i Heb 6, 12; Rom 4, 20.—j Heb 6, 12.—k Nm 23, 19; 1 Sm 15, 29; Jn 8, 17; 2 Tm 2, 13.—l Heb 10, 20; Ex 26, 31-33; Lv 16, 2.—m Heb 5, 10; Ps 110, 4.—n Gn 14, 17-20.—o Heb 4, 14; 6, 6; 10, 29.—p Gn 14, 20.—q Nm 18, 21 / Gn 35, 11.

6, 12: *Imitators of those . . . inheriting the promises:* the author urges the addressees to imitate the faith of the holy people of the Old Testament, who now possess the promised goods of which they lived in hope. This theme will be treated fully in ch 11.

6, 13: *He swore by himself:* God's promise to Abraham, which he confirmed by an oath ("I swear by myself," Gn 22, 16), was the basis for the hope of all Abraham's descendants.

6, 15: *He obtained the promise:* this probably refers not to Abraham's temporary possession of the land but to the eschatological blessings that Abraham and the other patriarchs have now come to possess.

6, 18: *Two immutable things:* the promise and the oath, both made by God.

6, 19: *Anchor . . . into the interior behind the veil:* a mixed metaphor. The Holy of Holies, beyond the veil that separates it from the Holy Place (Ex 26, 31-33), is seen as the earthly counterpart of the heavenly abode of God. This theme will be developed in ch 9.

7, 1-3: Recalling the meeting between Melchizedek and Abraham described in Gn 14, 17-20, the author enhances the significance of this priest by providing the popular etymological meaning of his name and that of the city over which he ruled (2). Since Genesis gives no information on the parentage or the death of Melchizedek, he is seen here as a type of Christ, representing a priesthood that is unique and eternal (3).

7, 1: The author here assumes that Melchizedek was a priest of the God of Israel (cf Gn 14, 22 and the note there).

7, 2: In Gn 14, the Hebrew text does not state explicitly who gave tithes to whom. The author of Heb supplies Abraham as the subject, according to a contemporary interpretation of the passage. This supports the argument of the midrash and makes it possible to see in Melchizedek a type of Jesus. The messianic blessings of righteousness and peace are foreshadowed in the names "Melchizedek" and "Salem."

7, 3: *Without father, mother, or ancestry, without beginning of days or end of life:* this is perhaps a quotation from a hymn about Melchizedek. The rabbis maintained that anything not mentioned in the Torah does not exist. Consequently, since the Old Testament nowhere mentions Melchizedek's ancestry, birth, or death, the conclusion can be drawn that he *remains . . . forever.*

7, 4-10: The tithe that Abraham gave to Melchizedek (4), a practice later followed by the levitical priesthood (5), was a gift (6) acknowledging a certain superiority in Melchizedek, the foreign priest (7). This is further indicated by the fact that the institution of the levitical priesthood was sustained by hereditary succession in the tribe of Levi, whereas the absence of any mention of Melchizedek's death in Gn implies that his personal priesthood is permanent (8). The levitical priesthood itself, through Abraham, its ancestor, paid tithes to Melchizedek, thus acknowledging the superiority of his priesthood over its own (9-10).

7, 7: *A lesser person is blessed by a greater:* though this sounds like a principle, there are some examples in the Old Testament that do not support it (cf 2 Sm 14, 22; Jb 31, 20). The author may intend it as a statement of a liturgical rule.

the one case, mortal men receive tithes; in the other, a man of whom it is testified that he lives on. [9] One might even say that Levi* himself, who receives tithes, was tithed through Abraham, [10] for he was still in his father's loins when Melchizedek met him.

[11] * If, then, perfection came through the levitical priesthood, on the basis of which the people received the law, what need would there still have been for another priest to arise according to the order of Melchizedek, and not reckoned according to the order of Aaron?[r] [12] When there is a change of priesthood, there is necessarily a change of law as well. [13] Now he of whom these things are said* belonged to a different tribe, of which no member ever officiated at the altar. [14] It is clear that our Lord arose from Judah,* and in regard to that tribe Moses said nothing about priests.[s] [15] * It is even more obvious if another priest is raised up after the likeness of Melchizedek, [16] who has become so, not by a law expressed in a commandment concerning physical descent but by the power of a life that cannot be destroyed.* [17] For it is testified:

> "You are a priest forever
>   according to the order of Melchizedek."[t]

r Heb 5, 6; Ps 110, 4.—s Gn 49, 10; Is 11, 1; Mt 1, 1-2.16.20; 2, 6; Lk 1, 27; 2, 4; Rom 1, 3; Rv 5, 5.—t Heb 5, 6; Ps 110, 4.—u Heb 10, 1.—v Ps 110, 4.—w Heb 8, 6-10; 9, 15-20; 10, 29; 12, 24; 13, 20.—x Heb 5, 6; 13, 8.—y Rom 8, 34; 1 Jn 2, 1; Rv 1, 18.—z Heb 4, 14.15.

7, 9: *Levi:* for the author this name designates not only the son of Jacob mentioned in Genesis but the priestly tribe that was thought to be descended from him.

7, 11-14: The levitical priesthood was not typified by the priesthood of Melchizedek, for Ps 110, 4 speaks of a priesthood of a new order, the order of Melchizedek, to arise in messianic times (11). Since the levitical priesthood served the Mosaic law, a new priesthood (12) would not come into being without a change in the law itself. Thus Jesus was not associated with the Old Testament priesthood, for he was a descendant of the tribe of Judah, which had never exercised the priesthood (13-14).

7, 13: *He of whom these things are said:* Jesus, the priest "according to the order of Melchizedek." According to the author's interpretation, Ps 110 spoke prophetically of Jesus.

7, 14: *Judah:* the author accepts the early Christian tradition that Jesus was descended from the family of David (cf Mt 1, 1-2.16.20; Lk 1, 27; 2, 4; Rom 1, 3). The Qumran community expected two Messiahs, one descended from Aaron and one from David; Heb shows no awareness of this view or at least does not accept it. Our author's view is not attested in contemporaneous Judaism.

7, 15-19: Jesus does not exercise a priesthood through family lineage but through his immortal existence (15-16), fulfilling Ps 110, 4 (17; cf Heb 7, 3). Thus he abolishes forever both the levitical priesthood and the law it serves, because neither could effectively sanctify people (18) by leading them into direct communication with God (19).

[18] On the one hand, a former commandment is annulled because of its weakness and uselessness,[u] [19] for the law brought nothing to perfection; on the other hand, a better hope* is introduced, through which we draw near to God. [20] * And to the degree that this happened not without the taking of an oath*—for others became priests without an oath, [21] but he with an oath, through the one who said to him:

> "The Lord has sworn, and he will not repent:[v]
>   'You are a priest forever' "—

[22] [w] to that same degree has Jesus [also] become the guarantee of an [even] better covenant.* [23] Those priests were many because they were prevented by death from remaining in office, [24] but he, because he remains forever, has a priesthood that does not pass away.[x] [25] Therefore, he is always able to save those who approach God through him, since he lives forever to make intercession* for them.[y]

[26] [z] It was fitting that we should have such a high priest:* holy, innocent, undefiled, separated from sinners, higher than the heavens.* [27] He has no need, as did the

7, 16: *A life that cannot be destroyed:* the life to which Jesus has attained by virtue of his resurrection; it is his exaltation rather than his divine nature that makes him priest. The Old Testament speaks of the Aaronic priesthood as eternal (see Ex 40, 15); our author does not explicitly consider this possible objection to his argument but implicitly refutes it in vv 23-24.

7, 19: *A better hope:* this hope depends upon the sacrifice of the Son of God; through it we "approach the throne of grace" (Heb 4, 16); cf Heb 6, 19.20.

7, 20-25: As was the case with the promise to Abraham (Heb 6, 13), though not with the levitical priesthood, the eternal priesthood of the order of Melchizedek was confirmed by God's oath (20-21); cf Ps 110, 4. Thus Jesus becomes the guarantee of a permanent covenant (22) that does not require a succession of priests as did the levitical priesthood (23) because his high priesthood is eternal and unchangeable (24). Consequently, Jesus is able to save all who draw near to God through him since he is their ever-living intercessor (25).

7, 20: *An oath:* God's oath in Ps 110, 4.

7, 22: *An [even] better covenant:* better than the Mosaic covenant because it will be eternal, like the priesthood of Jesus upon which it is based. Verse 12 argued that a change of priesthood involves a change of law; since "law" and "covenant" are used correlatively, a new covenant is likewise instituted.

7, 25: *To make intercession:* the intercession of the exalted Jesus, not the sequel to his completed sacrifice but its eternal presence in heaven; cf Rom 8, 34.

7, 26-28: Jesus is precisely the high priest whom the human race requires, holy and sinless, installed far above humanity (26); one having no need to offer sacrifice daily for sins but making a single offering of himself (27) once for all. The law could only appoint high priests with human limitations, but the fulfillment of God's oath regarding the priesthood of Melchizedek (Ps 110, 4) makes the Son of God the perfect priest forever (28).

7, 26: This verse with its list of attributes is reminiscent of v 3 and is perhaps a hymnic counterpart to it, contrasting the exalted Jesus with Melchizedek.

Heb

high priests, to offer sacrifice day after day,*a* first for his own sins and then for those of the people; he did that once for all when he offered himself.* 28 For the law appoints men subject to weakness to be high priests, but the word of the oath, which was taken after the law, appoints a son, who has been made perfect forever.*b*

CHAPTER 8

Heavenly Priesthood of Jesus.* 1 The main point of what has been said is this: we have such a high priest, who has taken his seat at the right hand of the throne of the Majesty in heaven,*c* 2 a minister of the sanctuary* and of the true tabernacle that the Lord, not man, set up.*d* 3 Now every high priest is appointed to offer gifts and sacrifices; thus the necessity for this one also to have something to offer.*e* 4 If then he were on earth, he would not be a priest, since there are those who offer gifts according to the law.*f* 5 They worship in a copy and shadow of the heavenly sanctuary, as Moses was warned when he was about to erect the tabernacle. For he says, "See that you make everything according to the pattern shown you on the mountain."*g* 6 Now he has obtained so much more excellent a ministry as he is mediator of a better covenant, enacted on better promises.*h*

Old and New Covenants.* 7 For if that first covenant had been faultless, no place would have been sought for a second one.

8 But he finds fault with them and says:*
"Behold, the days are coming, says the Lord,*i*
when I will conclude a new covenant with the house of Israel and the house of Judah.
9 It will not be like the covenant I made with their fathers
the day I took them by the hand to lead them forth from the land of Egypt;
for they did not stand by my covenant and I ignored them, says the Lord.
10 But this is the covenant I will establish with the house of Israel
after those days, says the Lord:
I will put my laws in their minds and I will write them upon their hearts.
I will be their God,
and they shall be my people.*j*
11 And they shall not teach, each one his fellow citizen
and kinsman, saying, 'Know the Lord,'
for all shall know me,
from least to greatest.
12 For I will forgive their evildoing and remember their sins no more."

13 *k* When he speaks of a "new" covenant, he declares the first one obsolete. And what has become obsolete and has grown old is close to disappearing.*

---

a Heb 5, 3; 9, 12.25-28; 10, 11-14; Ex 29, 38-39; Lv 16, 6.11.15-17; Nm 28, 3-4; Is 53, 10; Rom 6, 10.—b Heb 5, 1.2.9.—c Heb 1, 3; 4, 14; 7, 26-28.—d Heb 9, 11; Ex 33, 7; Nm 24, 6 LXX.—e Heb 5, 1.—f Heb 7, 13.—g Heb 9, 23; Ex 25, 40; Acts 7, 44; Col 2, 17.—h Heb 7, 22; 9, 15.—i Jer 31, 31-34.—j Heb 10, 16-17.—k Rom 10, 4.

7, 27: Such daily sacrifice is nowhere mentioned in the Mosaic law; only on the Day of Atonement is it prescribed that the high priest must *offer sacrifice . . . for his own sins and then for those of the people* (Lv 16, 11-19). *Once for all:* this translates the Greek words *ephapax/hapax* that occur eleven times in Heb.

8, 1-6: The Christian community has in Jesus the kind of high priest described in Heb 7, 26-28. In virtue of his ascension Jesus has taken his place at God's right hand in accordance with Ps 110, 1 (1), where he presides over the heavenly sanctuary established by God himself (2). Like every high priest, he has his offering to make (3; cf Heb 9, 12.14), but it differs from that of the levitical priesthood in which he had no share (4) and which was in any case but a shadowy reflection of the true offering in the heavenly sanctuary (5). But Jesus' ministry in the heavenly sanctuary is that of mediator of a superior covenant that accomplishes what it signifies (6).

8, 2: *The sanctuary:* the Greek term could also mean "holy things" but bears the meaning "sanctuary" elsewhere in Heb (Heb 9, 8.12.24.25; 10, 19; 13, 11). *The true tabernacle:* the heavenly tabernacle *that the Lord . . . set up* is contrasted with the earthly tabernacle that Moses set up in the desert. *True* means "real" in contradistinction to a mere "copy and shadow" (5); compare the Johannine usage (e.g., Jn 1, 9; 6, 32; 15, 1). The idea that the earthly sanctuary is a reflection of a heavenly model may be based upon Ex 25, 9, but probably also derives from the Platonic concept of a real world of which our observable world is merely a shadow.

8, 7-13: Since the first covenant was deficient in accomplishing what it signified, it had to be replaced (7), as Jeremiah (Jer 31, 31-34) had prophesied (8-12). Even in the time of Jeremiah, the first covenant was antiquated (13). In Heb 7, 22-24, the superiority of the new covenant was seen in the permanence of its priesthood; here the superiority is based on better promises, made explicit in the citation of Jer 31 (LXX: 38), 31-34, namely, in the immediacy of the people's knowledge of God (11) and in the forgiveness of sin (12).

8, 8-12: In citing Jer the author follows the Septuagint; some apparent departures from it may be the result of a different Septuagintal text rather than changes deliberately introduced.

8, 13: *Close to disappearing:* from the prophet's perspective, not that of the author of Heb.

CHAPTER 9

The Worship of the First Covenant.* [1]Now [even] the first covenant had regulations for worship and an earthly sanctuary. [2]For a tabernacle was constructed, the outer one,* in which were the lampstand, the table, and the bread of offering; this is called the Holy Place.[l] [3]Behind the second veil* was the tabernacle called the Holy of Holies,[m] [4]in which were the gold altar of incense* and the ark of the covenant entirely covered with gold. In it were the gold jar containing the manna, the staff of Aaron that had sprouted, and the tablets of the covenant.[n] [5]Above it were the cherubim of glory overshadowing the place of expiation.* Now is not the time to speak of these in detail.[o]

[6]With these arrangements for worship, the priests, in performing their service,* go into the outer tabernacle repeatedly,[p] [7]but the high priest alone goes into the inner one once a year, not without blood* that he offers for himself and for the sins of the people.[q] [8]In this way the holy Spirit shows that the way into the sanctuary had not yet been revealed while the outer tabernacle still had its place. [9]This is a symbol of the present time,* in which gifts and sacrifices are offered that cannot perfect the worshiper in conscience [10]but only in matters of food and drink and various ritual washings: regulations concerning the flesh, imposed until the time of the new order.[r]

Sacrifice of Jesus. [11] * But when Christ came as high priest of the good things that have come to be,* passing through the greater and more perfect tabernacle not made by hands, that is, not belonging to this creation,[s] [12]he entered once for all into the sanctuary, not with the blood of goats and calves but with his own blood, thus obtaining eternal redemption.[t] [13]For if the blood of goats and bulls and the sprinkling of a heifer's ashes* can sanctify those who are defiled so that their flesh is cleansed,[u] [14]how much more will the blood of Christ, who through the eternal spirit* offered himself unblemished to God, cleanse our consciences from dead works to worship the living God.[v]

---

l Ex 25, 23-30.—m Ex 26, 31-34.—n Ex 16, 32-34; 25, 10.16.21; 30, 1-10; Lv 16, 12-13; Nm 17, 2-7.16-26.—o Ex 25, 16-22; 26, 34; Lv 16, 14-15.—p Ex 27, 21; 30, 7; Lv 24, 8.—q Ex 30, 10; Lv 16, 1-14.—r Heb 13, 9; Lv 11; 14, 8; Nm 19, 11-21; Col 2, 16.—s Heb 4, 14; 10, 1.20.—t Heb 7, 27; Mt 26, 28.—u Heb 10, 4; Lv 16, 6-16; Nm, 19, 9.14-21.—v Heb 10, 10; Rom 5, 9; 1 Tm 3, 9; Ti 2, 14; 1 Pt 1, 18-19; 1 Jn 1, 7; Rv 1, 5.

9, 1-10: The regulations for worship under the old covenant permitted all the priests to enter the Holy Place (Heb 2, 6), but only the high priest to enter the Holy of Holies and then only once a year (3-5.7). The description of the sanctuary and its furnishings is taken essentially from Ex 25—26. This exclusion of the people from the Holy of Holies signified that they were not allowed to stand in God's presence (8) because their offerings and sacrifices, which were merely symbols of their need of spiritual renewal (10), could not obtain forgiveness of sins (9).

9, 2: *The outer one:* the author speaks of *the outer tabernacle* (6) and *the inner one* (7) rather than of one Mosaic tabernacle divided into two parts or sections.

9, 3: *The second veil:* what is meant is the veil that divided the Holy Place from the Holy of Holies. It is here called *the second,* because there was another veil at the entrance to the Holy Place, or "outer tabernacle" (Ex 26, 36).

9, 4: *The gold altar of incense:* Ex 30, 6 locates this altar in the Holy Place, i.e., the first tabernacle, rather than in the Holy of Holies. Neither is there any Old Testament support for the assertion that the jar of manna and the staff of Aaron were in the ark of the covenant. For the tablets of the covenant, see Ex 25, 16.

9, 5: *The place of expiation:* the gold "mercy seat" (Greek *hilastērion,* as in Rom 3, 25), where the blood of the sacrificial animals was sprinkled on the Day of Atonement (Lv 16, 14-15). This rite achieved "expiation" or atonement for the sins of the preceding year.

9, 6: *In performing their service:* the priestly services that had to be performed regularly in the Holy Place or *outer tabernacle* included burning incense on the incense altar twice each day (Ex 30, 7), replacing the loaves on the table of the bread of offering once each week (Lv 24, 8), and constantly caring for the lamps on the lampstand (Ex 27, 21).

9, 7: *Not without blood:* blood was essential to Old Testament sacrifice because it was believed that life was located in the blood. Hence blood was especially sacred, and its outpouring functioned as a meaningful symbol of cleansing from sin and reconciliation with God. Unlike Heb, the Old Testament never says that the blood is "offered." The author is perhaps retrojecting into his description of Mosaic ritual a concept that belongs to the New Testament antitype, as Paul does when he speaks of the Israelites' passage through the sea as a "baptism" (1 Cor 10, 2).

9, 9: *The present time:* this expression is equivalent to the "present age," used in contradistinction to the "age to come."

9, 11-14: Christ, the high priest of the spiritual blessings foreshadowed in the Old Testament sanctuary, has actually entered the true sanctuary of heaven that is not of human making (11). His place there is permanent, and his offering is his own blood that won eternal redemption (12). If the sacrifice of animals could bestow legal purification (13), how much more effective is the blood of the sinless, divine Christ who spontaneously offered himself to purge the human race of sin and render it fit for the service of God (14).

9, 11: *The good things that have come to be:* the majority of later manuscripts here read "the good things to come"; cf Heb 10, 1.

9, 13: *A heifer's ashes:* ashes from a red heifer that had been burned were mixed with water and used for the cleansing of those who had become ritually defiled by touching a corpse; see Nm 19, 9.14-21.

9, 14: *Through the eternal spirit:* this expression does not refer either to the holy Spirit or to the divine nature of Jesus but to the life of the risen Christ, "a life that cannot be destroyed" (Heb 7, 16).

Heb

[15] * For this reason he is mediator of a new covenant: since a death has taken place for deliverance from transgressions under the first covenant, those who are called may receive the promised eternal inheritance. [w] [16] * Now where there is a will, the death of the testator must be established. [17] For a will takes effect only at death; it has no force while the testator is alive. [18] Thus not even the first covenant was inaugurated without blood. [19] * When every commandment had been proclaimed by Moses to all the people according to the law, he took the blood of calves [and goats], together with water and crimson wool and hyssop, and sprinkled both the book itself and all the people, [x] [20] saying, "This is 'the blood of the covenant which God has enjoined upon you.' "[y] [21] In the same way, he sprinkled also the tabernacle* and all the vessels of worship with blood. [z] [22] According to the law almost everything is purified by blood, [a] and without the shedding of blood there is no forgiveness.*

[23] * Therefore, it was necessary for the copies of the heavenly things to be purified by these rites, but the heavenly things themselves by better sacrifices than these. [b] [24] For Christ did not enter into a sanctuary made by hands, a copy of the true one, but heaven itself, that he might now appear before God on our behalf. [c] [25] Not that he might offer himself repeatedly, as the high priest enters each year into the sanctuary with blood that is not his own; [26] if that were so, he would have had to suffer repeatedly from the foundation of the world. But now once for all he has appeared at the end of the ages* to take away sin by his sacrifice. [d] [27] Just as it is appointed that human beings die once, and after this the judgment, [e] [28] so also Christ, offered once to take away the sins of many,* will appear a second time, not to take away sin but to bring salvation to those who eagerly await him. [f]

---

w 1 Tm 2, 5.—x Heb 9, 12-13.—y Ex 24, 3-8; Mt 26, 28; Mk 14, 24.—z Ex 40, 9; Lv 8, 15.19.—a Lv 17, 11.—b Jb 15, 15.— c Heb 7, 25; Rom 8, 34; 1 Jn 2, 1-2.—d Heb 7, 27; Jn 1, 29; Gal 4, 4.—e Gn 3, 19.—f Heb 10, 10; Is 53, 12.

9, 15-22: Jesus' role as *mediator of the new covenant* is based upon his sacrificial *death* (cf Heb 8, 6). His death has effected *deliverance from transgressions*, i.e., deliverance from sins committed under the old covenant, which the Mosaic sacrifices were incapable of effacing. Until this happened, the *eternal inheritance* promised by God could not be obtained (15). This effect of his work follows the human pattern by which a last will and testament becomes effective only with the death of the testator (16-17). The Mosaic covenant was also associated with death, for Moses made use of blood to seal the pact between God and the people (18-21). In Old Testament tradition, guilt could normally not be remitted without the use of blood (22; cf Lv 17, 11).

9, 16-17: *A will . . . death of the testator:* the same Greek word *diathēkē*, meaning "covenant" in vv 15 and 18, is used here with the meaning *will*. The new covenant, unlike the old, is at the same time a will that requires *the death of the testator*. Jesus as eternal Son is the one who established the new covenant together with his Father, author of both covenants; at the same time he is the testator whose death puts his *will* into effect.

9, 19-20: A number of details here are different from the description of this covenant rite in Ex 24, 5-8. Exodus mentions only calves ("young bulls," NAB), not goats (but this addition in Heb is of doubtful authenticity), says nothing of the use of *water and crimson wool and hyssop* (these features probably came from a different rite; cf Lv 14, 3-7; Nm 19, 6-18), and describes Moses as splashing blood on the altar, whereas Heb says he sprinkled it on the book (but both book and altar are meant to symbolize the agreement of God). The words of Moses are also slightly different from those in Exodus and are closer to the words of Jesus at the Last Supper in Mk 14, 24 // Mt 26, 28.

9, 21: According to Ex, the tabernacle did not yet exist at the time of the covenant rite. Moreover, nothing is said of sprinkling it with blood at its subsequent dedication (Ex 40, 9-11).

9, 22: *Without the shedding of blood there is no forgiveness:* in fact, ancient Israel did envisage other means of obtaining forgiveness; the Old Testament mentions contrition of heart (Ps 51, 19), fasting (Jl 2, 12), and almsgiving (Sir 3, 29). The author is limiting his horizon to the sacrificial cult, which did always involve the shedding of blood for its expiatory and unitive value.

9, 23-28: Since the blood of animals became a cleansing symbol among Old Testament prefigurements, it was necessary that the realities foreshadowed be brought into being by a shedding of blood that was infinitely more effective by reason of its worth (23). Christ did not simply prefigure the heavenly realities (24) by performing an annual sacrifice with a blood not his own (25); he offered the single sacrifice of himself as the final annulment of sin (26). Just as death is the unrepeatable act that ends a person's life, so Christ's offering of himself for all is the unrepeatable sacrifice that has once for all achieved redemption (27-28).

9, 26: *At the end of the ages:* the use of expressions such as this shows that the author of Heb, despite his interest in the Platonic concept of an eternal world above superior to temporal reality here below, nevertheless still clings to the Jewish Christian eschatology with its sequence of "the present age" and "the age to come."

9, 28: *To take away the sins of many:* the reference is to Is 53, 12. Since the Greek verb *anapherō* can mean both "to take away" and "to bear," the author no doubt intended to play upon both senses: Jesus took away sin by bearing it himself. See the similar wordplay in Jn 1, 29. *Many* is used in the Semitic meaning of "all" in the inclusive sense, as in Mk 14, 24. *To those who eagerly await him:* Jesus will appear *a second time* at the parousia, as the high priest reappeared on the Day of Atonement, emerging from the Holy of Holies, which he had entered *to take away sin.* This dramatic scene is described in Sir 50, 5-11.

CHAPTER 10

One Sacrifice instead of Many. 1 * Since the law has only a shadow of the good things to come,* and not the very image of them, it can never make perfect those who come to worship by the same sacrifices that they offer continually each year.*g* 2 Otherwise, would not the sacrifices have ceased to be offered, since the worshipers, once cleansed, would no longer have had any consciousness of sins? 3 But in those sacrifices there is only a yearly remembrance of sins,*h* 4 for it is impossible that the blood of bulls and goats take away sins.*i* 5 For this reason, when he came into the world, he said:*

"Sacrifice and offering you did not desire,*j*
but a body you prepared for me;
6 holocausts and sin offerings you took no delight in.
7 Then I said, 'As is written of me in the scroll,
Behold, I come to do your will, O God.' "

8 First he says, "Sacrifices and offerings, holocausts and sin offerings,* you neither desired nor delighted in." These are offered according to the law.*k* 9 Then he says, "Behold, I come to do your will." He takes away the first to establish the second.*l* 10 By this "will," we have been consecrated through the offering of the body of Jesus Christ once for all.*m*

11 * Every priest stands daily at his ministry, offering frequently those same sacrifices that can never take away sins.*n* 12 But this one offered one sacrifice for sins, and took his seat forever at the right hand of God;*o* 13 now he waits until his enemies are made his footstool.* 14 For by one offering he has made perfect forever those who are being consecrated.*p* 15 The holy Spirit also testifies to us, for after saying:*

16 "This is the covenant I will establish with them after those days, says the Lord:
'I will put my laws in their hearts, and I will write them upon their minds,' "*q*
17 he also says:*

"Their sins and their evildoing I will remember no more."*r*
18 Where there is forgiveness of these, there is no longer offering for sin.

---

g Heb 8, 5; Col 2, 17.—h Lv 16, 21; Nm 5, 15 LXX.—i Is 1, 11; Mi 6, 6-8.— j 5-7: Ps 40, 7-9.—k Heb 10, 5-6; Ps 40, 7.—l Heb 10, 7; Ps 40, 8; Mt 26, 39; Mk 14, 36; Lk 22, 42; Jn 6, 38.—m Heb 9, 12.14.—n Heb 7, 27; Dt 10, 8; 18, 7.—o 12-13: Ps 110, 1.—p Heb 9, 28.—q Heb 8, 10; Jer 31, 33.—r Heb 8, 12; Jer 31, 34.

10, 1-10: Christian faith now realizes that the Old Testament sacrifices did not effect the spiritual benefits to come but only prefigured them (1). For if the sacrifices had actually effected the forgiveness of sin, there would have been no reason for their constant repetition (2). They were rather a continual reminder of the people's sins (3). It is not reasonable to suppose that human sins could be removed by the blood of animal sacrifices (4). Christ, therefore, is shown to understand his mission in terms of Ps 40, 6-8, cited according to the Septuagint (5-7). Jesus acknowledged that the Old Testament sacrifices did not remit the sins of the people and so, perceiving the will of God, offered his own body for this purpose (8-10).

10, 1: *A shadow of the good things to come:* the term *shadow* was used in Heb 8, 5 to signify the earthly counterpart of the Platonic heavenly reality. But here it means a prefiguration of what is to come in Christ, as it is used in the Pauline literature; cf Col 2, 17.

10, 5-7: A passage from Ps 40, 7-9a is placed in the mouth of the Son at his incarnation. As usual, the author follows the Septuagint text. There is a notable difference in v 5 (= Ps 40, 7b), where the Masoretic text reads "ears you have dug for me" ("ears open to obedience you gave me," NAB), but most Septuagint manuscripts have "a body you prepared for me," a reading obviously more suited to the interpretation of Heb.

10, 8: *Sacrifices and offerings, holocausts and sin offerings:* these four terms taken from the preceding passage of Ps 40 (with the first two changed to plural forms) are probably intended as equivalents to the four principal types of Old Testament sacrifices: peace offerings (Lv 3, here called *sacrifices*); cereal offerings (Lv 2, here called *offerings*); holocausts (Lv 1); and sin offerings (Lv 4—5). This last category includes the guilt offerings of Lv 5, 14-26.

10, 11-18: Whereas the levitical priesthood offered daily sacrifices that were ineffectual in remitting sin (11), Jesus offered a single sacrifice that won him a permanent place at God's right hand. There he has only to await the final outcome of his work (12-13; cf Ps 110, 1). Thus he has brought into being in his own person the new covenant prophesied by Jeremiah (Jer 31, 33-34) that has rendered meaningless all other offerings for sin (14-18).

10, 13: *Until his enemies are made his footstool:* Ps 110, 1 is again used; the reference here is to the period of time between the enthronement of Jesus and his second coming. The identity of the *enemies* is not specified; cf 1 Cor 15, 25-27.

10, 15-17: The testimony of the scriptures is now invoked to support what has just preceded. The passage cited is a portion of the new covenant prophecy of Jer 31, 31-34, which the author previously used in Heb 8, 8-12.

10, 17: *He also says:* these words are not in the Greek text, which has only *kai,* "also," but the expression *after saying* in v 15 seems to require such a phrase to divide the Jeremiah text into two sayings. Others understand "the Lord says" of v 16 (here rendered *says the Lord*) as outside the quotation and consider v 16b as part of the second saying. Two ancient versions and a number of minuscules introduce the words "then he said" or a similar expression at the beginning of v 17.

Heb

Recalling the Past.* ¹⁹Therefore, brothers, since through the blood of Jesus we have confidence of entrance into the sanctuaryˢ ²⁰by the new and living way he opened for us through the veil,ᵗ that is, his flesh,* ²¹ ᵘ and since we have "a great priest over the house of God,"* ²²let us approach with a sincere heart and in absolute trust, with our hearts sprinkled clean from an evil conscience* and our bodies washed in pure water.ᵛ ²³Let us hold unwaveringly to our confession that gives us hope, for he who made the promise is trustworthy.ʷ ²⁴We must consider how to rouse one another to love and good works. ²⁵We should not stay away from our assembly,* as is the custom of some, but encourage one another, and this all the more as you see the day drawing near.ˣ

²⁶ ʸ If we sin deliberately* after receiving knowledge of the truth, there no longer remains sacrifice for sins ²⁷but a fearful prospect of judgment and a flaming fire that is going to consume the adversaries.ᶻ ²⁸Anyone who rejects the law of Moses* is put to death without pity on the testimony of two or three witnesses.ᵃ ²⁹Do you not think that a much worse punishment is due the one who has contempt for the Son of God, considers unclean the covenant-blood

by which he was consecrated, and insults the spirit of grace?ᵇ ³⁰We know the one who said:

"Vengeance is mine; I will repay,"

and again:

"The Lord will judge his people."ᶜ

³¹It is a fearful thing to fall into the hands of the living God.ᵈ

³²Remember the days past when, after you had been enlightened,* you endured a great contest of suffering.ᵉ ³³At times you were publicly exposed to abuse and affliction; at other times you associated yourselves with those so treated.ᶠ ³⁴You even joined in the sufferings of those in prison and joyfully accepted the confiscation of your property, knowing that you had a better and lasting possession.ᵍ ³⁵Therefore, do not throw away your confidence; it will have great recompense.ʰ ³⁶You need endurance to do the will of God and receive what he has promised.ⁱ

³⁷ "For, after just a brief moment,*
    he who is to come shall come;
    he shall not delay.ʲ

³⁸ But my just one shall live by faith,
    and if he draws back I take no pleasure in him."ᵏ

³⁹We are not among those who draw back and perish, but among those who have faith and will possess life.

---

s Heb 3, 6; 4, 16; 6, 19-20; Eph 1, 7; 3, 12.—t Jn 14, 6 / Heb 6, 19-20; 9, 8.11-12; Mt 27, 51; Mk 15, 38; Lk 23, 45.—u Heb 3, 6.—v Heb 9, 13-14; Ez 36, 25; 1 Cor 6, 11; Ti 3, 5; 1 Pt 3, 21.—w Heb 3, 1.6; 4, 14; 1 Cor 10, 13.—x Rom 13, 12; 1 Cor 3, 13.—y Heb 3, 12; 6, 4-8.—z Heb 10, 31; 9, 27; Is 26, 11 LXX; Zep 1, 18.—a Dt 17, 6.—b Heb 6, 6.—c Dt 32, 35.36; Rom 12, 19.—d Heb 10, 27; Mt 10, 28; Lk 12, 4-5.—e Heb 6, 4.—f 1 Cor 4, 9.—g Heb 13, 3; Mt 6, 19-20; Lk 12, 33-34.—h Heb 4, 16.—i Lk 21, 19.—j Is 26, 20; Hb 2, 3.—k Hb 2, 4; Rom 1, 17; Gal 3, 11.

10, 19-39: Practical consequences from these reflections on the priesthood and the sacrifice of Christ should make it clear that Christians may now have direct and confident access to God through the person of Jesus (19-20), who rules God's house as high priest (21). They should approach God with sincerity and faith, in the knowledge that through baptism their sins have been remitted (22), reminding themselves of the hope they expressed in Christ at that event (23). They are to encourage one another to Christian love and activity (24), not refusing, no matter what the reason, to participate in the community's assembly, especially in view of the parousia (25; cf 1 Thes 4, 13-18). If refusal to participate in the assembly indicates rejection of Christ, no sacrifice exists to obtain forgiveness for so great a sin (26); only the dreadful judgment of God remains (27). For if violation of the Mosaic law could be punished by death, how much worse will be the punishment of those who have turned their backs on Christ by despising his sacrifice and disregarding the gifts of the holy Spirit (28-29). Judgment belongs to the Lord, and he enacts it by his living presence (30-31). There was a time when the spirit of their community caused them to welcome and share their sufferings (32-34). To revitalize that spirit is to share in the courage of the Old Testament prophets (cf Is 26, 20; Hb 2, 3-4), the kind of courage that must distinguish the faith of the Christian (35-39).

10, 20: *Through the veil, that is, his flesh:* the term *flesh* is used pejoratively. As the temple veil kept people from entering

the Holy of Holies (it was rent at Christ's death, Mk 15, 38), so the flesh of Jesus constituted an obstacle to approaching God.

10, 21: *The house of God:* this refers back to Heb 3, 6, "we are his house."

10, 22: *With our hearts sprinkled clean from an evil conscience:* as in Heb 9, 13 (see the note there), the sprinkling motif refers to the Mosaic rite of cleansing from ritual impurity. This could produce only an external purification, whereas sprinkling with the blood of Christ (Heb 9, 14) cleanses the *conscience.* *Washed in pure water:* baptism is elsewhere referred to as a washing; cf 1 Cor 6, 11; Eph 5, 26.

10, 25: *Our assembly:* the liturgical *assembly* of the Christian community, probably for the celebration of the Eucharist. *The day:* this designation for the parousia also occurs in the Pauline letters, e.g., Rom 2, 16; 1 Cor 3, 13; 1 Thes 5, 2.

10, 26: *If we sin deliberately:* verse 29 indicates that the author is here thinking of apostasy; cf Heb 3, 12; 6, 4-8.

10, 28: *Rejects the law of Moses:* evidently not any sin against the law, but idolatry. Dt 17, 2-7 prescribed capital punishment for idolaters who were convicted on the testimony of two or three witnesses.

10, 32: *After you had been enlightened:* "enlightenment" is an ancient metaphor for baptism (cf Eph 5, 14; Jn 9, 11), but see Heb 6, 4 and the note there.

10, 37-38: In support of his argument, the author uses Hb 2, 3-4 in a wording almost identical with the text of the Codex Alexandrinus of the Septuagint but with the first and second lines of v 4 inverted. He introduces it with a few words from Is 26, 20: *after just a brief moment.* Note the Pauline usage of Hb 2, 4 in Rom 1, 17; Gal 3, 11.

V. EXAMPLES, DISCIPLINE, DISOBEDIENCE

CHAPTER 11*

Faith of the Ancients. 1 Faith is the realization of what is hoped for and evidence* of things not seen.[l] 2 Because of it the ancients were well attested. 3 [m] By faith we understand that the universe was ordered by the word of God,* so that what is visible came into being through the invisible. 4 * By faith Abel offered to God a sacrifice greater than Cain's. Through this he was attested to be righteous, God bearing witness to his gifts, and through this, though dead, he still speaks.[n] 5 By faith Enoch was taken up so that he should not see death, and "he was found no more because God had taken him." Before he was taken up, he was attested to have pleased God.[o] 6 But without faith it is impossible to please him,[p] for anyone who approaches God must believe that he exists and that he rewards those who seek him.* 7 By faith Noah, warned about what was not yet seen, with reverence built an ark for the salvation of his household. Through this he condemned the world and inherited the righteousness that comes through faith.[q]

8 By faith Abraham obeyed when he was called to go out to a place that he was to receive as an inheritance; he went out, not knowing where he was to go.[r] 9 By faith he sojourned in the promised land as in a foreign country, dwelling in tents with Isaac and Jacob, heirs of the same promise;[s] 10 for he was looking forward to the city with foundations, whose architect and maker is God.[t] 11 By faith he received power to generate, even though he was past the normal age—and Sarah herself was sterile—for he thought that the one who had made the promise was trustworthy.[u] 12 So it was that there came forth from one man, himself as good as dead, descendants as numerous as the stars in the sky and as countless as the sands on the seashore.[v]

13 All these died in faith. They did not receive what had been promised but saw it and greeted it from afar and acknowledged themselves to be strangers and aliens on earth,[w] 14 for those who speak thus show that they are seeking a homeland. 15 If they had been thinking of the land from which they had come, they would have had opportunity to return. 16 But now they desire a better homeland, a heavenly one. Therefore, God is not ashamed to be called their God, for he has prepared a city for them.[x]

17 By faith Abraham, when put to the test, offered up Isaac, and he who had received the promises was ready to offer his only son,[y] 18 of whom it was said, "Through Isaac descendants shall bear

l Heb 1, 3; 3, 14; Rom 8, 24; 2 Cor 4, 18.—m Gn 1, 3; Ps 33, 6; Wis 9, 1; Jn 1, 3.—n Heb 12, 24; Gn 4, 4.10.—o Gn 5, 24; Sir 44, 16.—p Wis 4, 10.—q Gn 6, 8-22; Sir 44, 17-18; Mt 24, 37-39; Lk 17, 26-27; 1 Pt 3, 20; 2, Pt 2, 5.—r Gn 12, 1-4; 15, 7-21; Sir 44, 19-22; Acts 7, 2-8; Rom 4, 16-22.—s Gn 12, 8; 13, 12; 23, 4; 26, 3; 35, 27.—t Heb 12, 22; 13, 14; Rv 21, 10-22.—u Gn 17, 19; 21, 2; Rom 4, 19-21 / 1 Cor 10, 13.—v Gn 15, 5; 22, 17; 32, 13; Ex 32, 13; Dt 10, 22; Dn 3, 36 LXX.—w Gn 23, 4; Ps 39, 13.—x Heb 13, 14; Ex 3, 6.—y Gn 22, 1-10; Sir 44, 20; 1 Mc 2, 52; Jas 2, 21.

11, 1-40: This chapter draws upon the people and events of the Old Testament to paint an inspiring portrait of religious faith, firm and unyielding in the face of any obstacles that confront it. These pages rank among the most eloquent and lofty to be found in the Bible. They expand the theme announced in Heb 6, 12, to which the author now returns (Heb 10, 39). The material of this chapter is developed chronologically. Verses 3-7 draw upon the first nine chapters of Gn; vv 8-22, upon the period of the patriarchs; vv 23-31, upon the time of Moses; vv 32-38, upon the history of the judges, the prophets, and the Maccabean martyrs. The author gives the most extensive description of faith provided in the New Testament, though his interest does not lie in a technical, theological definition. In view of the needs of his audience he describes what authentic faith does, not what it is in itself. Through faith God guarantees the blessings to be hoped for from him, providing evidence in the gift of faith that what he promises will eventually come to pass (1). Because they accepted in faith God's guarantee of the future, the biblical personages discussed in vv 3-38 were themselves commended by God (2). Christians have even greater reason to remain firm in faith since they, unlike the Old Testament men and women of faith, have perceived the beginning of God's fulfillment of his messianic promises (39-40).

11, 1: *Faith is the realization . . . evidence:* the author is not attempting a precise definition. There is dispute about the meaning of the Greek words *hypostasis* and *elenchos,* here translated *realization* and *evidence,* respectively. *Hypostasis* usually means "substance," "being" (as translated in Heb 1, 3), or "reality" (as translated in Heb 3, 14); here it connotes something more subjective, and so *realization* has been chosen rather than "assurance" (RSV). *Elenchos,* usually "proof," is used here in an objective sense and so translated *evidence* rather than the transferred sense of "(inner) conviction" (RSV).

11, 3: *By faith . . . God:* this verse does not speak of the faith of the Old Testament men and women but is in the first person plural. Hence it seems out of place in the sequence of thought.

11, 4: The "Praise of the Ancestors" in Sir 44, 1—50, 21 gives a similar list of heroes. The Cain and Abel narrative in Gn 4, 1-16 does not mention Abel's faith. It says, however, that God "looked with favor on Abel and his offering" (Gn 4, 4); in view of v 6 the author probably understood God's favor to have been activated by Abel's faith. *Though dead, he still speaks:* possibly because his blood "cries out to me from the soil" (Gn 4, 10), but more probably a way of saying that the repeated story of Abel provides ongoing witness to faith.

11, 6: One must believe not only that God *exists* but that he is concerned about human conduct; the Old Testament defines folly as the denial of this truth; cf Ps 52, 2.

your name."z ¹⁹He reasoned that God was able to raise even from the dead,ᵃ and he received Isaac back as a symbol.* ²⁰By faith regarding things still to come Isaac* blessed Jacob and Esau.ᵇ ²¹By faith Jacob, when dying, blessed each of the sons of Joseph and "bowed in worship, leaning on the top of his staff."ᶜ ²²By faith Joseph, near the end of his life, spoke of the Exodus of the Israelites and gave instructions about his bones.ᵈ

²³ ᵉ By faith Moses was hidden by his parents for three months after his birth, because they saw that he was a beautiful child, and they were not afraid of the king's edict. ²⁴ * By faith Moses, when he had grown up, refused to be known as the son of Pharaoh's daughter;ᶠ ²⁵he chose to be ill-treated along with the people of God rather than enjoy the fleeting pleasure of sin. ²⁶He considered the reproach of the Anointed greater wealth than the treasures of Egypt, for he was looking to the recompense. ²⁷By faith he left Egypt, not fearing the king's fury, for he persevered as if seeing the one who is invisible.ᵍ ²⁸By faith he kept the Passover and sprinkled the blood, that the Destroyer of the firstborn might not touch them.ʰ ²⁹By faith they crossed the Red Sea as if it were dry land, but when the Egyptians attempted it they were drowned.ⁱ ³⁰By faith the walls of Jericho fell after being encircled for seven days.ʲ ³¹By faith Rahab the harlot did not perish with the disobedient, for she had received the spies in peace.ᵏ

³²What more shall I say? I have not time to tell of Gideon, Barak, Samson, Jephthah, of David and Samuel and the prophets,ˡ ³³who by faith conquered kingdoms, did what was righteous, obtained the promises; they closed the mouths of lions,ᵐ ³⁴put out raging fires, escaped the devouring sword; out of weakness they were made powerful, became strong in battle, and turned back foreign invaders.ⁿ ³⁵Women received back their dead through resurrection. Some were tortured and would not accept deliverance, in order to obtain a better resurrection.ᵒ ³⁶Others endured mockery, scourging, even chains and imprisonment.ᵖ ³⁷They were stoned, sawed in two, put to death at sword's point; they went about in skins of sheep or goats, needy, afflicted, tormented.ᑫ ³⁸The world was not worthy of them. They wandered about in deserts and on mountains, in caves and in crevices in the earth.ʳ

³⁹Yet all these, though approved because of their faith, did not receive what had been promised. ⁴⁰God had foreseen something better for us, so that without us they should not be made perfect.*

CHAPTER 12

God our Father.* ¹Therefore, since we are surrounded by so great a cloud of witnesses, let us rid ourselves of every burden and sin that clings to us* and persevere in running the race that lies before us ²while keeping our eyes fixed on Jesus, the leader and perfecter of faith. For the sake of the joy that lay before him he endured the cross, despising its shame, and has taken his seat at the right of the throne of God.ˢ ³Consider how he endured such opposition from sinners, in order that you may not grow weary and lose heart. ⁴In your struggle against sin you have not yet resisted to

z Gn 21, 12 LXX; Rom 9, 7.—a Rom 4, 16-22.—b Gn 27, 27-40.—c Gn 27, 38-40; 47, 31 LXX; 48, 15-16.—d Gn 50, 24-25.—e Ex 2, 2; Acts 7, 20.—f 24-25: Ex 2, 10-15; Acts 7, 23-29.—g Ex 2, 15; Acts 7, 29.—h Ex 12, 21-23; Wis 18, 25; 1 Cor 10, 10.—i Ex 14, 22-28.—j Jos 6, 12-21.—k Jos 2, 1-21; 6, 22-25; Jas 2, 25.—l Jgs 4, 6-22; 6, 11—8, 32; 11, 1—12, 7.—m Dn 6, 23.—n Dn 3, 22-25.49-50.—o 1 Kgs 17, 17-24; 2 Kgs 4, 18-37; 2 Mc 6, 18—7, 42.—p 2 Chr 36, 16; Jer 20, 2; 37, 15.—q 2 Chr 24, 21.—r 1 Mc 2, 28-30.—s Heb 2, 10; Ps 110, 1; Phil 2, 6-8.

11, 19: *As a symbol:* Isaac's "return from death" is seen as a *symbol* of Christ's resurrection. Others understand the words *en parabolē* to mean "in figure," i.e., the word *dead* is used figuratively of Isaac, since he did not really die. But in the one other place that *parabolē* occurs in Heb, it means symbol (Heb 9, 9).

11, 20-22: Each of these three patriarchs, Isaac, Jacob, and Joseph, had faith in the future fulfillment of God's promise and renewed this faith when near death.

11, 24-27: The reason given for Moses' departure from Egypt differs from the account in Ex 2, 11-15. The author also gives a christological interpretation of his decision to share the trials of his people.

11, 40: *So that without us they should not be made perfect:* the heroes of the Old Testament obtained their recompense only after the saving work of Christ had been accomplished. Thus they already enjoy what Christians who are still struggling do not yet possess in its fullness.

12, 1-13: Christian life is to be inspired not only by the Old Testament men and women of faith (1) but above all by Jesus. As the architect of Christian faith, he had himself to endure the cross before receiving the glory of his triumph (2). Reflection on his sufferings should give his followers courage to continue the struggle, if necessary even to the shedding of blood (3-4). Christians should regard their own sufferings as the affectionate correction of the Lord, who loves them as a father loves his children.

12, 1: *That clings to us:* the meaning is uncertain, since the Greek word *euperistatos,* translated *cling,* occurs only here. The papyrus P⁴⁶ and one minuscule read *euperispastos,* "easily distracting," which also makes good sense.

the point of shedding blood. [5] You have also forgotten the exhortation addressed to you as sons:

"My son, do not disdain the discipline of the Lord[t]
or lose heart when reproved by him;
[6] for whom the Lord loves, he disciplines;
he scourges every son he acknowledges."

[7] Endure your trials as "discipline"; God treats you as sons. For what "son" is there whom his father does not discipline?[u] [8] If you are without discipline, in which all have shared, you are not sons but bastards. [9] Besides this, we have had our earthly fathers to discipline us, and we respected them. Should we not [then] submit all the more to the Father of spirits and live?[v] [10] They disciplined us for a short time as seemed right to them, but he does so for our benefit, in order that we may share his holiness. [11] At the time, all discipline seems a cause not for joy but for pain, yet later it brings the peaceful fruit of righteousness to those who are trained by it.[w]

[12] So strengthen your drooping hands and your weak knees.[x] [13] Make straight paths for your feet, that what is lame may not be dislocated but healed.[y]

Penalties of Disobedience. [14] [z] Strive for peace with everyone, and for that holiness without which no one will see the Lord. [15] * See to it that no one be deprived of the grace of God, that no bitter root spring up and cause trouble, through which many may become defiled,[a] [16] that no one be an immoral or profane person like Esau, who sold his birthright for a single meal.[b] [17] For

you know that later, when he wanted to inherit his father's blessing, he was rejected because he found no opportunity to change his mind, even though he sought the blessing with tears.[c]

[18] * You have not approached that which could be touched[d] and a blazing fire and gloomy darkness and storm* [19] and a trumpet blast and a voice speaking words such that those who heard begged that no message be further addressed to them,[e] [20] for they could not bear to hear the command: "If even an animal touches the mountain, it shall be stoned."[f] [21] Indeed, so fearful was the spectacle that Moses said, "I am terrified and trembling."[g] [22] No, you have approached Mount Zion and the city of the living God, the heavenly Jerusalem, and countless angels in festal gathering,[h] [23] and the assembly of the firstborn enrolled in heaven,* and God the judge of all, and the spirits of the just made perfect,[i] [24] and Jesus, the mediator of a new covenant, and the sprinkled blood that speaks more eloquently* than that of Abel.[j]

[25] See that you do not reject the one who speaks. For if they did not escape when they refused the one who warned them on earth, how much more in our case if we turn away from the one who warns from heaven.[k] [26] His voice shook the earth at that time, but now he has promised, "I will once more shake not only earth but heaven."[l] [27] That phrase, "once more," points to [the] removal of shaken, created things, so that what is unshaken may remain.[m] [28] Therefore, we who are receiving the unshakable kingdom should have

Heb

---

t 5-6: Prv 3, 11-12 / Dt 8, 5; 1 Cor 11, 32.—u Prv 13, 24; Sir 30, 1.—v Nm 16, 22; 27, 16 LXX.—w 2 Cor 4, 17; Phil 1, 11; Jas 3, 18.—x Is 35, 3; Sir 25, 23; Jb 4, 3-4.—y Prv 4, 26 LXX.—z Rom 12, 18; 14, 19.—a Dt 29, 18 (17 LXX).—b Gn 25, 33.—c Gn 27, 34-38.—d Ex 19, 12-14; Dt 4, 11; 5, 22-23.—e Ex 19, 16.19; 20, 18-19.—f Ex 19, 12-13.—g Dt 9, 19.—h Gal 4, 26; Rv 21, 2.—i Lk 10, 20; Rv 5, 11.—j Heb 7, 22; 8, 6; 9, 15 / Heb 11, 4; Gn 4, 10.—k Ex 20, 19.—l Ex 19, 18; Jgs 5, 4-5; Ps 68, 9; Hg 2, 6.—m Is 66, 22; Mt 24, 35; Mk 13, 31; Lk 21, 33.

12, 15-17: Esau serves as an example in two ways: his *profane* attitude illustrates the danger of apostasy, and his inability to secure a blessing afterward illustrates the impossibility of repenting after falling away (see Heb 6, 4-6).

12, 18-29: As a final appeal for adherence to Christian teaching, the two covenants, of Moses and of Christ, are compared. The Mosaic covenant, the author argues, is shown to have originated in fear of God and threats of divine punishment (18-21). The covenant in Christ gives us direct access to God (22), makes us members of the Christian community, God's children, a sanctified

people (23), who have Jesus as mediator to speak for us (24). Not to heed the voice of the risen Christ is a graver sin than the rejection of the word of Moses (25-26). Though Christians fall away, God's kingdom in Christ will remain and his justice will punish those guilty of deserting it (28-29).

12, 18-24: This remarkably beautiful passage contrasts two great assemblies: that of the Israelites gathered at Mount Sinai for the sealing of the old covenant and the promulgation of the Mosaic law, and that of the followers of Jesus gathered at *Mount Zion, the heavenly Jerusalem,* the assembly of the *new covenant.* This latter scene, marked by the presence of *countless angels* and of *Jesus* with his redeeming *blood,* is reminiscent of the celestial liturgies of the Book of Revelation.

12, 23: *The assembly of the firstborn enrolled in heaven:* this expression may refer to the angels of v 22, or to the heroes of the Old Testament (see ch 11), or to the entire assembly of the new covenant.

12, 24: *Speaks more eloquently:* the blood of Abel, the first human blood to be shed, is contrasted with that of Jesus. Abel's blood cried out from the earth for vengeance, but the blood of Jesus has opened the way for everyone, providing cleansing and access to God (Heb 10, 19).

gratitude, with which we should offer worship pleasing to God in reverence and awe.[n] 29 For our God is a consuming fire.[o]

VI. FINAL EXHORTATION, BLESSING, GREETINGS

CHAPTER 13

1 * Let mutual love continue. 2 Do not neglect hospitality, for through it some have unknowingly entertained angels.[p] 3 Be mindful of prisoners as if sharing their imprisonment, and of the ill-treated as of yourselves, for you also are in the body.[q] 4 Let marriage be honored among all and the marriage bed be kept undefiled, for God will judge the immoral and adulterers.[r] 5 Let your life be free from love of money but be content with what you have, for he has said, "I will never forsake you or abandon you."[s] 6 Thus we may say with confidence:

"The Lord is my helper,
[and] I will not be afraid.
What can anyone do to me?"[t]

7 Remember your leaders who spoke the word of God to you. Consider the outcome of their way of life and imitate their faith. 8 Jesus Christ is the same yesterday, today, and forever.[u]

9 Do not be carried away by all kinds of strange teaching.* It is good to have our hearts strengthened by grace and not by foods, which do not benefit those who live by them.[v] 10 We have an altar* from which those who serve the tabernacle have no right to eat. 11 The bodies of the animals whose blood the high priest brings into the sanctuary as a sin offering are burned outside the camp.[w] 12 Therefore, Jesus also suffered outside the gate, to consecrate the people by his own blood.[x] 13 Let us then go to him outside the camp, bearing the reproach that he bore. 14 For here we have no lasting city, but we seek the one that is to come.[y] 15 Through him [then] let us continually offer God a sacrifice of praise, that is, the fruit of lips that confess his name.[z] 16 Do not neglect to do good and to share what you have; God is pleased by sacrifices of that kind.[a]

17 * Obey your leaders and defer to them, for they keep watch over you and will have to give an account, that they may fulfill their task with joy and not with sorrow, for that would be of no advantage to you.

18 Pray for us, for we are confident that we have a clear conscience, wishing to act rightly in every respect. 19 I especially ask for your prayers that I may be restored to you very soon.

20 * May the God of peace, who brought up from the dead the great shepherd of the sheep by the blood of the eternal covenant, Jesus our Lord,[b] 21 furnish you with all that is good, that you may do his will. May he carry out in you what is pleasing to him through Jesus Christ, to whom be glory forever [and ever]. Amen.

22 Brothers, I ask you to bear with this message of encouragement, for I have written to you rather briefly. 23 I must let you know that our brother Timothy has been set free. If he comes soon, I shall see you together with him.[c] 24 Greetings to all your leaders and to all the holy ones. Those from Italy send you greetings. 25 Grace be with all of you.[d]

n Dn 7, 14.18 / Rom 1, 9.—o Dt 4, 24; Is 33, 14.—p Gn 18, 3; 19, 2-3; Jgs 6, 11-22; Tb 5, 4.—q Mt 25, 36.—r 1 Cor 5, 13; Eph 5, 5.—s Dt 31, 6.8; Jos 1, 5.—t Pss 27, 1-3; 118, 6.—u Heb 1, 12; 7, 24; Rv 1, 17.—v Rom 14, 17; 1 Cor 8, 8; Eph 4, 14; Col 2, 16.—w Ex 29, 14; Lv 16, 27.—x Mt 21, 39; Mk 12, 8; Lk 20, 15; Jn 19, 17.—y Heb 11, 10.14.—z Hos 14, 3.—a Phil 4, 18.— b Is 63, 11; Zec 9, 11; Jn 10, 11; Acts 2, 24; Rom 15, 33.—c Acts 16, 1.—d Ti 3, 15.

13, 1-16: After recommendations on social and moral matters (1-6), the letter turns to doctrinal issues. The fact that the original leaders are dead should not cause the recipients of this letter to lose their faith (7), for Christ still lives and he remains always the same (8). They must not rely for their personal sanctification on regulations concerning foods (9), nor should they entertain the notion that Judaism and Christianity can be intermingled (10; cf the notes on Gal 2, 11-14 and Gal 2, 15-21). As Jesus died separated from his own people, so must the Christian community remain apart from the religious doctrines of Judaism (11-14). Christ must be the heart and center of the community (15-16).

13, 9: *Strange teaching:* this doctrine about *foods* probably refers to the Jewish food laws; in view of v 10, however, the author may be thinking of the Mosaic sacrificial banquets.

13, 10: *We have an altar:* this does not refer to the Eucharist, which is never clearly mentioned in Heb, but to the sacrifice of Christ.

13, 17-25: Recommending obedience to the leaders of the community, the author asks for prayers (17-19). The letter concludes with a blessing (20-21), a final request for the acceptance of its message (22), information regarding Timothy (23), and general greetings (24-25).

13, 20-21: These verses constitute one of the most beautiful blessings in the New Testament. The resurrection of Jesus is presupposed throughout Heb, since it is included in the author's frequently expressed idea of his exaltation, but this is the only place where it is explicitly mentioned.

THE CATHOLIC LETTERS

In addition to the thirteen letters attributed to Paul and the Letter to the Hebrews, the New Testament contains seven other letters. Three of these are attributed to John, two to Peter, and one each to James and Jude, all personages of the apostolic age. The term "catholic letter" first appears, with reference only to 1 John, in the writings of Apollonius of Ephesus, a second-century apologist, known only from a citation in Eusebius' *Ecclesiastical History*. Eusebius himself (A.D. 260-340) used the term to refer to all seven letters.

The reason for the term "catholic," which means "universal," was the perception that these letters, unlike those of Paul, which were directed to a particular local church, were apparently addressed more generally to the universal church. This designation is not entirely accurate, however. On the one hand, Hebrews has no specifically identified addressees, and originally this was probably true of Ephesians as well. On the other hand, 3 John is addressed to a named individual, 2 John to a specific, though unnamed, community, and 1 Peter to a number of churches that are specified as being located in Asia Minor.

While all seven of these writings begin with an epistolary formula, several of them do not appear to be real letters in the modern sense of the term. In the ancient world it was not unusual to cast an exhortation in the form of a letter for literary effect, a phenomenon comparable to the "open letter" that is sometimes used today.

With the exception of 1 Peter and 1 John, the ancient church showed reluctance to include the catholic letters in the New Testament canon. The reason for this was widespread doubt whether they had actually been written by the apostolic figures to whom they are attributed. The early Christians saw the New Testament as the depository of apostolic faith; therefore, they wished to include only the testimony of apostles. Today we distinguish more clearly between the authorship of a work and its canonicity: even though written by other, later witnesses than those whose names they bear, these writings nevertheless testify to the apostolic faith and constitute canonical scripture. By the late fourth or early fifth centuries, most objections had been overcome in both the Greek and the Latin churches (though not in the Syriac), and all seven of the catholic letters have since been acknowledged as canonical.

THE LETTER OF JAMES
INTRODUCTION

The person to whom this letter is ascribed can scarcely be one of the two members of the Twelve who bore the name James (see Mt 10, 2-3; Mk 3, 17-18; Lk 6, 14-15), for he is not identified as an apostle but only as "slave of God and of the Lord Jesus Christ" (1, 1). This designation most probably refers to the third New Testament personage named James, a relative of Jesus who is usually called "brother of the Lord" (see Mt 13, 55; Mk 6, 3). He was the leader of the Jewish Christian community in Jerusalem whom Paul acknowledged as one of the "pillars" (Gal 2, 9). In Acts he appears as the authorized spokesman for the Jewish Christian position in the early Church (Acts 12, 17; 15, 13-21). According to the Jewish historian Josephus (Antiquities 20, 9, 1 §§200-203), he was stoned to death by the Jews under the high priest Ananus II in A.D. 62.

The letter is addressed to "the twelve tribes in the dispersion." In Old Testament terminology the term "twelve tribes" designates the people of Israel; the "dispersion" or "diaspora" refers to the non-Palestinian Jews who had settled throughout the Greco-Roman world (see Jn 7, 35). Since in Christian thought the church is the new Israel, the address probably designates the Jewish Christian churches located in Palestine, Syria, and elsewhere. Or perhaps the letter is meant more generally for all Christian communities, and the "dispersion" has the symbolic meaning of exile from our true home, as it has in the address of 1 Peter (1, 1). The letter is so markedly Jewish in character that some scholars have regarded it as a Jewish document subsequently "baptized" by a few Christian insertions, but such an origin is scarcely tenable in view of the numerous contacts discernible between the Letter of James and other New Testament literature.

From the viewpoint of its literary form, James is a letter only in the most conventional sense; it has none of the characteristic features of a real letter except the address. It belongs rather to the genre of parenesis or exhortation and is concerned almost exclusively with ethical conduct. It therefore falls within the tradition of Jewish wisdom literature, such as can be found in the Old Testament (Proverbs, Sirach) and in the extracanonical Jewish literature (Testaments of the Twelve Patriarchs, the Books of Enoch, the Manual of Discipline found at Qumran). More specifically, it consists of sequences of didactic proverbs, comparable to Tb 4, 5-19, to many passages in Sirach, and to sequences of sayings in the synoptic gospels. Numerous passages in James treat of subjects that also appear in the synoptic sayings of Jesus, especially in Matthew's Sermon on the Mount, but the correspondences are too general to establish any literary dependence. James represents a type of early Christianity that emphasized sound teaching and responsible moral behavior. Ethical norms are derived not primarily from christology, as in Paul, but from a concept of salvation that involves conversion, baptism, forgiveness of sin, and expectation of judgment (1, 17; 4, 12).

Paradoxically, this very Jewish work is written in an excellent Greek style, which ranks among the best in the New Testament and appears to be the work of a trained Hellenistic writer. Those who continue to regard James of Jerusalem as its author are therefore obliged to suppose that a secretary must have put the letter into its present literary form. This assumption is not implausible in the light of ancient practice. Some regard the letter as one of the earliest writings in the New Testament and feel that its content accurately reflects what we would expect of the leader of Jewish Christianity. Moreover, they argue that the type of Jewish Christianity reflected in the letter cannot be situated historically after the fall of Jerusalem in A.D. 70.

Others, however, believe it more likely that James is a pseudonymous work of a later period. In addition to its Greek style, they observe further that (a) the prestige that the *writer is assumed to enjoy points to the later legendary reputation of James; (b) the discussion of the importance of good works seems to presuppose a debate subsequent to that in Paul's own day; (c) the author does not rely upon prescriptions of the Mosaic law, as we would expect from the historical James; (d) the letter contains no allusions to James's own history and to his relationship with Jesus or to the early Christian community of Jerusalem. For these reasons, many recent interpreters assign James to the period A.D. 90-100.*

The principal divisions of the Letter of James are the following:

    I.   *Address (1, 1)*
   II.   *The Value of Trials and Temptation (1, 2-18)*
  III.   *Exhortations and Warnings (1, 19—5, 12)*
  IV.   *The Power of Prayer (5, 13-20)*

I. ADDRESS

CHAPTER 1

¹ James, a slave of God and of the Lord Jesus Christ,* to the twelve tribes in the dispersion, greetings.ᵃ

II. THE VALUE OF TRIALS AND TEMPTATION

Perseverance in Trial. ² ᵇ Consider it all joy, my brothers, when you encounter various trials,* ³ for you know that the testing* of your faith produces perseverance. ⁴ And let perseverance be perfect, so that you may be perfect and complete, lacking in nothing. ⁵ But if any of you lacks wisdom,* he should ask God who gives to all generously and ungrudgingly, and he will be given it.ᶜ ⁶ But he should ask in faith, not doubting, for the one who doubts is like a wave of the sea that is driven and tossed about by the wind.ᵈ ⁷ For that person must not suppose that he will receive

anything from the Lord, ⁸ since he is a man of two minds, unstable in all his ways.

⁹ The brother in lowly circumstances* should take pride in his high standing,ᵉ ¹⁰ and the rich one in his lowliness, for he will pass away "like the flower of the field."ᶠ ¹¹ For the sun comes up with its scorching heat and dries up the grass, its flower droops, and the beauty of its appearance vanishes. So will the rich person fade away in the midst of his pursuits.

Temptation. ¹² ᵍ Blessed is the man who perseveres in temptation,* for when he has been proved he will receive the crown of life that he promised to those who love him. ¹³ * No one experiencing temptation should say, "I am being tempted by God"; for God is not subject to temptation to evil, and he himself tempts no one.ʰ ¹⁴ Rather, each person is tempted when he is lured and enticed by his own desire. ¹⁵ Then desire conceives and brings forth sin, and when sin reaches maturity it gives birth to death.

---

a Jn 7, 35; 1 Pt 1, 1.—b Rom 5, 3-5; 1 Pt 1, 6; 4, 13-16.—c Prv 2, 2-6; Wis 9, 4.9-12.—d Mt 7, 7; Mk 11, 24.—e Jas 2, 5.—f Is 40, 6-7.—g 1 Cor 9, 25; 2 Tm 4, 8; 1 Pt 5, 4; Rv 2, 10.—h Sir 15, 11-20; 1 Cor 10, 13.

1, 1: *James, a slave of God and of the Lord Jesus Christ:* a declaration of the writer's authority for instructing the Christian communities; cf Rom 1, 1. Regarding the identity of the author, see Introduction. *Dispersion:* see Introduction.

1, 2: *Consider it all joy . . . various trials:* a frequent teaching of the New Testament derived from the words and sufferings of Jesus (Mt 5, 10-12; Jn 10, 11; Acts 5, 41).

1, 3-8: The sequence of testing, perseverance, and being perfect and complete indicates the manner of attaining spiritual maturity and full preparedness for the coming of Christ (Jas 5, 7-12; cf 1 Pt 1, 6-7; Rom 5, 3-5). These steps require wisdom (5).

1, 5: *Wisdom:* a gift that God readily grants to all who ask in faith and that sustains the Christian in times of trial. It is a kind of knowledge or understanding not accessible to the unbeliever or

those who doubt, which gives the recipient an understanding of the real importance of events. In this way a Christian can deal with adversity with great calm and hope (cf 1 Cor 2, 6-12).

1, 9-11: Throughout his letter (see Jas 2, 5; 4, 10.13-16; 5, 1-6), the author reaffirms the teaching of Jesus that worldly prosperity is not necessarily a sign of God's favor but can even be a hindrance to proper humility before God (cf Lk 6, 20-25; 12, 16-21; 16, 19-31).

1, 12: *Temptation:* the Greek word used here is the same one used for "trials" in v 2. *The crown of life:* crowns or wreaths of flowers were worn at festive occasions as signs of joy and honor. In the Hellenistic world, wreaths were given as a reward to great statesmen, soldiers, athletes. *Life:* here means eternal life. *He promised:* some manuscripts read "God" or "the Lord," while the best witnesses do not specify the subject of "promised."

1, 13-15: It is contrary to what we know of God for God to be the author of human temptation (13). In the commission of a sinful act, one is first beguiled by passion (14), then consent is given, which in turn causes the sinful act. When sin permeates the entire person, it incurs the ultimate penalty of death (15).

Jas

16 * Do not be deceived, my beloved brothers: 17 all good giving and every perfect gift* is from above, coming down from the Father of lights, with whom there is no alteration or shadow caused by change. 18 *i* He willed to give us birth by the word of truth that we may be a kind of firstfruits of his creatures.*

III. EXHORTATIONS AND WARNINGS

Doers of the Word. 19 Know this, my dear brothers: everyone should be quick to hear,* slow to speak, slow to wrath,*j* 20 for the wrath of a man does not accomplish the righteousness of God.*k* 21 Therefore, put away all filth and evil excess and humbly welcome the word that has been planted in you and is able to save your souls.*l*

22 Be doers of the word and not hearers only, deluding yourselves.*m* 23 For if anyone is a hearer of the word and not a doer, he is like a man who looks at his own face in a mirror. 24 He sees himself, then goes off and promptly forgets what he looked like. 25 But the one who peers into the perfect law* of freedom and perseveres, and is not a hearer who forgets but a doer who acts, such a one shall be blessed in what he does.*n*

26 * If anyone thinks he is religious and does not bridle his tongue* but deceives his heart, his religion is vain.*o* 27 Religion that is pure and undefiled before God and the Father is this: to care for orphans and widows* in their affliction and to keep oneself unstained by the world.*p*

CHAPTER 2

Sin of Partiality.* 1 My brothers, show no partiality as you adhere to the faith in our glorious Lord Jesus Christ. 2 For if a man with gold rings on his fingers and in fine clothes comes into your assembly, and a poor person in shabby clothes also comes in, 3 and you pay attention to the one wearing the fine clothes and say, "Sit here, please," while you say to the poor one, "Stand there," or "Sit at my feet," 4 have you not made distinctions among yourselves and become judges with evil designs?*

5 Listen, my beloved brothers. Did not God choose those who are poor* in the world to be rich in faith and heirs of the kingdom that he promised to those who love him?*q* 6 But you dishonored the poor person. Are not the rich oppressing you? And do they themselves not haul you off to court? 7 Is it not they who blaspheme the noble name that was invoked over you?*r* 8 However, if you fulfill the royal* law according to the scripture, "You shall love your neighbor as yourself," you are doing well.*s* 9 But if you show partiality, you commit sin, and are convicted by the law as transgressors.*t* 10 For whoever keeps the whole law, but falls short in one particular, has become guilty in respect to all of it.*u* 11 For he who said, "You shall not commit

---

i Jn 1, 12-13; 1 Pt 1, 23.—j Prv 14, 17; Sir 5, 11.—k Eph 4, 26.—l Col 3, 8.—m Mt 7, 26; Rom 2, 13.—n Jas 2, 12; Ps 19, 8; Rom 8, 2.—o Jas 3, 2; Ps 34, 14.—p Ex 22, 21.—q 1 Cor 1, 26-28; Rv 2, 9.—r 1 Pt 4, 4.—s Lv 19, 18; Mt 22, 39; Rom 13, 9.—t Dt 1, 17.—u Gal 3, 10.

1, 16-18: The author here stresses that God is the source of all good and of good alone, and the evil of temptation does not come from him.

1, 17: *All good giving and every perfect gift* may be a proverb written in hexameter. *Father of lights:* God is here called the Father of the heavenly luminaries, i.e., the stars, sun, and moon that he created (Gn 1, 14-18). Unlike orbs moving from nadir to zenith, he never changes or diminishes in brightness.

1, 18: Acceptance of the gospel message, *the word of truth,* constitutes new birth (Jn 3, 5-6) and makes the recipient the *firstfruits* (i.e., the cultic offering of the earliest grains, symbolizing the beginning of an abundant harvest) of a new creation; cf 1 Cor 15, 20; Rom 8, 23.

1, 19-25: To *be quick to hear* the gospel is to accept it readily and to act in conformity with it, removing from one's soul whatever is opposed to it, so that it may take root and effect salvation (19-21). To listen to the gospel message but not practice it is failure to improve oneself (22-24). Only conformity of life to the perfect law of true freedom brings happiness (25).

1, 25: *Peers into the perfect law:* the image of a person doing this is paralleled to that of hearing God's word. The *perfect law* applies the Old Testament description of the Mosaic law to the gospel of Jesus Christ that brings freedom.

1, 26-27: A practical application of v 22 is now made.

1, 26: For control of the tongue, see the note on Jas 3, 1-12.

1, 27: In the Old Testament, orphans and widows are classical examples of the defenseless and oppressed.

2, 1-13: In the Christian community there must be no discrimination or favoritism based on status or wealth (2-4; cf Mt 5, 3; 11, 5; 23, 6; 1 Cor 1, 27-29). Divine favor rather consists in God's election and promises (5). The rich who oppress the poor blaspheme the name of Christ (6-7). By violating one law of love of neighbor, they offend against the whole law (8-11). On the other hand, conscious awareness of the final judgment helps the faithful to fulfill the whole law (12).

2, 4: When Christians show favoritism to the rich they are guilty of the worst kind of prejudice and discrimination. The author says that such Christians set themselves up as judges who judge not by divine law but by the basest, self-serving motives.

2, 5: The poor, "God's poor" of the Old Testament, were seen by Jesus as particularly open to God for belief in and reliance on him alone (Lk 6, 20). God's law cannot tolerate their oppression in any way (9).

2, 8: *Royal:* literally, "kingly"; because the Mosaic law came from God, the universal king. There may be an allusion to Jesus' uses of this commandment in his preaching of the kingdom of God (Mt 22, 39; Mk 12, 31; Lk 10, 27).

adultery," also said, "You shall not kill."*v* Even if you do not commit adultery but kill, you have become a transgressor of the law. 12 *w* So speak and so act as people who will be judged by the law of freedom.* 13 For the judgment is merciless to one who has not shown mercy; mercy triumphs over judgment.*x*

Faith and Works.* 14 What good is it, my brothers, if someone says he has faith but does not have works? Can that faith save him?*y* 15 If a brother or sister has nothing to wear and has no food for the day, 16 and one of you says to them, "Go in peace, keep warm, and eat well," but you do not give them the necessities of the body, what good is it?*z* 17 So also faith of itself, if it does not have works, is dead.

18 Indeed someone might say, "You have faith and I have works." Demonstrate your faith to me without works, and I will demonstrate my faith to you from my works. 19 You believe that God is one. You do well. Even the demons believe that and tremble. 20 Do you want proof, you ignoramus, that faith without works is useless? 21 Was not Abraham our father justified by works when he offered his son Isaac upon the altar?*a* 22 You see that faith was active along with his works, and faith was completed by the works. 23 Thus the scripture

---

v Ex 20, 13-14; Dt 5, 17-18.—w Jas 1, 25; Rom 8, 2.—x Mt 5, 7; 6, 14-15; 18, 32-33.—y Mt 25, 31-46; Gal 5, 6.—z 1 Jn 3, 17.—a Gn 22, 9-12; Heb 11, 17.—b Gn 15, 6; Rom 4, 3; Gal 3, 6 / 2 Chr 20, 7; Is 41, 8.—c Jos 2, 1-21.—d Jas 1, 26; Prv 13, 3; Sir 28, 12-26.—e Ps 140, 4.—f Mt 7, 16-17.—g Eph 4, 1-2.

2, 12-13: The law upon which the last judgment will be based is the law of freedom. As Jesus taught, mercy (which participates in God's own loving mercy) includes forgiveness of those who wrong us (see Mt 6, 12.14-15).

2, 14-26: The theme of these verses is the relationship of faith and works (deeds). It has been argued that the teaching here contradicts that of Paul (see especially Rom 4, 5-6). The problem can only be understood if the different viewpoints of the two authors are seen. Paul argues against those who claim to participate in God's salvation because of their good deeds as well as because they have committed themselves to trust in God through Jesus Christ (Paul's concept of faith). Paul certainly understands, however, the implications of true faith for a life of love and generosity (see Gal 5, 6.13-15). The author of James is well aware that proper conduct can only come about with an authentic commitment to God in faith (18.26). Many think he was seeking to correct a misunderstanding of Paul's view.

3, 1-12: The use and abuse of the important role of teaching in the church (1) are here related to the good and bad use of the tongue (9-12), the instrument through which teaching was chiefly conveyed (see Sir 5, 11—6, 1; 28, 12-26).

3, 13-18: This discussion of true wisdom is related to the previous reflection on the role of the teacher as one who is in control of his speech. The qualities of the wise man endowed from above are detailed (17-18; cf Gal 5, 22-23), in contrast to the qualities of earthbound wisdom (14-16; cf 2 Cor 12, 20).

---

was fulfilled that says, "Abraham believed God, and it was credited to him as righteousness," and he was called "the friend of God."*b* 24 See how a person is justified by works and not by faith alone. 25 And in the same way, was not Rahab the harlot also justified by works when she welcomed the messengers and sent them out by a different route?*c* 26 For just as a body without a spirit is dead, so also faith without works is dead.

CHAPTER 3

Power of the Tongue.* 1 Not many of you should become teachers, my brothers, for you realize that we will be judged more strictly, 2 for we all fall short in many respects. If anyone does not fall short in speech, he is a perfect man, able to bridle his whole body also.*d* 3 If we put bits into the mouths of horses to make them obey us, we also guide their whole bodies. 4 It is the same with ships: even though they are so large and driven by fierce winds, they are steered by a very small rudder wherever the pilot's inclination wishes. 5 In the same way the tongue is a small member and yet has great pretensions.

Consider how small a fire can set a huge forest ablaze. 6 The tongue is also a fire. It exists among our members as a world of malice, defiling the whole body and setting the entire course of our lives on fire, itself set on fire by Gehenna. 7 For every kind of beast and bird, of reptile and sea creature, can be tamed and has been tamed by the human species, 8 but no human being can tame the tongue. It is a restless evil, full of deadly poison.*e* 9 With it we bless the Lord and Father, and with it we curse human beings who are made in the likeness of God. 10 From the same mouth come blessing and cursing. This need not be so, my brothers. 11 Does a spring gush forth from the same opening both pure and brackish water? 12 Can a fig tree, my brothers, produce olives, or a grapevine figs? Neither can salt water yield fresh.*f*

True Wisdom.* 13 Who among you is wise and understanding? Let him show his works by a good life in the humility that comes from wisdom.*g* 14 But if you have bitter jealousy and selfish ambition in your hearts, do not boast and be false to the truth. 15 Wisdom of this kind does not come down from above but is earthly, un-

Jas

spiritual, demonic. [16] For where jealousy and selfish ambition exist, there is disorder and every foul practice. [17] But the wisdom from above is first of all pure, then peaceable, gentle, compliant, full of mercy and good fruits, without inconstancy or insincerity. [h] [18] And the fruit of righteousness is sown in peace for those who cultivate peace. [i]

CHAPTER 4

Causes of Division.* [1] Where do the wars and where do the conflicts among you come from? Is it not from your passions* that make war within your members? [j] [2] You covet but do not possess. You kill and envy but you cannot obtain; you fight and wage war. You do not possess because you do not ask. [3] You ask but do not receive, because you ask wrongly, to spend it on your passions. [4] Adulterers!* Do you not know that to be a lover of the world means enmity with God? Therefore, whoever wants to be a lover of the world makes himself an enemy of God. [k] [5] Or do you suppose that the scripture speaks without meaning when it says, "The spirit that he has made to dwell in us tends toward jealousy"?* [6] But he bestows a greater grace; therefore, it says: [l]

"God resists the proud, but gives grace to the humble."* [7] So submit yourselves to God. Resist the devil, and he will flee from you. [m] [8] Draw near to God, and he will draw near to you. Cleanse your hands, you sinners, and purify your hearts, you of two minds. [n] [9] Begin to lament, to mourn, to weep. Let your laughter be turned into mourning and your joy into dejection. [10] Humble yourselves before the Lord and he will exalt you. [o]

[11] Do not speak evil of one another, brothers. Whoever speaks evil of a brother or judges his brother speaks evil of the law and judges the law.* If you judge the law, you are not a doer of the law but a judge. [12] There is one lawgiver and judge who is able to save or to destroy. Who then are you to judge your neighbor? [p]

Warning against Presumption.* [13] Come now, you who say, "Today or tomorrow we shall go into such and such a town, spend a year there doing business, and make a profit"—[14] you have no idea what your life will be like tomorrow.* You are a puff of smoke that appears briefly and then disappears. [q] [15] Instead you should say, "If the Lord wills it,* we shall live to do this or that." [16] But now you are boasting in your arrogance. All such boasting is evil. [17] [r] So for one who knows the right thing to do and does not do it, it is a sin.*

---

h Jas 1, 17; Wis 7, 22-23.—i Mt 5, 9.—j Rom 7, 23; 1 Pt 2, 11.—k Mt 6, 24; Lk 16, 13; Rom 8, 7; 1 Jn 2, 15-16.—l Jb 22, 29; Prv 3, 34; Mt 23, 12; 1 Pt 5, 5.—m 1 Pt 5, 8-9.—n Zec 1, 3; Mal 3, 7.—o Jb 5, 11; Mt 23, 12; Lk 14, 11; 18, 14; 1 Pt 5, 6.—p Mt 7, 1; Rom 2, 1; 14, 4.—q Prv 27, 1 / Ps 39, 6-7.—r Lk 12, 47.

4, 1-12: The concern here is with the origin of conflicts in the Christian community. These are occasioned by love *of the world,* which *means enmity with God* (4). Further, the conflicts are bound up with failure to pray properly (cf Mt 7, 7-11; Jn 14, 13; 15, 7; 16, 23), that is, not asking God at all or using God's kindness only for one's pleasure (2-3). In contrast, the proper dispositions are submission to God, repentance, humility, and resistance to evil (7-10).

4,1: *Passions:* the Greek word here (literally, "pleasures") does not indicate that pleasure is evil. Rather, as the text points out (2-3), it is the manner in which one deals with needs and desires that determines good or bad. The motivation for any action can be wrong, especially if one does not pray properly but seeks only selfish enjoyment (3).

4, 4: *Adulterers:* a common biblical image for the covenant between God and his people is the marriage bond. In this image, breaking the covenant with God is likened to the unfaithfulness of adultery.

4, 5: The meaning of this saying is difficult because the author of Jas cites, probably from memory, a passage that is not in any extant manuscript of the Bible. Other translations of the text with

a completely different meaning are possible: "The Spirit that he (God) made to dwell in us yearns (for us) jealously," or, "He (God) yearns jealously for the spirit that he has made to dwell in us." If this last translation is correct, the author perhaps had in mind an apocryphal religious text that echoes the idea that God is zealous for his creatures; cf Ex 20, 5; Dt 4, 24; Zec 8, 2.

4, 6: The point of this whole argument is that God wants the happiness of all, but that selfishness and pride can make that impossible. We must work with him in humility (10).

4, 11: Slander of a fellow Christian does not break just one commandment but makes mockery of the authority of law in general and therefore of God.

4, 13-17: The uncertainty of life (14), its complete dependence on God, and the necessity of submitting to God's will (15) all help one know and do what is right (17). To disregard this is to live in pride and arrogance (16); failure to do what is right is a sin (17).

4, 14: Some important Greek manuscripts here have, "You who have no idea what tomorrow will bring. Why, what is your life?"

4, 15: *If the Lord wills it:* often in piety referred to as the *"conditio Jacobaea,"* the condition James says we should employ to qualify all our plans.

4, 17: *It is a sin:* those who live arrogantly, forgetting the contingency of life and our dependence on God (13-16), are guilty of sin.

CHAPTER 5

Warning to the Rich.* [1]Come now, you rich, weep and wail over your impending miseries.[s] [2]Your wealth has rotted away, your clothes have become moth-eaten,[t] [3]your gold and silver have corroded, and that corrosion will be a testimony against you; it will devour your flesh like a fire. You have stored up treasure for the last days.[u] [4]Behold, the wages you withheld from the workers who harvested your fields are crying aloud, and the cries of the harvesters have reached the ears of the Lord of hosts.[v] [5]You have lived on earth in luxury and pleasure; you have fattened your hearts for the day of slaughter.[w] [6]You have condemned; you have murdered the righteous one;[x] he offers you no resistance.*

Patience and Oaths. [7] * Be patient, therefore, brothers, until the coming of the Lord. See how the farmer waits for the precious fruit of the earth, being patient with it until it receives the early and the late rains.* [8]You too must be patient. Make your hearts firm, because the coming of the Lord is at hand.[y] [9]Do not complain, brothers, about one another, that you may not be judged. Behold, the Judge is standing before the gates. [10]Take as an example of hardship and patience, brothers, the prophets who spoke in the name of the Lord. [11]Indeed we call blessed those who have persevered. You have heard of the perseverance of Job, and you have seen the purpose of the Lord, because "the Lord is compassionate and merciful."[z]

[12] [a] But above all, my brothers, do not swear, either by heaven or by earth or with any other oath, but let your "Yes" mean "Yes" and your "No" mean "No," that you may not incur condemnation.*

IV. THE POWER OF PRAYER

Anointing of the Sick. [13]Is anyone among you suffering? He should pray. Is anyone in good spirits? He should sing praise. [14]Is anyone among you sick?* He should summon the presbyters of the church, and they should pray over him and anoint [him] with oil in the name of the Lord,[b] [15]and the prayer of faith will save the sick person, and the Lord will raise him up. If he has committed any sins, he will be forgiven.*

Confession and Intercession. [16]Therefore, confess your sins to one another and pray for one another, that you may be healed. The fervent prayer of a righteous person is very powerful. [17]Elijah was a human being like us; yet he prayed earnestly that it might not rain, and for three years and six months it did not rain upon the land.[c] [18]Then he prayed again, and the sky gave rain and the earth produced its fruit.[d]

Conversion of Sinners. [19] [e] My brothers, if anyone among you should stray from the truth and someone bring him back, [20] [f] he should know that whoever brings back a sinner from the error of his way will save his soul from death and will cover a multitude of sins.*

---

s Lk 6, 24.—t Mt 6, 19.—u Ps 21, 10; Prv 11, 4; Jdt 16, 17.—v Lv 19, 13; Dt 24, 14-15; Mal 3, 5.—w Jer 12, 3; Lk 16, 19-25.—x Wis 2, 10-20.—y Lk 21, 19; Heb 10, 36 / Heb 10, 25; 1 Pt 4, 7.—z Ex 34, 6; Ps 103, 8.—a Mt 5, 34-37.—b Mk 6, 13.—c 1 Kgs 17, 1; Lk 4, 25.—d 1 Kgs 18, 45.—e Mt 18, 15; Gal 6, 1.—f Prv 10, 12; 1 Pt 4, 8.

5, 1-6: Continuing with the theme of the transitory character of life on earth, the author points out the impending ruin of the godless. He denounces the unjust rich, whose victims cry to heaven for judgment on their exploiters (4-6). The decay and corrosion of the costly garments and metals, which symbolize wealth, prove them worthless and portend the destruction of their possessors (2-3).

5, 6: The author does not have in mind any specific crime in his readers' communities but rather echoes the Old Testament theme of the harsh oppression of the righteous poor (see Prv 1, 11; Wis 2, 10.12.20).

5, 7-11: Those oppressed by the unjust rich are reminded of the need for patience, both in bearing the sufferings of human life (9) and in their expectation of the coming of the Lord. It is then that they will receive their reward (7-8.10-11; cf Heb 10, 25; 1 Jn 2, 18).

5, 7: *The early and the late rains:* an expression related to the agricultural season in ancient Palestine (see Dt 11, 14; Jer 5, 24; Jl 2, 23).

5, 12: This is the threat of condemnation for the abuse of swearing oaths (cf Mt 5, 33-37). *By heaven or by earth:* these words were substitutes for the original form of an oath, to circumvent its binding force and to avoid pronouncing the holy name of God (see Ex 22, 10).

5, 14: In case of sickness a Christian should ask for the presbyters of the church, i.e., those who have authority in the church (cf Acts 15, 2.22-23; 1 Tm 5, 17; Ti 1, 5). They are to pray over the person and anoint with oil; oil was used for medicinal purposes in the ancient world (see Is 1, 6; Lk 10, 34). In Mk 6, 13, the Twelve anoint the sick with oil on their missionary journey. *In the name of the Lord:* by the power of Jesus Christ.

5, 15: The results of the prayer and anointing are physical health and forgiveness of sins. The Roman Catholic Church (Council of Trent, Session 14) declared that this anointing of the sick is a sacrament "instituted by Christ and promulgated by blessed James the apostle."

5, 20: When a Christian is instrumental in the conversion of a sinner, the result is forgiveness of sins and a reinstatement of the sinner to the life of grace.

Jas

THE FIRST LETTER OF PETER

INTRODUCTION

This letter begins with an address by Peter to Christian communities located in five provinces of Asia Minor (1, 1), including areas evangelized by Paul (Acts 16, 6-7; 18, 23). Christians there are encouraged to remain faithful to their standards of belief and conduct in spite of threats of persecution. Numerous allusions in the letter suggest that the churches addressed were largely of Gentile composition (1, 14.18; 2, 9-10; 4, 3-4), though considerable use is made of the Old Testament (1, 24; 2, 6-7.9-10.22; 3, 10-12).

The contents following the address both inspire and admonish these "chosen sojourners" (1, 1) who, in seeking to live as God's people, feel an alienation from their previous religious roots and the society around them. Appeal is made to Christ's resurrection and the future hope it provides (1, 3-5) and to the experience of baptism as new birth (1, 3.23-25; 3, 21). The suffering and death of Christ serve as both source of salvation and example (1, 19; 2, 21-25; 3, 18). What Christians are in Christ, as a people who have received mercy and are to proclaim and live according to God's call (2, 9-10), is repeatedly spelled out for all sorts of situations in society (2, 11-17), work (even as slaves, 2, 18-20), the home (3, 1-7), and general conduct (3, 8-12; 4, 1-11). But over all hangs the possibility of suffering as a Christian (3, 13-17). In 4, 12-19 persecution is described as already occurring, so that some have supposed the letter was addressed both to places where such a "trial by fire" was already present and to places where it might break out.

The letter constantly mingles moral exhortation (paraklēsis) with its catechetical summaries of mercies in Christ. Encouragement to fidelity in spite of suffering is based upon a vision of the meaning of Christian existence. The emphasis on baptism and allusions to various features of the baptismal liturgy suggest that the author has incorporated into his exposition numerous homiletic, credal, hymnic, and sacramental elements of the baptismal rite that had become traditional at an early date.

From Irenaeus in the late second century until modern times, Christian tradition regarded Peter the apostle as author of this document. Since he was martyred at Rome during the persecution of Nero between A.D. 64 and 67, it was supposed that the letter was written from Rome shortly before his death. This is supported by its reference to "Babylon" (5, 13), a code name for Rome in the early church.

Some modern scholars, however, on the basis of a number of features that they consider incompatible with Petrine authenticity, regard the letter as the work of a later Christian writer. Such features include the cultivated Greek in which it is written, difficult to attribute to a Galilean fisherman, together with its use of the Greek Septuagint translation when citing the Old Testament; the similarity in both thought and expression to the Pauline literature; and the allusions to widespread persecution of Christians, which did not occur until at least the reign of Domitian (A.D. 81-96). In this view the letter would date from the end of the first century or even the beginning of the second, when there is evidence for persecution of Christians in Asia Minor (the letter of Pliny the Younger to Trajan, A.D. 111-12).

Other scholars believe, however, that these objections can be met by appeal to use of a secretary, Silvanus, mentioned in 5, 12. Such secretaries often gave literary expression to the author's thoughts in their own style and language. The persecutions may refer to local harassment rather than to systematic repression by the state. Hence there is nothing in the document incompatible with Petrine authorship in the 60s.

Still other scholars take a middle position. The many literary contacts with the Pauline literature, James, and 1 John suggest a common fund of traditional formulations rather than direct dependence upon Paul. Such liturgical and catechetical traditions must have been very ancient and in some cases of Palestinian origin.

Yet it is unlikely that Peter addressed a letter to the Gentile churches of Asia Minor while Paul was still alive. This suggests a period after the death of the two apostles, perhaps A.D. 70-90. The author would be a disciple of Peter in Rome, representing a Petrine group that served as a bridge between the Palestinian origins of Christianity and its flowering in the Gentile world. The problem addressed would not be official persecution but the difficulty of living the Christian life in a hostile, secular environment that espoused different values and subjected the Christian minority to ridicule and oppression.

The principal divisions of the First Letter of Peter are the following:

    I.   Address (1, 1-2)
   II.   The Gift and Call of God in Baptism (1, 3—2, 10)
  III.   The Christian in a Hostile World (2, 11—4, 11)
  IV.   Advice to the Persecuted (4, 12—5, 11)
   V.   Conclusion (5, 12-14)

I. ADDRESS

CHAPTER 1

Greeting.* [1]Peter, an apostle of Jesus Christ, to the chosen sojourners of the dispersion* in Pontus, Galatia, Cappadocia, Asia, and Bithynia,[a] [2]in the foreknowledge of God the Father, through sanctification by the Spirit, for obedience and sprinkling with the blood of Jesus Christ: may grace and peace be yours in abundance.[b]

II. THE GIFT AND CALL OF GOD IN BAPTISM

Blessing. [3] * Blessed be the God and Father of our Lord Jesus Christ, who in his great mercy gave us a new birth to a living hope through the resurrection of Jesus Christ from the dead,[c] [4]to an inheritance that is imperishable, undefiled, and unfading, kept in heaven for you[d] [5]who by the power of God are safeguarded through faith, to a salvation that is ready to be re-

vealed in the final time. [6] * In this you rejoice, although now for a little while you may have to suffer through various trials,[e] [7]so that the genuineness of your faith, more precious than gold that is perishable even though tested by fire, may prove to be for praise, glory, and honor at the revelation of Jesus Christ.[f] [8]Although you have not seen him you love him; even though you do not see him now yet believe in him, you rejoice with an indescribable and glorious joy,[g] [9]as you attain the goal of [your] faith, the salvation of your souls.

[10] * Concerning this salvation, prophets who prophesied about the grace that was to be yours searched and investigated it, [11]investigating the time and circumstances that the Spirit of Christ within them indicated when it testified in advance to the sufferings destined for Christ and the glories to follow them.[h] [12]It was revealed to them that they were serving not themselves but you with regard to the things that have now been announced to you by those who preached the good news to you [through] the holy Spirit sent from heaven, things into which angels longed to look.

`1Pt`

---

a Jas 1, 1.—b Rom 8, 29.—c Ti 3, 5.—d Mt 6, 19-20.—e Jas 1, 2-3.—f 1 Cor 3, 13.—g 2 Cor 5, 6-7.—h Is 52, 13—53, 12; Dn 9, 24.

1, 1-2: The introductory formula names *Peter* as the writer (but see Introduction). In his comments to the presbyters (1 Pt 5, 1), the author calls himself a "fellow presbyter." He addresses himself to the Gentile converts of Asia Minor. Their privileged status as a *chosen* and sanctified people makes them worthy of God's *grace* and *peace*. In contrast is their actual existence as aliens and *sojourners*, scattered among pagans, far from their true country.

1, 1: *Dispersion:* literally, diaspora; see Jas 1, 1 and Introduction to that letter. *Pontus . . . Bithynia:* five provinces in Asia Minor, listed in clockwise order from the north, perhaps in the sequence in which a messenger might deliver the letter.

1, 3-5: A prayer of praise and thanksgiving to God who bestows the gift of new life and hope in baptism *(new birth,* 3) *through the resurrection of Jesus Christ from the dead.* The new birth is a sign of an *imperishable inheritance* (4), of *salvation* that is still in the future *(to be revealed in the final time,* 5).

1, 6-9: As the glory of Christ's resurrection was preceded by his sufferings and death, the new life of faith that it bestows is to be subjected to many *trials* (6) while achieving its goal: the glory of the fullness of *salvation* (9) at the coming of Christ (7).

1, 10-12: The *Spirit of Christ* (11) is here shown to have been present in the prophets, moving them to search, investigate, and prophesy about the *grace* of *salvation* that was to come (10), and in the apostles impelling them to preach the fulfillment of salvation in the message of Christ's sufferings and glory (12).

Obedience. 13 * Therefore, gird up the loins of your mind,* live soberly, and set your hopes completely on the grace to be brought to you at the revelation of Jesus Christ. 14 Like obedient children, do not act in compliance with the desires of your former ignorance* 15 but, as he who called you is holy, be holy yourselves in every aspect of your conduct,[i] 16 for it is written, "Be holy because I [am] holy."[j]

Reverence. 17 Now if you invoke as Father him who judges impartially according to each one's works, conduct yourselves with reverence during the time of your sojourning,[k] 18 realizing that you were ransomed from your futile conduct, handed on by your ancestors, not with perishable things like silver or gold[l] 19 but with the precious blood of Christ[m] as of a spotless unblemished lamb.* 20 He was known before the foundation of the world but revealed in the final time for you, 21 who through him believe in God who raised him from the dead and gave him glory, so that your faith and hope are in God.

Mutual Love. * 22 Since you have purified yourselves by obedience to the truth for sincere mutual love, love one another intensely from a [pure] heart.[n] 23 You have been born anew,[o] not from perishable but from imperishable seed, through the living and abiding word of God,* 24 for:

"All flesh is like grass,
    and all its glory like the flower of the field;

the grass withers,
    and the flower wilts;[p]
25 but the word of the Lord remains forever."

This is the word that has been proclaimed to you.

CHAPTER 2

God's House and People. 1 * Rid yourselves of all malice and all deceit, insincerity, envy, and all slander;[q] 2 like newborn infants, long for pure spiritual milk so that through it you may grow into salvation, 3 [r] for you have tasted that the Lord is good.* 4 Come to him, a living stone,* rejected by human beings but chosen and precious in the sight of God,[s] 5 and, like living stones, let yourselves be built* into a spiritual house to be a holy priesthood to offer spiritual sacrifices acceptable to God through Jesus Christ.[t] 6 For it says in scripture:

"Behold, I am laying a stone in Zion,
    a cornerstone, chosen and precious,
    and whoever believes in it shall not be put to shame."[u]

7 Therefore, its value is for you who have faith, but for those without faith:

"The stone which the builders rejected
    has become the cornerstone,"[v]

8 and

"A stone that will make people stumble,
    and a rock that will make them fall."

They stumble by disobeying the word, as is their destiny.[w]

---

i Mt 5, 48; 1 Jn 3, 3.—j Lv 11, 44; 19, 2.—k 1 Pt 2, 11.—l Is 52, 3; 1 Cor 6, 20.—m Ex 12, 5; Jn 1, 29; Heb 9, 14.—n Rom 12, 10.—o 1 Jn 3, 9.—p Is 40, 6-8.—q 1-2: Jas 1, 21.—r Ps 34, 9.—s Ps 118, 22; Mt 21, 42; Acts 4, 11.—t Eph 2, 21-22.—u Is 28, 16.—v Ps 118, 22; Mt 21, 42; Lk 20, 17; Acts 4, 11.—w Is 8, 14; Rom 9, 33.

1, 13-25: These verses are concerned with the call of God's people to holiness and to mutual love by reason of their redemption through the blood of Christ (18-21).

1, 13: *Gird up the loins of your mind:* a figure reminiscent of the rite of Passover when the Israelites were in flight from their oppressors (Ex 12, 11), and also suggesting the vigilance of the Christian people in expectation of the parousia of Christ (Lk 12, 35).

1, 14-16: The *ignorance* here referred to (14) was their former lack of knowledge of God, leading inevitably to godless conduct. Holiness (15-16), on the contrary, is the result of their call to the knowledge and love of God.

1, 19: Christians have received the redemption prophesied by Isaiah (Is 52, 3), through the blood (Jewish symbol of life) of the spotless lamb (Is 53, 7.10; Jn 1, 29; Rom 3, 24-25; cf 1 Cor 6, 20).

1, 22-25: The new birth of Christians (23) derives from Christ, the *imperishable seed* or sowing that produces a new and lasting existence in those who accept the gospel (24-25), with the consequent duty of loving *one another* (22).

1, 23: The *living and abiding word of God:* or, "the word of the living and abiding God."

2, 1-3: Growth toward salvation is seen here as two steps: first, stripping away all that is contrary to the new life in Christ; second, the nourishment (*pure spiritual milk*) that the newly baptized have received.

2, 3: *Tasted that the Lord is good:* cf Ps 34, 9.

2, 4-8: Christ is the cornerstone (cf Is 28, 16) that is the foundation of the spiritual edifice of the Christian community (5). To unbelievers, Christ is an obstacle and a stumbling block on which they are destined to fall (8); cf Rom 11, 11.

2, 5: *Let yourselves be built:* the form of the Greek word could also be indicative passive, "you are being built" (cf 9).

9 * But you are "a chosen race, a royal priesthood, a holy nation, a people of his own, so that you may announce the praises" of him who called you out of darkness into his wonderful light.x

10 Once you were "no people"
but now you are God's people;
you "had not received mercy"
but now you have received mercy.y

III. THE CHRISTIAN IN A HOSTILE WORLD

Christian Examples. 11 * Beloved, I urge you as aliens and sojourners* to keep away from worldly desires that wage war against the soul.z 12 Maintain good conduct among the Gentiles, so that if they speak of you as evildoers, they may observe your good works and glorify God on the day of visitation.

Christian Citizens. * 13 Be subject to every human institution for the Lord's sake, whether it be to the king as supremea 14 or to governors as sent by him for the punishment of evildoers and the approval of those who do good. 15 For it is the will of God that by doing good you may silence the ignorance of foolish people. 16 Be free, yet without using freedom as a pretext for evil, but as slaves of God.b 17 Give honor to all,

love the community, fear God, honor the king.c

Christian Slaves. 18 * Slaves, be subject to your masters with all reverence, not only to those who are good and equitable but also to those who are perverse.d 19 For whenever anyone bears the pain of unjust suffering because of consciousness of God, that is a grace. 20 But what credit is there if you are patient when beaten for doing wrong? But if you are patient when you suffer for doing what is good, this is a grace before God. 21 For to this you have been called, because Christ also suffered* for you, leaving you an example that you should follow in his footsteps.e

22 "He committed no sin,f
and no deceit was found in his
mouth."*

23 When he was insulted, he returned no insult; when he suffered, he did not threaten; instead, he handed himself over to the one who judges justly.g 24 He himself bore our sins in his body upon the cross, so that, free from sin, we might live for righteousness. By his wounds you have been healed.h 25 For you had gone astray like sheep,i but you have now returned to the shepherd and guardian of your souls.*

---

x Ex 19, 6; Is 61, 6; Rv 1, 6; 20, 6.—y Hos 1, 9; 2, 25 / Hos 1, 6.—z Gal 5, 24.—a Rom 13, 1-7.—b Gal 5, 13.—c Prv 24, 21; Mt 22, 21.—d Eph 6, 5.—e Mt 16, 24.—f Is 53, 9.—g Mt 5, 39.—h Is 53, 4.12 / Is 53, 5.—i Is 53, 6.

2, 9-10: The prerogatives of ancient Israel mentioned here are now more fully and fittingly applied to the Christian people: "a chosen race" (cf Is 43, 20-21) indicates their divine election (Eph 1, 4-6); "a royal priesthood" (cf Ex 19, 6) to serve and worship God in Christ, thus continuing the priestly functions of his life, passion, and resurrection; "a holy nation" (Ex 19, 6) reserved for God, a people he claims for his own (cf Mal 3, 17) in virtue of their baptism into his death and resurrection. This transcends all natural and national divisions and unites the people into one community to glorify the one who led them from the darkness of paganism to the light of faith in Christ. From being "no people" deprived of all mercy, they have become the very people of God, the chosen recipients of his mercy (cf Hos 1, 9; 2, 25).

2, 11—3, 12: After explaining the doctrinal basis for the Christian community, the author makes practical applications in terms of the virtues that should prevail in all the social relationships of the members of the community: good example to Gentile neighbors (1 Pt 2, 11-12); respect for human authority (1 Pt 2, 13-17); obedience, patience, and endurance of hardship in domestic relations (1 Pt 2, 18-25); Christian behavior of husbands and wives (1 Pt 3, 1-7); mutual charity (1 Pt 3, 8-12).

2, 11: Aliens and sojourners: no longer signifying absence from one's native land (Gn 23, 4), this image denotes rather their estrangement from the world during their earthly pilgrimage (see also 1 Pt 1, 1.17).

2, 13-17: True Christian freedom is the result of being servants of God (16; see the note on 1 Pt 2, 18-23). It includes reverence for God, esteem for every individual, and committed love for fellow Christians (17). Although persecution may threaten, subjection to human government is urged (13.17) and concern for the impact of Christians' conduct on those who are not Christians (12.15).

2, 18-21: Most of the labor in the commercial cities of first-century Asia Minor was performed by a working class of slaves. The sense of freedom contained in the gospel undoubtedly caused great tension among Christian slaves: witness the special advice given concerning them here and in 1 Cor 7, 21-24; Eph 6, 5-8; Col 3, 22-25; Phlm. The point made here does not have so much to do with the institution of slavery, which the author does not challenge, but with the nonviolent reaction (20) of slaves to unjust treatment. Their patient suffering is compared to that of Jesus (21), which won righteousness for all humanity.

2, 21: Suffered: some ancient manuscripts and versions read "died" (cf 1 Pt 3, 18).

2, 22-25: After the quotation of Is 53, 9b, the passage describes Jesus' passion with phrases concerning the Suffering Servant from Is 53, 4-12, perhaps as employed in an early Christian confession of faith; cf 1 Pt 1, 18-21 and 1 Pt 3, 18-22.

2, 25: The shepherd and guardian of your souls: the familiar shepherd and flock figures express the care, vigilance, and love of God for his people in the Old Testament (Ps 23; Is 40, 11; Jer 23, 4-5; Ez 34, 11-16) and of Jesus for all humanity in the New Testament (Mt 18, 10-14; Lk 15, 4-7; Jn 10, 1-16; Heb 13, 20).

1Pt

CHAPTER 3

Christian Spouses. [1] * Likewise, you wives should be subordinate to your husbands so that, even if some disobey the word, they may be won over without a word by their wives' conduct [2] when they observe your reverent and chaste behavior.[j] [3] Your adornment should not be an external one: braiding the hair, wearing gold jewelry, or dressing in fine clothes,[k] [4] but rather the hidden character of the heart, expressed in the imperishable beauty of a gentle and calm disposition, which is precious in the sight of God. [5] For this is also how the holy women who hoped in God once used to adorn themselves and were subordinate to their husbands; [6] thus Sarah obeyed Abraham, calling him "lord." You are her children when you do what is good and fear no intimidation.

[7] [l] Likewise, you husbands should live with your wives in understanding, showing honor to the weaker female sex, since we are joint heirs of the gift of life, so that your prayers may not be hindered.*

Christian Conduct.* [8] Finally, all of you, be of one mind, sympathetic, loving toward one another, compassionate, humble. [9] Do not return evil for evil, or insult for insult; but, on the contrary, a blessing, because to this you were called, that you might inherit a blessing.[m] [10] For:

"Whoever would love life[n]
　　and see good days
must keep the tongue from evil
　　and the lips from speaking deceit,
[11] must turn from evil and do good,
　　seek peace and follow after it.
[12] For the eyes of the Lord are on the righteous
　　and his ears turned to their prayer,
but the face of the Lord is against evildoers."

Christian Suffering.* [13] Now who is going to harm you if you are enthusiastic for what is good? [14] But even if you should suffer because of righteousness, blessed are you. Do not be afraid or terrified with fear of them, [15] but sanctify Christ as Lord in your hearts. Always be ready to give an explanation to anyone who asks you for a reason for your hope,[o] [16] but do it with gentleness and reverence, keeping your conscience clear, so that, when you are maligned, those who defame your good conduct in Christ may themselves be put to shame. [17] For it is better to suffer for doing good, if that be the will of God, than for doing evil.

[18] For Christ also suffered* for sins once, the righteous for the sake of the unrighteous, that he might lead you to God. Put to death in the flesh, he was brought to life in the spirit.[p] [19] In it he also went to preach to the spirits in prison,* [20] who had once been disobedient while God patiently waited in the days of Noah during the building of the ark, in which a few persons, eight in all, were saved through water.[q] [21] This prefigured baptism, which saves you now. It is not a removal of dirt from the body but an appeal to God* for a clear conscience, through the resurrection

---

j 1 Cor 7, 12-16; Eph 5, 22-24; Col 3, 18; 1 Tm 2, 9-15.—k 1 Tm 2, 9-10.—l Eph 5, 25-33; Col 3, 19.—m Mt 5, 44; Lk 6, 28; Rom 12, 14.—n 10-12: Ps 34, 13-17.—o Is 8, 12.—p 1 Cor 15, 45.—q Gn 7, 7.17; 2 Pt 2, 5.

3, 1-6: The typical marital virtues of women of the ancient world, obedience, reverence, and chastity (1-2), are outlined here by the author, who views them an entirely new motivation: Christian wives are to be virtuous so that they may be instrumental in the conversion of their husbands. In imitation of *holy women* in the past (5) they are to cultivate the interior life (4) instead of excessive concern with their appearance (3).

3, 7: Husbands who do not respect their wives will have as little success in prayer as those who, according to Paul, have no love: their prayers will be "a resounding gong or a clashing cymbal" (1 Cor 13, 1). Consideration for others is shown as a prerequisite for effective prayer also in Mt 5, 23-24; 1 Cor 11, 20-22; Jas 4, 3. After all, whatever the social position of women in the world and in the family, they are equal recipients of the gift of God's salvation. Paul is very clear on this point, too (see 1 Cor 11, 11-12; Gal 3, 28).

3, 8-12: For the proper ordering of Christian life in its various aspects as described in 1 Pt 2, 11—3, 9, there is promised the blessing expressed in Ps 34, 13-17. In the Old Testament this refers to longevity and prosperity; here, it also refers to eternal life.

3, 13-22: This exposition, centering on v 17, runs as follows: by his suffering and death Christ the righteous one saved the unrighteous (18); by his resurrection he received new life in the spirit, which he communicates to believers through the baptismal bath that cleanses their consciences from sin. As Noah's family was saved *through water*, so Christians are saved through the waters of baptism (19-22). Hence they need not share the fear of sinners; they should rather rejoice in suffering because of their hope in Christ. Thus their innocence disappoints their accusers (13-16; cf Mt 10, 28; Rom 8, 35-39).

3, 18: *Suffered:* very many ancient manuscripts and versions read "died." *Put to death in the flesh:* affirms that Jesus truly died as a human being. *Brought to life in the spirit:* that is, in the new and transformed existence freed from the limitations and weaknesses of natural human life (cf 1 Cor 15, 45).

3, 19: *The spirits in prison:* it is not clear just who these spirits are. They may be the spirits of the sinners who died in the flood, or angelic powers, hostile to God, who have been overcome by Christ (cf 1 Pt 3, 22; Gn 6, 4; Enoch 6-36, especially 21, 6; 2 Enoch 7, 1-5).

3, 21: *Appeal to God:* this could also be translated "pledge," that is, a promise on the part of Christians to live with a good conscience before God, or a pledge from God of forgiveness and therefore a good conscience for us.

of Jesus Christ,[r] 22who has gone into heaven and is at the right hand of God, with angels, authorities, and powers subject to him.[s]

CHAPTER 4

Christian Restraint.* 1Therefore, since Christ suffered in the flesh, arm yourselves also with the same attitude (for whoever suffers in the flesh has broken with sin), 2so as not to spend what remains of one's life in the flesh on human desires, but on the will of God. 3For the time that has passed is sufficient for doing what the Gentiles like to do: living in debauchery, evil desires, drunkenness, orgies, carousing, and wanton idolatry.[t] 4They are surprised that you do not plunge into the same swamp of profligacy, and they vilify you; 5but they will give an account to him who stands ready to judge the living and the dead.[u] 6For this is why the gospel was preached even to the dead* that, though condemned in the flesh in human estimation, they might live in the spirit in the estimation of God.

Christian Charity.* 7The end of all things is at hand. Therefore, be serious and sober for prayers. 8 [v] Above all, let your love for one another be intense, because love covers a multitude of sins.* 9Be hospitable to one another without complaining.[w] 10As each one has received a gift, use it to serve one another as good stewards of God's varied grace.[x] 11Whoever preaches, let it be with the words of God; whoever serves, let it be with the strength that God supplies, so that in all things God may be glorified through Jesus Christ,[y] to whom belong glory and dominion forever and ever. Amen.*

IV. ADVICE TO THE PERSECUTED

Trial of Persecution.* 12Beloved, do not be surprised that a trial by fire is occurring among you, as if something strange were happening to you.[z] 13But rejoice to the extent that you share in the sufferings of Christ, so that when his glory is revealed you may also rejoice exultantly.[a] 14If you are insulted for the name of Christ, blessed are you, for the Spirit of glory and of God rests upon you.[b] 15But let no one among you be made to suffer as a murderer, a thief, an evildoer, or as an intriguer. 16But whoever is made to suffer as a Christian should not be ashamed but glorify God because of the name. 17For it is time for the judgment to begin with the household of God; if it begins with us, how will it end for those who fail to obey the gospel of God?[c]

18 "And if the righteous one is barely saved,
   where will the godless and the sinner appear?"[d]

19As a result, those who suffer in accord with God's will hand their souls over to a faithful creator as they do good.

CHAPTER 5

Advice to Presbyters.* 1So I exhort the presbyters* among you, as a fellow presbyter and witness to the sufferings of Christ and one who has a share in the glory to be revealed. 2Tend the flock of God in your midst, [overseeing] not by constraint but willingly, as God would have it, not for

r Eph 5, 26; Heb 10, 22.—s Eph 1, 20-21.—t Eph 2, 2-3; 4, 17-19; Col 3, 7; Ti 3, 3.—u Acts 10, 42; 2 Tm 4, 1.—v Prv 10, 12; Jas 5, 20.—w Heb 13, 2.—x Rom 12, 6-8; 1 Cor 12, 4-11.—y 1 Cor 10, 31.—z 1 Pt 1, 6-7; 3, 14.17.—a Rom 5, 3-5; 8, 17; 2 Tm 2, 12.—b Acts 5, 41 / Is 11, 2.—c Lk 23, 31; 2 Thes 1, 8.—d Prv 11, 31 LXX.

4, 1-6: Willingness to suffer with Christ equips the Christian with the power to conquer sin (1). Christ is here portrayed as the judge to whom those guilty of pagan vices must render an account (5; cf Jn 5, 22-27; Acts 10, 42; 2 Tm 4, 1).

4, 6: *The dead:* these may be the sinners of the flood generation who are possibly referred to in 1 Pt 3, 19. But many scholars think that there is no connection between these two verses, and that *the dead* here are Christians who have died since hearing the preaching of the gospel.

4, 7-11: The inner life of the eschatological community is outlined as *the end* (the parousia of Christ) and the judgment draws near in terms of seriousness, sobriety, prayer, and love expressed through hospitality and the use of one's gifts for the glory of God and of Christ.

4, 8: *Love covers a multitude of sins:* a maxim based on Prv 10, 12; see also Ps 32, 1; Jas 5, 20.

4, 11: Some scholars feel that this doxology concludes the part of the homily addressed specifically to the newly baptized, begun in 1 Pt 1, 3; others that it concludes a baptismal liturgy. Such doxologies do occur within a New Testament letter, e.g., Rom 9, 5. Some propose that v 11 was an alternate ending, with 1 Pt 4, 12—5, 14 being read in places where persecution was more pressing. But such doxologies usually do not occur at the end of letters (the only examples are 2 Pt 3, 18, Jude 25, and Rom 16, 27, the last probably a liturgical insertion).

4, 12-19: The suffering to which the author has already frequently referred is presented in more severe terms. This has led some scholars to see these verses as referring to an actual persecution. Others see the heightening of the language as only a rhetorical device used at the end of the letter to emphasize the suffering motif.

5, 1-4: In imitation of Christ, the chief shepherd, those entrusted with a pastoral office are to tend the flock by their care and example.

5, 1: *Presbyters:* the officially appointed leaders and teachers of the Christian community (cf 1 Tm 5, 17-18; Ti 1, 5-8; Jas 5, 14).

1Pt

shameful profit but eagerly.[e] [3] Do not lord it over those assigned to you, but be examples to the flock. [4] [f] And when the chief Shepherd is revealed, you will receive the unfading crown of glory.*

Advice to the Community.* [5] Likewise, you younger members,* be subject to the presbyters. And all of you, clothe yourselves with humility in your dealings with one another, for:

"God opposes the proud
but bestows favor on the humble."[g]

[6] So humble yourselves under the mighty hand of God, that he may exalt you in due time. [h] [7] Cast all your worries upon him because he cares for you. [i]

---

e Acts 20, 28; Ti 1, 7.—f Wis 5, 15-16; 1 Cor 9, 25; 2 Tm 4, 8; Jas 1, 12.—g Prv 3, 34.—h Jb 22, 29; Jas 4, 10.—i Ps 55, 23; Mt 6, 25-33; Lk 12, 22-31; Phil 4, 6.—j 1 Thes 5, 6.—k Rom 8, 18; 2 Cor 4, 17.—l Rom 16, 16; 1 Cor 16, 20; 2 Cor 13, 12.

5, 4: See the note on 1 Pt 2, 25.

5, 5-11: The community is to be subject to the presbyters and to show humility toward one another and trust in God's love and care (5-7). With sobriety, alertness, and steadfast faith they must resist the evil one; their sufferings are shared with Christians everywhere (8-9). They will be strengthened and called to eternal glory (10-11).

5, 5: *Younger members:* this may be a designation for office-holders of lesser rank.

5, 12: *Silvanus:* the companion of Paul (see 2 Cor 1, 19; 1 Thes 1, 1; 2 Thes 1, 1). Jews and Jewish Christians, like Paul,

---

[8] Be sober and vigilant. Your opponent the devil is prowling around like a roaring lion looking for [someone] to devour.[j] [9] Resist him, steadfast in faith, knowing that your fellow believers throughout the world undergo the same sufferings. [10] The God of all grace who called you to his eternal glory through Christ [Jesus] will himself restore, confirm, strengthen, and establish you after you have suffered a little. [k] [11] To him be dominion forever. Amen.

V. CONCLUSION

[12] I write you this briefly through Silvanus,* whom I consider a faithful brother, exhorting you and testifying that this is the true grace of God. Remain firm in it. [13] The chosen one* at Babylon sends you greeting, as does Mark, my son. [14] Greet one another with a loving kiss. Peace to all of you who are in Christ. [l]

---

often had a Hebrew name (Saoul, Silas) and a Greek or Latin name (Paul, Silvanus). On Silvanus's possible role as amanuensis, see Introduction.

5, 13: *The chosen one:* feminine, referring to the Christian community *(ekklēsia)* at *Babylon,* the code name for Rome in Rv 14, 8; 17, 5; 18, 2. *Mark, my son:* traditionally a prominent disciple of Peter and co-worker at the church in Rome, perhaps the John Mark referred to in Acts 12, 12.25; 13, 5.13; and in Acts 15, 37-39, a companion of Barnabas. Perhaps this is the same Mark mentioned as Barnabas's cousin in Col 4, 10, a co-worker with Paul in Phlm 24 (see also 2 Tm 4, 11).

THE SECOND LETTER OF PETER

INTRODUCTION

This letter can be appreciated both for its positive teachings and for its earnest warnings. It seeks to strengthen readers in faith (1, 1), hope for the future (3, 1-10), knowledge (1, 2.6.8), love (1, 7), and other virtues (1, 5-6). This aim is carried out especially by warning against false teachers, the condemnation of whom occupies the long central section of the letter (2, 1-22). A particular crisis is the claim by "scoffers" that there will be no second coming of Jesus, a doctrine that the author vigorously affirms (3, 1-10). The concept of God's "promises" is particularly precious in the theology of 2 Peter (1, 4; 3, 4.9.13). Closing comments at 3, 17-18 well sum up the twin concerns: that you not "be led into" error and "fall" but instead "grow in grace" and "knowledge" of Jesus Christ.

Second Peter is clearly structured in its presentation of these points. It reminds its readers of the divine authenticity of Christ's teaching (1, 3-4), continues with reflections on Christian conduct (1, 5-15), then returns to the exalted dignity of Jesus by incorporating into the text the apostolic witness to his transfiguration (1, 16-18). It takes up the ques-

tion of the interpretation of scripture by pointing out that it is possible to misunderstand the sacred writings (1, 19-21) and that divine punishment will overtake false teachers (2, 1-22). It proclaims that the parousia is the teaching of the Lord and of the apostles and is therefore an eventual certainty (3, 1-13). At the same time, it warns that the meaning of Paul's writings on this question should not be distorted (3, 14-18).

In both content and style this letter is very different from 1 Peter, which immediately precedes it in the canon. The opening verse attributes it to "Symeon Peter, a slave and apostle of Jesus Christ." Moreover, the author in 3, 1 calls his work a "second letter," referring probably to 1 Peter as his first, and in 1, 18 counts himself among those present at the transfiguration of Jesus.

Nevertheless, acceptance of 2 Peter into the New Testament canon met with great resistance in the early church. The oldest certain reference to it comes from Origen in the early third century. While he himself accepted both Petrine letters as canonical, he testifies that others rejected 2 Peter. As late as the fifth century some local churches still excluded it from the canon, but eventually it was universally adopted. The principal reason for the long delay was the persistent doubt that the letter stemmed from the apostle Peter.

Among modern scholars there is wide agreement that 2 Peter is a pseudonymous work, i.e., one written by a later author who attributed it to Peter according to a literary convention popular at the time. It gives the impression of being more remote in time from the apostolic period than 1 Peter; indeed, many think it is the latest work in the New Testament and assign it to the first or even the second quarter of the second century.

The principal reasons for this view are the following. The author refers to the apostles and "our ancestors" as belonging to a previous generation, now dead (3, 2-4). A collection of Paul's letters exists and appears to be well known, but disputes have arisen about the interpretation of them (3, 14-16). The passage about false teachers (2, 1-18) contains a number of literary contacts with Jude 4-16, and it is generally agreed that 2 Peter depends upon Jude, not vice versa. Finally, the principal problem exercising the author is the false teaching of "scoffers" who have concluded from the delay of the parousia that the Lord is not going to return. This could scarcely have been an issue during the lifetime of Simon Peter.

The Christians to whom the letter is addressed are not identified, though it may be the intent of 3, 1 to identify them with the churches of Asia Minor to which 1 Peter was sent. Except for the epistolary greeting in 1, 1-2, 2 Peter does not have the features of a genuine letter at all, but is rather a general exhortation cast in the form of a letter. The author must have been a Jewish Christian of the dispersion for, while his Jewish heritage is evident in various features of his thought and style, he writes in the rather stilted literary Greek of the Hellenistic period. He appeals to tradition against the twin threat of doctrinal error and moral laxity, which appear to reflect an early stage of what later developed into full-blown gnosticism. Thus he forms a link between the apostolic period and the church of subsequent ages.

The principal divisions of the Second Letter of Peter are the following:

I. Address (1, 1-2)
II. Exhortation to Christian Virtue (1, 3-21)
III. Condemnation of the False Teachers (2, 1-22)
IV. The Delay of the Second Coming (3, 1-16)
V. Final Exhortation and Doxology (3, 17-18)

2Pt

I. ADDRESS

CHAPTER 1

Greeting. [1]Symeon Peter,* a slave and apostle of Jesus Christ, to those who have received a faith of equal value to ours through the righteousness of our God and savior Jesus Christ: [2]may grace and peace be yours in abundance through knowledge* of God and of Jesus our Lord.

II. EXHORTATION TO CHRISTIAN VIRTUE

The Power of God's Promise. [3] * His divine power has bestowed on us everything that makes for life and devotion, through the knowledge of him[a] who called us by his own glory and power.* [4]Through these, he has bestowed on us the precious and very great promises, so that through them you may come to share in the divine nature, after escaping from the corruption that is in the world because of evil desire.[b] [5] * For this very reason, make every effort to supplement your faith with virtue, virtue with knowledge,[c] [6]knowledge with self-control, self-control with endurance, endurance with devotion, [7]devotion with mutual affection, mutual affection with love. [8]If these are yours and increase in abundance, they will keep you from being idle or unfruitful in the knowledge of our Lord Jesus Christ. [9] [d] Anyone who lacks

them is blind and shortsighted, forgetful of the cleansing of his past sins. [10] * Therefore, brothers, be all the more eager to make your call and election firm, for, in doing so, you will never stumble. [11]For, in this way, entry into the eternal kingdom of our Lord and savior Jesus Christ will be richly provided for you.

Apostolic Witness. [12] * Therefore, I will always remind you of these things, even though you already know them and are established in the truth you have. [13]I think it right, as long as I am in this "tent,"* to stir you up by a reminder, [14]since I know that I will soon have to put it aside, as indeed our Lord Jesus Christ has shown me.[e] [15]I shall also make every effort to enable you always to remember these things after my departure.

[16]We did not follow cleverly devised myths when we made known to you the power and coming* of our Lord Jesus Christ, but we had been eyewitnesses of his majesty.[f] [17]For he received honor and glory from God the Father* when that unique declaration came to him from the majestic glory, "This is my Son, my beloved, with whom I am well pleased."[g] [18]We* ourselves heard this voice come from heaven while we were with him on the holy mountain. [19] [h] Moreover, we pos-

---

a 2 Cor 4, 6; 1 Pt 2, 9.—b 2 Cor 7, 1; 1 Jn 2, 15.—c 5-7: Gal 5, 22-23.—d 1 Jn 2, 9.11.—e Is 38, 12; Jn 21, 18-19.—f Lk 9, 28-36; Jn 1, 14.—g Ps 2, 7; Mt 17, 4-6.—h Lk 1, 78-79; Rv 2, 28..

1, 1: *Symeon Peter:* on the authorship of 2 Peter, see Introduction; on the spelling here of the Hebrew name *Šim'ôn*, cf Acts 15, 14. The greeting is especially similar to those in 1 Peter and Jude. The words translated *our God and savior Jesus Christ* could also be rendered "our God and the savior Jesus Christ"; cf 2 Pt 1, 11; 2, 20; 3, 2.18.

1, 2: *Knowledge:* a key term in the letter (2 Pt 1, 3.8; 2, 20; 3, 18), perhaps used as a Christian emphasis against gnostic claims.

1, 3-4: Christian life in its fullness is a gift of divine power effecting a knowledge of Christ and the bestowal of divine promises (2 Pt 3, 4.9). *To share in the divine nature,* escaping from a corrupt world, is a thought found elsewhere in the Bible but expressed only here in such Hellenistic terms, since it is said to be accomplished through *knowledge* (3); cf 2 Pt 1, 2; 2, 20; but see also Jn 15, 4; 17, 22-23; Rom 8, 14-17; Heb 3, 14; 1 Jn 1, 3; 3, 2.

1, 3: *By his own glory and power:* the most ancient papyrus and the best codex read "through glory and power."

1, 5-9: Note the climactic gradation of qualities (5-7), beginning with faith and leading to the fullness of Christian life, which is love; cf Rom 5, 3-4; Gal 5, 6.22 for a similar series of "virtues," though the program and sense here are different than in Paul. The fruit of these is knowledge of Christ (8) referred to in v 3; their absence is spiritual blindness (9).

1, 10-11: Perseverance in the Christian vocation is the best preventative against losing it and the safest provision for attaining its goal, the kingdom. *Kingdom of . . . Christ,* instead of "God," is unusual; cf Col 1, 13 and Mt 13, 41, as well as the *righteousness of . . . Christ* (1).

1, 12-19: The purpose in writing is to call to mind the apostle's witness to the truth, even as he faces the end of his life (12-15), his eyewitness testimony to Christ (16-18), and the true prophetic message (19) through the Spirit in scripture (20-21), in contrast to what false teachers are setting forth (ch 2).

1, 13: *Tent:* a biblical image for transitory human life (Is 38, 12), here combined with a verb that suggests not folding or packing up a tent but its being discarded in death (cf 2 Cor 5, 1-4).

1, 16: *Coming:* in Greek *parousia,* used at 2 Pt 3, 4.12 of the second coming of Christ. The word was used in the extrabiblical writings for the visitation of someone in authority; in Greek cult and Hellenistic Judaism it was used for the manifestation of the divine presence. What the apostles *made known* has been interpreted to refer to Jesus' transfiguration (17) or to his entire first coming or to his future coming in power (ch 3).

1, 17: The author assures the readers of the reliability of the apostolic message (including Jesus' power, glory, and coming; cf the note on 2 Pt 1, 16) by appeal to the transfiguration of Jesus in glory (cf Mt 17, 1-8 and parallels) and by appeal to the prophetic message (2 Pt 1, 19; perhaps Nm 24, 17). Here, as elsewhere, the New Testament insists on continued reminders as necessary to preserve the historical facts about Jesus and the truths of the faith; cf 2 Pt 3, 1-2; 1 Cor 11, 2; 15, 1-3. *My Son, my beloved:* or, "my beloved Son."

1, 18: *We:* at Jesus' transfiguration, referring to Peter, James, and John (Mt 17, 1).

sess the prophetic message that is altogether reliable. You will do well to be attentive to it, as to a lamp shining in a dark place, until day dawns and the morning star rises in your hearts. [20] * Know this first of all, that there is no prophecy of scripture that is a matter of personal interpretation, [21] for no prophecy ever came through human will; but rather human beings moved by the holy Spirit spoke under the influence of God.

III. CONDEMNATION OF THE FALSE TEACHERS

CHAPTER 2

False Teachers. * [1] There were also false prophets among the people, just as there will be false teachers among you, who will introduce destructive heresies and even deny the Master who ransomed them, bringing swift destruction on themselves.[i] [2] Many will follow their licentious ways, and because of them the way of truth will be reviled.[j] [3] In their greed they will exploit you with fabrications, but from of old their condemnation has not been idle and their destruction does not sleep.[k]

Lessons from the Past. [4] * For if God did not spare the angels when they sinned, but condemned them to the chains of Tartarus* and handed them over to be kept for judgment;[l] [5] * and if he did not spare the ancient world, even though he preserved

Noah, a herald of righteousness, together with seven others, when he brought a flood upon the godless world;[m] [6] and if he condemned the cities of Sodom and Gomorrah [to destruction], reducing them to ashes, making them an example for the godless [people] of what is coming;[n] [7] and if he rescued Lot, a righteous man oppressed by the licentious conduct of unprincipled people [8] (for day after day that righteous man living among them was tormented in his righteous soul at the lawless deeds that he saw and heard), [9] then the Lord knows how to rescue the devout from trial and to keep the unrighteous under punishment for the day of judgment,[o] [10] and especially those who follow the flesh with its depraved desire and show contempt for lordship.[p]

False Teachers Denounced. * Bold and arrogant, they are not afraid to revile glorious beings,* [11] whereas angels,[q] despite their superior strength and power, do not bring a reviling judgment against them from the Lord.* [12] But these people, like irrational animals born by nature for capture and destruction, revile things that they do not understand, and in their destruction they will also be destroyed,[r] [13] suffering wrong* as payment for wrongdoing. Thinking daytime revelry a delight, they are stains and defilements as they revel in their deceits while carousing with you.[s] [14] Their eyes are full of adultery and insatiable for sin. They seduce unstable people, and their hearts are trained in

---

i Mt 24, 11.24; 1 Tm 4, 1; Jude 4.—j Is 52, 5.—k Rom 16, 18.—l Jude 6.—m Gn 8, 15-19; Heb 11, 7.—n Gn 19, 24-25; Jude 7.—o 1 Cor 10, 13; Rv 3, 10.—p Jude 8.—q Jude 9.—r Ps 49, 13-15; Jude 10.—s Jude 12.

1, 20-21: Often cited, along with 2 Tm 3, 16, on the "inspiration" of scripture or against private interpretation, these verses in context are directed against the false teachers of ch 2 and clever tales (16). The prophetic word in scripture comes admittedly through *human beings* (21), but *moved by the holy Spirit*, not from their own interpretation, and is a matter of what the author and Spirit intended, not the *personal interpretation* of false teachers. Instead of *under the influence of God*, some manuscripts read "holy ones of God."

2, 1-3: The pattern of *false prophets* among the Old Testament people of God will recur through *false teachers* in the church. Such destructive opinions of heretical sects bring loss of faith in Christ, contempt for the way of salvation (cf 2 Pt 2, 21), and immorality.

2, 4-6: The false teachers will be punished just as surely and as severely as were the fallen *angels* (4; cf Jude 6; Gn 6, 1-4), the sinners of Noah's day (5; Gn 7, 21-23), and the inhabitants of the cities of the Plain (6; Jude 7; Gn 19, 25). Whereas there are three examples in Jude 5-7 (Exodus and wilderness; rebellious angels; Sodom and Gomorrah), 2 Peter omitted the first of these, has inserted a new illustration about Noah (5) between Jude's second and third examples, and listed the resulting three examples in their Old Testament order (Gn 6; 7; 19).

2, 4: *Chains of Tartarus:* cf Jude 6; other manuscripts in 2 Peter read "pits of Tartarus." *Tartarus:* a term borrowed from Greek mythology to indicate the infernal regions.

2, 5-10a: Although God did not spare the sinful, he kept and saved the righteous, such as *Noah* (5) and *Lot* (7), and he *knows how to rescue the devout* (9), who are contrasted with the false teachers of the author's day. On Noah, cf Gn 5, 32—9, 29, especially 7, 1. On Lot, cf Gn 13 and 19.

2, 10b-22: Some take 10b and 11 with the preceding paragraph. Others begin the new paragraph with 10a, supplying from v 9 *The Lord knows how . . . to keep . . . under punishment*, with reference to God and probably specifically Christ (1). The conduct of the false teachers is described and condemned in language similar to that of Jude 8-16. This arrogance knows no bounds; animal-like, they are due to be caught and destroyed. They seduce even those who have knowledge of Christ (20).

2, 10b: *Glorious beings:* literally, "glories"; cf Jude 8. While some think that illustrious personages are meant or even political officials behind whom (fallen) angels stand, it is more likely that the reference is to glorious angelic beings (cf Jude 9).

2, 11: *From the Lord:* some manuscripts read "before the Lord"; cf Jude 9.

2, 13: *Suffering wrong:* some manuscripts read "receiving a reward." *In their deceits:* some manuscripts read "in their love feasts" (Jude 12).

2Pt

greed. Accursed children! [15] Abandoning the straight road, they have gone astray, following the road of Balaam, the son of Bosor,* who loved payment for wrongdoing,[t] [16] but he received a rebuke for his own crime: a mute beast spoke with a human voice and restrained the prophet's madness.[u]

[17] These people are waterless springs and mists driven by a gale; for them the gloom of darkness has been reserved.[v] [18] For, talking empty bombast, they seduce with licentious desires of the flesh those who have barely escaped* from people who live in error.[w] [19] They promise them freedom, though they themselves are slaves of corruption, for a person is a slave of whatever overcomes him.[x] [20] For if they, having escaped the defilements of the world through the knowledge of [our] Lord and savior Jesus Christ, again become entangled and overcome by them, their last condition is worse than their first.[y] [21] For it would have been better for them not to have known the way of righteousness than after knowing it to turn back from the holy commandment handed down* to them.[z] [22] What is expressed in the true proverb has happened to them,[a] "The dog returns to its own vomit," and "A bathed sow returns to wallowing in the mire."*

---

t Nm 31, 16; Jude 11.—u Nm 22, 28-33.—v Jude 12-13.—w Jude 16.—x Jn 8, 34; Rom 6, 16-17.—y Mt 12, 45.—z Ez 3, 20.—a Prv 26, 11.—b Jude 17.—c 1 Tm 4, 1; 2 Tm 3, 1; Jude 18.—d Is 5, 19.—e Gn 1, 2.6.8; Ps 24, 2.—f Gn 7, 21.—g Is 51, 6; Mt 3, 12.—h Ps 90, 4.

2, 15: *Balaam, the son of Bosor:* in Nm 22, 5, Balaam is said to be the son of Beor, and it is this name that turns up in a few ancient Greek manuscripts by way of "correction" of the text. Balaam is not portrayed in such a bad light in Nm 22. His evil reputation and his *madness* (16), and possibly his surname Bosor, may have come from a Jewish tradition about him in the first/second century, of which we no longer have any knowledge.

2, 18: *Barely escaped:* some manuscripts read "really escaped."

2, 21: *Commandment handed down:* cf 2 Pt 3, 2 and Jude 3.

2, 22: The second proverb is of unknown origin, while the first appears in Prv 26, 11.

3, 1-4: The false teachers not only flout Christian morality (cf Jude 8-19); they also deny the second coming of Christ and the judgment (4; cf 2 Pt 3, 7). They seek to justify their licentiousness by arguing that the promised return of Christ has not been realized and the world is the same, no better than it was before (3-4). The author wishes to strengthen the faithful against such errors by reminding them in this *second letter* of the instruction in 1 Pt and of the teaching of the *prophets* and of Christ, conveyed through the *apostles* (1-2; cf Jude 17); cf 1 Pt 1, 10-12.16-21, especially 16-21; Eph 2, 20.

3, 3: *Scoffers:* cf Jude 18, where, however, only the passions of the scoffers are mentioned, not a denial on their part of Jesus' parousia.

IV. THE DELAY OF THE SECOND COMING

CHAPTER 3

Denial of the Parousia. [1] * This is now, beloved, the second letter I am writing to you; through them by way of reminder I am trying to stir up your sincere disposition, [2] to recall the words previously spoken by the holy prophets and the commandment of the Lord and savior through your apostles.[b] [3] Know this first of all, that in the last days scoffers* will come [to] scoff, living according to their own desires[c] [4] and saying, "Where is the promise of his coming?* From the time when our ancestors fell asleep, everything has remained as it was from the beginning of creation."[d] [5] They deliberately ignore the fact that the heavens existed of old and earth was formed out of water and through water* by the word of God;[e] [6] through these the world that then existed was destroyed,[f] deluged with water.* [7] The present heavens and earth have been reserved by the same word for fire, kept for the day of judgment and of destruction of the godless.[g]

[8] * But do not ignore this one fact, beloved, that with the Lord one day is like a thousand years* and a thousand years like one day.[h] [9] The Lord does not delay his promise, as some regard "delay," but he is patient with you, not wishing that any should perish but that all should come to

---

3, 4-7: The false teachers tried to justify their immorality by pointing out that the promised *coming (parousia)* of the Lord has not yet occurred, even though early Christians expected it in their day. They thus insinuate that God is not guiding the world's history anymore, since nothing has changed and the first generation of Christians, *our ancestors* (4), has all died by this time. The author replies that, just as God destroyed the earth by water in the flood (5-6, cf 2 Pt 2, 5), so he will destroy it along with the false teachers on judgment day (7). *The word of God,* which called the world into being (Gn 1; Ps 33, 6) and *destroyed* it by the waters of a flood, will destroy it again by fire on *the day of judgment* (5-7).

3, 5: *Formed out of water and through water:* Gn 1, 2.6-8 is reflected as well as Greek views that water was the basic element from which all is derived.

3, 6: *Destroyed, deluged with water:* cf 2 Pt 2, 5; Gn 7, 11—8, 2.

3, 8-10: The scoffers' objection (4) is refuted also by showing that *delay* of the Lord's second coming is not a failure to fulfill his word but rather a sign of his patience: God is giving time for repentance before the final judgment (cf Wis 11, 23-26; Ez 18, 23; 33, 11).

3, 8: Cf Ps 90, 4.

repentance.[i] [10]But the day of the Lord will come like a thief,* and then the heavens will pass away with a mighty roar and the elements will be dissolved by fire, and the earth and everything done on it will be found out.[j]

Exhortation to Preparedness.* [11]Since everything is to be dissolved in this way, what sort of persons ought [you] to be, conducting yourselves in holiness and devotion,[k] [12]waiting for and hastening the coming of the day of God,[l] because of which the heavens will be dissolved in flames and the elements melted by fire.* [13]But according to his promise we await new heavens and a new earth* in which righteousness dwells.[m]

[14]Therefore, beloved, since you await these things, be eager to be found without spot or blemish before him, at peace. [15]And consider the patience of our Lord as salvation, as our beloved brother Paul, according to the wisdom given to him, also wrote to you,[n] [16]speaking of these things* as he does in all his letters. In them there are some things hard to understand that the ignorant and unstable distort to their own destruction, just as they do the other scriptures.

V. FINAL EXHORTATION AND DOXOLOGY*

[17]Therefore, beloved, since you are forewarned, be on your guard not to be led into the error of the unprincipled and to fall from your own stability.[o] [18]But grow in grace and in the knowledge of our Lord and savior Jesus Christ. To him be glory now and to the day of eternity. [Amen.][p]

---

i Ez 18, 23; 1 Tm 2, 4.—j Is 66, 15-16; Mt 24, 29.—k Acts 3, 19-21.—l Is 34, 4; Heb 10, 27.—m Is 65, 17; 66, 22; Rom 8, 21; Rv 21, 1.27.—n Rom 8, 19; Jude 24.—o Mk 13, 5; Heb 2, 1.—p Rom 16, 27.

3, 10: *Like a thief:* Mt 24, 43; 1 Thes 5, 2; Rv 3, 3. *Will be found out:* cf 1 Cor 3, 13-15. Some few versions read, as the sense may demand, "will not be found out"; many manuscripts read "will be burned up"; there are further variants in other manuscripts, versions, and Fathers. Total destruction is assumed (11).

3, 11-16: The second coming of Christ and the judgment of the world are the doctrinal bases for the moral exhortation to readiness through vigilance and a virtuous life; cf Mt 24, 42.50-51; Lk 12, 40; 1 Thes 5, 1-11; Jude 20-21.

3, 12: *Flames . . . fire:* although this is the only New Testament passage about a final conflagration, the idea was common in apocalyptic and Greco-Roman thought. *Hastening:* eschatology is here used to motivate ethics (11), as elsewhere in the New Testament. Jewish sources and Acts 3, 19-20 assume that proper

ethical conduct can help bring the promised day of the Lord; cf 2 Pt 3, 9. Some render the phrase, however, "desiring it earnestly."

3, 13: *New heavens and a new earth:* cf Is 65, 17; 66, 22. The divine promises will be fulfilled after the day of judgment will have passed. The universe will be transformed by the reign of God's *righteousness* or justice; cf Is 65, 17-18; Acts 3, 21; Rom 8, 18-25; Rv 21, 1.

3, 16: *These things:* the teachings of this letter find parallels in Paul, e.g., God's will to save (Rom 2, 4; 9, 22-23; 1 Cor 1, 7-8), the coming of Christ (1 Thes 4, 16-17; 1 Cor 15, 23-52), and preparedness for the judgment (Col 1, 22-23; Eph 1, 4-14; 4, 30; 5, 5-14). *Other scriptures:* used to guide the faith and life of the Christian community. The letters of Paul are thus here placed on the same level as books of the Old Testament. Possibly other New Testament writings could also be included.

3, 17-18: To avoid the dangers of *error* and loss of *stability,* Christians are *forewarned* to be *on guard* and to *grow in grace and knowledge* (2 Pt 1, 2) of Christ. The doxology (18) recalls 1 Pt 4, 11. Some manuscripts add *Amen.*

THE FIRST LETTER OF JOHN

INTRODUCTION

Early Christian tradition identified this work as a letter of John the apostle. Because of its resemblance to the fourth gospel in style, vocabulary, and ideas, it is generally agreed that both works are the product of the same school of Johannine Christianity. The terminology and the presence or absence of certain theological ideas in 1 John suggest that it was written after the gospel; it may have been composed as a short treatise on ideas that were developed more fully in the fourth gospel. To others, the evidence suggests that 1 John was written after the fourth gospel as part of a debate on the proper interpretation of that gospel. Whatever its relation to the gospel, 1 John may be dated toward the end of the first century. Unlike 2 and 3 John, it lacks in form the salutation and epistolary conclusion of a letter. These features, its prologue, and its emphasis on doctrinal teaching make it more akin to a theological treatise than to most other New Testament letters.

The purpose of the letter is to combat certain false ideas, especially about Jesus, and to deepen the spiritual and social awareness of the Christian community (3, 17). Some former members (2, 19) of the community refused to acknowledge Jesus as the Christ (2,

1Jn

22) *and denied that he was a true man (4, 2). The specific heresy described in this letter cannot be identified exactly, but it is a form of docetism or gnosticism; the former doctrine denied the humanity of Christ to insure that his divinity was untainted, and the latter viewed the appearance of Christ as a mere stepping-stone to higher knowledge of God. These theological errors are rejected by an appeal to the reality and continuity of the apostolic witness to Jesus. The author affirms that authentic Christian love, ethics, and faith take place only within the historical revelation and sacrifice of Jesus Christ. The fullness of Christian life as fellowship with the Father must be based on true belief and result in charitable living; knowledge of God and love for one another are inseparable, and error in one area inevitably affects the other. Although the author recognizes that Christian doctrine presents intangible mysteries of faith about Christ, he insists that the concrete Christian life brings to light the deeper realities of the gospel.*

The structure and language of the letter are straightforward yet repetitious. The author sets forth the striking contrasts between light and darkness, Christians and the world, and truth and error to illustrate the threats and responsibilities of Christian life. The result is not one of theological argument but one of intense religious conviction expressed in simple truths. The letter is of particular value for its declaration of the humanity and divinity of Christ as an apostolic teaching and for its development of the intrinsic connection between Christian moral conduct and Christian doctrine.

The principal divisions of the First Letter of John are the following:

    I.   *Prologue (1, 1-4)*
   II.   *God as Light (1, 5—3, 10)*
  III.   *Love for One Another (3, 11—5, 12)*
  IV.   *Epilogue (5, 13-21)*

I. PROLOGUE

CHAPTER 1

The Word of Life*

1 What was from the beginning,
    what we have heard,
    what we have seen with our eyes,
    what we looked upon
    and touched with our hands
    concerns the Word of life—*a*
2 for the life was made visible;
    we have seen it and testify to it
    and proclaim to you the eternal life
    that was with the Father and was made
        visible to us—*b*
3 what we have seen and heard
    we proclaim now to you,

so that you too may have fellowship
        with us;
for our fellowship is with the Father
    and with his Son, Jesus Christ.*c*
4 We are writing this so that our joy may
        be complete.*d*

II. GOD AS LIGHT

God is Light. 5 Now this is the message that we have heard from him and proclaim to you: God is light,* and in him there is no darkness at all. 6 If we say, "We have fellowship with him," while we continue to walk in darkness, we lie and do not act in truth.*e* 7 But if we walk in the light as he is in the light, then we have fellowship with one another, and the blood of his Son Jesus cleanses us from all sin.*f* 8 If we say, "We are without sin," we deceive ourselves,*

---

a 1 Jn 2, 13; Jn 1, 1.14; 20, 20.25.27.—b Jn 15, 27; 17, 5.—c Jn 17, 21; Acts 4, 20.—d Jn 15, 11; 2 Jn 12.—e Jn 12, 35.—f Mt 26, 28; Rom 3, 24-25; Heb 9, 14; 1 Pt 1, 19; Rv 1, 5.

1, 1-4: There is a striking parallel to the prologue of the gospel of John (Jn 1, 1-18), but the emphasis here is not on the preexistent Word but rather on the apostles' witness to the incarnation of *life* by their experience of the historical Jesus. He is *the Word of life* (1; cf Jn 1, 4), *the eternal life that was with the Father and was made visible* (2; cf Jn 1, 14), and was *heard, seen, looked upon,* and *touched* by the apostles. The purpose of their teaching is to share that *life,* called *fellowship . . . with the Father and with his Son, Jesus Christ,* with those who receive their witness (3; Jn 1, 14.16).

1, 5-7: *Light* is to be understood here as truth and goodness; *darkness* here is error and depravity (cf Jn 3, 19-21; 17, 17; Eph 5, 8). To *walk* in light or darkness is to live according to truth or error, not merely intellectual but moral as well. Fellowship with God and with one another consists in a life according to the truth as found in God and in Christ.

1, 8-10: Denial of the condition of sin is self-deception and even contradictory of divine revelation; there is also the continual possibility of sin's recurrence. Forgiveness and deliverance from sin through Christ are assured through acknowledgment of them and repentance.

and the truth is not in us.^g ⁹If we acknowledge our sins, he is faithful and just and will forgive our sins and cleanse us from every wrongdoing.^h ¹⁰If we say, "We have not sinned," we make him a liar, and his word is not in us.ⁱ

CHAPTER 2

Christ and His Commandments. ¹My children,* I am writing this to you so that you may not commit sin. But if anyone does sin, we have an Advocate with the Father, Jesus Christ the righteous one.^j ²He is expiation for our sins, and not for our sins only but for those of the whole world.^k ³The way we may be sure* that we know him is to keep his commandments.^l ⁴Whoever says, "I know him," but does not keep his commandments is a liar, and the truth is not in him.^m ⁵But whoever keeps his word, the love of God is truly perfected in him. This is the way we may know that we are in union with him:ⁿ ⁶whoever claims to abide in him ought to live [just] as he lived.

The New Commandment.* ⁷Beloved, I am writing no new commandment to you but an old commandment that you had from the beginning. The old commandment is the word that you have heard.^o ⁸And yet I do write a new commandment to you, which holds true in him and among you,* for the darkness is passing away, and the true light is already shining.^p ⁹Whoever says he is in the light, yet hates his brother, is still in the darkness.^q ¹⁰Whoever loves his brother remains in the light, and there

is nothing in him to cause a fall.^r ¹¹Whoever hates his brother is in darkness; he walks in darkness and does not know where he is going because the darkness has blinded his eyes.

Members of the Community.* ¹²I am writing to you, children, because your sins have been forgiven^s for his name's sake.*

¹³I am writing to you, fathers, because you know him who is from the beginning.

I am writing to you, young men, because you have conquered the evil one.^t

¹⁴I write to you, children, because you know the Father.

I write to you, fathers, because you know him who is from the beginning.

I write to you, young men, because you are strong and the word of God remains in you, and you have conquered the evil one.

¹⁵Do not love the world or the things of the world.* If anyone loves the world, the love of the Father is not in him.^u ¹⁶For all that is in the world, sensual lust,* enticement for the eyes, and a pretentious life, is not from the Father but is from the world. ¹⁷Yet the world and its enticement are passing away. But whoever does the will of God remains forever.^v

Antichrists. ¹⁸Children, it is the last hour;* and just as you heard that the antichrist was coming, so now many antichrists have appeared. Thus we know this is the last hour.^w ¹⁹They went out from us, but they were not really of our number;* if

---

g 2 Chr 6, 36; Prv 20, 9.—h Prv 28, 13; Jas 5, 16.—i 1 Jn 5, 10.—j Jn 14, 16; Heb 7, 25.—k 1 Jn 4, 10.—l Jn 14, 15; 15, 10.—m 1 Jn 4, 20.—n Jn 14, 23.—o 1 Jn 3, 11; Dt 6, 5; Mt 22, 37-40.—p Jn 13, 34 / Jn 1, 5; Rom 13, 12.—q Jn 8, 12.—r Eccl 2, 14; Jn 11, 10.—s 1 Cor 6, 11.—t 1 Jn 1, 1; Jn 1, 1.—u Rom 8, 7-8; Jas 4, 4; 2 Pt 1, 4.—v Is 40, 8; Mt 7, 21; 1 Cor 7, 31; 1 Pt 4, 2.—w 1 Tim 4, 1.

2, 1: *Children:* like the term "beloved," this is an expression of pastoral love (cf Jn 13, 33; 21, 5; 1 Cor 4, 14). *Advocate:* for the use of the term, see Jn 14, 16. Forgiveness of sin is assured through Christ's intercession and expiation or "offering"; the death of Christ effected the removal of sin.

2, 3-6: *The way we may be sure:* to those who claim, "I have known Christ and therefore I know him," our author insists on not mere intellectual knowledge but obedience to God's commandments in a life conformed to the example of Christ; this confirms our knowledge of him and is *the love of God . . . perfected.* Disparity between moral life and the commandments proves improper belief.

2, 7-11: The author expresses the continuity and freshness of mutual charity in Christian experience. Through Christ the commandment of love has become the *light* defeating the *darkness* of evil in a new age. All hatred as darkness is incompatible with the light and Christian life. Note also the characteristic Johannine polemic in which a positive assertion is emphasized by the negative statement of its opposite.

2, 8: *Which holds true in him and among you:* literally, "a thing that holds true in him and in you."

2, 12-17: The Christian community that has experienced the grace of God through forgiveness of sin and knowledge of Christ is armed against the evil one.

2, 12: *For his name's sake:* because of Christ our sins are forgiven.

2, 15: *The world:* all that is hostile toward God and alienated from him. Love of the *world* and love of God are thus mutually exclusive; cf Jas 4, 4.

2, 16: *Sensual lust:* literally, "the lust of the flesh," inordinate desire for physical gratification. *Enticement for the eyes:* literally, "the lust of the eyes," avarice or covetousness; the eyes are regarded as the windows of the soul. *Pretentious life:* literally, "pride of life," arrogance or ostentation in one's earthly style of life that reflects a willful independence from God and others.

2, 18: *It is the last hour:* literally, "a last hour," the period between the death and resurrection of Christ and his second coming. *The antichrist:* opponent or adversary of Christ; the term appears only in 1-2 John, but "pseudochrists" (translated "false messiahs") in Mt 24, 24 and Mk 13, 22, and Paul's "lawless one" in 2 Thes 2, 3, are similar figures. *Many antichrists:* Mt, Mk, and Rv seem to indicate a collectivity of persons, here related to the false teachers.

2, 19: *Not really of our number:* the apostate teachers only proved their lack of faith by leaving the community.

1Jn

they had been, they would have remained with us. Their desertion shows that none of them was of our number. [20] But you have the anointing that comes from the holy one,* and you all have knowledge. [x] [21] I write to you not because you do not know the truth but because you do, and because every lie is alien to the truth. [y] [22] * Who is the liar? Whoever denies that Jesus is the Christ. Whoever denies the Father and the Son, this is the antichrist. [z] [23] No one who denies the Son has the Father, but whoever confesses the Son has the Father as well. [a]

Life from God's Anointing. [24] [b] Let what you heard from the beginning remain in you. If what you heard from the beginning remains in you, then you will remain in the Son and in the Father.* [25] And this is the promise that he made us: eternal life. [c] [26] I write you these things about those who would deceive you. [27] As for you, the anointing that you received from him remains in you, so that you do not need anyone to teach you. But his anointing teaches you about everything and is true and not false; just as it taught you, remain in him.

Children of God. [28] * And now, children, remain in him, so that when he appears we may have confidence and not be put to shame by him at his coming. [29] If you consider that he is righteous, you also know that everyone who acts in righteousness is begotten by him.

---

x Jn 14, 26.—y 1 Jn 3, 19; 2 Pt 1, 12.—z 2 Thes 2, 4.—a Jn 14, 7-9.—b Jn 14, 23.—c Jn 5, 24; 10, 28; 17, 2.—d Jn 1, 12; Eph 1, 5 / Jn 15, 21; 17, 25.—e Phil 3, 21.—f 1 Jn 2, 6.—g Is 53, 9; Jn 1, 29; 8, 46; 1 Pt 2, 22.—h Jn 8, 44; 12, 31-32.—i 1 Jn 2, 7; Jn 13, 34; 15, 12.17.

2, 20: *The anointing that comes from the holy one:* this anointing is in the Old Testament sense of receiving the Spirit of God. The *Holy One* probably refers to Christ. True knowledge is the gift of the Spirit (cf Is 11, 2), and the function of the Spirit is to lead Christians to the truth (Jn 14, 17.26; 16, 13).

2, 22-23: Certain gnostics denied that the earthly Jesus was the Christ; to deny knowledge of the Son is to deny the Father, since only through the Son has God been fully revealed (Jn 1, 18; 14, 8-9).

2, 24: Continuity with the apostolic witness as proclaimed in the prologue is the safeguard of right belief.

2, 28-29: Our confidence at his judgment is based on the daily assurance of salvation. Our actions reflect our true relation to him.

3, 1-3: The greatest sign of God's love is the gift of his Son (Jn 3, 16) that has made Christians true children of God. This relationship is a present reality and also part of the life to come; true knowledge of God will ultimately be gained, and Christians prepare themselves now by virtuous lives in imitation of the Son.

3, 2: *When it is revealed:* or "when he is revealed" (the subject of the verb could be Christ).

CHAPTER 3

[1] * See what love the Father has bestowed on us that we may be called the children of God. Yet so we are. The reason the world does not know us is that it did not know him. [d] [2] Beloved, we are God's children now; what we shall be has not yet been revealed. We do know that when it is revealed* we shall be like him, for we shall see him as he is. [e] [3] Everyone who has this hope based on him makes himself pure, as he is pure. [f]

Avoiding Sin. [4] Everyone who commits sin commits lawlessness, for sin is lawlessness.* [5] You know that he was revealed to take away sins, and in him there is no sin. [g] [6] No one who remains in him sins; no one who sins has seen him or known him. [7] Children, let no one deceive you. The person who acts in righteousness is righteous, just as he is righteous. [8] Whoever sins belongs to the devil, because the devil has sinned from the beginning. Indeed, the Son of God was revealed to destroy the works of the devil. [h] [9] No one who is begotten by God commits sin, because God's seed remains in him; he cannot sin because he is begotten by God.* [10] In this way, the children of God and the children of the devil are made plain; no one who fails to act in righteousness belongs to God, nor anyone who does not love his brother.

III. LOVE FOR ONE ANOTHER

[11] * For this is the message you have heard from the beginning: we should love one another, [i] [12] unlike Cain who belonged to the evil one and slaughtered his brother. Why did he slaughter him? Because his own works were evil, and those of his

---

3, 4: *Lawlessness:* a reference to the activity of the antichrist, so it is expressed as hostility toward God and a rejection of Christ. The author goes on to contrast the states of sin and righteousness. Christians do not escape sin but realize that when they sin they cease to have fellowship with God. Virtue and sin distinguish the children of God from the children of the devil.

3, 9: A habitual sinner is a child of the devil, while a child of God, who by definition is in fellowship with God, cannot sin. *Seed:* Christ or the Spirit who shares the nature of God with the Christian.

3, 11-18: Love, even to the point of self-sacrifice, is the point of the commandment. The story of Cain and Abel (12-15; Gn 4, 1-16) presents the rivalry of two brothers, in a contrast of evil and righteousness, where envy led to murder. For Christians, proof of deliverance is love toward others, after the example of Christ. This includes concrete acts of charity, out of our material abundance.

brother righteous.[j] [13] Do not be amazed, [then,] brothers, if the world hates you.[k] [14] We know that we have passed from death to life because we love our brothers. Whoever does not love remains in death.[l] [15] Everyone who hates his brother is a murderer, and you know that no murderer has eternal life remaining in him.[m] [16] The way we came to know love was that he laid down his life for us; so we ought to lay down our lives for our brothers.[n] [17] If someone who has worldly means sees a brother in need and refuses him compassion, how can the love of God remain in him?[o] [18] Children, let us love not in word or speech but in deed and truth.[p]

Confidence before God.* [19] [Now] this is how we shall know that we* belong to the truth and reassure our hearts before him [20] in whatever our hearts condemn, for God is greater than our hearts and knows everything. [21] Beloved, if [our] hearts do not condemn us, we have confidence in God [22] and receive from him whatever we ask, because we keep his commandments and do what pleases him.[q] [23] And his commandment is this: we should believe in the name of his Son, Jesus Christ, and love one another just as he commanded us.[r] [24] Those who keep his commandments remain in him, and he in them, and the way we know that he remains in us is from the Spirit that he gave us.[s]

CHAPTER 4

Testing the Spirits.* [1] Beloved, do not trust every spirit but test the spirits to see whether they belong to God, because many false prophets have gone out into the world.[t] [2] This is how you can know the Spirit of God: every spirit that acknowledges Jesus Christ come in the flesh belongs to God,[u] [3] and every spirit that does not acknowledge Jesus* does not belong to God. This is the spirit of the antichrist that, as you heard, is to come, but in fact is already in the world.[v] [4] You belong to God, children, and you have conquered them, for the one who is in you is greater than the one who is in the world. [5] They belong to the world; accordingly, their teaching belongs to the world, and the world listens to them.[w] [6] We belong to God, and anyone who knows God listens to us, while anyone who does not belong to God refuses to hear us. This is how we know the spirit of truth and the spirit of deceit.[x]

God's Love and Christian Life. [7] * Beloved, let us love one another, because love is of God; everyone who loves is begotten by God and knows God. [8] Whoever is without love does not know God, for God is love. [9] In this way the love of God was revealed to us: God sent his only Son into the world so that we might have life through him.[y] [10] In this is love: not that we have loved God, but that he loved us and sent his Son as expiation for our sins.[z] [11] Beloved, if God so loved us, we also must love one another. [12] No one has ever seen God. Yet, if we love one another, God remains in us, and his love is brought to perfection in us.[a]

[13] * This is how we know that we remain in him and he in us, that he has given us of his Spirit. [14] Moreover, we have seen and

---

j Gn 4, 8; Jude 11.—k Mt 24, 9; Jn 15, 18; 17, 14.—l Lv 19, 17; Jn 5, 24.—m Jn 8, 44.—n Mt 20, 28; Jn 10, 11; 15, 13.—o Dt 15, 7.11; Jas 2, 15-16.—p Jas 1, 22.—q 1 Jn 5, 15; Mt 7, 7-11; 21, 22; Jn 14, 13-14.—r Jn 13, 34; 15, 17.—s 1 Jn 4, 13; Jn 14, 21-23.—t 1 Jn 2, 18; Mt 24, 24.—u 1 Cor 12, 3; 1 Thes 5, 21.—v 1 Jn 1, 22.—w Jn 15, 19.—x Jn 8, 47; 10, 16.—y Jn 3, 16.—z Rom 5, 8.—a Jn 1, 18; 1 Tm 6, 16.

3, 19-24: Living a life of faith in Jesus and of Christian love assures us of abiding in God no matter what our feelings may at times tell us. Our obedience gives us confidence in prayer and trust in God's judgment. This obedience includes our belief in Christ and love for one another.

3, 19b-20: This difficult passage may also be translated "we shall be at peace before him in whatever our hearts condemn, for . . ." or "and before God we shall convince our hearts, if our hearts condemn us, that God is greater than our hearts."

4, 1-6: Deception is possible in spiritual phenomena and may be tested by its relation to Christian doctrine (cf 1 Cor 12, 3): those who fail to acknowledge Jesus Christ in the flesh are false prophets and belong to the antichrist. Even though these false prophets are well received in the world, the Christian who belongs to God has a greater power in the truth.

4, 3: *Does not acknowledge Jesus:* some ancient manuscripts add "Christ" and/or "to have come in the flesh" (cf 1 Jn 4, 2), and others read "every spirit that annuls (or severs) Jesus."

4, 7-12: Love as we share in it testifies to the nature of God and to his presence in our lives. One who loves shows that one is a child of God and knows God, for God's very being is love; one without love is without God. The revelation of the nature of God's love is found in the free gift of his Son to us, so that we may share life with God and be delivered from our sins. The love we have for one another must be of the same sort: authentic, merciful; this unique Christian love is our proof that we know God and can "see" the invisible God.

4, 13-21: The testimony of the Spirit and that of faith join the testimony of love to confirm our knowledge of God. Our love is grounded in the confession of Jesus as the Son of God and the example of God's love for us. Christian life is founded on the knowledge of God as love and on his continuing presence that relieves us from fear of judgment (16-18). What Christ is gives us confidence, even as we live and love in this world. Yet Christian love is not abstract but lived in the concrete manner of love for one another.

1Jn

testify that the Father sent his Son as savior of the world. [15]Whoever acknowledges that Jesus is the Son of God, God remains in him and he in God. [16]We have come to know and to believe in the love God has for us.

God is love, and whoever remains in love remains in God and God in him. [17]In this is love brought to perfection among us, that we have confidence on the day of judgment because as he is, so are we in this world.[b] [18]There is no fear in love, but perfect love drives out fear because fear has to do with punishment, and so one who fears is not yet perfect in love. [19]We love because he first loved us. [20]If anyone says, "I love God," but hates his brother, he is a liar; for whoever does not love a brother whom he has seen cannot love God* whom he has not seen.[c] [21]This is the commandment we have from him: whoever loves God must also love his brother.[d]

CHAPTER 5

Faith is Victory over the World. [1] * Everyone who believes that Jesus is the Christ is begotten by God, and everyone who loves the father loves [also] the one begotten by him.[e] [2]In this way we know that we love the children of God when we love God and obey his commandments. [3]For the love of God is this, that we keep his commandments. And his commandments are not burdensome,[f] [4]for whoever is begotten by God conquers the world. And the victory that conquers the world is our faith.[g] [5]Who [indeed] is the victor over the world but the one who believes that Jesus is the Son of God?[h]

[6]This is the one who came through water and blood,* Jesus Christ, not by water alone, but by water and blood. The Spirit is the one that testifies, and the Spirit is truth.[i] [7]So there are three that testify, [8]the Spirit, the water, and the blood, and the three are of one accord.[j] [9]If we accept human testimony, the testimony of God is surely greater. Now the testimony of God is this, that he has testified on behalf of his Son.[k] [10]Whoever believes in the Son of God has this testimony within himself. Whoever does not believe God has made him a liar by not believing the testimony God has given about his Son.[l] [11]And this is the testimony: God gave us eternal life, and this life is in his Son.[m] [12]Whoever possesses the Son has life; whoever does not possess the Son of God does not have life.

IV. EPILOGUE*

Prayer for Sinners. [13]I write these things to you so that you may know that you have eternal life, you who believe in the name of the Son of God.[n] [14]And we have this confidence in him, that if we ask anything according to his will, he hears us.[o] [15]And if we know that he hears us in regard to whatever we ask, we know that what we have asked him for is ours. [16]If anyone sees his brother sinning, if the sin is not deadly, he should pray to God and he will give him life. This is only for those whose sin is not deadly. There is such a thing as deadly sin, about which I do not say that you should pray.[p] [17]All wrongdoing is sin, but there is sin that is not deadly.

[18]We know that no one begotten by God sins; but the one begotten by God he protects, and the evil one cannot touch him.

b 1 Jn 2, 28.—c 1 Jn 2, 4.—d Jn 13, 34; 14, 15.21; 15, 17.—e Jn 8, 42; 1 Pt 1, 23.—f Jn 14, 15.—g Jn 16, 33.—h 1 Cor 15, 57.—i Jn 15, 26; 19, 34.—j Jn 5, 32.36; 15, 26.—k Jn 5, 32.37.—l 1 Jn 3, 33.—m 1 Jn 1, 2; Jn 1, 4; 5, 21.26; 17, 3.—n Jn 1, 12; 20, 31.—o 1 Jn 3, 21-22; Mt 7, 7; Jn 14, 13-14.—p Mt 12, 31.

4, 20: *Cannot love God:* some ancient manuscripts read "how can he love . . . ?"

5, 1-5: Children of God are identified not only by their love for others (1 Jn 4, 7-9) and for God (1 Jn 5, 1-2) but by their belief in the divine sonship of Jesus Christ. Faith, the acceptance of Jesus in his true character and the obedience in love to God's commands (3), is the source of the Christian's power in the world and conquers the world of evil (4-5), even as Christ overcame the world (Jn 16, 33).

5, 6-12: *Water and blood* (6) refers to Christ's baptism (Mt 3, 16-17) and to the shedding of his blood on the cross (Jn 19, 34). *The Spirit* was present at the baptism (Mt 3, 16; Mk 1, 10; Lk 3, 22; Jn 1, 32.34). *The testimony* to Christ as the Son of

God is confirmed by divine witness (7-9), greater by far than the two legally required human witnesses (Dt 17, 6). To deny this is to deny God's truth; cf Jn 8, 17-18. The gist of the divine witness or *testimony* is that *eternal life* (11-12) is given in Christ and nowhere else. To *possess the Son* is not acceptance of a doctrine but of a person who lives now and provides life.

5, 13-21: As children of God we have confidence in prayer because of our intimate relationship with him (14-15). In love, we pray (16-17) for those who are in *sin,* but not in *deadly sin* (literally, "sin unto death"), probably referring to apostasy or activities brought on under the antichrist; cf Mk 3, 29; Heb 6, 4-6; 10, 26-31. Even in the latter case, however, prayer, while not enjoined, is not forbidden. The letter concludes with a summary of the themes of the letter (18-20). There is a sharp antithesis between the children of God and those belonging to the world and to the evil one. The Son reveals the God of truth; Christians dwell in the true God, *in his Son,* and have eternal life. The final verse (21) voices a perennial warning about *idols,* any type of rival to God.

[19] We know that we belong to God, and the whole world is under the power of the evil one. [20] We also know that the Son of God

q Jer 24, 7; Jn 17, 3; Eph 1, 17.

has come and has given us discernment to know the one who is true. And we are in the one who is true, in his Son Jesus Christ. He is the true God and eternal life. [q] [21] Children, be on your guard against idols.

THE SECOND LETTER OF JOHN

INTRODUCTION

Written in response to similar problems, the Second and Third Letters of John are of the same length, perhaps determined by the practical consideration of the writing space on one piece of papyrus. In each letter the writer calls himself "the Presbyter," and their common authorship is further evidenced by internal similarities in style and wording, especially in the introductions and conclusions. The literary considerations that link 2 and 3 John also link them with the First Letter and the Gospel of John. The concern with "truth," christology, mutual love, the new commandment, antichrist, and the integrity of witness to the earthly Jesus mark these works as products of the Johannine school. The identity of the Presbyter is problematic. The use of the title implies more than age, and refers to his position of leadership in the early church. The absence of a proper name indicates that he was well known and acknowledged in authority by the communities to which he writes. Although traditionally attributed to John the apostle, these letters were probably written by a disciple or scribe of an apostle. The traditional place and date of composition, Ephesus at the end of the first century, are plausible for both letters.

The Second Letter is addressed to "the chosen Lady" and "to her children." This literary image of a particular Christian community reflects the specific destination and purpose of the letter. Unlike 1 John, this brief letter is not a theological treatise but a reply to problems within the church. The Johannine themes of love and truth are used to support practical advice on Christian living. The Presbyter encourages community members to show their Christianity by adhering to the great commandment of mutual love and to the historical truth about Jesus. The false teaching present among them is a spiritualizing christology that may tempt some members to discount teachings about the incarnation and death of Jesus the Christ; cf 1 Jn 4, 2. For their protection the Presbyter forbids hospitality toward unknown or "progressive" Christians to prevent their infiltration of the community. The Second Letter preserves the Johannine concerns of doctrinal purity and active love in the form of pastoral advice to a threatened community.

[1] [a] The Presbyter to the chosen Lady* and to her children whom I love in truth— and not only I but also all who know the truth—[2] because of the truth that dwells in

a Jn 8, 32; 3 Jn 1.

us and will be with us forever. [3] Grace, mercy, and peace* will be with us from God the Father and from Jesus Christ the Father's Son in truth and love.

1: *The chosen Lady:* literally "elected"; this could also be translated "Kyria (a woman's name) chosen (by God)" or "the lady Electa" or "Electa Kyria." The adjective "chosen" is applied to all Christians at the beginning of other New Testament letters (1 Pt 1, 1; Ti 1, 1). The description is of a specific community with "children" who are its members. *The truth:* the affirmation of Jesus in the flesh and in contrast to false teaching (7).

3: *Grace, mercy, and peace:* like 1 and 2 Tm this letter adds *mercy* to the terms used frequently in a salutation to describe Christian blessing; it appears only here in the Johannine writings. The author also puts the blessing in relation to *truth* and *love,* the watchwords of the Johannine teaching. *The Father's Son:* the title that affirms the close relationship of Christ to God; similar variations of this title occur elsewhere (Jn 1, 14; 3, 35), but the precise wording is not found elsewhere in the New Testament.

2Jn

[4] I rejoiced greatly to find some of your children* walking in the truth just as we were commanded by the Father.[b] [5] But now, Lady, I ask you, not as though I were writing a new commandment but the one we have had from the beginning: let us love one another.[c] [6] For this is love, that we walk according to his commandments;* this is the commandment, as you heard from the beginning, in which you should walk.[d]

[7] [e] Many deceivers have gone out into the world, those who do not acknowledge Jesus Christ as coming in the flesh; such is the deceitful one and the antichrist.* [8] Look to yourselves that you* do not lose what we worked for but may receive a full recompense. [9] [f] Anyone who is so "progressive"* as not to remain in the teaching of the Christ does not have God; whoever remains in the teaching has the Father and the Son. [10] * If anyone comes to you and does not bring this doctrine, do not receive him in your house or even greet him;[g] [11] for whoever greets him shares in his evil works.

[12] Although I have much to write to you, I do not intend to use paper and ink. Instead, I hope to visit you and to speak face to face so that our joy* may be complete.[h] [13] The children of your chosen sister* send you greetings.

---

b 3 Jn 3.—c Jn 13, 34; 15, 12; 1 Jn 4, 7.—d Jn 13, 34; 14, 15; 1 Jn 5, 3.—e 1 Jn 2, 22; 4, 2.—f Jn 8, 31; 1 Jn 2, 23; 4, 15.—g Rom 16, 17; 2 Thes 3, 6.—h Jn 15, 11; 1 Jn 1, 4; 3 Jn 13.

4: *Some of your children:* this refers to those whom the Presbyter has recently encountered, but it may also indicate the presence of false doctrine in the community: the Presbyter encourages those who have remained faithful. *Walking in the truth:* an expression used in the Johannine writings to describe a way of living in which the Christian faith is visibly expressed; cf 1 Jn 1, 6-7; 2, 6.11; 3 Jn 3.

6: *His commandments:* cf 1 Jn 3, 23; 2, 7-8; 4, 21; obedience to the commandment of faith and love includes all others.

7: *The antichrist:* see 1 Jn 2, 18-19.22; 4, 3.

8: *You* (plural): it is not certain whether this means the Christians addressed or includes the Presbyter, since some of the ancient Greek manuscripts and Greek Fathers have "we."

9: *Anyone who is so "progressive":* literally, "Anyone who goes ahead." Some gnostic groups held the doctrine of the Christ come in the flesh to be a first step in belief, which the more advanced and spiritual believer surpassed and abandoned in his knowledge of the spiritual Christ. The author affirms that fellowship with God may be gained only by holding to the complete doctrine of Jesus Christ (1 Jn 2, 22-23; 4, 2; 5, 5-6).

10-11: At this time false teachers were considered so dangerous and divisive as to be shunned completely. From this description they seem to be wandering preachers. We see here a natural suspicion of early Christians concerning such itinerants and can envisage the problems faced by missionaries such as those mentioned in 3 Jn 10.

12: *Our joy:* a number of other Greek manuscripts read "your joy."

13: *Chosen sister:* the community of which the Presbyter is now a part greets you (singular), the community of the Lady addressed.

THE THIRD LETTER OF JOHN

INTRODUCTION

The Third Letter of John preserves a brief glimpse into the problems of missionary activity and local autonomy in the early church. In contrast to the other two letters of John, this work was addressed to a specific individual, Gaius. This letter is less theological in content and purpose. The author's goal was to secure hospitality and material support for his missionaries, and the Presbyter is writing to another member of the church who has welcomed missionaries in the past. The Presbyter commends Gaius for his hospitality and encourages his future help. He indicates he may come to challenge the policy of Diotrephes that is based on evil gossip.

The problems of the Presbyter in this short letter provide us with valuable evidence of the flexible and personal nature of authority in the early church. The Presbyter writes to Gaius, whom perhaps he had converted or instructed, on the basis of their personal links. The brothers have also confirmed him as a loyal Christian in action and belief. Gaius accepted the missionaries from the Presbyter and presumably will accept Demetrius on the Presbyter's recommendation. In contrast, Diotrephes refuses to receive either letters or friends of the Presbyter. Although he is portrayed as ambitious and hostile, he perhaps exemplifies the cautious and sectarian nature of early Christianity; for its own protection the local community mistrusted missionaries as false teachers. Most interestingly, Diotrephes seems comfortable in ignoring the requests of the Presbyter. The Presbyter seems to acknowledge that only a personal confrontation with Diotrephes will remedy the situation (10). The division, however, may also rest on doctrinal disagreement in which Gaius and the other "friends" accept the teaching of the Presbyter, and Diotrephes does not; the missionaries are not received for suspicion of theological error. Diotrephes has thus been viewed by some as an overly ambitious local upstart trying to thwart the advance of orthodox Christianity, by others as an orthodox church official suspicious of the teachings of the Presbyter and those in the Johannine school who think as he does, or by still others as a local leader anxious to keep the debates in the Johannine community out of his own congregation.

This brief letter and the situation that it mirrors show us how little we know about some details of early development in the church: schools of opinion existed around which questions of faith and life were discussed, and personal ties as well as doctrine and authority played a role in what happened amid divisions and unity.

¹The Presbyter to the beloved Gaius* whom I love in truth. *a*

²Beloved, I hope you are prospering in every respect and are in good health, just as your soul is prospering. ³I rejoiced greatly when some of the brothers* came and testified to how truly you walk in the truth. *b* ⁴Nothing gives me greater joy than to hear that my children are walking in the truth. *c*

⁵Beloved, you are faithful in all you do* for the brothers, especially for strangers; *d* ⁶they have testified to your love before the church. *e* Please help them in a way worthy of God to continue their journey.* ⁷For they have set out for the sake of the Name* and are accepting nothing from the pagans. ⁸Therefore, we ought to support such persons, so that we may be co-workers in the truth.

⁹I wrote to the church, but Diotrephes, who loves to dominate,* does not acknowledge us. ¹⁰Therefore, if I come,* I will draw attention to what he is doing, spreading evil nonsense about us. And not content with that, he will not receive the brothers, hindering those who wish to do so and expelling them from the church.

¹¹Beloved, do not imitate evil* but imitate good. Whoever does what is good is of God; whoever does what is evil has never seen God. *f* ¹²Demetrius* receives a good report from all, even from the truth itself. We give our testimonial as well, and you know our testimony is true. *g*

¹³I have much to write to you, but I do not wish to write with pen and ink. *h* ¹⁴Instead, I hope to see you soon, when we can talk face to face. ¹⁵Peace be with you. The friends greet you; greet the friends* there each by name. *i*

a 2 Jn 1.—b 3 Jn 5; Gal 6, 10; 2 Jn 4.—c 1 Thes 2, 11-12; 1 Tm 1, 2; 2 Tm 1, 2; 1 Jn 2, 1; 2 Jn 4.—d Rom 12, 13; Gal 6, 10; Heb 13, 2.—e Acts 15, 3; Col 1, 10; 1 Thes 2, 12.—f 1 Jn 2, 29; 3, 6.10.—g Jn 19, 35; 21, 24; 1 Tm 3, 7.—h 2 Jn 12.—i Jn 20, 19.21.26; Eph 6, 23; 1 Pt 5, 14.

1: *Beloved Gaius:* a frequent form of address for fellow Christians in New Testament epistolary literature.

3: *The brothers:* in this letter, the term may refer to Christians who have been missionaries and received hospitality from Gaius (5-6). *Walk in the truth:* the common Johannine term to describe Christian living; this description presents Gaius as following the teachings of the Presbyter in contrast to Diotrephes.

5: *You are faithful in all you do:* Gaius's aid to the missionaries is a manifestation of his true Christian faith.

6: *Help them . . . to continue their journey:* the Presbyter asks Gaius not only to continue to welcome the missionaries to his community but also to equip them for further travels.

7: *The Name:* of Jesus Christ (cf Acts 5, 41; 1 Jn 2, 12; 3, 23; 5, 13). *Accepting nothing:* not expecting support from the pagans to whom they preach the gospel, so that they will not be considered as beggars; they required support from other Christians; cf Paul's complaints to the Corinthians (1 Cor 9, 3-12).

9: *Who loves to dominate:* the Presbyter does not deny Diotrephes' place as leader but indicates that his ambition may have caused him to disregard his letter and his influence.

10: *If I come:* the Presbyter may visit the community to challenge the actions of Diotrephes toward himself and the missionaries. *Will not receive the brothers:* Diotrephes may have been critical of the teachings of the Presbyter and sought to maintain doctrinal purity; cf 1 Jn 2, 19 and 2 Jn 10-11.

11: *Do not imitate evil:* Gaius should not be influenced by the behavior of Diotrephes.

12: *Demetrius:* because of the fear of false teachers, Demetrius, perhaps the bearer of the letter, is provided with a recommendation from the Presbyter; cf 2 Cor 3, 1; Rom 16, 1. *Even from the truth itself:* this refers probably to the manner of Demetrius's life that testifies to his true belief; cf Gaius above (v 3).

15: *Friends:* although a Johannine term for Christians (Jn 15, 15), the word here may refer to those in the community loyal to the Presbyter and to Gaius.

3Jn

THE LETTER OF JUDE

INTRODUCTION

This letter is by its address attributed to "Jude, a slave of Jesus Christ and brother of James" (1). Since he is not identified as an apostle, this designation can hardly be meant to refer to the Jude or Judas who is listed as one of the Twelve (Lk 6, 16; Acts 1, 13; cf Jn 14, 22). The person intended is almost certainly the other Jude, named in the gospels among the relatives of Jesus (Mt 13, 55; Mk 6, 3), and the James who is listed there as his brother is the one to whom the Letter of James is attributed (see the Introduction to James). Nothing else is known of this Jude, and the apparent need to identify him by reference to his better-known brother indicates that he was a rather obscure personage in the early church.

The letter is addressed in the most general terms to "those who are called, beloved in God the Father and kept safe for Jesus Christ" (1), hence apparently to all Christians. But since its purpose is to warn the addressees against false teachers, the author must have had in mind one or more specific Christian communities located in the unidentified region where the errors in question constituted a danger. While the letter contains some Semitic features, there is nothing to identify the addressees specifically as Jewish Christians; indeed, the errors envisaged seem to reflect an early form of gnosticism, opposed to law, that points rather to the cultural context of the Gentile world. Like James and 2 Peter, the Letter of Jude manifests none of the typical features of the letter form except the address.

There is so much similarity between Jude and 2 Peter, especially Jude 4-16 and 2 Peter 2, 1-18, that there must be a literary relationship between them. Since there is no evidence for the view that both authors borrowed from the same source, it is usually supposed that one of them borrowed from the other. Most scholars believe that Jude is the earlier of the two, principally because he quotes two apocryphal Jewish works, the Assumption of Moses (9) and the Book of Enoch (14-15), as part of his structured argument, whereas 2 Peter omits both references. Since there was controversy in the early church about the propriety of citing noncanonical literature that included legendary material, it is more probable that a later writer would omit such references than that he would add them.

Many interpreters today consider Jude a pseudonymous work dating from the end of the first century or even later. In support of this view they adduce the following arguments: (a) the apostles are referred to as belonging to an age that has receded into the past (17-18); (b) faith is understood as a body of doctrine handed down by a process of tradition (3); (c) the author's competent Greek style shows that he must have had a Hellenistic cultural formation; (d) the gnostic character of the errors envisaged fits better into the early second century than into a period several decades earlier. While impressive, these arguments are not entirely compelling and do not completely rule out the possibility of composition around the year A.D. 80, when the historical Jude may still have been alive.

This little letter is an urgent note by an author who intended to write more fully about salvation to an unknown group of readers, but who was forced by dangers from false teachers worming their way into the community (3-4) to dash off a warning against them (5-16) and to deliver some pressing Christian admonitions (17-23). The letter is justly famous for its majestic closing doxology (24-25).

Address and Greeting. [1] Jude, a slave of Jesus Christ and brother of James,* to those who are called, beloved in God the Father and kept safe for Jesus Christ:[a] [2] may mercy, peace, and love be yours in abundance.[b]

Occasion for Writing. [3] Beloved, although I was making every effort to write to you about our common salvation,* I now feel a need to write to encourage you to contend for the faith that was once for all handed down to the holy ones.[c] [4] For there have been some intruders, who long ago were designated for this condemnation, godless persons, who pervert the grace of our God into licentiousness and who deny our only Master and Lord, Jesus Christ.[d]

The False Teachers. [5] [e] I wish to remind you, although you know all things, that [the] Lord who once saved a people from the land of Egypt later destroyed those who did not believe.* [6] [f] The angels too, who did not keep to their own domain but deserted their proper dwelling, he has kept in eternal chains, in gloom, for the judgment of the great day.* [7] Likewise, Sodom, Gomorrah, and the surrounding towns, which, in the same manner as they, indulged in sexual promiscuity and practiced unnatural vice,* serve as an example by undergoing a punishment of eternal fire.[g]

[8] Similarly, these dreamers* nevertheless also defile the flesh, scorn lordship, and revile glorious beings. [9] Yet the archangel Michael, when he argued with the devil in a dispute over the body of Moses, did not venture to pronounce a reviling judgment* upon him but said, "May the Lord rebuke you!"[h] [10] But these people revile what they do not understand and are destroyed by what they know by nature like irrational animals.[i] [11] Woe to them![j] They followed the way of Cain, abandoned themselves to Balaam's error for the sake of gain, and perished in the rebellion of Korah.* [12] These are blemishes on your love feasts,* as they carouse fearlessly and look after themselves. They are waterless clouds blown about by winds, fruitless trees in late autumn, twice dead and uprooted.[k] [13] They are like wild waves of the sea, foaming up their shameless deeds, wandering stars for whom the gloom of darkness has been reserved forever.

[14] * Enoch, of the seventh generation from Adam, prophesied also about them when he said,[l] "Behold, the Lord has come with his countless holy ones [15] to execute judgment on all and to convict everyone for all the godless deeds that they committed and for all the harsh words godless sinners have uttered against him." [16] These

---

a Mt 13, 55; Mk 6, 3; Acts 12, 17; Rom 1, 7.—b Gal 6, 16; 1 Tm 1, 2; 2 Pt 1, 2.—c Jude 17.20; 1 Tm 6, 12.—d Gal 2, 4; 2 Tm 3, 6; 2 Pt 2, 1.—e Nm 14, 35; 1 Cor 10, 5; Heb 3, 16.17.—f 2 Pt 2, 4.9.—g Dt 29, 22-24; Mt 25, 41; 2 Thes 1, 8-9; 2 Pt 2, 6; 3, 7.—h Dn 10, 21; 12, 1.—i 2 Pt 2, 12.—j Gn 4, 8-16; 1 Jn 3, 12 / Nm 31, 15-16; 2 Pt 2, 15; Rv 2, 14 / Nm 16, 19-35.—k 2 Pt 2, 13.17.—l 14-15: Mt 16, 27; Heb 12, 22-23.

1: *Jude . . . brother of James:* for the identity of the author of this letter, see Introduction. *To those who are called:* the vocation to the Christian faith is God's free gift to those whom he loves and whom he safely protects in Christ until the Lord's second coming.

3-4: *Our common salvation:* the teachings of the Christian faith derived from the apostolic preaching and to be kept by the Christian community.

5: For this first example of divine punishment on those who had been saved but did not then keep faith, see Nm 14, 28-29 and the note there. Some manuscripts have the word "once" (*hapax* as at Jude 3) after "you know"; some commentators have suggested that it means "knowing one thing" or "you know all things once for all." Instead of "[the] Lord" manuscripts vary, having "Jesus," "God," or no subject stated.

6: This second example draws on Gn 6, 1-4 as elaborated in the apocryphal Book of Enoch (cf Jude 14): heavenly beings came to earth and had sexual intercourse with women. God punished them by casting them out of heaven into darkness and bondage.

7: *Practiced unnatural vice:* literally, "went after alien flesh." This example derives from Gn 19, 1-25, especially 4-11, when the townsmen of Sodom violated both hospitality and morality by demanding that Lot's two visitors (really messengers of Yahweh) be handed over to them so that they could abuse them

sexually. *Unnatural vice:* this refers to the desire for intimacies by human beings with angels (the reverse of the example in Jude 6). Sodom (whence "sodomy") and Gomorrah became proverbial as object lessons for God's punishment on sin (Is 1, 9; Jer 50, 40; Am 4, 11; Mt 10, 15; 2 Pt 2, 6).

8: *Dreamers:* the writer returns to the false teachers of v 4, applying charges from the three examples in vv 5, 6, 7. This may apply to claims they make for revelations they have received by night (to the author, hallucinations). *Defile the flesh:* this may mean bodily pollutions from the erotic dreams of sexual license (7). *Lordship . . . glorious beings:* these may reflect the Lord (5; Jesus, 4) whom they spurn and the angels (6; cf the note on 2 Pt 2, 10, here, as there, literally, "glories").

9: *The archangel Michael . . . judgment:* a reference to an incident in the apocryphal Assumption of Moses. Dt 34, 6 had said of Moses, literally in Greek, "they buried him" or "he (God?) buried him" (taken to mean "he was buried"). The later account tells how Michael, who was sent to bury him, was challenged by the devil's interest in the body. Our author draws out the point that if an archangel refrained from reviling even the devil, how wrong it is for mere human beings to revile glorious beings (angels).

11: *Cain . . . Balaam . . . Korah:* examples of rebellious men and of the punishment their conduct incurred; cf Gn 4, 8-16; Nm 16, 1-35; 31, 16. See the note on 2 Pt 2, 15.

12: *Blemishes on your love feasts:* or "hidden rocks" or "submerged reefs" (cf Jude 13). The opponents engaged in scandalous conduct in connection with community gatherings called *love feasts* (agape meals), which were associated with eucharistic celebrations at certain stages of early Christian practice; cf 1 Cor 11, 18-34 and the note on 2 Pt 2, 13.

14-15: Cited from the apocryphal Book of Enoch 1, 9.

Jude

people are complainers, disgruntled ones who live by their desires; their mouths utter bombast as they fawn over people to gain advantage.*m*

Exhortations. [17] But you, beloved, remember the words spoken beforehand by the apostles of our Lord Jesus Christ,*n* [18] for they told you,*o* "In [the] last time there will be scoffers who will live according to their own godless desires."* [19] These are the ones who cause divisions; they live on the natural plane, devoid of the Spirit.*p* [20] But you, beloved, build yourselves up in your most holy faith; pray in the holy Spirit.*q* [21] Keep yourselves in the love of

God and wait for the mercy of our Lord Jesus Christ that leads to eternal life.*r* [22] On those who waver, have mercy;* [23] save others by snatching them out of the fire; on others have mercy with fear,* abhorring even the outer garment stained by the flesh.

Doxology.* [24] To the one who is able to keep you from stumbling and to present you unblemished and exultant, in the presence of his glory,*s* [25] to the only God, our savior, through Jesus Christ our Lord be glory, majesty, power, and authority from ages past, now, and for ages to come. Amen.*t*

---

m Jude 18; 1 Cor 10, 10; 2 Pt 2, 10.18.—n Heb 2, 3; 2 Pt 3, 2.—o 1 Tm 4, 1; 2 Tm 3, 1-5; 2 Pt 3, 3.—p 1 Cor 2, 14; Jas 3, 15.—q Jude 2; Eph 6, 18; Col 2, 7.—r Ti 2, 13.—s 2 Cor 4, 14; 1 Pt 4, 13.—t Rom 11, 36; 1 Tm 1, 17.

18: This is the substance of much early Christian preaching rather than a direct quotation of any of the various New Testament passages on this theme (see Mk 13, 22; Acts 20, 30; 1 Tm 4, 1-3; 2 Pt 3, 3).

22: *Have mercy:* some manuscripts read "convince," "confute," or "reprove." Others have "even though you waver" or "doubt" instead of *who waver.*

23: *With fear:* some manuscripts connect the phrase "with fear" with the imperative "save" or with the participle "snatching." Other manuscripts omit the phrase "on others have mercy," so that only two groups are envisioned. Rescue of those led astray and caution in the endeavor are both enjoined. *Outer garment stained by the flesh:* the imagery may come from Zec 3, 3-5, just as that of *snatching. . . out of the fire* comes from Zec 3, 2; the very garments of the godless are to be abhorred because of their contagion.

24-25: With this liturgical statement about the power of God to keep the faithful from stumbling, and praise to him through Jesus Christ, the letter reaches its conclusion by returning to the themes with which it began (1-2).

THE BOOK OF REVELATION

INTRODUCTION

The Apocalypse, or Revelation to John, the last book of the Bible, is one of the most difficult to understand because it abounds in unfamiliar and extravagant symbolism, which at best appears unusual to the modern reader. Symbolic language, however, is one of the chief characteristics of apocalyptic literature, of which this book is an outstanding example. Such literature enjoyed wide popularity in both Jewish and Christian circles from ca. 200 B.C. to A.D. 200.

This book contains an account of visions in symbolic and allegorical language borrowed extensively from the Old Testament, especially Ezekiel, Zechariah, and Daniel. Whether or not these visions were real experiences of the author or simply literary conventions employed by him is an open question.

This much, however, is certain: symbolic descriptions are not to be taken as literal descriptions, nor is the symbolism meant to be pictured realistically. One would find it difficult and repulsive to visualize a lamb with seven horns and seven eyes; yet Jesus Christ is described in precisely such words (5, 6). The author used these images to suggest Christ's universal (seven) power (horns) and knowledge (eyes). A significant feature of apocalyptic writing is the use of symbolic colors, metals, garments (1, 13-16; 3, 18; 4, 4; 6, 1-8; 17, 4; 19, 8), and numbers (four signifies the world, six imperfection, seven totality of perfection, twelve Israel's tribes or the apostles, one thousand immensity). Finally the vindictive language in the book (6, 9-10; 18, 1—19, 4) is also to be understood symbolically and not literally. The cries for vengeance on the lips of Christian martyrs that sound so harsh are in fact literary devices the author employed to evoke in the reader and hearer a feeling of horror for apostasy and rebellion that will be severely punished by God.

The lurid descriptions of the punishment of Jezebel (2, 22) and of the destruction of the great harlot, Babylon (16, 9—19, 2), are likewise literary devices. The metaphor of Babylon as harlot would be wrongly construed if interpreted literally. On the other hand, the stylized figure of the woman clothed with the sun (12, 1-6), depicting the New Israel, may seem to be a negative stereotype. It is necessary to look beyond the literal meaning to see that these images mean to convey a sense of God's wrath at sin in the former case and trust in God's providential care over the church in the latter.

The Book of Revelation cannot be adequately understood except against the historical background that occasioned its writing. Like Daniel and other apocalypses, it was composed as resistance literature to meet a crisis. The book itself suggests that the crisis was ruthless persecution of the early church by the Roman authorities; the harlot Babylon symbolizes pagan Rome, the city on seven hills (17, 9). The book is, then, an exhortation and admonition to Christians of the first century to stand firm in the faith and to avoid compromise with paganism, despite the threat of adversity and martyrdom; they are to await patiently the fulfillment of God's mighty promises. The triumph of God in the world of men and women remains a mystery, to be accepted in faith and longed for in hope. It is a triumph that unfolded in the history of Jesus of Nazareth and continues to unfold in the history of the individual Christian who follows the way of the cross, even, if necessary, to a martyr's death.

Though the perspective is eschatological—ultimate salvation and victory are said to take place at the end of the present age when Christ will come in glory at the parousia—the book presents the decisive struggle of Christ and his followers against Satan and his

Rv

cohorts as already over. Christ's overwhelming defeat of the kingdom of Satan ushered in the everlasting reign of God (11, 15; 12, 10). Even the forces of evil unwittingly carry out the divine plan (17, 17), for God is the sovereign Lord of history.

The Book of Revelation had its origin in a time of crisis, but it remains valid and meaningful for Christians of all time. In the face of apparently insuperable evil, either from within or from without, all Christians are called to trust in Jesus' promise, "Behold, I am with you always, until the end of the age" (Mt 28, 20). Those who remain steadfast in their faith and confidence in the risen Lord need have no fear. Suffering, persecution, even death by martyrdom, though remaining impenetrable mysteries of evil, do not comprise an absurd dead end. No matter what adversity or sacrifice Christians may endure, they will in the end triumph over Satan and his forces because of their fidelity to Christ the victor. This is the enduring message of the book; it is a message of hope and consolation and challenge for all who dare to believe.

The author of the book calls himself John (1, 1.4.9; 22, 8), who because of his Christian faith has been exiled to the rocky island of Patmos, a Roman penal colony. Although he never claims to be John the apostle, whose name is attached to the fourth gospel, he was so identified by several of the early church Fathers, including Justin, Irenaeus, Clement of Alexandria, Tertullian, Cyprian, and Hippolytus. This identification, however, was denied by other Fathers, including Denis of Alexandria, Eusebius of Caesarea, Cyril of Jerusalem, Gregory Nazianzen, and John Chrysostom. Indeed, vocabulary, grammar, and style make it doubtful that the book could have been put into its present form by the same person(s) responsible for the fourth gospel. Nevertheless, there are definite linguistic and theological affinities between the two books. The tone of the letters to the seven churches (1, 4—3, 22) is indicative of the great authority the author enjoyed over the Christian communities in Asia. It is possible, therefore, that he was a disciple of John the apostle, who is traditionally associated with that part of the world. The date of the book in its present form is probably near the end of the reign of Domitian (A.D. 81-96), a fierce persecutor of the Christians.

The principal divisions of the Book of Revelation are the following:

I.   Prologue (1, 1-3)
II.   Letters to the Churches of Asia (1, 4—3, 22)
III.   God and the Lamb in Heaven (4, 1—5, 14)
IV.   The Seven Seals, Trumpets, and Plagues, with Interludes (6, 1—16, 21)
V.   The Punishment of Babylon and the Destruction of Pagan Nations (17, 1—20, 15)
VI.   The New Creation (21, 1—22, 5)
VII.   Epilogue (22, 6-21)

I. PROLOGUE*

CHAPTER 1

[1] The revelation of Jesus Christ, which God gave to him, to show his servants what must happen soon. He made it known by sending his angel to his servant John,[a]

[2] who gives witness to the word of God and to the testimony of Jesus Christ by reporting what he saw. [3] Blessed is the one* who reads aloud and blessed are those who listen to this prophetic message and heed what is written in it, for the appointed time is near.[b]

---

a Rv 22, 6-8.20; Dn 2, 28 / Rv 19, 10.—b Rv 22, 7 / Lk 11, 28.

1, 1-3: This prologue describes the source, contents, and audience of the book and forms an inclusion with the epilogue (Rv 22, 6-21), with its similar themes and expressions.

1, 3: *Blessed is the one:* this is the first of seven beatitudes in this book; the others are in Rv 14, 13; 16, 15; 19, 9; 20, 6; 22, 7.14. *This prophetic message:* literally, "the words of the prophecy"; so Rv 22, 7.10.18.19 by inclusion. *The appointed time:* when Jesus will return in glory; cf Rv 1, 7; 3, 11; 22, 7.10.12.20.

II. LETTERS TO THE CHURCHES OF ASIA

Greeting.* [4]John, to the seven churches in Asia:* grace to you and peace from him who is and who was and who is to come, and from the seven spirits before his throne,[c] [5]and from Jesus Christ, the faithful witness, the firstborn of the dead and ruler of the kings of the earth. To him who loves us and has freed us* from our sins by his blood,[d] [6]who has made us into a kingdom, priests for his God and Father, to him be glory and power forever [and ever]. Amen.[e]

[7] Behold, he is coming amid the clouds,
    and every eye will see him,
    even those who pierced him.
All the peoples of the earth will lament
    him.
    Yes. Amen.[f]

[8]"I am the Alpha and the Omega,"* says the Lord God, "the one who is and who was and who is to come, the almighty."[g]

The First Vision.* [9]I, John, your brother, who share with you the distress, the kingdom, and the endurance we have in Jesus, found myself on the island called Patmos* because I proclaimed God's word and gave testimony to Jesus. [10]I was caught up in spirit on the Lord's day* and heard behind me a voice as loud as a trumpet, [11]which said, "Write on a scroll* what you see and send it to the seven churches: to Ephesus, Smyrna, Pergamum, Thyatira, Sardis, Philadelphia, and Laodicea." [12] * Then I turned to see whose voice it was that spoke to me, and when I turned, I saw seven gold lampstands [13]and in the midst of the lampstands one like a son of man,* wearing an ankle-length robe, with a gold sash around his chest.[h] [14]The hair of his head was as white as white wool or as snow,* and his eyes were like a fiery flame. [15]His feet were like polished brass refined in a furnace,* and his voice was like the sound of rushing water. [16]In his right hand he held seven stars.* A sharp two-edged sword came out of his mouth, and his face shone like the sun at its brightest.[i]

[17]When I caught sight of him, I fell down at his feet as though dead.* He touched me with his right hand and said, "Do not be afraid. I am the first and the last,[j] [18]the one who lives. Once I was dead, but now I am alive forever and ever. I hold the keys to death and the netherworld.* [19]Write down, therefore, what

---

c Rv 1, 8; 4, 8; 11, 17; 16, 5; Ex 3, 14.—d Rv 3, 14; 1 Cor 15, 20; Col 1, 18 / Heb 9, 14; 1 Pt 1, 19; 1 Jn 1, 7.—e Ex 19, 6; 1 Pt 2, 9.—f Dn 7, 13 / Zec 12, 10; Mt 24, 30; Jn 19, 37.—g Rv 1, 17; 21, 6; 22, 13; Is 41, 4; 44, 6; 48, 12.—h Dn 7, 13; 10, 5.—i Heb 4, 12.—j Dn 8, 18 / Rv 1, 8.

1, 4-8: Although Revelation begins and ends (Rv 22, 21) with Christian epistolary formulae, there is nothing between chs 4 and 22 resembling a letter. The author here employs the standard word order for greetings in Greek letter writing: "N. to N., greetings . . ."; see the note on Rom 1, 1.

1, 4: *Seven churches in Asia:* Asia refers to the Roman province of that name in western Asia Minor (modern Turkey); these representative churches are mentioned by name in v 11, and each is the recipient of a message (Rv 2, 1—3, 22). *Seven* is the biblical number suggesting fullness and completeness; thus the seer is writing for the whole church.

1, 5: *Freed us:* the majority of Greek manuscripts and several early versions read "washed us"; but "freed us" is supported by the best manuscripts and fits well with Old Testament imagery, e.g., Is 40, 2.

1, 8: *The Alpha and the Omega:* the first and last letters of the Greek alphabet. In Rv 22, 13 the same words occur together with the expressions "the First and the Last, the Beginning and the End"; cf Rv 1, 17; 2, 8; 21, 6; Is 41, 4; 44, 6.

1, 9-20: In this first vision, the seer is commanded to write what he sees to the seven churches (9-11). He sees Christ in glory, whom he depicts in stock apocalyptic imagery (12-16), and hears him describe himself in terms meant to encourage Christians by emphasizing his victory over death (17-20).

1, 9: *Island called Patmos:* one of the Sporades islands in the Aegean Sea, some fifty miles south of Ephesus, used by the Romans as a penal colony. *Because I proclaimed God's word:* literally, "on account of God's word."

1, 10: *The Lord's day:* Sunday. *As loud as a trumpet:* the imagery is derived from the theophany at Sinai (Ex 19, 16.19; cf Heb 12, 19 and the trumpet in other eschatological settings in Is 27, 13; Jl 2, 1; Mt 24, 31; 1 Cor 15, 52; 1 Thes 4, 16).

1, 11: *Scroll:* a papyrus roll.

1, 12-16: A symbolic description of Christ in glory. The metaphorical language is not to be understood literally; cf Introduction.

1, 13: *Son of man:* see the note on Mk 8, 31. *Ankle-length robe:* Christ is priest; cf Ex 28, 4; 29, 5; Wis 18, 24; Zec 3, 4. *Gold sash:* Christ is king; cf Ex 28, 4; 1 Mc 10, 89; 11, 58; Dn 10, 5.

1, 14: *Hair . . . as white as white wool or as snow:* Christ is eternal, clothed with the dignity that belonged to the "Ancient of Days"; cf Rv 1, 18; Dn 7, 9. *His eyes were like a fiery flame:* Christ is portrayed as all-knowing; cf Rv 2, 23; Ps 7, 10; Jer 17, 10; and similar expressions in Rv 2, 18; 19, 12; cf Dn 10, 6.

1, 15: *His feet . . . furnace:* Christ is depicted as unchangeable; cf Ez 1, 27; Dn 10, 6. The Greek word translated "refined" is unconnected grammatically with any other word in the sentence. *His voice . . . water:* Christ speaks with divine authority; cf Ez 1, 24.

1, 16: *Seven stars:* in the pagan world, Mithras and the Caesars were represented with seven stars in their right hand, symbolizing their universal dominion. *A sharp two-edged sword:* this refers to the word of God (cf Eph 6, 17; Heb 4, 12) that will destroy unrepentant sinners; cf Rv 2, 16; 19, 15; Wis 18, 15; Is 11, 4; 49, 2. *His face . . . brightest:* this symbolizes the divine majesty of Christ; cf Rv 10, 1; 21, 23; Jgs 5, 31; Is 60, 19; Mt 17, 2.

1, 17: It was an Old Testament belief that for sinful human beings to see God was to die; cf Ex 19, 21; 33, 20; Jgs 6, 22-23; Is 6, 5.

1, 18: *Netherworld:* Greek Hades, Hebrew Sheol, the abode of the dead; cf Rv 20, 13-14; Nm 16, 33.

Rv

you have seen, and what is happening, and what will happen afterwards.* [20] This is the secret meaning* of the seven stars you saw in my right hand, and of the seven gold lampstands: the seven stars are the angels of the seven churches, and the seven lampstands are the seven churches.

CHAPTER 2

To Ephesus. [1] * "To the angel of the church* in Ephesus,* write this:

" 'The one who holds the seven stars in his right hand and walks in the midst of the seven gold lampstands says this: [2] "I know your works, your labor, and your endurance, and that you cannot tolerate the wicked; you have tested those who call themselves apostles but are not, and discovered that they are impostors.* [3] Moreover, you have endurance and have suffered for my name, and you have not grown weary. [4] Yet I hold this against you: you have lost the love you had at first. [5] Realize how far you have fallen. Repent, and do the works you did at first. Otherwise, I will come to you and remove your lampstand from its place, unless you repent. [6] But you have this in your favor: you

k Rv 2, 11.17.29; 3, 6.13.22; 13, 9; Mt 11, 15.—l Jas 2, 5.—m Rv 20, 6.14; 21, 8.

1, 19: *What you have seen, and what is happening, and what will happen afterwards:* the three parts of the Book of Revelation, the vision (10-20), the situation in the seven churches (chs 2-3), and the events of chs 6-22.

1, 20: *Secret meaning:* literally, "mystery." *Angels:* these are the presiding spirits of the seven churches. Angels were thought to be in charge of the physical world (cf Rv 7, 1; 14, 18; 16, 5) and of nations (Dn 10, 13; 12, 1), communities (the seven churches), and individuals (Mt 18, 10; Acts 12, 15). Some have seen in the "angel" of each of the seven churches its pastor or a personification of the spirit of the congregation.

2, 1—3, 22: Each of the seven letters follows the same pattern: address; description of the exalted Christ; blame and/or praise for the church addressed; threat and/or admonition; final exhortation and promise to all Christians.

2, 1-7: The letter to Ephesus praises the members of the church there for their works and virtues, including discerning false teachers (2-3), but admonishes them to repent and return to their former devotion (4-5). It concludes with a reference to the Nicolaitans (see the note on 6) and a promise that the victor will have access to eternal life (7).

2, 1: *Ephesus:* this great ancient city had a population of ca. 250,000; it was the capital of the Roman province of Asia and the commercial, cultural, and religious center of Asia. The other six churches were located in the same province, situated roughly in a circle; they were selected for geographical reasons rather than for the size of their Christian communities. *Walks in the midst of the seven gold lampstands:* this signifies that Christ is always present in the church; see the note on Rv 1, 4.

2, 2: *Who call themselves . . . impostors:* this refers to unauthorized and perverse missionaries; cf Acts 20, 29-30.

2, 6: *Nicolaitans:* these are perhaps the impostors of v 2; see the note on vv 14-15. There is little evidence for connecting this group with Nicolaus, the proselyte from Antioch, mentioned in Acts 6, 5.

hate the works of the Nicolaitans,* which I also hate.

[7] " ' "Whoever has ears ought to hear what the Spirit says to the churches. To the victor* I will give the right to eat from the tree of life that is in the garden of God." 'k

To Smyrna.* [8] "To the angel of the church in Smyrna,* write this:

" 'The first and the last, who once died but came to life, says this: [9] "I know your tribulation and poverty, but you are rich.* I know the slander of those who claim to be Jews and are not, but rather are members of the assembly of Satan.l [10] Do not be afraid of anything that you are going to suffer. Indeed, the devil will throw some of you into prison, that you may be tested, and you will face an ordeal for ten days. Remain faithful until death, and I will give you the crown of life.

[11] " ' "Whoever has ears ought to hear what the Spirit says to the churches.m The victor shall not be harmed by the second death." '*

To Pergamum.* [12] "To the angel of the church in Pergamum,* write this:

2, 7: *Victor:* referring to any Christian individual who holds fast to the faith and does God's will in the face of persecution. *The tree of life that is in the garden of God:* this is a reference to the tree in the primeval paradise (Gn 2, 9); cf Rv 22, 2.14.19. The decree excluding humanity from the tree of life has been revoked by Christ.

2, 8-11: The letter to Smyrna encourages the Christians in this important commercial center by telling them that although they are impoverished, they are nevertheless rich, and calls those Jews who are slandering them members of the assembly of Satan (9). There is no admonition; rather, the Christians are told that they will suffer much, even death, but the time of tribulation will be short compared to their eternal reward (10), and they will thus escape final damnation (11).

2, 8: *Smyrna:* modern Izmir, ca. thirty miles north of Ephesus, and the chief city of Lydia, with a temple to the goddess Roma. It was renowned for its loyalty to Rome, and it also had a large Jewish community very hostile toward Christians.

2, 9-10: The church in Smyrna was materially poor but spiritually rich. Accusations made by Jewish brethren there occasioned the persecution of Christians; cf Acts 14, 2.19; 17, 5.13.

2, 11: *The second death:* this refers to the eternal death, when sinners will receive their final punishment; cf Rv 20, 6.14-15; 21, 8.

2, 12-17: The letter to Pergamum praises the members of the church for persevering in their faith in Christ even in the midst of a pagan setting and in face of persecution and martyrdom (13). But it admonishes them about members who advocate an unprincipled morality (14; cf 2 Pt 2, 15; Jude 11) and others who follow the teaching of the Nicolaitans (15; see the note there). It urges them to repent (16) and promises them the hidden manna and Christ's amulet (17).

2, 12: *Pergamum:* modern Bergama, ca. forty-five miles northeast of Smyrna, a center for various kinds of pagan worship. It also had an outstanding library (the word *parchment* is derived from its name).

" 'The one with the sharp two-edged sword says this: [13]"I know that you live where Satan's throne* is, and yet you hold fast to my name and have not denied your faith in me, not even in the days of Antipas, my faithful witness, who was martyred among you, where Satan lives. [14] * Yet I have a few things against you. You have some people there who hold to the teaching of Balaam, who instructed Balak to put a stumbling block before the Israelites: to eat food sacrificed to idols and to play the harlot.[n] [15]Likewise, you also have some people who hold to the teaching of [the] Nicolaitans. [16]Therefore, repent. Otherwise, I will come to you quickly and wage war against them with the sword of my mouth.

[17]" ' "Whoever has ears ought to hear what the Spirit says to the churches. To the victor I shall give some of the hidden manna;* I shall also give a white amulet upon which is inscribed a new name, which no one knows except the one who receives it." '[o]

To Thyatira.* [18]"To the angel of the church in Thyatira,* write this:

" 'The Son of God, whose eyes are like a fiery flame and whose feet are like polished brass, says this: [19]"I know your works, your love, faith, service, and endurance, and that your last works are greater than the first. [20]Yet I hold this against you, that you tolerate the woman Jezebel, who calls herself a prophetess, who teaches and mis-

leads my servants to play the harlot and to eat food sacrificed to idols.* [21]I have given her time to repent, but she refuses to repent of her harlotry. [22]So I will cast her on a sickbed and plunge those who commit adultery with her into intense suffering unless they repent of her works. [23]I will also put her children* to death. Thus shall all the churches come to know that I am the searcher of hearts and minds and that I will give each of you what your works deserve.[p] [24]But I say to the rest of you in Thyatira, who do not uphold this teaching and know nothing of the so-called deep secrets of Satan:* on you I will place no further burden, [25]except that you must hold fast to what you have until I come.

[26] " ' "To the victor,* who keeps to my ways* until the end,
    I will give authority over the nations.[q]
[27] He will rule them with an iron rod.
    Like clay vessels will they be smashed,
[28]just as I received authority from my Father. And to him I will give the morning star.

[29]" ' "Whoever has ears ought to hear what the Spirit says to the churches." '

CHAPTER 3

To Sardis.* [1]"To the angel of the church in Sardis,* write this:

---

n Nm 22—24; 25, 1-3; 31, 16; 2 Pt 2, 15; Jude 11.—o Is 62, 2; 65, 15.—p 1 Sm 16, 7; Jer 11, 20; 17, 10.—q Rv 12, 5; Ps 2, 8-9.

2, 13: *Satan's throne:* the reference is to emperor worship and other pagan practices that flourished in Pergamum, perhaps specifically the white marble altar erected and dedicated to Zeus by Eumenes II (197-160 B.C.).

2, 14-15: Like Balaam, the biblical prototype of the religious compromiser (cf Nm 25, 1-3; 31, 16; 2 Pt 2, 15; Jude 11), the Nicolaitans in Pergamum and Ephesus (6) accommodated their Christian faith to paganism. They abused the principle of liberty enunciated by Paul (1 Cor 9, 19-23).

2, 17: *The hidden manna:* this is the food of life; cf Ps 78, 24-25. *White amulet:* literally, "white stone," on which was written a magical name, whose power could be tapped by one who knew the secret name. It is used here as a symbol of victory and joy; cf Rv 3, 4-5. *New name:* this is a reference to the Christian's rebirth in Christ; cf Rv 3, 12; 19, 12; Is 62, 2; 65, 15.

2, 18-29: The letter to Thyatira praises the progress in virtue of this small Christian community (19) but admonishes them for tolerating a false prophet who leads them astray (20). Her fate is sealed, but there is hope of repentance for her followers (21-22). Otherwise, they too shall die (23). They are warned against Satanic power or knowledge (24-25). Those who remain faithful will share in the messianic reign, having authority over nations (26-27), and will in fact possess Christ himself (28).

2, 18: *Thyatira:* modern Akhisar, ca. forty miles southeast of Pergamum, a frontier town famous for its workers' guilds (cf Acts 16, 14), membership in which may have involved festal meals in pagan temples.

2, 20: The scheming and treacherous Jezebel of old (cf 1 Kgs 19, 1-2; 21, 1-14; 2 Kgs 9, 22.30-34) introduced pagan customs into the religion of Israel; this new Jezebel was doing the same to Christianity.

2, 23: *Children:* spiritual descendants.

2, 24: *The so-called deep secrets of Satan:* literally, "the deep things of Satan," a scathing reference to the perverse teaching of the Nicolaitans (15).

2, 26-28: The Christian who perseveres in faith will share in Christ's messianic authority (cf Ps 2, 8-9) and resurrection victory over death, symbolized by the morning star; cf Rv 22, 16.

2, 26: *Who keeps to my ways:* literally, "who keeps my works."

3, 1-6: The letter to Sardis does not praise the community but admonishes its members to watchfulness, mutual support, and repentance (2-3). The few who have remained pure and faithful will share Christ's victory and will be inscribed in the book of life (4-5).

3, 1: *Sardis:* this city, located ca. thirty miles southeast of Thyatira, was once the capital of Lydia, known for its wealth at the time of Croesus (6th century B.C.). Its citadel, reputed to be unassailable, was captured by surprise, first by Cyrus and later by Antiochus. The church is therefore warned to be on guard.

Rv

" 'The one who has the seven spirits of God and the seven stars says this: "I know your works, that you have the reputation of being alive, but you are dead. ²Be watchful and strengthen what is left, which is going to die, for I have not found your works complete in the sight of my God. ³Remember then how you accepted and heard; keep it, and repent. If you are not watchful, I will come like a thief, and you will never know at what hour I will come upon you.ʳ ⁴However, you have a few people in Sardis who have not soiled their garments; they will walk with me dressed in white, because they are worthy.ˢ

⁵" ' "The victor will thus be dressed in white,* and I will never erase his name from the book of life but will acknowledge his name in the presence of my Father and of his angels.ᵗ

⁶" ' "Whoever has ears ought to hear what the Spirit says to the churches." '

To Philadelphia.* ⁷"To the angel of the church in Philadelphia,* write this:

" 'The holy one, the true,
    who holds the key of David,
    who opens and no one shall close,
    who closes and no one shall open,ᵘ
says this:

⁸" ' "I know your works (behold, I have left an open door* before you, which no one can close). You have limited strength, and yet you have kept my word and have not denied my name. ⁹Behold, I will make those of the assembly of Satan who claim to be Jews and are not, but are lying, behold I will make them come and fall prostrate at your feet, and they will realize that I love you.ᵛ ¹⁰Because you have kept my message of endurance,* I will keep you safe in the time of trial that is going to come to the whole world to test the inhabitants of the earth. ¹¹I am coming quickly. Hold fast to what you have, so that no one may take your crown.ʷ

¹²" ' "The victor I will make into a pillar* in the temple of my God, and he will never leave it again. On him I will inscribe the name of my God and the name of the city of my God, the new Jerusalem, which comes down out of heaven from my God, as well as my new name.ˣ

¹³" ' "Whoever has ears ought to hear what the Spirit says to the churches." '

To Laodicea.* ¹⁴"To the angel of the church in Laodicea,* write this:

" 'The Amen, the faithful and true witness, the source of God's creation, says this:ʸ ¹⁵"I know your works; I know that you are neither cold nor hot.* I wish you were either cold or hot. ¹⁶ * So, because you are lukewarm, neither hot nor cold, I

---

r Mt 24, 42-44; Mk 13, 33; 1 Thes 5, 2; 2 Pt 3, 10.—s Rv 7, 13-14.—t Ps 69, 29; Dn 12, 1 / Mt 10, 32.—u Is 22, 22; Mt 16, 19.—v Rv 2, 9 / Is 45, 14; 60, 14.—w Rv 2, 25; 22, 7.20.—x Rv 21, 2-3; Ez 48, 35 / Rv 19, 13.—y Rv 1, 5.

3, 5: *In white:* white is a sign of victory and joy as well as resurrection; see the note on Rv 2, 17. *The book of life:* the roll in which the names of the redeemed are kept; cf Rv 13, 8; 17, 8; 20, 12.15; 21, 27; Phil 4, 3; Dn 12, 1. They will be acknowledged by Christ in heaven; cf Mt 10, 32.

3, 7-13: The letter to Philadelphia praises the Christians there for remaining faithful even with their limited strength (8). Members of the assembly of Satan are again singled out (9; see Rv 2, 9 above). There is no admonition; rather, the letter promises that they will be kept safe at the great trial (10-11) and that the victors will become pillars of the heavenly temple, upon which three names will be inscribed: God, Jerusalem, and Christ (12).

3, 7: *Philadelphia:* modern Alasehir, ca. thirty miles southeast of Sardis, founded by Attalus II Philadelphus of Pergamum to be an "open door" (8) for Greek culture; it was destroyed by an earthquake in A.D. 17. Rebuilt by money from the Emperor Tiberius, the city was renamed Neo-Caesarea; this may explain the allusions to "name" in v 12. *Key of David:* to the heavenly city of David (cf Is 22, 22), "the new Jerusalem" (12), over which Christ has supreme authority.

3, 8: *An open door:* opportunities for sharing and proclaiming the faith; cf Acts 14, 27; 1 Cor 16, 9; 2 Cor 2, 12.

3, 10: *My message of endurance:* this does not refer to a saying of Jesus about patience but to the example of Christ's patient endurance. *The inhabitants of the earth:* literally, "those who live on the earth." This expression, which also occurs in Rv 6, 10; 8, 13; 11, 10; 13, 8.12.14; 17, 2.8, always refers to the pagan world.

3, 12: *Pillar:* this may be an allusion to the rebuilding of the city; see the note on v 7. *New Jerusalem:* it is described in Rv 21, 10—22, 5.

3, 14-22: The letter to Laodicea reprimands the community for being lukewarm (15-16), but no particular faults are singled out. Their material prosperity is contrasted with their spiritual poverty, the violet tunics that were the source of their wealth with the white robe of baptism, and their famous eye ointment with true spiritual perception (17-18). But Christ's chastisement is inspired by love and a desire to be allowed to share the messianic banquet with his followers in the heavenly kingdom (19-21).

3, 14: *Laodicea:* ca. forty miles southeast of Philadelphia and ca. eighty miles east of Ephesus, a wealthy industrial and commercial center, with a renowned medical school. It exported fine woolen garments and was famous for its eye salves. It was so wealthy that it was proudly rebuilt without outside aid after the devastating earthquake of A.D. 60/61. *The Amen:* this is a divine title (cf Hebrew text of Is 65, 16) applied to Christ; cf 2 Cor 1, 20. *Source of God's creation:* literally, "the beginning of God's creation," a concept found also in Jn 1, 3; Col 1, 16-17; Heb 1, 2; cf Prv 8, 22-31; Wis 9, 1-2.

3, 15-16: Halfhearted commitment to the faith is nauseating to Christ; cf Rom 12, 11.

3, 16: *Spit:* literally, "vomit." The image is that of a beverage that should be either hot or cold. Perhaps there is an allusion to the hot springs of Hierapolis across the Lycus river from Laodicea, which would have been lukewarm by the time they reached Laodicea.

will spit you out of my mouth. [17] *z* For you say, 'I am rich and affluent and have no need of anything,' and yet do not realize that you are wretched, pitiable, poor, blind, and naked.* [18] I advise you to buy from me gold refined by fire* so that you may be rich, and white garments to put on so that your shameful nakedness may not be exposed, and buy ointment to smear on your eyes so that you may see. [19] Those whom I love, I reprove and chastise. Be earnest, therefore, and repent. *a*

[20] " ' "Behold, I stand at the door and knock. If anyone hears my voice and opens the door, [then] I will enter his house and dine with him, and he with me.* [21] I will give the victor the right to sit with me on my throne, as I myself first won the victory and sit with my Father on his throne. *b*

[22] " ' "Whoever has ears ought to hear what the Spirit says to the churches." ' "

III. GOD AND THE LAMB
IN HEAVEN

CHAPTER 4

Vision of Heavenly Worship.* [1] After this I had a vision of an open door* to heaven, and I heard the trumpetlike voice that had spoken to me before, saying, "Come up here and I will show you what must happen afterwards." [2] * At once I was caught up in spirit. *c* A throne was there in heaven, and on the throne sat [3] one whose appearance sparkled like jasper and carnelian. Around the throne was a halo as brilliant as an emerald. [4] Surrounding the throne I saw

twenty-four other thrones on which twenty-four elders* sat, dressed in white garments and with gold crowns on their heads. *d* [5] From the throne came flashes of lightning, rumblings, and peals of thunder.* Seven flaming torches burned in front of the throne, which are the seven spirits of God. [6] *e* In front of the throne was something that resembled a sea of glass like crystal.*

In the center and around the throne, there were four living creatures covered with eyes in front and in back. [7] The first creature resembled a lion, the second was like a calf, the third had a face like that of a human being, and the fourth looked like an eagle* in flight. [8] The four living creatures, each of them with six wings,* were covered with eyes inside and out. Day and night they do not stop exclaiming:

"Holy, holy, holy is the Lord God almighty,
who was, and who is, and who is to come." *f*

[9] Whenever the living creatures give glory and honor and thanks to the one who sits on the throne, who lives forever and ever, [10] the twenty-four elders fall down before the one who sits on the throne and worship him, who lives forever and ever. They throw down their crowns before the throne, exclaiming:

[11] "Worthy are you, Lord our God,
to receive glory and honor and power,
for you created all things;
because of your will they came to be and were created." *g*

---

z Prv 13, 7; Lk 12, 21.—a Prv 3, 11-12; 1 Cor 11, 32; Heb 12, 5-11.—b Lk 22, 28-30; Mt 19, 28.—c 2-3: Is 6, 1 / Ez 1, 26-28.—d Is 24, 23.—e Ex 24, 10.—f Is 6, 2-3 / Rv 1, 4.8; 11, 17; 16, 5.—g Rom 4, 17; 16, 27.

3, 17: Economic prosperity occasioned spiritual bankruptcy.

3, 18: *Gold . . . fire:* God's grace. *White garments:* symbol of an upright life; the city was noted for its violet/purple cloth. *Ointment . . . eyes:* to remove spiritual blindness; one of the city's exports was eye ointment (see the note on Rv 3, 14).

3, 20: Christ invites all to the messianic banquet in heaven; cf Is 25, 6; Lk 14, 15; 22, 30.

4, 1-11: The seer now describes a vision of the heavenly court in worship of God enthroned. He reverently avoids naming or describing God but pictures twenty-four elders in priestly and regal attire (4) and God's throne and its surroundings made of precious gems and other symbols that traditionally express the majesty of God (5-6). Universal creation is represented by the four living creatures (6-7). Along with the twenty-four elders, they praise God unceasingly in humble adoration (8-11).

4, 1: The ancients viewed heaven as a solid vault, entered by way of actual doors.

4, 2-8: Much of the imagery here is taken from Ez 1 and 10.

4, 4: *Twenty-four elders:* these represent the twelve tribes of Israel and the twelve apostles; cf Rv 21, 12-14.

4, 5: *Flashes of lightning, rumblings, and peals of thunder:* as in other descriptions of God's appearance or activity; cf Rv 8, 5; 11, 19; 16, 18; Ex 19, 16; Ez 1, 4.13. *The seven spirits of God:* the seven "angels of the presence" as in Rv 8, 2 and Tb 12, 15.

4, 6: *A sea of glass like crystal:* an image adapted from Ez 1, 22-26. *Four living creatures:* these are symbols taken from Ez 1, 5-21; they are identified as cherubim in Ez 10, 20. *Covered with eyes:* these suggest God's knowledge and concern.

4, 7: *Lion . . . calf . . . human being . . . eagle:* these symbolize, respectively, what is noblest, strongest, wisest, and swiftest in creation. *Calf:* traditionally translated "ox," the Greek word refers to a heifer or young bull. Since the second century, these four creatures have been used as symbols of the evangelists Mark, Luke, Matthew, and John, respectively.

4, 8: *Six wings:* like the seraphim of Is 6, 2.

Rv

CHAPTER 5

The Scroll and the Lamb.* [1] I saw a scroll* in the right hand of the one who sat on the throne. It had writing on both sides and was sealed with seven seals.[h] [2] Then I saw a mighty angel who proclaimed in a loud voice, "Who is worthy to open the scroll and break its seals?" [3] But no one in heaven or on earth or under the earth was able to open the scroll or to examine it. [4] I shed many tears because no one was found worthy to open the scroll or to examine it. [5] One of the elders said to me, "Do not weep. The lion of the tribe of Judah, the root of David,* has triumphed, enabling him to open the scroll with its seven seals."[i]

[6] Then I saw standing in the midst of the throne and the four living creatures and the elders a Lamb* that seemed to have been slain. He had seven horns and seven eyes; these are the [seven] spirits of God sent out into the whole world.[j] [7] He came and received the scroll from the right hand of the one who sat on the throne. [8] When he took it, the four living creatures and the twenty-four elders fell down before the Lamb. Each of the elders held a harp and gold bowls filled with incense, which are the prayers of the holy ones. [9] They sang a new hymn:

"Worthy are you to receive the scroll
and to break open its seals,
for you were slain and with your
blood you purchased for God
those from every tribe and tongue,
people and nation.
[10] You made them a kingdom and priests
for our God,
and they will reign on earth."[k]

[11] I looked again and heard the voices of many angels who surrounded the throne and the living creatures and the elders. They were countless* in number,[l] [12] and they cried out in a loud voice:

"Worthy is the Lamb that was slain
to receive power and riches, wisdom
and strength,
honor and glory and blessing."

[13] Then I heard every creature in heaven and on earth and under the earth and in the sea, everything in the universe, cry out:

"To the one who sits on the throne and
to the Lamb
be blessing and honor, glory and
might,
forever and ever."

[14] The four living creatures answered, "Amen," and the elders fell down and worshiped.

IV. THE SEVEN SEALS, TRUMPETS, AND PLAGUES, WITH INTERLUDES*

CHAPTER 6*

The First Six Seals. [1] * Then I watched while the Lamb broke open the first of the seven seals, and I heard one of the four living creatures cry out in a voice like thunder, "Come forward." [2] I looked, and there was a white horse, and its rider had a

---

h Is 29, 11.—i Is 11, 1.10; Rom 15, 12.—j Jn 1, 29.—k Rv 1, 6; Ex 19, 6; Is 61, 6.—l Dn 7, 10; Jude 14-15.

5, 1-14: The seer now describes a papyrus roll in God's right hand (1) with seven seals indicating the importance of the message. A mighty angel asks who is worthy to open the scroll, i.e., who can accomplish God's salvific plan (2). There is despair at first when no one in creation can do it (3-4). But the seer is comforted by an elder who tells him that Christ, called the lion of the tribe of Judah, has won the right to open it (5). Christ then appears as a Lamb, coming to receive the scroll from God (6-7), for which he is acclaimed as at a coronation (8-10). This is followed by a doxology of the angels (11-12) and then finally by the heavenly church united with all of creation (13-14).

5, 1: *A scroll:* a papyrus roll possibly containing a list of afflictions for sinners (cf Ez 2, 9-10) or God's plan for the world. *Sealed with seven seals:* it is totally hidden from all but God. Only the Lamb (7-9) has the right to carry out the divine plan.

5, 5: *The lion of the tribe of Judah, the root of David:* these are the messianic titles applied to Christ to symbolize his victory; cf Rv 22, 16; Gn 49, 9; Is 11, 1.10; Mt 1, 1.

5, 6: Christ is the Paschal Lamb without blemish, whose blood saved the new Israel from sin and death; cf Ex 12; Is 53, 7; Jn 1, 29.36; Acts 8, 32; 1 Pt 1, 18-19. This is the main title for Christ in Rv, used twenty-eight times. *Seven horns and seven eyes:* Christ has the fullness (see the note on Rv 1, 4) of power (horns) and knowledge (eyes); cf Zec 4, 10. *[Seven] spirits:* as in Rv 1, 4; 3, 1; and 4, 5.

5, 11: *Countless:* literally, "100,000,000 plus 1,000,000," used by the author to express infinity.

6, 1—16, 21: A series of seven disasters now begins as each seal is broken (Rv 6, 1—8, 1), followed by a similar series as seven trumpets sound (Rv 8, 2—11, 19) and as seven angels pour

bowls on the earth causing plagues (Rv 15, 1—16, 21). These gloomy sequences are interrupted by longer or shorter scenes suggesting the triumph of God and his witnesses (e.g., chs 7, 10, 11, 12, 13, 14).

6, 1-17: This chapter provides a symbolic description of the contents of the sealed scroll. The breaking of the first four seals reveals four riders. The first rider (of a white horse) is a conquering power (1-2), the second (red horse) a symbol of bloody war (3-4), the third (black horse) a symbol of famine (5-6), the fourth (pale green horse) a symbol of Death himself, accompanied by Hades (the netherworld) as his page (7-8). Verse 8b summarizes the role of all four riders. The breaking of the fifth seal reveals Christian martyrs in an attitude of sacrifice as blood poured out at the foot of an altar begging God for vindication, which will come only when their quota is filled; but they are given a white robe symbolic of victory (9-11). The breaking of the sixth seal reveals typical apocalyptic signs in the sky and the sheer terror of all people at the imminent divine judgment (12-17).

6, 1-8: The imagery is adapted from Zec 1, 8-10; 6, 1-8.

bow.* He was given a crown, and he rode forth victorious to further his victories.[m]

³ When he broke open the second seal, I heard the second living creature cry out, "Come forward." ⁴ [n] Another horse came out, a red one. Its rider was given power to take peace away from the earth, so that people would slaughter one another. And he was given a huge sword.*

⁵ When he broke open the third seal, I heard the third living creature cry out, "Come forward." I looked, and there was a black horse,* and its rider held a scale in his hand. ⁶ I heard what seemed to be a voice in the midst of the four living creatures. It said, "A ration of wheat costs a day's pay,* and three rations of barley cost a day's pay. But do not damage the olive oil or the wine."[o]

⁷ When he broke open the fourth seal, I heard the voice of the fourth living creature cry out, "Come forward." ⁸ I looked, and there was a pale green* horse. Its rider was named Death, and Hades accompanied him. They were given authority over a quarter of the earth, to kill with sword, famine, and plague, and by means of the beasts of the earth.[p]

⁹ When he broke open the fifth seal, I saw underneath the altar* the souls of those who had been slaughtered because of the witness they bore to the word of God. ¹⁰ They cried out in a loud voice, "How long will it be, holy and true master,* before you sit in judgment and avenge our blood on the inhabitants of the earth?" ¹¹ Each of them was given a white robe, and they were told to be patient a little while longer until the number was filled of their fellow servants and brothers who were going to be killed as they had been.

¹² * Then I watched while he broke open the sixth seal, and there was a great earthquake; the sun turned as black as dark sackcloth* and the whole moon became like blood.[q] ¹³ The stars in the sky fell to the earth like unripe figs* shaken loose from the tree in a strong wind. ¹⁴ Then the sky was divided* like a torn scroll curling up, and every mountain and island was moved from its place.[r] ¹⁵ The kings of the earth, the nobles,* the military officers, the rich, the powerful, and every slave and free person hid themselves in caves and among mountain crags. ¹⁶ They cried out to the mountains and the rocks, "Fall on us and hide us from the face of the one who sits on the throne and from the wrath of the Lamb,[s] ¹⁷ because the great day of their* wrath has come and who can withstand it?"

CHAPTER 7*

The 144,000 Sealed. ¹ After this I saw four angels standing at the four corners of the earth,* holding back the four winds of

---

m Zec 1, 8-10; 6, 1-3.—n Ez 21, 14-16.—o Lv 26, 26; Ez 4, 16-17.—p Ez 14, 21.—q Jl 3, 4; Mt 24, 29.—r Is 34, 4 / Rv 16, 20.—s Is 2, 19; Hos 10, 8; Lk 23, 30.

6, 2: *White horse . . . bow:* this may perhaps allude specifically to the Parthians on the eastern border of the Roman empire. Expert in the use of the bow, they constantly harassed the Romans and won a major victory in A.D. 62; see the note on Rv 9, 13-21. But the Old Testament imagery typifies the history of oppression of God's people at all times.

6, 4: *Huge sword:* this is a symbol of war and violence; cf Ez 21, 14-17.

6, 5: *Black horse:* this is a symbol of famine, the usual accompaniment of war in antiquity; cf Lv 26, 26; Ez 4, 16-17. The *scale* is a symbol of shortage of food with a corresponding rise in price.

6, 6: *A day's pay:* literally, "a denarius," a Roman silver coin that constitutes a day's wage in Mt 20, 2. Because of the famine, food was rationed and sold at an exorbitant price. A liter of flour was considered a day's ration in the Greek historians Herodotus and Diogenes Laertius. *Barley:* food of the poor (Jn 6, 9.13; cf 2 Kgs 7, 1.16.18); it was also used to feed animals; cf 1 Kgs 5, 8. *Do not damage:* the olive and the vine are to be used more sparingly in time of famine.

6, 8: *Pale green:* symbol of death and decay; cf Ez 14, 21.

6, 9: *The altar:* this altar corresponds to the altar of holocausts in the temple in Jerusalem; see also Rv 11, 1. *Because of the witness . . . word of God:* literally, "because of the word of God and the witness they had borne."

6, 10: *Holy and true master:* Old Testament usage as well as the context indicates that this is addressed to God rather than to Christ.

6, 12-14: Symbolic rather than literal description of the cosmic upheavals attending the day of the Lord when the martyrs' prayer for vindication (10) would be answered; cf Am 8, 8-9; Is 34, 4; 50, 3; Jl 2, 10; 3, 3-4; Mt 24, 4-36; Mk 13, 5-37; Lk 21, 8-36.

6, 12: *Dark sackcloth:* for mourning, sackcloth was made from the skin of a black goat.

6, 13: *Unripe figs:* literally, "summer (or winter) fruit."

6, 14: *Was divided:* literally, "was split," like a broken papyrus roll torn in two, each half then curling up to form a roll on either side.

6, 15: *Nobles:* literally, "courtiers," "grandees." *Military officers:* literally, "commanders of 1,000 men," used in Josephus and other Greek authors as the equivalent of the Roman *tribunus militum.* The listing of various ranks of society represents the universality of terror at the impending doom.

6, 17: *Their:* this reading is attested in the best manuscripts, but the vast majority read "his" in reference to the wrath of the Lamb in the preceding verse.

7, 1-17: An interlude of two visions precedes the breaking of the seventh seal, just as two more will separate the sixth and seventh trumpets (ch 10). In the first vision (1-8), the elect receive the seal of the living God as protection against the coming cataclysm; cf Rv 14, 1; Ez 9, 4-6; 2 Cor 1, 22; Eph 1, 13; 4, 30. The second vision (9-17) portrays the faithful Christians before God's throne to encourage those on earth to persevere to the end, even to death.

7, 1: *The four corners of the earth:* the earth is seen as a table or rectangular surface.

Rv

the earth so that no wind could blow on land or sea or against any tree.[t] [2]Then I saw another angel come up from the East,* holding the seal of the living God. He cried out in a loud voice to the four angels who were given power to damage the land and the sea, [3]"Do not damage the land or the sea or the trees until we put the seal on the foreheads of the servants of our God."[u] [4]I heard the number of those who had been marked with the seal, one hundred and forty-four thousand marked* from every tribe of the Israelites:[v] [5]twelve thousand were marked from the tribe of Judah,* twelve thousand from the tribe of Reuben, twelve thousand from the tribe of Gad, [6]twelve thousand from the tribe of Asher, twelve thousand from the tribe of Naphtali, twelve thousand from the tribe of Manasseh, [7]twelve thousand from the tribe of Simeon, twelve thousand from the tribe of Levi, twelve thousand from the tribe of Issachar, [8]twelve thousand from the tribe of Zebulun, twelve thousand from the tribe of Joseph, and twelve thousand were marked from the tribe of Benjamin.

Triumph of the Elect. [9]After this I had a vision of a great multitude, which no one could count, from every nation, race, people, and tongue. They stood before the throne and before the Lamb, wearing white robes and holding palm branches* in their hands. [10]They cried out in a loud voice:

"Salvation comes from* our God, who is seated on the throne, and from the Lamb."

[11]All the angels stood around the throne and around the elders and the four living creatures. They prostrated themselves before the throne, worshiped God, [12]and exclaimed:

"Amen. Blessing and glory, wisdom and thanksgiving, honor, power, and might be to our God forever and ever. Amen."

[13]Then one of the elders spoke up and said to me, "Who are these wearing white robes, and where did they come from?" [14]I said to him, "My lord, you are the one who knows." He said to me, "These are the ones who have survived the time of great distress;* they have washed their robes and made them white in the blood of the Lamb.[w]

[15]"For this reason they stand before God's throne and worship him day and night in his temple. The one who sits on the throne will shelter them.

[16]They will not hunger or thirst anymore, nor will the sun or any heat strike them.[x]

[17]For the Lamb who is in the center of the throne will shepherd them and lead them to springs of life-giving water,* and God will wipe away every tear from their eyes."[y]

CHAPTER 8*

The Seven Trumpets. [1]When he broke open the seventh seal, there was silence in heaven* for about half an hour.[z] [2]And I saw that the seven angels who stood before God were given seven trumpets.[a]

---

t Jer 49, 36; Zec 6, 5.—u Ex 12, 7-14; Ez 9, 4; 2 Cor 1, 22; Eph 1, 13; 4, 30.—v Rv 14, 1.—w Mt 24, 21.—x Is 49, 10.—y Rv 21, 4; Is 25, 8.—z Hb 2, 20; Zep 1, 7; Zec 2, 17.—a Rv 4, 5; Tb 12, 15.

7, 2: *East:* literally, "rising of the sun." The east was considered the source of light and the place of paradise (Gn 2, 8). *Seal:* whatever was marked by the impression of one's signet ring belonged to that person and was under his protection.

7, 4-9: *One hundred and forty-four thousand:* the square of twelve (the number of Israel's tribes) multiplied by a thousand, symbolic of the new Israel (cf Rv 14, 1-5; Gal 6, 16; Jas 1, 1) that embraces people *from every nation, race, people, and tongue* (9).

7, 5-8: Judah is placed first because of Christ; cf "the Lion of the tribe of Judah" (Rv 5, 5). Dan is omitted because of a later tradition that the antichrist would arise from it.

7, 9: *White robes . . . palm branches:* symbols of joy and victory; see the note on Rv 3, 5.

7, 10: *Salvation comes from:* literally, "(let) salvation (be ascribed) to." A similar hymn of praise is found at the fall of the dragon (Rv 12, 10) and of Babylon (Rv 19, 1).

7, 14: *Time of great distress:* fierce persecution by the Romans; cf Introduction.

7, 17: *Life-giving water:* literally, "the water of life," God's grace, which flows from Christ; cf Rv 21, 6; 22, 1.17; Jn 4, 10.14.

8, 1-13: The breaking of the seventh seal produces at first silence and then seven symbolic disasters, each announced by a trumpet blast, of which the first four form a unit as did the first four seals. A minor liturgy (3-5) is enclosed by a vision of seven angels (2.6). Then follow the first four trumpet blasts, each heralding catastrophes modeled on the plagues of Egypt affecting the traditional prophetic third (cf Ez 5, 12) of the earth, sea, fresh water, and stars (7-12). Finally, there is a vision of an eagle warning of the last three trumpet blasts (13).

8, 1: *Silence in heaven:* as in Zep 1, 7, a prelude to the eschatological woes that are to follow; cf Introduction.

The Gold Censer. ³Another angel came and stood at the altar,* holding a gold censer. He was given a great quantity of incense to offer, along with the prayers of all the holy ones, on the gold altar that was before the throne.ᵇ ⁴The smoke of the incense along with the prayers of the holy ones went up before God from the hand of the angel. ⁵Then the angel took the censer, filled it with burning coals from the altar, and hurled it down to the earth. There were peals of thunder, rumblings, flashes of lightning, and an earthquake.ᶜ

The First Four Trumpets. ⁶The seven angels who were holding the seven trumpets prepared to blow them.ᵈ

⁷When the first one blew his trumpet, there came hail and fire mixed with blood, which was hurled down to the earth. A third of the land was burned up, along with a third of the trees and all green grass.*

⁸ * When the second angel blew his trumpet, something like a large burning mountain was hurled into the sea. A third of the sea turned to blood,ᵉ ⁹a third of the creatures living in the sea* died, and a third of the ships were wrecked.

¹⁰When the third angel blew his trumpet, a large star burning like a torch fell from the sky. It fell on a third of the rivers and on the springs of water.ᶠ ¹¹The star was called "Wormwood,"* and a third of all the water turned to wormwood. Many people died from this water, because it was made bitter.ᵍ

¹²When the fourth angel blew his trumpet, a third of the sun, a third of the moon, and a third of the stars were struck, so that a third of them became dark. The day lost its light for a third of the time, as did the night.ʰ

¹³Then I looked again and heard an eagle flying high overhead cry out in a loud voice, "Woe! Woe! Woe* to the inhabitants of the earth from the rest of the trumpet blasts that the three angels are about to blow!"

CHAPTER 9

The Fifth Trumpet.* ¹Then the fifth angel blew his trumpet, and I saw a star* that had fallen from the sky to the earth. It was given the key for the passage to the abyss. ²It opened the passage to the abyss,ⁱ and smoke came up out of the passage like smoke from a huge furnace. The sun and the air were darkened by the smoke from the passage.ʲ ³Locusts came out of the smoke onto the land, and they were given the same power as scorpions* of the earth.ᵏ ⁴They were told not to harm the grass of the earth or any plant or any tree, but only those people who did not have the seal of God on their foreheads. ⁵They were not allowed to kill them but only to torment them for five months;* the torment they inflicted was like that of a scorpion when it stings a person. ⁶During that time these people will seek death but will not find it, and they will long to die but death will escape them.ˡ

⁷ * The appearance of the locusts was like that of horses ready for battle. On their heads they wore what looked like crowns of gold; their faces were like human faces,ᵐ ⁸and they had hair like women's hair. Their teeth were like lions' teeth,ⁿ ⁹and they had chests like iron breastplates. The

---

b Ps 141, 2; Tb 12, 12.—c Ez 10, 2; Ps 11, 6 / Rv 4, 5; 11, 19; 16, 18.—d Rv 16, 1-21.—e Ex 7, 20.—f Is 14, 12.—g Jer 9, 14.—h Ex 10, 21-23.—i Rv 20, 1.—j Gn 19, 28.—k Ex 10, 12-15; Wis 16, 9.—l Jb 3, 21.—m Jl 2, 4.—n Jl 1, 6.

8, 3: *Altar:* there seems to be only one altar in the heavenly temple, corresponding to the altar of holocausts in Rv 6, 9, and here to the altar of incense in Jerusalem; cf also Rv 9, 13; 11, 1; 14, 18; 16, 7.

8, 7: This woe resembles the seventh plague of Egypt (Ex 9, 23-24); cf Jl 3, 3.

8, 8-11: The background of these two woes is the first plague of Egypt (Ex 7, 20-21).

8, 9: *Creatures living in the sea:* literally, "creatures in the sea that had souls."

8, 11: *Wormwood:* an extremely bitter and malignant plant symbolizing the punishment God inflicts on the ungodly; cf Jer 9, 12-14; 23, 15.

8, 13: *Woe! Woe! Woe:* each of the three woes pronounced by the angel represents a separate disaster; cf Rv 9, 12; 11, 14. The final woe, released by the seventh trumpet blast, includes the plagues of ch 16.

9, 1-12: The fifth trumpet heralds a woe containing elements from the eighth and ninth plagues of Egypt (Ex 10, 12-15.21-23) but specifically reminiscent of the invasion of locusts in Jl 1, 4—2, 10.

9, 1: *A star:* late Judaism represented fallen powers as stars (Is 14, 12-15; Lk 10, 18; Jude 13), but a comparison with Rv 1, 20 and Rv 20, 1 suggests that here it means an angel. *The passage to the abyss:* referring to Sheol, the netherworld, where Satan and the fallen angels are kept for a thousand years, to be cast afterwards into the pool of fire; cf Rv 20, 7-10. The abyss was conceived of as a vast subterranean cavern full of fire. Its only link with the earth was a kind of passage or mine shaft, which was kept locked.

9, 3: *Scorpions:* their poisonous sting was proverbial; Ez 2, 6; Lk 11, 12.

9, 5: *For five months:* more or less corresponding to the lifespan of locusts.

9, 7-10: Eight characteristics are listed to show the eschatological and diabolical nature of these locusts.

Rv

sound of their wings was like the sound of many horse-drawn chariots racing into battle. [10] They had tails like scorpions, with stingers; with their tails they had power to harm people for five months. [11] They had as their king the angel of the abyss, whose name in Hebrew is Abaddon* and in Greek Apollyon.

[12] The first woe has passed, but there are two more to come.

The Sixth Trumpet.* [13] Then the sixth angel blew his trumpet, and I heard a voice coming from the [four]* horns of the gold altar before God,*o* [14] telling the sixth angel who held the trumpet, "Release the four angels* who are bound at the banks of the great river Euphrates." [15] So the four angels were released, who were prepared for this hour, day, month, and year to kill a third of the human race. [16] The number of cavalry troops was two hundred million; I heard their number. [17] Now in my vision this is how I saw the horses and their riders. They wore red, blue,* and yellow breastplates, and the horses' heads were like heads of lions, and out of their mouths came fire, smoke, and sulfur.*p* [18] By these three plagues of fire, smoke, and sulfur that came out of their mouths a third of the human race was killed. [19] For the power of the horses is in their mouths and in their tails; for their tails are like snakes, with heads that inflict harm.

[20] The rest of the human race, who were not killed by these plagues, did not repent of the works of their hands,* to give up the worship of demons and idols made from gold, silver, bronze, stone, and wood,

which cannot see or hear or walk.*q* [21] Nor did they repent of their murders, their magic potions, their unchastity, or their robberies.

CHAPTER 10

The Angel with the Small Scroll. [1] * Then I saw another mighty angel come down from heaven wrapped in a cloud, with a halo around his head; his face was like the sun and his feet were like pillars of fire. [2] In his hand he held a small scroll that had been opened. He placed his right foot on the sea and his left foot on the land,* [3] and then he cried out in a loud voice as a lion roars. When he cried out, the seven thunders* raised their voices, too.*r* [4] When the seven thunders had spoken, I was about to write it down; but I heard a voice from heaven say, "Seal up what the seven thunders have spoken, but do not write it down." [5] Then the angel I saw standing on the sea and on the land raised his right hand to heaven [6] and swore by the one who lives forever and ever, who created heaven and earth and sea* and all that is in them, "There shall be no more delay.*s* [7] At the time when you hear the seventh angel blow his trumpet, the mysterious plan of God* shall be fulfilled, as he promised to his servants the prophets."*t*

[8] Then the voice that I had heard from heaven spoke to me again and said, "Go, take the scroll that lies open in the hand of the angel who is standing on the sea and on the land." [9] So I went up to the angel and told him to give me the small scroll. He

---

o Ex 30, 1-3.—p Jb 41, 10-13.—q Ps 135, 15-17; Is 17, 8; Dn 5, 4.—r Ps 29, 3-9; Jer 25, 30; Am 3, 8.—s Dt 32, 40; Dn 12, 7 / Ez 12, 28.—t Am 3, 7.

9, 11: *Abaddon:* Hebrew (more precisely, Aramaic) for destruction or ruin. *Apollyon:* Greek for the "Destroyer."

9, 13-21: The sixth trumpet heralds a woe representing another diabolical attack symbolized by an invasion by the Parthians living east of the Euphrates; see the note on Rv 6, 2. At the appointed time (15), the frightful horses act as God's agents of judgment. The imaginative details are not to be taken literally; see Introduction and the note on Rv 6, 12-14.

9, 13: *[Four]:* many Greek manuscripts and versions omit the word. The horns were situated at the four corners of the altar (Ex 27, 2; 30, 2-3); see the note on Rv 8, 3.

9, 14-15: *The four angels:* they are symbolic of the destructive activity that will be extended throughout the universe.

9, 17: *Blue:* literally, "hyacinth-colored." *Yellow:* literally, "sulfurous."

9, 20: *The works of their hands:* i.e., the gods their hands had made.

10, 1—11, 14: An interlude in two scenes (Rv 10, 1-11 and Rv 11, 1-14) precedes the sounding of the seventh trumpet; cf Rv 7, 1-17. The first vision describes an angel astride sea and land like a colossus, with a small scroll open, the contents of which indicate that the end is imminent (ch 10). The second vision is of the measuring of the temple and two witnesses, whose martyrdom means that the kingdom of God is about to be inaugurated.

10, 1-4: *The seven thunders:* God's voice announcing judgment and doom; cf Ps 29, 3-9, where thunder, as the voice of Yahweh, is praised seven times.

10, 2: *He placed . . . on the land:* this symbolizes the universality of the angel's message, as does the figure of the small scroll open to be read.

10, 6: *Heaven and earth and sea:* the three parts of the universe. *No more delay:* cf Dn 12, 7; Hb 2, 3.

10, 7: *The mysterious plan of God:* literally, "the mystery of God," the end of the present age when the forces of evil will be put down (Rv 17, 1—19, 4.11-21; 20, 7-10; cf 2 Thes 2, 6-12; Rom 16, 25-26), and the establishment of the reign of God when all creation will be made new (Rv 21, 1—22, 5).

10, 9-10: The small scroll was sweet because it predicted the final victory of God's people; it was sour because it also announced their sufferings. Cf Ez 3, 1-3.

said to me, "Take and swallow it. It will turn your stomach sour, but in your mouth it will taste as sweet* as honey." [10] I took the small scroll from the angel's hand and swallowed it. In my mouth it was like sweet honey, but when I had eaten it, my stomach turned sour.[u] [11] Then someone said to me, "You must prophesy again about many peoples, nations, tongues, and kings."*

CHAPTER 11

The Two Witnesses. [1] [v] Then I was given a measuring rod like a staff and I was told, "Come and measure the temple of God and the altar, and count those who are worshiping in it.* [2] But exclude the outer court* of the temple; do not measure it, for it has been handed over to the Gentiles, who will trample the holy city for forty-two months. [3] I will commission my two witnesses* to prophesy for those twelve hundred and sixty days, wearing sackcloth." [4] [w] These are the two olive trees and the two lampstands* that stand before the Lord of the earth. [5] * If anyone wants to harm them, fire comes out of their mouths and devours their enemies. In this way, anyone wanting to harm them is sure to be slain. [6] They have the power to close up the sky so that no rain can fall during the time of their prophesying. They also have power to turn water into blood and to afflict the earth with any plague as often as they wish.[x]

[7] When they have finished their testimony, the beast that comes up from the abyss* will wage war against them and conquer them and kill them.[y] [8] Their corpses will lie in the main street of the great city,* which has the symbolic names "Sodom" and "Egypt," where indeed their Lord was crucified. [9] * Those from every people, tribe, tongue, and nation will gaze on their corpses for three and a half days, and they will not allow their corpses to be buried. [10] The inhabitants of the earth will gloat over them and be glad and exchange gifts because these two prophets tormented the inhabitants of the earth. [11] But after the three and a half days, a breath of life from God entered them. When they stood on their feet, great fear fell on those who saw them.[z] [12] Then they heard a loud voice from heaven say to them, "Come up here." So they went up to heaven in a cloud as their enemies looked on.[a] [13] At that moment there was a great earthquake, and a tenth of the city fell in ruins. Seven thousand people* were killed during the earthquake; the rest were terrified and gave glory to the God of heaven.

[14] The second woe has passed, but the third is coming soon.

The Seventh Trumpet.* [15] Then the seventh angel blew his trumpet. There were loud voices in heaven, saying, "The kingdom of the world now belongs to our Lord and to his Anointed, and he will reign forever and ever." [16] The twenty-four elders who sat on their thrones before God

---

u Ez 3, 1-3.—v Ez 40, 3-5 / Zec 2, 5-9.—w Zec 4, 3.14.—x Ex 7, 17.—y Dn 7, 21.—z Ez 37, 5.10.—a 2 Kgs 2, 11.

10, 11: This further prophecy is contained in chs 12-22.

11, 1: The temple and altar symbolize the new Israel; see the note on Rv 7, 4-9. The worshipers represent Christians. The measuring of the temple (cf Ez 40, 3—42, 20; 47, 1-12; Zec 2, 5-6) suggests that God will preserve the faithful remnant (cf Is 4, 2-3) who remain true to Christ (Rv 14, 1-5).

11, 2: *The outer court:* the Court of the Gentiles. *Trample . . . forty-two months:* the duration of the vicious persecution of the Jews by Antiochus IV Epiphanes (Dn 7, 25; 12, 7); this persecution of three and a half years (half of seven, counted as 1260 days in Rv 11, 3; 12, 6) became the prototype of periods of trial for God's people; cf Lk 4, 25; Jas 5, 17. The reference here is to the persecution by the Romans; cf Introduction.

11, 3: The two witnesses, wearing sackcloth symbolizing lamentation and repentance, cannot readily be identified. Do they represent Moses and Elijah, or the Law and the Prophets, or Peter and Paul? Most probably they refer to the universal church, especially the Christian martyrs, fulfilling the office of witness (two because of Dt 19, 15; cf Mk 6, 7; Jn 8, 17).

11, 4: *The two olive trees and the two lampstands:* the martyrs who stand in the presence of the Lord; the imagery is taken from Zec 4, 1-3.11-14, where the olive trees refer to Zerubbabel and Joshua.

11, 5-6: These details are derived from stories of Moses, who turned *water into blood* (Ex 7, 17-20), and of Elijah, who called down fire from heaven (1 Kgs 18, 36-40; 2 Kgs 1, 10) and closed up the sky for three years (1 Kgs 17, 1; cf 1 Kgs 18, 1).

11, 7: *The beast . . . from the abyss:* the Roman emperor Nero, who symbolizes the forces of evil, or the antichrist (Rv 13, 1.8; 17, 8); cf Dn 7, 2-8.11-12.19-22 and Introduction.

11, 8: *The great city:* this expression is used constantly in Rv for Babylon, i.e., Rome; cf Rv 14, 8; 16, 19; 17, 18; 18, 2.10.21. *"Sodom" and "Egypt":* symbols of immorality (cf Is 1, 10) and oppression of God's people (cf Ex 1, 11-14). *Where indeed their Lord was crucified:* not the geographical but the symbolic Jerusalem that rejects God and his witnesses, i.e., Rome, called Babylon in chs 16-18; see the note on Rv 17, 9 and Introduction.

11, 9-12: Over the martyrdom (7) of the two witnesses, now called prophets, the ungodly rejoice *for three and a half days,* a symbolic period of time; see the note on v 2. Afterwards they go in triumph to heaven, as did Elijah (2 Kgs 2, 11).

11, 13: *Seven thousand people:* a symbolic sum to represent all social classes (seven) and large numbers (thousands); cf Introduction.

11, 15-19: The seventh trumpet proclaims the coming of God's reign after the victory over diabolical powers; see the note on Rv 10, 7.

prostrated themselves and worshiped God [17] and said:

"We give thanks to you, Lord God almighty,
who are and who were.
For you have assumed your great power
and have established your reign.
[18] The nations raged,
but your wrath has come,
and the time for the dead to be judged,
and to recompense your servants, the prophets,
and the holy ones and those who fear your name,
the small and the great alike,
and to destroy those who destroy the earth."[b]

[19] Then God's temple in heaven was opened, and the ark of his covenant could be seen in the temple. There were flashes of lightning, rumblings, and peals of thunder, an earthquake, and a violent hailstorm.

CHAPTER 12

The Woman and the Dragon. [1] * A great sign appeared in the sky, a woman* clothed with the sun, with the moon under her feet, and on her head a crown of twelve stars.[c] [2] She was with child and wailed aloud in pain as she labored to give birth.* [3] Then another sign appeared in the sky; it was a huge red dragon,* with seven heads and ten horns, and on its heads were seven diadems.[d] [4] Its tail swept away a third of the stars in the sky and hurled them down to the earth. Then the dragon stood before the woman about to give birth, to devour her child when she gave birth.[e] [5] She gave birth to a son, a male child, destined to rule all the nations with an iron rod.* Her child was caught up to God and his throne.[f] [6] The woman herself fled into the desert where she had a place prepared by God, that there she might be taken care of for twelve hundred and sixty days.*

[7] * Then war broke out in heaven; Michael* and his angels battled against the dragon. The dragon and its angels fought back, [8] but they did not prevail and there was no longer any place for them in heaven. [9] The huge dragon, the ancient serpent,* who is called the Devil and Satan, who deceived the whole world, was thrown down to earth, and its angels were thrown down with it.[g]

[10] Then I heard a loud voice in heaven say:

"Now have salvation and power come,
and the kingdom of our God
and the authority of his Anointed.
For the accuser* of our brothers is cast out,
who accuses them before our God day and night.
[11] They conquered him by the blood of the Lamb
and by the word of their testimony;

---

b Ps 2, 1.5 / Am 3, 7.—c Gn 37, 9.—d Dn 7, 7.—e Dn 8, 10.—f Is 66, 7 / Ps 2, 9.—g Gn 3, 1-4 / Lk 10, 18.

12, 1—14, 20: This central section of Rv portrays the power of evil, represented by a dragon, in opposition to God and his people. First, the dragon pursues the woman about to give birth, but her son is saved and "caught up to God and his throne" (Rv 12, 5). Then Michael and his angels cast the dragon and his angels out of heaven (Rv 12, 7-9). After this, the dragon tries to attack the boy indirectly by attacking members of his church (Rv 12, 13-18). A beast, symbolizing the Roman empire, then becomes the dragon's agent, mortally wounded but restored to life and worshiped by all the world (Rv 13, 1-10). A second beast arises from the land, symbolizing the antichrist, which leads people astray by its prodigies to idolize the first beast (Rv 13, 11-18). This is followed by a vision of the Lamb and his faithful ones, and the proclamation of imminent judgment upon the world in terms of the wine of God's wrath (Rv 14, 1-20).

12, 1-6: The woman adorned with the sun, the moon, and the stars (images taken from Gn 37, 9-10) symbolizes God's people in the Old and the New Testament. The Israel of old gave birth to the Messiah (5) and then became the new Israel, the church, which suffers persecution by the dragon (6.13-17); cf Is 50, 1; 66, 7; Jer 50, 12. This corresponds to a widespread myth throughout the ancient world that a goddess pregnant with a savior was pursued by a horrible monster; by miraculous intervention, she bore a son who then killed the monster.

12, 2: Because of Eve's sin, the woman gives birth in distress and pain (Gn 3, 16; cf Is 66, 7-14).

12, 3: *Huge red dragon:* the Devil or Satan (cf Rv 12, 9; 20, 2), symbol of the forces of evil, a mythical monster known also as Leviathan (Ps 74, 13-14) or Rahab (Jb 26, 12-13; Ps 89, 11). *Seven diadems:* these are symbolic of the fullness of the dragon's sovereignty over the kingdoms of this world; cf Christ with many diadems (Rv 19, 12).

12, 5: *Rule . . . iron rod:* fulfilled in Rv 19, 15; cf Ps 2, 9. *Was caught up to God:* reference to Christ's ascension.

12, 6: God protects the persecuted church in the desert, the traditional Old Testament place of refuge for the afflicted, according to the typology of the Exodus; see the note on Rv 11, 2.

12, 7-12: Michael, mentioned only here in Rv, wins a victory over the dragon. A hymn of praise follows.

12, 7: *Michael:* the archangel, guardian and champion of Israel; cf Dn 10, 13.21; 12, 1; Jude 9. In Hebrew, the name Michael means "Who can compare with God?"; cf Rv 13, 4.

12, 9: *The ancient serpent:* who seduced Eve (Gn 3, 1-6), mother of the human race; cf Rv 20, 2; Eph 6, 11-12. *Was thrown down:* allusion to the expulsion of Satan from heaven; cf Lk 10, 18.

12, 10: *The accuser:* the meaning of the Hebrew word "Satan," found in v 9; Jb 1—2; Zec 3, 1; 1 Chr 21, 1; he continues to accuse Christ's disciples.

love for life did not deter them from death.

12 Therefore, rejoice, you heavens,
and you who dwell in them.
But woe to you, earth and sea,
for the Devil has come down to you
in great fury,
for he knows he has but a short
time."

13 When the dragon saw that it had been thrown down to the earth, it pursued the woman who had given birth to the male child. *h* 14 But the woman was given the two wings of the great eagle,* so that she could fly to her place in the desert, where, far from the serpent, she was taken care of for a year, two years, and a half-year. *i* 15 The serpent,* however, spewed a torrent of water out of his mouth after the woman to sweep her away with the current. 16 But the earth helped the woman and opened its mouth and swallowed the flood that the dragon spewed out of its mouth. 17 Then the dragon became angry with the woman and went off to wage war against the rest of her offspring, those who keep God's commandments and bear witness to Jesus.* 18 It took its position* on the sand of the sea. *j*

CHAPTER 13

The First Beast.* 1 Then I saw a beast come out of the sea with ten horns and seven heads; on its horns were ten diadems, and on its heads blasphemous name[s]. *k* 2 The beast I saw was like a leopard, but it had feet like a bear's, and its mouth was like the mouth of a lion. *l* To it the dragon gave its own power and throne,

along with great authority.* 3 I saw that one of its heads seemed to have been mortally wounded, but this mortal wound was healed.* Fascinated, the whole world followed after the beast. 4 They worshiped the dragon because it gave its authority to the beast; they also worshiped the beast* and said, "Who can compare with the beast or who can fight against it?"

5 * The beast was given a mouth uttering proud boasts and blasphemies, *m* and it was given authority to act for forty-two months.* 6 It opened its mouth to utter blasphemies against God, blaspheming his name and his dwelling and those who dwell in heaven. 7 It was also allowed to wage war against the holy ones and conquer them, and it was granted authority over every tribe, people, tongue, and nation. *n* 8 All the inhabitants of the earth will worship it, all whose names were not written from the foundation of the world in the book of life, which belongs to the Lamb who was slain. *o*

9 Whoever has ears ought to hear these words. *p*
10 Anyone destined for captivity goes into captivity.
Anyone destined to be slain by the sword shall be slain by the sword. *q*
Such is the faithful endurance of the holy ones.

The Second Beast.* 11 Then I saw another beast come up out of the earth; it had two horns like a lamb's but spoke like a dragon. 12 It wielded all the authority of the first beast in its sight and made the earth and its inhabitants worship the first beast, whose mortal wound had been healed. 13 It

---

h Gn 3, 15.—i Ex 19, 4; Dn 7, 25; 12, 7.—j Gn 3, 15.—k 2 Thes 2, 3-12.—l Dn 7, 3-6.—m Dn 7, 8.11.25; 8, 14; 9, 27; 11, 36; 12, 7.—n Dn 7, 21.—o Rv 3, 5; 17, 8; 20, 12.—p Mt 13, 9.—q Jer 15, 2.

12, 14: *Great eagle:* symbol of the power and swiftness of divine help; cf Ex 19, 4; Dt 32, 11; Is 40, 31.

12, 15: The serpent is depicted as the sea monster; cf Rv 13, 1; Is 27, 1; Ez 32, 2; Ps 74, 13-14.

12, 17: Although the church is protected by God's special providence (16), the individual Christian is to expect persecution and suffering.

12, 18: *It took its position:* many later manuscripts and versions read "I took my position," thus connecting the sentence to the following paragraph.

13, 1-10: This wild beast, combining features of the four beasts in Dn 7, 2-28, symbolizes the Roman empire; the seven heads represent the emperors; see the notes on Rv 17, 10 and Rv 17, 12-14. The blasphemous names are the divine titles assumed by the emperors.

13, 2: Satan (Rv 12, 9), the prince of this world (Jn 12, 31), commissioned the beast to persecute the church (5-7).

13, 3: This may be a reference to the popular legend that Nero would come back to life and rule again after his death (which occurred in A.D. 68 from a self-inflicted stab wound in the throat); cf Rv 13, 14; 17, 8. Domitian (A.D. 81-96) embodied all the cruelty and impiety of Nero. Cf Introduction.

13, 4: *Worshiped the beast:* allusion to emperor worship, which Domitian insisted upon and ruthlessly enforced. *Who can compare with the beast:* perhaps a deliberate parody of the name Michael; see the note on Rv 12, 7.

13, 5-6: Domitian, like Antiochus IV Epiphanes (Dn 7, 8.11.25), demanded that he be called by divine titles such as "our lord and god" and "Jupiter." See the note on Rv 11, 2.

13, 5: *Forty-two months:* this is the same duration as the profanation of the holy city (Rv 11, 2), the prophetic mission of the two witnesses (Rv 11, 3), and the retreat of the woman into the desert (Rv 12, 6.14).

13, 11-18: The second beast is described in terms of the false prophets (cf Rv 16, 13; 19, 20; 20, 10) who accompany the false messiahs (the first beast); cf Mt 24, 24; Mk 13, 22; 2 Thes 2, 9; cf also Dt 13, 2-4. Christians had either to worship the emperor and his image or to suffer martyrdom.

Rv

performed great signs, even making fire come down from heaven to earth in the sight of everyone.ʳ ¹⁴It deceived the inhabitants of the earth with the signs it was allowed to perform in the sight of the first beast, telling them to make an image for the beast who had been wounded by the sword and revived. ¹⁵It was then permitted to breathe life into the beast's image, so that the beast's image could speak and [could] have anyone who did not worship it put to death.ˢ ¹⁶It forced all the people, small and great, rich and poor, free and slave, to be given a stamped image on their right hands or their foreheads,ᵗ ¹⁷so that no one could buy or sell except one who had the stamped image of the beast's name or the number that stood for its name.

¹⁸ ᵘ Wisdom is needed here; one who understands can calculate the number of the beast, for it is a number that stands for a person. His number is six hundred and sixty-six.*

CHAPTER 14

The Lamb's Companions.* ¹Then I looked and there was the Lamb standing on Mount Zion,* and with him a hundred and forty-four thousand who had his name and his Father's name written on their foreheads.ᵛ ²I heard a sound from heaven like the sound of rushing water or a loud peal of thunder. The sound I heard was like that of harpists playing their harps. ³They were singing [what seemed to be] a new hymn before the throne, before the four living creatures and the elders. No one could learn this hymn except the hundred and forty-four thousand who had been ransomed from the earth.ʷ ⁴These are they who were not defiled with women; they are virgins* and these are the ones who follow the Lamb wherever he goes. They have been ransomed as the firstfruits of the human race for God and the Lamb.ˣ ⁵On their lips no deceit* has been found; they are unblemished.ʸ

The Three Angels.* ⁶Then I saw another angel flying high overhead, with everlasting good news* to announce to those who dwell on earth, to every nation, tribe, tongue, and people. ⁷He said in a loud voice, "Fear God and give him glory, for his time has come to sit in judgment. Worship him who made heaven and earth and sea and springs of water."ᶻ

⁸A second angel followed, saying:

"Fallen, fallen is Babylon the great,ᵃ
    that made all the nations drink
    the wine of her licentious passion."*

⁹A third angel followed them and said in a loud voice, "Anyone who worships the beast or its image, or accepts its mark on forehead or hand, ¹⁰will also drink the wine of God's fury,* poured full strength into the cup of his wrath, and will be tormented in burning sulfur before the holy angels and before the Lamb. ¹¹The smoke of the fire that torments them will rise forever and ever, and there will be no relief day or night for those who worship the

---

r Dt 13, 2-4; Mt 24, 24; 2 Thes 2, 9-10.—s Dn 3, 5-7.15.—t Rv 14, 9; 16, 2; 19, 20; 20, 4.—u Rv 17, 9.—v Jl 3, 5; Ob 17; Acts 2, 21.—w Pss 33, 3; 96, 1; 98, 1; Is 42, 10.—x Jer 2, 2; Jas 1, 18.—y Zep 3, 13.—z Rv 2, 10; Mt 10, 28.—a Rv 18, 2-3; Is 21, 9; Jer 51, 8 / Is 51, 17; Jer 25, 15-17.

13, 18: Each of the letters of the alphabet in Hebrew as well as in Greek has a numerical value. Many possible combinations of letters will add up to 666, and many candidates have been nominated for this infamous number. The most likely is the emperor Caesar Nero (see the note on Rv 13, 3), the Greek form of whose name in Hebrew letters gives the required sum. (The Latin form of this name equals 616, which is the reading of a few manuscripts.) Nero personifies the emperors who viciously persecuted the church. It has also been observed that "6" represents imperfection, falling short of the perfect number "7," and is represented here in a triple or superlative form.

14, 1-5: Now follows a tender and consoling vision of the Lamb and his companions.

14, 1: *Mount Zion:* in Jerusalem, the traditional place where the true remnant, the Israel of faith, is to be gathered in the messianic reign; cf 2 Kgs 19, 30-31; Jl 3, 5; Ob 17; Mi 4, 6-8; Zep 3, 12-20. *A hundred and forty-four thousand:* see the note on Rv 7, 4-9. *His Father's name . . . foreheads:* in contrast to the pagans who were marked with the name or number of the beast (Rv 13, 16-17).

14, 4: *Virgins:* metaphorical, because they never indulged in any idolatrous practices, which are considered in the Old Testament to be adultery and fornication (Rv 2, 14-15.20-22; 17, 1-6; cf Ez 16, 1-58; 23, 1-49). The parallel passages (Rv 7, 3; 22, 4) indicate that the 144,000 whose foreheads are sealed represent all Christian people.

14, 5: *No deceit:* because they did not deny Christ or do homage to the beast. Lying is characteristic of the opponents of Christ (Jn 8, 44), but the Suffering Servant spoke no falsehood (Is 53, 9; 1 Pt 2, 22). *Unblemished:* a cultic term taken from the vocabulary of sacrificial ritual.

14, 6-13: Three angels proclaim imminent judgment on the pagan world, calling all peoples to worship God the creator. Babylon (Rome) will fall, and its supporters will be tormented forever.

14, 6: *Everlasting good news:* that God's eternal reign is about to begin; see the note on Rv 10, 7.

14, 8: This verse anticipates the lengthy dirge over Babylon (Rome) in Rv 18, 1—19, 4. The oracle of Is 21, 9 to Babylon is applied here.

14, 10-11: *The wine of God's fury:* image taken from Is 51, 17; Jer 25, 15-16; 49, 12; 51, 7; Ez 23, 31-34. Eternal punishment in the fiery pool of burning sulfur (or "fire and brimstone"; cf Gn 19, 24) is also reserved for the Devil, the beast, and the false prophet (Rv 19, 20; 20, 10; 21, 8).

beast or its image or accept the mark of its name."[b] [12] Here is what sustains the holy ones who keep God's commandments[c] and their faith in Jesus.*

[13] [d] I heard a voice from heaven say, "Write this: Blessed are the dead who die in the Lord from now on." "Yes," said the Spirit, "let them find rest from their labors, for their works accompany them."*

The Harvest of the Earth.* [14] Then I looked and there was a white cloud, and sitting on the cloud one who looked like a son of man, with a gold crown on his head and a sharp sickle in his hand.[e] [15] Another angel came out of the temple, crying out in a loud voice to the one sitting on the cloud, "Use your sickle and reap the harvest, for the time to reap has come, because the earth's harvest is fully ripe."[f] [16] So the one who was sitting on the cloud swung his sickle over the earth, and the earth was harvested.

[17] Then another angel came out of the temple in heaven who also had a sharp sickle. [18] Then another angel [came] from the altar,* [who] was in charge of the fire, and cried out in a loud voice to the one who had the sharp sickle, "Use your sharp sickle and cut the clusters from the earth's vines, for its grapes are ripe." [19] So the angel swung his sickle over the earth and cut the earth's vintage. He threw it into the great wine press of God's fury.[g] [20] The wine press was trodden outside the city and blood poured out of the wine press to the height of a horse's bridle for two hundred miles.*

b Rv 19, 3.—c Rv 12, 17.—d Mt 11, 28-29; 2 Thes 1, 7; Heb 4, 10.—e Rv 1, 7; Dn 7, 13.—f Jl 4, 13; Mt 13, 36-43.—g Rv 19, 15; Is 63, 1-6.—h Rv 7, 9.14; 13, 15-18.—i Pss 92, 6; 98, 1 / Dt 32, 4; Ps 145, 17.—j Ps 86, 9-10; Jer 10, 7.—k Rv 19, 8.—l 1 Kgs 8, 10; Is 6, 4.

14, 12: In addition to *faith in Jesus,* the seer insists upon the necessity and value of works, as in Rv 2, 23; 20, 12-13; 22, 12; cf Mt 16, 27; Rom 2, 6.

14, 13: See the note on Rv 1, 3. According to Jewish thought, people's actions followed them as witnesses before the court of God.

14, 14-20: The reaping of the harvest symbolizes the gathering of the elect in the final judgment, while the reaping and treading of the grapes symbolizes the doom of the ungodly (cf Jl 4, 12-13; Is 63, 1-6) that will come in Rv 19, 11-21.

14, 18: *Altar:* there was only one altar in the heavenly temple; see the notes above on Rv 6, 9; 8, 3; 11, 1.

14, 20: *Two hundred miles:* literally sixteen hundred stades. The *stadion,* a Greek unit of measurement, was about 607 feet in length, approximately the length of a furlong.

CHAPTER 15

The Seven Last Plagues. [1] * Then I saw in heaven another sign,* great and awe-inspiring: seven angels with the seven last plagues, for through them God's fury is accomplished.

[2] Then I saw something like a sea of glass mingled with fire.* On the sea of glass were standing those who had won the victory over the beast and its image and the number that signified its name. They were holding God's harps,[h] [3] and they sang the song of Moses,* the servant of God, and the song of the Lamb:

"Great and wonderful are your works,
　　Lord God almighty.
Just and true are your ways,
　　O king of the nations.[i]
[4]　Who will not fear you, Lord,
　　or glorify your name?
For you alone are holy.
　　All the nations will come
　　and worship before you,
　　for your righteous acts have been revealed."[j]

[5] * After this I had another vision. The temple that is the heavenly tent of testimony* opened, [6] and the seven angels with the seven plagues came out of the temple. They were dressed in clean white linen, with a gold sash around their chests.[k] [7] One of the four living creatures gave the seven angels seven gold bowls filled with the fury of God, who lives forever and ever. [8] Then the temple became so filled with the smoke from God's glory and might that no one could enter it until the seven plagues of the seven angels had been accomplished.[l]

15, 1—16, 21: The seven bowls, the third and last group of seven after the seven seals and the seven trumpets, foreshadow the final cataclysm. Again, the series is introduced by a heavenly prelude, in which the victors over the beast sing the canticle of Moses (15, 2-4).

15, 1-4: A vision of the victorious martyrs precedes the vision of woe in Rv 15, 5—16, 21; cf Rv 7, 9-12.

15, 2: *Mingled with fire:* fire symbolizes the sanctity involved in facing God, reflected in the trials that have prepared the victorious Christians or in God's wrath.

15, 3: *The song of Moses:* the song that Moses and the Israelites sang after their escape from the oppression of Egypt (Ex 15, 1-18). The martyrs have escaped from the oppression of the Devil. *Nations:* many other Greek manuscripts and versions read "ages."

15, 5-8: Seven angels receive the bowls of God's wrath.

15, 5: *Tent of testimony:* the name of the meeting tent in the Greek text of Ex 40. Cf 2 Mc 2, 4-7.

Rv

CHAPTER 16

The Seven Bowls.* [1]I heard a loud voice speaking from the temple to the seven angels, "Go and pour out the seven bowls of God's fury upon the earth."

[2]The first angel went and poured out his bowl on the earth. Festering and ugly sores broke out on those who had the mark of the beast or worshiped its image.*

[3] * The second angel poured out his bowl on the sea. The sea turned to blood like that from a corpse; every creature living in the sea died.

[4]The third angel poured out his bowl on the rivers and springs of water. These also turned to blood.[m] [5]Then I heard the angel in charge of the waters say:

"You are just, O Holy One,
  who are and who were,
  in passing this sentence.[n]
[6] For they have shed the blood of the
    holy ones and the prophets,
  and you [have] given them blood to
    drink;
  it is what they deserve."[o]

[7]Then I heard the altar cry out,

"Yes, Lord God almighty,
  your judgments are true and
    just."[p]

[8]The fourth angel poured out his bowl on the sun. It was given the power to burn people with fire. [9]People were burned by the scorching heat and blasphemed the name of God who had power over these plagues, but they did not repent or give him glory.[q]

[10] [r] The fifth angel poured out his bowl on the throne of the beast.* Its kingdom

was plunged into darkness, and people bit their tongues in pain [11]and blasphemed the God of heaven because of their pains and sores. But they did not repent of their works.[s]

[12]The sixth angel emptied his bowl on the great river Euphrates. Its water was dried up to prepare the way for the kings of the East.* [13]I saw three unclean spirits like frogs* come from the mouth of the dragon, from the mouth of the beast, and from the mouth of the false prophet.[t] [14]These were demonic spirits who performed signs. They went out to the kings of the whole world to assemble them for the battle on the great day of God the almighty.[u] [15]("Behold, I am coming like a thief."* Blessed is the one who watches and keeps his clothes ready, so that he may not go naked and people see him exposed.)[v] [16]They then assembled the kings in the place that is named Armageddon* in Hebrew.

[17]The seventh angel poured out his bowl into the air. A loud voice came out of the temple from the throne, saying, "It is done."[w] [18]Then there were lightning flashes, rumblings, and peals of thunder, and a great earthquake. It was such a violent earthquake that there has never been one like it since the human race began on earth.[x] [19]The great city* was split into three parts, and the gentile cities fell. But God remembered great Babylon, giving it the cup filled with the wine of his fury and wrath. [20] * Every island fled, and mountains disappeared. [21]Large hailstones like huge weights came down from the sky on people, and they blasphemed God for the plague of hail because this plague was so severe.[y]

---

m Ex 7, 14-24.—n Rv 1, 4.—o Ez 35, 6; Mt 23, 34-35.—p Dn 3, 27; Tb 3, 2.—q Am 4, 6.—r Ex 10, 21-23.—s Ex 9, 8-11 / Jer 5, 3.—t Ex 8, 2-3.—u 1 Cor 1, 8.—v Mt 24, 42-44 / Rv 3, 17.— w Is 66, 6.—x Mk 13, 19.—y Ex 9, 22-26.

16, 1-21: These seven bowls, like the seven seals (Rv 6, 1-17; 8, 1) and the seven trumpets (Rv 8, 2—9, 21; 11, 15-19), bring on a succession of disasters modeled in part on the plagues of Egypt (Ex 7—12). See the note on Rv 6, 12-14.

16, 2: Like the sixth Egyptian plague (Ex 9, 8-11).

16, 3-4: Like the first Egyptian plague (Ex 7, 20-21). The same woe followed the blowing of the second trumpet (Rv 8, 8-9).

16, 10: *The throne of the beast:* symbol of the forces of evil. *Darkness:* like the ninth Egyptian plague (Ex 10, 21-23); cf Rv 9, 2.

16, 12: *The kings of the East:* Parthians; see the notes on Rv 6, 2 and Rv 17, 12-13. *East:* literally, "rising of the sun," as in Rv 7, 2.

16, 13: *Frogs:* possibly an allusion to the second Egyptian plague (Ex 7, 26—8, 11). *The false prophet:* identified with the two-horned second beast (Rv 13, 11-18 and the note there).

16, 15: *Like a thief:* as in Rv 3, 3 (cf Mt 24, 42-44; 1 Thes 5, 2). *Blessed:* see the note on Rv 1, 3.

16, 16: *Armageddon:* in Hebrew, this means "Mountain of Megiddo." Since Megiddo was the scene of many decisive battles in antiquity (Jgs 5, 19-20; 2 Kgs 9, 27; 2 Chr 35, 20-24), the town became the symbol of the final disastrous rout of the forces of evil.

16, 19: *The great city:* Rome and the empire.

16, 20-21: See the note on Rv 6, 12-14. *Hailstones:* as in seventh Egyptian plague (Ex 9, 23-24); cf Rv 8, 7. *Like huge weights:* literally, "weighing a talent," about one hundred pounds.

V. THE PUNISHMENT OF BABYLON AND THE DESTRUCTION OF PAGAN NATIONS

CHAPTER 17

Babylon the Great. 1 * Then one of the seven angels who were holding the seven bowls came and said to me, "Come here. I will show you the judgment on the great harlot* who lives near the many waters.ᶻ 2 The kings of the earth have had intercourse with her,ᵃ and the inhabitants of the earth became drunk on the wine of her harlotry."* 3 Then he carried me away in spirit to a deserted place where I saw a woman seated on a scarlet beast* that was covered with blasphemous names, with seven heads and ten horns.ᵇ 4 The woman was wearing purple and scarlet and adorned with gold, precious stones, and pearls.ᶜ She held in her hand a gold cup that was filled with the abominable and sordid deeds of her harlotry.* 5 On her forehead was written a name, which is a mystery, "Babylon the great, the mother of harlots and of the abominations of the earth." 6 I saw that the woman was drunk on the blood of the holy ones and on the blood of the witnesses to Jesus.

Meaning of the Beast and Harlot.* When I saw her I was greatly amazed. 7 The angel said to me, "Why are you amazed? I will explain to you the mystery of the woman and of the beast that carries her, the beast with the seven heads and the ten horns. 8 ᵈ The beast that you saw existed once but now exists no longer. It will come up from the abyss and is headed for destruction. The inhabitants of the earth whose names have not been written in the book of life from the foundation of the world shall be amazed when they see the beast, because it existed once but exists no longer, and yet it will come again.* 9 Here is a clue* for one who has wisdom. The seven heads represent seven hills upon which the woman sits. They also represent seven kings:ᵉ 10 five have already fallen, one still lives, and the last has not yet come,* and when he comes he must remain only a short while. 11 The beast* that existed once but exists no longer is an eighth king, but really belongs to the seven and is headed for destruction. 12 The ten horns that you saw represent ten kings who have not yet been crowned;* they will receive royal authority along with the beast for one hour.ᶠ 13 They are of one mind and will give their power and authority to the beast. 14 They will fight with the Lamb, but the Lamb will conquer them, for he is Lord of lords and king of kings, and those with him are called, chosen, and faithful."ᵍ

15 Then he said to me, "The waters that you saw where the harlot lives represent large numbers of peoples, nations, and tongues. 16 The ten horns* that you saw and the beast will hate the harlot; they will leave her desolate and naked; they will eat her flesh and consume her with fire.ʰ 17 For God has put it into their minds to carry out his purpose and to make them come to an agreement to give their kingdom to the beast until the words of God are accomplished. 18 The woman whom you saw represents the great city that has sovereignty over the kings of the earth."

---

z Jer 50, 38; 51, 13.—a Jer 51, 7.—b Rv 13, 1.—c Rv 18, 16.—d Rv 13, 3-4 / Rv 3, 5; 13, 8; 20, 12.—e Rv 13, 18.—f Dn 7, 24.—g Rv 19, 11-21; 2 Mc 13, 4; 1 Tm 6, 15 / Rom 1, 6; 1 Pt 2, 9; Jude 1.—h Ez 16, 37-41; 23, 25-29.

17, 1—19, 10: The punishment of Babylon is now described as a past event and, metaphorically, under the image of the great harlot who leads people astray into idolatry.

17, 1-6: Babylon, the symbolic name (5) of Rome, is graphically described as "the great harlot."

17, 2: *Intercourse . . . harlotry:* see the note on Rv 14, 4. The pagan kings subject to Rome adopted the cult of the emperor.

17, 3: *Scarlet beast:* see the note on Rv 13, 1-10. *Blasphemous names:* divine titles assumed by the Roman emperors; see the note on Rv 13, 5-6.

17, 4: Reference to the great wealth and idolatrous cults of Rome.

17, 6b-18: An interpretation of the vision is here given.

17, 8: Allusion to the belief that the dead Nero would return to power (11); see the note on Rv 13, 3.

17, 9: *Here is a clue:* literally, "Here a mind that has wisdom." *Seven hills:* of Rome.

17, 10: There is little agreement as to the identity of the Roman emperors alluded to here. The number seven (9) suggests that all the emperors are meant; see the note on Rv 1, 4.

17, 11: *The beast:* Nero; see the note on Rv 17, 8.

17, 12-13: *Ten kings who have not yet been crowned:* perhaps Parthian satraps who are to accompany the revived Nero (the beast) in his march on Rome to regain power; see the note on Rv 13, 3. In Rv 19, 11-21, the Lamb and his companions will conquer them.

17, 16-18: *The ten horns:* the ten pagan kings (12) who unwittingly fulfill God's will against harlot Rome, the great city; cf Ez 16, 37.

Rv

CHAPTER 18

The Fall of Babylon.* [1]After this I saw another angel coming down from heaven, having great authority, and the earth became illumined by his splendor.[i] [2]He cried out in a mighty voice:

"Fallen, fallen is Babylon the great.[j]
  She has become a haunt for demons.
She is a cage for every unclean spirit,
  a cage for every unclean bird,
  [a cage for every unclean] and disgusting [beast].*
[3] For all the nations have drunk*
  the wine of her licentious passion.
The kings of the earth had intercourse with her,
  and the merchants of the earth grew rich from her drive for luxury."[k]

[4]Then I heard another voice from heaven say:

"Depart from her,* my people,
  so as not to take part in her sins
  and receive a share in her plagues,[l]
[5] for her sins are piled up to the sky,
  and God remembers her crimes.[m]
[6] Pay her back as she has paid others.
  Pay her back double for her deeds.
Into her cup pour double what she poured.[n]
[7] To the measure of her boasting and wantonness
  repay her in torment and grief;
for she said to herself,
  'I sit enthroned as queen;
I am no widow,
  and I will never know grief.'[o]
[8] Therefore, her plagues will come in one day,
  pestilence, grief, and famine;
she will be consumed by fire.
For mighty is the Lord God who judges her."

[9]The kings of the earth who had intercourse with her in their wantonness will weep and mourn over her when they see the smoke of her pyre. [10]They will keep their distance for fear of the torment inflicted on her, and they will say:

"Alas, alas, great city,
  Babylon, mighty city.
In one hour your judgment has come."

[11]The merchants of the earth will weep and mourn for her, because there will be no more markets* for their cargo: [12]their cargo of gold, silver, precious stones, and pearls; fine linen, purple silk, and scarlet cloth; fragrant wood of every kind, all articles of ivory and all articles of the most expensive wood, bronze, iron, and marble; [13]cinnamon, spice,* incense, myrrh, and frankincense; wine, olive oil, fine flour, and wheat; cattle and sheep, horses and chariots, and slaves, that is, human beings.

[14] "The fruit you craved
  has left you.
All your luxury and splendor are gone,
  never again will one find them."[p]

[15]The merchants who deal in these goods, who grew rich from her, will keep their distance for fear of the torment inflicted on her. Weeping and mourning, [16]they cry out:

"Alas, alas, great city,
  wearing fine linen, purple and scarlet,
  adorned [in] gold, precious stones, and pearls.[q]
[17] In one hour this great wealth has been ruined."

Every captain of a ship, every traveler at sea, sailors, and seafaring merchants stood at a distance [18]and cried out when they saw the smoke of her pyre, "What city could compare with the great city?" [19] [r] They threw dust on their heads and cried out, weeping and mourning:

---

i Ez 43, 2.—j Rv 14, 8; Is 21, 9; Jer 50, 2-3; 51, 8.—k Rv 17, 2; Jer 51, 7.—l Is 48, 20; Jer 50, 8.—m Jer 51, 9.—n Jer 50, 15 / Jer 16, 18.—o Is 47, 8-9.—p Hos 10, 5 / Am 6, 7.—q Rv 17, 4.—r Ez 27, 27-32.

18, 1—19, 4: A stirring dirge over the fall of Babylon-Rome. The perspective is prophetic, as if the fall of Rome had already taken place. The imagery here, as elsewhere in this book, is not to be taken literally. The vindictiveness of some of the language, borrowed from the scathing Old Testament prophecies against Babylon, Tyre, and Nineveh (Is 23; 24; 27; Jer 50—51; Ez 26—27), is meant to portray symbolically the inexorable demands of God's holiness and justice; cf Introduction. The section concludes with a joyous canticle on the future glory of heaven.

  18, 2: Many Greek manuscripts and versions omit *a cage for every unclean . . . beast.*

  18, 3-24: Rome is condemned for her immorality, symbol of idolatry (see the note on Rv 14, 4), and for persecuting the church; cf Rv 19, 2.

  18, 4: *Depart from her:* not evacuation of the city but separation from sinners, as always in apocalyptic literature.

  18, 11: Ironically, the merchants weep not so much for Babylon-Rome, but for their lost markets; cf Ez 27, 36.

  18, 13: *Spice:* an unidentified spice plant called in Greek *amōmon.*

"Alas, alas, great city,
   in which all who had ships at sea
   grew rich from her wealth.
In one hour she has been ruined.
20 Rejoice over her, heaven,
   you holy ones, apostles, and prophets.
For God has judged your case against
   her."[s]

21 A mighty angel picked up a stone like a huge millstone and threw it into the sea and said:

"With such force will Babylon the great
   city be thrown down,
   and will never be found again.[t]
22 No melodies of harpists and musicians,
   flutists and trumpeters,
   will ever be heard in you again.
No craftsmen in any trade
   will ever be found in you again.
No sound of the millstone
   will ever be heard in you again.[u]
23 No light from a lamp
   will ever be seen in you again.
No voices of bride and groom
   will ever be heard in you again.
Because your merchants were the great
   ones of the world,
all nations were led astray by your
   magic potion.[v]
24 In her was found the blood of prophets
   and holy ones
   and all who have been slain on the
   earth."[w]

---

s Rv 19, 1-2; Dt 32, 43.—t Jer 51, 63-64; Ez 26, 21.—u Is 24, 8; Ez 26, 13.—v Jer 7, 34; 16, 9; 25, 10.—w Rv 16, 6.—x Dn 3, 27 / Jer 51, 48-49.—y Rv 14, 11; Is 34, 10.—z Rv 11, 18; Ps 115, 13.—a Mt 22, 9; Eph 5, 27.—b Rv 15, 6; Is 61, 10; Mt 22, 11-12.—c Mt 8, 11; Lk 14, 15.—d Rv 22, 8-9.

19, 1.3.4.6: *Alleluia:* found only here in the New Testament, this frequent exclamation of praise in the Hebrew psalms was important in Jewish liturgy.

19, 5-10: A victory song follows, sung by the entire church, celebrating the marriage of the Lamb, the union of the Messiah with the community of the elect.

19, 7: *The wedding day of the Lamb:* symbol of God's reign about to begin (Rv 21, 1—22, 5); see the note on Rv 10, 7. *His bride:* the church; cf 2 Cor 11, 2; Eph 5, 22-27. Marriage is one of the biblical metaphors used to describe the covenant relationship between God and his people; cf Hos 2, 16-22; Is 54, 5-6; 62, 5; Ez 16, 6-14. Hence, idolatry and apostasy are viewed as adultery and harlotry (Hos 2, 4-15; Ez 16, 15-63); see the note on Rv 14, 4.

19, 8: See the note on Rv 14, 12.

19, 9: *Blessed:* see the note on Rv 1, 3.

19, 10: *The spirit of prophecy:* as the prophets were inspired to proclaim God's word, so the Christian is called to give witness to the Word of God (13) made flesh; cf Rv 1, 2; 6, 9; 12, 17.

19, 11-16: Symbolic description of the exalted Christ (cf Rv 1, 13-16) who together with the armies of heaven overcomes the beast and its followers; cf Rv 17, 14.

CHAPTER 19

1 After this I heard what sounded like the loud voice of a great multitude in heaven, saying:

"Alleluia!*
Salvation, glory, and might belong to
   our God,
2   for true and just are his judgments.
He has condemned the great harlot
   who corrupted the earth with her
   harlotry.
He has avenged on her the blood of his
   servants."[x]

3 They said a second time:

"Alleluia! Smoke will rise from her
   forever and ever."[y]

4 The twenty-four elders and the four living creatures fell down and worshiped God who sat on the throne, saying, "Amen. Alleluia."

The Victory Song. * 5 A voice coming from the throne said:

"Praise our God, all you his servants,
   [and] you who revere him, small and
   great."[z]

6 Then I heard something like the sound of a great multitude or the sound of rushing water or mighty peals of thunder, as they said:

"Alleluia!
The Lord has established his reign,
   [our] God, the almighty.
7 Let us rejoice and be glad
   and give him glory.
For the wedding day of the Lamb* has
   come,
   his bride has made herself ready.[a]
8 She was allowed to wear
   a bright, clean linen garment."[b]

(The linen represents the righteous deeds of the holy ones.)*

9 Then the angel said to me, "Write this: Blessed* are those who have been called to the wedding feast of the Lamb." And he said to me, "These words are true; they come from God."[c] 10 I fell at his feet to worship him. But he said to me, "Don't! I am a fellow servant of yours and of your brothers who bear witness to Jesus. Worship God.[d] Witness to Jesus is the spirit of prophecy."*

The King of Kings. 11 * Then I saw the heavens opened, and there was a white horse; its rider was [called] "Faithful and

True." He judges and wages war in righteousness.[e] [12]His eyes were [like] a fiery flame, and on his head were many diadems. He had a name* inscribed that no one knows except himself.[f] [13]He wore a cloak that had been dipped in* blood, and his name was called the Word of God.[g] [14]The armies of heaven followed him, mounted on white horses and wearing clean white linen.[h] [15]Out of his mouth came a sharp sword to strike the nations. He will rule them with an iron rod, and he himself will tread out in the wine press* the wine of the fury and wrath of God the almighty.[i] [16]He has a name written on his cloak and on his thigh, "King of kings and Lord of lords."[j]

[17] * Then I saw an angel standing on the sun. He cried out [in] a loud voice to all the birds flying high overhead, "Come here. Gather for God's great feast, [18]to eat the flesh of kings, the flesh of military officers, and the flesh of warriors, the flesh of horses and of their riders, and the flesh of all, free and slave, small and great."[k] [19]Then I saw the beast and the kings of the earth and their armies gathered to fight against the one riding the horse and against his army. [20]The beast was caught and with it the false prophet* who had performed in its sight the signs by which he led astray those who had accepted the mark of the beast and those who had worshiped its image. The two were thrown alive into the fiery pool burning with sulfur.[l] [21]The rest were killed by the sword that came out of the mouth of the one riding the horse, and all the birds gorged themselves on their flesh.

CHAPTER 20

The Thousand-year Reign. [1] * Then I saw an angel come down from heaven, holding in his hand the key to the abyss* and a heavy chain.[m] [2]He seized the dragon, the ancient serpent, which is the Devil or Satan,* and tied it up for a thousand years[n] [3]and threw it into the abyss, which he locked over it and sealed, so that it could no longer lead the nations astray until the thousand years are completed. After this, it is to be released for a short time.

[4]Then I saw thrones; those who sat on them were entrusted with judgment. I also saw the souls of those who had been beheaded for their witness to Jesus and for the word of God, and who had not worshiped the beast or its image nor had accepted its mark* on their foreheads or hands. They came to life and they reigned with Christ for a thousand years.[o] [5]The rest of the dead did not come to life until the thousand years were over. This is the first resurrection. [6]Blessed* and holy is the one who shares in the first resurrection. The second death has no power over these; they will be priests of God and of Christ, and they will reign with him for [the] thousand years.

[7] * When the thousand years are completed, Satan will be released from his prison. [8]He will go out to deceive the nations at the four corners of the earth, Gog and Magog,* to gather them for battle; their number is like the sand of the sea.[p] [9]They invaded the breadth of the earth* and surrounded the camp of the holy ones

---

e Is 11, 4.—f Rv 1, 14-16; 2, 18 / Lk 10, 22.—g Is 63, 1 / Jn 1, 1.—h Rv 15, 6; 19, 8.—i Rv 14, 20; Is 63, 3.—j Rv 17, 14; 2 Mc 13, 4.—k Ez 39, 17-20.—l Rv 14, 10.—m Rv 9, 1.—n Gn 3, 1.—o Mt 19, 28.—p Ez 38, 2.9.16.

19, 12: *A name:* in Semitic thought, the name conveyed the reality of the person; cf Mt 11, 27; Lk 10, 22.

19, 13: *Had been dipped in:* other Greek manuscripts and versions read "had been sprinkled with"; cf Rv 19, 15. *The Word of God:* Christ is the revelation of the Father; cf Jn 1, 1.14; 1 Jn 2, 14.

19, 15: The treading of the wine press is a prophetic symbol used to describe the destruction of God's enemies; cf Is 63, 1-6; Jl 4, 13.

19, 17-21: The certainty of Christ's victory is proclaimed by an angel, followed by a reference to the mustering of enemy forces and a fearsome description of their annihilation. The gruesome imagery is borrowed from Ez 39, 4.17-20.

19, 20: *Beast . . . false prophet:* see the notes on ch 13. *The fiery pool . . . sulfur:* symbol of God's punishment (Rv 14, 10; 20, 10.14-15), different from the abyss; see the note on Rv 9, 1.

20, 1-6: Like the other numerical values in this book, the thousand years are not to be taken literally; they symbolize the long period of time between the chaining up of Satan (a symbol for Christ's resurrection-victory over death and the forces of evil) and the end of the world. During this time God's people share in the glorious reign of God that is present to them by virtue of their baptismal victory over death and sin; cf Rom 6, 1-8; Jn 5, 24-25; 16, 33; 1 Jn 3, 14; Eph 2, 1.

20, 1: *Abyss:* see the note on Rv 9, 1.

20, 2: *Dragon . . . serpent . . . Satan:* see the notes on Rv 12, 3.9.10.15.

20, 4: *Beast . . . mark:* see ch 13 and its notes.

20, 6: *Blessed:* see the note on Rv 1, 3. *Second death:* see the note on Rv 2, 11. *Priests:* as in Rv 1, 6; 5, 10; cf 1 Pt 2, 9.

20, 7-10: A description of the symbolic battle to take place when Satan is released at the end of time, when the thousand years are over; see the note on Rv 20, 1-6.

20, 8: *Gog and Magog:* symbols of all pagan nations; the names are taken from Ez 38, 1—39, 20.

20, 9: *The breadth of the earth:* Palestine. *The beloved city:* Jerusalem; see the note on Rv 14, 1.

and the beloved city. But fire came down from heaven and consumed them.*q* 10 The Devil who had led them astray was thrown into the pool of fire and sulfur, where the beast and the false prophet were. There they will be tormented day and night forever and ever.

The Large White Throne.* 11 Next I saw a large white throne and the one who was sitting on it. The earth and the sky fled from his presence and there was no place for them.*r* 12 I saw the dead, the great and the lowly, standing before the throne, and scrolls were opened. Then another scroll was opened, the book of life.* The dead were judged according to their deeds, by what was written in the scrolls.*s* 13 The sea gave up its dead; then Death and Hades* gave up their dead. All the dead were judged according to their deeds. 14 *t* Then Death and Hades were thrown into the pool of fire. (This pool of fire is the second death.*) 15 Anyone whose name was not found written in the book of life was thrown into the pool of fire.

VI. THE NEW CREATION*

CHAPTER 21

The New Heaven and the New Earth. 1 *u* Then I saw a new heaven and a new earth. The former heaven and the former earth had passed away, and the sea was no more.* 2 I also saw the holy city, a new Jerusalem,* coming down out of heaven from God, prepared as a bride adorned for her husband.*v* 3 I heard a loud voice from the throne saying, "Behold, God's dwelling is with the human race.*w* He will dwell with them and they will be his people* and God himself will always be with them [as their God].* 4 He will wipe every tear from their eyes, and there shall be no more death or mourning, wailing or pain, [for] the old order has passed away."*x*

5 The one who sat on the throne* said, "Behold, I make all things new." Then he said, "Write these words down, for they are trustworthy and true."*y* 6 He said to me, "They are accomplished.* I [am] the Alpha and the Omega, the beginning and the end. To the thirsty I will give a gift from the spring of life-giving water.*z* 7 The victor* will inherit these gifts, and I shall be his God, and he will be my son.*a* 8 But as for cowards,* the unfaithful, the depraved, murderers, the unchaste, sorcerers, idol-worshipers, and deceivers of every sort, their lot is in the burning pool of fire and sulfur, which is the second death."*b*

The New Jerusalem.* 9 One of the seven angels who held the seven bowls filled with the seven last plagues came and said to me, "Come here. I will show you the bride, the wife of the Lamb."* 10 He took me in spirit to a great, high mountain and showed me the holy city Jerusalem coming down out of heaven from God.*c* 11 It gleamed with the splendor of God. Its radiance was like that of a precious stone, like jasper, clear as crystal.*d* 12 It had a massive, high wall, with twelve gates where twelve angels were stationed and on which names were inscribed, [the names] of the twelve tribes of the Israelites. 13 There were three gates facing east, three north, three south, and three west.*e* 14 The wall of the city had

---

q Ez 38, 22.—r 2 Pt 3, 7.10.12.—s Rom 2, 6.—t 1 Cor 15, 26.54-55.—u Is 65, 17; 66, 22; Rom 8, 19-23; 2 Pt 3, 13.—v Rv 19, 7-9.—w Ez 37, 27.—x Rv 7, 17; Is 25, 8; 35, 10.—y Is 43, 19; 2 Cor 5, 17.—z Rv 22, 17; Ps 36, 8-9; Is 55, 1.—a 2 Sm 7, 14.—b Rv 22, 15; Rom 1, 29-32.—c Ez 40, 2.—d Heb 11, 10.—e Ez 48, 31-35.

20, 11-15: A description of the final judgment. After the intermediate reign of Christ, all the dead are raised and judged, thus inaugurating the new age.

20, 12: *The book of life:* see the note on Rv 3, 5. *Judged . . . scrolls:* see the note on Rv 14, 12.

20, 13: *Hades:* the netherworld; see the note on Rv 1, 18.

20, 14: *Second death:* see the note on Rv 2, 11.

21, 1—22, 5: A description of God's eternal kingdom in heaven under the symbols of a new heaven and a new earth; cf Is 65, 17-25; 66, 22; Mt 19, 28.

21, 1: *Sea . . . no more:* because as home of the dragon it was doomed to disappear; cf Jb 7, 12.

21, 2: *New Jerusalem . . . bride:* symbol of the church (Gal 4, 26); see the note on Rv 19, 7.

21, 3: *People:* other ancient manuscripts read a plural, "peoples."

21, 3-4: Language taken from Ez 37, 27; Is 25, 8; 35, 10; cf Rv 7, 17.

21, 5: *The one . . . on the throne:* God himself; cf Rv 4, 1-11.

21, 6: *They are accomplished:* God's reign has already begun; see the note on Rv 20, 1-6. *Alpha . . . Omega:* see the note on Rv 1, 8. *Life-giving water:* see the note on Rv 7, 17.

21, 7: *The victor:* over the forces of evil; see the conclusions of the seven letters (Rv 2, 7.11.17.26; 3, 5.12.21). *He will be my son:* the victorious Christian enjoys divine affiliation by adoption (Gal 4, 4-7; Rom 8, 14-17); see the note on Rv 2, 26-28.

21, 8: *Cowards:* their conviction is so weak that they deny Christ in time of trial and become traitors. *Second death:* see the note on Rv 2, 11.

21, 9—22, 5: Symbolic descriptions of the new Jerusalem, the church. Most of the images are borrowed from Ez 40—48.

21, 9: *The bride, the wife of the Lamb:* the church (2), the new Jerusalem (10); cf 2 Cor 11, 2.

Rv

twelve courses of stones as its foundation, on which were inscribed the twelve names of the twelve apostles* of the Lamb.*f*

15 * The one who spoke to me held a gold measuring rod to measure the city, its gates, and its wall. 16 The city was square, its length the same as [also] its width. He measured the city with the rod and found it fifteen hundred miles* in length and width and height. 17 He also measured its wall: one hundred and forty-four cubits* according to the standard unit of measurement the angel used. 18 * The wall was constructed of jasper, while the city was pure gold, clear as glass. 19 The foundations of the city wall were decorated with every precious stone; the first course of stones was jasper, the second sapphire, the third chalcedony, the fourth emerald,*g* 20 the fifth sardonyx, the sixth carnelian, the seventh chrysolite, the eighth beryl, the ninth topaz, the tenth chrysoprase, the eleventh hyacinth, and the twelfth amethyst. 21 The twelve gates were twelve pearls, each of the gates made from a single pearl; and the street of the city was of pure gold, transparent as glass.

22 *h* I saw no temple in the city, for its temple is the Lord God almighty and the Lamb.* 23 The city had no need of sun or moon to shine on it,*i* for the glory of God gave it light, and its lamp was the Lamb.* 24 The nations will walk by its light,* and to it the kings of the earth will bring their treasure.*j* 25 During the day its gates will never be shut, and there will be no night there. 26 The treasure and wealth of the nations will be brought there, 27 but nothing unclean will enter it, nor any[one] who

does abominable things or tells lies. Only those will enter whose names are written in the Lamb's book of life.*k*

CHAPTER 22

1 Then the angel showed me the river of life-giving water,* sparkling like crystal, flowing from the throne of God and of the Lamb*l* 2 down the middle of its street. On either side of the river grew the tree of life* that produces fruit twelve times a year, once each month; the leaves of the trees serve as medicine for the nations. 3 Nothing accursed will be found there anymore. The throne of God and of the Lamb will be in it, and his servants will worship him. 4 They will look upon his face,* and his name will be on their foreheads. 5 Night will be no more, nor will they need light from lamp or sun, for the Lord God shall give them light, and they shall reign forever and ever.*m*

VII. EPILOGUE*

6 And he said to me, "These words are trustworthy and true, and the Lord, the God of prophetic spirits, sent his angel to show his servants what must happen soon."*n* 7 "Behold, I am coming soon."* Blessed* is the one who keeps the prophetic message of this book.*o*

8 It is I, John, who heard and saw these things, and when I heard and saw them I fell down to worship at the feet of the angel who showed them to me. 9 But he said to me, "Don't! I am a fellow servant of yours and of your brothers the prophets and of

---

f Eph 2, 20.—g Is 54, 11-12.—h Jn 2, 19-20.—i Is 60, 1-2.19-20.—j Is 60, 11.—k Is 35, 8; 52, 1; Zec 13, 2 / Rv 3, 5; 20, 12.—l Ez 47, 1-12.—m Is 60, 20.—n Rv 1, 1.—o Rv 22, 12.20 / Rv 1, 3.

21, 14: *Courses of stones . . . apostles:* literally, "twelve foundations"; cf Eph 2, 19-20.

21, 15-17: The city is shaped like a gigantic cube, a symbol of perfection (cf 1 Kgs 6, 19-20). The measurements of the city and its wall are multiples of the symbolic number twelve; see the note on Rv 7, 4-9.

21, 16: *Fifteen hundred miles:* literally, twelve thousand stades, about 12,000 furlongs (see the note on Rv 14, 20); the number is symbolic: twelve (the apostles as leaders of the new Israel) multiplied by 1,000 (the immensity of Christians); cf Introduction. *In length and width and height:* literally, "its length and width and height are the same."

21, 17: *One hundred and forty-four cubits:* the cubit was about eighteen inches in length. *Standard unit of measurement the angel used:* literally, "by a human measure, i.e., an angel's."

21, 18-21: The gold and precious gems symbolize the beauty and excellence of the church; cf Ex 28, 15-21; Tb 13, 16-17; Is 54, 11-12.

21, 22: Christ is present throughout the church; hence, no temple is needed as an earthly dwelling for God; cf Mt 18, 20; 28, 20; Jn 4, 21.

21, 23: *Lamp . . . Lamb:* cf Jn 8, 12.

21, 24-27: All men and women of good will are welcome in the church; cf Is 60, 1.3.5.11. *The . . . book of life:* see the note on Rv 3, 5.

22, 1.17: *Life-giving water:* see the note on Rv 7, 17.

22, 2: *The tree of life:* cf Rv 22, 14; see the note on Rv 2, 7. *Fruit . . . medicine:* cf Ez 47, 12.

22, 4: *Look upon his face:* cf Mt 5, 8; 1 Cor 13, 12; 1 Jn 3, 2.

22, 6-21: The book ends with an epilogue consisting of a series of warnings and exhortations and forming an inclusion with the prologue by resuming its themes and expressions; see the note on Rv 1, 1-3.

22, 7.12.20: *I am coming soon:* Christ is the speaker; see the note on Rv 1, 3.

22, 7.14: *Blessed:* see the note on Rv 1, 3.

those who keep the message of this book. Worship God."*p*

¹⁰Then he said to me, "Do not seal up the prophetic words of this book, for the appointed time* is near. ¹¹Let the wicked still act wickedly, and the filthy still be filthy. The righteous must still do right, and the holy still be holy."

¹²"Behold, I am coming soon. I bring with me the recompense I will give to each according to his deeds.*q* ¹³I am the Alpha and the Omega,*r* the first and the last, the beginning and the end."*

¹⁴Blessed are they who wash their robes so as to have the right to the tree of life and enter the city* through its gates.*s* ¹⁵Outside are the dogs, the sorcerers, the unchaste, the murderers, the idol-worshipers, and all who love and practice deceit.*t*

¹⁶"I, Jesus, sent my angel to give you this testimony for the churches. I am the root and offspring of David,* the bright morning star."*u*

¹⁷The Spirit and the bride* say, "Come." Let the hearer say, "Come." Let the one who thirsts come forward, and the one who wants it receive the gift of life-giving water.*v*

¹⁸I warn everyone who hears the prophetic words in this book: if anyone adds to them, God will add to him the plagues described in this book, ¹⁹and if anyone takes away from the words in this prophetic book, God will take away his share in the tree of life and in the holy city described in this book.*w*

²⁰ *x* The one who gives this testimony says, "Yes, I am coming soon." Amen! Come, Lord Jesus!*

²¹The grace of the Lord Jesus be with all.

---

p Rv 19, 10.—q Rv 22, 7.20 / Ps 62, 12; 2 Tm 4, 14.—r Rv 1, 8; 21, 6; Is 41, 4; 44, 6.—s Rv 7, 14-15; 22, 2.—t Rv 21, 8; Rom 1, 29-32.—u Rv 1, 1.11-12; 22, 6 / Rv 2, 28.—v Rv 21, 6; Is 55, 1.—w Dt 4, 2.—x Rv 22, 7.12 / Acts 3, 20-21; 1 Cor 15, 23; 16, 22.

22, 10: *The appointed time:* see the note on Rv 1, 3.

22, 13: Christ applies to himself words used by God in Rv 1, 8.

22, 14: *The city:* heavenly Jerusalem; see the note on Rv 21, 2.

22, 16: *The root . . . of David:* see the note on Rv 5, 5. *Morning star:* see the note on Rv 2, 26-28.

22, 17: *Bride:* the church; see the note on Rv 21, 2.

22, 20: *Come, Lord Jesus:* a liturgical refrain, similar to the Aramaic expression *Marana tha*—"Our Lord, come!"—in 1 Cor 16, 22; cf the note there. It was a prayer for the coming of Christ in glory at the parousia; see the note on Rv 1, 3.

THE MIRACLES OF JESUS DURING HIS PUBLIC LIFE

Water Made Wine: Jn 2, 1-11.

The Royal Official's Son: Jn 4, 46-54.

The Catch of Fishes: Lk 5, 1-11.

The Cure of a Demoniac: Mk 1, 23-28; Lk 4, 33-37.

Peter's Mother-in-law: Mt 8, 14-15; Mk 1, 29-31; Lk 4, 38-39.

The Leper: Mt 8, 1-4; Mk 1, 40-45; Lk 5, 12-19.

The Paralytic at Capernaum: Mt 9, 1-8; Mk 2, 1-12; Lk 5, 18-26.

The Cure at Bethesda: Jn 5, 1-15.

The Man with a Shriveled Hand: Mt 12, 9-13; Mk 3, 1-6; Lk 6, 6-11.

The Centurion's Servant: Mt 8, 5-13; Lk 7, 1-10.

The Widow's Son: Lk 7, 11-17.

The Blind and Dumb Demoniac: Mt 12, 22.

Calming of the Storm: Mt 8, 23-27; Mk 4, 35-41; Lk 8, 22-25.

Expulsion of the Demons in Gadara: Mt 8, 29-34; Mk 5, 1-20; Lk 8, 26-39.

Jairus' Daughter: Mt 9, 18-26; Mk 5, 21-43; Lk 8, 40-56.

The Woman in the Crowd: Mt 9, 20-22; Mk 5, 24-34; Lk 8, 43-48.

Two Blind Men: Mt 9, 27-31.

The Possessed Mute: Mt 9, 32-34.

Five Thousand Fed: Mt 14, 31-21; Mk 6, 34-44; Lk 9, 12-17; Jn 6, 1-15.

Jesus Walks on the Water: Mt 14, 22; Mk 6, 45-52; Jn 6, 16-21.

The Canaanite Woman: Mt 15, 21-28; Mk 7, 24-30.

Healing of a Deaf-Mute: Mk 7, 31-37.

Four Thousand Fed: Mt 15, 32-38; Mk 8, 1-9.

The Blind Man at Bethsaida: Mk 8, 22.

A Possessed Boy: Mt 17, 14-21; Mk 9, 13-28; Lk 9, 37-43.

The Temple Tax Provided: Mt 17, 23-26.

The Man Born Blind: Jn 9, 1-38.

The Crippled, Blind and Mute: Mt 15, 29.

A Woman Cured: Lk 13, 10-17.

The Raising of Lazarus: Jn 11, 1-44.

The Man with the Dropsy: Lk 14, 1-6.

Ten Lepers: Lk 17, 11-19.

The Blind Men at Jericho: Mt 20, 29-34; Mk 10, 46-52; Lk 18, 35-43.

The Fig Tree Cursed: Mt 21, 18-22; Mk 11, 12-14.

The Servant's Ear Healed: Lk 22, 49-51.

The Catch of Fishes: Jn 21, 1-14.

THE PRINCIPAL PARABLES OF JESUS

Children, The Wayward, Mt 11, 16-19; Lk 7, 31-35.

Debtors, The Two, Lk 7, 41-42.

Fig Tree, A Sign of Summer, Mt 24, 32-35; Mk 13, 28f; Lk 21, 29-31.

Fig Tree, The Barren, Lk 13, 6-9.

Judge, The Corrupt, Lk 18, 1-8.

Kingdom, A Divided, Mt 12, 25-27; Mk 3, 23-26; Lk 11, 17f.

Laborers in the Vineyard, Mt 20, 1-16.

Merciless Official, The, Lk 18, 21-35.

Mustard Seed and the Leaven, Mt 13, 31f; Mk 4, 30-32; Lk 13, 18f.

Net, Parable of The, Mt 13, 47-50.

Pharisee and the Tax Collector, Lk 18, 9-14.

Rich Man and Lazarus, Lk 16, 19-31.

Rich Man, The Foolish, Lk 12, 16-21.

Samaritan, The Good, Lk 10, 29-27.

Seat, The Lowest, Lk 14, 7-14.

Seed, The, Mt 13, 3-23; Mk 4, 3-20; Lk 8, 4-15.

Seed, The Growing, Mk 4, 26-29.

Servant, The Faithful and the Worthless, Mt 24, 45-51; Lk 12, 42-48.

Servants, The Useless, Lk 17, 7-10.

Sheep, The Straying, Mt 18, 12-14; Lk 15, 3-7.

Shepherd, The Good, Jn 10, 1-21.

Silver Pieces, The, Mt 25, 14-30.

Son, The Prodigal, Lk 15, 11-32.

Sons, The Two, Mt 21, 28-32.

Sums of Money, Parable of, Lk 19, 11-27.

Tenants, The, Mt 21, 33-46; Mk 12, 1-12; Lk 20, 9-19.

Treasure and the Pearl, Mt 13, 44-46.

Vigilance, Exhortation to, Mt 24, 43f; Lk 12, 39f.

Vine, and the Branches, The, Jn 15, 1-17.

Watchfulness, The Need for, Mark 13, 34-37; Lk 12, 36-38.

Wedding Banquet, The, Mt 22, 1-14; Lk 14, 16-24.

Weeds, The, Mt 13, 24-30.

Wily Manager, The, Lk 16, 1-13.

Yeast, The, Mt 13, 33.

STUDY GUIDE

THE MEANING AND MESSAGE OF THE NEW TESTAMENT

By KATHRYN SULLIVAN, R.S.C.J.

The texts presented here are prepared for reading or prayer in the hope that the person of Jesus and his life-giving words as cherished in the apostolic church may bring strength and light.

The first table contains a list of topics related to Jesus and his words. The second table contains an amplification of each topic and references to specific passages in the gospels. The third table contains a list of topics related to the life and teaching of the early days of the Church. The fourth table contains references to relevant passages in the Acts of the Apostles and the epistles and Book of Revelation. The fifth table contains sixty themes that are to be found in the New Testament. The sixth table contains an amplification of each theme and references to relevant passages in the whole New Testament.

Those who wish to deepen their understanding of the meaning of the New Testament are urged to consult the recommended passages and make these inspired words the subject of prayerful reflection. These passages contain much more than each table indicates. It would also be profitable to examine any references found in the notes to the New Testament, especially those to other passages of the New Testament where the thought is related but is not exactly the same.

TABLE NUMBER ONE

The Person of Jesus Christ and His Life-giving Words

1. IN THE GOSPELS WE SEE that Jesus is true God.
2. He wishes all men to know the Father.
3. He teaches that God is good.
4. He explains that God loves all men.
5. He offers salvation to all men.
6. IN THE GOSPEL WE SEE that Jesus is true man.
7. He brings life to the world.
8. He seeks the poor.
9. He saves sinners.
10. He comforts the troubled.
11. IN THE GOSPELS WE SEE that Jesus preaches the Kingdom of God.
12. He overcomes Satan the adversary.
13. He promises men his body and blood.
14. He proclaims an ethic based on love.
15. He prays to his Father and teaches men how to pray.
16. IN THE GOSPELS WE SEE that Jesus is the Light and Life of the world.
17. He preaches to men in parables.
18. He heals the sick.
19. He goes about doing good.
20. He tells men who he is.
21. IN THE GOSPELS WE SEE that Jesus is the way to the Father.
22. He taught men how to live.
23. He helped them to be true witnesses.
24. He gave his life for men.
25. He will return one day to judge the living and the dead.

TABLE NUMBER TWO

The Person of Jesus Christ and His Life-giving Words

RECOMMENDED GOSPEL PASSAGES

1. IN THE GOSPELS WE SEE that Jesus is true God, the Son of the Father
  (1) The words of the Father from heaven, Mt 3, 17; 17, 5
  (2) In the beginning was the Word, Jn 1, 1-14
  (3) Only the Son knows the Father, Mt 11, 25-27
  (4) Before Abraham was I am, Jn 8, 54-57
  (5) Who do men say that I am?, Mt 16, 16
  (6) He comes from the Father, Jn 16, 26-28; 17, 5
  (7) All that the Father has is his, Jn 16, 13-15; 17, 9
  (8) He and the Father are one, Jn 10, 29
  (9) To see him is to see the Father, Jn 14, 9
  (10) The Father has given him all power, Mt 11, 27
  (11) Father and Son love one another, Jn 5, 20
  (12) His divine power will be revealed at the end of time, Mt 24, 30
  (13) His words are the words of him who sent him, Jn 14, 24
  (14) He returns to his Father and our Father, Jn 20, 17

411

2. He wishes all men to know the Father

(1) Do you not know that I must be about my Father's work?, Lk 2, 9

(2) The Father is in me and I am in the Father, Jn 10, 35-39; 14, 8-11

(3) My Father works until now and I work, Jn 5, 17f

(4) Only the Son knows the Father and those to whom he has made this revelation, Mt 11, 27

(5) He who has seen me sees the Father, Jn 14, 9

(6) He makes known what he has learned from the Father, Jn 15, 15

(7) His word is the word of the Father, Jn 14, 24

(8) The Father always hears his prayer, Jn 11, 41

(9) He who receives me receives him who sent me, Mk 9, 37

(10) The Father loves the Son, the Son loves the Father, Jn 5, 20; 14, 30

(11) He returns to his Father and our Father, Jn 20, 17

(12) He gives all to the Father, Lk 23, 46

3. He teaches that God is good

(1) God so loved the world that he sent his only Son to save the world, Jn 3, 17

(2) God alone is good, Mk 10, 18

(3) God wishes all men to be saved, Mt 18, 12-14

(4) God hears the prayers of those who pray together, Mt 18, 19

(5) God is merciful, Lk 6, 36

(6) God rejoices when a single sinner repents, Lk 15, 7

(7) God is all-perfect, Mt 5, 48

(8) God is the most-high, Lk 1, 32. 35. 76; 6, 35

(9) God is the one true God, Mk 12, 29; Jn 17, 3

(10) God is all-powerful, Lk 1, 49; Mt 26, 64

(11) God is holy and just, Jn 17, 25

(12) God allows those whom he loves to suffer, Mt 6, 19ff; Lk 12, 33f

(13) God allowed his own Son to suffer, Lk 9, 22; 17, 25; 24, 7. 26

(14) God is love, Jn 4, 8. 16

4. He explains that God loves all men

(1) God is concerned about all that concerns men, Mt 10, 29-31

(2) God knows what each one needs, Mt 6, 8. 32

(3) God looks after the good and the bad, Lk 6, 35

(4) God shows his love by giving all power to his Son, Jn 3, 35

(5) God wishes that there be one flock and one shepherd, Jn 10, 16

(6) God asks all peoples to place their trust in Jesus, Mt 12, 18-21

(7) God desires all men to have an abundance of life, Jn 10, 10

(8) God wishes all men to hear the word of Jesus, Jn 14, 23

(9) God has given all to the Son through love of men, Jn 5, 20; 17, 9

(10) God is the God of Israel, not only of the Christians, Lk 1, 68; Mt 15, 31

(11) God is the God of Abraham, Isaac and Joseph, Mt 22, 32

(12) God show his love by keeping his promises, Lk 1, 70-73

5. He offers salvation to all men

(1) God is our Savior, Lk 1, 47

(2) God sent his Son to save the world, Jn 3, 17

(3) God does not want anyone to be lost, Mt 18, 12-14

(4) God has power over life and death, Jn 5, 21. 26

(5) God wishes his Son to be called Jesus because he is the Savior, Mt 1, 21

(6) God sends his Son to find those who are lost, Lk 19, 10

(7) God's power alone makes salvation possible, Mt 19, 25f

(8) Jesus reveals that he is the Savior by significant acts, Mt 9, 21; Mk 3, 4; 5, 23

(9) Faith in Jesus brings salvation to men, Lk 8, 48; 17, 19; 18, 42

(10) All who will be saved must accept the gospel, Lk 8, 12

(11) Salvation is offered to men in a paradox, Mt 10, 39; Lk 9, 24; Jn 12, 25

(12) Jesus has come to save and not to condemn, Jn 12, 47

(13) All men who wish to be saved must do penance, Lk 13, 3. 5

(14) All who will be saved must persevere until the end, Mt 24, 13

6. IN THE GOSPELS WE SEE that Jesus is true man

(1) The message of the angel to the Blessed Virgin Mary, Lk 1, 26-38

(2) A meditation on the incarnation: the Magnificat, Lk 1, 39-55

(3) The birth of Jesus in Bethlehem, Lk 2, 1-7. 16-19

(4) The prophecy of Simeon, Lk 2, 33-35

(5) Mary and the child Jesus, Mt 2, 11. 13. 20f; Lk 2, 30-52

(6) The testimony of the neighbors, Mk 6, 3; Jn 6, 41f; 7, 5

(7) Jesus loved and wept, Jn 11, 3. 35f; 13, 23; Lk 19, 41

(8) Jesus was filled with pity and moved to anger, Mt 9, 36; Mk 10, 13-16

(9) Jesus ate and drank, was tired and troubled, Mt 4, 2; 9, 10f; Jn 4, 6; 12, 27

(10) Jesus loved to pray, Mk 1, 35; Lk 6, 12f

(11) Jesus experienced anguish, Mt 26, 39-44; 27, 46

(12) Jesus experienced joy, Lk 10, 21

(13) The Word was made flesh and dwelt in our midst, Jn 1, 14

(14) He died on the cross, Mk 15, 37

7. He brings life to the world

(1) The importance of life, Mk 3, 4; 12, 27; Mt 6, 25

(2) Jesus' power over life, Jn 11, 15. 21

(3) The relation of sin and life, Mt 9, 6

(4) True life, Mt 7, 14; 18, 8f; 19, 16. 29

(5) In Jesus is life, Jn 1, 4

(6) He is the way, the truth and the life, Jn 14, 6

(7) He is the resurrection and the life, Jn 11, 25

(8) He is the light of life, Jn 8, 12

(9) He is the bread of life, Jn 6, 27-58

(10) To believe in Jesus is to pass from death to life, Jn 5, 24; 11, 25f

(11) Jesus gives life by laying down his life, Jn 10, 11-18

(12) To know the Father and the Son is to have eternal life, Jn 17, 3

8. He seeks the poor

(1) The privileged place of the poor in the kingdom, Mt 5, 3; Lk 6, 20

(2) Mary's understanding of the poor, Lk 1, 46-55

(3) Jesus' role of the Messiah of the poor, Lk 4, 18

(4) Jesus' poverty at Bethlehem and Nazareth, Lk 2, 7; Mt 13, 55

(5) Jesus' poverty during his public life, Mt 8, 20

(6) Jesus' poverty on the cross, Mt 27, 35. 43. 46

(7) The invitation addressed to the poor, Mt 11, 29

(8) The poverty of Jesus' triumph, Mt 21, 5

(9) Poverty and the spirit of childhood, Mt 19, 13-24; Lk 18, 15f

(10) Voluntary poverty, Mt 19, 21. 27; Lk 12, 33

(11) Apostolic poverty, Mt 10, 9

(12) The mystery of the service of the poor, Mt 25, 34-46; 26, 11

9. He saves sinners

(1) Jesus came into the world to save sinners, Mk 2, 17

(2) He teaches the inner quality of sin, Mk 7, 21ff

(3) He condemns the mere external fulfillment of the law, Mt 5, 20

(4) He proclaims in parable God's merciful love for the sinner, Lk 15, 11-32

(5) He welcomes and forgives the sinful woman, Lk 7, 36-50

(6) He dines with sinners, Lk 19, 1-10

(7) He allows no one to condemn the sinner, Jn 8, 1-11

(8) He gives his life as a ransom for many, Mk 10, 45

(9) He dies to bring together the scattered children of God, Jn 11, 50-52

(10) He prays for sinners, Lk 23, 34

(11) He is known as the friend of sinners, Mt 11, 19; Lk 15, 1f

(12) He brings light to a sinful world, Jn 3, 19

(13) He promised paradise to a sinner, Lk 23, 42f

(14) He loved sinners and served them until the very end, Jn 13, 1-17; Lk 22, 24-27

10. He comforts the troubled

(1) He asks all who are troubled to come to him, Mt 11, 28-30

(2) He knows the meaning of opposition, Mk 3, 5

(3) He has been rejected by those he tried to help, Lk 19, 41; Mt 19, 22

(4) He has sorrowed over the death of one he loved, Jn 11, 35-38

(5) He felt anguish, Mt 26, 37f

(6) He promised comfort to those who weep, Lk 6, 21

(7) He foresaw the joy of those who suffer now, Jn 16, 20

(8) He asks those who love him not to be troubled, Jn 14, 1-31

(9) He knows that love is stronger than sorrow, Jn 15, 18-27

(10) He prays for those who are troubled, Jn 17, 1-26

(11) He explained the Scriptures to those who were sad, Lk 24, 13-35

(12) Risen from the dead, he promised to give joy, Jn 17, 13; 20, 20

11. IN THE GOSPELS WE SEE that Jesus preaches the kingdom of God

(1) The primacy of the kingdom in his preaching, Mt 4, 23; 9, 35

(2) Miracles are the signs of the presence of the kingdom, Mt 11, 4f

(3) The coming of the kingdom puts an end to Satan's dominion, Mt 12, 28

(4) The apostles are told to preach the kingdom, Mt 10, 7

(5) The kingdom is to be revealed to the little ones, Mt 11, 25

(6) The kingdom is to be compared to grain scattered on the earth, Mt 13, 3-9. 18-23

(7) The kingdom will grow, Mk 4, 26-29

(8) The kingdom is preached first to the Jews, Lk 12, 32

(9) The kingdom will shelter all the nations of the world, Mt 13, 31

(10) The coming of the kingdom is mysterious, Lk 17, 20f

(11) The kingdom is not of this world, Jn 6, 15

(12) To Peter are entrusted the keys of the kingdom, Mt 16, 18f

(13) Members of the kingdom have certain signs, Mt 5, 3; 6, 33; 13, 44; 19, 23

(14) The king of the kingdom, Jn 18, 36f; cf Mt 21, 1-11; Lk 23, 2

12. He overcomes Satan the adversary

(1) In the desert he triumphs over the adversary, Lk 4, 1-13

(2) He rejected Satan's suggestions of a messianism of wealth, glory, power, Mt 4, 1-11

(3) Before beginning his ministry Satan tempted him, Mk 1, 12f

(4) Satan is identified as the evil one, Mt 5, 37; 6, 13

(5) Satan is father of lies, Jn 8, 41-44

(6) Satan is the tempter, Mt 4, 1-11

(7) Satan is overcome on many occasions, Mk 1, 23-27; Mt 12, 22ff; Lk 6, 18; 7, 21

(8) Satan has no power over Jesus, Jn 14, 30

(9) Satan was active during the passion of Jesus, Jn 13, 2. 27

(10) The coming of the kingdom marks the end of Satan's dominion, Mk 3, 22ff

(11) Satan has been condemned, Jn 16, 11

(12) In our struggles with Satan it is good to remember that Jesus has overcome him, Jn 16, 33

13. He promises men his body and blood

(1) The meaning of the multiplication of loaves, Mt 14, 13-21; Mk 6, 32-44; Lk 9, 10-17; Jn 6, 1-15

(2) The discourse in the synagogue of Capernaum, Jn 6, 22. 71

(3) The Last Supper according to Matthew, 26, 26-29

(4) The Last Supper according to Mark, 14, 22-25

(5) The Last Supper according to Luke, 22, 15-20

(6) The Last Supper according to Paul, 1 Cor 11, 23-34

(7) Those who eat this bread and drink this wine will never hunger, Jn 6, 34

(8) Eternal life will be given to those who receive the eucharist, Jn 6, 53

(9) Many found this promise of Jesus "a hard saying," Jn 6, 60

(10) The eucharist is memorial and promise, Mk 14, 25; Lk 22, 15

(11) The eucharist is a sign of Christ's redemptive death, Mt 26, 27; Mk 14, 24; Lk 22, 19

(12) Humility and charity are a prerequisite for the eucharist, Jn 13, 2-20

14. He proclaims an ethic based on love

(1) Love of God is the greatest commandment, Mt 22, 35-38; Lk 10, 25-28

(2) He reproaches the Pharisees for neglecting the love of God, Lk 11, 42

(3) He insists that God alone is to be adored, Mt 4, 8-10

(4) True adorers are those who adore the Father in spirit and truth, Jn 4, 20-24

(5) He asks that prayer be made unostentatiously, Mt 6, 5f

(6) Keeping the commandments is a sign of the love of God, Jn 14, 15. 21; 15, 14f

(7) The love of one's neighbor is inseparable from the love of God, Mt 22, 40

(8) Love must extend to one's enemies, Mt 5, 43-48; Lk 6, 27-36

(9) Love must be proved by deeds, Mt 7, 12; Lk 6, 36-38; 21, 1-4

(10) Love is the sign by which men will know his followers, Jn 13, 34f; 15, 12. 17

(11) The Father loves all who love his Son, Jn 16, 27f

(12) All who love should be one, Jn 17, 21-26

15. He prays and teaches men how to pray

(1) Before daybreak he prays, Mk 1, 35

(2) In lonely mountain places he prays, Mk 6, 46; Lk 9, 28

(3) Before important decisions he spends the night in prayer, Lk 6, 12f

(4) His disciples ask him to teach them how to pray, Lk 11, 1-4

(5) At the close of his discourse at the Last Supper, he prays to the Father, Jn 17, 1-26

(6) During his agony he prays, Mt 26, 39-44

(7) He prays for those who will be tempted, Lk 22, 31f

(8) He prays for those given him by the Father, Jn 17, 9

(9) He prays for those who believe in him, Jn 17, 20

(10) He thanks the Father for always hearing his prayer, Jn 11, 41f

(11) He thanks the Father for the joy given by the Spirit, Lk 10, 21f

(12) On the cross he prays for those who have made him suffer, Lk 23, 34

(13) On the cross he cries out to the Father, Mt 27, 46

(14) On the cross he surrenders himself to the Father, Lk 23, 46

16. IN THE GOSPELS WE SEE that Jesus is the Light and Life of the world

(1) Jesus is the light foretold by the prophets, Mt 4, 12-17

(2) Zechariah recognized in him the shining in the darkness, Lk 1, 78f

(3) Simeon thanked God that he had seen the light illuminating all peoples, Lk 2, 32

(4) Jesus assured men that he was the light of life, Jn 8, 12

(5) He is the resurrection and the life, Jn 11, 25

(6) He is the way, the truth and the life, Jn 14, 6

(7) To those who believe in him, he gives the living water that leads to eternal life, Jn 4, 14

(8) Those who receive the bread of life, share in his life, Jn 6, 27-58

(9) To believe is to enter into life, Jn 11, 25f

(10) He is the light that overcomes the darkness, Jn 12, 46

(11) He gives life superabundantly, Jn 10, 10

(12) Jesus worked many signs in the presence of the disciples so that those who believe may have life in his name, Jn 20, 31

17. He preaches to men in parables

(1) The reason for preaching in parables, Mt 13, 10-17; Mk 4, 10-12; Lk 8, 9f; Jn 16, 25

(2) The kingdom of God, Mt 13, 3-23; Mk 4, 3-20; Lk 8, 4-15

(3) The growth of the kingdom despite its insignificance, Mt 13, 31; Lk 13, 20

(4) The presence of good and bad, Mt 13, 47-50

(5) The condition of an absolute and total commitment, Lk 9, 62; 14, 28-33

(6) The necessity of detachment, Lk 12, 16-21

(7) Man's responsibility, Mt 7, 16-20; 25, 14-30; Lk 19, 12-27

(8) The value of vigilance, Mt 24, 43f; Lk 12, 35-48

(9) The lesson of perfect love, Lk 10, 29-37

(10) The practice of humility, Lk 6, 37-42; 14, 7-11; 18, 9-14

(11) The beauty of trust, Mt 6, 26-30; Lk 11, 5-8

(12) The meaning of mercy, Mt 18, 12-14; Lk 15, 3-32

(13) The importance of God's call, Mt 20, 1-16

(14) The final reckoning, Mt 24, 45-51; Lk 12, 42-46

18. He heals the sick

(1) Why he works miracles, Mt 11, 3-6

(2) Signs of the messianic reign, Mt 11, 2; Lk 7, 18-23

(3) Unlimited cures, Mt 4, 23f; 8, 16f; 14, 14; 15, 13; Lk 9, 11; Mk 1, 32-34

(4) The son of an official, Jn 4, 43-54

(5) A leper, Mt 8, 2-4; Mk 1, 40-45; Lk 5, 12-16

(6) A paralytic, Mt 9, 1-8; Mk 2, 1-12; Lk 5, 17-26

(7) Two blind men, Mt 9, 27-31

(8) The woman with a hemorrhage, Mt 9, 20-22; Mk 5, 24-34; Lk 8, 43-48

(9) A deaf-mute, Mk 7, 31-37

(10) The man born blind, Jn 9, 1-40

(11) Ten lepers, Lk 17, 11-19

(12) Malchus, Lk 22, 50f; Jn 8, 10

(13) Healings are meant to awaken faith and lead to life, Jn 20, 31

(14) He gives the apostles the power to heal others, Mt 10, 1. 8; Mk 6, 13

19. He goes about doing good

(1) He invites men to follow him, Mt 4, 18-22; Mk 3, 13-19; Jn 1, 35-51

(2) He helps his host, Jn 2, 1-11

(3) He multiplies the loaves as a sign of the bread of life, Jn 6, 26-35

(4) He warns against the dangers of riches, Lk 12, 16-21

(5) He rewarded the trust of the centurion, Mt 8, 5-13

(6) He helped the sick, Mk 16, 18

(7) He corrected the presumption of Peter, Mt 26, 33-35. 69-75

(8) He taught his disciples to pray, Mt 6, 9-13; Lk 11, 2-4

(9) He cures souls and bodies, Mt 9, 6; Jn 5, 14

(10) He calms a storm, Mt 8, 23-27; Mk 4, 35-41; Lk 8, 22-25

(11) He restores life, Mk 5, 35-43; Lk 7, 11-17; Jn 11, 1-44

(12) He prepares his disciples for the passion, Mk 8, 31-33; 9, 30-32; 10, 32-34

20. He tells men who he is

(1) The Messiah, Mt 16, 16; Mk 14, 61

(2) The Son of Man, Mt 8, 20; 11, 19; 16, 13; Jn 3, 13f; 12, 34

(3) The Son of God, Mt 16, 16; 26, 63

(4) The good shepherd, Jn 10, 11-16

(5) The living water, Jn 4, 10-15; 7, 37-39

(6) The grain of wheat, Jn 12, 24

(7) The light of the world, Jn 8, 12; 9, 5; 12, 46

(8) The life, Jn 11, 25

(9) The way, the truth and the life, Jn 14, 4-6

(10) The bread of life, Jn 6, 35

(11) The gate, Jn 10, 1-10

(12) The vine, Jn 15, 1-8

(13) The king, Jn 18, 33-37

(14) The judge, Mt 24, 1-44; Lk 17, 22-37

21. IN THE GOSPELS WE SEE that Jesus is the way to the Father

(1) He establishes his Church, Mt 16, 18f

(2) He is in the midst of those who pray, Mt 18, 19f

(3) He is the shepherd of the flock, Jn 10, 16

(4) He is the vine and we are the branches, Jn 15, 1-6

(5) He is the king and we are members of his kingdom, Lk 12, 32

(6) He invites us to follow him, Jn 15, 16

(7) He teaches us what the Father has told him, Jn 15, 15

(8) He asks for newness of life, Lk 5, 31f; 13, 1-5

(9) He prays for all who believe in him, Jn 17, 20

(10) He died that we might be one, Jn 11, 51f

(11) He will always be with us until the end of the world, Mt 28, 20

(12) He wishes all men to be united in his love for the Father, Jn 17, 20-26

22. He taught men how to live

(1) The importance of prayer, Mt 6, 9-13; 7, 7-11; Lk 11, 2-4; 18, 1-8

(2) Submission of will, Mt 6, 10; 21, 28-31; Mk 3, 31-35; Lk 11, 27f; Jn 9, 31

(3) Keeping the commandments, Mt 19, 16f

(4) The law of life through death, Jn 12, 25

(5) The meaning of the kingdom, Mt 6, 32f

(6) The proof of good works, Mt 5, 14-16

(7) The following of Christ, Mt 4, 18-22

(8) The commandment of love, Lk 6, 27-36

(9) The beauty of childhood, Mt 18, 1-4; Lk 6, 20

(10) The inevitability of suffering, Jn 16, 33

(11) The problem of sickness, Mt 8, 16

(12) The missionary responsibility of every Christian, Mt 28, 18-20

(13) This life is a preparation for the life to come, Mt 6, 19-21; Mk 10, 21; Lk 12, 13-21

(14) An eternal life of joy is prepared for those who love the Lord, Mt 25, 31-46

23. He helped them to be true witnesses

(1) Repentance, Lk 13, 1-5

(2) Faith, Mt 21, 21; Mk 11, 22f; Jn 20, 29

(3) Baptism, Jn 3, 3-8

(4) Childlikeness, Jn 1, 11-13

(5) Light, Jn 8, 12

(6) Joy, Jn 15, 11; 16, 21f; 17, 13

(7) Peace, Jn 14, 27

(8) Eucharist, Jn 6, 50

(9) Love, Mt 22, 35-38; Lk 10, 25-28; Mk 12, 28-34

(10) Prayer, Mt 6, 5f

(11) Thanksgiving, Lk 1, 46-55

(12) Almsgiving, Mt 6, 1-4

24. He gave his life for men

(1) Jesus prepared his disciples for his sufferings, Mk 8, 31-33; 9, 30-32; 10, 32-34

(2) He promised to give his life as a ransom for many, Mk 10, 45

(3) He desired to die for others, Mk 10, 38; Lk 12, 50

(4) At the prospect of death he was in agony, Jn 12, 27; Mt 26, 36-46; Mk 14, 32-42; Lk 22, 40-45

(5) He prayed for his disciples at the Last Supper, Jn 13, 1-17. 26

(6) He was arrested, Mt 26, 47-56; Mk 14, 43-52; Lk 22, 47-53; Jn 18, 2-11

(7) He was brought before his judges, Mt 26, 57—27, 16; Mk 14, 53—15, 22; Lk 22, 63—23, 25; Jn 18, 1—19, 16

(8) He was crucified, Mt 27, 37-56; Mk 15, 25-27; Lk 23, 33-46; Jn 19, 17-37

(9) He was buried, Mt 27, 57-60; Mk 15, 42-46; Lk 23, 50-54; Jn 19, 38-42

(10) He rose from the dead, Mt 28, 1-8; Mk 16, 1-8; Lk 24, 1-11; Jn 20, 1-2

(11) He appeared for forty days, Mt 28, 9-15; Mk 16, 9-13; Lk 24, 12-35; Jn 20, 3—21, 25

(12) He ascended into glory, giving his disciples a mission, Mt 28, 16-20; Mk 16, 14-20; Lk 24, 36-53

25. He will return one day to judge the living and the dead

(1) He will return and bring us to himself, Mt 24, 1-44; 25, 4

(2) No one knows when this will be, Mt 25, 13

(3) Watch, Mt 24, 42-44

(4) As he has risen, so will we rise, Jn 6, 39f; 11, 23-26

(5) The dead will hear the voice of the Son of God, Jn 5, 25. 28

(6) The Son of Man will come in glory, Mt 25, 31-46

(7) He will know those who have been loyal to him, Mt 10, 32f; Jn 10, 14f. 27-29

(8) Sorrow will give place to joy, Jn 16, 21f

(9) The Spirit will remind men of all that Jesus taught, Jn 14, 26

(10) In times of trouble he will send the Spirit to help men, Mt 10, 17-20

(11) On that day men will know the union of the Father and Son, Jn 14, 18-20

(12) On that day men will see the glory of the Father and Son, Jn 17, 1-3. 24-26

TABLE NUMBER THREE

The Life and Teaching of the Early Church

TOPICS

In the Acts of the Apostles and in the epistles and Book of Revelation we learn the meaning of Christian life today by considering:

1. The first days of the early Church
2. The harmony of the first Christians
3. Persecution and troubles
4. The role of Peter
5. The power of the apostles
6. The conversion of Paul
7. Paul's missionary activity (1)
8. Paul's missionary activity (2)
9. Paul's captivity
10. Paul the apostle
11. The apostolic message
12. God—Father, Son, Spirit
13. The Son of God
14. The Spirit of God
15. The Lord Jesus—Savior
16. The coming of the Lord
17. The meaning of man
18. "In Christ"
19. Faith
20. Hope
21. Charity
22. The Body of Christ
23. Apostolic communities
24. The Old Testament in the early Church
25. Resurrection

TABLE NUMBER FOUR

The Life and Teaching of the Early Church

RECOMMENDED PASSAGES FROM THE ACTS OF THE APOSTLES,
THE EPISTLES AND BOOK OF REVELATION

1. The first days of the early Church

(1) The ascension of the Lord, Acts 1, 6-11

(2) Waiting in the upper room, Acts 1, 12-14

(3) The election of Matthias, Acts 1, 15-26

(4) The coming of the Spirit on the first Christian Pentecost, Acts 2, 1-13

(5) Peter's discourse, Acts 2, 14-36

(6) First conversions, Acts 2, 37-41

(7) First cure, Acts 3, 1-10

(8) Peter's second discourse, Acts 3, 11-26

(9) The arrest and trial of Peter and John, Acts 4, 1-22

(10) The prayer of the Christians, Acts 4, 23-31

(11) An ideal community, Acts 2, 42-47; 4, 32-35

(12) The example of Barnabas, Acts 4, 36-37

(13) The deception of Ananias and Sapphira, Acts 5, 1-11

(14) Gamaliel's advice, Acts 5, 34-42

2. The harmony of the first Christians

(1) The unity of the early Church, Acts 1, 14; 2, 46; 4, 24. 32; 5, 12

(2) The meaning of baptism, Acts 2, 41; 9, 18; 10, 44-48; 16, 13-15; 18, 8; 19, 5

(3) Attentive to the apostolic teaching, Acts 2, 42; 15, 35-36; 20, 11. 20

(4) Fidelity to Jewish services, Acts 2, 46; 3, 1

(5) Fidelity to Christian worship, Acts 1, 14. 24; 2, 42; 4, 24-30; 6, 4; 13, 2; 20, 36

(6) Fidelity to the breaking of bread, Acts 2, 46; 20, 7-12; 27, 35

(7) Sharing all things, Acts 2, 42; 4, 32; 5, 1-11

(8) The consolation of the Scriptures, Acts 9, 22; 13, 14-15; 17, 2-3; 26, 22-23; 28, 23

(9) The strengthening of the Spirit, Acts 9, 31; 13, 5

(10) The power of the name of Jesus, Acts 2, 21; 4, 12; 9, 14

(11) Their joy, Acts 2, 46; 8, 8; 13, 52; 16, 34

(12) The presence of the Spirit, Acts 9, 31; 13, 52

3. Persecution and troubles

(1) The troubles of the first Pentecost, Acts 2, 5-13

(2) Peter and John appear before the Sanhedrin, Acts 4, 1-22

(3) The loyalty and fervor of the Christians during persecution, Acts 4, 23-31

(4) Arrest and miraculous release of the apostles, Acts 5, 17-41

(5) The complaints of the Hellenists, Acts 6, 1-6

(6) Stephen's arrest, Acts 6, 8—7, 54

(7) The first martyr, Acts 7, 55-60

(8) Persecution in Jerusalem, Acts 8, 1-3

(9) The spread of the gospel, Acts 8, 4-8

(10) The Roman centurion, Acts 10, 1-34

(11) Peter and the baptism of pagans, Acts 11, 1-18

(12) Herod's attack and the result, Acts 12, 1-23

4. The role of Peter

(1) The election of Matthias, Acts 1, 15-26

(2) Peter's Pentecostal sermon, Acts 2, 14-36

(3) Peter's advice to the first converts, Acts 2, 37-41

(4) Peter and the lame man at the temple gate, Acts 3, 1-9

(5) Peter's second sermon, Acts 3, 11-26

(6) The consequences, Acts 4, 1-31

(7) Peter's miraculous release, Acts 5, 17-21

(8) Peter's answer to the Sanhedrin, Acts 5, 29-33

(9) Peter cures a paralytic at Lydda, Acts 9, 32-35

(10) Peter restores a woman in Joppa, Acts 9, 36-43

(11) Peter and Cornelius, Acts 10, 1-43

(12) The baptism of the first pagans, Acts 10, 44-48

(13) Peter and the brethren in Jerusalem, Acts 11, 1-18

(14) Peter's arrest and miraculous release, Acts 12, 1-19

5. The power of the apostles

(1) The presence of the Spirit, Acts 1, 5. 8; 2, 1-13; 4, 8; 6, 3; 9, 17; 11, 24

(2) The act of witnessing, Acts 2, 4; 7, 55; 8, 29; 10, 19; 11, 12; 16, 6; 20, 22-28

(3) The preaching of the word, Acts 4, 19-20; 8, 25; 10, 36; 13, 26; 15, 35; 20, 7

(4) The preparation of the world for the coming of Christ, Acts 4, 24; 7, 20-50; 13, 22-25

(5) Their understanding of Christ, Acts 3, 22-23; 7, 35-39; 10, 38; 13, 29; 17, 3; 26, 23

(6) The evangelization of the Hellenists, Acts 8, 1-26; 9, 2. 30; 11, 19-20

(7) The work of Philip, Acts 6, 5; 8, 5; 21, 8

(8) The apostolate of Barnabas, Acts 4, 36; 9, 27; 11, 22; 13, 1-3; 14, 3; 15, 2

(9) The mission of John Mark, Acts 12, 25; 13, 5; 15, 37-39; cf 12, 12

(10) The Jerusalem Council, Acts 15, 1-18

(11) Miracles, Acts 3, 1-10; 8, 7-8; 8, 9-25; 9, 33-43

(12) Signs of growth, Acts 6, 7; 12, 24; 13, 49; 19, 20; 20, 18

(13) Growth and persecution, Acts 4, 27-30; 5, 40-42; 8, 4; 11, 19; 12, 17; 13, 50-51; 16, 6-10; 17, 10; 18, 6; 19, 8; 20, 18; 21, 11-14; 23, 11; 28, 30-31

6. The conversion of Paul

(1) Saul the Pharisee, Acts 22, 3; 26, 4; Phil 3, 5; Rom 11, 1; 2 Cor 11, 22

(2) The persecutor of the Church, 1 Cor 25, 9; Gal 1, 13. 23

(3) The Damascus experience, Acts 9, 1-19; 22, 1-16; 26, 9-19

(4) The revelation of the Son, 2 Cor 3, 15; Gal 1, 15-16; Eph 3, 3

(5) The act of re-evaluation, Phil 3, 7-9; Gal 2, 15-21

(6) The power of the resurrection and the fellowship of his sufferings, Phil 3, 10-11; Rom 6, 3f

(7) A witness before all peoples, Acts 9, 15-16; 22, 14-15; 26, 22-23; 1 Cor 15, 9

(8) The preaching of the gospel, Rom 1, 1-5; Eph 3, 7-11

(9) Servant, Phil 1, 1; Gal 1, 10; Rom 1, 1; 1 Cor 3, 5

(10) The inevitability of persecution, Acts 9, 16; 18, 9-10

(11) The meaning of the new covenant, 2 Cor 3, 6-11

(12) The vision of the risen Lord, Acts 9, 17; 22, 14-15; 26, 16; 1 Cor 15, 8

7. Paul's missionary activity (1)

(1) Beginnings in Damascus, Acts 9, 19-25; 26, 20; 2 Cor 11, 32-33; Gal 1, 17

(2) Journey to Jerusalem, Acts 9, 26-29; 22, 17-21; 26, 20; Gal 1, 18-21

(3) Return to Tarsus, Acts 9, 30; 11, 25; Gal 2, 21

(4) A year in Antioch, Acts 11, 25-30; 12, 24-25

(5) Barnabas, Paul and John Mark go to Cyprus, Acts 13, 4-13

(6) Barnabas and Paul continue to Pisidian Antioch, Acts 13, 14-52

(7) Success in Iconium and sudden departure for Lycaonia, Acts 14, 1-26

(8) Controversy in Antioch, Acts 14, 27—15, 2

(9) Further discussions in Jerusalem, Acts 15, 3-29

(10) More plans in Antioch, Acts 15, 30-40

(11) Paul, Silas and Timothy in Lycaonia, Acts 15, 40—16, 5

(12) Working in Asia Minor, Acts 16, 6-8

(13) The call to Macedonia, Acts 16, 9-10

(14) Arrival in Philippi, Acts 16, 11-18

8. Paul's missionary activity (2)

(1) Imprisonment in Philippi and miraculous deliverance, Acts 16, 19-40

(2) Problems in Thessalonica, Acts 17, 1-10

(3) Initial success followed by difficulties in Beroea, Acts 17, 10-14

(4) Arrival in Athens, Acts 17, 15-21

(5) Address before the Areopagus, Acts 17, 22-34

(6) Foundation of the church in Corinth, Acts 18, 1-18

(7) Return to Antioch, Acts 18, 19-22

(8) Journey to Ephesus, Acts 18, 23—19, 22

(9) Trouble in Ephesus, Acts 19, 23—20, 1

(10) Visit to Troas, Acts 20, 2-12

(11) Farewell discourse to Ephesian elders at Miletus, Acts 20, 13-38

(12) Return to Jerusalem, Acts 21, 1-16

9. Paul's captivity

(1) Welcome and warnings in Jerusalem, Acts 21, 17-25
(2) Arrest in the temple, Acts 21, 26-40
(3) Discourse before the Jews in Jerusalem, Acts 22, 1-30
(4) Before the Sanhedrin, Acts 23, 1-15
(5) Night flight, Acts 23, 16-35
(6) The trial in Caesarea, Acts 24, 1-9
(7) Discourse before Felix, Acts 24, 10-22
(8) Felix and Festus, Acts 24, 23—25, 21
(9) Discourse before King Agrippa, Acts 25, 22—26, 32
(10) Storm and shipwreck, Acts 27, 1-44
(11) Welcome rest in Malta, Acts 28, 1-10
(12) "And so we came to Rome," Acts 28, 11-16
(13) Discussion with the Jews in Rome, Acts 28, 17-29
(14) Paul's two-year apostolate in Rome, Acts 28, 30-31

10. Paul the apostle

(1) Courage in difficulties, 1 Cor 4, 9-13; 2 Cor 4, 7-12; Phil 4, 11-12; Rom 8, 35
(2) Love for his converts, 1 Thes 2, 11-12; 1 Cor 4, 14-15; 2 Cor 6, 11-13; 1 Tm 1, 2
(3) Tenderness, 1 Thes 2, 7-8; Gal 4, 19-20; 1 Cor 3, 1-2
(4) Zeal for their progress, 2 Cor 13, 9; Phil 1, 9; 4, 1
(5) Personal affection, 2 Cor 1, 15; 9, 3-5; Phil 1, 25-26; 2 Tm 1, 4
(6) Willingness to give his life, Phil 2, 17-18; Col 2, 24; 2 Tm 4, 6-7
(7) His desire to please God, 1 Thes 2, 4; 2 Cor 5, 9-10
(8) Firmness, 2 Thes 2, 14-15; 1 Cor 4, 19-21; 2 Cor 10, 1-10; Gal 4, 8-11; Col 2, 8
(9) Tears and sorrows, 2 Cor 2, 1; Rom 8, 35; 9, 2
(10) Humility, 1 Cor 15, 8-10; 2 Cor 2, 14-16; Eph 3, 8
(11) Joy, 1 Thes 2, 19-20; 2 Cor 1, 3-7; Phil 1, 18; 2, 2; 4, 1; Rom 1, 12; Eph 6, 19-20
(12) Confidence, 1 Phil 1, 5; 2 Thes 3, 4; Phil 1, 20; Rom 8, 35-39; Eph 6, 19-20; Phlm 8, 21

11. The apostolic message

(1) God loved us and chose us in Christ before the creation of the world, Rom 8, 29; 11, 2; Eph 1, 4
(2) He hopes to see in us the image of his Son, Rom 9, 11; Eph 1, 5; 3, 11
(3) In Christ we are freed from our sins, Eph 1, 7; Col 1, 14; Gal 3, 13; Rom 3, 24
(4) His death reconciled us with God, Rom 5, 9-11; 2 Cor 5, 18; Eph 1, 10; Col 1, 20
(5) He has brought peace to Jews and Gentiles, Eph 2, 14-18
(6) Through his grace we are saved, Eph 2, 3-6
(7) He has justified us, Rom 1, 17; 3, 21-26; 5, 15-21; 8, 30; 10, 9-10; 2 Cor 3, 9; Eph 4, 24
(8) He has called us in the gospel, Rom 1, 6-7; 9, 24; 1 Cor 1, 2; 7, 24; Gal 5, 8
(9) The gift of the Spirit, Eph 1, 13-14; 4, 30
(10) He has made us sons of God, Rom 8, 14-17; 2 Cor 3, 17-18; 4, 3-6
(11) We are meant to turn to God, 1 Thes 1, 9; 2 Cor 3, 16; Eph 4, 22
(12) We are made new creatures, 2 Cor 5, 17; Gal 5, 25; Ti 3, 4-7
(13) We are called to live and to die in Christ, 1 Thes 4, 16; 1 Cor 15, 18; Rom 6, 23
(14) We are glorified in Christ, Rom 5, 1-11; 8, 11-17; Eph 4, 30

12. God—Father, Son, Spirit

(1) There is but one God, Rom 3, 30; 1 Cor 8, 4; 1 Tm 1, 17; 2, 5
(2) He is the creator, Rom 1, 25; 4, 17; Col 3, 10; Eph 3, 9
(3) He is all-powerful, Rom 1, 20; 4, 21; 9, 17-22; 2 Cor 6, 18; Eph 1, 19-20; 3, 7; 2 Tm 1, 8
(4) He is the God of peace, 1 Thes 5, 23; 1 Cor 14, 33; 2 Cor 13, 11; Phil 4, 7-9
(5) He is the God of mercy, Rom 9, 15-16; 2 Cor 1, 3; Phil 2, 27; Eph 2, 4
(6) He is faithful, 1 Thes 5, 24; 1 Cor 1, 9; 10, 13; 2 Cor 1, 18-20
(7) He is loving, Rom 5, 5; 8, 31-39; 2 Cor 13, 11; Phil 2, 1; Eph 1, 4-6; Ti 3, 4
(8) He is patient, Rom 2, 4; 9, 22; 11, 22
(9) He is the giver of life, 1 Thes 1, 9; 2 Cor 6, 16; Rom 8, 26; 1 Tm 3, 15; 4, 10
(10) He is eternal, Rom 1, 23; 16, 26
(11) He is the consoler, Rom 15, 5; 2 Thes 2, 16; 2 Cor 1, 3-7
(12) He is our Father, 1 Thes 1, 3; 3, 11-13; 2 Thes 1, 1; 2, 16; 1 Cor 1, 3; 2 Cor 1, 2; Gal 1, 4; Rom 1, 7; Phil 4, 20; Col 1, 2; Eph 1, 2; Phlm 3

13. The Son of God

(1) The image of God, Rom 8, 29; 1 Cor 15, 49; 2 Cor 3, 18; Col 3, 10

(2) The first-born of all creatures, Col 1, 15-17

(3) The beloved of the Father, Col 1, 13; Eph 1, 6

(4) The mediator, Rom 5, 18; Eph 2, 14-21

(5) The wisdom of God, 1 Cor 1, 17-25; 2, 7-9; Eph 3, 2-12

(6) The justice of God, 1 Cor 1, 30

(7) The power of God, 1 Cor 1, 18-24; 2 Cor 12, 9

(8) The Savior, 1 Thes 1, 10; Rom 11, 26; Phil 3, 20-21; Eph 5, 23

(9) The revelation of the Father's love, Rom 5, 5-8; 2 Thes 2, 16; Eph 2, 4-6

(10) The head of all creation, Col 1, 18; 2, 19; 5, 23-24

(11) The giver of glory, 2 Thes 2, 14; 1 Cor 2, 7-9

(12) The sign of the fidelity of God, 2 Cor 1, 19-20

(13) The Lord, Phil 2, 6-11

(14) The plenitude of the divinity, Col 1, 9

14. The Spirit of God

(1) Union of Father, Son and Spirit, 1 Cor 12, 4-6; 2 Cor 13, 13; Phil 2, 1; Eph 4, 4-6

(2) The Spirit of the Son, Gal 4, 6; Rom 8, 9; Phil 1, 19

(3) The first-fruits and the pledge of our inheritance, 2 Cor 1, 22; Eph 1, 13-14; Rom 8, 23

(4) The giver of love, Rom 5, 5

(5) The power of God, Rom 8, 11; 2 Cor 13, 4; Phil 3, 10

(6) The life of the Spirit, Rom 8, 1-13

(7) Children of God and the Spirit, Rom 8, 14-17

(8) Diversity and unity of charisms in the Spirit, 1 Cor 12, 4-11

(9) The source of new life, Rom 7, 6; 2 Cor 3, 6

(10) The helper, Rom 8, 26-27

(11) The law of the Spirit, Rom 7, 18. 25; 8, 2-4

(12) The fruits of the Spirit, Gal 5, 19-23

15. The Lord Jesus — Savior

(1) The Son of God, Rom 1, 4; 5, 10; 8, 3; 1 Cor 1, 9; Col 1, 13

(2) The Lord, 1 Cor 15, 25; Col 3, 1; Eph 1, 20; Phil 2, 10

(3) The role of the servant, Phil 2, 5-11

(4) Mediator, Gal 3, 15-18; Col 1, 16

(5) Savior, Eph 5, 23; 1 Thes 1, 10; Rom 11, 26

(6) The sign of the Father's love, Gal 4, 4; Rom 8, 3

(7) The beloved of the Father, Col 1, 13; Eph 1, 6

(8) The first-born of all creation, Col 1, 15-16; Rom 8, 29

(9) The image of the invisible God, Col 1, 15

(10) The new covenant, 1 Cor 11, 25

(11) Our Passover, 1 Cor 5, 7

(12) Victory over sin, Rom 5, 1-11; 6, 5; 2 Cor 5, 17

(13) Victory over death, 2 Tm 1, 10

(14) The triumph of the ascension, Col 3, 1-3

16. The coming of the Lord

(1) The attitude of the Christian, 1 Cor 16, 22; Phil 4, 5

(2) The spirit of vigilance, 1 Thes 5, 1-11

(3) The coming of the adversary, 2 Thes 2, 3-12

(4) Preparation for the Lord's coming, 1 Thes 3, 11-13

(5) No reason for fear, 1 Cor 1, 7-9

(6) The resurrection of the dead, 1 Thes 4, 13-16; 1 Cor 15, 22

(7) The transformation, 1 Cor 15, 35-53

(8) The victory over death, 1 Cor 15, 26. 54-57

(9) The judgment of the Lord, 1 Cor 4, 4-5; 6, 2-3; 2 Cor 5, 10; Rom 2, 2-5

(10) The justice of the judgment, 2 Thes 1, 6-10; 2, 12; 1 Cor 3, 8-15; Gal 6, 7-9

(11) The basis of the judgment, Rom 2, 12-16

(12) Jesus and the Father, 1 Cor 15, 24; Eph 5, 5

17. The meaning of man

(1) Created by God, 1 Cor 11, 9; 2 Cor 5, 17

(2) Dust from dust, 1 Cor 15, 47

(3) Relationship with the body, Rom 12, 3-13

(4) The first Adam and sin, Rom 5, 12-20

(5) The consequences of sin, Rom 5, 16-18; 6, 23; 1 Cor 15, 21-26

(6) Pagans, Rom 1, 21-28; 3, 25

(7) Jews, Rom 2, 17-24; Eph 2, 3

(8) The coming of Christ, Rom 8, 3; Col 1, 22; Eph 2, 14

(9) The obedience of Christ, Rom 5, 18-19; Phil 2, 6-8

(10) The sacrifice of Christ, Rom 3, 25; 4, 25; Eph 5, 2

(11) The liberation of the Christian, Rom 7, 1-6; 1 Cor 15, 56-57; Col 2, 11-13; Eph 2, 4-6

(12) The indwelling Spirit, 1 Cor 3, 16; Rom 8, 9

(13) Future glory, Rom 8, 23

(14) Heirs of the kingdom, Rom 18, 14-17; Gal 4, 4-7

18. "In Christ"

(1) God's love for man manifested in Christ, Rom 8, 39; Eph 2, 7

(2) God's grace bestowed on man in Christ, 1 Cor 1, 4; Rom 5, 15; Eph 4, 32

(3) Redemption in Christ, Rom 3, 24; Col 1, 14; Eph 1, 7

(4) Justification in Christ, Gal 2, 17; 1 Cor 1, 2

(5) A new creature in Christ, 2 Cor 5, 17; Col 3, 3-4

(6) Living in Christ, 1 Cor 1, 17; 2 Cor 1, 21; 1 Thes 3, 8; Phil 4, 1

(7) Dying in Christ, 2 Tm 2, 11; Rom 6, 4; Col 2, 12

(8) Suffering in Christ, Rom 8, 17; 2 Cor 1, 5; Phil 3, 10; Col 1, 24

(9) Rising in Christ, Col 2, 12; 3, 1; Eph 2, 6

(10) Perfected in Christ, Col 1, 28

(11) Reigning in Christ, 2 Tm 2, 12

(12) Christ in us, 2 Cor 13, 5; Gal 2, 20; Rom 8, 10; Col 3, 11; Eph 3, 17

19. Faith

(1) The knowledge of the mystery of Christ, Eph 3; 2-12. 16-19

(2) The knowledge of the truth, 1 Tm 2, 4; 4, 3; Ti 1, 1

(3) Faith in God, Gal 3, 6-7; Rom 4, 3-24; 10, 9; Col 2, 12

(4) Faith in Jesus, Lord and Savior, Gal 2, 16; 3, 22-26; Rom 3, 22-26; Phil 1, 29

(5) Effect of faith, Rom 9, 33; 10, 11

(6) Faith in the gospel, 2 Thes 1, 10; 2, 12; Rom 10, 16; Phil 1, 17; Eph 1, 13

(7) Confession of faith, Rom 10, 9-10; 1 Tm 6, 12

(8) Courage of faith, Rom 1, 16; 1 Tm 5, 8; 2 Tm 1, 8

(9) Justification by faith and not by law, Gal 2, 15-21; Rom 3, 21-30; 9, 30-32

(10) Faith and good works, Gal 3, 10-12; 1 Thes 1, 3; 2 Thes 1, 11; Col 1, 10; Eph 2, 8-10

(11) Growth in faith, 2 Cor 10, 15; Col 1, 10

(12) Faith and charity, Gal 5, 6; 1 Cor 13, 13

(13) Limitations of faith, 2 Cor 5, 10

(14) Faith and the Holy Spirit, Gal 3, 2-5

20. Hope

(1) The Christian lives in hope, 1 Thes 1, 10; 1 Cor 1, 7; Phil 3, 20

(2) The Christian does not live like those without hope, 1 Thes 4, 13; Eph 2, 12

(3) The gift of the Spirit and hope, Rom 5, 5; 8, 23; 2 Cor 3, 3; Gal 5, 5; Eph 4, 4

(4) The Christian is saved in hope, Rom 8, 24; Eph 2, 5-6; 1 Cor 1, 18-21; 2 Cor 2, 15-16

(5) Hope is a gift of God, 2 Thes 2, 16

(6) Christians must hope when tested, Rom 5, 4; 1 Thes 2, 4; 1 Cor 9, 27

(7) Hope and perseverance, 1 Thes 1, 3; 2 Thes 1, 4; 1 Cor 13, 7; 2 Cor 1, 6; Rom 5, 3-4

(8) Hope and prayer, Rom 15, 30

(9) Hope and the armor of the Christian, 1 Thes 5, 8; 2 Cor 6, 7; Rom 6, 13

(10) Christian hope and Abraham, Rom 4, 18-25

(11) Christian hope and the example of Paul, 2 Cor 5, 4; Rom 8, 23

(12) Hope and charity, 1 Cor 13, 13

21. Charity

(1) The perfection of the law, Gal 5, 14; Rom 13, 8-10

(2) Charity is a gift of the Spirit, Gal 5, 16; Rom 5, 5; 15, 30; Col 1, 8; 2 Tm 1, 7

(3) Charity enables us to love as God loves, Eph 5, 1-2

(4) Charity, faith and hope, 1 Thes 1, 3; 1 Cor 13, 7; Gal 5, 5-6; Rom 5, 1-5; 12, 6-12

(5) Charity and constancy, 2 Thes 3, 5; 1 Cor 13, 7; Rom 5, 3-5

(6) Charity and sincerity, 2 Cor 6, 6; Rom 12, 9; Eph 4, 25

(7) Charity and kindness, 1 Cor 13, 4; 2 Cor 6, 6; Eph 4, 32

(8) Charity and service, Gal 4, 2; 1 Cor 8, 1-13; Gal 6, 1-5; Rom 14, 1-15

(9) Charity and edification, 1 Cor 8, 1; 10, 23-24; Rom 14, 19-20

(10) Charity and patience, 1 Thes 5, 14; 1 Cor 13, 4; 2 Cor 6, 6

(11) Charity and God, 1 Thes 2, 4; 1 Cor 2, 9; Gal 1, 10; Rom 8, 28

(12) Charity and neighbor, 1 Cor 16, 15-16; 2 Cor 8, 2-6; Gal 5, 13; Rom 12, 13

(13) Charity and forgiveness, Col 3, 13; Eph 4, 32; 2 Cor 2, 7-10

(14) Charity here and hereafter, 1 Cor 13, 13

22. The Body of Christ

(1) The eucharist and the body of Christ, 1 Cor 10, 16-22
(2) The Greek fable, 1 Cor 12, 14-26
(3) Baptism and the body of Christ, 1 Cor 12, 13-27
(4) The function of each member, 1 Cor 12, 27-30; Rom 12, 4
(5) Christ, the head of the body, Col 1, 18
(6) The cosmic Christ, Eph 1, 22
(7) Christ's love for the Church, Eph 5, 23. 28
(8) Christ's proof of his love, Eph 5, 25
(9) The pleroma, Eph 1, 23; Col 1, 24
(10) Christ and the unity of the body, Col 2, 19
(11) The body of the Christian and the body of Christ, 1 Cor 6, 19
(12) The glory of the body of Christ, Phil 3, 20-21

23. Apostolic communities

(1) Prayer, Gal 4, 6; Rom 8, 15; 1 Cor 16, 22; Phil 4, 5. 20; 2 Cor 1, 20
(2) Hymns and spiritual canticles, 1 Cor 14, 16-18; 2 Cor 9, 11-12; Phil 4, 6
(3) Thanksgiving, 1 Thes 5, 18; 1 Cor 14, 16-18; 2 Cor 9, 11-12; Phil 4, 6; Col 3, 15-17; Eph 5, 4
(4) Sacred Scripture, 1 Thes 5, 27; Col 4, 16
(5) Liturgical assembly, 1 Cor 16, 2
(6) "The holy kiss," 1 Thes 5, 26; 1 Cor 16, 20; 2 Cor 13, 12; Rom 16, 16
(7) The gospel, 1 Thes 2, 13; 1 Cor 15, 1-11; Gal 1, 11-12; Col 2, 6-8
(8) Loyalty to tradition, 1 Tm 6, 20; 2 Tm 1, 14; Ti 1, 9
(9) The desire to please God, 1 Thes 2, 4; 2 Cor 5, 9-10; Gal 1, 8-10
(10) Availability, 1 Cor 9, 19-23; 10, 33
(11) A desire not to be a burden, 1 Thes 2, 5-7; 2 Thes 3, 7-9; 1 Cor 9, 1-15
(12) Courage in trials, 2 Cor 6, 4; Rom 15, 3-6
(13) Understanding of the paschal mystery, Phil 3, 10-11
(14) Perseverance until the end, Phil 2, 12-16

24. The Old Testament in the early Church

(1) The veil over the Old Testament, 2 Cor 3, 12-18; Rom 11, 7-10
(2) The understanding of the Scripture, 1 Cor 2, 6-16; 2 Cor 3, 4-6; Eph 3, 2
(3) Old Testament Scripture may be an allegory, Gal 4, 24
(4) Old Testament may be a "mystery," Eph 5, 31-32
(5) Love of one's enemies, Rom 12, 20
(6) Gladly giving, 2 Cor 9, 7-10; 8, 15
(7) The Christian warrior, 1 Thes 5, 8; Eph 6, 14. 17
(8) The message of the prophets, Rom 1, 1-2; 16, 25-27; 1 Cor 15, 3
(9) The law and Christ, Rom 10, 4-8; 1 Cor 9, 21
(10) The new temple, 1 Cor 3, 10-17; 6, 19-20
(11) The new sacrifice, Eph 5, 2
(12) The resurrection and the victory, 1 Cor 15, 4

25. Resurrection

(1) Baptism and resurrection, Rom 6, 4
(2) Purification and Christ's resurrection, Rom 4, 6; 1 Cor 5, 7-8
(3) Figures of the resurrection, 1 Cor 10, 6. 11
(4) A new creature, 2 Cor 5, 17
(5) A new life, Gal 2, 20; Col 3, 4
(6) The recognition of the Father, Phil 2, 9-10
(7) Risen with Christ, Eph 2, 6; Col 3, 1-2
(8) Life through Christ, 1 Cor 15, 20-22
(9) The truth of the resurrection according to the Scriptures, 1 Cor 15, 4
(10) The action of God, 1 Thes 1, 10; 1 Cor 6, 14; 15, 15; 2 Cor 4, 14; Phil 3, 10; Rom 1, 4
(11) Seating at the right hand of the Father, Rom 8, 34; Col 3, 1; Eph 1, 20; 2, 6
(12) Exaltation, Phil 2, 9-11; Eph 4, 8-9; 1 Tm 3, 16

TABLE NUMBER FIVE

New Testament Themes

LISTING

1. Adoption	21. Fasting	41. Law
2. Almsgiving	22. Father	42. Light
3. Amen	23. Fear	43. Life
4. Apostle	24. Forgiveness	44. Love
5. Atonement	25. Freedom	45. Miracle
6. Authority	26. Glory	46. Mystery
7. Baptism	27. Gospel	47. Name
8. Birth	28. Grace	48. Name of Jesus
9. Blessing	29. Harvest	49. Neighbor
10. Bread	30. Heaven	50. Parable
11. Body	31. Hope	51. Peace
12. Blindness	32. Image	52. Poor
13. Brother	33. Idolatry	53. Praise
14. Call	34. Inheritance	54. Redemption
15. City	35. Joy	55. Repentance
16. Conversion	36. Judgment	56. Sacrifice
17. Covenant	37. Justice	57. Salvation
18. Cross	38. Justification	58. Truth
19. Disciple	39. King	59. Wisdom
20. Faith	40. Kingdom	60. Worship

TABLE NUMBER SIX

New Testament Themes

AMPLIFICATION AND REFERENCES

1. Adoption

Adoption of a child from one family into another was a practice well known in the Greek and Roman world. Paul uses this word to explain God's love for all men.

(1) The Spirit empowers man to cry out "Abba, Father" (Rom 8, 14)
(2) The Christian looks forward to the full freedom of a child of God (Rom 8, 21)
(3) Adoption confers special privileges (Rom 9, 4)
(4) God sent his Son so that we might be adopted as sons and heirs (Gal 4, 5)
(5) Adoption means for us a participation in the Sonship of Christ (Gal 4, 6)
(6) In God's plan of salvation we have been freely chosen for adoption without any claim on our part (Eph 1, 5)

2. Almsgiving

Generosity to those in need is stressed in the Old Testament: "I command you to open your hand to your poor and needy kinsman in your country" (Dt 15, 11). Christ made this one of the signs of his followers.

(1) Almsgiving should be done simply, secretly, purely (Mt 6, 1-4)
(2) More blessed is the one who gives than he who receives (Acts 20, 35)
(3) In the early Church all possessions were shared (Acts 4, 32. 34)
(4) Paul asked his converts to set aside money for the poor every Sunday (1 Cor 16, 1-4)
(5) Christians should remember Christ's generosity and follow his example (2 Cor 8, 6-9)
(6) Readiness to give alms makes a man pleasing to God (2 Cor 8, 11)
(7) Man should give generously and above all cheerfully (2 Cor 9, 6-12)

3. Amen

This Hebrew word which has been transliterated into almost every language has the same root as truth. It means that which is sure, certain, secure. More than 94 times in the gospels Jesus uses this word to introduce a solemn statement. In John (25 times) the word is always doubled. In both Old and New Testaments it usually is the liturgical expression of assent to or approval of a prayer or a wish.

(1) It marks the end of the Our Father (Mt 6, 13)

(2) It closes Christ's final commission to the disciples (Mt 28, 20)

(3) Paul uses it at the close of many of his prayers (Gal 1, 5; Eph 3, 21; 1 Cor 14, 16)
  Other epistles employ it in the same way, 1 Pt 5, 11; 2 Pt 3, 18

(5) The heavenly Christ is called "The Amen" (that is, "The truly reliable one") (Rv 3, 14)

(6) Paul says Christ is the "Yes" to all God's promises, so that it is through him that we say "Amen" to the praise of God (2 Cor 2, 19-22)

4. Apostle

The word refers to the 12 or the 11 original apostles plus Matthias. Later the term has a wider application. An apostle is one who is sent, a messenger, an agent, a representative, a herald, a preacher.

(1) Jesus selects 12 men, sends them to preach (Mk 3, 14; 6, 30)

(2) The apostle is to be received as Christ (Mt 10, 40)

(3) Those whom Jesus sends enjoy his authority (Mk 2, 10; 3, 15)

(4) Some falsely claim this title and should be rejected (2 Cor 11, 13)

(5) Paul's right to be an apostle comes from Jesus and the Father (Gal 1, 1)

(6) When in Corinth Paul worked "the signs of an apostle" (1 Cor 12, 28)

(7) Preaching Christ is the apostles' chief task (Gal 1, 16)

(8) Christ is acclaimed as "the apostle and high priest" (Heb 3, 1)

(9) In the heavenly Jerusalem the apostles are specially honored (Rv 21, 14)

5. Atonement

The English word atonement is really "at-one-ment." This is a rich concept including ideas of reconciliation, sacrificial expiation, intercession, ransom, release.

(1) Without God in the world men are estranged and prone to evil (Col 1, 21)

(2) Jesus was recognized as the friend of sinners (Mk 10, 45; Rom 5, 8)

(3) Through his total self-giving we can go to the Father (Eph 2, 8; Heb 10, 20)

(4) Man is now at peace with God (Rom 14, 9; 2 Cor 5, 15)

(5) Christ's obedience is an example for all men (Phil 2, 5-11)

(6) The barrier separating man from God is now removed (Jn 1, 29; Rom 8, 23; Col 1, 7)

6. Authority

In the New Testament Jesus revealed the true nature of divine authority. Authority is closely connected with power and refers to its rightful use. In the Bible all power is in God's hands.

(1) Jesus, unlike the scribes or the prophets, taught with authority (Mk 1, 22)

(2) He showed his power by forgiving sins (Mk 2, 10)

(3) He was supreme over forces of evil (Lk 11, 14-20)

(4) His power knows no limits of time or space (2 Pt 1, 11)

(5) Christ shared his power with his disciples (Mt 16, 19; Lk 9, 1; Jn 20, 23)

7. Baptism

The antecedents of baptism are found in Jewish customs. John the Baptist preached a baptism of repentance and forgiveness of sins. Since the time of the early Church baptism has been the sign of the followers of Christ.

(1) Jesus gave his followers an example by his own baptism (Mk 1, 9-11; Jn 1, 32-34)

(2) On the day of Pentecost the first Christians were baptized (Acts 2, 38-41)

(3) Baptism was administered in the name of Jesus (Acts 10, 48; 19, 5)

(4) Incorporation in the body of Christ is by means of baptism (1 Cor 12, 12-13)

(5) Sonship and faith are connected with baptism (Gal 3, 26-29)

(6) Baptism brings transformation (1 Pt 3, 21)

8. Blessings

Blessings in the experience of the chosen people often conditioned a whole life. They were a sign of divine favor, communicating to the one blessed God's strength.

(1) The beatitudes are the blessings offered to those who live under the new covenant (Mt 5, 3-12)

(2) God's blessings are for all men (Rom 4, 6-9)

(3) Thanksgiving is an appropriate response to God's blessings (Eph 1, 3-14)

(4) It is good to recall God's blessings (Heb 1, 1-4)

(5) Those who read or listen to the Book of Revelation are promised a blessing (Rv 1, 3)

9. Body of Christ

This beautiful term expresses the strength and importance of the relations between Jesus Christ and those who belong to him, and their relations with one another. All who are united with him share in the power of the resurrection.

(1) Oneness with him is begun by baptism (Rom 6, 1-11; 1 Cor 12, 12-13; Eph 4, 4-5; Col 2, 9-19)

(2) Christ loves, strengthens, sanctifies and fills his body with glory (Eph 1, 23-29; Col 1, 19; 2, 9)

(3) Within one body, the gifts of the Spirit are given (Rom 12, 4-8)

(4) Here there is no division between Jew and Gentile (1 Cor 12-13; Eph 2, 11-18; Col 3, 11)

(5) In Pauline thought this body is linked with the Church (Eph 1, 22; 5, 23; Col 1, 18)

10. Blood

In biblical thought blood was considered sacred because it was believed to be the vital principle of all living beings: "The life of a living body is in its blood" (Lv 17, 11). All life comes from God, so he has special rights over the blood of men and animals.

(1) Without the shedding of blood there can be no forgiveness (Heb 9, 22)

(2) Christ's death is a redeeming sacrifice (Eph 1, 7; 5, 2)

(3) Just as the old covenant was ratified by the shedding of blood in sacrifice by Moses (Ex 24, 5-8), so the new covenant was ratified by the blood Jesus shed on the cross (Mt 26, 28; 1 Cor 11, 25; Heb 10, 29)

(4) The blood of Jesus justifies us (Rom 5, 9), brings us peace (Eph 2, 13), cleanses us (Heb 9, 14), sanctifies us (1 Pt 1, 2)

(5) In the eucharist we share in the flesh and blood of Jesus (Jn 6, 54; 1 Cor 10, 16)

11. Bread

In the Bible "bread" is often used for food in general. As part of the diet of an agricultural people many times it is mentioned in the Old Testament. Its most beautiful meanings in the New Testament refer to Christ.

(1) Jesus calls himself "the real heavenly bread" (Jn 6, 31-33)

(2) He promises that those who eat this bread will live (Jn 6, 35-51)

(3) In the Lord's Prayer he teaches us to ask for our daily bread (Mt 6, 11)

(4) All four evangelists report Christ's multiplication of bread (Mt 14, 13-21; Mk 6, 32-44; Lk 9, 10-17; Jn 6, 1-15)

(5) Christ chose bread and wine at the Last Supper to be his gift (Mt 26, 26-28; Mk 14, 22-24; Lk 22, 19-20; 1 Cor 11, 23-25)

12. Brother

This term has a much wider meaning in Hebrew than in English. It includes blood relations of many degrees, clansmen, tribesmen, countrymen, friends.

(1) Jesus gives this title to all who do the will of his Father (Mk 3, 35; Lk 8, 21)

(2) His apostles and disciples are called brothers (Jn 20, 17)

(3) All those whom he has redeemed are given this name (Heb 2, 11)

(4) Brotherly love can lead to the giving of our life (1 Jn 3, 16)

(5) Our love for one another should be brotherly, full of sincerity and respect (Rom 12, 9f)

13. Call

God's call is the beginning of the People of God (Dt 4, 37). Not all responded to this call, but it was repeated in the Church (Mt 24, 22; Lk 18, 7; Jn 15, 16)

(1) Those whom God calls are specially graced (1 Pt 2, 9; Gal 3, 29)

(2) This call is never a cause for self-glorying but a pure gift (Mt 8, 12; 20, 16; 22, 14)

(3) This call is a sign of God's love (1 Cor 1, 2. 9; Jude 1)

(4) The entire economy of salvation is involved (2 Thes 2, 14)

(5) This call unites us with all others who have received the same call (Eph 4, 4; Col 3, 15)

(6) This call brings us into holiness 1 Thes 4, 7), eternal life (1 Tm 6, 12), apostolic life (Rom 1, 1; 1 Cor 1, 1; Acts 13, 2; 16, 10)

14. City

Although the city is sometimes the expression of man's sin in biblical thought, the story of man which begins in a garden in Genesis ends in a heavenly city in the Book of Revelation.

(1) The Church on earth finds here no lasting city but seeks one that is above (Heb 13, 14)

(2) Members of the Church recall their heavenly citizenship (Phil 3, 20; Heb 12, 22)

(3) The new Jerusalem will be a perfect city (Rv 21, 1—22, 5)

(4) The city of David, Bethlehem, the birthplace of Jesus (Lk 2, 4)

(5) The city of David, Jerusalem, the center of the life of Jesus, Lk 2, 22-52; Jn 7, 2; 10, 21-39; 12, 12—19, 42

(6) The city and the Christians, Acts 1, 12—8, 3

15. Contentment

The loving acceptance of life and its conditions as the wise providence of an all-good and all-powerful God who loves us.

(1) This may seem a passive attitude opposed to social reform (e.g. Lk 3, 14) but the teaching of the prophets and the transcendence of barriers of sex, race, class (Gal 3, 28) correct this.

(2) The Sermon of the Mount specifies contentment (Mt 16, 19-34)

(3) A warning against the discontentment arising from money is appropriate in every age (1 Tm 6, 6-8; Heb 13, 5) in a Christian who trusts God.

(4) We must share what we have to provide for the contentment of others (2 Cor 9, 6-10)

(5) Contentment can be acquired Phil 4, 11-13)

(6) Contentment requires a right perspective (Phil 3, 8f)

16. Conversion

A turning or a returning to God, often in the sense of repentance.

(1) True repentance involves regret for the past and firm resolve for the future (2 Cor 7, 10)

(2) John the Baptizer called for repentance and insisted on its fruits (Lk 3, 3-8)

(3) Jesus asked those who would follow him to repent (Mk 1, 15; 2, 17)

(4) Repentance is closely related to forgiveness (Lk 24, 47; Acts 5, 31)

(5) Conversion leads to a new life (Acts 11, 18)

(6) Conversion is linked with faith (Acts 20, 21; Heb 6, 1)

17. Covenant

A solemn agreement made between God and men, men and men. It is made binding by an oath which may take the form of a formula or a symbolic act.

(1) In the accounts of the Last Supper Jesus refers to the new covenant (Mt 26, 28; Mk 14, 24; Lk 22, 20; 1 Cor 11, 25)

(2) There is a vast difference between the old and the new covenant (Gal 4, 21-28)

(3) The epistle to the Hebrews points to the abrogation of the old covenant by the new (Heb 7, 1—9, 22)

(4) Jesus speaks of himself as the mediator of the new covenant (Lk 22, 50; 1 Cor 11, 25)

(5) The new covenant is a freeing of man from sin (Heb 9, 14f; Rom 8, 5) through the paschal mystery (Rom 4, 25)

(6) The new covenant is sealed by the gift of the Spirit (Acts 1, 4f; 2, 14ff)

18. Cross

The centrality of the mystery of the cross in the New Testament is evident in reference to both the physical object used in Christ's crucifixion and its metaphorical value as a term expressing our redemption.

(1) The cross in the life of Jesus is described by all the evangelists (Mt 27, 32ff; Mk 15, 21ff; Lk 23, 26; Jn 19, 17ff)

(2) To the Jews the cross is a stumbling block, shocking as it was to think the Messiah would be put to death by the Romans (Gal 5, 11)

(3) To Christians, too, the cross is a challenge and a paradox (1 Cor 1, 17-24; Col 2, 14)

(4) Jesus insisted that all his followers should take up the cross (Mt 10, 38; Mk 8, 34; Lk 14, 27)

(5) This following is meant to lead to perfect union with Christ crucified (Rom 6, 6)

(6) The Christian should never separate the cross from the resurrection (Phil 3, 10)

19. Disciple

The word disciple is used many times in the New Testament to denote those who believe in Jesus. It is not a specific reference to the Twelve but to all who love him.

(1) Fidelity to Jesus' word leads to the disciple's freedom (Jn 8, 31)
(2) Total self-surrender and the yielding of all possessions is required of the disciple (Lk 14, 26)
(3) Suffering is inseparable from true discipleship (Lk 14, 27)
(4) Jesus promised the love of the Father to those whose discipleship bears much fruit (Jn 15, 8-9)
(5) The fervor of the early disciples is described in Acts (1—5)
(6) Paul asks God to bless the true followers of Jesus (Rom 16, 25-27)

20. Faith

With the coming of Christ and the fulfullment of the messianic prophecies, faith is more than mere trust in God but the full submission of heart and mind and will to Christ.

(1) Faith is a rich and complex act (2 Cor 10, 5; Rom 4, 1-25; Heb 11, 6)
(2) Divine grace is required for this act (Eph 2, 8)
(3) Faith leads to untroubled peace (Jn 14, 1-12)
(4) Faith leads to eternal life (Jn 3, 14-18)
(5) Faith may be tempered by many trials (1 Pt 1, 7; Jas 1, 2-4)
(6) Faith should be living (Gal 2, 20; Ti 3, 8; 1 Tm 5, 8)
(7) Beautiful examples of faith (Mt 8, 10; 9, 21; 15, 28; Lk 1, 45; Heb 10, 32-36)

21. Fasting

Days and prolonged periods of fasting were frequent in Old Testament times. Moments of national sorrow were marked by special forms of abstinence. This may also be observed in the New Testament (Lk 2, 37; Acts 23, 21; 27, 9)

(1) Jesus set the example for all Christians by his fast in the desert (Mt 4, 2; Mk 1, 12-13; Lk 4, 2)
(2) While he was with his disciples Jesus did not wish them to fast (Mt 9, 14-15; Mk 2, 18-20; Lk 5, 33-35)

(3) Fasting may at times be necessary (Mt 17, 20; Mk 9, 28)
(4) The Christian should never be ostentatious in his fasting (Mt 6, 16-17)
(5) The early Christians fasted to learn God's will (Acts 13, 2-3)
(6) Paul recognized the value of fasting (2 Cor 6, 5; 11, 27)

22. Father

In the Old Testament God is frequently addressed as "Father." Israel was recognized as his first-born son. In the New Testament the believer becomes an adopted son of God (Rom 8, 15; Gal 4, 6). Jesus often refers to Father, sometimes saying: "My Father" or "Your Father" and once: "My Father and your Father" (Jn 20, 17), to distinguish his special relationship from ours.

23. Fear

The fear of the Lord is a prevailing Old Testament concept. It is a basic response of man in the presence of greatness, majesty, power, holiness. Man's guilt, compromises, divided loyalties deepen this estrangement which Christ came to heal.

(1) Exhortations not to fear (Lk 1, 13. 30; 2, 10; Mt 28, 5; Mk 5, 36; Lk 8, 50)
(2) The first missionaries were told to preach fearlessly (Mt 10, 26. 28. 31)
(3) When Christ walked on the water he bade his disciples to be unafraid (Mt 14, 27)
(4) Christ demands fortitude of his followers (Lk 12, 4-5)
(5) Those who are filled with zeal need not fear (1 Pt 3, 13-15)
(6) Paul was told to preach courageously (Acts 18, 9)
(7) John was told to be unafraid (Rv 1, 17-19)

24. Forgiveness

In both Old and New Testaments forgiveness and repentance are related. The reestablishment of a right relationship between God and man is stressed in the preaching and in the life of Jesus.

(1) There is no limit to forgiveness (Mt 18, 20-21)
(2) Forgiveness by God calls for our willingness to forgive (Mt 6, 12; Lk 11, 4)
(3) This willingness to be merciful is imperative (Mt 18, 21-35)
(4) Jesus asks men to forgive (Mt 5, 23-24; Lk 6, 37)

(5) On the cross Jesus taught the lesson of forgiveness (Lk 23, 34)

(6) Jesus claimed the divine prerogative of forgiving sin (Mt 9, 2-7)

(7) Paul stresses the necessity of our forgiving others (Eph 4, 32; Col 3, 13)

25. Freedom

Liberation from moral or political servitude is a deep desire of every human heart. External freedom will avail little if there is not an inner freedom. Christ's coming inaugurated an era of freedom from anxiety, from sin, from fear of death.

(1) Christ purchased our freedom at a great price (1 Cor 6, 20; 7, 23)

(2) The Holy Spirit is given to us now as a pledge of our freedom (Eph 1, 14; 4, 30)

(3) Baptism frees the believer from sin (Rom 6, 17-22; 8, 2)

(4) Christ has broken the wall separating Jew and Gentile (Eph 2, 14)

(5) Christ broke the domination of Satan (Col 1, 13-14) but we must preserve our freedom by spiritual warfare (Eph 6, 12)

(6) A truly free life should be lived according to the Spirit (Rom 8, 1; 2 Cor 3, 17)

(7) A truly free life leads to a service in love (1 Pt 2, 16)

26. Glory

The primary meaning of the Hebrew word is greatness, wealth, dignity. Later the idea of brightness was added. All these commanded respect, admiration, and in the course of centuries became associated with the idea of God's presence. The glory of God shone on the shepherds when the birth of Christ was announced to them.

(1) Jesus is the glory of God made visible on earth (Jn 1, 14)

(2) His miracles are a sign of his glory (Jn 2, 11)

(3) Through him we learn of the glory of God (2 Cor 2, 6)

(4) His glory is in us (Col 1, 27)

(5) Christians should frequently give glory to God in their prayer (Rom 11, 36; 16, 27; Gal 1, 5; Eph 3, 21; Phil 4, 20; 1 Tm 1, 17)

(6) Glory is for Christians a partly fulfilled reality into which we can grow (2 Cor 3, 18)

27. Gospel

Gospel is literally the good tidings that Jesus has fulfilled the Old Testament promises of his coming. Jesus himself used the term "to preach the gospel" and the early Church adopted these words to describe the saving message of the Old Testament as we find it in the message of Jesus and in his own person (Rom 1, 1; Gal 3, 8)

(1) The gospel lovingly accepted enables his followers to serve him (2 Cor 12, 9-10; Eph 6, 10-12)

(2) Those who accept the gospel will suffer as Christ suffered (Rom 8, 17; 2 Cor 4, 10; Eph 3, 13)

(3) The gospel is one of grace and peace (1 Pt 1, 13; Eph 6, 14)

(4) Christians are called to be witnesses to the gospel (Mt 10, 18; 24, 14; Mk 13, 9; Acts 1, 8; 3, 15)

(5) Paul, despite his unworthiness, was called to be a minister of the gospel (Eph 3, 7-12)

(6) The gospel is meant for all men (Mt 28, 16-20 Jn 21, 1-23; Lk 24, 47; Acts 1, 8)

28. Grace

In the Old Testament grace was a characteristic in man that was pleasing. It enabled him to find favor in the eyes of God and man. In the New Testament it means attractiveness and much more. It means the reality of God's love for man and the results in man of this love.

(1) Grace makes men pleasing to God (Rom 3, 24; Ti 3, 7)

(2) Grace appeared to men in the incarnation (Ti 2, 11)

(3) Grace gives power (Acts 6, 8; Rom 1, 5; 12, 3; 1 Cor 3, 10; Eph 3, 7-12)

(4) Grace is meant to be given to more and more people (2 Cor 4, 13-15)

(5) The Holy Spirit is the giver of grace (Heb 10, 29)

(6) Christians should appeal frequently to the throne of grace (Heb 4, 16)

29. Harvest

To the Israelite the time of harvesting was a time of feasting and merry-making. Three major Old Testament feasts were connected with the annual gathering in of the fruits of the field and vine. Mechanized agriculture and urban life have shorn this image of much of its biblical beauty.

(1) The harvest is a figure of the fruitfulness of the kingdom (Mt 9, 37-38)

(2) The apostle reaps what Jesus has sown (Jn 4, 31-38)

(3) The end of the world and the final judgment is likened by Jesus to the harvest (Mt 13, 39)

(4) In the Book of Revelation the angel at the end of time will reap the earth (Rv 4, 15-16)

30. Heaven

The opening of the heavens signified the coming of the Lord in the Old Testament. Heaven thus became the dwelling place of God (Mt 6, 9) which was sometimes used in the Bible as a substitute made through reverence for the name of God. Mark and Luke do not hesitate to speak of the kingdom of God but Matthew almost always refers to the kingdom of heaven. In the use of heaven there is no sense of place or direction.

(1) In the incarnation Jesus is said to come from heaven (Jn 3, 13-31; 6, 38)

(2) During his lifetime the heavens opened (Mt 3, 16f; Mk 1, 10f; Lk 3, 21f; Jn 1, 32)

(3) His ascension and second coming are associated with heaven (Mt 26, 64; Mk 16, 62; 1 Thes 1, 10)

(4) The Christian's treasure and reward are said to be in heaven (Mt 5, 12; 6, 20)

(5) The Christian is a citizen of heaven, his home (Jn 14, 1-3; Phil 3, 20)

(6) All who rise with Christ will be taken to heaven (1 Thes 4, 16-17; 1 Cor 15, 42-49)

31. Hope

The whole Old Testament is a book of hope which finds its fulfillment in Christ who is the bringer of our hope (1 Tm 1, 1). Christian hope is rooted in the paschal mystery: "We have been born anew to a living hope through the resurrection of Jesus Christ from the dead" (1 Pt 1, 3)

(1) Abraham is a model of hope (Rom 4, 18)

(2) Christians are saved through hope (Rom 8, 24; 12, 12)

(3) The object and the motive of hope are unseen (Heb 3, 6)

(4) Patient suffering and reading the Bible lead to hope (Rom 5, 4; 15, 4)

(5) Christians should always be ready to explain their hope to others (1 Pt 3, 15) widow

(6) Hope is related to faith and love (1 Cor 13, 13)

32. Image

The earliest pages of the Bible state that God made man to his own image and likeness. The New Testament develops this idea of man's resemblance to God in his finest qualities, his powers of self-awareness and self-determination.

(1) Paul speaks of Christ as the image of God (2 Cor 4, 4; Col 1, 15)

(2) The Christian is invited to be changed into this image (2 Cor 3, 18)

(3) This image requires the generous service of God (Col 1, 9-13)

(4) Charity is at the root of this growing likeness to God (Eph 3, 14-21)

33. Inheritance

This is an important theological concept in the Bible. It is related in the Old Testament to Yahweh's promise that his people would inherit the land. In the New Testament it is connected with the fact that Jesus, the Son of God and heir, wishes to share his inheritance with us.

(1) The inheritance is described as the kingdom, eternal life, blessing (Mt 25, 34; Mk 10, 17; Lk 10, 25; 1 Pt 3, 9; Heb 12, 17)

(2) To inherit, the Christian must become a true son (Mt 21, 38; Mk 12, 7; Lk 20, 14; Heb 1, 2)

(3) Paul spoke beautifully of our responsibility as co-heirs (Rom 8, 17; Gal 3, 29; 4, 7)

(4) All men are called to share in this inheritance (Eph 3, 6)

34. Joy

This is a biblical concept often associated with those who belong to Israel or to the Church. It is not a transient experience but an integral quality of the true servant of the Lord.

(1) Joy is a sign of membership in the kingdom (Rom 14, 17)

(2) Joy is connected with peace and hope (Rom 15, 13)

(3) Jesus during his lifetime took part in many joyous celebrations (Jn 2, 1-11; 3, 29; 17, 3)

(4) According to the Book of Revelation there is joy in heaven (Rv 19, 7)

(5) Jesus wishes his followers to be filled with joy (Mt 9, 15; Jn 15, 11)

(6) The resurrection is a cause of our joy (Jn 16, 20. 22)

(7) Paul counseled his followers to rejoice (Phil 3, 1; 4, 4; 1 Thes 5, 16)

(8) Joy is the fruit of the Spirit and proceeds from the Spirit (1 Thes 1, 6; Gal 5, 22; Rom 14, 17; 15, 13)

35. Judgment

In the Old Testament God is recognized as the judge of the whole world who will render justice. He loves justice and his coming means both condemnation and vindication. His love and mercy are expressed in the incarnation.

(1) The day of final judgment is coming (Mt 10, 15; 12, 36; Lk 11, 22. 24)

(2) Jesus came primarily not to judge but to save (Jn 3, 17)

(3) Judgment at any moment is man's response to God (Jn 3, 18; 5, 24)

(4) Christians should prepare for the coming judgment (Mt 24, 42-44; Mk 13, 33-37; Lk 12, 41-48)

(5) No Christian should judge another (Mt 7, 1-2; Rom 14, 10; 1 Cor 4, 5)

(6) Christians should look forward with confidence in God to the coming judgment (1 Jn 2, 28; 4, 16-17; 1 Pt 1, 5-7; 4, 16-19)

36. King

The kingship of Jesus is not one of the dominant New Testament themes but it has an Old Testament foundation in the prophecies about the coming of a royal messiah. In every instance the unworldly character of his kingship is stressed.

(1) The infant Jesus is honored as king (Mt 2, 1-12)

(2) Jesus' divinity and kingship should always be combined (Jn 1, 47-49)

(3) Entering Jerusalem Jesus is hailed as king (Jn 12, 12-16)

(4) During the passion allusion is made, mockingly, to his kingship (Mt 27, 29. 37. 42; Mk 15, 9; Lk 23, 37-38; Jn 19, 3. 14-15. 19. 21)

(5) After his resurrection he spoke to his disciples about his kingdom (Acts 1, 3)

(6) The early church believed in his kingship (1 Cor 15, 23-28; Rv 11, 15)

37. Kingdom of God

This is the central theme of the gospel message. To understand its meaning is to understand who he is and what he came to do. Matthew prefers to speak of the kingdom of heaven, reflecting the reverence of Jews for the divine name.

(1) Many of the parables contain lessons about the kingdom (Mt 13; 18, 23-35; Mk 4, 26-29; Lk 14, 28-32)

(2) The miracles of Jesus point to the coming of the kingdom (Mt 11, 20-21; Mk 3, 22-30; Lk 11, 17-23)

(3) The kingdom was announced by John the Baptizer (Mt 4, 23; 9, 35; Lk 4, 43; 16, 16)

(4) Jesus tells his followers to proclaim the kingdom, to seek it, to pray for it (Mt 3, 2; 4, 17; 6, 10; Lk 8, 10; 11, 2)

(5) The kingdom is a mystery (Mt 13, 11; Mk 4, 11; Lk 8, 10)

(6) The kingdom is a double reality; it is already here, yet it is to come in its fullness hereafter (Mt 25, 1-13; Lk 13, 18-21)

(7) The kingdom will not come easily (Mt 11, 12; 16, 16)

(8) Righteousness, peace and joy are signs of the kingdom given by the Father to his Son (Mt 6, 33; Lk 12, 31; Rom 14, 17; 1 Cor 15, 24; Col 1, 13)

38. Law

Reverence for the commandments of God is to be found in the life and in the teaching of Jesus. This same reverence he asked his followers to observe.

(1) The kingdom of God is to be entered by those who keep God's commandments (Mt 5, 17-20; 19, 16-19)

(2) The whole law can be summarized in the commandment of love of God and neighbor (Mt 22, 34-40; Mk 12, 28-34; Lk 10, 25-28)

(3) To be "in Christ" is to keep God's commandments (Rom 3, 31)

(4) Life and holiness come through love of Christ's law (Gal 2, 21)

39. Light

In the Bible light has often a figurative sense and can mean purity or knowledge, sometimes prosperity and happiness. It is often used as a sign of God's presence or his revelation (Mt 17, 5; Lk 2, 9)

(1) The early Christians spoke of God as light (1 Jn 1, 5-7)
(2) Jesus told his followers that he was the light of the world (Jn 8, 12; 9. 5)
(3) Jesus gives light to every man (Jn 1, 9)
(4) His followers are children of light (Lk 16, 8; Jn 12, 36; 1 Thes 5, 5; Eph 5, 8)
(5) Jesus is the light needed by all men (Jn 3, 19; 12, 35-36; 1 Jn 2, 8-10)
(6) The Father dwells in inaccessible light (1 Tm 6, 16)
(7) The coming of light means the coming of life (Eph 5, 14; Col 1, 12: 1 Pt 2, 9)

40. Life

In the Bible life means more than existence and well-being here. The acclamation "Long live the king" signified more than length of life. Eternal life is explained more clearly in the New Testament than in the Old.

(1) Jesus is life for man in the fullest possible sense (1 Jn 1, 2-3)
(2) To keep the commandments is to have life (Mt 19, 16-17; Mk 10, 17-19; Lk 10, 28)
(3) Paul teaches that life is God's gift for which one must work (Rom 2, 7; 6, 22-23)
(4) Life comes through believing, hoping, seeking (Ti 1, 2; 3, 7; 1 Tm 1, 16; 6, 12)
(5) Our true life is a life in the risen Lord (Rom 8, 11)
(6) The Christian no longer lives but Jesus lives in him (Gal 2, 20; cf Rom 6, 11; Eph 4, 18)

41. Lord's Prayer

The Lord's Prayer is given us as a plan on which to base our prayer. Some suggestions are given here of passages in the New Testament that are related to the petitions of the prayer taught by Jesus to his followers when they asked how they were to pray.

(1) The prayer is given in two forms in the New Testament (Mt 6, 9-13; Lk 11, 2-4)
(2) The address to the Father (Mt 11, 25-26; Mk 14, 36; Lk 22, 42)
(3) First petition (Rom 2, 24; 10, 13-15)
(4) Second petition (Mt 16, 28; Mk 9, 1; Lk 9, 27)
(5) Third petition (Mk 14, 36)
(6) Fourth petition (Jn 14, 13-14)
(7) Fifth petition (Mt 18, 20-21)
(8) Sixth petition (Jn 14, 1-4)

42. Love

Love is the biblical word that denotes the perfect relationship between persons. It is not something sentimental but involves reverence, responsibility, loyalty, knowledge, service. Because of the covenant God made with man, man in the Old Testament was sure of God's love. The incarnation is our proof of this continuing love (1 Jn 4, 10-11)

(1) Love is the gift of the Spirit (Gal 5, 22)
(2) It is inseparable from faith and hope (Gal 5, 6; 1 Thes 3, 6; 1 Tm 1, 14; 2 Tm 1, 13)
(3) It is the bond of perfection (Col 3, 12-14)
(4) Other charisms are valueless without it (1 Cor 13, 1-3)
(5) It is found in all its beauty in Jesus (Rom 8, 39)
(6) It will always remain, even in the next life (1 Cor 13, 13)

43. Love of God

These words may be understood in two ways. They may denote the love of God for man or the love of man for God.

(1) Jesus is the Son loved by God (Mt 3, 17; 17, 5; Jn 3, 6; 17, 24)
(2) God's love is all-embracing (Mt 6, 26-28; Lk 6, 35; Acts 10, 34)
(3) The qualities of God's love (Rom 9, 12-13)
(4) Love is man's response to God's love for him (Mt 22, 36-38; Mk 12, 29-30; Lk 10, 27; Rom 13, 10; 1 Jn 3, 14)
(5) Love is expressed in the keeping of the commandments (1 Jn 5, 3; 2 Jn 6)
(6) Our model of the true love of God is Jesus (Jn 15, 9; 17, 26)

44. Love of neighbor

Closely related to our love of God—in fact inseparable from this love—is our love for one another.

(1) Jesus insisted on the necessity of our love for our neighbor (Mt 19, 19; Lk 10, 27)

(2) Love of God and neighbor are one (Mt 22, 37-40; Mk 12, 30-32)

(3) Love is Christ's "new commandment" (Jn 13, 34; 1 Jn 2, 7-8)

(4) Love is a fruit of the Spirit and possible only in union with Jesus (Col 1, 8; 1 Cor 16, 24)

(5) Fraternal love is a proof of true Christian life (1 Jn 3, 9-10; 2 Pt 1, 7)

(6) This love extends to all, even our enemies (Lk 10, 29-37; Mt 5, 43-48)

45. Miracle

Manifestations of divine power are frequent in the Bible. They attest God's love for man. The working of wonders is only one of the many forms in which his power and his love are revealed.

(1) Jesus is the power of God (Rom 1, 4; 1 Cor 1, 24)

(2) His words are the power of God (Rom 1, 16; 1 Cor 1, 18)

(3) Jesus manifested his power in the world of nature (Mt 15, 32-39; Mk 6, 45-52; Lk 8, 22-25; Jn 2, 1-11)

(4) Jesus manifested his power in miracles of healing (Mt 8, 1-4; Mk 7, 31-37; Lk 13, 10-17; Jn 5, 1-18)

(5) Jesus manifested his power over demons (Mt 17, 14-20; Mk 5, 1-20; Lk 4, 31-37)

(6) Jesus manifested his power by raising the dead (Mt 9, 18-26; Mk 5, 22-43; Lk 7, 11-17; Jn 11, 1-44)

46. Mystery

Paul uses this word to denote God's plan for the salvation of the world which has been and is being disclosed to man. This revelation is divine and it will always be beyond man's full understanding.

(1) The kingdom of God is a mystery (Mk 4, 11)

(2) The mystery of God's will is to bring all into unity in Christ (Eph 1, 9-10)

(3) This plan includes the saving of men through Christ's death (Eph 3, 6-9)

(4) The mission of the apostles is to reveal this plan (Eph 6, 19)

(5) Christ's dwelling in us is part of the mystery (Eph 1, 26-27)

(6) Belief in Christ is "the mystery of faith" (1 Tm 3, 9)

47. Name

In the Bible "name" is often more than a sign of identification. It is identified in some way wth the hearer. To know a person's name gives a certain control over that person. "The Name" was one of the popular substitutes for the sacred name of Yahweh.

(1) To believe in Jesus' name is to believe that he is the Son of God (Jn 3, 18)

(2) Prayer made in the name of Jesus will always be heard (Jn 14, 13-14; 15, 16)

(3) He is in the midst of those who come together for his sake (Mt 18, 20)

(4) To be baptized in his name is to become his possession (1 Cor 1, 13-15)

(5) To reveal the Father's name is to reveal his true character (Jn 17, 6. 26)

(6) To glorify the Father's name is to glorify his divinity (Jn 12, 28)

48. Name of Jesus

To know the name of Yahweh meant to have an experience of the reality of who he is and what he expects of man. This theology of the name finds a beautiful presentation in the truths about "the name of Jesus."

(1) The name of Jesus is a name of power (Mk 16, 17; Lk 10, 17; Acts 3, 6; 4, 12; 1 Cor 6, 11; 1 Jn 2, 12)

(2) This name is above all others (Phil 2, 9-11; Eph 1, 21)

(3) Christians are those who invoke the name of Jesus (Acts 2, 38; Rom 6, 3)

(4) To preach the name of Jesus is to proclaim who he is (Acts 5, 40; 9, 20)

(5) Christian faith is belief in his name (Jn 3, 18; 1 Jn 5, 13)

(6) Christians accept hardship and suffering in his name (Mt 19, 29; Jn 15, 21)

(7) The Christian lives in the name of Jesus (Mt 18, 5-20; Jn 14, 13; 16, 26; 1 Cor 12, 3; 2 Thes 3, 6; Col 3, 17)

49. Neighbor

The Old Testament meaning was often restricted to those dwelling in the land given to the people of God. In the New Testament the meaning is extended.

(1) In the parable of the Good Samaritan the neighbor is the one who showed compassion, not the one who received it (Lk 10, 25-27)

(2) The law of universal love (Mt 5, 42-48)

(3) The whole law requires love of God and neighbor (Mt 22, 36-40)

(4) To be a good neighbor is to be generous (2 Cor 9, 7)

(5) Love of God and neighbor are inseparable (1 Jn 3, 17; 4, 20-21)

50. Parable

Teaching in parables meant the telling of a story that held the hearer's interest and challenged him to make a suitable response. The incredulous and indifferent never discover "the meaning behind the meaning of the parables."

(1) Jesus taught in parables (Mt 13, 14-15; Mk 4, 12; Lk 8, 10)

(2) Many parables deal with the kingdom of God (Mt 13, 3-23; Mk 4, 26-29; Lk 13, 18-21)

(3) Some parables concentrate on the members of the kingdom (Mt 11, 16-19; Mk 7, 27-28; Lk 5, 33-35)

(4) Other parables express the duties of those in the kingdom (Mt 7, 9-11; Mk 4, 21; Lk 15, 4-32)

51. Peace

Shalom, the Hebrew word for peace, means totality, wholeness, well-being, prosperity, freedom from violence or misfortune. It was central in the Old Testament and was expected to be a dominant characteristic of the kingdom established by the Messiah.

(1) It was the work of John the Baptizer to prepare for this peace (Lk 1, 79)

(2) The birth of Jesus was the beginning of peace (Lk 2, 14)

(3) Jesus hailed as the bringer of peace (Lk 19, 38)

(4) Peace is the greeting of the risen Jesus (Jn 20. 19-26)

(5) The message of Jesus is "a gospel of peace" (Acts 10, 36; Eph 6, 15)

(6) God is the God of peace (Rom 15, 33; 16, 20; 1 Cor 14, 33; Phil 4, 9; Heb 13, 20)

(7) Peace should mark Christian life (Eph 4, 3; 2 Tm 2, 22-23; Jas 3, 16-18)

52. Poor

The example as well as the words of Jesus points to the importance of a life of simplicity, free from ostentation, a life lived for others.

(1) The renunciation of wealth is a condition for the following of Jesus (Mt 19, 27-29; Mk 10, 28-30; Lk 18, 28-30)

(2) Jesus condemns the stingy giver (Mt 12, 41-44)

(3) Jesus taught "evangelical poverty" (Mt 19, 16-22; Mk 10, 17-22; Lk 18, 18-23)

(4) The rich man is condemned for living luxuriously when there were poor who needed his help (Lk 16, 19-21)

(5) The poor are blessed (Mt 5, 3; Lk 6, 20)

(6) To them is brought the gospel and they are admitted to the kingdom (Mt 11, 5; Lk 4, 18; 14, 15; 16, 19-31)

53. Praise

The extolling of God's perfections is found from one end of the Bible to the other. This is a Christian's obligation and privilege.

(1) Singing and blessing God should be constant (Col 3, 16; Heb 13, 15)

(2) The example of praising God is given by Mary (Lk 1, 46-55)

(3) Other examples of praise (Lk 1, 68-79; 2, 14; 20, 29-32)

(4) Christ taught the necessity of praise (Mt 21, 19; Lk 17, 18)

(5) Praise characterized the prayer of the early Church (Acts 2, 46-47; 16, 25; Rom 1, 25; 2 Cor 11, 31; Eph 1, 3-14; Rv 1, 6)

54. Redemption

In the New Testament this word usually refers to the saving work of Jesus. It is a proof of the Father's love. It is expressed in many beautiful ways.

(1) Redemption and the giving of life (Mk 10, 45)

(2) The costliness of the redemption (Gal 1, 4; 2, 20; Eph 5, 2; Col 1, 14)

(3) Redemption and sanctification (Rom 3, 24)

(4) The results of redemption (Heb 9, 14; 1 Jn 1, 7. 9)

(5) Christians now enjoy the first-fruits of redemption (Rom 8, 19-23)

(6) The future of those redeemed (Rv 1, 5; 5, 10)

55. Repentance

The moral change by which a man turns from what is less pleasing to what is more pleasing to God was the message of the prophets that was repeated by John the Baptist and made a basic part of the following of Christ.

(1) Repentance was the Baptist's theme (Mt 3, 1-12)

(2) Repentance is the preparation for the kingdom (Mt 4, 17; Mk 1, 15)

(3) Ideal types of repentance are presented by Jesus (Lk 15, 11-32; 18, 9-14)

(4) Repentance was understood to be essential by the early Church (Acts 2, 38; 3, 19; 5, 31; 8, 22; 11, 18; 17, 30; 20, 21)

(5) True repentance comes from God (2 Tm 2, 25)

(6) True repentance is constant, i.e., "unrepentant" (2 Cor 7, 10)

56. Sacrifice

The setting-apart and the destruction of precious objects have marked man's response to God since the earliest times. The Old Testament sacrificial system was elaborate and the prophets continually pointed to its defects. Jesus gave man a new form of sacrifice.

(1) The recognition of the inadequacy of the old covenant sacrifices (Heb 10, 4)

(2) The repetition of prophetic castigations (Mt 9, 13; 12, 7)

(3) The value of the sacrifice of the new covenant (Heb 9—10)

(4) The motivation of love in Christ's sacrifice (Eph 5, 2)

(5) The institution of the eucharistic sacrifice (Mt 26, 26-29; Mk 14, 22-25; Lk 22, 15-20; 1 Cor 11, 23-26)

(6) The Christian's obligation for sacrifice (Rom 12, 1; 1 Pt 2, 5)

57. Suffering

The problem of suffering has challenged men of every century. Is suffering vindictive, punitive, disciplinary, purifying? The Old Testament had no complete answer. It pointed to the perfect answer which is to be seen in an innocent Savior suffering for sinners.

(1) All who follow Christ will have a share in his sufferings (Jn 15, 20)

(2) Jesus offered his life for others (Heb 13, 12; 1 Pt 2, 19-23)

(3) Suffering is not the direct result of some sin (Lk 13, 1-5; Jn 9, 2)

(4) Suffering is a kind of testing (Jas 1, 3. 12)

(5) Suffering should be a cause of rejoicing (Rom 5, 3)

(6) The paradox of Christian suffering (2 Cor 12, 7-10)

58. Truth

In the Old Testament the Hebrew idea of truth is related to reliable, dependable, trustworthy. The Greek idea of truth means that which really exists as opposed to what merely seems to be or that which is temporary or inauthentic. In the New Testament both of these ideas are represented.

(1) To speak the truth is a frequently recurring phrase in the New Testament (Mk 5, 33; Lk 4, 25; Jn 5, 31; Acts 26, 25)

(2) The apostle is called to be a teacher in truth (1 Tm 2, 7)

(3) Truth and righteousness are synonymus (Eph 4, 24; 5, 9; 6, 14)

(4) Truth and the real (1 Thes 1, 9; Rv 6, 10)

(5) Jesus is the truth (Jn 1, 9; 15, 1; 6, 55)

(6) All who belong to the truth hear his voice (Jn 18, 37)

59. Wisdom

Understanding, skill in right thinking and right doing are all connected with the Hebrew words for wisdom. In the New Testament it is a charismatic gift that opens up the meaning of the mysteries and truths of faith.

(1) Christ is the wisdom of God (1 Cor 1, 24)

(2) Christ is our wisdom (1 Cor 1, 30)

(3) In Christ are hidden all the treasures of wisdom (Col 2, 1-3)

(4) Christ grew in wisdom as a child (Lk 2, 52)

(5) The wise of this world must seek God's wisdom (1 Cor 3, 18-19)

(6) Christians should admonish one another wisely (Col 3, 16)

60. Worship

Worship under the Old Law involved both liturgical service and an inward attitude. This tension between the ritual and the personal aspects continues in the New Testament and is resolved by Jesus who asks both of his followers.

(1) To God alone is due our supreme worship (Mt 4, 10; Lk 4, 8)

(2) True worship is adoring, obedient love (Lk 10, 25-28)

(3) Every well-intentioned act is an act of worship (Mt 25, 34-40; Jas 1, 27)

(4) All worship should be well ordered (1 Cor 14, 23-40)

(5) Music and singing have a place in worship (Col 3, 16; Eph 5, 19)

(6) True worship is of God the Father and the Son (Jn 5, 23; Phil 2, 5-11)

THE SUNDAY GOSPELS (3-year Cycle)

See p. 438 for feasts of the year that displace the Mass of Sunday.

Year A

Year B

Year C

MAJOR FEASTS OF THE YEAR

BIBLE DICTIONARY

ABEL. The religious and just son of Adam and Eve whose sacrifice pleased God, yet aroused the murderous envy of his brother Cain. He was a shepherd and offered the firstlings of his flock to the Lord (Gn 4, 2-8).

ABRAHAM. "Father of believers." At God's command he left his home in Ur of the Chaldees about 2000 B.C. and settled in Palestine. God made a covenant with him and promised him a great posterity. In his old age his wife Sarah bore him a son (Isaac) in fulfillment of God's promise (Gn 11—25).

ABYSS. In the Old Testament this word refers to the primordial ocean of the ancient Semitic cosmogony. After God's creative activity this vast body forms the salt-water seas (Gn 1, 9f); part of it is the fresh water under the earth (Ps 33, 7), which wells forth on the earth as springs and fountains (Gn 7, 11). Part of it, "the upper water" (Ps 148, 4), is held up by the dome of the sky (Gn 1, 6f), from which rain descends on the earth (Gn 7, 11). In the New Testament this word is used to describe the depths of the earth, variously considered the abode of the dead (Rom 10, 7) or of the demons (Lk 8, 3; Rv 9, 1ff; 11, 7; 17, 8; 20, 1.3). Sheol, Pool of Fire, Gehenna and the nether world are similar conceptions.

ADONAI. One of the names of God. It is a plural of majesty and signifies "my lord." In Jewish tradition, it is the word which designates God and replaces the "ineffable Name" (YHWH), which no one was permitted to pronounce. See **LORD. NAME. YAHWEH.**

ALLELUIA. Triumphal acclamation signifying: "Praise God," which is often found at the beginning or the end of certain psalms (105-107; 135; Rv 19, 1). It has passed over, untranslated, into the Catholic liturgy.

ALPHA AND OMEGA. The first and last letters of the Greek alphabet. The Hebrews used these two letters to symbolize the fulness, the eternity of God. The Christians inherited this tradition and used alpha and omega to express their belief that in Jesus, the Son of God, is to be found all grace and truth (Rv 1, 8; 21, 6; 22, 13).

ALTAR. A stone or pile of stones, or any structure or place on which sacrifices were burned or incense was offered to God. In the temple at Jerusalem there was an altar of bronze. Solomon had a special altar constructed for burning incense (2 Chr 4, 1).

AMEN. A Hebrew word meaning, "certainly, truly," used to give assent to a statement, a curse, a blessing, a prayer, or the like; in this sense of "so be it," the term came to be employed in Jewish worship and as such the Christian liturgy also uses it after prayers and blessings. In the Gospels, Jesus uses it to give force to his statements (Mt 5, 18. 26). However, the present translation does not reproduce "Amen" but translates it according to the sense of the context.

ANANIAS. Three persons bear this name in the New Testament: (1) the husband of Sapphira (Acts 5); (2) a Christian who received Paul after his conversion (Acts 9 and 22); (3) a high priest who ordered St. Paul to be slapped (Acts 23) and was later assassinated (66 A.D.).

ANATHEMA (DOOMED). In Hebrew: *herem*, which originally signified some thing (or person) set aside from profane use and made sacred to the Lord (Dt 12, 12ff; Jos 11, 11. 14). Hence, it could not be appropriated by anyone; in a good number of cases, the obligation existed to destroy it. This often barbaric custom expressed God's absolute rights over every creature. In the course of time, the term was softened and came to refer to nothing more than objects offered to God (Lv 27, 28; Ez 44, 27; Mk 7, 11). The Greek term *anathema* in the New Testament is used in the sense of "cursed," "separated from God." Later Christianity used this word in the sense of "excommunication" (1 Cor 12, 3: "let a curse be upon him").

ANCIENTS. The forebears of Israel, whose traditions were supposed to be the authority for the unwritten law (Mt 5, 27-33; 15, 2). See **ELDERS.**

ANGEL OF THE LORD. Someone who has received a divine delegation, through whom God reveals himself, says, or does something (Jgs 6, 11ff). In numerous biblical texts, the word designates the visible manifestation of God (Gn 16, 7-13; Zec 3, 1ff). In the New Testament, *angels* are heavenly spirits (Heb 1, 7).

ANGER (WRATH) OF GOD. This expression is to be compared with other similar expressions: repentance, jealousy, hand and arm of God. It is an "anthropomorphism," a figure of speech, an image. Seeking to explain the external phenomena supposedly produced by God (storms, floods, earthquakes, catastrophes), we attribute to him sentiments or attitudes which would be found in similar circumstances among men (Ps 78; Dt 32, 15ff; Is 1, 18-20; Lk 13, 3-5).

ANTICHRIST. This word, which is found only in the Epistles of St. John (1 Jn 2, 18-22; 4, 3; 2 Jn 7), designates a personage who is at once both an enemy of Christ and his evildoing imitator. The idea stems from the Jewish writers of the age preceding Christianity. These described the Messiah as having to appear at the end of times to renew all things, but as having to take part in a very violent struggle against a mysterious Adversary. This idea is found throughout the New Testament. Paul calls him "the man of lawlessness," "the son of perdition and adversity" (2 Thes 2, 3. 8; 2 Cor 6, 15). Matthew, Mark and Revelation seem to refer to a collectivity of persons (Mt 24, 23f; Mk 13, 14-20; Rv 13, 17; 17, 7-14).

ANTIOCH. Capital of the Roman province of Syria, it was the most active center of early Christianity (Acts 11, 26).

APOCRYPHA. Religious books used by both Jews and Christians which were not included in the collection of inspired writings. In the Protestant Church, this term designates the books of Tobit, Judith, Maccabees, Wisdom, Baruch, and Ecclesiasticus, which were introduced rather late into the collection of the Bible. Catholics call them "deuterocanonical" books.

APOSTLES. Twelve men chosen by Christ to enjoy special jurisdiction and to teach. They are: Peter, Andrew, James, John, Philip, Bartholomew, Thomas, Matthew, James the Less, Jude, Simon the Zealot and Judas, who was replaced by Matthias. Within the circle of Jesus' disciples, the Twelve were given a privileged position. They alone were present with him at the Last Supper (Mk 14, 17). Later they exercised leadership over the primitive community in Jerusalem (Acts 1, 26; 2, 14; 5, 20f), and were responsible for the information about Jesus that developed into the gospel tradition (Acts 6, 2. 4). Paul and Barnabas are also called Apostles (Gal 2, 7ff), which means literally "one who is sent" (Lk 24, 35. 48; Mt 28, 19-20).

ARK OF THE COVENANT. Wooden chest, overlaid with gold, fashioned by Moses, which contained the two tablets of the law (Ex 25, 10-16; 37, 1-5). It was the symbol of the covenant and God's presence among his people. God was pictured as resting his feet on its golden lid (called "propitiatory"). The ark was placed in the sanctuary of the temple (1 Kgs 8, 1-9) in Jerusalem and disappeared in its ruin at the destruction of the city by the Chaldeans in 586 B.C. (2 Kgs 25, 1-21).

ARMOR. Leather or metal covering which was worn by warriors. It included a helmet, breastplate and shield (Eph 6, 13-17).

ASIA. In the New Testament, used of the Roman Province of Asia, which included only the western third of what is now Asia Minor. Ephesus was its capital, and of its other important cities and districts many are mentioned in the New Testament. The evangelization of the province was accomplished by St. Paul on his third missionary journey (Acts 18—21), St. Peter addressed the churches of Asia (1 Pt 1, 7), and the Book of Revelation conveys messages to each of its most important cities, the "seven churches" (Rv 1, 4ff).

ASSYRIA. A country occupying the northern and middle part of Mesopotamia, including Babylonia and Chaldea. The Assyrians were probably of Semitic origin, descendants of Asshur, one of the sons of Shem (Gn 10, 22). An independent kingdom began about the seventeenth century B.C. In 605 B.C. Nineveh was destroyed by the Medes and Babylonians, and Assyria became a province of these countries.

ASTARTE. Phoenician goddess of fertility, often associated with Baal. Her cult experienced great success in Palestine and her attraction frequently led the Hebrews into idolatry (Jgs 2, 13; 10, 6; 2 Kgs 17, 16).

AZYMES. Unleavened bread which was the only kind permitted during the week of the Jewish Passover. They recalled at the same time the agricultural feast of the barley harvest and the exodus from Egypt, when the Hebrews in their haste were unable to have their dough leavened (Ex 34, 25; 23, 18).

BAAL. This Hebrew word is translated as master, lord. It designates the chief god of the Canaanites and the Phoenicians. His cult was preserved by the Hebrews in Palestine, in spite of the efforts of the prophets (1 Kgs 16, 31-33). The word Baal also designates small local gods (Jgs 2, 11).

BABYLON. Capital of Babylonia, to which many Jewish captives were deported after the fall of Jerusalem in 586 B.C.; this is known as the Babylonian Captivity (2 Kgs 25, 7ff). The name was then applied to any nation hostile to God (Rv 14; 17; etc.).

BALANCES. Scales for weighing money and other items. The moral necessity of a just balance and true weights and the iniquity of false ones are frequently emphasized by the prophets (Am 8, 5; Mi 6, 11).

BAPTISM. The baptism of John the Baptist (Mt 3, 1) is thought to stem from the rabbinical custom of baptizing proselytes who had converted to the faith of Israel (Mt 21, 25). This seems to be a remembrance of the baptism the Jewish people received in crossing the sea (1 Cor 10, 1-2) to acquire the law at Sinai and to attain the promised land. The events of the Exodus foreshadowed the imminent coming of the Lord. Jesus himself underwent baptism to inaugurate his mission (Mt 3, 13ff; Jn 1, 32). He thus became one with the Jewish people and took personal charge of them (Is 53). In this sense, baptism was a preparation for the cross (Mk 10, 38; Lk 12, 50). After the Redemption, baptism became a sacrament for entering a new state of grace (Mt 28, 19; Acts 2, 38-41), the way of regeneration to the divine life.

BEELZEBUL (BAALZEBUB). Name of the god of the nation of Canaan. In the Old Testament it appears under the form *Baalzebub*, "Baal (Lord) of Flies." Later association with the Aramaic *beeldebaba*, "enemy," gave the ancient name its connotation of "devil," and the New Testament uses Beelzebul to refer to the prince of demons (Mt 10, 25; 12, 24; Lk 11, 15).

BETHEL. In Hebrew: house of God. This town was originally called Luz. It is there that Abraham established one of the first sanctuaries and that Jacob had the famous vision of the ladder (Gn 12, 8; 13, 3 and 28, 10). King Jeroboam established the idol of the golden calf here after the schism of the northern tribes (1 Kgs 12, 26-30). The prophets saw therein the symbol of idolatry and gave it the surname of *Bethaven*, house of iniquity (Hos 4, 15).

BISHOP. Greek word signifying "overseer." From the beginning, it has designated the heads of the Christian communities, also called "presbyters" or "elders" (1 Tm 3, 1-7).

BLESSING. The word *bless* changes its meaning according to whether its subject is God or man. Man blesses God by his acts of adoration and thanksgiving (Ps 103, 1. 2); men bless other men by wishing them well or happiness (Mt 5, 44). The ancient Hebrews believed that such wishes were always efficacious (belief in magic) just as they did in the case of maledictions which are the opposite of blessings.

God blesses men by giving them material or spiritual benefits (Gn 24, 1).

Finally, man pronounces blessings on objects, on nourishment, to consecrate them to God (1 Cor 10, 16) or on persons, to sanctify them (Gn 49).

BLOOD. According to the ancients, blood is the seat and sign of life over which only God has power and so must be respected (Gn 9, 4). It is forbidden to consume it in the various offerings (Lv 1-7). This abstention was extended to the consummation of all fleshly nourishment. In the solemn sacrifice of the Day of Atonement, the blood of the victim was spilled over the ark of the convenant. Hence, the blood of Christ, who died for men, has in the eyes of Christians taken on an expiatory value (Heb 9, 28).

BREAD. In an extended sense, this often designates all that is necessary for subsistence. In the Gospels, we find the expression "bread of life," and "living bread" (Jn 6, 31-35), an image by which Jesus affirms that he is the principle of eternal life; at the same time it suggests the use of the Eucharist. Bread of heaven refers first of all to manna and secondly to the sacrament of the Eucharist.

In the Acts of the Apostles, the rite of breaking bread designates the Eucharist (Acts 2, 42).

BREAK BREAD. Among the Jews, the person who presided at the repast would break bread and distribute it to those at table. This is what Jesus did at the multiplication of the loaves (Mt 14, 19) and the Last Supper (Mt 26, 26).

BROTHERS OF THE LORD. Persons who formed part of Jesus' entourage. Among them are James, Joseph, Jude, and Simon. They are "relatives" of Jesus. For Greek-speaking Semites used the terms *adelphos* and *adelphe* not only in the ordinary sense of blood brother and sister but also for nephew, niece, half-brother, half-sister and cousin. Since, according to tradition, Jesus was Mary's only child, this expression is understood in the sense of "cousin," as belonging to the same blood (Mk 6, 1-6).

CAIAPHAS. High priest functioning at Jerusalem from the year 18 to 36 A.D. He was the son-in-law of the former high priest Annas and involved in the conspiracy to destroy Jesus (Jn 11, 49; Mt 26, 57). He was deposed by the legate of Syria, Vitellius, after the recall of Pontius Pilate in 36 A.D.

CALENDAR. (1) The civil *day* was reckoned from sunset to sunset, and hence Jewish Sabbaths and feasts began with the setting of the sun. (2) The *hours* of the day were twelve, beginning at about our 6:00 A.M. and ending at 6:00 P.M. The third, sixth, ninth and twelfth hours were specially sacred to prayer. The night was divided into four watches, the evening watch beginning at 6:00 P.M., the midnight watch at 9:00, "cockcrow" at 12:00, the morning watch at 3:00 A.M. (3) The *week* contained seven days ending in the sabbath, or "Rest." The "first day of the week" became sacred for Christians because of Christ's Resurrection (Jn 20, 19; Acts 20, 7). (4) The *year* consisted of twelve lunar months of twenty-nine or thirty days — i.e., 354 days. The month began with the new moon, and this first day was observed as a holy day. To preserve the proper relation between the lunar and solar calendars, an extra lunar month was intercalated every two or three years. The first month, Nisan, always began on the new moon nearest to and preceding the vernal equinox, March 21.

CANAANITE. Inhabitant of the country of Canaan situated east•of the Jordan River (Mt 15, 22). At the time of Jesus, a variant of this word ("Canaanean," translated from the Greek as "Zealot") signified a political party which laid claim to national independence. The apostle Simon was a member of this movement (Mt 10, 4).

CAPTIVITY. This word denotes the exile and deportation of the northern kingdom into Babylonia in 721 (2 Kgs 17—18) and more especially of the southern kingdom in 586 (2 Kgs 25). After the latter date, Israel continually asks God for deliverance from her slavery, the return of the exiles, and the restoration of the chosen people. In 539 Cyrus the Great conquered Babylonia and allowed the Israelites to return home (Ezr 1, 1-4). From then on the Babylonian captivity became a symbol of man's state after Adam's sin from which Jesus has delivered him (Heb 2, 14-15).

CENTURION. Officer in charge of a century (originally 100 men), sixtieth part of the Roman legion. Legionnaires in Palestine were recruited locally, but officers were Roman (Mt 8, 5-13).

CHALICE-CUP. These words are often taken in a figurative sense. For a cup contains either a bitter beverage, symbol of trial (the cup of the divine wrath, for example) (Rv 15, 7) or a sweet beverage, symbol of divine blessing (Rv 5, 8). Since the Last Supper, in which it contained Christ's blood, it has become the expression for the eucharistic mystery (1 Cor 10, 21). In another sense, the word signifies man's destiny, fixed by God. Indeed, in an apportionment the lots to be drawn were in a cup (Ps 16, 5-6).

CHARISM. Word copied from the Greek. It designates, in the Epistles of St. Paul, certain extraordinary spiritual gifts, enabling Christians to collaborate fruitfully in the building up of the mystical body of Christ. For example, the gifts of healing, preaching, and teaching (1 Cor 13).

CHARITY. Word taken from the Latin *caritas* but translating the Greek term *agape*. It designates a very elevated and pure love similar to the love of God for men and the love of Christians for God and their brothers. This word is not to be confused with the sense of almsgiving, or charitable work. The fraternal meals of the first Christians often followed by the Eucharist received the name *agape* (Jude 12; 2 Pt 2, 13) translated by "feast" in this Bible.

CHRIST. This word, derived from the Greek, signifies "anointed" and translates the Hebrew word for *Messiah*. The Hebrew king was anointed with holy oil: so was the high priest (2 Sm 12, 7; Ex 29, 21). In the Bible, it is the title given to the one who, in the future, will come to restore Israel (Dn 9, 25-26). Jesus presents himself as the expected Messiah (Mk 14, 62). St. Paul and the first Christians gave him the name *Christos* (past participle of the verb) which quickly became a proper name: Jesus Christ, Christ Jesus, or simply Christ (Acts 17, 3). *See* **JESUS.**

CHRISTIAN. This word is derived from *Christ*. It was used for the first time at Antioch around 35 A.D. to designate the disciples of Jesus Christ who until then had been called *Nazoreans* (Acts 11, 26).

CHURCH. (1) Among the Hebrews, this word designates the sacred assembly of the Israelites (cf Jgs 21, 8 where it is translated "assembly"). (2) In the New Testament, it refers first to the assembly of the Christians of Jerusalem (Acts 5, 11). Later, the word was applied to each of the communities founded by St. Paul (1 Cor 1, 2). Finally, it designates the totality of Christians and that ideal church which will be fully realized only at the end of times. In this sense, the church is the body of Christ (Mt 16, 18).

CIRCUMCISION. Removal of the prepuce. It is a very ancient ethical practice which the Hebrews converted into a religious rite. Abraham received it as a sign of the covenant (Gn 17, 10ff). Later, the prophets stressed the fact that this bodily mark has no value unless it is accompanied by an "internal circumcision" signifying moral purity (Jer 9, 25f).

COMING. Translation of the Greek word *parousia*. This word designates the second coming of Christ for the last judgment (Mt 24, 3; 1 Thes 4, 15). The belief in a twofold messianic coming distinguishes the Christian mentality from Jewish messianism.

COMMUNION. State in which the faithful is united to God, is close to God, and enjoys his intimacy. Christianity has as its object to place us in communion with the Father and the Son through the action of the Holy Spirit, that is, to give us a share in the divine life (Jn 15). In the Bible, the word never signifies sacramental communion in the Eucharist.

CONSECRATE. Withdrawal of an object or person from secular use so as to transfer it into the domain of God and keep it there (Ex 13, 1; 30, 29).

CONVERSION. This word is frequently associated with other terms of repentance and penitence. It signifies changing one's life. In their preaching, the apostles ask that their hearers be converted (repent) and be baptized (Acts 2, 38). In the Bible, the word conversion is never used in the sense of "changing one's religion."

COVENANT. Man has always sought to place himself in contact with the divinity. In sacred history, this contact has taken the form of a kind of contract between God and the people of Israel. But there had already been a personal covenant between God and Noah (Gn 6, 18-22), and between God and Abraham (with the sign of circumcision: Gn 17, 10-14). This covenant is made by God without the opinion of the other party being asked. It is therefore gratuitous. But it is bilateral by reason of the promises of the contracting parties: the people promise to observe the law, and God promises to reward fidelity (Ex 19, 4-8; Dt 5, 1-21).

Unfortunately, the people were often unfaithful. It is then that the prophets promise (for the messianic times) a new covenant in which the union between God and man will no longer be solely in a national religion but in an interior and spiritual piety (Jer 31, 31-34; 11, 1-17).

This hope is realized by the Gospel in Jesus Christ, in whom Christians receive the grace promised (Mt 26, 28; Heb 10, 9-18).

Hence, the two parts of the Bible were designated by the first Christians with the terms Old Covenant, New Covenant. However, since the Greek word *diatheke* (covenant) also signifies testament, the custom arose (we do not know why) in Latin and the modern languages of using this latter word, even though the meaning is almost incomprehensible.

CREATION. This notion is at the basis of the faith of Israel. It is presented not only as an abstract notion (2 Mc 7, 28), but also as the corollary to the existence of an active Creator, present in the world (Ps 104; Jb 38). It expresses itself in popular cosmological descriptions of the time (Gn 1—3) and establishes the fundamental relation between man and God in the Judaeo-Christian religion. The revelation and redemption of the Messiah sometimes appears as a re-creation: "new world," "new heaven" (Is 45, 8), reestablishing the order and first destiny of things and of men, lost through sin.

CROSS. This instrument of Roman torture reserved for slaves was particularly infamous. It was known to Jesus who preached a type of detachment to his disciples which would go as far as this humiliation of the cross (Mt 10, 38). He himself followed this way of self-denial out of love and obedience (Phil 2, 8). The death on the cross of the Messiah, Son of God, is a scandal, the paradox which will become the most incontestable historical and spiritual center of the work of salvation accomplished by Jesus (1 Cor 1, 18-23). By his abasement on the cross which paid men's debt to sin and crushed the devil (1 Cor 2, 8; Col 2, 14) Jesus is elevated (2 Cor 13, 4) and the wood of infamy has become a tree of life (Rv 2, 7). Crucified with Christ through baptism and the life of faith (Gal 2, 19; Rom 6, 6), the Christian must glory only in the cross of Jesus (Gal 6, 12-15).

DAGON. Word derived from the root *dag*: fish. It is the name originally of a Mesopotamian deity who became the principal god of the Philistines. His body was half-man and half-fish (Jgs 16, 23).

DAMASCUS. Capital of Syria, destroyed in 732 B.C. (2 Kgs 16, 9), which had a large Jewish population. It was the scene of Paul's conversion (Acts 9, 1-27).

DARKNESS. Absence of light. In the Bible God, who is eternal truth, is considered the true light and the source of all light (Is 10, 17); therefore darkness becomes a symbol of estrangement from God. Jesus said that those who followed him would not walk in darkness (John 8, 12), i.e., he would show them clearly the truth.

DAY OF THE LORD (JUDGMENT). This is the day on which God will judge. The judgment is often conceived of as a punishment. The "day of the Lord" was announced by the prophets as affecting chiefly the pagan nations, who were guilty of attacking and enslaving the people of God (Is 2, 12-22). Later, the same prophets will affirm that the judgment will also touch Israel (Zep 1, 7. 14-18) and, at the end of times, all mankind (Zec 14, 1-7). In the New Testament, this idea persists, and it is toward this glorious manifestation of Christ that the whole of Christian hope tends (1 Cor 1, 8; 1 Thes 5, 2. 4).

DEACON. This word signifies: server, assistant. It has taken on a particular meaning with the institution of the deacons in the early church to serve the poor and assist the apostles (Acts 6, 1-6).

DEMON. The Jews recognized the existence of destructive evil spirits, wicked powers dedicated to doing harm. These are the demons, enslaved by Satan, who dwell within and stir up those who are possessed (Mt 8, 28-32).

DESERT. This word holds a major place in biblical thought: it is in the desert that the people has experienced divine intimacy (Ex 19). The desert symbolizes the desolate sojourn of the times of trial. Jesus withdraws to the desert before beginning his ministry (Mt 4, 1).

DIASPORA (DISPERSION). This word designates the Jews scattered throughout the pagan regions of the Roman Empire (Jn 7, 35).

DIVORCE. The Bible presents marriage as a union of the natural order, indissoluble and allowable once for each couple, in order to assure the mutual complement of man and woman (Gn 2, 24). Moses, for reasons of "hardness of heart" and in order to limit the abuses of polygamy, codified the custom of repudiation then in use, exacting a tribute, that is, a written piece of paper which the married man had to give his wife signifying that her freedom was restored. He was not allowed to take her back again (Dt 24, 1-4). Our Lord, in bringing the law of charity and a higher moral order, renewed the natural precept of Gn 2, 24, and gave marriage its original unity and indissolubility (Mt 19, 3; 5, 32; Mk 10, 2; Lk 16, 18).

ELDER. In the Old Testament the word refers to an official class having both civil and religious jurisdiction (Ex 3, 16; 24, 1). In the New Testament it refers to an official of the early Christian church, such as a bishop or priest (Acts 20, 17. 28; Jas 5, 14).

ELECT, ELECTION. This refers to the divine choice. (1) Abraham is chosen and taken from his family and country. This election culminates in the election of Israel (Gn 12, 1-7; Ex 19, 1-9). (2) Certain persons are said to be chosen (David, the Messiah) (2 Sm 7, 14ff). (3) Jesus is called the elect ("chosen one") of God (Lk 23, 35). (4) Christ chooses his apostles (Mt 10, 2-4). (5) All Christians are the object of a divine election (Rom 1, 6).

ELOHIM. Ordinary Hebrew word for God. It is the plural of majesty. Elohim ordinarily designates God in his action on the world in contrast to Yahweh which is used of the God of the covenant (Ex 3, 14).

ESSENES. The Dead Sea Scrolls have indicated that the Essenes ranked in importance with the Pharisees and Sadducees. There were about 4000 Essenes although only 200 lived in Qumran, their most important center. A member had to undergo a one-year "postulancy" and a three-year "novitiate." He then vowed to be reverent, just, hate sinners, help the just, obey his superiors, tell the truth, share his property, and keep Essene teaching secret. Meals and ritual baths were of great importance. Some think that John the Baptist was a member of this sect (Lk 1, 80; 3, 1-21).

ETERNAL. This corresponds to the Hebrew word *olam*, signifying a long period of time; these terms indicate primarily something that perdures throughout the centuries (Gn 17, 8); then something that has neither beginning nor end, like God (Gn 21, 33); and, finally, something outside of time (1 Jn 5, 11-12).

EXPIATION-PROPITIATION. Translation of the Hebrew *Kippur* signifying pardon or suppression of sin. Jesus is called "expiation" because he assures pardon of all sins (Rom 3, 25).

FAITH. In the Old Testament, faith is rarely mentioned. Its essential component is trust in God. Thus, Abraham's trust becomes the type of true faith (Gal 3, 6). In the New Testament, faith holds a predominant place: Jesus requires faith in himself which presupposes the acceptance of his message and trust in the person of the Master (Jn 6, 29-40) In St. Paul, faith is the chief element of his tĕaching and the key to salvation (Rom 1, 16).

FASTS. The chief Jewish fast was that of the Day of Atonement known as "the (autumn) fast" (Acts 27, 9). The especially devout customarily fasted on the second and fifth days of the week (Mt 9, 14; Lk 18, 12). Our Lord's great fast (Mt 4, 2) was foreshadowed by those of Moses (Ex 24, 18) and Elijah (1 Kgs 19, 8).

FEAR OF GOD. (1) Feeling experienced before any kind of divine manifestation: dread, fear, dismay (Ex 20, 18ff). (2) The same word also serves to denote the service of God, religion (Dt 4, 10). (3) The term "God-fearer" was used of a pagan who had adopted Jewish religious practices, without however belonging completely to the religion of Israel (Acts 10, 1).

FEASTS. In memory of the rest of God after the work of creation, the Jews kept as sacred the seventh day, or sabbath, the seventh month, the seventh or sabbatical year, and the fiftieth or jubilee year (Gn 2, 1-3; Lv 25, 1-22).

The weekly sabbath was observed by special sacrifices, by rest from servile work, and by attendance at religious instruction (Ex 20, 8-11; Lv 23, 2f).

The first day of the month, the New Moon, was a holy day on which special offerings were made (Nm 28, 11-15; Col 2, 16).

The three major feasts of the year, on which male Israelites were required to go to the temple, were Passover, in March or April, Pentecost, fifty days later, and Tabernacles, toward the end of September.

Passover began on the evening of the fourteenth Nisan with the eating of the lamb. On the fourteenth, after all leaven had been removed from the house, the lamb was sacrificed at the temple, and then brought home for cooking. It was eaten with herbs and unleavened bread in memory of the going out of Israel from Egypt (Lv 23, 5f; Heb 11, 27-29). The following week was known as the days of the Unleavened Bread (Lv 23, 6-8). The eve of the sabbath within this week was the Preparation Day (Mt 27, 62). During this week the first-fruits of the barley harvest were presented as the opening of the seven weeks of harvest.

Pentecost recalled the giving of the law, and it offered in thanks the first-fruits of the wheat harvest (Lv 23, 15-11). At Pentecost the Holy Spirit came upon the apostles and the others gathered in the Upper Room (Acts 2, 1ff).

Tabernacles was celebrated in the month of Tishri. The first day of that month was the feast of Trumpets, the civil New Year. On the tenth fell the Day of Atonement, a day of fast and of expiatory sacrifices, when the high priest entered the holy of holies to sprinkle blood (Lv 16; 23, 23-36; Nm 29, 7-11). From the fifteenth to the twenty-first of the month the feast of Tabernacles (Booths) was celebrated. It recalled the wanderings of the Israelites in the desert. This week marked the end of the harvest of fruit, wine and oil (Lv 23, 39-43). The last day of the feast was a day of rest on which were observed the ceremonies of water libation and the lighting of the four great golden candelabra (Jn 7, 37; 8, 12).

Two minor feasts were kept during the winter, Dedication and Purim (Lots). The former was held in our December, and was a joyous commemoration of the rededication of the temple by Judas Maccabeus (1 Mc 4, 56-59). It was also known as the feast of Lights, since during it the temple was illuminated (Jn 10, 22). Purim, held at the close of winter, recalled the rescue of the Jews by Esther when Haman cast lots to determine the day on which they should be destroyed (Est 9, 20-32; 2 Mc 15, 36).

FIGURE (TYPE). A person, event, or object which in God's intention signifies or foreshadows something else. Many realities of the Old Testament foreshadowed those of the New (Heb 7, 1-22).

FIRE. This is used as a symbol to express the divinity which radiates and consumes at the same time, with a joyous or terrifying aspect: God present in the fire on Mt. Sinai, in a storm (Ex 19, 18). On the altar of the temple, there was a perpetual fire (Lv 6, 5; 2 Chr 4, 1). God, a devouring fire, consumes Sodom and Gomorrah (Gn 19, 24-25). Jesus is said to baptize "with fire," that is, with the Holy Spirit (Mt 3, 11).

FIRST-BORN. By right, every first-born male must be reserved for God. He must be either immolated or (since infant-sacrifice was abolished by the Hebrews) redeemed (Ex 13, 2; Nm 3, 11-13). The title "first-born" could be given to the boy even if he had no brother or sister. And it entailed the privilege of "birthright," entitling him to a position of honor in the family and to a double share in the possessions inherited from the father (Ex 25, 31). Jesus is called the first-born of creation because of his position as the head of mankind (Heb 1, 6).

FIRST-FRUITS. The first fruits of the season which out of obligation were offered to God (Ex 23, 19). Paul calls Jesus "the first fruits" of the dead, showing that his resurrection will be followed by theirs (1 Cor 15, 20. 23).

FLESH. (1) First meaning: the flesh of an animal in contrast to the blood and bones (Gn 9, 3ff). (2) Everything that has life (Gn 6, 13). (3) Man in contrast to God by reason of his weakness; hence, the person, human nature (Mt 26, 41). (4) Especially in St. Paul's Epistles, natural man, without grace, with his weaknesses and tendencies toward sin, in contrast to the "spirit" which designates the faculty that enables man to share in the Holy Spirit through the new birth of baptism (Rom 7, 14).

FOREIGNERS. Term reserved for those who were not of Hebrew stock, the Gentiles (Ex 12, 44).

GALILEE. The most northerly region of Palestine and the most favored by nature. Among its flourishing towns were Cana, Chorazin, Nazareth, Capernaum, Bethsaida, Tiberias. The population was predominantly Jewish, but there was a noticeable Galilean dialect (Mt 26, 73). The Galileans were very loyal to their religion and nation, though regarded by the Judeans as ignorant and lawless (Jn 7, 41; Mk 14, 70). Our Lord was reared in Galilee, he spent most of his time preaching there, and all but one of his apostles were from Galilee.

GALILEE, SEA OF. A lake which formed the eastern boundary of Galilee. It was also called the Lake of Gennesaret, from the plain on its northwest corner (Lk 5, 1), and the Sea of Tiberias, from the city of this name, the residence of Herod Antipas (Jn 6, 1). The lake is about thirteen miles long and six broad.

GEHENNA. This comes from the Hebrew "Valley of Hinnom," a place near Jerusalem where ritual infant-sacrifices had been practiced (2 Chr 28, 3). This place was later used as a depot for refuse. The word became synonymous with place of malediction (Jer 7, 31) and then in the New Testament with the abode of the damned, a place of torment, unquenchable fire and the consuming worm (Mt 5, 29; 10, 28; 18, 8f; Mk 9, 44ff). *See* **SHEOL**.

GETHSEMANI. This word, which signifies "oil press," became the name for a plantation of olive trees located opposite the temple of Jerusalem, east of the torrent of Kidron. This is the "mount of Olives," scene of Christ's agony and betrayal (Mt 26, 36-56).

GLORY. A very important notion in biblical theology. In Hebrew *(kabod)*, the word designates "to be heavy," "to be illustrious." It often denotes the radiant manifestation of God in his grandeur (Ez 1, 28). This divine glory is possessed by Jesus (Jn 1, 14). According to St. Paul, every Christian shares in this divine glory already here below (Phil 3, 21).

GOEL. *See* **KIN, NEXT OF**.

GOLGOTHA. Aramaic word signifying "skull place." It was the name of a little hill located northwest of the city of Jerusalem. Those condemned were executed there, and it was here that Jesus suffered crucifixion (Mt 27, 33). The Latin rendering of this word is *Calvaria* which is the origin of our "Calvary."

GOOD NEWS. *See* **GOSPEL**.

GOSPEL. In Greek, this word signifies good news, and specifically the good news of the Kingdom of God (Heb 4, 2; Mt 4, 23). St. Paul uses the word to indicate his preaching; later, the same word will be applied to the accounts of Christ's life (1 Cor 9, 16; Rom 1, 3).

GRACE. This word (in Greek: *doxa*) has a great variety of meanings: favor, benevolence, benefit. Hence, it signifies God's gratuitous love which makes the creature its acceptable beneficiary (Rom 11, 5. 6). The grace par excellence is salvation, justification (Eph 2, 5). In the plural—graces—it signifies the supernatural gifts and helps given to each one by the Holy Spirit.

HASIDEANS. This word is derived from the Hebrew word *hasidim*, "pious ones," and designates the faithful servants of God. They are mentioned in the book of Proverbs (2, 8) and in the Psalms (40, 5; 50, 5; 148, 14). They played a leading part during the resistance directed by Judas Maccabeus (1 Mc 2, 42 and 7, 6; 2 Mc 14, 6). They are undoubtedly at the origin of the Essenes, the brotherhood established in the monastery of Qumran which left us the famous Dead Sea Scrolls.

HEART. The Hebrews regarded the heart as the seat not only of emotions but also of thoughts and voluntary acts. Thus, the heart represents the whole man (Jl, 2, 13; 1 Pt 3, 4).

HEAVEN. This word has several meanings: (1) the firmament in which the stars are perceived (Gn 1, 14-17); (2) the region of the atmosphere where the birds fly (Dt 4, 17); (3) the place of God's residence, the throne-room where the Everlasting One is seated surrounded by the angels (Mt 5, 12; 24, 36). Jewish tradition had imagined several heavens or firmaments superimposed on one another, populated with various kinds of angels. It is in this sense that they spoke of the "heavenly host" and that St. Paul spoke of having been caught up in ecstasy "to the third heaven" (2 Cor 12, 2).

HELL. The place of eternal punishment, also called Gehenna. *See* **GEHENNA. SHEOL.**

HELLENIST. A Jew, or a Jew turned Christian, living in a foreign land and speaking Greek (Acts 6, 1).

HERITAGE. *See* **INHERITANCE.**

HEROD. The Herodian family, though Jewish in religion, was Idumean in origin. Herod "the Great" (B.C. 62 to 4) was appointed by Rome as king of Judea in B.C. 40, to the exclusion of the native Hasmonean line. He rebuilt the temple, and was in general an efficient ruler, but his cruelties made him odious. He slaughtered the infants at Bethlehem (Mt 2, 16-18). Four of his children are mentioned in the New Testament: Archelaus, Antipas and two named Philip.

Archelaus, ethnarch of Judea (4 B.C.-6 A.D.), was deposed on account of his cruelty and exiled to Vienne in Gaul.

Antipas, tetrarch of Galilee and Perea, was deposed in 39 A.D. He divorced his wife, the daughter of King Aretas, and married Herodias, the wife of his brother Philip, who resided in Rome. He imprisoned and later beheaded John the Baptizer (Mt 14, 1ff). He was present in Jerusalem at the time of our Lord's trial (Lk 23, 7-12).

Philip, tetrarch of Trachonitis (4 B.C.—34 A.D.) unlike his brothers, was a moderate and peaceful ruler.

Two other descendants of Herod are also mentioned in the New Testament. Herod Agrippa I, grandson of Herod the Great, was king of all Palestine from 41 to 44 A.D. He was a strict observer of Judaism, and a persecutor of Christianity (Acts 12, 1ff). His death is mentioned in Acts 12, 23. His son, Agrippa II, ruled in Trachonitis until his death in 100 A.D. This Agrippa and his sister Bernice heard St. Paul's defense (Acts 25—26). Another sister, Drusilla, was married to the procurator Felix (Acts 24, 24).

HERODIANS. These were partisans and courtiers of the reigning dynasty of the Herods. Though they were Jews in religion, their spirit was Gentile. They conspired with their enemies the Pharisees against Christ (Mt 22, 16).

HERODIAS. Daughter of Aristobulus and granddaughter of Herod the Great and Mariamme. She was the wife of Philip but left him to marry Antipas. Her daughter Salome (who has unfortunately achieved some notoriety) resulted from the first marriage (Mt 14, 6-10).

HIGH PLACES. In Hebrew *bamoth* designates the sanctuaries ordinarily built on the heights by the inhabitants of Canaan (Nm 33, 52) as well as the Hebrews before the temple was built (1 Kgs 3, 2). However, later they became the symbol of idolatry for Israel, a symbol to which the ancient Jewish people constantly returned, in spite of the prohibition of Deuteronomy (12, 4ff), and the constant condemnations of the prophets (Ez 6, 3-6).

HIGH PRIEST. The chief of the sacred ministers among the Jews. He was supreme in religious matters, and to him was reserved the exclusive right of offering the great sacrifice of expiation and of entering the holy of holies (Heb 9, 7). Through him at times God announced things to come (Jn 11, 51). He was a member of the Sanhedrin and ordinarily presided over its deliberations (Mt 26, 57; Acts 4, 5f; 5, 27; etc.). Induction into this high priesthood was by anointing or by investiture in the precious robes of the office. The dignity descended at first by primogeniture from Aaron and the elder branch of Aaron's family and was held for life. But in the days of Christ the high priests were appointed and removed at will by the Herods and the Roman procurators. During the lifetime of our Lord some fifteen different individuals held the office, the most noted of whom were Annas (6-5 A.D.) and his son-in-law Caiaphas (18-36 A.D.). Annas and Caiaphas, often named together, judged Christ (Jn 18, 13. 24), Peter and John (Acts 4, 6), then all the Apostles (Acts 5, 17ff) and St. Stephen (Acts 6, 12ff), while Ananias acted against Paul (Acts 23, 2; 24, 1).

HOLOCAUST. In the ancient sacrifices only the blood and certain parts of the victim were offered to God; the rest was divided among the priest and faithful who had offered it (Lv 7, 11-21). A holocaust (from the Greek "wholly burned") was a sacrifice in which an entire animal except its hide was consumed in the fire on the altar, with the primary purpose of rendering glory to God (Lv 1, 1ff).

HOLY (SANCTIFY). The term "holy" is applied to anything that is consecrated to God, and hence withdrawn from all (secular) human use. In this sense, holy or sacred implies that no one can touch the object, for such contact would entail an "impurity" (1 Kgs 8, 4). God is "holy," because he is completely apart from any contact with the universe; but also because he possesses moral perfection. The people of Israel was to be "holy" in order to resemble God (Lv 20, 7. 26). Christians are "holy" because they have been consecrated to God by baptism. They are thus called to achieve moral perfection (Rom 6, 3ff). To

sanctify means to consecrate something or someone to the service of God (Heb 13, 12). God shows himself to be holy by manifesting his justice (Is 5, 16).

HOPE. The messianic hope is at the center of the life of Israel, the source of all its unity, its action, and influence on others. The Hebrew terms which designate it express the tension of a bow ready to shoot its arrow to infinity (Zec 9, 13-14); this hope thus represents a search, an absolute confidence and a concentration of all one's energy flowing from God's covenant with Israel. It does not rest on human resources and initiative, but on the all-powerful Presence of God (Ps 18; 7). It is unshakable in spite of all the vicissitudes of the history of Israel (Mi 7, 7-9; Ps 22, 5-6; Jer 30, 7). It is the constant on which many of the words of the prophets are predicated (Mi 4—5; Is 40ff; Jer 30—33; Ez 40ff). This hope was confirmed and reinforced by the coming of the Messiah, the incarnation and redemption of Christ. Christian hope takes its character from this absolute witness of love and God's fidelity to his promises. It brings the gospel to the far corners of the world as well as souls to a more complete assurance of salvation (Rom 5, 1-11; Heb 6, 18-20) until the end of time (1 Pt 1, 3-5).

HORNS. These are the symbol of power and strength (1 Sm 2, 1). The Bible often speaks of the horns of the altar, ornaments jutting out over the four corners of the altar of the temple of Jerusalem (1 Kgs 1, 50).

HOSANNA Hebrew expression signifying: "may God save," used in the course of Jewish feasts (Ps 118, 25f). It served as an acclamation during Christ's entrance into Jerusalem, in the sense of "Long live," and it is always chanted during the course of Catholic liturgy (Mt 21, 9).

HOSTS. Translation of the Hebrew word *sabaoth* which signifies armies. These armies are either a warrior grouping (material sense) (Ex 14, 17) or the multitude (such as an army) of stars (Ps 33, 6) or angelic beings that express God's glory (Jb 25, 3).

IMPOSITION OF HANDS. The customary Jewish way of designating a person for a task and invoking upon him the divine blessing and power to perform it (Nm 8, 10-11). Jesus used it when healing (Mk 6, 5). By the imposition of hands, the apostles conferred the Holy Spirit (Acts 8, 17), the diaconate (Acts 6, 6), and the priesthood (1 Tm 4, 14).

INHERITANCE. The corresponding Greek indicates a portion (of a share) as the result of drawing lots. This word designates the various parts of the promised land chosen for each Israelite tribe (Jos 15, 1). The word is retained in the New Testament in reference to Jesus who has been constituted by God as the heir of all things (Heb 1, 2); and in reference to Christians, sons and heirs of God, through Jesus Christ (Rom 4, 13-16; 8, 17).

ISRAEL. Proper name signifying "one who struggles with God." The popular explanation of this glorious surname recalling Jacob's struggle (Gn 32, 29) then passes on to his posterity and designates the People of the Promise (Ex 3, 16).

JEALOUS (GOD). This is the translation used for a Hebrew verb which contains the concept of ardor; it can characterize the divine justice as ardent, zealous, and prompt to chastise sinners (Ex 20, 5). God is also termed jealous because since he is unique he cannot allow man not to render single-minded worship to him (Ex 34, 14).

JERUSALEM. In Hebrew, *Yerushalaim*, vision of peace. But the origin of the name seems to be *Ursalim* which signifies "foundation of Salem," a Canaanite divinity. The city was a citadel of the Jebusites (Jgs 1, 8). It was conquered by David who made it his capital (2 Sm 5; 6). Destroyed in 586 B.C., it was rebuilt by the Jews who returned from the exile, in the fifth century before the Christian era (2 Kgs 25, 1-21; Ezr 3—6). It was besieged and destroyed for the second time by the emperor Titus in 70 A.D. At the time of Christ, Jerusalem was the chief city of Palestine and the religious center of Judaism. Situated on a plateau, its walls looked down into deep ravines, the Kidron on the east and the Valley of Hinnom on the south and west. Within the walls the city was divided by the Valley of the Tyropoean, and sloped gradually toward the southeast.

The northeastern part of the city rested on Mount Moriah and was occupied chiefly by the temple and the fortress Antonia. North of the temple were the Sheep Gate and the Pool of Bethesda (Jn 5, 2). The Golden Gate, in the eastern wall of the city, opened on the road to Gethsemani, Mount Olivet, Bethany and Jericho. On its western side the temple had a bridge that led over the Tyropoean to the Upper City. The southeastern section of the city was the ancient city of David, whose walls contained the tower of Siloam (Lk 13, 4) and the various gates that led to the fountains outside the walls. This part of the city was inhabitated largely by priests. The southwestern section of the city contained the business districts, the palaces of Annas and Caiaphas, of Herod and of the Hasmoneans. To the east of it was the Pool of Siloam (Jn 9, 7), and to the south the Valley of Hinnom (a place for refuse) and Akeldama ("Blood Field") (Mt 27, 8; Acts 1, 19).

Another section of the city lay to the northwest, across from the temple. Beyond its walls were fields, gardens and places of burial. The Ephraim Gate which opened here on the highway to Jaffa was not far from the place of the Crucifixion, which lay just outside the city (Jn 19, 17-20; Heb 13, 12).

JESUS. This name, which was common in Israel, signifies "God saves." It was bestowed by God (Lk 1, 31) on the son of the Virgin Mary—who was truly man (Acts 2, 22, 32) and later recognized as Lord (Phil 2, 11) and Savior (2 Tm 1, 10)—in consequence of his mission (Mt 1, 21).

But before being recognized as the Messiah and Son of God, Jesus of Nazareth is taken for the son of Joseph and Mary, and he appears in history at the moment when John the Baptizer is preaching repentance in Judea (Lk 3, 1ff). Jesus wins the admiration of the crowds by his preaching and healing, proclaiming the good news of the kingdom of God and doing good. He is soon followed by numerous disciples and like John his precursor becomes a sign of contradiction for the Judaism of his time (Mt 10, 34; Lk 4, 15; 11, 27). He speaks with authority in the synagogues and is called Teacher and Rabbi. He criticizes the formalism of certain religious practices (the sabbath, ablutions), questions the worship tied down to the perdurance of the temple, and overturns social barriers (publicans and sinners draw near to him). He allows himself to be called Messiah and Son of David by the enthusiastic crowds. However, Jesus knows that this is an ambiguous messianism and so he reveals his true identity to a few of those chosen for their faith (Mt 16, 16; Jn 6, 67-70).

Jesus is condemned as a blasphemer by those who hand him over to the Roman authority to be crucified (Mt 26, 65). Under the Roman procurator Pontius Pilate (26-36 A.D.) he is put to death for the crime of having made himself "King of the Jews."

All the direct testimonies about Jesus and his work (the New Testament) concern firstly his resurrection and the divine character of his person. Foretold by the prophets and all the Scriptures (Lk 18, 31; 24, 25-27; Heb 1, 1ff), Jesus can be known only in the light of the Spirit of God. He will be understood only after his resurrection when he has sent forth this Spirit to the witnesses of his work, chosen by him. They will then recognize him as the Suffering Servant (Mt 3, 17; Phil 2, 7), the Son of David (Jn 7, 41-42), the High Priest and Mediator of the new Covenant (Jn 16, 26; Heb 3, 1; 8, 6), the Son of Man manifested as the savior at the time willed by God (1 Tm 1, 1-5), the Lord, image and Son of God, and God himself (Acts 2, 36; 11, 20; Rom 8, 29; 9, 5; Phil 2, 11; Heb 1, 3); the one who has come from God in the humility of the flesh (Jn 1; 7, 15-16. 27; 8, 14; Phil 2, 6-7) and, after his death, has been exalted by the Father whom he has revealed (Jn 3, 14; 12, 32).

All these titles—Word, Elect or Holy One of God, Lamb of God, Rabbi, Messiah, Son of God, Son of Man, King of Israel—are gathered together by John in the introduction accorded Jesus in the first chapter of his Gospel. But his name Jesus is henceforth above every name (Phil 2, 9). Lord of the universe and head of the church, he is the salvation which he brings to us (Lk 1, 71); thus the one who believes in him will desire to be worthy to die for his name (Acts 15, 26; 21, 13).

JORDAN. The foremost river of Palestine. From the Lebanons to the Dead Sea it covers a distance of 125 miles, though with its meanderings the stream itself is more than double that. The width varies from 80 to 150 feet, and the depth in summer from 4 to 12 feet. The river is generally hidden by a thick growth of willow. There are many fords which allow passage from the one bank to the other (Jos 2, 7; Mt 3, 13).

JUBILEE. Year of joy and amnesty, celebrated at the end of each 49 year period, in the course of which one's debts must be remitted and slaves set free (Lv 25, 8-55).

JUDGMENT. In the Old Testament, judgment is related to the covenant. Judges and kings were established to maintain or reestablish the faithfulness to the covenant in the midst of national difficulties and in matters concerning the observation of the law (1 Kgs 3, 6). They represented the supreme Judge (Is 11, 3-5). Referring to God, judgment designates divine intervention, sometimes to assure his people victory or deliverance and at other times to condemn and punish them after an infidelity (Dt 32, 36; Jer 30, 11ff).

In the Psalms Yahweh appears as the supreme Judge above all in the great deeds of the "Day of the Lord" *(see this term)* and his power extends over all the earth. Among the prophets this perspective becomes more and more connected with the eschatological plane (Zec 14; Dn 7, 12).

In the New Testament, judgment is connected with the work of Christ, accepted by the faithful or rejected by the unbelievers. It is already present and marks a difference between groups of people (Jn 3, 17-21; 8, 15; 12, 31). Hence, it is necessary to be on one's guard, because judgment is coming. It will be made evident at the last day, which will be marked by the definitive triumph of Christ (Mt 25, 31; 1 Thes 4, 16; 2 Thes 2, 3-10).

JUST (JUSTICE). The just man is one who is virtuous, faithful to God and to the law of Moses (Mt 19, 17-20). In the New Testament the "just" man is one who does the will of God (Mt 7, 21). In the teachings of St. Paul, the terms justice and justification appear often: God makes man "just," free from sin and pleasing to God through grace (grace attested by faith) (Rom 3, 20-30).

KINGDOM (REIGN) OF GOD. The Kingdom will be established by the Messiah, over Israel first (Zep 3, 14-15), and then over all the nations of the earth (Zec 14, 9). "Kingdom" signifies a state of things in which God is recognized as King to whom everything must be submitted: Kingdom of God and Kingdom of heaven are equivalent. The Kingdom is proclaimed by John the Baptizer (Mt 3, 2), inaugurated by Jesus (Mt 12, 25-28), continued in the church (Mt 10, 7; 16, 19), and will be definitively accomplished in the glory of Christ's return (Mt 24, 26-31). The members of the Kingdom are children of God and even in this life enjoy that eternal life which will be completely expanded in the future world (Jn 3, 15-16; Rv 22, 2).

KIN (NEXT OF), AVENGER OF BLOOD, GOEL. *See* LEVIRATE.

KISHON. Name of a brook flowing at the foot of Mt. Tabor. It witnessed several violent scenes and battles (Jgs 4, 13, 1 Kgs 18, 40).

KITTIM. This name referred originally to inhabitants of Kiti, capital of the isle of Cyprus, then to any Cypriots (Gn 10, 4; Is 23, 1; Jer 2, 10), later to Greeks in general (Nm 24, 24), and finally even to Romans (Dn 11, 30).

KNOW. God knows everything, since he is the Creator (Jb 37, 16). He knows his people, since he has chosen it (Gn 18, 19). On his part, man seeks to know God in faith (Dt 29, 3; Jer 31, 31-34). The word "know" has a third meaning in the Bible: man "knows" his wife; he has carnal relations with her (Gn 4, 1).

LAW OF MOSES. The law, respected by all Jews as from God, consisted of the five books of Moses. These formed the basis of the Scripture reading and instruction in the synagogue services. In addition the Pharisees observed a traditional law, the *Mishna*, which they taught also had its author in Moses. Our Lord observed the Mosaic law and promulgated for his followers its essential element, the Ten Commandments (Mt 5, 17). He criticized the Pharisees for their neglect of it in favor of their traditions (Mt 15, 2-9).

LEBANON. Mountainous chain north of Palestine. Its name, derived from *laban* which signifies "to be white," alludes to its tops covered with permanent snows (Jer 18, 14).

LEVIATHAN. A mythological sea monster symbolizing the chaos that existed in the beginning of creation. Also used for a crocodile or a whale (Ps 74, 14).

LEVIRATE. This word, derived from the Latin *levir* (brother-in-law) designates an ancient Israelite custom (Gn 38, 8ff), codified in the Bible: when a man dies without leaving a male child, the closest relative of the deceased—generally, his brother—must marry the widow who is his sister-in-law and thus perpetuate the line. The first son born of this union would be considered the son and heir of the dead man (Dt 25, 5-10).

LEVITES. Sacred ministers of lowest rank among the Jews. Unlike the priests, they were members of the tribe of Levi who did not belong to the house of Aaron. While on duty they wore a distinctive linen dress, but they entered only the inner court and not the holy place of the temple. The higher levites assisted the officiating priests, others had charge of the music during the services, and still others acted as doorkeepers and overseers of the temple (1 Chr 23, 4-6).

LIGHT. Has various meanings in Scripture: (1) material sense of outward light or daybreak (Gn 1, 3); (2) symbol of God (showing his incorporeal, pure and holy nature) (1 Jn 1, 5); (3) symbol of Christ (Jn 8, 12); (4) Christians are children of light because they have received the spiritual light of truth and grace, and are to radiate it in the world by their good example (Mt 5, 14; Eph 5, 8).

LORD. Originally, this title signified nothing more than "sir." From the 3rd century B.C. onward, the Jews replaced the ineffable name *Yahweh* with *Adonai* (Lord) in reading the Bible. Applied to Jesus by the first Christians, the name "Lord" was thus equivalent to an affirmation of his divinity (Acts 2, 36). *See* **ADONAI. NAME. YAHWEH.**

LOVE. In the Old Testament, the love of God expresses itself in his many interventions of creation (Gn 1, 3; Jb 38ff) and the history of Israel (Dt 4, 37; Ps 41, 12). It is a freely-given elective love (Dt 7, 7) working for the salvation of mankind, ever merciful in the face of human infidelity (Hos 11, 1-4). The New Testament explores these first glimmerings more fully. The love of God is historical because God has not spared his own Son and has delivered him to death in order to save us (Jn 3, 16). It is also freely-given and elective by the work of Christ, which was in perfect correspondence with the will of the Father and which made the faithful the beloved ones of God (Jn 5, 20-25; Col 3, 12). Finally, this love in action is merciful, as shown above all by the cross and explained in the parables (Jn 15, 13; Lk 15, 11-32).

The love of man for God is thus a love which is returned. It must be sealed by a total obedience to the Commandments, a fidelity to the covenant. In the New Testament it must respond without limit to the prior love of God and Christ (1 Jn 3, 1-16; 4, 10-19).

MAGI. In the texts of the Old Testament, they are often associated with sorcerers and diviners. They seem to have been a Persian religious caste of royal advisers (Jer 39, 2: "princes"), and were regarded as wise men, astrologers. In the Gospel of Matthew, many think it refers to learned men from Babylon who had contact with Jewish Messianism (cf Dn 2, 2). In the Acts of the Apostles, the word is taken in the pejorative sense in the case of a magician who sets himself up as an adversary of Paul the Apostle (Acts 8, 9).

MEDIATOR. In its primary sense, the word signifies an intermediary, a third person who intervenes between other parties to bring them together or reconcile them. Moses was thus a mediator between God and the people (Nm 14, 13-20). Applied to Jesus, the term takes on an even more profound meaning, for Jesus is at the same time God and man; he belongs, at once, to the two parties. Through Christ we have access to the Father, and through Christ the Father gives himself to mankind (Heb 9, 11-25; 12, 24).

MERCY. This word is found in both Testaments, but retains all the primitive value of the Hebrew word *hesed*, which suggests love more than pity (Jas 2, 1-13).

MESSIAH. Hebrew word signifying "one who has been anointed." The kings of Israel were anointed in the name of God (1 Sm 9, 16). The term Messiah later was used to designate a "future king" who would make all things new (Dn 9, 25-26). This son of David, expected by the Jewish nation, was the Messiah par exellence (Mk 10, 47-48), a term that has been rendered in Greek by *Christos*. This was a common name that ultimately became a title for Jesus the Savior (Rom 1, 1). *See* **CHRIST. JESUS.**

MIRACLES. This word corresponds to two biblical words: sign and wonder. In the sense of "sign," a miracle is an unaccustomed and unexpected event which serves as a motive for credibility by manifesting the power of Christ, and leads the spectator to believe in his person (Jn 2, 11).

MISSION. Out of love the Father sends his only Son into the world. Jesus speaks in this way of his "mission" which is to save men by giving them Life (Jn 16, 27-28). Then, just as the Father has sent the Son into the world, so Jesus sends the apostles into the world (Jn 20, 21). This second mission is a prolongation of the former one.

MONEY. In the time of our Lord the coins current in Palestine were Roman, Greek, Syrian and Jewish. The Jews might issue coins only in bronze.

1) Large sums were expressed in *talents* and *mnas*. The talent equalled about $1920.00 in United States currency. The mna was one-sixtieth of a talent, or about $32.00. The units of Luke 19, 13ff were mnas.

2) Silver coins mentioned in the New Testament are: the Syrian *stater* (51 cents), the Roman *denarius* (about 17 cents), the Greek *drachme*, equivalent to the denarius. The stater was accepted as equal to the Jewish *shekel*, one-fiftieth of a mna

(about 64 cents), the temple tax for two persons (Mt 17, 26). The denarius was the usual day's wage for a laborer in the field, and it was the coin of the tax to the Emperor (Mt 20, 2; 22, 19).

3) Bronze coins referred to are the Roman *assarion* (one cent) and *quadrans* (one-fourth of a cent), the Jewish *perutah* or *lepton* (one-eighth of a cent), the coin of the "widow's mite" (Mt 10, 29; 5, 26; Mk 12, 42).

It should be remembered that the coin values here given are only approximate, and that the purchasing power of money was much greater in ancient times than today.

MOUNTAIN (MOUNT). A mountain is regarded as the dwelling place of divinity. Sanctuaries were set up on a good many mounts. It was on mountains that God chose to give his revelations (Sinai, Tabor) (Dt 33, 2; Mt 17, 1ff). Zion is called the "mountain God has chosen" (Ps 68, 17).

MUSICAL INSTRUMENTS. The Hebrews were devoted to music and used it for both secular and religious purposes. Various types of instruments are mentioned in the Bible — stringed, wind and percussive instruments (Ps 150, 3-5).

MYSTERY. The origin of this word is Greek. It signified first of all the place where religious ceremonies took place which were reserved only to those who had been "initiated." In the plural, it signified the rites themselves. In a derived sense, the word is synonymous with divine secret. St. Paul uses it in the sense of divine plan (inaccessible to man, secret, but revealed by Jesus Christ), having the salvation of men as its object (Rom 16, 25-26). In Scripture it must never be taken in the sense (to which the catechism has accustomed us) of revealed truth incomprehensible to the human intelligence (for example, the mystery of the Blessed Trinity).

NAME. According to the conception of the ancients, the *Name* designates more than the external person; it tends to express his basic character, his personality (Gn 21, 3ff). We might say it is an emanation of the person himself. Change of vocation entailed changing one's name (Mt 16, 16-19). In the ancient texts of the Bible, to name or give a name can signify "to have power over" (Gn 2, 19-21). The "name of God" thus signifies God himself. Hence, we find the expressions: God acting for his name's sake — to glorify and sanctify his name (Ez 20, 14; Is 29, 23). In the same way sin profanes the name of God (Lv 18, 21). Among the Israelites, the veneration which came to be accorded to the name of God approached superstition. The Israelites did not dare pronounce this name and forbade even the use of the name *Yahweh.* In place of this word whose consonants were written out, the reader had to read *Adonai* (Lord). This custom continues to exist in present-day Judaism. Hence, the first Christians surrounded the name of Jesus with great veneration and the expressions: "in the name of Jesus" and "for the name of Jesus" occur frequently in the sense of: "acting in such an intention in dependence on Jesus" and "by authority of Jesus" (Col 3, 17). In John's Gospel, we are urged to pray "in the name of Jesus" (Jn 14, 13). Moreover, this manner of speaking has been retained until our own day; for example, we say: "In the name of the Father, and of the Son, and of the Holy Spirit." In the Our Father, the expression: "Hallowed be thy name," signifies that we pray for God's holiness to be acknowledged and adored by all men.

NATIONS. The Israelites distinguished themselves from foreign peoples. They designated the latter by the Hebrew term *goïm;* this word, which includes a certain nuance of scorn, is often translated in our modern languages as "nations" or "Gentiles" (Is 49, 6). *See* **FOREIGNERS.**

NAZIRITE. This term stems from the Hebrew word *nazir,* meaning "set apart as sacred, dedicated, vowed." The nazirite vow could be either for a limited period or for life. Those bound by this vow had to abstain from all the products of the grapevine, from cutting or shaving their hair, and from contact with a corpse. They were regarded as men of God like the prophets; cf Am 2, 11f. Examples of lifelong nazirites were Samson (Jgs 13, 4f. 7; 16, 17), Samuel (1 Sm 1, 11), and John the Baptizer (Lk 1, 15). At the time of Christ the practice of taking the nazirite vow for a limited period seems to have been quite common, even among the early Christians; cf Acts 18, 18; 21, 23f. 26.

NAZOREAN. A title of Jesus which the Gospel derives from the name of the town of Nazareth (Mt 2, 23). The Christians were called Nazoreans for a long time (Acts 24, 5). In Hebrew this word has a certain resemblance with the word *nezer* which signifies "shoot." Primitive Christian tradition thus saw in this an allusion to a passage of Isaiah (11, 11) in which the Messiah is presented as the shoot par excellence of David, son of Jesse.

NUMBERS. In the Bible, numbers often have a symbolic value. For example 7 (seven days, seven angels, seven lights . .); 12 (tribes, apostles); 40 (days of rain, days of prayer on Sinai, days of fast, period before the Ascension); 144,000 (the elect, in the Book of Revelation). It must also be noted that in the ancient accounts numbers must be regarded in accord with Oriental custom and they are subject to poetic approximation: *thousand* can signify a group or family. In the military accounts, most numbers are considerably exaggerated (Dt 32, 30).

PARACLETE (COUNSELLOR). Word derived from the Greek. It is used only in John's Gospel and signifies "advocate or defender." This word is applied either to Christ, who fulfilled this role toward his disciples, or to the Holy Spirit, who continues to exercise it with Christ himself (Jn 14, 16).

PARADISE. Word of Persian origin, which passed over into Hebrew and then Greek, used to designate a garden; in particular, the garden of Eden (Gn 2, 15). Later, it signified the eternal abode of the just (Lk 23, 43).

PASSOVER. *See* **FEASTS.**

PASTOR. *See* **SHEPHERD.**

PEACE. This word is used in the Bible to express two ideas: (1) peace with God,

reestablished by the covenant, often a synonym for reconciliation, and (2) peace between individuals and peoples.

The promises of the messianic covenant are often accompanied by the announcement of peace. Thus the Messiah will be called the "Prince of Peace" (Is 9, 5). The word "peace" is contained in the literal translation of the word Jerusalem (Salem) (Heb 7, 2). Peace demands faithfulness to the covenant and justice among men (Ps 72, 3-7) so often invoked by the prophets. Christ came to bring peace (Lk 2, 14) and to render it effective by a reconciliation of mankind to God (Jn 14, 27; Eph 2, 14-17). The extension of the peaceful reign of Christ is thus for the true Christian the condition and source of true peace and true justice between individuals and between nations.

PEOPLE OF GOD. This is how Israel is designated throughout the Bible. God has gratuitously chosen her and she is his own possession (Ex 25, 8). God dwells in her midst (Ex 25, 8). The people is thus holy and set apart from other peoples (Lv 20, 24). In its turn, Christianity is also called the People "[God] claims for his own," but it rejects any kind of national particularism (1 Pt 2, 9).

PERFECT. In the ancient text, this word indicates someone who avoids sin' and practices the law. The passage in which Jesus says: "Be perfected as your heavenly Father is perfect" (Mt 5, 48) signifies — according to its context — that one must imitate the divine mercy and impartiality. In a single passage (Mt 19, 21) Jesus speaks of the perfection of the disciple who goes beyond his ordinary duties. St. Paul uses the term perfect of the "spiritually mature" Christians who know true wisdom and want all men to be perfect in Christ (1 Cor 2, 6ff).

PHARISEES. A religious sect of the Jews that numbered about 6000 in the time of Christ. Originating in the days of the Greek conquest of Palestine, they sought above all to preserve the Jews from the contamination of foreign religion, and to this end insisted upon strict separation from the Gentiles. They insisted also on strict loyalty to the Scriptures and to the traditions of the rabbis. Among many Pharisaic hedges about the law, ceremonial purity and payment of religious dues were emphasized. In doctrine the Pharisees were inclined to fatalism, but on the other hand they strongly upheld the resurrection and the future life. By the time of Christ their primitive zeal had degenerated into fanaticism and hypocrisy. They took a leading part in the opposition to Christ, and he scathingly rebuked their insincerity (Mt 23, 25; Lk 11, 39; 18, 9-14). That they were not all bad is evidenced by such men as Gamaliel (Acts 5, 34).

PHILADELPHIA. A city of Lydia in Asia Minor, founded by Attalus II Philadelphus, king of Pergamum. The book of Revelation alludes to it twice (1, 11 and 3, 7).

PHILISTINES. Non-Semitic invaders who gave their name to all of Palestine although they occupied only its southwestern plains. They were subdued by David (2 Sm 5, 17-25), but became practically independent under the separated kingdom and disappeared as a people after the time of the Maccabees.

PIETY. In Hebrew as in English, account must be taken of the relationship between this word *piety* and *pity* (in the sense of goodness). God is called pious, that is, good (Is 1, 4). Men are termed pious, that is, faithful, just and devoted to God (Acts 10, 7).

POOR. Originally, this word had merely an economic and social meaning. Gradually, it took on the meaning of humble, modest, small, the little people often oppressed by the rich and powerful but who remained faithful to God (Am 2, 6-7). It was in this sense that Jesus said: "Blest are the poor in spirit" (Mt 5, 3).

PRESBYTER. *See* **ELDER.**

PRIESTS, JEWISH. Sacred ministers, whose duty it was to offer sacrifice at the altar of holocausts, and to enter morning and evening into the holy place to burn incense at the golden altar (Heb 7, 27; 10, 11). They also had care of the loaves of proposition (Mt 12, 4) and certified the cure of lepers (Lk 17, 13f). They were divided into twenty-four classes, each of which in turn officiated for a week at the temple (Lk 1, 5). During the three great feasts all the classes ministered together. Their dress comprised a long linen tunic, ornamented sash and turban. The priesthood was hereditary, by descent from the tribe of Levi through the younger branch of Aaron's family (Heb 7, 5). For their support the priests received tithes and other offerings.

PROMISE. This term of Greek origin is employed only in the New Testament. It designates and interprets the meaning of all the previous prophetic history of the chosen people in their messianic mission. The Old Testament gave promise of Christ. But it is in Christ that all this preparatory and figurative history finds its perfect fulfillment (Mt 5, 17; Acts 13, 32-33; Rom 15, 8; 2 Cor 1, 20; Gal 3, 14). An analogous relationship exists between Christ's work of the Redemption and his second coming which, at the end of time, will asssure the glorious consummation of all things (Acts 1, 4-5; 2, 16-21) and fulfill the promise of Christ's work.

PROPHET. One who speaks to another on the part of God (Dt 18, 18). Prophets are also called "seers" by reason of their gift of reading thoughts. Prophet does not necessarily signify that one foretells the future and there were prophets in the first Christian communities (1 Cor 12, 28ff).

PUBLICANS. Management of imperial taxation was farmed by the Roman government to the highest bidders, who in turn entrusted the collection in the provinces to native agents by whom the privilege had been purchased with advance payments. These agents are the "publicans." They were often guilty of merciless extortion, and were universally hated as plunderers of their own people. Among the Jews they were also considered as disloyal to their religion, since they cooperated with Gentiles and exacted tribute from the race that God had made free (Jn 8, 33; Mt 22, 17). Like the Baptizer, our Lord condemned the injustice of the publicans, but did not reject those who were sincerely repentant (Mt 5, 46; 21, 31f). Two publicans are distinguished in the Gospels, Zacchaeus (Lk 19, 2) and Matthew (Mt 10, 3), who became an apostle and evangelist.

PURITY (RITUAL). State of the man who fulfills the conditions imposed by the Mosaic law on every one of the faithful who appeared for worship (Lv 7, 19-21). Certain bodily functions, contact with forbidden animals, and with corpses forbade participation in worship; anyone who was guilty of such things was "impure" or "unclean" (Nm 19, 1-10). "Purity" could be recovered by various rites: · sacrifices, washings, aspersions, etc. (Nm 19, 19). There is no relation between this term and what we call "purity" in the sense of chastity.

REDEMPTION. This word comes from the Latin *redimere* which signifies to buy back or redeem. The corresponding Hebrew term was used in the Bible for the first time with reference to the exodus from Egypt (Ex 15, 13). God has redeemed his people from the bondage of Egypt, gratuitously, just as a master sets free his slave (Lv 19, 20). In the New Testament, it signifies that God, through Jesus Christ (gratuitously), redeems his people in order to establish his kingdom (Rom 3, 24).

REMNANT. An expression often used by the prophets. It designates the survivors of great catastrophes: the flood, the exile (Gn 7, 1f; Is 6, 13). God reserves this remnant for himself to help in the restoration (Is 37, 31). It is they who are and will remain the depositaries of the promise (Mi 4, 6-7). In the New Testament, the church is presented as fulfilling the function of the faithful Remnant and the "Israel after the flesh" is contrasted with the "Israel of God" which is the church (Rom 9, 27; 1 Cor 10, 18; Gal 6, 16); and this interpretation follows the teaching of the Old Testament.

RESURRECTION. The Bible does not have this unique and specific term. It uses the verbs to awake, to raise up, to cure, or the intransitive verbs, to get up, to appear, to show (one's self) sometimes as an act showing the power of God, sometimes as a manifestation of the victory of life over death. In the Old Testament, the idea is made known little by little at first in the perspective of the entire people (Ez 37, 1, 14), then for the Servant of Yahweh (Is 53) but always in a very limited fashion (Pss 16, 10ff; 49, 16; 73, 26; 17, 15). In the New Testament, this idea takes on an elemental importance through the resurrection of Jesus, which became the fundamental historical fact, the principal witness of his divinity (1 Cor 15, 4. 12). The Resurrection is also the divine judgment which has ordered the defeat of death and pledges salvation and resurrection to all the faithful (Rom 4, 25; Col 2, 12ff; Eph 2, 1-7). This resurrection in grace is the prelude to the final and glorious resurrection (1 Cor 15, 2ff; 1 Thes 4, 14ff).

SACRED. The same Hebrew word has both the active meaning of "holy," that is, keeping oneself free from profane impurities, and the passive meaning of "sacred," that is, set apart from what is profane and therefore treated with religious reverence (Lv 21, 6).

SACRIFICE. The supreme form of divine worship, by which some creature is offered to God and used in adoration as an acknowledgment of his majesty and the creature's subjection. True sacrifices were offered in the Old Law (Heb 9, 1ff), but they were only preparations for the perfect sacrifice of Christ on the cross (Heb 9, 11).

SADDUCEES. A religious sect of the Jews, less numerous than their rivals the Pharisees, but very influential on account of the many noble and wealthy persons who belonged to their ranks (Acts 4, 1; 5, 17). They set aside traditions and even rejected truths taught in the Sacred Books themselves. They insisted upon human free will, but denied immortality, the resurrection and the existence of angels (Mt 22, 23; Mk 12, 18; Lk 20, 27; Acts 23, 8). They were denounced by John the Baptizer (Mt 3, 7) and by our Lord (Mt 16, 6). Though less prominent in their opposition to Christ than the Pharisees, they nevertheless sought to entrap him (Mt 16, 1; 22, 23), and through their representatives joined in his condemnation by the Sanhedrin. They also strongly opposed the early church because the apostles proclaimed our Lord's Resurrection (Acts 4, 1f; etc.).

SALVATION, SAVIOR. Inasmuch as the terms express redemption (cf. **REDEMPTION**) and appear as a cause of salvation, the Hebrew uses one word: *Yacha*, which means to be generous, to deliver from slavery or from distress. This term in the Old Testament expresses the Work of God, assuring the deliverance of his people as a whole (Hos 5, 13; Is 31, 1; Ps 33, 16-17) and then personal salvation (Ps 51, 14) — the whole bound up in the messianic and eschatological perspective. This term provides the substantive "machia," translated as Savior (Is 45, 21). In the New Testament, the term is employed very frequently for a cure, the health of the body, but often, in connection with faith, of the soul (Mk 5, 34; Lk 8, 48; 18, 42). Thus, the work of the New Testament even in its temporal action is entirely oriented toward the work of spiritual salvation, of remission of sins (Lk 17, 19) and the liberation from the servitude that sin brings to man (Mt 1, 21; Lk 1, 77; Acts 5, 31, etc.) and leading the Christian to his highest destiny (Rom 1, 16; 5, 9-10; 1 Cor 15, 2; Jas 1, 21). This work will be definitively manifested at the last judgment (Rom 8, 22-25).

SAMARITANS. The inhabitants of Samaria were a mixed race, descended from intermarriage of Israelites and Assyrian colonists. The enmity between the Jews and the Samaritans was so great that travelers between Galilee and Judea often had to cross the Jordan into Perea for safety. In various uprisings this race was almost exterminated, and only a small remnant survives today.

In religion the Samaritans acknowledged the Pentateuch, Joshua and Judges, but not the additional revelation or Jewish traditional doctrine. They looked for the Messiah who would teach all truth (Jn 4, 25f). In practice they worshiped the same God as the Jews, and in such matters as sabbaths and feasts, circumcision and worship, they did not dissent. But through vying with the Jews in the strict observance of Mosaic regulations, they disowned the Jerusalem temple and priesthood. The rival sanctuary of Gerizim they revered as their holy place (Jn 4, 20). Our Lord passed through their country more than once, and preached and worked miracles among the people. He also spoke well of them (Lk 10, 30-37), defended them (Lk 9, 51-56), and commanded that the gospel be preached to them. This was done with success, and a Christian community was early formed among the Samaritans (Acts 8, 4-17; 9, 31; 15, 3).

SANHEDRIN. Literally *session*, a council, national or local, endowed with authority to pass on cases ecclesiastical or civil.

1) The national Sanhedrin, or Great Council, of the Jews met at Jerusalem. The high priest himself seems to have presided as a rule. The full membership was seventy-two, representing equally the three groups of priests, scribes and elders. This council took cognizance of grave matters of a doctrinal, judicial or administrative character affecting the Jewish religion and nation. The Romans acknowledged the decrees of the Sanhedrin, and guards attended the meetings to fulfill the orders of the judges (Mt 26, 58). Sentence of death, however, was reserved for the Roman authority (Jn 18, 31).

2) Local tribunals, subordinate to the supreme Sanhedrin, were found in the towns of Palestine. Their membership varied from three to twenty-three, according to the size of the male population of the place. The "Sanhedrin" of Mt 5, 22 probably refers to one of these lower tribunals.

SAVIOR. Exact translation of the word *Yehoshua* which has become "Jesus" (Lk 1, 31ff). See **SALVATION**.

SCRIBES. Literally this title means a writer, but in the New Testament the reference is to the learned class among the Jews, the official authorities on the written law and oral traditions. One who had made successful studies became a scribe at the age of thirty by receiving imposition of hands with the delivery of a tablet and key.

As the function of the priests was ritualistic, that of the scribes was doctrinal. These latter were interpreters of the Scriptures (Mt 2, 4; 17, 10; Mk 12, 35), but our Lord condemned them for their burdensome additions to the divine law (Mt 23). They taught by quoting the celebrated doctors of the past (Mk 1, 22). In our Lord's day the chief rival schools among the scribes were those of the liberal Hillel and the severe Shammai. Generally the scribes opposed the Sadducees (Lk 20, 39) and upheld the Pharisees. Like the Pharisees, the scribes were noted for hypocrisy, pride, and contradiction of Christ (Mt 23, 2ff; Mk 12, 28-30; Lk 20, 46; Mt 9, 3). But there were noble and sincere characters among them (Mt 8, 19), especially Nicodemus and Gamaliel (Jn 3; Acts 5, 34).

SCRIPTURES. (1) The inspired books, the work of the Holy Spirit. They were customarily divided into three series: the Law, the Prophets, and the Writings. (2) Christianity added its own writings: the Gospels and the Letters of the Apostles.

SEPTUAGINT. Translation into Greek of the Hebrew and Aramaic Old Testament (including the deuterocanonical books) made in Egypt by various authors during the period between 250 B.C. and 100 B.C. Its name comes from the fact that legend ascribes the work to a group of seventy-two scholars and it is designated by the Roman numerals LXX. It is by far the most important ancient version of the Old Testament and until recently was our sole witness for the state of the original text of the Hebrew Old Testament before the Christian era. The Septuagint was the version used by the Hebrews in Christ's time, by the apostles and New Testament writers, and by the Greek Fathers of the Church; it is still the official text of the Greek Church.

SHEOL. The ancient concept of the abode of the dead (*the nether world*, in Hebrew, *Sheol*) supposed no activity or lofty emotion among the deceased, who were pictured as surrounded by the darkness of oblivion (Nm 16, 30ff; Ps 6, 6). The Hebrews shared in this common idea almost to the time of Christ, when God revealed a clearer notion of the hearafter (Wis 3). It is at this time that belief in the resurrection of the dead was introduced (Dn 12, 2). Some (for example, the Sadducees) refused to believe it; but the people embraced it like some great revelation. In the New Testament, the whole concept is transfigured in the light of Christ's resurrection. His body did not see corruption in Hades; he has the keys of death and the nether world (Rv 1, 18). The word "Gehenna" (hell) is used of the nether world when punishment is involved (Mt 5, 29; 10, 28). *See* **GEHENNA.**

SIN. In the Old Testament sin is not so much a wrong action in one's conscience as something which disrupts the order of the world wished by God, and particularly the covenant fixed by the law. Thus the Israelite did not search himself for deep causes or establish its relationship with original sin; it is necessary to wait for the book of Wisdom to find such an allusion (2 ,24). The New Testament describes sin as relating to original sin and tells of the universal sorrow because of sin (Rom 1—5) erased by the Redemption (Rom 5—8). It describes responsibility for it. This conception of sin thus became linked with the ideas of faith and love which gave life to Christians (Rom 13, 8ff; 1 Cor 5, 9; 13, 4ff).

SON. In Hebrew, this word is used to designate diverse relations or dependencies: (1) relations of direct descendence (Ex 1, 1-5); (2) relations of disciples to their master (Prv 1, 8); (3) relations of origin or analogy (Jb 1, 3; 42, 13); (4) moral relations (Jos 7, 19).

SON OF MAN. An enigmatic title. Jewish apocryphal tradition (1 Henoch, 2 Esdras, 2 Baruch) uses it to describe a unique religious personage, a messiah with extraordinary spiritual endowments. Jesus' use of it seems to derive from Ez 2, where it is a title of humility, and Dn 7, 13f, where it indicates a clearly messianic figure. It expresses for him his twofold destiny, of suffering (Mk 8, 31; 9, 11. 31; 10, 33; 12, 31; 14, 21) and of glory (Mk 8, 38; 12, 36; 14, 62). Peter, along with the other disciples, fails (despite his confession) to grasp the association of suffering and death with the office of Messiah. Only after the resurrection does the Christian community endow it with its messianic meaning (Acts 7, 56; Rv 1, 3).

SOUL. In its first sense, the Hebrew word *nephesh* signifies breath, life, the principle of animal life (Gn 1, 20). It was only much later (toward the beginning of the Christian era) that the Hebrews adopted the distinction (of Greek philosophy) of soul and body (Rv 6, 9; 20, 4).

SPIRIT. Literally, breath. It is an element with as little materiality as possible; it is the innermost part of man, more subtle than his soul. The Old Testament attributes to the Spirit of God both external and internal actions that surpass human powers (Nm 11, 24-29). The Spirit is a person distinct from the Father and the Son

(Jn 14, 26). Each Christian possesses the Spirit. He is the principle of life and a pledge of resurrection (Rom 8, 2. 11).

SYNAGOGUES. Minor places of religious assembly among the Jews, used also as schools, libraries and halls of judgment. The central place of worship was the temple, the one national sanctuary and the only place of sacrifice. The synagogue served local communities or separate congregations for less solemn religious functions. Every considerable Jewish community, whether in or out of Palestine, had at least one synagogue. The building, commonly rectangular, was erected on the plan of the temple. There was a gallery reserved for women, another space for men, and the worshipers faced toward Jerusalem and the holy of holies. In front was a platform on which stood the holy ark containing the Scriptures and an eight-branch candlestick burning before it. Nearest the platform were the chief seats, where sat the leading men facing the congregation (Mt 23, 6; Mk 12, 39; Lk 11, 43; 20, 46). Among these leading men were the ruler of the synagogue and the elders, and various functionaries whom they appointed.

TEMPLE. The sacred place of worship on Mount Moriah, including all buildings and courts. The first temple was built by Solomon, in 967 to 964 B.C., but was destroyed by the Chaldeans in 586 B.C. The second was erected by Zerubbabel in 515 B.C., but was profaned in 167 B.C. by the Syrians. Herod the Great began a magnificent restoration of this temple. It is his structure that is the temple referred to in the time of our Lord. In a more restricted sense, the term applies only to the "House" in which were the holy place and the holy of holies, or to the immediate precincts of this "House." The space covered by the temple and its courts was about 585 by 6 100 feet.
The temple proper (Naos) measured 30 feet north to south, and 90 feet east to west. The innermost part of this building was the holy of holies, set apart from the outer room, the holy place, by a double curtain (Mt 27, 51). The holy of holies contained the stone on which once rested the ark of the covenant. It was entered once a year by the high priest (Heb 9, 3-5). The holy place had within it the golden altar of incense (Lk 1, 11), and the table of loaves (Mt 12, 4). About the Naos ran an uncovered court reserved to the priests. In front of the entrance to the holy place stood the altar of holocausts (Ex 27, 1-8). The lay Israelite might approach this altar only to bring his sacrifice to the priests (Mt 5, 23).
Outside this court of the priests, toward the east, was the court of the Israelites, where the laity could assist at the services. Beyond this was an outer court known as the court of the women, since to it women were admitted. This court was surrounded by rooms, one of which was the treasury with thirteen boxes for contributions (Lk 21, 1ff). To these courts only Jews were admitted, inscriptions warning non-Jews not to enter under pain of death (Acts 21, 28). By a staircase of fifteen steps one descended to the outer court which was known as that of the Gentiles. This outside court was surrounded by walls with high towers. The court of the Gentiles was open to all, and it was used for buying and selling (Mk 11, 15). Against the walls of this court on the

interior were porches or colonnades where the people listened to religious teachers (Lk 2, 46; Mt 26, 55). The porch attached to the eastern wall was known as Solomon's (Jn 10, 23; Acts 3, 11; 5, 12). At its northwestern corner this court was adjacent to the fortress Antonia, whose garrison was ready to keep order among the crowds (Acts 21, 30ff). But the Jews had also their own temple police, with captains and officers, who patrolled the whole area day and night (Lk 22, 52; Acts 4, 1).

TIME. In Hebrew, *olam* designates a very long and indefinite period. In Greek, this word has been translated by two terms: "world" and "age" which are often taken for one another. Hence, one says: this world, the next world or the ages to come. In the plural, ages is practically equivalent to eternity (Mt 12, 32; Eph 2, 7).

TONGUES (SPEAK IN). Two passages of the New Testament speak of the *gift of tongues* (Acts 2 and 1 Cor 14). In the first, we find the mention of the miracle by which the apostles suddenly began to speak in tongues foreign to them—or by which their auditors each understand in their own language what the apostles said to them in the apostles' tongue. In the second, it is a case of a phenomenon that is difficult to describe and analyze: this was a manner of expressing oneself in inarticulate sounds or cries, proper to certain states of mystical exaltation.

TRUTH. This word, in Hebrew *emeth*, designates something firm and solid, hence something faithful. The adjective "true" signifies not only what is true and authentic but also what is the principle of this truth and this authenticity (Gn 32, 10; Ps 12, 1-2).

VULGATE. The official Latin translation of the Bible which was prepared almost entirely by St. Jerome from 382 to 405 A.D. Jerome borrowed heavily from Origen in translating the Psalter and took Ecclesiasticus, Baruch and both books of Maccabees from Old Latin texts. He translated everything else from the existing Hebrew, Aramaic or Greek manuscripts. The Council of Trent declared the Vulgate to be "authentic in public readings, disputations, preachings and exposition" because it conforms to the original texts and contains no errors in faith or morals. Since 1907 the Benedictine Order has, at the request of St. Pius X, been working on a revised edition of the modern Vulgate text to make it conform as closely as possible to the text of St. Jerome, and several parts have already been published.

YAHWEH. The proper personal name of the God of Israel, signifying, "I am who am" (Ex 3, 14-15). It is commonly explained in reference to God as the absolute and necessary Being. It may be understood of God as the Source of all created beings. Out of reverence for this name, the term *Adonai*, "my Lord," was later used as a substitute. The word Lord in the present version represents this traditional usage. The word "Jehovah" arose from a false reading of this name as it is written in the current Hebrew text. *See* **ADONAI. NAME.**

Other subjects will be found in the Bible Dictionary, pp. 439ff. The cross references to the passages cited below should also be consulted.

Absolution, the power promised and given to the pastors of the church, Mt 16, 19; 18, 18; Jn 20, 22f.

Abstinence, from flesh with its blood, forbidden, Acts 15, 29; □ observed by St. John the Baptist, Lk 1, 15; □ even permitted food to be abstained from, so as not to scandalize others, Rom 4, 20f; 1 Cor 8, 13.

Adoption, of Israel by God, Rom 9, 4; □ of children of God described, Rom 8, 14-17; Gal 3, 26-29; 4, 1-7; Eph 1, 5; Heb 2, 10; □ effects, 2 Cor 6, 17. 18; 7, 1; Heb 12, 5-11; 1 Jn 3, 2-5; □ of Gentiles, Rom 9, 24-26; Acts 15, 17.

Affliction, days of afflictions shortened on account of the elect, Mt 24, 22; Mk 13, 20; □ no proportion between the affliction of this life and the glory to come, Rom 8, 18.

Agriculture, serves as an example for spiritual lessons, Mt 13, 3-43; 2 Cor 9, 6; Gal 6, 7-9.

Almsgiving, Mt 6, 3; 10, 42; 19, 21; 25, 35. 42; Lk 3, 11; 6, 35; 11, 41; 12, 33; 14, 13.

Altar, place where faithful achieve communion with God, 1 Cor 10, 18; □ to be respected, Mt 2, 23f; 23, 18-20; □ Christians have an altar that has supplanted the previous ones, Heb 13, 10; the Lord's table, 1 Cor 10, 16-21.

Angels, they have a charge over us, Mt 18, 10; Heb 1, 14; □ pray for us, Rv 8, 4; □ communion with, Heb 12, 22; □ fall of, Lk 10, 18; Jude 6; Rv 12, 4; 20, 9.

Anger, Mt 5, 22; Eph 4, 26. 31; Jas 1, 19f.

Animals, seen in a vision by St. Peter, Acts 10, 12.

Apostles, chosen from the disciples, Lk 6, 13; □ sent to announce the kingdom of God in Judea, Mt 10; □ sent to evangelize the whole world, Mt 18, 19; Mk 16, 15; Lk 24, 46; Jn 15, 16. 27; 20, 21; Acts 1, 8; 10, 42.

Apostolical Traditions, 1 Cor 11, 2; 2 Thes 2, 15; 3, 6; 2 Tm 1, 13; 2, 2; 3, 14.

Avarice, Lk 12, 15-21; 1 Cor 5, 11; 6, 9f; Eph 5, 3. 5; Col 3, 5; 1 Tm 6, 9; Heb 13, 5.

Beasts, of the Apocalypse, Rv 17, 3.

Beatitudes, Mt 5, 3-11; Lk 6, 20-23.

Bishop, at Ephesus, Acts 20, 28; □ at Philippi, Phil 1, 1; □ qualities required of, 1 Tm 3, 1-7; Ti 1, 6-9.

Blasphemy, punished, Rom 2, 24; 1 Tm 1, 20; Jude 8; □ against Jesus Christ, Mt 27, 39; Lk 23, 39; □ against the Holy Spirit, not forgiven, Mt 12, 31.

Blessings, by which creatures are consecrated and sanctified, 1 Tm 4, 5; Heb 19, 2f; □ spiritual blessings: Acts 4, 12; presence of God, Mt 28, 20; strength, Col 1, 11; help, Heb 2, 18; joy, Ps 40, 4; Acts 13, 52; peace, Jn 14, 27; Phil 4, 7; □ of praise, 1 Cor 1, 9.

Blindness, cured by Christ, Mt 9, 27-30; 12, 22; 20, 30-34; Jn 9; □ inflicted as a punishment, Jn 12, 40; Acts 28, 26; Rom 11, 8. 10; Gn 19, 11; 2 Kgs 6, 18; Acts 13, 11; □ inflicted by Satan, 2 Cor 4, 4.

Body, of Christian is temple of Holy Spirit, 1 Cor 3, 16. 17; 2 Cor 6, 16, and member of Christ, 1 Cor 6, 15; 12, 27; □ Church is body of Christ, Eph 1, 22. 23; Col 3, 15; 1 Cor 10, 17; □ of man will be raised up, Mt 22, 23-32; 1 Cor 15, 12-57; □ Word of God received a human body, Mt 1, 18-23; Jn 1, 14; Heb 10, 5; □ which was crucified, Jn 19, 17-18. 33; and raised again, 1 Cor 15, 3-8.

Bread, Jesus, the bread which came down from heaven, Jn 4, 31; 1 Cor 10, 16; 11, 27; see Eucharist; □ multiplied by Christ, Mt 16, 19; Mk 6, 41; 8, 20; Lk 9, 13; Jn 6, 11.

Ceremonies, at prayer, 1 Cor 11, 4; □ signs of things to come, 1 Cor 10, 11; 2 Cor 3, 13; Heb 7, 8, 5; 9, 1; 10, 1.

Charity, a virtue more excellent than faith, Mt 23, 38; 1 Cor 13, 13; □ fraternal, Mt 7, 3; 19, 19; 23, 38; Jn 13, 14. 34; 15, 12; Rom 12, 10; 13, 9; 1 Cor 13; Gal 5, 14; Eph 4, 15; 5, 2; Phil 2, 2; Col 3, 13f; 1 Thes 4, 9; 1 Tm 1, 5; Heb 13; 1 Pt 4, 8; 1 Jn 3, 23; 4, 7; □ toward our enemies, Mt 5, 44; Lk 6, 27. 35; 23, 33; Acts 7, 60; Rom 12, 20; □ produced by the Holy Spirit, Col 1, 8; □ exemplified by Jesus, Jn 13, 1—16, 34; 15, 12; Eph 5, 2. 25; Rv 1, 5.

Chastity, virginity preferable to marriage, Mt 22, 30; □ evangelical perfection, Mt 19, 12; 1 Cor 7, 25; □ recommended to ministers of the church, 1 Tm 3, 2. 8; □ recommended to women, Ti 2, 5.

Children, massacred by Herod, Mt 2, 16; □ blessed by our Lord, Mt 10, 16; Lk 18, 17; □ duty to parents, Mt 10, 35; 19, 19; Mk 10, 19; Lk 2, 51; Acts 7, 14; Col 3, 20; 1 Pt 5, 5.

Christ, Jesus, foretold in Old Testament, Lk 24, 27; □ Son of Man, Mt 9, 6; 26, 64; Mk 8, 31; Lk 19, 10; Jn 3, 13-14; 5, 27; Acts 7, 55; □ Son of David, Mt 1, 1; 9, 27; Jn 7, 42; □ Son of Mary, Mt 1, 21; Lk 2, 7; Jn 19, 25; Acts 1, 14; □ Son of God, Mt 3, 17; 4, 3; 14, 33; 16, 16; Mk 1, 1; Lk 1, 32; Jn 1, 34; 10, 36; Rom 1, 3; □ the same God with his Father, and

equal to Him, Jn 5, 18. 19. 23; 10, 30; 14, 1. 9; 16, 14f; 17, 10; Phil 2, 5f; □ true God, Mt 1, 23; Lk 1, 16f; Jn 1, 1; 20, 28f; Acts 20, 25; Rom 9, 5; Ti 2, 13; Heb 1, 8; 1 Jn 5, 20; □ Creator of all things, Jn 1, 3. 10f; Col 1, 16f; Heb 1, 2. 10-12; 3, 4; □ the Lord of glory, 1 Cor 2, 8; □ the King of kings and Lord of lords, Rv 17, 14; 19, 16; □ the Alpha and Omega, the beginning and the end, Rv 1, 7f. 17f; 2, 8; 22, 12f; □ circumcised, Lk 2, 21; □ baptized in the Jordan, Mt 3, 16; Mk 1, 9; Lk 3, 21; □ preached the kingdom, Mt 3, 2; Mk 1, 15; Acts 2, 38; □ performed many signs, Mt 4, 23f; Lk 7, 21f; □ obedient to the Father, Mt 11, 25; Mk 14, 36; Lk 2, 49; Jn 4, 34; Phil 2, 8; □ immune from sin, Jn 8, 46; 2 Cor 5, 21; Heb 4, 15; 1 Pt 2, 22; □ he died for all, Jn 3, 16f; Rom 5, 18; 2 Cor 5, 14f; 1 Tm 2, 3-6; 4, 10; Heb 2, 9; 1 Jn 2, 1f; □ even for the reprobate, Rom 14, 15; 1 Cor 8, 11; 2 Pt 2, 1; □ rose from the dead and appeared to many, Mt 12, 39f; 28, 6; Acts 1, 22; 2, 24; Rom 4, 24; 1 Cor 15, 4. 14; □ is seated at the right hand of the Father, Mk 14, 62; 16, 19; Acts 7, 55; Rom 8, 34; Eph 1, 20; Col 3, 6; Heb 1, 3; 1 Pt 3, 22; □ will come to judge all human beings, Mt 19, 28; 24, 30-51; 25, 31-46; Jn 5, 22; Acts 10, 42; Rom 14, 10; 2 Cor 5, 10; □ designated by various titles; Lamb of God, Jn 1, 29; good shepherd, Jn 10, 11; light of the world, Jn 8, 12; image of God, 2 Cor 4, 4; eternal priest, Heb 7, 24; mediator of the new covenant, Heb 9, 15; head of the Church, Col 1, 18.

Church, of God, 1 Cor 1, 2. 10. 32; 11, 22; 1 Thes 1, 4; 1 Tm 3, 5. 15; □ and of Christ, Mt 16, 18; Acts 20, 28; □ body of Christ, 1 Cor 12, 12f. 27; Rom 12, 5; Eph 1, 22f; □ God's building and temple, 1 Cor 3, 9. 10. 16; □ royal priesthood, 1 Tm 2, 1; 1 Pt 2, 5, 9; □ bride, 2 Cor 11, 2; Eph 5, 25. 27. 29; Rv 19, 7; □ flock, Lk 12, 32; Jn 10, 3-5. 11; □ founded on Christ, 1 Cor 3, 11; □ will last forever, Mt 16, 18; □ possesses the means of salvation, Eph 4, 11. 12; □ organization and government, Acts 6, 2-6; 14, 23; 1 Tm 3, 8-13; 1 Cor 12, 4-11; Eph 4, 11-13; □ infallible in matters of faith or morals; this follows from the promises, Mt 16, 18; 28, 19f; Lk 22, 32; Jn 14, 16f. 26; 16, 13; 17, 11. 20; 1 Tm 3, 14f; 1 Jn 2, 27; Is 35, 8; 54, 9f; 59, 19-21.

Church Guides, and their authority, Mt 18, 17f; 28, 18-20; Lk 10, 16; Jn 14, 16f. 26; 16, 13; 20, 21; Eph 4, 11f; Heb 13, 7. 17; 1 Jn 4, 6.

Circumcision, ceased under the New Testament, Rom 2, 26-29; 3, 30; Col 2, 11; □ of the heart, Rom 2, 29; Col 2, 11.

Commandments, to be kept in order to gain eternal life, Mt 19, 17; Mk 10, 18f; Lk 18, 19f; 10, 26; 1 Cor 7, 19; □ the first and greatest Commandment, Mt 22, 36f; Mk 12, 28; Lk 10, 25; 18, 18; □ the second Commandment, Mt 22, 39; □ the new Commandment of love, Jn 13, 34.

Communion in One Kind, sufficient for salvation, Jn 6, 51. 57. 58; □ body and blood of Christ now inseparable, Rom 6, 9; □ mention of one kind alone, Lk 24, 30f; Acts 2, 42; 20, 7; 1 Cor 10, 17.

Concupiscence, forbidden and punished, Mt 5, 28; Mk 4, 19; Gal 5, 16; Col 3, 5; 1 Thes 4, 3; 1 Tm 5, 6. 11; 2 Tm 2, 22; 1 Cor 10, 6; 2 Pt 1, 4; 1 Jn 2, 16; Jas 1, 14; 4, 1.

Confession of Sins, Mt 3, 6; Acts 19, 18; Jas 5, 16; □ obligation of confession is gathered from the judiciary power of binding and loosing, forgiving and retaining sins, given to the pastors of Christ's Church, Mt 18, 18; Jn 20, 22f.

Confidence in God, Lk 12, 32; Jn 14, 1; 16, 33.

Conscience, the happiness of a good, 1 Jn 3, 21; 2 Cor 1, 12; □ of others must be respected, Rom 14, 1-4. 10. 13. 15. 16. 21.

Conscientious Objection, Mt 5, 39. 44; Lk 6, 27-29. 31-33. 35; Acts 4, 19; 5, 29; Rom 12, 17-21; 1 Thes 5, 15; Heb 10, 30; 12, 14; 1 Pt 3, 9.

Consulting, the Lord and his ministers when in doubt, Lk 16, 29.

Continency, possible, Mt 19, 11f; □ breach of vow of, 1 Tm 5, 12; □ practice commended, 1 Cor 7, 7f. 27. 37. 38. 40; □ for the clergy, 1 Cor 7, 32. 33. 35.

Contrition, commended and preached, Mt 3, 2; 4, 17; Lk 13, 3; 24, 47; Acts 2, 38; 3, 19; 8, 22; 17, 30; 20, 21; 26, 20; □ remission of sins promised to true contrition, Acts 3, 19; 26, 18. 20.

Conversion, comes from God, Rom 15, 18; □ prayer for, Lk 18, 13; of Jews, Acts 2, 41-47; 3, 25-26; 4, 4. 32; □ of Paul, Acts 9, 1-22; □ of Gentiles accomplished, Acts 8, 26-39; 10, 11-13; Eph 2, 11-17.

Correction, fraternal, Mt 18, 15; Gal 2, 11; 1 Tm 5, 20; Heb 3, 13; Jas 5, 19; □ qualities for correcting, Mt 7, 3; Jn 8, 7; Ti 1, 6-9.

Councils of the Church, gathered in Christ's name are assisted by Christ, Mt 18, 20; □ assisted by the Holy Spirit, Acts 15, 28; □ decrees diligently to be observed by the faithful, Acts 15, 41; 16, 4. **See** Church Guides.

Creation, brought into being by God, Jn 1, 3f; Acts 7, 50; □ for the glory of God, Rom 8, 39; □ of the world, Acts 17,

24; Heb 11, 3; □ of human beings, 1 Cor 15, 45; Eph 2, 10; 1 Tm 2, 13; □ beauty of, 1 Tm 4, 3-5; □ renewed, Rom 8, 19-22; Rv 21, 5.

Cross and Tribulation, lot of all who wish to live piously, Mt 16, 24; 1 Thes 3, 3; 2 Tm 3, 12; □ folly of the cross, 1 Cor 1, 18; □ crosses sent us by God for our good, 2 Cor 11, 30; 1 Pt 3, 14, 17; 4, 12-18; □ cross to be borne patiently and joyfully, Mt 5, 12; 10, 38; 16, 24; Jas 1, 2.

Damnation, eternal, prepared for the devil and the reprobate, Mt 3, 12; 5, 29; 13, 50; 22, 13; Lk 3, 17; 16, 22ff; Heb 10, 27; 2 Pt 2, 4; Rv 19, 20; 20, 10f; 21, 8.

Dance, effects of, Mt 14, 6.

Day, of light, Jn 9, 4; 11, 9; □ epoch, Lk 19, 42; □ day of rest, the sabbath, Lk 6, 6-10; □ day of the Lord (Jesus), 1 Cor 1, 8; 1 Thes 5, 2. 4; □ day of judgment, Mt 10, 15; 12, 36. 41f; Lk 10, 14; Acts 17, 31; 2 Pt 2, 9; 1 Jn 4, 17; Jude 6; □ last day, Jn 6, 39; 11, 24; 12, 48; □ last days, Acts 2, 17; 2 Tm 3, 1; 2 Pt 3, 3.

Dead, mourning for the, Jn 11, 35; □ resurrection of, Jn 5, 25. 28f; 1 Cor 15, 12. 42.

Death, Jn 9, 4; Rom 5, 12; 1 Cor 15, 21f. 26.

Despair, causes of, Rom 7, 23f; Rv 6, 16; 16, 10; □ remedy for, Lk 18, 1; 2 Cor 4, 8f; Gal 6, 9; Heb 12, 2f.

Detraction, forbidden and punished, Rom 1, 30; 2 Cor 12, 20; 1 Pt 2, 1; Jas 4, 11.

Devil, always seeks to injure men, Lk 8, 12; Acts 13, 8; Eph 6, 11; Rv 2, 10; 12, 9; □ tempts our Lord, Mt 4, 1-11; □ transforms himself into an angel of light, 2 Cor 11, 4; □ his empire destroyed by Christ, Mt 12, 25-29; Lk 10, 18; 11, 20-22; Jn 12, 31; Col 1, 13; 2 Tm 1, 10; Heb 2, 14; 1 Jn 3, 8; Rv 20, 9.

Divorce, allowed in the Old Law but forbidden in the New, Mt 5, 31f; 19, 3-9; Mk 10, 2-12; Lk 16, 18; 1 Cor 7, 10-13.

Drunkenness, calls forth the ire of God, 1 Cor 6, 10; □ causes one to lose his reason, Eph 5, 18.

Ecumenism, Jn 17, 9-11. 20-23; Eph 4, 3-16; 1 Cor 10, 17; 12, 12-27; Rom 12, 5; 9, 6-8; Mt 7, 21-23.

Elect, Christ, Lk 23, 35; 1 Pt 2, 4. 6 (Is 42, 1); □ the Church, Mt 24, 22. 24. 31; Lk 18, 7; Rom 8, 33; 2 Tm 2, 10; 1 Pt 1, 2; 2, 9.

Enemies, attitude toward, Mt 5, 24. 38f; Lk 6, 29; Rom 12, 17ff; □ God saves from enemies, Acts 16, 19-40; □ punishment for enemies of God, 2 Thes 1, 6-9; Rv 21, 8.

Envy, Mt 27, 18; Acts 5, 17; Phil 1, 15.

Eternity of Hell's Torments, Mt 3, 12; 25, 41. 46; Mk 9, 43-46. 48; Lk 3, 17;

2 Thes 1, 7-9; Jude 6-7; Rv 14, 10f; 20, 10.

Eucharist, real presence of the body and blood of Christ, Mt 26, 26-28; Mk 14, 22-24; Lk 22, 19f; Jn 6, 51f; 1 Cor 10, 16; 11, 24f. 27. 29.

Excommunication, used by the Apostles, 1 Cor 5, 3-5. 9-13; 2 Thes 3, 6. 14; 1 Tm 1, 20; Ti 3, 10f; □ of the Pharisees, Jn 9, 22. 34; 12, 42; 16, 2.

Expiation, effected under the old law, Heb 9, 7. 13; □ effected by Christ, Lk 19, 22; Jn 1, 29. 36; Rom 5, 6-10; 1 Cor 1, 30; Gal 4, 5; Eph 2, 13-18; Heb 9, 12. 14. 28; 1 Pt 3, 8.

Faith, necessary to salvation, Mk 16, 16; Acts 2, 44-47; 4, 12; Heb 11, 6; □ without good works is dead, Jas 2, 14, 17. 20; □ alone, does not justify, Jas 2, 24; □ working with charity, Gal 5, 6; □ does not imply an absolute assurance of our being in grace; much less of our eternal salvation, Rom 11, 20-22; 1 Cor 9, 27; 10, 12; Phil 2, 12; Rv 3, 11.

Fasting, of great efficacy against the devil, Mt 9, 15; Mk 2, 20; Lk 5, 35; **See** also Acts 13, 3; 14, 22; 2 Cor 6, 5; 11, 27; □ the obligation of, Mt 6, 16; Mk 2, 20; Lk 2, 36f; 5, 35; Acts 13, 2f; 14, 22; Rom 13, 13f; 2 Cor 6, 5; 11, 27; Eph 5, 18; 1 Thes 5, 6; 1 Pt 1, 13; 5, 8; □ merits of, Mt 6, 17; Lk 2, 37; 1 Sm 31, 13; 2 Sm 1, 12; □ Christ fasting for forty days, Mt 4, 2;

Fear of God, and keep him always before our eyes, Mt 10, 28; Lk 12, 5; 1 Pt 2, 17; Rv 14, 7; □ fruit of the fear of God and his praise, Acts 9, 31; □ not opposed to faith, Rom 11, 20; Heb 3, 14; 4, 1.

Fidelity, demanded by God of his servants, Mt 24, 45f; 25, 21. 23; Lk 12, 42-46; 1 Cor 4, 2; □ toward others, Lk 16, 10; 1 Tm 3, 11; Ti 2, 10; □ God's fidelity, Rom 3, 3.

Fornication, provokes God's anger, 1 Cor 6, 9; Heb 13, 4; □ desire of, forbidden, Mt 5, 28.

Fraud, condemned, Mk 7, 21f; Acts 5, 2; Rom 1, 29.

Free-Will, often resists the grace of God, Mt 23, 37; Lk 13, 34; Acts 7, 51; Heb 12, 15; 2 Pt 3, 9; Rv 20, 4.

Gentiles, conversion of, Mt 8, 11; Jn 10, 16; Acts 8, 26; 1 Cor 12, 12f.

Gifts of God, Jesus, Jn 3, 16; 2 Cor 9, 15; □ the Holy Spirit, Lk 11, 13; Acts 2, 38; □ salvation, Eph 2, 8; □ eternal life, Jn 10, 28; Rom 6, 23; 1 Jn 5, 11; □ grace and glory, Jas 4, 6; □ various spiritual gifts, 1 Cor 1, 7; 12, 1-11; Jas 1, 17.

Glory, of God, to be sought in all things, Mt 6, 9; Jn 17, 4; Acts 3, 13; 12, 23; 1 Cor 6, 20; 10, 31; Phil 1, 20; Col 3, 17; Ti 2, 10.

Gluttony, Heb 12, 16f.

God, a pure spirit and self-existent, Jn 4, 24; □ he is one, Eph 4, 5f; □ there are three persons in one God, the Father, Jn 6, 27; the Son, Heb 1, 8-10; the Spirit, revealed at the baptism of Jesus, Mt 3, 16f; at the transfiguration, Lk 9, 28-35; by Jesus, Mt 28, 19; Jn 3, 16; 5, 21-23; 14, 16f; □ he is eternal, Rm 1, 20; 1 Tm 1, 17; 6, 15; Rv 4, 8; □ unchangeable, Jas 1, 17; □ omniscient, 1 Cor 2, 10; Heb 4, 13; 1 Jn 3, 20; □ almighty, Lk 1, 37; Acts 26, 8; Rv 19, 6; □ Creator of all things, Jn 1, 3; Acts 17, 24; Col 1, 16; Heb 3, 4; 11, 3; Rv 4, 11; □ his fidelity, 1 Cor 1, 9; 2 Thes 3, 3; Heb 10, 23; 1 Jn 1, 9; □ his justice, Acts 10, 34f; Rom 11, 22. 33; □ his mercy, Lk 1, 50; Jas 2, 13; □ his grace, Lk 2, 40; Acts 13, 43; 20, 24; Rom 9, 15; 2 Cor 12, 9; 1 Pt 5, 10; □ loves all human beings, Jn 3, 16; 16, 27; Rom 5, 8f; 8, 32; 1 Tm 2, 4; □ wills all to be saved, Mt 23, 37; Jn 6, 39f; 1 Tm 2, 4.

Good Works, meritorious, Mt 5, 11f; 10, 42; 16, 27; 1 Cor 3, 8; 2 Tm 4, 8.

Gospel, the preaching of, Mt 1, 21; 11, 28; 28, 19f; Mk 16, 15; Lk 2, 10; 24; 46f; Jn 3, 16; 6, 35; 8, 12; 10, 9; 12, 46; Rom 1, 16; 3, 21. 24f; 8, 3; 1 Cor 1, 17. 23; 4, 15; 15, 1; 2 Cor 5, 18; Gal 1, 6. 11; Eph 1, 13; 1 Tm 1, 15; 2 Tm 1, 8; 2, 8; 1 Pt 4, 17.

Grace, spoken of in Scripture as a favor, Acts 2, 47; 25, 9; □ as a reward expected from God, Lk 6, 33; 1 Pt 2, 19; □ as a supernatural gift, Lk 1, 28; 2, 40; Jn 1, 16; Rom 1, 7; 1 Cor 16, 23, 2 Cor 1, 12; Gal 5, 4f; Heb 13, 9, Jas 4, 6; □ before and after meals, Mt 14, 19; 15, 36; 26, 26; Mk 6, 41; 8, 6; 14, 22; Lk 9, 16; Jn 6, 11. 23; Acts 27, 35; Rom 14, 6; 1 Cor 10, 30; 1 Tm 4, 3.

Gratitude, recommended, Acts 4, 21; Eph 5, 19f; Phil 4, 6; Col 2, 7; 3, 15.

Happiness, condition for, Mt 5, 1-12; Lk 11, 28; Jn 13, 17; Rom 4, 7f.

Hardness, of heart, insensibility punished, Mt 18, 30. 34; 25, 42; Jas 2, 13; □ of the rich man (Dives), Lk 16, 21.

Hatred, reconciliation enjoined, Mt 5, 23f; □ of the world for the disciples of Christ, Mk 13, 13.

Heart, purified and sanctified by our Lord, Jn 13, 10; 15, 3; Acts 15, 9; 1 Cor 6, 11; Heb 1, 3; 9, 14; 10, 14; 13, 12; □ God accepts a person's heart or good will as an action, Mt 15, 8; Mk 12, 41-44; Lk 21, 1-4; 2 Cor 8, 12.

Heaven, joys of, Mt 5, 12; 13, 43; Jn 12, 26; 14, 3; 17, 24; 1 Cor 13, 12; Rv 7, 16; □ those who will attain it, Mt 5, 8; 25, 33-40; Rom 8, 17; Phil 4, 3; Heb 12, 23; Rv 3, 5; □ new heaven, 2 Pt 3, 13; Rv 21, 1.

· **Hell,** pains of, Mt 8, 12; Lk 13, 28; Rv 14, 10; □ proportioned to sins, Lk 16, 25;

Rv 18, 7; □ endless, Mt 25, 41; 2 Thes 1, 9.

Holy Scripture, divinely inspired, 2 Tm 3, 16f; 2 Pt 1, 21; □ purpose of, to instruct, Rom 15, 4; give spiritual nourishment, Mt 4, 4; 1 Pt 2, 2; lead to faith, Jn 20, 31; sanctify, Jn 17, 17; Eph 5, 26; edify, Acts 20, 32; 2 Tm 3, 16f; □ fulfilled by Christ, Mt 5, 17; Lk 24, 25-27; Jn 19, 30; □ explained by the apostles, Acts 2, 16-21. 25-36; Rom 3, 10-18; □ danger of rejecting them, Jn 12, 48; Heb 2, 2-4; 10, 28-31.

Holy Spirit, his divinity, Acts 5, 3f; 28, 25f; 1 Cor 2, 10f; 6, 11. 19f. **See** also Mt 12, 31f; Acts 13, 2; 20, 28; 2 Cor 13, 13; and the solemn form of baptism, Mt 28, 19f; □ proceeds from the Father and the Son, Jn 15, 26; □ his works, Jn 3, 3-8; 6, 63; 14, 16f. 26; 16, 12-14; Rom 5, 5; 8, 14. 26; Gal 5, 18; Eph 6, 18; Phil 3, 3; □ governs the work of the Church, Acts 13, 2. 4; 20, 22. 28; □ dwells within the followers of Christ, Jn 14, 16f.

Hope, in God, Rom 15, 13; Acts 24, 15; 1 Tm 4, 10; □ in Christ, Acts 28, 20; 1 Cor 15, 19; 1 Tm 1, 1; □ effects of, Rom 5, 5; 12, 12; 2 Cor 3, 12; Heb 3, 6; 1 Jn 3, 3.

Hospitality, commended, Lk 14, 13; Rom 12, 13; 1 Tm 3, 2; 3 Jn 5.

Humility, agreeable to God, Mt 3, 11; Mk 9, 34; Jn 13, 4f; Acts 10, 25; Rom 11, 20; 12, 16; 1 Cor 4, 6; Phil 2, 3; Col 3, 12; Heb 11, 24-26; 1 Pt 5, 5; Jas 1, 9; 4, 10; Rv 4, 10f; 19, 10.

Hypocrisy, described, Mt 23, 14; Col 2, 18; 2 Tm 3, 5; □ condemned, Mt 23, 13-36; □ exhortations to avoid, Mt 6, 2; Jas 3, 17; 1 Pt 2, 1.

Idolatry, wicked practice of, Rom 1, 24-27; 1 Cor 10, 7-8; 1 Pt 4, 3-4; Rv 2, 14. 20-22; 17, 1-6; □ denunciations against, Acts 15, 29; Rom 1, 25; 1 Cor 6, 9; 10, 14; 1 Jn 5, 21; Rv 21, 8.

Ignorance, dangers of, Acts 3, 17; 17, 29-31; Eph 4, 18f; 1 Pt 1, 14; □ mercy of God for the ignorant, Acts 17, 30; 1 Tm 1, 13; Heb 5, 2.

Image, human beings created in God's, 1 Cor 11, 7; □ Christ is image of God, 2 Cor 4, 4; Phil 2, 6; Col 1, 15; Heb 1, 3.

Immortality, of God, 1 Tm 1, 17; 6, 16; 2 Tm 1, 10. □ of human beings, Rom 2, 7; 1 Cor 15, 53

Imposition, of hands, Mk 10, 16; □ in confirmation, Acts 8, 17; 19, 6; □ in holy orders, Acts 6, 6; 13, 3; 1 Tm 4, 14; 5, 22; 2 Tm 1, 6.

Infidelity, punished, Mt 8, 28ff; 14, 39; 17, 17-19; 24, 25; Jn 3, 18. 36; 8, 24; 12, 48; 20, 27; Rom 11, 20; Heb 3, 18; 4, 2; 11, 6; Rv 21, 8.

Ingratitude, punishment for, Mt 11, 20; Lk 17, 18; Jn 11, 46; Rom 1, 21; 2 Tm 3, 2.

Injustice, not to be attributed to God, Jn 7, 18; Rom 3, 5f; □ not to be committed, Lk 16, 10; □ retribution, 2 Thes 2, 12; 2 Pt 2, 9.

Jews, their reprobation announced by St. Paul, Rom 10, 1; □ persecute the apostles, Acts 5, 18; □ three thousand converted, Acts 2, 41; □ five thousand converted, Acts 4, 4; □ Greek Jews murmur as to alms, Acts 6, 1; □ rise against St. Stephen, Acts 7; □ gospel preached to, Acts 11, 19; □ resist St. Paul, Acts 13, 45; □ abandoned for the Gentiles, Acts 13, 46; □ persecute St. Paul, Acts 13, 50; □ do themselves what they condemn, Rom 2, 1; □ their privileges over the Gentiles, Rom 3, 1; □ their salvation excites St. Paul's zeal, Rom 9, 1. 3; □ their fall does not make void God's promises, Rom 9, 6; □ zeal of the ignorant Jews, Rom 10, 2; □ their incredulity opposed, Rom 10, 21; □ their future recall, Rom 11, 26; □ Christ promised to them, Rom 15, 5; □ the cross a scandal to them, 1 Cor 1, 23; □ in tutelage under the law, Gal 4, 2; □ their union with the Gentiles, Eph 2, 19; □ true Jews, Rom 2, 28f.

Joy, of the People of God, Mt 2, 10; Jn 15, 11; Acts 2, 46; Rom 14, 17; 2 Cor 8, 2; □ follows afflictions, Jn 16, 20-22; Jas 1, 2-4; □ sources of, Lk 10, 20f; Acts 2, 28; Rom 15, 13; □ in heaven over repentant sinners, Lk 15, 7. 10.

Judgment, we must not judge rashly, Mt 7, 1; 12, 7; Lk 7, 33f; Jn 7, 24; 9, 16; Acts 28, 3-6; Rom 14, 4. 13; 1 Cor 4, 5; 1 Tm 5, 21; □ last judgment announced by our Lord, and reserved to him alone, Jn 5, 22; □ last judgment described, Mt 25, 31-46; Rv 6, 14-17; 7; 8, 9; □ particular judgment, Lk 16, 19-31; Heb 9, 27; 10, 31.

Justification, through faith, Rom 1, 17; 3, 20-30; 4; 5; Gal 3, 11; Acts 13, 39.

Kingdom, of God, Mt 6, 10; Lk 11, 2; Acts 1, 3; □ of Christ, Mt 26, 29; Jn 18, 36f; □ of heaven, Mt 3, 2; 5, 19; 7, 21; 23, 13; □ parables of, Mt 13, 1-52; 20, 1-16; 22, 2-14; 25.

Law, the Old and the New, Rom 3, 20; 4, 15; 5, 20; 7, 1-7; Gal 3, 19; 1 Tm 1, 8; Heb 7, 18-27; □ the natural, Rom 1, 18-23; 2, 12-16; □ ceremonies of the, abrogated by Christ, Mt 15, 1-20; Mk 15, 38; Acts 13, 38; 15, 11; Rom 6, 14; 7, 4; 8, 3; Gal 3, 13; 4, 5; Eph 2, 13; Col 2, 14; 1 Pt 1, 11-19.

Lepers, healed, Mt 8, 2f; Mk 1, 40-42; Lk 17, 12-14.

Liberty, evangelical, Jn 8, 32; Rom 6, 18; 8, 2. 21; Gal 5, 13; 1 Pt 1, 18; 2, 16; 2 Pt 2, 19.

Light, Jesus Christ is the light of the world, Jn 1, 5; 8, 12; 9, 5; 12, 36. 46; 1 Jn 1, 5; 2, 8 □ how Christians are, Mt 5, 14; Rom 2, 19; Phil 2, 15.

Magic, condemned, Acts 13, 6-11; 19, 19; Gal 5, 20; Rv 21, 8; 22, 15.

Man, creation and dignity, 1 Cor 11, 7; □ his fall, 2 Cor 11, 3; □ his sinful state, Rom 3, 13-18; 7, 18; 1 Jn 1, 8; □ his weakness, Mt 6, 27; 1 Cor 3, 7; □ his redemption, Rom 5; 1 Cor 1, 30; Gal 3, 14; Eph 3; Col 1, 12-29; Heb 2, 9-18; 1 Pt 1, 18f; □ lot of the child of God, Acts 13, 48; 22, 14; 1 Thes 3, 5; 1 Pt 1, 3-5.

Mary, called mother of our Lord, Lk 1, 43; □ mother of Jesus, Mt 2, 13; □ the angel Gabriel sent to, Lk 1, 26; □ visits St. Elizabeth, Lk 1, 39f; □ composes her canticle, the Magnificat, Lk 1, 46; □ gives birth to our Savior, Mt 1, 16; Lk 2, 7; □ presents Jesus in the temple, Lk 2, 22; □ sorrows prophesied to her, Lk 2, 34f; □ flees into Egypt, Mt 2, 13f; □ returns to Nazareth, Mt 2, 20-23; □ loses Jesus in the temple, Lk 2, 42-51; □ at the foot of the cross, Jn 19, 25; □ St. John given to her as a son, Jn 19, 26f; □ remains with the apostles, Acts 1, 14.

Mass, instituted by Christ, Lk 22, 19f; □ attested, 1 Cor 10, 16. 18-21; Heb 13, 10. **See** Eucharist.

Meekness, commended, Mt 5, 4; Gal 6, 1; Eph 4, 2; Col 3, 12; Ti 3, 2; □ especially to ministers of the Lord, 2 Tm 2, 24f; □ one of the fruits of the Holy Spirit, Gal 5, 23; □ example of Christ, Mt 11, 29.

Mercy, Mt 5, 7; 9, 13; 10, 42; 18, 33. 35; 25, 40; Rom 12, 13; Eph 4, 32; Col 3, 12; 1 Tm 5, 10. **See** Almsgiving.

Messiah, foretold in Old Testament, Lk 24, 27; □ called the Christ, Jn 1, 41; 4, 25; 7, 41; 11, 27; Mt 26, 63f; Acts 17, 3; 18, 28; □ he is the Lamb of God, Jn 1, 29. 36.

Moses, appears in the transfiguration of Christ, Mt 17, 3; Lk 9, 30f.

Name, of God, to be venerated, Lk 1, 49; 1 Tm 6, 1. □ of Christ, to be confessed, Act 9, 15. 28; 19, 17; 2 Thes 1, 12; 2 Tm 2, 19; □ actions done in Christ's name, Mt 28, 19; Mk 9, 41; Jn 14, 13; 16, 23f; Acts 3, 6; 4, 10; 1 Cor 5, 4f; Eph 5, 20; Col 3, 17; Heb 13, 15; □ salvation in Christ's name, Acts 2, 21; Rom 10, 13; 1 Cor 6, 11; 1 Jn 3, 23; 5, 13.

Neighbor, duties toward, Lk 10, 25-37; Rom 3, 9; Gal 5, 14; Jas 2, 8.

Obedience, Rom 6, 16; 13, 5; 1 Pt 1, 22; □ to God, Acts 4, 19; □ to parents, Mt 15, 4; 19, 19; Mk 7, 10; Eph 6, 1-14; 2 Tm 3, 2; Heb 12, 7; □ to masters and those in authority, Eph 6, 5-9; Heb 13, 17; □ of Christ, Lk 2, 51; Phil 2, 8; Heb 5, 8f.

Original Sin, Rom 3, 9. 23; 5, 12; □ its effects, Rom 5, 12. 17; 6, 23; 8, 6-8. 11. 13. 17; Gal 5, 17; Eph 2, 3.

Parables, see p. 410.

Pardon, granted by God alone, Mk 2, 7; Lk 5, 21. □ granted in virtue of Christ's blood, Mt 26, 28; Eph 1, 7; Heb 9, 12. 22; 1 Pt 1, 18f; as a result of faith in Jesus, Acts 10, 43; 26, 18; in Christ, Eph 4, 32; Col 1, 14; after repentance, Mk 1, 4; Lk 3, 3; 24, 47; Acts 5, 31; through baptism, Acts 2, 38; □ power to pardon granted by Jesus to disciples, Jn 20, 23; □ happiness of those pardoned, Rom 4, 7; □ pardon one another, Mt 6, 14f; 18, 23-35; Mk 11, 25f; Lk 6, 37; 2 Cor 2, 7; Eph 4, 32; Col 3, 13; Jas 2, 13.

Parents, their duties, Mt 10, 37; Eph 6, 4; Col 3, 21; 2 Tm 3, 15; Ti 2, 4.

Peace, of God, Rom 1, 7; 2 Cor 1, 2; Phil 4, 7; □ of Christ, Lk 7, 50; 8, 48; Jn 14, 27; Rom 5, 1; 1 Cor 1, 3; Gal 1, 3; 2 Thes 3, 16; □ fruit of the Spirit, Rom 8, 6; Gal 5, 22; Eph 2, 17; □ peace with God, Acts 10, 34-36; Rom 5, 1; 2 Cor 5, 18-20; Eph 2, 12-18; □ no peace for the wicked, Rom 3, 17; Rv 6, 4.

Penance, satisfaction for sins, Mt 3, 8; Lk 3, 8; Acts 2, 38; 8, 22; 2 Cor 7-10; □ is preached, Mt 3, 2. 4. 8; Lk 3, 3. 8; 13, 3; 24, 47; Acts 2, 38; 3, 19; 8, 21; 17, 30; 20, 21; 26, 20; □ examples of true, Mt 26, 75; Lk 7, 37-44; 15, 18; 18, 13; 19, 8; 22, 62; 23, 41; Acts 2, 37-41; □ examples of false, Mt 27, 4; Acts 8, 13-23; Heb 12, 17.

People of God, privileges and blessings, Lk 1, 17; Rom 11; 1 Pt 2, 9; Rv 21, 3-7; □ belongs to God, Ti 2, 14; Heb 8, 10; □ saved, Mt 1, 21; Rv 5, 9; □ the rest of God, Heb 4, 9-11.

Persecution, foretold, Mt 5, 11; 13, 21; 23, 34; Mk 10, 30; Lk 10, 49; 21, 12; Jn 15, 20; 2 Tm 3, 12; □ how to be endured, Mt 5, 12. 44; 10, 23; Acts 5, 41; Rom 12, 14; Heb 10, 34; 1 Pt 4, 12-19; □ blessings of, Mt 5, 11f; 1 Thes 1, 4-7; Rv 6, 9-11.

Perseverance, exhortations to, Mt 10, 22; 24, 13; Lk 9, 62; Acts 13, 43; 1 Cor 15, 58; Eph 6, 18; Heb 3, 6. 13; 10, 23. 28; 2 Pt 3, 17; □ rewarded, Is 56, 4-7; Lk 8, 15; Rom 2, 7; 15, 4; Heb 6, 15; Jas 1, 25; □ examples of, Acts 1, 14; 2, 42; 1 Cor 15, 1; Rv 1, 9.

Poor, not to be oppressed, Jas 2, 2-6; □ duties toward, Mt 5, 42; Lk 3, 11; Gal 2, 10; Eph 4, 28; 1 Tm 6, 18; 1 Jn 3, 17; □ promises of God for, 2 Cor 8, 9; □ to be consoled by the Church, Acts 6, 1; 11, 29f; 1 Cor 16, 1; 2 Cor 8, 1-3; 9, 11-13; Gal 2, 10; Heb 13, 16; □ blessed are the poor in spirit, Mt 5, 3; Lk 6, 20.

Pope, or chief bishop, St. Peter, by Christ's ordinance, was raised to this dignity, Mt 16, 18f; Lk 22, 31f; Jn 21, 15; 17. **See** also Mt 10, 2; Acts 5, 29; Gal 2, 7f.

Prayer, Mt 6, 5-13; 7, 7-11; 18, 19f; Mk 14, 24-26; Lk 11, 2-13; 18, 1; Jn 14, 13f; 15, 7; 16, 23f; Rom 8, 26f; Eph 6, 18; Phil 4, 6; Col 4, 2; 1 Thes 5, 17; 1 Tm 2, 1-3; Jas 4, 3; 5, 16-18; 1 Jn 3, 22; 5, 14f; □ the Lord's, Mt 6, 9-13; Lk 11, 2-4; □ of Christ for his disciples, Jn 17; □ of the apostles, Acts 4, 24-30.

Preaching, of repentance, Mt 3, 1-12; 4, 17; 12, 41; Mk 1, 4-8. 14; Lk 3, 3-20; □ of the gospel, by Jesus, Mt 4, 23; 5; 6; 7; Mk 1, 14; Lk 4, 18-27; by the apostles, Mt 28, 19f; Mk 16, 15; Lk 24, 47; Acts 2, 14-40; 3, 12-26; 4, 8-12; 10, 34-48; 13, 16-41; 17, 22-31; 26, 1-19.

Presumption, Jas 4, 13-16.

Pride, Mt 23, 12; Lk 1, 51f; 18, 9-14; Gal 6, 3; Jas 4, 6. 16; 1 Pt 5, 5.

Promises, of God, inviolable, 2 Cor 1, 20; Heb 6, 17f; obtained by faith and perseverance, Heb 6, 12; 10, 36; Rom 4, 13; Lk 1, 45; of a celestial inheritance, 1 Pt 1, 3f; □ of Christ, to his disciples, Mt 6, 4. 6. 18; 7, 7-10; 16, 8. 19, 15. 28; Lk 11, 9f; 12, 31f; Jn 14, 15; 16; 20, 21-23; about his return, Mt 24, 30. 44; Mk 13, 26; Lk 12, 40; 21; 27; Jn 14, 3; Acts 1, 11.

Prophecy, gift of God, Lk 1, 70; of the Spirit, 1 Cor 12, 9f; 1 Pt 1, 21; of Jesus, Eph 4, 11; Rv 1, 1; 11, 3; □ how to receive it, Lk 24, 25; 1 Thes 5, 20; 2 Pt 1, 19; Rv 1, 3; 22, 7; □ prophecies concerning Jesus the Messiah and their fulfillment:
Gn 12, 3; 18, 18 / Acts 3, 25f; Dt 18, 15. 18 / Acts 3, 22f; Ps 2, 1f / Acts 4, 25-28; Ps 2, 7 / Acts 13, 33 / Heb 1, 5; Ps 22, 2 / Mt 27, 46 / Mk 15, 34; Ps 22, 19 / Mt 27, 35 / Jn 19, 23; Ps 69, 22 / Mt 27, 34. 48; Is 7, 14 / Mt 1, 18-23; Is 8, 23—9, 1 / Mt 4, 15f; Is 53, 12 / Mk 15, 27f / Lk 23, 33f; Mi 5, 1 / Mt 2, 1. 5f; Zec 9, 9 / Mt 21, 1-9; Zec 11, 13 / Mt 27, 3-10; Zec 13, 7 / Mt 26, 31. 56; Mal 3, 1 / Mt 11, 7-10; Mal 4, 5f / Mt 11, 13f & 17, 10.

Prophecies, pronounced by Jesus about his death and resurrection, Mt 12, 40; 17, 22f; 20, 18f; Jn 2, 19-22; 12, 32f; about Judas' betrayal, Mt 26, 21-25; Jn 6, 70f; 13, 18f; about Peter's denial, Mt 26, 34; Jn 13, 38; about the sending of the Holy Spirit, Jn 14, 16; Lk 24, 49; Acts 1, 5. 8; about the preaching of the gospel, Mt 24, 14; 26, 13; Mk 13, 10; about persecutions, Mt 10, 17-25; Jn 16, 2. 32f; about destruction of Jerusalem, Mt 24; Mk 13; Lk 19, 43f; 21.

Prudence, exhortations to, Mt 24, 45; 25, 13; 26, 41; Lk 12, 35; 21, 36; 1 Cor 10, 12; 1 Thes 5, 6; 2 Tm 4, 5; 1 Pt 4, 7; 5, 8.

Purgatory, or a middle state of souls, suffering for a time on account of their sins, is shown by those many texts of Scripture which affirm that God will render to every man according to his works, so that such as die in lesser sins shall not escape without punishment, Mt 5, 25f; 12, 32; Lk 12, 58f; 1 Cor 3, 15; 1 Pt 3, 18-20; 1 Jn 5, 16; Rv 5, 3. 13.

Purifications, water jars for purifying, Jn 2, 6; □ dispute between John's disciples and the Jews concerning purifications, Jn 3, 25.

Quarrels, to be avoided, 1 Cor 6, 6f; Phil 2, 14f; 2 Tm 2, 23f.

Questions, useless questions to be avoided, Jn 21, 21; Acts 1, 16f; 1 Tm 1, 4; 6, 3f; 2 Tm 2, 16; Ti 3, 9.

Redemption, Lk 21, 28; Rom 3, 24; 1 Cor 6, 20; 7, 23; 15, 55; 2 Cor 5, 15; 1 Tm 2, 5f; 2 Tm 1, 9; Ti 2, 14; Heb 9, 11f; 1 Pt 1, 18f; Rv 1, 5; 5, 9.

Relics, miraculous, Mt 9, 20f; Acts 19, 11f.

Repentance, preached by John the Baptist, Mt 3, 2; 8, 11; Mk 1, 4; Lk 3, 3. 8. 19; □ preached by Jesus, Mt 4, 17; Mk 1, 15; Lk 15; 24, 27; □ preached by the disciples, Mk 6, 12; Acts 2, 38; 3, 19; 17, 30; □ exhortations to, Mt 3, 3; 4, 17; Rv 2, 5. 16. 21; 3, 3. 19.

Revelation, communications to human being of hidden things, Mt 11; 25; Rom 8, 18; 1 Cor 2, 9f; 1 Pt 1, 5, 12; Rom 16, 25; Col 1, 26; □ God the author of, Mt 16, 17; □ through the Spirit, 1 Cor 2, 10; Eph 3, 5; □ depositaries of, chosen by God and Christ, Mt 11, 25-27; Lk 10, 22; Jn 11, 38-40; Gal 1, 15f; □ Jesus reveals God, Jn 1, 18; Col 1, 15; Mt 11, 27; Lk 10, 22; his justice, Rom 8, 19; his love, 1 Jn 4, 9; Jn 3, 16.

Reward, promised to the just, Mt 10, 41f; Lk 6, 35; □ promised to those unjustly persecuted, Mt 5, 11f; □ promised to each according to his works, 1 Cor 3, 8; Col 3, 23f; 2 Jn 8; Rv 22, 12.

Riches, dangers of, Mt 6, 19; Lk 12, 15; 1 Tm 6, 9. 17; Jas 2, 6; □ evils brought on by, Mt 10, 22f; 13, 22; 19, 23f; Mk 10, 22; 1 Tm 6, 10; □ true riches, Mt 6, 20; Lk 12, 33; Col 3, 1f; 1 Tm 6, 19; Rv 2, 9; 3, 18; Rom 11, 33; □ duties imposed by, Mt 19, 21; 1 Tm 6, 18f; 1 Jn 3, 17.

Sacraments, they produce Grace, Jn 6, 57ff; Acts 2, 37f; 19, 5; 8, 17; 1 Pt 3, 20f;

BAPTISM, commanded by Christ, Mt 28, 19; Mk 16, 16; Jn 3, 5; □ taught and administered by the apostles, Acts 2, 38. 41; Acts 8, 12, 38; 9, 18; 10, 48; 16, 15, etc; □ the laver of regeneration, 1 Pt 2, 21; Ti 3, 5; □ takes away all sin, Mk 1, 4; 16, 16; Jn 3, 5; 1, 33; Acts 2, 38; 8,

12f; 16, 33; Rom 6, 3-6; Gal 3, 27; 1 Cor 6, 11; Eph 5, 26; Col 2, 12-14; Lk 3, 3; Heb 10, 22; □ not to be repeated, Eph 4, 5; Heb 6, 4-6; 10, 26; □ signifies passion or suffering, Mk 10, 38; Lk 12, 50; □ to be administered to children, Mt 18, 14; 19, 13f; Mk 10, 13-16; Lk 18, 15. 17; Jn 3, 5; Acts 2, 39; 16, 15. 33; 1 Cor 1, 16; 15, 22; □ persons baptized receive the Holy Spirit, Acts 2, 38; 19, 5f; □ the baptized put on Christ, Gal 3, 27; □ Christians are baptized in Christ's death, Rom 6, 3; □ are baptized in one body, 1 Cor 12, 13. 27;

CONFIRMATION, Acts 19, 6. 20; 8, 17; Heb 6, 2; 2 Cor 1, 21f; Eph 1, 13;

HOLY EUCHARIST, promised, Jn 32-60; □ instituted, Mt 26, 26-28; Mk 14, 22-24; Lk 22, 19f; 1 Cor 11, 23-27; 10, 16; 11, 27. 29; □ should be frequently received, Acts 2, 42; 20, 7; □ Eucharist under one kind, Lk 24, 30f; Jn 6, 59. **See** also verses 33, 38, 51, 52, 58; Acts 2, 42; 20, 7; 1 Cor 11, 27;

PENANCE, Mt 18, 18; 16, 19; Jn 20, 22f; 2 Cor 5, 20. **See** verses 18, 19;

ANOINTING OF THE SICK, Jas 5, 14f; Mk 6, 12f;

HOLY ORDERS, instituted by Christ, Lk 22, 19; Jn 20, 22f. □ conferred by imposition of hands, Acts 6, 6; 13, 3; 14, 22; □ give grace, 1 Tm 4, 14; 2 Tm 1, 6.

MATRIMONY, Eph 5, 25. 31f; Mt 19, 5; Mk 10, 7; 1 Thes 4, 4; 1 Tm 2, 15.

Saints, departed, assist us by their prayers, Lk 16, 9; 1 Cor 12, 12. 20f; Rv 5, 8; □ we have a communion with them, 1 Cor 12, 26; Heb 12, 22f; □ they have power over nations, Rv 2, 26f; 5, 10; □ they are with Christ in heaven, before the general resurrection, 2 Cor 5, 1. 6-8; Phil 1, 23f; Rv 4, 4; 6, 9; 7, 9. 14. 15; 14, 1. 3f; 19, 1. 4-6; 20, 4; □ their invocation, consult the texts quoted above with relation to angels, and such as testify to the great power which the prayers of God's servants have with him, and which authorize us to call for their prayers. For which **see** Rom 15, 30; Eph 6, 18f; 1 Thes 5, 25; Heb 13, 18; Jas 5, 16.

Sin, against the Holy Spirit, Mt 12, 31; Mk 3, 29; Lk 11, 15; 12, 10; Heb 6, 4-6; 10, 26; 1 Jn 5, 16; □ crying for vengeance, Jas 5, 4.

Sinner, prayer of, for pardon, Mt 8, 2; Lk 15, 17-19; 18, 13.

Spirit (Divining), girl with a, delivered from the devil, Acts 16, 16-18.

Spouses, relations with each other, Mt 19, 4-6; Mk 10, 6-9; 1 Cor 7, 3-5; Eph 5, 22-24; Col 3, 18; 1 Pt 3, 7; □ fidelity owed each other, Mk 10, 12; Lk 18, 20; Rom 7, 2f; □ love one another, Eph 5, 25-33; Col 3, 19; □ figure of Christ and

the Church, Mt 9, 15; 25, 1-13; 2 Cor 11, 2; Eph 5, 23. 24; Rv 19, 7.

Temptation, of Jesus by the devil, Mt 4, 1-11; Mk 1, 12f; Lk 4, 1-13; □ of the People of God, Lk 22, 31f. 40; 1 Cor 7, 5; Jas 1, 12; 1 Pt 1, 7; 4, 12; □ God's help in, Mt 6, 13; Lk 11, 4; 1 Cor 10, 13; Heb 2, 18; Rv 3, 10; □ need for watchfulness and prayer, Mt 26, 41; Mk 14, 38; Lk 22, 46; Gal 6, 1.

Trinity, Mt 3, 16; 10, 20; 17, 5; 28, 19; Lk 4, 18; Jn 3, 34f; 14, 16. 26; 1 Jn 5, 7.

Unbelief, sin of, Mk 16, 14; Jn 16, 9; Ti 1, 15; 1 Jn 5, 10; □ whence it comes, Lk 8, 12; 24, 25; Jn 10, 26; 12, 38-40; Acts 19, 9; 2 Cor 4, 4; 2 Thes 2, 11f; Heb 3, 12; □ effects of, Jn 5, 38; 12, 37; 16, 9; Acts 14, 2; Heb 4, 2.

Wicked, lot of, 2 Pt 3, 7; □ Christ died for the, Rom 4, 5; 5, 6.

Will, accommodated to the divine will, Mt 6, 10; 26, 39; Mk 14, 35; Lk 22, 42; Acts 21, 14; 1 Cor 4, 19; Heb 6, 3; Jas 4, 15.

Will of God, Mt 7, 21; 12, 50; Mk 3, 36; Jn 6, 39; Rom 12, 2; Eph 5, 17; Col 1, 9; 1 Thes 4, 3; 1 Tm 2, 4; 1 Jn 2, 17.

Women, celebrated in salvation history, Mt 1, 1-17; Lk 2, 36f; 1 Pt 3, 5; □ religious privileges of, among early Christians, Acts 1, 14; 12, 12f; 1 Cor 11, 5; 14, 34; 1 Tm 2, 11; □ rules for dress of Christian, 1 Tm 2, 9f; 1 Pt 3, 3f; □ complement of man, Mt 19, 4; 1 Cor 11, 7; □ condition of, 1 Cor 14, 34; Eph 5, 22; Col 3, 18; 1 Tm 2, 12; □ emancipation of, Lk 10, 38; 24, 22; Acts 1, 14; 16, 13; 3, 28; □ love for, Mk 10, 7f; □ as poets, Elizabeth, Lk 1, 42-45; Mary, Lk 1, 46-55; □ as prophets, Anna, Lk 36-38; Philip's daughter, Acts 21, 9; □ sold for husband's debts, Mt 18, 25; □ last at the Cross, Mt 27, 55f; Mk 15, 40f; □ first to whom risen Christ appeared, Mk 16, 9; Jn 20, 14-18; □ social status of in Roman customs, Acts 24, 24; 25, 13. 23; 26, 30.

Word of God, one of names given to Jesus, Jn 1, 1. 14; 1 Jn 1, 1; Rv 19, 16; **see** also Holy Spirit.

Works, of God, inadequacy of works of law, Rom 3, 20; Gal 2, 16; Eph 2, 9; □ demonstrate faith, Acts 26, 20; Jas 2, 14-26; □ exhortations to good works, Mt 5, 16; Acts 9, 36; 2 Cor 8, 9; Eph 2, 10; Phil 2, 12; 1 Thes 4, 11f; 2 Thes 2, 17; 3, 7-13; Heb 10, 24; 1 Pt 2, 13.

World, creation of, Mt 13, 35; Jn 1, 10; Acts 17, 24; Rom 1, 20; Heb 1, 2; 11, 3.

Worship, to be offered to God alone, Mt 4, 10; Lk 4, 8; Acts 10, 26; □ manner of offering, Jn 4, 23f; Eph 5, 19; Col 3, 16.

454

COLLABORATORS ON THE REVISED NEW TESTAMENT OF THE NEW AMERICAN BIBLE

BISHOPS' AD HOC COMMITTEE

Most Rev. Theodore E. McCarrick, D.D.
Most Rev. Richard J. Sklba, D.D.
Most Rev. J. Francis Stafford, D.D.
Most Rev. John F. Whealon, D.D., *Chairman*

BOARD OF EDITORS

Rev. Msgr. Myles M. Bourke
Rev. Francis T. Gignac, S.J., *Chairman*
Rev. Stephen J. Hartdegen, O.F.M., *Secretary*
Rev. Claude J. Peifer, O.S.B.
Rev. John H. Reumann

REVISERS

Rev. Msgr. Myles M. Bourke
Rev. Frederick W. Danker
Rev. Alexander A. Di Lella, O.F.M.
Rev. Charles H. Giblin, S.J.
Rev. Francis T. Gignac, S.J.
Rev. Stephen J. Hartdegen, O.F.M.
Dr. Maurya P. Horgan
Rev. John R. Keating, S.J.
Rev. John Knox
Dr. Paul J. Kobelski
Dr. J. Rebecca Lyman
Bro. Elliott C. Maloney, O.S.B.
Dr. Janet A. Timbie

CONSULTANTS

Rev. Joseph Jensen, O.S.B.
Rev. Aidan Kavanagh, O.S.B.
Dr. Marianne Sawicki

BUSINESS MANAGER

Charles A. Buggé

WORD PROCESSOR

Suzanna Jordan